Contents

About the Authors

Dr. Christopher Kendris has worked as interpreter and translator of French for the
U.S. State Department at the American Embassy in Paris. He earned his B.S. and M.S.
degrees at Columbia University in the City of New York, where he held a New York State
Scholarship, and his M.A. and Ph.D. degrees at Northwestern University in Evanston,
Illinois, where he held a Teaching Assistantship and Tutorial Fellowship during four years.
He also earned two diplomas with *Mention très Honorable* at the Université de Paris (en
Sorbonne), Faculté des Lettres, École Supérieure de Préparation et de Perfectionnement
des Professeurs de Français à l'Étranger, and at the Institut de Phonétique, Paris. In
1986 he was one of 95 teachers in the United States awarded a Rockefeller Foundation
Fellowship for Teachers of Foreign Languages in American High Schools. He has taught
French at the College of the University of Chicago as visiting summer lecturer, at Colby
College, Duke University, Rutgers—The State University of New Jersey, and the State
University of New York at Albany. He was Chairman of the Department of Foreign
Languages and Supervisor of 16 foreign language teachers on the secondary level at
Farmingdale High School, Farmingdale, New York, where he was also a teacher of all
levels of French and Spanish, and prepared students for the New York State French and
Spanish Regents, SAT exams, and AP tests. Dr. Kendris is the author of 22 school and
college books, workbooks, and other language guides of French and Spanish. He is
listed in *Contemporary Authors* and the *Directory of American Scholars*.

Dr. Theodore Kendris earned his B.A. degree in Modern Languages at Union College,
Schenectady, New York, where he received the Thomas J. Judson Memorial Award for
modern language study. He went on to earn his M.A. degree in French Language and
Literature at Northwestern University, Evanston, Illinois, where he held a Teaching
Assistantship. He earned his Ph.D. degree in French Literature at Université Laval in
Quebec City, where he studied the Middle Ages and Renaissance. While at Université
Laval he taught French writing skills as a *chargé de cours* in the French as a Second
Language program and, in 1997, he was awarded a doctoral scholarship by the *Fondation
de l'Université Laval*. He has also taught in the Department of English and Foreign Lan-
guages at the University of St. Francis in Joliet, Illinois, as well as the Hazleton Campus
of Penn State University.

Preface to the Sixth Edition

This new edition of *501 French Verbs* has been completely rearranged to help you find the information that you need more quickly. We have also updated the verb lists to account for the ever-changing technological advances in our modern world. We have therefore added to both the French-English and English-French lists of verbs conjugated like model verbs. The model verbs themselves have been revised and include extra material for certain Essential Verbs. These are verbs that we believe will be helpful to students because they represent an important conjugation group or because they are useful in many everyday situations and idiomatic expressions. If you have used *501 French Verbs* in the past, you will notice that you can now find all the learning material before the list of 501 fully conjugated verbs. We have also placed the defective and impersonal verbs in a separate section immediately following the 501 fully conjugated verbs. The numerous verb lists can be found in the back part of the book with handy tabs to help you save time as you study. Don't forget to take advantage of the verb drills and tests with answers explained, beginning on page 50. You will need a lot of practice in French verb forms and tenses in a variety of tests to determine your strengths and weaknesses and to make some things clearer in your mind. You should also review the section on definitions of basic grammatical terms. Many students who study a foreign language are at a disadvantage because they do not understand certain grammatical terms. If you understand these terms you will be able to communicate better in French.

If you can't remember the French verb you need to use, don't forget to refer to the English-French verb index, which starts on page 705. We have made it more comprehensive so that you will rarely need to look elsewhere for what you need.

We are very pleased to offer our new *501 French Verb* CD-ROM activities, which you will find in the back of the book. Have some fun while you practice conjugating French verbs!

We hope that you will make full use of all the features of this new edition and that you will enjoy your exploration of French language and culture.

C.K. and T.K.

Introduction

This self-teaching book of 501 commonly used French verbs for students and travelers provides fingertip access to correct verb forms.

Verb conjugations are usually found scattered in French grammar books and they are difficult to find quickly when needed. Verbs have always been a major problem for students no matter what system or approach the teacher uses. You will master French verb forms if you study this book a few minutes every day.

This book has been compiled in order to help make your work easier and at the same time to teach you French verb forms systematically. It is a useful book because it provides a quick and easy way to find the full conjugation of many French verbs.

The 501 verbs included here are arranged alphabetically by infinitive at the top of each page. The book contains many common verbs of high frequency, both reflexive and non-reflexive, which you need to know. It also contains many other frequently used verbs which are irregular in some way. Beginning on page 733 you can find an additional 2,600 French verbs that are conjugated in the same way as model verbs among the 501. If the verb you have in mind is not given among the 501, consult this list.

The subject pronouns have been omitted from the conjugations in order to emphasize the verb forms. You can find the subject pronouns on page 103. Turn to that page now and become acquainted with them.

The first thing to do when you use this book is to become familiar with it from cover to cover—in particular, the front and back pages where you will find valuable and useful information to make your work easier and more enjoyable. Take a minute right now and familiarize yourself with the following features:

(a)   On page 6 there is an explanation of which verbs are conjugated with *avoir* or *être* to form a compound tense. Study page 6 and refer to it frequently until you master those verbs.

(b)   On page 3 you will find how to form a present participle regularly in French and we give you examples. We also give you the common irregular present participles.

(c)   On page 3 we do the same for past participles, with examples. The present and past participles of each verb are at the top of the page where verb forms are given for a particular verb.

(d)   On page 7 you will find the principal parts of some important verbs, which, in French, are called *Les Temps primitifs.* This is useful because if you know these you can easily form all the tenses and moods from them.

(e)   On pages 4 and 5 there are two tables showing the derivation of tenses of a typical verb conjugated with *avoir* and another conjugated with *être.* These are presented as in a picture so that you can see what tenses are derived from the principal parts.

(f)   On pages 8 and 9 a sample English verb conjugation gives you an idea of the way a verb is expressed in the English tenses. Many people do not know one tense from another because they have never learned the use of verb tenses in a systematic and organized way—not even in English! How can you know, for example, that you need the conditional form of a verb in French when you want to say "*I would go* to the movies if . . ." or the pluperfect tense in French if you want to say "*I had gone* . . ."? The sample English verb conjugation with the names of the tenses and their numerical ranking will help you to distinguish one tense from another so that you will know what tense you need to express a verb in French.

(g) Beginning on page 10 is a summary of meanings and uses of French verb tenses and moods as related to English verb tenses and moods. That section is very important and useful because the seven simple tenses are separated from the seven compound tenses. The name of each tense is given in French and English starting with the present indicative, which is called tense No. 1, because it is the tense most frequently used. A number is assigned to each tense name so that you can fix each one in your mind and associate the tense names and numbers in their logical order. There is a brief explanation of what each tense is and when you use it, and there are examples using verbs in sentences in French and English.

(h) On page 21 is a summary of all the fourteen tenses in French with English equivalents, which have been divided into the seven simple tenses and the seven compound tenses. After referring to that summary frequently, you will soon know that tense No. 1 is the present indicative, tense No. 2 is the imperfect indicative, and so on.

(i) On page 22 you are shown how to form the seven simple tenses for regular verbs and here, again, the same number has been assigned to each tense name. We also explain how each compound tense is based on each simple tense in the table on page 23 and on page 24. Try to see these two divisions as two frames, two pictures, with the seven simple tenses in one frame and the seven compound tenses in another frame. Place them side by side in your mind, and you will see how tense No. 8 is related to tense No. 1, tense No. 9 to tense No. 2, and so on. If you study the numerical arrangement of each of the seven simple tenses and associate the tense number with the tense name, you will find it very easy to learn the names of the seven compound tenses, how they rank numerically according to use, how they are formed, and when they are used. Spend at least ten minutes every day studying these preliminary pages to help you understand better the fourteen tenses in French.

Finally, in the back pages of this book there are useful indexes, an additional 2,600 French verbs that are conjugated like model verbs among the 501, as well as verbs that require certain prepositions. If you refer to these each time you look up verb tense forms for a particular verb, you will increase your knowledge of French vocabulary by leaps and bounds.

Note that each verb that is listed in the Alphabetical Listing of 501 French Verbs is followed by a number in parentheses. This number is the verb number for the purpose of easy cross-referencing in this book.

We sincerely hope that this book will be of some help to you in learning and using French verbs.

Christopher Kendris and Theodore Kendris

Present and past participles in French— Formation

Formation of the present participle in French

The present participle is regularly formed in the following way. Take the **nous** form of the present indicative of the verb you have in mind, drop the ending **-ons** and add **-ant**. That ending is the equivalent to *-ing* in English. Examples:

chantons, chantant   vendons, vendant   allons, allant

finissons, finissant   mangeons, mangeant   travaillons, travaillant

Common irregular present participles

The three common irregular present participles are: **ayant** from **avoir**; **étant** from **être**; **sachant** from **savoir**.

Formation of the past participle in French

The past participle is regularly formed from the infinitive:

-er ending verbs, drop the **-er** and add **é**:   **donner, donné**
-ir ending verbs, drop the **-ir** and add **i**:   **finir, fini**
-re ending verbs, drop the **-re** and add **u**:   **vendre, vendu**

Common irregular past participles

INFINITIVE	PAST PARTICIPLE	INFINITIVE	PAST PARTICIPLE
apprendre	appris	naître	né
asseoir	assis	offrir	offert
avoir	eu	ouvrir	ouvert
boire	bu	paraître	paru
comprendre	compris	permettre	permis
conduire	conduit	plaire	plu
connaître	connu	pleuvoir	plu
construire	construit	pouvoir	pu
courir	couru	prendre	pris
couvrir	couvert	promettre	promis
craindre	craint	recevoir	reçu
croire	cru	revenir	revenu
devenir	devenu	rire	ri
devoir	dû, due	savoir	su
dire	dit	suivre	suivi
écrire	écrit	taire	tu
être	été	tenir	tenu
faire	fait	valoir	valu
falloir	fallu	venir	venu
lire	lu	vivre	vécu
mettre	mis	voir	vu
mourir	mort	vouloir	voulu

Derivation of tenses: Verbs conjugated with *avoir* and *être*

Verbs Conjugated with *avoir*

INFINITIF	PARTICIPE PRÉSENT	PARTICIPE PASSÉ	PRÉSENT DE L'INDICATIF	PASSÉ SIMPLE
donner	donnant	donné	je donne	je donnai

FUTUR	IMPARFAIT DE L'INDICATIF	PASSÉ COMPOSÉ	PRÉSENT DE L'INDICATIF	PASSÉ SIMPLE
donnerai		ai donné		donnai
donneras	donnais	as donné	donne	donnas
donnera	donnais	a donné	donnes	donna
donnerons	donnait	avons donné	donne	donnâmes
donnerez	donnions	avez donné	donnons	donnâtes
donneront	donniez	ont donné	donnez	donnèrent
	donnaient		donnent	

CONDITIONNEL		PLUS-QUE-PARFAIT DE L'INDICATIF	IMPÉRATIF	IMPARFAIT DU SUBJONCTIF
donnerais		avais donné	donne	donnasse
donnerais		avais donné	donnons	donnasses
donnerait		avait donné	donnez	donnât
donnerions		avions donné		donnassions
donneriez		aviez donné	PRÉSENT DU SUBJONCTIF	donnassiez
donneraient		avaient donné		donnassent
			donne	
		PASSÉ ANTÉRIEUR	donnes	
		eus donné	donne	
		eus donné	donnions	
		eut donné	donniez	
		eûmes donné	donnent	
		eûtes donné		
		eurent donné		

FUTUR ANTÉRIEUR	CONDITIONNEL PASSÉ	PASSÉ DU SUBJONCTIF	PLUS-QUE-PARFAIT DU SUBJONCTIF
aurai donné	aurais donné	aie donné	eusse donné
auras donné	aurais donné	aies donné	eusses donné
aura donné	aurait donné	ait donné	eût donné
aurons donné	aurions donné	ayons donné	eussions donné
aurez donné	auriez donné	ayez donné	eussiez donné
auront donné	auraient donné	aient donné	eussent donné

INFINITIF	PARTICIPE PRÉSENT	PARTICIPE PASSÉ	PRÉSENT DE L'INDICATIF	PASSÉ SIMPLE
arriver	arrivant	arrivé	j'arrive	j'arrivai

FUTUR	IMPARFAIT DE L'INDICATIF	PASSÉ COMPOSÉ	PRÉSENT DE L'INDICATIF	PASSÉ SIMPLE
arriverai		suis arrivé(e)		arrivai
arriveras	arrivais	es arrivé(e)	arrive	arrivas
arrivera	arrivais	est arrivé(e)	arrives	arriva
arriverons	arrivait	sommes arrivé(e)s	arrive	arrivâmes
arriverez	arrivions	êtes arrivé(e)(s)	arrivons	arrivâtes
arriveront	arriviez	sont arrivé(e)s	arrivez	arrivèrent
	arrivaient		arrivent	

CONDITIONNEL		PLUS-QUE-PARFAIT DE L'INDICATIF	IMPÉRATIF	IMPARFAIT DU SUBJONCTIF
arriverais		étais arrivé(e)	arrive	arrivasse
arriverais		étais arrivé(e)	arrivons	arrivasses
arriverait		était arrivé(e)	arrivez	arrivât
arriverions		étions arrivé(e)s		arrivassions
arriveriez		étiez arrivé(e)(s)	PRÉSENT DU SUBJONCTIF	arrivassiez
arriveraient		étaient arrivé(e)s	arrive	arrivassent
			arrives	
		PASSÉ ANTÉRIEUR	arrive	
		fus arrivé(e)	arrivions	
		fus arrivé(e)	arriviez	
		fut arrivé(e)	arrivent	
		fûmes arrivé(e)s		
		fûtes arrivé(e)(s)		
		furent arrivé(e)s		

FUTUR ANTÉRIEUR	CONDITIONNEL PASSÉ	PASSÉ DU SUBJONCTIF	PLUS-QUE-PARFAIT DU SUBJONCTIF
serai arrivé(e)	serais arrivé(e)	sois arrivé(e)	fusse arrivé(e)
seras arrivé(e)	serais arrivé(e)	sois arrivé(e)	fusses arrivé(e)
sera arrivé(e)	serait arrivé(e)	soit arrivé(e)	fût arrivé(e)
serons arrivé(e)s	serions arrivé(e)s	soyons arrivé(e)s	fussions arrivé(e)s
serez arrivé(e)(s)	seriez arrivé(e)(s)	soyez arrivé(e)(s)	fussiez arrivé(e)(s)
seront arrivé(e)s	seraient arrivé(e)s	soient arrivé(e)s	fussent arrivé(e)s

Verbs conjugated with *avoir* or *être* to form a compound tense

(a) Generally speaking, a French verb is conjugated with *avoir* to form a compound tense.

(b) All reflexive verbs, for example, *se laver*, are conjugated with *être*.

(c) The following is a list of common non-reflexive verbs that are conjugated with *être*. The verbs marked with asterisks (*) are conjugated with *avoir* when used with a direct object.

1. aller   to go
   Elle est allée au cinéma.
2. arriver   to arrive
   Elle est arrivée à une heure.
3. *descendre   to go down, come down
   Elle est descendue vite.   *She came down quickly.*
   BUT: *Elle a descendu la valise.   *She brought down the suitcase.*
4. devenir   to become
   Elle est devenue docteur.
5. entrer   to enter, go in, come in
   Elle est entrée dans l'école.   *She entered the school.*
   BUT: *Elle a entré la clé dans la serrure.   *She put the key in the lock.*
6. *monter   to go up, come up
   Elle est montée vite.   *She went up quickly.*
   BUT: *Elle a monté l'escalier.   *She went up the stairs.*
7. mourir   to die
   Elle est morte hier.
8. naître   to be born
   Elle est née hier.
9. partir   to leave
   Elle est partie vite.

10. *passer   to go by, to pass by
    Elle est passée chez moi.   *She came by my house.*
    BUT: *Elle m'a passé le sel.   *She passed me the salt.*

    AND: *Elle a passé un examen.   *She took an exam.*

11. *rentrer   to go in again, to return (home)
    Elle est rentrée tôt.   *She returned home early.*
    BUT: *Elle a rentré le chat dans la maison.   *She brought (took) the cat into the house.*

12. rester   to remain, to stay
    Elle est restée chez elle.
13. retourner   to return, to go back
    Elle est retournée à sa place.
14. revenir   to come back
    Elle est revenue hier.
15. *sortir   to go out
    Elle est sortie hier soir.   *She went out last night.*
    BUT: *Elle a sorti son mouchoir.   *She took out her handkerchief.*

16. tomber   to fall
    Elle est tombée.
17. venir   to come
    Elle est venue ce matin.

Principal parts of some important verbs

(*Les Temps primitifs de quelques verbes importants*)

The principal parts of a verb are very important to know because from them you can easily form all the tenses. See the following pages where two tables are given, one showing the derivation of tenses of a verb conjugated with **avoir** and the other with **être**. Note that the headings at the top of each column are the same as the following headings.

INFINITIF	PARTICIPE PRÉSENT	PARTICIPE PASSÉ	PRÉSENT DE L'INDICATIF	PASSÉ SIMPLE
aller	allant	allé	je vais	j'allai
avoir	ayant	eu	j'ai	j'eus
battre	battant	battu	je bats	je battis
boire	buvant	bu	je bois	je bus
craindre	craignant	craint	je crains	je craignis
croire	croyant	cru	je crois	je crus
devoir	devant	dû, due	je dois	je dus
dire	disant	dit	je dis	je dis
écrire	écrivant	écrit	j'écris	j'écrivis
être	étant	été	je suis	je fus
faire	faisant	fait	je fais	je fis
lire	lisant	lu	je lis	je lus
mettre	mettant	mis	je mets	je mis
mourir	mourant	mort	je meurs	je mourus
naître	naissant	né	je nais	je naquis
ouvrir	ouvrant	ouvert	j'ouvre	j'ouvris
porter	portant	porté	je porte	je portai
pouvoir	pouvant	pu	je peux *or* je puis	je pus
prendre	prenant	pris	je prends	je pris
recevoir	recevant	reçu	je reçois	je reçus
savoir	sachant	su	je sais	je sus
venir	venant	venu	je viens	je vins
vivre	vivant	vécu	je vis	je vécus
voir	voyant	vu	je vois	je vis
voler	volant	volé	je vole	je volai

Tip

In the Present indicative (*Présent de l'indicatif*) and the simple past (*Passé simple*) columns above, only the 1st person singular (**je**) forms are given just to get you started. If you cannot recall the remaining verb forms in the *Présent de l'indicatif* and the *Passé simple* of the verbs listed above in the first column under Infinitive (*Infinitif*), please practice them by looking them up in this book, where the infinitive form of the verb is listed alphabetically at the top of each page from verb 1 to 501. When you find them, say them aloud at the same time you practice writing them in French. This is a very useful exercise to do.

Sample English verb conjugation

INFINITIVE to go—aller
PRESENT PARTICIPLE going   *PAST PARTICIPLE* gone

Tense no.	The seven simple tenses
1 *Present indicative*	I go, you go, he (she, it) goes; we go, you go, they go
	or: I do go, you do go, he (she, it) does go; we do go, you do go, they do go
	or: I am going, you are going, he (she, it) is going; we are going, you are going, they are going
2 *Imperfect indicative*	I was going, you were going, he (she, it) was going; we were going, you were going, they were going
	or: I went, you went, he (she, it) went; we went, you went, they went
	or: I used to go, you used to go, he (she, it) used to go; we used to go, you used to go, they used to go
3 *Passé simple*	I went, you went, he (she, it) went; we went, you went, they went
	or: I did go, you did go, he (she, it) did go; we did go, you did go, they did go
4 *Future*	I shall (will) go, you will go, he (she, it) will go; we shall (will) go, you will go, they will go
5 *Conditional*	I would go, you would go, he (she, it) would go; we would go, you would go, they would go
6 *Present subjunctive*	that I may go, that you may go, that he (she, it) may go; that we may go, that you may go, that they may go
7 *Imperfect subjunctive*	that I might go, that you might go, that he (she, it) might go; that we might go, that you might go, that they might go

INFINITIVE to go—aller
PRESENT PARTICIPLE going   *PAST PARTICIPLE* gone

Tense no.	The seven compound tenses
8 *Passé compose*	I have gone, you have gone, he (she, it) has gone; we have gone, you have gone, they have gone
	or: I went, you went, he (she, it) went; we went, you went, they went
	or: I did go, you did go, he (she, it) did go; we did go, you did go, they did go
9 *Pluperfect or Past perfect indicative*	I had gone, you had gone, he (she, it) had gone; we had gone, you had gone, they had gone *deja*
10 *Past anterior*	I had gone, you had gone, he (she, it) had gone; we had gone, you had gone, they had gone
11 *Future perfect or Future anterior*	I shall (will) have gone, you will have gone, he (she, it) will have gone; we shall (will) have gone, you will have gone, they will have gone
12 *Conditional perfect*	I would have gone, you would have gone, he (she, it) would have gone; we would have gone, you would have gone, they would have gone
13 *Past subjunctive*	that I may have gone, that you may have gone, that he (she, it) may have gone; that we may have gone, that you may have gone, that they may have gone
14 *Pluperfect or Past perfect subjunctive*	that I might have gone, that you might have gone, that he (she, it) might have gone; that we might have gone, that you might have gone, that they might have gone
Imperative (Command)	Go! (sing.) Let's go! Go! (pl.)

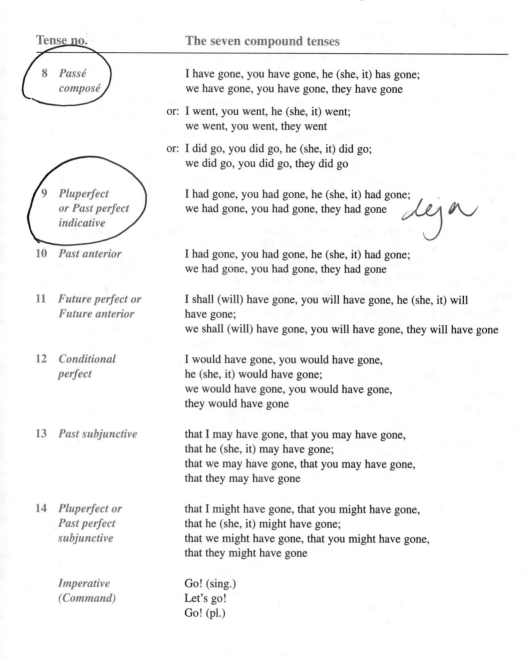

A summary of French verb tenses and moods

A verb is where the action is! A verb is a word that expresses an action (like *go, eat, write*) or a state of being (like *think, believe, be*). Tense means time. French and English verb tenses are divided into three main groups of time: past, present, and future. A verb tense shows if an action or state of being took place, is taking place, or will take place.

French and English verbs are also used in three moods (or modes). Mood has to do with the *way* a person regards an action or a state. For example, a person may merely make a statement or ask a question—this is the Indicative Mood, which we use most of the time in French and English. A person may say that he *would do* something if something else were possible or that he *would have done* something if something else had been possible—this is the Conditional Tense. A person may use a verb *in such a way* to indicate a wish, a fear, a regret, a supposition, or something of this sort—this is the Subjunctive Mood. The Subjunctive Mood is used in French much more than in English. A person may command that something be done—this is the Imperative Mood. (There is also the Infinitive Mood, but we are not concerned with that here.)

There are six tenses in English: Present, Past, Future, Present Perfect, Past Perfect, and Future Perfect. The first three are simple tenses. The other three are compound tenses and are based on the simple tenses. In French, however, there are fourteen tenses, seven of which are simple and seven of which are compound.

In the pages that follow, the tenses and moods are given in French and the equivalent name or names in English are given in parenthesis. Each tense name has been numbered for easy reference and recognition. Although some of the names given in English are not considered to be tenses (there are only six), they are given for the purpose of identification as they are related to the French names. The comparison includes only the essential points you need to know about the meanings and uses of French verb tenses and moods as related to English usage.

The examples serve to illustrate their meanings and uses. See page 22 for the formation of the seven simple tenses for regular verbs.

THE SEVEN SIMPLE TENSES

Tense No. 1   **Le Présent de l'indicatif**
              (Present indicative)

This tense is used most of the time in French and English. It indicates:

(a) An action or a state of being at the present time.
    EXAMPLES:
    1. Je vais à l'école maintenant. I *am going* to school now.
    2. Je pense; donc, je suis. I *think*; therefore, I *am*.

(b) Habitual action.

EXAMPLE:

1. Je **vais** à la bibliothéque tous les jours.
2. I *go* to the library every day, or I *do go* to the library every day.

(c) A general truth, something which is permanently true.

EXAMPLES:

1. Deux et deux **font** quatre. Two and two *are* four.
2. Voir c'**est** croire. Seeing *is* believing.

(d) Vividness when talking or writing about past events. This is called the *historical present*.

EXAMPLE:

Marie-Antoinette **est** condamnée à mort. Elle **monte** dans la charrette et **est** en route pour la guillotine.

Marie-Antoinette *is* condemned to die. She *gets* into the cart and *is* on her way to the guillotine.

(e) A near future.

EXAMPLE:

Il **arrive** demain. He *arrives* tomorrow.

(f) An action or state of being that occurred in the past and *continues up to the present*. In English, this tense is the Present Perfect, which is formed with the present tense of *to have* (*have* or *has*) plus the past participle of the verb you are using.

EXAMPLES:

1. Je **suis** ici depuis dix minutes.
   I *have been* here for ten minutes. (I am still here at present)
2. Elle **est** malade depuis trois jours.
   She *has been* sick for three days. (She is still sick at present)
3. J'**attends** l'autobus depuis dix minutes.
   I *have been waiting* for the bus for ten minutes.

NOTE: In this last example the formation of the English verb tense is slightly different from the other two examples in English. The present participle (*waiting*) is used instead of the past participle (*waited*).

NOTE ALSO: For the formation of this tense for regular verbs see page 22.

Tense No. 2   L'Imparfait de l'indicatif
(Imperfect indicative)

This is a past tense. It is used to indicate:

(a) An action that was going on in the past at the same time as another action.

EXAMPLE:

Il **lisait** pendant que j'**écrivais**. He *was reading* while I *was writing*.

(b) An action that was going on in the past when another action occurred.

EXAMPLE:

Il **lisait** quand je suis entré. He *was reading* when I came in.

..ction that a person did habitually in the past.

EXAMPLE:

Nous **allions** à la plage tous les jours. We *used to go* to the beach every day.

OR:

We *would go* to the beach every day.

(d) A description of a mental or physical condition in the past.

EXAMPLES :

(mental condition)   Il **était** triste quand je l'ai vu.
description   He *was* sad when I saw him.
(physical condition) Quand ma mère **était** jeune, elle **était** belle.
description   When my mother *was* young, she *was* beautiful.

(e) An action or state of being that occurred in the past and *lasted for a certain length of time* prior to another past action. In English, it is usually translated as a pluperfect tense and is formed with *had been* plus the present participle of the verb you are using. It is like the special use of the **Présent de l'indicatif** described in the above section (Tense No. 1) in paragraph (f), except that the action or state of being no longer exists at present.

EXAMPLE:

J'**attendais** l'autobus depuis dix minutes quand il est arrivé.

I *had been waiting* for the bus for ten minutes when it arrived.

NOTE: For the formation of this tense for regular verbs see page 22.

Tense No. 3 Le Passé simple
(Past definite or Simple past)

This past tense is not ordinarily used in conversational French or in informal writing. It is a literary tense. It is used in formal writing, such as history and literature. You should be able merely to recognize this tense when you see it in your French readings. It should be noted that French writers use the **Passé simple** less and less these days. The **Passé composé** (Tense No. 8) is taking its place in literature, except for **avoir** and **être**, which you must know in this tense.

EXAMPLES:

(a) Il **alla** en Afrique. He *went* to Africa.
(b) Il **voyagea** en Amérique. He *traveled* to America.
(c) Elle **fut** heureuse. She *was* happy.
(d) Elle **eut** un grand bonheur. She *had* great happiness.

NOTE: For the formation of this tense for regular verbs see page 22.

Tense No. 4 Le Futur
(Future)

In French and English this tense is used to express an action or a state of being which will take place at some time in the future.

EXAMPLES:

(a) J'**irai** en France l'été prochain.
I *shall go* to France next summer.
OR:
I *will go* to France next summer.

(c) Je **partirai** dès qu'il arrivera.
I *shall leave* as soon as he arrives

(d) Je te **dirai** tout quand tu seras ici.
I *shall tell* you all when you are here.

(b) J'y penserai.
I *shall think* about it.
OR:
I *will think* about it.

If the action of the verb you are using is not past or present and if future time is implied, the future tense is used when the clause begins with any of the following conjunctions: aussitôt que (as soon as), dès que (as soon as), quand (when), lorsque (when), and tant que (as long as).

NOTE: For the formation of this tense for regular verbs see page 22.

Another way to express the future is le Futur proche (the Near Future). As one may guess, the Futur proche is used when talking about something that will take place in the near future. In French, the near future is formed by using aller with the infinitive of the verb that you want to use. In English you use *to go* with the infinitive of the verb that you want to use.

Demain, je vais acheter un ordinateur.
Tomorrow I *am going to buy* a computer.
Nous allons manger en ville.
We are *going to eat* downtown.

Tense No. 5 Le Conditionnel présent
(Conditional)

The Conditional is used in French and English to express:
(a) An action that you would do if something else were possible.
EXAMPLE:
Je ferais le travail si j'avais le temps.
I *would do* the work if I had the time.

(b) A conditional desire. This is the Conditional of courtesy in French.
EXAMPLES:
J'aimerais du thé. I *would like* some tea.
Je voudrais du café. I *would like* some coffee.

(c) An obligation or duty.
EXAMPLE:
Je devrais étudier pour l'examen. I *should* study for the examination.
OR: I *ought* to study for the examination.

NOTE (1): The French verb devoir plus the infinitive is used to express the idea of *should* when you mean *ought to*.

NOTE (2): When the Conditional of the verb pouvoir is used in French, it is translated into English as *could* or *would be able*.
EXAMPLE:
Je pourrais venir après le dîner. I *could come* after dinner.
OR: I *would be able* to come after dinner.

NOTE: For the formation of this tense for regular verbs see page 22.

Tense No. 6   Le Présent du subjonctif
(Present subjunctive)

The Subjunctive Mood is used in French much more than in English. It is disappearing in English, except for the following major uses:

(a) The Subjunctive is used in French and English to express a command.
EXAMPLE:
Soyez à l'heure! *Be* on time!
NOTE: In English, the form in the Subjunctive applies mainly to the verb *to be*. Also, note that all verbs in French are not in the Subjunctive when expressing a command. See l'Impératif on pages 20–21.

(b) The Subjunctive is commonly used in English to express a condition contrary to fact.
EXAMPLE:
If I *were* you, I would not do it.
NOTE: In French the Subjunctive is not used in this instance. Instead, the Imparfait de l'indicatif is used if what precedes is *si* (*if*). Same example in French: Si j'étais vous, je ne le ferais pas.

(c) The Present subjunctive is used in French and English after a verb that expresses some kind of insistence, preference, or suggestion.
EXAMPLES:
1. Je préfère qu'il fasse le travail maintenant. I prefer that *he do* the work now.
2. J'exige qu'il soit puni. I demand that *he be* punished.

(d) The Subjunctive is used in French after a verb that expresses doubt, fear, joy, sorrow, or some other emotion. Notice in the following examples that the Subjunctive is not used in English but it is in French.
EXAMPLES:
1. Je doute qu'il vienne.
   I doubt that he *is coming*.   OR: I doubt that he *will come*.
2. Je suis heureux qu'il vienne.
   I'm happy that he *is coming*.
3. Je regrette qu'il soit malade.
   I'm sorry that he *is* sick.
4. J'ai peur qu'il ne soit malade.
   I'm afraid that he *is* sick.
NOTE: After a verb that expresses fear (used in the affirmative), you should add *ne* before the verb that is in the subjunctive. If the statement is negative, do not add *ne*.

(e) The Present subjunctive is used in French after certain conjunctions. Notice, however, that the Subjunctive is not always used in English.
EXAMPLES:
1. Je resterai jusqu'à ce qu'il vienne.
   I shall stay until he *comes*.
2. Quoiqu'elle soit belle, il ne l'aime pas.
   Although she *is* beautiful, he does not love her.
3. Je l'explique pour qu'elle comprenne.
   I'm explaining it *so that she may understand*.
4. Je partirai à moins qu'il ne vienne.
   I shall leave unless he *comes*.
NOTE: After a verb that expresses the possibility of an obstacle (or of a precaution), you may add *ne* before the verb that is in the subjunctive.

(f) The Present subjunctive is used in French after certain impersonal expressions that show a need, doubt, possibility or impossibility. Notice, however, that the Subjunctive is not always used in English in the following examples:

1. Il est urgent qu'il **vienne**.
   It is urgent that he *come*.
2. Il vaut mieux qu'il **vienne**.
   It is better that he *come*.
3. Il est possible qu'il **vienne**.
   It is possible that he *will come*.
4. Il est douteux qu'il **vienne**.
   It is doubtful that he *will come*.
5. Il est nécessaire qu'il **vienne**.
   It is necessary that he *come*. OR: He must come.
6. Il faut qu'il **vienne**.
   It is necessary that he *come*. OR: He must come.
7. Il est important que vous **fassiez** le travail.
   It is important that you *do* the work.
8. Il est indispensable qu'elle **fasse** le travail.
   It is required that she *do* the work.

NOTE: For the formation of this tense for regular verbs see page 23.
See also the note about the Subjunctive which begins on page 26.

Tense No. 7 L'Imparfait du subjonctif
(Imperfect subjunctive)

L'Imparfait du subjonctif is used for the same reasons as the Présent du subjonctif—that is, after certain verbs, conjunctions, and impersonal expressions which were used in examples above under the section, le Présent du subjonctif. The main difference between these two is the time of the action. If present, use the Présent du subjonctif (Tense No. 6). If the action is related to the past, the Imparfait du subjonctif (this tense) is used, provided that the action was *not* completed. If the action was completed, the Plus-que-parfait du subjonctif is used. See below under the section, Plus-que-parfait du subjonctif (Tense No. 14).

Since the Subjunctive Mood is troublesome in French and English, you may be pleased to know that this tense is rarely used in English. It is used in French, however, but only in formal writing and in literature. For that reason, you should merely be familiar with it so you can recognize it when you see it in your French readings. In conversational French and in informal writing, l'Imparfait du subjonctif is avoided. Use, instead, the Présent du subjonctif.

Notice that the Imparfait du subjonctif is used in French in both of the following examples, but is used in English only in the second example (b):

EXAMPLES:
(a) Je voulais qu'il **vînt**. I wanted him to come.
   (action not completed; he did not come while I wanted him to come)
   NOTE: The Subjunctive of venir is used because the verb that precedes is one that requires the Subjunctive *after* it—in this example it is vouloir. In conversational French and informal writing, the Imparfait du subjonctif is avoided. Use, instead, the Présent du subjonctif: Je voulais qu'il **vienne**.

(b) Je le lui expliquais *pour qu'elle le comprît*.

I was explaining it to her *so that she might understand it*.

(action not completed; the understanding was not completed at the time of the explaining)

NOTE: The Subjunctive of comprendre is used because the conjunction that precedes is one that requires the Subjunctive *after* it—in this example it is pour que. In conversational French and informal writing, the Imparfait du subjonctif is avoided. Use, instead, the Présent du subjonctif: Je le lui expliquais pour qu'elle le comprenne.

NOTE: For the formation of this tense for regular verbs see page 23.
See also the note about the Subjunctive which begins on page 26.

THE SEVEN COMPOUND TENSES

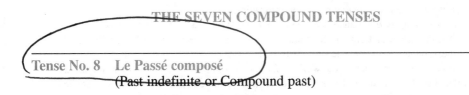

Tense No. 8 Le Passé composé
(Past indefinite or Compound past)

The past tense is used in conversational French, correspondence, and other informal writing. The Passé composé is used more and more in literature these days and is taking the place of the Passé simple (Tense No. 3). It is a compound tense because it is formed with the Présent de l'indicatif (Tense No. 1) of *avoir* or *être* (depending on which of these two auxiliaries is required to form a compound tense) plus the past participle. See page 6 for the distinction made between verbs conjugated with *avoir* or *être*.

EXAMPLES:
1. Il est allé à l'école. He *went* to school.
2. Il est allé à l'école. He *did go* to school.
3. Il est allé à l'école. He *has gone* to school.
4. J'ai mangé dans ce restaurant beaucoup de fois.
   I *have eaten* in this restaurant many times.

NOTE: In examples 3 and 4 in English the verb is formed with the Present tense of *to have* (*have* or *has*) plus the past participle of the verb you are using. In English, this form is called the Present Perfect.

5. J'ai parlé au garçon. I *spoke* to the boy. OR: I *have spoken* to the boy.
   OR: I *did speak* to the boy.

Tense No. 9 Le Plus-que-parfait de l'indicatif
(Pluperfect or Past perfect indicative)

In French and English this tense is used to express an action which happened in the past *before* another past action. Since it is used in relation to another past action, the other past action is expressed in either the Passé composé (Tense No. 8) or the Imparfait de l'indicatif (Tense No. 2) in French. This tense is used in formal writing and literature as well as in conversational French and informal writing. The correct use of this tense is strictly observed in French. In English, however, too often we neglect to use it correctly. It is a compound tense because it is formed with the Impar-fait de l'indicatif of *avoir* or *être* (depending on which of these two auxiliaries is required to form a compound tense) plus the past participle. See page 6 for the distinction made between verbs con-jugated with *avoir* or *être*. In English, this tense is formed with the Past Tense of *to have* (*had*) plus the past participle of the verb you are using.

EXAMPLES:

(a) Je me suis rappelé que j'avais oublié de le lui dire.
I remembered that I *had forgotten* to tell him.

NOTE: It would be incorrect in English to say: I remembered that I *forgot* to tell him. The point here is that *first* I forgot; then, I remembered. Both actions are in the past. The action that occurred in the past *before* the other past action is in the Pluperfect. And in this example it is *I had forgotten* (j'avais oublié).

(b) J'avais étudié la leçon que le professeur a expliquée.
I *had studied* the lesson which the teacher explained.

NOTE: *First* I studied the lesson; then, the teacher explained it. Both actions are in the past. The action that occurred in the past *before* the other past action is in the Pluperfect. And in this example it is *I had studied* (j'avais étudié). If you say J'ai étudié la leçon que le professeur avait expliquée, you are saying that you *studied* the lesson which the teacher *had explained*. In other words, the teacher explained the lesson first and then you studied it.

(c) J'étais fatigué ce matin parce que je n'avais pas dormi.
I was tired this morning because I *had* not *slept*.

Tense No. 10   Le Passé antérieur
                (Past anterior)

This tense is similar to the Plus-que-parfait de l'indicatif (Tense No. 9). The main difference is that in French it is a literary tense; that is, it is used in formal writing, such as history and literature. More and more French writers today use the Plus-que-parfait de l'indicatif instead of this tense. Generally speaking, the Passé antérieur is to the Plus-que-parfait what the Passé simple is to the Passé composé. The Passé antérieur is a compound tense. In French, it is formed with the Passé simple of *avoir* or *être* (depending on which of these two auxiliaries is required to form a com-pound tense—see page 6) plus the past participle. In English, it is formed in the same way as the Pluperfect or Past Perfect. This tense is ordinarily introduced by conjunctions of time: après que, aussitôt que, dès que, lorsque, quand.

EXAMPLE:
Quand il eut mangé son dessert, il partit. When he *had eaten* his dessert, he left.

NOTE: In conversational French and informal writing, the Plus-que-parfait de l'indicatif is used instead: Quand il avait mangé son dessert, il est parti. The translation into English is the same.

Tense No. 11 Le Futur antérieur
(Future perfect or Future anterior)

In French and English this tense is used to express an action which will happen in the future *before* another future action. Since it is used in relation to another future action, the other future action is expressed in the simple Future in French, but not always in the simple Future in English. In French, it is used in conversation and informal writing as well as in formal writing and in literature. It is a compound tense because it is formed with the **Futur** of *avoir* or *être* (depending on which of these two auxiliaries is required to form a compound tense—see page 6) plus the past participle of the verb you are using. In English, it is formed by using *shall have* or *will have* plus the past participle of the verb you are using.

EXAMPLES:
(a) Elle arrivera demain et j'**aurai fini** le travail.
She will arrive tomorrow and I *shall have finished* the work.

NOTE: First, I shall finish the work; then, she will arrive. The action that will occur in the future *before* the other future action is in the **Futur antérieur.**

(b) Quand elle arrivera demain, j'**aurai fini** le travail.
When she arrives tomorrow, I *shall have finished* the work.

NOTE: The idea of future time here is the same as in example (a) above. In English, the Present tense is used (*When she arrives . . .*) to express a near future. In French, the **Futur** is used (**Quand elle arrivera . . .**) because **quand** precedes and the action will take place in the future. Study Tense No. 4 on pages 12–13.

Tense No. 12 Le Conditionnel passé
(Conditional perfect)

This is used in French and English to express an action that you *would have done* if something else had been possible; that is, you would have done something *on condition* that something else had been possible. It is a compound tense because it is formed with the **Conditionnel présent** of *avoir* or *être* plus the past participle of the verb you are using. In English, it is formed by using *would have* plus the past participle. Observe the difference between the following examples and the one given for the use of the **Conditionnel présent** which was explained and illustrated in Tense No. 5 above.

EXAMPLES:
(a) J'**aurais fait** le travail si j'avais étudié.
I *would have done* the work if I had studied.

(b) J'**aurais fait** le travail si j'avais eu le temps.
I *would have done* the work if I had had the time.

NOTE: Review the **Plus-que-parfait de l'indicatif** which was explained above in Tense No. 9 in order to understand the use of *if I had studied* (si j'avais étudié) and *if I had had the time* (si j'avais eu le temps).

NOTE FURTHER: The French verb **devoir** plus the infinitive is used to express the idea of *should* when you mean *ought to*. The past participle of **devoir** is **dû**. It is conjugated with **avoir.**

EXAMPLE:
J'**aurais dû** étudier.
I *should have* studied. OR: I *ought to have* studied.

Tense No. 13   Le Passé du subjonctif
(Past or Perfect subjunctive)

This tense is used to express an action which took place in the past in relation to the present time. It is like the **Passé composé**, except that the auxiliary verb (*avoir* or *être*) is in the **Présent du subjonctif.** The Subjunctive is used (as was noted in the previous sections of verb tenses in the Subjunctive) because what precedes is a certain verb, a certain conjunction, or a certain impersonal expression. The **Passé du subjonctif** is also used in relation to a future time when another action will be completed. This tense is rarely used in English. In French, however, this tense is used in formal writing and in literature as well as in conversational French and informal writing. It is a compound tense because it is formed with the **Présent du subjonctif** of *avoir* or *être* as the auxiliary plus the past participle of the verb you are using.

EXAMPLES:
(a) A past action in relation to the present
Il est possible qu'elle **soit partie.**
It is possible that she *may have left.* OR: It is possible that she *has left.*
Je doute qu'il **ait fait** cela.
I doubt that he *did* that.

(b) An action that will take place in the future

J'insiste que vous **soyez rentré** avant dix heures.
I insist that you *be back* before ten o'clock.

See also the note about the Subjunctive which begins on page 26.

Tense No. 14   Le Plus-que-parfait du subjonctif
(Pluperfect or Past perfect subjunctive)

This tense is used for the same reasons as the **Imparfait du subjonctif** (Tense No. 7)—that is, after certain verbs, conjunctions, and impersonal expressions which were used in examples previously under **le Présent du subjonctif.** The main difference between the **Imparfait du subjonctif** and this tense is the time of the action in the past. If the action was *not* completed, the **Imparfait du subjonctif** is used. If the action was completed, this tense is used. It is rarely used in English. In French, it is used only in formal writing and in literature. For that reason, you should merely be familiar with it so you can recognize it in your readings in French literature. In conversational French and in informal writing, this tense is avoided. Use, instead, the **Passé du subjonctif** (Tense No. 13).

This is a compound tense. It is formed by using the Imparfait du subjonctif of *avoir* or *être* plus the past participle. This tense is like the Plus-que-parfait de l'indicatif, except that the auxiliary verb (*avoir* or *être*) is in the Imparfait du subjonctif. Review the uses of the Subjunctive Mood in Tense No. 6.

EXAMPLES:

(a) Il était possible qu'elle fût partie.
It was possible that she *might have left.*

NOTE: Avoid this tense in conversational and informal French. Use, instead, le Passé du subjonctif:
Il était possible qu'elle soit partie.

(b) Je ne croyais pas qu'elle eût dit cela.
I did not believe that she *had said* that.

NOTE: Avoid this tense in conversational and informal French. Use, instead, le Passé du subjonctif:
Je ne croyais pas qu'elle ait dit cela.

(c) Je n'ai pas cru qu'elle eût dit cela.
I did not believe that she *had said* that.

NOTE: Avoid this tense in conversational and informal French. Use, instead, le Passé du subjonctif:
Je n'ai pas cru qu'elle ait dit cela.

(d) J'ai craint que vous ne fussiez tombé.
I was afraid that you *had fallen.*

NOTE: Avoid this tense in conversational and informal French. Use, instead, le Passé du subjonctif:
J'ai craint que vous ne soyez tombé.

NOTE: After a verb that expresses fear (used in the affirmative), you should add *ne* before the verb that is in the subjunctive. If the statement is negative, do not add *ne*.

See also the note about the Subjunctive which begins on page 26.

L'Impératif
(Imperative or Command)

The Imperative Mood is used in French and English to express a command or a request. It is also used to express an indirect request made in the third person, as in (e) and (f) below. In both languages it is formed by dropping the subject pronoun and using the present tense. Remember that you must drop the final *s* in the second person singular of an *-er* verb (Tu danses—Danse!) There are a few exceptions in both languages when the Présent du subjonctif is used.

EXAMPLES:

(a) Sortez! Get out!

(b) Entrez! Come in!

(c) Buvons! Let's drink!

(d) Soyez à l'heure! *Be* on time! (Subjunctive is used.)

(e) Dieu le veuille! May God *grant* it! or *God willing!* (Subjunctive is used.)

(f) Qu'ils mangent du gâteau! Let them *eat* cake! (Subjunctive is used.)

(g) Asseyez-vous! Sit down!

(h) Levez-vous! Get up!

(i) Ne vous asseyez pas! Don't sit down!

(j) Ne vous levez pas! Don't get up!

NOTE: The Imperative is not a tense. It is a mood.

NOTE FURTHER: If you use a reflexive verb in the Imperative, drop the subject pronoun but keep the reflexive pronoun. Example: Lavez-vous! Wash yourself! See also examples (g) through (j).

Summary of verb tenses and moods in French with English equivalents

Les sept temps simples *The seven simple tenses*		Les sept temps composés *The seven compound tenses*	
Tense No.	Tense Name	Tense No.	Tense Name
1	Présent de l'indicatif *Present indicative*	8	Passé composé
2	Imparfait de l'indicatif *Imperfect indicative*	9	Plus-que-parfait de l'indicatif *Pluperfect indicative*
3	Passé simple *Past definite or Simple past*	10	Passé antérieur *Past anterior*
4	Futur *Future*	11	Futur antérieur *Future perfect*
5	Conditionnel *Conditional*	12	Conditionnel passé *Conditional perfect*
6	Présent du subjonctif *Present subjunctive*	13	Passé du subjonctif *Past subjunctive*
7	Imparfait du subjonctif *Imperfect subjunctive*	14	Plus-que-parfait du subjonctif *Pluperfect subjunctive*

The imperative is not a tense; it is a mood.

nple tenses and seven compound tenses. A simple tense
nsists of one word. A compound tense is a verb form that con-
iary verb and the past participle). The auxiliary verb is also
French it is any of the seven simple tenses of avoir or être.

: SEVEN SIMPLE TENSES FOR REGULAR VERBS

Tense No. 1 Présent de l'indicatif
(Present indicative)

-er verbs: drop -er and add e, es, e; ons, ez, ent

-ir verbs: drop -ir and add is, is, it; issons, issez, issent

-re verbs: drop -re and add s, s, -; ons, ez, ent

Tense No. 2 Imparfait de l'indicatif
(Imperfect indicative)

Was reading?

For -er, -ir, -re verbs, take the "nous" form in the present indicative of the verb you have
in mind, drop the ending -ons and add: ais, ais, ait; ions, iez, aient

---

Tense No. 3 Passé simple
(Past definite or Simple past)

For all -er verbs, drop -er and add ai, as, a; âmes, âtes, èrent
For -ir and -re verbs, drop the ending of the Infinitive and add is, is, it; îmes, îtes, irent

---

Tense No. 4 Futur
(Future)

Add the following endings to the whole infinitive, but for -re verbs drop e in -re before
adding the future endings, which are: ai, as, a; ons, ez, ont. Note that these endings are
based on the Present indicative of avoir.

Tense No. 5 Conditionnel
(Conditional)

would, could, should might to

Add the following endings to the whole infinitive, but for -re verbs drop e in -re before
adding the conditional endings, which are: ais, ais, ait; ions, iez, aient. Note that these
endings are the same as those for the Imperfect indicative (Tense No. 2).

Tense No. 6 Présent du subjonctif
(Present subjunctive)

Drop -ant ending of the present participle of the verb you have in mind and add e, es, e; ions, iez, ent

Tense No. 7 Imparfait du subjonctif
(Imperfect subjunctive)

There is a shortcut to finding the forms of this difficult tense. Go straight to the 3d person, singular, Passé simple tense of the verb you have in mind. If the ending is -a, as in parla (parler), drop -a and add -asse, -asses, -ât; -assions, -assiez, -assent. If the ending is -it, as in finit (finir) or vendit (vendre), drop -it and add -isse, -isses, -ît; -issions, -issiez, -issent. If you find the ending -ut, as in many irregular -re verbs (lire/lut), drop -ut and add -usse, -usses, -ût; -ussions, -ussiez, -ussent. Note the accent mark (ˆ) on -ât, -ît, and -ût.

NOTE:
(a) For the forms of irregular verbs, *e.g.*, avoir, être, faire, aller, and many others, turn to the page where the verb you have in mind is given in this book. All verbs are listed alphabetically at the top of each page.
(b) For the uses of the seven simple tenses, see pages 10–16.
(c) For the formation of the seven compound tenses and their uses, see pages 16–20 and the section below.

FORMATION OF THE SEVEN COMPOUND TENSES

An Easy Way to Form the Seven Compound Tenses in French

avoir or être* in the following simple tenses **+** PLUS the past participle of the verb you have in mind** **=** EQUALS the following compound tenses

1. Présent de l'indicatif	8. Passé composé
2. Imparfait de l'indicatif	9. Plus-que-parfait de l'indicatif
3. Passé simple	10. Passé antérieur
4. Futur	11. Futur antérieur
5. Conditionnel	12. Conditionnel passé
6. Présent du subjonctif	13. Passé du subjonctif
7. Imparfait du subjonctif	14. Plus-que-parfait du subjonctif

* To know if avoir or être is required, see page 6.
** To know how to form a past participle, see page 3.

Each compound tense is based on each simple tense. The fourteen tenses given on page 23 are arranged in a logical order, which is numerical.

Here is how you form each of the seven compound tenses:

Tense No. 8 is based on Tense No. 1 of avoir or être; in other words, you form the Passé composé by using the auxiliary avoir or être (whichever is appropriate) in the Présent de l'indicatif plus the past participle of the verb you have in mind. Examples: j'ai parlé; je suis allé(e).

Tense No. 9 is based on Tense No. 2 of avoir or être; in other words, you form the Plus-que-parfait de l'indicatif by using the auxiliary avoir or être (whichever is appropriate) in the Imparfait de l'indicatif plus the past participle of the verb you have in mind. Examples: j'avais parlé; j'étais allé(e).

Tense No. 10 is based on Tense No. 3 of avoir or être; in other words, you form the Passé antérieur by using the auxiliary avoir or être (whichever is appropriate) in the Passé simple plus the past participle of the verb you have in mind. Examples: j'eus parlé; je fus allé(e).

Tense No. 11 is based on Tense No. 4 of avoir or être; in other words, you form the Futur antérieur by using the auxiliary avoir or être (whichever is appropriate) in the Futur plus the past participle of the verb you have in mind. Examples: j'aurai parlé; je serai allé(e).

Tense No. 12 is based on Tense No. 5 of avoir or être; in other words, you form the Conditionnel passé by using the auxiliary avoir or être (whichever is appropriate) in the Conditionnel plus the past participle of the verb you have in mind. Examples: j'aurais parlé; je serais allé(e).

Tense No. 13 is based on Tense No. 6 of avoir or être; in other words, you form the Passé du subjonctif by using the auxiliary avoir or être (whichever is appropriate) in the Présent du subjonctif plus the past participle of the verb you have in mind. Examples: que j'aie parlé; que je sois allé(e). This tense is like the Passé composé (tense number 8), except that the auxiliary verb avoir or être is in the present subjunctive.

Tense No. 14 is based on Tense No. 7 of avoir or être; in other words, you form the Plus-que-parfait du subjonctif by using the auxiliary avoir or être (whichever is appropriate) in the Imparfait du subjonctif plus the past participle of the verb you have in mind. Examples: que j'eusse parlé; que je fusse allé(e).

If you ever expect to know or even recognize the meaning of any of the seven compound tenses, or to know how to form them, you certainly have to know avoir and être in the seven simple tenses. If you do not, you cannot form the seven compound tenses—and they are the easiest to form. This is one perfect example to illustrate that learning French verb forms is a cumulative experience because in order to know the seven compound tenses, you must first know the forms of avoir and être in the seven simple tenses. They are verbs 62 and 211 in this book.

To know which verbs are conjugated with avoir or être to form the seven compound tenses, see page 6. To understand the uses of the seven simple tenses, see pages 10–16. To understand the uses of the seven compound tenses, see pages 16–20. To know the translation of all fourteen tenses into English, see pages 8–9.

A Note about the *Passé surcomposé* verb tense

There is another verb tense in French but it is rarely used. It is called *le Passé surcomposé*. It gets its name from the fact that the auxiliary (helping) verb is already stated in a *Passé composé* form. In other words, it is "extra" passé composé, just as surchauffé means *overheated* or surnatural means *supernatural*. The *Surcomposé* contains two auxiliary verbs and it is used in the subordinate clause when the verb of the main clause is in a compound tense. Examples: j'ai eu (*I have had*, or *I had*); j'ai été (*I have been*, or *I was*). To change the compound form into a *Surcomposé*, the past participle of the verb you have in mind is stated with the double helping verb. Examples: Mon ami est arrivé quand j'ai eu fini la leçon / *My friend arrived when I (have had) finished the lesson*. The verb form in the subordinate clause with a double helping verb (j'ai eu fini) is what makes the form *Surcomposé*. In English, some people call it *double* or *super compound*. It has also been used in other compound tenses with avoir or être as the helping verb. Nowadays, one hardly ever hears this unusual verb form, but it's worth being aware of in case you come across it in your readings in French literature.

A summary of sequence of verb tenses— *Si* clauses

WHEN THE VERB IN THE
SI CLAUSE IS: THE VERB IN THE MAIN OR RESULT CLAUSE IS:

(a) present indicative   present indicative, or future, or imperative
(b) imperfect indicative   conditional
(c) pluperfect indicative   conditional perfect

NOTE: By si we mean *if*. Sometimes si can mean *whether*, and in that case this summary of what tenses are used does not apply. When si means *whether*, there are no restrictions about the tenses. By the way, the sequence of tenses with a si clause in French is the same as it is in English with an *if* clause.

Example:
   (a) Si elle arrive, je pars.   If she arrives, I'm leaving.
       Si elle arrive, je partirai.   If she arrives, I will leave.
       Si elle arrive, partez!   If she arrives, leave!

   (b) Si elle arrivait, je partirais.   If she arrived, I would leave.

   (c) Si elle était arrivée, je serais parti.   If she had arrived, I would have left.

The Subjunctive

The subjunctive is not a tense; it is a mood, or mode. Usually, when we speak in French or English, we use the indicative mood. We use the subjunctive mood in French for certain reasons. The following are the principal reasons.

After certain conjunctions

When the following conjunctions introduce a new clause, the verb in that new clause is normally in the subjunctive mood:

à condition que   on condition that; **Je vous prêterai l'argent à condition que vous me le rendiez le plutôt possible.**

à moins que   unless; **Je pars à six heures précises à moins qu'il (n') y ait un orage.** [Expletive ne is optional]

afin que   in order that, so that; **Je vous explique clairement afin que vous compreniez.**

attendre que   to wait until; **Attendez que je finisse mon dîner.**

au cas que   in case; **Au cas qu'il vienne, je pars tout de suite.**

autant que   **Autant que je le sache . . .**   As far as I know . . .

avant que   before; **Ne me dites rien avant qu'il vienne.** [Expletive ne is optional]

bien que   although; **Bien que Madame Cartier soit malade, elle a toujours bon appétit.**

de crainte que   for fear that; **La mère a dit à sa petite fille de rester dans la maison de crainte qu'elle ne se fasse mal dans la rue.** [Expletive ne is required]

de façon que   so that, in a way that, in such a way that; **Barbara étudie de façon qu'elle puisse réussir.**

de manière que   so that, in a way that, in such a way that; **Joseph travaille dans la salle de classe de manière qu'il puisse réussir.**

de peur que   for fear that; **Je vous dis de rester dans la maison aujourd'hui de peur que vous ne glissiez sur la glace.** [Expletive **ne** is required]

de sorte que   so that, in a way that, in such a way that; **Nettoyez la chambre de sorte que tout soit propre.**

en attendant que   until; **Nous allons rester ici en attendant qu'elle vienne.**

jusqu'à ce que   until; **Je vais attendre jusqu'à ce que vous finissiez.**

malgré que   although; **Malgré que Madame Cartier soit malade, elle a toujours bon appétit.** (NOTE: It is preferable to use **bien que**, as in the example given with **bien que** above on this list)

pour autant que   as far as, as much as; **Pour autant que je me souvienne . . .** As far as I remember (NOTE: It is preferable to use **autant que**, as in the example given with **autant que** above on this list)

pour que   in order that, so that; **Expliquez-vous mieux, s'il vous plaît, pour que je comprenne.**

pourvu que   provided that; **Vous pouvez parler librement pourvu que vous me laissiez faire de même.**

que . . . ou non   whether . . . or not; **Qu'il vienne ou non, cela m'est égal.**

quoique   although; **Quoiqu'il soit vieux, il a l'agilité d'un jeune homme.**

sans que . . . ou que   whether . . . or; either . . . or; **Soit qu'elle comprenne ou qu'elle ne comprenne pas, cela m'est égal.**

soit que . . . soit que   whether . . . or whether; **Soit que vous le fassiez, soit que vous ne le fassiez pas, cela m'est égal.**

tâcher que   to try to, to attempt to; **Tâchez que le bébé soit bien nourri.**

veiller à ce que   to see to it that; **Veillez à ce que la porte soit fermée à clef pendant mon absence.**

After indefinite expressions

où que   wherever; **Où que vous alliez, cela ne m'importe pas.**

quel que   whatever; **Je vous aiderai, quelles que soient vos ambitions** / I will help you, whatever your ambitions may be. (NOTE that the appropriate form of **quel** is needed in this indefinite expression because you are dealing with a noun (**ambitions**) and **quel** functions as an adjective)

qui que   whoever; **Qui que vous soyez, je ne veux pas vous écouter** / Whoever you are (Whoever you may be), I don't want to listen to you.

quoi que   whatever, no matter what; **Quoi que cet homme dise, je ne le crois pas** / No matter what this man says, I do not believe him.

Si + adj. + que   however; **Si bavarde qu'elle soit, elle ne dit jamais de bêtises** / However talkative she may be, she never says anything stupid.

After an indefinite antecedent

The reason why the subjunctive is needed after an indefinite antecedent is that the person or thing desired may possibly not exist; or, if it does exist, you may never find it.

(a) **Je cherche une personne qui soit honnête** / I am looking for a person who is honest.

(b) **Je cherche un appartement qui ne soit pas trop cher** / I am looking for an apartment that is not too expensive.

(c) **Connaissez-vous quelqu'un qui puisse réparer mon téléviseur une fois pour toutes?** / Do you know someone who can repair my TV set once and for all?

(d) **Y a-t-il un élève qui comprenne le subjonctif?** / Is there a student who understands the subjunctive?

BUT IF THE PERSON OR THING YOU ARE LOOKING FOR DOES EXIST, USE THE INDICATIVE MOOD:

(a) **J'ai trouvé une personne qui est honnête.**

(b) **J'ai un appartement qui n'est pas trop cher.**

(c) **Je connais une personne qui peut réparer votre téléviseur.**

After a superlative expressing an opinion

Those superlatives expressing an opinion are commonly: le seul, la seule (the only), le premier, la première (the first), le dernier, la dernière (the last), le plus petit, la plus petite (the smallest), le plus grand, la plus grande, *etc.*

(a) **A mon avis, Marie est la seule étudiante qui comprenne le subjonctif parfaitement.**

(b) **A mon opinion, Henriette est la plus jolie élève que j'aie jamais vue.**

After Que, meaning *let* or *may* to express a wish, an order, a command in the 3d person singular or plural

(a) **Qu'il parte!** / Let him leave!

(b) **Que Dieu nous pardonne!** / May God forgive us! (NOTE that the form ***pardonne*** is the same in the 3d pers. subjunctive as in the indicative)

(c) **Qu'ils s'en aillent!** / Let them go away!
(NOTE that what is understood in front of Que here is (Je veux) que . . .)

After certain impersonal expressions

c'est dommage que   it's a pity that; it's too bad that; C'est dommage qu'elle soit morte.

il est à souhaiter que   it is to be desired that; Il est à souhaiter qu'elle soit guérie.

il est bizarre que   it is odd that; Il est bizarre qu'il soit parti sans rien dire.

il est bon que   it is good that; Il est bon que vous restiez au lit.

il est convenable que   it is fitting (proper) that; Il est convenable qu'il vienne me voir.

il est douteux que   it is doubtful that; Il est douteux qu'il soit présent au concert ce soir.

il est essentiel que   it is essential that; Il est essentiel que vous veniez me voir le plus tôt possible.

il est étonnant que   it is astonishing that; Il est étonnant qu'elle soit sortie sans rien dire.

il est étrange que   it is strange that; Il est étrange qu'il n'ait pas répondu à ta lettre.

il est faux que   it is false (it is not true) that; Il est faux que vous ayez vu ma soeur dans ce cabaret.

il est heureux que   it is fortunate that; Il est très heureux que Madame Piquet soit guérie.

il est honteux que   it is shameful (a shame) that; Il est honteux que vous trichiez.

il est important que   it is important that; Il est important que vous arriviez à l'heure.

il est impossible que   it is impossible that; Il est impossible que je sois chez vous avant trois heures.

il est juste que   it is right that; Il est juste que le criminel soit puni pour son crime.

il est naturel que   it is natural that; Il est naturel qu'on ait peur dans un moment dangereux.

il est nécessaire que   it is necessary that; Il est nécessaire que tu finisses la leçon de français avant d'aller au cinéma.

il est possible que   it is possible that; Il est possible que Madame Paquet soit déjà partie.

il est rare que   it is rare that; Il est rare qu'elle sorte.

il est regrettable que   it is regrettable that; Il est regrettable que cet homme riche ait perdu tout au jeu.

il est surprenant que   it is surprising that; Il est surprenant que tu n'aies pas fait ton devoir aujourd'hui.

il est temps que   it is time that; Il est temps que tu fasses tes devoirs tous les jours.

il est urgent que   it is urgent that; Il est urgent que le docteur vienne immédiatement.

il faut que   it is necessary that; Il faut que tu sois ici à neuf heures précises.

il importe que   it is important that; Il importe que tu me dises toute la vérité.

il se peut que   it may be that; Il se peut qu'elle soit sortie.

il semble que   it seems that, it appears that; Il semble que Madame Gervaise soit déjà partie.

il suffit que   it is enough that, it suffices that; Il suffit qu'il soit informé tout simplement.

il vaut mieux que   it is better that; Il vaut mieux que vous soyez présent quand le docteur est ici.

After the following impersonal expressions (in English, the subject is *It*) used in the negative or interrogative because they suggest some kind of doubt, uncertainty, hesitation . . .

Il ne me semble pas que . . .	Il ne paraît pas que . . .
Me semble-t-il que . . . ?	Paraît-il que . . . ?
Il n'est pas clair que . . .	Il n'est pas vrai que . . .
Est-il clair que . . . ?	Est-il vrai que . . . ?

Il n'est pas évident que . . .　　　　Il n'est pas sûr que . . .
Est-il évident que . . . ?　　　　　　Est-il sûr que . . . ?

Il n'est pas certain que . . .　　　　Il n'est pas probable que . . .
Est-il certain que . . . ?　　　　　　Est-il probable que . . . ?

After certain verbs expressing doubt, emotion, wishing

aimer que . . .
　to like that . . .
aimer mieux que . . .
　to prefer that . . .
s'attendre à ce que . . .
　to expect that . . .
avoir peur que . . .
　to be afraid that . . .
　[expletive **ne** is required]
craindre que . . .
　to fear that . . .
　[expletive **ne** is required]
défendre que . . .
　to forbid that . . .
désirer que . . .
　to desire that . . .
douter que . . .
　to doubt that . . .
empêcher que . . .
　to prevent that . . .
s'étonner que . . .
　to be astonished that . . .
s'étonner de ce que . . .
　to be astonished at the fact that . . .
être bien aise que . . .
　to be pleased that . . .
être content que . . .
　to be glad that . . .
être désolé que . . .
　to be distressed that . . .
être étonné que . . .
　to be astonished that . . .

être heureux que . . .
　to be happy that . . .
être joyeux que . . .
　to be joyful that . . .
être malheureux que . . .
　to be unhappy that . . .
être ravi que . . .
　to be delighted that . . .
être surpris que . . .
　to be surprised that . . .
être triste que . . .
　to be sad that . . .
exiger que . . .
　to demand that . . .
se fâcher que . . .
　to be angry that . . .
ordonner que . . .
　to order that . . .
préférer que . . .
　to prefer that . . .
regretter que . . .
　to regret that . . .
souhaiter que . . .
　to wish that . . .
tenir à ce que . . .
　to insist upon . . .
trembler que . . .
　to tremble that . . .
　[expletive **ne** is required]
vouloir que . . .
　to want that . . .

SOME EXAMPLES:
　J'aimerais que vous restiez ici / I would like you to stay here.
　J'aime mieux que vous restiez ici / I prefer that you stay here.
　Je m'attends à ce qu'elle vienne immédiatement / I expect her to come
　　immediately.

J'ai peur qu'il ne soit malade / I am afraid that he may be sick. [expletive **ne** is required]

Je crains qu'elle ne soit gravement malade / I fear that she may be seriously ill. [expletive **ne** is required]

Je m'étonne qu'elle ne soit pas venue me voir / I am astonished that she has not come to see me.

Je m'étonne de ce qu'il ne soit pas parti / I am astonished (at the fact that) he has not left.

Ta mère est contente que tu sois heureux / Your mother is glad that you are happy.

Madame Poulet est désolée que son mari ait perdu toute sa fortune / Mrs. Poulet is distressed that her husband has lost his entire fortune.

After verbs of believing and thinking, such as **croire, penser, trouver** (meaning *to think, to have an impression*), and **espérer** when used in the negative OR interrogative but not when both interrogative AND negative . . .

EXAMPLES:

Je ne pense pas qu'il soit coupable / I don't think that he is guilty. **Croyez-vous qu'il dise la vérité?** / Do you believe he is telling the truth?

BUT: **Ne croyez-vous pas qu'il dit la vérité?** / Don't you think that he is telling the truth?

Trouvez-vous qu'il y ait beaucoup de crimes dans la société d'aujourd'hui? Do you find (think) that there are many crimes in today's society?

BUT: **Ne trouvez-vous pas que ce livre est intéressant?** / Don't you think (*or:* Don't you find) that this book is interesting?

Note: The subjunctive forms in Tense No. 6 (**présent du subjonctif**), Tense No. 7 (**imparfait du subjonctif**), Tense No. 13 (**passé du subjonctif**), and Tense No. 14 (**plus-que-parfait du subjonctif**) of any verb are normally preceded by **que** (that); for example, **que je sois** / that I may be, **que tu ailles** / that you may go.

Orthographically changing verbs— verb forms that change in spelling

Verbs that end in -cer in the infinitive form change c to ç when in front of the vowels a, o or u in order to keep the s sound in the infinitive form and retain its identity. That little mark under the c (ç) is called une cédille. Actually it is the lower part of the letter s which is used in order to tell the reader that the ç should be pronounced as an s. Without that mark, the letter c in front of the vowels a, o and u must be pronounced as a k sound. Since the c in the ending -cer is pronounced like an s, the same sound must be retained in all its forms.

(1) Some common verbs that end in -cer in the infinitive form are:

annoncer / to announce
avancer / to advance
commencer / to begin, to start
divorcer / to divorce
effacer / to erase, to efface

lancer / to launch, to hurl
menacer / to threaten
placer / to place, to set
prononcer / to pronounce
remplacer / to replace

(2) Examples of when this change occurs:

Present indicative: nous annonçons, nous avançons, nous commençons, nous divorçons, nous effaçons, nous lançons, nous menaçons, nous prononçons, nous remplaçons.

Imperfect indicative: j'annonçais, tu annonçais, il (elle, on) annonçait; ils (elles) annonçaient [You do the same for the other -cer type verbs given above in (1).]

Passé simple: j'annonçai, tu annonças, il (elle, on) annonça; nous annonçâmes, vous annonçâtes [You do the same for the other -cer type verbs given above in (1).]

Imperfect subjunctive: que j'annonçasse, que tu annonçasses, qu'il (qu'elle, qu'on) annonçât; que nous annonçassions, que vous annonçassiez, qu'ils (qu'elles) annonçassent [Now you do the same for the other -cer type verbs given above in (1).]

(3) Verbs that end in -ger in the infinitive form change g to ge in front of the vowels a, o or u in order to keep the soft sound of g in the infinitive form and retain its identity; otherwise, g in front of a, o or u is normally pronounced hard, as in go.

(4) Some common verbs that end in -ger in the infinitive form are:

arranger / to arrange
changer / to change
corriger / to correct
déranger / to disturb
manger / to eat
nager / to swim
neiger / to snow

obliger / to oblige
partager / to divide, to share
plonger / to dive, to plunge
ranger / to arrange by row, put
   in order
songer / to think, to dream
voyager / to travel

(5) Examples of when this change occurs:

Present indicative: nous arrangeons, nous changeons, nous corrigeons, nous dérangeons [Now you do the same for the other -ger type verbs given above in (4).]

Imperfect indicative: j'arrangeais, tu arrangeais, il (elle, on) arrangeait; ils (elles) arrangeaient [Now you do the same for the other -ger type verbs given above in (4).]

Passé simple: j'arrangeai, tu arrangeas, il (elle, on) arrangea; nous arrangeâmes, vous arrangeâtes [Now you do the same for the other -ger type verbs given above in (4).]

Imperfect subjunctive: que j'arrangeasse, que tu arrangeasses, qu'il (qu'elle, qu'on) arrangeât; que nous arrangeassions, que vous arrangeassiez, qu'ils (qu'elles) arrangeassent [Just for the fun of it, do the same for the other -ger type verbs given above.]

(6) Verbs that end in -oyer or -uyer in the infinitive form must change y to i in front of mute e.

(7) Common verbs that end in -oyer or -uyer in the infinitive form are:

-OYER	-UYER
choyer / to fondle, to coddle	ennuyer / to bore, to annoy
employer / to employ, to use	essuyer / to wipe
envoyer / to send	
nettoyer / to clean	

(8) Verbs that end in -AYER in the infinitive form may change y to i or may keep y in front of mute e.

Two common verbs that end in -ayer in the infinitive form are: essayer / to try, to try on; and payer / to pay, to pay for.

(9) Examples of when this change occurs:

Present indicative: j'emploie, tu emploies, il (elle, on) emploie; ils (elles) emploient.

Future: j'emploierai, tu emploieras, il (elle, on) emploiera; nous emploierons, vous emploierez, ils (elles) emploieront.

Conditional: j'emploierais, tu emploierais, il (elle, on) emploierait; nous emploierions, vous emploieriez, ils (elles) emploieraient.

Present subjunctive: que j'emploie, que tu emploies, qu'il (qu'elle, qu'on) emploie; qu'ils (qu'elles) emploient.

(10) Verbs that contain a mute e in the syllable before the infinitive ending -er:

acheter / to buy	lever / to raise, to lift
achever / to complete	se lever / to get up
amener / to bring, to lead	mener / to lead
élever / to raise	peser / to weigh
emmener / to lead away, to take away	promener / to walk (a person or an animal)
enlever / to remove, to take off	se promener / to take a walk (for yourself)
geler / to freeze	

(11) These verbs, given above in (10), change mute e to è when, in a verb form, the syllable after it contains another mute e.

(12) This change occurs because that mute e in the stem of the infinitive now becomes pronounced clearly in some verb forms. Examples:

Present indicative: j'achète, tu achètes, il (elle, on) achète; ils (elles) achètent.

Future: j'achèterai, tu achèteras, il (elle, on) achètera; nous achèterons, vous achèterez, ils (elles) achèteront.

Conditional: j'achèterais, tu achèterais, il (elle, on) achèterait; nous achèterions, vous achèteriez, ils (elles) achèteraient.

Present subjunctive: que j'achète, que tu achètes, qu'il (qu'elle, qu'on) achète; qu'ils (qu'elles) achètent.

(13) Instead of changing like the verbs above in (10)–(12) the following verbs double the consonant in the syllable that contains the mute e in the stem:

appeler / to call	jeter / to throw
rappeler / to recall	rejeter / to throw again, to throw back
se rappeler / to remember	

Examples of when this spelling change occurs:

Present indicative: je m'appelle, tu t'appelles, il (elle, on) s'appelle; ils (elles) s'appellent.

Future: je m'appellerai, tu t'appelleras, il (elle, on) s'appellera; nous nous appellerons, vous vous appellerez, ils (elles) s'appelleront.

Conditional: je m'appellerais, tu t'appellerais, il (elle, on) s'appellerait; nous nous appellerions, vous vous appelleriez, ils (elles) s'appelleraient.

Present subjunctive: que je m'appelle, que tu t'appelles, qu'il (qu'elle, qu'on) s'appelle; qu'ils (qu'elles) s'appellent.

(14) Verbs that contain é in the syllable before the infinitive ending -er:

céder / to cede, to yield, to give up	posséder / to possess, to own
célébrer / to celebrate	préférer / to prefer
concéder / to concede, to give up	protéger / to protect
considérer / to consider	répéter / to repeat
espérer / to hope	suggérer / to suggest

(15) These verbs, given above in (14), change é to è when, in a verb form, the syllable after it contains mute e.

Examples of when this spelling change occurs:

Present indicative: je préfère, tu préfères, il (elle, on) préfère: ils (elles) préfèrent.

Present subjunctive: que je préfère, que tu préfères, qu'il (qu'elle, qu'on) préfère; qu'ils (qu'elles) préfèrent.

Definitions of basic grammatical terms with examples

active voice   When we speak or write in the active voice, the subject of the verb performs the action. The action falls on the direct object.

*Everyone loves Janine / **Tout le monde aime Janine.***

The subject is *everyone*. The verb is *loves*. The direct object is *Janine*. See also *passive voice* in this list. Compare the above sentence with the example in the passive voice.

adjective   An adjective is a word that modifies a noun or a pronoun. In grammar, to modify a word means to describe, limit, expand, or make the meaning particular.

*a beautiful garden / **un beau jardin;** she is pretty / **elle est jolie.***

The adjective *beautiful/**beau*** modifies the noun *garden/**jardin.*** The adjective *pretty/**jolie*** modifies the pronoun *she/**elle.*** In French there are different kinds of adjectives. *See also* comparative adjective, demonstrative adjective, descriptive adjective, interrogative adjective, limiting adjective, possessive adjective, superlative adjective.

adverb   An adverb is a word that modifies a verb, an adjective, or another adverb. An adverb says something about how, when, where, to what extent, or in what way.

*Jane runs swiftly / **Jeanne court rapidement.***

The adverb *swiftly/**rapidement*** modifies the verb *runs/**court.*** The adverb shows *how* she runs.

*Jack is a very good friend / **Jacques est un très bon ami.***

The adverb *very/**très*** modifies the adjective *good/**bon.*** The adverb shows *how good* a friend he is.

*The boy is eating too fast now / **Le garçon mange trop vite maintenant.***

The adverb *too/**trop*** modifies the adverb *fast/**vite.*** The adverb shows *to what extent* he is eating *fast.* The adverb *now/**maintenant*** tells us *when.*

*The post office is there / **Le bureau de poste est là.***

The adverb *there/**là*** modifies the verb *is/**est.*** It tells us *where* the post office is.

*Mary writes carefully / **Marie écrit soigneusement.***

The adverb *carefully/**soigneusement*** modifies the verb *writes/**écrit.*** It tells us *in what way* she writes.

affirmative statement, negative statement   A statement in the affirmative is expressed positively. To negate an affirmative statement is to make it negative.

Affirmative: *I like chocolate ice cream / **J'aime la glace au chocolat.***

Negative: *I do not like chocolate ice cream / **Je n'aime pas la glace au chocolat.***

agreement of adjective with noun   Agreement is made on the adjective with the noun it modifies in gender (masculine or feminine) and number (singular or plural).

*a white house / **une maison blanche.***

The adjective **blanche** is feminine singular because the noun **une maison** is feminine singular.

*two white houses / **deux maisons blanches.***

The adjective **blanches** is feminine plural because the noun **maisons** is feminine plural.

agreement of past participle of a reflexive verb with its reflexive pronoun

Agreement is made on the past participle of a reflexive verb with its reflexive pronoun in gender (masculine or feminine) and number (singular or plural) if that pronoun is the *direct object* of the verb. The agreement is determined by looking at the subject to see its gender and number, which is the same as its reflexive pronoun. If the reflexive pronoun is the *indirect object*, an agreement is *not* made. *See* se laver and se lever.

She washed herself / Elle s'est lavée.

There is a feminine agreement on the past participle lavée (added e) with the reflexive pronoun se (here, s') because it serves as a direct object pronoun. What or whom did she wash? Herself, which is expressed in se (s').

But:

She washed her hair / Elle s'est lavé les cheveux.

There is no feminine agreement on the past participle lavé here because the reflexive pronoun (se, here, s') serves as an *indirect object*. The direct object is les cheveux and it is stated *after* the verb. What did she wash? She washed her hair *on herself (s')*. *See also* reflexive pronoun and reflexive verb.

agreement of past participle with its direct object   Agreement is made on the past participle with its direct object in gender (masculine or feminine) and number (singular or plural) when the verb is conjugated with avoir in the compound tenses. Agreement is made when the direct object, if there is one, *precedes* the verb.

Where are the little cakes? Paul ate them / Où sont les petits gâteaux?
Paul les a mangés.

The verb a mangés is in the *passé composé*; manger is conjugated with avoir. There is a plural agreement on the past participle mangés (added s) because the *preceding* direct object *them/les* is masculine plural, referring to *les petits gâteaux*, which is masculine plural.

Who wrote the letters? Robert wrote them / Qui a écrit les lettres?
Robert les a écrites.

The verb a écrites is in the *passé composé*; écrire is conjugated with avoir. There is a feminine plural agreement on the past participle écrites (added e and s) because the *preceding*-direct object *them/les* is feminine plural, referring to *les lettres*, which is feminine plural. A past participle functions as an adjective.

An agreement in gender and number is *not* made with *an indirect object*. *See* indirect object noun, indirect object pronoun. Review the regular formation of past participles and irregular past participles on page 3. *See also* direct object noun, direct object pronoun.

agreement of past participle with the subject   Agreement is made on the past participle with the subject in gender (masculine or feminine) and number (singular or plural) when the verb is conjugated with être in the compound tenses.

She went to Paris / Elle est allée à Paris.

The verb est allée is in the *passé composé*; aller is conjugated with être. There is a feminine agreement on the past participle allée (added e) because the subject elle is feminine singular.

The boys have arrived / Les garçons sont arrivés.

The verb sont arrivés is in the *passé composé*; arriver is conjugated with être. There is a plural agreement on the past participle arrivés (added s) because the subject les garçons is masculine plural.

Review page 6 to find out about verbs conjugated with either avoir or être to form the seven compound tenses. *See* aller and arriver. *See also* past participle and subject.

agreement of verb with its subject   A verb agrees in person (1st, 2d, or 3d) and in number (singular or plural) with its subject.

Does he always tell the truth? / Dit-il toujours la vérité?

The verb **dit** (of **dire**) is 3d person singular because the subject *il/he* is 3d person singular.

Where are they going? / Où vont-ils?

The verb **vont** (of **aller**) is 3d person plural because the subject *ils/they* is 3d person plural. For subject pronouns in the singular and plural, review page 103.

antecedent   An antecedent is a word to which a relative pronoun refers. It comes *before* the pronoun.

The girl who is laughing over there is my sister /
La jeune fille qui rit là-bas est ma soeur.

The antecedent is *girl/la jeune fille*. The relative pronoun *who/qui* refers to the girl.

The car that I bought is expensive / La voiture que j'ai achetée est chère.

The antecedent is *car/la voiture*. The relative pronoun *that/que* refers to the car. Note also that the past participle *achetée* is fem. sing. because it refers to *la voiture* (fem. sing.), which precedes the verb. Review **acheter** and **rire**. *See also* relative pronoun.

auxiliary verb   An auxiliary verb is a helping verb. In English grammar it is *to have*. In French grammar it is **avoir** (to have) or **être** (to be). An auxiliary verb is used to help form the seven compound tenses.

I have eaten /J'ai mangé; she has left / elle est partie.

Review page 6 to find out about verbs conjugated with **avoir** or **être** as helping verbs. Also, review **manger** and **partir**.

cardinal number   A cardinal number is a number that expresses an amount, such as *one, two, three,* and so on. *See also* ordinal number.

causative faire   In English grammar a causative verb causes something to be done. In French grammar the idea is the same. The subject of the verb causes the action expressed in the verb to be carried out by someone else.

Mrs. Roth makes her students work in French class /
Madame Roth fait travailler ses élèves dans la classe de français.

Mr. Smith is having a house built / Monsieur Smith fait construire une maison.

Review **construire**, **faire**, and **travailler**.

clause   A clause is a group of words that contains a subject and a predicate. A predicate may contain more than one word. A conjugated verb form is revealed in the predicate.

Mrs. Coty lives in a small apartment /
Madame Coty demeure dans un petit appartement.

The subject is *Mrs. Coty/Madame Coty*. The predicate is *lives in a small apartment/demeure dans un petit appartement*. The verb is *lives/demeure*. *See also* dependent clause, independent clause.

comparative adjective   When making a comparison between two persons or things, an adjective is used to express the degree of comparison in the following ways.

Same degree of comparison:

Raymond is as tall as his father / Raymond est aussi grand que son père.

Lesser degree of comparison:

Monique is less intelligent than her sister / Monique est moins intelligente que sa soeur.

Higher degree of comparison:

This apple is more delicious than that apple /
Cette pomme-ci est plus délicieuse que cette pomme-là.

See also superlative adjective.

comparative adverb   An adverb is compared in the same way as an adjective is compared. *See* comparative adjective.

Same degree of comparison:

Mr. Bernard speaks as fast as Mr. Claude /
Monsieur Bernard parle aussi vite que Monsieur Claude.

Lesser degree of comparison:

Alice studies less seriously than her sister /
Alice étudie moins sérieusement que sa soeur.

Higher degree of comparison:

Albert works more slowly than his brother /
Albert travaille plus lentement que son frère.

See also superlative adverb.

complex sentence   A complex sentence contains one independent clause and one or more dependent clauses.

One independent clause and one dependent clause:

Jack is handsome but his brother isn't / Jacques est beau mais son frère ne l'est pas.
The independent clause is *Jack is handsome*. It makes sense when it stands alone because it expresses a complete thought. The dependent clause is *but his brother isn't*. The dependent clause, which is introduced by the conjunction *but*, does not make complete sense when it stands alone because it *depends* on the thought expressed in the independent clause.

One independent clause and two dependent clauses:

Mary gets good grades in school because she studies but her sister never studies /
Marie reçoit de bonnes notes à l'école parce
qu'elle étudie mais sa soeur n'étudie jamais.

The independent clause is *Mary gets good grades in school*. It makes sense when it stands alone because it expresses a complete thought. The first dependent clause is *because she studies*. This dependent clause, which is introduced by the conjunction *because*, does not make complete sense when it stands alone because it *depends* on the thought expressed in the independent clause. The second dependent clause is *but her sister never studies*. That dependent clause, which is introduced by the conjunction *but*, does not make complete sense either when it stands alone because it *depends* on the thought expressed in the independent clause. *See also* dependent clause, independent clause.

compound sentence   A compound sentence contains two or more independent clauses.

Mrs. Dubois went to the supermarket, she bought some groceries, and then
she returned home / Madame Dubois est allée au supermarché, elle a acheté des
provisions, et puis elle est rentrée chez elle.

This compound sentence contains three independent clauses. They are independent because they make sense when they stand alone. Review the *passé composé* on page 16. *See also* independent clause.

conditional perfect tense   In French grammar the conditional used to be considered a mood. Grammarians now regard it as a tense of the indicative mood. This tense is defined with examples on pages 18 and 19.

conditional present tense   In French grammar the conditional used to be considered a mood. Grammarians now regard it as a tense of the indicative mood. This tense is defined with examples on page 13.

conjugation   The conjugation of a verb is the fixed order of all its forms showing their inflections (changes) in the three persons of the singular and plural in a particular tense.

conjunction   A conjunction is a word that connects words or groups of words.
and/et, or/ou, but/mais
You and I are going downtown / Toi et moi, nous allons en ville.
You can stay home or you can come with us /
Tu peux rester à la maison ou tu peux venir avec nous.

declarative sentence   A declarative sentence makes a statement.
I have finished the work / J'ai fini le travail.
Review **finir**.

definite article   The definite article in French has four forms and they all mean *the*.
They are: **le, la, l', les**, as in:
le livre/the book, la maison/the house, l'école/the school,
les enfants/the children
The definite articles are also used as direct object pronouns. *See* direct object pronoun.

demonstrative adjective   A demonstrative adjective is an adjective that points out. It is placed in front of a noun.
this book/ce livre; this hotel/cet hôtel; this child/cet enfant; this house/cette maison;
these flowers/ces fleurs

demonstrative pronoun   A demonstrative pronoun is a pronoun that points out. It takes the place of a noun. It agrees in gender and number with the noun it replaces.
I have two apples; do you prefer this one or that one?
J'ai deux pommes; préférez-vous celle-ci ou celle-là?
Sorry, but I prefer those / Je regrette, mais je préfère celles-là.
Do you like the ones that are on the table? / Aimez-vous celles qui sont sur la table?
For demonstrative pronouns that are neuter, *see* neuter.

dependent clause   A dependent clause is a group of words that contains a subject and a predicate. It does not express a complete thought when it stands alone. It is called *dependent* because it depends on the independent clause for a complete meaning. Subordinate clause is another term for dependent clause.
Mary is absent today because she is sick /
Marie est absente aujourd'hui parce qu'elle est malade.
The independent clause is *Mary is absent today*. The dependent clause is *because she is sick*.
See also clause, independent clause.

descriptive adjective   A descriptive adjective is an adjective that describes a person, place, or thing.
a pretty girl/une jolie jeune fille; a handsome boy/un beau garçon;
a small house/une petite maison; a big city/une grande ville;
an expensive car/une voiture chère.
See also adjective.

direct object noun   A direct object noun receives the action of the verb *directly*. That is why it is called a direct object, as opposed to an indirect object. A direct object noun is normally placed *after* the verb.

I am writing a letter / J'écris une lettre.

The subject is *I/Je*. The verb is *am writing/écris*. The direct object is the noun *letter/une lettre*. *See also* direct object pronoun.

direct object pronoun   A direct object pronoun receives the action of the verb *directly*. It takes the place of a direct object noun. In French a pronoun that is a direct object of a verb is ordinarily placed *in front of* the verb.

I am reading it [the letter] / Je la lis.

A direct object pronoun is placed *after* the verb and joined with a hyphen *in the affirmative imperative.*

Write it [the letter] now / Écrivez-la maintenant.

The direct object pronouns are:

Person	Singular	Plural
1st	*me (m')* me	*nous* us
2d	*te (t')* you (fam.)	*vous* you (sing. polite or pl.)
3d	*le (l')* him, it (person or thing) *la (l')* her, it (person or thing)	*les* them (persons or things)

Review écrire and lire. *See also* imperative.

disjunctive pronoun   In French grammar a disjunctive pronoun is a pronoun that is stressed; in other words, emphasis is placed on it.

I speak well; he does not speak well / Moi, je parle bien; lui, il ne parle pas bien.

Talk to me / Parlez-moi.

A disjunctive pronoun is also object of a preposition:

She is talking with me / Elle parle avec moi.

I always think of you / Je pense toujours à toi.

The disjunctive pronouns are:

Person	Singular	Plural
1st	*moi* me, I	*nous* us, we
2d	*toi* you (fam.)	*vous* you (sing. polite or pl.)
3d	*soi* oneself *lui* him, he *elle* her, she	*eux* them, they (m.) *elles* them, they (f.)

ending of a verb   In French grammar the ending of a verb form changes according to the person and number of the subject and the tense of the verb.

For example, to form the present indicative tense of a regular -er type verb like **parler**, drop **er** of the infinitive and add the following endings: **-e, -es, -e** for the 1st, 2d, and 3d persons of the singular; **-ons, -ez, -ent** for the 1st, 2d, and 3d persons of the plural. You then get:

je parle, tu parles, il (elle, on) parle;
nous parlons, vous parlez, ils (elles) parlent

Review pages 22 and 23. *See also* stem of a verb.

feminine   In French grammar the gender of a noun, pronoun, or adjective is feminine or masculine, not male or female.

Masculine			Feminine		
noun	pronoun	adjective	noun	pronoun	adjective
le garçon	*il*	*grand*	*la femme*	*elle*	*grande*
the boy	*he*	*tall*	*the woman*	*she*	*tall*
le livre	*il*	*petit*	*la voiture*	*elle*	*petite*
the book	*it*	*small*	*the car*	*it*	*small*

See also gender.

futur proche, le   In English the **futur proche** is called the near future. As one may guess, the near future is used when talking about something that will take place in the near future. The formation is similar in French and English. In French, the near future is formed by using **aller** with the infinitive of the verb that you want to use. In English, you use *to go* with the infinitive of the verb that you want to use.

Demain, je **vais acheter** un ordinateur.
Tomorrow, I *am going to buy* a computer.

future perfect tense   This tense is defined with examples on page 18.

future tense   This tense is defined with examples on pages 12–13.

gender   In French grammar gender means masculine or feminine.

Masculine: *the boy/le garçon; he, it/il; the rooster/le coq; the book/le livre*
Feminine: *the girl/la jeune fille; she, it/elle;*
the hen/la poule; the house/la maison

gerund   In English grammar a gerund is a word formed from a verb. It ends in *ing*. Actually, it is the present participle of a verb. But it is not used as a verb. It is used as a noun.

Seeing is believing / Voir c'est croire.

However, in French grammar the infinitive form of the verb is used, as in the above example, when the verb is used as a noun. In French, *seeing is believing* is expressed as *to see is to believe.*

The French gerund is also a word formed from a verb. It ends in *ant*. It is also the present participle of a verb. As a gerund, it is normally preceded by the preposition **en**.

En partant, il a fait ses excuses / While leaving, he made his excuses.

See also present participle.

if (si) clause   An "if" clause is defined with examples at the top of page 26. *See also* clause.

imperative   The imperative is a mood, not a tense. It is used to express a command. In French it is used in the 2d person of the singular (tu), the 2d person of the plural (vous), and in the 1st person of the plural (nous). Review the imperative with examples on pages 20 and 21. Also review the three imperative forms of **donner**. *See also* person (1st, 2d, 3d).

imperfect indicative tense   This tense is defined with examples on pages 11 and 12.

imperfect subjunctive tense   This tense is defined with examples on pages 15 and 16.

indefinite article   In English the indefinite articles are *a, an,* as in *a book, an apple.* They are indefinite because they do not refer to any definite or particular noun.
 In French there are two indefinite articles in the singular: one in the masculine form (un) and one in the feminine form (une).

Masculine singular: *un ami/a friend*

Feminine singular: *une pomme/an apple*

In French they both change to des in the plural.

I have a brother/J'ai un frère; I have brothers/J'ai des frères.

I have a sister/J'ai une soeur; I have sisters/J'ai des soeurs.

I have an apple/J'ai une pomme; I have apples/J'ai des pommes.

See also definite article.

indefinite pronoun   An indefinite pronoun is a pronoun that does not refer to any definite or particular noun.

something/quelque chose; someone, somebody/quelqu'un, quelqu'une;

each one/chacun, chacune; anything/n'importe quoi

independent clause   An independent clause is a group of words that contains a subject and a predicate. It expresses a complete thought when it stands alone.

The cat is sleeping under the bed / Le chat dort sous le lit.

See also clause, dependent clause, predicate.

indicative mood   The indicative mood is used in sentences that make a statement or ask a question. The indicative mood is used most of the time when we speak or write in English or French.

I am going home now/Je vais chez moi maintenant.

Where are you going?/Où allez-vous?

indirect object noun   An indirect object noun receives the action of the verb *indirectly. I am writing a letter to Mary or I am writing Mary a letter / J'écris une lettre à Marie.* The subject is *I/Je.* The verb is *am writing/écris.* The direct object noun is *a letter/une lettre.* The indirect object noun is *Mary/Marie.* An agreement is not made with an indirect object noun. *See also* indirect object pronoun, direct object noun, direct object pronoun.

indirect object pronoun   An indirect object pronoun takes the place of an indirect object noun. It receives the action of the verb *indirectly.* In French a pronoun that is the indirect object of a verb is ordinarily placed *in front of* the verb.

I am writing a letter to her or I am writing her a letter / Je lui écris une lettre.

The indirect object pronoun is *(to) her/lui.* An agreement is not made with an indirect object pronoun.
An indirect object pronoun is placed *after* the verb and joined with a hyphen *in the affirmative imperative.*

Write to her now / Écris-lui maintenant.

The indirect object pronouns are:

Person	Singular	Plural
1st	*me (m') to me*	*nous to us*
2d	*te (t') to you (fam.)*	*vous to you (sing. polite or pl.)*
3d	*lui to him, to her*	*leur to them*

See also indirect object noun.

infinitive   An infinitive is a verb form. In English it is normally stated with the preposition *to*, as in *to talk, to finish, to sell*. In French the infinitive form of a verb consists of three major types: those of the 1st conjugation that end in **-er**, those of the 2d conjugation that end in **-ir**, and those of the 3d conjugation that end in **-re**.

> *parler/to talk, to speak; finir/to finish; vendre/to sell*

All the verbs in this book are given in the infinitive form at the top of each page where they are arranged alphabetically.

interjection   An interjection is a word that expresses emotion, a feeling of joy, of sadness, an exclamation of surprise, and other exclamations consisting of one or two words.

> *Ah!/Ah! Oh!/Oh! Darn it!/Zut! Whew!/Ouf! My God!/Mon Dieu!*

interrogative adjective   An interrogative adjective is an adjective that is used in a question. It agrees in gender and number with the noun it modifies.

> *What book do you want? / Quel livre désirez-vous?*
> *What time is it? / Quelle heure est-il?*

interrogative adverb   An interrogative adverb is an adverb that introduces a question. As an adverb, it modifies the verb.

> *How are you? / Comment allez-vous?*
> *How much does this book cost? / Combien coûte ce livre?*
> *When will you arrive? / Quand arriverez-vous?*

interrogative pronoun   An interrogative pronoun is a pronoun that asks a question. There are interrogative pronouns that refer to persons and those that refer to things.

> *Who is on the phone? / Qui est à l'appareil?*
> *What are you saying? / Que dites-vous?*

interrogative sentence   An interrogative sentence asks a question.

> *What are you doing? / Que faites-vous?*

intransitive verb   An intransitive verb is a verb that does not take a direct object.

> *The professor is talking loudly / Le professeur parle fort.*

An intransitive verb takes an indirect object.

> *The professor is talking to us / Le professeur nous parle.*

See also indirect object pronoun.

irregular verb   An irregular verb is a verb that does not follow a fixed pattern in its conjugation in the various verb tenses.

Basic irregular verbs in French:

aller/to go   *avoir*/to have   *être*/to be   *faire*/to do, to make

Review these verbs. *See also* conjugation, regular verb.

limiting adjective   A limiting adjective is an adjective that limits a quantity.

three tickets/*trois billets*; *a few candies*/*quelques bonbons*

main clause   Main clause is another term for independent clause. *See* independent clause.

masculine   In French grammar the gender of a noun, pronoun, or adjective is masculine or feminine, not male or female. *See also* gender and feminine.

mood of verbs   Some grammarians use the term *the mode* instead of *the mood* of a verb. Either term means *the manner or way* a verb is expressed. In English and in French grammar a verb expresses an action or state of being in the following three moods (modes, *ways*): the indicative mood, the imperative mood, and the subjunctive mood. In French grammar there is also the infinitive mood when the whole infinitive is used, e.g., **voir**, **croire**, as in **Voir c'est croire**/*Seeing is believing (to see is to believe)*. Most of the time, in English and French, we speak and write in the indicative mood.

near future   See *futur proche, le.*

negative statement, affirmative statement

see **affirmative statement, negative statement**

neuter   A word that is neuter is neither masculine nor feminine. Common neuter demonstrative pronouns are ce (c')/*it*, ceci/*this*, cela/*that*, ça/*that*. They are invariable, which means they do not change in gender and number.

It's not true/*Ce n'est pas vrai*; *it is true*/*c'est vrai*; *this is true*/*ceci est vrai*; *that is true*/*cela est vrai*; *what is that?*/*qu'est-ce que c'est que ça?*

For demonstrative pronouns that are not neuter, *see* demonstrative pronoun. There is also the neuter pronoun le, as in: *Je le crois / I believe it*; *Je le pense / I think so.*

noun   A noun is a word that names a person, animal, place, thing, condition or state, or quality.

the man/*l'homme*, *the woman*/*la femme*, *the horse*/*le cheval*, *the house*/*la maison*
the book/*le livre*, *happiness*/*le bonheur*, *excellence*/*l'excellence*

In French the noun **le nom** is the word for name and noun.

number   In English and French grammar, number means singular or plural.
Masc. sing.:

the boy/*le garçon; the arm*/*le bras; the eye*/*l'oeil*

Masc. pl.:

the boys/*les garçons; the arms*/*les bras; the eyes*/*les yeux*

Fem. sing.:

the girl/*la jeune fille; the house*/*la maison; the hen*/*la poule*

Fem. pl.:

the girls/*les jeunes filles; the houses*/*les maisons; the hens*/*les poules*

ordinal number   An ordinal number is a number that expresses position in a series, such as *first, second, third,* and so on. In English and French grammar we talk about 1st person, 2d person, 3d person singular or plural regarding subjects and verbs. *See also* cardinal number and person (1st, 2d, 3d).

orthographical changes in verb forms   An orthographical change in a verb form is a change in spelling.

The second letter c in the verb *commencer/to begin* changes to ç if the letter after it is a, o, or u, as in *nous commençons/we begin*. The reason for this spelling change is to preserve the sound of *s* as it is pronounced in the infinitive form **commencer**. When a, o, or u follow the letter c, the c is pronounced as in the sound of k. The mark under the letter ç is called *une cédille/cedilla*. Some linguists say it is the lower part of the letter s and it tells you to pronounce ç as an s sound. Other linguists say that ç was borrowed from the Greek alphabet, which represents the sound of s when it is the last letter of a Greek word.

The verb *s'appeler/to call oneself, to be named* contains a single l. When a verb form is stressed on the syllable containing one l, it doubles, as in *je m'appelle . . ./I call myself . . . , my name is . . . .*

partitive   In French grammar the partitive denotes a *part* of a whole. In English we express the partitive by saying *some* or *any* in front of the noun. In French we use the following partitive forms in front of the noun:
Masculine singular: **du** or **de l'**   Feminine singular: **de la** or **de l'**
Masculine or feminine plural: **des**
I have some coffee / J'ai du café.
I'd like some water / J'aimerais de l'eau.
I'd like some meat / J'aimerais de la viande.
Do you have any candies? / Avez-vous des bonbons?
In the negative, these partitive forms change to **de** or **d'**:
I don't have any coffee / Je n'ai pas de café.
I don't want any water / Je ne veux pas d'eau.
I wouldn't like any meat / Je n'aimerais pas de viande.
No, I don't have any candies / Non, je n'ai pas de bonbons.

passive voice   When we speak or write in the active voice and change to the passive voice, the direct object becomes the subject, the subject becomes object of a preposition, and the verb becomes *to be* plus the past participle of the active verb. The past participle functions as an adjective.
Janine is loved by everyone / Janine est aimée de tout le monde.
The subject is *Janine*. The verb is *is/est*. The object of the preposition *by/de* is *everyone/tout le monde. See also* active voice. Compare the above sentence with the example in the active voice.

past anterior tense   This tense is defined with examples on page 17.

past definite or simple past tense   This tense is defined with examples on page 12. In French it is the *passé simple*.

past indefinite tense   This tense is defined with examples on page 16. In French it is the *passé composé*.

past participle   A past participle is derived from a verb. It is used to form the compound tenses. Its auxiliary verb in English is *to have*. In French the auxiliary verb is **avoir**/to *have* or **être**/to be. It is part of the verb tense.
With **avoir** as the auxiliary verb: *Elle a mangé / She has eaten.*

Definitions of basic grammatical terms with examples   45

The subject is *elle/she*. The verb is *a mangé/has eaten*. The tense of the verb is the *passé composé*. The auxiliary verb is *a/has*. The past participle is *mangé/eaten*.

With **être** as the auxiliary verb: *Elle est arrivée / She has arrived.*

The verb is *est arrivée/has arrived*. The tense of the verb is the *passé composé*. The auxiliary verb is *est*. The past participle is *arrivée/arrived*.

Review page 3 for the regular formation of a past participle and a list of basic irregular past participles. Review page 6 to find out about verbs conjugated with either **avoir** or **être**. *See also* auxiliary verb and agreement of past participle with the subject.

past perfect tense   This tense is also called the pluperfect indicative tense. Review pages 16 and 17 for a definition with examples.

past simple tense   This tense is defined with examples on page 12. It is also called the simple past tense or past definite tense. In French it is the *passé simple*.

past subjunctive tense   This tense is also called the perfect subjunctive tense. It is defined with examples on page 19.

person (1st, 2d, 3d)   Verb forms in a particular tense are learned systematically according to person (1st, 2d, 3d) and number (singular, plural).

Present indicative tense of the verb **aller**/to go:

Singular	Plural
1st person: *je vais*	1st person: *nous allons*
2d person: *tu vas*	2d person: *vous allez*
3d person: *il, elle, on va*	3d person: *ils, elles vont*

personal pronoun   A personal pronoun refers to a person. The pronoun *it/il* or *elle* is in this category. Review the subject pronouns on page 103. For examples of other types of pronouns, *see also* demonstrative pronoun, direct object pronoun, disjunctive pronoun, indefinite pronoun, indirect object pronoun, interrogative pronoun, possessive pronoun, reflexive pronoun, relative pronoun.

pluperfect indicative tense   This tense is also called the past perfect indicative tense. It is defined with examples on pages 16–17.

pluperfect subjunctive tense   This tense is also called the past perfect subjunctive tense. It is defined with examples on pages 19–20.

plural   Plural means more than one. *See also* person (1st, 2d, 3d) and singular.

possessive adjective   A possessive adjective is an adjective that is placed in front of a noun to show possession. In French their forms change in gender (masculine or feminine) and number (singular or plural) to agree with the noun they modify.

my book/mon livre   my books/mes livres   my dress/ma robe

possessive pronoun   A possessive pronoun is a pronoun that shows possession. It takes the place of a possessive adjective with the noun. Its form agrees in gender (masculine or feminine) and number (singular or plural) with what it is replacing.

English:

mine, yours, his, hers, its, ours, theirs

French:

Possessive adjective	Possessive pronoun
my book/mon livre	*mine/le mien*
my dress/ma robe	*mine/la mienne*
my shoes/mes chaussures	*mine/les miennes*

predicate   The predicate is that part of the sentence that tells us something about the subject. The main word of the predicate is the verb.

The tourists are waiting for the tour bus / Les touristes attendent l'autocar.
The subject is *the tourists/les touristes*. The predicate is *are waiting for the tour bus/attendent l'autocar*. The verb is *are waiting/attendent*. The direct object is *the tour bus/l'autocar.*

preposition   A preposition is a word that establishes a rapport between words.
English:

with, in, on, at, between

French:

with me/avec moi; in the drawer/dans le tiroir; on the table/sur la table
at six o'clock/à six heures; between him and her/entre lui et elle
Review verbs with prepositions beginning on page 690.

present indicative tense   This tense is defined with examples on pages 10 and 11.

present participle   A present participle is derived from a verb form. In French it is regularly formed like this: take the **nous** form of the present indicative tense of the verb you have in mind, then drop the ending **ons** and add **ant**. In English a present participle ends in *ing*.

Infinitive	Present Indicative **nous** form	Present participle
chanter	*nous chantons*	*chantant*
to sing	*we sing*	*singing*
finir	*nous finissons*	*finissant*
to finish	*we finish*	*finishing*
vendre	*nous vendons*	*vendant*
to sell	*we sell*	*selling*

For the regular formation of present participles and to find out what the three common irregular present participles are, review page 3.

present subjunctive tense   This tense is defined with examples on pages 14 and 15.

pronoun   A pronoun is a word that takes the place of a noun.

l'homme/il	*la femme/elle*	*l'arbre/il*	*la voiture/elle*
the man/he	*the woman/she*	*the tree/it*	*the car/it*

reflexive pronoun and reflexive verb   In English a reflexive pronoun is a personal pronoun that contains *self* or *selves*. In French and English a reflexive pronoun is used with a verb that is called reflexive because the action of the verb falls on the reflexive pronoun.

In French there is a required set of reflexive pronouns for a reflexive verb.

se laver	*Je me lave.*	*Se blesser*	*Elle s'est blessée.*
to wash oneself	*I wash myself.*	*to hurt oneself*	*She hurt herself.*

In French a reflexive verb is conjugated with être to form the compound tenses. The French term for a reflexive verb is **un verbe pronominal** because a pronoun goes with the verb. Review the reflexive verbs s'appeler (verb 39), se blesser (verb 74), se laver (verb 277), and se lever (verb 279). *See also* agreement of past participle of a reflexive verb with its reflexive pronoun.

regular verb A regular verb is a verb that is conjugated in the various tenses according to a fixed pattern. For examples, review pages 22 to 25. *See also* conjugation, irregular verb.

relative pronoun A relative pronoun is a pronoun that refers to its antecedent.
The girl who is laughing over there is my sister /
La jeune fille qui rit là-bas est ma soeur.
The antecedent is *girl/la jeune fille*. The relative pronoun *who/qui* refers to the girl. *See also* antecedent.

sentence A sentence is a group of words that contains a subject and a predicate. The verb is contained in the predicate. A sentence expresses a complete thought.
The train leaves from the North Station at two o'clock in the afternoon /
Le train part de la Gare du Nord à deux heures de l'après-midi.
The subject is *train/le train*. The predicate is *leaves from the North Station at two o'clock in the afternoon/part de la Gare du Nord à deux heures de l'après-midi*. The verb is *leaves/part*. *See also* complex sentence, compound sentence, simple sentence.

simple sentence A simple sentence is a sentence that contains one subject and one predicate. The verb is the core of the predicate. The verb is the most important word in a sentence because it tells us what the subject is doing.
Mary is eating an apple from her garden / Marie mange une pomme de son jardin.
The subject is *Mary/Marie*. The predicate is *is eating an apple from her garden/mange une pomme de son jardin*. The verb is *is eating/mange*. The direct object is *an apple/une pomme*. *From her garden/de son jardin* is an adverbial phrase. It tells you from where the apple came. *See also* complex sentence, compound sentence.

singular Singular means one. *See also* plural.

stem of a verb The stem of a verb is what is left after we drop the ending of its infinitive form. It is necessary to add to it the required endings of a regular verb in a particular verb tense.

Infinitive	Ending of infinitive	Stem
donner/to give	*er*	*donn*
choisir/to choose	*ir*	*chois*
vendre/to sell	*re*	*vend*

See also ending of a verb.

subject A subject is that part of a sentence that is related to its verb. The verb says something about the subject.
Clara and Isabel are beautiful / Clara et Isabel sont belles.

subjunctive mood The subjunctive mood is the mood of a verb that is used in specific cases, *e.g.*, after certain verbs expressing a wish, doubt, emotion, fear, joy, uncertainty, an indefinite expression, an indefinite antecedent, certain conjunctions, and others. The subjunctive mood is used more frequently in French than in English. Review the uses of the subjunctive mood with examples on pages 26 to 31. *See also* mood of verbs.

subordinate clause   Subordinate clause is another term for dependent clause. *See* dependent clause.

superlative adjective   A superlative adjective is an adjective that expresses the highest degree when making a comparison of more than two persons or things.

Adjective	Comparative	Superlative
bon/good	*meilleur*/better	*le meilleur*/best
mauvais/bad	*plus mauvais*/worse	*le plus mauvais*/worst

See also comparative adjective.

superlative adverb   A superlative adverb is an adverb that expresses the highest degree when making a comparison of more than two persons or things.

Adverb	Comparative	Superlative
vite/quickly	*plus vite*/more quickly	*le plus vite*/most quickly
	moins vite/less quickly	*le moins vite*/least quickly

See also comparative adverb.

tense of verb   In English and French grammar, tense means time. The tense of the verb indicates the time of the action or state of being. The three major segments of time are past, present, and future. In French there are fourteen verb tenses, of which seven are simple tenses and seven are compound. Review pages 21 and 23 for the names of the fourteen tenses in French and English.

transitive verb   A transitive verb is a verb that takes a direct object.
I am closing the window / Je ferme la fenêtre.
The subject is *Il/Je*. The verb is *am closing / ferme*. The direct object is *the window/la fenêtre*.
See also intransitive verb.

verb   A verb is a word that expresses action or a state of being.
Action: *Les oiseaux volent / The birds are flying.*
The verb is *volent/are flying*.
State of being: *La jeune fille est heureuse / The girl is happy.*
The verb is *est/is*.

Verb drills and tests with answers explained

The hundreds of verb forms in this part of the book will immerse you in the practice and improvement of your knowledge of French verb forms, tenses, and uses. You will find a variety of types of questions to make your experience interesting, challenging, and rewarding. All verb forms used in the drills and tests are found in the preliminary pages, among the 501 verbs, and in the back pages of this book.

The answers and explanations begin on page 81. The explanations are brief and to the point, including references to pages in this book for study and review.

Tips: To figure out the correct verb form of the required tense, examine each sentence carefully. Take a good look at the subject of the verb. Is it 1st, 2d, or 3d person? Is it singular or plural? Is it masculine or feminine? Look for a possible preceding noun or pronoun direct object, agreement on the past participle if necessary, and key elements that precede or follow the verb to determine the verb form and tense.

Also, look for other key words, such as yesterday, last week, today, at this moment, tomorrow, next year, certain conjunctions, and other key elements that indicate the need for the indicative or subjunctive moods in the required tense. The correct verb form depends on the sense and grammatical structure of the sentence. The best way to learn irregular forms in the seven simple tenses is from study, practice, and experience. For the formation of present and past participles, including irregulars, consult page 3. As for the formation of regular verb forms, consult pages 22 to 25. From time to time study and review pages 10 to 21.

Verb Test 1

SENTENCE COMPLETION

Directions: *Each of the following sentences contains a missing verb form. From the choices given, select the verb form of the tense that is required, according to the sense of the sentence, and write the letter of your choice on the line. At times, only the infinitive form is needed or a present or past participle. Answers and explanations begin on page 81.*

1. Hier, Marguerite _____ allée au théâtre avec ses amis.
   A. a   B. est   C. avait   D. était

2. Madame Céléstine ne _____ pas lire parce qu'elle a besoin de ses lunettes.
   A. pouvons   B. peuvent   C. peux   D. peut

3. Quand j'étais enfant, j' _____ beaucoup de camarades à l'école.
   A. ai   B. eus   C. avais   D. aurai

4. La petite fille _____ parce qu'elle est heureuse.
   A. sourit   B. souris   C. ait souri   D. eût souri

5. Hier soir, j'ai bien ri pendant que je _____ un film comique à la télé.
   A. regardait B. regardais   C. ai regardé   D. regarderais

6. À cause du grand bruit qui vient de la rue, je ne peux pas _____ .
A. dormir   B. dors   C. dormant   D. dormirai

7. Asseyez-vous, s'il vous plaît. Le docteur _____ d'arriver.
A. viens   B. vient   C. est venu   D. était venu

8. Robert, je te demande de _____ ta chambre parce qu'elle est bien sale.
A. nettoie   B. nettoyant   C. nettoyer   D. nettoyez

9. Le tonnerre va _____ peur aux enfants.
A. faire   B. faisant   C. fait   D. font

10. Il commence à pleuvoir et Hélène a _____ son parapluie.
A. oublié   B. oubliée   C. oublie   D. oublia

11. Chéri, aimes-tu les chaussures que j'ai _____ aujourd'hui?
A. acheté   B. achetée   C. achetés   D. achetées

12. La semaine prochaine j' _____ en France.
A. irai   B. alla   C. allais   D. irais

13. Si j'avais assez d'argent, j' _____ en Italie.
A. irai   B. irais   C. allais   D. aille

14. Si j'ai assez d'argent, j' _____ au Canada.
A. irai   B. irais   C. allais   D. aille

15. Ce matin Paulette _____ .
A. s'est lavé   B. s'est lavée   C. se sont lavés   D. se sont lavées

16. Ce matin Gertrude _____ les cheveux.
A. s'est lavé   B. s'est lavée   C. se sont lavés   D. se sont lavées

17. Je _____ à l'école en ce moment.
A. suis allé   B. étais allé   C. vais   D. serais allé

18. Je _____ à la bibliothèque tous les jours.
A. vais   B. étais allé   C. serai allé   D. serais allé

19. Deux et deux _____ quatre.
A. fait   B. font   C. feraient   D. faisaient

20. Depuis combien de temps êtes-vous ici? Moi? Je _____ ici depuis dix minutes.
A. étais   B. serai   C. serais   D. suis

DIALOGUE

Directions: *In the following dialogue there are blank spaces indicating missing verb forms. Select the appropriate verb form according to the sense of what the speakers are saying and write the letter of your choice on the line. The situation is given below. First, read the entire selection once. During the second reading, make your choices.*

Situation: You just got off an airplane. You go to the baggage room to claim your suitcase but you can't find it. An employee talks to you.

L'employé: Y a-t-il quelque chose qui ne va pas, mademoiselle?
Vous: Je ne _____ pas ma valise.

1. A. trouve   B. trouverai   C. trouverais   D. trouvais

L'employé: Donnez-moi votre ticket de bagages, s'il vous plaît.
Vous: Une seconde, s'il vous plaît. _____ qu'il est dans ma poche.

2. A. J'ai cru   B. Je croirai   C. Je croirais   D. Je crois

L'employé: Une minute. Je vais voir ce qui se passe.
Vous: J' _____ que ma valise n'est pas perdue!

3. A. espère   B. espérer   C. espères   D. espérais

L'employé: Votre valise est dans l'avion qui arrive cet après-midi.
Vous: _____ bien contente.

4. A. J'ai été   B. J'avais été   C. J'aurais été   D. Je suis

L'employé: Votre valise sera ici vers cinq heures, mademoiselle.
Vous: Je _____ la chercher. Merci bien, monsieur.

5. A. viendrai   B. suis venue   C. suis venu   D. viendrais

PATTERN RESPONSES

Directions: *Answer the following questions in French in complete sentences in the affirmative, using a pronoun for the subject. Add* aussi *(also).*

Model: François apprend bien. Et vos frères?
You write: **Ils apprennent bien aussi.**

1. Pierre comprend bien. Et vos frères?

   _____

2. Robert écrit bien. Et vos soeurs?

   _____

3. Anne va bien. Et ses amis?

   _____

4. Juliette lit un livre dans le lit. Et toi?

   _____

5. Catherine voit bien. Et tes amis?

   _____

6. Richard est allé au cinéma. Et Suzanne?

   _____

7. Jean a bien mangé. Et nous?

   _____

8. Jeanne s'est assise. Et les autres jeunes filles?

   _____

9. Monsieur Dufy s'est lavé. Et sa femme?

   _____

10. Monsieur Durand s'est lavé les cheveux. Et sa femme?

    _____

11. Tu as rougi. Et les enfants?

    _____

12. Monsieur Bertrand choisit une auto. Et Monsieur et Madame Duval?

    _____

13. Tu finis la leçon. Et Pierre?

    _____

14. Les enfants ont fait les devoirs. Et toi?

    _____

15. Ce soldat défend la patrie. Et les autres soldats?

    _____

16. Vous répondez à la question. Et Jacques?

_____

17. Vous vous couchez à dix heures. Et vos parents?

_____

18. Les enfants se sont amusés. Et Marie?

_____

19. Jacqueline s'est reposée. Et vous?

_____

20. Annie s'est levée tôt. Et nous?

_____

Verb Test 4

SENTENCE COMPLETION

Directions: _Each of the following sentences contains a missing verb form. From the choices given, select the verb form of the tense that is required, according to the sense of the sentence, and write the letter of your choice on the line._

1. Je partirai quand mon amie _____ .
   A. arrive   B. arrivera   C. est arrivé   D. est arrivée

2. Je voudrais vous _____ ces fleurs.
   A. donnez   B. donner   C. donnerais   D. donnerez

3. Avez-vous lu les deux livres que je vous ai _____ la semaine dernière?
   A. donner   B. donné   C. donnés   D. donnez

4. Voici la lettre que _____ hier.
   A. je reçois   B. j'ai reçu   C. je recevrais   D. j'ai reçue

5. Hier _____ une lettre à des amis en France.
   A. j'ai envoyé   B. j'ai envoyée   C. j'enverrai   D. j'enverrais

6. J'irais en France si _____ assez d'argent.
   A. j'ai   B. j'aurais   C. j'aurai   D. j'avais

7. J'irai en France quand _____ assez d'argent.
   A. j'aurai   B. j'aurais   C. j'ai eu   D. j'avais

8. J'insiste que tu _____ ici avant cinq heures.
   A. es   B. sois   C. soit   D. soyez

9. Quand un enfant grandit, cela _____ dire qu'il devient plus grand.

    A. veuille   B. voulût   C. veux   D. veut

10. Pour bien apprendre dans la classe de français, _____ faire attention.

    A. il faut   B. il est   C. il pleut   D. il fend

11. Mon frère lisait pendant que j' _____ .

    A. écris   B. écrive   C. ai écrit   D. écrivais

12. Les étudiants lisaient quand _____ dans la salle de classe.

    A. je suis entré   B. j'entre   C. j'étais entré   D. j'entrerai

13. Quand j'étais petit, ma famille et moi _____ à la plage en été.

    A. allons   B. allions   C. allaient   D. irons

14. Richard _____ triste quand je l'ai vu.

    A. est   B. sera   C. était   D. serait

15. Quand ma mère était jeune, elle _____ jolie.

    A. était   B. est   C. a été   D. serait

16. À minuit, Pierre _____ et il a dit à son frère: "Lève-toi!"

    A. se réveille   B. s'est réveillé   C. s'est réveillée   D. se réveillera

17. J'entends _____ quelqu'un en bas dans la salle à manger!

    A. marchant   B. marché   C. marcher   D. a marché

18. En général, on _____ froid en hiver.

    A. est   B. fait   C. tient   D. a

19. L'année dernière nous _____ en France.

    A. est allé   B. est allée   C. sommes allés   D. irons

20. Voici les livres que vous avez _____ .

    A. désiré   B. désirée   C. désirés   D. désirer

Verb Test 5

DIALOGUE

Directions: *In the following dialogue there are blank spaces indicating missing verb forms. Select the appropriate verb form according to the sense of what the speakers are saying and write the letter of your choice on the line. The conversation is taking place at the present time. First, read the entire selection once. During the second reading, make your choices.*

Situation: It's the morning of the year-end French exam in school. You and Jeanne are talking about the exams and your plans for summer vacation.

Jeanne: Il me reste encore un examen pour demain, puis les vacances vont commencer.
Vous: Mon dernier examen _____ lieu après-demain.

1. A. est   B. sera   C. aura   D. avait

Jeanne: J'espère réussir à tous mes examens.
Vous: Il n'y _____ rien à craindre. Tu reçois toujours de bonnes notes.

2. A. ait   B. soit   C. a eu   D. a

Jeanne: Ma famille et moi nous allons faire un voyage à Québec en juillet.
Vous: Moi, je devrai _____ ici à travailler.

3. A. reste   B. rester   C. restera   D. resterai

Jeanne: L'été passé nous sommes allés dans les montagnes.
Vous: Alors, tu _____ faire un voyage tous les étés!

4. A. pouvez   B. puis   C. peux   D. put

Jeanne: Alors, je te souhaite bonne chance dans tes examens.
Vous: Merci. Et je te _____ la même chose!

5. A. souhaite   B. souhaites   C. souhaité   D. souhaitai

Verb Test 6

CHANGING FROM ONE VERB TO ANOTHER

Directions: *The verb forms in the following statements are all in the imperative. Change each sentence by replacing the verb with the proper form of the verb in parentheses, keeping the imperative form. The verb form you write must be in the same person as the one you are replacing. In other words, you must recognize if the given verb form is 2d person singular (tu), 1st person plural (nous), or 2d person plural, polite singular (vous). See the index of common irregular French verb forms, in the Appendixes, for irregular verb forms that you cannot identify.*

Model: Prononcez le mot. (écrire)

You write: Écrivez le mot.

1. Lisez la phrase. (dire)

   _____

2. Prends le lait. (boire)

   _____

3. Venez tout de suite. (partir)

   _____

4. Ouvre la fenêtre. (fermer)

5. Mets la valise là-bas. (prendre)

6. Lisons la lettre. (écrire)

7. Apprenez le poème. (lire)

8. Partons maintenant. (sortir)

9. Soyez à l'heure! (revenir)

10. Voyons la leçon. (faire)

11. Asseyez-vous, s'il vous plaît. (se lever)

12. Accepte l'argent. (refuser)

13. Vends le vélo. (acheter)

14. Venez à l'heure. (être)

15. Reste dans la maison. (aller)

16. Lave-toi. (se lever)

17. Cachons-nous. (se dépêcher)

18. Arrête-toi. (s'amuser)

19. Vends la maison. (acheter)

20. Mange. (venir)

CHANGING FROM ONE TENSE TO ANOTHER

Directions: *The following verb forms are all in the **future tense**. Change them to the **conditional**, keeping the same subject. See the index of common irregular French verb forms, in the Appendixes, for irregular verb forms that you cannot identify.*

Model: J'aurai   **You write: J'aurais**

1. J'irai _____

2. Je partirai _____

3. J'aurai _____

4. Je serai _____

5. Tu aimeras _____

6. Tu feras _____

7. Il aura _____

8. Il sera _____

9. Il ira _____

10. On dira _____

11. Vous serez _____

12. Elle lira _____

13. J'ouvrirai _____

14. Nous saurons _____

15. Ils viendront _____

16. On boira _____

17. Ils courront _____

18. Ils liront _____

19. Elle mettra _____

20. Il apprendra _____

21. Je couvrirai _____

22. Il deviendra _____

23. Nous devrons _____

24. Vous direz _____

25. Vous irez _____

26. J'aimerai _____

27. Il faudra _____

28. Ils seront _____

29. Elles feront _____

30. On choisira _____

PATTERN RESPONSES

Directions: Answer the following questions in the negative in complete French sentences. In answer (a), use **non**. *In answer (b), use* **non plus** *(either). Study models (a) and (b) carefully. Use a pronoun as subject in your answers. Place* **non plus** *at the end of the sentence.*

Models: (a) **Est-ce que vous dansez?**   You write: (a) **Non, je ne danse pas.**
        (Do you dance?)   (No, I don't dance.)

       (b) **Et Charles?**   You write: (b) **Il ne danse pas non plus.**
        (And Charles?)   (He doesn't dance either.)

1. (a) Est-ce que vous travaillez?

_____

(b) Et Paul?

_____

2. (a) Est-ce que Jacqueline étudie?

_____

(b) Et les grands garçons?

_____

3. (a) Est-ce qu'Anne va au match?

_____

(b) Et toi?

_____

4. (a) Est-ce que les enfants crient?

_____

(b) Et toi et tes amis?

_____

5. (a) Est-ce que l'avion arrive?

_____

(b) Et les trains?

_____

6. (a) Est-ce que tu es occupé?

_____

(b) Et tes parents?

_____

7. (a) As-tu fermé la fenêtre?

_____

(b) Et Pierre?

_____

8. (a) Avez-vous assisté à la conférence?

_____

(b) Et vos amis?

_____

9. (a) Monsieur Durand est-il allé au supermarché?

_____

(b) Et sa femme?

_____

10. (a) Madame Coty est-elle allée à la piscine?

_____

(b) Et les enfants?

_____

Verb Test 9

DIALOGUE

Directions: _In the following dialogue there are blank spaces indicating missing verb forms. Select the appropriate verb form according to the sense of what the speakers are saying and write the letter of your choice on the line. The situation is given below. The conversation is taking place at the present time. First, read the entire selection once. During the second reading, make your choices._

Situation: You are seated in a train about to leave for Paris. A young man approaches and asks if he can sit next to you.

Le jeune homme: Vous permettez?
Vous: Mais, bien sûr! Je vous en _____ .

1. A. prie B. priez C. pries D. prions

Le jeune homme: J'espère que nous _____ un voyage agréable.

2. A. faisons B. fassions C. avons fait D. ferons

Vous: Je l' _____ bien aussi.

3. A. espérer B. ai espéré C. avais espéré D. espère

Le jeune homme: Savez-vous à quelle heure le train _____ à Paris?

4. A. est arrivé B. arriverait C. arrivera D. arrivait

60 Verb drills and tests

| Vous: | Vers une heure et quart. |
| Le jeune homme: | Il semble qu'il _____ beau temps. |

5.   A. a fait   B. va faire   C. faisait   D. fasse

Vous: Oui, on _____ une belle journée pour aujourd'hui.

6.   A. prévoit   B. prévois   C. prévoira   D. prévoie

Le jeune homme: Je suppose que le train _____ bientôt.

7.   A. est parti   B. sera parti   C. va partir   D. partir

Vous: En effet, je _____ que nous sommes déjà en route.

8.   A. crus   B. croit   C. croyais   D. crois

Verb Test 10

SENTENCE COMPLETION

Directions: Each of the following sentences contains a missing verb form. From the choices given, select the verb form of the tense that is required, according to the sense of the sentence, and write the letter of your choice on the line. At times, only the infinitive form is needed or a present or past participle.

1. J'ai besoin de _____ mais je n'ai pas de savon.
A. laver   B. se laver   C. me laver   D. me laverai

2. Quand Lisa _____ dans le salon, elle a vu un vase de jolies fleurs.
A. entre   B. entrera   C. est entré   D. est entrée

3. Si j'ai le temps, _____ le travail.
A. j'ai fait   B. je ferai   C. je ferais   D. je faisais

4. Si j'avais le temps, _____ le travail.
A. je ferais   B. je ferai   C. j'aurais fait   D. j'ai fait

5. Si j'avais eu le temps, _____ le travail.
A. j'ai fait   B. j'aurai fait   C. j'aurais fait   D. je faisais

6. Mademoiselle, un café pour mon ami, s'il vous plaît. Moi, _____ un thé.
A. j'aimerais   B. j'ai aimé   C. j'aimai   D. j'aimais

7. À quelle heure pourriez-vous venir? Je _____ venir après le dîner.
A. pouvais   B. pourrais   C. pouvons   D. puisse

8. Si j'étais vous, je ne le _____ pas.
   A. ferai   B. ferais   C. faisais   D. fasse

9. Je doute que Jeanne _____ ce soir.
   A. viendra   B. vienne   C. viendrait   D. vient

10. J'ai peur qu'il ne _____ malade.
    A. sois   B. soit   C. sera   D. serait

11. Je regrette que tu _____ malade.
    A. es   B. est   C. soit   D. sois

12. Je partirai à moins qu'il ne _____ .
    A. vienne   B. viennent   C. viendra   D. vient

13. Quoiqu'elle _____ belle, il ne l'aime pas.
    A. est   B. soit   C. serait   D. sera

14. Je le lui explique pour qu'elle _____ .
    A. comprendra B. comprenne   C. comprennent   D. comprend

15. Je partirai dès qu'elle _____ .
    A. arrive   B. arrivera   C. arriverait   D. est arrivée

16. Il est urgent que vous _____ .
    A. pars   B. partez   C. partiez   D. partirez

17. Tout d'un coup, je me suis rappelé que _____ de le lui dire.
    A. j'ai oublié B. j'oublie   C. j'oublierai   D. j'avais oublié

18. J'étais fatigué ce matin parce que _____ dormi.
    A. je n'ai pas B. je n'aurai pas C. je n'avais pas D. j'ai

19. Je suis fatigué maintenant parce que _____ dormi.
    A. j'ai   B. je n'ai pas   C. je vais   D. je n'avais pas

20. Quand elle arrivera demain _____ le travail.
    A. j'aurai fini B. j'ai fini   C. j'avais fini   D. je finisse

CHANGING FROM ONE TENSE TO ANOTHER

Directions: *The following verb forms are all in the present indicative tense. Change them to the passé composé, keeping the same subject. Consult the index of common irregular French verb forms, in the Appendixes, for irregular verb forms that you cannot identify. Keep in mind that to form the passé composé you need to use the present indicative tense of either avoir or être (depending on which of the two helping verbs is required) plus the past participle of the verb you are working with. If you feel uncertain about this, consult page 6 about when to use avoir or être as a helping verb.*

Model: Elle mange.

You write: Elle a mangé.

1. Elle va. _____

2. Il a. _____

3. Je m'assieds. _____

4. Ils ont. _____

5. Tu es. _____

6. Il va. _____

7. Nous allons. _____

8. Nous avons. _____

9. Je parle. _____

10. Elles viennent. _____

11. Je bois. _____

12. Ils boivent. _____

13. Vous buvez. _____

14. Je crois. _____

15. Tu dis. _____

16. Je peux. _____

17. Il faut. _____

18. Vous lisez. _____

19. Vous dites. _____

20. Tu mets. _____

21. Elle naît. _____

22. Elle meurt. _____

23. Elle vend. _____

24. Ils s'amusent. _____

25. Elle entre. _____

26. On finit. _____

27. Elles courent. _____

28. Ils prennent. _____

29. On apprend. _____

30. Elles arrivent. _____

COMPLETION OF VERB FORMS
(in the Seven Simple Tenses)

Directions: *Complete each verb form in the tenses indicated by writing the correct letter or letters on the blank lines.*

Présent de l'indicatif (Tense No. 1)

1. (aimer) J'aim _____
2. (chanter) Tu chant _____
3. (étudier)Il/elle/on étudi _____
4. (choisir) Janine chois _____
5. (entendre) J'entend _____

6. (attendre) Nous attend _____
7. (manger) Vous mang _____
8. (vendre) Ils/elles vend _____
9. (finir) Richard et moi fin _____
10. (donner) Marie et Jeanne donn _____

Imparfait de l'indicatif (Tense No. 2)

1. (parler) Je parl _____
2. (finir) Tu finiss _____
3. (vendre) Il/elle/on vend _____
4. (être) Madeleine ét _____
5. (avoir) Il/elle/on av _____

6. (venir) Nous ven _____
7. (faire) Vous fais _____
8. (aller) Ils/elles all _____
9. (jouer) Paul et Henri jou _____
10. (donner) Tu donn _____

Passé simple (Tense No. 3)
(*This tense is not used in conversation. It is used in literary style.*)

1. (parler) Je parl _____
2. (finir) Tu fin _____
3. (vendre) Il/elle/on vend _____
4. (écrire) Catherine écriv _____
5. (aller) Ils/elles all _____

6. (donner) Nous donn _____
7. (choisir) Vous chois _____
8. (comprendre) Ils/elles compr _____
9. (désirer) Hélène et Raymond désir _____
10. (danser) Il/elle/on dans _____

Futur (Tense No. 4)

1. (manger) Je manger _____
2. (finir) Tu finir _____
3. (vendre) Il/elle/on vendr _____
4. (écrire) La femme écrir _____
5. (aller) J'ir _____

6. (donner) Nous donner _____
7. (choisir) Vous choisir _____
8. (comprendre) Ils/elles comprendr _____
9. (jouer) Les garçons jouer _____
10. (avoir) J'aur _____

Conditionnel (Tense No. 5)

1. (aller) J'ir _____
2. (finir) Tu finir _____
3. (faire) Il/elle/on fer _____
4. (manger) Je manger _____
5. (pouvoir) Vous pourr _____

6. (parler) Nous parler _____
7. (être) Vous ser _____
8. (avoir) Ils/elles aur _____
9. (prendre) Je prendr _____
10. (dîner) Vous dîner _____

Présent du subjonctif (Tense No. 6)

1. (parler) que je parl _____
2. (donner) que tu donn _____
3. (oser) qu'il/elle/on os _____
4. (choisir) que je choisiss _____
5. (manger) que tu mang _____

6. (partir) que nous part _____
7. (vendre) que vous vend _____
8. (prendre) qu'ils/elles prenn _____
9. (finir) que nous finiss _____
10. (fermer) qu'il/elle/on ferm _____

Imparfait du subjonctif (Tense No. 7)

1. (parler) que je parl _____
2. (donner) que tu donn _____
3. (ouvrir) qu'il/elle/on ouvr _____

4. (partir) que nous part _____
5. (vouloir) que vous voul _____
6. (finir) qu'ils/elles fin _____

Verb Test 13

PAST PARTICIPLES

Directions: *In this crossword puzzle (mots-croisés) write the past participle for each of the verbs given below. Most of them are irregular. Past participles are important to know because they are needed to form the seven compound tenses, for example, the passé composé.*

Horizontalement
1. donner
5. pouvoir
7. fuir
8. rire
9. devoir (*backwards*)
10. taire
11. savoir
13. lire
15. savoir
18. naître
19. rire (*backwards*)
21. taire
22. tuer

Verticalement
1. devoir
2. naître
3. lire
4. vendre
5. prendre
6. dire
7. falloir
12. user
14. finir
16. mourir
17. être
20. avoir

Verb Test 14

DRILLING THE VERB *AVOIR*
(in the Seven Simple Tenses)

Note: You definitely must know the verb **avoir** in the seven simple tenses because they are needed to form the seven compound tenses of verbs conjugated with **avoir**, for example, the passé composé (Tense No. 8), as in **j'ai mangé** (I have eaten). Practice these by writing them every day until you know them thoroughly. If you don't know them, see verb 62. Also, read about **avoir** verbs on page 6. Review pages 23 to 25.

Directions: Write the verb forms of *avoir* in the seven simple tenses indicated.

1. Présent de l'indicatif (Tense No. 1)

Singular	Plural
j' _____	nous _____
tu _____	vous _____
il/elle/on/(*or a noun*) _____	ils/elles/(*or a noun*) _____

2. Imparfait de l'indicatif (Tense No. 2)

j' _____	nous _____
tu _____	vous _____
il/elle/on/(*or a noun*) _____	ils/elles/(*or a noun*) _____

3. Passé simple (Tense No. 3)

j' _____	nous _____
tu _____	vous _____
il/elle/on/(*or a noun*) _____	ils/elles/(*or a noun*) _____

4. Futur (Tense No. 4)

j' _____	nous _____
tu _____	vous _____
il/elle/on/(*or a noun*) _____	ils/elles/(*or a noun*) _____

5. Conditionnel (Tense No. 5)

j' _____	nous _____
tu _____	vous _____
il/elle/on/(*or a noun*) _____	ils/elles/(*or a noun*) _____

6. Présent du subjonctif (Tense No. 6)

que j' _____	que nous _____
que tu _____	que vous _____
qu'il/elle/on/(*or a noun*) _____	qu'ils/elles/(*or a noun*) _____

7. Imparfait du subjonctif (Tense No. 7)

que j' _____	que nous _____
que tu _____	que vous _____
qu'il/elle/on/(*or a noun*) _____	qu'ils/elles/(*or a noun*) _____

DRILLING THE VERB *ÊTRE*
(in the Seven Simple Tenses)

Note: You must know the verb **être** in the seven simple tenses because they are needed to form the seven compound tenses of verbs conjugated with **être**, for example, the **passé composé** (Tense No. 8), as in **elle est arrivée** (she has arrived). Practice these by writing them every day until you know them thoroughly. If you don't know them, see verb 211. Also, read about **être** verbs on page 6. Review pages 23 to 25.

Directions: Write the verb forms of **être** in the seven simple tenses indicated.

1. Présent de l'indicatif (Tense No. 1)

<u>Singular</u>   <u>Plural</u>

je _____   nous _____
tu _____   vous _____
il/elle/on/(*or a noun*) _____   ils/elles/(*or a noun*) _____

2. Imparfait de l'indicatif (Tense No. 2)

j' _____   nous _____
tu _____   vous _____
il/elle/on/(*or a noun*) _____   ils/elles/(*or a noun*) _____

3. Passé simple (Tense No. 3)

je _____   nous _____
tu _____   vous _____
il/elle/on/(*or a noun*) _____   ils/elles/(*or a noun*) _____

4. Futur (Tense No. 4)

je _____   nous _____
tu _____   vous _____
il/elle/on/(*or a noun*) _____   ils/elles/(*or a noun*) _____

5. Conditionnel (Tense No. 5)

je _____   nous _____
tu _____   vous _____
il/elle/on/(*or a noun*) _____   ils/elles/(*or a noun*) _____

6. Présent du subjonctif (Tense No. 6)

que je ——————————— que nous ————————————

que tu ——————————— que vous ————————————

qu'il/elle/on/(*or a noun*) ———— qu'ils/elles/(*or a noun*) ————————

7. Imparfait du subjonctif (Tense No. 7)

que je ——————————— que nous ————————————

que tu ——————————— que vous ————————————

qu'il/elle/on/(*or a noun*) ———— qu'ils/elles/(*or a noun*) ————————

Verb Test 16

CHANGING FROM ONE TENSE TO ANOTHER

Directions: *The following verb forms are all in the* passé composé *(Tense No. 8). Change them to the* plus-que-parfait de l'indicatif *(Tense No. 9), keeping the same subject. Keep in mind that to form the* plus-que-parfait de l'indicatif *you need to use the imperfect indicative tense of either* avoir *or* être *(depending on which of the two helping verbs is required) plus the past participle of the verb you are working with. If you feel uncertain about this, consult page 6 about when to use* avoir *or* être *as a helping verb. Review the formation of the past participles on page 3. Also, review Verb Tests 14 and 15.*

Passé composé	Plus-que-parfait de l'indicatif
Model: Elle a mangé.	**You write:** Elle avait mangé.
(She has eaten.)	(She had eaten.)
Elle est arrivée.	Elle était arrivée.
(She has arrived.)	(She had arrived.)

1. Elle est allée. ————————   **16.** J'ai pu. ————————

2. Il a eu. ————————   **17.** Il a fallu. ————————

3. Je me suis assis. ————————   **18.** Vous avez lu. ————————

4. Ils ont eu. ————————   **19.** Vous avez dit. ————————

5. Tu as été. ————————   **20.** Tu as mis. ————————

6. Il est allé. ————————   **21.** Elle est née. ————————

7. Nous sommes allés. ————————   **22.** Elle est morte. ————————

8. Nous avons eu. ————————   **23.** Elle s'est lavée. ————————

9. J'ai parlé. ————————   **24.** Elles se sont lavées. ————————

10. Elle est venue. ————————   **25.** Je suis entré. ————————

11. J'ai bu. ————————   **26.** On a parlé. ————————

12. Ils se sont tus. ————————   **27.** Ils ont couru. ————————

13. J'ai fait. ————————   **28.** Ils ont pris. ————————

14. Tu as dû. ————————   **29.** On a dit. ————————

15. Vous avez dit. ————————   **30.** J'ai compris. ————————

SENTENCE COMPLETION

Directions: *Each of the following sentences contains a missing verb form. From the choices given, select the verb form of the tense that is required, according to the sense of the sentence, and write the letter of your choice on the line. At times only the infinitive form is needed or a present or past participle.*

1. Il est possible qu'elle _____ partie.
    A. est   B. soit   C. a   D. ait

2. Je doute que Laurent _____ fait cela.
    A. a   B. est   C. ait   D. soit

3. Je ne peux pas _____ maintenant parce qu'il fait un temps affreux.
    A. sort   B. sortant   C. sortir   D. sors

4. Joséphine est tombée en _____ dans la cuisine.
    A. entrer   B. entrant   C. entrée   D. entre

5. Simone a _____ la table.
    A. essuyer   B. essuyé   C. essuyée   D. essuyant

6. Françoise s'est _____ à écrire une lettre à sa tante.
    A. mis   B. mise   C. mettre   D. mettant

7. Les enfants _____ dire bonsoir aux invités.
    A. vouloir   B. voulu   C. voulus   D. veulent

8. Voici les fleurs que j'ai _____ .
    A. acheté   B. achetés   C. achetées   D. acheter

9. Quand Raymond eut mangé, il _____ .
    A. partit   B. partis   C. partir   D. partira

10. J' _____ fait le travail si j'avais eu le temps.
    A. aurait   B. aurais   C. avais   D. ai

PRESENT PARTICIPLES

Directions: In this word puzzle, find the present participle of each of the verbs listed below and draw a line around each one. To get you started, the first verb on the list (*aller*), whose present participle is *allant*, is already done. The present participles are written horizontally, vertically, or backwards.

aller
avoir
chanter
choisir
croire
dire
être
faire
finir

lire
naître
oser
prendre
tenir
vendre
venir
voir

C	H	A	N	T	A	N	T	A	T
H	F	Y	T	N	V	E	A	P	N
O	A	A	N	A	E	F	V	R	A
I	I	N	A	N	A	I	E	E	Y
S	S	T	Y	E	N	N	N	N	O
I	A	A	O	T	T	I	D	A	V
S	N	N	R	D	I	S	A	N	T
S	T	T	C	T	E	S	N	T	N
A	L	L	A	N	T	A	T	O	A
N	A	I	S	S	A	N	T	S	N
T	N	O	S	A	N	T	F	A	E
L	I	S	A	N	T	T	A	N	V

DIALOGUE

Directions: In the following dialogue there are blank spaces indicating missing verb forms. Select the appropriate verb form according to the sense of what the speakers are saying and write the letter of your choice on the line. The situation is given below.

Situation: You are a tourist in Paris. You are talking with the desk clerk in a hotel about a room.

L'employé: Bonjour. Vous désirez une chambre?
Vous: Oui, je désire _____ une petite chambre avec salle de bains.
1.   A. louer   B. loué   C. louée   D. louant

L'employé: C'est pour combien de personnes, s'il vous plaît?
Vous: _____ pour moi seulement.
2.   A. C'était   B. C'est   C. Ce fut   D. Ce fût

L'employé: Il me reste seulement une chambre à 150 euros la nuit, petit déjeuner compris.
Vous: D'accord. Je la _____ .
3.   A. prend   B. prends   C. pris   D. prenne

L'employé: C'est pour combien de temps?
Vous: Probablement pour une semaine, je _____ .
4. A. croit B. crus C. croie D. crois

L'employé: Bon. Signez ici et _____-moi votre passeport, s'il vous plaît.
5. A. montres B. montez C. montrez D. montrerez

Verb Test 20

CHANGING FROM ONE VERB TO ANOTHER

Directions: *The verb forms in the following statements are all in the passé composé. Change each sentence by replacing the verb in the sentence with the proper form of the verb in parentheses. Keep the passé composé, of course. Rewrite the statement in French.*

Models: **Madeleine** *est arrivée.* **(partir)** **You write:** **Madeleine** *est partie.*
Simone *a mangé* **le gâteau. (faire)** **Simone** *a fait* **le gâteau.**

1. Richard *a appris* la leçon. (écrire)

_____

2. Elle *s'est assise.* (se lever)

_____

3. J'*ai écrit* la lettre. (lire)

_____

4. Elle *a fermé* la fenêtre. (ouvrir)

_____

5. Hélène *est arrivée.* (mourir)

_____

6. *Avez-vous acheté* un cadeau? (offrir)

_____

7. Marguerite *est sortie.* (venir)

_____

8. *Nous avons écouté* l'histoire. (croire)

_____

9. *Ils ont visité* Paris. (voir)

_____

10. Les enfants *ont pleuré.* (rire)

_____

11. *As-tu commandé* les frites? (prendre)

_____

12. *Ils sont allés* à Paris. (rester)

_____

13. L'étudiant *n'a pas compris* la réponse. (savoir)

_____

14. L'enfant *a mangé* un bon repas. (avoir)

_____

15. J'*ai envoyé* la lettre. (recevoir)

_____

16. *Avez-vous voyagé* en France? (être)

_____

17. *A-t-il ouvert* la boîte? (couvrir)

_____

18. Les enfants *se sont lavés*. (se taire)

_____

19. Louise *a désiré* venir chez moi. (vouloir)

_____

20. Qui *a entendu* le bruit? (faire)

_____

Verb Test 21

TRANSLATING VERB FORMS OF *ALLER*

Directions: *Translate the following verb forms of* aller *with their subjects into English. Keep in mind that some verb tenses can be translated into English in more than one way. For example, depending on the thought expressed in a particular situation,* Je vais *can mean I go, I do go, or I am going.*

1. Nous allons	_____	**8.** Elle est allée	_____
2. Tu allais	_____	**9.** Elles étaient allées	_____
3. Il alla	_____	**10.** Nous fûmes allés	_____
4. Nous irons	_____	**11.** Tu seras allé	_____
5. Vous iriez	_____	**12.** Vous seriez allé	_____
6. Que j'aille	_____	**13.** Qu'il soit allé	_____
7. Que j'allasse	_____	**14.** Qu'elle fût allée	_____

Now, let's try a few other verbs. The infinitive form is given in parentheses in case you do not recognize the verb form. Remember that all verb forms used in these drills and tests are in this book among the 501 French verbs, in the preliminary pages, and in the back pages.

15. (savoir) Je sais _____	**23.** (faire) Nous ferons _____
16. (être) Il fut _____	**24.** (venir) Je serais venu _____
17. (avoir) Elle aura _____	**25.** (s'en aller) Allez-vous-en! _____
18. (avoir) Nous aurions _____	**26.** (vendre) Vous avez vendu _____
19. (être) que je sois _____	**27.** (finir) Nous aurons fini _____
20. (avoir) Il eut _____	**28.** (boire) Tu avais bu _____
21. (avoir) J'ai eu _____	**29.** (monter) Elle est montée _____
22. (mettre) J'ai mis _____	**30.** (rester) Nous sommes restés_____

Verb Test 22

PRESENT INDICATIVE

Directions: In this word puzzle, find the verb form in the present indicative tense for each infinitive given in parentheses in the sentences below. When you find them, draw a line around each one. The verb form in the present tense of *faire* in the first statement given below is *faites*. It has already been done to get you started. The words are written horizontally, vertically, diagonally, or backwards.

- Que (**faire**)-vous ce soir?
- Que me (**dire**)-vous?
- J' (**aimer**) danser.
- Moi, je (**aller**) chez moi.
- Les garçons (**avoir**)-ils assez d'argent pour aller au cinéma?
- Nous (**aller**) en France l'été prochain.
- Quand (**partir**)-tu?
- Et vous, (**être**)-vous heureux?
- Tes parents (**pouvoir**)-ils venir avec nous?
- Que (**devoir**)-tu faire maintenant?
- Pourquoi (**courir**)-tu?
- (**Vendre**)-ils leur maison?
- Est-ce que nous (**finir**) le travail aujourd'hui?

A	I	M	E	B	A	L	I	T	A
C	D	A	L	O	S	E	T	I	D
O	O	E	F	I	O	A	E	G	I
U	I	E	A	A	L	L	O	N	S
R	S	V	S	I	O	U	E	A	U
S	A	I	R	E	U	Ê	T	E	S
I	L	N	A	P	S	U	V	L	O
A	E	I	P	E	U	V	E	N	T
E	O	N	T	N	E	D	N	E	V
L	U	I	A	L	L	E	Z	O	N
F	A	T	E	Z	V	A	V	A	I
F	I	N	I	S	S	O	N	S	S

TRANSLATING VERB FORMS
(from English into French)

Directions: *Translate the following verb forms with their subjects into French. In Test 21 you did the opposite. This is good practice because it helps you to master verb forms in French and English.*

1. We are going

_____

2. You (*tu*) were going

_____

3. He went (*Tense No. 3*)

_____

4. We will go

_____

5. You (*vous*) would go

_____

6. that I may go

_____

7. that I might go (*Tense No. 7*)

_____

8. She has gone

_____

9. They (*fem.*) had gone

_____

10. We had gone (*Tense No. 10*)

_____

11. You (*tu*) will have gone

_____

12. You (*vous*) would have gone

_____

13. that he may have gone

_____

14. that she might have gone (*Tense No. 14*)

_____

15. I know (*savoir*)

_____

16. He was (*Tense No. 3*)

_____

17. She will have

_____

18. We would have

_____

19. that I may be

_____

20. He had (*Tense No. 3*)

_____

21. I have had

_____

22. I have put

_____

23. We will do

_____

24. I would have come

_____

25. Go away! (*vous*)

_____

26. You (*vous*) sold

_____

27. We will have finished

_____

28. You (*tu*) had drunk

_____

29. She went up

_____

30. We stayed

_____

DRILLING THE VERB *AVOIR* AGAIN
(in the Seven Simple Tenses)

Note: In Test 14 you drilled the verb **avoir** in the seven simple tenses. Now, do it again here because you must know them in order to form the seven compound tenses of verbs conjugated with **avoir**. Practice these by writing them every day until you know them thoroughly. If you don't know them yet, see verb 62. Also, read about **avoir** verbs on page 6. Review pages 23 to 25 again.

Directions: Write the verb forms of avoir in the tenses indicated.

<u>Singular</u>   <u>Plural</u>

1. Présent de l'indicatif (Tense No. 1)

j' _____   nous _____
tu _____   vous _____
il/elle/on/(*or a noun*) _____   ils/elles/(*or a noun*) _____

2. Imparfait de l'indicatif (Tense No. 2)

j' _____   nous _____
tu _____   vous _____
il/elle/on/(*or a noun*) _____   ils/elles/(*or a noun*) _____

3. Passé simple (Tense No. 3)

j' _____   nous _____
tu _____   vous _____
il/elle/on/(*or a noun*) _____   ils/elles/(*or a noun*) _____

4. Futur (Tense No. 4)

j' _____   nous _____
tu _____   vous _____
il/elle/on/(*or a noun*) _____   ils/elles/(*or a noun*) _____

5. Conditionnel (Tense No. 5)

j' _____   nous _____
tu _____   vous _____
il/elle/on/(*or a noun*) _____   ils/elles/(*or a noun*) _____

6. Présent du subjonctif (Tense No. 6)

que j' _____	que nous _____
que tu _____	que vous _____
qu'il/elle/on/(*or a noun*) _____	qu'ils/elles/(*or a noun*) _____

7. Imparfait du subjonctif (Tense No. 7)

que j' _____	que nous _____
que tu _____	que vous _____
qu'il/elle/on/(*or a noun*) _____	qu'ils/elles/(*or a noun*) _____

Verb Test 25

DRILLING THE VERB *ÊTRE* AGAIN
(in the Seven Simple Tenses)

Note: In Test 15 you drilled the verb être in the seven simple tenses. We would like you to do it again here because you must know them in order to form the seven compound tenses of verbs conjugated with être. Practice these by writing them every day until you know them thoroughly. If you don't know them yet, see verb 211. Also, read the statement about être verbs on page 6. Review again pages 23 to 25.

Directions: *Write the verb forms of être in the tenses indicated.*

1. Présent de l'indicatif (Tense No. 1)

<u>Singular</u>	<u>Plural</u>
je _____	nous _____
tu _____	vous _____
il/elle/on/(*or a noun*) _____	ils/elles/(*or a noun*) _____

2. Imparfait de l'indicatif (Tense No. 2)

j' _____	nous _____
tu _____	vous _____
il/elle/on/(*or a noun*) _____	ils/elles/(*or a noun*) _____

3. Passé simple (Tense No. 3)

je _____   nous _____
tu _____   vous _____
il/elle/on/(*or a noun*) _____   ils/elles/(*or a noun*) _____

4. Futur (Tense No. 4)

je _____   nous _____
tu _____   vous _____
il/elle/on/(*or a noun*) _____   ils/elles/(*or a noun*) _____

5. Conditionnel (Tense No. 5)

je _____   nous _____
tu _____   vous _____
il/elle/on/(*or a noun*) _____   ils/elles/(*or a noun*) _____

6. Présent du subjonctif (Tense No. 6)

que je _____   que nous _____
que tu _____   que vous _____
qu'il/elle/on/(*or a noun*) _____   qu'ils/elles/(*or a noun*) _____

7. Imparfait du subjonctif (Tense No. 7)

que je _____   que nous _____
que tu _____   que vous _____
qu'il/elle/on/(*or a noun*) _____   qu'ils/elles/(*or a noun*) _____

LE PASSÉ COMPOSÉ

Directions: *This crossword puzzle (mots-croisés) tests your knowledge of the passé composé. The missing words in the sentences below are the present tense of avoir or être, or the correct form of the past participle, or a subject pronoun.*

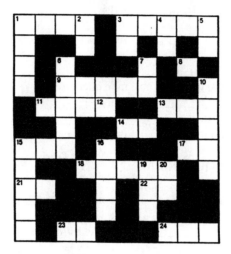

Horizontalement

1. Hier, je _____ allé au cinéma.
3. Marie est _____ (aller) à Paris.
8. Pierre _____ lu un livre.
9. Ils ont _____ (vouloir) partir.
11. _____ avez bien parlé.
13. La lettre? Je l'ai _____ (lire).
14. Paul s'est _____ (taire).
15. J'ai _____ (mettre) du sucre dans le café.
17. J'ai _____ (devoir) (*backwards*) partir.
18. Les lettres? Je les ai _____ (mettre) sur le bureau.
21. Nous avons bien _____ (rire).
22. Avez-vous _____ (savoir) la réponse?
23. Victor a-t- _____ compris?
24. Qu'a-t-elle _____ (dire)?

Verticalement

1. Je _____ tombé en montant l'escalier.
2. J'ai _____ (savoir) la réponse.
3. Hier soir, j' _____ beaucoup mangé.
4. Simone a _____ (lire) un livre.
5. Ce matin j'ai _____ (avoir) un petit accident.
6. Nous _____ pris le train.
7. Les enfants ont _____ (pouvoir) venir.
10. Nous avons _____ (vendre) la maison.
12. A-t-il _____ (savoir) (*backwards*) la réponse?
15. Madame Durand est _____ (mourir) hier soir.
16. Tu as _____ (finir) la leçon?
19. Jacqueline _____ restée à la maison.
20. Tu as _____ (savoir) cela, n'est-ce pas?

IDENTIFYING VERB FORMS
(in a Passage from French Literature)

Directions: *Read the following literary passage twice. Then, identify the verb forms with their subjects printed in **bold face** by giving (a) the infinitive of the verb form, (b) the name of the tense in French, and (c) the person and number of the verb form.*

Example: je vois   You write: (a) **voir**
(b) **présent de l'indicatif**
(c) **1st person singular**

Pourquoi donc ne vous **vois-je** pas, mon cher ami? **Je suis** inquiète de vous. **Vous** m'**aviez** tant **promis** de ne faire qu'aller et venir de l'Hermitage ici! Sur cela je vous **ai laissé** libre; et point du tout, **vous laissez** passer huit jours. Si **on** ne m'**avait** pas **dit** que **vous étiez** en bonne santé, **je** vous **croirais** malade. Je vous **attendais** avant-hier ou hier, et **je** ne vous **vois** point arriver.

Mon Dieu! qu'**avez-vous** donc? **Vous** n'**avez** point d'affaires; **vous** n'**avez** pas non plus de chagrins, car **je me flatte** que **vous seriez venu** sur-le-champ me les confier. **Vous êtes** donc malade! **Tirez**-moi d'inquiétude bien vite, **je** vous en **prie**. Adieu, mon cher ami.

Lettre de Madame d'Épinay à Jean-Jacques Rousseau,
Selection from *Les Confessions* by Jean-Jacques Rousseau

1. vois-je

(a) _____

(b) _____

(c) _____

2. je suis

(a) _____

(b) _____

(c) _____

3. vous aviez promis

(a) _____

(b) _____

(c) _____

4. j'ai laissé

(a) _____

(b) _____

(c) _____

5. vous laissez

(a) _____

(b) _____

(c) _____

6. on avait dit

(a) _____

(b) _____

(c) _____

7. vous étiez

(a) _____

(b) _____

(c) _____

8. je croirais

(a) _____

(b) _____

(c) _____

9. vous avez

(a) _____

(b) _____

(c) _____

10. j'attendais

(a) _____

(b) _____

(c) _____

11. je vois

(a) _____

(b) _____

(c) _____

12. avez-vous

(a) _____

(b) _____

(c) _____

13. vous avez

(a) _____

(b) _____

(c) _____

14. je me flatte

(a) _____

(b) _____

(c) _____

15. vous seriez venu

(a) _____

(b) _____

(c) _____

16. vous êtes

(a) _____

(b) _____

(c) _____

17. tirez

(a) _____

(b) _____

(c) _____

18. je prie

(a) _____

(b) _____

(c) _____

Answers to verb tests with explanations

Test 1

1. B The verb **aller** is conjugated with **être** to form a compound tense. Review page 6. A and C are not correct because they are forms of **avoir**. You need the *passé composé* because of **hier**/yesterday. In D, **était** is imperfect indicative, which makes the verb form **était allée** pluperfect indicative. Review the uses of the *passé composé* on page 16 and the *plus-que-parfait de l'indicatif* on pages 16 to 17. Review **aller**.

2. D The subject is 3d person sing. In D, **peut** is 3d person sing. A, B, and C are not 3d person sing. Review **pouvoir**.

3. C The tenses of **avoir** in A, B, and D would not make sense here because you need the imperfect indicative, which is in C. Review the imperfect tense on pages 11 and 12. Review **avoir**.

4. A You need the 3d person sing., present tense, of **sourire** because the subject is 3d person sing. The tenses in C and D do not make any sense here because there is nothing in the sentence to require the subjunctive. The verb form in B is not 3d person sing. Review **sourire**.

5. B The tenses of **regarder** in C and D would not make sense here because you need the imperfect indicative, which is in B. The verb form in A is 3d person sing. and you are dealing with the subject **je**, which is 1st person, sing. Besides, C is not a good choice because **je** would be **j'** in front of **ai regardé**. Review the uses of the imperfect indicative tense on pages 11 and 12. Review **regarder**.

6. A You need the infinitive form **dormir** because it is right after the verb form **peux** in **je ne peux pas** (I am not able to sleep). The forms in B, C, and D would make no sense. Review those forms of **dormir**.

7. B The situation is in the present. The subject, **le docteur**, is 3d person sing. and so is **vient** in B. In A, **viens** is not 3d person sing. C and D are not in the present tense. Review **venir** and **venir de**. Also review *Verbs with prepositions* in the Appendixes, specifically **venir de + inf**.

8. C The infinitive **nettoyer** is needed because of the preposition **de** in front of it. Review *Verbs with prepositions* in the Appendixes, specifically **demander de + inf**. Review the other forms of **nettoyer** in A, B, and D.

9. A The infinitive **faire** is needed because **va** (a form of **aller**) precedes it. Review **aller + inf**. in the section on *Verbs with prepositions* in the Appendixes, and the other forms of **faire** in B, C, and D.

10. A You need the past participle to complete the *passé composé* where you see the helping verb **a** in front of the blank space. The past participle in B is feminine but there is no preceding feminine direct object. Review the forms of **oublier** in C and D.

11. D You need the fem. pl. form of the past participle (**achetées**) because there is a preceding fem. pl. direct object noun (**les chaussures**). The other past participles are masc. sing. in A, fem. sing. in B, and masc. pl. in C.

12. A The subject is 1st pers. sing. **j'** and it requires **irai**, the future of **aller**. **La semaine prochaine** indicates future time. Review the other tenses of **aller** in B, C, and D.

13. B   You need the 1st pers. sing. conditional of **aller** because the subordinate clause begins with **si** (if) and the verb in that clause is imperfect indicative (**j'avais**). Review **si** clauses, a summary of sequence of verb tenses at the top of page 26 where there are examples. Review the other tenses of **aller** in A, C, and D. Study, practice, and experience will help you recognize French verb forms and tenses.

14. A   You need the 1st pers. sing. future of **aller** because the subordinate clause begins with **si** (if) and the verb in that clause is present indicative (**j'ai**). Review **si** clauses, a summary of sequence of verb tenses at the top of page 26 where there are examples. Review the other tenses of **aller** in B, C, and D.

15. B   You need the fem. sing. form of the past participle (**lavée**) because the verb is reflexive (**se laver**/to wash oneself) and the fem. sing. agreement on the past participle is made with the reflexive pronoun **s'** (herself). We know it's fem. because the subject is **Paulette**. The reflexive pronoun **s'** in this sentence serves as a preceding direct object because Paulette washed *herself*. However, if there were a direct object *after* the verb, e.g., her feet, hair (as in sentence 16 below), there would be no agreement on the past participle. The other past participles in this sentence are masc. sing. in A, masc. pl. in C, and fem. pl. in D. Review also page 6.

16. A   You need the masc. sing. form of the past participle (**lavé**) because in this sentence the reflexive pronoun **s'** in **s'est lavé** is an indirect object, not a direct object. A past participle never agrees in gender (masc. or fem.) or number (sing. or pl.) with an indirect object. In other words, Gertrude washed her hair (**les cheveux**), which is *on herself*. Compare this sentence with number 15 above.

17. C   You need the present indicative of **aller** because the sentence states **en ce moment**/at this moment. Review the other tenses of **aller** in A, B, and D. Review the uses of the present indicative tense and the examples on pages 10 and 11.

18. A   You need the present indicative of **aller** because the sentence states **tous les jours** (every day), which is habitual action. Review the uses of the present indicative tense and the examples on page 10, in particular, the example in (b) at the top of page 11.

19. B   You need the present tense, 3d person pl. of **faire** because the subject is 3d person pl. Review the examples in (c) at the top of page 11. Also, review the other tenses of **faire** in A, C, and D.

20. D   You need the present tense, 1st person sing. of **être** because the subject is 1st person sing. Review the examples in (f) on page 11. Also, review the other tenses of **être** in A, B, and C.

Test 2

1. A   The situation is in the present. Review the other tenses of **trouver** in B, C, and D.

2. D   You need the present tense because the action is going on in the present. Do you recognize the other tenses in A, B, and C? Review **croire**.

3. A   Again, the present tense. Review the forms of **espérer**.

4. D   If you cannot identify the tenses, review **être**.

5. A   You need the future tense of **venir** because the clerk says that the suitcase will be available around five o'clock. You will come to get it at that time. Review the tenses of **venir**.

Test 3

1. **Ils comprennent bien aussi.** Study the forms of **comprendre**.
2. **Elles écrivent bien aussi.** Study the forms of **écrire**.
3. **Ils vont bien aussi.** Study the forms of **aller**.
4. **Je lis un livre dans le lit aussi.** Study the forms of **lire**.
5. **Ils voient bien aussi.** Study the forms of **voir**.
6. **Elle est allée au cinéma aussi.** You need to add **e** on the past participle for fem. agreement with the subject **elle**. Study the nonreflexive verbs conjugated with **être** to form the compound tenses on page 6. Also, study the forms of **aller**.
7. **Nous avons bien mangé aussi.** Study the *passé composé* of **manger**.
8. **Elles se sont assises aussi.** You need the fem. pl. agreement on the past participle of this reflexive verb **s'asseoir** because the reflexive pronoun **se** is a preceding direct object and the subject is **elles**. In other words, they *sat themselves*. Review the explanation in number 15 in Test 1. Review the forms of **s'asseoir**.
9. **Elle s'est lavée aussi.** Review the explanation in number 15 in Test 1. It's the same idea here. Review the *passé composé* of **se laver**.
10. **Elle s'est lavé les cheveux aussi.** Review the explanation in number 16 in Test 1. It's the same idea here.
11. **Ils ont rougi aussi.** Review the *passé composé* of **rougir**.
12. **Ils choisissent une auto aussi.** Study the present tense of **choisir**.
13. **Il finit la leçon aussi.** Study the present tense of **finir**.
14. **J'ai fait les devoirs aussi.** Study the *passé composé* of **faire**.
15. **Ils défendent la patrie aussi.** Study the present tense of **défendre**.
16. **Il répond à la question aussi.** Study the present tense of **répondre** and **répondre à** + noun, in the section on *Verbs with prepositions* in the Appendixes.
17. **Ils se couchent à dix heures aussi.** Study the forms of the reflexive verb **se coucher**.
18. **Elle s'est amusée aussi.** She amused *herself*. Review the explanation in number 15 in Test 1. It's the same idea here. Also, study the *passé composé* of the reflexive verb **s'amuser**.
19. **Je me suis reposé(e) aussi.** **Je** tells you if it is fem. or masc., depending on the context. If **me** (myself) is fem., add **e** to the past participle for fem. agreement with it. The idea here is the same as in the explanation in number 15 in Test 1. Study the *passé composé* of **se reposer**.
20. **Nous nous sommes levés tôt aussi.** Same idea here as in number 19 above. Review **se lever**.

Test 4

1. B   You need the future tense because **quand** introduces the clause and the verb in the main clause is future tense. Review the uses and examples of the future tense on pages 12–13 and the formation of the future on page 22. Study the verb forms of **arriver** in A, C, and D.
2. B   You need the infinitive form because there is no subject preceding the blank space. Here, **vous** is an indirect object pronoun meaning *to you*. (I would like to give these flowers to you.) Study the verb forms of **donner** in A, C, and D.

3. C You need the masc. pl. form of the past participle because **donner** is conjugated with **avoir** to form the *passé composé*, a compound tense, and it must agree with the preceding direct object **livres**. Here, **que** is a relative pronoun (*that* or *which*) and it refers to **les deux livres**. In other words, *Did you read the two books that I gave (to) you last week?*

4. D Same idea here as in number 3 above. Do you think you understand this construction by now? You need the fem. sing. form of the past participle because it refers to **que**, which relates to **la lettre**. In other words, *Here is the letter that I received yesterday.* Review the forms of **recevoir**.

5. A You need the *passé composé* because the sentence begins with **hier**/yesterday. In B the past participle is fem. because of the added **e**. There is no need for a fem. past participle because there is no *preceding* fem. direct object. The direct object is **une lettre**, which comes *after* the verb. Review the verb forms in C and D of **envoyer**.

6. D The clause where a verb form is needed begins with **si**/if. The verb in the main clause is conditional (**j'irais**/I would go). For those two reasons you need the imperfect indicative in D. Review **si** clauses where there are examples at the top of page 26. If you reversed the two clauses, the idea would be the same: **Si j'avais assez d'argent j'irais en France**/If I had enough money I would go to France. Review the verb forms in A, B, and C of **avoir**.

7. A You need the future tense of **avoir** because **quand** (when) precedes the required verb form and the verb in the main clause is future (**j'irai**). Review the uses and examples of the future on pages 12–13, in particular, example (d). Also, review the other forms of **avoir** in B, C, and D.

8. B You need the present subjunctive of **être** (**que tu** *sois*) because the verb in the preceding main clause is **j'insiste**. Here, the need for the subjunctive is the same in English, too, when we say: *I insist that you be here before five o'clock.* Review the uses and examples of the present subjunctive on page 14, especially example (c). Study the other forms of **être** in A, C, and D.

9. D You need the 3d person sing. present tense **veut** because the subject (**cela**/that) is 3d person sing. The form **veux** in C is 1st or 2d person sing. present tense of **vouloir**. There is nothing in the sentence to require the present subjunctive in A or the imperfect subjunctive in B. Review the forms of **vouloir**.

10. A You must know the impersonal expression **il faut**/it is necessary. Review the forms of **falloir** in the section on *Defective and impersonal verbs* in the Appendixes, and the expressions on the bottom of that page. Also, review the section on *Verbs with prepositions* in the Appendixes, in particular, **falloir** + inf. In B review **être**. In C review **il pleut (pleuvoir)** in the section on *Defective and impersonal verbs*, in the Appendixes, and the examples on the bottom of that page. In D review **il fend (fendre)**.

11. D The conjunction **pendant que** (while) precedes the subject and required verb form. This indicates that two actions were going on at the same time in the past: *My brother was reading while I was writing.* For that reason the imperfect indicative is needed. Review the imperfect tense on pages 11 and 12, especially example (a). Also, review the other forms of **écrire** in A, B, and C. See page 22 for the regular formation of the imperfect.

12. A An action was going on in the past when another action occurred: *The students were reading when I entered the classroom.* Review the imperfect tense on pages 11 and 12, especially example (b). Review the other forms of **entrer** in B, C, and D.

13. B You need the imperfect indicative tense because a habitual action took place in the past: *When I was little, my family and I used to go to the beach in the summer.* Review the imperfect tense on pages 11 and 12, especially example (c). Review the other forms of **aller** in A, C, and D.

14. C You need the imperfect indicative tense because the sentence contains a description in the past: *Richard was sad when I saw him.* Review the imperfect tense on pages 11 and 12, especially example (d). Also, review the other forms of **être** in A, B, and D.

15. A The reason for the imperfect indicative tense here is the same as in number 14 above. Do you think you understand this construction now?

16. B You need the *passé composé* because the action took place in the past: *At midnight, Peter woke up and said to his brother: "Get up!"* In C the past participle is fem. sing., but there is no need for it because the subject is masc. Review agreement on the past participle of a reflexive verb in numbers 15 and 16, Test 1. Review the other forms of **se réveiller** in A, C, and D.

17. C You need the infinitive form **marcher** because it is right after the verb **entendre**. Review **entendre** + inf. in the section on *Verbs with prepositions* in the Appendixes. Review the other forms of **marcher** in A, B, and D.

18. D You are dealing with **avoir froid**/to feel cold. Review the verb **avoir**. Review the forms of **avoir**. In A review **être**, **faire** in B, **tenir** in C, and the idiomatic expressions on the bottom of those pages.

19. C The subject of the verb is **nous**, 1st person pl. You need the *passé composé* because of **l'année dernière**/last year. The plural **s** is needed on **allés** because it is conjugated with **être** and the subject is plural. Review the other forms of **aller** in A, B, and D. Also, review page 6.

20. C The explanation here is the same as in numbers 3 and 4 above in this test.

Test 5

1. C You are dealing with **avoir lieu**/to take place. Review the verb **avoir**, especially **avoir lieu**. You need the future of **avoir** because the exam will take place after tomorrow. Review **avoir** and the forms of **être** in A and B.

2. D You are dealing with **avoir** in the idiomatic expression **il y a**/there is . . ., there are: *There is nothing to fear.* Review the verb **avoir**, especially **il y a**. Review the other forms of **avoir** in A and C. Review also **être** for **soit** in B.

3. B You need the infinitive form **rester** because it is right after the verb **devrai** (**devoir**). Review **devoir** and **devoir** + inf. in the section on *Verbs with prepositions* in the Appendixes. See **rester** for the other forms in A, C, and D.

4. C Review **pouvoir** for the forms in A, B, C, and D.

5. A Review **souhaiter** for the forms in A, B, C, and D.

Test 6

Note: In this test, the verb form you are given in each sentence is the imperative (command) mood. Review the *impératif* on pages 20 and 21. The forms of the imperative are given near the bottom of each page among the 501 verbs fully conjugated in all the tenses in this book. They are the *tu*, *nous*, and *vous* forms; for example: **donne!**/give! (*tu* understood), **donnons!**/let's give! (*nous* understood), **donnez!**/give! (*vous* understood). You have to look at the ending of the verb form to see if the subject understood is 2d person sing. (*tu*), 1st person pl. (*nous*), or 2d person pl., polite sing. (*vous*).

In the imperative, er verbs, like **donner**, drop the s in the 2d person sing. (*tu* form) of the present indicative, for example: **Marie, donne-moi le chocolat!**/Marie, give me the chocolate! But the s remains if the word that follows is en or y to facilitate a liaison in pronunciation, making the s sound as z, for example: **Robert, donnes-en aux enfants!**/ Robert, give some to the children! If you need to improve your pronunciation of French— in particular, verb forms—consult Barron's book *Pronounce It Perfectly in French*.

1. **Dites la phrase.** Study the forms of **lire** and **dire**.
2. **Bois le lait.** Study the forms of **prendre** and **boire**.
3. **Partez tout de suite.** Study the forms of **venir** and **partir**.
4. **Ferme la fenêtre.** Study the forms of **ouvrir** and **fermer**.
5. **Prends la valise là-bas.** Study the forms of **mettre** and **prendre**.
6. **Écrivons la lettre.** Study the forms of **lire** and **écrire**.
7. **Lisez le poème.** Study the forms of **apprendre** and **lire**.
8. **Sortons maintenant.** Study the forms of **partir** and **sortir**.
9. **Revenez à l'heure!** Study the forms of **être** (for *soyez*) and **revenir**. Note that in the imperative être uses the forms of the present subjunctive. See example (d) at the top of page 21.
10. **Faisons la leçon.** Study the forms of **voir** and **faire**.
11. **Levez-vous, s'il vous plaît.** Study the forms of the reflexive verb **s'asseoir** and **se lever**. Note that when you use a reflexive verb in the imperative, drop the subject pronoun, of course, but keep the reflexive pronoun **nous** or **vous**, placing it after the verb with a hyphen. **Tu** changes to **toi** in the affirmative imperative; for example: **Lève-toi!**/Get up! Under the *Impératif* for these two verbs note where the reflexive pronoun is placed when the imperative is negative.
12. **Refuse l'argent.** Study the forms of **accepter** and **refuser**.
13. **Achète le vélo.** Study the forms of **vendre** and **acheter**. Read the note above for an explanation of when s drops or is kept on er verbs in the *tu* form of the imperative.
14. **Soyez à l'heure.** Study the forms of **venir** and **être** (for *soyez*). Note that in the imperative être uses the forms of the present subjunctive. See example (d) at the top of page 21.
15. **Va dans la maison.** Study the forms of **aller** and **rester**. Note that s drops in the 2d person sing. (*tu* form) of the present indicative of **aller** when used in the imperative. But the s remains if the word that follows is y to facilitate a liaison in pronunciation, making the s sound as z, for example: **Robert, vas-y!**/ Robert, go to it!
16. **Lève-toi.** Study the forms of **se laver** in the imperative and **se lever**. Read our note of explanation in sentence number 11 above.

17. **Dépêchons-nous.** Study the forms of the imperative of **se cacher** and **se dépêcher**.
18. **Amuse-toi.** Study the forms of the imperative of **s'arrêter** and **s'amuser**. Read the explanation about reflexive verbs in the imperative, affirmative, and negative, above in number 11.
19. **Achète la maison.** Study the forms of the imperative of **vendre** and **acheter**. Review the explanation in number 13 above.
20. **Viens.** Study the imperative of **manger** and **venir**.

Test 7

Note: For all verb forms in this test, review the uses and examples of the future and conditional on pages 12–13. For the formation of the future and conditional of regular verbs, review page 22.

Also, review the future and conditional of each of the verbs given below.

1. J'irais. See aller.
2. Je partirais. See partir.
3. J'aurais. See avoir.
4. Je serais. See être.
5. Tu aimerais. See aimer.
6. Tu ferais. See faire.
7. Il aurait. See avoir.
8. Il serait. See être.
9. Il irait. See aller.
10. On dirait. See dire.
11. Vous seriez. See être.
12. Elle lirait. See lire.
13. J'ouvrirais. See ouvrir.
14. Nous saurions. See savoir.
15. Ils viendraient. See **venir**.
16. On boirait. See boire.
17. Ils courraient. See courir.
18. Ils liraient. See lire.
19. Elle mettrait. See mettre.
20. Il apprendrait. See apprendre.
21. Je couvrirais. See couvrir.
22. Il deviendrait. See devenir.
23. Nous devrions. See devoir.
24. Vous diriez. See dire.
25. Vous iriez. See aller.
26. J'aimerais. See aimer.
27. Il faudrait. See falloir.
28. Ils seraient. See être.
29. Elles feraient. See faire.
30. On choisirait. See choisir.

Test 8

Note: For the formation of the present indicative tense of regular verbs, review page 22. For the formation of the *passé composé* and other compound tenses, review pages 23 to 25. Note the position of **ne** and **pas** in the following negative sentences.

1. (a) Non, je ne travaille pas. (b) Il ne travaille pas non plus.
   Review the present indicative of **travailler**.
2. (a) Non, elle n'étudie pas. (b) Ils n'étudient pas non plus.
   Review the present indicative of **étudier**.
3. (a) Non, elle ne va pas au match. (b) Je ne vais pas au match non plus.
   Review the present indicative of **aller**.
4. (a) Non, ils ne crient pas. (b) Nous ne crions pas non plus.
   Review the present indicative of **crier**.
5. (a) Non, il n'arrive pas. (b) Ils n'arrivent pas non plus.
   Review the present indicative of **arriver**.

6. (a) **Non, je ne suis pas occupé.** (b) **Ils ne sont pas occupés non plus.**
Review the present indicative of **être**. Note the expression **être occupé** (to be busy) under the verb **occuper**. Note also that **occupés** contains **s** to make it masc. pl. because it is an adjective that describes the subject **ils**, which is masc. pl. If the subject were **elles**, the sentence would be **elles ne sont pas occupées non plus.**

7. (a) **Non, je n'ai pas fermé la fenêtre.** (b) **Il n'a pas fermé la fenêtre non plus.**
Review the *passé composé* of **fermer**. Note the position of **ne** and **pas** in a compound tense.

8. (a) **Non, je n'ai pas assisté à la conférence.** (b) **Ils n'ont pas assisté à la conférence non plus.**
Review the *passé composé* of **assister** and note the expression **assister à**. Note also the position of **ne** and **pas** in a compound tense. Also review the use of **assister à**.

9. (a) **Non, il n'est pas allé au supermarché.** (b) **Elle n'est pas allée au supermarché non plus.**
Review the *passé composé* of **aller**. Note the need for the addition of **e** on the past participle **allée**. The fem. sing. agreement must be made on it because **aller** is conjugated with **être** to form a compound tense. The agreement is made with the subject, which is **elle**, fem. sing. Review page 6.

10. (a) **Non, elle n'est pas allée à la piscine.** (b) **Ils ne sont pas allés à la piscine non plus.**
Read the explanation in number 9 above. It's the same idea here.

Test 9

Note: From time to time practice the formation of the seven simple tenses for regular verbs on pages 22 and 23 and the formation of the seven compound tenses on pages 23 to 25.

1. A The subject is **je**; therefore, you need the 1st person sing. of **prier**. Review the forms of **prier** in the present indicative tense and the words and expressions related to that verb.

2. D You need the 1st person pl. of **faire** because the subject is **nous**. The future tense is needed because of the sense of the statement. The other verb forms in A, B, and C would not make any sense here. If you do not recognize those forms, review **faire**.

3. D You need the 1st person sing. of **espérer** because the subject is **je**. The tenses of **espérer** in B and C would make no sense here. In A the infinitive form of the verb cannot be used here because there is a subject. Review **espérer**. If you want to know why the *accent aigu* on **espérer** sometimes changes to *accent grave*, as in **j'espère**, review the section on orthographically changing verbs (those that change in spelling) on pages 32–34, in particular, examples (14) and (15) on page 34.

4. C You need the 3d person sing. because the subject is **le train**, 3d person sing. The future tense is needed because the tenses in A, B, and D would make no sense. A is the *passé composé*. B is the conditional. D is the imperfect indicative. Can you recognize those tenses from the endings of the verb forms? If not, review them on pages 12–13, and under **arriver**. Also, if you are not sure of how they are translated into English, review pages 8 and 9 where you will find English translations of all the tenses using the verb *to go* as an example. Just substitute the verb *to arrive* in place of *to go*.

5. B The only sensible verb tense here is in B: *It seems that it is going to be beautiful weather*. A is the *passé composé* of **faire** but the speakers are not talking about what the weather was like in the past. C is the imperfect indicative of **faire** but the speakers are not talking about what the weather was like at any particular time in the past. D is the present subjunctive of **faire** and there is nothing in the sentence that requires the subjunctive. Review the tenses of **faire** and the expressions regarding weather on the bottom of that page.

6. A The subject is **on**, 3d person sing. The verb form in A is also 3d person sing. As for the tenses of the verb forms in B, C, and D, review the verb **prévoir**.

7. C You cannot use the infinitive form in D because **le train**, 3d person sing., is the subject. As for the tenses of the verb forms in A and B, review the verb **partir**. The speaker supposes that the train *is going to leave* soon.

8. D You need the 1st person sing. of **croire** because the subject is **je**. B is 3d person sing. A is the *passé simple*, which is not used in conversation. C is the imperfect indicative of **croire**, which is a past tense, and the speakers are talking about things happening now. Review the verb forms of **croire**.

Test 10

1. C You need the infinitive form of the reflexive verb **se laver** because the preposition **de** is in front of the blank space where a verb form is required. For that reason, D is not a correct choice because it is not an infinitive. In C the form *me* **laver** (to wash myself) is needed because the subject is **je**. A is not a reflexive verb. B is reflexive but you cannot use **se laver** because the subject is **je**. When you use a reflexive verb, its pronoun (**me, te, se, nous, vous, se**) must agree with the subject; for example: **je me . . . , tu te . . . , il se . . .** and so on. Review the forms of **se laver**. Also, review **avoir besoin de** under **avoir**.

2. D You need the *passé composé* of **entrer** because of the sense of the statement and the use of **a vu** (*passé composé* of **voir**) in the sentence. When Lisa entered the living room, she saw a vase of pretty flowers. In D the past participle **entrée** is fem. sing. because the verb is conjugated with **être** and the subject is fem. sing. Review page 6. In C the past participle **entré** is masc. sing. A is the present tense and B is the future, neither of which makes any sense from the point of view of time because the action is in the past. Review the forms of **entrer**.

3. B The sentence means *If I have the time, I will do the work*. Review the verb tenses in **si** (if) clauses at the top of page 26, example (a). Review the verb **faire** where you will find the *passé composé* in choice A, the future in B, the conditional in C, and the imperfect indicative in D.

4. A The sentence means *If I had the time, I would do the work*. Review the verb tenses in **si** (if) clauses at the top of page 26, example (b). Review the verb **faire** where you will find the conditional in A, the future in B, the conditional perfect in C, and the *passé composé* in D.

5. C The sentence means *If I had had the time, I would have done the work*. Review the verb tenses in **si** (if) clauses at the top of page 26, example (c). Review the verb **faire** where you will find the *passé composé* in A, the future perfect in B, the conditional perfect in C, and the imperfect indicative in D. Also, see page 18, example (b) on the bottom of the page where the uses of the conditional perfect are explained with examples.

6. A This is the conditional of courtesy. See page 13, example (b) on the bottom of the page where the uses of the conditional are explained with examples. Review the verb **aimer** where you will find the conditional in A, the *passé composé* in B, the *passé simple* in C, and the imperfect indicative in D.

7. B At what time *would you be able* to come? The reply to the question contains the same verb (**pouvoir**) in the same tense. Review the English translation of the conditional on page 8. See also the explanation on the bottom of page 13 in note (2) with the example. Study the verb forms of **pouvoir**.

8. B The verb in the **si** (if) clause is imperfect indicative of **être**; for that reason, the verb form in the other clause must be conditional. See the note in example (b) on page 14. See also example (b) at the top of page 26. Review **faire** for the other forms in A, C, and D.

9. B **Je doute** expresses doubt and it requires the subjunctive of **venir** in the clause that follows. Review the subjunctive that begins in the middle of page 26, specifically **douter que** on page 30. Review **venir** for the other forms in A, C, and D.

10. B **Avoir peur** expresses fear and it requires the subjunctive of **être** in the clause that follows. Review the subjunctive that begins in the middle of page 26, specifically **avoir peur que** on page 30, and the last example on the bottom of that page. Review **être** for the other forms in A, C, and D. Review idiomatic expressions with **avoir** under that verb.

11. D **Je regrette** expresses regret and it requires the subjunctive of the verb in the following clause. Review the subjunctive that begins in the middle of page 26, specifically **regretter que** on page 30. Review **être** for the other forms in A, B, and C.

12. A The conjunction **à moins que** (unless) requires the subjunctive of the verb in the clause it introduces. Review the subjunctive that begins in the middle of page 26, specifically **à moins que** listed under certain conjunctions on that page. Review **venir** for the other forms in B, C, and D.

13. B The conjunction **quoique** (although) requires the subjunctive of the verb in the clause it introduces. Review the subjunctive that begins in the middle of page 26, specifically **quoique** listed under certain conjunctions on page 27. Review **être** for the other forms in A, C, and D.

14. B The conjunction **pour que** (in order that, so that) requires the subjunctive of the verb in the clause it introduces. Review the subjunctive that begins in the middle of page 26, specifically **pour que** listed under certain conjunctions on page 27. Review **comprendre** for the other forms in A, C, and D.

15. B The conjunction **dès que** requires the future of the verb in the clause it introduces, provided that the verb in the main clause implies future time. In this sentence, **je partirai** is future. Review the future tense on pages 12–13 and the example in (c). Review **arriver** for the forms in A, B, C, and D.

16. C The impersonal expression **il est urgent que . . .** (it is urgent that . . .) requires the subjunctive of the verb in the clause it introduces. Review the subjunctive that begins in the middle of page 26, specifically **il est urgent que** on page 29. Review **partir** for the forms in A, B, C, and D.

17. D You need the pluperfect indicative tense of **oublier** because this past action occurred *before* the other past action in the sentence (*I remembered that I had forgotten*). Review the explanation and uses of the pluperfect indicative tense on

the bottom of page 16 to page 17. Review **oublier** for the forms in A, B, C, and D. Also, review **se rappeler**.

18. C You need the pluperfect indicative tense of **dormir**. Review, again, the explanation and uses of the pluperfect indicative tense on the bottom of page 16 to page 17. Review **dormir**.

19. B You need the *passé composé* of **dormir**. You are saying that you are tired *now* (**maintenant**) because you did not sleep. Review the explanation and uses of the *passé composé* with examples on page 16.

20. A You need the future perfect of **finir** because the verb in the other clause is in the future (**elle arrivera**) and it is introduced by the conjunction **quand** (when). Both actions will take place in the future. The action that will happen in the future *before* another future action is in the future perfect tense. Review the explanation and uses of the future perfect, with examples, on page 18. Review the verb forms of **finir**. If you did not recognize **arrivera** as future, review **arriver**.

Test 11

Note: For all verb forms in this test, review the uses and examples of the present indicative on pages 10 and 11 and the *passé composé* on page 16. For the formation of the present indicative of regular verbs, review page 22. For the formation of the *passé composé*, review the bottom of page 23 and Tense No. 8 at the top of page 24.

For the formation of regular and irregular past participles, see page 3.

Also, review the present indicative and the *passé composé* of the verbs given below.

1. Elle est allée.
   See aller.

2. Il a eu.
   See avoir.

3. Je me suis assis.
   See s'asseoir.

4. Ils ont eu.
   See avoir.

5. Tu as été.
   See être.

6. Il est allé.
   See aller.

7. Nous sommes allés.
   See aller.

8. Nous avons eu.
   See avoir.

9. J'ai parlé.
   See parler.

10. Elles sont venues.
   See venir.

11. J'ai bu.
   See boire.

12. Ils ont bu.
   See boire.

13. Vous avez bu.
   See boire.

14. J'ai cru.
   See croire.

15. Tu as dit.
   See dire.

16. J'ai pu.
   See pouvoir.

17. Il a fallu.
   See falloir.

18. Vous avez lu.
   See lire.

19. Vous avez dit.
   See dire.

20. Tu as mis.
   See mettre.

21. Elle est née.
   See naître.

22. Elle est morte.
   See mourir.

23. Elle a vendu.
   See vendre.

24. Ils se sont amusés.
   See s'amuser.

25. Elle est entrée.
   See entrer.

26. On a fini.
   See finir.

27. Elles ont couru.
   See courir.

28. Ils ont pris.
   See prendre.

29. On a appris.
   See apprendre.

30. Elles sont arrivées.
   See arriver.

Test 12

Note: This test is a good exercise to practice the formation of the seven simple tenses by using the required endings for regular -er, -ir, and -re verbs. The explanations and endings are on pages 22 and 23. For irregular verbs, see the verbs arranged alphabetically at the top of each page among the 501 verbs fully conjugated in all the tenses in this book.

Présent de l'indicatif (Tense No. 1)
1. J'aime.
2. Tu chantes.
3. Il/elle/on étudie.
4. Janine choisit.
5. J'entends.
6. Nous attendons.
7. Vous mangez.
8. Ils/elles vendent.
9. Richard et moi finissons.
10. Marie et Jeanne donnent.

Imparfait de l'indicatif (Tense No. 2)
1. Je parlais.
2. Tu finissais.
3. Il/elle/on vendait.
4. Madeleine était.
5. Il/elle/on avait.
6. Nous venions.
7. Vous faisiez.
8. Ils/elles allaient.
9. Paul et Henri jouaient.
10. Tu donnais.

Passé simple (Tense No. 3)
1. Je parlai.
2. Tu finis.
3. Il/elle/on vendit.
4. Catherine écrivit.
5. Ils/elles allèrent.
6. Nous donnâmes.
7. Vous choisîtes.
8. Ils/elles comprirent.
9. Hélène et Raymond désirèrent.
10. Il/elle/on dansa.

Futur (Tense No. 4)
1. Je mangerai.
2. Tu finiras.
3. Il/elle/on vendra.
4. La femme écrira.
5. J'irai.
6. Nous donnerons.
7. Vous choisirez.
8. Ils/elles comprendront.
9. Les garçons joueront.
10. J'aurai.

Conditionnel (Tense No. 5)
1. J'irais.
2. Tu finirais.
3. Il/elle/on ferait.
4. Je mangerais.
5. Vous pourriez.
6. Nous parlerions.
7. Vous seriez.
8. Ils/elles auraient.
9. Je prendrais.
10. Vous dîneriez.

Présent du subjonctif (Tense No. 6)
1. que je parle
2. que tu donnes
3. qu'il/elle/on ose
4. que je choisisse
5. que tu manges
6. que nous partions
7. que vous vendiez
8. qu'ils/elles prennent
9. que nous finissions
10. qu'il/elle/on ferme

Imparfait du subjonctif (Tense No. 7)

1. que je parlasse
2. que tu donnasses
3. qu'il/elle/on ouvrît
4. que nous partissions
5. que vous voulussiez
6. qu'ils/elles finissent

Test 13

Note: Review the regular and irregular past participles on page 3.

Test 14

Note: You must know the verb avoir in the seven simple tenses because they are needed to form the seven compound tenses of verbs conjugated with avoir. If you did not do well on this test, study them and write them for practice until you are sure that you know them. Review the seven compound tenses of a verb conjugated with avoir, for example, parler. If you drop the past participle parlé, you will see that what is left is the verb avoir in the seven simple tenses.

1. Présent de l'indicatif
   (Tense No. 1)

j'ai	nous avons
tu as	vous avez
il/elle/on a	ils/elles ont

2. Imparfait de l'indicatif
   (Tense No. 2)

j'avais	nous avions
tu avais	vous aviez
il/elle/on avait	ils/elles avaient

3. Passé simple
   (Tense No. 3)

j'eus	nous eûmes
tu eus	vous eûtes
il/elle/on eut	ils/elles eurent

4. Futur
   (Tense No. 4)

j'aurai	nous aurons
tu auras	vous aurez
il/elle/on aura	ils/elles auront

5. Conditionnel
(Tense No. 5)

j'aurais	nous aurions
tu aurais	vous auriez
il/elle/on aurait	ils/elles auraient

7. Imparfait du subjonctif
(Tense No. 7)

que j'eusse	que nous eussions
que tu eusses	que vous eussiez
qu'il/elle/on eût	qu'ils/elles eussent

6. Présent du subjonctif
(Tense No. 6)

que j'aie	que nous ayons
que tu aies	que vous ayez
qu'il/elle/on ait	qu'ils/elles aient

Test 15

Note: You must know the verb être in the seven simple tenses because they are needed to form the seven compound tenses of verbs conjugated with être. If you did not do well on this test, study them and write them for practice until you are sure that you know them. Review the seven compound tenses of a verb conjugated with être, for example, aller. If you drop the past participle allé, you will see that what is left is the verb être in the seven simple tenses.

1. Présent de l'indicatif
(Tense No. 1)

je suis	nous sommes
tu es	vous êtes
il/elle/on est	ils/elles sont

5. Conditionnel
(Tense No. 5)

je serais	nous serions
tu serais	vous seriez
il/elle/on serait	ils/elles seraient

2. Imparfait de l'indicatif
(Tense No. 2)

j'étais	nous étions
tu étais	vous étiez
il/elle/on était	ils/elles étaient

6. Présent du subjonctif
(Tense No. 6)

que je sois	que nous soyons
que tu sois	que vous soyez
qu'il/elle/on soit	qu'ils/elles soient

3. Passé simple
(Tense No. 3)

je fus	nous fûmes
tu fus	vous fûtes
il/elle/on fut	ils/elles furent

7. Imparfait du subjonctif
(Tense No. 7)

que je fusse	que nous fussions
que tu fusses	que vous fussiez
qu'il/elle/on fût	qu'ils/elles fussent

4. Futur
(Tense No. 4)

je serai	nous serons
tu seras	vous serez
il/elle/on sera	ils/elles seront

Test 16

Note: This test is another example to show that it is very important for you to know the present indicative of **avoir** and **être** so that you can form the *passé composé*. It also shows that you must know the imperfect indicative of **avoir** and **être** so that you can form the pluperfect indicative (*le plus-que-parfait de l'indicatif*). For the English translations of both these tenses, review the *passé composé* and the *plus-que-parfait de l'indicatif* on pages 16–17, where you will find explanations and examples in French and English.

Review the *passé composé* and the *plus-que-parfait de l'indicatif* of the verbs given below.

1. Elle était allée.
   See aller.
2. Il avait eu.
   See avoir.
3. Je m'étais assis.
   See s'asseoir.
4. Ils avaient eu.
   See avoir.
5. Tu avais été.
   See être.
6. Il était allé.
   See aller.
7. Nous étions allés.
   See aller.
8. Nous avions eu.
   See avoir.
9. J'avais parlé.
   See parler.
10. Elle était venue.
    See venir.

11. J'avais bu.
    See boire.
12. Ils s'étaient tus.
    See se taire.
13. J'avais fait.
    See faire.
14. Tu avais dû.
    See devoir.
15. Vous aviez dit.
    See dire.
16. J'avais pu.
    See pouvoir.
17. Il avait fallu.
    See falloir.
18. Vous aviez lu.
    See lire.
19. Vous aviez dit.
    See dire.
20. Tu avais mis.
    See mettre.

21. Elle était née.
    See naître.
22. Elle était morte.
    See mourir.
23. Elle s'était lavée.
    See se laver.
24. Elles s'étaient lavées.
    See se laver.
25. J'étais entré.
    See entrer.
26. On avait parlé.
    See parler.
27. Ils avaient couru.
    See courir.
28. Ils avaient pris.
    See prendre.
29. On avait dit.
    See dire.
30. J'avais compris.
    See comprendre.

Test 17

1. B Partir is conjugated with être to form a compound tense, so C and D are not appropriate choices because they are forms of avoir. You need the present subjunctive of être in B because of the impersonal expression il est possible que in the beginning of the sentence. Review the section on the uses of the subjunctive that begins in the middle of page 26, in particular, il est possible que on page 29. Review also partir in the *passé du subjonctif* (Tense No. 13). Refresh your memory by reading about the *passé du subjonctif* with explanations and examples in French and English on page 19.

2. C Faire is conjugated with avoir to form a compound tense; so B and D are not appropriate choices because they are forms of être. You need the present subjunctive of avoir in C because the verb in the main clause is douter. Review the section on the uses of the subjunctive that begins in the middle of page 26, in particular, douter que on page 30. Review also faire in the *passé du subjonctif* (Tense No. 13). Refresh your memory by reading about the *passé du subjonctif* with explanations and examples in French and English on page 19.

3. C In front of the blank space there is a verb form (je ne peux pas/I can't). That is why you need the infinitive form in C (*I am not able to go out*). Review pouvoir + inf. in the section on *Verbs with prepositions* in the Appendixes. Review the other forms of sortir in A, B, and D. As for il fait un temps affreux, review *Verbs used in weather expressions* in the Appendixes, specifically (b), on page 688.

4. B You need the present participle entrant because it is preceded by en. Josephine fell *while entering* (*en entrant*) the kitchen. Review regular and irregular present participles on page 3. Review the other forms of entrer in A, C, and D.

5. B Simone wiped the table. You need the past participle essuyé to complete the *passé composé*. There is no need for the fem. agreement in C because there is no fem. sing. direct object that *precedes* the verb. A is the infinitive form. D is the present participle. Review essuyer.

6. B To complete the *passé composé* you need mise, which is fem. sing. because the reflexive pronoun s' (se/herself) serves as the preceding direct object pronoun and it refers to Françoise, the subject, which is fem. sing. Review se mettre à + inf. in the section on *Verbs with prepositions* in the Appendixes. Review the forms of se mettre and the examples on the bottom of that page.

7. D The subject, les enfants, is 3d person pl. The only verb form that is also 3d person pl. among the choices is in D. Review the forms of vouloir.

8. C To complete the *passé composé* you need achetées, which is fem. pl. because the relative pronoun que (which or that) refers to the preceding direct object, les fleurs, which is fem. pl. The past participle in A is masc. sing. In B it is masc. pl. The infinitive in D cannot be used because you must complete the *passé composé*. Review acheter and the examples on the bottom of that page.

9. A The verb form in the clause beginning with quand is in the *passé antérieur* (past anterior), which is used in literary style. Review the explanation and examples of that tense on page 17. Since that tense is used in the subordinate clause, you need to use the *passé simple* in the main clause, which is in choice A. You need the 3d person sing. (partit) because the subject (il) is 3d person sing. Review the uses and explanation of the *passé simple* on page 12 and the examples in French and English. Also, review the *passé antérieur* (Tense No. 10) of manger and the *passé simple* (Tense No. 3) of partir as well as the other forms in the choices. Remember that the *passé simple* and the *passé antérieur* are literary tenses. They are not normally used in conversational French. These two tenses are occasionally used in these tests so you can become aware of them when reading French literature.

10. B To complete the *conditionnel passé* (Tense No. 12) of faire, you need the conditional (Tense No. 5) of avoir, which is aurais, 1st person sing., since the subject je is 1st person sing. As for j'aurais fait (I would have done), review the uses and explanation of the *conditionnel passé* on page 18 and the examples in French and English, as well as Tense No. 12 of faire. As for j'avais eu (I had had) review the *plus-que-parfait de l'indicatif* (Tense No. 9) on pages 16–17, and under the verb avoir. Also, review si (if) clauses at the top of page 26.

Test 18

Note: Review the regular and irregular present participles on page 3.

```
C H A N T A N T A T
H F Y T N V E A P N
O A A N A E F V R A
I I N A N A I E E Y
S S T Y E N N N N O
I A A O T T I D A V
S N N R D I S A N T
S T T C T É S N T N
A L L A N T A T O A
N A I S S A N T S N
T N O S A N T F A E
L I S A N T T A N V
```

Test 19

Note: From time to time practice the formation of the seven simple tenses for regular verbs on pages 22 and 23 and the formation of the seven compound tenses on pages 23 to 25.

1. A   The infinitive form is needed because the blank space is preceded by a verb form and a subject (**Je désire**). Review **désirer** + inf. in the section on *Verbs with prepositions* in the Appendixes. In B, **loué** is a masc. sing. past participle. In C, **louée** is a fem. sing. past participle. There is no need for a past participle here because there is no helping verb in the sentence to require the completion of a compound tense. In D, **louant** is a present participle and there is no need for that because it would make no sense. Review **louer**.

2. B   You need the present indicative tense (**C'est**/It is) because the conversation is taking place right now. Review the other forms of **être** in A, C, and D.

3. B   By now we hope that you are able to recognize the ending of a verb form that agrees with the subject in person (1st, 2d, or 3d) and number (sing. or pl.). For example: **je prends, tu prends, il prend**, and so forth. There is nothing in the sentence to require the present subjunctive **prenne**. Review the verb forms and tenses of **prendre**.

4. D   Same here. The ending of a verb form agrees with the subject in person and number. See number 3 above. There is nothing in the sentence to require the present subjunctive **croie**. Review the verb forms and tenses of **croire**.

5. C   The clerk at the hotel desk started the conversation by using the polite **vous** form while talking to you. That is why you need the **vous** form, **montrez**, in C. The clerk also tells you **"Signez"** in the same statement. You are dealing with the imperative (command) because he is telling you to do something. In the imperative the subject is not stated. Review the imperative on pages 20 and 21. In B the infinitive of the verb form **montez** is **monter**/to go up. Review the forms of **montrer**.

Test 20

Note: Review page 6. Review regular and irregular past participles on page 3. Study the formation and uses of the *passé composé* with examples in French and English on page 16. Also, review the *passé composé* of the verbs given after each answer.

1. Richard a écrit la leçon. Review apprendre and écrire.
2. Elle s'est levée. Review s'asseoir and se lever.
3. J'ai lu la lettre. Review écrire and lire.
4. Elle a ouvert la fenêtre. Review fermer and ouvrir.
5. Hélène est morte. Review arriver and mourir.
6. Avez-vous offert un cadeau? Review acheter and offrir.
7. Marguerite est venue. Review sortir and venir.
8. Nous avons cru l'histoire. Review écouter and croire.
9. Ils ont vu Paris. Review visiter and voir.
10. Les enfants ont ri. Review pleurer and rire.
11. As-tu pris les frites? Review commander and prendre.
12. Ils sont restés à Paris. Review aller and rester.
13. L'étudiant n'a pas su la réponse. Review comprendre and savoir.
14. L'enfant a eu un bon repas. Review manger and avoir.
15. J'ai reçu la lettre. Review envoyer and recevoir.
16. Avez-vous été en France? Review voyager and être.
17. A-t-il couvert la boîte? Review ouvrir and couvrir.
18. Les enfants se sont tus. Review se laver and se taire.
19. Louise a voulu venir chez moi. Review désirer and vouloir.
20. Qui a fait le bruit? Review entendre and faire.

Test 21

Note: Review the two-page spread on pages 8 and 9 to be sure you can translate into English the seven simple tenses, the seven compound tenses, and the imperative. The model verb on those two pages is *to go* (*aller*). Keep those two pages open flat and flip back and forth to aller, where you see all the forms in all the tenses of aller. Compare the forms in English and French. As a guide, follow the tense No. and the name of the tense in both languages as you make your comparison. For practice, you can apply this procedure to other verbs by merely substituting an English verb for a French one, e.g., *to drink* (*boire*).

The asterisks in front of each of the English verb forms below designate the following:
*The French verb forms in Tense No. 3 (*le passé simple*) are used in literary style, formal writing. In French conversation and informal writing use the *passé composé* (Tense No. 8) instead of this tense.
**The French verb forms in Tense No. 7 (*l'imparfait du subjonctif*) are used in literary style, formal writing. In French conversation and informal writing use the *présent du subjonctif* (Tense No. 6) instead of this tense.
***The French verb forms in Tense No. 10 (*le passé antérieur*) are used in literary style, formal writing. In French conversation and informal writing, use *le plus-que-parfait de l'indicatif* (Tense No. 9) instead of this tense.

****The French verb forms in Tense No. 14 (*le plus-que-parfait du subjonctif*) are used in literary style, formal writing. In French conversation and informal writing, use *le passé du subjonctif* (Tense No. 13) instead of this tense.

1. we go, we do go, we are going
2. you were going, you went, you used to go
*3. he went, he did go
4. we shall go, we will go
5. you would go
6. that I may go
**7. that I might go
8. she has gone, she went, she did go
9. they had gone
***10. we had gone
11. you will have gone

12. you would have gone
13. that he may have gone
****14. that she might have gone

15. I know, I do know

*16. he was
17. she will have
18. we would have
19. that I may be
*20. he had
21. I have had, I had, I did have
22. I put, I have put, I did put
23. we will do, we will make
24. I would have come
25. Go away!
26. You have sold, you sold, you did sell
27. We will have finished
28. You had drunk
29. She has gone up, she went up, she did go up
30. We have stayed, we stayed, we did stay

Test 22

Note: Verify the verb forms in the present indicative tense by looking up the verbs in this test on the pages where they appear among the 501 verbs in this book.

A	I	M	E	B	A	L	I	T	A
C	D	A	L	O	S	E	T	I	D
O	O	E	F	I	O	A	E	G	I
U	I	E	A	A	L	L	O	N	S
R	S	V	S	I	O	U	E	A	U
S	A	I	R	E	U	E	T	E	S
I	L	N	A	P	S	U	V	L	O
A	E	I	P	E	U	V	E	N	T
E	O	N	T	N	E	D	N	E	V
L	U	I	A	L	L	E	Z	O	N
F	A	T	E	Z	V	A	V	A	I
F	I	N	I	S	S	O	N	S	S

Test 23

Note: In Test 21 you translated verb forms in a variety of tenses from French to English. In this test you are translating English verb forms in a variety of tenses back into French.

1. Nous allons	16. Il fut
2. Tu allais	17. Elle aura
3. Il alla	18. Nous aurions
4. Nous irons	19. Que je sois
5. Vous iriez	20. Il eut
6. Que j'aille	21. J'ai eu
7. Que j'allasse	22. J'ai mis
8. Elle est allée	23. Nous ferons
9. Elles étaient allées	24. Je serais venu
10. Nous fûmes allés	25. Allez-vous-en!
11. Tu seras allé	26. Vous avez vendu
12. Vous seriez allé	27. Nous aurons fini
13. Qu'il soit allé	28. Tu avais bu
14. Qu'elle fût allée	29. Elle est montée
15. Je sais	30. Nous sommes restés

Test 24

Note: This is a repeat of Test 14 because you must know thoroughly the verb forms of avoir in the seven simple tenses. They are needed to form the seven compound tenses. Go to Test 14 in this answers section and correct your work. Also, review the verb avoir where you will find all the forms. Review again the formation of the seven compound tenses on pages 23 to 25.

Test 25

Note: This is a repeat of Test 15 because you must know thoroughly the verb forms of être in the seven simple tenses. They are needed to form the seven compound tenses. Go to Test 15 in this answers section and correct your work. Also, review the verb être where you will find all the forms. Review again the formation of the seven compound tenses on pages 23 to 25.

Test 26

Note: Verify the verb forms in the *passé composé* by looking up the verbs in this test on the pages where they appear among the 501 verbs in this book.

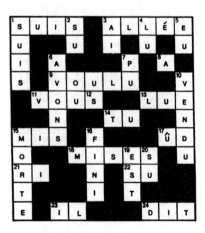

1. (a) voir
   (b) présent de l'indicatif
   (c) 1st pers., sing.
2. (a) être
   (b) présent de l'indicatif
   (c) 1st pers., sing.
3. (a) promettre
   (b) plus-que-parfait de l'indicatif
   (c) 2d pers., pl.
4. (a) laisser
   (b) passé composé
   (c) 1st pers., sing.
5. (a) laisser
   (b) présent de l'indicatif
   (c) 2d pers., pl.
6. (a) dire
   (b) plus-que-parfait de l'indicatif
   (c) 3d pers., sing.
7. (a) être
   (b) imparfait de l'indicatif
   (c) 2d pers., pl.
8. (a) croire
   (b) conditionnel
   (c) 1st pers., sing.
9. (a) avoir
   (b) présent de l'indicatif
   (c) 2d pers., pl.

10. (a) attendre
    (b) imparfait de l'indicatif
    (c) 1st pers., sing.
11. (a) voir
    (b) présent de l'indicatif
    (c) 1st pers., sing.
12. (a) avoir
    (b) présent de l'indicatif
    (c) 2d pers., pl.
13. (a) avoir
    (b) présent de l'indicatif
    (c) 2d pers., pl.
14. (a) se flatter
    (b) présent de l'indicatif
    (c) 1st pers., sing.
15. (a) venir
    (b) conditionnel passé
    (c) 2d pers., pl.
16. (a) être
    (b) présent de l'indicatif
    (c) 2d pers., pl.
17. (a) tirer
    (b) impératif
    (c) 2d pers., pl.
18. (a) prier
    (b) présent de l'indicatif
    (c) 1st pers., sing.

Essential 55 verb list

Beginning students should pay careful attention to the verbs in this list. We have chosen them because they represent important spelling changes and popular usage. If you study these key verbs you will be able to conjugate just about any verb you come across and express yourself in correct idiomatic French.

acheter	garder
aimer	jouer
aller/s'en aller	laver/se laver
(Verb Pair)	*(Verb Pair)*
apprendre	se lever
attendre	lire
avoir	manger
boire	mettre/se mettre
chanter	*(Verb Pair)*
choisir	monter
commencer	parler
connaître	partir
courir	payer
couvrir	perdre
se débrouiller	pouvoir
devoir	prendre
dire	rendre
donner	rentrer
dormir	savoir
écrire	sentir
entendre	sortir
entrer	tenir
envoyer	tomber
éteindre	vendre
être	venir
étudier	voir
faire	vouloir
finir	

Alphabetical Listing of 501 French
Verbs Fully Conjugated
in All the Tenses and Moods

Regular **-er** verb   to lower, to reduce, to humiliate, to humble

The Seven Simple Tenses		The Seven Compound Tenses	
Singular	Plural	Singular	Plural

1 présent de l'indicatif

abaisse	abaissons
abaisses	abaissez
abaisse	abaissent

8 passé composé

ai abaissé	avons abaissé
as abaissé	avez abaissé
a abaissé	ont abaissé

2 imparfait de l'indicatif

abaissais	abaissions
abaissais	abaissiez
abaissait	abaissaient

9 plus-que-parfait de l'indicatif

avais abaissé	avions abaissé
avais abaissé	aviez abaissé
avait abaissé	avaient abaissé

3 passé simple

abaissai	abaissâmes
abaissas	abaissâtes
abaissa	abaissèrent

10 passé antérieur

eus abaissé	eûmes abaissé
eus abaissé	eûtes abaissé
eut abaissé	eurent abaissé

4 futur

abaisserai	abaisserons
abaisseras	abaisserez
abaissera	abaisseront

11 futur antérieur

aurai abaissé	aurons abaissé
auras abaissé	aurez abaissé
aura abaissé	auront abaissé

5 conditionnel

abaisserais	abaisserions
abaisserais	abaisseriez
abaisserait	abaisseraient

12 conditionnel passé

aurais abaissé	aurions abaissé
aurais abaissé	auriez abaissé
aurait abaissé	auraient abaissé

6 présent du subjonctif

abaisse	abaissions
abaisses	abaissiez
abaisse	abaissent

13 passé du subjonctif

aie abaissé	ayons abaissé
aies abaissé	ayez abaissé
ait abaissé	aient abaissé

7 imparfait du subjonctif

abaissasse	abaissassions
abaissasses	abaissassiez
abaissât	abaissassent

14 plus-que-parfait du subjonctif

eusse abaissé	eussions abaissé
eusses abaissé	eussiez abaissé
eût abaissé	eussent abaissé

Impératif
abaisse
abaissons
abaissez

Words and expressions related to this verb

abaisser le store   to pull down the (venetian) blind, shade
abaisser les yeux   to cast one's eyes down, to look down
un abaissement   abasement, lowering
abaisser qqn   to humiliate someone
abaisser la valeur de qqch   to bring down the value of something

un abaisse-langue   tongue depressor
un rabais   reduction
vendre au rabais   to sell at a discount
Il est important d'abaisser votre taux de cholestérol.   It's important to lower your cholesterol level.

See also **s'abaisser** and **baisser.**

The subject pronouns are found on page 103.   **107**

to humble oneself, to lower oneself,   Reflexive regular -er verb
to condescend, to slope

The Seven Simple Tenses		The Seven Compound Tenses	
Singular	Plural	Singular	Plural
1 présent de l'indicatif		8 passé composé	
m'abaisse	nous abaissons	me suis abaissé(e)	nous sommes abaissé(e)s
t'abaisses	vous abaissez	t'es abaissé(e)	vous êtes abaissé(e)(s)
s'abaisse	s'abaissent	s'est abaissé(e)	se sont abaissé(e)s
2 imparfait de l'indicatif		9 plus-que-parfait de l'indicatif	
m'abaissais	nous abaissions	m'étais abaissé(e)	nous étions abaissé(e)s
t'abaissais	vous abaissiez	t'étais abaissé(e)	vous étiez abaissé(e)(s)
s'abaissait	s'abaissaient	s'était abaissé(e)	s'étaient abaissé(e)s
3 passé simple		10 passé antérieur	
m'abaissai	nous abaissâmes	me fus abaissé(e)	nous fûmes abaissé(e)s
t'abaissas	vous abaissâtes	te fus abaissé(e)	vous fûtes abaissé(e)(s)
s'abaissa	s'abaissèrent	se fut abaissé(e)	se furent abaissé(e)s
4 futur		11 futur antérieur	
m'abaisserai	nous abaisserons	me serai abaissé(e)	nous serons abaissé(e)s
t'abaisseras	vous abaisserez	te seras abaissé(e)	vous serez abaissé(e)(s)
s'abaissera	s'abaisseront	se sera abaissé(e)	se seront abaissé(e)s
5 conditionnel		12 conditionnel passé	
m'abaisserais	nous abaisserions	me serais abaissé(e)	nous serions abaissé(e)s
t'abaisserais	vous abaisseriez	te serais abaissé(e)	vous seriez abaissé(e)(s)
s'abaisserait	s'abaisseraient	se serait abaissé(e)	se seraient abaissé(e)s
6 présent du subjonctif		13 passé du subjonctif	
m'abaisse	nous abaissions	me sois abaissé(e)	nous soyons abaissé(e)s
t'abaisses	vous abaissiez	te sois abaissé(e)	vous soyez abaissé(e)(s)
s'abaisse	s'abaissent	se soit abaissé(e)	se soient abaissé(e)s
7 imparfait du subjonctif		14 plus-que-parfait du subjonctif	
m'abaissasse	nous abaissassions	me fusse abaissé(e)	nous fussions abaissé(e)s
t'abaissasses	vous abaissassiez	te fusses abaissé(e)	vous fussiez abaissé(e)(s)
s'abaissât	s'abaissassent	se fût abaissé(e)	se fussent abaissé(e)s

Impératif
abaisse-toi; ne t'abaisse pas
abaissons-nous; ne nous abaissons pas
abaissez-vous; ne vous abaissez pas

Words and expressions related to this verb
s'abaisser   to decline, to go down
s'abaisser à   to stoop to
s'abaisser devant qqn   to humble oneself before someone
Le taux de chômage s'est abaissé.   The unemployment rate declined.
Car quiconque s'élève sera abaissé, et celui qui s'abaisse sera élevé.   For whoever exalts
  himself will be humbled, and he who humbles himself will be exalted. (Luke 14:11)

See also abaisser and baisser.

Regular **-ir** verb   to daze, to deafen, to stun, to bewilder, to stupefy

The Seven Simple Tenses		The Seven Compound Tenses	
Singular	Plural	Singular	Plural

A

1 présent de l'indicatif		8 passé composé	
abasourdis	**abasourdissons**	**ai abasourdi**	**avons abasourdi**
abasourdis	**abasourdissez**	**as abasourdi**	**avez abasourdi**
abasourdit	**abasourdissent**	**a abasourdi**	**ont abasourdi**

2 imparfait de l'indicatif		9 plus-que-parfait de l'indicatif	
abasourdissais	**abasourdissions**	**avais abasourdi**	**avions abasourdi**
abasourdissais	**abasourdissiez**	**avais abasourdi**	**aviez abasourdi**
abasourdissait	**abasourdissaient**	**avait abasourdi**	**avaient abasourdi**

3 passé simple		10 passé antérieur	
abasourdis	**abasourdîmes**	**eus abasourdi**	**eûmes abasourdi**
abasourdis	**abasourdîtes**	**eus abasourdi**	**eûtes abasourdi**
abasourdit	**abasourdirent**	**eut abasourdi**	**eurent abasourdi**

4 futur		11 futur antérieur	
abasourdirai	**abasourdirons**	**aurai abasourdi**	**aurons abasourdi**
abasourdiras	**abasourdirez**	**auras abasourdi**	**aurez abasourdi**
abasourdira	**abasourdiront**	**aura abasourdi**	**auront abasourdi**

5 conditionnel		12 conditionnel passé	
abasourdirais	**abasourdirions**	**aurais abasourdi**	**aurions abasourdi**
abasourdirais	**abasourdiriez**	**aurais abasourdi**	**auriez abasourdi**
abasourdirait	**abasourdiraient**	**aurait abasourdi**	**auraient abasourdi**

6 présent du subjonctif		13 passé du subjonctif	
abasourdisse	**abasourdissions**	**aie abasourdi**	**ayons abasourdi**
abasourdisses	**abasourdissiez**	**aies abasourdi**	**ayez abasourdi**
abasourdisse	**abasourdissent**	**ait abasourdi**	**aient abasourdi**

7 imparfait du subjonctif		14 plus-que-parfait du subjonctif	
abasourdisse	**abasourdissions**	**eusse abasourdi**	**eussions abasourdi**
abasourdisses	**abasourdissiez**	**eusses abasourdi**	**eussiez abasourdi**
abasourdît	**abasourdissent**	**eût abasourdi**	**eussent abasourdi**

Impératif
abasourdis
abasourdissons
abasourdissez

Words and expressions related to this verb
assourdir   to deafen, to deaden a sound, to muffle
s'assourdir   to soften the sound of a consonant, to unvoice a consonant
abasourdissant, abasourdissante   astounding, amazing
sourd, sourde   deaf
devenir sourd   to become deaf

faire la sourde oreille   to turn a deaf ear, not to listen
être sourd à   to be deaf to
la surdité   deafness
un abasourdissement   amazement, astonishment, bewilderment
Ce que j'ai vu à la télé m'a abasourdi.   I was stunned by what I saw on TV.

The *s* in **abasourdir** is pronounced as if it were written *z*.

The subject pronouns are found on page 103.
109

abattre (4)

Part. pr. **abattant**   Part. passé **abattu**

to dishearten, to strike down, to cut down,
to knock down, to slaughter

Irregular verb in 1s, 2s,
3s present indicative

The Seven Simple Tenses		The Seven Compound Tenses	
Singular	Plural	Singular	Plural
1 présent de l'indicatif		8 passé composé	
abats	abattons	ai abattu	avons abattu
abats	abattez	as abattu	avez abattu
abat	abattent	a abattu	ont abattu
2 imparfait de l'indicatif		9 plus-que-parfait de l'indicatif	
abattais	abattions	avais abattu	avions abattu
abattais	abattiez	avais abattu	aviez abattu
abattait	abattaient	avait abattu	avaient abattu
3 passé simple		10 passé antérieur	
abattis	abattîmes	eus abattu	eûmes abattu
abattis	abattîtes	eus abattu	eûtes abattu
abattit	abattirent	eut abattu	eurent abattu
4 futur		11 futur antérieur	
abattrai	abattrons	aurai abattu	aurons abattu
abattras	abattrez	auras abattu	aurez abattu
abattra	abattront	aura abattu	auront abattu
5 conditionnel		12 conditionnel passé	
abattrais	abattrions	aurais abattu	aurions abattu
abattrais	abattriez	aurais abattu	auriez abattu
abattrait	abattraient	aurait abattu	auraient abattu
6 présent du subjonctif		13 passé du subjonctif	
abatte	abattions	aie abattu	ayons abattu
abattes	abattiez	aies abattu	ayez abattu
abatte	abattent	ait abattu	aient abattu
7 imparfait du subjonctif		14 plus-que-parfait du subjonctif	
abattisse	abattissions	eusse abattu	eussions abattu
abattisses	abattissiez	eusses abattu	eussiez abattu
abattît	abattissent	eût abattu	eussent abattu

Impératif
abats
abattons
abattez

Words and expressions related to this verb
l'abattage *m.*   slaughtering of animals
un abattoir   slaughterhouse
rabattre   to pull down, to turn down, to knock
down, to beat down
un rabat-joie   killjoy, "wet blanket"; (des
rabat-joie)
un abatteur   slaughterer of animals

à bas!   down with! à bas les devoirs!   down
with homework!
un abat-jour   lampshade
un abat-son   louver
Le gangster fut abattu dans la rue.   The
gangster was struck down (killed) in
the street.

See also battre, se battre, and combattre.

110

The Seven Simple Tenses		The Seven Compound Tenses	
Singular	Plural	Singular	Plural

1 présent de l'indicatif

abolis	abolissons		
abolis	abolissez		
abolit	abolissent		

8 passé composé

ai aboli	avons aboli
as aboli	avez aboli
a aboli	ont aboli

2 imparfait de l'indicatif

abolissais	abolissions
abolissais	abolissiez
abolissait	abolissaient

9 plus-que-parfait de l'indicatif

avais aboli	avions aboli
avais aboli	aviez aboli
avait aboli	avaient aboli

3 passé simple

abolis	abolîmes
abolis	abolîtes
abolit	abolirent

10 passé antérieur

eus aboli	eûmes aboli
eus aboli	eûtes aboli
eut aboli	eurent aboli

4 futur

abolirai	abolirons
aboliras	abolirez
abolira	aboliront

11 futur antérieur

aurai aboli	aurons aboli
auras aboli	aurez aboli
aura aboli	auront aboli

5 conditionnel

abolirais	abolirions
abolirais	aboliriez
abolirait	aboliraient

12 conditionnel passé

aurais aboli	aurions aboli
aurais aboli	auriez aboli
aurait aboli	auraient aboli

6 présent du subjonctif

abolisse	abolissions
abolisses	abolissiez
abolisse	abolissent

13 passé du subjonctif

aie aboli	ayons aboli
aies aboli	ayez aboli
ait aboli	aient aboli

7 imparfait du subjonctif

abolisse	abolissions
abolisses	abolissiez
abolît	abolissent

14 plus-que-parfait du subjonctif

eusse aboli	eussions aboli
eusses aboli	eussiez aboli
eût aboli	eussent aboli

Impératif
abolis
abolissons
abolissez

Sentences using this verb and words related to this verb
Le législateur a soumis un projet de loi abolissant la peine de mort.
The legislator submitted a bill abolishing the death penalty.
l'abolition *f.* abolition
l'abolitionnisme *m.* abolitionism
abolitionniste abolitionist
Les abolitionnistes ont réussi à éliminer l'esclavage.
The abolitionists succeeded in eliminating slavery.

absoudre (6)

Part. pr. absolvant   **Part. passé** absous (absoute)

to absolve

Irregular verb   *Tense Nos. 3 and 7 of this verb are rarely used.

The Seven Simple Tenses		The Seven Compound Tenses	
Singular	Plural	Singular	Plural

1 présent de l'indicatif

		8 passé composé	
absous	absolvons	ai absous	avons absous
absous	absolvez	as absous	avez absous
absout	absolvent	a absous	ont absous

2 imparfait de l'indicatif

		9 plus-que-parfait de l'indicatif	
absolvais	absolvions	avais absous	avions absous
absolvais	absolviez	avais absous	aviez absous
absolvait	absolvaient	avait absous	avaient absous

*3 passé simple

		10 passé antérieur	
absolus	absolûmes	eus absous	eûmes absous
absolus	absolûtes	eus absous	eûtes absous
absolut	absolurent	eut absous	eurent absous

4 futur

		11 futur antérieur	
absoudrai	absoudrons	aurai absous	aurons absous
absoudras	absoudrez	auras absous	aurez absous
absoudra	absoudront	aura absous	auront absous

5 conditionnel

		12 conditionnel passé	
absoudrais	absoudrions	aurais absous	aurions absous
absoudrais	absoudriez	aurais absous	auriez absous
absoudrait	absoudraient	aurait absous	auraient absous

6 présent du subjonctif

		13 passé du subjonctif	
absolve	absolvions	aie absous	ayons absous
absolves	absolviez	aies absous	ayez absous
absolve	absolvent	ait absous	aient absous

*7 imparfait du subjonctif

		14 plus-que-parfait du subjonctif	
absolusse	absolussions	eusse absous	eussions absous
absolusses	absolussiez	eusses absous	eussiez absous
absolût	absolussent	eût absous	eussent absous

Impératif
absous
absolvons
absolvez

Words and expressions related to this verb

une absolution   absolution (of a sin)
donner l'absolution à un pécheur   to absolve a sinner (of his sins)
une absoute   recitation of prayers for the dead
absolument   absolutely; Je le veux absolument.   I really insist upon it.

une confiance absolue   complete confidence
un refus absolu   absolute (flat) refusal
absolument pas!   certainly not!
absolument rien!   absolutely nothing!

The *b* in absoudre is pronounced as if it were written *p*. See also résoudre.

Get acquainted with what preposition goes with what verb. See *Verbs with prepositions* in the Appendixes.

Reflexive irregular verb   to abstain

The Seven Simple Tenses		The Seven Compound Tenses	
Singular	Plural	Singular	Plural
1 présent de l'indicatif		**8 passé composé**	
m'abstiens	nous abstenons	me suis abstenu(e)	nous sommes abstenu(e)s
t'abstiens	vous abstenez	t'es abstenu(e)	vous êtes abstenu(e)(s)
s'abstient	s'abstiennent	s'est abstenu(e)	se sont abstenu(e)s
2 imparfait de l'indicatif		**9 plus-que-parfait de l'indicatif**	
m'abstenais	nous abstenions	m'étais abstenu(e)	nous étions abstenu(e)s
t'abstenais	vous absteniez	t'étais abstenu(e)	vous étiez abstenu(e)(s)
s'abstenait	s'abstenaient	s'était abstenu(e)	s'étaient abstenu(e)s
3 passé simple		**10 passé antérieur**	
m'abstins	nous abstînmes	me fus abstenu(e)	nous fûmes abstenu(e)s
t'abstins	vous abstîntes	te fus abstenu(e)	vous fûtes abstenu(e)(s)
s'abstint	s'abstinrent	se fut abstenu(e)	se furent abstenu(e)s
4 futur		**11 futur antérieur**	
m'abstiendrai	nous abstiendrons	me serai abstenu(e)	nous serons abstenu(e)s
t'abstiendras	vous abstiendrez	te seras abstenu(e)	vous serez abstenu(e)(s)
s'abstiendra	s'abstiendront	se sera abstenu(e)	se seront abstenu(e)s
5 conditionnel		**12 conditionnel passé**	
m'abstiendrais	nous abstiendrions	me serais abstenu(e)	nous serions abstenu(e)s
t'abstiendrais	vous abstiendriez	te serais abstenu(e)	vous seriez abstenu(e)(s)
s'abstiendrait	s'abstiendraient	se serait abstenu(e)	se seraient absttenu(e)s
6 présent du subjonctif		**13 passé du subjonctif**	
m'abstienne	nous abstenions	me sois abstenu(e)	nous soyons abstenu(e)s
t'abstiennes	vous absteniez	te sois abstenu(e)	vous soyez abstenu(e)(s)
s'abstienne	s'abstiennent	se soit abstenu(e)	se soient abstenu(e)s
7 imparfait du subjonctif		**14 plus-que-parfait du subjonctif**	
m'abstinsse	nous abstinssions	me fusse abstenu(e)	nous fussions abstenu(e)s
t'abstinsses	vous abstinssiez	te fusses abstenu(e)	vous fussiez abstenu(e)(s)
s'abstînt	s'abstinssent	se fût abstenu(e)	se fussent abstenu(e)s

Impératif
abstiens-toi; ne t'abstiens pas
abstenons-nous; ne nous abstenons pas
abstenez-vous; ne vous abstenez pas

Words and expressions related to this verb

s'abstenir de   to abstain from, to refrain from
l'abstinence f.   abstinence
l'abstention f.   abstention
abstinent, abstinente   abstinent

faire abstinence de   to abstain from
un abstentionniste   abstentionist
s'abstenir de faire   to refrain from doing
Je m'abstiens de fumer dans la bibliothèque.
    I refrain from smoking in the library.

The *b* in s'abstenir is pronounced as if it were written *p*.

How are you doing? Find out with the verb drills and tests with answers explained on pages 50–101.

accepter (8)
Part. pr. **acceptant**   Part. passé **accepté**

to accept

Regular **-er** verb

The Seven Simple Tenses		The Seven Compound Tenses	
Singular	Plural	Singular	Plural
1 présent de l'indicatif		**8 passé composé**	
accepte	acceptons	ai accepté	avons accepté
acceptes	acceptez	as accepté	avez accepté
accepte	acceptent	a accepté	ont accepté
2 imparfait de l'indicatif		**9 plus-que-parfait de l'indicatif**	
acceptais	acceptions	avais accepté	avions accepté
acceptais	acceptiez	avais accepté	aviez accepté
acceptait	acceptaient	avait accepté	avaient accepté
3 passé simple		**10 passé antérieur**	
acceptai	acceptâmes	eus accepté	eûmes accepté
acceptas	acceptâtes	eus accepté	eûtes accepté
accepta	acceptèrent	eut accepté	eurent accepté
4 futur		**11 futur antérieur**	
accepterai	accepterons	aurai accepté	aurons accepté
accepteras	accepterez	auras accepté	aurez accepté
acceptera	accepteront	aura accepté	auront accepté
5 conditionnel		**12 conditionnel passé**	
accepterais	accepterions	aurais accepté	aurions accepté
accepterais	accepteriez	aurais accepté	auriez accepté
accepterait	accepteraient	aurait accepté	auraient accepté
6 présent du subjonctif		**13 passé du subjonctif**	
accepte	acceptions	aie accepté	ayons accepté
acceptes	acceptiez	aies accepté	ayez accepté
accepte	acceptent	ait accepté	aient accepté
7 imparfait du subjonctif		**14 plus-que-parfait du subjonctif**	
acceptasse	acceptassions	eusse accepté	eussions accepté
acceptasses	acceptassiez	eusses accepté	eussiez accepté
acceptât	acceptassent	eût accepté	eussent accepté

Impératif
accepte
acceptons
acceptez

Words and expressions related to this verb

acceptable   acceptable, satisfactory
une acceptation   acceptance
accepter une invitation   to accept an
   invitation
l'acception *f.*   sense, meaning
accepter de fair qqch   to agree to do
   something

**Michel a accepté de travailler dimanche
   prochain.**   Michael agreed to work next
   Sunday.
Acceptez-vous les cartes bancaires?   Do you
   accept credit cards?

Regular **-er** verb   to acclaim, to applaud, to cheer

The Seven Simple Tenses		The Seven Compound Tenses	
Singular	Plural	Singular	Plural

1 présent de l'indicatif		8 passé composé	
acclame	acclamons	ai acclamé	avons acclamé
acclames	acclamez	as acclamé	avez acclamé
acclame	acclament	a acclamé	ont acclamé

2 imparfait de l'indicatif		9 plus-que-parfait de l'indicatif	
acclamais	acclamions	avais acclamé	avions acclamé
acclamais	acclamiez	avais acclamé	aviez acclamé
acclamait	acclamaient	avait acclamé	avaient acclamé

3 passé simple		10 passé antérieur	
acclamai	acclamâmes	eus acclamé	eûmes acclamé
acclamas	acclamâtes	eus acclamé	eûtes acclamé
acclama	acclamèrent	eut acclamé	eurent acclamé

4 futur		11 futur antérieur	
acclamerai	acclamerons	aurai acclamé	aurons acclamé
acclameras	acclamerez	auras acclamé	aurez acclamé
acclamera	acclameront	aura acclamé	auront acclamé

5 conditionnel		12 conditionnel passé	
acclamerais	acclamerions	aurais acclamé	aurions acclamé
acclamerais	acclameriez	aurais acclamé	auriez acclamé
acclamerait	acclameraient	aurait acclamé	auraient acclamé

6 présent du subjonctif		13 passé du subjonctif	
acclame	acclamions	aie acclamé	ayons acclamé
acclames	acclamiez	aies acclamé	ayez acclamé
acclame	acclament	ait acclamé	aient acclamé

7 imparfait du subjonctif		14 plus-que-parfait du subjonctif	
acclamasse	acclamassions	eusse acclamé	eussions acclamé
acclamasses	acclamassiez	eusses acclamé	eussiez acclamé
acclamât	acclamassent	eût acclamé	eussent acclamé

Impératif
acclame
acclamons
acclamez

Words and expressions related to this verb
l'**acclamation** *f.* acclamation, cheering
nommer par acclamation to name by
    acclamation
réclamer to demand, to ask for
une réclame advertisement, commercial
élire par acclamation to elect by acclamation

se faire acclamer to be cheered, hailed
une réclamation complaint
Jean-Claude a été acclamé pour tout ce qu'il
    avait fait pour l'équipe. Jean-Claude was
    cheered for all that he had done for the team.

It's important that you be familiar with the subjunctive. See pages 26–31.

The Seven Simple Tenses		The Seven Compound Tenses	
Singular	Plural	Singular	Plural
1 présent de l'indicatif		8 passé composé	
accompagne	accompagnons	ai accompagné	avons accompagné
accompagnes	accompagnez	as accompagné	avez accompagné
accompagne	accompagnent	a accompagné	ont accompagné
2 imparfait de l'indicatif		9 plus-que-parfait de l'indicatif	
accompagnais	accompagnions	avais accompagné	avions accompagné
accompagnais	accompagniez	avais accompagné	aviez accompagné
accompagnait	accompagnaient	avait accompagné	avaient accompagné
3 passé simple		10 passé antérieur	
accompagnai	accompagnâmes	eus accompagné	eûmes accompagné
accompagnas	accompagnâtes	eus accompagné	eûtes accompagné
accompagna	accompagnèrent	eut accompagné	eurent accompagné
4 futur		11 futur antérieur	
accompagnerai	accompagnerons	aurai accompagné	aurons accompagné
accompagneras	accompagnerez	auras accompagné	aurez accompagné
accompagnera	accompagneront	aura accompagné	auront accompagné
5 conditionnel		12 conditionnel passé	
accompagnerais	accompagnerions	aurais accompagné	aurions accompagné
accompagnerais	accompagneriez	aurais accompagné	auriez accompagné
accompagnerait	accompagneraient	aurait accompagné	auraient accompagné
6 présent du subjonctif		13 passé du subjonctif	
accompagne	accompagnions	aie accompagné	ayons accompagné
accompagnes	accompagniez	aies accompagné	ayez accompagné
accompagne	accompagnent	ait accompagné	aient accompagné
7 imparfait du subjonctif		14 plus-que-parfait du subjonctif	
accompagnasse	accompagnassions	eusse accompagné	eussions accompagné
accompagnasses	accompagnassiez	eusses accompagné	eussiez accompagné
accompagnât	accompagnassent	eût accompagné	eussent accompagné

Impératif
accompagne
accompagnons
accompagnez

Words and expressions related to this verb
une compagnie company, theatrical troupe
raccompagner quelqu'un to see someone out, see someone off
un animal de compagnie (animal domestique) a pet
Il vaut mieux être seul qu'en mauvaise compagnie! It's better to be alone than in bad company!

s'accompagner de to be accompanied by
un accompagnement accompanying, accompaniment (music)
un accompagnateur, une accompagnatrice accompanist (music)
un compagnon, une compagne companion

Get acquainted with what preposition goes with what verb. See *Verbs with prepositions* in the Appendixes.

Regular **-er** verb   to accord, to grant, to reconcile, to admit

The Seven Simple Tenses	The Seven Compound Tenses

Singular	Plural	Singular	Plural

1 présent de l'indicatif

accorde	accordons
accordes	accordez
accorde	accordent

8 passé composé

ai accordé	avons accordé
as accordé	avez accordé
a accordé	ont accordé

2 imparfait de l'indicatif

accordais	accordions
accordais	accordiez
accordait	accordaient

9 plus-que-parfait de l'indicatif

avais accordé	avions accordé
avais accordé	aviez accordé
avait accordé	avaient accordé

3 passé simple

accordai	accordâmes
accordas	accordâtes
accorda	accordèrent

10 passé antérieur

eus accordé	eûmes accordé
eus accordé	eûtes accordé
eut accordé	eurent accordé

4 futur

accorderai	accorderons
accorderas	accorderez
accordera	accorderont

11 futur antérieur

aurai accordé	aurons accordé
auras accordé	aurez accordé
aura accordé	auront accordé

5 conditionnel

accorderais	accorderions
accorderais	accorderiez
accorderait	accorderaient

12 conditionnel passé

aurais accordé	aurions accordé
aurais accordé	auriez accordé
aurait accordé	auraient accordé

6 présent du subjonctif

accorde	accordions
accordes	accordiez
accorde	accordent

13 passé du subjonctif

aie accordé	ayons accordé
aies accordé	ayez accordé
ait accordé	aient accordé

7 imparfait du subjonctif

accordasse	accordassions
accordasses	accordassiez
accordât	accordassent

14 plus-que-parfait du subjonctif

eusse accordé	eussions accordé
eusses accordé	eussiez accordé
eût accordé	eussent accordé

Impératif
accorde
accordons
accordez

Words and expressions related to this verb
un accord   agreement, consent
d'accord   agreed, okay
mettre d'accord   to reconcile
se mettre d'accord   to come to an agreement
l'accord entre le sujet et le verbe   subject-verb agreement
une concordance   similarity, concordance
un accordage   tuning (music)
un accordéon   accordion (music)

un, une accordéoniste   accordionist
s'accorder   to be on good terms; to come to terms, to agree
cordialement   cordially, heartily
donner son accord   to agree, consent
Le verbe s'accorde en personne et en nombre avec le sujet.   The verb agrees in person and number with the subject.

The subject pronouns are found on page 103.   **117**

to run to, to run up to, to come (go) running to   Irregular verb

This verb is conjugated with either **avoir** or **être** to form the compound tenses.

The Seven Simple Tenses		The Seven Compound Tenses	
Singular	Plural	Singular	Plural

1   présent de l'indicatif

		8 passé composé	
accours	accourons	ai accouru	avons accouru
accours	accourez	as accouru	avez accouru
accourt	accourent	a accouru	ont accouru

2   imparfait de l'indicatif

		9 plus-que-parfait de l'indicatif	
accourais	accourions	avais accouru	avions accouru
accourais	accouriez	avais accouru	aviez accouru
accourait	accouraient	avait accouru	avaient accouru

3   passé simple

		10 passé antérieur	
accourus	accourûmes	eus accouru	eûmes accouru
accourus	accourûtes	eus accouru	eûtes accouru
accourut	accoururent	eut accouru	eurent accouru

4   futur

		11 futur antérieur	
accourrai	accourrons	aurai accouru	aurons accouru
accourras	accourrez	auras accouru	aurez accouru
accourra	accourront	aura accouru	auront accouru

5   conditionnel

		12 conditionnel passé	
accourrais	accourrions	aurais accouru	aurions accouru
accourrais	accourriez	aurais accouru	auriez accouru
accourrait	accourraient	aurait accouru	auraient accouru

6   présent du subjonctif

		13 passé du subjonctif	
accoure	accourions	aie accouru	ayons accouru
accoures	accouriez	aies accouru	ayez accouru
accoure	accourent	ait accouru	aient accouru

7   imparfait du subjonctif

		14 plus-que-parfait du subjonctif	
accourusse	accourussions	eusse accouru	eussions accouru
accourusses	accourussiez	eusses accouru	eussiez accouru
accourût	accourussent	eût accouru	eussent accouru

Impératif
accours
accourons
accourez

Words and expressions related to this verb

accourir vers qqn   to go (come) running toward someone

J'ai accouru vers la pauvre vieille dame pour l'aider à se relever.   I went running up to the poor old lady to help her get on her feet.

courir   to run

concourir   to compete

encourir   to incur

secourir   to aid, help

la course et la marche   running and walking

la course au pouvoir   the race for power

Le bon Samaritain a accouru pour aider les victimes de l'accident.   The good Samaritan ran to help the accident victims.

See also **courir**.

Regular **-er** verb   to hang (up), to hook (on a hanger, nail, *e.g.*, a coat)

The Seven Simple Tenses		The Seven Compound Tenses	
Singular	Plural	Singular	Plural

A

1 présent de l'indicatif		8 passé composé	
accroche	accrochons	ai accroché	avons accroché
accroches	accrochez	as accroché	avez accroché
accroche	accrochent	a accroché	ont accroché

2 imparfait de l'indicatif		9 plus-que-parfait de l'indicatif	
accrochais	accrochions	avais accroché	avions accroché
accrochais	accrochiez	avais accroché	aviez accroché
accrochait	accrochaient	avait accroché	avaient accroché

3 passé simple		10 passé antérieur	
accrochai	accrochâmes	eus accroché	eûmes accroché
accrochas	accrochâtes	eus accroché	eûtes accroché
accrocha	accrochèrent	eut accroché	eurent accroché

4 futur		11 futur antérieur	
accrocherai	accrocherons	aurai accroché	aurons accroché
accrocheras	accrocherez	auras accroché	aurez accroché
accrochera	accrocheront	aura accroché	auront accroché

5 conditionnel		12 conditionnel passé	
accrocherais	accrocherions	aurais accroché	aurions accroché
accrocherais	accrocheriez	aurais accroché	auriez accroché
accrocherait	accrocheraient	aurait accroché	auraient accroché

6 présent du subjonctif		13 passé du subjonctif	
accroche	accrochions	aie accroché	ayons accroché
accroches	accrochiez	aies accroché	ayez accroché
accroche	accrochent	ait accroché	aient accroché

7 imparfait du subjonctif		14 plus-que-parfait du subjonctif	
accrochasse	accrochassions	eusse accroché	eussions accroché
accrochasses	accrochassiez	eusses accroché	eussiez accroché
accrochât	accrochassent	eût accroché	eussent accroché

Impératif
accroche
accrochons
accrochez

Words and expressions related to this verb

accrocher son manteau   to hang up one's coat
un accrocheur, une accrocheuse   leech (a person who clings, "hangs on" to another person, and is difficult to shake off)
un accroche-plat   plate hanger
un accroche-coeur   curl of hair against the temple of one's head (kiss curl); **des accroche-coeurs**
Accroche-toi!   Hang on! Hang in there!

décrocher   to unhook, to pick up the receiver of a telephone; **raccrocher**   to hang up
décrocher une bonne place   to land a soft job
le décrochage   unhooking
un crochet   hook, hanger
crocheter   to hook in, to pick a lock
faire du crochet   to crochet
Félicité a accroché le chapeau au miroir.
Felicity hung the hat on the mirror.

The subject pronouns are found on page 103.
                                                   119

accroître (14) Part. pr. accroissant Part. passé accru

to increase, to make greater, to enlarge   Irregular verb

The Seven Simple Tenses		The Seven Compound Tenses	
Singular	Plural	Singular	Plural
1 présent de l'indicatif		8 passé composé	
accrois	accroissons	ai accru	avons accru
accrois	accroissez	as accru	avez accru
accroît	accroissent	a accru	ont accru
2 imparfait de l'indicatif		9 plus-que-parfait de l'indicatif	
accroissais	accroissions	avais accru	avions accru
accroissais	accroissiez	avais accru	aviez accru
accroissait	accroissaient	avait accru	avaient accru
3 passé simple		10 passé antérieur	
accrus	accrûmes	eus accru	eûmes accru
accrus	accrûtes	eus accru	eûtes accru
accrut	accrurent	eut accru	eurent accru
4 futur		11 futur antérieur	
accroîtrai	accroîtrons	aurai accru	aurons accru
accroîtras	accroîtrez	auras accru	aurez accru
accroîtra	accroîtront	aura accru	auront accru
5 conditionnel		12 conditionnel passé	
accroîtrais	accroîtrions	aurais accru	aurions accru
accroîtrais	accroîtriez	aurais accru	auriez accru
accroîtrait	accroîtraient	aurait accru	auraient accru
6 présent du subjonctif		13 passé du subjonctif	
accroisse	accroissions	aie accru	ayons accru
accroisses	accroissiez	aies accru	ayez accru
accroisse	accroissent	ait accru	aient accru
7 imparfait du subjonctif		14 plus-que-parfait du subjonctif	
accrusse	accrussions	eusse accru	eussions accru
accrusses	accrussiez	eusses accru	eussiez accru
accrût	accrussent	eût accru	eussent accru

Impératif
accrois
accroissons
accroissez

Words related to this verb
un accroissement growth, increase, accumulation, accretion
une accrue increase, accretion
s'accroître to accrue, to increase
accroître son pouvoir to increase one's power
accroître sa production to increase one's production
Note: Accroître is not conjugated exactly like croître. In many of the simple tenses croître has an
added circumflex accent to distinguish it from croire (to believe): je crois (croître), je crois (croire).

See also croître and décroître.

Irregular verb

to greet, welcome

The Seven Simple Tenses | The Seven Compound Tenses

Singular	Plural	Singular	Plural
1 présent de l'indicatif		8 passé composé	
accueille	**accueillons**	**ai accueilli**	**avons accueilli**
accueilles	**accueillez**	**as accueilli**	**avez accueilli**
accueille	**accueillent**	**a accueilli**	**ont accueilli**
2 imparfait de l'indicatif		9 plus-que-parfait de l'indicatif	
accueillais	**accueillions**	**avais accueilli**	**avions accueilli**
accueillais	**accueilliez**	**avais accueilli**	**aviez accueilli**
accueillait	**accueillaient**	**avait accueilli**	**avaient accueilli**
3 passé simple		10 passé antérieur	
accueillis	**accueillîmes**	**eus accueilli**	**eûmes accueilli**
accueillis	**accueillîtes**	**eus accueilli**	**eûtes accueilli**
accueillit	**accueillirent**	**eut accueilli**	**eurent accueilli**
4 futur		11 futur antérieur	
accueillerai	**accueillerons**	**aurai accueilli**	**aurons accueilli**
accueilleras	**accueillerez**	**auras accueilli**	**aurez accueilli**
accueillera	**accueilleront**	**aura accueilli**	**auront accueilli**
5 conditionnel		12 conditionnel passé	
accueillerais	**accueillerions**	**aurais accueilli**	**aurions accueilli**
accueillerais	**accueilleriez**	**aurais accueilli**	**auriez accueilli**
accueillerait	**accueilleraient**	**aurait accueilli**	**auraient accueilli**
6 présent du subjonctif		13 passé du subjonctif	
accueille	**accueillions**	**aie accueilli**	**ayons accueilli**
accueilles	**accueilliez**	**aies accueilli**	**ayez accueilli**
accueille	**accueillent**	**ait accueilli**	**aient accueilli**
7 imparfait du subjonctif		14 plus-que-parfait du subjonctif	
accueillisse	**accueillissions**	**eusse accueilli**	**eussions accueilli**
accueillisses	**accueillissiez**	**eusses accueilli**	**eussiez accueilli**
accueillît	**accueillissent**	**eût accueilli**	**eussent accueilli**

Impératif
accueille
accueillons
accueillez

Words and expressions related to this verb

accueillir chaleureusement   to give a warm welcome
accueillir froidement   to give a cool reception
faire bon accueil   to give a warm welcome
l'accueil *m.*/**le bureau d'accueil**   reception desk
un accueil   welcome, reception;
   un accueil chaleureux   warm welcome

accueillant, accueillante   hospitable;
   l'accueil des touristes   accommodating the tourists
Avez-vous jamais été accueilli aimablement?
   Have you ever been welcomed kindly?

For other words and expressions related to this verb, see **cueillir.**

Grammar putting you in a tense mood? Review the definitions of basic grammatical terms with examples on pages 35–49.

The subject pronouns are found on page 103.

to accuse

The Seven Simple Tenses		The Seven Compound Tenses	
Singular	Plural	Singular	Plural
1 présent de l'indicatif		**8 passé composé**	
accuse	accusons	ai accusé	avons accusé
accuses	accusez	as accusé	avez accusé
accuse	accusent	a accusé	ont accusé
2 imparfait de l'indicatif		**9 plus-que-parfait de l'indicatif**	
accusais	accusions	avais accusé	avions accusé
accusais	accusiez	avais accusé	aviez accusé
accusait	accusaient	avait accusé	avaient accusé
3 passé simple		**10 passé antérieur**	
accusai	accusâmes	eus accusé	eûmes accusé
accusas	accusâtes	eus accusé	eûtes accusé
accusa	accusèrent	eut accusé	eurent accusé
4 futur		**11 futur antérieur**	
accuserai	accuserons	aurai accusé	aurons accusé
accuseras	accuserez	auras accusé	aurez accusé
accusera	accuseront	aura accusé	auront accusé
5 conditionnel		**12 conditionnel passé**	
accuserais	accuserions	aurais accusé	aurions accusé
accuserais	accuseriez	aurais accusé	auriez accusé
accuserait	accuseraient	aurait accusé	auraient accusé
6 présent du subjonctif		**13 passé du subjonctif**	
accuse	accusions	aie accusé	ayons accusé
accuses	accusiez	aies accusé	ayez accusé
accuse	accusent	ait accusé	aient accusé
7 imparfait du subjonctif		**14 plus-que-parfait du subjonctif**	
accusasse	accusassions	eusse accusé	eussions accusé
accusasses	accusassiez	eusses accusé	eussiez accusé
accusât	accusassent	eût accusé	eussent accusé

Impératif
accuse
accusons
accusez

Words and expressions related to this verb

accuser réception de qqch to acknowledge receipt of something

une accusation accusation, charge, indictment

porter une accusation contre to bring charges against

un accusateur, une accusatrice accuser; **l'accusateur public** public prosecutor

s'accuser de to accuse oneself of

un accusé de réception acknowledgment/confirmation of receipt

Proverb: **Qui s'excuse, s'accuse.** A guilty conscience needs no accuser.

Don't forget to check the list of 2,600 additional verbs keyed to the 501 model verbs. It's in the Appendixes!

to buy, to purchase

Regular **-er** verb endings; spelling change:
e changes to **è** before syllable with mute **e**

The Seven Simple Tenses		The Seven Compound Tenses	
Singular	Plural	Singular	Plural

1   présent de l'indicatif

achète	achetons
achètes	achetez
achète	achètent

8   passé composé

ai acheté	avons acheté
as acheté	avez acheté
a acheté	ont acheté

2   imparfait de l'indicatif

achetais	achetions
achetais	achetiez
achetait	achetaient

9   plus-que-parfait de l'indicatif

avais acheté	avions acheté
avais acheté	aviez acheté
avait acheté	avaient acheté

3   passé simple

achetai	achetâmes
achetas	achetâtes
acheta	achetèrent

10   passé antérieur

eus acheté	eûmes acheté
eus acheté	eûtes acheté
eut acheté	eurent acheté

4   futur

achèterai	achèterons
achèteras	achèterez
achètera	achèteront

11   futur antérieur

aurai acheté	aurons acheté
auras acheté	aurez acheté
aura acheté	auront acheté

5   conditionnel

achèterais	achèterions
achèterais	achèteriez
achèterait	achèteraient

12   conditionnel passé

aurais acheté	aurions acheté
aurais acheté	auriez acheté
aurait acheté	auraient acheté

6   présent du subjonctif

achète	achetions
achètes	achetiez
achète	achètent

13   passé du subjonctif

aie acheté	ayons acheté
aies acheté	ayez acheté
ait acheté	aient acheté

7   imparfait du subjonctif

achetasse	achetassions
achetasses	achetassiez
achetât	achetassent

14   plus-que-parfait du subjonctif

eusse acheté	eussions acheté
eusses acheté	eussiez acheté
eût acheté	eussent acheté

Impératif
achète
achetons
achetez

Acheter is an essential verb for beginning students because it is useful in many situations and in a number of idiomatic expressions.

Sentences using acheter

Je voudrais acheter des aspirines et des pastilles contre la toux. I would like to buy some aspirin and some cough drops.

J'aimerais acheter quelques pâtisseries. I would like to buy some pastries.

J'achète ce journal et ce magazine. I'm buying this newspaper and this magazine.

Ce vélo? Je l'ai acheté à Michel. This bike? I bought it from Michael.

L'amitié ne s'achète pas. Friendship cannot be bought.

Achetons une nouvelle voiture! Let's buy a new car!

Achetez deux et recevez-en un troisième gratuitement! Buy two and get the third one free!

Le criminel s'est racheté en aidant les pauvres. The criminal redeemed himself by helping the poor.

Il y a plus d'acheteurs que de connaisseurs. There are more buyers than connoisseurs.

Words and expressions related to this verb

un achat **purchase**

faire un achat **to make a purchase**

un achat en ligne **on-line purchase**

un achat électronique **electronic purchase (Internet)**

acheter qqch à qqn **to buy something from someone**

acheter comptant **to buy for cash**

acheter à crédit **to buy on credit**

un acheteur, une acheteuse **buyer, purchaser**

achetable **purchasable**

Acheter has a tricky spelling change before a syllable with a mute **e**. If you can conjugate **acheter** you can also conjugate the following verbs.

corseter **to corset, constrict**

fureter **to ferret out, pry into, snoop, search**

haleter (aspirate h) **to pant, gasp**

racheter **to buy more, buy back, ransom, redeem, atone**

se racheter **to redeem oneself (helping verb** être**)**

Regular **-er** verb endings; spelling change:
e changes to **è** before syllable with mute **e**

to achieve, to finish,
to complete, to end

The Seven Simple Tenses | | The Seven Compound Tenses

A

Singular	Plural	Singular	Plural
1 présent de l'indicatif		8 passé composé	
achève	achevons	ai achevé	avons achevé
achèves	achevez	as achevé	avez achevé
achève	achèvent	a achevé	ont achevé
2 imparfait de l'indicatif		9 plus-que-parfait de l'indicatif	
achevais	achevions	avais achevé	avions achevé
achevais	acheviez	avais achevé	aviez achevé
achevait	achevaient	avait achevé	avaient achevé
3 passé simple		10 passé antérieur	
achevai	achevâmes	eus achevé	eûmes achevé
achevas	achevâtes	eus achevé	eûtes achevé
acheva	achevèrent	eut achevé	eurent achevé
4 futur		11 futur antérieur	
achèverai	achèverons	aurai achevé	aurons achevé
achèveras	achèverez	auras achevé	aurez achevé
achèvera	achèveront	aura achevé	auront achevé
5 conditionnel		12 conditionnel passé	
achèverais	achèverions	aurais achevé	aurions achevé
achèverais	achèveriez	aurais achevé	auriez achevé
achèverait	achèveraient	aurait achevé	auraient achevé
6 présent du subjonctif		13 passé du subjonctif	
achève	achevions	aie achevé	ayons achevé
achèves	acheviez	aies achevé	ayez achevé
achève	achèvent	ait achevé	aient achevé
7 imparfait du subjonctif		14 plus-que-parfait du subjonctif	
achevasse	achevassions	eusse achevé	eussions achevé
achevasses	achevassiez	eusses achevé	eussiez achevé
achevât	achevassent	eût achevé	eussent achevé

Impératif
achève
achevons
achevez

Words and expressions related to this verb
achever de faire qqch   to finish doing something
s'achever   to come to an end, to close, to be fulfilled
un idiot achevé, une idiote achevée   a complete idiot
un achèvement   completion, end, conclusion; **l'achèvement du travail**   completion of the work
Pierre a commencé son roman en 1980, et il l'a achevé vingt ans plus tard.   Peter started his
   novel in 1980, and he finished it twenty years later.

The subject pronouns are found on page 103.
                                                                                                125

to acquire, to obtain

The Seven Simple Tenses		The Seven Compound Tenses	
Singular	Plural	Singular	Plural
1 présent de l'indicatif		8 passé composé	
acquiers	**acquérons**	**ai acquis**	**avons acquis**
acquiers	**acquérez**	**as acquis**	**avez acquis**
acquiert	**acquièrent**	**a acquis**	**ont acquis**
2 imparfait de l'indicatif		9 plus-que-parfait de l'indicatif	
acquérais	**acquérions**	**avais acquis**	**avions acquis**
acquérais	**acquériez**	**avais acquis**	**aviez acquis**
acquérait	**acquéraient**	**avait acquis**	**avaient acquis**
3 passé simple		10 passé antérieur	
acquis	**acquîmes**	**eus acquis**	**eûmes acquis**
acquis	**acquîtes**	**eus acquis**	**eûtes acquis**
acquit	**acquirent**	**eut acquis**	**eurent acquis**
4 futur		11 futur antérieur	
acquerrai	**acquerrons**	**aurai acquis**	**aurons acquis**
acquerras	**acquerrez**	**auras acquis**	**aurez acquis**
acquerra	**acquerront**	**aura acquis**	**auront acquis**
5 conditionnel		12 conditionnel passé	
acquerrais	**acquerrions**	**aurais acquis**	**aurions acquis**
acquerrais	**acquerriez**	**aurais acquis**	**auriez acquis**
acquerrait	**acquerraient**	**aurait acquis**	**auraient acquis**
6 présent du subjonctif		13 passé du subjonctif	
acquière	**acquérions**	**aie acquis**	**ayons acquis**
acquières	**acquériez**	**aies acquis**	**ayez acquis**
acquière	**acquièrent**	**ait acquis**	**aient acquis**
7 imparfait du subjonctif		14 plus-que-parfait du subjonctif	
acquisse	**acquissions**	**eusse acquis**	**eussions acquis**
acquisses	**acquissiez**	**eusses acquis**	**eussiez acquis**
acquît	**acquissent**	**eût acquis**	**eussent acquis**

Impératif
acquiers
acquérons
acquérez

Words and expressions related to this verb
s'acquérir to accrue; to improve; to be gained or obtained
une acquisition acquisition, purchase; **faire l'acquisition de** to acquire
un acquit receipt; release
acquis, acquise acquired
conquérir to conquer
tenir quelque chose pour acquis to take something for granted
Il ne faut rien prendre/tenir pour acquis. One must not take anything for granted.

Get acquainted with what preposition goes with what verb. See *Verbs with prepositions* in the Appendixes.

The Seven Simple Tenses		The Seven Compound Tenses

A

Singular	Plural	Singular	Plural
1 présent de l'indicatif		8 passé composé	
admets	**admettons**	**ai admis**	**avons admis**
admets	**admettez**	**as admis**	**avez admis**
admet	**admettent**	**a admis**	**ont admis**
2 imparfait de l'indicatif		9 plus-que-parfait de l'indicatif	
admettais	**admettions**	**avais admis**	**avions admis**
admettais	**admettiez**	**avais admis**	**aviez admis**
admettait	**admettaient**	**avait admis**	**avaient admis**
3 passé simple		10 passé antérieur	
admis	**admîmes**	**eus admis**	**eûmes admis**
admis	**admîtes**	**eus admis**	**eûtes admis**
admit	**admirent**	**eut admis**	**eurent admis**
4 futur		11 futur antérieur	
admettrai	**admettrons**	**aurai admis**	**aurons admis**
admettras	**admettrez**	**auras admis**	**aurez admis**
admettra	**admettront**	**aura admis**	**auront admis**
5 conditionnel		12 conditionnel passé	
admettrais	**admettrions**	**aurais admis**	**aurions admis**
admettrais	**admettriez**	**aurais admis**	**auriez admis**
admettrait	**admettraient**	**aurait admis**	**auraient admis**
6 présent du subjonctif		13 passé du subjonctif	
admette	**admettions**	**aie admis**	**ayons admis**
admettes	**admettiez**	**aies admis**	**ayez admis**
admette	**admettent**	**ait admis**	**aient admis**
7 imparfait du subjonctif		14 plus-que-parfait du subjonctif	
admisse	**admissions**	**eusse admis**	**eussions admis**
admisses	**admissiez**	**eusses admis**	**eussiez admis**
admît	**admissent**	**eût admis**	**eussent admis**

Impératif
admets
admettons
admettez

Words and expressions related to this verb
admis, admise   admitted, accepted
une admission   admission, admittance
l'admissibilité *f.*   acceptability
se faire admettre dans un club   to be admitted to a club
admissible   acceptable
C'est une idée folle, je l'admets.   It's a crazy idea, I admit it.

See also **commettre, mettre, permettre, promettre, remettre,** and **soumettre.**

to admire

The Seven Simple Tenses		The Seven Compound Tenses	
Singular	Plural	Singular	Plural
1 présent de l'indicatif		8 passé composé	
admire	admirons	ai admiré	avons admiré
admires	admirez	as admiré	avez admiré
admire	admirent	a admiré	ont admiré
2 imparfait de l'indicatif		9 plus-que-parfait de l'indicatif	
admirais	admirions	avais admiré	avions admiré
admirais	admiriez	avais admiré	aviez admiré
admirait	admiraient	avait admiré	avaient admiré
3 passé simple		10 passé antérieur	
admirai	admirâmes	eus admiré	eûmes admiré
admiras	admirâtes	eus admiré	eûtes admiré
admira	admirèrent	eut admiré	eurent admiré
4 futur		11 futur antérieur	
admirerai	admirerons	aurai admiré	aurons admiré
admireras	admirerez	auras admiré	aurez admiré
admirera	admireront	aura admiré	auront admiré
5 conditionnel		12 conditionnel passé	
admirerais	admirerions	aurais admiré	aurions admiré
admirerais	admireriez	aurais admiré	auriez admiré
admirerait	admireraient	aurait admiré	auraient admiré
6 présent du subjonctif		13 passé du subjonctif	
admire	admirions	aie admiré	ayons admiré
admires	admiriez	aies admiré	ayez admiré
admire	admirent	ait admiré	aient admiré
7 imparfait du subjonctif		14 plus-que-parfait du subjonctif	
admirasse	admirassions	eusse admiré	eussions admiré
admirasses	admirassiez	eusses admiré	eussiez admiré
admirât	admirassent	eût admiré	eussent admiré

Impératif
admire
admirons
admirez

Words and expressions related to this verb
une admiration admiration, wonder
admirativement admiringly
admiratif, admirative admiring
un admirateur, une admiratrice admirer
un mirage mirage, illusion
un miroir mirror

remplir quelqu'un d'admiration to fill someone with admiration
être admirable de courage to show great courage
admirablement admirably, wonderfully
être en admiration devant to be filled with admiration for

See also **mirer.**

Regular **-er** verb

to worship, to adore

The Seven Simple Tenses		The Seven Compound Tenses	
Singular	Plural	Singular	Plural
1 présent de l'indicatif		**8 passé composé**	
adore	adorons	ai adoré	avons adoré
adores	adorez	as adoré	avez adoré
adore	adorent	a adoré	ont adoré
2 imparfait de l'indicatif		**9 plus-que-parfait de l'indicatif**	
adorais	adorions	avais adoré	avions adoré
adorais	adoriez	avais adoré	aviez adoré
adorait	adoraient	avait adoré	avaient adoré
3 passé simple		**10 passé antérieur**	
adorai	adorâmes	eus adoré	eûmes adoré
adoras	adorâtes	eus adoré	eûtes adoré
adora	adorèrent	eut adoré	eurent adoré
4 futur		**11 futur antérieur**	
adorerai	adorerons	aurai adoré	aurons adoré
adoreras	adorerez	auras adoré	aurez adoré
adorera	adoreront	aura adoré	auront adoré
5 conditionnel		**12 conditionnel passé**	
adorerais	adorerions	aurais adoré	aurions adoré
adorerais	adoreriez	aurais adoré	auriez adoré
adorerait	adoreraient	aurait adoré	auraient adoré
6 présent du subjonctif		**13 passé du subjonctif**	
adore	adorions	aie adoré	ayons adoré
adores	adoriez	aies adoré	ayez adoré
adore	adorent	ait adoré	aient adoré
7 imparfait du subjonctif		**14 plus-que-parfait du subjonctif**	
adorasse	adorassions	eusse adoré	eussions adoré
adorasses	adorassiez	eusses adoré	eussiez adoré
adorât	adorassent	eût adoré	eussent adoré

Impératif
adore
adorons
adorez

Sentences using this verb and words related to it
Laure adore sa nièce.   Laura adores her niece.
Madeleine est une fille adorable. Elle adore écouter la musique québécoise.
   Madeleine is an adorable girl. She adores listening to Québécois music.

une adoration   adoration, worship
adorablement   adorably
un adorateur, une adoratrice   adorer, worshipper

adorable   adorable, charming, delightful
un village adorable   delightful village
une robe adorable   lovely dress

The subject pronouns are found on page 103.   **129**

to address   Regular **-er** verb

The Seven Simple Tenses		The Seven Compound Tenses	
Singular	Plural	Singular	Plural
1 présent de l'indicatif		**8 passé composé**	
adresse	adressons	ai adressé	avons adressé
adresses	adressez	as adressé	avez adressé
adresse	adressent	a adressé	ont adressé
2 imparfait de l'indicatif		**9 plus-que-parfait de l'indicatif**	
adressais	adressions	avais adressé	avions adressé
adressais	adressiez	avais adressé	aviez adressé
adressait	adressaient	avait adressé	avaient adressé
3 passé simple		**10 passé antérieur**	
adressai	adressâmes	eus adressé	eûmes adressé
adressas	adressâtes	eus adressé	eûtes adressé
adressa	adressèrent	eut adressé	eurent adressé
4 futur		**11 futur antérieur**	
adresserai	adresserons	aurai adressé	aurons adressé
adresseras	adresserez	auras adressé	aurez adressé
adressera	adresseront	aura adressé	auront adressé
5 conditionnel		**12 conditionnel passé**	
adresserais	adresserions	aurais adressé	aurions adressé
adresserais	adresseriez	aurais adressé	auriez adressé
adresserait	adresseraient	aurait adressé	auraient adressé
6 présent du subjonctif		**13 passé du subjonctif**	
adresse	adressions	aie adressé	ayons adressé
adresses	adressiez	aies adressé	ayez adressé
adresse	adressent	ait adressé	aient adressé
7 imparfait du subjonctif		**14 plus-que-parfait du subjonctif**	
adressasse	adressassions	eusse adressé	eussions adressé
adressasses	adressassiez	eusses adressé	eussiez adressé
adressât	adressassent	eût adressé	eussent adressé

Impératif
adresse
adressons
adressez

Words and expressions related to this verb
une adresse   address; skill, adroitness
adresser qqn à   to refer someone to
adresser la parole à   to direct your words to,
   to speak to
s'adresser à   to apply to, to talk to
un tour d'adresse   feat of skill
avec adresse   skillfully

dresser   to tame, to erect
redresser   to straighten up
une adresse électronique   e-mail address
**Pour d'autres renseignements, adressez-vous
   au service à la clientèle.**   For more
   information, talk to customer service.

130

Regular **-er** verb endings; spelling change:
c changes to **ç** before **a** or **o** to keep **s** sound

to annoy, to irritate,
to pester, to vex

A

The Seven Simple Tenses		The Seven Compound Tenses	
Singular	Plural	Singular	Plural
1 présent de l'indicatif		**8 passé composé**	
agace	agaçons	ai agacé	avons agacé
agaces	agacez	as agacé	avez agacé
agace	agacent	a agacé	ont agacé
2 imparfait de l'indicatif		**9 plus-que-parfait de l'indicatif**	
agaçais	agacions	avais agacé	avions agacé
agaçais	agaciez	avais agacé	aviez agacé
agaçait	agaçaient	avait agacé	avaient agacé
3 passé simple		**10 passé antérieur**	
agaçai	agaçâmes	eus agacé	eûmes agacé
agaças	agaçâtes	eus agacé	eûtes agacé
agaça	agacèrent	eut agacé	eurent agacé
4 futur		**11 futur antérieur**	
agacerai	agacerons	aurai agacé	aurons agacé
agaceras	agacerez	auras agacé	aurez agacé
agacera	agaceront	aura agacé	auront agacé
5 conditionnel		**12 conditionnel passé**	
agacerais	agacerions	aurais agacé	aurions agacé
agacerais	agaceriez	aurais agacé	auriez agacé
agacerait	agaceraient	aurait agacé	auraient agacé
6 présent du subjonctif		**13 passé du subjonctif**	
agace	agacions	aie agacé	ayons agacé
agaces	agaciez	aies agacé	ayez agacé
agace	agacent	ait agacé	aient agacé
7 imparfait du subjonctif		**14 plus-que-parfait du subjonctif**	
agaçasse	agaçassions	eusse agacé	eussions agacé
agaçasses	agaçassiez	eusses agacé	eussiez agacé
agaçât	agaçassent	eût agacé	eussent agacé

Impératif
agace
agaçons
agacez

Words and expressions related to this verb
un agacement irritation
Cela est agaçant! That's irritating!
agacer les nerfs de qqn to get on someone's nerves
s'agacer to get annoyed, irritated
Cela m'agace! It's getting on my nerves!
Tu m'agaces! You're getting on my nerves!

Don't forget to check the list of 2,600 additional verbs keyed to the 501 model verbs.

The subject pronouns are found on page 103.

to act, to behave, to take effect

Regular **-ir** verb

The Seven Simple Tenses		The Seven Compound Tenses	
Singular	Plural	Singular	Plural
1 présent de l'indicatif		8 passé composé	
agis	agissons	ai agi	avons agi
agis	agissez	as agi	avez agi
agit	agissent	a agi	ont agi
2 imparfait de l'indicatif		9 plus-que-parfait de l'indicatif	
agissais	agissions	avais agi	avions agi
agissais	agissiez	avais agi	aviez agi
agissait	agissaient	avait agi	avaient agi
3 passé simple		10 passé antérieur	
agis	agîmes	eus agi	eûmes agi
agis	agîtes	eus agi	eûtes agi
agit	agirent	eut agi	eurent agi
4 futur		11 futur antérieur	
agirai	agirons	aurai agi	aurons agi
agiras	agirez	auras agi	aurez agi
agira	agiront	aura agi	auront agi
5 conditionnel		12 conditionnel passé	
agirais	agirions	aurais agi	aurions agi
agirais	agiriez	aurais agi	auriez agi
agirait	agiraient	aurait agi	auraient agi
6 présent du subjonctif		13 passé du subjonctif	
agisse	agissions	aie agi	ayons agi
agisses	agissiez	aies agi	ayez agi
agisse	agissent	ait agi	aient agi
7 imparfait du subjonctif		14 plus-que-parfait du subjonctif	
agisse	agissions	eusse agi	eussions agi
agisses	agissiez	eusses agi	eussiez agi
agît	agissent	eût agi	eussent agi

Impératif
agis
agissons
agissez

Words and expressions related to this verb
faire agir   to set in motion, to call into action
bien agir   to behave well; **mal agir**   to behave badly
agir sur   to bear upon, to influence, to act upon
agir contre   to sue, to take action against

faire agir la loi   to put the law into effect
un agitateur, une agitatrice   agitator
agiter   to rouse, to stir up; to agitate, to shake
réagir   to react
agir à la légère   to act thoughtlessly

See also **s'agir** in the *Defective and impersonal verb* section.

Get acquainted with what preposition goes with what verb. See *Verbs with prepositions* in the Appendixes.

Part. pr. **aidant**   Part. passé **aidé**

Regular **-er** verb   to aid, to ~~h~~

The Seven Simple Tenses		The Seven Compound Tenses	
Singular	Plural	Singular	Plural
1 présent de l'indicatif		8 passé composé	
aide	**aidons**	**ai aidé**	**avons aidé**
aides	**aidez**	**as aidé**	**avez aidé**
aide	**aident**	**a aidé**	**ont aidé**
2 imparfait de l'indicatif		9 plus-que-parfait de l'indicatif	
aidais	**aidions**	**avais aidé**	**avions aidé**
aidais	**aidiez**	**avais aidé**	**aviez aidé**
aidait	**aidaient**	**avait aidé**	**avaient aidé**
3 passé simple		10 passé antérieur	
aidai	**aidâmes**	**eus aidé**	**eûmes aidé**
aidas	**aidâtes**	**eus aidé**	**eûtes aidé**
aida	**aidèrent**	**eut aidé**	**eurent aidé**
4 futur		11 futur antérieur	
aiderai	**aiderons**	**aurai aidé**	**aurons aidé**
aideras	**aiderez**	**auras aidé**	**aurez aidé**
aidera	**aideront**	**aura aidé**	**auront aidé**
5 conditionnel		12 conditionnel passé	
aiderais	**aiderions**	**aurais aidé**	**aurions aidé**
aiderais	**aideriez**	**aurais aidé**	**auriez aidé**
aiderait	**aideraient**	**aurait aidé**	**auraient aidé**
6 présent du subjonctif		13 passé du subjonctif	
aide	**aidions**	**aie aidé**	**ayons aidé**
aides	**aidiez**	**aies aidé**	**ayez aidé**
aide	**aident**	**ait aidé**	**aient aidé**
7 imparfait du subjonctif		14 plus-que-parfait du subjonctif	
aidasse	**aidassions**	**eusse aidé**	**eussions aidé**
aidasses	**aidassiez**	**eusses aidé**	**eussiez aidé**
aidât	**aidassent**	**eût aidé**	**eussent aidé**

Impératif
aide
aidons
aidez

Sentences using this verb and words related to it

Tous les soirs Daniel aide Matthieu, son petit frère, à faire sa leçon de mathématiques.
Every evening Daniel helps his little brother Matthew do his math lesson.
Ce soir, Matthieu lui demande: This evening, Matthew asks him:
—Après cette leçon, veux-tu m'aider à écrire une composition?   After this lesson, would you
   like to help me write a composition?
—Aide-toi et le ciel t'aidera, lui répond Daniel.   Heaven helps those who help themselves,
   answers Daniel.

aider qqn à faire qqch   to help someone do   un aide-mémoire   handbook, memory aid
   something   À l'aide tout de suite!   Get help right away!
s'aider   to help oneself; to help each other   Je peux vous aider?   May I help you?
une aide   aid, assistance, help; à l'aide de   s'entraider   to help each other
   with the help of

Note that **se servir** should be used when speaking of food or drink: **Sers-toi!** (Help yourself!)
Servez-vous! (Help yourself/yourselves!) See also **servir** and **se servir**.

The subject pronouns are found on page 103.   **133**

Regular **-er** verb

aider (26)
help, to assist

A

The Seven Compound Tenses

Singular	Plural

aime   aiment

8   passé composé

ai aimé	avons aimé
as aimé	avez aimé
a aimé	ont aimé

2   imparfait de l'indicatif

aimais	aimions
aimais	aimiez
aimait	aimaient

9   plus-que-parfait de l'indicatif

avais aimé	avions aimé
avais aimé	aviez aimé
avait aimé	avaient aimé

3   passé simple

aimai	aimâmes
aimas	aimâtes
aima	aimèrent

10   passé antérieur

eus aimé	eûmes aimé
eus aimé	eûtes aimé
eut aimé	eurent aimé

4   futur

aimerai	aimerons
aimeras	aimerez
aimera	aimeront

11   futur antérieur

aurai aimé	aurons aimé
auras aimé	aurez aimé
aura aimé	auront aimé

5   conditionnel

aimerais	aimerions
aimerais	aimeriez
aimerait	aimeraient

12   conditionnel passé

aurais aimé	aurions aimé
aurais aimé	auriez aimé
aurait aimé	auraient aimé

6   présent du subjonctif

aime	aimions
aimes	aimiez
aime	aiment

13   passé du subjonctif

aie aimé	ayons aimé
aies aimé	ayez aimé
ait aimé	aient aimé

7   imparfait du subjonctif

aimasse	aimassions
aimasses	aimassiez
aimât	aimassent

14   plus-que-parfait du subjonctif

eusse aimé	eussions aimé
eusses aimé	eussiez aimé
eût aimé	eussent aimé

Impératif
aime
aimons
aimez

AN ESSENTIAL
55 VERB

AN ESSENTIAL 55 VERB

Aimer is a very useful verb. It has often been thought of as the model of a regular -er verb.

Sentences using aimer and related words

Greg aime faire du vélo. Greg loves to bike.

Est-ce que David aime les cigarettes?
Does David like cigarettes?

Je n'aime pas les ascenseurs! Je préfère monter l'escalier. I don't like elevators! I prefer to walk up the stairs.

Vous êtes bien aimable. You are very kind.

J'aimerais acheter quelques pâtisseries. I would *WNld* like to buy some pastries.

Moi, je n'aime pas le poulet. Je préfère un steak bien cuit. As for me, I don't like chicken. I prefer a steak well-done.

Veuillez avoir l'amabilité de . . . Please be so kind as to . . .

Je t'aimais, je t'aime et je t'aimerai. I loved you, I love you and I will love you. (Francis Cabrel, French singer)

Required sentence
J'aime le français. I love French.

Words and expressions related to this verb

amour *m.* **love**

une chanson d'amour **love song (song of love)**

aimer bien qqn **to like somebody**

aimer (à) faire qqch **to enjoy doing something**

aimer mieux **to prefer, to like better**

s'entr'aimer **to love each other**

l'amabilité *f.* **kindness**

aimable **friendly, amiable, pleasant**

un amant, une amante **lover**

amoureux, amoureuse de **in love with**

tomber amoureux, amoureuse **to fall in love**

Proverb

Choisissez un travail que vous aimez et vous n'aurez pas à travailler un seul jour de votre vie. **Choose a job you love and you will never have to work a day in your life. (Confucius)**

The subject pronouns are found on page 103.

Regular **-er** verb

The Seven Simple Tenses		The Seven Compound Tenses	
Singular	Plural	Singular	Plural
1 présent de l'indicatif		**8 passé composé**	
ajoute	ajoutons	ai ajouté	avons ajouté
ajoutes	ajoutez	as ajouté	avez ajouté
ajoute	ajoutent	a ajouté	ont ajouté
2 imparfait de l'indicatif		**9 plus-que-parfait de l'indicatif**	
ajoutais	ajoutions	avais ajouté	avions ajouté
ajoutais	ajoutiez	avais ajouté	aviez ajouté
ajoutait	ajoutaient	avait ajouté	avaient ajouté
3 passé simple		**10 passé antérieur**	
ajoutai	ajoutâmes	eus ajouté	eûmes ajouté
ajoutas	ajoutâtes	eus ajouté	eûtes ajouté
ajouta	ajoutèrent	eut ajouté	eurent ajouté
4 futur		**11 futur antérieur**	
ajouterai	ajouterons	aurai ajouté	aurons ajouté
ajouteras	ajouterez	auras ajouté	aurez ajouté
ajoutera	ajouteront	aura ajouté	auront ajouté
5 conditionnel		**12 conditionnel passé**	
ajouterais	ajouterions	aurais ajouté	aurions ajouté
ajouterais	ajouteriez	aurais ajouté	auriez ajouté
ajouterait	ajouteraient	aurait ajouté	auraient ajouté
6 présent du subjonctif		**13 passé du subjonctif**	
ajoute	ajoutions	aie ajouté	ayons ajouté
ajoutes	ajoutiez	aies ajouté	ayez ajouté
ajoute	ajoutent	ait ajouté	aient ajouté
7 imparfait du subjonctif		**14 plus-que-parfait du subjonctif**	
ajoutasse	ajoutassions	eusse ajouté	eussions ajouté
ajoutasses	ajoutassiez	eusses ajouté	eussiez ajouté
ajoutât	ajoutassent	eût ajouté	eussent ajouté

Impératif
ajoute
ajoutons
ajoutez

Sentences using this verb and words related to it
Une gousse d'ail ajoute du goût à votre ragoût.   A clove of garlic adds flavor to your ragout.

un ajout   addition (of words in a manuscript or page proofs)
ajouter foi à   to add credence to, to give credence to

jouter   to tilt, to joust; to dispute, to fight
une joute   contest, tournament
rajouter   to add more
un rajout   an addition

Don't forget to check the list of 2,600 additional verbs keyed to the 501 model verbs. It's in the Appendixes!

The Seven Simple Tenses		The Seven Compound Tenses	
Singular	Plural	Singular	Plural
1 présent de l'indicatif		8 passé composé	
vais	**allons**	**suis allé(e)**	**sommes allé(e)s**
vas	**allez**	**es allé(e)**	**êtes allé(e)(s)**
va	**vont**	**est allé(e)**	**sont allé(e)s**
2 imparfait de l'indicatif		9 plus-que-parfait de l'indicatif	
allais	**allions**	**étais allé(e)**	**étions allé(e)s**
allais	**alliez**	**étais allé(e)**	**étiez allé(e)(s)**
allait	**allaient**	**était allé(e)**	**étaient allé(e)s**
3 passé simple		10 passé antérieur	
allai	**allâmes**	**fus allé(e)**	**fûmes allé(e)s**
allas	**allâtes**	**fus allé(e)**	**fûtes allé(e)(s)**
alla	**allèrent**	**fut allé(e)**	**furent allé(e)s**
4 futur		11 futur antérieur	
irai	**irons**	**serai allé(e)**	**serons allé(e)s**
iras	**irez**	**seras allé(e)**	**serez allé(e)(s)**
ira	**iront**	**sera allé(e)**	**seront allé(e)s**
5 conditionnel		12 conditionnel passé	
irais	**irions**	**serais allé(e)**	**serions allé(e)s**
irais	**iriez**	**serais allé(e)**	**seriez allé(e)(s)**
irait	**iraient**	**serait allé(e)**	**seraient allé(e)s**
6 présent du subjonctif		13 passé du subjonctif	
aille	**allions**	**sois allé(e)**	**soyons allé(e)s**
ailles	**alliez**	**sois allé(e)**	**soyez allé(e)(s)**
aille	**aillent**	**soit allé(e)**	**soient allé(e)s**
7 imparfait du subjonctif		14 plus-que-parfait du subjonctif	
allasse	**allassions**	**fusse allé(e)**	**fussions allé(e)s**
allasses	**allassiez**	**fusses allé(e)**	**fussiez allé(e)(s)**
allât	**allassent**	**fût allé(e)**	**fussent allé(e)s**

Impératif
va
allons
allez

Can't recognize an irregular verb form? Check out the index of common irregular French verb forms in the Appendixes.

Aller and s'en aller

Aller and **s'en aller** are an essential pair of verbs for beginning students. They are used in many everyday situations and common idiomatic expressions.

Sentences using aller and related words

Comment allez-vous? How are you?

Je vais bien, merci. I'm fine, thank you.

Je vais mal. I'm not well.

Je vais mieux maintenant. I'm feeling better now.

Ça va? Is everything O.K.?

Oui, ça va! Yes, everything's O.K.!

Ça va sans dire. That goes without saying.

Allez-y! (polite) Vas-y! (familiar) Go ahead!

Allons donc! Come on, now! Nonsense!

S'il te plaît, pourrais-tu aller chercher Madeleine à l'école? Could you please go get Madeleine at school?

Est-ce que je vais tout droit pour arriver au Château Frontenac? Do I go straight ahead to arrive at the Château Frontenac?

The verb **s'en aller** has the following idiomatic meaning: to move away (from one residence to another), to die, to pass away, to steal away.

Monsieur et Madame Moreau n'habitent plus ici. Ils s'en sont allés. Je crois qu'ils sont maintenant à Bordeaux. Mr. and Mrs. Moreau don't live here anymore. They went away. I believe that they are in Bordeaux now.

Madame Morel est gravement malade; elle s'en va. Mrs. Morel is gravely ill; she's dying.

Le cambrioleur s'en est allé furtivement avec l'argent et les bijoux. The burglar went away stealthily with the money and the jewelry.

Idiomatic expressions related to these verbs

aller à la chasse to go hunting
aller à la pêche to go fishing
aller à la rencontre de quelqu'un to go to meet someone
aller au-devant de quelqu'un to go to meet someone
aller à pied to walk, to go on foot
aller à quelqu'un to be becoming, to fit, to suit someone
aller au fond des choses to get to the bottom of things
aller aux urnes to vote
aller avec quelque chose to match something
aller chercher to go get
aller de pair avec . . . to go hand in hand with . . .
aller de soi to go without saying, to be obvious
aller en voiture to ride in a car
aller sans dire to go without saying
aller tout droit to go straight ahead

Aller is often used to express the future (instead of Tense No. 4):

Nous allons dîner en ville. We are going to have dinner downtown.

Je vais partir demain soir. I'm going to leave tomorrow evening.

Words and expressions using *aller*

un billet aller-retour a round-trip ticket
aller-retour round-trip
aller simple one-way

The Seven Simple Tenses		The Seven Compound Tenses	
Singular	Plural	Singular	Plural
1 présent de l'indicatif		**8 passé composé**	
m'en vais	**nous en allons**	**m'en suis allé(e)**	**nous en sommes allé(e)s**
t'en vas	**vous en allez**	**t'en es allé(e)**	**vous en êtes allé(e)(s)**
s'en va	**s'en vont**	**s'en est allé(e)**	**s'en sont allé(e)s**
2 imparfait de l'indicatif		**9 plus-que-parfait de l'indicatif**	
m'en allais	**nous en allions**	**m'en étais allé(e)**	**nous en étions allé(e)s**
t'en allais	**vous en alliez**	**t'en étais allé(e)**	**vous en étiez allé(e)(s)**
s'en allait	**s'en allaient**	**s'en était allé(e)**	**s'en étaient allé(e)s**
3 passé simple		**10 passé antérieur**	
m'en allai	**nous en allâmes**	**m'en fus allé(e)**	**nous en fûmes allé(e)s**
t'en allas	**vous en allâtes**	**t'en fus allé(e)**	**vous en fûtes allé(e)(s)**
s'en alla	**s'en allèrent**	**s'en fut allé(e)**	**s'en furent allé(e)s**
4 futur		**11 futur antérieur**	
m'en irai	**nous en irons**	**m'en serai allé(e)**	**nous en serons allé(e)s**
t'en iras	**vous en irez**	**t'en seras allé(e)**	**vous en serez allé(e)(s)**
s'en ira	**s'en iront**	**s'en sera allé(e)**	**s'en seront allé(e)s**
5 conditionnel		**12 conditionnel passé**	
m'en irais	**nous en irions**	**m'en serais allé(e)**	**nous en serions allé(e)s**
t'en irais	**vous en iriez**	**t'en serais allé(e)**	**vous en seriez allé(e)(s)**
s'en irait	**s'en iraient**	**s'en serait allé(e)**	**s'en seraient allé(e)s**
6 présent du subjonctif		**13 passé du subjonctif**	
m'en aille	**nous en allions**	**m'en sois allé(e)**	**nous en soyons allé(e)s**
t'en ailles	**vous en alliez**	**t'en sois allé(e)**	**vous en soyez allé(e)(s)**
s'en aille	**s'en aillent**	**s'en soit allé(e)**	**s'en soient allé(e)s**
7 imparfait du subjonctif		**14 plus-que-parfait du subjonctif**	
m'en allasse	**nous en allassions**	**m'en fusse allé(e)**	**nous en fussions allé(e)s**
t'en allasses	**vous en allassiez**	**t'en fusses allé(e)**	**vous en fussiez allé(e)(s)**
s'en allât	**s'en allassent**	**s'en fût allé(e)**	**s'en fussent allé(e)s**

Impératif
va-t'en; ne t'en va pas
allons-nous-en; ne nous en allons pas
allez-vous-en; ne vous en allez pas

AN ESSENTIAL
55 VERB

The subject pronouns are found on page 103.

139

amener (31) Part. pr. **amenant** Part. passé **amené**

to bring, to lead

Regular **-er** verb endings; spelling change:
e changes to **è** before syllable with mute **e**

The Seven Simple Tenses		The Seven Compound Tenses	
Singular	Plural	Singular	Plural
1 présent de l'indicatif		**8 passé composé**	
amène	amenons	ai amené	avons amené
amènes	amenez	as amené	avez amené
amène	amènent	a amené	ont amené
2 imparfait de l'indicatif		**9 plus-que-parfait de l'indicatif**	
amenais	amenions	avais amené	avions amené
amenais	ameniez	avais amené	aviez amené
amenait	amenaient	avait amené	avaient amené
3 passé simple		**10 passé antérieur**	
amenai	amenâmes	eus amené	eûmes amené
amenas	amenâtes	eus amené	eûtes amené
amena	amenèrent	eut amené	eurent amené
4 futur		**11 futur antérieur**	
amènerai	amènerons	aurai amené	aurons amené
amèneras	amènerez	auras amené	aurez amené
amènera	amèneront	aura amené	auront amené
5 conditionnel		**12 conditionnel passé**	
amènerais	amènerions	aurais amené	aurions amené
amènerais	amèneriez	aurais amené	auriez amené
amènerait	amèneraient	aurait amené	auraient amené
6 présent du subjonctif		**13 passé du subjonctif**	
amène	amenions	aie amené	ayons amené
amènes	ameniez	aies amené	ayez amené
amène	amènent	ait amené	aient amené
7 imparfait du subjonctif		**14 plus-que-parfait du subjonctif**	
amenasse	amenassions	eusse amené	eussions amené
amenasses	amenassiez	eusses amené	eussiez amené
amenât	amenassent	eût amené	eussent amené

Impératif
amène
amenons
amenez

Sentences using this verb and words related to it

Aujourd'hui ma mère a amené ma petite soeur chez le dentiste. Quand elles sont entrées chez lui, le dentiste leur a demandé:—Quel bon vent vous amène ici?

amener une conversation   to direct, lead a
  conversation
amène   pleasant, agreeable

des propos peu amènes   unkind words
un exemple bien amené   well-introduced
  example

See also **emmener** and **mener**.

How are you doing? Find out with the verb drills and tests with answers explained on pages 50–101.

The Seven Simple Tenses | | The Seven Compound Tenses | |

Singular	Plural	Singular	Plural

A

1   présent de l'indicatif

amuse	amusons	**8 passé composé**	
amuses	amusez	ai amusé	avons amusé
amuse	amusent	as amusé	avez amusé
		a amusé	ont amusé

2   imparfait de l'indicatif

amusais	amusions	**9 plus-que-parfait de l'indicatif**	
amusais	amusiez	avais amusé	avions amusé
amusait	amusaient	avais amusé	aviez amusé
		avait amusé	avaient amusé

3   passé simple

amusai	amusâmes	**10 passé antérieur**	
amusas	amusâtes	eus amusé	eûmes amusé
amusa	amusèrent	eus amusé	eûtes amusé
		eut amusé	eurent amusé

4   futur

amuserai	amuserons	**11 futur antérieur**	
amuseras	amuserez	aurai amusé	aurons amusé
amusera	amuseront	auras amusé	aurez amusé
		aura amusé	auront amusé

5   conditionnel

amuserais	amuserions	**12 conditionnel passé**	
amuserais	amuseriez	aurais amusé	aurions amusé
amuserait	amuseraient	aurais amusé	auriez amusé
		aurait amusé	auraient amusé

6   présent du subjonctif

amuse	amusions	**13 passé du subjonctif**	
amuses	amusiez	aie amusé	ayons amusé
amuse	amusent	aies amusé	ayez amusé
		ait amusé	aient amusé

7   imparfait du subjonctif

amusasse	amusassions	**14 plus-que-parfait du subjonctif**	
amusasses	amusassiez	eusse amusé	eussions amusé
amusât	amusassent	eusses amusé	eussiez amusé
		eût amusé	eussent amusé

Impératif
amuse
amusons
amusez

Sentences using this verb and words related to it

Cet acteur sait bien jouer son rôle. Il amuse les spectateurs. C'est un comédien accompli. Il est amusant, n'est-ce pas?

amusant, amusante   amusing
un amuseur   amuser, entertainer
un amuse-gueule, un amuse-bouche   tidbit, titbit, snack
une amusette   diversion, pastime, idle pleasure

un amusement   amusement, entertainment
Tes remarques ne m'amusent pas.   Your remarks don't amuse me.
C'est pour l'amusement des enfants.   It's for the children's entertainment.
le museau   muzzle, snout

See also s'amuser.

The subject pronouns are found on page 103.

to have a good time, to amuse
oneself, to enjoy oneself

Reflexive regular **-er** verb

The Seven Simple Tenses		The Seven Compound Tenses	
Singular	Plural	Singular	Plural
1 présent de l'indicatif		8 passé composé	
m'amuse	nous amusons	me suis amusé(e)	nous sommes amusé(e)s
t'amuses	vous amusez	t'es amusé(e)	vous êtes amusé(e)(s)
s'amuse	s'amusent	s'est amusé(e)	se sont amusé(e)s
2 imparfait de l'indicatif		9 plus-que-parfait de l'indicatif	
m'amusais	nous amusions	m'étais amusé(e)	nous étions amusé(e)s
t'amusais	vous amusiez	t'étais amusé(e)	vous étiez amusé(e)(s)
s'amusait	s'amusaient	s'était amusé(e)	s'étaient amusé(e)s
3 passé simple		10 passé antérieur	
m'amusai	nous amusâmes	me fus amusé(e)	nous fûmes amusé(e)s
t'amusas	vous amusâtes	te fus amusé(e)	vous fûtes amusé(e)(s)
s'amusa	s'amusèrent	se fut amusé(e)	se furent amusé(e)s
4 futur		11 futur antérieur	
m'amuserai	nous amuserons	me serai amusé(e)	nous serons amusé(e)s
t'amuseras	vous amuserez	te seras amusé(e)	vous serez amusé(e)(s)
s'amusera	s'amuseront	se sera amusé(e)	se seront amusé(e)s
5 conditionnel		12 conditionnel passé	
m'amuserais	nous amuserions	me serais amusé(e)	nous serions amusé(e)s
t'amuserais	vous amuseriez	te serais amusé(e)	vous seriez amusé(e)(s)
s'amuserait	s'amuseraient	se serait amusé(e)	se seraient amusé(e)s
6 présent du subjonctif		13 passé du subjonctif	
m'amuse	nous amusions	me sois amusé(e)	nous soyons amusé(e)s
t'amuses	vous amusiez	te sois amusé(e)	vous soyez amusé(e)(s)
s'amuse	s'amusent	se soit amusé(e)	se soient amusé(e)s
7 imparfait du subjonctif		14 plus-que-parfait du subjonctif	
m'amusasse	nous amusassions	me fusse amusé(e)	nous fussions amusé(e)s
t'amusasses	vous amusassiez	te fusses amusé(e)	vous fussiez amusé(e)(s)
s'amusât	s'amusassent	se fût amusé(e)	se fussent amusé(e)s

Impératif
amuse-toi; ne t'amuse pas
amusons-nous; ne nous amusons pas
amusez-vous; ne vous amusez pas

Sentences using this verb and words related to it

Il y a des élèves qui s'amusent à mettre le professeur en colère. Est-ce que vous vous amusez dans la classe de français? Moi, je m'amuse beaucoup dans cette classe.

Hier soir je suis allé au cinéma et j'ai vu un film très amusant. Je me suis bien amusé. Mon amie, Françoise, s'est bien amusée aussi.

Que faites-vous pour vous amuser?

Amuse-toi bien!   Have a great time!   **s'amuser de**   to make fun of
s'amuser à + inf.   to enjoy oneself + pres. part.   **s'amuser avec**   to play with

See also **amuser.**

A

to announce

Regular **-er** verb endings; spelling change: **c** changes to **ç** before **a** or **o** to keep **s** sound

The Seven Simple Tenses		The Seven Compound Tenses	
Singular	Plural	Singular	Plural

1 présent de l'indicatif		8 passé composé	
annonce	**annonçons**	**ai annoncé**	**avons annoncé**
annonces	**annoncez**	**as annoncé**	**avez annoncé**
annonce	**annoncent**	**a annoncé**	**ont annoncé**

2 imparfait de l'indicatif		9 plus-que-parfait de l'indicatif	
annonçais	**annoncions**	**avais annoncé**	**avions annoncé**
annonçais	**annonciez**	**avais annoncé**	**aviez annoncé**
annonçait	**annonçaient**	**avait annoncé**	**avaient annoncé**

3 passé simple		10 passé antérieur	
annonçai	**annonçâmes**	**eus annoncé**	**eûmes annoncé**
annonças	**annonçâtes**	**eus annoncé**	**eûtes annoncé**
annonça	**annoncèrent**	**eut annoncé**	**eurent annoncé**

4 futur		11 futur antérieur	
annoncerai	**annoncerons**	**aurai annoncé**	**aurons annoncé**
annonceras	**annoncerez**	**auras annoncé**	**aurez annoncé**
annoncera	**annonceront**	**aura annoncé**	**auront annoncé**

5 conditionnel		12 conditionnel passé	
annoncerais	**annoncerions**	**aurais annoncé**	**aurions annoncé**
annoncerais	**annonceriez**	**aurais annoncé**	**auriez annoncé**
annoncerait	**annonceraient**	**aurait annoncé**	**auraient annoncé**

6 présent du subjonctif		13 passé du subjonctif	
annonce	**annoncions**	**aie annoncé**	**ayons annoncé**
annonces	**annonciez**	**aies annoncé**	**ayez annoncé**
annonce	**annoncent**	**ait annoncé**	**aient annoncé**

7 imparfait du subjonctif		14 plus-que-parfait du subjonctif	
annonçasse	**annonçassions**	**eusse annoncé**	**eussions annoncé**
annonçasses	**annonçassiez**	**eusses annoncé**	**eussiez annoncé**
annonçât	**annonçassent**	**eût annoncé**	**eussent annoncé**

Impératif
annonce
annonçons
annoncez

Words and expressions related to this verb
une annonce   announcement, notification
demander par annonce   to advertise for
un annonceur   advertiser, announcer, speaker
un annoncier, une annoncière   advertising
  manager

s'annoncer bien   to look promising;
  Cela s'annonce bien   That looks promising
les petites annonces d'un journal   newspaper
  classified advertisements
s'annoncer   to announce (introduce) oneself

See also **prononcer.**

Note that **annoncer** can also mean to predict (weather, event): **J'ai amené mon parapluie parce qu'ils avaient annoncé de la pluie.** I brought my umbrella because rain had been predicted.

to perceive

Irregular verb with spelling change: **c** changes to **ç** before **o** or **u** to keep **s** sound

The Seven Simple Tenses		The Seven Compound Tenses	
Singular	Plural	Singular	Plural
1 présent de l'indicatif		8 passé composé	
aperçois	apercevons	ai aperçu	avons aperçu
aperçois	apercevez	as aperçu	avez aperçu
aperçoit	aperçoivent	a aperçu	ont aperçu
2 imparfait de l'indicatif		9 plus-que-parfait de l'indicatif	
apercevais	apercevions	avais aperçu	avions aperçu
apercevais	aperceviez	avais aperçu	aviez aperçu
apercevait	apercevaient	avait aperçu	avaient aperçu
3 passé simple		10 passé antérieur	
aperçus	aperçûmes	eus aperçu	eûmes aperçu
aperçus	aperçûtes	eus aperçu	eûtes aperçu
aperçut	aperçurent	eut aperçu	eurent aperçu
4 futur		11 futur antérieur	
apercevrai	apercevrons	aurai aperçu	aurons aperçu
apercevras	apercevrez	auras aperçu	aurez aperçu
apercevra	apercevront	aura aperçu	auront aperçu
5 conditionnel		12 conditionnel passé	
apercevrais	apercevrions	aurais aperçu	aurions aperçu
apercevrais	apercevriez	aurais aperçu	auriez aperçu
apercevrait	apercevraient	aurait aperçu	auraient aperçu
6 présent du subjonctif		13 passé du subjonctif	
aperçoive	apercevions	aie aperçu	ayons aperçu
aperçoives	aperceviez	aies aperçu	ayez aperçu
aperçoive	aperçoivent	ait aperçu	aient aperçu
7 imparfait du subjonctif		14 plus-que-parfait du subjonctif	
aperçusse	aperçussions	eusse aperçu	eussions aperçu
aperçusses	aperçussiez	eusse aperçu	eussiez aperçu
aperçût	aperçussent	eût aperçu	eussent aperçu

Impératif
aperçois
apercevons
apercevez

Words and expressions related to this verb

sans s'en apercevoir without taking any notice (of it)
la perception perception, collection (tax)
perceptiblement perceptibly
à peine perceptible scarcely perceptible
un aperçu glimpse, glance, outline

s'apercevoir de to become aware of, to notice
la perceptibilité perceptibility
perceptif, perceptive perceptive
entr'apercevoir to glimpse
percevoir to perceive, to sense

Don't forget to check the list of 2,600 additional verbs keyed to the 501 model verbs. It's in the Appendixes!

The Seven Simple Tenses | The Seven Compound Tenses

A

Singular	Plural	Singular	Plural
1 présent de l'indicatif		**8 passé composé**	
apparais	**apparaissons**	**ai apparu**	**avons apparu**
apparais	**apparaissez**	**as apparu**	**avez apparu**
apparaît	**apparaissent**	**a apparu**	**ont apparu**
2 imparfait de l'indicatif		**9 plus-que-parfait de l'indicatif**	
apparaissais	**apparaissions**	**avais apparu**	**avions apparu**
apparaissais	**apparaissiez**	**avais apparu**	**aviez apparu**
apparaissait	**apparaissaient**	**avait apparu**	**avaient apparu**
3 passé simple		**10 passé antérieur**	
apparus	**apparûmes**	**eus apparu**	**eûmes apparu**
apparus	**apparûtes**	**eus apparu**	**eûtes apparu**
apparut	**apparurent**	**eut apparu**	**eurent apparu**
4 futur		**11 futur antérieur**	
apparaîtrai	**apparaîtrons**	**aurai apparu**	**aurons apparu**
apparaîtras	**apparaîtrez**	**auras apparu**	**aurez apparu**
apparaîtra	**apparaîtront**	**aura apparu**	**auront apparu**
5 conditionnel		**12 conditionnel passé**	
apparaîtrais	**apparaîtrions**	**aurais apparu**	**aurions apparu**
apparaîtrais	**apparaîtriez**	**aurais apparu**	**auriez apparu**
apparaîtrait	**apparaîtraient**	**aurait apparu**	**auraient apparu**
6 présent du subjonctif		**13 passé du subjonctif**	
apparaisse	**apparaissions**	**aie apparu**	**ayons apparu**
apparaisses	**apparaissiez**	**aies apparu**	**ayez apparu**
apparaisse	**apparaissent**	**ait apparu**	**aient apparu**
7 imparfait du subjonctif		**14 plus-que-parfait du subjonctif**	
apparusse	**apparussions**	**eusse apparu**	**eussions apparu**
apparusses	**apparussiez**	**eusses apparu**	**eussiez apparu**
apparût	**apparussent**	**eût apparu**	**eussent apparu**

Impératif
apparais
apparaissons
apparaissez

Words and expressions related to this verb

apparemment   apparently

apparent, apparente   apparent

une apparition   apparition

une apparence   appearance

This verb can be conjugated with *avoir* or *être* to form the seven compound tenses (Nos. 8 to 14) above. The seven simple tense forms (1 to 7) remain as they are above. The past participle remains *apparu*. Just use the appropriate forms of *être* as the auxiliary instead of *avoir* and make the required agreements in gender (masc. or fem.) and number (s. or pl.) as you would when you conjugate the verb *aller*. Example, Tense No. 8: elle a apparu *or* elle est apparue. Summary: this verb is conjugated with *avoir* when it expresses an action; it is conjugated with *être* when it expresses the state resulting from the accomplished action.

See also paraître, disparaître, and reparaître.

Grammar putting you in a tense mood? Review the definitions of basic grammatical terms with examples on pages 35–49.

to belong, to pertain

Irregular verb

The Seven Simple Tenses		The Seven Compound Tenses	
Singular	Plural	Singular	Plural
1 présent de l'indicatif		**8 passé composé**	
appartiens	appartenons	ai appartenu	avons appartenu
appartiens	appartenez	as appartenu	avez appartenu
appartient	appartiennent	a appartenu	ont appartenu
2 imparfait de l'indicatif		**9 plus-que-parfait de l'indicatif**	
appartenais	appartenions	avais appartenu	avions appartenu
appartenais	apparteniez	avais appartenu	aviez appartenu
appartenait	appartenaient	avait appartenu	avaient appartenu
3 passé simple		**10 passé antérieur**	
appartins	appartînmes	eus appartenu	eûmes appartenu
appartins	appartîntes	eus appartenu	eûtes appartenu
appartint	appartinrent	eut appartenu	eurent appartenu
4 futur		**11 futur antérieur**	
appartiendrai	appartiendrons	aurai appartenu	aurons appartenu
appartiendras	appartiendrez	auras appartenu	aurez appartenu
appartiendra	appartiendront	aura appartenu	auront appartenu
5 conditionnel		**12 conditionnel passé**	
appartiendrais	appartiendrions	aurais appartenu	aurions appartenu
appartiendrais	appartiendriez	aurais appartenu	auriez appartenu
appartiendrait	appartiendraient	aurait appartenu	auraient appartenu
6 présent du subjonctif		**13 passé du subjonctif**	
appartienne	appartenions	aie appartenu	ayons appartenu
appartiennes	apparteniez	aies appartenu	ayez appartenu
appartienne	appartiennent	ait appartenu	aient appartenu
7 imparfait du subjonctif		**14 plus-que-parfait du subjonctif**	
appartinsse	appartinssions	eusse appartenu	eussions appartenu
appartinsses	appartinssiez	eusses appartenu	eussiez appartenu
appartînt	appartinssent	eût appartenu	eussent appartenu

Impératif
appartiens
appartenons
appartenez

Words and expressions related to this verb

appartenir à   to belong to, to pertain to, to appertain to

Il appartient que . . .   It is fitting that . . .

appartenir à qqn de + inf.   to behoove someone to; **Il lui appartient de dire la vérité.**

une appartenance   appurtenance; **appartenant, appartenante**   appertaining, belonging

un sentiment d'appartenance   feeling of belonging

A TOUS CEUX QU'IL APPARTIENDRA   TO WHOM IT MAY CONCERN

s'appartenir   to be independent

appartenir à qqn de faire qqch   to be up to someone to do something

Get acquainted with what preposition goes with what verb. See *Verbs with prepositions* in the Appendixes.

Regular **-er** verb endings; spelling change:
l becomes **ll** before syllable with a mute **e**

to call, to name, to appeal

The Seven Simple Tenses		The Seven Compound Tenses	
Singular	Plural	Singular	Plural

A

1 présent de l'indicatif		8 passé composé	
appelle	appelons	ai appelé	avons appelé
appelles	appelez	as appelé	avez appelé
appelle	appellent	a appelé	ont appelé

2 imparfait de l'indicatif		9 plus-que-parfait de l'indicatif	
appelais	appelions	avais appelé	avions appelé
appelais	appeliez	avais appelé	aviez appelé
appelait	appelaient	avait appelé	avaient appelé

3 passé simple		10 passé antérieur	
appelai	appelâmes	eus appelé	eûmes appelé
appelas	appelâtes	eus appelé	eûtes appelé
appela	appelèrent	eut appelé	eurent appelé

4 futur		11 futur antérieur	
appellerai	appellerons	aurai appelé	aurons appelé
appelleras	appellerez	auras appelé	aurez appelé
appellera	appelleront	aura appelé	auront appelé

5 conditionnel		12 conditionnel passé	
appellerais	appellerions	aurais appelé	aurions appelé
appellerais	appelleriez	aurais appelé	auriez appelé
appellerait	appelleraient	aurait appelé	auraient appelé

6 présent du subjonctif		13 passé du subjonctif	
appelle	appelions	aie appelé	ayons appelé
appelles	appeliez	aies appelé	ayez appelé
appelle	appellent	ait appelé	aient appelé

7 imparfait du subjonctif		14 plus-que-parfait du subjonctif	
appelasse	appelassions	eusse appelé	eussions appelé
appelasses	appelassiez	eusses appelé	eussiez appelé
appelât	appelassent	eût appelé	eussent appelé

Impératif
appelle
appelons
appelez

Sentences using this verb and words related to it

Madame Dubois va appeler le médecin parce qu'elle ne va pas bien aujourd'hui.
—As-tu appelé le docteur, chérie? lui demande son mari.
—Non, mon chéri—répond sa femme. Je souffre. Veux-tu l'appeler, s'il te plaît?

une appellation appellation; **un appel**
appeal, call
en appeler à qqn to appeal to someone
rappeler to call back, to remind, to recall
appellation contrôlée French government
approval of the quality of a wine or cheese
un appel call; **appel téléphonique**
telephone call; **faire l'appel** to call the roll

faire un appel de phares to flash the high
beams (of a vehicle)
être appelé à qqch to be destined for
something, to have a calling (vocation, career)
Appelez un taxi, s'il vous plaît. Please call a
taxi.

See also **s'appeler.**

The subject pronouns are found on page 103.

147

s'appeler (39)

Part. pr. s'appelant   **Part. passé** appelé(e)(s)

to be named, to
call oneself

Reflexive verb; regular **-er** verb endings; spelling
change: **l** becomes **ll** before syllable with a mute **e**

The Seven Simple Tenses | The Seven Compound Tenses

Singular	Plural	Singular	Plural
1 présent de l'indicatif		8 passé composé	
m'appelle	nous appelons	me suis appelé(e)	nous sommes appelé(e)s
t'appelles	vous appelez	t'es appelé(e)	vous êtes appelé(e)(s)
s'appelle	s'appellent	s'est appelé(e)	se sont appelé(e)s
2 imparfait de l'indicatif		9 plus-que-parfait de l'indicatif	
m'appelais	nous appelions	m'étais appelé(e)	nous étions appelé(e)s
t'appelais	vous appeliez	t'étais appelé(e)	vous étiez appelé(e)(s)
s'appelait	s'appelaient	s'était appelé(e)	s'étaient appelé(e)s
3 passé simple		10 passé antérieur	
m'appelai	nous appelâmes	me fus appelé(e)	nous fûmes appelé(e)s
t'appelas	vous appelâtes	te fus appelé(e)	vous fûtes appelé(e)(s)
s'appela	s'appelèrent	se fut appelé(e)	se furent appelé(e)s
4 futur		11 futur antérieur	
m'appellerai	nous appellerons	me serai appelé(e)	nous serons appelé(e)s
t'appelleras	vous appellerez	te seras appelé(e)	vous serez appelé(e)(s)
s'appellera	s'appelleront	se sera appelé(e)	se seront appelé(e)s
5 conditionnel		12 conditionnel passé	
m'appellerais	nous appellerions	me serais appelé(e)	nous serions appelé(e)s
t'appellerais	vous appelleriez	te serais appelé(e)	vous seriez appelé(e)(s)
s'appellerait	s'appelleraient	se serait appelé(e)	se seraient appelé(e)s
6 présent du subjonctif		13 passé du subjonctif	
m'appelle	nous appelions	me sois appelé(e)	nous soyons appelé(e)s
t'appelles	vous appeliez	te sois appelé(e)	vous soyez appelé(e)(s)
s'appelle	s'appellent	se soit appelé(e)	se soient appelé(e)s
7 imparfait du subjonctif		14 plus-que-parfait du subjonctif	
m'appelasse	nous appelassions	me fusse appelé(e)	nous fussions appelé(e)s
t'appelasses	vous appelassiez	te fusses appelé(e)	vous fussiez appelé(e)(s)
s'appelât	s'appelassent	se fût appelé(e)	se fussent appelé(e)s

Impératif
appelle-toi; ne t'appelle pas
appelons-nous; ne nous appelons pas
appelez-vous; ne vous appelez pas

Sentences using this verb and words related to it

—Bonjour, mon enfant. Comment t'appelles-tu?

—Je m'appelle Henri.

—As-tu des frères et des soeurs?

—Oui, j'ai deux frères et trois soeurs. Ils s'appellent Joseph, Bernard, Thérèse, Paulette,
et Andrée.

Permettez-moi de me présenter. Je m'appelle . . . Please allow me to introduce myself.
My name is . . .

For other words and expressions related to this verb, see appeler, rappeler, and se rappeler.

Don't miss orthographically changing verbs on pages 32–34.

The Seven Simple Tenses		The Seven Compound Tenses	
Singular	Plural	Singular	Plural

A

1 présent de l'indicatif

apporte	apportons		
apportes	apportez		
apporte	apportent		

8 passé composé

ai apporté	avons apporté		
as apporté	avez apporté		
a apporté	ont apporté		

2 imparfait de l'indicatif

apportais	apportions
apportais	apportiez
apportait	apportaient

9 plus-que-parfait de l'indicatif

avais apporté	avions apporté
avais apporté	aviez apporté
avait apporté	avaient apporté

3 passé simple

apportai	apportâmes
apportas	apportâtes
apporta	apportèrent

10 passé antérieur

eus apporté	eûmes apporté
eus apporté	eûtes apporté
eut apporté	eurent apporté

4 futur

apporterai	apporterons
apporteras	apporterez
apportera	apporteront

11 futur antérieur

aurai apporté	aurons apporté
auras apporté	aurez apporté
aura apporté	auront apporté

5 conditionnel

apporterais	apporterions
apporterais	apporteriez
apporterait	apporteraient

12 conditionnel passé

aurais apporté	aurions apporté
aurais apporté	auriez apporté
aurait apporté	auraient apporté

6 présent du subjonctif

apporte	apportions
apportes	apportiez
apporte	apportent

13 passé du subjonctif

aie apporté	ayons apporté
aies apporté	ayez apporté
ait apporté	aient apporté

7 imparfait du subjonctif

apportasse	apportassions
apportasses	apportassiez
apportât	apportassent

14 plus-que-parfait du subjonctif

eusse apporté	eussions apporté
eusses apporté	eussiez apporté
eût apporté	eussent apporté

Impératif
apporte
apportons
apportez

Sentences using this verb and words related to it

Hier soir, j'ai dîné dans un restaurant français. Quand le garçon m'a apporté mon repas, je lui ai dit:—Apportez-moi du pain, aussi, s'il vous plaît et n'oubliez pas de m'apporter un verre de vin rouge.

—Tout de suite, monsieur—il m'a répondu. Voulez-vous que je vous apporte l'addition maintenant ou après le dîner? Aimez-vous la salade que je vous ai apportée?

un apport something brought; **un apport dotal** wife's dowry
un apporteur a person who brings something (usually news); **un apporteur de bonnes nouvelles** bearer of good news

See also **porter** and **supporter**.

The subject pronouns are found on page 103.   **149**

apprécier (41)

Part. pr. **appréciant**   Part. passé **apprécié**

to appreciate

The Seven Simple Tenses		The Seven Compound Tenses	
Singular	Plural	Singular	Plural
1 présent de l'indicatif		8 passé composé	
apprécie	apprécions	ai apprécié	avons apprécié
apprécies	appréciez	as apprécié	avez apprécié
apprécie	apprécient	a apprécié	ont apprécié
2 imparfait de l'indicatif		9 plus-que-parfait de l'indicatif	
appréciais	appréciions	avais apprécié	avions apprécié
appréciais	appréciiez	avais apprécié	aviez apprécié
appréciait	appréciaient	avait apprécié	avaient apprécié
3 passé simple		10 passé antérieur	
appréciai	appréciâmes	eus apprécié	eûmes apprécié
apprécias	appréciâtes	eus apprécié	eûtes apprécié
apprécia	apprécièrent	eut apprécié	eurent apprécié
4 futur		11 futur antérieur	
apprécierai	apprécierons	aurai apprécié	aurons apprécié
apprécieras	apprécierez	auras apprécié	aurez apprécié
appréciera	apprécieront	aura apprécié	auront apprécié
5 conditionnel		12 conditionnel passé	
apprécierais	apprécierions	aurais apprécié	aurions apprécié
apprécierais	apprécieriez	aurais apprécié	auriez apprécié
apprécierait	apprécieraient	aurait apprécié	auraient apprécié
6 présent du subjonctif		13 passé du subjonctif	
apprécie	appréciions	aie apprécié	ayons apprécié
apprécies	appréciiez	aies apprécié	ayez apprécié
apprécie	apprécient	ait apprécié	aient apprécié
7 imparfait du subjonctif		14 plus-que-parfait du subjonctif	
appréciasse	appréciassions	eusse apprécié	eussions apprécié
appréciasses	appréciassiez	eusses apprécié	eussiez apprécié
appréciât	appréciassent	eût apprécié	eussent apprécié

Impératif
apprécie
apprécions
appréciez

Sentences using this verb and words related to it
Simon n'apprécie pas le goût de ce fromage.
Simon does not appreciate (like) the taste of this cheese.
Il n'y a pas de différence appréciable entre ces deux ordinateurs.
There isn't an appreciable difference between these two computers.

Words and expressions related to this verb
appréciable appreciable
appréciation *f.* appreciation, assessment

déprécier to depreciate
dépréciation depreciation

Note: To say that you are grateful, use the adjective **reconnaissant/reconnaissante. Merci de m'avoir aidé. J'en suis très reconnaissant.** Thank you for helping me. I'm very grateful for it. (I appreciate it.)

A

The Seven Simple Tenses		The Seven Compound Tenses	
Singular	Plural	Singular	Plural
1　présent de l'indicatif		8　passé composé	
apprends	apprenons	ai appris	avons appris
apprends	apprenez	as appris	avez appris
apprend	apprennent	a appris	ont appris
2　imparfait de l'indicatif		9　plus-que-parfait de l'indicatif	
apprenais	apprenions	avais appris	avions appris
apprenais	appreniez	avais appris	aviez appris
apprenait	apprenaient	avait appris	avaient appris
3　passé simple		10　passé antérieur	
appris	apprîmes	eus appris	eûmes appris
appris	apprîtes	eus appris	eûtes appris
apprit	apprirent	eut appris	eurent appris
4　futur		11　futur antérieur	
apprendrai	apprendrons	aurai appris	aurons appris
apprendras	apprendrez	auras appris	aurez appris
apprendra	apprendront	aura appris	auront appris
5　conditionnel		12　conditionnel passé	
apprendrais	apprendrions	aurais appris	aurions appris
apprendrais	apprendriez	aurais appris	auriez appris
apprendrait	apprendraient	aurait appris	auraient appris
6　présent du subjonctif		13　passé du subjonctif	
apprenne	apprenions	aie appris	ayons appris
apprennes	appreniez	aies appris	ayez appris
apprenne	apprennent	ait appris	aient appris
7　imparfait du subjonctif		14　plus-que-parfait du subjonctif	
apprisse	apprissions	eusse appris	eussions appris
apprisses	apprissiez	eusses appris	eussiez appris
apprît	apprissent	eût appris	eussent appris

Impératif
apprends
apprenons
apprenez

AN ESSENTIAL
55 VERB

AN ESSENTIAL 55 VERB

Apprendre

Apprendre is an important verb for beginning students because it is used in many everyday situations and idiomatic expressions. **Apprendre** is also useful for talking about school.

Sentences using apprendre **and related words**

J'aime bien ce poème de Verlaine. Je l'ai appris par coeur. I like this poem by Verlaine. I learned it by heart (memorized it).

À l'école j'apprends à lire en français. In school I am learning to read in French.

Tu apprends à écrire et à parler? Formidable! You're learning to write and speak? Wonderful!

Demain nous apprendrons la conjugaison du verbe *apprendre*. Tomorrow we will learn the conjugation of the verb *apprendre*.

François m'a appris à réparer ma voiture. Francis taught me to fix my car.

Sais-tu que Roland est malade? Je l'ai appris ce matin. Did you know that Roland is sick? I found out this morning.

Enseigner, c'est apprendre deux fois. To teach is to learn two times. (Joseph Joubert)

Words and expressions related to this verb

apprendre par coeur **to learn by heart, memorize**

apprendre à qqn à faire qqch **to teach somebody to do something**

apprendre qqch à qqn **to inform someone of something; to teach someone something**

apprendre à faire qqch **to learn to do something**

un apprentissage **apprenticeship, learning**

un apprenti, une apprentie **apprentice**

See also **comprendre, entreprendre, se méprendre, prendre, reprendre,** and **surprendre.**

Proverb

Sage et prudent celui qui apprend aux dépens d'autrui. **He who learns at someone else's expense is both wise and prudent.**

152

Regular **-er** verb

to approach, to come near, to bring near

The Seven Simple Tenses		The Seven Compound Tenses	
Singular	Plural	Singular	Plural
1 présent de l'indicatif		8 passé composé	
approche	**approchons**	**ai approché**	**avons approché**
approches	**approchez**	**as approché**	**avez approché**
approche	**approchent**	**a approché**	**ont approché**
2 imparfait de l'indicatif		9 plus-que-parfait de l'indicatif	
approchais	**approchions**	**avais approché**	**avions approché**
approchais	**approchiez**	**avais approché**	**aviez approché**
approchait	**approchaient**	**avait approché**	**avaient approché**
3 passé simple		10 passé antérieur	
approchai	**approchâmes**	**eus approché**	**eûmes approché**
approchas	**approchâtes**	**eus approché**	**eûtes approché**
approcha	**approchèrent**	**eut approché**	**eurent approché**
4 futur		11 futur antérieur	
approcherai	**approcherons**	**aurai approché**	**aurons approché**
approcheras	**approcherez**	**auras approché**	**aurez approché**
approchera	**approcheront**	**aura approché**	**auront approché**
5 conditionnel		12 conditionnel passé	
approcherais	**approcherions**	**aurais approché**	**aurions approché**
approcherais	**approcheriez**	**aurais approché**	**auriez approché**
approcherait	**approcheraient**	**aurait approché**	**auraient approché**
6 présent du subjonctif		13 passé du subjonctif	
approche	**approchions**	**aie approché**	**ayons approché**
approches	**approchiez**	**aies approché**	**ayez approché**
approche	**approchent**	**ait approché**	**aient approché**
7 imparfait du subjonctif		14 plus-que-parfait du subjonctif	
approchasse	**approchassions**	**eusse approché**	**eussions approché**
approchasses	**approchassiez**	**eusses approché**	**eussiez approché**
approchât	**approchassent**	**eût approché**	**eussent approché**

Impératif
approche
approchons
approchez

Words and expressions related to this verb
s'approcher de qqn ou qqch   to approach someone or something
se rapprocher de   to come closer to
rapprocher   to bring closer, nearer
reprocher qqch à qqn   to reproach someone with something; **un reproche**   reproach; **faire des reproches à**   to reproach; **sans reproche**   without blame, blameless
proche   close, near; **la pharmacie la plus proche**   the nearest pharmacy
prochain, prochaine   next; **la semaine prochaine**   next week; **la prochaine fois**   the next time

Don't forget to check the list of 2,600 additional verbs keyed to the 501 model verbs. It's in the Appendixes!

The subject pronouns are found on page 103.
153

to approve (of)

Regular **-er** verb

The Seven Simple Tenses		The Seven Compound Tenses	
Singular	Plural	Singular	Plural
1　présent de l'indicatif		8　passé composé	
approuve	approuvons	ai approuvé	avons approuvé
approuves	approuvez	as approuvé	avez approuvé
approuve	approuvent	a approuvé	ont approuvé
2　imparfait de l'indicatif		9　plus-que-parfait de l'indicatif	
approuvais	approuvions	avais approuvé	avions approuvé
approuvais	approuviez	avais approuvé	aviez approuvé
approuvait	approuvaient	avait approuvé	avaient approuvé
3　passé simple		10　passé antérieur	
approuvai	approuvâmes	eus approuvé	eûmes approuvé
approuvas	approuvâtes	eus approuvé	eûtes approuvé
approuva	approuvèrent	eut approuvé	eurent approuvé
4　futur		11　futur antérieur	
approuverai	approuverons	aurai approuvé	aurons approuvé
approuveras	approuverez	auras approuvé	aurez approuvé
approuvera	approuveront	aura approuvé	auront approuvé
5　conditionnel		12　conditionnel passé	
approuverais	approuverions	aurais approuvé	aurions approuvé
approuverais	approuveriez	aurais approuvé	auriez approuvé
approuverait	approuveraient	aurait approuvé	auraient approuvé
6　présent du subjonctif		13　passé du subjonctif	
approuve	approuvions	aie approuvé	ayons approuvé
approuves	approuviez	aies approuvé	ayez approuvé
approuve	approuvent	ait approuvé	aient approuvé
7　imparfait du subjonctif		14　plus-que-parfait du subjonctif	
approuvasse	approuvassions	eusse approuvé	eussions approuvé
approuvasses	approuvassiez	eusses approuvé	eussiez approuvé
approuvât	approuvassent	eût approuvé	eussent approuvé

Impératif
approuve
approuvons
approuvez

Words and expressions related to this verb

approuver qqn de faire qqch　to approve of someone's doing something

acheter à condition　to buy on approval

avec approbation　approvingly

la désapprobation　disapproval, disapprobation

J'approuve votre décision de continuer l'étude de la langue française.

l'approbation f.　approval

un approbateur, une approbatrice　approver

désapprouver　to disapprove, to disapprove of

See also **éprouver** and **prouver.**

Soak up some verbs used in weather expressions. There's a list in the Appendixes!

Regular **-er** verb   to pull up, to pull out, to uproot

The Seven Simple Tenses		The Seven Compound Tenses	
Singular	Plural	Singular	Plural

A

1 présent de l'indicatif		8 passé composé	
arrache	arrachons	ai arraché	avons arraché
arraches	arrachez	as arraché	avez arraché
arrache	arrachent	a arraché	ont arraché

2 imparfait de l'indicatif		9 plus-que-parfait de l'indicatif	
arrachais	arrachions	avais arraché	avions arraché
arrachais	arrachiez	avais arraché	aviez arraché
arrachait	arrachaient	avait arraché	avaient arraché

3 passé simple		10 passé antérieur	
arrachai	arrachâmes	eus arraché	eûmes arraché
arrachas	arrachâtes	eus arraché	eûtes arraché
arracha	arrachèrent	eut arraché	eurent arraché

4 futur		11 futur antérieur	
arracherai	arracherons	aurai arraché	aurons arraché
arracheras	arracherez	auras arraché	aurez arraché
arrachera	arracheront	aura arraché	auront arraché

5 conditionnel		12 conditionnel passé	
arracherais	arracherions	aurais arraché	aurions arraché
arracherais	arracheriez	aurais arraché	auriez arraché
arracherait	arracheraient	aurait arraché	auraient arraché

6 présent du subjonctif		13 passé du subjonctif	
arrache	arrachions	aie arraché	ayons arraché
arraches	arrachiez	aies arraché	ayez arraché
arrache	arrachent	ait arraché	aient arraché

7 imparfait du subjonctif		14 plus-que-parfait du subjonctif	
arrachasse	arrachassions	eusse arraché	eussions arraché
arrachasses	arrachassiez	eusses arraché	eussiez arraché
arrachât	arrachassent	eût arraché	eussent arraché

Impératif
arrache
arrachons
arrachez

Common idiomatic expressions using this verb and words related to it
arracher qqch des mains de qqn   to grab something out of someone's hands
faire qqch d'arrache-pied   to do something without interruption
s'arracher à   to tear oneself away from
un arrache-clou   nail puller (extractor) (**des arrache-clous**)
s'arracher les yeux   to have a violent quarrel (to scratch each other's eyes out)
d'arrache-pied   relentlessly

How are you doing? Find out with the verb drills and tests with answers explained on pages 50–101.

arranger (46)
Part. pr. **arrangeant**   Part. passé **arrangé**

to arrange

Regular **-er** verb endings; spelling change: retain the **ge** before **a** or **o** to keep the soft **g** sound of the verb

The Seven Simple Tenses		The Seven Compound Tenses	
Singular	Plural	Singular	Plural
1 présent de l'indicatif		**8 passé composé**	
arrange	arrangeons	ai arrangé	avons arrangé
arranges	arrangez	as arrangé	avez arrangé
arrange	arrangent	a arrangé	ont arrangé
2 imparfait de l'indicatif		**9 plus-que-parfait de l'indicatif**	
arrangeais	arrangions	avais arrangé	avions arrangé
arrangeais	arrangiez	avais arrangé	aviez arrangé
arrangeait	arrangeaient	avait arrangé	avaient arrangé
3 passé simple		**10 passé antérieur**	
arrangeai	arrangeâmes	eus arrangé	eûmes arrangé
arrangeas	arrangeâtes	eus arrangé	eûtes arrangé
arrangea	arrangèrent	eut arrangé	eurent arrangé
4 futur		**11 futur antérieur**	
arrangerai	arrangerons	aurai arrangé	aurons arrangé
arrangeras	arrangerez	auras arrangé	aurez arrangé
arrangera	arrangeront	aura arrangé	auront arrangé
5 conditionnel		**12 conditionnel passé**	
arrangerais	arrangerions	aurais arrangé	aurions arrangé
arrangerais	arrangeriez	aurais arrangé	auriez arrangé
arrangerait	arrangeraient	aurait arrangé	auraient arrangé
6 présent du subjonctif		**13 passé du subjonctif**	
arrange	arrangions	aie arrangé	ayons arrangé
arranges	arrangiez	aies arrangé	ayez arrangé
arrange	arrangent	ait arrangé	aient arrangé
7 imparfait du subjonctif		**14 plus-que-parfait du subjonctif**	
arrangeasse	arrangeassions	eusse arrangé	eussions arrangé
arrangeasses	arrangeassiez	eusses arrangé	eussiez arrangé
arrangeât	arrangeassent	eût arrangé	eussent arrangé

Impératif
arrange
arrangeons
arrangez

Sentences using this verb and words related to it

J'aime beaucoup un joli arrangement de fleurs. Aimez-vous les fleurs que j'ai arrangées dans ce vase? Les Japonais savent bien arranger les fleurs. Quand mon père apporte des fleurs à ma mère, nous les arrangeons dans un joli vase.

arranger qqch   to arrange, contrive something
arranger l'affaire   to straighten out a matter
s'arranger   to come to an agreement

arranger qqn   to accommodate, suit someone;
Ça m'arrange bien   That suits me fine; Ça
s'arrangera   It will turn out all right.

Regular **-er** verb

to arrest, to stop (someone or something), to halt

The Seven Simple Tenses		The Seven Compound Tenses	
Singular	Plural	Singular	Plural

A

1 présent de l'indicatif		8 passé composé	
arrête	**arrêtons**	**ai arrêté**	**avons arrêté**
arrêtes	**arrêtez**	**as arrêté**	**avez arrêté**
arrête	**arrêtent**	**a arrêté**	**ont arrêté**

2 imparfait de l'indicatif		9 plus-que-parfait de l'indicatif	
arrêtais	**arrêtions**	**avais arrêté**	**avions arrêté**
arrêtais	**arrêtiez**	**avais arrêté**	**aviez arrêté**
arrêtait	**arrêtaient**	**avait arrêté**	**avaient arrêté**

3 passé simple		10 passé antérieur	
arrêtai	**arrêtâmes**	**eus arrêté**	**eûmes arrêté**
arrêtas	**arrêtâtes**	**eus arrêté**	**eûtes arrêté**
arrêta	**arrêtèrent**	**eut arrêté**	**eurent arrêté**

4 futur		11 futur antérieur	
arrêterai	**arrêterons**	**aurai arrêté**	**aurons arrêté**
arrêteras	**arrêterez**	**auras arrêté**	**aurez arrêté**
arrêtera	**arrêteront**	**aura arrêté**	**auront arrêté**

5 conditionnel		12 conditionnel passé	
arrêterais	**arrêterions**	**aurais arrêté**	**aurions arrêté**
arrêterais	**arrêteriez**	**aurais arrêté**	**auriez arrêté**
arrêterait	**arrêteraient**	**aurait arrêté**	**auraient arrêté**

6 présent du subjonctif		13 passé du subjonctif	
arrête	**arrêtions**	**aie arrêté**	**ayons arrêté**
arrêtes	**arrêtiez**	**aies arrêté**	**ayez arrêté**
arrête	**arrêtent**	**ait arrêté**	**aient arrêté**

7 imparfait du subjonctif		14 plus-que-parfait du subjonctif	
arrêtasse	**arrêtassions**	**eusse arrêté**	**eussions arrêté**
arrêtasses	**arrêtassiez**	**eusses arrêté**	**eussiez arrêté**
arrêtât	**arrêtassent**	**eût arrêté**	**eussent arrêté**

Impératif
arrête
arrêtons
arrêtez

Sentences using this verb and words related to it

L'agent de police a arrêté les voitures pour laisser les piétons traverser la rue. Il a crié:— Arrêtez! Arrêtez! The police officer stopped the cars to let the pedestrians cross the street. He shouted: Stop! Stop!

Arrêtez-la/le/les! Stop her/him/them!

un arrêt halt, stop, arrest; **sans arrêt** continually
arrêt d'autobus bus stop
un arrêté ministériel decree
arrêter qqn de faire qqch to stop someone from doing something
une arrestation arrest, apprehension; **être en état d'arrestation** to be under arrest
arrêter un jour to set a date; **arrêter un marché** to make a deal

See also **s'arrêter.**

The subject pronouns are found on page 103.   **157**

to stop (oneself, itself), to pause   Reflexive regular **-er** verb

The Seven Simple Tenses		The Seven Compound Tenses	
Singular	Plural	Singular	Plural
1 présent de l'indicatif		8 passé composé	
m'arrête	**nous arrêtons**	**me suis arrêté(e)**	**nous sommes arrêté(e)s**
t'arrêtes	**vous arrêtez**	**t'es arrêté(e)**	**vous êtes arrêté(e)(s)**
s'arrête	**s'arrêtent**	**s'est arrêté(e)**	**se sont arrêté(e)s**
2 imparfait de l'indicatif		9 plus-que-parfait de l'indicatif	
m'arrêtais	**nous arrêtions**	**m'étais arrêté(e)**	**nous étions arrêté(e)s**
t'arrêtais	**vous arrêtiez**	**t'étais arrêté(e)**	**vous étiez arrêté(e)(s)**
s'arrêtait	**s'arrêtaient**	**s'était arrêté(e)**	**s'étaient arrêté(e)s**
3 passé simple		10 passé antérieur	
m'arrêtai	**nous arrêtâmes**	**me fus arrêté(e)**	**nous fûmes arrêté(e)s**
t'arrêtas	**vous arrêtâtes**	**te fus arrêté(e)**	**vous fûtes arrêté(e)(s)**
s'arrêta	**s'arrêtèrent**	**se fut arrêté(e)**	**se furent arrêté(e)s**
4 futur		11 futur antérieur	
m'arrêterai	**nous arrêterons**	**me serai arrêté(e)**	**nous serons arrêté(e)s**
t'arrêteras	**vous arrêterez**	**te seras arrêté(e)**	**vous serez arrêté(e)(s)**
s'arrêtera	**s'arrêteront**	**se sera arrêté(e)**	**se seront arrêté(e)s**
5 conditionnel		12 conditionnel passé	
m'arrêterais	**nous arrêterions**	**me serais arrêté(e)**	**nous serions arrêté(e)s**
t'arrêterais	**vous arrêteriez**	**te serais arrêté(e)**	**vous seriez arrêté(e)(s)**
s'arrêterait	**s'arrêteraient**	**se serait arrêté(e)**	**se seraient arrêté(e)s**
6 présent du subjonctif		13 passé du subjonctif	
m'arrête	**nous arrêtions**	**me sois arrêté(e)**	**nous soyons arrêté(e)s**
t'arrêtes	**vous arrêtiez**	**te sois arrêté(e)**	**vous soyez arrêté(e)(s)**
s'arrête	**s'arrêtent**	**se soit arrêté(e)**	**se soient arrêté(e)s**
7 imparfait du subjonctif		14 plus-que-parfait du subjonctif	
m'arrêtasse	**nous arrêtassions**	**me fusse arrêté(e)**	**nous fussions arrêté(e)s**
t'arrêtasses	**vous arrêtassiez**	**te fusses arrêté(e)**	**vous fussiez arrêté(e)(s)**
s'arrêtât	**s'arrêtassent**	**se fût arrêté(e)**	**se fussent arrêté(e)s**

Impératif
arrête-toi; ne t'arrête pas
arrêtons-nous; ne nous arrêtons pas
arrêtez-vous; ne vous arrêtez pas

Sentences using this verb and words related to it

Madame Dumont s'est arrêtée devant une pâtisserie pour acheter une belle tarte aux cerises. Deux autres dames se sont arrêtées derrière elle et les trois sont entrées dans le magasin.

s'arrêter de faire qqch   to desist from doing something

s'arrêter de fumer   to stop smoking

See also **arrêter.**

sans s'arrêter   without stopping

Madame Martin s'est arrêtée pour se reposer.   Mrs. Martin stopped to rest.

Don't forget to use the English-French verb index. It's in the Appendixes.

The Seven Simple Tenses		The Seven Compound Tenses	
Singular	Plural	Singular	Plural

1 présent de l'indicatif		8 passé composé	
arrive	**arrivons**	**suis arrivé(e)**	**sommes arrivé(e)s**
arrives	**arrivez**	**es arrivé(e)**	**êtes arrivé(e)(s)**
arrive	**arrivent**	**est arrivé(e)**	**sont arrivé(e)s**

2 imparfait de l'indicatif		9 plus-que-parfait de l'indicatif	
arrivais	**arrivions**	**étais arrivé(e)**	**étions arrivé(e)s**
arrivais	**arriviez**	**étais arrivé(e)**	**étiez arrivé(e)(s)**
arrivait	**arrivaient**	**était arrivé(e)**	**étaient arrivé(e)s**

3 passé simple		10 passé antérieur	
arrivai	**arrivâmes**	**fus arrivé(e)**	**fûmes arrivé(e)s**
arrivas	**arrivâtes**	**fus arrivé(e)**	**fûtes arrivé(e)(s)**
arriva	**arrivèrent**	**fut arrivé(e)**	**furent arrivé(e)s**

4 futur		11 futur antérieur	
arriverai	**arriverons**	**serai arrivé(e)**	**serons arrivé(e)s**
arriveras	**arriverez**	**seras arrivé(e)**	**serez arrivé(e)(s)**
arrivera	**arriveront**	**sera arrivé(e)**	**seront arrivé(e)s**

5 conditionnel		12 conditionnel passé	
arriverais	**arriverions**	**serais arrivé(e)**	**serions arrivé(e)s**
arriverais	**arriveriez**	**serais arrivé(e)**	**seriez arrivé(e)(s)**
arriverait	**arriveraient**	**serait arrivé(e)**	**seraient arrivé(e)s**

6 présent du subjonctif		13 passé du subjonctif	
arrive	**arrivions**	**sois arrivé(e)**	**soyons arrivé(e)s**
arrives	**arriviez**	**sois arrivé(e)**	**soyez arrivé(e)(s)**
arrive	**arrivent**	**soit arrivé(e)**	**soient arrivé(e)s**

7 imparfait du subjonctif		14 plus-que-parfait du subjonctif	
arrivasse	**arrivassions**	**fusse arrivé(e)**	**fussions arrivé(e)s**
arrivasses	**arrivassiez**	**fusses arrivé(e)**	**fussiez arrivé(e)(s)**
arrivât	**arrivassent**	**fût arrivé(e)**	**fussent arrivé(e)s**

	Impératif
	arrive
	arrivons
	arrivez

Sentences using this verb and words related to it
  À quelle heure est-ce que l'avion arrive à Paris?   At what time does the plane arrive in Paris?
  Le train pour Québec arrivera à 15h22.   The train to Québec will arrive at 3:22 P.M.
  Qu'est-ce qui arrive?   What's happening? What's going on?
  Qu'est-ce qui est arrivé?   What happened?
  Quoi qu'il arrive . . .   Come what may . . .

arriver à faire qqch   to succeed in + pres. part.; to manage to do something
arriver à   to happen to; Cela n'arrive qu'à moi!   It's just my luck! That would happen to me!
J'arrive!   I'm coming!

The subject pronouns are found on page 103.   **159**

assaillir (50)

to attack, to beset, to assail

Part. pr. assaillant Part. passé assailli

Irregular verb

The Seven Simple Tenses		The Seven Compound Tenses	
Singular	Plural	Singular	Plural
1 présent de l'indicatif		**8 passé composé**	
assaille	assaillons	ai assailli	avons assailli
assailles	assaillez	as assailli	avez assailli
assaille	assaillent	a assailli	ont assailli
2 imparfait de l'indicatif		**9 plus-que-parfait de l'indicatif**	
assaillais	assaillions	avais assailli	avions assailli
assaillais	assailliez	avais assailli	aviez assailli
assaillait	assaillaient	avait assailli	avaient assailli
3 passé simple		**10 passé antérieur**	
assaillis	assaillîmes	eus assailli	eûmes assailli
assaillis	assaillîtes	eus assailli	eûtes assailli
assaillit	assaillirent	eut assailli	eurent assailli
4 futur		**11 futur antérieur**	
assaillirai	assaillirons	aurai assailli	aurons assailli
assailliras	assaillirez	auras assailli	aurez assailli
assaillira	assailliront	aura assailli	auront assailli
5 conditionnel		**12 conditionnel passé**	
assaillirais	assaillirions	aurais assailli	aurions assailli
assaillirais	assailliriez	aurais assailli	auriez assailli
assaillirait	assailliraient	aurait assailli	auraient assailli
6 présent du subjonctif		**13 passé du subjonctif**	
assaille	assaillions	aie assailli	ayons assailli
assailles	assailliez	aies assailli	ayez assailli
assaille	assaillent	ait assailli	aient assailli
7 imparfait du subjonctif		**14 plus-que-parfait du subjonctif**	
assaillisse	assaillissions	eusse assailli	eussions assailli
assaillisses	assaillissiez	eusses assailli	eussiez assailli
assaillît	assaillissent	eût assailli	eussent assailli

Impératif
assaille
assaillons
assaillez

Sentences using this verb and words related to it
Leurs ennemis les ont assaillis pendant la nuit.   Their enemies attacked them during the night.
Le coup de tonnerre m'a fait tressaillir.   The thunderclap made me jump.

Words and expressions related to this verb
un assaillant, une assaillante   assailant
saillir   to project (conj. like **assaillir**, 3ᵈ person and infinitive); to mate (conj. like **finir**, 3ᵈ person and present participle)
saillant, saillante   protruding, prominent
une saillie   projection, ledge
tressaillir   to jump, flinch

Don't forget to check the list of 2,600 additional verbs keyed to the 501 model verbs. It's in the Appendixes!

The Seven Simple Tenses		The Seven Compound Tenses	
Singular	Plural	Singular	Plural

1 présent de l'indicatif

m'assieds	nous asseyons	
t'assieds	vous asseyez	
s'assied	s'asseyent	

8 passé composé

me suis assis(e)	nous sommes assis(es)
t'es assis(e)	vous êtes assis(e)(es)
s'est assis(e)	se sont assis(es)

2 imparfait de l'indicatif

m'asseyais	nous asseyions
t'asseyais	vous asseyiez
s'asseyait	s'asseyaient

9 plus-que-parfait de l'indicatif

m'étais assis(e)	nous étions assis(es)
t'étais assis(e)	vous étiez assis(e)(es)
s'était assis(e)	s'étaient assis(es)

3 passé simple

m'assis	nous assîmes
t'assis	vous assîtes
s'assit	s'assirent

10 passé antérieur

me fus assis(e)	nous fûmes assis(es)
te fus assis(e)	vous fûtes assis(e)(es)
se fut assis(e)	se furent assis(es)

4 futur

m'assiérai	nous assiérons
t'assiéras	vous assiérez
s'assiéra	s'assiéront

11 futur antérieur

me serai assis(e)	nous serons assis(es)
te seras assis(e)	vous serez assis(e)(es)
se sera assis(e)	se seront assis(es)

5 conditionnel

m'assiérais	nous assiérions
t'assiérais	vous assiériez
s'assiérait	s'assiéraient

12 conditionnel passé

me serais assis(e)	nous serions assis(es)
te serais assis(e)	vous seriez assis(e)(es)
se serait assis(e)	se seraient assis(es)

6 présent du subjonctif

m'asseye	nous asseyions
t'asseyes	vous asseyiez
s'asseye	s'asseyent

13 passé du subjonctif

me sois assis(e)	nous soyons assis(es)
te sois assis(e)	vous soyez assis(e)(es)
se soit assis(e)	se soient assis(es)

7 imparfait du subjonctif

m'assisse	nous assissions
t'assisses	vous assissiez
s'assît	s'assissent

14 plus-que-parfait du subjonctif

me fusse assis(e)	nous fussions assis(es)
te fusses assis(e)	vous fussiez assis(e)(es)
se fût assis(e)	se fussent assis(es)

Impératif
assieds-toi; ne t'assieds pas
asseyons-nous; ne nous asseyons pas
asseyez-vous; ne vous asseyez pas

Common idiomatic expressions using this verb and words related to it

Quand je voyage en train, je m'assieds toujours près d'une fenêtre si c'est possible.
Une fois, pendant un voyage, une belle jeune fille s'est approchée de moi et m'a demandé:
—Puis-je m'asseoir ici? Est-ce que cette place est libre?
—Certainement, j'ai répondu—asseyez-vous, je vous en prie.
Elle s'est assise auprès de moi et nous nous sommes bien amusés à raconter des histoires drôles.

asseoir qqn to seat someone
rasseoir to seat again, to reseat; se rasseoir to sit down again
s'asseoir à califourchon to sit astride

See also seoir.

The subject pronouns are found on page 103.
                                                                      161

to besiege, to lay siege to

Regular -er verb endings; spelling changes: retain the **ge** before **a** or **o** to keep the soft **g** sound of the verb; **e** changes to **è** before syllable with mute **e**

The Seven Simple Tenses		The Seven Compound Tenses	
Singular	Plural	Singular	Plural
1 présent de l'indicatif		**8 passé composé**	
assiège	assiégeons	ai assiégé	avons assiégé
assièges	assiégez	as assiégé	avez assiégé
assiège	assiègent	a assiégé	ont assiégé
2 imparfait de l'indicatif		**9 plus-que-parfait de l'indicatif**	
assiégeais	assiégions	avais assiégé	avions assiégé
assiégeais	assiégiez	avais assiégé	aviez assiégé
assiégeait	assiégeaient	avait assiégé	avaient assiégé
3 passé simple		**10 passé antérieur**	
assiégeai	assiégeâmes	eus assiégé	eûmes assiégé
assiégeas	assiégeâtes	eus assiégé	eûtes assiégé
assiégea	assiégèrent	eut assiégé	eurent assiégé
4 futur		**11 futur antérieur**	
assiégerai	assiégerons	aurai assiégé	aurons assiégé
assiégeras	assiégerez	auras assiégé	aurez assiégé
assiégera	assiégeront	aura assiégé	auront assiégé
5 conditionnel		**12 conditionnel passé**	
assiégerais	assiégerions	aurais assiégé	aurions assiégé
assiégerais	assiégeriez	aurais assiégé	auriez assiégé
assiégerait	assiégeraient	aurait assiégé	auraient assiégé
6 présent du subjonctif		**13 passé du subjonctif**	
assiège	assiégions	aie assiégé	ayons assiégé
assièges	assiégiez	aies assiégé	ayez assiégé
assiège	assiègent	ait assiégé	aient assiégé
7 imparfait du subjonctif		**14 plus-que-parfait du subjonctif**	
assiégeasse	assiégeassions	eusse assiégé	eussions assiégé
assiégeasses	assiégeassiez	eusses assiégé	eussiez assiégé
assiégeât	assiégeassent	eût assiégé	eussent assiégé

Impératif
assiège
assiégeons
assiégez

Words and expressions related to this verb
assiégeant, assiégeante *adj.*　besieging
le siège　seat, siege
siéger　to sit (committee, government)
Les barbares nous assiègent. Ils sont aux portes de la ville.　The barbarians are laying siege to us. They are at the gates of the city.

If you can conjugate assiéger you can also conjugate:
abréger　to shorten
agréger　to agglomerate
alléger　to lighten
piéger　to trap

The Seven Simple Tenses		The Seven Compound Tenses	
Singular	Plural	Singular	Plural

1   présent de l'indicatif

assiste	assistons
assistes	assistez
assiste	assistent

8   passé composé

ai assisté	avons assisté
as assisté	avez assisté
a assisté	ont assisté

2   imparfait de l'indicatif

assistais	assistions
assistais	assistiez
assistait	assistaient

9   plus-que-parfait de l'indicatif

avais assisté	avions assisté
avais assisté	aviez assisté
avait assisté	avaient assisté

3   passé simple

assistai	assistâmes
assistas	assistâtes
assista	assistèrent

10   passé antérieur

eus assisté	eûmes assisté
eus assisté	eûtes assisté
eut assisté	eurent assisté

4   futur

assisterai	assisterons
assisteras	assisterez
assistera	assisteront

11   futur antérieur

aurai assisté	aurons assisté
auras assisté	aurez assisté
aura assisté	auront assisté

5   conditionnel

assisterais	assisterions
assisterais	assisteriez
assisterait	assisteraient

12   conditionnel passé

aurais assisté	aurions assisté
aurais assisté	auriez assisté
aurait assisté	auraient assisté

6   présent du subjonctif

assiste	assistions
assistes	assistiez
assiste	assistent

13   passé du subjonctif

aie assisté	ayons assisté
aies assisté	ayez assisté
ait assisté	aient assisté

7   imparfait du subjonctif

assistasse	assistassions
assistasses	assistassiez
assistât	assistassent

14   plus-que-parfait du subjonctif

eusse assisté	eussions assisté
eusses assisté	eussiez assisté
eût assisté	eussent assisté

Impératif
assiste
assistons
assistez

Sentences using this verb

Lundi prochain, j'assisterai à une conférence de presse.   Next Monday, I will attend a press conference.

L'année dernière j'ai assisté à la même conférence de presse et il y avait beaucoup de monde.   Last year I attended the same press conference and there were a lot of people.

Words and expressions using this verb

assistance *f.*   assistance, help; attendance; audience
assister à   to be present at, to attend
les services de l'Assistance publique   health and social security services
les assistants   those present; spectators

The subject pronouns are found on page 103.   **163**

to assure, to ensure, to insure, to guarantee

Regular -er verb

The Seven Simple Tenses		The Seven Compound Tenses	
Singular	Plural	Singular	Plural
1 présent de l'indicatif		8 passé composé	
assure	assurons	ai assuré	avons assuré
assures	assurez	as assuré	avez assuré
assure	assurent	a assuré	ont assuré
2 imparfait de l'indicatif		9 plus-que-parfait de l'indicatif	
assurais	assurions	avais assuré	avions assuré
assurais	assuriez	avais assuré	aviez assuré
assurait	assuraient	avait assuré	avaient assuré
3 passé simple		10 passé antérieur	
assurai	assurâmes	eus assuré	eûmes assuré
assuras	assurâtes	eus assuré	eûtes assuré
assura	assurèrent	eut assuré	eurent assuré
4 futur		11 futur antérieur	
assurerai	assurerons	aurai assuré	aurons assuré
assureras	assurerez	auras assuré	aurez assuré
assurera	assureront	aura assuré	auront assuré
5 conditionnel		12 conditionnel passé	
assurerais	assurerions	aurais assuré	aurions assuré
assurerais	assureriez	aurais assuré	auriez assuré
assurerait	assureraient	aurait assuré	auraient assuré
6 présent du subjonctif		13 passé du subjonctif	
assure	assurions	aie assuré	ayons assuré
assures	assuriez	aies assuré	ayez assuré
assure	assurent	ait assuré	aient assuré
7 imparfait du subjonctif		14 plus-que-parfait du subjonctif	
assurasse	assurassions	eusse assuré	eussions assuré
assurasses	assurassiez	eusses assuré	eussiez assuré
assurât	assurassent	eût assuré	eussent assuré

Impératif
assure
assurons
assurez

Words and expressions related to this verb
assurer qqn de qqch   to assure someone of something; sûr, sûre   sure
assurable   insurable, assurable; sûrement   surely; sûrement pas   certainly not
rassurer   to reassure; la sûreté   safety
se rassurer   to be reassured
assuré, assurée   certain

See also s'assurer.

How are you doing? Find out with the verb drills and tests with answers explained on pages 50–101.

Reflexive regular **-er** verb

to make sure, to assure oneself,
to insure oneself

The Seven Simple Tenses

Singular	Plural
1 présent de l'indicatif	
m'assure	**nous assurons**
t'assures	**vous assurez**
s'assure	**s'assurent**
2 imparfait de l'indicatif	
m'assurais	**nous assurions**
t'assurais	**vous assuriez**
s'assurait	**s'assuraient**
3 passé simple	
m'assurai	**nous assurâmes**
t'assuras	**vous assurâtes**
s'assura	**s'assurèrent**
4 futur	
m'assurerai	**nous assurerons**
t'assureras	**vous assurerez**
s'assurera	**s'assureront**
5 conditionnel	
m'assurerais	**nous assurerions**
t'assurerais	**vous assureriez**
s'assurerait	**s'assureraient**
6 présent du subjonctif	
m'assure	**nous assurions**
t'assures	**vous assuriez**
s'assure	**s'assurent**
7 imparfait du subjonctif	
m'assurasse	**nous assurassions**
t'assurasses	**vous assurassiez**
s'assurât	**s'assurassent**

The Seven Compound Tenses

Singular	Plural
8 passé composé	
me suis assuré(e)	**nous sommes assuré(e)s**
t'es assuré(e)	**vous êtes assuré(e)(s)**
s'est assuré(e)	**se sont assuré(e)s**
9 plus-que-parfait de l'indicatif	
m'étais assuré(e)	**nous étions assuré(e)s**
t'étais assuré(e)	**vous étiez assuré(e)(s)**
s'était assuré(e)	**s'étaient assuré(e)s**
10 passé antérieur	
me fus assuré(e)	**nous fûmes assuré(e)s**
te fus assuré(e)	**vous fûtes assuré(e)(s)**
se fut assuré(e)	**se furent assuré(e)s**
11 futur antérieur	
me serai assuré(e)	**nous serons assuré(e)s**
te seras assuré(e)	**vous serez assuré(e)(s)**
se sera assuré(e)	**se seront assuré(e)s**
12 conditionnel passé	
me serais assuré(e)	**nous serions assuré(e)s**
te serais assuré(e)	**vous seriez assuré(e)(s)**
se serait assuré(e)	**se seraient assuré(e)s**
13 passé du subjonctif	
me sois assuré(e)	**nous soyons assuré(e)s**
te sois assuré(e)	**vous soyez assuré(e)(s)**
se soit assuré(e)	**se soient assuré(e)s**
14 plus-que-parfait du subjonctif	
me fusse assuré(e)	**nous fussions assuré(e)s**
te fusses assuré(e)	**vous fussiez assuré(e)(s)**
se fût assuré(e)	**se fussent assuré(e)s**

A

Impératif
assure-toi; ne t'assure pas
assurons-nous; ne nous assurons pas
assurez-vous; ne vous assurez pas

Sentences using this verb and words related to it

Pour s'assurer que la porte était bien fermée, Madame Lafontaine l'a fermée à clef. Puis elle a fermé toutes les fenêtres pour avoir de l'assurance et un sentiment de sécurité.

Assurément, elle a raison. Il y a des cambrioleurs dans le voisinage.

assurément   assuredly
assurance *f.*   assurance, insurance
un assureur   insurer
s'assurer de la protection de qqn   to secure
   someone's protection

l'assurance-vie *f.*   life insurance, life
   assurance
l'assurance automobile *f.*   car insurance

See also **assurer.**

The subject pronouns are found on page 103.   **165**

to attain

The Seven Simple Tenses		The Seven Compound Tenses	
Singular	Plural	Singular	Plural

1 présent de l'indicatif		8 passé composé	
atteins	atteignons	ai atteint	avons atteint
atteins	atteignez	as atteint	avez atteint
atteint	atteignent	a atteint	ont atteint

2 imparfait de l'indicatif		9 plus-que-parfait de l'indicatif	
atteignais	atteignions	avais atteint	avions atteint
atteignais	atteigniez	avais atteint	aviez atteint
atteignait	atteignaient	avait atteint	avaient atteint

3 passé simple		10 passé antérieur	
atteignis	atteignîmes	eus atteint	eûmes atteint
atteignis	atteignîtes	eus atteint	eûtes atteint
atteignit	atteignirent	eut atteint	eurent atteint

4 futur		11 futur antérieur	
atteindrai	atteindrons	aurai atteint	aurons atteint
atteindras	atteindrez	auras atteint	aurez atteint
atteindra	atteindront	aura atteint	auront atteint

5 conditionnel		12 conditionnel passé	
atteindrais	atteindrions	aurais atteint	aurions atteint
atteindrais	atteindriez	aurais atteint	auriez atteint
atteindrait	atteindraient	aurait atteint	auraient atteint

6 présent du subjonctif		13 passé du subjonctif	
atteigne	atteignions	aie atteint	ayons atteint
atteignes	atteigniez	aies atteint	ayez atteint
atteigne	atteignent	ait atteint	aient atteint

7 imparfait du subjonctif		14 plus-que-parfait du subjonctif	
atteignisse	atteignissions	eusse atteint	eussions atteint
atteignisses	atteignissiez	eusses atteint	eussiez atteint
atteignît	atteignissent	eût atteint	eussent atteint

Impératif
atteins
atteignons
atteignez

Words and expressions related to this verb
atteindre le but/la cible to hit the target
atteindre à to reach
une atteinte reach; attack
hors d'atteinte beyond reach
être atteint (atteinte) de to suffer from

Don't forget to check the list of 2,600 additional verbs keyed to the 501 model verbs. It's in the Appendixes!

Regular **-re** verb   to wait, to wait for, to expect

A

The Seven Simple Tenses		The Seven Compound Tenses	
Singular	Plural	Singular	Plural

1 présent de l'indicatif

attends	**attendons**		
attends	**attendez**		
attend	**attendent**		

8 passé composé

ai attendu		**avons attendu**	
as attendu		**avez attendu**	
a attendu		**ont attendu**	

2 imparfait de l'indicatif

attendais	**attendions**
attendais	**attendiez**
attendait	**attendaient**

9 plus-que-parfait de l'indicatif

avais attendu	**avions attendu**
avais attendu	**aviez attendu**
avait attendu	**avaient attendu**

3 passé simple

attendis	**attendîmes**
attendis	**attendîtes**
attendit	**attendirent**

10 passé antérieur

eus attendu	**eûmes attendu**
eus attendu	**eûtes attendu**
eut attendu	**eurent attendu**

4 futur

attendrai	**attendrons**
attendras	**attendrez**
attendra	**attendront**

11 futur antérieur

aurai attendu	**aurons attendu**
auras attendu	**aurez attendu**
aura attendu	**auront attendu**

5 conditionnel

attendrais	**attendrions**
attendrais	**attendriez**
attendrait	**attendraient**

12 conditionnel passé

aurais attendu	**aurions attendu**
aurais attendu	**auriez attendu**
aurait attendu	**auraient attendu**

6 présent du subjonctif

attende	**attendions**
attendes	**attendiez**
attende	**attendent**

13 passé du subjonctif

aie attendu	**ayons attendu**
aies attendu	**ayez attendu**
ait attendu	**aient attendu**

7 imparfait du subjonctif

attendisse	**attendissions**
attendisses	**attendissiez**
attendît	**attendissent**

14 plus-que-parfait du subjonctif

eusse attendu	**eussions attendu**
eusses attendu	**eussiez attendu**
eût attendu	**eussent attendu**

Impératif
attends
attendons
attendez

AN ESSENTIAL
55 VERB

AN ESSENTIAL
55 VERB

Attendre

Attendre is a regular **-re** verb that is used in many everyday situations and expressions.

Sentences using attendre **and related words**

J'attends l'autobus depuis vingt minutes! I have been waiting for the bus for twenty minutes!

Hier, j'ai attendu dix minutes. Yesterday, I waited for ten minutes.

Quand le bus arrivera, je m'attendrai à trouver une place libre. When the bus arrives, I will expect to find an empty seat.

Georges ne s'attendait pas à gagner. George wasn't expecting to win.

Cela peut attendre! It can wait!

Sa réaction était complètement inattendu. His reaction was completely unexpected.

M. Godot n'est pas encore arrivé. En attendant, prenons un café. Mr. Godot hasn't arrived yet. In the meantime, let's have a coffee.

Manon a manqué le bus. Il faut qu'elle attende le prochain. Manon missed the bus. She has to wait for the next one.

Bob et Katie attendent un enfant. Bob and Katie are expecting a child.

Words and expressions related to this verb

l'attente *f.* **wait, waiting**

une salle d'attente waiting room

faire attendre qqch à qqn to make someone wait for something; to keep someone waiting for something

en attendant meanwhile, in the meantime

s'attendre à to expect

inattendu, inattendue *adj.* **unexpected**

If you can conjugate attendre you can also conjugate the following verbs:

détendre to relax, loosen	**prétendre to claim**
se détendre to relax (use être **for auxiliary)**	**retendre to retighten**
distendre to stretch	**sous-tendre to underlie, subtend**
entendre to hear	**tendre to tighten, offer**
étendre to spread	

168

| The Seven Simple Tenses | | The Seven Compound Tenses | |

Singular	Plural	Singular	Plural

A

1 présent de l'indicatif

attire	**attirons**
attires	**attirez**
attire	**attirent**

8 passé composé

ai attiré	**avons attiré**
as attiré	**avez attiré**
a attiré	**ont attiré**

2 imparfait de l'indicatif

attirais	**attirions**
attirais	**attiriez**
attirait	**attiraient**

9 plus-que-parfait de l'indicatif

avais attiré	**avions attiré**
avais attiré	**aviez attiré**
avait attiré	**avaient attiré**

3 passé simple

attirai	**attirâmes**
attiras	**attirâtes**
attira	**attirèrent**

10 passé antérieur

eus attiré	**eûmes attiré**
eus attiré	**eûtes attiré**
eut attiré	**eurent attiré**

4 futur

attirerai	**attirerons**
attireras	**attirerez**
attirera	**attireront**

11 futur antérieur

aurai attiré	**aurons attiré**
auras attiré	**aurez attiré**
aura attiré	**auront attiré**

5 conditionnel

attirerais	**attirerions**
attirerais	**attireriez**
attirerait	**attireraient**

12 conditionnel passé

aurais attiré	**aurions attiré**
aurais attiré	**auriez attiré**
aurait attiré	**auraient attiré**

6 présent du subjonctif

attire	**attirions**
attires	**attiriez**
attire	**attirent**

13 passé du subjonctif

aie attiré	**ayons attiré**
aies attiré	**ayez attiré**
ait attiré	**aient attiré**

7 imparfait du subjonctif

attirasse	**attirassions**
attirasses	**attirassiez**
attirât	**attirassent**

14 plus-que-parfait du subjonctif

eusse attiré	**eussions attiré**
eusses attiré	**eussiez attiré**
eût attiré	**eussent attiré**

Impératif
attire
attirons
attirez

Common idiomatic expressions using this verb and words related to it

attirant, attirante attractive
le tirage drawing, pulling; printing of a publication
premier tirage first printing
à gros tirage large number of copies printed
une attraction attraction

tirer to pull
un tirage limité limited number of copies
les attraits *m.* charms, beauty
Do not confuse **un tirage** with **un triage**, which means sorting, selecting.

See also **retirer, se retirer,** and **tirer.**

Use the guide to French pronunciation. It's in the Appendixes.

The subject pronouns are found on page 103.   **169**

to catch

Regular **-er** verb

The Seven Simple Tenses		The Seven Compound Tenses	
Singular	Plural	Singular	Plural

1   présent de l'indicatif

		8 passé composé	
attrape	**attrapons**	**ai attrapé**	**avons attrapé**
attrapes	**attrapez**	**as attrapé**	**avez attrapé**
attrape	**attrapent**	**a attrapé**	**ont attrapé**

2   imparfait de l'indicatif

		9 plus-que-parfait de l'indicatif	
attrapais	**attrapions**	**avais attrapé**	**avions attrapé**
attrapais	**attrapiez**	**avais attrapé**	**aviez attrapé**
attrapait	**attrapaient**	**avait attrapé**	**avaient attrapé**

3   passé simple

		10 passé antérieur	
attrapai	**attrapâmes**	**eus attrapé**	**eûmes attrapé**
attrapas	**attrapâtes**	**eus attrapé**	**eûtes attrapé**
attrapa	**attrapèrent**	**eut attrapé**	**eurent attrapé**

4   futur

		11 futur antérieur	
attraperai	**attraperons**	**aurai attrapé**	**aurons attrapé**
attraperas	**attraperez**	**auras attrapé**	**aurez attrapé**
attrapera	**attraperont**	**aura attrapé**	**auront attrapé**

5   conditionnel

		12 conditionnel passé	
attraperais	**attraperions**	**aurais attrapé**	**aurions attrapé**
attraperais	**attraperiez**	**aurais attrapé**	**auriez attrapé**
attraperait	**attraperaient**	**aurait attrapé**	**auraient attrapé**

6   présent du subjonctif

		13 passé du subjonctif	
attrape	**attrapions**	**aie attrapé**	**ayons attrapé**
attrapes	**attrapiez**	**aies attrapé**	**ayez attrapé**
attrape	**attrapent**	**ait attrapé**	**aient attrapé**

7   imparfait du subjonctif

		14 plus-que-parfait du subjonctif	
attrapasse	**attrapassions**	**eusse attrapé**	**eussions attrapé**
attrapasses	**attrapassiez**	**eusses attrapé**	**eussiez attrapé**
attrapât	**attrapassent**	**eût attrapé**	**eussent attrapé**

Impératif
attrape
attrapons
attrapez

Common idiomatic expressions using this verb

—Si tu ne veux pas attraper un rhume, mets ton manteau parce qu'il fait froid dehors.
If you don't want to catch cold, put on your coat because it's cold outside.

—Je n'ai pas le temps maintenant, maman—je dois attraper l'autobus.   I don't have the
time right now, Mom—I have to catch the bus.

attraper un rhume to catch cold	**une attrape** trick
attraper qqn à qqch to catch someone at something (to surprise)	**un attrape-mouche** flypaper (sticky paper to catch flies), fly trap
s'attraper to be catching, infectious	**une trappe** trap

Get acquainted with what preposition goes with what verb. See *Verbs with prepositions*
in the Appendixes.

Regular **-er** verb   to augment, to increase

The Seven Simple Tenses | The Seven Compound Tenses

Singular	Plural	Singular	Plural	**A**

1   présent de l'indicatif

augmente	**augmentons**
augmentes	**augmentez**
augmente	**augmentent**

8   passé composé

ai augmenté	**avons augmenté**
as augmenté	**avez augmenté**
a augmenté	**ont augmenté**

2   imparfait de l'indicatif

augmentais	**augmentions**
augmentais	**augmentiez**
augmentait	**augmentaient**

9   plus-que-parfait de l'indicatif

avais augmenté	**avions augmenté**
avais augmenté	**aviez augmenté**
avait augmenté	**avaient augmenté**

3   passé simple

augmentai	**augmentâmes**
augmentas	**augmentâtes**
augmenta	**augmentèrent**

10   passé antérieur

eus augmenté	**eûmes augmenté**
eus augmenté	**eûtes augmenté**
eut augmenté	**eurent augmenté**

4   futur

augmenterai	**augmenterons**
augmenteras	**augmenterez**
augmentera	**augmenteront**

11   futur antérieur

aurai augmenté	**aurons augmenté**
auras augmenté	**aurez augmenté**
aura augmenté	**auront augmenté**

5   conditionnel

augmenterais	**augmenterions**
augmenterais	**augmenteriez**
augmenterait	**augmenteraient**

12   conditionnel passé

aurais augmenté	**aurions augmenté**
aurais augmenté	**auriez augmenté**
aurait augmenté	**auraient augmenté**

6   présent du subjonctif

augmente	**augmentions**
augmentes	**augmentiez**
augmente	**augmentent**

13   passé du subjonctif

aie augmenté	**ayons augmenté**
aies augmenté	**ayez augmenté**
ait augmenté	**aient augmenté**

7   imparfait du subjonctif

augmentasse	**augmentassions**
augmentasses	**augmentassiez**
augmentât	**augmentassent**

14   plus-que-parfait du subjonctif

eusse augmenté	**eussions augmenté**
eusses augmenté	**eussiez augmenté**
eût augmenté	**eussent augmenté**

Impératif
augmente
augmentons
augmentez

Words and expressions related to this verb
augmentation *f.*   increase, augmentation; **augmentation de salaire**   increase in salary
l'augmentation de la mémoire vive   RAM increase (computer)
une augmentation des impôts   tax increase
augmenter une douleur   to aggravate a pain
augmenter les prix   to increase prices

Grammar putting you in a tense mood? Review the definitions of basic grammatical terms with examples on pages 35–49.

The subject pronouns are found on page 103.
171

to advance, to
go forward

Regular **-er** verb endings; spelling change:
c changes to **ç** before **a** or **o** to keep **s** sound

The Seven Simple Tenses		The Seven Compound Tenses	
Singular	Plural	Singular	Plural

1 présent de l'indicatif

		8 passé composé	
avance	avançons	ai avancé	avons avancé
avances	avancez	as avancé	avez avancé
avance	avancent	a avancé	ont avancé

2 imparfait de l'indicatif

		9 plus-que-parfait de l'indicatif	
avançais	avancions	avais avancé	avions avancé
avançais	avanciez	avais avancé	aviez avancé
avançait	avançaient	avait avancé	avaient avancé

3 passé simple

		10 passé antérieur	
avançai	avançâmes	eus avancé	eûmes avancé
avanças	avançâtes	eus avancé	eûtes avancé
avança	avancèrent	eut avancé	eurent avancé

4 futur

		11 futur antérieur	
avancerai	avancerons	aurai avancé	aurons avancé
avanceras	avancerez	auras avancé	aurez avancé
avancera	avanceront	aura avancé	auront avancé

5 conditionnel

		12 conditionnel passé	
avancerais	avancerions	aurais avancé	aurions avancé
avancerais	avanceriez	aurais avancé	auriez avancé
avancerait	avanceraient	aurait avancé	auraient avancé

6 présent du subjonctif

		13 passé du subjonctif	
avance	avancions	aie avancé	ayons avancé
avances	avanciez	aies avancé	ayez avancé
avance	avancent	ait avancé	aient avancé

7 imparfait du subjonctif

		14 plus-que-parfait du subjonctif	
avançasse	avançassions	eusse avancé	eussions avancé
avançasses	avançassiez	eusses avancé	eussiez avancé
avançât	avançassent	eût avancé	eussent avancé

Impératif
avance
avançons
avancez

Sentences using this verb and words related to it
   Le docteur a dit au petit garçon:—Ouvre la bouche et avance la langue.
   Le garçon n'a pas ouvert la bouche et il n'a pas avancé la langue.
   Le docteur a insisté:—Ouvrons la bouche et avançons la langue!

une avance   advance; **faire des avances à qqn**
   to make advances to somebody
à l'avance, d'avance   in advance, beforehand
arriver en avance   to arrive early
s'avancer   to advance (oneself)
l'avant *m.*   front

Ta montre avance.   Your watch is fast.
avancer une théorie   to promote a theory
Comment avance le travail?   How is the
   work coming along?
en avant   ahead, in front
devancer   to arrive ahead

The Seven Simple Tenses		The Seven Compound Tenses	
Singular	Plural	Singular	Plural

A

1 présent de l'indicatif		8 passé composé	
ai	**avons**	**ai eu**	**avons eu**
as	**avez**	**as eu**	**avez eu**
a	**ont**	**a eu**	**ont eu**

2 imparfait de l'indicatif		9 plus-que-parfait de l'indicatif	
avais	**avions**	**avais eu**	**avions eu**
avais	**aviez**	**avais eu**	**aviez eu**
avait	**avaient**	**avait eu**	**avaient eu**

3 passé simple		10 passé antérieur	
eus	**eûmes**	**eus eu**	**eûmes eu**
eus	**eûtes**	**eus eu**	**eûtes eu**
eut	**eurent**	**eut eu**	**eurent eu**

4 futur		11 futur antérieur	
aurai	**aurons**	**aurai eu**	**aurons eu**
auras	**aurez**	**auras eu**	**aurez eu**
aura	**auront**	**aura eu**	**auront eu**

5 conditionnel		12 conditionnel passé	
aurais	**aurions**	**aurais eu**	**aurions eu**
aurais	**auriez**	**aurais eu**	**auriez eu**
aurait	**auraient**	**aurait eu**	**auraient eu**

6 présent du subjonctif		13 passé du subjonctif	
aie	**ayons**	**aie eu**	**ayons eu**
aies	**ayez**	**aies eu**	**ayez eu**
ait	**aient**	**ait eu**	**aient eu**

7 imparfait du subjonctif		14 plus-que-parfait du subjonctif	
eusse	**eussions**	**eusse eu**	**eussions eu**
eusses	**eussiez**	**eusses eu**	**eussiez eu**
eût	**eussent**	**eût eu**	**eussent eu**

Impératif
aie
ayons
ayez

AN ESSENTIAL
55 VERB

The subject pronouns are found on page 103.
                                                              173

AN ESSENTIAL 55 VERB

Avoir

Avoir is a very important verb. First of all, it is used as the auxiliary for the compound tenses of most French verbs. So, if you can conjugate **avoir** in the seven simple tenses (1–7) all you need is a verb's past participle and you can create the seven compound tenses (8–14). Secondly, **avoir** is used in a vast number of idiomatic expressions. That's why **avoir** gets an extra page of examples!

Avoir is used in a great number of idiomatic expressions. Here are a few of the more useful ones with sample sentences:

Avoir by itself can mean to have something the matter.
Qu'est-ce que vous avez? What's the matter with you?
Qu'est-ce qu'il y a? What's the matter?

avoir . . . ans to be . . . years old
Quel âge avez-vous? How old are you?
J'ai seize ans. I'm sixteen.

avoir à + inf. to have to, to be obliged to + inf.
J'ai quelque chose à vous dire. I have something to tell you.

avoir beau + inf. to be useless + inf., to do something in vain
Vous avez beau parler; je ne vous écoute pas. You're talking in vain (uselessly); I'm not listening to you.

avoir besoin de to need, to have need of
Vous avez l'air fatigué; vous avez besoin de repos. You look tired; you need some rest.

avoir bonne mine to look well, to look good (persons)
Joseph a bonne mine aujourd'hui, ne trouvez-vous pas? Joseph looks good today, don't you think so?

avoir chaud to be (feel) warm (persons)
J'ai chaud; ouvrez la fenêtre, s'il vous plaît. I feel warm; open the window, please.

avoir congé to have a day off, a holiday from work or school
Demain nous avons congé et nous allons à la plage. Tomorrow we have the day off and we're going to the beach.

avoir de la chance to be lucky
Tu as trouvé une pièce de monnaie?! Tu as de la chance! You found a coin?! You're lucky!

avoir de quoi + inf. to have the material, means, enough + inf.
As-tu de quoi manger? Have you something (enough) to eat?

avoir envie de to feel like, to have a desire to
Madame Loisel a toujours envie de danser. Mrs. Loisel always feels like dancing.

avoir faim to be hungry
As-tu faim, Anne? Bon, alors je vais te donner à manger. Are you hungry, Anne? Good, then I'm going to give you something to eat.

avoir froid to be (feel) cold (persons)
J'ai froid; fermez la fenêtre, s'il vous plaît. I feel cold; close the window, please.

avoir l'air + adj. to seem, to appear, to look + adj.
Vous avez l'air malade; asseyez-vous. You look sick; sit down.

Expressions using *avoir*

Qui ne risque rien n'a rien.
Nothing ventured, nothing gained.

Les murs ont des oreilles.
The walls have ears.

avoir l'air de + inf. to appear + inf.
Vous avez l'air d'être malade; couchez-vous. You appear to be sick; lie down.

avoir l'habitude de + inf. to be accustomed to, to be in the habit of
J'ai l'habitude de faire mes devoirs avant le dîner. I'm in the habit of doing my homework before dinner.

avoir lieu to take place
Le match aura lieu demain. The game will take place tomorrow.

avoir mal to feel sick
Qu'est-ce que tu as, Robert? What's the matter, Robert?
J'ai mal. I feel sick.

avoir mal à + (place where it hurts) to have a pain or ache in . . .
J'ai mal à la jambe. My leg hurts.
J'ai mal à la tête. I have a headache.

avoir mauvaise mine to look ill, not to look well
Qu'est-ce que tu as, Janine? What's the matter, Janine?
Tu as mauvaise mine. You don't look well.

avoir qqn to get the better of someone
Je t'ai eu! I got you!

en avoir marre to be fed up, to be bored stiff, to be sick and tired of something
J'en ai marre! I'm fed up! I've had it!

en avoir par-dessus la tête to have enough of it, to be sick and tired of it, to have it up to here
J'en ai par-dessus la tête! I've had it up to here!

il y a + length of time ago
Madame Duclos est partie il y a un mois. Mrs. Duclos left a month ago.
Il y a dix minutes que j'attends l'autobus. I have been waiting for the bus for ten minutes.
Il n'y a pas de quoi. You're welcome.

n'avoir qu'à + inf. to have only + inf.
Tu n'as qu'à appuyer sur le bouton et la machine se met en marche. All you have to do is press the button and the machine starts itself.

More idiomatic expressions using avoir

avoir affaire à quelqu'un **to deal with someone**
avoir des nouvelles **to receive news, to hear (from someone)**
avoir droit à **to be entitled to**
avoir du savoir-faire **to have tact**
avoir du savoir-vivre **to have good manners, etiquette**
avoir hâte **to be in a hurry**
avoir hâte de faire qqch **to be anxious to do something, to look forward to doing something**
avoir honte **to be (feel) ashamed**
avoir l'idée de + inf. **to have a notion + inf.**
avoir l'impression **to be under the impression**
avoir l'intention de **to intend + inf.**
avoir l'occasion de + inf. **to have the opportunity + inf.**
avoir l'occasion de faire qqch **to have the opportunity to do something**
avoir la bonté de + inf. **to have the kindness + inf.**
avoir la langue bien pendue **to have the gift of gab**
avoir la parole **to have the floor (to speak)**
avoir le cafard **to feel downhearted (downcast), to have the blues**
avoir le coeur gros **to be heartbroken**
avoir le droit de faire qqch **to be entitled (have the right) to do something**
avoir le temps de + inf. **to have (the) time + inf.**
avoir mal au coeur **to feel nauseous**
avoir peine à + inf. **to have difficulty in + pres. part.**
avoir peur de **to be afraid of**
avoir raison **to be right (persons)**
avoir rendez-vous avec qqn **to have a date (appointment) with someone**
avoir soif **to be thirsty**
avoir sommeil **to be (feel) sleepy**
avoir son mot à dire **to have one's way**
avoir tendance à faire qqch **to tend to do something**
avoir tort **to be wrong (persons)**
avoir trait à qqch **to have to do with something**
avoir une faim de loup **to be starving**
en avoir assez **to have enough of it**
il y a . . . there is . . ., there are . . .
il y avait . . . there was . . ., there were . . .
il y a eu . . . there was . . ., there were . . .
il y aura . . . there will be . . .
il y aurait . . . there would be . . .
Il y a lieu de croire que . . . **There is reason to believe that . . .**

A

The subject pronouns are found on page 103.

to lower, to sink

The Seven Simple Tenses		The Seven Compound Tenses	
Singular	Plural	Singular	Plural
1 présent de l'indicatif		**8 passé composé**	
baisse	baissons	ai baissé	avons baissé
baisses	baissez	as baissé	avez baissé
baisse	baissent	a baissé	ont baissé
2 imparfait de l'indicatif		**9 plus-que-parfait de l'indicatif**	
baissais	baissions	avais baissé	avions baissé
baissais	baissiez	avais baissé	aviez baissé
baissait	baissaient	avait baissé	avaient baissé
3 passé simple		**10 passé antérieur**	
baissai	baissâmes	eus baissé	eûmes baissé
baissas	baissâtes	eus baissé	eûtes baissé
baissa	baissèrent	eut baissé	eurent baissé
4 futur		**11 futur antérieur**	
baisserai	baisserons	aurai baissé	aurons baissé
baisseras	baisserez	auras baissé	aurez baissé
baissera	baisseront	aura baissé	auront baissé
5 conditionnel		**12 conditionnel passé**	
baisserais	baisserions	aurais baissé	aurions baissé
baisserais	baisseriez	aurais baissé	auriez baissé
baisserait	baisseraient	aurait baissé	auraient baissé
6 présent du subjonctif		**13 passé du subjonctif**	
baisse	baissions	aie baissé	ayons baissé
baisses	baissiez	aies baissé	ayez baissé
baisse	baissent	ait baissé	aient baissé
7 imparfait du subjonctif		**14 plus-que-parfait du subjonctif**	
baissasse	baissassions	eusse baissé	eussions baissé
baissasses	baissassiez	eusses baissé	eussiez baissé
baissât	baissassent	eût baissé	eussent baissé

Impératif
baisse
baissons
baissez

Common idiomatic expressions using this verb
baisser la voix to lower one's voice
baisser les yeux to look down, cast one's eyes down
baisser les bras to admit defeat, to give in

See also **abaisser** and **s'abaisser**.

se jeter tête baissée dans qqch to do something blindly, headlong
se baisser to bend (stoop) down
rabaisser to depreciate, to humble, to lower
un rabais discount

Don't forget to use the English-French verb index. It's in the Appendixes.

Part. pr. **balançant**   Part. passé **balancé**   **balancer (64)**

Regular **-er** verb endings; spelling change:
c changes to **ç** before **a** or **o** to keep **s** sound

to balance, to sway, to swing,
to weigh, to throw away

The Seven Simple Tenses | The Seven Compound Tenses

B

Singular	Plural	Singular	Plural
1 présent de l'indicatif		8 passé composé	
balance	balançons	ai balancé	avons balancé
balances	balancez	as balancé	avez balancé
balance	balancent	a balancé	ont balancé
2 imparfait de l'indicatif		9 plus-que-parfait de l'indicatif	
balançais	balancions	avais balancé	avions balancé
balançais	balanciez	avais balancé	aviez balancé
balançait	balançaient	avait balancé	avaient balancé
3 passé simple		10 passé antérieur	
balançai	balançâmes	eus balancé	eûmes balancé
balanças	balançâtes	eus balancé	eûtes balancé
balança	balancèrent	eut balancé	eurent balancé
4 futur		11 futur antérieur	
balancerai	balancerons	aurai balancé	aurons balancé
balanceras	balancerez	auras balancé	aurez balancé
balancera	balanceront	aura balancé	auront balancé
5 conditionnel		12 conditionnel passé	
balancerais	balancerions	aurais balancé	aurions balancé
balancerais	balanceriez	aurais balancé	auriez balancé
balancerait	balanceraient	aurait balancé	auraient balancé
6 présent du subjonctif		13 passé du subjonctif	
balance	balancions	aie balancé	ayons balancé
balances	balanciez	aies balancé	ayez balancé
balance	balancent	ait balancé	aient balancé
7 imparfait du subjonctif		14 plus-que-parfait du subjonctif	
balançasse	balançassions	eusse balancé	eussions balancé
balançasses	balançassiez	eusses balancé	eussiez balancé
balançât	balançassent	eût balancé	eussent balancé

Impératif
balance
balançons
balancez

Words and expressions related to this verb
une balançoire   see-saw, swing
une balance   weight scale
la balance des pouvoirs   the balance of
  powers
le balancement   balancing, rocking

Il a balancé la bouteille par la vitre de l'auto.
  He tossed the bottle out of the car window.
faire pencher la balance   to favor someone
balancer le pour et le contre   to weigh the
  pros and cons

Don't forget to use the English-French verb index. It's in the Appendixes!

The subject pronouns are found on page 103.   **177**

to sweep

Regular **-er** verb endings; spelling change: **-ayer** verbs may change **y** to **i** in front of a mute **e** or may keep **y**

The Seven Simple Tenses		The Seven Compound Tenses	
Singular	Plural	Singular	Plural
1 présent de l'indicatif		8 passé composé	
balaye	balayons	ai balayé	avons balayé
balayes	balayez	as balayé	avez balayé
balaye	balayent	a balayé	ont balayé
2 imparfait de l'indicatif		9 plus-que-parfait de l'indicatif	
balayais	balayions	avais balayé	avions balayé
balayais	balayiez	avais balayé	aviez balayé
balayait	balayaient	avait balayé	avaient balayé
3 passé simple		10 passé antérieur	
balayai	balayâmes	eus balayé	eûmes balayé
balayas	balayâtes	eus balayé	eûtes balayé
balaya	balayèrent	eut balayé	eurent balayé
4 futur		11 futur antérieur	
balayerai	balayerons	aurai balayé	aurons balayé
balayeras	balayerez	auras balayé	aurez balayé
balayera	balayeront	aura balayé	auront balayé
5 conditionnel		12 conditionnel passé	
balayerais	balayerions	aurais balayé	aurions balayé
balayerais	balayeriez	aurais balayé	auriez balayé
balayerait	balayeraient	aurait balayé	auraient balayé
6 présent du subjonctif		13 passé du subjonctif	
balaye	balayions	aie balayé	ayons balayé
balayes	balayiez	aies balayé	ayez balayé
balaye	balayent	ait balayé	aient balayé
7 imparfait du subjonctif		14 plus-que-parfait du subjonctif	
balayasse	balayassions	eusse balayé	eussions balayé
balayasses	balayassiez	eusses balayé	eussiez balayé
balayât	balayassent	eût balayé	eussent balayé

Impératif
balaye
balayons
balayez

Sentences using this verb and words related to it
—Marie, as-tu balayé ta chambre?
—Non, maman.
—Et pourquoi pas?
—Parce que je n'ai pas de balai, je n'ai pas de balayette, et je ne suis pas balayeuse. Voilà pourquoi!
—Quelle fille!

un balai broom; une balayette small brush, whiskbroom; un balayeur, une balayeuse sweeper
un balai d'essuie-glace windshield wiper blade

Regular **-ir** verb   to build, to construct

The Seven Simple Tenses		The Seven Compound Tenses	
Singular	Plural	Singular	Plural
1 présent de l'indicatif		**8 passé composé**	
bâtis	bâtissons	ai bâti	avons bâti
bâtis	bâtissez	as bâti	avez bâti
bâtit	bâtissent	a bâti	ont bâti
2 imparfait de l'indicatif		**9 plus-que-parfait de l'indicatif**	
bâtissais	bâtissions	avais bâti	avions bâti
bâtissais	bâtissiez	avais bâti	aviez bâti
bâtissait	bâtissaient	avait bâti	avaient bâti
3 passé simple		**10 passé antérieur**	
bâtis	bâtîmes	eus bâti	eûmes bâti
bâtis	bâtîtes	eus bâti	eûtes bâti
bâtit	bâtirent	eut bâti	eurent bâti
4 futur		**11 futur antérieur**	
bâtirai	bâtirons	aurai bâti	aurons bâti
bâtiras	bâtirez	auras bâti	aurez bâti
bâtira	bâtiront	aura bâti	auront bâti
5 conditionnel		**12 conditionnel passé**	
bâtirais	bâtirions	aurais bâti	aurions bâti
bâtirais	bâtiriez	aurais bâti	auriez bâti
bâtirait	bâtiraient	aurait bâti	auraient bâti
6 présent du subjonctif		**13 passé du subjonctif**	
bâtisse	bâtissions	aie bâti	ayons bâti
bâtisses	bâtissiez	aies bâti	ayez bâti
bâtisse	bâtissent	ait bâti	aient bâti
7 imparfait du subjonctif		**14 plus-que-parfait du subjonctif**	
bâtisse	bâtissions	eusse bâti	eussions bâti
bâtisses	bâtissiez	eusses bâti	eussiez bâti
bâtît	bâtissent	eût bâti	eussent bâti

Impératif
bâtis
bâtissons
bâtissez

Words and expressions related to this verb
un bâtiment building, edifice, ship; **un bâtisseur** builder
bâtir to baste (sewing term; when basting food, use **arroser**); **du fil à bâtir** basting thread
un bâtiment de guerre warship
rebâtir to rebuild
bâtir des châteaux en Espagne to build castles in the air
bâtir sur le sable to build on sand
bien bâti, bien bâtie well built
Sergio est bien bâti parce qu'il est culturiste. Sergio is well built because he is a bodybuilder.

to beat, to hit, to strike

Irregular verb in 1s, 2s, 3s present indicative

The Seven Simple Tenses		The Seven Compound Tenses	
Singular	Plural	Singular	Plural
1 présent de l'indicatif		8 passé composé	
bats	**battons**	**ai battu**	**avons battu**
bats	**battez**	**as battu**	**avez battu**
bat	**battent**	**a battu**	**ont battu**
2 imparfait de l'indicatif		9 plus-que-parfait de l'indicatif	
battais	**battions**	**avais battu**	**avions battu**
battais	**battiez**	**avais battu**	**aviez battu**
battait	**battaient**	**avait battu**	**avaient battu**
3 passé simple		10 passé antérieur	
battis	**battîmes**	**eus battu**	**eûmes battu**
battis	**battîtes**	**eus battu**	**eûtes battu**
battit	**battirent**	**eut battu**	**eurent battu**
4 futur		11 futur antérieur	
battrai	**battrons**	**aurai battu**	**aurons battu**
battras	**battrez**	**auras battu**	**aurez battu**
battra	**battront**	**aura battu**	**auront battu**
5 conditionnel		12 conditionnel passé	
battrais	**battrions**	**aurais battu**	**aurions battu**
battrais	**battriez**	**aurais battu**	**auriez battu**
battrait	**battraient**	**aurait battu**	**auraient battu**
6 présent du subjonctif		13 passé du subjonctif	
batte	**battions**	**aie battu**	**ayons battu**
battes	**battiez**	**aies battu**	**ayez battu**
batte	**battent**	**ait battu**	**aient battu**
7 imparfait du subjonctif		14 plus-que-parfait du subjonctif	
battisse	**battissions**	**eusse battu**	**eussions battu**
battisses	**battissiez**	**eusses battu**	**eussiez battu**
battît	**battissent**	**eût battu**	**eussent battu**

Impératif
bats
battons
battez

Sentences using this verb and words related to it
Il faut battre le fer quand il est chaud.   You have to strike while the iron is hot.

battre des mains   to clap, to applaud
battre la campagne   to scour the countryside
le battant   leaf, flap (of a table)
une porte à deux battants   double door
une batte   bat, beater

le battement   banging (of a door);
  throbbing, flutter, beating
un batteur   whisk, beater
le battage   beating

See also **abattre**, **se battre**, and **combattre**.

Review the Subjunctive clearly and simply on pages 26–31.

Reflexive irregular verb in 1s, 2s, 3s present indicative

to fight

The Seven Simple Tenses | The Seven Compound Tenses

B

Singular	Plural	Singular	Plural
1 présent de l'indicatif		**8 passé composé**	
me bats	**nous battons**	**me suis battu(e)**	**nous sommes battu(e)s**
te bats	**vous battez**	**t'es battu(e)**	**vous êtes battu(e)(s)**
se bat	**se battent**	**s'est battu(e)**	**se sont battu(e)s**
2 imparfait de l'indicatif		**9 plus-que-parfait de l'indicatif**	
me battais	**nous battions**	**m'étais battu(e)**	**nous étions battu(e)s**
te battais	**vous battiez**	**t'étais battu(e)**	**vous étiez battu(e)(s)**
se battait	**se battaient**	**s'était battu(e)**	**s'étaient battu(e)s**
3 passé simple		**10 passé antérieur**	
me battis	**nous battîmes**	**me fus battu(e)**	**nous fûmes battu(e)s**
te battis	**vous battîtes**	**te fus battu(e)**	**vous fûtes battu(e)(s)**
se battit	**se battirent**	**se fut battu(e)**	**se furent battu(e)s**
4 futur		**11 futur antérieur**	
me battrai	**nous battrons**	**me serai battu(e)**	**nous serons battu(e)s**
te battras	**vous battrez**	**te seras battu(e)**	**vous serez battu(e)(s)**
se battra	**se battront**	**se sera battu(e)**	**se seront battu(e)s**
5 conditionnel		**12 conditionnel passé**	
me battrais	**nous battrions**	**me serais battu(e)**	**nous serions battu(e)s**
te battrais	**vous battriez**	**te serais battu(e)**	**vous seriez battu(e)(s)**
se battrait	**se battraient**	**se serait battu(e)**	**se seraient battu(e)s**
6 présent du subjonctif		**13 passé du subjonctif**	
me batte	**nous battions**	**me sois battu(e)**	**nous soyons battu(e)s**
te battes	**vous battiez**	**te sois battu(e)**	**vous soyez battu(e)(s)**
se batte	**se battent**	**se soit battu(e)**	**se soient battu(e)s**
7 imparfait du subjonctif		**14 plus-que-parfait du subjonctif**	
me battisse	**nous battissions**	**me fusse battu(e)**	**nous fussions battu(e)s**
te battisses	**vous battissiez**	**te fusses battu(e)**	**vous fussiez battu(e)(s)**
se battît	**se battissent**	**se fût battu(e)**	**se fussent battu(e)s**

Impératif
bats-toi; ne te bats pas
battons-nous; ne nous battons pas
battez-vous; ne vous battez pas

Sentences using this verb and words related to it

Ecoutez! Nos voisins commencent à se battre. Ils se battent toujours. La dernière fois ils se sont battus à coups de poings. Il y a toujours un grand combat chez eux.

For other words and expressions related to this verb, see abattre, battre, and combattre.

Don't forget to check the list of 2,600 additional verbs keyed to the 501 model verbs. It's in the Appendixes!

to chat, to chatter, to babble, to gossip

Regular **-er** verb

The Seven Simple Tenses		The Seven Compound Tenses	
Singular	Plural	Singular	Plural
1 présent de l'indicatif		8 passé composé	
bavarde	bavardons	ai bavardé	avons bavardé
bavardes	bavardez	as bavardé	avez bavardé
bavarde	bavardent	a bavardé	ont bavardé
2 imparfait de l'indicatif		9 plus-que-parfait de l'indicatif	
bavardais	bavardions	avais bavardé	avions bavardé
bavardais	bavardiez	avais bavardé	aviez bavardé
bavardait	bavardaient	avait bavardé	avaient bavardé
3 passé simple		10 passé antérieur	
bavardai	bavardâmes	eus bavardé	eûmes bavardé
bavardas	bavardâtes	eus bavardé	eûtes bavardé
bavarda	bavardèrent	eut bavardé	eurent bavardé
4 futur		11 futur antérieur	
bavarderai	bavarderons	aurai bavardé	aurons bavardé
bavarderas	bavarderez	auras bavardé	aurez bavardé
bavardera	bavarderont	aura bavardé	auront bavardé
5 conditionnel		12 conditionnel passé	
bavarderais	bavarderions	aurais bavardé	aurions bavardé
bavarderais	bavarderiez	aurais bavardé	auriez bavardé
bavarderait	bavarderaient	aurait bavardé	auraient bavardé
6 présent du subjonctif		13 passé du subjonctif	
bavarde	bavardions	aie bavardé	ayons bavardé
bavardes	bavardiez	aies bavardé	ayez bavardé
bavarde	bavardent	ait bavardé	aient bavardé
7 imparfait du subjonctif		14 plus-que-parfait du subjonctif	
bavardasse	bavardassions	eusse bavardé	eussions bavardé
bavardasses	bavardassiez	eusses bavardé	eussiez bavardé
bavardât	bavardassent	eût bavardé	eussent bavardé

Impératif
bavarde
bavardons
bavardez

Sentences using this verb and words related to it

Aimez-vous les personnes qui bavardent tout le temps? Je connais un homme qui est bavard. Sa femme est bavarde aussi. Elle aime à parler avec abondance. Moi, je n'aime pas le bavardage. Je ne bavarde pas parce que je n'aime pas perdre mon temps.

le bavardage chitchat, chattering, talkativeness

bavard, bavarde talkative, loquacious, garrulous

perdre son temps à bavarder to waste one's time babbling

la bave drool, dribble

baver to drool

le clavardage chat (Internet); combination of **le clavier** (keyboard) and **le bavardage**

clavarder to chat (Internet)

Regular **-ir** verb

to bless, to consecrate

B

The Seven Simple Tenses		The Seven Compound Tenses	
Singular	Plural	Singular	Plural
1 présent de l'indicatif		8 passé composé	
bénis	bénissons	ai béni	avons béni
bénis	bénissez	as béni	avez béni
bénit	bénissent	a béni	ont béni
2 imparfait de l'indicatif		9 plus-que-parfait de l'indicatif	
bénissais	bénissions	avais béni	avions béni
bénissais	bénissiez	avais béni	aviez béni
bénissait	bénissaient	avait béni	avaient béni
3 passé simple		10 passé antérieur	
bénis	bénîmes	eus béni	eûmes béni
bénis	bénîtes	eus béni	eûtes béni
bénit	bénirent	eut béni	eurent béni
4 futur		11 futur antérieur	
bénirai	bénirons	aurai béni	aurons béni
béniras	bénirez	auras béni	aurez béni
bénira	béniront	aura béni	auront béni
5 conditionnel		12 conditionnel passé	
bénirais	bénirions	aurais béni	aurions béni
bénirais	béniriez	aurais béni	auriez béni
bénirait	béniraient	aurait béni	auraient béni
6 présent du subjonctif		13 passé du subjonctif	
bénisse	bénissions	aie béni	ayons béni
bénisses	bénissiez	aies béni	ayez béni
bénisse	bénissent	ait béni	aient béni
7 imparfait du subjonctif		14 plus-que-parfait du subjonctif	
bénisse	bénissions	eusse béni	eussions béni
bénisses	bénissiez	eusses béni	eussiez béni
bénît	bénissent	eût béni	eussent béni

Impératif
bénis
bénissons
bénissez

Words and expressions related to this verb
de l'eau bénite   holy (blessed) water; **du pain bénit**   holy (blessed) bread
le bénitier   holy water font
une bénédiction   blessing
dire le bénédicité   to say grace (before a meal)

Do not confuse **bénir** with **blesser**, which means *to wound*.

Don't forget to study the section on defective and impersonal verbs. It's right after this main list.

The subject pronouns are found on page 103.   **183**

to blame

The Seven Simple Tenses		The Seven Compound Tenses	
Singular	Plural	Singular	Plural
1 présent de l'indicatif		8 passé composé	
blâme	**blâmons**	**ai blâmé**	**avons blâmé**
blâmes	**blâmez**	**as blâmé**	**avez blâmé**
blâme	**blâment**	**a blâmé**	**ont blâmé**
2 imparfait de l'indicatif		9 plus-que-parfait de l'indicatif	
blâmais	**blâmions**	**avais blâmé**	**avions blâmé**
blâmais	**blâmiez**	**avais blâmé**	**aviez blâmé**
blâmait	**blâmaient**	**avait blâmé**	**avaient blâmé**
3 passé simple		10 passé antérieur	
blâmai	**blâmâmes**	**eus blâmé**	**eûmes blâmé**
blâmas	**blâmâtes**	**eus blâmé**	**eûtes blâmé**
blâma	**blâmèrent**	**eut blâmé**	**eurent blâmé**
4 futur		11 futur antérieur	
blâmerai	**blâmerons**	**aurai blâmé**	**aurons blâmé**
blâmeras	**blâmerez**	**auras blâmé**	**aurez blâmé**
blâmera	**blâmeront**	**aura blâmé**	**auront blâmé**
5 conditionnel		12 conditionnel passé	
blâmerais	**blâmerions**	**aurais blâmé**	**aurions blâmé**
blâmerais	**blâmeriez**	**aurais blâmé**	**auriez blâmé**
blâmerait	**blâmeraient**	**aurait blâmé**	**auraient blâmé**
6 présent du subjonctif		13 passé du subjonctif	
blâme	**blâmions**	**aie blâmé**	**ayons blâmé**
blâmes	**blâmiez**	**aies blâmé**	**ayez blâmé**
blâme	**blâment**	**ait blâmé**	**aient blâmé**
7 imparfait du subjonctif		14 plus-que-parfait du subjonctif	
blâmasse	**blâmassions**	**eusse blâmé**	**eussions blâmé**
blâmasses	**blâmassiez**	**eusses blâmé**	**eussiez blâmé**
blâmât	**blâmassent**	**eût blâmé**	**eussent blâmé**

Impératif
blâme
blâmons
blâmez

Words and expressions related to this verb
être blâmé (blâmée)   to be blamed
le blâme   blame
blasphémer   to blaspheme

se blâmer   to blame oneself
blâmable   blameworthy, blamable
le blasphème   blasphemy

Don't forget to use the English-French verb index. It's in the Appendixes.

Regular **-ir** verb   to whiten, to launder, to exonerate

The Seven Simple Tenses		The Seven Compound Tenses	
Singular	Plural	Singular	Plural
1 présent de l'indicatif		8 passé composé	
blanchis	**blanchissons**	**ai blanchi**	**avons blanchi**
blanchis	**blanchissez**	**as blanchi**	**avez blanchi**
blanchit	**blanchissent**	**a blanchi**	**ont blanchi**
2 imparfait de l'indicatif		9 plus-que-parfait de l'indicatif	
blanchissais	**blanchissions**	**avais blanchi**	**avions blanchi**
blanchissais	**blanchissiez**	**avais blanchi**	**aviez blanchi**
blanchissait	**blanchissaient**	**avait blanchi**	**avaient blanchi**
3 passé simple		10 passé antérieur	
blanchis	**blanchîmes**	**eus blanchi**	**eûmes blanchi**
blanchis	**blanchîtes**	**eus blanchi**	**eûtes blanchi**
blanchit	**blanchirent**	**eut blanchi**	**eurent blanchi**
4 futur		11 futur antérieur	
blanchirai	**blanchirons**	**aurai blanchi**	**aurons blanchi**
blanchiras	**blanchirez**	**auras blanchi**	**aurez blanchi**
blanchira	**blanchiront**	**aura blanchi**	**auront blanchi**
5 conditionnel		12 conditionnel passé	
blanchirais	**blanchirions**	**aurais blanchi**	**aurions blanchi**
blanchirais	**blanchiriez**	**aurais blanchi**	**auriez blanchi**
blanchirait	**blanchiraient**	**aurait blanchi**	**auraient blanchi**
6 présent du subjonctif		13 passé du subjonctif	
blanchisse	**blanchissions**	**aie blanchi**	**ayons blanchi**
blanchisses	**blanchissiez**	**aies blanchi**	**ayez blanchi**
blanchisse	**blanchissent**	**ait blanchi**	**aient blanchi**
7 imparfait du subjonctif		14 plus-que-parfait du subjonctif	
blanchisse	**blanchissions**	**eusse blanchi**	**eussions blanchi**
blanchisses	**blanchissiez**	**eusses blanchi**	**eussiez blanchi**
blanchît	**blanchissent**	**eût blanchi**	**eussent blanchi**

Impératif
blanchis
blanchissons
blanchissez

Common idiomatic expressions using this verb and words related to it

le blanc   white
le blanc d'oeil   the white of the eye
la bille blanche   white billiard ball
du vin blanc   white wine
la blanchisserie   laundry
   (store where clothes are washed)
carte blanche   unlimited privileges and authority
blanc comme neige   as white as snow

Blanche-Neige   Snow White
un chèque en blanc   blank check
un verre de blanc   a glass of white wine
le blanchissage   washing
Le maire a été blanchi des accusations de
   corruption.   The mayor was cleared of the
charges of corruption.

to harm, to hurt, to injure, to wound, to offend
               Regular **-er** verb

The Seven Simple Tenses		The Seven Compound Tenses	
Singular	Plural	Singular	Plural
1 présent de l'indicatif		8 passé composé	
blesse	blessons	ai blessé	avons blessé
blesses	blessez	as blessé	avez blessé
blesse	blessent	a blessé	ont blessé
2 imparfait de l'indicatif		9 plus-que-parfait de l'indicatif	
blessais	blessions	avais blessé	avions blessé
blessais	blessiez	avais blessé	aviez blessé
blessait	blessaient	avait blessé	avaient blessé
3 passé simple		10 passé antérieur	
blessai	blessâmes	eus blessé	eûmes blessé
blessas	blessâtes	eus blessé	eûtes blessé
blessa	blessèrent	eut blessé	eurent blessé
4 futur		11 futur antérieur	
blesserai	blesserons	aurai blessé	aurons blessé
blesseras	blesserez	auras blessé	aurez blessé
blessera	blesseront	aura blessé	auront blessé
5 conditionnel		12 conditionnel passé	
blesserais	blesserions	aurais blessé	aurions blessé
blesserais	blesseriez	aurais blessé	auriez blessé
blesserait	blesseraient	aurait blessé	auraient blessé
6 présent du subjonctif		13 passé du subjonctif	
blesse	blessions	aie blessé	ayons blessé
blesses	blessiez	aies blessé	ayez blessé
blesse	blessent	ait blessé	aient blessé
7 imparfait du subjonctif		14 plus-que-parfait du subjonctif	
blessasse	blessassions	eusse blessé	eussions blessé
blessasses	blessassiez	eusses blessé	eussiez blessé
blessât	blessassent	eût blessé	eussent blessé

Impératif
blesse
blessons
blessez

Sentences using this verb and words related to it
   Ma sœur est tombée sur un rocher qui l'a blessée au visage. Ce fut* une blessure grave.

blesser à mort to wound mortally   **être blessé à la jambe (au bras)** to be injured
une blessure wound, injury   in the leg (in the arm)
une parole blessante a cutting word
See also **se blesser.**

   *The verb form **fut** is the **passé simple** of être.

Do not confuse **blesser** with **bénir,** which means *to bless.*

Reflexive regular **-er** verb   to hurt oneself, to injure oneself, to wound oneself

The Seven Simple Tenses		The Seven Compound Tenses	
Singular	Plural	Singular	Plural

B

1 présent de l'indicatif		8 passé composé	
me blesse	nous blessons	me suis blessé(e)	nous sommes blessé(e)s
te blesses	vous blessez	t'es blessé(e)	vous êtes blessé(e)(s)
se blesse	se blessent	s'est blessé(e)	se sont blessé(e)s

2 imparfait de l'indicatif		9 plus-que-parfait de l'indicatif	
me blessais	nous blessions	m'étais blessé(e)	nous étions blessé(e)s
te blessais	vous blessiez	t'étais blessé(e)	vous étiez blessé(e)(s)
se blessait	se blessaient	s'était blessé(e)	s'étaient blessé(e)s

3 passé simple		10 passé antérieur	
me blessai	nous blessâmes	me fus blessé(e)	nous fûmes blessé(e)s
te blessas	vous blessâtes	te fus blessé(e)	vous fûtes blessé(e)(s)
se blessa	se blessèrent	se fut blessé(e)	se furent blessé(e)s

4 futur		11 futur antérieur	
me blesserai	nous blesserons	me serai blessé(e)	nous serons blessé(e)s
te blesseras	vous blesserez	te seras blessé(e)	vous serez blessé(e)(s)
se blessera	se blesseront	se sera blessé(e)	se seront blessé(e)s

5 conditionnel		12 conditionnel passé	
me blesserais	nous blesserions	me serais blessé(e)	nous serions blessé(e)s
te blesserais	vous blesseriez	te serais blessé(e)	vous seriez blessé(e)(s)
se blesserait	se blesseraient	se serait blessé(e)	se seraient blessé(e)s

6 présent du subjonctif		13 passé du subjonctif	
me blesse	nous blessions	me sois blessé(e)	nous soyons blessé(e)s
te blesses	vous blessiez	te sois blessé(e)	vous soyez blessé(e)(s)
se blesse	se blessent	se soit blessé(e)	se soient blessé(e)s

7 imparfait du subjonctif		14 plus-que-parfait du subjonctif	
me blessasse	nous blessassions	me fusse blessé(e)	nous fussions blessé(e)s
te blessasses	vous blessassiez	te fusses blessé(e)	vous fussiez blessé(e)(s)
se blessât	se blessassent	se fût blessé(e)	se fussent blessé(e)s

Impératif
blesse-toi; ne te blesse pas
blessons-nous; ne nous blessons pas
blessez-vous; ne vous blessez pas

Sentences using this verb and words related to it
   Madame Leblanc est tombée dans la rue et elle s'est blessée au genou. Ce fut* une blessure légère, heureusement.

se blesser de   to take offense at   **se blesser pour un rien**   to be easily offended

For other words and expressions related to this verb, see **blesser**.

   *The verb form **fut** is the **passé simple** of **être**.

Do not confuse **blesser** and **se blesser** with **bénir**, which means *to bless*.

The subject pronouns are found on page 103.   **187**

The Seven Simple Tenses		The Seven Compound Tenses	
Singular	Plural	Singular	Plural
1 présent de l'indicatif		8 passé composé	
bois	**buvons**	**ai bu**	**avons bu**
bois	**buvez**	**as bu**	**avez bu**
boit	**boivent**	**a bu**	**ont bu**
2 imparfait de l'indicatif		9 plus-que-parfait de l'indicatif	
buvais	**buvions**	**avais bu**	**avions bu**
buvais	**buviez**	**avais bu**	**aviez bu**
buvait	**buvaient**	**avait bu**	**avaient bu**
3 passé simple		10 passé antérieur	
bus	**bûmes**	**eus bu**	**eûmes bu**
bus	**bûtes**	**eus bu**	**eûtes bu**
but	**burent**	**eut bu**	**eurent bu**
4 futur		11 futur antérieur	
boirai	**boirons**	**aurai bu**	**aurons bu**
boiras	**boirez**	**auras bu**	**aurez bu**
boira	**boiront**	**aura bu**	**auront bu**
5 conditionnel		12 conditionnel passé	
boirais	**boirions**	**aurais bu**	**aurions bu**
boirais	**boiriez**	**aurais bu**	**auriez bu**
boirait	**boiraient**	**aurait bu**	**auraient bu**
6 présent du subjonctif		13 passé du subjonctif	
boive	**buvions**	**aie bu**	**ayons bu**
boives	**buviez**	**aies bu**	**ayez bu**
boive	**boivent**	**ait bu**	**aient bu**
7 imparfait du subjonctif		14 plus-que-parfait du subjonctif	
busse	**bussions**	**eusse bu**	**eussions bu**
busses	**bussiez**	**eusses bu**	**eussiez bu**
bût	**bussent**	**eût bu**	**eussent bu**

Impératif
bois
buvons
buvez

AN ESSENTIAL
55 VERB

AN ESSENTIAL 55 VERB

Boire

Boire is a very useful verb for a beginning French student. Pay attention to its irregular conjugation pattern.

Sentences using boire and related words

Boire un petit coup, c'est agréable! It's pleasant to have a little drink. (French song)

Il pleut à boire debout! It's raining hard! (It's raining so hard you could drink standing up.)

—René, as-tu bu ton lait?
—Non, maman, je ne l'ai pas bu.
—Bois-le tout de suite, je te dis.
—Tous les jours je bois du lait. N'y a-t-il pas d'autres boissons dans la maison?
—Si, il y a d'autres boissons dans la maison mais les bons garçons comme toi boivent du lait.

(Note that si is used instead of oui for *yes* in answer to a question in the negative.)

—René, did you drink your milk?
—No, Mother, I didn't drink it.
—I'm telling you: drink it right away.
—I drink milk every day. Aren't there other drinks in the house?
—Yes, there are other drinks in the house, but good boys like you drink milk.

Words and expressions related to this verb

boire à la santé de qqn **to drink to someone's health**

boire à la bouteille **to drink right out of the bottle**

boire à sa soif **to drink to one's heart's content**

boire comme un trou **to drink too much (alcohol)**

un buveur, une buveuse **drinker**

une buvette **bar**

un buvard **ink blotter**

boire un coup **to have a drink**

une boisson **drink**

une boisson gazeuse **carbonated drink**

un breuvage **beverage**

The subject pronouns are found on page 103.

189

to budge, to move

Regular -**er** verb endings; spelling change: retain the **ge** before **a** or **o** to keep the soft **g** sound of the verb

The Seven Simple Tenses		The Seven Compound Tenses	
Singular	Plural	Singular	Plural
1 présent de l'indicatif		8 passé composé	
bouge	bougeons	ai bougé	avons bougé
bouges	bougez	as bougé	avez bougé
bouge	bougent	a bougé	ont bougé
2 imparfait de l'indicatif		9 plus-que-parfait de l'indicatif	
bougeais	bougions	avais bougé	avions bougé
bougeais	bougiez	avais bougé	aviez bougé
bougeait	bougeaient	avait bougé	avaient bougé
3 passé simple		10 passé antérieur	
bougeai	bougeâmes	eus bougé	eûmes bougé
bougeas	bougeâtes	eus bougé	eûtes bougé
bougea	bougèrent	eut bougé	eurent bougé
4 futur		11 futur antérieur	
bougerai	bougerons	aurai bougé	aurons bougé
bougeras	bougerez	auras bougé	aurez bougé
bougera	bougeront	aura bougé	auront bougé
5 conditionnel		12 conditionnel passé	
bougerais	bougerions	aurais bougé	aurions bougé
bougerais	bougeriez	aurais bougé	auriez bougé
bougerait	bougeraient	aurait bougé	auraient bougé
6 présent du subjonctif		13 passé du subjonctif	
bouge	bougions	aie bougé	ayons bougé
bouges	bougiez	aies bougé	ayez bougé
bouge	bougent	ait bougé	aient bougé
7 imparfait du subjonctif		14 plus-que-parfait du subjonctif	
bougeasse	bougeassions	eusse bougé	eussions bougé
bougeasses	bougeassiez	eusses bougé	eussiez bougé
bougeât	bougeassent	eût bougé	eussent bougé

Impératif
bouge
bougeons
bougez

Words and expressions related to this verb

avoir la bougeotte   to be on the move; to be restless, to move about restlessly; to be fidgety
    La terre a bougé.   The ground shook.
ne pas bouger   not to make a move; **Personne n'a bougé.**   Nobody moved.

Get acquainted with what preposition goes with what verb. See *Verbs with prepositions* in the Appendixes.

Don't miss orthographically changing verbs on pages 32–34.

Irregular verb   to boil

The Seven Simple Tenses		The Seven Compound Tenses	
Singular	Plural	Singular	Plural

1   présent de l'indicatif

		8 passé composé	
bous	bouillons	ai bouilli	avons bouilli
bous	bouillez	as bouilli	avez bouilli
bout	bouillent	a bouilli	ont bouilli

2   imparfait de l'indicatif

		9 plus-que-parfait de l'indicatif	
bouillais	bouillions	avais bouilli	avions bouilli
bouillais	bouilliez	avais bouilli	aviez bouilli
bouillait	bouillaient	avait bouilli	avaient bouilli

3   passé simple

		10 passé antérieur	
bouillis	bouillîmes	eus bouilli	eûmes bouilli
bouillis	bouillîtes	eus bouilli	eûtes bouilli
bouillit	bouillirent	eut bouilli	eurent bouilli

4   futur

		11 futur antérieur	
bouillirai	bouillirons	aurai bouilli	aurons bouilli
bouilliras	bouillirez	auras bouilli	aurez bouilli
bouillira	bouilliront	aura bouilli	auront bouilli

5   conditionnel

		12 conditionnel passé	
bouillirais	bouillirions	aurais bouilli	aurions bouilli
bouillirais	bouilliriez	aurais bouilli	auriez bouilli
bouillirait	bouilliraient	aurait bouilli	auraient bouilli

6   présent du subjonctif

		13 passé du subjonctif	
bouille	bouillions	aie bouilli	ayons bouilli
bouilles	bouilliez	aies bouilli	ayez bouilli
bouille	bouillent	ait bouilli	aient bouilli

7   imparfait du subjonctif

		14 plus-que-parfait du subjonctif	
bouillisse	bouillissions	eusse bouilli	eussions bouilli
bouillisses	bouillissiez	eusses bouilli	eussiez bouilli
bouillît	bouillissent	eût bouilli	eussent bouilli

Impératif
bous
bouillons
bouillez

Words and expressions related to this verb

faire bouillir to boil	**faire donner un bouillon** to bring to boil
le bouillon broth; bubble	**une bulle de savon** soap bubble
une bulle *(ewn bewl)* bubble, blister	**une bouilloire** kettle
faire des bulles to blow bubbles	**réduire en bouillie** to beat to a pulp
la bouillabaisse fish soup (chowder)	**la bouillie** baby food, cereal, porridge
le bouillonnement bubbling, boiling	**manger de la bouillie** to speak badly, mumble

Use the guide to French pronunciation. It's in the Appendixes.

See the summary of sequence of tenses with **si** (*if*) clauses on page 26.

The subject pronouns are found on page 103.
     191

brancher (78)

Part. pr. **branchant** Part. passé **branché**

to plug in, to connect

The Seven Simple Tenses		The Seven Compound Tenses	
Singular	Plural	Singular	Plural
1 présent de l'indicatif		8 passé composé	
branche	branchons	ai branché	avons branché
branches	branchez	as branché	avez branché
branche	branchent	a branché	ont branché
2 imparfait de l'indicatif		9 plus-que-parfait de l'indicatif	
branchais	branchions	avais branché	avions branché
branchais	branchiez	avais branché	aviez branché
branchait	branchaient	avait branché	avaient branché
3 passé simple		10 passé antérieur	
branchai	branchâmes	eus branché	eûmes branché
branchas	branchâtes	eus branché	eûtes branché
brancha	branchèrent	eut branché	eurent branché
4 futur		11 futur antérieur	
brancherai	brancherons	aurai branché	aurons branché
brancheras	brancherez	auras branché	aurez branché
branchera	brancheront	aura branché	auront branché
5 conditionnel		12 conditionnel passé	
brancherais	brancherions	aurais branché	aurions branché
brancherais	brancheriez	aurais branché	auriez branché
brancherait	brancheraient	aurait branché	auraient branché
6 présent du subjonctif		13 passé du subjonctif	
branche	branchions	aie branché	ayons branché
branches	branchiez	aies branché	ayez branché
branche	branchent	ait branché	aient branché
7 imparfait du subjonctif		14 plus-que-parfait du subjonctif	
branchasse	branchassions	eusse branché	eussions branché
branchasses	branchassiez	eusses branché	eussiez branché
branchât	branchassent	eût branché	eussent branché

Impératif
branche
branchons
branchez

Sentences using this verb and words related to it
Pierre est branché sur le jardinage. Pierre is into gardening.
Branche ton modem sur le bon port de ton ordinateur. Plug your modem into the correct port
  on your computer.

Words and expressions related to this verb
débrancher to unplug, disconnect
une branche branch
ma vieille branche my old friend

Don't forget to study the section on defective and impersonal verbs. It's right after this main list.

B

The Seven Simple Tenses		The Seven Compound Tenses	
Singular	Plural	Singular	Plural
1 présent de l'indicatif		8 passé composé	
brosse	**brossons**	**ai brossé**	**avons brossé**
brosses	**brossez**	**as brossé**	**avez brossé**
brosse	**brossent**	**a brossé**	**ont brossé**
2 imparfait de l'indicatif		9 plus-que-parfait de l'indicatif	
brossais	**brossions**	**avais brossé**	**avions brossé**
brossais	**brossiez**	**avais brossé**	**aviez brossé**
brossait	**brossaient**	**avait brossé**	**avaient brossé**
3 passé simple		10 passé antérieur	
brossai	**brossâmes**	**eus brossé**	**eûmes brossé**
brossas	**brossâtes**	**eus brossé**	**eûtes brossé**
brossa	**brossèrent**	**eut brossé**	**eurent brossé**
4 futur		11 futur antérieur	
brosserai	**brosserons**	**aurai brossé**	**aurons brossé**
brosseras	**brosserez**	**auras brossé**	**aurez brossé**
brossera	**brosseront**	**aura brossé**	**auront brossé**
5 conditionnel		12 conditionnel passé	
brosserais	**brosserions**	**aurais brossé**	**aurions brossé**
brosserais	**brosseriez**	**aurais brossé**	**auriez brossé**
brosserait	**brosseraient**	**aurait brossé**	**auraient brossé**
6 présent du subjonctif		13 passé du subjonctif	
brosse	**brossions**	**aie brossé**	**ayons brossé**
brosses	**brossiez**	**aies brossé**	**ayez brossé**
brosse	**brossent**	**ait brossé**	**aient brossé**
7 imparfait du subjonctif		14 plus-que-parfait du subjonctif	
brossasse	**brossassions**	**eusse brossé**	**eussions brossé**
brossasses	**brossassiez**	**eusses brossé**	**eussiez brossé**
brossât	**brossassent**	**eût brossé**	**eussent brossé**

Impératif
brosse
brossons
brossez

Sentences using this verb and words related to it
—**Henriette, as-tu brossé tes souliers?**
—**Non, maman, je ne les ai pas brossés.**
—**Et pourquoi pas, ma petite?**
—**Parce que je n'ai pas de brosse.**

une brosse   brush; **brosse à chaussures**   shoebrush; **brosse à dents**   toothbrush; **brosse à ongles**   nailbrush
donner un coup de brosse   to brush
le brossage brushing

See also se **brosser**.

If you don't know the French verb for an English verb you have in mind, try the index in the Appendixes.

se brosser (80)

to brush oneself

Part. pr. **se brossant**   Part. passé **brossé(e)(s)**

Reflexive regular **-er** verb

The Seven Simple Tenses		The Seven Compound Tenses	
Singular	Plural	Singular	Plural
1 présent de l'indicatif		8 passé composé	
me brosse	nous brossons	me suis brossé(e)	nous sommes brossé(e)s
te brosses	vous brossez	t'es brossé(e)	vous êtes brossé(e)(s)
se brosse	se brossent	s'est brossé(e)	se sont brossé(e)s
2 imparfait de l'indicatif		9 plus-que-parfait de l'indicatif	
me brossais	nous brossions	m'étais brossé(e)	nous étions brossé(e)s
te brossais	vous brossiez	t'étais brossé(e)	vous étiez brossé(e)(s)
se brossait	se brossaient	s'était brossé(e)	s'étaient brossé(e)s
3 passé simple		10 passé antérieur	
me brossai	nous brossâmes	me fus brossé(e)	nous fûmes brossé(e)s
te brossas	vous brossâtes	te fus brossé(e)	vous fûtes brossé(e)(s)
se brossa	se brossèrent	se fut brossé(e)	se furent brossé(e)s
4 futur		11 futur antérieur	
me brosserai	nous brosserons	me serai brossé(e)	nous serons brossé(e)s
te brosseras	vous brosserez	te seras brossé(e)	vous serez brossé(e)(s)
se brossera	se brosseront	se sera brossé(e)	se seront brossé(e)s
5 conditionnel		12 conditionnel passé	
me brosserais	nous brosserions	me serais brossé(e)	nous serions brossé(e)s
te brosserais	vous brosseriez	te serais brossé(e)	vous seriez brossé(e)(s)
se brosserait	se brosseraient	se serait brossé(e)	se seraient brossé(e)s
6 présent du subjonctif		13 passé du subjonctif	
me brosse	nous brossions	me sois brossé(e)	nous soyons brossé(e)s
te brosses	vous brossiez	te sois brossé(e)	vous soyez brossé(e)(s)
se brosse	se brossent	se soit brossé(e)	se soient brossé(e)s
7 imparfait du subjonctif		14 plus-que-parfait du subjonctif	
me brossasse	nous brossassions	me fusse brossé(e)	nous fussions brossé(e)s
te brossasses	vous brossassiez	te fusses brossé(e)	vous fussiez brossé(e)(s)
se brossât	se brossassent	se fût brossé(e)	se fussent brossé(e)s

Impératif
brosse-toi; ne te brosse pas
brossons-nous; ne nous brossons pas
brossez-vous; ne vous brossez pas

Sentences using this verb and words related to it

—Tina Marie, est-ce que tu t'es brossée?

—Non, maman, je ne me suis pas brossée.

—Et pourquoi pas? Brosse-toi vite!

—Parce que je n'ai pas de brosse à habits, je n'ai pas de brosse à cheveux, je n'ai pas de brosse à chaussures. Je n'ai aucune brosse. Je n'ai pas de brosse à dents, non plus.

—Quelle fille!

se brosser les dents, les cheveux, etc.   to brush one's teeth, hair, etc.

For other words and expressions related to this verb, see brosser.

If you want to see a sample English verb fully conjugated in all the tenses, check out pages 8 and 9.

The Seven Simple Tenses		The Seven Compound Tenses	
Singular	Plural	Singular	Plural
1 présent de l'indicatif		**8 passé composé**	
brûle	brûlons	ai brûlé	avons brûlé
brûles	brûlez	as brûlé	avez brûlé
brûle	brûlent	a brûlé	ont brûlé
2 imparfait de l'indicatif		**9 plus-que-parfait de l'indicatif**	
brûlais	brûlions	avais brûlé	avions brûlé
brûlais	brûliez	avais brûlé	aviez brûlé
brûlait	brûlaient	avait brûlé	avaient brûlé
3 passé simple		**10 passé antérieur**	
brûlai	brûlâmes	eus brûlé	eûmes brûlé
brûlas	brûlâtes	eus brûlé	eûtes brûlé
brûla	brûlèrent	eut brûlé	eurent brûlé
4 futur		**11 futur antérieur**	
brûlerai	brûlerons	aurai brûlé	aurons brûlé
brûleras	brûlerez	auras brûlé	aurez brûlé
brûlera	brûleront	aura brûlé	auront brûlé
5 conditionnel		**12 conditionnel passé**	
brûlerais	brûlerions	aurais brûlé	aurions brûlé
brûlerais	brûleriez	aurais brûlé	auriez brûlé
brûlerait	brûleraient	aurait brûlé	auraient brûlé
6 présent du subjonctif		**13 passé du subjonctif**	
brûle	brûlions	aie brûlé	ayons brûlé
brûles	brûliez	aies brûlé	ayez brûlé
brûle	brûlent	ait brûlé	aient brûlé
7 imparfait du subjonctif		**14 plus-que-parfait du subjonctif**	
brûlasse	brûlassions	eusse brûlé	eussions brûlé
brûlasses	brûlassiez	eusses brûlé	eussiez brûlé
brûlât	brûlassent	eût brûlé	eussent brûlé

Impératif
brûle
brûlons
brûlez

Sentences using this verb and words related to it
—Joséphine, avez-vous brûlé les vieux papiers que je vous ai donnés?
—Oui, madame, et je me suis brûlée. J'ai une brûlure aux doigts.

une brûlure   burn
un brûleur   burner, roaster
brûler d'amour   to be madly in love
brûler de faire qqch   to be eager to do something

brûler un feu rouge   to pass through a red traffic light
une crème brûlée   a crème brûlée (dessert)

It's important that you be familiar with the Subjunctive. See pages 26–31.

to hide

Regular **-er** verb

The Seven Simple Tenses		The Seven Compound Tenses	
Singular	Plural	Singular	Plural
1 présent de l'indicatif		8 passé composé	
cache	cachons	ai caché	avons caché
caches	cachez	as caché	avez caché
cache	cachent	a caché	ont caché
2 imparfait de l'indicatif		9 plus-que-parfait de l'indicatif	
cachais	cachions	avais caché	avions caché
cachais	cachiez	avais caché	aviez caché
cachait	cachaient	avait caché	avaient caché
3 passé simple		10 passé antérieur	
cachai	cachâmes	eus caché	eûmes caché
cachas	cachâtes	eus caché	eûtes caché
cacha	cachèrent	eut caché	eurent caché
4 futur		11 futur antérieur	
cacherai	cacherons	aurai caché	aurons caché
cacheras	cacherez	auras caché	aurez caché
cachera	cacheront	aura caché	auront caché
5 conditionnel		12 conditionnel passé	
cacherais	cacherions	aurais caché	aurions caché
cacherais	cacheriez	aurais caché	auriez caché
cacherait	cacheraient	aurait caché	auraient caché
6 présent du subjonctif		13 passé du subjonctif	
cache	cachions	aie caché	ayons caché
caches	cachiez	aies caché	ayez caché
cache	cachent	ait caché	aient caché
7 imparfait du subjonctif		14 plus-que-parfait du subjonctif	
cachasse	cachassions	eusse caché	eussions caché
cachasses	cachassiez	eusses caché	eussiez caché
cachât	cachassent	eût caché	eussent caché

Impératif
cache
cachons
cachez

Sentences using this verb and words related to it
—Pierre, qu'est-ce que tu as caché derrière toi?
—Rien, papa.
—Ne me dis pas ça. Tu caches quelque chose.
—Voilà, papa, c'est un petit chat que j'ai trouvé dans le parc.

une cache, une cachette   hiding place
la cache   cache (computer)
un cachet   seal, mark
un cachetage   sealing
cacheter   to seal up

le cache-cache   hide-and-seek
le vin cacheté   vintage wine
cacher qqch à qqn   to hide something from someone
un cache-nez   muffler
en cachette   in secret

See also se cacher.

Part. pr. **se cachant**   Part. passé **caché(e)(s)**   **se cacher (83)**

Reflexive regular **-er** verb   to hide oneself

The Seven Simple Tenses	The Seven Compound Tenses

Singular	Plural	Singular	Plural
1 présent de l'indicatif		**8 passé composé**	
me cache	nous cachons	me suis caché(e)	nous sommes caché(e)s
te caches	vous cachez	t'es caché(e)	vous êtes caché(e)(s)
se cache	se cachent	s'est caché(e)	se sont caché(e)s
2 imparfait de l'indicatif		**9 plus-que-parfait de l'indicatif**	
me cachais	nous cachions	m'étais caché(e)	nous étions caché(e)s
te cachais	vous cachiez	t'étais caché(e)	vous étiez caché(e)(s)
se cachait	se cachaient	s'était caché(e)	s'étaient caché(e)s
3 passé simple		**10 passé antérieur**	
me cachai	nous cachâmes	me fus caché(e)	nous fûmes caché(e)s
te cachas	vous cachâtes	te fus caché(e)	vous fûtes caché(e)(s)
se cacha	se cachèrent	se fut caché(e)	se furent caché(e)s
4 futur		**11 futur antérieur**	
me cacherai	nous cacherons	me serai caché(e)	nous serons caché(e)s
te cacheras	vous cacherez	te seras caché(e)	vous serez caché(e)(s)
se cachera	se cacheront	se sera caché(e)	se seront caché(e)s
5 conditionnel		**12 conditionnel passé**	
me cacherais	nous cacherions	me serais caché(e)	nous serions caché(e)s
te cacherais	vous cacheriez	te serais caché(e)	vous seriez caché(e)(s)
se cacherait	se cacheraient	se serait caché(e)	se seraient caché(e)s
6 présent du subjonctif		**13 passé du subjonctif**	
me cache	nous cachions	me sois caché(e)	nous soyons caché(e)s
te caches	vous cachiez	te sois caché(e)	vous soyez caché(e)(s)
se cache	se cachent	se soit caché(e)	se soient caché(e)s
7 imparfait du subjonctif		**14 plus-que-parfait du subjonctif**	
me cachasse	nous cachassions	me fusse caché(e)	nous fussions caché(e)s
te cachasses	vous cachassiez	te fusses caché(e)	vous fussiez caché(e)(s)
se cachât	se cachassent	se fût caché(e)	se fussent caché(e)s

Impératif
cache-toi; ne te cache pas
cachons-nous; ne nous cachons pas
cachez-vous; ne vous cachez pas

Sentences using this verb and words related to it

J'ai un petit chien que j'appelle Coco. Quelquefois je ne peux pas le trouver parce qu'il se cache sous mon lit ou derrière l'arbre dans le jardin. La semaine dernière il s'est caché sous le chapeau de mon père. Il aime jouer à cache-cache. Il est très intelligent.

une cache, une cachette   hiding place
un cachet   seal, mark
un cachetage   sealing
se cacher de qqn   to hide from someone
cacheter   to seal up

le cache-cache   hide-and-seek
le vin cacheté   vintage wine
un cachot   cell, prison; dungeon
en cachette de qqn   behind someone's back

See also cacher.

The subject pronouns are found on page 103.

to break

The Seven Simple Tenses		The Seven Compound Tenses	
Singular	Plural	Singular	Plural
1 présent de l'indicatif		**8 passé composé**	
casse	cassons	ai cassé	avons cassé
casses	cassez	as cassé	avez cassé
casse	cassent	a cassé	ont cassé
2 imparfait de l'indicatif		**9 plus-que-parfait de l'indicatif**	
cassais	cassions	avais cassé	avions cassé
cassais	cassiez	avais cassé	aviez cassé
cassait	cassaient	avait cassé	avaient cassé
3 passé simple		**10 passé antérieur**	
cassai	cassâmes	eus cassé	eûmes cassé
cassas	cassâtes	eus cassé	eûtes cassé
cassa	cassèrent	eut cassé	eurent cassé
4 futur		**11 futur antérieur**	
casserai	casserons	aurai cassé	aurons cassé
casseras	casserez	auras cassé	aurez cassé
cassera	casseront	aura cassé	auront cassé
5 conditionnel		**12 conditionnel passé**	
casserais	casserions	aurais cassé	aurions cassé
casserais	casseriez	aurais cassé	auriez cassé
casserait	casseraient	aurait cassé	auraient cassé
6 présent du subjonctif		**13 passé du subjonctif**	
casse	cassions	aie cassé	ayons cassé
casses	cassiez	aies cassé	ayez cassé
casse	cassent	ait cassé	aient cassé
7 imparfait du subjonctif		**14 plus-que-parfait du subjonctif**	
cassasse	cassassions	eusse cassé	eussions cassé
cassasses	cassassiez	eusses cassé	eussiez cassé
cassât	cassassent	eût cassé	eussent cassé

Impératif
casse
cassons
cassez

Sentences using this verb and words related to it
—Jean, c'est toi qui as cassé mon joli vase?   John, is it you who broke my pretty vase?
—Non, maman, c'est Mathilde.   No, Mother, it was Mathilda.
—Mathilde, c'est toi qui as cassé mon joli vase?   Mathilda, is it you who broke my pretty vase?
—Non, maman, c'est Jean.   No, Mother, it was John.
—Quels enfants!   What children!

une casse   breakage, damage
un casse-croûte   snack
un casse-noisettes, un casse-noix   nutcracker
casser la croûte   to have a snack
un casse-pieds   a bore, a pain in the neck
un cassement de tête   puzzle, worry

See also se casser.

un casse-tête   puzzle
concasser   to crush (cereal, sugar lumps, stones)
casser la tête à qqn   to pester someone
casser les oreilles à qqn   to bore someone stiff
   (by talking too much)
casser les pieds à qqn   to be a pain in the neck to someone

Reflexive regular **-er** verb

to break (a part of one's body, *e.g.*, leg, arm, nose)

The Seven Simple Tenses | The Seven Compound Tenses

Singular	Plural	Singular	Plural
1 présent de l'indicatif		8 passé composé	
me casse	**nous cassons**	**me suis cassé(e)**	**nous sommes cassé(e)s**
te casses	**vous cassez**	**t'es cassé(e)**	**vous êtes cassé(e)(s)**
se casse	**se cassent**	**s'est cassé(e)**	**se sont cassé(e)s**
2 imparfait de l'indicatif		9 plus-que-parfait de l'indicatif	
me cassais	**nous cassions**	**m'étais cassé(e)**	**nous étions cassé(e)s**
te cassais	**vous cassiez**	**t'étais cassé(e)**	**vous étiez cassé(e)(s)**
se cassait	**se cassaient**	**s'était cassé(e)**	**s'étaient cassé(e)s**
3 passé simple		10 passé antérieur	
me cassai	**nous cassâmes**	**me fus cassé(e)**	**nous fûmes cassé(e)s**
te cassas	**vous cassâtes**	**te fus cassé(e)**	**vous fûtes cassé(e)(s)**
se cassa	**se cassèrent**	**se fut cassé(e)**	**se furent cassé(e)s**
4 futur		11 futur antérieur	
me casserai	**nous casserons**	**me serai cassé(e)**	**nous serons cassé(e)s**
te casseras	**vous casserez**	**te seras cassé(e)**	**vous serez cassé(e)(s)**
se cassera	**se casseront**	**se sera cassé(e)**	**se seront cassé(e)s**
5 conditionnel		12 conditionnel passé	
me casserais	**nous casserions**	**me serais cassé(e)**	**nous serions cassé(e)s**
te casserais	**vous casseriez**	**te serais cassé(e)**	**vous seriez cassé(e)(s)**
se casserait	**se casseraient**	**se serait cassé(e)**	**se seraient cassé(e)s**
6 présent du subjonctif		13 passé du subjonctif	
me casse	**nous cassions**	**me sois cassé(e)**	**nous soyons cassé(e)s**
te casses	**vous cassiez**	**te sois cassé(e)**	**vous soyez cassé(e)(s)**
se casse	**se cassent**	**se soit cassé(e)**	**se soient cassé(e)s**
7 imparfait du subjonctif		14 plus-que-parfait du subjonctif	
me cassasse	**nous cassassions**	**me fusse cassé(e)**	**nous fussions cassé(e)s**
te cassasses	**vous cassassiez**	**te fusses cassé(e)**	**vous fussiez cassé(e)(s)**
se cassât	**se cassassent**	**se fût cassé(e)**	**se fussent cassé(e)s**

Impératif
casse-toi . . . ; ne te casse pas . . .
cassons-nous . . . ; ne nous cassons pas . . .
cassez-vous . . . ; ne vous cassez pas . . .

Sentences using this verb and words related do it

Pendant les vacances d'hiver, nous sommes allés faire du ski dans les montagnes. Mon père s'est cassé le bras, ma mère s'est cassé la jambe, et moi, je me suis cassé le pied.   During winter vacation we went skiing in the mountains. My father broke his arm, my mother broke her leg, and I broke my foot.

se casser la tête   to rack one's brains
se casser le nez   to find nobody answering the door
casser la tête à qqn   to annoy someone; **un casse-cou**   daredevil, reckless person

See also **casser**.

How are you doing? Find out with the verb drills and tests with answers explained on pages 50–101.

Part. pr. **causant**   Part. passé **causé**

Regular **-er** verb

The Seven Simple Tenses		The Seven Compound Tenses	
Singular	Plural	Singular	Plural
1 présent de l'indicatif		8 passé composé	
cause	**causons**	**ai causé**	**avons causé**
causes	**causez**	**as causé**	**avez causé**
cause	**causent**	**a causé**	**ont causé**
2 imparfait de l'indicatif		9 plus-que-parfait de l'indicatif	
causais	**causions**	**avais causé**	**avions causé**
causais	**causiez**	**avais causé**	**aviez causé**
causait	**causaient**	**avait causé**	**avaient causé**
3 passé simple		10 passé antérieur	
causai	**causâmes**	**eus causé**	**eûmes causé**
causas	**causâtes**	**eus causé**	**eûtes causé**
causa	**causèrent**	**eut causé**	**eurent causé**
4 futur		11 futur antérieur	
causerai	**causerons**	**aurai causé**	**aurons causé**
causeras	**causerez**	**auras causé**	**aurez causé**
causera	**causeront**	**aura causé**	**auront causé**
5 conditionnel		12 conditionnel passé	
causerais	**causerions**	**aurais causé**	**aurions causé**
causerais	**causeriez**	**aurais causé**	**auriez causé**
causerait	**causeraient**	**aurait causé**	**auraient causé**
6 présent du subjonctif		13 passé du subjonctif	
cause	**causions**	**aie causé**	**ayons causé**
causes	**causiez**	**aies causé**	**ayez causé**
cause	**causent**	**ait causé**	**aient causé**
7 imparfait du subjonctif		14 plus-que-parfait du subjonctif	
causasse	**causassions**	**eusse causé**	**eussions causé**
causasses	**causassiez**	**eusses causé**	**eussiez causé**
causât	**causassent**	**eût causé**	**eussent causé**

Impératif
cause
causons
causez

Sentences using this verb and words related to it

Quand je voyage, j'aime beaucoup causer avec les passagers. Est-ce que vous causez avec vos voisins dans la salle de classe? En français, bien sûr! Je connais un garçon qui n'est pas très causant.

causant, causante talkative	une cause célèbre famous trial
causatif, causative causative	une causerie chat, informal talk
une cause cause, reason	causeur, causeuse talkative
causer de la pluie et du beau temps to chat about the weather	une causeuse love seat
une causette chat	causer de la peine à qqn to hurt someone

Don't forget to use the English-French verb index. It's in the Appendixes.

Regular **-er** verb endings; spelling change: **to yield, to cede**
é changes to **è** before syllable with mute **e**

The Seven Simple Tenses | The Seven Compound Tenses

Singular	Plural	Singular	Plural
1 présent de l'indicatif		8 passé composé	
cède	**cédons**	**ai cédé**	**avons cédé**
cèdes	**cédez**	**as cédé**	**avez cédé**
cède	**cèdent**	**a cédé**	**ont cédé**
2 imparfait de l'indicatif		9 plus-que-parfait de l'indicatif	
cédais	**cédions**	**avais cédé**	**avions cédé**
cédais	**cédiez**	**avais cédé**	**aviez cédé**
cédait	**cédaient**	**avait cédé**	**avaient cédé**
3 passé simple		10 passé antérieur	
cédai	**cédâmes**	**eus cédé**	**eûmes cédé**
cédas	**cédâtes**	**eus cédé**	**eûtes cédé**
céda	**cédèrent**	**eut cédé**	**eurent cédé**
4 futur		11 futur antérieur	
céderai	**céderons**	**aurai cédé**	**aurons cédé**
céderas	**céderez**	**auras cédé**	**aurez cédé**
cédera	**céderont**	**aura cédé**	**auront cédé**
5 conditionnel		12 conditionnel passé	
céderais	**céderions**	**aurais cédé**	**aurions cédé**
céderais	**céderiez**	**aurais cédé**	**auriez cédé**
céderait	**céderaient**	**aurait cédé**	**auraient cédé**
6 présent du subjonctif		13 passé du subjonctif	
cède	**cédions**	**aie cédé**	**ayons cédé**
cèdes	**cédiez**	**aies cédé**	**ayez cédé**
cède	**cèdent**	**ait cédé**	**aient cédé**
7 imparfait du subjonctif		14 plus-que-parfait du subjonctif	
cédasse	**cédassions**	**eusse cédé**	**eussions cédé**
cédasses	**cédassiez**	**eusses cédé**	**eussiez cédé**
cédât	**cédassent**	**eût cédé**	**eussent cédé**

Impératif
cède
cédons
cédez

Sentences using this verb and words related to it

Hier soir j'ai pris l'autobus pour rentrer chez moi. J'ai pris la dernière place libre. Après quelques minutes, une vieille dame est entrée dans l'autobus et j'ai cédé ma place à cette aimable personne.

céder à   to give up, give in, yield to
accéder à   to accede to, to comply with
concéder à   to concede to, to grant
décéder   to pass away

céder le pas à qqn   to give way to someone
céder qqch à qqn   to let somebody have something

NOTE: The Académie française now allows the accent grave (`) in the future (*e.g.*, **je cèderai**) and conditional (*e.g.*, **je cèderais**) of this verb.

to cease

The Seven Simple Tenses		The Seven Compound Tenses	
Singular	Plural	Singular	Plural
1 présent de l'indicatif		8 passé composé	
cesse	cessons	ai cessé	avons cessé
cesses	cessez	as cessé	avez cessé
cesse	cessent	a cessé	ont cessé
2 imparfait de l'indicatif		9 plus-que-parfait de l'indicatif	
cessais	cessions	avais cessé	avions cessé
cessais	cessiez	avais cessé	aviez cessé
cessait	cessaient	avait cessé	avaient cessé
3 passé simple		10 passé antérieur	
cessai	cessâmes	eus cessé	eûmes cessé
cessas	cessâtes	eus cessé	eûtes cessé
cessa	cessèrent	eut cessé	eurent cessé
4 futur		11 futur antérieur	
cesserai	cesserons	aurai cessé	aurons cessé
cesseras	cesserez	auras cessé	aurez cessé
cessera	cesseront	aura cessé	auront cessé
5 conditionnel		12 conditionnel passé	
cesserais	cesserions	aurais cessé	aurions cessé
cesserais	cesseriez	aurais cessé	auriez cessé
cesserait	cesseraient	aurait cessé	auraient cessé
6 présent du subjonctif		13 passé du subjonctif	
cesse	cessions	aie cessé	ayons cessé
cesses	cessiez	aies cessé	ayez cessé
cesse	cessent	ait cessé	aient cessé
7 imparfait du subjonctif		14 plus-que-parfait du subjonctif	
cessasse	cessassions	eusse cessé	eussions cessé
cessasses	cessassiez	eusses cessé	eussiez cessé
cessât	cessassent	eût cessé	eussent cessé

Impératif
cesse
cessons
cessez

Sentences using this verb and words related to it
Proverb: **Quand le sage est en colère, il cesse d'être sage.**   When the wise man is angry, he stops being wise.

une cesse   cease, ceasing; **cesser de faire qqch**   to stop doing something
sans cesse   constantly
incessant   incessant, ceaseless
cesser de se voir   to stop seeing each other; **Il n'a pas cessé de neiger depuis hier.**   It has not stopped snowing since yesterday.
cesser le feu   to cease fire; **un cessez-le-feu**   cease-fire

For **je me tais,** see **se taire.** See also **bavarder.**

Regular **-er** verb endings; spelling change: retain the
ge before **a** or **o** to keep the soft **g** sound of the verb

to change

The Seven Simple Tenses		The Seven Compound Tenses	
Singular	Plural	Singular	Plural

1 présent de l'indicatif		8 passé composé	
change	changeons	ai changé	avons changé
changes	changez	as changé	avez changé
change	changent	a changé	ont changé

2 imparfait de l'indicatif		9 plus-que-parfait de l'indicatif	
changeais	changions	avais changé	avions changé
changeais	changiez	avais changé	aviez changé
changeait	changeaient	avait changé	avaient changé

3 passé simple		10 passé antérieur	
changeai	changeâmes	eus changé	eûmes changé
changeas	changeâtes	eus changé	eûtes changé
changea	changèrent	eut changé	eurent changé

4 futur		11 futur antérieur	
changerai	changerons	aurai changé	aurons changé
changeras	changerez	auras changé	aurez changé
changera	changeront	aura changé	auront changé

5 conditionnel		12 conditionnel passé	
changerais	changerions	aurais changé	aurions changé
changerais	changeriez	aurais changé	auriez changé
changerait	changeraient	aurait changé	auraient changé

6 présent du subjonctif		13 passé du subjonctif	
change	changions	aie changé	ayons changé
changes	changiez	aies changé	ayez changé
change	changent	ait changé	aient changé

7 imparfait du subjonctif		14 plus-que-parfait du subjonctif	
changeasse	changeassions	eusse changé	eussions changé
changeasses	changeassiez	eusses changé	eussiez changé
changeât	changeassent	eût changé	eussent changé

Impératif
change
changeons
changez

Common idiomatic expressions using this verb

Je vais changer de vêtements maintenant parce que je prends le train pour Paris, et là, je vais changer de train pour aller à Marseille.

changer d'avis   to change one's mind
changer de route   to take another road
un changement soudain   a sudden change
une pièce/un pneu de rechange   spare part/tire
échanger   to exchange
Plus ça change, plus c'est la même chose.
   The more things change, the more they
   remain the same.

changer de train   to change trains
changer de vêtements   to change clothes
changer de l'argent   to exchange some money
le bureau de change   money exchange desk
   (office)
Je désire changer de l'argent.   I would like to
   exchange some money.

The subject pronouns are found on page 103.   **203**

The Seven Simple Tenses		The Seven Compound Tenses	
Singular	Plural	Singular	Plural

1 présent de l'indicatif

		8 passé composé	
chante	chantons	ai chanté	avons chanté
chantes	chantez	as chanté	avez chanté
chante	chantent	a chanté	ont chanté

2 imparfait de l'indicatif

		9 plus-que-parfait de l'indicatif	
chantais	chantions	avais chanté	avions chanté
chantais	chantiez	avais chanté	aviez chanté
chantait	chantaient	avait chanté	avaient chanté

3 passé simple

		10 passé antérieur	
chantai	chantâmes	eus chanté	eûmes chanté
chantas	chantâtes	eus chanté	eûtes chanté
chanta	chantèrent	eut chanté	eurent chanté

4 futur

		11 futur antérieur	
chanterai	chanterons	aurai chanté	aurons chanté
chanteras	chanterez	auras chanté	aurez chanté
chantera	chanteront	aura chanté	auront chanté

5 conditionnel

		12 conditionnel passé	
chanterais	chanterions	aurais chanté	aurions chanté
chanterais	chanteriez	aurais chanté	auriez chanté
chanterait	chanteraient	aurait chanté	auraient chanté

6 présent du subjonctif

		13 passé du subjonctif	
chante	chantions	aie chanté	ayons chanté
chantes	chantiez	aies chanté	ayez chanté
chante	chantent	ait chanté	aient chanté

7 imparfait du subjonctif

		14 plus-que-parfait du subjonctif	
chantasse	chantassions	eusse chanté	eussions chanté
chantasses	chantassiez	eusses chanté	eussiez chanté
chantât	chantassent	eût chanté	eussent chanté

Impératif
chante
chantons
chantez

AN ESSENTIAL
55 VERB

C

Chanter is a regular **-er** verb that is used in many common expressions and situations. If you can conjugate **chanter**, you can conjugate any regular **-er** verb.

Sentences using chanter and words related to it

Madame Chanteclaire aime bien chanter en jouant du piano. Mrs. Chanteclaire likes to sing while playing the piano.

Marie donne des leçons de chant. Mary gives singing lessons.

C'est une autre chanson! That's another story!

Mais qu'est-ce que vous chantez là? What are you talking about?

Demain, je vais me lever au chant du coq pour attraper le bus. Tomorrow I'm going to get up at the crack of dawn to catch the bus.

Claire a étudié l'ancien français pour lire les chansons de geste. Claire studied Old French in order to read epic poems.

Words and expressions related to this verb

une chanson **song**

une chanson d'amour **love song**

une chanson de geste **epic poem**

chansons! **nonsense! fiddlesticks!**

Si ça vous chante . . . **If you are in the mood for it . . .**

Ça ne me chante pas. **I'm not in the mood.**

un chant **carol, chant, singing**

le chantage **blackmail**

faire chanter qqn **to blackmail someone**

un chanteur, une chanteuse **singer**

chanter ô ma belle **to cry out in pain (Antilles)**

enchanter **to enchant**

Enchanté! **Pleased to meet you!**

au chant du coq **at the crack of dawn (when the rooster crows)**

Proverbs

C'est la poule qui chante qui a fait l'oeuf. **It's the hen who sings who made (laid) the egg.**

Vous chantiez? j'en suis fort aise: Eh bien! dansez maintenant. **You were singing? I'm very delighted about it. Well! Now dance.** (La Fontaine, *La Cigale et la Fourmi*)

Don't forget to check the list of 2,600 additional verbs keyed to the 501 model verbs. It's in the Appendixes!

The subject pronouns are found on page 103.

205

charger (91)

Part. pr. chargeant **Part. passé chargé**

to burden, to
charge, to load

Regular **-er** verb endings; spelling change: retain the
ge before **a** or **o** to keep the soft **g** sound of the verb

The Seven Simple Tenses		The Seven Compound Tenses	
Singular	Plural	Singular	Plural
1 présent de l'indicatif		**8 passé composé**	
charge	chargeons	ai chargé	avons chargé
charges	chargez	as chargé	avez chargé
charge	chargent	a chargé	ont chargé
2 imparfait de l'indicatif		**9 plus-que-parfait de l'indicatif**	
chargeais	chargions	avais chargé	avions chargé
chargeais	chargiez	avais chargé	aviez chargé
chargeait	chargeaient	avait chargé	avaient chargé
3 passé simple		**10 passé antérieur**	
chargeai	chargeâmes	eus chargé	eûmes chargé
chargeas	chargeâtes	eus chargé	eûtes chargé
chargea	chargèrent	eut chargé	eurent chargé
4 futur		**11 futur antérieur**	
chargerai	chargerons	aurai chargé	aurons chargé
chargeras	chargerez	auras chargé	aurez chargé
chargera	chargeront	aura chargé	auront chargé
5 conditionnel		**12 conditionnel passé**	
chargerais	chargerions	aurais chargé	aurions chargé
chargerais	chargeriez	aurais chargé	auriez chargé
chargerait	chargeraient	aurait chargé	auraient chargé
6 présent du subjonctif		**13 passé du subjonctif**	
charge	chargions	aie chargé	ayons chargé
charges	chargiez	aies chargé	ayez chargé
charge	chargent	ait chargé	aient chargé
7 imparfait du subjonctif		**14 plus-que-parfait du subjonctif**	
chargeasse	chargeassions	eusse chargé	eussions chargé
chargeasses	chargeassiez	eusses chargé	eussiez chargé
chargeât	chargeassent	eût chargé	eussent chargé

Impératif
charge
chargeons
chargez

Common idiomatic expressions using this verb

**Je connais une dame qui charge son mari de paquets chaque fois qu'ils vont faire des
emplettes. Une fois quand je les ai vus en ville, il a chargé sa femme de malédictions.**

une charge   a load, burden
chargé d'impôts   heavily taxed
un chargé d'affaires   envoy
Je m'en charge.   I'll take care of it.
télécharger   to download (computer)

charger de malédictions   to curse
charger de louanges   to overwhelm with
   praises
un chargeur de batterie   battery charger
décharger   to unload

Grammar putting you in a tense mood? Review the definitions of basic grammatical terms with
examples on pages 35–49.

Regular **-er** verb   to hunt, to pursue, to chase, to drive out

The Seven Simple Tenses		The Seven Compound Tenses	
Singular	Plural	Singular	Plural
1 présent de l'indicatif		**8 passé composé**	
chasse	chassons	ai chassé	avons chassé
chasses	chassez	as chassé	avez chassé
chasse	chassent	a chassé	ont chassé
2 imparfait de l'indicatif		**9 plus-que-parfait de l'indicatif**	
chassais	chassions	avais chassé	avions chassé
chassais	chassiez	avais chassé	aviez chassé
chassait	chassaient	avait chassé	avaient chassé
3 passé simple		**10 passé antérieur**	
chassai	chassâmes	eus chassé	eûmes chassé
chassas	chassâtes	eus chassé	eûtes chassé
chassa	chassèrent	eut chassé	eurent chassé
4 futur		**11 futur antérieur**	
chasserai	chasserons	aurai chassé	aurons chassé
chasseras	chasserez	auras chassé	aurez chassé
chassera	chasseront	aura chassé	auront chassé
5 conditionnel		**12 conditionnel passé**	
chasserais	chasserions	aurais chassé	aurions chassé
chasserais	chasseriez	aurais chassé	auriez chassé
chasserait	chasseraient	aurait chassé	auraient chassé
6 présent du subjonctif		**13 passé du subjonctif**	
chasse	chassions	aie chassé	ayons chassé
chasses	chassiez	aies chassé	ayez chassé
chasse	chassent	ait chassé	aient chassé
7 imparfait du subjonctif		**14 plus-que-parfait du subjonctif**	
chassasse	chassassions	eusse chassé	eussions chassé
chassasses	chassassiez	eusses chassé	eussiez chassé
chassât	chassassent	eût chassé	eussent chassé

Impératif
chasse
chassons
chassez

Words and expressions related to this verb
pourchasser   to chase, pursue
un chasse-neige   snowplow
un chasse-mouches   fly swatter
tirer la chasse d'eau   to flush the toilet

Proverb:
Je chasse toujours les arcs-en-ciel.   I'm always chasing rainbows.

Pronounce out loud this tongue twister as fast as you can: **Le chasseur, sachant* chasser sans son chien, chassera.** (The hunter, knowing how to hunt without his dog, will hunt.)
*Sachant is the pres. part. of **savoir**.

The subject pronouns are found on page 103.   **207**

The Seven Simple Tenses		The Seven Compound Tenses	
Singular	Plural	Singular	Plural

1 présent de l'indicatif		8 passé composé	
cherche	cherchons	ai cherché	avons cherché
cherches	cherchez	as cherché	avez cherché
cherche	cherchent	a cherché	ont cherché

2 imparfait de l'indicatif		9 plus-que-parfait de l'indicatif	
cherchais	cherchions	avais cherché	avions cherché
cherchais	cherchiez	avais cherché	aviez cherché
cherchait	cherchaient	avait cherché	avaient cherché

3 passé simple		10 passé antérieur	
cherchai	cherchâmes	eus cherché	eûmes cherché
cherchas	cherchâtes	eus cherché	eûtes cherché
chercha	cherchèrent	eut cherché	eurent cherché

4 futur		11 futur antérieur	
chercherai	chercherons	aurai cherché	aurons cherché
chercheras	chercherez	auras cherché	aurez cherché
cherchera	chercheront	aura cherché	auront cherché

5 conditionnel		12 conditionnel passé	
chercherais	chercherions	aurais cherché	aurions cherché
chercherais	chercheriez	aurais cherché	auriez cherché
chercherait	chercheraient	aurait cherché	auraient cherché

6 présent du subjonctif		13 passé du subjonctif	
cherche	cherchions	aie cherché	ayons cherché
cherches	cherchiez	aies cherché	ayez cherché
cherche	cherchent	ait cherché	aient cherché

7 imparfait du subjonctif		14 plus-que-parfait du subjonctif	
cherchasse	cherchassions	eusse cherché	eussions cherché
cherchasses	cherchassiez	eusses cherché	eussiez cherché
cherchât	cherchassent	eût cherché	eussent cherché

Impératif
cherche
cherchons
cherchez

Sentences using this verb and words related to it

—Monsieur, monsieur, j'ai perdu mon livre de français. J'ai cherché partout et je n'arrive pas à le trouver.

—Continue à chercher parce que demain je donnerai un examen.

se chercher   to look for one another
chercheur   seeker, investigator, researcher
aller chercher   to go and get
chercher à   to attempt to, try to
aller chercher qqn ou qqch   to go get someone or something
rechercher   to investigate, to seek, to look for again

faire des travaux de recherches   to carry out research work
envoyer chercher   to send for
un moteur de recherche   search engine (Internet)
Je vais envoyer chercher le médecin.   I am going to send for the doctor.

208

Regular **-ir** verb   to cherish

The Seven Simple Tenses		The Seven Compound Tenses	
Singular	Plural	Singular	Plural
1 présent de l'indicatif		8 passé composé	
chéris	**chérissons**	**ai chéri**	**avons chéri**
chéris	**chérissez**	**as chéri**	**avez chéri**
chérit	**chérissent**	**a chéri**	**ont chéri**
2 imparfait de l'indicatif		9 plus-que-parfait de l'indicatif	
chérissais	**chérissions**	**avais chéri**	**avions chéri**
chérissais	**chérissiez**	**avais chéri**	**aviez chéri**
chérissait	**chérissaient**	**avait chéri**	**avaient chéri**
3 passé simple		10 passé antérieur	
chéris	**chérîmes**	**eus chéri**	**eûmes chéri**
chéris	**chérîtes**	**eus chéri**	**eûtes chéri**
chérit	**chérirent**	**eut chéri**	**eurent chéri**
4 futur		11 futur antérieur	
chérirai	**chérirons**	**aurai chéri**	**aurons chéri**
chériras	**chérirez**	**auras chéri**	**aurez chéri**
chérira	**chériront**	**aura chéri**	**auront chéri**
5 conditionnel		12 conditionnel passé	
chérirais	**chéririons**	**aurais chéri**	**aurions chéri**
chérirais	**chéririez**	**aurais chéri**	**auriez chéri**
chérirait	**chériraient**	**aurait chéri**	**auraient chéri**
6 présent du subjonctif		13 passé du subjonctif	
chérisse	**chérissions**	**aie chéri**	**ayons chéri**
chérisses	**chérissiez**	**aies chéri**	**ayez chéri**
chérisse	**chérissent**	**ait chéri**	**aient chéri**
7 imparfait du subjonctif		14 plus-que-parfait du subjonctif	
chérisse	**chérissions**	**eusse chéri**	**eussions chéri**
chérisses	**chérissiez**	**eusses chéri**	**eussiez chéri**
chérît	**chérissent**	**eût chéri**	**eussent chéri**

Impératif
chéris
chérissons
chérissez

Words and expressions related to this verb
cher, chère   dear; expensive
Ça coûte cher!   That costs a lot!
chéri, chérie   darling, dear
chèrement   dearly
renchérir   to go up in cost, to make a higher
  bid

acheter cher   to buy at a high price
vendre cher   to sell at a high price
Vous me le paierez cher!   You will pay dearly
  for it!
un renchérissement   increase

Don't forget to study the section on defective and impersonal verbs. It's right after this main list.

The subject pronouns are found on page 103.   **209**

to choose, to select, to pick

Regular **-ir** verb

The Seven Simple Tenses		The Seven Compound Tenses	
Singular	Plural	Singular	Plural
1 présent de l'indicatif		**8 passé composé**	
choisis	choisissons	ai choisi	avons choisi
choisis	choisissez	as choisi	avez choisi
choisit	choisissent	a choisi	ont choisi
2 imparfait de l'indicatif		**9 plus-que-parfait de l'indicatif**	
choisissais	choisissions	avais choisi	avions choisi
choisissais	choisissiez	avais choisi	aviez choisi
choisissait	choisissaient	avait choisi	avaient choisi
3 passé simple		**10 passé antérieur**	
choisis	choisîmes	eus choisi	eûmes choisi
choisis	choisîtes	eus choisi	eûtes choisi
choisit	choisirent	eut choisi	eurent choisi
4 futur		**11 futur antérieur**	
choisirai	choisirons	aurai choisi	aurons choisi
choisiras	choisirez	auras choisi	aurez choisi
choisira	choisiront	aura choisi	auront choisi
5 conditionnel		**12 conditionnel passé**	
choisirais	choisirions	aurais choisi	aurions choisi
choisirais	choisiriez	aurais choisi	auriez choisi
choisirait	choisiraient	aurait choisi	auraient choisi
6 présent du subjonctif		**13 passé du subjonctif**	
choisisse	choisissions	aie choisi	ayons choisi
choisisses	choisissiez	aies choisi	ayez choisi
choisisse	choisissent	ait choisi	aient choisi
7 imparfait du subjonctif		**14 plus-que-parfait du subjonctif**	
choisisse	choisissions	eusse choisi	eussions choisi
choisisses	choisissiez	eusses choisi	eussiez choisi
choisît	choisissent	eût choisi	eussent choisi

Impératif
choisis
choisissons
choisissez

AN ESSENTIAL
55 VERB

AN ESSENTIAL 55 VERB

Choisir

We have chosen **choisir** as a key verb because it is a regular **-ir** verb and because **choisir** is used in numerous everyday situations and idiomatic expressions.

Sentences using choisir and related words

Au restaurant français j'ai choisi la crêpe Suzette et Raymond a choisi le filet mignon. Joseph a choisi d'aller au fast-food quand il a vu les prix. At the French restaurant I chose the crêpe suzette and Raymond chose the filet mignon. Joseph chose to go to the fast food restaurant when he saw the prices.

Il n'y a pas grand choix.
There's not much choice.

Choisissez bien vos amis.
Choose your friends well.

Words and expressions related to this verb

un choix **choice**

faire un bon choix **to make a good choice**

faire un mauvais choix **to make a bad choice**

faire choix de **to make choice of**

l'embarras du choix **too much to choose from**

savoir choisir ses amis **to know how to choose one's friends**

au choix **optional, elective**

If you can conjugate **choisir** you can also conjugate the following verbs (and many others):

adoucir **to reduce, soften, mellow**

grossir **to gain weight, grow larger**

moisir **to get moldy**

radoucir **to soften**

réussir **to succeed**

Proverb

Choisissez un travail que vous aimez et vous n'aurez pas à travailler un seul jour de votre vie. **Choose a job you love and you will never have to work a day in your life. (Confucius)**

Don't forget to check the list of 2,600 additional verbs keyed to the 501 model verbs. It's in the Appendixes!

The subject pronouns are found on page 103.

211

to whisper

The Seven Simple Tenses		The Seven Compound Tenses	
Singular	Plural	Singular	Plural
1 présent de l'indicatif		8 passé composé	
chuchote	chuchotons	ai chuchoté	avons chuchoté
chuchotes	chuchotez	as chuchoté	avez chuchoté
chuchote	chuchotent	a chuchoté	ont chuchoté
2 imparfait de l'indicatif		9 plus-que-parfait de l'indicatif	
chuchotais	chuchotions	avais chuchoté	avions chuchoté
chuchotais	chuchotiez	avais chuchoté	aviez chuchoté
chuchotait	chuchotaient	avait chuchoté	avaient chuchoté
3 passé simple		10 passé antérieur	
chuchotai	chuchotâmes	eus chuchoté	eûmes chuchoté
chuchotas	chuchotâtes	eus chuchoté	eûtes chuchoté
chuchota	chuchotèrent	eut chuchoté	eurent chuchoté
4 futur		11 futur antérieur	
chuchoterai	chuchoterons	aurai chuchoté	aurons chuchoté
chuchoteras	chuchoterez	auras chuchoté	aurez chuchoté
chuchotera	chuchoteront	aura chuchoté	auront chuchoté
5 conditionnel		12 conditionnel passé	
chuchoterais	chuchoterions	aurais chuchoté	aurions chuchoté
chuchoterais	chuchoteriez	aurais chuchoté	auriez chuchoté
chuchoterait	chuchoteraient	aurait chuchoté	auraient chuchoté
6 présent du subjonctif		13 passé du subjonctif	
chuchote	chuchotions	aie chuchoté	ayons chuchoté
chuchotes	chuchotiez	aies chuchoté	ayez chuchoté
chuchote	chuchotent	ait chuchoté	aient chuchoté
7 imparfait du subjonctif		14 plus-que-parfait du subjonctif	
chuchotasse	chuchotassions	eusse chuchoté	eussions chuchoté
chuchotasses	chuchotassiez	eusses chuchoté	eussiez chuchoté
chuchotât	chuchotassent	eût chuchoté	eussent chuchoté

Impératif
chuchote
chuchotons
chuchotez

Common idiomatic expressions using this verb and words related to it
un chuchoteur, une chuchoteuse whisperer
chuchoter à l'oreille de qqn to whisper in someone's ear
souffler to prompt (in a stage whisper)
le chuchotement whispering
une chuchoterie a conversation in whispering tones so that others may not hear

Get acquainted with what preposition goes with what verb. See *Verbs with prepositions* in the Appendixes.

Irregular verb in 1s, 2s, 3s present indicative

to combat, to fight

The Seven Simple Tenses		The Seven Compound Tenses	
Singular	Plural	Singular	Plural

1 présent de l'indicatif

combats	combattons		
combats	combattez		
combat	combattent		

8 passé composé

ai combattu	avons combattu		
as combattu	avez combattu		
a combattu	ont combattu		

2 imparfait de l'indicatif

combattais	combattions
combattais	combattiez
combattait	combattaient

9 plus-que-parfait de l'indicatif

avais combattu	avions combattu
avais combattu	aviez combattu
avait combattu	avaient combattu

3 passé simple

combattis	combattîmes
combattis	combattîtes
combattit	combattirent

10 passé antérieur

eus combattu	eûmes combattu
eus combattu	eûtes combattu
eut combattu	eurent combattu

4 futur

combattrai	combattrons
combattras	combattrez
combattra	combattront

11 futur antérieur

aurai combattu	aurons combattu
auras combattu	aurez combattu
aura combattu	auront combattu

5 conditionnel

combattrais	combattrions
combattrais	combattriez
combattrait	combattraient

12 conditionnel passé

aurais combattu	aurions combattu
aurais combattu	auriez combattu
aurait combattu	auraient combattu

6 présent du subjonctif

combatte	combattions
combattes	combattiez
combatte	combattent

13 passé du subjonctif

aie combattu	ayons combattu
aies combattu	ayez combattu
ait combattu	aient combattu

7 imparfait du subjonctif

combattisse	combattissions
combattisses	combattissiez
combattît	combattissent

14 plus-que-parfait du subjonctif

eusse combattu	eussions combattu
eusses combattu	eussiez combattu
eût combattu	eussent combattu

Impératif
combats
combattons
combattez

Words and expressions related to this verb
un combat   fight, struggle
hors de combat   out of the fight
combattant, combattante   fighting
un non-combattant, une non-combattante
   noncombatant

un combat aérien   aerial combat
combatif, combative   pugnacious, aggressive

For other words and expressions related to this verb, see **abattre**, **battre**, and **se battre**.

Don't forget to study the section on defective and impersonal verbs. It's right after this main list.

to command, to order

Regular **-er** verb

The Seven Simple Tenses		The Seven Compound Tenses	
Singular	Plural	Singular	Plural
1 présent de l'indicatif		8 passé composé	
commande	commandons	ai commandé	avons commandé
commandes	commandez	as commandé	avez commandé
commande	commandent	a commandé	ont commandé
2 imparfait de l'indicatif		9 plus-que-parfait de l'indicatif	
commandais	commandions	avais commandé	avions commandé
commandais	commandiez	avais commandé	aviez commandé
commandait	commandaient	avait commandé	avaient commandé
3 passé simple		10 passé antérieur	
commandai	commandâmes	eus commandé	eûmes commandé
commandas	commandâtes	eus commandé	eûtes commandé
commanda	commandèrent	eut commandé	eurent commandé
4 futur		11 futur antérieur	
commanderai	commanderons	aurai commandé	aurons commandé
commanderas	commanderez	auras commandé	aurez commandé
commandera	commanderont	aura commandé	auront commandé
5 conditionnel		12 conditionnel passé	
commanderais	commanderions	aurais commandé	aurions commandé
commanderais	commanderiez	aurais commandé	auriez commandé
commanderait	commanderaient	aurait commandé	auraient commandé
6 présent du subjonctif		13 passé du subjonctif	
commande	commandions	aie commandé	ayons commandé
commandes	commandiez	aies commandé	ayez commandé
commande	commandent	ait commandé	aient commandé
7 imparfait du subjonctif		14 plus-que-parfait du subjonctif	
commandasse	commandassions	eusse commandé	eussions commandé
commandasses	commandassiez	eusses commandé	eussiez commandé
commandât	commandassent	eût commandé	eussent commandé

Impératif
commande
commandons
commandez

Common idiomatic expressions using this verb

   Hier soir mes amis et moi avons dîné dans un restaurant chinois. Nous avons commandé beaucoup de choses intéressantes.

un commandant   commanding officer
une commande   an order
commander à qqn de faire qqch   to order someone to do something
recommander   to recommend; **recommander à qqn de faire qqch**   to advise someone to do
   something
décommander un rendez-vous   to cancel a date, an appointment

Try the verb drills and verb tests with answers explained on pages 50–101.

Regular **-er** verb endings; spelling change:
c changes to **ç** before **a** or **o** to keep **s** sound

to begin, to start,
to commence

The Seven Simple Tenses		The Seven Compound Tenses	
Singular	Plural	Singular	Plural

1 présent de l'indicatif		8 passé composé	
commence	commençons	ai commencé	avons commencé
commences	commencez	as commencé	avez commencé
commence	commencent	a commencé	ont commencé

2 imparfait de l'indicatif		9 plus-que-parfait de l'indicatif	
commençais	commencions	avais commencé	avions commencé
commençais	commenciez	avais commencé	aviez commencé
commençait	commençaient	avait commencé	avaient commencé

3 passé simple		10 passé antérieur	
commençai	commençâmes	eus commencé	eûmes commencé
commenças	commençâtes	eus commencé	eûtes commencé
commença	commencèrent	eut commencé	eurent commencé

4 futur		11 futur antérieur	
commencerai	commencerons	aurai commencé	aurons commencé
commenceras	commencerez	auras commencé	aurez commencé
commencera	commenceront	aura commencé	auront commencé

5 conditionnel		12 conditionnel passé	
commencerais	commencerions	aurais commencé	aurions commencé
commencerais	commenceriez	aurais commencé	auriez commencé
commencerait	commenceraient	aurait commencé	auraient commencé

6 présent du subjonctif		13 passé du subjonctif	
commence	commencions	aie commencé	ayons commencé
commences	commenciez	aies commencé	ayez commencé
commence	commencent	ait commencé	aient commencé

7 imparfait du subjonctif		14 plus-que-parfait du subjonctif	
commençasse	commençassions	eusse commencé	eussions commencé
commençasses	commençassiez	eusses commencé	eussiez commencé
commençât	commençassent	eût commencé	eussent commencé

Impératif
commence
commençons
commencez

AN ESSENTIAL
55 VERB

Get acquainted with what preposition goes with what verb. See *Verbs with prepositions*
in the Appendixes.

Commencer is an essential verb for beginning students because of its spelling change and because it is used in a number of everyday situations.

Sentences using commencer and related words

Dépêche-toi! Le film commence à midi! Hurry up! The movie starts at noon!

Nous commençons à nous inquiéter parce que Marie-Ève n'est pas encore revenue. We are beginning to worry because Marie-Eve hasn't come back yet.

Commençons au commencement. Let's begin at the beginning.

—Alexandre, as-tu commencé tes devoirs pour la classe de français?
—Non, maman, pas encore. Je vais faire une promenade maintenant.
—Tu ne vas pas faire une promenade parce qu'il commence à pleuvoir. Commence à faire tes devoirs tout de suite!

—Alexander, have you begun your homework for French class?
—No, Mother, not yet. I'm going to take a walk now.
—You are not going to take a walk because it is beginning to rain. Start to do your homework immediately!

> **Words and expressions related to this verb**
> _____
>
> commencer à + inf. **to begin + inf.**
>
> le commencement **the beginning**
>
> au commencement **in the beginning**
>
> du commencement à la fin **from beginning to end**
>
> pour commencer **to begin with**
>
> commencer par **to begin by**
>
> recommencer à **to begin again + inf.**
>
> un recommencement **a new start**

The **c** before the **-er** ending in **commencer** takes a cedilla before the letters **a** and **o**. This is done to retain the sound of **s** in **-cer**. Otherwise, **c** before **a** would sound like **k** as in **camion** (truck) and **coûter** (to cost). If you can conjugate **commencer** you can also conjugate:

annoncer **to announce**	financer **to finance**
balancer **to balance**	lancer **to throw**
cadencer **to give rhythm, cadence**	prononcer **to pronounce**
concurrencer **to compete**	recommencer **to begin again**
dénoncer **to denounce**	

The Seven Simple Tenses		The Seven Compound Tenses	
Singular	Plural	Singular	Plural

C

1   présent de l'indicatif

		8 passé composé	
commets	commettons	ai commis	avons commis
commets	commettez	as commis	avez commis
commet	commettent	a commis	ont commis

2   imparfait de l'indicatif

		9 plus-que-parfait de l'indicatif	
commettais	commettions	avais commis	avions commis
commettais	commettiez	avais commis	aviez commis
commettait	commettaient	avait commis	avaient commis

3   passé simple

		10 passé antérieur	
commis	commîmes	eus commis	eûmes commis
commis	commîtes	eus commis	eûtes commis
commit	commirent	eut commis	eurent commis

4   futur

		11 futur antérieur	
commettrai	commettrons	aurai commis	aurons commis
commettras	commettrez	auras commis	aurez commis
commettra	commettront	aura commis	auront commis

5   conditionnel

		12 conditionnel passé	
commettrais	commettrions	aurais commis	aurions commis
commettrais	commettriez	aurais commis	auriez commis
commettrait	commettraient	aurait commis	auraient commis

6   présent du subjonctif

		13 passé du subjonctif	
commette	commettions	aie commis	ayons commis
commettes	commettiez	aies commis	ayez commis
commette	commettent	ait commis	aient commis

7   imparfait du subjonctif

		14 plus-que-parfait du subjonctif	
commisse	commissions	eusse commis	eussions commis
commisses	commissiez	eusses commis	eussiez commis
commît	commissent	eût commis	eussent commis

Impératif
commets
commettons
commettez

Words and expressions related to this verb

commettre un péché   to commit a sin
être commis à   to be committed to
commis aux soins de   to be placed under the care of
se commettre   to commit oneself

commettre qqch à qqn   to entrust something to someone
commettre qqn à qqn   to entrust someone to someone, to place someone under someone's care

See also **mettre, permettre, promettre, remettre, soumettre,** and **transmettre.**

Soak up some verbs used in weather expressions. There's a list in the Appendixes!

The subject pronouns are found on page 103.

to compare

The Seven Simple Tenses		The Seven Compound Tenses	
Singular	Plural	Singular	Plural

1 présent de l'indicatif		8 passé composé	
compare	comparons	ai comparé	avons comparé
compares	comparez	as comparé	avez comparé
compare	comparent	a comparé	ont comparé

2 imparfait de l'indicatif		9 plus-que-parfait de l'indicatif	
comparais	comparions	avais comparé	avions comparé
comparais	compariez	avais comparé	aviez comparé
comparait	comparaient	avait comparé	avaient comparé

3 passé simple		10 passé antérieur	
comparai	comparâmes	eus comparé	eûmes comparé
comparas	comparâtes	eus comparé	eûtes comparé
compara	comparèrent	eut comparé	eurent comparé

4 futur		11 futur antérieur	
comparerai	comparerons	aurai comparé	aurons comparé
compareras	comparerez	auras comparé	aurez comparé
comparera	compareront	aura comparé	auront comparé

5 conditionnel		12 conditionnel passé	
comparerais	comparerions	aurais comparé	aurions comparé
comparerais	comparereiz	aurais comparé	auriez comparé
comparerait	compareraient	aurait comparé	auraient comparé

6 présent du subjonctif		13 passé du subjonctif	
compare	comparions	aie comparé	ayons comparé
compares	compariez	aies comparé	ayez comparé
compare	comparent	ait comparé	aient comparé

7 imparfait du subjonctif		14 plus-que-parfait du subjonctif	
comparasse	comparassions	eusse comparé	eussions comparé
comparasses	comparassiez	eusses comparé	eussiez comparé
comparât	comparassent	eût comparé	eussent comparé

Impératif
compare
comparons
comparez

Words and expressions related to this verb

comparer à to compare to (when some equality exists between the two compared)

comparer avec to compare with (when one is considered to be of a higher degree than the rest)

sans comparaison without comparison

une comparaison comparison

comparativement comparatively

comparatif, comparative comparative

par comparaison avec comparatively to

comparable à comparable to

en comparaison de in comparison with

For an explanation of meanings and uses of French and English verb tenses and moods, see pages 10–21.

Irregular verb

to understand, to include

The Seven Simple Tenses		The Seven Compound Tenses	
Singular	Plural	Singular	Plural

1 présent de l'indicatif

comprends	comprenons		
comprends	comprenez		
comprend	comprennent		

8 passé composé

ai compris	avons compris		
as compris	avez compris		
a compris	ont compris		

2 imparfait de l'indicatif

comprenais	comprenions
comprenais	compreniez
comprenait	comprenaient

9 plus-que-parfait de l'indicatif

avais compris	avions compris
avais compris	aviez compris
avait compris	avaient compris

3 passé simple

compris	comprîmes
compris	comprîtes
comprit	comprirent

10 passé antérieur

eus compris	eûmes compris
eus compris	eûtes compris
eut compris	eurent compris

4 futur

comprendrai	comprendrons
comprendras	comprendrez
comprendra	comprendront

11 futur antérieur

aurai compris	aurons compris
auras compris	aurez compris
aura compris	auront compris

5 conditionnel

comprendrais	comprendrions
comprendrais	comprendriez
comprendrait	comprendraient

12 conditionnel passé

aurais compris	aurions compris
aurais compris	auriez compris
aurait compris	auraient compris

6 présent du subjonctif

comprenne	comprenions
comprennes	compreniez
comprenne	comprennent

13 passé du subjonctif

aie compris	ayons compris
aies compris	ayez compris
ait compris	aient compris

7 imparfait du subjonctif

comprisse	comprissions
comprisses	comprissiez
comprît	comprissent

14 plus-que-parfait du subjonctif

eusse compris	eussions compris
eusses compris	eussiez compris
eût compris	eussent compris

Impératif
comprends
comprenons
comprenez

Sentences using this verb and expressions related to it

Je ne comprends jamais le prof de biologie. Je n'ai pas compris la leçon d'hier, je ne comprends pas la leçon d'aujourd'hui, et je ne comprendrai jamais rien.

faire comprendre à qqn que . . .   to make it clear to someone that . . .
la compréhension   comprehension, understanding
Ça se comprend.   Of course; That is understood.
y compris   included, including
y compris la taxe   tax included
service compris, y compris le service   service included (no tip necessary)
Est-ce que le service est compris?   Is the service (tip) included?
compréhensif, compréhensive *adj.*   understanding

See also **apprendre, entreprendre, se méprendre, prendre, reprendre,** and **surprendre.**

to count, to intend, to expect to

The Seven Simple Tenses		The Seven Compound Tenses	
Singular	Plural	Singular	Plural
1 présent de l'indicatif		8 passé composé	
compte	comptons	ai compté	avons compté
comptes	comptez	as compté	avez compté
compte	comptent	a compté	ont compté
2 imparfait de l'indicatif		9 plus-que-parfait de l'indicatif	
comptais	comptions	avais compté	avions compté
comptais	comptiez	avais compté	aviez compté
comptait	comptaient	avait compté	avaient compté
3 passé simple		10 passé antérieur	
comptai	comptâmes	eus compté	eûmes compté
comptas	comptâtes	eus compté	eûtes compté
compta	comptèrent	eut compté	eurent compté
4 futur		11 futur antérieur	
compterai	compterons	aurai compté	aurons compté
compteras	compterez	auras compté	aurez compté
comptera	compteront	aura compté	auront compté
5 conditionnel		12 conditionnel passé	
compterais	compterions	aurais compté	aurions compté
compterais	compteriez	aurais compté	auriez compté
compterait	compteraient	aurait compté	auraient compté
6 présent du subjonctif		13 passé du subjonctif	
compte	comptions	aie compté	ayons compté
comptes	comptiez	aies compté	ayez compté
compte	comptent	ait compté	aient compté
7 imparfait du subjonctif		14 plus-que-parfait du subjonctif	
comptasse	comptassions	eusse compté	eussions compté
comptasses	comptassiez	eusses compté	eussiez compté
comptât	comptassent	eût compté	eussent compté

Impératif
compte
comptons
comptez

Common idiomatic expressions using this verb

Je compte aller en France l'été prochain avec ma femme pour voir nos amis français.

la comptabilité bookkeeping, accounting
comptable accountable
le comptage counting
payer comptant to pay cash
compter faire qqch to expect to do something
compter sur to count (rely) on; **Puis-je y compter?** Can I depend on it?

escompter to discount; **un escompte** a discount
donner sans compter to give generously
sans compter . . . to say nothing of . . .
le comptoir counter (in a store)

to conceive

Irregular verb with spelling change:
c changes to **ç** before **o** or **u** to keep **s** sound

The Seven Simple Tenses		The Seven Compound Tenses	
Singular	Plural	Singular	Plural

C

1 présent de l'indicatif		8 passé composé	
conçois	concevons	ai conçu	avons conçu
conçois	concevez	as conçu	avez conçu
conçoit	conçoivent	a conçu	ont conçu

2 imparfait de l'indicatif		9 plus-que-parfait de l'indicatif	
concevais	concevions	avais conçu	avions conçu
concevais	conceviez	avais conçu	aviez conçu
concevait	concevaient	avait conçu	avaient conçu

3 passé simple		10 passé antérieur	
conçus	conçûmes	eus conçu	eûmes conçu
conçus	conçûtes	eus conçu	eûtes conçu
conçut	conçurent	eut conçu	eurent conçu

4 futur		11 futur antérieur	
concevrai	concevrons	aurai conçu	aurons conçu
concevras	concevrez	auras conçu	aurez conçu
concevra	concevront	aura conçu	auront conçu

5 conditionnel		12 conditionnel passé	
concevrais	concevrions	aurais conçu	aurions conçu
concevrais	concevriez	aurais conçu	auriez conçu
concevrait	concevraient	aurait conçu	auraient conçu

6 présent du subjonctif		13 passé du subjonctif	
conçoive	concevions	aie conçu	ayons conçu
conçoives	conceviez	aies conçu	ayez conçu
conçoive	conçoivent	ait conçu	aient conçu

7 imparfait du subjonctif		14 plus-que-parfait du subjonctif	
conçusse	conçussions	eusse conçu	eussions conçu
conçusses	conçussiez	eusses conçu	eussiez conçu
conçût	conçussent	eût conçu	eussent conçu

Impératif
conçois
concevons
concevez

Words and expressions related to this verb
concevoir des idées   to form ideas
concevable   conceivable
une conception   concept, idea
un concepteur, une conceptrice   designer

ainsi conçu   written as follows
Je ne peux même pas concevoir . . .   I just
can't even imagine . . .

Don't forget to use the English-French verb index. It's in the Appendixes.

The subject pronouns are found on page 103.
                                                                                    221

Part. pr. **concluant**   Part. passé **conclu**

to conclude

Irregular verb

The Seven Simple Tenses		The Seven Compound Tenses	
Singular	Plural	Singular	Plural

1 présent de l'indicatif

conclus	concluons	
conclus	concluez	
conclut	concluent	

8 passé composé

ai conclu	avons conclu
as conclu	avez conclu
a conclu	ont conclu

2 imparfait de l'indicatif

concluais	concluions
concluais	concluiez
concluait	concluaient

9 plus-que-parfait de l'indicatif

avais conclu	avions conclu
avais conclu	aviez conclu
avait conclu	avaient conclu

3 passé simple

conclus	conclûmes
conclus	conclûtes
conclut	conclurent

10 passé antérieur

eus conclu	eûmes conclu
eus conclu	eûtes conclu
eut conclu	eurent conclu

4 futur

conclurai	conclurons
concluras	conclurez
conclura	concluront

11 futur antérieur

aurai conclu	aurons conclu
auras conclu	aurez conclu
aura conclu	auront conclu

5 conditionnel

conclurais	conclurions
conclurais	concluriez
conclurait	concluraient

12 conditionnel passé

aurais conclu	aurions conclu
aurais conclu	auriez conclu
aurait conclu	auraient conclu

6 présent du subjonctif

conclue	concluions
conclues	concluiez
conclue	concluent

13 passé du subjonctif

aie conclu	ayons conclu
aies conclu	ayez conclu
ait conclu	aient conclu

7 imparfait du subjonctif

conclusse	conclussions
conclusses	conclussiez
conclût	conclussent

14 plus-que-parfait du subjonctif

eusse conclu	eussions conclu
eusses conclu	eussiez conclu
eût conclu	eussent conclu

Impératif
conclus
concluons
concluez

Words and expressions related to this verb

la conclusion   conclusion
en conclusion   in conclusion
exclure   to exclude
exclu, exclue   excluded
un film en exclusivité   a first-run motion
  picture
See also inclure.

inclure   to enclose, to include (part. passé:
  inclus, incluse); une photo ci-incluse
  a photo enclosed herewith; jusqu'à la
  page 100 incluse   up to and including
  page 100

Soak up some verbs used in weather expressions. There's a list in the Appendixes.

Irregular verb   to lead, to drive, to conduct, to

C

The Seven Simple Tenses		The Seven Compound Tenses	
Singular	Plural	Singular	Plural
1 présent de l'indicatif		**8 passé composé**	
conduis	conduisons	ai conduit	avons conduit
conduis	conduisez	as conduit	avez conduit
conduit	conduisent	a conduit	ont conduit
2 imparfait de l'indicatif		**9 plus-que-parfait de l'indicatif**	
conduisais	conduisions	avais conduit	avions conduit
conduisais	conduisiez	avais conduit	aviez conduit
conduisait	conduisaient	avait conduit	avaient conduit
3 passé simple		**10 passé antérieur**	
conduisis	conduisîmes	eus conduit	eûmes conduit
conduisis	conduisîtes	eus conduit	eûtes conduit
conduisit	conduisirent	eut conduit	eurent conduit
4 futur		**11 futur antérieur**	
conduirai	conduirons	aurai conduit	aurons conduit
conduiras	conduirez	auras conduit	aurez conduit
conduira	conduiront	aura conduit	auront conduit
5 conditionnel		**12 conditionnel passé**	
conduirais	conduirions	aurais conduit	aurions conduit
conduirais	conduiriez	aurais conduit	auriez conduit
conduirait	conduiraient	aurait conduit	auraient conduit
6 présent du subjonctif		**13 passé du subjonctif**	
conduise	conduisions	aie conduit	ayons conduit
conduises	conduisiez	aies conduit	ayez conduit
conduise	conduisent	ait conduit	aient conduit
7 imparfait du subjonctif		**14 plus-que-parfait du subjonctif**	
conduisisse	conduisissions	eusse conduit	eussions conduit
conduisisses	conduisissiez	eusses conduit	eussiez conduit
conduisît	conduisissent	eût conduit	eussent conduit

Impératif
conduis
conduisons
conduisez

Sentences using this verb and words related to it

—Savez-vous conduire?

—Oui, je sais conduire. Je conduis une voiture, je dirige un orchestre, et hier j'ai conduit quelqu'un à la gare. Attendez, je vais vous conduire à la porte.

—Merci, vous êtes très aimable.

un conducteur, une conductrice driver	**conduire une voiture** to drive a car
la conduite conduct, behavior	**se conduire** to conduct (behave) oneself
induire to induce	**un permis de conduire** driver's license
induire en to lead into	**enduire** to coat, spread

See also **déduire, introduire, produire, réduire, reproduire, séduire,** and **traduire.**

connaître (106)
to know, to manage

acquainted with, to
ntance of

Irregular verb

Tenses		The Seven Compound Tenses	
	Plural	Singular	Plural

catif

1 présent de l'indicatif

connais	connaissons
connais	connaissez
connaît	connaissent

8 passé composé

ai connu	avons connu
as connu	avez connu
a connu	ont connu

2 imparfait de l'indicatif

connaissais	connaissions
connaissais	connaissiez
connaissait	connaissaient

9 plus-que-parfait de l'indicatif

avais connu	avions connu
avais connu	aviez connu
avait connu	avaient connu

3 passé simple

connus	connûmes
connus	connûtes
connut	connurent

10 passé antérieur

eus connu	eûmes connu
eus connu	eûtes connu
eut connu	eurent connu

4 futur

connaîtrai	connaîtrons
connaîtras	connaîtrez
connaîtra	connaîtront

11 futur antérieur

aurai connu	aurons connu
auras connu	aurez connu
aura connu	auront connu

5 conditionnel

connaîtrais	connaîtrions
connaîtrais	connaîtriez
connaîtrait	connaîtraient

12 conditionnel passé

aurais connu	aurions connu
aurais connu	auriez connu
aurait connu	auraient connu

6 présent du subjonctif

connaisse	connaissions
connaisses	connaissiez
connaisse	connaissent

13 passé du subjonctif

aie connu	ayons connu
aies connu	ayez connu
ait connu	aient connu

7 imparfait du subjonctif

connusse	connussions
connusses	connussiez
connût	connussent

14 plus-que-parfait du subjonctif

eusse connu	eussions connu
eusses connu	eussiez connu
eût connu	eussent connu

Impératif
connais
connaissons
connaissez

AN ESSENTIAL
55 VERB

224

Connaître

Connaître is an important verb to know. It is used in a number of expressions and in many everyday situations.

Sample sentences using connaître

—Connaissez-vous quelqu'un qui puisse m'aider?
—Je suis touriste et je ne connais pas cette ville.
—Non, je ne connais personne. Je suis touriste aussi.
—Voulez-vous aller prendre un café? Nous pouvons faire connaissance.
—Pas du tout! Je ne vous connais pas!

—Do you know someone who can help me?
—I am a tourist and I don't know this city.
—No, I don't know anyone. I'm a tourist too.
—Would you like to go have a coffee? We could get acquainted.
—Not at all! I don't know you!

À ma connaissance, il est impossible de dépasser la vitesse de la lumière. As far as I know, it is impossible to go beyond the speed of light.

Michel et Dorothea sont de vrais connaisseurs en vin. Michael and Dorothy are real wine connoisseurs.

Il a connu beaucoup de difficultés pendant son adolescence. He experienced many difficulties (problems) during his adolescence.

Ce film a connu un grand succès en Europe. This movie was very successful (well received) in Europe.

Ça me connaît! I know that well!/I know about that! (Note: This is a rare construction.)

Mon père a connu ma mère à New York. My father met my mother in New York.

Words and expressions related to this verb

la connaissance **knowledge, understanding, acquaintance**

à ma connaissance **as far as I know**

connaisseur, connaisseuse *adj.* **expert**

un connaisseur, une connaisseuse **connoisseur**

se connaître **to know each other, to know oneself**

faire connaissance **to get acquainted**

avoir des connaissances en **to be knowledgeable in**

The subject pronouns are found on page 103.

to conquer

Irregular verb

The Seven Simple Tenses		The Seven Compound Tenses	
Singular	Plural	Singular	Plural
1 présent de l'indicatif		8 passé composé	
conquiers	conquérons	ai conquis	avons conquis
conquiers	conquérez	as conquis	avez conquis
conquiert	conquièrent	a conquis	ont conquis
2 imparfait de l'indicatif		9 plus-que-parfait de l'indicatif	
conquérais	conquérions	avais conquis	avions conquis
conquérais	conquériez	avais conquis	aviez conquis
conquérait	conquéraient	avait conquis	avaient conquis
3 passé simple		10 passé antérieur	
conquis	conquîmes	eus conquis	eûmes conquis
conquis	conquîtes	eus conquis	eûtes conquis
conquit	conquirent	eut conquis	eurent conquis
4 futur		11 futur antérieur	
conquerrai	conquerrons	aurai conquis	aurons conquis
conquerras	conquerrez	auras conquis	aurez conquis
conquerra	conquerront	aura conquis	auront conquis
5 conditionnel		12 conditionnel passé	
conquerrais	conquerrions	aurais conquis	aurions conquis
conquerrais	conquerriez	aurais conquis	auriez conquis
conquerrait	conquerraient	aurait conquis	auraient conquis
6 présent du subjonctif		13 passé du subjonctif	
conquière	conquérions	aie conquis	ayons conquis
conquières	conquériez	aies conquis	ayez conquis
conquière	conquièrent	ait conquis	aient conquis
7 imparfait du subjonctif		14 plus-que-parfait du subjonctif	
conquisse	conquissions	eusse conquis	eussions conquis
conquisses	conquissiez	eusses conquis	eussiez conquis
conquît	conquissent	eût conquis	eussent conquis

Impératif
conquiers
conquérons
conquérez

Words and expressions related to this verb
conquérir l'affection de qqn to win someone's affection
conquérir une femme to win over a woman; **conquérir un homme** to win over a man
la conquête conquest; **la conquête du pouvoir** conquest of power
avoir un air conquérant to seem pretentious
Guillaume le Conquérant William the Conqueror

Conquer your fear of the Subjunctive. See pages 26–31.

Regular **-er** verb   to advise, to counsel, to **recommend**

The Seven Simple Tenses		The Seven Compound Tenses	
Singular	Plural	Singular	Plural

1   présent de l'indicatif

conseille	**conseillons**	
conseilles	**conseillez**	
conseille	**conseillent**	

8   passé composé

ai conseillé	**avons conseillé**
as conseillé	**avez conseillé**
a conseillé	**ont conseillé**

2   imparfait de l'indicatif

conseillais	**conseillions**
conseillais	**conseilliez**
conseillait	**conseillaient**

9   plus-que-parfait de l'indicatif

avais conseillé	**avions conseillé**
avais conseillé	**aviez conseillé**
avait conseillé	**avaient conseillé**

3   passé simple

conseillai	**conseillâmes**
conseillas	**conseillâtes**
conseilla	**conseillèrent**

10   passé antérieur

eus conseillé	**eûmes conseillé**
eus conseillé	**eûtes conseillé**
eut conseillé	**eurent conseillé**

4   futur

conseillerai	**conseillerons**
conseilleras	**conseillerez**
conseillera	**conseilleront**

11   futur antérieur

aurai conseillé	**aurons conseillé**
auras conseillé	**aurez conseillé**
aura conseillé	**auront conseillé**

5   conditionnel

conseillerais	**conseillerions**
conseillerais	**conseilleriez**
conseillerait	**conseilleraient**

12   conditionnel passé

aurais conseillé	**aurions conseillé**
aurais conseillé	**auriez conseillé**
aurait conseillé	**auraient conseillé**

6   présent du subjonctif

conseille	**conseillions**
conseilles	**conseilliez**
conseille	**conseillent**

13   passé du subjonctif

aie conseillé	**ayons conseillé**
aies conseillé	**ayez conseillé**
ait conseillé	**aient conseillé**

7   imparfait du subjonctif

conseillasse	**conseillassions**
conseillasses	**conseillassiez**
conseillât	**conseillassent**

14   plus-que-parfait du subjonctif

eusse conseillé	**eussions conseillé**
eusses conseillé	**eussiez conseillé**
eût conseillé	**eussent conseillé**

Impératif
conseille
conseillons
conseillez

Words and expressions related to this verb
conseiller qqch à qqn   to recommend something to someone
conseiller à qqn de faire qqch   to advise someone to do something
un conseiller (un conseilleur), une conseillère (une conseilleuse)   counselor, adviser
un conseil   counsel, advice; **sur le conseil de**   on the advice of
déconseiller   to advise, warn against; **déconseiller qqch à qqn**   to advise someone against
    something

We recommend that you try the verb drills and tests with answers explained on pages 50–101.

The subject pronouns are found on page 103.   **227**

Part. pr consentant **Part. passé** consenti

Irregular verb

The Seven Simple Tenses		The Seven Compound Tenses	
Singular	Plural	Singular	Plural
1 présent de l'indicatif		8 passé composé	
consens	consentons	ai consenti	avons consenti
consens	consentez	as consenti	avez consenti
consent	consentent	a consenti	ont consenti
2 imparfait de l'indicatif		9 plus-que-parfait de l'indicatif	
consentais	consentions	avais consenti	avions consenti
consentais	consentiez	avais consenti	aviez consenti
consentait	consentaient	avait consenti	avaient consenti
3 passé simple		10 passé antérieur	
consentis	consentîmes	eus consenti	eûmes consenti
consentis	consentîtes	eus consenti	eûtes consenti
consentit	consentirent	eut consenti	eurent consenti
4 futur		11 futur antérieur	
consentirai	consentirons	aurai consenti	aurons consenti
consentiras	consentirez	auras consenti	aurez consenti
consentira	consentiront	aura consenti	auront consenti
5 conditionnel		12 conditionnel passé	
consentirais	consentirions	aurais consenti	aurions consenti
consentirais	consentiriez	aurais consenti	auriez consenti
consentirait	consentiraient	aurait consenti	auraient consenti
6 présent du subjonctif		13 passé du subjonctif	
consente	consentions	aie consenti	ayons consenti
consentes	consentiez	aies consenti	ayez consenti
consente	consentent	ait consenti	aient consenti
7 imparfait du subjonctif		14 plus-que-parfait du subjonctif	
consentisse	consentissions	eusse consenti	eussions consenti
consentisses	consentissiez	eusses consenti	eussiez consenti
consentît	consentissent	eût consenti	eussent consenti

Impératif
consens
consentons
consentez

Words and expressions related to this verb

consentir à faire qqch   to agree to do
   something
le consentement   consent, approval
consentant, consentante   agreeable, willing

consentir à qqch   to consent to something
consentir au mariage   to consent to marriage
donner son consentement   to give one's
   consent, agreement

See also sentir.

Grammar putting you in a tense mood? Review the definitions of basic grammatical terms on pages 35–49.

Irregular verb

to construct, to build

The Seven Simple Tenses		The Seven Compound Tenses	
Singular	Plural	Singular	Plural
1 présent de l'indicatif		8 passé composé	
construis	**construisons**	**ai construit**	**avons construit**
construis	**construisez**	**as construit**	**avez construit**
construit	**construisent**	**a construit**	**ont construit**
2 imparfait de l'indicatif		9 plus-que-parfait de l'indicatif	
construisais	**construisions**	**avais construit**	**avions construit**
construisais	**construisiez**	**avais construit**	**aviez construit**
construisait	**construisaient**	**avait construit**	**avaient construit**
3 passé simple		10 passé antérieur	
construisis	**construisîmes**	**eus construit**	**eûmes construit**
construisis	**construisîtes**	**eus construit**	**eûtes construit**
construisit	**construisirent**	**eut construit**	**eurent construit**
4 futur		11 futur antérieur	
construirai	**construirons**	**aurai construit**	**aurons construit**
construiras	**construirez**	**auras construit**	**aurez construit**
construira	**construiront**	**aura construit**	**auront construit**
5 conditionnel		12 conditionnel passé	
construirais	**construirions**	**aurais construit**	**aurions construit**
construirais	**construiriez**	**aurais construit**	**auriez construit**
construirait	**construiraient**	**aurait construit**	**auraient construit**
6 présent du subjonctif		13 passé du subjonctif	
construise	**construisions**	**aie construit**	**ayons construit**
construises	**construisiez**	**aies construit**	**ayez construit**
construise	**construisent**	**ait construit**	**aient construit**
7 imparfait du subjonctif		14 plus-que-parfait du subjonctif	
construisisse	**construisissions**	**eusse construit**	**eussions construit**
construisisses	**construisissiez**	**eusses construit**	**eussiez construit**
construisît	**construisissent**	**eût construit**	**eussent construit**

Impératif
construis
construisons
construisez

Sentences using this verb and words related to it

—Je vois que vous êtes en train de construire quelque chose. Qu'est-ce que vous construisez?

—Je construis une tour comme la Tour Eiffel. Aimez-vous ce bateau que j'ai construit?

un constructeur   a manufacturer, builder, constructor
une construction   construction, building
reconstruire   to reconstruct, to rebuild; **en construction**   under construction

For an explanation of meanings and uses of French and English verb tenses and moods, see pages 10–21.

The subject pronouns are found on page 103.
     229

to contain   Irregular verb

The Seven Simple Tenses		The Seven Compound Tenses	
Singular	Plural	Singular	Plural
1 présent de l'indicatif		8 passé composé	
contiens	contenons	ai contenu	avons contenu
contiens	contenez	as contenu	avez contenu
contient	contiennent	a contenu	ont contenu
2 imparfait de l'indicatif		9 plus-que-parfait de l'indicatif	
contenais	contenions	avais contenu	avions contenu
contenais	conteniez	avais contenu	aviez contenu
contenait	contenaient	avait contenu	avaient contenu
3 passé simple		10 passé antérieur	
contins	contînmes	eus contenu	eûmes contenu
contins	contîntes	eus contenu	eûtes contenu
contint	continrent	eut contenu	eurent contenu
4 futur		11 futur antérieur	
contiendrai	contiendrons	aurai contenu	aurons contenu
contiendras	contiendrez	auras contenu	aurez contenu
contiendra	contiendront	aura contenu	auront contenu
5 conditionnel		12 conditionnel passé	
contiendrais	contiendrions	aurais contenu	aurions contenu
contiendrais	contiendriez	aurais contenu	auriez contenu
contiendrait	contiendraient	aurait contenu	auraient contenu
6 présent du subjonctif		13 passé du subjonctif	
contienne	contenions	aie contenu	ayons contenu
contiennes	conteniez	aies contenu	ayez contenu
contienne	contiennent	ait contenu	aient contenu
7 imparfait du subjonctif		14 plus-que-parfait du subjonctif	
continsse	continssions	eusse contenu	eussions contenu
continsses	continssiez	eusses contenu	eussiez contenu
contînt	continssent	eût contenu	eussent contenu

Impératif
contiens
contenons
contenez

Common idiomatic expressions using this verb and words related to it

contenir ses émotions   to contain (dominate)
   one's emotions

être content (contente)   to be content,
   satisfied

être content (contente) des autres   to be
   content (satisfied) with others

se contenir   to contain oneself, to dominate
   (control) oneself

un contenant   container

le contenu   contents

être content (contente) de soi   to be self-satisfied

avoir l'air content   to seem pleased

See also **obtenir, retenir,** and **tenir.**

Don't forget to check the list of 2,600 additional verbs keyed to the 501 model verbs. It's in the Appendixes!

Regular **-er** verb   to relate, to narrate

The Seven Simple Tenses		The Seven Compound Tenses	
Singular	Plural	Singular	Plural
1 présent de l'indicatif		**8 passé composé**	
conte	contons	ai conté	avons conté
contes	contez	as conté	avez conté
conte	content	a conté	ont conté
2 imparfait de l'indicatif		**9 plus-que-parfait de l'indicatif**	
contais	contions	avais conté	avions conté
contais	contiez	avais conté	aviez conté
contait	contaient	avait conté	avaient conté
3 passé simple		**10 passé antérieur**	
contai	contâmes	eus conté	eûmes conté
contas	contâtes	eus conté	eûtes conté
conta	contèrent	eut conté	eurent conté
4 futur		**11 futur antérieur**	
conterai	conterons	aurai conté	aurons conté
conteras	conterez	auras conté	aurez conté
contera	conteront	aura conté	auront conté
5 conditionnel		**12 conditionnel passé**	
conterais	conterions	aurais conté	aurions conté
conterais	conteriez	aurais conté	auriez conté
conterait	conteraient	aurait conté	auraient conté
6 présent du subjonctif		**13 passé du subjonctif**	
conte	contions	aie conté	ayons conté
contes	contiez	aies conté	ayez conté
conte	content	ait conté	aient conté
7 imparfait du subjonctif		**14 plus-que-parfait du subjonctif**	
contasse	contassions	eusse conté	eussions conté
contasses	contassiez	eusses conté	eussiez conté
contât	contassent	eût conté	eussent conté

Impératif
conte
contons
contez

C

Sentences using this verb and words related to it

Notre professeur de français nous conte toujours des histoires intéressantes. Son conte favori est *Un coeur simple* **de Flaubert.**

un conte   a story, tale
un conte de fées   fairy tale
un conte à dormir debout   cock-and-bull
   story

un conteur, une conteuse   writer of short
   stories
Contez-moi vos malheurs.   Tell me about
   your troubles.

See also **raconter.**

Use the guide to French pronunciation. It's in the Appendixes.

The subject pronouns are found on page 103.   **231**

to continue

The Seven Simple Tenses		The Seven Compound Tenses	
Singular	Plural	Singular	Plural
1 présent de l'indicatif		8 passé composé	
continue	continuons	ai continué	avons continué
continues	continuez	as continué	avez continué
continue	continuent	a continué	ont continué
2 imparfait de l'indicatif		9 plus-que-parfait de l'indicatif	
continuais	continuions	avais continué	avions continué
continuais	continuiez	avais continué	aviez continué
continuait	continuaient	avait continué	avaient continué
3 passé simple		10 passé antérieur	
continuai	continuâmes	eus continué	eûmes continué
continuas	continuâtes	eus continué	eûtes continué
continua	continuèrent	eut continué	eurent continué
4 futur		11 futur antérieur	
continuerai	continuerons	aurai continué	aurons continué
continueras	continuerez	auras continué	aurez continué
continuera	continueront	aura continué	auront continué
5 conditionnel		12 conditionnel passé	
continuerais	continuerions	aurais continué	aurions continué
continuerais	continueriez	aurais continué	auriez continué
continuerait	continueraient	aurait continué	auraient continué
6 présent du subjonctif		13 passé du subjonctif	
continue	continuions	aie continué	ayons continué
continues	continuiez	aies continué	ayez continué
continue	continuent	ait continué	aient continué
7 imparfait du subjonctif		14 plus-que-parfait du subjonctif	
continuasse	continuassions	eusse continué	eussions continué
continuasses	continuassiez	eusses continué	eussiez continué
continuât	continuassent	eût continué	eussent continué

Impératif
continue
continuons
continuez

Sentences using this verb and words related to it
—Allez-vous continuer à étudier le français l'année prochaine?
—Certainement. Je compte étudier cette belle langue continuellement.

la continuation   continuation
continuel, continuelle   continual
continuellement   continually
continuer à + inf.   to continue + inf.

continuer de + inf.   to continue (persist) in;
Cet ivrogne continue de boire.   This
drunkard persists in drinking (habit).

Get acquainted with what preposition goes with what verb. See *Verbs with prepositions* in the Appendixes.

Irregular verb   to constrain, to restrain, to compel

The Seven Simple Tenses		The Seven Compound Tenses	
Singular	Plural	Singular	Plural
1 présent de l'indicatif		8 passé composé	
contrains	**contraignons**	**ai contraint**	**avons contraint**
contrains	**contraignez**	**as contraint**	**avez contraint**
contraint	**contraignent**	**a contraint**	**ont contraint**
2 imparfait de l'indicatif		9 plus-que-parfait de l'indicatif	
contraignais	**contraignions**	**avais contraint**	**avions contraint**
contraignais	**contraigniez**	**avais contraint**	**aviez contraint**
contraignait	**contraignaient**	**avait contraint**	**avaient contraint**
3 passé simple		10 passé antérieur	
contraignis	**contraignîmes**	**eus contraint**	**eûmes contraint**
contraignis	**contraignîtes**	**eus contraint**	**eûtes contraint**
contraignit	**contraignirent**	**eut contraint**	**eurent contraint**
4 futur		11 futur antérieur	
contraindrai	**contraindrons**	**aurai contraint**	**aurons contraint**
contraindras	**contraindrez**	**auras contraint**	**aurez contraint**
contraindra	**contraindront**	**aura contraint**	**auront contraint**
5 conditionnel		12 conditionnel passé	
contraindrais	**contraindrions**	**aurais contraint**	**aurions contraint**
contraindrais	**contraindriez**	**aurais contraint**	**auriez contraint**
contraindrait	**contraindraient**	**aurait contraint**	**auraient contraint**
6 présent du subjonctif		13 passé du subjonctif	
contraigne	**contraignions**	**aie contraint**	**ayons contraint**
contraignes	**contraigniez**	**aies contraint**	**ayez contraint**
contraigne	**contraignent**	**ait contraint**	**aient contraint**
7 imparfait du subjonctif		14 plus-que-parfait du subjonctif	
contraignisse	**contraignissions**	**eusse contraint**	**eussions contraint**
contraignisses	**contraignissiez**	**eusses contraint**	**eussiez contraint**
contraignît	**contraignissent**	**eût contraint**	**eussent contraint**

C

Impératif
contrains
contraignons
contraignez

Words and expressions related to this verb

se contraindre à faire qqch   to constrain oneself from doing something
avoir l'air contraint   to have a constrained expression (on one's face)
parler sans contrainte   to speak freely
contraint, contrainte   constrained, forced

être contraint (contrainte) à faire qqch   to be constrained to doing something
la contrainte   constraint
tenir qqn dans la contrainte   to hold someone in constraint

Check out the principal parts of some important French verbs on page 7.

The subject pronouns are found on page 103.
                                                                                 233

The Seven Simple Tenses		The Seven Compound Tenses	
Singular	Plural	Singular	Plural

1 présent de l'indicatif		8 passé composé	
contredis	contredisons	ai contredit	avons contredit
contredis	contredisez	as contredit	avez contredit
contredit	contredisent	a contredit	ont contredit

2 imparfait de l'indicatif		9 plus-que-parfait de l'indicatif	
contredisais	contredisions	avais contredit	avions contredit
contredisais	contredisiez	avais contredit	aviez contredit
contredisait	contredisaient	avait contredit	avaient contredit

3 passé simple		10 passé antérieur	
contredis	contredîmes	eus contredit	eûmes contredit
contredis	contredîtes	eus contredit	eûtes contredit
contredit	contredirent	eut contredit	eurent contredit

4 futur		11 futur antérieur	
contredirai	contredirons	aurai contredit	aurons contredit
contrediras	contredirez	auras contredit	aurez contredit
contredira	contrediront	aura contredit	auront contredit

5 conditionnel		12 conditionnel passé	
contredirais	contredirions	aurais contredit	aurions contredit
contredirais	contrediriez	aurais contredit	auriez contredit
contredirait	contrediraient	aurait contredit	auraient contredit

6 présent du subjonctif		13 passé du subjonctif	
contredise	contredisions	aie contredit	ayons contredit
contredises	contredisiez	aies contredit	ayez contredit
contredise	contredisent	ait contredit	aient contredit

7 imparfait du subjonctif		14 plus-que-parfait du subjonctif	
contredisse	contredissions	eusse contredit	eussions contredit
contredisses	contredissiez	eusses contredit	eussiez contredit
contredît	contredissent	eût contredit	eussent contredit

Impératif
contredis
contredisons
contredisez

Words and expressions related to this verb

se **contredire**   to contradict oneself, to contradict each other (one another)
un **contredit**   contradiction; sans **contredit** unquestionably
une **contradiction**   contradiction

contradictoire   contradictory
contradicteur, contradictrice   contradictor
contradictoirement   contradictorily
en **contradiction avec**   inconsistent with

See also **dire, interdire, maudire, médire,** and **prédire.**

It's important that you be familiar with the Subjunctive. See pages 26–31.

The Seven Simple Tenses		The Seven Compound Tenses	
Singular	Plural	Singular	Plural
1 présent de l'indicatif		**8 passé composé**	
convaincs	**convainquons**	**ai convaincu**	**avons convaincu**
convaincs	**convainquez**	**as convaincu**	**avez convaincu**
convainc	**convainquent**	**a convaincu**	**ont convaincu**
2 imparfait de l'indicatif		**9 plus-que-parfait de l'indicatif**	
convainquais	**convainquions**	**avais convaincu**	**avions convaincu**
convainquais	**convainquiez**	**avais convaincu**	**aviez convaincu**
convainquait	**convainquaient**	**avait convaincu**	**avaient convaincu**
3 passé simple		**10 passé antérieur**	
convainquis	**convainquîmes**	**eus convaincu**	**eûmes convaincu**
convainquis	**convainquîtes**	**eus convaincu**	**eûtes convaincu**
convainquit	**convainquirent**	**eut convaincu**	**eurent convaincu**
4 futur		**11 futur antérieur**	
convaincrai	**convaincrons**	**aurai convaincu**	**aurons convaincu**
convaincras	**convaincrez**	**auras convaincu**	**aurez convaincu**
convaincra	**convaincront**	**aura convaincu**	**auront convaincu**
5 conditionnel		**12 conditionnel passé**	
convaincrais	**convaincrions**	**aurais convaincu**	**aurions convaincu**
convaincrais	**convaincriez**	**aurais convaincu**	**auriez convaincu**
convaincrait	**convaincraient**	**aurait convaincu**	**auraient convaincu**
6 présent du subjonctif		**13 passé du subjonctif**	
convainque	**convainquions**	**aie convaincu**	**ayons convaincu**
convainques	**convainquiez**	**aies convaincu**	**ayez convaincu**
convainque	**convainquent**	**ait convaincu**	**aient convaincu**
7 imparfait du subjonctif		**14 plus-que-parfait du subjonctif**	
convainquisse	**convainquissions**	**eusse convaincu**	**eussions convaincu**
convainquisses	**convainquissiez**	**eusses convaincu**	**eussiez convaincu**
convainquît	**convainquissent**	**eût convaincu**	**eussent convaincu**

Impératif
convaincs
convainquons
convainquez

Words and expressions related to this verb

convaincre qqn de qqch   to convince
  (persuade) someone of something
se laisser convaincre   to allow oneself to be
  persuaded

d'un ton convaincu   in a convincing tone
convaincant, convaincante   convincing
se convaincre   to convince oneself, to realize

See also **vaincre**.

How are you doing? Find out with the verb drills and tests with answers explained on pages 50–101.

convenir (118)

Part. pr. convenant   **Part. passé** convenu

to suit, to be suitable, to be appropriate,
to agree, to acknowledge

Irregular verb

The Seven Simple Tenses		The Seven Compound Tenses	
Singular	Plural	Singular	Plural
1 présent de l'indicatif		8 passé composé	
conviens	convenons	ai convenu	avons convenu
conviens	convenez	as convenu	avez convenu
convient	conviennent	a convenu	ont convenu
2 imparfait de l'indicatif		9 plus-que-parfait de l'indicatif	
convenais	convenions	avais convenu	avions convenu
convenais	conveniez	avais convenu	aviez convenu
convenait	convenaient	avait convenu	avaient convenu
3 passé simple		10 passé antérieur	
convins	convînmes	eus convenu	eûmes convenu
convins	convîntes	eus convenu	eûtes convenu
convint	convinrent	eut convenu	eurent convenu
4 futur		11 futur antérieur	
conviendrai	conviendrons	aurai convenu	aurons convenu
conviendras	conviendrez	auras convenu	aurez convenu
conviendra	conviendront	aura convenu	auront convenu
5 conditionnel		12 conditionnel passé	
conviendrais	conviendrions	aurais convenu	aurions convenu
conviendrais	conviendriez	aurais convenu	auriez convenu
conviendrait	conviendraient	aurait convenu	auraient convenu
6 présent du subjonctif		13 passé du subjonctif	
convienne	convenions	aie convenu	ayons convenu
conviennes	conveniez	aies convenu	ayez convenu
convienne	conviennent	ait convenu	aient convenu
7 imparfait du subjonctif		14 plus-que-parfait du subjonctif	
convinsse	convinssions	eusse convenu	eussions convenu
convinsses	convinssiez	eusses convenu	eussiez convenu
convînt	convinssent	eût convenu	eussent convenu

Impératif
conviens
convenons
convenez

Common idiomatic expressions using this verb

convenir à   to please, to suit (conjugated with avoir); **Cela lui a convenu.**   That suited him.

convenir de qqch   to agree on something (conjugated with **être**); **Ils sont convenus d'aller au cinéma.**   They agreed to go to the movies.

J'en conviens.   I agree to it.

Ce n'est pas convenable.   That's not appropriate.

Faites ce qui convient.   Do what is suitable.

convenir de faire qqch   to agree to do something; **Mon père et moi, nous avons convenu de venir chez vous à 8 h. du soir.**   My father and I agreed to come to your place at 8 in the evening.

Il faut convenir que vous avez raison.   Admittedly, you are right (One must admit that you are right).

Cela ne me convient pas.   That does not suit me.

See also **devenir, prévenir, revenir, se souvenir,** and **venir.**

to correct

Regular **-er** verb endings; spelling change: retain the
ge before **a** or **o** to keep the soft **g** sound of the verb

The Seven Simple Tenses		The Seven Compound Tenses	
Singular	Plural	Singular	Plural

1 présent de l'indicatif		8 passé composé	
corrige	corrigeons	ai corrigé	avons corrigé
corriges	corrigez	as corrigé	avez corrigé
corrige	corrigent	a corrigé	ont corrigé

2 imparfait de l'indicatif		9 plus-que-parfait de l'indicatif	
corrigeais	corrigions	avais corrigé	avions corrigé
corrigeais	corrigiez	avais corrigé	aviez corrigé
corrigeait	corrigeaient	avait corrigé	avaient corrigé

3 passé simple		10 passé antérieur	
corrigeai	corrigeâmes	eus corrigé	eûmes corrigé
corrigeas	corrigeâtes	eus corrigé	eûtes corrigé
corrigea	corrigèrent	eut corrigé	eurent corrigé

4 futur		11 futur antérieur	
corrigerai	corrigerons	aurai corrigé	aurons corrigé
corrigeras	corrigerez	auras corrigé	aurez corrigé
corrigera	corrigeront	aura corrigé	auront corrigé

5 conditionnel		12 conditionnel passé	
corrigerais	corrigerions	aurais corrigé	aurions corrigé
corrigerais	corrigeriez	aurais corrigé	auriez corrigé
corrigerait	corrigeraient	aurait corrigé	auraient corrigé

6 présent du subjonctif		13 passé du subjonctif	
corrige	corrigions	aie corrigé	ayons corrigé
corriges	corrigiez	aies corrigé	ayez corrigé
corrige	corrigent	ait corrigé	aient corrigé

7 imparfait du subjonctif		14 plus-que-parfait du subjonctif	
corrigeasse	corrigeassions	eusse corrigé	eussions corrigé
corrigeasses	corrigeassiez	eusses corrigé	eussiez corrigé
corrigeât	corrigeassent	eût corrigé	eussent corrigé

Impératif
corrige
corrigeons
corrigez

Sentences using this verb and words related to it

Dans la classe de français nous corrigeons toujours nos devoirs en classe. Le (La) prof de français écrit les corrections au tableau.

une correction   correction; **la correction**
  accuracy, correctness; **recorriger**   to correct
  again
corriger qqn de   to correct someone of
se corriger de   to correct one's ways

corrigible   corrigible; **incorrigible**   incorrigible
incorrectement   inaccurately, incorrectly
la correction automatique   automatic
  correction (comp.)
un correcteur, une correctrice   proofreader

The subject pronouns are found on page 103.

to corrupt

Regular **-re** verb endings; spelling change:
3rd person sing. of Tense No. 1 adds **t**

The Seven Simple Tenses		The Seven Compound Tenses	
Singular	Plural	Singular	Plural

1   présent de l'indicatif

corromps	**corrompons**	
corromps	**corrompez**	
corrompt	**corrompent**	

8   passé composé

ai corrompu	**avons corrompu**
as corrompu	**avez corrompu**
a corrompu	**ont corrompu**

2   imparfait de l'indicatif

corrompais	**corrompions**
corrompais	**corrompiez**
corrompait	**corrompaient**

9   plus-que-parfait de l'indicatif

avais corrompu	**avions corrompu**
avais corrompu	**aviez corrompu**
avait corrompu	**avaient corrompu**

3   passé simple

corrompis	**corrompîmes**
corrompis	**corrompîtes**
corrompit	**corrompirent**

10   passé antérieur

eus corrompu	**eûmes corrompu**
eus corrompu	**eûtes corrompu**
eut corrompu	**eurent corrompu**

4   futur

corromprai	**corromprons**
corrompras	**corromprez**
corrompra	**corrompront**

11   futur antérieur

aurai corrompu	**aurons corrompu**
auras corrompu	**aurez corrompu**
aura corrompu	**auront corrompu**

5   conditionnel

corromprais	**corromprions**
corromprais	**corrompriez**
corromprait	**corrompraient**

12   conditionnel passé

aurais corrompu	**aurions corrompu**
aurais corrompu	**auriez corrompu**
aurait corrompu	**auraient corrompu**

6   présent du subjonctif

corrompe	**corrompions**
corrompes	**corrompiez**
corrompe	**corrompent**

13   passé du subjonctif

aie corrompu	**ayons corrompu**
aies corrompu	**ayez corrompu**
ait corrompu	**aient corrompu**

7   imparfait du subjonctif

corrompisse	**corrompissions**
corrompisses	**corrompissiez**
corrompît	**corrompissent**

14   plus-que-parfait du subjonctif

eusse corrompu	**eussions corrompu**
eusses corrompu	**eussiez corrompu**
eût corrompu	**eussent corrompu**

Impératif
corromps
corrompons
corrompez

Sentences using this verb and words related to it

corrompre qqch   to corrupt something;
   Je connais un élève qui corrompt la
   prononciation de la langue française.
   I know a student who corrupts the
   pronunciation of the French language.
corruptible   corruptible
se laisser corrompre   to allow oneself to be
   corrupted

corrompre qqn   to corrupt someone; **Les**
   spectacles ignobles à la télévision
   corrompent la jeunesse de ce pays.   The
   disgraceful shows on television corrupt the
   youth of this country.
la corruption   corruption
un corrupteur, une corruptrice   corrupter

See also **interrompre** and **rompre**.

Can't recognize an irregular verb form? Check out the index of common irregular French verb
forms, in the Appendixes.

Regular **-er** verb   to put to bed, to lay, to flatten

The Seven Simple Tenses		The Seven Compound Tenses	
Singular	Plural	Singular	Plural
1 présent de l'indicatif		8 passé composé	
couche	couchons	ai couché	avons couché
couches	couchez	as couché	avez couché
couche	couchent	a couché	ont couché
2 imparfait de l'indicatif		9 plus-que-parfait de l'indicatif	
couchais	couchions	avais couché	avions couché
couchais	couchiez	avais couché	aviez couché
couchait	couchaient	avait couché	avaient couché
3 passé simple		10 passé antérieur	
couchai	couchâmes	eus couché	eûmes couché
couchas	couchâtes	eus couché	eûtes couché
coucha	couchèrent	eut couché	eurent couché
4 futur		11 futur antérieur	
coucherai	coucherons	aurai couché	aurons couché
coucheras	coucherez	auras couché	aurez couché
couchera	coucheront	aura couché	auront couché
5 conditionnel		12 conditionnel passé	
coucherais	coucherions	aurais couché	aurions couché
coucherais	coucheriez	aurais couché	auriez couché
coucherait	coucheraient	aurait couché	auraient couché
6 présent du subjonctif		13 passé du subjonctif	
couche	couchions	aie couché	ayons couché
couches	couchiez	aies couché	ayez couché
couche	couchent	ait couché	aient couché
7 imparfait du subjonctif		14 plus-que-parfait du subjonctif	
couchasse	couchassions	eusse couché	eussions couché
couchasses	couchassiez	eusses couché	eussiez couché
couchât	couchassent	eût couché	eussent couché

Impératif
couche
couchons
couchez

Words and expressions related to this verb
C'est l'heure du coucher.   It's time for bed.
le coucher et la nourriture   bed and board
au coucher du soleil   at sunset
découcher   to sleep somewhere other than in one's own bed
coucher à l'hôtel   to sleep in a hotel

accoucher de   to give birth to a child; **Elle a accouché d'une fille.**   She has given birth to a girl.
recoucher   to put back to bed
Ils couchent ensemble.   They sleep together.

See also **se coucher.**

Can't find the verb you're looking for? Check the back pages of this book for a list of over 2,600 additional verbs!

The subject pronouns are found on page 103.
                    239

se coucher (122)

Part. pr. se couchant **Part. passé** couché(e)(s)

to go to bed, to lie down

Reflexive regular -er verb

The Seven Simple Tenses		The Seven Compound Tenses	
Singular	Plural	Singular	Plural

1 présent de l'indicatif		8 passé composé	
me couche	nous couchons	me suis couché(e)	nous sommes couché(e)s
te couches	vous couchez	t'es couché(e)	vous êtes couché(e)(s)
se couche	se couchent	s'est couché(e)	se sont couché(e)s

2 imparfait de l'indicatif		9 plus-que-parfait de l'indicatif	
me couchais	nous couchions	m'étais couché(e)	nous étions couché(e)s
te couchais	vous couchiez	t'étais couché(e)	vous étiez couché(e)(s)
se couchait	se couchaient	s'était couché(e)	s'étaient couché(e)s

3 passé simple		10 passé antérieur	
me couchai	nous couchâmes	me fus couché(e)	nous fûmes couché(e)s
te couchas	vous couchâtes	te fus couché(e)	vous fûtes couché(e)(s)
se coucha	se couchèrent	se fut couché(e)	se furent couché(e)s

4 futur		11 futur antérieur	
me coucherai	nous coucherons	me serai couché(e)	nous serons couché(e)s
te coucheras	vous coucherez	te seras couché(e)	vous serez couché(e)(s)
se couchera	se coucheront	se sera couché(e)	se seront couché(e)s

5 conditionnel		12 conditionnel passé	
me coucherais	nous coucherions	me serais couché(e)	nous serions couché(e)s
te coucherais	vous coucheriez	te serais couché(e)	vous seriez couché(e)(s)
se coucherait	se coucheraient	se serait couché(e)	se seraient couché(e)s

6 présent du subjonctif		13 passé du subjonctif	
me couche	nous couchions	me sois couché(e)	nous soyons couché(e)s
te couches	vous couchiez	te sois couché(e)	vous soyez couché(e)(s)
se couche	se couchent	se soit couché(e)	se soient couché(e)s

7 imparfait du subjonctif		14 plus-que-parfait du subjonctif	
me couchasse	nous couchassions	me fusse couché(e)	nous fussions couché(e)s
te couchasses	vous couchassiez	te fusses couché(e)	vous fussiez couché(e)(s)
se couchât	se couchassent	se fût couché(e)	se fussent couché(e)s

Impératif
couche-toi; ne te couche pas
couchons-nous; ne nous couchons pas
couchez-vous; ne vous couchez pas

Sentences using this verb and words related to it
—Couche-toi, Hélène! Il est minuit. Hier soir tu t'es couchée tard.
—Donne-moi ma poupée pour coucher ensemble.

le coucher du soleil   sunset
une couche   a layer
une couchette   bunk, cot
Le soleil se couche.   The sun is setting.
se recoucher   to go back to bed

se coucher tôt   to go to bed early
Comme on fait son lit on se couche!   You've made your bed; now lie in it!
un sac de couchage   sleeping bag
un couche-tard   night owl

See also coucher.

Irregular verb

to sew, to stitch

The Seven Simple Tenses		The Seven Compound Tenses	
Singular	Plural	Singular	Plural
1 présent de l'indicatif		8 passé composé	
couds	cousons	ai cousu	avons cousu
couds	cousez	as cousu	avez cousu
coud	cousent	a cousu	ont cousu
2 imparfait de l'indicatif		9 plus-que-parfait de l'indicatif	
cousais	cousions	avais cousu	avions cousu
cousais	cousiez	avais cousu	aviez cousu
cousait	cousaient	avait cousu	avaient cousu
3 passé simple		10 passé antérieur	
cousis	cousîmes	eus cousu	eûmes cousu
cousis	cousîtes	eus cousu	eûtes cousu
cousit	cousirent	eut cousu	eurent cousu
4 futur		11 futur antérieur	
coudrai	coudrons	aurai cousu	aurons cousu
coudras	coudrez	auras cousu	aurez cousu
coudra	coudront	aura cousu	auront cousu
5 conditionnel		12 conditionnel passé	
coudrais	coudrions	aurais cousu	aurions cousu
coudrais	coudriez	aurais cousu	auriez cousu
coudrait	coudraient	aurait cousu	auraient cousu
6 présent du subjonctif		13 passé du subjonctif	
couse	cousions	aie cousu	ayons cousu
couses	cousiez	aies cousu	ayez cousu
couse	cousent	ait cousu	aient cousu
7 imparfait du subjonctif		14 plus-que-parfait du subjonctif	
cousisse	cousissions	eusse cousu	eussions cousu
cousisses	cousissiez	eusses cousu	eussiez cousu
cousît	cousissent	eût cousu	eussent cousu

Impératif
couds
cousons
cousez

Words and expressions related to this verb
recoudre   to sew again, to sew up
la couture   sewing; dressmaking
la couture à la machine   machine sewing
découdre   to unstitch, to rip up some sewing
une machine à coudre   sewing machine
un couturier, une couturière   fashion designer

la haute couture   high fashion
décousu, décousue   unstitched, unsewn; incoherent   **Mon professeur d'algèbre explique les leçons d'une manière décousue.**

Don't forget to study the section on defective and impersonal verbs. It's right after this main list.

The subject pronouns are found on page 103.

Regular **-er** verb

The Seven Simple Tenses		The Seven Compound Tenses	
Singular	Plural	Singular	Plural
1 présent de l'indicatif		**8 passé composé**	
coupe	coupons	ai coupé	avons coupé
coupes	coupez	as coupé	avez coupé
coupe	coupent	a coupé	ont coupé
2 imparfait de l'indicatif		**9 plus-que-parfait de l'indicatif**	
coupais	coupions	avais coupé	avions coupé
coupais	coupiez	avais coupé	aviez coupé
coupait	coupaient	avait coupé	avaient coupé
3 passé simple		**10 passé antérieur**	
coupai	coupâmes	eus coupé	eûmes coupé
coupas	coupâtes	eus coupé	eûtes coupé
coupa	coupèrent	eut coupé	eurent coupé
4 futur		**11 futur antérieur**	
couperai	couperons	aurai coupé	aurons coupé
couperas	couperez	auras coupé	aurez coupé
coupera	couperont	aura coupé	auront coupé
5 conditionnel		**12 conditionnel passé**	
couperais	couperions	aurais coupé	aurions coupé
couperais	couperiez	aurais coupé	auriez coupé
couperait	couperaient	aurait coupé	auraient coupé
6 présent du subjonctif		**13 passé du subjonctif**	
coupe	coupions	aie coupé	ayons coupé
coupes	coupiez	aies coupé	ayez coupé
coupe	coupent	ait coupé	aient coupé
7 imparfait du subjonctif		**14 plus-que-parfait du subjonctif**	
coupasse	coupassions	eusse coupé	eussions coupé
coupasses	coupassiez	eusses coupé	eussiez coupé
coupât	coupassent	eût coupé	eussent coupé

Impératif
coupe
coupons
coupez

Common idiomatic expressions using this verb
   Ce morceau de pain est trop grand. Je vais le couper en deux.

un coupon   coupon
une coupure   cut, gash, crack
couper les cheveux en quatre   to split hairs
se faire couper les cheveux   to have one's hair cut
Aïe! Je me suis coupé le doigt!   Ouch! I cut my finger!

découper   to cut out
entrecouper   to interrupt
couper la fièvre   to reduce the fever
une coupe (de cheveux)   haircut
une coupe croisée   crosscut

How are you doing? Find out with the verb drills and tests with answers explained on pages 50–101.

Irregular verb

The Seven Simple Tenses		The Seven Compound Tenses

Singular	Plural	Singular	Plural
1 présent de l'indicatif		**8 passé composé**	
cours	courons	ai couru	avons couru
cours	courez	as couru	avez couru
court	courent	a couru	ont couru
2 imparfait de l'indicatif		**9 plus-que-parfait de l'indicatif**	
courais	courions	avais couru	avions couru
courais	couriez	avais couru	aviez couru
courait	couraient	avait couru	avaient couru
3 passé simple		**10 passé antérieur**	
courus	courûmes	eus couru	eûmes couru
courus	courûtes	eus couru	eûtes couru
courut	coururent	eut couru	eurent couru
4 futur		**11 futur antérieur**	
courrai	courrons	aurai couru	aurons couru
courras	courrez	auras couru	aurez couru
courra	courront	aura couru	auront couru
5 conditionnel		**12 conditionnel passé**	
courrais	courrions	aurais couru	aurions couru
courrais	courriez	aurais couru	auriez couru
courrait	courraient	aurait couru	auraient couru
6 présent du subjonctif		**13 passé du subjonctif**	
coure	courions	aie couru	ayons couru
coures	couriez	aies couru	ayez couru
coure	courent	ait couru	aient couru
7 imparfait du subjonctif		**14 plus-que-parfait du subjonctif**	
courusse	courussions	eusse couru	eussions couru
courusses	courussiez	eusses couru	eussiez couru
courût	courussent	eût couru	eussent couru

Impératif
cours
courons
courez

AN ESSENTIAL
55 VERB

Courir is an important verb for a beginning student because, even though it is considered to be an irregular verb, there are several verbs that are conjugated like it.

Sentences using courir

Les enfants sont toujours prêts à courir.
  Children are always ready to run.

Quand on est jeune, on court sans se fatiguer.
  When you're young (one is young), you run
  (one runs) without getting tired.

Michel a couru de la maison jusqu'à l'école.
  Michael ran from home to school.

Si tu cours dans la maison tu cours le risque de
  te faire mal. If you run in the house you run
  the risk of hurting yourself.

Rien ne sert de courir; il faut partir à point.
  (La Fontaine, *Le Lièvre et la Tortue*) It's no use
  running; you have to leave at the right moment.
  (La Fontaine, *The Tortoise and the Hare*)

Le facteur est arrivé en courant pour nous livrer
  notre courrier, mais le courrier électronique
  est toujours plus rapide. The mail carrier
  arrived in a hurry to deliver our mail to us, but
  e-mail is still faster.

If you can conjugate **courir** you can also
conjugate these verbs:

accourir **to come running**

concourir **to compete**

discourir **to discourse, talk at length**

encourir **to incur**

parcourir **to go through, to travel through,
  to cover (distance), to skim (reading)**

recourir **to run again**

secourir **to help**

Words and expressions related to this verb

un coureur, une coureuse **runner**

faire courir un bruit **to spread a
  rumor**

courir une course **to run a race**

courir le monde **to roam all over the
  world**

recourir à qqn **to turn to someone
  (for help)**

recourir à qqch **to resort to something**

accourir vers **to come running
  toward**

courir les rues **to run about the
  streets**

par le temps qui court **these days,
  nowadays**

faire les courses **to do the shopping**

un cheval de course **racehorse**

le courrier **mail, messenger, courier**

le courriel, le courrier électronique
  e-mail, electronic mail

courir le risque, courir un risque **to
  run the risk, to run a risk, to risk**

Cela/Ça court les rues. **That's
  common/dull.**

Cela/Ça ne court pas les rues. **That's
  unusual/uncommon.**

244

Irregular verb

C

The Seven Simple Tenses		The Seven Compound Tenses	
Singular	Plural	Singular	Plural
1 présent de l'indicatif		8 passé composé	
couvre	couvrons	ai couvert	avons couvert
couvres	couvrez	as couvert	avez couvert
couvre	couvrent	a couvert	ont couvert
2 imparfait de l'indicatif		9 plus-que-parfait de l'indicatif	
couvrais	couvrions	avais couvert	avions couvert
couvrais	couvriez	avais couvert	aviez couvert
couvrait	couvraient	avait couvert	avaient couvert
3 passé simple		10 passé antérieur	
couvris	couvrîmes	eus couvert	eûmes couvert
couvris	couvrîtes	eus couvert	eûtes couvert
couvrit	couvrirent	eut couvert	eurent couvert
4 futur		11 futur antérieur	
couvrirai	couvrirons	aurai couvert	aurons couvert
couvriras	couvrirez	auras couvert	aurez couvert
couvrira	couvriront	aura couvert	auront couvert
5 conditionnel		12 conditionnel passé	
couvrirais	couvririons	aurais couvert	aurions couvert
couvrirais	couvririez	aurais couvert	auriez couvert
couvrirait	couvriraient	aurait couvert	auraient couvert
6 présent du subjonctif		13 passé du subjonctif	
couvre	couvrions	aie couvert	ayons couvert
couvres	couvriez	aies couvert	ayez couvert
couvre	couvrent	ait couvert	aient couvert
7 imparfait du subjonctif		14 plus-que-parfait du subjonctif	
couvrisse	couvrissions	eusse couvert	eussions couvert
couvrisses	couvrissiez	eusses couvert	eussiez couvert
couvrît	couvrissent	eût couvert	eussent couvert

Impératif
couvre
couvrons
couvrez

AN ESSENTIAL
55 VERB

Couvrir

Couvrir is an important verb for you to study because, even though it is considered to be irregular, there are many verbs that are conjugated in the same way. Pay special attention to the past participle, which ends in -ert.

Sentences using couvrir **and related words**

Le temps se couvre aujourd'hui. It's getting overcast today.

Le ciel est couvert aujourd'hui. The sky is overcast today.

Avant de quitter la maison, Madame Champlain a couvert le lit d'un couvre-lit. Before leaving the house, Mrs. Champlain covered the bed with a bedspread.

Dans ce cours nous couvrirons l'histoire du monde, de l'an mil jusqu'à présent. In this course we will cover the history of the world, from the year one thousand to the present.

Couvre-toi. Il pleut aujourd'hui. Put on your hat. It's raining today.

À cause des émeutes la police a imposé un couvre-feu. Because of the riots the police imposed a curfew.

J'ai couvert la marmite pour laisser le ragoût mijoter. I covered the cooking pot to let the stew simmer.

N'oublie pas de mettre le couvert. Don't forget to set the table.

Words and expressions related to this verb

le couvre-feu **curfew**

un couvre-lit **bedspread**

une couverture **blanket**

un couvert **place setting (spoon, knife, fork, etc.)**

acheter des couverts **to buy cutlery**

se couvrir **to cover oneself, to put on one's hat**

If you can conjugate couvrir you can also conjugate these verbs:

découvrir **to discover, to disclose, to uncover**

entrouvrir **to open halfway**

ouvrir **to open**

recouvrir **to cover, to cover again**

rouvrir **to reopen, to open again**

Irregular verb

to fear, to be afraid

C

The Seven Simple Tenses		The Seven Compound Tenses	
Singular	Plural	Singular	Plural
1 présent de l'indicatif		8 passé composé	
crains	**craignons**	**ai craint**	**avons craint**
crains	**craignez**	**as craint**	**avez craint**
craint	**craignent**	**a craint**	**ont craint**
2 imparfait de l'indicatif		9 plus-que-parfait de l'indicatif	
craignais	**craignions**	**avais craint**	**avions craint**
craignais	**craigniez**	**avais craint**	**aviez craint**
craignait	**craignaient**	**avait craint**	**avaient craint**
3 passé simple		10 passé antérieur	
craignis	**craignîmes**	**eus craint**	**eûmes craint**
craignis	**craignîtes**	**eus craint**	**eûtes craint**
craignit	**craignirent**	**eut craint**	**eurent craint**
4 futur		11 futur antérieur	
craindrai	**craindrons**	**aurai craint**	**aurons craint**
craindras	**craindrez**	**auras craint**	**aurez craint**
craindra	**craindront**	**aura craint**	**auront craint**
5 conditionnel		12 conditionnel passé	
craindrais	**craindrions**	**aurais craint**	**aurions craint**
craindrais	**craindriez**	**aurais craint**	**auriez craint**
craindrait	**craindraient**	**aurait craint**	**auraient craint**
6 présent du subjonctif		13 passé du subjonctif	
craigne	**craignions**	**aie craint**	**ayons craint**
craignes	**craigniez**	**aies craint**	**ayez craint**
craigne	**craignent**	**ait craint**	**aient craint**
7 imparfait du subjonctif		14 plus-que-parfait du subjonctif	
craignisse	**craignissions**	**eusse craint**	**eussions craint**
craignisses	**craignissiez**	**eusses craint**	**eussiez craint**
craignît	**craignissent**	**eût craint**	**eussent craint**

Impératif
crains
craignons
craignez

Sentences using this verb and words related to it

Le petit garçon **craint** de traverser le parc pendant la nuit. Il a raison parce que c'est dangereux. Il a des **craintes**.

une crainte	fear, dread	de crainte que + subj.	for fear that, for fear of
craindre pour sa vie	to be in fear of one's life	Kevin a mis ses lunettes de soleil, de crainte	
sans crainte	fearless	qu'on ne le reconnaisse. Kevin put on his	
craintif, craintive	fearful	sunglasses, for fear that someone might	
craintivement	fearfully	recognize him.	
avec crainte	fearfully		

Use the guide to French pronunciation. It's in the Appendixes.

créer (128)	Part. pr. **créant**	Part. passé **créé**

to create

The Seven Simple Tenses		The Seven Compound Tenses	
Singular	Plural	Singular	Plural

1 présent de l'indicatif

		8 passé composé	
crée	créons	ai créé	avons créé
crées	créez	as créé	avez créé
crée	créent	a créé	ont créé

2 imparfait de l'indicatif / **9 plus-que-parfait de l'indicatif**

créais	créions	avais créé	avions créé
créais	créiez	avais créé	aviez créé
créait	créaient	avait créé	avaient créé

3 passé simple / **10 passé antérieur**

créai	créâmes	eus créé	eûmes créé
créas	créâtes	eus créé	eûtes créé
créa	créèrent	eut créé	eurent créé

4 futur / **11 futur antérieur**

créerai	créerons	aurai créé	aurons créé
créeras	créerez	auras créé	aurez créé
créera	créeront	aura créé	auront créé

5 conditionnel / **12 conditionnel passé**

créerais	créerions	aurais créé	aurions créé
créerais	créeriez	aurais créé	auriez créé
créerait	créeraient	aurait créé	auraient créé

6 présent du subjonctif / **13 passé du subjonctif**

crée	créions	aie créé	ayons créé
crées	créiez	aies créé	ayez créé
crée	créent	ait créé	aient créé

7 imparfait du subjonctif / **14 plus-que-parfait du subjonctif**

créasse	créassions	eusse créé	eussions créé
créasses	créassiez	eusses créé	eussiez créé
créât	créassent	eût créé	eussent créé

Impératif
crée
créons
créez

Sentences using this verb and words related to it

Madame Imbert, professeur de mathématiques, est une drôle de créature. Tout ce qu'elle fait manque d'originalité. Quelle misérable créature!

drôle de créature funny, queer person
la création creation; **depuis la création du monde** since the creation of the world
la créativité creativity; **la récréation** recreation

une créature creature
recréer to create again; **récréer** to enliven
un créateur, une créatrice creator

Don't forget to use the English-French verb index. It's in the Appendixes.

Regular **-er** verb   to shout, to cry out

The Seven Simple Tenses		The Seven Compound Tenses	
Singular	Plural	Singular	Plural
1 présent de l'indicatif		**8 passé composé**	
crie	**crions**	**ai crié**	**avons crié**
cries	**criez**	**as crié**	**avez crié**
crie	**crient**	**a crié**	**ont crié**
2 imparfait de l'indicatif		**9 plus-que-parfait de l'indicatif**	
criais	**criions**	**avais crié**	**avions crié**
criais	**criiez**	**avais crié**	**aviez crié**
criait	**criaient**	**avait crié**	**avaient crié**
3 passé simple		**10 passé antérieur**	
criai	**criâmes**	**eus crié**	**eûmes crié**
crias	**criâtes**	**eus crié**	**eûtes crié**
cria	**crièrent**	**eut crié**	**eurent crié**
4 futur		**11 futur antérieur**	
crierai	**crierons**	**aurai crié**	**aurons crié**
crieras	**crierez**	**auras crié**	**aurez crié**
criera	**crieront**	**aura crié**	**auront crié**
5 conditionnel		**12 conditionnel passé**	
crierais	**crierions**	**aurais crié**	**aurions crié**
crierais	**crieriez**	**aurais crié**	**auriez crié**
crierait	**crieraient**	**aurait crié**	**auraient crié**
6 présent du subjonctif		**13 passé du subjonctif**	
crie	**criions**	**aie crié**	**ayons crié**
cries	**criiez**	**aies crié**	**ayez crié**
crie	**crient**	**ait crié**	**aient crié**
7 imparfait du subjonctif		**14 plus-que-parfait du subjonctif**	
criasse	**criassions**	**eusse crié**	**eussions crié**
criasses	**criassiez**	**eusses crié**	**eussiez crié**
criât	**criassent**	**eût crié**	**eussent crié**

Impératif
crie
crions
criez

Words and expressions related to this verb
un cri   a shout, a cry
pousser un cri   to utter a cry
crier à tue-tête   to shout one's head off
un crieur   hawker
un crieur de journaux   newsboy
décrier   to decry, criticize

un criailleur, une criailleuse   nagger
un criard, une criarde   someone who constantly shouts, nags, scolds; screecher
un portrait criant de vérité   a portrait strikingly true to life

Pour attraper l'autobus qui était en train de partir, Monsieur Duval a crié à tue-tête.
    To catch the bus that was about to leave, Mr. Duval shouted at the top of his voice.

The subject pronouns are found on page 103.   **249**

croire (130)

Part. pr. **croyant**   Part. passé **cru**

to believe

Irregular verb

The Seven Simple Tenses		The Seven Compound Tenses	
Singular	Plural	Singular	Plural
1 présent de l'indicatif		**8 passé composé**	
crois	croyons	ai cru	avons cru
crois	croyez	as cru	avez cru
croit	croient	a cru	ont cru
2 imparfait de l'indicatif		**9 plus-que-parfait de l'indicatif**	
croyais	croyions	avais cru	avions cru
croyais	croyiez	avais cru	aviez cru
croyait	croyaient	avait cru	avaient cru
3 passé simple		**10 passé antérieur**	
crus	crûmes	eus cru	eûmes cru
crus	crûtes	eus cru	eûtes cru
crut	crurent	eut cru	eurent cru
4 futur		**11 futur antérieur**	
croirai	croirons	aurai cru	aurons cru
croiras	croirez	auras cru	aurez cru
croira	croiront	aura cru	auront cru
5 conditionnel		**12 conditionnel passé**	
croirais	croirions	aurais cru	aurions cru
croirais	croiriez	aurais cru	auriez cru
croirait	croiraient	aurait cru	auraient cru
6 présent du subjonctif		**13 passé du subjonctif**	
croie	croyions	aie cru	ayons cru
croies	croyiez	aies cru	ayez cru
croie	croient	ait cru	aient cru
7 imparfait du subjonctif		**14 plus-que-parfait du subjonctif**	
crusse	crussions	eusse cru	eussions cru
crusses	crussiez	eusses cru	eussiez cru
crût	crussent	eût cru	eussent cru

Impératif
crois
croyons
croyez

Sentences using this verb and words related to it

Est-ce que vous croyez tout ce que vous entendez? Avez-vous cru l'histoire que je vous ai racontée?

Croyez-m'en!   Take my word for it!
se croire   to think oneself; to consider oneself
Paul se croit beau.   Paul thinks himself handsome.
croyable   believable
incroyable   unbelievable

croire à qqch   to believe in something
croire en qqn   to believe in someone
croire en Dieu   to believe in God
Je crois que oui.   I think so.
Je crois que non.   I don't think so.

Get acquainted with what preposition goes with what verb. See *Verbs with prepositions* in the Appendixes.

250

Irregular verb   to grow, to increase

The Seven Simple Tenses		The Seven Compound Tenses	
Singular	Plural	Singular	Plural
1 présent de l'indicatif		**8 passé composé**	
croîs	**croissons**	**ai crû**	**avons crû**
croîs	**croissez**	**as crû**	**avez crû**
croît	**croissent**	**a crû**	**ont crû**
2 imparfait de l'indicatif		**9 plus-que-parfait de l'indicatif**	
croissais	**croissions**	**avais crû**	**avions crû**
croissais	**croissiez**	**avais crû**	**aviez crû**
croissait	**croissaient**	**avait crû**	**avaient crû**
3 passé simple		**10 passé antérieur**	
crûs	**crûmes**	**eus crû**	**eûmes crû**
crûs	**crûtes**	**eus crû**	**eûtes crû**
crût	**crûrent**	**eut crû**	**eurent crû**
4 futur		**11 futur antérieur**	
croîtrai	**croîtrons**	**aurai crû**	**aurons crû**
croîtras	**croîtrez**	**auras crû**	**aurez crû**
croîtra	**croîtront**	**aura crû**	**auront crû**
5 conditionnel		**12 conditionnel passé**	
croîtrais	**croîtrions**	**aurais crû**	**aurions crû**
croîtrais	**croîtriez**	**aurais crû**	**auriez crû**
croîtrait	**croîtraient**	**aurait crû**	**auraient crû**
6 présent du subjonctif		**13 passé du subjonctif**	
croisse	**croissions**	**aie crû**	**ayons crû**
croisses	**croissiez**	**aies crû**	**ayez crû**
croisse	**croissent**	**ait crû**	**aient crû**
7 imparfait du subjonctif		**14 plus-que-parfait du subjonctif**	
crûsse	**crûssions**	**eusse crû**	**eussions crû**
crûsses	**crûssiez**	**eusses crû**	**eussiez crû**
crût	**crûssent**	**eût crû**	**eussent crû**

Impératif
croîs
croissons
croissez

Words and expressions related to this verb

un croissant   crescent (shape of moon); name of a pastry in crescent shape: **Au petit déjeuner, les Français aiment prendre un café et un croissant.** / For breakfast, French people like to have coffee and a croissant (crescent shaped roll).

la croissance   growth; **un accroissement**   increase

crescendo   crescendo (progressive increase in intensity of sound in music; an Italian word related to **croître**).

Note: In many of the simple tenses **croître** has an added circumflex accent to distinguish it from **croire** (to believe): **je croîs (croître), je crois (croire).**

See also **accroître** and **décroître.**

The subject pronouns are found on page 103.
251

to gather, to pick

The Seven Simple Tenses		The Seven Compound Tenses	
Singular	Plural	Singular	Plural
1 présent de l'indicatif		**8 passé composé**	
cueille	cueillons	ai cueilli	avons cueilli
cueilles	cueillez	as cueilli	avez cueilli
cueille	cueillent	a cueilli	ont cueilli
2 imparfait de l'indicatif		**9 plus-que-parfait de l'indicatif**	
cueillais	cueillions	avais cueilli	avions cueilli
cueillais	cueilliez	avais cueilli	aviez cueilli
cueillait	cueillaient	avait cueilli	avaient cueilli
3 passé simple		**10 passé antérieur**	
cueillis	cueillîmes	eus cueilli	eûmes cueilli
cueillis	cueillîtes	eus cueilli	eûtes cueilli
cueillit	cueillirent	eut cueilli	eurent cueilli
4 futur		**11 futur antérieur**	
cueillerai	cueillerons	aurai cueilli	aurons cueilli
cueilleras	cueillerez	auras cueilli	aurez cueilli
cueillera	cueilleront	aura cueilli	auront ceuilli
5 conditionnel		**12 conditionnel passé**	
cueillerais	cueillerions	aurais cueilli	aurions cueilli
cueillerais	cueilleriez	aurais cueilli	auriez cueilli
cueillerait	cueilleraient	aurait cueilli	auraient cueilli
6 présent du subjonctif		**13 passé du subjonctif**	
cueille	cueillions	aie cueilli	ayons cueilli
cueilles	cueilliez	aies cueilli	ayez cueilli
cueille	cueillent	ait cueilli	aient cueilli
7 imparfait du subjonctif		**14 plus-que-parfait du subjonctif**	
cueillisse	cueillissions	eusse cueilli	eussions cueilli
cueillisses	cueillissiez	eusses cueilli	eussiez cueilli
cueillît	cueillissent	eût cueilli	eussent cueilli

Impératif
cueille
cueillons
cueillez

Sentences using this verb and words related to it
   Je vois que tu cueilles des fleurs. As-tu cueilli toutes les fleurs qui sont dans ce vase?

un cueilleur, une cueilleuse gatherer, picker
la cueillaison, la cueillette gathering, picking
un cueilloir basket for picking fruit;
   instrument for picking fruit on high branches

Cueillez, cueillez votre jeunesse. (Ronsard:
   Make the most of your youth.)   Seize the
   day. (Horace: *Carpe diem*)

For other words related to this verb, see accueillir and recueillir.

Grammar putting you in a tense mood? Review the definitions of basic grammatical terms with examples on pages 35–49.

Irregular verb   to cook

The Seven Simple Tenses		The Seven Compound Tenses	
Singular	Plural	Singular	Plural
1 présent de l'indicatif		8 passé composé	
cuis	**cuisons**	**ai cuit**	**avons cuit**
cuis	**cuisez**	**as cuit**	**avez cuit**
cuit	**cuisent**	**a cuit**	**ont cuit**
2 imparfait de l'indicatif		9 plus-que-parfait de l'indicatif	
cuisais	**cuisions**	**avais cuit**	**avions cuit**
cuisais	**cuisiez**	**avais cuit**	**aviez cuit**
cuisait	**cuisaient**	**avait cuit**	**avaient cuit**
3 passé simple		10 passé antérieur	
cuisis	**cuisîmes**	**eus cuit**	**eûmes cuit**
cuisis	**cuisîtes**	**eus cuit**	**eûtes cuit**
cuisit	**cuisirent**	**eut cuit**	**eurent cuit**
4 futur		11 futur antérieur	
cuirai	**cuirons**	**aurai cuit**	**aurons cuit**
cuiras	**cuirez**	**auras cuit**	**aurez cuit**
cuira	**cuiront**	**aura cuit**	**auront cuit**
5 conditionnel		12 conditionnel passé	
cuirais	**cuirions**	**aurais cuit**	**aurions cuit**
cuirais	**cuiriez**	**aurais cuit**	**auriez cuit**
cuirait	**cuiraient**	**aurait cuit**	**auraient cuit**
6 présent du subjonctif		13 passé du subjonctif	
cuise	**cuisions**	**aie cuit**	**ayons cuit**
cuises	**cuisiez**	**aies cuit**	**ayez cuit**
cuise	**cuisent**	**ait cuit**	**aient cuit**
7 imparfait du subjonctif		14 plus-que-parfait du subjonctif	
cuisisse	**cuisissions**	**eusse cuit**	**eussions cuit**
cuisisses	**cuisissiez**	**eusses cuit**	**eussiez cuit**
cuisît	**cuisissent**	**eût cuit**	**eussent cuit**

Impératif
cuis
cuisons
cuisez

Sentences using this verb and words related to it
   Qui a cuit ce morceau de viande? C'est dégoûtant! Il est trop cuit. Ne savez-vous pas faire cuire un bon morceau de viande? Vous n'êtes pas bon cuisinier.

Moi, je n'aime pas le poulet. Je préfère un steak bien cuit.   As for me, I don't like chicken.
   I prefer a steak well-done.

la cuisine   kitchen
cuisinier, cuisinière   cook
faire cuire à la poêle   to pan fry
Il est cuit.   He's done for; His goose is
   cooked.
une cuisinière   kitchen range (stove)

un cuiseur   pressure cooker
trop cuit   overcooked, overdone
la cuisson   cooking (time)
bien cuit   well done

The subject pronouns are found on page 103.   **253**

danser (134)

Part. pr. dansant   **Part. passé dansé**

to dance

Regular **-er** verb

The Seven Simple Tenses		The Seven Compound Tenses	
Singular	Plural	Singular	Plural
1 présent de l'indicatif		**8 passé composé**	
danse	dansons	ai dansé	avons dansé
danses	dansez	as dansé	avez dansé
danse	dansent	a dansé	ont dansé
2 imparfait de l'indicatif		**9 plus-que-parfait de l'indicatif**	
dansais	dansions	avais dansé	avions dansé
dansais	dansiez	avais dansé	aviez dansé
dansait	dansaient	avait dansé	avaient dansé
3 passé simple		**10 passé antérieur**	
dansai	dansâmes	eus dansé	eûmes dansé
dansas	dansâtes	eus dansé	eûtes dansé
dansa	dansèrent	eut dansé	eurent dansé
4 futur		**11 futur antérieur**	
danserai	danserons	aurai dansé	aurons dansé
denseras	danserez	auras dansé	aurez dansé
dansera	danseront	aura dansé	auront dansé
5 conditionnel		**12 conditionnel passé**	
danserais	danserions	aurais dansé	aurions dansé
danserais	danseriez	aurais dansé	auriez dansé
danserait	danseraient	aurait dansé	auraient dansé
6 présent du subjonctif		**13 passé du subjonctif**	
danse	dansions	aie dansé	ayons dansé
danses	dansiez	aies dansé	ayez dansé
danse	dansent	ait dansé	aient dansé
7 imparfait du subjonctif		**14 plus-que-parfait du subjonctif**	
dansasse	dansassions	eusse dansé	eussions dansé
dansasses	dansassiez	eusses dansé	eussiez dansé
dansât	dansassent	eût dansé	eussent dansé

Impératif
danse
dansons
dansez

Sentences using this verb and words related to it
René: Veux-tu danser avec moi?
Renée: Je ne sais pas danser.
René: Je suis bon danseur. Je vais t'apprendre à danser. Viens! Dansons!

danser de joie   to dance for joy
une soirée dansante   evening dancing party
un thé dansant   dancing at teatime (usually 5 o'clock); tea dance
Le chat parti, les souris dansent.   When the cat's away the mice will play.

un danseur, une danseuse   dancer
une danse   dance; un bal   ball (dance)
danseur, danseuse de claquettes   tap dancer
la danse macabre   dance of death

Don't forget to study the section on defective and impersonal verbs. It's right after this main list.

Reflexive regular **-er** verb   to manage, to improvise, to get by

The Seven Simple Tenses		The Seven Compound Tenses	
Singular	Plural	Singular	Plural
1 présent de l'indicatif		**8 passé composé**	
me débrouille	nous débrouillons	me suis débrouillé(e)	nous sommes débrouillé(e)s
te débrouilles	vous débrouillez	t'es débrouillé(e)	vous êtes débrouillé(e)(s)
se débrouille	se débrouillent	s'est débrouillé(e)	se sont débrouillé(e)s
2 imparfait de l'indicatif		**9 plus-que-parfait de l'indicatif**	
me débrouillais	nous débrouillions	m'étais débrouillé(e)	nous étions débrouillé(e)s
te débrouillais	vous débrouilliez	t'étais débrouillé(e)	vous étiez débrouillé(e)(s)
se débrouillait	se débrouillaient	s'était débrouillé(e)	s'étaient débrouillé(e)s
3 passé simple		**10 passé antérieur**	
me débrouillai	nous débrouillâmes	me fus débrouillé(e)	nous fûmes débrouillé(e)s
te débrouillas	vous débrouillâtes	te fus débrouillé(e)	vous fûtes débrouillé(e)(s)
se débrouilla	se débrouillèrent	se fut débrouillé(e)	se furent débrouillé(e)s
4 futur		**11 futur antérieur**	
me débrouillerai	nous débrouillerons	me serai débrouillé(e)	nous serons débrouillé(e)s
te débrouilleras	vous débrouillerez	te seras débrouillé(e)	vous serez débrouillé(e)(s)
se débrouillera	se débrouilleront	se sera débrouillé(e)	se seront débrouillé(e)s
5 conditionnel		**12 conditionnel passé**	
me débrouillerais	nous débrouillerions	me serais débrouillé(e)	nous serions débrouillé(e)s
te débrouillerais	vous débrouilleriez	te serais débrouillé(e)	vous seriez débrouillé(e)(s)
se débrouillerait	se débrouilleraient	se serait débrouillé(e)	se seraient débrouillé(e)s
6 présent du subjonctif		**13 passé du subjonctif**	
me débrouille	nous débrouillions	me sois débrouillé(e)	nous soyons débrouillé(e)s
te débrouilles	vous débrouilliez	te sois débrouillé(e)	vous soyez débrouillé(e)(s)
se débrouille	se débrouillent	se soit débrouillé(e)	se soient débrouillé(e)s
7 imparfait du subjonctif		**14 plus-que-parfait du subjonctif**	
me débrouillasse	nous débrouillassions	me fusse débrouillé(e)	nous fussions débrouillé(e)s
te débrouillasses	vous débrouillassiez	te fusses débrouillé(e)	vous fussiez débrouillé(e)(s)
se débrouillât	se débrouillassent	se fût débrouillé(e)	se fussent débrouillé(e)s

Impératif
débrouille-toi; ne te débrouille pas
débrouillons-nous; ne nous débrouillons pas
débrouillez-vous; ne vous débrouillez pas

AN ESSENTIAL
55 VERB

Se débrouiller

Se débrouiller is an essential verb because it is used in many everyday expressions and situations. The "Système D" has long been an important part of French culture and it is known throughout the francophone world.

Sentences using se débrouiller

Jean-Claude est très débrouillard. Jean-Claude is very resourceful.

Je ne parle pas japonais, mais je me débrouille. I don't know Japanese, but I get by.

C'est ton problème. Débrouille-toi! It's your problem. Straighten it out yourself!

Mon oncle a acheté les billets, grâce au Système D. My uncle bought the tickets, thanks to his ability to work around the system.

Laisse-le se débrouiller tout seul. Let him manage alone.

Words and expressions related to this verb

brouiller **to mix up, confuse, cloud, scramble (eggs)**

le brouillard **fog, mist**

débrouiller **to disentangle**

embrouiller **to tangle, complicate**

débrouillard **resourceful**

un débrouillard, une débrouillarde **a resourceful person**

le système D (le système des débrouillards) **resourcefulness, ability to work around the system**

la débrouillardise **resourcefulness**

le débrouillage **untangling**

Can't find the verb you're looking for? Check the back pages of this book for a list of over 2,600 additional verbs!

Irregular verb; spelling change: **c** changes
to **ç** before **o** or **u** to keep **s** sound

The Seven Simple Tenses | | The Seven Compound Tenses |

Singular	Plural	Singular	Plural
1 présent de l'indicatif		8 passé composé	
déçois	décevons	ai déçu	avons déçu
déçois	décevez	as déçu	avez déçu
déçoit	déçoivent	a déçu	ont déçu
2 imparfait de l'indicatif		9 plus-que-parfait de l'indicatif	
décevais	décevions	avais déçu	avions déçu
décevais	déceviez	avais déçu	aviez déçu
décevait	décevaient	avait déçu	avaient déçu
3 passé simple		10 passé antérieur	
déçus	déçûmes	eus déçu	eûmes déçu
déçus	déçûtes	eus déçu	eûtes déçu
déçut	déçurent	eut déçu	eurent déçu
4 futur		11 futur antérieur	
décevrai	décevrons	aurai déçu	aurons déçu
décevras	décevrez	auras déçu	aurez déçu
décevra	décevront	aura déçu	auront déçu
5 conditionnel		12 conditionnel passé	
décevrais	décevrions	aurais déçu	aurions déçu
décevrais	décevriez	aurais déçu	auriez déçu
décevrait	décevraient	aurait déçu	auraient déçu
6 présent du subjonctif		13 passé du subjonctif	
déçoive	décevions	aie déçu	ayons déçu
déçoives	déceviez	aies déçu	ayez déçu
déçoive	déçoivent	ait déçu	aient déçu
7 imparfait du subjonctif		14 plus-que-parfait du subjonctif	
déçusse	déçussions	eusse déçu	eussions déçu
déçusses	déçussiez	eusses déçu	eussiez déçu
déçût	déçussent	eût déçu	eussent déçu

Impératif
déçois
décevons
décevez

Words and expressions related to this verb
décevoir la confiance de qqn to deceive someone's confidence (trust)
décevant, décevante disappointing, deceptive
être déçu to be disappointed
décevoir les espoirs de qqn to disappoint someone's hopes

la déception disappointment; **la tromperie** deceit
Vous m'avez déçu. You have disappointed me.
Quelle déception! What a disappointment!

The subject pronouns are found on page 103.   **257**

déchirer (137)

Part. pr. déchirant

Part. passé déchiré

to rip, to tear, to rend

Regular **-er** verb

The Seven Simple Tenses		The Seven Compound Tenses	
Singular	Plural	Singular	Plural
1 présent de l'indicatif		8 passé composé	
déchire	**déchirons**	**ai déchiré**	**avons déchiré**
déchires	**déchirez**	**as déchiré**	**avez déchiré**
déchire	**déchirent**	**a déchiré**	**ont déchiré**
2 imparfait de l'indicatif		9 plus-que-parfait de l'indicatif	
déchirais	**déchirions**	**avais déchiré**	**avions déchiré**
déchirais	**déchiriez**	**avais déchiré**	**aviez déchiré**
déchirait	**déchiraient**	**avait déchiré**	**avaient déchiré**
3 passé simple		10 passé antérieur	
déchirai	**déchirâmes**	**eus déchiré**	**eûmes déchiré**
déchiras	**déchirâtes**	**eus déchiré**	**eûtes déchiré**
déchira	**déchirèrent**	**eut déchiré**	**eurent déchiré**
4 futur		11 futur antérieur	
déchirerai	**déchirerons**	**aurai déchiré**	**aurons déchiré**
déchireras	**déchirerez**	**auras déchiré**	**aurez déchiré**
déchirera	**déchireront**	**aura déchiré**	**auront déchiré**
5 conditionnel		12 conditionnel passé	
déchirerais	**déchirerions**	**aurais déchiré**	**aurions déchiré**
déchirerais	**déchireriez**	**aurais déchiré**	**auriez déchiré**
déchirerait	**déchireraient**	**aurait déchiré**	**auraient déchiré**
6 présent du subjonctif		13 passé du subjonctif	
déchire	**déchirions**	**aie déchiré**	**ayons déchiré**
déchires	**déchiriez**	**aies déchiré**	**ayez déchiré**
déchire	**déchirent**	**ait déchiré**	**aient déchiré**
7 imparfait du subjonctif		14 plus-que-parfait du subjonctif	
déchirasse	**déchirassions**	**eusse déchiré**	**eussions déchiré**
déchirasses	**déchirassiez**	**eusses déchiré**	**eussiez déchiré**
déchirât	**déchirassent**	**eût déchiré**	**eussent déchiré**

Impératif
déchire
déchirons
déchirez

Words and expressions related to this verb

déchirer qqn à belles dents to tear someone apart

déchirer le voile to discover the truth

une déchirure laceration, tear

une déchiqueteuse de papier paper shredder

déchirer en lambeaux to tear into shreds

se déchirer to tear each other apart

un déchirement tearing; **un déchirement du coeur** heartbreak

déchiqueter to cut to pieces

Grammar putting you in a tense mood? Review the definitions of basic grammatical terms with examples on pages 35–49.

The Seven Simple Tenses		The Seven Compound Tenses	
Singular	Plural	Singular	Plural

1 présent de l'indicatif

décide	décidons
décides	décidez
décide	décident

8 passé composé

ai décidé	avons décidé
as décidé	avez décidé
a décidé	ont décidé

2 imparfait de l'indicatif

décidais	décidions
décidais	décidiez
décidait	décidaient

9 plus-que-parfait de l'indicatif

avais décidé	avions décidé
avais décidé	aviez décidé
avait décidé	avaient décidé

3 passé simple

décidai	décidâmes
décidas	décidâtes
décida	décidèrent

10 passé antérieur

eus décidé	eûmes décidé
eus décidé	eûtes décidé
eut décidé	eurent décidé

4 futur

déciderai	déciderons
décideras	déciderez
décidera	décideront

11 futur antérieur

aurai décidé	aurons décidé
auras décidé	aurez décidé
aura décidé	auront décidé

5 conditionnel

déciderais	déciderions
déciderais	décideriez
déciderait	décideraient

12 conditionnel passé

aurais décidé	aurions décidé
aurais décidé	auriez décidé
aurait décidé	auraient décidé

6 présent du subjonctif

décide	décidions
décides	décidiez
décide	décident

13 passé du subjonctif

aie décidé	ayons décidé
aies décidé	ayez décidé
ait décidé	aient décidé

7 imparfait du subjonctif

décidasse	décidassions
décidasses	décidassiez
décidât	décidassent

14 plus-que-parfait du subjonctif

eusse décidé	eussions décidé
eusses décidé	eussiez décidé
eût décidé	eussent décidé

Impératif
décide
décidons
décidez

Words and expressions related to this verb
une décision decision; **prendre une décision** to make (come to) a decision
décidément decidedly
décider de faire qqch to decide to do something; **J'ai décidé de partir.** I decided to leave.
se décider à faire qqch to make up one's mind, to resolve to do something; **Le docteur Malaise s'est décidé à faire l'opération.**
Décidez-vous! Make up your mind!

Get acquainted with what preposition goes with what verb. See *Verbs with prepositions* in the Appendixes.

discover, to uncover

The Seven Simple Tenses		The Seven Compound Tenses	
Singular	Plural	Singular	Plural
1 présent de l'indicatif		**8 passé composé**	
découvre	découvrons	ai découvert	avons découvert
découvres	découvrez	as découvert	avez découvert
découvre	découvrent	a découvert	ont découvert
2 imparfait de l'indicatif		**9 plus-que-parfait de l'indicatif**	
découvrais	découvrions	avais découvert	avions découvert
découvrais	découvriez	avais découvert	aviez découvert
découvrait	découvraient	avait découvert	avaient découvert
3 passé simple		**10 passé antérieur**	
découvris	découvrîmes	eus découvert	eûmes découvert
découvris	découvrîtes	eus découvert	eûtes découvert
découvrit	découvrirent	eut découvert	eurent découvert
4 futur		**11 futur antérieur**	
découvrirai	découvrirons	aurai découvert	aurons découvert
découvriras	découvrirez	auras découvert	aurez découvert
découvrira	découvriront	aura découvert	auront découvert
5 conditionnel		**12 conditionnel passé**	
découvrirais	découvririons	aurais découvert	aurions découvert
découvrirais	découvririez	aurais découvert	auriez découvert
découvrirait	découvriraient	aurait découvert	auraient découvert
6 présent du subjonctif		**13 passé du subjonctif**	
découvre	découvrions	aie découvert	ayons découvert
découvres	découvriez	aies découvert	ayez découvert
découvre	découvrent	ait découvert	aient découvert
7 imparfait du subjonctif		**14 plus-que-parfait du subjonctif**	
découvrisse	découvrissions	eusse découvert	eussions découvert
découvrisses	découvrissiez	eusses découvert	eussiez découvert
découvrît	découvrissent	eût découvert	eussent découvert

Impératif
découvre
découvrons
découvrez

Sentences using this verb and words related to it
Ce matin j'ai couvert ce panier de fruits et maintenant il est découvert. Qui l'a découvert?

un découvreur discoverer
une découverte a discovery, invention
un découvert overdraft
se découvrir to take off one's clothes; to take off one's hat

aller à la découverte to explore
Découvrir saint Pierre pour couvrir saint Paul. To rob Peter to pay Paul.

See also couvrir.

Can't find the verb you're looking for? Check the back pages of this book for a list of over 2,600 additional verbs!

The Seven Simple Tenses

Singular	Plural
1 présent de l'indicatif	
décris	décrivons
décris	décrivez
décrit	décrivent
2 imparfait de l'indicatif	
décrivais	décrivions
décrivais	décriviez
décrivait	décrivaient
3 passé simple	
décrivis	décrivîmes
décrivis	décrivîtes
décrivit	décrivirent
4 futur	
décrirai	décrirons
décriras	décrirez
décrira	décriront
5 conditionnel	
décrirais	décririons
décrirais	décririez
décrirait	décriraient
6 présent du subjonctif	
décrive	décrivions
décrives	décriviez
décrive	décrivent
7 imparfait du subjonctif	
décrivisse	décrivissions
décrivisses	décrivissiez
décrivît	décrivissent

The Seven Compound Tenses

Singular	Plural
8 passé composé	
ai décrit	avons décrit
as décrit	avez décrit
a décrit	ont décrit
9 plus-que-parfait de l'indicatif	
avais décrit	avions décrit
avais décrit	aviez décrit
avait décrit	avaient décrit
10 passé antérieur	
eus décrit	eûmes décrit
eus décrit	eûtes décrit
eut décrit	eurent décrit
11 futur antérieur	
aurai décrit	aurons décrit
auras décrit	aurez décrit
aura décrit	auront décrit
12 conditionnel passé	
aurais décrit	aurions décrit
aurais décrit	auriez décrit
aurait décrit	auraient décrit
13 passé du subjonctif	
aie décrit	ayons décrit
aies décrit	ayez décrit
ait décrit	aient décrit
14 plus-que-parfait du subjonctif	
eusse décrit	eussions décrit
eusses décrit	eussiez décrit
eût décrit	eussent décrit

Impératif
décris
décrivons
décrivez

Sentences using this verb and words related to it

Quel beau paysage! Je le décrirai dans une lettre à mon ami. Je ferai une description en détail.

une description description
indescriptible indescribable
écrire to write
proscrire to proscribe

prescrire to prescribe, stipulate
une prescription prescription (medical prescription: **une ordonnance**)

See also **écrire**.

How are you doing? Find out with the verb drills and tests with answers explained on pages 50–101.

décroître (141)

to decrease, to diminish

Part. pr. décroissant   **Part. passé décru**

Irregular verb

The Seven Simple Tenses		The Seven Compound Tenses	
Singular	Plural	Singular	Plural
1 présent de l'indicatif		8 passé composé	
décrois	décroissons	ai décru	avons décru
décrois	décroissez	as décru	avez décru
décroît	décroissent	a décru	ont décru
2 imparfait de l'indicatif		9 plus-que-parfait de l'indicatif	
décroissais	décroissions	avais décru	avions décru
décroissais	décroissiez	avais décru	aviez décru
décroissait	décroissaient	avait décru	avaient décru
3 passé simple		10 passé antérieur	
décrus	décrûmes	eus décru	eûmes décru
décrus	décrûtes	eus décru	eûtes décru
décrut	décrurent	eut décru	eurent décru
4 futur		11 futur antérieur	
décroîtrai	décroîtrons	aurai décru	aurons décru
décroîtras	décroîtrez	auras décru	aurez décru
décroîtra	décroîtront	aura décru	auront décru
5 conditionnel		12 conditionnel passé	
décroîtrais	décroîtrions	aurais décru	aurions décru
décroîtrais	décroîtriez	aurais décru	auriez décru
décroîtrait	décroîtraient	aurait décru	auraient décru
6 présent du subjonctif		13 passé du subjonctif	
décroisse	décroissions	aie décru	ayons décru
décroisses	décroissiez	aies décru	ayez décru
décroisse	décroissent	ait décru	aient décru
7 imparfait du subjonctif		14 plus-que-parfait du subjonctif	
décrusse	décrussions	eusse décru	eussions décru
décrusses	décrussiez	eusses décru	eussiez décru
décrût	décrussent	eût décru	eussent décru

Impératif
décrois
décroissons
décroissez

Words and expressions related to this verb
le décroît de la lune   waning of the moon
la décroissance   decrease
être en décroissance   to be diminishing
une décrue   decrease (water level)
décroissant, décroissante   decreasing,
   diminishing

un croissant   crescent shaped roll; crescent (of
   the moon)
la croissance   increase, growth
croître   to grow, to increase

Note: **Décroître** is not conjugated exactly like **croître**. In many of the simple tenses **croître** has an added circumflex accent to distinguish it from **croire** (to believe): **je croîs (croître), je crois (croire)**.

See also **accroître** and **croître.**

Irregular verb   to deduce, to infer, to deduct

D

The Seven Simple Tenses		The Seven Compound Tenses	
Singular	Plural	Singular	Plural
1 présent de l'indicatif		8 passé composé	
déduis	**déduisons**	**ai déduit**	**avons déduit**
déduis	**déduisez**	**as déduit**	**avez déduit**
déduit	**déduisent**	**a déduit**	**ont déduit**
2 imparfait de l'indicatif		9 plus-que-parfait de l'indicatif	
déduisais	**déduisions**	**avais déduit**	**avions déduit**
déduisais	**déduisiez**	**avais déduit**	**aviez déduit**
déduisait	**déduisaient**	**avait déduit**	**avaient déduit**
3 passé simple		10 passé antérieur	
déduisis	**déduisîmes**	**eus déduit**	**eûmes déduit**
déduisis	**déduisîtes**	**eus déduit**	**eûtes déduit**
déduisit	**déduisirent**	**eut déduit**	**eurent déduit**
4 futur		11 futur antérieur	
déduirai	**déduirons**	**aurai déduit**	**aurons déduit**
déduiras	**déduirez**	**auras déduit**	**aurez déduit**
déduira	**déduiront**	**aura déduit**	**auront déduit**
5 conditionnel		12 conditionnel passé	
déduirais	**déduirions**	**aurais déduit**	**aurions déduit**
déduirais	**déduiriez**	**aurais déduit**	**auriez déduit**
déduirait	**déduiraient**	**aurait déduit**	**auraient déduit**
6 présent du subjonctif		13 passé du subjonctif	
déduise	**déduisions**	**aie déduit**	**ayons déduit**
déduises	**déduisiez**	**aies déduit**	**ayez déduit**
déduise	**déduisent**	**ait déduit**	**aient déduit**
7 imparfait du subjonctif		14 plus-que-parfait du subjonctif	
déduisisse	**déduisissions**	**eusse déduit**	**eussions déduit**
déduisisses	**déduisissiez**	**eusses déduit**	**eussiez déduit**
déduisît	**déduisissent**	**eût déduit**	**eussent déduit**

Impératif
déduis
déduisons
déduisez

Words and expressions related to this verb
une déduction   deduction, inference;
    allowance
déductif, déductive   deductive
se déduire   to be deduced

une réduction   reduction
réduire   to reduce
à prix réduit   at a reduced price
déductible   deductible

See also **conduire, introduire, produire, réduire, reproduire, séduire,** and **traduire.**

It's important that you be familiar with the Subjunctive. See pages 26–31.

to undo, to untie Irregular verb

The Seven Simple Tenses		The Seven Compound Tenses	
Singular	Plural	Singular	Plural
1 présent de l'indicatif		8 passé composé	
défais	défaisons	ai défait	avons défait
défais	défaites	as défait	avez défait
défait	défont	a défait	ont défait
2 imparfait de l'indicatif		9 plus-que-parfait de l'indicatif	
défaisais	défaisions	avais défait	avions défait
défaisais	défaisiez	avais défait	aviez défait
défaisait	défaisaient	avait défait	avaient défait
3 passé simple		10 passé antérieur	
défis	défîmes	eus défait	eûmes défait
défis	défîtes	eus défait	eûtes défait
défit	défirent	eut défait	eurent défait
4 futur		11 futur antérieur	
déferai	déferons	aurai défait	aurons défait
déferas	déferez	auras défait	aurez défait
défera	déferont	aura défait	auront défait
5 conditionnel		12 conditionnel passé	
déferais	déferions	aurais défait	aurions défait
déferais	déferiez	aurais défait	auriez défait
déferait	déferaient	aurait défait	auraient défait
6 présent du subjonctif		13 passé du subjonctif	
défasse	défassions	aie défait	ayons défait
défasses	défassiez	aies défait	ayez défait
défasse	défassent	ait défait	aient défait
7 imparfait du subjonctif		14 plus-que-parfait du subjonctif	
défisse	défissions	eusse défait	eussions défait
défisses	défissiez	eusses défait	eussiez défait
défît	défissent	eût défait	eussent défait

Impératif
défais
défaisons
défaites

Common idiomatic expressions using this verb and words related to it

défaire un lit   to strip a bed
défaire une malle, une valise, etc.   to unpack
  a trunk, suitcase, etc.
une défaite   (military) defeat
avoir le visage défait   to look pale
défaire les boutons   to unbutton, to undo the
  buttons

défaire la table   to clear the table
se défaire de qqch   to rid oneself of
  something
se défaire d'une habitude   to break a habit
le défaitisme   defeatism
des cheveux défaits   dishevelled hair

See also faire and satisfaire.

Regular **-re** verb   to defend, to forbid, to prohibit

The Seven Simple Tenses		The Seven Compound Tenses	
Singular	Plural	Singular	Plural
1 présent de l'indicatif		**8 passé composé**	
défends	**défendons**	**ai défendu**	**avons défendu**
défends	**défendez**	**as défendu**	**avez défendu**
défend	**défendent**	**a défendu**	**ont défendu**
2 imparfait de l'indicatif		**9 plus-que-parfait de l'indicatif**	
défendais	**défendions**	**avais défendu**	**avions défendu**
défendais	**défendiez**	**avais défendu**	**aviez défendu**
défendait	**défendaient**	**avait défendu**	**avaient défendu**
3 passé simple		**10 passé antérieur**	
défendis	**défendîmes**	**eus défendu**	**eûmes défendu**
défendis	**défendîtes**	**eus défendu**	**eûtes défendu**
défendit	**défendirent**	**eut défendu**	**eurent défendu**
4 futur		**11 futur antérieur**	
défendrai	**défendrons**	**aurai défendu**	**aurons défendu**
défendras	**défendrez**	**auras défendu**	**aurez défendu**
défendra	**défendront**	**aura défendu**	**auront défendu**
5 conditionnel		**12 conditionnel passé**	
défendrais	**défendrions**	**aurais défendu**	**aurions défendu**
défendrais	**défendriez**	**aurais défendu**	**auriez défendu**
défendrait	**défendraient**	**aurait défendu**	**auraient défendu**
6 présent du subjonctif		**13 passé du subjonctif**	
défende	**défendions**	**aie défendu**	**ayons défendu**
défendes	**défendiez**	**aies défendu**	**ayez défendu**
défende	**défendent**	**ait défendu**	**aient défendu**
7 imparfait du subjonctif		**14 plus-que-parfait du subjonctif**	
défendisse	**défendissions**	**eusse défendu**	**eussions défendu**
défendisses	**défendissiez**	**eusses défendu**	**eussiez défendu**
défendît	**défendissent**	**eût défendu**	**eussent défendu**

Impératif
défends
défendons
défendez

Sentences using this verb and words related to it
    Le père: Je te défends de fumer. C'est une mauvaise habitude.
    Le fils: Alors, pourquoi fumes-tu, papa?

une défense defense
Défense de . . . No . . . Allowed
Défense d'afficher Post No Bills (signs)
Défense d'entrer Keep Out/No Entry
Défense de fumer No Smoking
défendable justifiable
défendre qqch à qqn to forbid someone
    something

se défendre to defend oneself
défensif, défensive defensive
défensivement defensively
se défendre d'avoir fait qqch to deny having
    done something

The subject pronouns are found on page 103.   **265**

dégager (145)

Part. pr. dégageant   **Part. passé dégagé**

to free, to clear (out), to remove, to give off, to emit

Regular **-er** verb endings; spelling change: retain the **ge** before **a** or **o** to keep the soft **g** sound of the verb

The Seven Simple Tenses		The Seven Compound Tenses	
Singular	Plural	Singular	Plural
1 présent de l'indicatif		8 passé composé	
dégage	dégageons	ai dégagé	avons dégagé
dégages	dégagez	as dégagé	avez dégagé
dégage	dégagent	a dégagé	ont dégagé
2 imparfait de l'indicatif		9 plus-que-parfait de l'indicatif	
dégageais	dégagions	avais dégagé	avions dégagé
dégageais	dégagiez	avais dégagé	aviez dégagé
dégageait	dégageaient	avait dégagé	avaient dégagé
3 passé simple		10 passé antérieur	
dégageai	dégageâmes	eus dégagé	eûmes dégagé
dégageas	dégageâtes	eus dégagé	eûtes dégagé
dégagea	dégagèrent	eut dégagé	eurent dégagé
4 futur		11 futur antérieur	
dégagerai	dégagerons	aurai dégagé	aurons dégagé
dégageras	dégagerez	auras dégagé	aurez dégagé
dégagera	dégageront	aura dégagé	auront dégagé
5 conditionnel		12 conditionnel passé	
dégagerais	dégagerions	aurais dégagé	aurions dégagé
dégagerais	dégageriez	aurais dégagé	auriez dégagé
dégagerait	dégageraient	aurait dégagé	auraient dégagé
6 présent du subjonctif		13 passé du subjonctif	
dégage	dégagions	aie dégagé	ayons dégagé
dégages	dégagiez	aies dégagé	ayez dégagé
dégage	dégagent	ait dégagé	aient dégagé
7 imparfait du subjonctif		14 plus-que-parfait du subjonctif	
dégageasse	dégageassions	eusse dégagé	eussions dégagé
dégageasses	dégageassiez	eusses dégagé	eussiez dégagé
dégageât	dégageassent	eût dégagé	eussent dégagé

Impératif
dégage
dégageons
dégagez

Sentences using this verb and words related to it

Paul m'a répondu d'un ton dégagé.   Paul answered me casually.

Dégage!   Go away! Take off!

Nous ne pouvons pas partir; ils n'ont pas encore dégagé la route.   We can't leave; they haven't cleared the road yet.

Stéphane, il y a une odeur désagréable qui se dégage de ta chambre.   Steven, there's an unpleasant odor emanating from your room.

On annonce un ciel dégagé cet après-midi.   They're predicting a clear sky this afternoon.

Words and expressions related to this verb

d'un air dégagé, d'un ton dégagé *adv.*   casually
engager   to commit, to begin, to hire, to insert
s'engager   to begin, to commit
le dégagement   release, clearing (out)

Don't forget to study the section on defective and impersonal verbs. It's right after this main list.

266

Regular **-er** verb

to lunch, to have lunch, breakfast

The Seven Simple Tenses		The Seven Compound Tenses	
Singular	Plural	Singular	Plural
1 présent de l'indicatif		8 passé composé	
déjeune	**déjeunons**	**ai déjeuné**	**avons déjeuné**
déjeunes	**déjeunez**	**as déjeuné**	**avez déjeuné**
déjeune	**déjeunent**	**a déjeuné**	**ont déjeuné**
2 imparfait de l'indicatif		9 plus-que-parfait de l'indicatif	
déjeunais	**déjeunions**	**avais déjeuné**	**avions déjeuné**
déjeunais	**déjeuniez**	**avais déjeuné**	**aviez déjeuné**
déjeunait	**déjeunaient**	**avait déjeuné**	**avaient déjeuné**
3 passé simple		10 passé antérieur	
déjeunai	**déjeunâmes**	**eus déjeuné**	**eûmes déjeuné**
déjeunas	**déjeunâtes**	**eus déjeuné**	**eûtes déjeuné**
déjeuna	**déjeunèrent**	**eut déjeuné**	**eurent déjeuné**
4 futur		11 futur antérieur	
déjeunerai	**déjeunerons**	**aurai déjeuné**	**aurons déjeuné**
déjeuneras	**déjeunerez**	**auras déjeuné**	**aurez déjeuné**
déjeunera	**déjeuneront**	**aura déjeuné**	**auront déjeuné**
5 conditionnel		12 conditionnel passé	
déjeunerais	**déjeunerions**	**aurais déjeuné**	**aurions déjeuné**
déjeunerais	**déjeuneriez**	**aurais déjeuné**	**auriez déjeuné**
déjeunerait	**déjeuneraient**	**aurait déjeuné**	**auraient déjeuné**
6 présent du subjonctif		13 passé du subjonctif	
déjeune	**déjeunions**	**aie déjeuné**	**ayons déjeuné**
déjeunes	**déjeuniez**	**aies déjeuné**	**ayez déjeuné**
déjeune	**déjeunent**	**ait déjeuné**	**aient déjeuné**
7 imparfait du subjonctif		14 plus-que-parfait du subjonctif	
déjeunasse	**déjeunassions**	**eusse déjeuné**	**eussions déjeuné**
déjeunasses	**déjeunassiez**	**eusses déjeuné**	**eussiez déjeuné**
déjeunât	**déjeunassent**	**eût déjeuné**	**eussent déjeuné**

Impératif
déjeune
déjeunons
déjeunez

Sentences using this verb and words related to it

Tous les matins je me lève et je prends mon petit déjeuner à sept heures et demie. A midi je déjeune avec mes camarades à l'école. Avec qui déjeunez-vous?

le déjeuner   lunch
le petit déjeuner   breakfast
jeûner   to fast
le jeûne   fast, fasting

rompre le jeûne   to break one's fast
un jour de jeûne   a day of fasting
le déjeuner sur l'herbe   picnic lunch (on the grass)

NOTE: The French tend to say **le petit déjeuner** (breakfast), **le déjeuner** (lunch), and **le dîner** (evening meal) or **le souper** (late evening snack). However, in some French-speaking regions, the meals one eats during the day are **le déjeuner** (breakfast), **le dîner** (lunch), and **le souper** (supper).

The subject pronouns are found on page 103.

to ask (for), to request

The Seven Simple Tenses		The Seven Compound Tenses	
Singular	Plural	Singular	Plural
1 présent de l'indicatif		8 passé composé	
demande	demandons	ai demandé	avons demandé
demandes	demandez	as demandé	avez demandé
demande	demandent	a demandé	ont demandé
2 imparfait de l'indicatif		9 plus-que-parfait de l'indicatif	
demandais	demandions	avais demandé	avions demandé
demandais	demandiez	avais demandé	aviez demandé
demandait	demandaient	avait demandé	avaient demandé
3 passé simple		10 passé antérieur	
demandai	demandâmes	eus demandé	eûmes demandé
demandas	demandâtes	eus demandé	eûtes demandé
demanda	demandèrent	eut demandé	eurent demandé
4 futur		11 futur antérieur	
demanderai	demanderons	aurai demandé	aurons demandé
demanderas	demanderez	auras demandé	aurez demandé
demandera	demanderont	aura demandé	auront demandé
5 conditionnel		12 conditionnel passé	
demanderais	demanderions	aurais demandé	aurions demandé
demanderais	demanderiez	aurais demandé	auriez demandé
demanderait	demanderaient	aurait demandé	auraient demandé
6 présent du subjonctif		13 passé du subjonctif	
demande	demandions	aie demandé	ayons demandé
demandes	demandiez	aies demandé	ayez demandé
demande	demandent	ait demandé	aient demandé
7 imparfait du subjonctif		14 plus-que-parfait du subjonctif	
demandasse	demandassions	eusse demandé	eussions demandé
demandasses	demandassiez	eusses demandé	eussiez demandé
demandât	demandassent	eût demandé	eussent demandé

Impératif
demande
demandons
demandez

Sentences using this verb and words related to it

J'ai demandé à une passante où s'arrête l'autobus. Elle m'a répondu:—Je ne sais pas, monsieur. Demandez à l'agent de police.   I asked a passerby where the bus stops. She answered me:—I don't know, Sir. Ask the police officer.

une demande a request
sur demande on request, on application
faire une demande de to apply for
Si votre fils demande un morceau de pain, lui donnerez-vous une pierre? If your son asks for a piece of bread, will you give him a stone? (Matthew 7:9) See "if" clauses, top of page 26.

se demander to wonder
mander to send word by letter
un mandat mandate; un mandat-lettre letter money order; un mandat-poste postal money order
une demande d'emploi job application

Regular **-er** verb   to reside, to live, to remain, to stay

The Seven Simple Tenses		The Seven Compound Tenses	
Singular	Plural	Singular	Plural
1 présent de l'indicatif		8 passé composé	
demeure	demeurons	ai demeuré	avons demeuré
demeures	demeurez	as demeuré	avez demeuré
demeure	demeurent	a demeuré	ont demeuré
2 imparfait de l'indicatif		9 plus-que-parfait de l'indicatif	
demeurais	demeurions	avais demeuré	avions demeuré
demeurais	demeuriez	avais demeuré	aviez demeuré
demeurait	demeuraient	avait demeuré	avaient demeuré
3 passé simple		10 passé antérieur	
demeurai	demeurâmes	eus demeuré	eûmes demeuré
demeuras	demeurâtes	eus demeuré	eûtes demeuré
demeura	demeurèrent	eut demeuré	eurent demeuré
4 futur		11 futur antérieur	
demeurerai	demeurerons	aurai demeuré	aurons demeuré
demeureras	demeurerez	auras demeuré	aurez demeuré
demeurera	demeureront	aura demeuré	auront demeuré
5 conditionnel		12 conditionnel passé	
demeurerais	demeurerions	aurais demeuré	aurions demeuré
demeurerais	demeureriez	aurais demeuré	auriez demeuré
demeurerait	demeureraient	aurait demeuré	auraient demeuré
6 présent du subjonctif		13 passé du subjonctif	
demeure	demeurions	aie demeuré	ayons demeuré
demeures	demeuriez	aies demeuré	ayez demeuré
demeure	demeurent	ait demeuré	aient demeuré
7 imparfait du subjonctif		14 plus-que-parfait du subjonctif	
demeurasse	demeurassions	eusse demeuré	eussions demeuré
demeurasses	demeurassiez	eusses demeuré	eussiez demeuré
demeurât	demeurassent	eût demeuré	eussent demeuré

Impératif
demeure
demeurons
demeurez

Sentences using this verb and words related to it
—**Où demeurez-vous?**
—**Je demeure dans un appartement, rue des Jardins.**

une demeure dwelling, residence
au demeurant incidentally
demeurer couché to stay in bed
demeurer court to stop short

demeurer à un hôtel to stay at a hotel
une mise en demeure injunction
demeurer fidèle to remain faithful

When **demeurer** means "to remain" or "to stay" the auxiliary is **être**.
Marcel est demeuré muet devant les accusations. Marcel remained silent in the face of the charges.

The subject pronouns are found on page 103.   **269**

to demolish

Regular **-ir** verb

The Seven Simple Tenses		The Seven Compound Tenses	
Singular	Plural	Singular	Plural

1 présent de l'indicatif		8 passé composé	
démolis	démolissons	ai démoli	avons démoli
démolis	démolissez	as démoli	avez démoli
démolit	démolissent	a démoli	ont démoli

2 imparfait de l'indicatif		9 plus-que-parfait de l'indicatif	
démolissais	démolissions	avais démoli	avions démoli
démolissais	démolissiez	avais démoli	aviez démoli
démolissait	démolissaient	avait démoli	avaient démoli

3 passé simple		10 passé antérieur	
démolis	démolîmes	eus démoli	eûmes démoli
démolis	démolîtes	eus démoli	eûtes démoli
démolit	démolirent	eut démoli	eurent démoli

4 futur		11 futur antérieur	
démolirai	démolirons	aurai démoli	aurons démoli
démoliras	démolirez	auras démoli	aurez démoli
démolira	démoliront	aura démoli	auront démoli

5 conditionnel		12 conditionnel passé	
démolirais	démolirions	aurais démoli	aurions démoli
démolirais	démoliriez	aurais démoli	auriez démoli
démolirait	démoliraient	aurait démoli	auraient démoli

6 présent du subjonctif		13 passé du subjonctif	
démolisse	démolissions	aie démoli	ayons démoli
démolisses	démolissiez	aies démoli	ayez démoli
démolisse	démolissent	ait démoli	aient démoli

7 imparfait du subjonctif		14 plus-que-parfait du subjonctif	
démolisse	démolissions	eusse démoli	eussions démoli
démolisses	démolissiez	eusses démoli	eussiez démoli
démolît	démolissent	eût démoli	eussent démoli

Impératif
démolis
démolissons
démolissez

Words and expressions related to this verb
une démolition demolition
un démolisseur, une démolisseuse
  demolisher

se démolir   to fall apart, to fall to pieces
démolir l'estomac   to ruin one's stomach

Grammar putting you in a tense mood? Review the definitions of basic grammatical terms with examples on pages 35–49.

Regular **-er** verb   to pass, to go past, to go beyond, to exceed

The Seven Simple Tenses		The Seven Compound Tenses	
Singular	Plural	Singular	Plural
1 présent de l'indicatif		8 passé composé	
dépasse	dépassons	ai dépassé	avons dépassé
dépasses	dépassez	as dépassé	avez dépassé
dépasse	dépassent	a dépassé	ont dépassé
2 imparfait de l'indicatif		9 plus-que-parfait de l'indicatif	
dépassais	dépassions	avais dépassé	avions dépassé
dépassais	dépassiez	avais dépassé	aviez dépassé
dépassait	dépassaient	avait dépassé	avaient dépassé
3 passé simple		10 passé antérieur	
dépassai	dépassâmes	eus dépassé	eûmes dépassé
dépassas	dépassâtes	eus dépassé	eûtes dépassé
dépassa	dépassèrent	eut dépassé	eurent dépassé
4 futur		11 futur antérieur	
dépasserai	dépasserons	aurai dépassé	aurons dépassé
dépasseras	dépasserez	auras dépassé	aurez dépassé
dépassera	dépasseront	aura dépassé	auront dépassé
5 conditionnel		12 conditionnel passé	
dépasserais	dépasserions	aurais dépassé	aurions dépassé
dépasserais	dépasseriez	aurais dépassé	auriez dépassé
dépasserait	dépasseraient	aurait dépassé	auraient dépassé
6 présent du subjonctif		13 passé du subjonctif	
dépasse	dépassions	aie dépassé	ayons dépassé
dépasses	dépassiez	aies dépassé	ayez dépassé
dépasse	dépassent	ait dépassé	aient dépassé
7 imparfait du subjonctif		14 plus-que-parfait du subjonctif	
dépassasse	dépassassions	eusse dépassé	eussions dépassé
dépassasses	dépassassiez	eusses dépassé	eussiez dépassé
dépassât	dépassassent	eût dépassé	eussent dépassé

Impératif
dépasse
dépassons
dépassez

Words and expressions related to this verb
le dépassement   passing, exceeding
dépassé, dépassée   outdated
se dépasser   to outdo oneself

passer   to pass, to spend (time)
passable   passable, adequate
une passoire   colander

Fais attention! Tu dépasses la limite de vitesse!   Watch out! You're going over the speed limit!

Can't find the verb you're looking for? Check the back pages of this book for a list of over 2,600 additional verbs!

The subject pronouns are found on page 103.   **271**

se dépêcher (151) Part. pr. se dépêchant   Part. passé dépêché(e)(s)

to hurry, to hasten

Reflexive regular -er verb

The Seven Simple Tenses		The Seven Compound Tenses	
Singular	Plural	Singular	Plural
1 présent de l'indicatif		**8 passé composé**	
me dépêche	nous dépêchons	me suis dépêché(e)	nous sommes dépêché(e)s
te dépêches	vous dépêchez	t'es dépêché(e)	vous êtes dépêché(e)(s)
se dépêche	se dépêchent	s'est dépêché(e)	se sont dépêché(e)s
2 imparfait de l'indicatif		**9 plus-que-parfait de l'indicatif**	
me dépêchais	nous dépêchions	m'étais dépêché(e)	nous étions dépêché(e)s
te dépêchais	vous dépêchiez	t'étais dépêché(e)	vous étiez dépêché(e)(s)
se dépêchait	se dépêchaient	s'était dépêché(e)	s'étaient dépêché(e)s
3 passé simple		**10 passé antérieur**	
me dépêchai	nous dépêchâmes	me fus dépêché(e)	nous fûmes dépêché(e)s
te dépêchas	vous dépêchâtes	te fus dépêché(e)	vous fûtes dépêché(e)(s)
se dépêcha	se dépêchèrent	se fut dépêché(e)	se furent dépêché(e)s
4 futur		**11 futur antérieur**	
me dépêcherai	nous dépêcherons	me serai dépêché(e)	nous serons dépêché(e)s
te dépêcheras	vous dépêcherez	te seras dépêché(e)	vous serez dépêché(e)(s)
se dépêchera	se dépêcheront	se sera dépêché(e)	se seront dépêché(e)s
5 conditionnel		**12 conditionnel passé**	
me dépêcherais	nous dépêcherions	me serais dépêché(e)	nous serions dépêché(e)s
te dépêcherais	vous dépêcheriez	te serais dépêché(e)	vous seriez dépêché(e)(s)
se dépêcherait	se dépêcheraient	se serait dépêché(e)	se seraient dépêché(e)s
6 présent du subjonctif		**13 passé du subjonctif**	
me dépêche	nous dépêchions	me sois dépêché(e)	nous soyons dépêché(e)s
te dépêches	vous dépêchiez	te sois dépêché(e)	vous soyez dépêché(e)(s)
se dépêche	se dépêchent	se soit dépêché(e)	se soient dépêché(e)s
7 imparfait du subjonctif		**14 plus-que-parfait du subjonctif**	
me dépêchasse	nous dépêchassions	me fusse dépêché(e)	nous fussions dépêché(e)s
te dépêchasses	vous dépêchassiez	te fusses dépêché(e)	vous fussiez dépêché(e)(s)
se dépêchât	se dépêchassent	se fût dépêché(e)	se fussent dépêché(e)s

Impératif
dépêche-toi; ne te dépêche pas
dépêchons-nous; ne nous dépêchons pas
dépêchez-vous; ne vous dépêchez pas

Sentences using this verb and words related to it
En me dépêchant pour attraper l'autobus, je suis tombé et je me suis fait mal au genou.
Je me dépêchais de venir chez vous pour vous dire quelque chose de très important.

une dépêche   a telegram, a dispatch
dépêcher   to dispatch
faire les courses en se dépêchant   to do the shopping hurriedly

See also **empêcher.**

Don't forget to study the section on defective and impersonal verbs. It's right after this main list.

Irregular verb   to depict, to describe, to portray

D

The Seven Simple Tenses | The Seven Compound Tenses

Singular	Plural	Singular	Plural
1 présent de l'indicatif		8 passé composé	
dépeins	**dépeignons**	**ai dépeint**	**avons dépeint**
dépeins	**dépeignez**	**as dépeint**	**avez dépeint**
dépeint	**dépeignent**	**a dépeint**	**ont dépeint**
2 imparfait de l'indicatif		9 plus-que-parfait de l'indicatif	
dépeignais	**dépeignions**	**avais dépeint**	**avions dépeint**
dépeignais	**dépeigniez**	**avais dépeint**	**aviez dépeint**
dépeignait	**dépeignaient**	**avait dépeint**	**avaient dépeint**
3 passé simple		10 passé antérieur	
dépeignis	**dépeignîmes**	**eus dépeint**	**eûmes dépeint**
dépeignis	**dépeignîtes**	**eus dépeint**	**eûtes dépeint**
dépeignit	**dépeignirent**	**eut dépeint**	**eurent dépeint**
4 futur		11 futur antérieur	
dépeindrai	**dépeindrons**	**aurai dépeint**	**aurons dépeint**
dépeindras	**dépeindrez**	**auras dépeint**	**aurez dépeint**
dépeindra	**dépeindront**	**aura dépeint**	**auront dépeint**
5 conditionnel		12 conditionnel passé	
dépeindrais	**dépeindrions**	**aurais dépeint**	**aurions dépeint**
dépeindrais	**dépeindriez**	**aurais dépeint**	**auriez dépeint**
dépeindrait	**dépeindraient**	**aurait dépeint**	**auraient dépeint**
6 présent du subjonctif		13 passé du subjonctif	
dépeigne	**dépeignions**	**aie dépeint**	**ayons dépeint**
dépeignes	**dépeigniez**	**aies dépeint**	**ayez dépeint**
dépeigne	**dépeignent**	**ait dépeint**	**aient dépeint**
7 imparfait du subjonctif		14 plus-que-parfait du subjonctif	
dépeignisse	**dépeignissions**	**eusse dépeint**	**eussions dépeint**
dépeignisses	**dépeignissiez**	**eusses dépeint**	**eussiez dépeint**
dépeignît	**dépeignissent**	**eût dépeint**	**eussent dépeint**

Impératif
dépeins
dépeignons
dépeignez

Words and expressions related to this verb
dépeindre une scène   to depict a scene
peindre   to paint
une peinture à l'huile   oil painting
la peinture   painting

peinturer   to daub
un peintre   painter; **une femme peintre**
   woman artist
repeindre   to repaint

For other words and expressions related to this verb, see **peindre.**

Soak up some verbs used in weather expressions. There's a list in the Appendixes!

dépendre (153)

Part. pr. **dépendant**   Part. passé **dépendu**

to depend (on), to be dependent (on), to
take down (something that is hanging)

The Seven Simple Tenses | The Seven Compound Tenses

Singular	Plural	Singular	Plural
1 présent de l'indicatif		**8 passé composé**	
dépends	dépendons	ai dépendu	avons dépendu
dépends	dépendez	as dépendu	avez dépendu
dépend	dépendent	a dépendu	ont dépendu
2 imparfait de l'indicatif		**9 plus-que-parfait de l'indicatif**	
dépendais	dépendions	avais dépendu	avions dépendu
dépendais	dépendiez	avais dépendu	aviez dépendu
dépendait	dépendaient	avait dépendu	avaient dépendu
3 passé simple		**10 passé antérieur**	
dépendis	dépendîmes	eus dépendu	eûmes dépendu
dépendis	dépendîtes	eus dépendu	eûtes dépendu
dépendit	dépendirent	eut dépendu	eurent dépendu
4 futur		**11 futur antérieur**	
dépendrai	dépendrons	aurai dépendu	aurons dépendu
dépendras	dépendrez	auras dépendu	aurez dépendu
dépendra	dépendront	aura dépendu	auront dépendu
5 conditionnel		**12 conditionnel passé**	
dépendrais	dépendrions	aurais dépendu	aurions dépendu
dépendrais	dépendriez	aurais dépendu	auriez dépendu
dépendrait	dépendraient	aurait dépendu	auraient dépendu
6 présent du subjonctif		**13 passé du subjonctif**	
dépende	dépendions	aie dépendu	ayons dépendu
dépendes	dépendiez	aies dépendu	ayez dépendu
dépende	dépendent	ait dépendu	aient dépendu
7 imparfait du subjonctif		**14 plus-que-parfait du subjonctif**	
dépendisse	dépendissions	eusse dépendu	eussions dépendu
dépendisses	dépendissiez	eusses dépendu	eussiez dépendu
dépendît	dépendissent	eût dépendu	eussent dépendu

Impératif
dépends
dépendons
dépendez

Common idiomatic expressions using this verb and words related to it

dépendre de   to depend on, to be dependent
on
la dépendance   dependence
l'indépendance   independence
être sous la dépendance de   to be dependent
on

See also **pendre** (to hang).

Il dépend de vous de + inf.   It depends on you
+ inf.
indépendamment de   independently of
dépendant de   depending on, subject to
indépendant, indépendante   independent
Cela dépend!   That depends!

Get acquainted with what preposition goes with what verb. See *Verbs with prepositions*
in the Appendixes.

The Seven Simple Tenses		The Seven Compound Tenses	
Singular	Plural	Singular	Plural
1 présent de l'indicatif		8 passé composé	
dépense	**dépensons**	**ai dépensé**	**avons dépensé**
dépenses	**dépensez**	**as dépensé**	**avez dépensé**
dépense	**dépensent**	**a dépensé**	**ont dépensé**
2 imparfait de l'indicatif		9 plus-que-parfait de l'indicatif	
dépensais	**dépensions**	**avais dépensé**	**avions dépensé**
dépensais	**dépensiez**	**avais dépensé**	**aviez dépensé**
dépensait	**dépensaient**	**avait dépensé**	**avaient dépensé**
3 passé simple		10 passé antérieur	
dépensai	**dépensâmes**	**eus dépensé**	**eûmes dépensé**
dépensas	**dépensâtes**	**eus dépensé**	**eûtes dépensé**
dépensa	**dépensèrent**	**eut dépensé**	**eurent dépensé**
4 futur		11 futur antérieur	
dépenserai	**dépenserons**	**aurai dépensé**	**aurons dépensé**
dépenseras	**dépenserez**	**auras dépensé**	**aurez dépensé**
dépensera	**dépenseront**	**aura dépensé**	**auront dépensé**
5 conditionnel		12 conditionnel passé	
dépenserais	**dépenserions**	**aurais dépensé**	**aurions dépensé**
dépenserais	**dépenseriez**	**aurais dépensé**	**auriez dépensé**
dépenserait	**dépenseraient**	**aurait dépensé**	**auraient dépensé**
6 présent du subjonctif		13 passé du subjonctif	
dépense	**dépensions**	**aie dépensé**	**ayons dépensé**
dépenses	**dépensiez**	**aies dépensé**	**ayez dépensé**
dépense	**dépensent**	**ait dépensé**	**aient dépensé**
7 imparfait du subjonctif		14 plus-que-parfait du subjonctif	
dépensasse	**dépensassions**	**eusse dépensé**	**eussions dépensé**
dépensasses	**dépensassiez**	**eusses dépensé**	**eussiez dépensé**
dépensât	**dépensassent**	**eût dépensé**	**eussent dépensé**

Impératif
dépense
dépensons
dépensez

Sentences using this verb and words related to it
   Mon père m'a dit que je dépense sottement. Je lui ai répondu que je n'ai rien dépensé cette semaine.

dépensier, dépensière extravagant, unthrifty,
   spendthrift
dépenser sottement to spend money foolishly

aux dépens de quelqu'un at someone's
   expense
les dépenses du ménage household expenses

How are you doing? Find out with the verb drills and tests with answers explained on pages 50–101.

to displease

The Seven Simple Tenses		The Seven Compound Tenses	
Singular	Plural	Singular	Plural
1 présent de l'indicatif		**8 passé composé**	
déplais	déplaisons	ai déplu	avons déplu
déplais	déplaisez	as déplu	avez déplu
déplaît	déplaisent	a déplu	ont déplu
2 imparfait de l'indicatif		**9 plus-que-parfait de l'indicatif**	
déplaisais	déplaisions	avais déplu	avions déplu
déplaisais	déplaisiez	avais déplu	aviez déplu
déplaisait	déplaisaient	avait déplu	avaient déplu
3 passé simple		**10 passé antérieur**	
déplus	déplûmes	eus déplu	eûmes déplu
déplus	déplûtes	eus déplu	eûtes déplu
déplut	déplurent	eut déplu	eurent déplu
4 futur		**11 futur antérieur**	
déplairai	déplairons	aurai déplu	aurons déplu
déplairas	déplairez	auras déplu	aurez déplu
déplaira	déplairont	aura déplu	auront déplu
5 conditionnel		**12 conditionnel passé**	
déplairais	déplairions	aurais déplu	aurions déplu
déplairais	déplairiez	aurais déplu	auriez déplu
déplairait	déplairaient	aurait déplu	auraient déplu
6 présent du subjonctif		**13 passé du subjonctif**	
déplaise	déplaisions	aie déplu	ayons déplu
déplaises	déplaisiez	aies déplu	ayez déplu
déplaise	déplaisent	ait déplu	aient déplu
7 imparfait du subjonctif		**14 plus-que-parfait du subjonctif**	
déplusse	déplussions	eusse déplu	eussions déplu
déplusses	déplussiez	eusses déplu	eussiez déplu
déplût	déplussent	eût déplu	eussent déplu

Impératif
déplais
déplaisons
déplaisez

Common idiomatic expressions using this verb
Cela me déplaît   I don't like that.
Il me déplaît de + inf.   I don't like + inf.
Plaise à Dieu . . .   May God grant that . . .
le plaisir   pleasure
le déplaisir   displeasure
plaire à qqn   to please someone

A Dieu ne plaise!   God forbid!
Plaît-il?   Pardon me? I beg your pardon?
   What did you say?
déplaisant, déplaisante   displeasing, offensive
déplaire à qqn   to displease someone

See also **plaire.**

Use the guide to French pronunciation. It's in the Appendixes.

Regular **-er** verb endings; spelling change: retain the
ge before **a** or **o** to keep the soft **g** sound of the verb

to disturb, to derange

D

The Seven Simple Tenses		The Seven Compound Tenses	
Singular	Plural	Singular	Plural
1 présent de l'indicatif		8 passé composé	
dérange	dérangeons	ai dérangé	avons dérangé
déranges	dérangez	as dérangé	avez dérangé
dérange	dérangent	a dérangé	ont dérangé
2 imparfait de l'indicatif		9 plus-que-parfait de l'indicatif	
dérangeais	dérangions	avais dérangé	avions dérangé
dérangeais	dérangiez	avais dérangé	aviez dérangé
dérangeait	dérangeaient	avait dérangé	avaient dérangé
3 passé simple		10 passé antérieur	
dérangeai	dérangeâmes	eus dérangé	eûmes dérangé
dérangeas	dérangeâtes	eus dérangé	eûtes dérangé
dérangea	dérangèrent	eut dérangé	eurent dérangé
4 futur		11 futur antérieur	
dérangerai	dérangerons	aurai dérangé	aurons dérangé
dérangeras	dérangerez	auras dérangé	aurez dérangé
dérangera	dérangeront	aura dérangé	auront dérangé
5 conditionnel		12 conditionnel passé	
dérangerais	dérangerions	aurais dérangé	aurions dérangé
dérangerais	dérangeriez	aurais dérangé	auriez dérangé
dérangerait	dérangeraient	aurait dérangé	auraient dérangé
6 présent du subjonctif		13 passé du subjonctif	
dérange	dérangions	aie dérangé	ayons dérangé
déranges	dérangiez	aies dérangé	ayez dérangé
dérange	dérangent	ait dérangé	aient dérangé
7 imparfait du subjonctif		14 plus-que-parfait du subjonctif	
dérangeasse	dérangeassions	eusse dérangé	eussions dérangé
dérangeasses	dérangeassiez	eusses dérangé	eussiez dérangé
dérangeât	dérangeassent	eût dérangé	eussent dérangé

Impératif
dérange
dérangeons
dérangez

Sentences using this verb and words related to it
Le professeur: Entrez!
L'élève: Excusez-moi, monsieur. Est-ce que je
vous dérange?
Le professeur: Non, tu ne me déranges pas.
Qu'est-ce que tu veux?
L'élève: Je veux savoir si nous avons un jour
de congé demain.
NE PAS DÉRANGER   DO NOT DISTURB

dérangé, dérangée   upset, out of order, broken
down
une personne dérangée   a deranged person
un dérangement   disarrangement, disorder,
inconvenience
se déranger   to inconvenience oneself
Je vous en prie, ne vous dérangez pas!   I beg
you (please), don't disturb yourself!

The subject pronouns are found on page 103.

to go down, to descend, to take down, to bring down   Regular **-re** verb

The Seven Simple Tenses		The Seven Compound Tenses	
Singular	Plural	Singular	Plural
1 présent de l'indicatif		8 passé composé	
descends	descendons	suis descendu(e)	sommes descendu(e)s
descends	descendez	es descendu(e)	êtes descendu(e)(s)
descend	descendent	est descendu(e)	sont descendu(e)s
2 imparfait de l'indicatif		9 plus-que-parfait de l'indicatif	
descendais	descendions	étais descendu(e)	étions descendu(e)s
descendais	descendiez	étais descendu(e)	étiez descendu(e)(s)
descendait	descendaient	était descendu(e)	étaient descendu(e)s
3 passé simple		10 passé antérieur	
descendis	descendîmes	fus descendu(e)	fûmes descendu(e)s
descendis	descendîtes	fus descendu(e)	fûtes descendu(e)(s)
descendit	descendirent	fut descendu(e)	furent descendu(e)s
4 futur		11 futur antérieur	
descendrai	descendrons	serai descendu(e)	serons descendu(e)s
descendras	descendrez	seras descendu(e)	serez descendu(e)(s)
descendra	descendront	sera descendu(e)	seront descendu(e)s
5 conditionnel		12 conditionnel passé	
descendrais	descendrions	serais descendu(e)	serions descendu(e)s
descendrais	descendriez	serais descendu(e)	seriez descendu(e)(s)
descendrait	descendraient	serait descendu(e)	seraient descendu(e)s
6 présent du subjonctif		13 passé du subjonctif	
descende	descendions	sois descendu(e)	soyons descendu(e)s
descendes	descendiez	sois descendu(e)	soyez descendu(e)(s)
descende	descendent	soit descendu(e)	soient descendu(e)s
7 imparfait du subjonctif		14 plus-que-parfait du subjonctif	
descendisse	descendissions	fusse descendu(e)	fussions descendu(e)s
descendisses	descendissiez	fusses descendu(e)	fussiez descendu(e)(s)
descendît	descendissent	fût descendu(e)	fussent descendu(e)s

Impératif
descends
descendons
descendez

Words and expressions related to this verb
descendre à un hôtel   to stop (stay over) at a hotel
descendre le store   to pull down the window shade
une descente   slope
Aidez-moi à descendre mes bagages, s'il vous plaît.   Please help me bring down my luggage.

See also the verb **monter.**

This verb is conjugated with *avoir* when it has a direct object.

Examples: **J'ai descendu l'escalier**   I went down the stairs.
               J'ai descendu les valises   I brought down the suitcases.
BUT: **Elle est descendue vite**   She came down quickly.

The Seven Simple Tenses | | The Seven Compound Tenses

Singular   Plural   Singular   Plural

1 présent de l'indicatif
désire   **désirons**
désires   **désirez**
désire   **désirent**

8 passé composé
ai désiré   **avons désiré**
as désiré   **avez désiré**
a désiré   **ont désiré**

2 imparfait de l'indicatif
désirais   **désirions**
désirais   **désiriez**
désirait   **désiraient**

9 plus-que-parfait de l'indicatif
avais désiré   **avions désiré**
avais désiré   **aviez désiré**
avait désiré   **avaient désiré**

3 passé simple
désirai   **désirâmes**
désiras   **désirâtes**
désira   **désirèrent**

10 passé antérieur
eus désiré   **eûmes désiré**
eus désiré   **eûtes désiré**
eut désiré   **eurent désiré**

4 futur
désirerai   **désirerons**
désireras   **désirerez**
désirera   **désireront**

11 futur antérieur
aurai désiré   **aurons désiré**
auras désiré   **aurez désiré**
aura désiré   **auront désiré**

5 conditionnel
désirerais   **désirerions**
désirerais   **désireriez**
désirerait   **désireraient**

12 conditionnel passé
aurais désiré   **aurions désiré**
aurais désiré   **auriez désiré**
aurait désiré   **auraient désiré**

6 présent du subjonctif
désire   **désirions**
désires   **désiriez**
désire   **désirent**

13 passé du subjonctif
aie désiré   **ayons désiré**
aies désiré   **ayez désiré**
ait désiré   **aient désiré**

7 imparfait du subjonctif
désirasse   **désirassions**
désirasses   **désirassiez**
désirât   **désirassent**

14 plus-que-parfait du subjonctif
eusse désiré   **eussions désiré**
eusses désiré   **eussiez désiré**
eût désiré   **eussent désiré**

Impératif
désire
désirons
désirez

Sentences using this verb and words related to it

La vendeuse: **Bonjour, monsieur. Vous désirez?**
Le client: **Je désire acheter une cravate.**
La vendeuse: **Bien, monsieur. Vous pouvez choisir. Voici toutes nos cravates.**
un désir desire, wish; **la désirabilité** desirability
désirable desirable; **désireux, désireuse** desirous

indésirable undesirable
un désir de plaire a desire to please
laisser à désirer to leave much to be desired; **le désir de faire qqch** the desire to do something
Je désire changer de l'argent. I would like to exchange some money.
Combien désirez-vous changer? How much do you want to exchange?

dessiner (159)

Part. pr. dessinant **Part. passé dessiné**

to draw, to sketch

Regular -er verb

The Seven Simple Tenses		The Seven Compound Tenses	
Singular	Plural	Singular	Plural
1 présent de l'indicatif		**8 passé composé**	
dessine	dessinons	ai dessiné	avons dessiné
dessines	dessinez	as dessiné	avez dessiné
dessine	dessinent	a dessiné	ont dessiné
2 imparfait de l'indicatif		**9 plus-que-parfait de l'indicatif**	
dessinais	dessinions	avais dessiné	avions dessiné
dessinais	dessiniez	avais dessiné	aviez dessiné
dessinait	dessinaient	avait dessiné	avaient dessiné
3 passé simple		**10 passé antérieur**	
dessinai	dessinâmes	eus dessiné	eûmes dessiné
dessinas	dessinâtes	eus dessiné	eûtes dessiné
dessina	dessinèrent	eut dessiné	eurent dessiné
4 futur		**11 futur antérieur**	
dessinerai	dessinerons	aurai dessiné	aurons dessiné
dessineras	dessinerez	auras dessiné	aurez dessiné
dessinera	dessineront	aura dessiné	auront dessiné
5 conditionnel		**12 conditionnel passé**	
dessinerais	dessinerions	aurais dessiné	aurions dessiné
dessinerais	dessineriez	aurais dessiné	auriez dessiné
dessinerait	dessineraient	aurait dessiné	auraient dessiné
6 présent du subjonctif		**13 passé du subjonctif**	
dessine	dessinions	aie dessiné	ayons dessiné
dessines	dessiniez	aies dessiné	ayez dessiné
dessine	dessinent	ait dessiné	aient dessiné
7 imparfait du subjonctif		**14 plus-que-parfait du subjonctif**	
dessinasse	dessinassions	eusse dessiné	eussions dessiné
dessinasses	dessinassiez	eusses dessiné	eussiez dessiné
dessinât	dessinassent	eût dessiné	eussent dessiné

Impératif
dessine
dessinons
dessinez

Words and expressions related to this verb
dessiner au crayon   to draw with a pencil
un dessinateur, une dessinatrice   sketcher;
— de journal   cartoonist; — de modes
dress designer; — de dessins animés
cartoonist
une bande dessinée   comic strip
un dessin animé   cartoon

dessiner très vite   to do a quick sketch
se dessiner   to take shape, to stand out
un dessin   drawing, sketch
un dessin à la plume   pen and ink sketch
le dessin assisté par ordinateur   CAD
(computer-aided design)

Do not confuse **un dessin** (sketch, drawing) with **un dessein** (plan, project, purpose).

Regular **-er** verb

to detest, to dislike, to hate

The Seven Simple Tenses		The Seven Compound Tenses	
Singular	Plural	Singular	Plural
1 présent de l'indicatif		**8 passé composé**	
déteste	détestons	ai détesté	avons détesté
détestes	détestez	as détesté	avez détesté
déteste	détestent	a détesté	ont détesté
2 imparfait de l'indicatif		**9 plus-que-parfait de l'indicatif**	
détestais	détestions	avais détesté	avions détesté
détestais	détestiez	avais détesté	aviez détesté
détestait	détestaient	avait détesté	avaient détesté
3 passé simple		**10 passé antérieur**	
détestai	détestâmes	eus détesté	eûmes détesté
détestas	détestâtes	eus détesté	eûtes détesté
détesta	détestèrent	eut détesté	eurent détesté
4 futur		**11 futur antérieur**	
détesterai	détesterons	aurai détesté	aurons détesté
détesteras	détesterez	auras détesté	aurez détesté
détestera	détesteront	aura détesté	auront détesté
5 conditionnel		**12 conditionnel passé**	
détesterais	détesterions	aurais détesté	aurions détesté
détesterais	détesteriez	aurais détesté	auriez détesté
détesterait	détesteraient	aurait détesté	auraient détesté
6 présent du subjonctif		**13 passé du subjonctif**	
déteste	détestions	aie détesté	ayons détesté
détestes	détestiez	aies détesté	ayez détesté
déteste	détestent	ait détesté	aient détesté
7 imparfait du subjonctif		**14 plus-que-parfait du subjonctif**	
détestasse	détestassions	eusse détesté	eussions détesté
détestasses	détestassiez	eusses détesté	eussiez détesté
détestât	détestassent	eût détesté	eussent détesté

Impératif
déteste
détestons
détestez

Sentences using this verb and words related to it

Je déteste la médiocrité, je déteste le mensonge, et je déteste la calomnie. Ce sont des choses détestables.

détestable   loathsome, hateful, dreadful
détestablement   detestably

How are you doing? Find out with the verb drills and tests with answers explained on pages 50–101.

The subject pronouns are found on page 103.

to turn aside, to turn away, to divert

Regular **-er** verb

The Seven Simple Tenses		The Seven Compound Tenses	
Singular	Plural	Singular	Plural
1 présent de l'indicatif		8 passé composé	
détourne	détournons	ai détourné	avons détourné
détournes	détournez	as détourné	avez détourné
détourne	détournent	a détourné	ont détourné
2 imparfait de l'indicatif		9 plus-que-parfait de l'indicatif	
détournais	détournions	avais détourné	avions détourné
détournais	détourniez	avais détourné	aviez détourné
détournait	détournaient	avait détourné	avaient détourné
3 passé simple		10 passé antérieur	
détournai	détournâmes	eus détourné	eûmes détourné
détournas	détournâtes	eus détourné	eûtes détourné
détourna	détournèrent	eut détourné	eurent détourné
4 futur		11 futur antérieur	
détournerai	détournerons	aurai détourné	aurons détourné
détourneras	détournerez	auras détourné	aurez détourné
détournera	détourneront	aura détourné	auront détourné
5 conditionnel		12 conditionnel passé	
détournerais	détournerions	aurais détourné	aurions détourné
détournerais	détourneriez	aurais détourné	auriez détourné
détournerait	détourneraient	aurait détourné	auraient détourné
6 présent du subjonctif		13 passé du subjonctif	
détourne	détournions	aie détourné	ayons détourné
détournes	détourniez	aies détourné	ayez détourné
détourne	détournent	ait détourné	aient détourné
7 imparfait du subjonctif		14 plus-que-parfait du subjonctif	
détournasse	détournassions	eusse détourné	eussions détourné
détournasses	détournassiez	eusses détourné	eussiez détourné
détournât	détournassent	eût détourné	eussent détourné

Impératif
détourne
détournons
détournez

Words and expressions related to this verb
détourner les yeux   to look away
détourner qqn de faire qqch   to discourage
   someone from doing something
un chemin détourné   side road

se détourner de   to turn oneself away from
un détour   detour; **faire un détour**   to make
   a detour
tourner   to turn

See also **retourner** and **tourner**.

Can't find the verb you're looking for? Check the back pages of this book for a list of over 2,600 additional verbs!

The Seven Simple Tenses		The Seven Compound Tenses	
Singular	Plural	Singular	Plural
1 présent de l'indicatif		8 passé composé	
détruis	détruisons	ai détruit	avons détruit
détruis	détruisez	as détruit	avez détruit
détruit	détruisent	a détruit	ont détruit
2 imparfait de l'indicatif		9 plus-que-parfait de l'indicatif	
détruisais	détruisions	avais détruit	avions détruit
détruisais	détruisiez	avais détruit	aviez détruit
détruisait	détruisaient	avait détruit	avaient détruit
3 passé simple		10 passé antérieur	
détruisis	détruisîmes	eus détruit	eûmes détruit
détruisis	détruisîtes	eus détruit	eûtes détruit
détruisit	détruisirent	eut détruit	eurent détruit
4 futur		11 futur antérieur	
détruirai	détruirons	aurai détruit	aurons détruit
détruiras	détruirez	auras détruit	aurez détruit
détruira	détruiront	aura détruit	auront détruit
5 conditionnel		12 conditionnel passé	
détruirais	détruirions	aurais détruit	aurions détruit
détruirais	détruiriez	aurais détruit	auriez détruit
détruirait	détruiraient	aurait détruit	auraient détruit
6 présent du subjonctif		13 passé du subjonctif	
détruise	détruisions	aie détruit	ayons détruit
détruises	détruisiez	aies détruit	ayez détruit
détruise	détruisent	ait détruit	aient détruit
7 imparfait du subjonctif		14 plus-que-parfait du subjonctif	
détruisisse	détruisissions	eusse détruit	eussions détruit
détruisisses	détruisissiez	eusses détruit	eussiez détruit
détruisît	détruisissent	eût détruit	eussent détruit

Impératif
détruis
détruisons
détruisez

Words related to this verb
la **destruction**   destruction
destructif, destructive   destructive
destructeur, destructrice *adj.*   destructive;
  n. destroyer
la **destructivité**   destructiveness
destructible   destructible

se détruire   to destroy (to do away with)
  oneself
Les drogues ont détruit sa vie.   Drugs
  destroyed his/her life.

It's important that you be familiar with the Subjunctive. See pages 26–31.

The subject pronouns are found on page 103.   **283**

to develop, to spread out

The Seven Simple Tenses		The Seven Compound Tenses	
Singular	Plural	Singular	Plural
1 présent de l'indicatif		8 passé composé	
développe	développons	ai développé	avons développé
développes	développez	as développé	avez développé
développe	développent	a développé	ont développé
2 imparfait de l'indicatif		9 plus-que-parfait de l'indicatif	
développais	développions	avais développé	avions développé
développais	développiez	avais développé	aviez développé
développait	développaient	avait développé	avaient développé
3 passé simple		10 passé antérieur	
développai	développâmes	eus développé	eûmes développé
développas	développâtes	eus développé	eûtes développé
développa	développèrent	eut développé	eurent développé
4 futur		11 futur antérieur	
développerai	développerons	aurai développé	aurons développé
développeras	développerez	auras développé	aurez développé
développera	développeront	aura développé	auront développé
5 conditionnel		12 conditionnel passé	
développerais	développerions	aurais développé	aurions développé
développerais	développeriez	aurais développé	auriez développé
développerait	développeraient	aurait développé	auraient développé
6 présent du subjonctif		13 passé du subjonctif	
développe	développions	aie développé	ayons développé
développes	développiez	aies développé	ayez développé
développe	développent	ait développé	aient développé
7 imparfait du subjonctif		14 plus-que-parfait du subjonctif	
développasse	développassions	eusse développé	eussions développé
développasses	développassiez	eusses développé	eussiez développé
développât	développassent	eût développé	eussent développé

	Impératif
	développe
	développons
	développez

Words related to this verb

un développement   development
un enveloppement   envelopment, wrapping up; **enveloppement sinapisé**   mustard poultice
envelopper   to envelop, to wrap up
une enveloppe   envelope
développer une pellicule   to develop film

Don't forget to use the English-French verb index. It's in the Appendixes.

Irregular verb   to become

The Seven Simple Tenses		The Seven Compound Tenses	
Singular	Plural	Singular	Plural
1 présent de l'indicatif		**8 passé composé**	
deviens	devenons	suis devenu(e)	sommes devenu(e)s
deviens	devenez	es devenu(e)	êtes devenu(e)(s)
devient	deviennent	est devenu(e)	sont devenu(e)s
2 imparfait de l'indicatif		**9 plus-que-parfait de l'indicatif**	
devenais	devenions	étais devenu(e)	étions devenu(e)s
devenais	deveniez	étais devenu(e)	étiez devenu(e)(s)
devenait	devenaient	était devenu(e)	étaient devenu(e)s
3 passé simple		**10 passé antérieur**	
devins	devînmes	fus devenu(e)	fûmes devenu(e)s
devins	devîntes	fus devenu(e)	fûtes devenu(e)(s)
devint	devinrent	fut devenu(e)	furent devenu(e)s
4 futur		**11 futur antérieur**	
deviendrai	deviendrons	serai devenu(e)	serons devenu(e)s
deviendras	deviendrez	seras devenu(e)	serez devenu(e)(s)
deviendra	deviendront	sera devenu(e)	seront devenu(e)s
5 conditionnel		**12 conditionnel passé**	
deviendrais	deviendrions	serais devenu(e)	serions devenu(e)s
deviendrais	deviendriez	serais devenu(e)	seriez devenu(e)(s)
deviendrait	deviendraient	serait devenu(e)	seraient devenu(e)s
6 présent du subjonctif		**13 passé du subjonctif**	
devienne	devenions	sois devenu(e)	soyons devenu(e)s
deviennes	deveniez	sois devenu(e)	soyez devenu(e)(s)
devienne	deviennent	soit devenu(e)	soient devenu(e)s
7 imparfait du subjonctif		**14 plus-que-parfait du subjonctif**	
devinsse	devinssions	fusse devenu(e)	fussions devenu(e)s
devinsses	devinssiez	fusses devenu(e)	fussiez devenu(e)(s)
devînt	devinssent	fût devenu(e)	fussent devenu(e)s

Impératif
deviens
devenons
devenez

Common idiomatic expressions using this verb

J'ai entendu dire que Claudette est devenue docteur. Et vous, qu'est-ce que vous voulez devenir?

devenir fou, devenir folle   to go mad, crazy; **devenir vieux/grand**   to grow old/tall
Qu'est devenue votre soeur?   What has become of your sister?

See also **convenir, prévenir, revenir, se souvenir,** and **venir.**

Don't forget to study the section on defective and impersonal verbs. It's right after this main list.

to have to, must, ought, owe, should   Irregular verb

The Seven Simple Tenses		The Seven Compound Tenses	
Singular	Plural	Singular	Plural
1 présent de l'indicatif		**8 passé composé**	
dois	devons	ai dû	avons dû
dois	devez	as dû	avez dû
doit	doivent	a dû	ont dû
2 imparfait de l'indicatif		**9 plus-que-parfait de l'indicatif**	
devais	devions	avais dû	avions dû
devais	deviez	avais dû	aviez dû
devait	devaient	avait dû	avaient dû
3 passé simple		**10 passé antérieur**	
dus	dûmes	eus dû	eûmes dû
dus	dûtes	eus dû	eûtes dû
dut	durent	eut dû	eurent dû
4 futur		**11 futur antérieur**	
devrai	devrons	aurai dû	aurons dû
devras	devrez	auras dû	aurez dû
devra	devront	aura dû	auront dû
5 conditionnel		**12 conditionnel passé**	
devrais	devrions	aurais dû	aurions dû
devrais	devriez	aurais dû	auriez dû
devrait	devraient	aurait dû	auraient dû
6 présent du subjonctif		**13 passé du subjonctif**	
doive	devions	aie dû	ayons dû
doives	deviez	aies dû	ayez dû
doive	doivent	ait dû	aient dû
7 imparfait du subjonctif		**14 plus-que-parfait du subjonctif**	
dusse	dussions	eusse dû	eussions dû
dusses	dussiez	eusses dû	eussiez dû
dût	dussent	eût dû	eussent dû

Impératif
dois
devons
devez

AN ESSENTIAL 55 VERB

Devoir is a verb that you ought to know. It is useful in numerous everyday situations.

D

Sentences using devoir and words related to it

Cette grosse somme d'argent est due lundi. This large amount of money is due Monday.

Combien je vous dois? How much do I owe you?

Vous me devez cent euros. You owe me 100 euros.

J'ai dû attendre deux heures! I had to wait two hours!

Avant quelle heure dois-je quitter la chambre? Before what time must I leave (check out of) the room?

Hier soir, je suis allé au cinéma avec mes amis. Vous auriez dû venir avec nous. Le film était excellent. Yesterday evening I went to the movies with my friends. You should have come with us. The film was excellent.

—Où sont tes devoirs, Robert?
—Un lézard a mangé mes devoirs!
—Tu dois arrêter de dire des bêtises, Robert!

—Where is your homework, Robert?
—A lizard ate my homework!
—You should stop talking nonsense, Robert!

Words and expressions related to this verb

le devoir **duty, obligation**

les devoirs **homework**

faire ses devoirs **to do one's homework**

Don't forget to check the list of 2,600 additional verbs keyed to the 501 model verbs. It's in the Appendixes!

The subject pronouns are found on page 103.

to diminish, to decrease, to lessen

Regular **-er** verb

The Seven Simple Tenses		The Seven Compound Tenses	
Singular	Plural	Singular	Plural
1 présent de l'indicatif		8 passé composé	
diminue	diminuons	ai diminué	avons diminué
diminues	diminuez	as diminué	avez diminué
diminue	diminuent	a diminué	ont diminué
2 imparfait de l'indicatif		9 plus-que-parfait de l'indicatif	
diminuais	diminuions	avais diminué	avions diminué
diminuais	diminuiez	avais diminué	aviez diminué
diminuait	diminuaient	avait diminué	avaient diminué
3 passé simple		10 passé antérieur	
diminuai	diminuâmes	eus diminué	eûmes diminué
diminuas	diminuâtes	eus diminué	eûtes diminué
diminua	diminuèrent	eut diminué	eurent diminué
4 futur		11 futur antérieur	
diminuerai	diminuerons	aurai diminué	aurons diminué
diminueras	diminuerez	auras diminué	aurez diminué
diminuera	diminueront	aura diminué	auront diminué
5 conditionnel		12 conditionnel passé	
diminuerais	diminuerions	aurais diminué	aurions diminué
diminuerais	diminueriez	aurais diminué	auriez diminué
diminuerait	diminueraient	aurait diminué	auraient diminué
6 présent du subjonctif		13 passé du subjonctif	
diminue	diminuions	aie diminué	ayons diminué
diminues	diminuiez	aies diminué	ayez diminué
diminue	diminuent	ait diminué	aient diminué
7 imparfait du subjonctif		14 plus-que-parfait du subjonctif	
diminuasse	diminuassions	eusse diminué	eussions diminué
diminuasses	diminuassiez	eusses diminué	eussiez diminué
diminuât	diminuassent	eût diminué	eussent diminué

Impératif
diminue
diminuons
diminuez

Words and expressions related to this verb

une diminution   decrease, diminution, reduction
Le prix du café n'a pas diminué.   The price of coffee has not gone down.
Votre travail a diminué de moitié.   Your work has decreased by half.

diminutif, diminutive   diminutive
faire diminuer   to lower, to decrease
la diminution d'un prix   lowering of a price
se diminuer   to lower oneself

Don't forget to study the section on defective and impersonal verbs. It's right after this main list.

Regular **-er** verb   to dine, to have dinner

The Seven Simple Tenses | The Seven Compound Tenses

Singular	Plural	Singular	Plural
1 présent de l'indicatif		8 passé composé	
dîne	**dînons**	**ai dîné**	**avons dîné**
dînes	**dînez**	**as dîné**	**avez dîné**
dîne	**dînent**	**a dîné**	**ont dîné**
2 imparfait de l'indicatif		9 plus-que-parfait de l'indicatif	
dînais	**dînions**	**avais dîné**	**avions dîné**
dînais	**dîniez**	**avais dîné**	**aviez dîné**
dînait	**dînaient**	**avait dîné**	**avaient dîné**
3 passé simple		10 passé antérieur	
dînai	**dînâmes**	**eus dîné**	**eûmes dîné**
dînas	**dînâtes**	**eus dîné**	**eûtes dîné**
dîna	**dînèrent**	**eut dîné**	**eurent dîné**
4 futur		11 futur antérieur	
dînerai	**dînerons**	**aurai dîné**	**aurons dîné**
dîneras	**dînerez**	**auras dîné**	**aurez dîné**
dînera	**dîneront**	**aura dîné**	**auront dîné**
5 conditionnel		12 conditionnel passé	
dînerais	**dînerions**	**aurais dîné**	**aurions dîné**
dînerais	**dîneriez**	**aurais dîné**	**auriez dîné**
dînerait	**dîneraient**	**aurait dîné**	**auraient dîné**
6 présent du subjonctif		13 passé du subjonctif	
dîne	**dînions**	**aie dîné**	**ayons dîné**
dînes	**dîniez**	**aies dîné**	**ayez dîné**
dîne	**dînent**	**ait dîné**	**aient dîné**
7 imparfait du subjonctif		14 plus-que-parfait du subjonctif	
dînasse	**dînassions**	**eusse dîné**	**eussions dîné**
dînasses	**dînassiez**	**eusses dîné**	**eussiez dîné**
dînât	**dînassent**	**eût dîné**	**eussent dîné**

Impératif
dîne
dînons
dînez

Common idiomatic expressions using this verb

    Lundi j'ai dîné chez des amis. Mardi tu as dîné chez moi. Mercredi nous avons dîné chez Pierre. J'aurais dû dîner seul.

le dîner dinner	**un dîneur** diner
une dînette child's tea party	**donner un dîner** to give a dinner
l'heure du dîner dinner time	**dîner en ville** to dine out
j'aurais dû I should have	**J'aurais dû dîner.** I should have had dinner.

Try reading aloud this play on sounds (the letter **d**) as fast as you can:
Denis a dîné du dos d'un dindon dodu.
Dennis dined on (ate) the back of a plump turkey.

The subject pronouns are found on page 103.   **289**

to say, to tell   Irregular verb

The Seven Simple Tenses		The Seven Compound Tenses	
Singular	Plural	Singular	Plural
1 présent de l'indicatif		**8 passé composé**	
dis	disons	ai dit	avons dit
dis	dites	as dit	avez dit
dit	disent	a dit	ont dit
2 imparfait de l'indicatif		**9 plus-que-parfait de l'indicatif**	
disais	disions	avais dit	avions dit
disais	disiez	avais dit	aviez dit
disait	disaient	avait dit	avaient dit
3 passé simple		**10 passé antérieur**	
dis	dîmes	eus dit	eûmes dit
dis	dîtes	eus dit	eûtes dit
dit	dirent	eut dit	eurent dit
4 futur		**11 futur antérieur**	
dirai	dirons	aurai dit	aurons dit
diras	direz	auras dit	aurez dit
dira	diront	aura dit	auront dit
5 conditionnel		**12 conditionnel passé**	
dirais	dirions	aurais dit	aurions dit
dirais	diriez	aurais dit	auriez dit
dirait	diraient	aurait dit	auraient dit
6 présent du subjonctif		**13 passé du subjonctif**	
dise	disions	aie dit	ayons dit
dises	disiez	aies dit	ayez dit
dise	disent	ait dit	aient dit
7 imparfait du subjonctif		**14 plus-que-parfait du subjonctif**	
disse	dissions	eusse dit	eussions dit
disses	dissiez	eusses dit	eussiez dit
dît	dissent	eût dit	eussent dit

Impératif
dis
disons
dites

See also **contredire, interdire, maudire, médire, prédire,** and note the different *vous* form in the *présent de l'indicatif* and the *impératif.*

AN ESSENTIAL
55 VERB

Dire

D

Dire is an important verb for a beginning student because it is useful in many idiomatic expressions and situations and because there are many verbs conjugated like it.

Sentences using dire

J'entends dire que Tina s'est mariée avec
   Alexandre. I hear that Tina married Alexander.

Qu'est-ce que vous avez dit? What did you say?

Dites-moi comment ouvrir cette porte, s'il vous
   plaît. Please tell me how to open this door.

Qui l'aurait dit? Who would have thought so?

Que veut dire ce mot? What does this word mean?

Cela va sans dire. That goes without saying.

Cela me dit qqch. That rings a bell.

Words and expressions related to this verb

à ce qu'on dit . . . **according to what they say** . . .

à vrai dire **to tell the truth**

aussitôt dit, aussitôt fait **no sooner said than done**

avoir son mot à dire **to have one's say (in something)**

c'est-à-dire **that is, that is to say**

dire du bien de **to speak well of**

dire du mal de **to speak ill of**

Dis donc . . . **Say now . . .; Hey . . .**

entendre dire que **to hear it said that, to hear tell that**

soi-disant **so-called**

vouloir dire **to mean**

If you can conjugate **dire** you can also conjugate the following verbs:

contredire **to contradict**

se dédire **to retract, to go back on one's word** (être **for compound tenses**)

interdire **to forbid**

maudire **to curse**

médire de **to speak ill (badly) of**

prédire **to predict**

redire **to repeat, to say again**

Proverbs

Dis-moi ce que tu manges, je te dirai ce que tu es. **(Brillat-Savarin) Tell me what you eat and I will tell you what you are.**

Bien faire et laisser dire. **Do your work well and never mind the critics.**

Qui ne dit mot consent. **If you don't speak up you agree.**

The subject pronouns are found on page 103.

Part. pr. discutant   **Part. passé discuté**

to discuss, to argue

The Seven Simple Tenses		The Seven Compound Tenses	
Singular	Plural	Singular	Plural
1 présent de l'indicatif		**8 passé composé**	
discute	discutons	ai discuté	avons discuté
discutes	discutez	as discuté	avez discuté
discute	discutent	a discuté	ont discuté
2 imparfait de l'indicatif		**9 plus-que-parfait de l'indicatif**	
discutais	discutions	avais discuté	avions discuté
discutais	discutiez	avais discuté	aviez discuté
discutait	discutaient	avait discuté	avaient discuté
3 passé simple		**10 passé antérieur**	
discutai	discutâmes	eus discuté	eûmes discuté
discutas	discutâtes	eus discuté	eûtes discuté
discuta	discutèrent	eut discuté	eurent discuté
4 futur		**11 futur antérieur**	
discuterai	discuterons	aurai discuté	aurons discuté
discuteras	discuterez	auras discuté	aurez discuté
discutera	discuteront	aura discuté	auront discuté
5 conditionnel		**12 conditionnel passé**	
discuterais	discuterions	aurais discuté	aurions discuté
discuterais	discuteriez	aurais discuté	auriez discuté
discuterait	discuteraient	aurait discuté	auraient discuté
6 présent du subjonctif		**13 passé du subjonctif**	
discute	discutions	aie discuté	ayons discuté
discutes	discutiez	aies discuté	ayez discuté
discute	discutent	ait discuté	aient discuté
7 imparfait du subjonctif		**14 plus-que-parfait du subjonctif**	
discutasse	discutassions	eusse discuté	eussions discuté
discutasses	discutassiez	eusses discuté	eussiez discuté
discutât	discutassent	eût discuté	eussent discuté

Impératif
discute
discutons
discutez

Words and expressions related to this verb
une discussion discussion
discutable disputable, questionable
discuter avec to argue with; **discuter de** to argue about
un groupe de discussion newsgroup (Internet)

Get acquainted with what preposition goes with what verb. See *Verbs with prepositions*
in the Appendixes.

Irregular verb   to disappear

The Seven Simple Tenses		The Seven Compound Tenses	
Singular	Plural	Singular	Plural
1 présent de l'indicatif		**8 passé composé**	
disparais	disparaissons	ai disparu	avons disparu
disparais	disparaissez	as disparu	avez disparu
disparaît	disparaissent	a disparu	ont disparu
2 imparfait de l'indicatif		**9 plus-que-parfait de l'indicatif**	
disparaissais	disparaissions	avais disparu	avions disparu
disparaissais	disparaissiez	avais disparu	aviez disparu
disparaissait	disparaissaient	avait disparu	avaient disparu
3 passé simple		**10 passé antérieur**	
disparus	disparûmes	eus disparu	eûmes disparu
disparus	disparûtes	eus disparu	eûtes disparu
disparut	disparurent	eut disparu	eurent disparu
4 futur		**11 futur antérieur**	
disparaîtrai	disparaîtrons	aurai disparu	aurons disparu
disparaîtras	disparaîtrez	auras disparu	aurez disparu
disparaîtra	disparaîtront	aura disparu	auront disparu
5 conditionnel		**12 conditionnel passé**	
disparaîtrais	disparaîtrions	aurais disparu	aurions disparu
disparaîtrais	disparaîtriez	aurais disparu	auriez disparu
disparaîtrait	disparaîtraient	aurait disparu	auraient disparu
6 présent du subjonctif		**13 passé du subjonctif**	
disparaisse	disparaissions	aie disparu	ayons disparu
disparaisses	disparaissiez	aies disparu	ayez disparu
disparaisse	disparaissent	ait disparu	aient disparu
7 imparfait du subjonctif		**14 plus-que-parfait du subjonctif**	
disparusse	disparussions	eusse disparu	eussions disparu
disparusses	disparussiez	eusses disparu	eussiez disparu
disparût	disparussent	eût disparu	eussent disparu

Impératif
disparais
disparaissons
disparaissez

Words and expressions related to this verb
faire disparaître aux regards to hide from
   sight
notre cher ami disparu (notre chère amie
   disparue) our dear departed friend

la disparition disappearance, disappearing
disparu, disparue en mer lost at sea
être porté disparu to be declared missing
un disparu missing person

See also **apparaître, paraître,** and **reparaître.**

Grammar putting you in a tense mood? Review the definitions of basic grammatical terms with examples on pages 35–49.

The subject pronouns are found on page 103.

to give

The Seven Simple Tenses		The Seven Compound Tenses	
Singular	Plural	Singular	Plural
1 présent de l'indicatif		8 passé composé	
donne	donnons	ai donné	avons donné
donnes	donnez	as donné	avez donné
donne	donnent	a donné	ont donné
2 imparfait de l'indicatif		9 plus-que-parfait de l'indicatif	
donnais	donnions	avais donné	avions donné
donnais	donniez	avais donné	aviez donné
donnait	donnaient	avait donné	avaient donné
3 passé simple		10 passé antérieur	
donnai	donnâmes	eus donné	eûmes donné
donnas	donnâtes	eus donné	eûtes donné
donna	donnèrent	eut donné	eurent donné
4 futur		11 futur antérieur	
donnerai	donnerons	aurai donné	aurons donné
donneras	donnerez	auras donné	aurez donné
donnera	donneront	aura donné	auront donné
5 conditionnel		12 conditionnel passé	
donnerais	donnerions	aurais donné	aurions donné
donnerais	donneriez	aurais donné	auriez donné
donnerait	donneraient	aurait donné	auraient donné
6 présent du subjonctif		13 passé du subjonctif	
donne	donnions	aie donné	ayons donné
donnes	donniez	aies donné	ayez donné
donne	donnent	ait donné	aient donné
7 imparfait du subjonctif		14 plus-que-parfait du subjonctif	
donnasse	donnassions	eusse donné	eussions donné
donnasses	donnassiez	eusses donné	eussiez donné
donnât	donnassent	eût donné	eussent donné

Impératif
donne
donnons
donnez

AN ESSENTIAL
55 VERB

AN ESSENTIAL
55 VERB

Donner

Donner is an important verb for you to know because it is used in many everyday situations and idiomatic expressions. It is a regular **-er** verb.

Sentences using donner

La salle à manger donne sur le jardin. The dining room looks out on (faces) the garden.

Donnez-moi, s'il vous plaît, cet éclair et deux beignets aux pommes. Please give me this eclair and two apple fritters.

J'aimerais une chambre qui donne sur la rue. I would like a room that looks out on the street.

Proverbs and expressions

Il y a plus de bonheur à donner qu'à recevoir. It is better to give than to receive.

Ce qui est donné est donné. What is given is given. (Never take back what you have given.)

La façon de donner vaut mieux que ce qu'on donne. (Corneille) The way you give is worth more than what you give.

Words and expressions related to this verb

donner rendez-vous à qqn **to make an appointment (a date) with someone**

donner sur **to look out on**

donner à boire à qqn **to give someone something to drink**

donner à manger à qqn **to give someone something to eat**

donner congé à **to grant leave to**

donner du chagrin à qqn **to give someone grief**

donner un cours **to give a course, to lecture**

une base de données **database (computer)**

If you can conjugate **donner** you can also conjugate the following verbs (and any regular **-er** verb):

abandonner **to abandon**

amidonner **to starch**

se désabonner **to cancel a subscription (helping verb être)**

ordonner **to order, to prescribe**

pardonner **to pardon, to forgive**

randonner **to hike**

rognonner **to grumble**

ronronner **to purr**

Can't find the verb you're looking for? Check the back pages of this book for a list of over 2,600 additional verbs!

to sleep   Irregular verb

The Seven Simple Tenses		The Seven Compound Tenses	
Singular	Plural	Singular	Plural
1 présent de l'indicatif		8 passé composé	
dors	**dormons**	**ai dormi**	**avons dormi**
dors	**dormez**	**as dormi**	**avez dormi**
dort	**dorment**	**a dormi**	**ont dormi**
2 imparfait de l'indicatif		9 plus-que-parfait de l'indicatif	
dormais	**dormions**	**avais dormi**	**avions dormi**
dormais	**dormiez**	**avais dormi**	**aviez dormi**
dormait	**dormaient**	**avait dormi**	**avaient dormi**
3 passé simple		10 passé antérieur	
dormis	**dormîmes**	**eus dormi**	**eûmes dormi**
dormis	**dormîtes**	**eus dormi**	**eûtes dormi**
dormit	**dormirent**	**eut dormi**	**eurent dormi**
4 futur		11 futur antérieur	
dormirai	**dormirons**	**aurai dormi**	**aurons dormi**
dormiras	**dormirez**	**auras dormi**	**aurez dormi**
dormira	**dormiront**	**aura dormi**	**auront dormi**
5 conditionnel		12 conditionnel passé	
dormirais	**dormirions**	**aurais dormi**	**aurions dormi**
dormirais	**dormiriez**	**aurais dormi**	**auriez dormi**
dormirait	**dormiraient**	**aurait dormi**	**auraient dormi**
6 présent du subjonctif		13 passé du subjonctif	
dorme	**dormions**	**aie dormi**	**ayons dormi**
dormes	**dormiez**	**aies dormi**	**ayez dormi**
dorme	**dorment**	**ait dormi**	**aient dormi**
7 imparfait du subjonctif		14 plus-que-parfait du subjonctif	
dormisse	**dormissions**	**eusse dormi**	**eussions dormi**
dormisses	**dormissiez**	**eusses dormi**	**eussiez dormi**
dormît	**dormissent**	**eût dormi**	**eussent dormi**

Impératif
dors
dormons
dormez

Dormir

Dormir is an important verb for you to know because, although it is irregular, several verbs are conjugated like it. **Dormir** is also used in many idiomatic expressions and situations.

Sentences using dormir

As-tu bien dormi, chéri? Did you sleep well, darling?

J'ai acheté des bouche-oreilles et maintenant je dors comme une bûche. I bought some earplugs and now I sleep like a log.

La semaine prochaine nous allons faire du camping. J'aime bien dormir à la belle étoile. Next week we are going camping. I like to sleep outdoors.

Madeleine s'est endormie à une heure du matin. Madeleine fell asleep at one o'clock in the morning.

Words and expressions related to this verb

dormir toute la nuit to sleep through the night

parler en dormant to talk in one's sleep

empêcher de dormir to keep from sleeping

la dormition dormition (falling asleep)

le dortoir dormitory

dormir à la belle étoile to sleep outdoors

dormir sur les deux oreilles to sleep soundly

dormir comme une bûche to sleep like a log

avoir envie de dormir to feel like sleeping

un conte à dormir debout a cock-and-bull story

Proverb

Bon dîneur, mauvais dormeur. If you eat too much you won't sleep well.

If you can conjugate **dormir** you can also conjugate:

endormir to put to sleep

s'endormir to fall asleep (helping verb être)

redormir to sleep again, to sleep a little

more

rendormir to put to sleep again

se rendormir to fall asleep again (helping verb être)

The subject pronouns are found on page 103.

to doubt

Regular **-er** verb

The Seven Simple Tenses		The Seven Compound Tenses	
Singular	Plural	Singular	Plural
1 présent de l'indicatif		8 passé composé	
doute	**doutons**	**ai douté**	**avons douté**
doutes	**doutez**	**as douté**	**avez douté**
doute	**doutent**	**a douté**	**ont douté**
2 imparfait de l'indicatif		9 plus-que-parfait de l'indicatif	
doutais	**doutions**	**avais douté**	**avions douté**
doutais	**doutiez**	**avais douté**	**aviez douté**
doutait	**doutaient**	**avait douté**	**avaient douté**
3 passé simple		10 passé antérieur	
doutai	**doutâmes**	**eus douté**	**eûmes douté**
doutas	**doutâtes**	**eus douté**	**eûtes douté**
douta	**doutèrent**	**eut douté**	**eurent douté**
4 futur		11 futur antérieur	
douterai	**douterons**	**aurai douté**	**aurons douté**
douteras	**douterez**	**auras douté**	**aurez douté**
doutera	**douteront**	**aura douté**	**auront douté**
5 conditionnel		12 conditionnel passé	
douterais	**douterions**	**aurais douté**	**aurions douté**
douterais	**douteriez**	**aurais douté**	**auriez douté**
douterait	**douteraient**	**aurait douté**	**auraient douté**
6 présent du subjonctif		13 passé du subjonctif	
doute	**doutions**	**aie douté**	**ayons douté**
doutes	**doutiez**	**aies douté**	**ayez douté**
doute	**doutent**	**ait douté**	**aient douté**
7 imparfait du subjonctif		14 plus-que-parfait du subjonctif	
doutasse	**doutassions**	**eusse douté**	**eussions douté**
doutasses	**doutassiez**	**eusses douté**	**eussiez douté**
doutât	**doutassent**	**eût douté**	**eussent douté**

Impératif
doute
doutons
doutez

Common idiomatic expressions using this verb
Je doute que cet homme soit coupable. Il n'y a pas de doute qu'il est innocent.

le doute   doubt
sans doute   no doubt
sans aucun doute   undoubtedly
d'un air de doute   dubiously
redouter   to dread, to fear

ne douter de rien   to doubt nothing, to be too
   credulous
ne se douter de rien   to suspect nothing
se douter de   to suspect
douteux, douteuse   doubtful

It's important that you be familiar with the Subjunctive. See pages 26–31.

Regular **-er** verb   to escape, to avoid

The Seven Simple Tenses		The Seven Compound Tenses	
Singular	Plural	Singular	Plural
1 présent de l'indicatif		8 passé composé	
échappe	échappons	ai échappé	avons échappé
échappes	échappez	as échappé	avez échappé
échappe	échappent	a échappé	ont échappé
2 imparfait de l'indicatif		9 plus-que-parfait de l'indicatif	
échappais	échappions	avais échappé	avions échappé
échappais	échappiez	avais échappé	aviez échappé
échappait	échappaient	avait échappé	avaient échappé
3 passé simple		10 passé antérieur	
échappai	échappâmes	eus échappé	eûmes échappé
échappas	échappâtes	eus échappé	eûtes échappé
échappa	échappèrent	eut échappé	eurent échappé
4 futur		11 futur antérieur	
échapperai	échapperons	aurai échappé	aurons échappé
échapperas	échapperez	auras échappé	aurez échappé
échappera	échapperont	aura échappé	auront échappé
5 conditionnel		12 conditionnel passé	
échapperais	échapperions	aurais échappé	aurions échappé
échapperais	échapperiez	aurais échappé	auriez échappé
échapperait	échapperaient	aurait échappé	auraient échappé
6 présent du subjonctif		13 passé du subjonctif	
échappe	échappions	aie échappé	ayons échappé
échappes	échappiez	aies échappé	ayez échappé
échappe	échappent	ait échappé	aient échappé
7 imparfait du subjonctif		14 plus-que-parfait du subjonctif	
échappasse	échappassions	eusse échappé	eussions échappé
échappasses	échappassiez	eusses échappé	eussiez échappé
échappât	échappassent	eût échappé	eussent échappé

Impératif
échappe
échappons
échappez

Words and expressions related to this verb
échapper à to avoid; **échapper de** to escape from
l'échapper belle to have a narrow escape; **Je l'ai échappé belle.** I had a narrow escape.
Cela m'a échappé. I did not notice it.
Cela m'est échappé. It slipped my mind (I forgot it).
laisser échapper to let slip, to overlook
s'échapper de to escape from
une échappée de lumière a glimmer of light
l'échappement *m.* exhaust
le pot d'échappement muffler (auto)

Check out the principal parts of some important French verbs on page 7.

échouer (175) Part. pr. échouant Part. passé échoué

to fail, to run aground

Regular **-er** verb

The Seven Simple Tenses		The Seven Compound Tenses	
Singular	Plural	Singular	Plural
1 présent de l'indicatif		**8 passé composé**	
échoue	échouons	ai échoué	avons échoué
échoues	échouez	as échoué	avez échoué
échoue	échouent	a échoué	ont échoué
2 imparfait de l'indicatif		**9 plus-que-parfait de l'indicatif**	
échouais	échouions	avais échoué	avions échoué
échouais	échouiez	avais échoué	aviez échoué
échouait	échouaient	avait échoué	avaient échoué
3 passé simple		**10 passé antérieur**	
échouai	échouâmes	eus échoué	eûmes échoué
échouas	échouâtes	eus échoué	eûtes échoué
échoua	échouèrent	eut échoué	eurent échoué
4 futur		**11 futur antérieur**	
échouerai	échouerons	aurai échoué	aurons échoué
échoueras	échouerez	auras échoué	aurez échoué
échouera	échoueront	aura échoué	auront échoué
5 conditionnel		**12 conditionnel passé**	
échouerais	échouerions	aurais échoué	aurions échoué
échouerais	échoueriez	aurais échoué	auriez échoué
échouerait	échoueraient	aurait échoué	auraient échoué
6 présent du subjonctif		**13 passé du subjonctif**	
échoue	échouions	aie échoué	ayons échoué
échoues	échouiez	aies échoué	ayez échoué
échoue	échouent	ait échoué	aient échoué
7 imparfait du subjonctif		**14 plus-que-parfait du subjonctif**	
échouasse	échouassions	eusse échoué	eussions échoué
échouasses	échouassiez	eusses échoué	eussiez échoué
échouât	échouassent	eût échoué	eussent échoué

Impératif
échoue
échouons
échouez

Common idiomatic expressions using this verb
échouer à qqch to fail (flunk) at something
échouer à un examen to flunk an exam
échouer to touch bottom (accidentally), to fail
Tous mes espoirs ont échoué. All my hopes have touched bottom (have failed).
Le bateau a échoué sur un banc de sable. The ship ran aground on a shoal.

Can't find the verb you're looking for? Check the back pages of this book for a list of over 2,600 additional verbs!

300

Regular **-er** verb   to listen (to)

The Seven Simple Tenses		The Seven Compound Tenses	
Singular	Plural	Singular	Plural
1 présent de l'indicatif		8 passé composé	
écoute	écoutons	ai écouté	avons écouté
écoutes	écoutez	as écouté	avez écouté
écoute	écoutent	a écouté	ont écouté
2 imparfait de l'indicatif		9 plus-que-parfait de l'indicatif	
écoutais	écoutions	avais écouté	avions écouté
écoutais	écoutiez	avais écouté	aviez écouté
écoutait	écoutaient	avait écouté	avaient écouté
3 passé simple		10 passé antérieur	
écoutai	écoutâmes	eus écouté	eûmes écouté
écoutas	écoutâtes	eus écouté	eûtes écouté
écouta	écoutèrent	eut écouté	eurent écouté
4 futur		11 futur antérieur	
écouterai	écouterons	aurai écouté	aurons écouté
écouteras	écouterez	auras écouté	aurez écouté
écoutera	écouteront	aura écouté	auront écouté
5 conditionnel		12 conditionnel passé	
écouterais	écouterions	aurais écouté	aurions écouté
écouterais	écouteriez	aurais écouté	auriez écouté
écouterait	écouteraient	aurait écouté	auraient écouté
6 présent du subjonctif		13 passé du subjonctif	
écoute	écoutions	aie écouté	ayons écouté
écoutes	écoutiez	aies écouté	ayez écouté
écoute	écoutent	ait écouté	aient écouté
7 imparfait du subjonctif		14 plus-que-parfait du subjonctif	
écoutasse	écoutassions	eusse écouté	eussions écouté
écoutasses	écoutassiez	eusses écouté	eussiez écouté
écoutât	écoutassent	eût écouté	eussent écouté

Impératif
écoute
écoutons
écoutez

Common idiomatic expressions using this verb and words related to it
Ecoutez-vous le professeur quand il explique la leçon? L'avez-vous écouté ce matin en classe?

aimer à s'écouter parler   to love to hear one's own voice
un écouteur   telephone receiver (earpiece)
être à l'écoute   to be listening in
être aux écoutes   to be on the watch, to eavesdrop

n'écouter personne   not to heed anyone
savoir écouter   to be a good listener
écouter aux portes   to eavesdrop, to listen secretly
Ecoutez-moi.   Listen to me.
Je vous écoute.   I'm listening to you.
Parlez donc!   Speak up!

Don't forget to study the section on defective and impersonal verbs. It's right after this main list.

The subject pronouns are found on page 103.   **301**

Part. pr. **écrivant**   Part. passé **écrit**

Irregular verb

The Seven Simple Tenses		The Seven Compound Tenses	
Singular	Plural	Singular	Plural
1 présent de l'indicatif		**8 passé composé**	
écris	écrivons	ai écrit	avons écrit
écris	écrivez	as écrit	avez écrit
écrit	écrivent	a écrit	ont écrit
2 imparfait de l'indicatif		**9 plus-que-parfait de l'indicatif**	
écrivais	écrivions	avais écrit	avions écrit
écrivais	écriviez	avais écrit	aviez écrit
écrivait	écrivaient	avait écrit	avaient écrit
3 passé simple		**10 passé antérieur**	
écrivis	écrivîmes	eus écrit	eûmes écrit
écrivis	écrivîtes	eus écrit	eûtes écrit
écrivit	écrivirent	eut écrit	eurent écrit
4 futur		**11 futur antérieur**	
écrirai	écrirons	aurai écrit	aurons écrit
écriras	écrirez	auras écrit	aurez écrit
écrira	écriront	aura écrit	auront écrit
5 conditionnel		**12 conditionnel passé**	
écrirais	écririons	aurais écrit	aurions écrit
écrirais	écririez	aurais écrit	auriez écrit
écrirait	écriraient	aurait écrit	auraient écrit
6 présent du subjonctif		**13 passé du subjonctif**	
écrive	écrivions	aie écrit	ayons écrit
écrives	écriviez	aies écrit	ayez écrit
écrive	écrivent	ait écrit	aient écrit
7 imparfait du subjonctif		**14 plus-que-parfait du subjonctif**	
écrivisse	écrivissions	eusse écrit	eussions écrit
écrivisses	écrivissiez	eusses écrit	eussiez écrit
écrivît	écrivissent	eût écrit	eussent écrit

Impératif
écris
écrivons
écrivez

AN ESSENTIAL
55 VERB

Écrire is a very useful verb for a beginning French student. There are several verbs that are conjugated like **écrire**.

E

Sentences using écrire

Jean: As-tu écrit ta composition pour la classe de français?
Jeanne: Non, je ne l'ai pas écrite.
Jean: Écris-la tout de suite!

John: Did you write your composition for French class?
Jean: No, I didn't write it.
John: Write it right away!

J'ai oublié mon stylo. Pourrais-tu me prêter de quoi écrire? I forgot my pen. Could you lend me something to write with?

C'est un nom bizarre. Comment est-ce que cela s'écrit? That's a strange name. How is it written?

Avant donc d'écrire, apprenez à penser. (Boileau) Before writing, learn to think.

Words and expressions related to this verb

un écrivain writer

une femme écrivain female writer; **une écrivaine (Québec)** female writer

écriture f. handwriting, writing

par écrit in writing

écrivasser to write badly

une machine à écrire a typewriter

de quoi écrire something to write with

écrire un petit mot à qqn to write a note to someone

If you can conjugate **écrire** you can also conjugate these verbs:

circonscrire **to limit, circumscribe**

décrire **to describe**

inscrire **to inscribe, write down**

prescrire **to prescribe**

proscrire **to proscribe, ban, outlaw**

récrire, réécrire **to rewrite**

retranscrire **to retranscribe**

souscrire à **to subscribe to**

transcrire **to transcribe**

to frighten

Regular **-er** verb endings; spelling change: **-ayer** verbs may change **y** to **i** in front of a mute **e** or may keep **y**

The Seven Simple Tenses		The Seven Compound Tenses	
Singular	Plural	Singular	Plural
1 présent de l'indicatif		8 passé composé	
effraye	effrayons	ai effrayé	avons effrayé
effrayes	effrayez	as effrayé	avez effrayé
effraye	effrayent	a effrayé	ont effrayé
2 imparfait de l'indicatif		9 plus-que-parfait de l'indicatif	
effrayais	effrayions	avais effrayé	avions effrayé
effrayais	effrayiez	avais effrayé	aviez effrayé
effrayait	effrayaient	avait effrayé	avaient effrayé
3 passé simple		10 passé antérieur	
effrayai	effrayâmes	eus effrayé	eûmes effrayé
effrayas	effrayâtes	eus effrayé	eûtes effrayé
effraya	effrayèrent	eut effrayé	eurent effrayé
4 futur		11 futur antérieur	
effrayerai	effrayerons	aurai effrayé	aurons effrayé
effrayeras	effrayerez	auras effrayé	aurez effrayé
effrayera	effrayeront	aura effrayé	auront effrayé
5 conditionnel		12 conditionnel passé	
effrayerais	effrayerions	aurais effrayé	aurions effrayé
effrayerais	effrayeriez	aurais effrayé	auriez effrayé
effrayerait	effrayeraient	aurait effrayé	auraient effrayé
6 présent du subjonctif		13 passé du subjonctif	
effraye	effrayions	aie effrayé	ayons effrayé
effrayes	effrayiez	aies effrayé	ayez effrayé
effraye	effrayent	ait effrayé	aient effrayé
7 imparfait du subjonctif		14 plus-que-parfait du subjonctif	
effrayasse	effrayassions	eusse effrayé	eussions effrayé
effrayasses	effrayassiez	eusses effrayé	eussiez effrayé
effrayât	effrayassent	eût effrayé	eussent effrayé

Impératif
effraye
effrayons
effrayez

Sentences using this verb and words related to it

Le tigre a effrayé l'enfant. L'enfant a effrayé le singe. Le singe effraiera le bébé. C'est effrayant!

effrayant, effrayante frightful, awful
effrayé, effrayée frightened
l'effroi *m.* fright, terror

effroyable dreadful, fearful
effroyablement dreadfully, fearfully

Don't forget to check the list of 2,600 additional verbs keyed to the 501 model verbs. It's in the Appendixes!

Regular **-er** verb endings; spelling change: **-ayer** verbs
may change **y** to **i** in front of a mute **e** or may keep **y**

to amuse, to cheer up,
to enliven, to entertain

The Seven Simple Tenses		The Seven Compound Tenses	
Singular	Plural	Singular	Plural
1 présent de l'indicatif		**8 passé composé**	
égaye	égayons	ai égayé	avons égayé
égayes	égayez	as égayé	avez égayé
égaye	égayent	a égayé	ont égayé
2 imparfait de l'indicatif		**9 plus-que-parfait de l'indicatif**	
égayais	égayions	avais égayé	avions égayé
égayais	égayiez	avais égayé	aviez égayé
égayait	égayaient	avait égayé	avaient égayé
3 passé simple		**10 passé antérieur**	
égayai	égayâmes	eus égayé	eûmes égayé
égayas	égayâtes	eus égayé	eûtes égayé
égaya	égayèrent	eut égayé	eurent égayé
4 futur		**11 futur antérieur**	
égayerai	égayerons	aurai égayé	aurons égayé
égayeras	égayerez	auras égayé	aurez égayé
égayera	égayeront	aura égayé	auront égayé
5 conditionnel		**12 conditionnel passé**	
égayerais	égayerions	aurais égayé	aurions égayé
égayerais	égayeriez	aurais égayé	auriez égayé
égayerait	égayeraient	aurait égayé	auraient égayé
6 présent du subjonctif		**13 passé du subjonctif**	
égaye	égayions	aie égayé	ayons égayé
égayes	égayiez	aies égayé	ayez égayé
égaye	égayent	ait égayé	aient égayé
7 imparfait du subjonctif		**14 plus-que-parfait du subjonctif**	
égayasse	égayassions	eusse égayé	eussions égayé
égayasses	égayassiez	eusses égayé	eussiez égayé
égayât	égayassent	eût égayé	eussent égayé

Impératif
égaye
égayons
égayez

Words related to this verb

égayant, égayante   lively
un égaiement   amusement
s'égayer aux dépens de   to amuse oneself at
   someone's expense

gai, gaie   gay, cheerful, merry
gaiement   gaily, cheerfully

Grammar putting you in a tense mood? Review the definitions of basic grammatical terms on pages 35–49.

The subject pronouns are found on page 103.

to raise, to rear, to bring up

Regular **-er** verb endings; spelling change:
e changes to **è** before syllable with mute **e**

The Seven Simple Tenses		The Seven Compound Tenses	
Singular	Plural	Singular	Plural
1 présent de l'indicatif		8 passé composé	
élève	élevons	ai élevé	avons élevé
élèves	élevez	as élevé	avez élevé
élève	élèvent	a élevé	ont élevé
2 imparfait de l'indicatif		9 plus-que-parfait de l'indicatif	
élevais	élevions	avais élevé	avions élevé
élevais	éleviez	avais élevé	aviez élevé
élevait	élevaient	avait élevé	avaient élevé
3 passé simple		10 passé antérieur	
élevai	élevâmes	eus élevé	eûmes élevé
élevas	élevâtes	eus élevé	eûtes élevé
éleva	élevèrent	eut élevé	eurent élevé
4 futur		11 futur antérieur	
élèverai	élèverons	aurai élevé	aurons élevé
élèveras	élèverez	auras élevé	aurez élevé
élèvera	élèveront	aura élevé	auront élevé
5 conditionnel		12 conditionnel passé	
élèverais	élèverions	aurais élevé	aurions élevé
élèverais	élèveriez	aurais élevé	auriez élevé
élèverait	élèveraient	aurait élevé	auraient élevé
6 présent du subjonctif		13 passé du subjonctif	
élève	élevions	aie élevé	ayons élevé
élèves	éleviez	aies élevé	ayez élevé
élève	élèvent	ait élevé	aient élevé
7 imparfait du subjonctif		14 plus-que-parfait du subjonctif	
élevasse	élevassions	eusse élevé	eussions élevé
élevasses	élevassiez	eusses élevé	eussiez élevé
élevât	élevassent	eût élevé	eussent élevé

Impératif
élève
élevons
élevez

Words and expressions related to this verb
un, une élève   pupil, student; **un, une élève
   professeur**   student teacher
élevage *m.*   breeding, rearing; **occuper une
   position élevée**   to hold a high position

élévation *f.*   elevation, raising; **La musique
   élève l'âme.**   Music uplifts the soul.
bien élevé   well-bred, well brought up
mal élevé   ill-bred, badly brought up

Car quiconque s'élève sera abaissé, et celui qui s'abaisse sera élevé.   For whoever exalts
   himself will be humbled, and he who humbles himself will be exalted. (Luke 14:11)

See also **enlever** and **lever**.

Irregular verb   to elect, to choose

The Seven Simple Tenses		The Seven Compound Tenses	
Singular	Plural	Singular	Plural
1 présent de l'indicatif		**8 passé composé**	
élis	**élisons**	**ai élu**	**avons élu**
élis	**élisez**	**as élu**	**avez élu**
élit	**élisent**	**a élu**	**ont élu**
2 imparfait de l'indicatif		**9 plus-que-parfait de l'indicatif**	
élisais	**élisions**	**avais élu**	**avions élu**
élisais	**élisiez**	**avais élu**	**aviez élu**
élisait	**élisaient**	**avait élu**	**avaient élu**
3 passé simple		**10 passé antérieur**	
élus	**élûmes**	**eus élu**	**eûmes élu**
élus	**élûtes**	**eus élu**	**eûtes élu**
élut	**élurent**	**eut élu**	**eurent élu**
4 futur		**11 futur antérieur**	
élirai	**élirons**	**aurai élu**	**aurons élu**
éliras	**élirez**	**auras élu**	**aurez élu**
élira	**éliront**	**aura élu**	**auront élu**
5 conditionnel		**12 conditionnel passé**	
élirais	**élirions**	**aurais élu**	**aurions élu**
élirais	**éliriez**	**aurais élu**	**auriez élu**
élirait	**éliraient**	**aurait élu**	**auraient élu**
6 présent du subjonctif		**13 passé du subjonctif**	
élise	**élisions**	**aie élu**	**ayons élu**
élises	**élisiez**	**aies élu**	**ayez élu**
élise	**élisent**	**ait élu**	**aient élu**
7 imparfait du subjonctif		**14 plus-que-parfait du subjonctif**	
élusse	**élussions**	**eusse élu**	**eussions élu**
élusses	**élussiez**	**eusses élu**	**eussiez élu**
élût	**élussent**	**eût élu**	**eussent élu**

Impératif
élis
élisons
élisez

Words and expressions related to this verb
Car il y a beaucoup d'appelés mais peu d'élus. For many are called but few are chosen.
    (Matthew 22:14)
une élection election, choice
le jour des élections election day
électif, élective elective
un électeur, une électrice voter
se rendre aux urnes to vote, go to the polls

Don't forget to use the English-French verb index. It's in the Appendixes.

The subject pronouns are found on page 103.   **307**

to move away, to go away, to withdraw,
to step back, to keep back, to keep away

Reflexive regular -er verb

The Seven Simple Tenses		The Seven Compound Tenses	
Singular	Plural	Singular	Plural
1 présent de l'indicatif		8 passé composé	
m'éloigne	nous éloignons	me suis éloigné(e)	nous sommes éloigné(e)s
t'éloignes	vous éloignez	t'es éloigné(e)	vous êtes éloigné(e)(s)
s'éloigne	s'éloignent	s'est éloigné(e)	se sont éloigné(e)s
2 imparfait de l'indicatif		9 plus-que-parfait de l'indicatif	
m'éloignais	nous éloignions	m'étais éloigné(e)	nous étions éloigné(e)s
t'éloignais	vous éloigniez	t'étais éloigné(e)	vous étiez éloigné(e)(s)
s'éloignait	s'éloignaient	s'était éloigné(e)	s'étaient éloigné(e)s
3 passé simple		10 passé antérieur	
m'éloignai	nous éloignâmes	me fus éloigné(e)	nous fûmes éloigné(e)s
t'éloignas	vous éloignâtes	te fus éloigné(e)	vous fûtes éloigné(e)(s)
s'éloigna	s'éloignèrent	se fut éloigné(e)	se furent éloigné(e)s
4 futur		11 futur antérieur	
m'éloignerai	nous éloignerons	me serai éloigné(e)	nous serons éloigné(e)s
t'éloigneras	vous éloignerez	te seras éloigné(e)	vous serez éloigné(e)(s)
s'éloignera	s'éloigneront	se sera éloigné(e)	se seront éloigné(e)s
5 conditionnel		12 conditionnel passé	
m'éloignerais	nous éloignerions	me serais éloigné(e)	nous serions éloigné(e)s
t'éloignerais	vous éloigneriez	te serais éloigné(e)	vous seriez éloigné(e)(s)
s'éloignerait	s'éloigneraient	se serait éloigné(e)	se seraient éloigné(e)s
6 présent du subjonctif		13 passé du subjonctif	
m'éloigne	nous éloignions	me sois éloigné(e)	nous soyons éloigné(e)s
t'éloignes	vous éloigniez	te sois éloigné(e)	vous soyez éloigné(e)(s)
s'éloigne	s'éloignent	se soit éloigné(e)	se soient éloigné(e)s
7 imparfait du subjonctif		14 plus-que-parfait du subjonctif	
m'éloignasse	nous éloignassions	me fusse éloigné(e)	nous fussions éloigné(e)s
t'éloignasses	vous éloignassiez	te fusses éloigné(e)	vous fussiez éloigné(e)(s)
s'éloignât	s'éloignassent	se fût éloigné(e)	se fussent éloigné(e)s

Impératif
éloigne-toi; ne t'éloigne pas
éloignons-nous; ne nous éloignons pas
éloignez-vous; ne vous éloignez pas

Words and expressions related to this verb
éloigner de   to keep away from, to keep at a distance
s'éloigner de   to keep one's distance from, to move away from
s'éloigner en courant   to run away, to move away while running
loin   far; lointain, lointaine   distant
loin de là, loin de ça   far from it
Loin des yeux, loin du coeur.   Out of sight, out of mind.
Eloignez-vous, s'il vous plaît!   Stay back! Keep your distance, please!
l'éloignement m.   distance

Regular **-er** verb

to kiss, to embrace

The Seven Simple Tenses		The Seven Compound Tenses	
Singular	Plural	Singular	Plural

1 présent de l'indicatif		8 passé composé	
embrasse	embrassons	ai embrassé	avons embrassé
embrasses	embrassez	as embrassé	avez embrassé
embrasse	embrassent	a embrassé	ont embrassé

2 imparfait de l'indicatif		9 plus-que-parfait de l'indicatif	
embrassais	embrassions	avais embrassé	avions embrassé
embrassais	embrassiez	avais embrassé	aviez embrassé
embrassait	embrassaient	avait embrassé	avaient embrassé

3 passé simple		10 passé antérieur	
embrassai	embrassâmes	eus embrassé	eûmes embrassé
embrassas	embrassâtes	eus embrassé	eûtes embrassé
embrassa	embrassèrent	eut embrassé	eurent embrassé

4 futur		11 futur antérieur	
embrasserai	embrasserons	aurai embrassé	aurons embrassé
embrasseras	embrasserez	auras embrassé	aurez embrassé
embrassera	embrasseront	aura embrassé	auront embrassé

5 conditionnel		12 conditionnel passé	
embrasserais	embrasserions	aurais embrassé	aurions embrassé
embrasserais	embrasseriez	aurais embrassé	auriez embrassé
embrasserait	embrasseraient	aurait embrassé	auraient embrassé

6 présent du subjonctif		13 passé du subjonctif	
embrasse	embrassions	aie embrassé	ayons embrassé
embrasses	embrassiez	aies embrassé	ayez embrassé
embrasse	embrassent	ait embrassé	aient embrassé

7 imparfait du subjonctif		14 plus-que-parfait du subjonctif	
embrassasse	embrassassions	eusse embrassé	eussions embrassé
embrassasses	embrassassiez	eusses embrassé	eussiez embrassé
embrassât	embrassassent	eût embrassé	eussent embrassé

Impératif
embrasse
embrassons
embrassez

Sentences using this verb and words related to it
—Embrasse-moi. Je t'aime. Ne me quitte pas.
—Je t'embrasse. Je t'aime aussi. Je ne te quitte pas. Embrassons-nous.

le bras   arm
un embrassement   embracement, embrace
s'embrasser   to embrace each other, to hug each other
embrasseur, embrasseuse   a person who likes to kiss a lot

How are you doing? Find out with the verb drills and tests with answers explained on pages 50–101.

emmener (184)   Part. pr. **emmenant**   Part. passé **emmené**

to lead, to lead away, to take away (persons)

Regular **-er** verb endings; spelling change: **e** changes to **è** before syllable with mute **e**

The Seven Simple Tenses		The Seven Compound Tenses	
Singular	Plural	Singular	Plural
1 présent de l'indicatif		8 passé composé	
emmène	emmenons	ai emmené	avons emmené
emmènes	emmenez	as emmené	avez emmené
emmène	emmènent	a emmené	ont emmené
2 imparfait de l'indicatif		9 plus-que-parfait de l'indicatif	
emmenais	emmenions	avais emmené	avions emmené
emmenais	emmeniez	avais emmené	aviez emmené
emmenait	emmenaient	avait emmené	avaient emmené
3 passé simple		10 passé antérieur	
emmenai	emmenâmes	eus emmené	eûmes emmené
emmenas	emmenâtes	eus emmené	eûtes emmené
emmena	emmenèrent	eut emmené	eurent emmené
4 futur		11 futur antérieur	
emmènerai	emmènerons	aurai emmené	aurons emmené
emmèneras	emmènerez	auras emmené	aurez emmené
emmènera	emmèneront	aura emmené	auront emmené
5 conditionnel		12 conditionnel passé	
emmènerais	emmènerions	aurais emmené	aurions emmené
emmènerais	emmèneriez	aurais emmené	auriez emmené
emmènerait	emmèneraient	aurait emmené	auraient emmené
6 présent du subjonctif		13 passé du subjonctif	
emmène	emmenions	aie emmené	ayons emmené
emmènes	emmeniez	aies emmené	ayez emmené
emmène	emmènent	ait emmené	aient emmené
7 imparfait du subjonctif		14 plus-que-parfait du subjonctif	
emmenasse	emmenassions	eusse emmené	eussions emmené
emmenasses	emmenassiez	eusses emmené	eussiez emmené
emmenât	emmenassent	eût emmené	eussent emmené

Impératif
emmène
emmenons
emmenez

Sentences using this verb and words related to it

Quand j'emmène une personne d'un lieu dans un autre, je mène cette personne avec moi.
Mon père nous emmènera au cinéma lundi prochain. Samedi dernier il nous a emmenés au théâtre.

Le train m'a emmené à Paris.   The train took me to Paris.
Un agent de police a emmené l'assassin.   A policeman took away the assassin.

See also **mener** and **amener**.

Can't find the verb you're looking for? Check the back pages of this book for a list of over 2,600 additional verbs!

Irregular verb   to move, to touch, to excite, to arouse

The Seven Simple Tenses		The Seven Compound Tenses	
Singular	Plural	Singular	Plural
1 présent de l'indicatif		8 passé composé	
émeus	émouvons	ai ému	avons ému
émeus	émouvez	as ému	avez ému
émeut	émeuvent	a ému	ont ému
2 imparfait de l'indicatif		9 plus-que-parfait de l'indicatif	
émouvais	émouvions	avais ému	avions ému
émouvais	émouviez	avais ému	aviez ému
émouvait	émouvaient	avait ému	avaient ému
3 passé simple		10 passé antérieur	
émus	émûmes	eus ému	eûmes ému
émus	émûtes	eus ému	eûtes ému
émut	émurent	eut ému	eurent ému
4 futur		11 futur antérieur	
émouvrai	émouvrons	aurai ému	aurons ému
émouvras	émouvrez	auras ému	aurez ému
émouvra	émouvront	aura ému	auront ému
5 conditionnel		12 conditionnel passé	
émouvrais	émouvrions	aurais ému	aurions ému
émouvrais	émouvriez	aurais ému	auriez ému
émouvrait	émouvraient	aurait ému	auraient ému
6 présent du subjonctif		13 passé du subjonctif	
émeuve	émouvions	aie ému	ayons ému
émeuves	émouviez	aies ému	ayez ému
émeuve	émeuvent	ait ému	aient ému
7 imparfait du subjonctif		14 plus-que-parfait du subjonctif	
émusse	émussions	eusse ému	eussions ému
émusses	émussiez	eusses ému	eussiez ému
émût	émussent	eût ému	eussent ému

Impératif
émeus
émouvons
émouvez

Words and expressions related to this verb
s'émouvoir de to be moved (touched) by
une émeute insurrection, insurgency
un émeutier, une émeutière insurrectionist, insurgent, rioter
être ému(e) to be moved

émouvant, émouvante moving, touching
fort émouvant thrilling
émouvoir la pitié de qqn to move someone to pity
l'émotion *f.* feeling

Don't forget to check the list of 2,600 additional verbs keyed to the 501 model verbs. It's in the Appendixes!

to hinder, to prevent

Regular **-er** verb

The Seven Simple Tenses		The Seven Compound Tenses	
Singular	Plural	Singular	Plural
1 présent de l'indicatif		8 passé composé	
empêche	empêchons	ai empêché	avons empêché
empêches	empêchez	as empêché	avez empêché
empêche	empêchent	a empêché	ont empêché
2 imparfait de l'indicatif		9 plus-que-parfait de l'indicatif	
empêchais	empêchions	avais empêché	avions empêché
empêchais	empêchiez	avais empêché	aviez empêché
empêchait	empêchaient	avait empêché	avaient empêché
3 passé simple		10 passé antérieur	
empêchai	empêchâmes	eus empêché	eûmes empêché
empêchas	empêchâtes	eus empêché	eûtes empêché
empêcha	empêchèrent	eut empêché	eurent empêché
4 futur		11 futur antérieur	
empêcherai	empêcherons	aurai empêché	aurons empêché
empêcheras	empêcherez	auras empêché	aurez empêché
empêchera	empêcheront	aura empêché	auront empêché
5 conditionnel		12 conditionnel passé	
empêcherais	empêcherions	aurais empêché	aurions empêché
empêcherais	empêcheriez	aurais empêché	auriez empêché
empêcherait	empêcheraient	aurait empêché	auraient empêché
6 présent du subjonctif		13 passé du subjonctif	
empêche	empêchions	aie empêché	ayons empêché
empêches	empêchiez	aies empêché	ayez empêché
empêche	empêchent	ait empêché	aient empêché
7 imparfait du subjonctif		14 plus-que-parfait du subjonctif	
empêchasse	empêchassions	eusse empêché	eussions empêché
empêchasses	empêchassiez	eusses empêché	eussiez empêché
empêchât	empêchassent	eût empêché	eussent empêché

Impératif
empêche
empêchons
empêchez

Sentences using this verb and words related to it
Georgette a empêché son frère de finir ses devoirs parce qu'elle jouait des disques en même temps. Le bruit était un vrai empêchement.

un empêchement   impediment, hindrance
en cas d'empêchement   in case of prevention
empêcher qqn de faire qqch   to prevent someone from doing something
empêcher d'entrer   to keep from entering

s'empêcher de faire qqch   to refrain from doing something
Je n'ai pas pu m'empêcher de rire.
   I couldn't help laughing.

See also **dépêcher**.

Get acquainted with what preposition (if any) goes with what verb. There's a list in the Appendixes.

Regular **-er** verb endings; spelling change: **-oyer** verbs must change **y** to **i** in front of a mute **e**

to use, to employ

The Seven Simple Tenses		The Seven Compound Tenses	
Singular	Plural	Singular	Plural
1 présent de l'indicatif		8 passé composé	
emploie	employons	ai employé	avons employé
emploies	employez	as employé	avez employé
emploie	emploient	a employé	ont employé
2 imparfait de l'indicatif		9 plus-que-parfait de l'indicatif	
employais	employions	avais employé	avions employé
employais	employiez	avais employé	aviez employé
employait	employaient	avait employé	avaient employé
3 passé simple		10 passé antérieur	
employai	employâmes	eus employé	eûmes employé
employas	employâtes	eus employé	eûtes employé
employa	employèrent	eut employé	eurent employé
4 futur		11 futur antérieur	
emploierai	emploierons	aurai employé	aurons employé
emploieras	emploierez	auras employé	aurez employé
emploiera	emploieront	aura employé	auront employé
5 conditionnel		12 conditionnel passé	
emploierais	emploierions	aurais employé	aurions employé
emploierais	emploieriez	aurais employé	auriez employé
emploierait	emploieraient	aurait employé	auraient employé
6 présent du subjonctif		13 passé du subjonctif	
emploie	employions	aie employé	ayons employé
emploies	employiez	aies employé	ayez employé
emploie	emploient	ait employé	aient employé
7 imparfait du subjonctif		14 plus-que-parfait du subjonctif	
employasse	employassions	eusse employé	eussions employé
employasses	employassiez	eusses employé	eussiez employé
employât	employassent	eût employé	eussent employé

Impératif
emploie
employons
employez

Words and expressions related to this verb
un employé, une employée   employee
un employeur, une employeuse   employer
sans emploi   jobless
un emploi   employment
une demande d'emploi   job application

s'employer à faire qqch   to occupy oneself
  doing something
employer son temps   to spend one's time
un emploi nouveau   a new use

It's important that you use the Subjunctive correctly. See pages 26–31.

to borrow

Regular **-er** verb

The Seven Simple Tenses		The Seven Compound Tenses	
Singular	Plural	Singular	Plural
1 présent de l'indicatif		8 passé composé	
emprunte	empruntons	ai emprunté	avons emprunté
empruntes	empruntez	as emprunté	avez emprunté
emprunte	empruntent	a emprunté	ont emprunté
2 imparfait de l'indicatif		9 plus-que-parfait de l'indicatif	
empruntais	empruntions	avais emprunté	avions emprunté
empruntais	empruntiez	avais emprunté	aviez emprunté
empruntait	empruntaient	avait emprunté	avaient emprunté
3 passé simple		10 passé antérieur	
empruntai	empruntâmes	eus emprunté	eûmes emprunté
empruntas	empruntâtes	eus emprunté	eûtes emprunté
emprunta	empruntèrent	eut emprunté	eurent emprunté
4 futur		11 futur antérieur	
emprunterai	emprunterons	aurai emprunté	aurons emprunté
emprunteras	emprunterez	auras emprunté	aurez emprunté
empruntera	emprunteront	aura emprunté	auront emprunté
5 conditionnel		12 conditionnel passé	
emprunterais	emprunterions	aurais emprunté	aurions emprunté
emprunterais	emprunteriez	aurais emprunté	auriez emprunté
emprunterait	emprunteraient	aurait emprunté	auraient emprunté
6 présent du subjonctif		13 passé du subjonctif	
emprunte	empruntions	aie emprunté	ayons emprunté
empruntes	empruntiez	aies emprunté	ayez emprunté
emprunte	empruntent	ait emprunté	aient emprunté
7 imparfait du subjonctif		14 plus-que-parfait du subjonctif	
empruntasse	empruntassions	eusse emprunté	eussions emprunté
empruntasses	empruntassiez	eusses emprunté	eussiez emprunté
empruntât	empruntassent	eût emprunté	eussent emprunté

Impératif
emprunte
empruntons
empruntez

Words related to this verb

emprunteur, emprunteuse   a person who makes a habit of borrowing
un emprunt   loan, borrowing
emprunter quelque chose à quelqu'un   to borrow something from someone
   Monsieur Leblanc a emprunté de l'argent à mon père.   Mr. Leblanc borrowed some money
   from my father.
faire un emprunt pour payer ses dettes de jeu   to take out a loan to pay one's gambling debts

Don't confuse **emprunter** with **prêter** (*to lend*).

to encourage

Regular **-er** verb endings; spelling change: retain the
ge before **a** or **o** to keep the soft **g** sound of the verb

The Seven Simple Tenses		The Seven Compound Tenses	
Singular	Plural	Singular	Plural

1   présent de l'indicatif

encourage	encourageons		
encourages	encouragez		
encourage	encouragent		

8   passé composé

ai encouragé	avons encouragé		
as encouragé	avez encouragé		
a encouragé	ont encouragé		

2   imparfait de l'indicatif

encourageais	encouragions
encourageais	encouragiez
encourageait	encourageaient

9   plus-que-parfait de l'indicatif

avais encouragé	avions encouragé
avais encouragé	aviez encouragé
avait encouragé	avaient encouragé

3   passé simple

encourageai	encourageâmes
encourageas	encourageâtes
encouragea	encouragèrent

10   passé antérieur

eus encouragé	eûmes encouragé
eus encouragé	eûtes encouragé
eut encouragé	eurent encouragé

4   futur

encouragerai	encouragerons
encourageras	encouragerez
encouragera	encourageront

11   futur antérieur

aurai encouragé	aurons encouragé
auras encouragé	aurez encouragé
aura encouragé	auront encouragé

5   conditionnel

encouragerais	encouragerions
encouragerais	encourageriez
encouragerait	encourageraient

12   conditionnel passé

aurais encouragé	aurions encouragé
aurais encouragé	auriez encouragé
aurait encouragé	auraient encouragé

6   présent du subjonctif

encourage	encouragions
encourages	encouragiez
encourage	encouragent

13   passé du subjonctif

aie encouragé	ayons encouragé
aies encouragé	ayez encouragé
ait encouragé	aient encouragé

7   imparfait du subjonctif

encourageasse	encourageassions
encourageasses	encourageassiez
encourageât	encourageassent

14   plus-que-parfait du subjonctif

eusse encouragé	eussions encouragé
eusses encouragé	eussiez encouragé
eût encouragé	eussent encouragé

Impératif
encourage
encourageons
encouragez

Words and expressions related to this verb

encourager qqn à faire qqch   to encourage
    someone to do something
encourageant, encourageante   encouraging;
    des paroles encourageantes   encouraging
    words
Bon courage!   Good luck! (Take heart!)

l'encouragement *m.*   encouragement
le découragement   discouragement
le courage   courage
décourager   to discourage
se décourager   to become discouraged

Don't forget to study the section on defective and impersonal verbs. It's right after this main list.

The subject pronouns are found on page 103.

315

to run away, to slip away,   Reflexive irregular verb
to escape, to flee, to fly away

The Seven Simple Tenses | The Seven Compound Tenses

Singular	Plural	Singular	Plural
1　présent de l'indicatif		8　passé composé	
m'enfuis	nous enfuyons	me suis enfui(e)	nous sommes enfui(e)s
t'enfuis	vous enfuyez	t'es enfui(e)	vous êtes enfui(e)(s)
s'enfuit	s'enfuient	s'est enfui(e)	se sont enfui(e)s
2　imparfait de l'indicatif		9　plus-que-parfait de l'indicatif	
m'enfuyais	nous enfuyions	m'étais enfui(e)	nous étions enfui(e)s
t'enfuyais	vous enfuyiez	t'étais enfui(e)	vous étiez enfui(e)(s)
s'enfuyait	s'enfuyaient	s'était enfui(e)	s'étaient enfui(e)s
3　passé simple		10　passé antérieur	
m'enfuis	nous enfuîmes	me fus enfui(e)	nous fûmes enfui(e)s
t'enfuis	vous enfuîtes	te fus enfui(e)	vous fûtes enfui(e)(s)
s'enfuit	s'enfuirent	se fut enfui(e)	se furent enfui(e)s
4　futur		11　futur antérieur	
m'enfuirai	nous enfuirons	me serai enfui(e)	nous serons enfui(e)s
t'enfuiras	vous enfuirez	te seras enfui(e)	vous serez enfui(e)(s)
s'enfuira	s'enfuiront	se sera enfui(e)	se seront enfui(e)s
5　conditionnel		12　conditionnel passé	
m'enfuirais	nous enfuirions	me serais enfui(e)	nous serions enfui(e)s
t'enfuirais	vous enfuiriez	te serais enfui(e)	vous seriez enfui(e)(s)
s'enfuirait	s'enfuiraient	se serait enfui(e)	se seraient enfui(e)s
6　présent du subjonctif		13　passé du subjonctif	
m'enfuie	nous enfuyions	me sois enfui(e)	nous soyons enfui(e)s
t'enfuies	vous enfuyiez	te sois enfui(e)	vous soyez enfui(e)(s)
s'enfuie	s'enfuient	se soit enfui(e)	se soient enfui(e)s
7　imparfait du subjonctif		14　plus-que-parfait du subjonctif	
m'enfuisse	nous enfuissions	me fusse enfui(e)	nous fussions enfui(e)s
t'enfuisses	vous enfuissiez	te fusses enfui(e)	vous fussiez enfui(e)(s)
s'enfuît	s'enfuissent	se fût enfui(e)	se fussent enfui(e)s

Impératif
enfuis-toi; ne t'enfuis pas
enfuyons-nous; ne nous enfuyons pas
enfuyez-vous; ne vous enfuyez pas

Common idiomatic expressions using this verb and words related to it
s'enfuir d'un endroit　to flee from a place
prendre la fuite　to take to flight
laid à faire fuir　ugly enough to make you run off
fuir　to flee

faire fuir　to put to flight
la fuite　flight
fuir devant un danger　to run away from danger
Le temps fuit.　Time flies.

See also **fuir**.

Can't find the verb you're looking for? Check the back pages of this book for a list of over 2,600 additional verbs!

Regular **-er** verb endings; spelling change:
e changes to **è** before syllable with mute **e**

to carry away, to take
away, to remove

The Seven Simple Tenses | The Seven Compound Tenses

E

Singular	Plural	Singular	Plural
1 présent de l'indicatif		8 passé composé	
enlève	**enlevons**	**ai enlevé**	**avons enlevé**
enlèves	**enlevez**	**as enlevé**	**avez enlevé**
enlève	**enlèvent**	**a enlevé**	**ont enlevé**
2 imparfait de l'indicatif		9 plus-que-parfait de l'indicatif	
enlevais	**enlevions**	**avais enlevé**	**avons enlevé**
enlevais	**enleviez**	**avais enlevé**	**aviez enlevé**
enlevait	**enlevaient**	**avait enlevé**	**avaient enlevé**
3 passé simple		10 passé antérieur	
enlevai	**enlevâmes**	**eus enlevé**	**eûmes enlevé**
enlevas	**enlevâtes**	**eus enlevé**	**eûtes enlevé**
enleva	**enlevèrent**	**eut enlevé**	**eurent enlevé**
4 futur		11 futur antérieur	
enlèverai	**enlèverons**	**aurai enlevé**	**aurons enlevé**
enlèveras	**enlèverez**	**auras enlevé**	**aurez enlevé**
enlèvera	**enlèveront**	**aura enlevé**	**auront enlevé**
5 conditionnel		12 conditionnel passé	
enlèverais	**enlèverions**	**aurais enlevé**	**aurions enlevé**
enlèverais	**enlèveriez**	**aurais enlevé**	**auriez enlevé**
enlèverait	**enlèveraient**	**aurait enlevé**	**auraient enlevé**
6 présent du subjonctif		13 passé du subjonctif	
enlève	**enlevions**	**aie enlevé**	**ayons enlevé**
enlèves	**enleviez**	**aies enlevé**	**ayez enlevé**
enlève	**enlèvent**	**ait enlevé**	**aient enlevé**
7 imparfait du subjonctif		14 plus-que-parfait du subjonctif	
enlevasse	**enlevassions**	**eusse enlevé**	**eussions enlevé**
enlevasses	**enlevassiez**	**eusses enlevé**	**eussiez enlevé**
enlevât	**enlevassent**	**eût enlevé**	**eussent enlevé**

Impératif
enlève
enlevons
enlevez

Sentences using this verb and words related to it

Madame Dubac est entrée dans sa maison. Elle a enlevé son chapeau, son manteau et ses gants. Puis, elle est allée directement au salon pour enlever une chaise et la mettre dans la salle à manger. Après cela, elle a enlevé les ordures.

enlever les ordures   to take the garbage out
un enlèvement   lifting, carrying off, removal
enlèvement d'un enfant   baby snatching, kidnapping
un enlevage   spurt (sports)

See also **élever** and **lever**.

Don't miss orthographically changing verbs on pages 32–34.

to bore, to annoy, to weary

Regular **-er** verb endings; spelling change: **-uyer** verbs must change **y** to **i** in front of mute **e**

The Seven Simple Tenses

The Seven Compound Tenses

Singular	Plural	Singular	Plural
1 présent de l'indicatif		8 passé composé	
ennuie	ennuyons	ai ennuyé	avons ennuyé
ennuies	ennuyez	as ennuyé	avez ennuyé
ennuie	ennuient	a ennuyé	ont ennuyé
2 imparfait de l'indicatif		9 plus-que-parfait de l'indicatif	
ennuyais	ennuyions	avais ennuyé	avions ennuyé
ennuyais	ennuyiez	avais ennuyé	aviez ennuyé
ennuyait	ennuyaient	avait ennuyé	avaient ennuyé
3 passé simple		10 passé antérieur	
ennuyai	ennuyâmes	eus ennuyé	eûmes ennuyé
ennuyas	ennuyâtes	eus ennuyé	eûtes ennuyé
ennuya	ennuyèrent	eut ennuyé	eurent ennuyé
4 futur		11 futur antérieur	
ennuierai	ennuierons	aurai ennuyé	aurons ennuyé
ennuieras	ennuierez	auras ennuyé	aurez ennuyé
ennuiera	ennuieront	aura ennuyé	auront ennuyé
5 conditionnel		12 conditionnel passé	
ennuierais	ennuierions	aurais ennuyé	aurions ennuyé
ennuierais	ennuieriez	aurais ennuyé	auriez ennuyé
ennuierait	ennuieraient	aurait ennuyé	auraient ennuyé
6 présent du subjonctif		13 passé du subjonctif	
ennuie	ennuyions	aie ennuyé	ayons ennuyé
ennuies	ennuyiez	aies ennuyé	ayez ennuyé
ennuie	ennuient	ait ennuyé	aient ennuyé
7 imparfait du subjonctif		14 plus-que-parfait du subjonctif	
ennuyasse	ennuyassions	eusse ennuyé	eussions ennuyé
ennuyasses	ennuyassiez	eusses ennuyé	eussiez ennuyé
ennuyât	ennuyassent	eût ennuyé	eussent ennuyé

Impératif
ennuie
ennuyons
ennuyez

Sentences using this verb and words related to it

—**Est-ce que je vous ennuie?** — Am I boring you?
—**Oui, vous m'ennuyez. Allez-vous-en!** — Yes, you're boring me. Go away!

un ennui   weariness, boredom, ennui
des ennuis   worries, troubles
ennuyeux, ennuyeuse   boring
s'ennuyer de quelqu'un   to miss someone

mourir d'ennui   to be bored to tears
s'ennuyer   to become bored, to get bored
Quel ennui!   What a nuisance!

to be bored

Reflexive verb; regular **-er** verb endings; spelling change:
-uyer verbs must change **y** to **i** in front of mute **e**

The Seven Simple Tenses		The Seven Compound Tenses	
Singular	Plural	Singular	Plural
1 présent de l'indicatif		8 passé composé	
m'ennuie	nous ennuyons	me suis ennuyé(e)	nous sommes ennuyé(e)s
t'ennuies	vous ennuyez	t'es ennuyé(e)	vous êtes ennuyé(e)(s)
s'ennuie	se ennuient	s'est ennuyé(e)	se sont ennuyé(e)s
2 imparfait de l'indicatif		9 plus-que-parfait de l'indicatif	
m'ennuyais	nous ennuyions	m'étais ennuyé(e)	nous étions ennuyé(e)s
t'ennuyais	vous ennuyiez	t'étais ennuyé(e)	vous étiez ennuyé(e)(s)
s'ennuyait	s'ennuyaient	s'était ennuyé(e)	s'étaient ennuyé(e)s
3 passé simple		10 passé antérieur	
m'ennuyai	nous ennuyâmes	me fus ennuyé(e)	nous fûmes ennuyé(e)s
t'ennuyas	vous ennuyâtes	te fus ennuyé(e)	vous fûtes ennuyé(e)(s)
s'ennuya	s'ennuyèrent	se fut ennuyé(e)	se furent ennuyé(e)s
4 futur		11 futur antérieur	
m'ennuierai	nous ennuierons	me serai ennuyé(e)	nous serons ennuyé(e)s
t'ennuieras	vous ennuierez	te seras ennuyé(e)	vous serez ennuyé(e)(s)
s'ennuiera	s'ennuieront	se sera ennuyé(e)	se seront ennuyé(e)s
5 conditionnel		12 conditionnel passé	
m'ennuierais	nous ennuierions	me serais ennuyé(e)	nous serions ennuyé(e)s
t'ennuierais	vous ennuieriez	te serais ennuyé(e)	vous seriez ennuyé(e)(s)
s'ennuierait	s'ennuieraient	se serait ennuyé(e)	se seraient ennuyé(e)s
6 présent du subjonctif		13 passé du subjonctif	
m'ennuie	nous ennuyions	me sois ennuyé(e)	nous soyons ennuyé(e)s
t'ennuies	vous ennuyiez	te sois ennuyé(e)	vous soyez ennuyé(e)(s)
s'ennuie	s'ennuient	se soit ennuyé(e)	se soient ennuyé(e)s
7 imparfait du subjonctif		14 plus-que-parfait du subjonctif	
m'ennuyasse	nous ennuyassions	me fusse ennuyé(e)	nous fussions ennuyé(e)s
t'ennuyasses	vous ennuyassiez	te fusses ennuyé(e)	vous fussiez ennuyé(e)(s)
s'ennuyât	s'ennuyassent	se fût ennuyé(e)	se fussent ennuyé(e)s

Impératif
ennuie-toi; ne t'ennuie pas
ennuyons-nous; ne nous ennuyons pas
ennuyez-vous; ne vous ennuyez pas

Sentences using this verb and words related to it
   Quelle barbe! On s'ennuie à 100 sous de l'heure dans cette classe!   How boring! We're really bored in this class!
   Je m'ennuie de toi.   I miss you.
Proverb
   Un ennui ne vient jamais seul. (Similar to: **Jamais deux sans trois.**)   Bad luck comes in threes.
Words and expressions related to this verb

s'ennuyer de qqn   to miss someone
l'ennui *m.*   boredom, trouble
s'ennuyer à 100 sous de l'heure   to be very bored (Literally, to be bored at 100 cents per

hour. One hundred sous used to make up five francs; **un franc** was the former monetary unit in France, replaced by **un euro**.)
ennuyeux, ennuyeuse *adj.*   boring

to teach

The Seven Simple Tenses		The Seven Compound Tenses	
Singular	Plural	Singular	Plural
1　présent de l'indicatif		8　passé composé	
enseigne	enseignons	ai enseigné	avons enseigné
enseignes	enseignez	as enseigné	avez enseigné
enseigne	enseignent	a enseigné	ont enseigné
2　imparfait de l'indicatif		9　plus-que-parfait de l'indicatif	
enseignais	enseignions	avais enseigné	avions enseigné
enseignais	enseigniez	avais enseigné	aviez enseigné
enseignait	enseignaient	avait enseigné	avaient enseigné
3　passé simple		10　passé antérieur	
enseignai	enseignâmes	eus enseigné	eûmes enseigné
enseignas	enseignâtes	eus enseigné	eûtes enseigné
enseigna	enseignèrent	eut enseigné	eurent enseigné
4　futur		11　futur antérieur	
enseignerai	enseignerons	aurai enseigné	aurons enseigné
enseigneras	enseignerez	auras enseigné	aurez enseigné
enseignera	enseigneront	aura enseigné	auront enseigné
5　conditionnel		12　conditionnel passé	
enseignerais	enseignerions	aurais enseigné	aurions enseigné
enseignerais	enseigneriez	aurais enseigné	auriez enseigné
enseignerait	enseigneraient	aurait enseigné	auraient enseigné
6　présent du subjonctif		13　passé du subjonctif	
enseigne	enseignions	aie enseigné	ayons enseigné
enseignes	enseigniez	aies enseigné	ayez enseigné
enseigne	enseignent	ait enseigné	aient enseigné
7　imparfait du subjonctif		14　plus-que-parfait du subjonctif	
enseignasse	enseignassions	eusse enseigné	eussions enseigné
enseignasses	enseignassiez	eusses enseigné	eussiez enseigné
enseignât	enseignassent	eût enseigné	eussent enseigné

Impératif
enseigne
enseignons
enseignez

Sentences using this verb and words and expressions related to it
J'enseigne aux élèves à lire en français. L'enseignement est une belle profession.

enseigner quelque chose à quelqu'un　to teach something to someone
une enseigne　sign; une enseigne lumineuse neon sign
les enseignements du Christ/de Moïse/de Mahomet/du Bouddha　the teachings of Christ/of Moses/of Mohammed/of Buddha

l'enseignement m.　teaching
l'enseignement à distance　distance education
renseigner qqn de qqch　to inform someone about something
se renseigner　to get information, to inquire
un renseignement, des renseignements information

Regular **-re** verb   to hear, to understand

The Seven Simple Tenses		The Seven Compound Tenses	
Singular	Plural	Singular	Plural
1 présent de l'indicatif		**8 passé composé**	
entends	entendons	ai entendu	avons entendu
entends	entendez	as entendu	avez entendu
entend	entendent	a entendu	ont entendu
2 imparfait de l'indicatif		**9 plus-que-parfait de l'indicatif**	
entendais	entendions	avais entendu	avions entendu
entendais	entendiez	avais entendu	aviez entendu
entendait	entendaient	avait entendu	avaient entendu
3 passé simple		**10 passé antérieur**	
entendis	entendîmes	eus entendu	eûmes entendu
entendis	entendîtes	eus entendu	eûtes entendu
entendit	entendirent	eut entendu	eurent entendu
4 futur		**11 futur antérieur**	
entendrai	entendrons	aurai entendu	aurons entendu
entendras	entendrez	auras entendu	aurez entendu
entendra	entendront	aura entendu	auront entendu
5 conditionnel		**12 conditionnel passé**	
entendrais	entendrions	aurais entendu	aurions entendu
entendrais	entendriez	aurais entendu	auriez entendu
entendrait	entendraient	aurait entendu	auraient entendu
6 présent du subjonctif		**13 passé du subjonctif**	
entende	entendions	aie entendu	ayons entendu
entendes	entendiez	aies entendu	ayez entendu
entende	entendent	ait entendu	aient entendu
7 imparfait du subjonctif		**14 plus-que-parfait du subjonctif**	
entendisse	entendissions	eusse entendu	eussions entendu
entendisses	entendissiez	eusses entendu	eussiez entendu
entendît	entendissent	eût entendu	eussent entendu

Impératif
entends
entendons
entendez

Entendre is a very useful verb for a beginning French student. **Entendre** is a regular -re verb so many verbs are conjugated like it.

Sentences using entendre

—As-tu entendu quelque chose?
—Non, chéri, je n'ai rien entendu.
—J'ai entendu un bruit . . . de la cuisine . . . silence . . . je l'entends encore. C'est un cambrioleur!
—Non, chéri, c'est notre chien que tu entends.

—Did you hear something?
—No, dear, I didn't hear anything.
—I heard a noise . . . from the kitchen . . . quiet . . . I still hear it. It's a burglar!
—No, dear, it's our dog that you hear.

C'est entendu! It's understood! Agreed!

Je m'entends bien avec ma soeur. I get along well with my sister.

J'ai entendu dire qu'on mange bien dans ce restaurant. I've heard that a person can have a good meal in this restaurant.

Qu'entendez-vous par là?! What do you mean by that?!

J'ai entendu parler d'un grand changement dans l'administration de cette école. I've heard about a big change in the administration of this school.

Je ne peux pas vous entendre. Parlez plus fort, s'il vous plaît. I can't hear you. Please speak more loudly.

Words and expressions related to this verb

un entendement **understanding**

une entente **understanding**

une mésentente **disagreement**

malentendant, malentendante **hard of hearing**

bien entendu **of course**

laisser entendre **to hint**

entendre raison **to listen to reason**

ne pas entendre malice **not to mean any harm**

entendre parler de **to hear about, to hear of**

un sous-entendu **innuendo**

If you can conjugate **entendre** you can also conjugate these verbs:

s'entendre avec qqn **to get along with someone, to understand each other**

s'entendre à merveille **to get along with each other marvelously**

sous-entendre **to imply**

Regular **-er** verb   to bury

The Seven Simple Tenses		The Seven Compound Tenses	
Singular	Plural	Singular	Plural
1 présent de l'indicatif		8 passé composé	
enterre	enterrons	ai enterré	avons enterré
enterres	enterrez	as enterré	avez enterré
enterre	enterrent	a enterré	ont enterré
2 imparfait de l'indicatif		9 plus-que-parfait de l'indicatif	
enterrais	enterrions	avais enterré	avions enterré
enterrais	enterriez	avais enterré	aviez enterré
enterrait	enterraient	avait enterré	avaient enterré
3 passé simple		10 passé antérieur	
enterrai	enterrâmes	eus enterré	eûmes enterré
enterras	enterrâtes	eus enterré	eûtes enterré
enterra	enterrèrent	eut enterré	eurent enterré
4 futur		11 futur antérieur	
enterrerai	enterrerons	aurai enterré	aurons enterré
enterreras	enterrerez	auras enterré	aurez enterré
enterrera	enterreront	aura enterré	auront enterré
5 conditionnel		12 conditionnel passé	
enterrerais	enterrerions	aurais enterré	aurions enterré
enterrerais	enterreriez	aurais enterré	auriez enterré
enterrerait	enterreraient	aurait enterré	auraient enterré
6 présent du subjonctif		13 passé du subjonctif	
enterre	enterrions	aie enterré	ayons enterré
enterres	enterriez	aies enterré	ayez enterré
enterre	enterrent	ait enterré	aient enterré
7 imparfait du subjonctif		14 plus-que-parfait du subjonctif	
enterrasse	enterrassions	eusse enterré	eussions enterré
enterrasses	enterrassiez	eusses enterré	eussiez enterré
enterrât	enterrassent	eût enterré	eussent enterré

Impératif
enterre
enterrons
enterrez

Words and expressions related to this verb
enterrer un cadavre   to bury a corpse
s'enterrer   to bury oneself
enterrer une affaire   to abandon a matter
enterrer sa vie de garçon   to hold a bachelor's party (for a man about to be married)
la terre   earth, soil

enterrer une chose   to bury something, to forget about something, to shelve something
un enterrement   burial, interment
s'enterrer dans un endroit   to bury oneself in a place, to isolate oneself from the rest of the world

Soak up some verbs used in weather expressions. There's a list in the Appendixes!

The subject pronouns are found on page 103.
                                                                   323

to undertake, to engage upon
Irregular verb

The Seven Simple Tenses		The Seven Compound Tenses	
Singular	Plural	Singular	Plural
1 présent de l'indicatif		8 passé composé	
entreprends	entreprenons	ai entrepris	avons entrepris
entreprends	entreprenez	as entrepris	avez entrepris
entreprend	entreprennent	a entrepris	ont entrepris
2 imparfait de l'indicatif		9 plus-que-parfait de l'indicatif	
entreprenais	entreprenions	avais entrepris	avions entrepris
entreprenais	entrepreniez	avais entrepris	aviez entrepris
entreprenait	entreprenaient	avait entrepris	avaient entrepris
3 passé simple		10 passé antérieur	
entrepris	entreprîmes	eus entrepris	eûmes entrepris
entrepris	entreprîtes	eus entrepris	eûtes entrepris
entreprit	entreprirent	eut entrepris	eurent entrepris
4 futur		11 futur antérieur	
entreprendrai	entreprendrons	aurai entrepris	aurons entrepris
entreprendras	entreprendrez	auras entrepris	aurez entrepris
entreprendra	entreprendront	aura entrepris	auront entrepris
5 conditionnel		12 conditionnel passé	
entreprendrais	entreprendrions	aurais entrepris	aurions entrepris
entreprendrais	entreprendriez	aurais entrepris	auriez entrepris
entreprendrait	entreprendraient	aurait entrepris	auraient entrepris
6 présent du subjonctif		13 passé du subjonctif	
entreprenne	entreprenions	aie entrepris	ayons entrepris
entreprennes	entrepreniez	aies entrepris	ayez entrepris
entreprenne	entreprennent	ait entrepris	aient entrepris
7 imparfait du subjonctif		14 plus-que-parfait du subjonctif	
entreprisse	entreprissions	eusse entrepris	eussions entrepris
entreprisses	entreprissiez	eusses entrepris	eussiez entrepris
entreprît	entreprissent	eût entrepris	eussent entrepris

Impératif
entreprends
entreprenons
entreprenez

Words and expressions related to this verb

entreprendre de faire qqch to undertake to do something

avoir un esprit entreprenant to be bold, daring, enterprising

une entreprise enterprise; **une entreprise rémunératrice** profitable enterprise

entreprenant, entreprenante enterprising

un entrepreneur, une entrepreneuse contractor

une entreprise de déménagement moving company

See also **apprendre, comprendre, se méprendre, prendre, reprendre,** and **surprendre.**

Don't forget to use the English-French verb index. It's in the Appendixes.

324

The Seven Simple Tenses		The Seven Compound Tenses	
Singular	Plural	Singular	Plural
1 présent de l'indicatif		**8 passé composé**	
entre	**entrons**	**suis entré(e)**	**sommes entré(e)s**
entres	**entrez**	**es entré(e)**	**êtes entré(e)(s)**
entre	**entrent**	**est entré(e)**	**sont entré(e)s**
2 imparfait de l'indicatif		**9 plus-que-parfait de l'indicatif**	
entrais	**entrions**	**étais entré(e)**	**étions entré(e)s**
entrais	**entriez**	**étais entré(e)**	**étiez entré(e)(s)**
entrait	**entraient**	**était entré(e)**	**étaient entré(e)s**
3 passé simple		**10 passé antérieur**	
entrai	**entrâmes**	**fus entré(e)**	**fûmes entré(e)s**
entras	**entrâtes**	**fus entré(e)**	**fûtes entré(e)(s)**
entra	**entrèrent**	**fut entré(e)**	**furent entré(e)s**
4 futur		**11 futur antérieur**	
entrerai	**entrerons**	**serai entré(e)**	**serons entré(e)s**
entreras	**entrerez**	**seras entré(e)**	**serez entré(e)(s)**
entrera	**entreront**	**sera entré(e)**	**seront entré(e)s**
5 conditionnel		**12 conditionnel passé**	
entrerais	**entrerions**	**serais entré(e)**	**serions entré(e)s**
entrerais	**entreriez**	**serais entré(e)**	**seriez entré(e)(s)**
entrerait	**entreraient**	**serait entré(e)**	**seraient entré(e)s**
6 présent du subjonctif		**13 passé du subjonctif**	
entre	**entrions**	**sois entré(e)**	**soyons entré(e)s**
entres	**entriez**	**sois entré(e)**	**soyez entré(e)(s)**
entre	**entrent**	**soit entré(e)**	**soient entré(e)s**
7 imparfait du subjonctif		**14 plus-que-parfait du subjonctif**	
entrasse	**entrassions**	**fusse entré(e)**	**fussions entré(e)s**
entrasses	**entrassiez**	**fusses entré(e)**	**fussiez entré(e)(s)**
entrât	**entrassent**	**fût entré(e)**	**fussent entré(e)s**

	Impératif
	entre
	entrons
	entrez

AN ESSENTIAL
55 VERB

Entrer

Entrer is an essential verb for a beginning student of French. Pay attention to the choice of helping verb when you use **entrer** in the compound tenses. It is usually conjugated with *être*, unless there is a direct object. In that case, you should use *avoir*, as noted below.

Sentences using entrer

Le cambrioleur est entré par la fenêtre.
The burglar entered through the window.

Entrez donc!
Do come in!

Entrons voir.
Let's go in and see.

This verb is conjugated with *avoir* when it has a direct object.

Example:
Ma mère a entré la clé dans la serrure pour ouvrir la porte.
My mother put the key in the lock to open the door.

BUT:
Ma mère est entrée dans la maison.
My mother went in the house.

Words and expressions related to this verb

l'entrée *f.* **entrance**

entrée interdite **no entry**

l'entrée *f.* des données **data input, data entry**

entrer par la fenêtre **to enter through the window**

entrer dans + noun **to enter (into) + noun**

entrer dans le décor **to drive off the road and have an accident (le décor/scenery)**

une entrée gratuite **free admission**

entrer des données **to enter/input data (computer)**

faire entrer qqn **to show somebody in**

entrer comme dans un moulin **to have free access**

entrer dans le vif du sujet **to get to the heart of the matter**

entrer dans une famille **to marry into a family**

entrer dans les détails **to go into the details**

Can't find the verb you're looking for? Check the back pages of this book for a list of over 2,600 additional verbs!

Reflexive regular **-er** verb

to fly off, to fly away, to take flight, to take wing (birds), to take off (airplane)

The Seven Simple Tenses		The Seven Compound Tenses	
Singular	Plural	Singular	Plural

1   présent de l'indicatif

m'envole	nous envolons	
t'envoles	vous envolez	
s'envole	s'envolent	

8   passé composé

me suis envolé(e)	nous sommes envolé(e)s
t'es envolé(e)	vous êtes envolé(e)(s)
s'est envolé(e)	se sont envolé(e)s

2   imparfait de l'indicatif

m'envolais	nous envolions
t'envolais	vous envoliez
s'envolait	s'envolaient

9   plus-que-parfait de l'indicatif

m'étais envolé(e)	nous étions envolé(e)s
t'étais envolé(e)	vous étiez envolé(e)(s)
s'était envolé(e)	s'étaient envolé(e)s

3   passé simple

m'envolai	nous envolâmes
t'envolas	vous envolâtes
s'envola	s'envolèrent

10   passé antérieur

me fus envolé(e)	nous fûmes envolé(e)s
te fus envolé(e)	vous fûtes envolé(e)(s)
se fut envolé(e)	se furent envolé(e)s

4   futur

m'envolerai	nous envolerons
t'envoleras	vous envolerez
s'envolera	s'envoleront

11   futur antérieur

me serai envolé(e)	nous serons envolé(e)s
te seras envolé(e)	vous serez envolé(e)(s)
se sera envolé(e)	se seront envolé(e)s

5   conditionnel

m'envolerais	nous envolerions
t'envolerais	vous envoleriez
s'envolerait	s'envoleraient

12   conditionnel passé

me serais envolé(e)	nous serions envolé(e)s
te serais envolé(e)	vous seriez envolé(e)(s)
se serait envolé(e)	se seraient envolé(e)s

6   présent du subjonctif

m'envole	nous envolions
t'envoles	vous envoliez
s'envole	s'envolent

13   passé du subjonctif

me sois envolé(e)	nous soyons envolé(e)s
te sois envolé(e)	vous soyez envolé(e)(s)
se soit envolé(e)	se soient envolé(e)s

7   imparfait du subjonctif

m'envolasse	nous envolassions
t'envolasses	vous envolassiez
s'envolât	s'envolassent

14   plus-que-parfait du subjonctif

me fusse envolé(e)	nous fussions envolé(e)s
te fusses envolé(e)	vous fussiez envolé(e)(s)
se fût envolé(e)	se fussent envolé(e)s

Impératif
envole-toi; ne t'envole pas
envolons-nous; ne nous envolons pas
envolez-vous; ne vous envolez pas

Words and expressions related to this verb
une envolée   flying off
un envol   flight of a bird; take-off of an airplane
voler   to fly, to steal

See also **voler.**

le vol   flight, theft
Les paroles s'envolent.   Spoken words fly away.

Don't forget to check the list of 2,600 additional verbs keyed to the 501 model verbs. It's in the Appendixes!

The subject pronouns are found on page 103.

to send   Regular **-er** verb endings; spelling change: **-oyer** verbs must change **y** to **i** in front of a mute **e**, future and conditional stem is **enverr-**

The Seven Simple Tenses		The Seven Compound Tenses	
Singular	Plural	Singular	Plural
1 présent de l'indicatif		8 passé composé	
envoie	envoyons	ai envoyé	avons envoyé
envoies	envoyez	as envoyé	avez envoyé
envoie	envoient	a envoyé	ont envoyé
2 imparfait de l'indicatif		9 plus-que-parfait de l'indicatif	
envoyais	envoyions	avais envoyé	avions envoyé
envoyais	envoyiez	avais envoyé	aviez envoyé
envoyait	envoyaient	avait envoyé	avaient envoyé
3 passé simple		10 passé antérieur	
envoyai	envoyâmes	eus envoyé	eûmes envoyé
envoyas	envoyâtes	eus envoyé	eûtes envoyé
envoya	envoyèrent	eut envoyé	eurent envoyé
4 futur		11 futur antérieur	
enverrai	enverrons	aurai envoyé	aurons envoyé
enverras	enverrez	auras envoyé	aurez envoyé
enverra	enverront	aura envoyé	auront envoyé
5 conditionnel		12 conditionnel passé	
enverrais	enverrions	aurais envoyé	aurions envoyé
enverrais	enverriez	aurais envoyé	auriez envoyé
enverrait	enverraient	aurait envoyé	auraient envoyé
6 présent du subjonctif		13 passé du subjonctif	
envoie	envoyions	aie envoyé	ayons envoyé
envoies	envoyiez	aies envoyé	ayez envoyé
envoie	envoient	ait envoyé	aient envoyé
7 imparfait du subjonctif		14 plus-que-parfait du subjonctif	
envoyasse	envoyassions	eusse envoyé	eussions envoyé
envoyasses	envoyassiez	eusses envoyé	eussiez envoyé
envoyât	envoyassent	eût envoyé	eussent envoyé

Impératif
envoie
envoyons
envoyez

AN ESSENTIAL
55 VERB

Envoyer

Envoyer is an important verb because it has an interesting spelling change and because it is very useful for a beginning French student.

Sentences using envoyer and related words and expressions

Hier j'ai envoyé une lettre à des amis en France. Yesterday I sent a letter to some friends in France.

Demain j'enverrai une lettre à mes amis au Canada. Tomorrow I will send a letter to my friends in Canada.

J'enverrais une lettre en Italie mais je ne connais personne dans ce pays. I would send a letter to Italy but I don't know anyone in that country.

Mon père a envoyé chercher le docteur parce que mon petit frère est malade. My father sent for the doctor because my little brother is sick.

Où est-ce que je peux envoyer un courriel/un courrier électronique? Where can I send an e-mail?

Marc a été renvoyé de l'école. Mark was kicked out of school.

Words and expressions related to this verb

envoyer chercher **to send for**

un envoi **envoi (poetry), sending**

envoyer promener qqn **to send someone packing**

envoyeur, envoyeuse **sender**

un envoyé, une envoyée **envoy, messenger**

le renvoi **return, call forwarding**

renvoyer **to send away (back), to discharge someone, to sack someone**

Don't forget to study the section on defective and impersonal verbs. It's right after this main list.

The Seven Simple Tenses		The Seven Compound Tenses	
Singular	Plural	Singular	Plural
1 présent de l'indicatif		8 passé composé	
épouse	épousons	ai épousé	avons épousé
épouses	épousez	as épousé	avez épousé
épouse	épousent	a épousé	ont épousé
2 imparfait de l'indicatif		9 plus-que-parfait de l'indicatif	
épousais	épousions	avais épousé	avions épousé
épousais	épousiez	avais épousé	aviez épousé
épousait	épousaient	avait épousé	avaient épousé
3 passé simple		10 passé antérieur	
épousai	épousâmes	eus épousé	eûmes épousé
épousas	épousâtes	eus épousé	eûtes épousé
épousa	épousèrent	eut épousé	eurent épousé
4 futur		11 futur antérieur	
épouserai	épouserons	aurai épousé	aurons épousé
épouseras	épouserez	auras épousé	aurez épousé
épousera	épouseront	aura épousé	auront épousé
5 conditionnel		12 conditionnel passé	
épouserais	épouserions	aurais épousé	aurions épousé
épouserais	épouseriez	aurais épousé	auriez épousé
épouserait	épouseraient	aurait épousé	auraient épousé
6 présent du subjonctif		13 passé du subjonctif	
épouse	épousions	aie épousé	ayons épousé
épouses	épousiez	aies épousé	ayez épousé
épouse	épousent	ait épousé	aient épousé
7 imparfait du subjonctif		14 plus-que-parfait du subjonctif	
épousasse	épousassions	eusse épousé	eussions épousé
épousasses	épousassiez	eusses épousé	eussiez épousé
épousât	épousassent	eût épousé	eussent épousé

Impératif
épouse
épousons
épousez

Sentences using this verb and words related to it

J'ai trois frères. Le premier a épousé une jolie jeune fille française. Le deuxième a épousé une belle jeune fille italienne, et le troisième a épousé une jolie fille espagnole. Elles sont très intelligentes.

un époux   husband, spouse
une épouse   wife, spouse
les nouveaux mariés   the newlyweds

épouser une grosse fortune   to marry into money
se marier avec quelqu'un   to get married to someone

Can't remember the French verb you need? Check the back pages of this book for the English-French verb index!

Regular **-er** verb   to try, to test, to put to the test, to feel, to experience

The Seven Simple Tenses		The Seven Compound Tenses	
Singular	Plural	Singular	Plural
1 présent de l'indicatif		8 passé composé	
éprouve	**éprouvons**	**ai éprouvé**	**avons éprouvé**
éprouves	**éprouvez**	**as éprouvé**	**avez éprouvé**
éprouve	**éprouvent**	**a éprouvé**	**ont éprouvé**
2 imparfait de l'indicatif		9 plus-que-parfait de l'indicatif	
éprouvais	**éprouvions**	**avais éprouvé**	**avions éprouvé**
éprouvais	**éprouviez**	**avais éprouvé**	**aviez éprouvé**
éprouvait	**éprouvaient**	**avait éprouvé**	**avaient éprouvé**
3 passé simple		10 passé antérieur	
éprouvai	**éprouvâmes**	**eus éprouvé**	**eûmes éprouvé**
éprouvas	**éprouvâtes**	**eus éprouvé**	**eûtes éprouvé**
éprouva	**éprouvèrent**	**eut éprouvé**	**eurent éprouvé**
4 futur		11 futur antérieur	
éprouverai	**éprouverons**	**aurai éprouvé**	**aurons éprouvé**
éprouveras	**éprouverez**	**auras éprouvé**	**aurez éprouvé**
éprouvera	**éprouveront**	**aura éprouvé**	**auront éprouvé**
5 conditionnel		12 conditionnel passé	
éprouverais	**éprouverions**	**aurais éprouvé**	**aurions éprouvé**
éprouverais	**éprouveriez**	**aurais éprouvé**	**auriez éprouvé**
éprouverait	**éprouveraient**	**aurait éprouvé**	**auraient éprouvé**
6 présent du subjonctif		13 passé du subjonctif	
éprouve	**éprouvions**	**aie éprouvé**	**ayons éprouvé**
éprouves	**éprouviez**	**aies éprouvé**	**ayez éprouvé**
éprouve	**éprouvent**	**ait éprouvé**	**aient éprouvé**
7 imparfait du subjonctif		14 plus-que-parfait du subjonctif	
éprouvasse	**éprouvassions**	**eusse éprouvé**	**eussions éprouvé**
éprouvasses	**éprouvassiez**	**eusses éprouvé**	**eussiez éprouvé**
éprouvât	**éprouvassent**	**eût éprouvé**	**eussent éprouvé**

Impératif
éprouve
éprouvons
éprouvez

Common idiomatic expressions using this verb and words related to it

éprouver des doutes   to have doubts, to feel doubtful

éprouver qqn   to put someone to the test

mettre qqn à l'épreuve   to put someone to the test

éprouver un regret   to feel a regret

éprouver de la sympathie pour qqn   to feel sympathy for someone

mettre à l'épreuve   to put to the test

une épreuve   test, proof, page proof

une épreuve écrite   written test

une épreuve orale   oral test

éprouver de la honte   to experience shame

How are you doing? Find out with the verb drills and tests with answers explained on pages 50–101.

espérer (203)　　　　　Part. pr. **espérant**　　Part. passé **espéré**

to hope

Regular **-er** verb endings; spelling change:
é changes to **è** before syllable with mute **e**

The Seven Simple Tenses		The Seven Compound Tenses	
Singular	Plural	Singular	Plural
1　présent de l'indicatif		8　passé composé	
espère	espérons	ai espéré	avons espéré
espères	espérez	as espéré	avez espéré
espère	espèrent	a espéré	ont espéré
2　imparfait de l'indicatif		9　plus-que-parfait de l'indicatif	
espérais	espérions	avais espéré	avions espéré
espérais	espériez	avais espéré	aviez espéré
espérait	espéraient	avait espéré	avaient espéré
3　passé simple		10　passé antérieur	
espérai	espérâmes	eus espéré	eûmes espéré
espéras	espérâtes	eus espéré	eûtes espéré
espéra	espérèrent	eut espéré	eurent espéré
4　futur		11　futur antérieur	
espérerai	espérerons	aurai espéré	aurons espéré
espéreras	espérerez	auras espéré	aurez espéré
espérera	espéreront	aura espéré	auront espéré
5　conditionnel		12　conditionnel passé	
espérerais	espérerions	aurais espéré	aurions espéré
espérerais	espéreriez	aurais espéré	auriez espéré
espérerait	espéreraient	aurait espéré	auraient espéré
6　présent du subjonctif		13　passé du subjonctif	
espère	espérions	aie espéré	ayons espéré
espères	espériez	aies espéré	ayez espéré
espère	espèrent	ait espéré	aient espéré
7　imparfait du subjonctif		14　plus-que-parfait du subjonctif	
espérasse	espérassions	eusse espéré	eussions espéré
espérasses	espérassiez	eusses espéré	eussiez espéré
espérât	espérassent	eût espéré	eussent espéré

Impératif
espère
espérons
espérez

Sentences using this verb and words and expressions related to it

J'espère que Paul viendra mais je n'espère pas que son frère vienne.

l'espérance *f.*　hope, expectation
plein d'espérance　hopeful, full of hope
l'espoir *m.*　hope
avoir bon espoir de réussir　to have good hopes of succeeding
désespérer de　to despair of; **se désespérer**　to be in despair
le désespoir　despair; **un désespoir d'amour**　disappointed love

Don't forget to check the list of 2,600 additional verbs keyed to the 501 model verbs. It's in the Appendixes!

Regular **-er** verb endings; spelling change: **-ayer** verbs
may change **y** to **i** in front of a mute **e** or may keep **y**

to try, to try on

The Seven Simple Tenses		The Seven Compound Tenses	
Singular	Plural	Singular	Plural
1 présent de l'indicatif		8 passé composé	
essaye	essayons	ai essayé	avons essayé
essayes	essayez	as essayé	avez essayé
essaye	essayent	a essayé	ont essayé
2 imparfait de l'indicatif		9 plus-que-parfait de l'indicatif	
essayais	essayions	avais essayé	avions essayé
essayais	essayiez	avais essayé	aviez essayé
essayait	essayaient	avait essayé	avaient essayé
3 passé simple		10 passé antérieur	
essayai	essayâmes	eus essayé	eûmes essayé
essayas	essayâtes	eus essayé	eûtes essayé
essaya	essayèrent	eut essayé	eurent essayé
4 futur		11 futur antérieur	
essayerai	essayerons	aurai essayé	aurons essayé
essayeras	essayerez	auras essayé	aurez essayé
essayera	essayeront	aura essayé	auront essayé
5 conditionnel		12 conditionnel passé	
essayerais	essayerions	aurais essayé	aurions essayé
essayerais	essayeriez	aurais essayé	auriez essayé
essayerait	essayeraient	aurait essayé	auraient essayé
6 présent du subjonctif		13 passé du subjonctif	
essaye	essayions	aie essayé	ayons essayé
essayes	essayiez	aies essayé	ayez essayé
essaye	essayent	ait essayé	aient essayé
7 imparfait du subjonctif		14 plus-que-parfait du subjonctif	
essayasse	essayassions	eusse essayé	eussions essayé
essayasses	essayassiez	eusses essayé	eussiez essayé
essayât	essayassent	eût essayé	eussent essayé

Impératif
essaye
essayons
essayez

E

Sentences using this verb and words related to it

   Marcel a essayé d'écrire un essai sur la vie des animaux sauvages mais il n'a pas pu réussir
à écrire une seule phrase. Alors, il est allé dans la chambre de son grand frère pour travailler
avec lui.

   Puis-je essayer cette robe?   May I try on this dress?

un essai   essay
essayiste   essayist
essayer de faire qqch   to try to do something

une salle/un salon d'essayage   fitting room
essayeur, essayeuse   fitter (clothing)
essayage *m.*   fitting (clothing)

to wipe

Regular -er verb endings; spelling change: -uyer verbs must change y to i in front of a mute e

The Seven Simple Tenses		The Seven Compound Tenses	
Singular	Plural	Singular	Plural
1 présent de l'indicatif		8 passé composé	
essuie	essuyons	ai essuyé	avons essuyé
essuies	essuyez	as essuyé	avez essuyé
essuie	essuient	a essuyé	ont essuyé
2 imparfait de l'indicatif		9 plus-que-parfait de l'indicatif	
essuyais	essuyions	avais essuyé	avions essuyé
essuyais	essuyiez	avais essuyé	aviez essuyé
essuyait	essuyaient	avait essuyé	avaient essuyé
3 passé simple		10 passé antérieur	
essuyai	essuyâmes	eus essuyé	eûmes essuyé
essuyas	essuyâtes	eus essuyé	eûtes essuyé
essuya	essuyèrent	eut essuyé	eurent essuyé
4 futur		11 futur antérieur	
essuierai	essuierons	aurai essuyé	aurons essuyé
essuieras	essuierez	auras essuyé	aurez essuyé
essuiera	essuieront	aura essuyé	auront essuyé
5 conditionnel		12 conditionnel passé	
essuierais	essuierions	aurais essuyé	aurions essuyé
essuierais	essuieriez	aurais essuyé	auriez essuyé
essuierait	essuieraient	aurait essuyé	auraient essuyé
6 présent du subjonctif		13 passé du subjonctif	
essuie	essuyions	aie essuyé	ayons essuyé
essuies	essuyiez	aies essuyé	ayez essuyé
essuie	essuient	ait essuyé	aient essuyé
7 imparfait du subjonctif		14 plus-que-parfait du subjonctif	
essuyasse	essuyassions	eusse essuyé	eussions essuyé
essuyasses	essuyassiez	eusses essuyé	eussiez essuyé
essuyât	essuyassent	eût essuyé	eussent essuyé

Impératif
essuie
essuyons
essuyez

Words and expressions related to this verb
un essuie-mains hand towel
un essuie-glace windshield wiper
l'essuyage *m.* wiping

un essuie-verres glass cloth
s'essuyer to wipe oneself
s'essuyer le front to wipe one's brow

S'il vous plaît, essuyez vos pieds avant d'entrer. Please wipe your feet before entering.
Notre équipe a essuyé une défaite dans le championnat. Our team suffered a defeat in the championship. (Note: This does not mean "wiped defeat.")

Soak up some verbs used in weather expressions. There's a list in the Appendixes!

Regular **-ir** verb   to establish, to set up, to draw up

The Seven Simple Tenses		The Seven Compound Tenses	
Singular	Plural	Singular	Plural
1 présent de l'indicatif		**8 passé composé**	
établis	**établissons**	**ai établi**	**avons établi**
établis	**établissez**	**as établi**	**avez établi**
établit	**établissent**	**a établi**	**ont établi**
2 imparfait de l'indicatif		**9 plus-que-parfait de l'indicatif**	
établissais	**établissions**	**avais établi**	**avions établi**
établissais	**établissiez**	**avais établi**	**aviez établi**
établissait	**établissaient**	**avait établi**	**avaient établi**
3 passé simple		**10 passé antérieur**	
établis	**établîmes**	**eus établi**	**eûmes établi**
établis	**établîtes**	**eus établi**	**eûtes établi**
établit	**établirent**	**eut établi**	**eurent établi**
4 futur		**11 futur antérieur**	
établirai	**établirons**	**aurai établi**	**aurons établi**
établiras	**établirez**	**auras établi**	**aurez établi**
établira	**établiront**	**aura établi**	**auront établi**
5 conditionnel		**12 conditionnel passé**	
établirais	**établirions**	**aurais établi**	**aurions établi**
établirais	**établiriez**	**aurais établi**	**auriez établi**
établirait	**établiraient**	**aurait établi**	**auraient établi**
6 présent du subjonctif		**13 passé du subjonctif**	
établisse	**établissions**	**aie établi**	**ayons établi**
établisses	**établissiez**	**aies établi**	**ayez établi**
établisse	**établissent**	**ait établi**	**aient établi**
7 imparfait du subjonctif		**14 plus-que-parfait du subjonctif**	
établisse	**établissions**	**eusse établi**	**eussions établi**
établisses	**établissiez**	**eusses établi**	**eussiez établi**
établît	**établissent**	**eût établi**	**eussent établi**

Impératif
établis
établissons
établissez

Words related to this verb
rétablir   to reestablish, to restore
s'établir   to settle down, to start a business
se rétablir   to recover one's health
un établissement   establishment
Bon rétablissement!   Get well soon!

Grammar putting you in a tense mood? Review the definitions of basic grammatical terms with examples on pages 35–49.

The subject pronouns are found on page 103.
335

to extinguish, to shut down (computer), to turn off   Irregular verb

The Seven Simple Tenses		The Seven Compound Tenses	
Singular	Plural	Singular	Plural
1 présent de l'indicatif		8 passé composé	
éteins	éteignons	ai éteint	avons éteint
éteins	éteignez	as éteint	avez éteint
éteint	éteignent	a éteint	ont éteint
2 imparfait de l'indicatif		9 plus-que-parfait de l'indicatif	
éteignais	éteignions	avais éteint	avions éteint
éteignais	éteigniez	avais éteint	aviez éteint
éteignait	éteignaient	avait éteint	avaient éteint
3 passé simple		10 passé antérieur	
éteignis	éteignîmes	eus éteint	eûmes éteint
éteignis	éteignîtes	eus éteint	eûtes éteint
éteignit	éteignirent	eut éteint	eurent éteint
4 futur		11 futur antérieur	
éteindrai	éteindrons	aurai éteint	aurons éteint
éteindras	éteindrez	auras éteint	aurez éteint
éteindra	éteindront	aura éteint	auront éteint
5 conditionnel		12 conditionnel passé	
éteindrais	éteindrions	aurais éteint	aurions éteint
éteindrais	éteindriez	aurais éteint	auriez éteint
éteindrait	éteindraient	aurait éteint	auraient éteint
6 présent du subjonctif		13 passé du subjonctif	
éteigne	éteignions	aie éteint	ayons éteint
éteignes	éteigniez	aies éteint	ayez éteint
éteigne	éteignent	ait éteint	aient éteint
7 imparfait du subjonctif		14 plus-que-parfait du subjonctif	
éteignisse	éteignissions	eusse éteint	eussions éteint
éteignisses	éteignissiez	eusses éteint	eussiez éteint
éteignît	éteignissent	eût éteint	eussent éteint

Impératif
éteins
éteignons
éteignez

Éteindre is an important verb for you to know because, although it is irregular, there are a number of verbs that are conjugated like it. Pay attention to the past participle.

E

Sentences using éteindre

J'éteins la lumière. Bonne nuit! I'm turning out the light. Good night!

N'oublie pas d'enregistrer (sauver) le document que tu as créé avant d'éteindre ton ordinateur. Don't forget to save the document you created before shutting down your computer.

Julie est triste parce que sa tante s'est éteinte hier. Julie is sad because her aunt passed away yesterday.

On pourra m'ôter cette vie, mais on n'éteindra pas mon chant. (Aragon) You can take this life from me, but you will not kill my song.

Les pompiers ont éteint l'incendie après une lutte de trois heures. The firemen put out the fire after a three-hour struggle.

Words and expressions related to this verb

éteint, éteinte extinct, extinguished

un éteignoir snuffer, extinguisher

s'éteindre to flicker out, to die out, to die

éteindre le feu to put out the fire

éteindre la lumière to turn off the light

un extincteur fire extinguisher

Arriver pour éteindre les cierges. To arrive in time to put out the altar candles. (To arrive too late. To arrive after the church service.)

If you can conjugate **éteindre** you can also conjugate the following verbs:

étreindre to hug

restreindre to restrict

déteindre to rub off, lose color

reteindre to dye again

to stretch oneself, to stretch out, to lie down   Reflexive regular **-re** verb

The Seven Simple Tenses		The Seven Compound Tenses	
Singular	Plural	Singular	Plural
1 présent de l'indicatif		8 passé composé	
m'étends	nous étendons	me suis étendu(e)	nous sommes étendu(e)s
t'étends	vous étendez	t'es étendu(e)	vous êtes étendu(e)(s)
s'étend	s'étendent	s'est étendu(e)	se sont étendu(e)s
2 imparfait de l'indicatif		9 plus-que-parfait de l'indicatif	
m'étendais	nous étendions	m'étais étendu(e)	nous étions étendu(e)s
t'étendais	vous étendiez	t'étais étendu(e)	vous étiez étendu(e)(s)
s'étendait	s'étendaient	s'était étendu(e)	s'étaient étendu(e)s
3 passé simple		10 passé antérieur	
m'étendis	nous étendîmes	me fus étendu(e)	nous fûmes étendu(e)s
t'étendis	vous étendîtes	te fus étendu(e)	vous fûtes étendu(e)(s)
s'étendit	s'étendirent	se fut étendu(e)	se furent étendu(e)s
4 futur		11 futur antérieur	
m'étendrai	nous étendrons	me serai étendu(e)	nous serons étendu(e)s
t'étendras	vous étendrez	te seras étendu(e)	vous serez étendu(e)(s)
s'étendra	s'étendront	se sera étendu(e)	se seront étendu(e)s
5 conditionnel		12 conditionnel passé	
m'étendrais	nous étendrions	me serais étendu(e)	nous serions étendu(e)s
t'étendrais	vous étendriez	te serais étendu(e)	vous seriez étendu(e)(s)
s'étendrait	s'étendraient	se serait étendu(e)	se seraient étendu(e)s
6 présent du subjonctif		13 passé du subjonctif	
m'étende	nous étendions	me sois étendu(e)	nous soyons étendu(e)s
t'étendes	vous étendiez	te sois étendu(e)	vous soyez étendu(e)(s)
s'étende	s'étendent	se soit étendu(e)	se soient étendu(e)s
7 imparfait du subjonctif		14 plus-que-parfait du subjonctif	
m'étendisse	nous étendissions	me fusse étendu(e)	nous fussions étendu(e)s
t'étendisses	vous étendissiez	te fusses étendu(e)	vous fussiez étendu(e)(s)
s'étendît	s'étendissent	se fût étendu(e)	se fussent étendu(e)s

Impératif
étends-toi; ne t'étends pas
étendons-nous; ne nous étendons pas
étendez-vous; ne vous étendez pas

Sentences using this verb and words and expressions related to it
   Ma mère était si fatiguée quand elle est rentrée à la maison après avoir fait du shopping, qu'elle est allée directement au lit et elle s'est étendue.

étendre le linge   to hang out the wash   l'étendue *f.*   area, extent
étendre d'eau   to water down   s'étendre   to stretch
s'étendre sur qqch   to dwell on something

Regular **-er** verb   to amaze, to astonish, to stun, to surprise

The Seven Simple Tenses		The Seven Compound Tenses	
Singular	Plural	Singular	Plural
1 présent de l'indicatif		8 passé composé	
étonne	étonnons	ai étonné	avons étonné
étonnes	étonnez	as étonné	avez étonné
étonne	étonnent	a étonné	ont étonné
2 imparfait de l'indicatif		9 plus-que-parfait de l'indicatif	
étonnais	étonnions	avais étonné	avions étonné
étonnais	étonniez	avais étonné	aviez étonné
étonnait	étonnaient	avait étonné	avaient étonné
3 passé simple		10 passé antérieur	
étonnai	étonnâmes	eus étonné	eûmes étonné
étonnas	étonnâtes	eus étonné	eûtes étonné
étonna	étonnèrent	eut étonné	eurent étonné
4 futur		11 futur antérieur	
étonnerai	étonnerons	aurai étonné	aurons étonné
étonneras	étonnerez	auras étonné	aurez étonné
étonnera	étonneront	aura étonné	auront étonné
5 conditionnel		12 conditionnel passé	
étonnerais	étonnerions	aurais étonné	aurions étonné
étonnerais	étonneriez	aurais étonné	auriez étonné
étonnerait	étonneraient	aurait étonné	auraient étonné
6 présent du subjonctif		13 passé du subjonctif	
étonne	étonnions	aie étonné	ayons étonné
étonnes	étonniez	aies étonné	ayez étonné
étonne	étonnent	ait étonné	aient étonné
7 imparfait du subjonctif		14 plus-que-parfait du subjonctif	
étonnasse	étonnassions	eusse étonné	eussions étonné
étonnasses	étonnassiez	eusses étonné	eussiez étonné
étonnât	étonnassent	eût étonné	eussent étonné

Impératif
étonne
étonnons
étonnez

Words related to this verb
étonnant, étonnante   astonishing
C'est bien étonnant!   It's quite astonishing!
l'étonnement *m.*   astonishment, amazement
s'étonner de   to be astonished at

Cela m'étonne!   That astonishes me!
Cela ne m'étonne pas!   That does not surprise
me!

Don't be caught by surprise. Try the verb drills and tests with answers explained on pages
50–101.

to daze, to stun, to make dizzy, to deafen, to bewilder

Regular **-ir** verb

The Seven Simple Tenses		The Seven Compound Tenses	
Singular	Plural	Singular	Plural
1 présent de l'indicatif		**8 passé composé**	
étourdis	étourdissons	ai étourdi	avons étourdi
étourdis	étourdissez	as étourdi	avez étourdi
étourdit	étourdissent	a étourdi	ont étourdi
2 imparfait de l'indicatif		**9 plus-que-parfait de l'indicatif**	
étourdissais	étourdissions	avais étourdi	avions étourdi
étourdissais	étourdissiez	avais étourdi	aviez étourdi
étourdissait	étourdissaient	avait étourdi	avaient étourdi
3 passé simple		**10 passé antérieur**	
étourdis	étourdîmes	eus étourdi	eûmes étourdi
étourdis	étourdîtes	eus étourdi	eûtes étourdi
étourdit	étourdirent	eut étourdi	eurent étourdi
4 futur		**11 futur antérieur**	
étourdirai	étourdirons	aurai étourdi	aurons étourdi
étourdiras	étourdirez	auras étourdi	aurez étourdi
étourdira	étourdiront	aura étourdi	auront étourdi
5 conditionnel		**12 conditionnel passé**	
étourdirais	étourdirions	aurais étourdi	aurions étourdi
étourdirais	étourdiriez	aurais étourdi	auriez étourdi
étourdirait	étourdiraient	aurait étourdi	auraient étourdi
6 présent du subjonctif		**13 passé du subjonctif**	
étourdisse	étourdissions	aie étourdi	ayons étourdi
étourdisses	étourdissiez	aies étourdi	ayez étourdi
étourdisse	étourdissent	ait étourdi	aient étourdi
7 imparfait du subjonctif		**14 plus-que-parfait du subjonctif**	
étourdisse	étourdissions	eusse étourdi	eussions étourdi
étourdisses	étourdissiez	eusses étourdi	eussiez étourdi
étourdît	étourdissent	eût étourdi	eussent étourdi

Impératif
étourdis
étourdissons
étourdissez

Words and expressions related to this verb
s'étourdir   to lose one's senses in some kind of outlet
une étourderie   thoughtlessness, carelessness
un étourdissement   giddiness; temporary loss of one's senses

étourdiment   thoughtlessly
étourdi, étourdie   thoughtless, giddy
par étourderie   by an oversight
étourdissant, étourdissante   staggering, deafening

Are you bewildered by the Subjunctive? Read pages 26–31.

Irregular verb

The Seven Simple Tenses		The Seven Compound Tenses	
Singular	Plural	Singular	Plural
1 présent de l'indicatif		**8 passé composé**	
suis	sommes	ai été	avons été
es	êtes	as été	avez été
est	sont	a été	ont été
2 imparfait de l'indicatif		**9 plus-que-parfait de l'indicatif**	
étais	étions	avais été	avions été
étais	étiez	avais été	aviez été
était	étaient	avait été	avaient été
3 passé simple		**10 passé antérieur**	
fus	fûmes	eus été	eûmes été
fus	fûtes	eus été	eûtes été
fut	furent	eut été	eurent été
4 futur		**11 futur antérieur**	
serai	serons	aurai été	aurons été
seras	serez	auras été	aurez été
sera	seront	aura été	auront été
5 conditionnel		**12 conditionnel passé**	
serais	serions	aurais été	aurions été
serais	seriez	aurais été	auriez été
serait	seraient	aurait été	auraient été
6 présent du subjonctif		**13 passé du subjonctif**	
sois	soyons	aie été	ayons été
sois	soyez	aies été	ayez été
soit	soient	ait été	aient été
7 imparfait du subjonctif		**14 plus-que-parfait du subjonctif**	
fusse	fussions	eusse été	eussions été
fusses	fussiez	eusses été	eussiez été
fût	fussent	eût été	eussent été

Impératif
sois
soyons
soyez

AN ESSENTIAL
55 VERB

The subject pronouns are found on page 103.

AN ESSENTIAL 55 VERB

Être is an obvious choice to be a key verb. It is used as an auxiliary in compound tenses for a number of verbs (see page 6) and it is used in a seemingly endless list of idiomatic expressions.

Sentences using être

Ma soeur est en train d'écrire un courriel à son petit ami. My sister is busy writing an e-mail to her boyfriend.

Je suis à vous. I am at your service.

Madame Paquet est toujours bien mise. Mrs. Paquet is always well dressed.

Je ne suis pas dans mon assiette aujourd'hui. I'm not feeling up to par (quite myself) today.

À quelle heure ta mère sera-t-elle de retour? At what time will your mother be back?

Ma mère est très malade; elle n'est pas en état de vous parler maintenant. My mother is very sick; she isn't able to talk to you now.

Vous êtes toujours le bienvenu chez nous. You are always welcome in our home.

Dépêchons-nous parce que le train est sur le point de partir. Let's hurry because the train is about to leave.

—**Quelle heure est-il?** What time is it?
—**Il est une heure.** It is one o'clock.
—**Il est trois heures.** It is three o'clock.

Ça y est! That's it!

—**À qui est ce livre?** Whose book is this?
—**Ce livre est à moi.** This book is mine.

Madame Beaupuy est au courant de tout. Mrs. Beaupuy is informed on (knows about) everything.

Est-ce que vous êtes bien dans cette chaise? Are you comfortable in this chair?

Ainsi soit-il! So be it!

Words and expressions using this verb

le bien-être well-being
être à qqn to belong to someone
être à l'heure to be on time
être à temps to be in time
être au courant de to be informed about
être bien to be comfortable
être bien aise (de) to be very glad (to)
être bien mis (mise) to be well dressed
être d'accord avec to agree with
être dans son assiette to feel up to par
être de bonne (mauvaise) humeur to be in a good (bad) mood
être de retour to be back
être en (bonne) forme to be in (good) shape
être en état de + inf. to be able + inf.
être en panne to be broken down, out of order (machine, auto)
être pressé, être pressée to be in a hurry
être en retard to be late
être en train de + inf. to be in the act of + pres. part., to be in the process of, to be busy + pres. part.
être en vacances to be on vacation
être en vie to be alive
être enrhumé to have a cold
être hors de soi to be beside oneself, to be upset
être le bienvenu (la bienvenue) to be welcome
être sur le point de + inf. to be about + inf.
être temps de + inf. to be time to + inf.
De quelle couleur est (sont) . . .? What color is (are) . . .?
Il était une fois . . . Once upon a time there was . . .
un être humain human being

342

The Seven Simple Tenses		The Seven Compound Tenses	
Singular	Plural	Singular	Plural
1 présent de l'indicatif		8 passé composé	
étudie	étudions	ai étudié	avons étudié
étudies	étudiez	as étudié	avez étudié
étudie	étudient	a étudié	ont étudié
2 imparfait de l'indicatif		9 plus-que-parfait de l'indicatif	
étudiais	étudiions	avais étudié	avions étudié
étudiais	étudiiez	avais étudié	aviez étudié
étudiait	étudiaient	avait étudié	avaient étudié
3 passé simple		10 passé antérieur	
étudiai	étudiâmes	eus étudié	eûmes étudié
étudias	étudiâtes	eus étudié	eûtes étudié
étudia	étudièrent	eut étudié	eurent étudié
4 futur		11 futur antérieur	
étudierai	étudierons	aurai étudié	aurons étudié
étudieras	étudierez	auras étudié	aurez étudié
étudiera	étudieront	aura étudié	auront étudié
5 conditionnel		12 conditionnel passé	
étudierais	étudierions	aurais étudié	aurions étudié
étudierais	étudieriez	aurais étudié	auriez étudié
étudierait	étudieraient	aurait étudié	auraient étudié
6 présent du subjonctif		13 passé du subjonctif	
étudie	étudiions	aie étudié	ayons étudié
étudies	étudiiez	aies étudié	ayez étudié
étudie	étudient	ait étudié	aient étudié
7 imparfait du subjonctif		14 plus-que-parfait du subjonctif	
étudiasse	étudiassions	eusse étudié	eussions étudié
étudiasses	étudiassiez	eusses étudié	eussiez étudié
étudiât	étudiassent	eût étudié	eussent étudié

Impératif
étudie
étudions
étudiez

AN ESSENTIAL
55 VERB

Étudier

Étudier is a very useful verb for a beginning French student. As you study this verb, be careful about the **ii** in the **nous** and **vous** forms of the **imparfait** and the **présent du subjonctif**.

Sentences using étudier and related words

Ma tante étudie le piano depuis dix ans. My aunt has been studying piano for ten years.

Le dossier de Monsieur Pompier est à l'étude. Mr. Pompier's file is under study.

Thomas fait ses études à l'Université de Grenoble. Thomas is studying at the University of Grenoble.

—Depuis combien de temps étudiez-vous le français? How long have you been studying French?

—J'étudie le français depuis deux ans. I have been studying French for two years.

Words and expressions using this verb

un étudiant, une étudiante **student**

l'étude *f.* **study**

les études *f.* **studies**

une salle d'études **study hall**

étudier à fond **to study thoroughly**

faire ses études **to study, to go to school**

à l'étude **under consideration, under study**

s'étudier **to analyze oneself**

étudier qqch de près **to study something closely**

s'amuser au lieu d'étudier **to have a good time instead of studying**

If you can conjugate **étudier** you can also conjugate these verbs:

apprécier **to appreciate**	copier **to copy**
balbutier **to stammer**	identifier **to identify**
certifier **to guarantee**	justifier **to justify**
clarifier **to clarify**	planifier **to plan**
classifier **to classify**	skier **to ski**

Regular **-er** verb   to evaluate, to appraise, to assess, to estimate

The Seven Simple Tenses		The Seven Compound Tenses	
Singular	Plural	Singular	Plural
1 présent de l'indicatif		**8 passé composé**	
évalue	**évaluons**	**ai évalué**	**avons évalué**
évalues	**évaluez**	**as évalué**	**avez évalué**
évalue	**évaluent**	**a évalué**	**ont évalué**
2 imparfait de l'indicatif		**9 plus-que-parfait de l'indicatif**	
évaluais	**évaluions**	**avais évalué**	**avions évalué**
évaluais	**évaluiez**	**avais évalué**	**aviez évalué**
évaluait	**évaluaient**	**avait évalué**	**avaient évalué**
3 passé simple		**10 passé antérieur**	
évaluai	**évaluâmes**	**eus évalué**	**eûmes évalué**
évaluas	**évaluâtes**	**eus évalué**	**eûtes évalué**
évalua	**évaluèrent**	**eut évalué**	**eurent évalué**
4 futur		**11 futur antérieur**	
évaluerai	**évaluerons**	**aurai évalué**	**aurons évalué**
évalueras	**évaluerez**	**auras évalué**	**aurez évalué**
évaluera	**évalueront**	**aura évalué**	**auront évalué**
5 conditionnel		**12 conditionnel passé**	
évaluerais	**évaluerions**	**aurais évalué**	**aurions évalué**
évaluerais	**évalueriez**	**aurais évalué**	**auriez évalué**
évaluerait	**évalueraient**	**aurait évalué**	**auraient évalué**
6 présent du subjonctif		**13 passé du subjonctif**	
évalue	**évaluions**	**aie évalué**	**ayons évalué**
évalues	**évaluiez**	**aies évalué**	**ayez évalué**
évalue	**évaluent**	**ait évalué**	**aient évalué**
7 imparfait du subjonctif		**14 plus-que-parfait du subjonctif**	
évaluasse	**évaluassions**	**eusse évalué**	**eussions évalué**
évaluasses	**évaluassiez**	**eusses évalué**	**eussiez évalué**
évaluât	**évaluassent**	**eût évalué**	**eussent évalué**

E

Impératif
évalue
évaluons
évaluez

Words and expressions related to this verb
une évaluation evaluation, estimate, assessment
de valeur valuable, of value
valable valid
mettre en valeur to emphasize, to enhance

faire évaluer qqch par un expert to have something appraised by an expert
valablement validly
valeureusement valorously
la valeur value, valor

Can't find the verb you're looking for? Check the back pages of this book for a list of over 2,600 additional verbs!

The subject pronouns are found on page 103.   **345**

to faint, to lose consciousness,
to swoon, to vanish

The Seven Simple Tenses		The Seven Compound Tenses	
Singular	Plural	Singular	Plural
1 présent de l'indicatif		**8 passé composé**	
m'évanouis	nous évanouissons	me suis évanoui(e)	nous sommes évanoui(e)s
t'évanouis	vous évanouissez	t'es évanoui(e)	vous êtes évanoui(e)(s)
s'évanouit	s'évanouissent	s'est évanoui(e)	se sont évanoui(e)s
2 imparfait de l'indicatif		**9 plus-que-parfait de l'indicatif**	
m'évanouissais	nous évanouissions	m'étais évanoui(e)	nous étions évanoui(e)s
t'évanouissais	vous évanouissiez	t'étais évanoui(e)	vous étiez évanoui(e)(s)
s'évanouissait	s'évanouissaient	s'était évanoui(e)	s'étaient évanoui(e)s
3 passé simple		**10 passé antérieur**	
m'évanouis	nous évanouîmes	me fus évanoui(e)	nous fûmes évanoui(e)s
t'évanouis	vous évanouîtes	te fus évanoui(e)	vous fûtes évanoui(e)(s)
s'évanouit	s'évanouirent	se fut évanoui(e)	se furent évanoui(e)s
4 futur		**11 futur antérieur**	
m'évanouirai	nous évanouirons	me serai évanoui(e)	nous serons évanoui(e)s
t'évanouiras	vous évanouirez	te seras évanoui(e)	vous serez évanoui(e)(s)
s'évanouira	s'évanouiront	se sera évanoui(e)	se seront évanoui(e)s
5 conditionnel		**12 conditionnel passé**	
m'évanouirais	nous évanouirions	me serais évanoui(e)	nous serions évanoui(e)s
t'évanouirais	vous évanouiriez	te serais évanoui(e)	vous seriez évanoui(e)(s)
s'évanouirait	s'évanouiraient	se serait évanoui(e)	se seraient évanoui(e)s
6 présent du subjonctif		**13 passé du subjonctif**	
m'évanouisse	nous évanouissions	me sois évanoui(e)	nous soyons évanoui(e)s
t'évanouisses	vous évanouissiez	te sois évanoui(e)	vous soyez évanoui(e)(s)
s'évanouisse	s'évanouissent	se soit évanoui(e)	se soient évanoui(e)s
7 imparfait du subjonctif		**14 plus-que-parfait du subjonctif**	
m'évanouisse	nous évanouissions	me fusse évanoui(e)	nous fussions évanoui(e)s
t'évanouisses	vous évanouissiez	te fusses évanoui(e)	vous fussiez évanoui(e)(s)
s'évanouît	s'évanouissent	se fût évanoui(e)	se fussent évanoui(e)s

Impératif
évanouis-toi; ne t'évanouis pas
évanouissons-nous; ne nous évanouissons pas
évanouissez-vous; ne vous évanouissez pas

Words and expressions related to this verb
un évanouissement   faint, fading
un rêve évanoui   vanished dream
tomber évanoui, évanouie   to faint, to pass out

évanoui, évanouie   unconscious, fainted, in a faint; vanished
revenir d'un évanouissement   to come out of a faint

Grammar putting you in a tense mood? Review the definitions of basic grammatical terms with examples on pages 35–49.

Regular **-er** verb   to avoid

The Seven Simple Tenses		The Seven Compound Tenses	
Singular	Plural	Singular	Plural
1 présent de l'indicatif		8 passé composé	
évite	**évitons**	**ai évité**	**avons évité**
évites	**évitez**	**as évité**	**avez évité**
évite	**évitent**	**a évité**	**ont évité**
2 imparfait de l'indicatif		9 plus-que-parfait de l'indicatif	
évitais	**évitions**	**avais évité**	**avions évité**
évitais	**évitiez**	**avais évité**	**aviez évité**
évitait	**évitaient**	**avait évité**	**avaient évité**
3 passé simple		10 passé antérieur	
évitai	**évitâmes**	**eus évité**	**eûmes évité**
évitas	**évitâtes**	**eus évité**	**eûtes évité**
évita	**évitèrent**	**eut évité**	**eurent évité**
4 futur		11 futur antérieur	
éviterai	**éviterons**	**aurai évité**	**aurons évité**
éviteras	**éviterez**	**auras évité**	**aurez évité**
évitera	**éviteront**	**aura évité**	**auront évité**
5 conditionnel		12 conditionnel passé	
éviterais	**éviterions**	**aurais évité**	**aurions évité**
éviterais	**éviteriez**	**aurais évité**	**auriez évité**
éviterait	**éviteraient**	**aurait évité**	**auraient évité**
6 présent du subjonctif		13 passé du subjonctif	
évite	**évitions**	**aie évité**	**ayons évité**
évites	**évitiez**	**aies évité**	**ayez évité**
évite	**évitent**	**ait évité**	**aient évité**
7 imparfait du subjonctif		14 plus-que-parfait du subjonctif	
évitasse	**évitassions**	**eusse évité**	**eussions évité**
évitasses	**évitassiez**	**eusses évité**	**eussiez évité**
évitât	**évitassent**	**eût évité**	**eussent évité**

Impératif
évite
évitons
évitez

Words and expressions related to this verb
éviter de faire qqch   to avoid doing something
éviter à qqn la peine de faire qqch   to spare someone the trouble of doing something
évitable   avoidable
inévitable   inevitable, unavoidable
inévitablement   inevitably, unavoidably

Get acquainted with what preposition goes with what verb. See *Verbs with prepositions* in the Appendixes.

The subject pronouns are found on page 103.   **347**

to excuse

Regular **-er** verb

The Seven Simple Tenses		The Seven Compound Tenses	
Singular	Plural	Singular	Plural

1 présent de l'indicatif		8 passé composé	
excuse	excusons	ai excusé	avons excusé
excuses	excusez	as excusé	avez excusé
excuse	excusent	a excusé	ont excusé

2 imparfait de l'indicatif		9 plus-que-parfait de l'indicatif	
excusais	excusions	avais excusé	avions excusé
excusais	excusiez	avais excusé	aviez excusé
excusait	excusaient	avait excusé	avaient excusé

3 passé simple		10 passé antérieur	
excusai	excusâmes	eus excusé	eûmes excusé
excusas	excusâtes	eus excusé	eûtes excusé
excusa	excusèrent	eut excusé	eurent excusé

4 futur		11 futur antérieur	
excuserai	excuserons	aurai excusé	aurons excusé
excuseras	excuserez	auras excusé	aurez excusé
excusera	excuseront	aura excusé	auront excusé

5 conditionnel		12 conditionnel passé	
excuserais	excuserions	aurais excusé	aurions excusé
excuserais	excuseriez	aurais excusé	auriez excusé
excuserait	excuseraient	aurait excusé	auraient excusé

6 présent du subjonctif		13 passé du subjonctif	
excuse	excusions	aie excusé	ayons excusé
excuses	excusiez	aies excusé	ayez excusé
excuse	excusent	ait excusé	aient excusé

7 imparfait du subjonctif		14 plus-que-parfait du subjonctif	
excusasse	excusassions	eusse excusé	eussions excusé
excusasses	excusassiez	eusses excusé	eussiez excusé
excusât	excusassent	eût excusé	eussent excusé

Impératif
excuse
excusons
excusez

Words and expressions related to this verb

excuser de   to excuse from (for)
excuser qqn de faire qqch   to excuse someone from doing something; to excuse someone's doing something
se faire excuser   to ask to be excused
une excuse   excuse
faire ses excuses à qqn pour qqch   to apologize to someone for something
Mille excuses!   Excuse me! (a thousand pardons)

See also s'excuser.

Can't remember the French verb you need? Check the back pages of this book for the English-French verb index!

Reflexive regular **-er** verb   to excuse oneself, to apologize

The Seven Simple Tenses		The Seven Compound Tenses	
Singular	Plural	Singular	Plural
1 présent de l'indicatif		**8 passé composé**	
m'excuse	nous excusons	me suis excusé(e)	nous sommes excusé(e)s
t'excuses	vous excusez	t'es excusé(e)	vous êtes excusé(e)(s)
s'excuse	s'excusent	s'est excusé(e)	se sont excusé(e)s
2 imparfait de l'indicatif		**9 plus-que-parfait de l'indicatif**	
m'excusais	nous excusions	m'étais excusé(e)	nous étions excusé(e)s
t'excusais	vous excusiez	t'étais excusé(e)	vous étiez excusé(e)(s)
s'excusait	s'excusaient	s'était excusé(e)	s'étaient excusé(e)s
3 passé simple		**10 passé antérieur**	
m'excusai	nous excusâmes	me fus excusé(e)	nous fûmes excusé(e)s
t'excusas	vous excusâtes	te fus excusé(e)	vous fûtes excusé(e)(s)
s'excusa	s'excusèrent	se fut excusé(e)	se furent excusé(e)s
4 futur		**11 futur antérieur**	
m'excuserai	nous excuserons	me serai excusé(e)	nous serons excusé(e)s
t'excuseras	vous excuserez	te seras excusé(e)	vous serez excusé(e)(s)
s'excusera	s'excuseront	se sera excusé(e)	se seront excusé(e)s
5 conditionnel		**12 conditionnel passé**	
m'excuserais	nous excuserions	me serais excusé(e)	nous serions excusé(e)s
t'excuserais	vous excuseriez	te serais excusé(e)	vous seriez excusé(e)(s)
s'excuserait	s'excuseraient	se serait excusé(e)	se seraient excusé(e)s
6 présent du subjonctif		**13 passé du subjonctif**	
m'excuse	nous excusions	me sois excusé(e)	nous soyons excusé(e)s
t'excuses	vous excusiez	te sois excusé(e)	vous soyez excusé(e)(s)
s'excuse	s'excusent	se soit excusé(e)	se soient excusé(e)s
7 imparfait du subjonctif		**14 plus-que-parfait du subjonctif**	
m'excusasse	nous excusassions	me fusse excusé(e)	nous fussions excusé(e)s
t'excusasses	vous excusassiez	te fusses excusé(e)	vous fussiez excusé(e)(s)
s'excusât	s'excusassent	se fût excusé(e)	se fussent excusé(e)s

Impératif
excuse-toi; ne t'excuse pas
excusons-nous; ne nous excusons pas
excusez-vous; ne vous excusez pas

Sentences using this verb and words and expressions related to it

L'élève: **Je m'excuse, madame. Excusez-moi. Je m'excuse de vous déranger.**
            Est-ce que vous m'excusez? Est-ce que je vous dérange?
La maîtresse: **Oui, je t'excuse. Non, tu ne me déranges pas. Que veux-tu?**
L'élève: **Est-ce que je peux quitter la salle de classe pour aller aux toilettes?**
La maîtresse: **Oui, vas-y.**

s'excuser de   to apologize for
Veuillez m'excuser.   Please (Be good enough to) excuse me.
Qui s'excuse s'accuse.   A guilty conscience needs no accuser.

Don't forget to study the section on defective and impersonal verbs. It's right after this main list.

to demand, to require

Regular **-er** verb endings; spelling change: retain the **ge** before **a** or **o** to keep the soft **g** sound of the verb

The Seven Simple Tenses		The Seven Compound Tenses	
Singular	Plural	Singular	Plural
1 présent de l'indicatif		8 passé composé	
exige	exigeons	ai exigé	avons exigé
exiges	exigez	as exigé	avez exigé
exige	exigent	a exigé	ont exigé
2 imparfait de l'indicatif		9 plus-que-parfait de l'indicatif	
exigeais	exigions	avais exigé	avions exigé
exigeais	exigiez	avais exigé	aviez exigé
exigeait	exigeaient	avait exigé	avaient exigé
3 passé simple		10 passé antérieur	
exigeai	exigeâmes	eus exigé	eûmes exigé
exigeas	exigeâtes	eus exigé	eûtes exigé
exigea	exigèrent	eut exigé	eurent exigé
4 futur		11 futur antérieur	
exigerai	exigerons	aurai exigé	aurons exigé
exigeras	exigerez	auras exigé	aurez exigé
exigera	exigeront	aura exigé	auront exigé
5 conditionnel		12 conditionnel passé	
exigerais	exigerions	aurais exigé	aurions exigé
exigerais	exigeriez	aurais exigé	auriez exigé
exigerait	exigeraient	aurait exigé	auraient exigé
6 présent du subjonctif		13 passé du subjonctif	
exige	exigions	aie exigé	ayons exigé
exiges	exigiez	aies exigé	ayez exigé
exige	exigent	ait exigé	aient exigé
7 imparfait du subjonctif		14 plus-que-parfait du subjonctif	
exigeasse	exigeassions	eusse exigé	eussions exigé
exigeasses	exigeassiez	eusses exigé	eussiez exigé
exigeât	exigeassent	eût exigé	eussent exigé

Impératif
exige
exigeons
exigez

Sentences using this verb and words related to it

La maîtresse de français: **Paul, viens ici. Ta composition est pleine de fautes.**
                 J'exige que tu la refasses. Rends-la-moi dans dix minutes.
L'élève: **Ce n'est pas de ma faute, madame. C'est mon père qui l'a écrite.**
          Dois-je la refaire?

exigeant, exigeante   exacting   **exiger des soins attentifs**   to demand great care
l'exigence *f.*   exigency   **les exigences**   requirements

Soak up some verbs used in weather expressions. There's a list in the Appendixes!

The Seven Simple Tenses		The Seven Compound Tenses	
Singular	Plural	Singular	Plural

1   présent de l'indicatif

explique	expliquons	8 passé composé	
expliques	expliquez	**ai expliqué**	**avons expliqué**
explique	expliquent	**as expliqué**	**avez expliqué**
		a expliqué	**ont expliqué**

2   imparfait de l'indicatif

expliquais	expliquions	9 plus-que-parfait de l'indicatif	
expliquais	expliquiez	**avais expliqué**	**avions expliqué**
expliquait	expliquaient	**avais expliqué**	**aviez expliqué**
		avait expliqué	**avaient expliqué**

3   passé simple

expliquai	expliquâmes	10 passé antérieur	
expliquas	expliquâtes	**eus expliqué**	**eûmes expliqué**
expliqua	expliquèrent	**eus expliqué**	**eûtes expliqué**
		eut expliqué	**eurent expliqué**

4   futur

expliquerai	expliquerons	11 futur antérieur	
expliqueras	expliquerez	**aurai expliqué**	**aurons expliqué**
expliquera	expliqueront	**auras expliqué**	**aurez expliqué**
		aura expliqué	**auront expliqué**

5   conditionnel

expliquerais	expliquerions	12 conditionnel passé	
expliquerais	expliqueriez	**aurais expliqué**	**aurions expliqué**
expliquerait	expliqueraient	**aurais expliqué**	**auriez expliqué**
		aurait expliqué	**auraient expliqué**

6   présent du subjonctif

explique	expliquions	13 passé du subjonctif	
expliques	expliquiez	**aie expliqué**	**ayons expliqué**
explique	expliquent	**aies expliqué**	**ayez expliqué**
		ait expliqué	**aient expliqué**

7   imparfait du subjonctif

expliquasse	expliquassions	14 plus-que-parfait du subjonctif	
expliquasses	expliquassiez	**eusse expliqué**	**eussions expliqué**
expliquât	expliquassent	**eusses expliqué**	**eussiez expliqué**
		eût expliqué	**eussent expliqué**

Impératif
explique
expliquons
expliquez

Words related to this verb
explicite   explicit
explicitement   explicitly
l'explication *f.*   explanation
une explication de texte   interpretation,
  critical analysis of a text

explicable   explainable
explicatif, explicative   explanatory
s'expliciter   to be explicit

Note the difference in meaning in the following two sentences. See page 17 (b).

J'ai étudié la leçon que le professeur avait expliquée.   I studied the lesson that the teacher had explained.
J'avais étudié la leçon que le professeur a expliquée.   I had studied the lesson that the teacher explained.

to express

Regular **-er** verb

The Seven Simple Tenses		The Seven Compound Tenses	
Singular	Plural	Singular	Plural
1 présent de l'indicatif		8 passé composé	
exprime	exprimons	ai exprimé	avons exprimé
exprimes	exprimez	as exprimé	avez exprimé
exprime	expriment	a exprimé	ont exprimé
2 imparfait de l'indicatif		9 plus-que-parfait de l'indicatif	
exprimais	exprimions	avais exprimé	avions exprimé
exprimais	exprimiez	avais exprimé	aviez exprimé
exprimait	exprimaient	avait exprimé	avaient exprimé
3 passé simple		10 passé antérieur	
exprimai	exprimâmes	eus exprimé	eûmes exprimé
exprimas	exprimâtes	eus exprimé	eûtes exprimé
exprima	exprimèrent	eut exprimé	eurent exprimé
4 futur		11 futur antérieur	
exprimerai	exprimerons	aurai exprimé	aurons exprimé
exprimeras	exprimerez	auras exprimé	aurez exprimé
exprimera	exprimeront	aura exprimé	auront exprimé
5 conditionnel		12 conditionnel passé	
exprimerais	exprimerions	aurais exprimé	aurions exprimé
exprimerais	exprimeriez	aurais exprimé	auriez exprimé
exprimerait	exprimeraient	aurait exprimé	auraient exprimé
6 présent du subjonctif		13 passé du subjonctif	
exprime	exprimions	aie exprimé	ayons exprimé
exprimes	exprimiez	aies exprimé	ayez exprimé
exprime	expriment	ait exprimé	aient exprimé
7 imparfait du subjonctif		14 plus-que-parfait du subjonctif	
exprimasse	exprimassions	eusse exprimé	eussions exprimé
exprimasses	exprimassiez	eusses exprimé	eussiez exprimé
exprimât	exprimassent	eût exprimé	eussent exprimé

Impératif
exprime
exprimons
exprimez

Words and expressions related to this verb
exprimer ses vœux to express (convey) one's wishes
exprimable expressible
une expression expression; **expression des sentiments** expression of feelings

Closing of letter:
Agréez, Monsieur (Madame), l'expression de mes sentiments distingués   Sincerely
s'exprimer to express oneself
s'exprimer par gestes to express oneself with gestures

Reflexive regular **-er** verb   to become angry, to get angry

The Seven Simple Tenses		The Seven Compound Tenses	
Singular	Plural	Singular	Plural
1 présent de l'indicatif		**8 passé composé**	
me fâche	nous fâchons	me suis fâché(e)	nous sommes fâché(e)s
te fâches	vous fâchez	t'es fâché(e)	vous êtes fâché(e)(s)
se fâche	se fâchent	s'est fâché(e)	se sont fâché(e)s
2 imparfait de l'indicatif		**9 plus-que-parfait de l'indicatif**	
me fâchais	nous fâchions	m'étais fâché(e)	nous étions fâché(e)s
te fâchais	vous fâchiez	t'étais fâché(e)	vous étiez fâché(e)(s)
se fâchait	se fâchaient	s'était fâché(e)	s'étaient fâché(e)s
3 passé simple		**10 passé antérieur**	
me fâchai	nous fâchâmes	me fus fâché(e)	nous fûmes fâché(e)s
te fâchas	vous fâchâtes	te fus fâché(e)	vous fûtes fâché(e)(s)
se fâcha	se fâchèrent	se fut fâché(e)	se furent fâché(e)s
4 futur		**11 futur antérieur**	
me fâcherai	nous fâcherons	me serai fâché(e)	nous serons fâché(e)s
te fâcheras	vous fâcherez	te seras fâché(e)	vous serez fâché(e)(s)
se fâchera	se fâcheront	se sera fâché(e)	se seront fâché(e)s
5 conditionnel		**12 conditionnel passé**	
me fâcherais	nous fâcherions	me serais fâché(e)	nous serions fâché(e)s
te fâcherais	vous fâcheriez	te serais fâché(e)	vous seriez fâché(e)(s)
se fâcherait	se fâcheraient	se serait fâché(e)	se seraient fâché(e)s
6 présent du subjonctif		**13 passé du subjonctif**	
me fâche	nous fâchions	me sois fâché(e)	nous soyons fâché(e)s
te fâches	vous fâchiez	te sois fâché(e)	vous soyez fâché(e)(s)
se fâche	se fâchent	se soit fâché(e)	se soient fâché(e)s
7 imparfait du subjonctif		**14 plus-que-parfait du subjonctif**	
me fâchasse	nous fâchassions	me fusse fâché(e)	nous fussions fâché(e)s
te fâchasses	vous fâchassiez	te fusses fâché(e)	vous fussiez fâché(e)(s)
se fâchât	se fâchassent	se fût fâché(e)	se fussent fâché(e)s

Impératif
fâche-toi; ne te fâche pas
fâchons-nous; ne nous fâchons pas
fâchez-vous; ne vous fâchez pas

Words and expressions related to this verb

fâcher qqn   to anger someone, to offend someone

se fâcher contre qqn   to become angry at someone

une fâcherie   tiff, quarrel

C'est fâcheux!   It's a nuisance! It's annoying!

fâcheusement   awkwardly, unfortunately

se fâcher tout rouge   to turn red with anger

How are you doing? Find out with the verb drills and tests with answers explained on pages 50–101.

The subject pronouns are found on page 103.   **353**

faillir (222)

Part. pr. faillant   **Part. passé failli**

to fail, to almost (do something)

Irregular verb

The Seven Simple Tenses		The Seven Compound Tenses	
Singular	Plural	Singular	Plural
1 présent de l'indicatif		**8 passé composé**	
faux	**faillons**	**ai failli**	**avons failli**
faux	**faillez**	**as failli**	**avez failli**
faut	**faillent**	**a failli**	**ont failli**
2 imparfait de l'indicatif		**9 plus-que-parfait de l'indicatif**	
faillais	**faillions**	**avais failli**	**avions failli**
faillais	**failliez**	**avais failli**	**aviez failli**
faillait	**faillaient**	**avait failli**	**avaient failli**
3 passé simple		**10 passé antérieur**	
faillis	**faillîmes**	**eus failli**	**eûmes failli**
faillis	**faillîtes**	**eus failli**	**eûtes failli**
faillit	**faillirent**	**eut failli**	**eurent failli**
4 futur		**11 futur antérieur**	
faillirai or faudrai	**faillirons or faudrons**	**aurai failli**	**aurons failli**
failliras or faudras	**faillirez or faudrez**	**auras failli**	**aurez failli**
faillira or faudra	**failliront or faudront**	**aura failli**	**auront failli**
5 conditionnel		**12 conditionnel passé**	
faillirais or faudrais	**faillirions or faudrions**	**aurais failli**	**aurions failli**
faillirais or faudrais	**failliriez or faudriez**	**aurais failli**	**auriez failli**
faillirait or faudrait	**failliraient or faudraient**	**aurait failli**	**auraient failli**
6 présent du subjonctif		**13 passé du subjonctif**	
faille	**faillions**	**aie failli**	**ayons failli**
failles	**failliez**	**aies failli**	**ayez failli**
faille	**faillent**	**ait failli**	**aient failli**
7 imparfait du subjonctif		**14 plus-que-parfait du subjonctif**	
faillisse	**faillissions**	**eusse failli**	**eussions failli**
faillisses	**faillissiez**	**eusses failli**	**eussiez failli**
faillît	**faillissent**	**eût failli**	**eussent failli**

Impératif
[not in use]

Words and expressions related to this verb
la faillite   bankruptcy, failure
failli, faillie   bankrupt
faillir + inf.   to almost do something
J'ai failli tomber.   I almost fell.
faire faillite   to go bankrupt

défaillir   to weaken, to faint
défaillant, défaillante   feeble
une défaillance   faint (swoon)
être en faillite   to be bankrupt

The conjugated forms of this verb are used most of the time in the **passé simple** and compound tenses. The other tenses are rarely used.

Irregular verb   to do, to make

The Seven Simple Tenses		The Seven Compound Tenses	
Singular	Plural	Singular	Plural
1 présent de l'indicatif		**8 passé composé**	
fais	faisons	ai fait	avons fait
fais	faites	as fait	avez fait
fait	font	a fait	ont fait
2 imparfait de l'indicatif		**9 plus-que-parfait de l'indicatif**	
faisais	faisions	avais fait	avions fait
faisais	faisiez	avais fait	aviez fait
faisait	faisaient	avait fait	avaient fait
3 passé simple		**10 passé antérieur**	
fis	fîmes	eus fait	eûmes fait
fis	fîtes	eus fait	eûtes fait
fit	firent	eut fait	eurent fait
4 futur		**11 futur antérieur**	
ferai	ferons	aurai fait	aurons fait
feras	ferez	auras fait	aurez fait
fera	feront	aura fait	auront fait
5 conditionnel		**12 conditionnel passé**	
ferais	ferions	aurais fait	aurions fait
ferais	feriez	aurais fait	auriez fait
ferait	feraient	aurait fait	auraient fait
6 présent du subjonctif		**13 passé du subjonctif**	
fasse	fassions	aie fait	ayons fait
fasses	fassiez	aies fait	ayez fait
fasse	fassent	ait fait	aient fait
7 imparfait du subjonctif		**14 plus-que-parfait du subjonctif**	
fisse	fissions	eusse fait	eussions fait
fisses	fissiez	eusses fait	eussiez fait
fît	fissent	eût fait	eussent fait

Impératif
fais
faisons
faites

F

Faire is a verb that a beginning French student should find very useful. It is so useful that we have given it an extra page!

Sentences using faire

Cela ne fait rien. That doesn't matter. That makes no difference.

Ma mère a fait faire une jolie robe. My mother had a pretty dress made.

Quel temps fait-il? What's the weather like?

Il fait beau aujourd'hui. The weather's nice today.

Il fait très froid ce matin. It's very cold this morning.

Il a fait très chaud hier. It was very warm yesterday.

Faites comme chez vous! (formal, plural) Make yourself/yourselves at home!

Fais comme chez toi! (informal) Make yourself at home!

Cela lui fera du bien. That will do her (him) some good.

Que faire? What is to be done?

Mon père a fait venir le médecin parce que ma mère est malade. My father had the doctor come because my mother is sick.

Faisons le tour du parc. Let's go around the park.

Ce grand garçon-là a fait mal à mon petit frère. That big boy hurt my little brother.

Je leur ai fait part du mariage de mon fils. I notified them of the marriage of my son.

Proverb

Bien faire et laisser dire. **Do your work well and never mind the critics.**

Faites suivre mes lettres, s'il vous plaît. Forward my letters please.

Ma fille fait ses études à l'Université de Montréal. My daughter is studying at the University of Montreal.

Est-il nécessaire de faire la correspondance? Dans quelle direction? Is it necessary to transfer (change trains)? In what direction?

Words and expressions related to this verb

aussitôt dit aussitôt fait (aussitôt dit que fait) **no sooner said than done**

Comment se fait-il . . .? **How come . . .?**

en faire autant **to do the same, to do as much**

faire + inf. **to have something done**

Note: When you use faire with another verb, this is the causative faire (see page 37). Example: Mon père fait peindre la maison. My father is having the house painted. [That is, someone else does the action.]

faire faire **to have something made (done)**

faire à sa tête **to have one's way**

faire attention (à) **to pay attention (to)**

faire beau **to be pleasant, nice weather**

faire mauvais **to be bad weather**

faire bon accueil **to welcome**

faire chaud **to be warm (weather)**

(Continued on next page)

faire comme chez soi **to make oneself at home**

faire d'une pierre deux coups **to kill two birds with one stone**

faire de l'autostop, faire du pouce **to hitchhike**

faire de la peine à qqn **to hurt someone (morally, emotionally)**

faire de son mieux **to do one's best**

faire des châteaux en Espagne **to build castles in the air**

faire des cours **to give courses, to lecture**

faire des emplettes, faire des courses, faire des achats, faire du shopping **to go shopping**

faire des progrès **to make progress**

faire du bien à qqn **to do good for someone**

faire du ski **to ski**

faire du sport **to play sports**

faire du vélo **to ride a bike**

faire exprès **to do on purpose**

faire face à **to oppose**

faire fi **to scorn**

faire froid **to be cold (weather)**

faire jour **to be daylight**

faire la bête **to act like a fool**

faire la connaissance de qqn **to make the acquaintance of someone, to meet someone for the first time**

faire la cuisine **to do the cooking**

faire la grasse matinée **to sleep late in the morning**

faire la lessive **to do the laundry**

faire la malle **to pack the trunk**

faire la queue **to line up, to get in line, to stand in line, to queue up**

faire la sourde oreille **to turn a deaf ear, to pretend not to hear**

faire la vaisselle **to do (wash) the dishes**

faire le ménage **to do housework**

faire le tour de **to take a stroll, to go around**

faire les bagages **to pack the baggage, luggage**

faire les valises **to pack the suitcases, valises**

faire mal à qqn **to hurt, to harm someone**

faire mon affaire **to suit me, to be just the thing for me**

faire nuit **to be night(time)**

faire part à qqn **to inform someone**

faire part de qqch à qqn **to let someone know about something, to inform, to notify someone of something**

faire partie de **to be a part of**

faire peur à qqn **to frighten someone**

faire plaisir à qqn **to please someone**

faire sa toilette **to wash up**

faire savoir qqch à qqn **to inform someone of something**

faire semblant de + inf. **to pretend + inf.**

faire ses adieux **to say goodbye**

faire ses amitiés à qqn **to give one's regards to someone**

faire ses études à **to study at**

faire son lit **to make one's bed**

faire son possible **to do one's best (utmost)**

faire suivre **to forward mail**

faire un appel (téléphonique) **to make a (telephone) call**

faire un cours **to give a course, to lecture**

faire un tour **to go for a stroll**

faire un voyage **to take a trip**

faire une partie de **to play a game of**

faire une plainte **to make a complaint**

faire une promenade **to take a walk**

faire une promenade en voiture **to go for a drive**

faire une question **to ask (to pose) a question**

faire une réclamation **to make a complaint**

faire une visite **to pay a visit**

faire venir qqn **to have someone come**

faire venir l'eau à la bouche **to make one's mouth water**

F

The subject pronouns are found on page 103.

to feign, to make believe, to pretend, to simulate　　　Irregular verb

The Seven Simple Tenses		The Seven Compound Tenses	
Singular	Plural	Singular	Plural
1 présent de l'indicatif		**8 passé composé**	
feins	feignons	ai feint	avons feint
feins	feignez	as feint	avez feint
feint	feignent	a feint	ont feint
2 imparfait de l'indicatif		**9 plus-que-parfait de l'indicatif**	
feignais	feignions	avais feint	avions feint
feignais	feigniez	avais feint	aviez feint
feignait	feignaient	avait feint	avaient feint
3 passé simple		**10 passé antérieur**	
feignis	feignîmes	eus feint	eûmes feint
feignis	feignîtes	eus feint	eûtes feint
feignit	feignirent	eut feint	eurent feint
4 futur		**11 futur antérieur**	
feindrai	feindrons	aurai feint	aurons feint
feindras	feindrez	auras feint	aurez feint
feindra	feindront	aura feint	auront feint
5 conditionnel		**12 conditionnel passé**	
feindrais	feindrions	aurais feint	aurions feint
feindrais	feindriez	aurais feint	auriez feint
feindrait	feindraient	aurait feint	auraient feint
6 présent du subjonctif		**13 passé du subjonctif**	
feigne	feignions	aie feint	ayons feint
feignes	feigniez	aies feint	ayez feint
feigne	feignent	ait feint	aient feint
7 imparfait du subjonctif		**14 plus-que-parfait du subjonctif**	
feignisse	feignissions	eusse feint	eussions feint
feignisses	feignissiez	eusses feint	eussiez feint
feignît	feignissent	eût feint	eussent feint

Impératif
feins
feignons
feignez

Words and expressions related to this verb

feint, feinte feigned, pretended　　　**feignant, feignante** lazy
la feinte pretense, sham　　　　　　**fainéant, fainéante** lazy
feinter to feint, to fake　　　　　　**sans feinte** without pretense
feindre la colère to pretend to be angry　**feinter qqn** to fool someone
　　　　　　　　　　　　　　　　　faire une feinte à qqn to fool someone

Can't find the verb you're looking for? Check the back pages of this book for a list of over 2,600 additional verbs!

Regular **-er** verb

to congratulate

The Seven Simple Tenses		The Seven Compound Tenses	
Singular	Plural	Singular	Plural
1 présent de l'indicatif		8 passé composé	
félicite	**félicitons**	**ai félicité**	**avons félicité**
félicites	**félicitez**	**as félicité**	**avez félicité**
félicite	**félicitent**	**a félicité**	**ont félicité**
2 imparfait de l'indicatif		9 plus-que-parfait de l'indicatif	
félicitais	**félicitions**	**avais félicité**	**avions félicité**
félicitais	**félicitiez**	**avais félicité**	**aviez félicité**
félicitait	**félicitaient**	**avait félicité**	**avaient félicité**
3 passé simple		10 passé antérieur	
félicitai	**félicitâmes**	**eus félicité**	**eûmes félicité**
félicitas	**félicitâtes**	**eus félicité**	**eûtes félicité**
félicita	**félicitèrent**	**eut félicité**	**eurent félicité**
4 futur		11 futur antérieur	
féliciterai	**féliciterons**	**aurai félicité**	**aurons félicité**
féliciteras	**féliciterez**	**auras félicité**	**aurez félicité**
félicitera	**féliciteront**	**aura félicité**	**auront félicité**
5 conditionnel		12 conditionnel passé	
féliciterais	**féliciterions**	**aurais félicité**	**aurions félicité**
féliciterais	**féliciteriez**	**aurais félicité**	**auriez félicité**
féliciterait	**féliciteraient**	**aurait félicité**	**auraient félicité**
6 présent du subjonctif		13 passé du subjonctif	
félicite	**félicitions**	**aie félicité**	**ayons félicité**
félicites	**félicitiez**	**aies félicité**	**ayez félicité**
félicite	**félicitent**	**ait félicité**	**aient félicité**
7 imparfait du subjonctif		14 plus-que-parfait du subjonctif	
félicitasse	**félicitassions**	**eusse félicité**	**eussions félicité**
félicitasses	**félicitassiez**	**eusses félicité**	**eussiez félicité**
félicitât	**félicitassent**	**eût félicité**	**eussent félicité**

Impératif
félicite
félicitons
félicitez

Words and expressions related to this verb

féliciter qqn de qqch to congratulate someone for something
Je vous félicite! I congratulate you!
la félicitation congratulation
Félicitations! Congratulations!
se féliciter de qqch to congratulate oneself about something
la félicité bliss, felicity, happiness

Don't forget to study the section on defective and impersonal verbs. It's right after this main list.

fendre (226)

Part. pr. fendant **Part. passé fendu**

to split, to crack, to cleave

The Seven Simple Tenses		The Seven Compound Tenses	
Singular	Plural	Singular	Plural
1 présent de l'indicatif		**8 passé composé**	
fends	fendons	ai fendu	avons fendu
fends	fendez	as fendu	avez fendu
fend	fendent	a fendu	ont fendu
2 imparfait de l'indicatif		**9 plus-que-parfait de l'indicatif**	
fendais	fendions	avais fendu	avions fendu
fendais	fendiez	avais fendu	aviez fendu
fendait	fendaient	avait fendu	avaient fendu
3 passé simple		**10 passé antérieur**	
fendis	fendîmes	eus fendu	eûmes fendu
fendis	fendîtes	eus fendu	eûtes fendu
fendit	fendirent	eut fendu	eurent fendu
4 futur		**11 futur antérieur**	
fendrai	fendrons	aurai fendu	aurons fendu
fendras	fendrez	auras fendu	aurez fendu
fendra	fendront	aura fendu	auront fendu
5 conditionnel		**12 conditionnel passé**	
fendrais	fendrions	aurais fendu	aurions fendu
fendrais	fendriez	aurais fendu	auriez fendu
fendrait	fendraient	aurait fendu	auraient fendu
6 présent du subjonctif		**13 passé du subjonctif**	
fende	fendions	aie fendu	ayons fendu
fendes	fendiez	aies fendu	ayez fendu
fende	fendent	ait fendu	aient fendu
7 imparfait du subjonctif		**14 plus-que-parfait du subjonctif**	
fendisse	fendissions	eusse fendu	eussions fendu
fendisses	fendissiez	eusses fendu	eussiez fendu
fendît	fendissent	eût fendu	eussent fendu

Impératif
fends
fendons
fendez

Common idiomatic expressions using this verb and words related to it

fendre un mur   to make a crack in a wall
une fente   crack, split, slot
se fendre de chagrin   to feel heartbroken
fendre du bois   to split wood

fendre son coeur   to break one's heart
un fendoir   cleaver
à fendre l'âme   enough to break one's spirit,
   to crush one's heart

Grammar putting you in a tense mood? Review the definitions of basic grammatical terms on pages 35–49.

Part. pr. **fermant**   Part. passé **fermé**   **fermer (227)**

Regular **-er** verb   to close

The Seven Simple Tenses		The Seven Compound Tenses	
Singular	Plural	Singular	Plural
1 présent de l'indicatif		**8 passé composé**	
ferme	fermons	ai fermé	avons fermé
fermes	fermez	as fermé	avez fermé
ferme	ferment	a fermé	ont fermé
2 imparfait de l'indicatif		**9 plus-que-parfait de l'indicatif**	
fermais	fermions	avais fermé	avions fermé
fermais	fermiez	avais fermé	aviez fermé
fermait	fermaient	avait fermé	avaient fermé
3 passé simple		**10 passé antérieur**	
fermai	fermâmes	eus fermé	eûmes fermé
fermas	fermâtes	eus fermé	eûtes fermé
ferma	fermèrent	eut fermé	eurent fermé
4 futur		**11 futur antérieur**	
fermerai	fermerons	aurai fermé	aurons fermé
fermeras	fermerez	auras fermé	aurez fermé
fermera	fermeront	aura fermé	auront fermé
5 conditionnel		**12 conditionnel passé**	
fermerais	fermerions	aurais fermé	aurions fermé
fermerais	fermeriez	aurais fermé	auriez fermé
fermerait	fermeraient	aurait fermé	auraient fermé
6 présent du subjonctif		**13 passé du subjonctif**	
ferme	fermions	aie fermé	ayons fermé
fermes	fermiez	aies fermé	ayez fermé
ferme	ferment	ait fermé	aient fermé
7 imparfait du subjonctif		**14 plus-que-parfait du subjonctif**	
fermasse	fermassions	eusse fermé	eussions fermé
fermasses	fermassiez	eusses fermé	eussiez fermé
fermât	fermassent	eût fermé	eussent fermé

Impératif
ferme
fermons
fermez

Sentences using this verb and words and expressions related to it

Je fermais la porte quand j'ai entendu le téléphone sonner.   I was closing the door when I heard the phone ring.

Fermez la porte, s'il vous plaît.   Please close the door.

enfermer   to shut in
fermer à clef   to lock
fermer au verrou   to bolt
Ferme-la!   Shut up! Zip it!
fermer le robinet   to turn off the tap
fermer un programme   to close a program (computer)

renfermer   to enclose
Ça sent le renfermé.   It's musty in here.
une fermeture   closing, shutting
une fermeture éclair, une fermeture à glissière   zipper
l'heure de fermer   closing time

The subject pronouns are found on page 103.   **361**

se fier (228)

Part. pr. se fiant   **Part. passé fié(e)(s)**

to depend on, to rely on, to trust in

Reflexive regular **-er** verb

The Seven Simple Tenses		The Seven Compound Tenses	
Singular	Plural	Singular	Plural
1 présent de l'indicatif		8 passé composé	
me fie	nous fions	me suis fié(e)	nous sommes fié(e)s
te fies	vous fiez	t'es fié(e)	vous êtes fié(e)(s)
se fie	se fient	s'est fié(e)	se sont fié(e)s
2 imparfait de l'indicatif		9 plus-que-parfait de l'indicatif	
me fiais	nous fiions	m'étais fié(e)	nous étions fié(e)s
te fiais	vous fiiez	t'étais fié(e)	vous étiez fié(e)(s)
se fiait	se fiaient	s'était fié(e)	s'étaient fié(e)s
3 passé simple		10 passé antérieur	
me fiai	nous fiâmes	me fus fié(e)	nous fûmes fié(e)s
te fias	vous fiâtes	te fus fié(e)	vous fûtes fié(e)(s)
se fia	se fièrent	se fut fié(e)	se furent fié(e)s
4 futur		11 futur antérieur	
me fierai	nous fierons	me serai fié(e)	nous serons fié(e)s
te fieras	vous fierez	te seras fié(e)	vous serez fié(e)(s)
se fiera	se fieront	se sera fié(e)	se seront fié(e)s
5 conditionnel		12 conditionnel passé	
me fierais	nous fierions	me serais fié(e)	nous serions fié(e)s
te fierais	vous fieriez	te serais fié(e)	vous seriez fié(e)(s)
se fierait	se fieraient	se serait fié(e)	se seraient fié(e)s
6 présent du subjonctif		13 passé du subjonctif	
me fie	nous fiions	me sois fié(e)	nous soyons fié(e)s
te fies	vous fiiez	te sois fié(e)	vous soyez fié(e)(s)
se fie	se fient	se soit fié(e)	se soient fié(e)s
7 imparfait du subjonctif		14 plus-que-parfait du subjonctif	
me fiasse	nous fiassions	me fusse fié(e)	nous fussions fié(e)s
te fiasses	vous fiassiez	te fusses fié(e)	vous fussiez fié(e)(s)
se fiât	se fiassent	se fût fié(e)	se fussent fié(e)s

Impératif
fie-toi; ne te fie pas
fions-nous; ne nous fions pas
fiez-vous; ne vous fiez pas

Words and expressions related to this verb
la confiance   confidence, trust
avoir confiance en soi   to be self-confident
confier à   to confide to
se méfier de   to mistrust, to distrust, to beware of
fiable   reliable, trustworthy
la méfiance   mistrust, distrust
se fier à   to depend on, to trust in, to rely on
se confier à   to trust to, to confide in
Ne vous fiez pas aux apparences.   Don't trust appearances.

Get acquainted with what preposition goes with what verb. See *Verbs with prepositions* in the Appendixes.

Regular **-ir** verb   to finish, to end, to terminate, to complete

The Seven Simple Tenses		The Seven Compound Tenses	
Singular	Plural	Singular	Plural
1 présent de l'indicatif		**8 passé composé**	
finis	finissons	ai fini	avons fini
finis	finissez	as fini	avez fini
finit	finissent	a fini	ont fini
2 imparfait de l'indicatif		**9 plus-que-parfait de l'indicatif**	
finissais	finissions	avais fini	avions fini
finissais	finissiez	avais fini	aviez fini
finissait	finissaient	avait fini	avaient fini
3 passé simple		**10 passé antérieur**	
finis	finîmes	eus fini	eûmes fini
finis	finîtes	eus fini	eûtes fini
finit	finirent	eut fini	eurent fini
4 futur		**11 futur antérieur**	
finirai	finirons	aurai fini	aurons fini
finiras	finirez	auras fini	aurez fini
finira	finiront	aura fini	auront fini
5 conditionnel		**12 conditionnel passé**	
finirais	finirions	aurais fini	aurions fini
finirais	finiriez	aurais fini	auriez fini
finirait	finiraient	aurait fini	auraient fini
6 présent du subjonctif		**13 passé du subjonctif**	
finisse	finissions	aie fini	ayons fini
finisses	finissiez	aies fini	ayez fini
finisse	finissent	ait fini	aient fini
7 imparfait du subjonctif		**14 plus-que-parfait du subjonctif**	
finisse	finissions	eusse fini	eussions fini
finisses	finissiez	eusses fini	eussiez fini
finît	finissent	eût fini	eussent fini

Impératif
finis
finissons
finissez

F

AN ESSENTIAL
55 VERB

The subject pronouns are found on page 103.
                                                                                        363

Finir

Finir is a very useful verb because it is a regular **-ir** verb and many **-ir** verbs are conjugated like it. There are also many common words and expressions related to **finir**.

Sentences using finir

J'ai fini de travailler pour aujourd'hui. I have finished working for today.

Louis a fini par épouser une femme plus riche que lui. Louis ended up by marrying a woman richer than he.

Tout est bien qui finit bien. All's well that ends well.

Le psychologue a aidé ce pauvre homme qui voulait mettre fin à ses jours. The psychologist helped this poor man who wanted to put an end to his days.

Finissons-en avec la pauvreté! Let's put an end to poverty!

La fin justifie les moyens. The end justifies the means.

Words and expressions related to this verb

finir de + inf. **to finish + pr. part.**

finir par + inf. **to end up by + pr. part.**

la fin **the end**

la fin de semaine **weekend**

afin de **in order to**

enfin **finally**

finalement **finally**

mettre fin à **to put an end to**

en finir avec qqch **to get something over with**

en finir avec qqn **to be finished/done with someone**

final, finale **final**

la finition **finish (of a piece of work)**

If you can conjugate **finir** you can also conjugate these verbs (and any regular **-ir** verb):

définir **to define**

redéfinir **to redefine**

The Seven Simple Tenses		The Seven Compound Tenses	
Singular	Plural	Singular	Plural
1 présent de l'indicatif		8 passé composé	
fonde	fondons	ai fondé	avons fondé
fondes	fondez	as fondé	avez fondé
fonde	fondent	a fondé	ont fondé
2 imparfait de l'indicatif		9 plus-que-parfait de l'indicatif	
fondais	fondions	avais fondé	avions fondé
fondais	fondiez	avais fondé	aviez fondé
fondait	fondaient	avait fondé	avaient fondé
3 passé simple		10 passé antérieur	
fondai	fondâmes	eus fondé	eûmes fondé
fondas	fondâtes	eus fondé	eûtes fondé
fonda	fondèrent	eut fondé	eurent fondé
4 futur		11 futur antérieur	
fonderai	fonderons	aurai fondé	aurons fondé
fonderas	fonderez	auras fondé	aurez fondé
fondera	fonderont	aura fondé	auront fondé
5 conditionnel		12 conditionnel passé	
fonderais	fonderions	aurais fondé	aurions fondé
fonderais	fonderiez	aurais fondé	auriez fondé
fonderait	fonderaient	aurait fondé	auraient fondé
6 présent du subjonctif		13 passé du subjonctif	
fonde	fondions	aie fondé	ayons fondé
fondes	fondiez	aies fondé	ayez fondé
fonde	fondent	ait fondé	aient fondé
7 imparfait du subjonctif		14 plus-que-parfait du subjonctif	
fondasse	fondassions	eusse fondé	eussions fondé
fondasses	fondassiez	eusses fondé	eussiez fondé
fondât	fondassent	eût fondé	eussent fondé

Impératif
fonde
fondons
fondez

Common idiomatic expressions using this verb and words related to it

se fonder sur to be based on
un fondateur, une fondatrice founder
le fond bottom; background
à fond thoroughly
du fond du coeur from the bottom of one's heart
de fond en comble from top to bottom (from bottom to top)

le fondement foundation of a building
la fondation foundation, endowment
bien fondé well founded; **mal fondé** ill founded
au fond in the bottom, in the back, in the rear; at bottom, after all
manquer de fond to be shallow

Can't remember the French verb you need? Check the back pages of this book for the English-French verb index!

fondre (231) Part. pr. **fondant**   Part. passé **fondu**

to melt, to dissolve, to mix colors

Regular **-re** verb

The Seven Simple Tenses		The Seven Compound Tenses	
Singular	Plural	Singular	Plural
1 présent de l'indicatif		8 passé composé	
fonds	fondons	ai fondu	avons fondu
fonds	fondez	as fondu	avez fondu
fond	fondent	a fondu	ont fondu
2 imparfait de l'indicatif		9 plus-que-parfait de l'indicatif	
fondais	fondions	avais fondu	avions fondu
fondais	fondiez	avais fondu	aviez fondu
fondait	fondaient	avait fondu	avaient fondu
3 passé simple		10 passé antérieur	
fondis	fondîmes	eus fondu	eûmes fondu
fondis	fondîtes	eus fondu	eûtes fondu
fondit	fondirent	eut fondu	eurent fondu
4 futur		11 futur antérieur	
fondrai	fondrons	aurai fondu	aurons fondu
fondras	fondrez	auras fondu	aurez fondu
fondra	fondront	aura fondu	auront fondu
5 conditionnel		12 conditionnel passé	
fondrais	fondrions	aurais fondu	aurions fondu
fondrais	fondriez	aurais fondu	auriez fondu
fondrait	fondraient	aurait fondu	auraient fondu
6 présent du subjonctif		13 passé du subjonctif	
fonde	fondions	aie fondu	ayons fondu
fondes	fondiez	aies fondu	ayez fondu
fonde	fondent	ait fondu	aient fondu
7 imparfait du subjonctif		14 plus-que-parfait du subjonctif	
fondisse	fondissions	eusse fondu	eussions fondu
fondisses	fondissiez	eusses fondu	eussiez fondu
fondît	fondissent	eût fondu	eussent fondu

Impératif
fonds
fondons
fondez

Words and expressions related to this verb
confondre   to confound, to confuse; **se confondre**   to merge, to mingle
refondre   to recast, to remelt; **se fondre**   to melt, to dissolve
la refonte   recasting, remelting of metal
du beurre fondu   melted butter; **du fromage fondu**   melted cheese
fondre en larmes   to burst into tears

How are you doing? Find out with the verb drills and tests with answers explained on pages 50–101.

Part. pr. **forçant**   Part. passé **forcé**   **forcer (232)**

Regular **-er** verb endings; spelling change: **c** changes
to **ç** before **a** or **o** to keep **s** sound

The Seven Simple Tenses | The Seven Compound Tenses

Singular	Plural	Singular	Plural
1 présent de l'indicatif		**8 passé composé**	
force	forçons	ai forcé	avons forcé
forces	forcez	as forcé	avez forcé
force	forcent	a forcé	ont forcé
2 imparfait de l'indicatif		**9 plus-que-parfait de l'indicatif**	
forçais	forcions	avais forcé	avions forcé
forçais	forciez	avais forcé	aviez forcé
forçait	forçaient	avait forcé	avaient forcé
3 passé simple		**10 passé antérieur**	
forçai	forçâmes	eus forcé	eûmes forcé
forças	forçâtes	eus forcé	eûtes forcé
força	forcèrent	eut forcé	eurent forcé
4 futur		**11 futur antérieur**	
forcerai	forcerons	aurai forcé	aurons forcé
forceras	forcerez	auras forcé	aurez forcé
forcera	forceront	aura forcé	auront forcé
5 conditionnel		**12 conditionnel passé**	
forcerais	forcerions	aurais forcé	aurions forcé
forcerais	forceriez	aurais forcé	auriez forcé
forcerait	forceraient	aurait forcé	auraient forcé
6 présent du subjonctif		**13 passé du subjonctif**	
force	forcions	aie forcé	ayons forcé
forces	forciez	aies forcé	ayez forcé
force	forcent	ait forcé	aient forcé
7 imparfait du subjonctif		**14 plus-que-parfait du subjonctif**	
forçasse	forçassions	eusse forcé	eussions forcé
forçasses	forçassiez	eusses forcé	eussiez forcé
forçât	forçassent	eût forcé	eussent forcé

Impératif
force
forçons
forcez

Words and expressions related to this verb
forcer la porte de qqn to force one's way
  into someone's house
être forcé de faire qqch to be obliged to do
  something
se forcer la voix to strain one's voice
à force de by dint of, by means of
A force d'essayer, il a réussi. By dint of
  trying, he succeeded.

la force strength, force; **avec force**
  forcefully, with force
forcément necessarily, inevitably
forcer qqn à faire qqch to force someone to
  do something
un forçat a convict

The subject pronouns are found on page 103.   **367**

to dig deeply, to excavate, to go deep into, to search

Regular **-er** verb

The Seven Simple Tenses		The Seven Compound Tenses	
Singular	Plural	Singular	Plural
1 présent de l'indicatif		8 passé composé	
fouille	**fouillons**	**ai fouillé**	**avons fouillé**
fouilles	**fouillez**	**as fouillé**	**avez fouillé**
fouille	**fouillent**	**a fouillé**	**ont fouillé**
2 imparfait de l'indicatif		9 plus-que-parfait de l'indicatif	
fouillais	**fouillions**	**avais fouillé**	**avions fouillé**
fouillais	**fouilliez**	**avais fouillé**	**aviez fouillé**
fouillait	**fouillaient**	**avait fouillé**	**avaient fouillé**
3 passé simple		10 passé antérieur	
fouillai	**fouillâmes**	**eus fouillé**	**eûmes fouillé**
fouillas	**fouillâtes**	**eus fouillé**	**eûtes fouillé**
fouilla	**fouillèrent**	**eut fouillé**	**eurent fouillé**
4 futur		11 futur antérieur	
fouillerai	**fouillerons**	**aurai fouillé**	**aurons fouillé**
fouilleras	**fouillerez**	**auras fouillé**	**aurez fouillé**
fouillera	**fouilleront**	**aura fouillé**	**auront fouillé**
5 conditionnel		12 conditionnel passé	
fouillerais	**fouillerions**	**aurais fouillé**	**aurions fouillé**
fouillerais	**fouilleriez**	**aurais fouillé**	**auriez fouillé**
fouillerait	**fouilleraient**	**aurait fouillé**	**auraient fouillé**
6 présent du subjonctif		13 passé du subjonctif	
fouille	**fouillions**	**aie fouillé**	**ayons fouillé**
fouilles	**fouilliez**	**aies fouillé**	**ayez fouillé**
fouille	**fouillent**	**ait fouillé**	**aient fouillé**
7 imparfait du subjonctif		14 plus-que-parfait du subjonctif	
fouillasse	**fouillassions**	**eusse fouillé**	**eussions fouillé**
fouillasses	**fouillassiez**	**eusses fouillé**	**eussiez fouillé**
fouillât	**fouillassent**	**eût fouillé**	**eussent fouillé**

Impératif
fouille
fouillons
fouillez

Words and expressions related to this verb
fouiller la maision to search the house
fouiller dans les poches to search around
  (to rummage) in one's pockets

fouiller qqn to frisk (search) someone
la fouille excavation
un fouilleur, une fouilleuse searcher

Don't forget to check the list of 2,600 additional verbs keyed to the 501 model verbs. It's in the Appendixes!

Regular **-ir** verb   to furnish, to supply

The Seven Simple Tenses		The Seven Compound Tenses	
Singular	Plural	Singular	Plural
1 présent de l'indicatif		8 passé composé	
fournis	**fournissons**	**ai fourni**	**avons fourni**
fournis	**fournissez**	**as fourni**	**avez fourni**
fournit	**fournissent**	**a fourni**	**ont fourni**
2 imparfait de l'indicatif		9 plus-que-parfait de l'indicatif	
fournissais	**fournissions**	**avais fourni**	**avions fourni**
fournissais	**fournissiez**	**avais fourni**	**aviez fourni**
fournissait	**fournissaient**	**avait fourni**	**avaient fourni**
3 passé simple		10 passé antérieur	
fournis	**fournîmes**	**eus fourni**	**eûmes fourni**
fournis	**fournîtes**	**eus fourni**	**eûtes fourni**
fournit	**fournirent**	**eut fourni**	**eurent fourni**
4 futur		11 futur antérieur	
fournirai	**fournirons**	**aurai fourni**	**aurons fourni**
fourniras	**fournirez**	**auras fourni**	**aurez fourni**
fournira	**fourniront**	**aura fourni**	**auront fourni**
5 conditionnel		12 conditionnel passé	
fournirais	**fournirions**	**aurais fourni**	**aurions fourni**
fournirais	**fourniriez**	**aurais fourni**	**auriez fourni**
fournirait	**fourniraient**	**aurait fourni**	**auraient fourni**
6 présent du subjonctif		13 passé du subjonctif	
fournisse	**fournissions**	**aie fourni**	**ayons fourni**
fournisses	**fournissiez**	**aies fourni**	**ayez fourni**
fournisse	**fournissent**	**ait fourni**	**aient fourni**
7 imparfait du subjonctif		14 plus-que-parfait du subjonctif	
fournisse	**fournissions**	**eusse fourni**	**eussions fourni**
fournisses	**fournissiez**	**eusses fourni**	**eussiez fourni**
fournît	**fournissent**	**eût fourni**	**eussent fourni**

Impératif
fournis
fournissons
fournissez

Words and expressions related to this verb
fournir qqch à qqn   to supply somebody with something
se fournir de   to provide oneself with
un fournisseur   supplier
fournir à   to provide for; **fournir de**   to furnish with
la fourniture   supplying; **les fournitures**   supplies

Don't forget to study the section on defective and impersonal verbs. It's right after this main list.

The subject pronouns are found on page 103.   **369**

to knock, to hit, to frap, to rap, to strike (hit)

Regular **-er** verb

The Seven Simple Tenses		The Seven Compound Tenses	
Singular	Plural	Singular	Plural
1 présent de l'indicatif		8 passé composé	
frappe	**frappons**	**ai frappé**	**avons frappé**
frappes	**frappez**	**as frappé**	**avez frappé**
frappe	**frappent**	**a frappé**	**ont frappé**
2 imparfait de l'indicatif		9 plus-que-parfait de l'indicatif	
frappais	**frappions**	**avais frappé**	**avions frappé**
frappais	**frappiez**	**avais frappé**	**aviez frappé**
frappait	**frappaient**	**avait frappé**	**avaient frappé**
3 passé simple		10 passé antérieur	
frappai	**frappâmes**	**eus frappé**	**eûmes frappé**
frappas	**frappâtes**	**eus frappé**	**eûtes frappé**
frappa	**frappèrent**	**eut frappé**	**eurent frappé**
4 futur		11 futur antérieur	
frapperai	**frapperons**	**aurai frappé**	**aurons frappé**
frapperas	**frapperez**	**auras frappé**	**aurez frappé**
frappera	**frapperont**	**aura frappé**	**auront frappé**
5 conditionnel		12 conditionnel passé	
frapperais	**frapperions**	**aurais frappé**	**aurions frappé**
frapperais	**frapperiez**	**aurais frappé**	**auriez frappé**
frapperait	**frapperaient**	**aurait frappé**	**auraient frappé**
6 présent du subjonctif		13 passé du subjonctif	
frappe	**frappions**	**aie frappé**	**ayons frappé**
frappes	**frappiez**	**aies frappé**	**ayez frappé**
frappe	**frappent**	**ait frappé**	**aient frappé**
7 imparfait du subjonctif		14 plus-que-parfait du subjonctif	
frappasse	**frappassions**	**eusse frappé**	**eussions frappé**
frappasses	**frappassiez**	**eusses frappé**	**eussiez frappé**
frappât	**frappassent**	**eût frappé**	**eussent frappé**

Impératif
frappe
frappons
frappez

Common idiomatic expressions using this verb and words related to it

se **frapper la poitrine**   to beat one's chest
le **frappage**   striking (medals, coins)
une **faute de frappe**   a typing mistake
frapper à la porte   to knock on the door
frapper du pied   to stamp one's foot
entrer sans frapper   enter without knocking

C'est frappant!   It's striking!
frappé (frappée) de   stricken with
le **frappement**   beating, striking
frappé à mort   mortally wounded
un **lait frappé**   milkshake

It's important that you be familiar with the Subjunctive. See pages 26–31.

Regular **-ir** verb   to shudder, to quiver, to tremble

The Seven Simple Tenses		The Seven Compound Tenses	
Singular	Plural	Singular	Plural
1 présent de l'indicatif		8 passé composé	
frémis	**frémissons**	**ai frémi**	**avons frémi**
frémis	**frémissez**	**as frémi**	**avez frémi**
frémit	**frémissent**	**a frémi**	**ont frémi**
2 imparfait de l'indicatif		9 plus-que-parfait de l'indicatif	
frémissais	**frémissions**	**avais frémi**	**avions frémi**
frémissais	**frémissiez**	**avais frémi**	**aviez frémi**
frémissait	**frémissaient**	**avait frémi**	**avaient frémi**
3 passé simple		10 passé antérieur	
frémis	**frémîmes**	**eus frémi**	**eûmes frémi**
frémis	**frémîtes**	**eus frémi**	**eûtes frémi**
frémit	**frémirent**	**eut frémi**	**eurent frémi**
4 futur		11 futur antérieur	
frémirai	**frémirons**	**aurai frémi**	**aurons frémi**
frémiras	**frémirez**	**auras frémi**	**aurez frémi**
frémira	**frémiront**	**aura frémi**	**auront frémi**
5 conditionnel		12 conditionnel passé	
frémirais	**frémirions**	**aurais frémi**	**aurions frémi**
frémirais	**frémiriez**	**aurais frémi**	**auriez frémi**
frémirait	**frémiraient**	**aurait frémi**	**auraient frémi**
6 présent du subjonctif		13 passé du subjonctif	
frémisse	**frémissions**	**aie frémi**	**ayons frémi**
frémisses	**frémissiez**	**aies frémi**	**ayez frémi**
frémisse	**frémissent**	**ait frémi**	**aient frémi**
7 imparfait du subjonctif		14 plus-que-parfait du subjonctif	
frémisse	**frémissions**	**eusse frémi**	**eussions frémi**
frémisses	**frémissiez**	**eusses frémi**	**eussiez frémi**
frémît	**frémissent**	**eût frémi**	**eussent frémi**

F

Impératif
frémis
frémissons
frémissez

Words and expressions related to this verb
frémir de colère   to shake with anger
le frémissement   quivering, rustling,
  shuddering; **le frémissement des feuilles**
  rustling of leaves
faire frémir qqn   to give someone the shivers

une histoire à faire frémir   a horror story,
  a chiller thriller
frémissant, frémissante   rustling, quivering,
  shuddering
de l'eau frémissante   simmering water

Don't forget to use the English-French verb index. It's in the Appendixes.

to flee, to fly off, to shun, to leak

Irregular verb

The Seven Simple Tenses		The Seven Compound Tenses	
Singular	Plural	Singular	Plural
1 présent de l'indicatif		8 passé composé	
fuis	**fuyons**	**ai fui**	**avons fui**
fuis	**fuyez**	**as fui**	**avez fui**
fuit	**fuient**	**a fui**	**ont fui**
2 imparfait de l'indicatif		9 plus-que-parfait de l'indicatif	
fuyais	**fuyions**	**avais fui**	**avions fui**
fuyais	**fuyiez**	**avais fui**	**aviez fui**
fuyait	**fuyaient**	**avait fui**	**avaient fui**
3 passé simple		10 passé antérieur	
fuis	**fuîmes**	**eus fui**	**eûmes fui**
fuis	**fuîtes**	**eus fui**	**eûtes fui**
fuit	**fuirent**	**eut fui**	**eurent fui**
4 futur		11 futur antérieur	
fuirai	**fuirons**	**aurai fui**	**aurons fui**
fuiras	**fuirez**	**auras fui**	**aurez fui**
fuira	**fuiront**	**aura fui**	**auront fui**
5 conditionnel		12 conditionnel passé	
fuirais	**fuirions**	**aurais fui**	**aurions fui**
fuirais	**fuiriez**	**aurais fui**	**auriez fui**
fuirait	**fuiraient**	**aurait fui**	**auraient fui**
6 présent du subjonctif		13 passé du subjonctif	
fuie	**fuyions**	**aie fui**	**ayons fui**
fuies	**fuyiez**	**aies fui**	**ayez fui**
fuie	**fuient**	**ait fui**	**aient fui**
7 imparfait du subjonctif		14 plus-que-parfait du subjonctif	
fuisse	**fuissions**	**eusse fui**	**eussions fui**
fuisses	**fuissiez**	**eusses fui**	**eussiez fui**
fuît	**fuissent**	**eût fui**	**eussent fui**

Impératif
fuis
fuyons
fuyez

Common idiomatic expressions using this verb
faire fuir to put to flight
la fuite flight, escape
prendre la fuite to take to flight
une fuite de gaz gas leak
s'enfuir de to flee from, to run away from

fugitif, fugitive fugitive, fleeting, runaway
fugitivement fugitively
une fuite d'huile oil leak
faire une fugue to run away, to elope

See also s'enfuir.

Grammar putting you in a tense mood? Review the definitions of basic grammatical terms with examples on pages 35–49.

Regular **-er** verb

to smoke, to steam

The Seven Simple Tenses		The Seven Compound Tenses	
Singular	Plural	Singular	Plural

1 présent de l'indicatif		8 passé composé	
fume	fumons	ai fumé	avons fumé
fumes	fumez	as fumé	avez fumé
fume	fument	a fumé	ont fumé

2 imparfait de l'indicatif		9 plus-que-parfait de l'indicatif	
fumais	fumions	avais fumé	avions fumé
fumais	fumiez	avais fumé	aviez fumé
fumait	fumaient	avait fumé	avaient fumé

3 passé simple		10 passé antérieur	
fumai	fumâmes	eus fumé	eûmes fumé
fumas	fumâtes	eus fumé	eûtes fumé
fuma	fumèrent	eut fumé	eurent fumé

4 futur		11 futur antérieur	
fumerai	fumerons	aurai fumé	aurons fumé
fumeras	fumerez	auras fumé	aurez fumé
fumera	fumeront	aura fumé	auront fumé

5 conditionnel		12 conditionnel passé	
fumerais	fumerions	aurais fumé	aurions fumé
fumerais	fumeriez	aurais fumé	auriez fumé
fumerait	fumeraient	aurait fumé	auraient fumé

6 présent du subjonctif		13 passé du subjonctif	
fume	fumions	aie fumé	ayons fumé
fumes	fumiez	aies fumé	ayez fumé
fume	fument	ait fumé	aient fumé

7 imparfait du subjonctif		14 plus-que-parfait du subjonctif	
fumasse	fumassions	eusse fumé	eussions fumé
fumasses	fumassiez	eusses fumé	eussiez fumé
fumât	fumassent	eût fumé	eussent fumé

Impératif
fume
fumons
fumez

Sentences using this verb and words related to it

Le père: **Je te défends de fumer. C'est une mauvaise habitude.**   I forbid you to smoke. It's a bad habit.

Le fils: **Alors, pourquoi fumes-tu, papa?**   Then why do you smoke, Dad?

Il n'y a pas de fumée sans feu.   Where there's smoke, there's fire.

Défense de fumer No smoking allowed	**fumeux, fumeuse** smoky
la fumée smoke	**un fume-cigare** cigar holder
un rideau de fumée smoke screen	**un fume-cigarette** cigarette holder
parfumer to perfume	**un fumeur, une fumeuse** smoker (person who
non-fumeur nonsmoking	smokes)

The subject pronouns are found on page 103.

to win, to earn, to gain

The Seven Simple Tenses		The Seven Compound Tenses	
Singular	Plural	Singular	Plural
1 présent de l'indicatif		**8 passé composé**	
gagne	gagnons	ai gagné	avons gagné
gagnes	gagnez	as gagné	avez gagné
gagne	gagnent	a gagné	ont gagné
2 imparfait de l'indicatif		**9 plus-que-parfait de l'indicatif**	
gagnais	gagnions	avais gagné	avions gagné
gagnais	gagniez	avais gagné	aviez gagné
gagnait	gagnaient	avait gagné	avaient gagné
3 passé simple		**10 passé antérieur**	
gagnai	gagnâmes	eus gagné	eûmes gagné
gagnas	gagnâtes	eus gagné	eûtes gagné
gagna	gagnèrent	eut gagné	eurent gagné
4 futur		**11 futur antérieur**	
gagnerai	gagnerons	aurai gagné	aurons gagné
gagneras	gagnerez	auras gagné	aurez gagné
gagnera	gagneront	aura gagné	auront gagné
5 conditionnel		**12 conditionnel passé**	
gagnerais	gagnerions	aurais gagné	aurions gagné
gagnerais	gagneriez	aurais gagné	auriez gagné
gagnerait	gagneraient	aurait gagné	auraient gagné
6 présent du subjonctif		**13 passé du subjonctif**	
gagne	gagnions	aie gagné	ayons gagné
gagnes	gagniez	aies gagné	ayez gagné
gagne	gagnent	ait gagné	aient gagné
7 imparfait du subjonctif		**14 plus-que-parfait du subjonctif**	
gagnasse	gagnassions	eusse gagné	eussions gagné
gagnasses	gagnassiez	eusses gagné	eussiez gagné
gagnât	gagnassent	eût gagné	eussent gagné

Impératif
gagne
gagnons
gagnez

Common idiomatic expressions using this verb and words related to it

gagner sa vie   to earn one's living
gagner du poids   to gain weight
gagner de l'argent   to earn money
gagnable   obtainable
gagner du temps   to save time

regagner   to regain, to recover, to win back
regagner le temps perdu   to make up (to recover) lost time
un gagne-pain   a job
un gagnant, une gagnante   a winner

How are you doing? Find out with the verb drills and tests with answers explained on pages 50–101.

Regular **-er** verb   to guard, to keep, to retain

The Seven Simple Tenses		The Seven Compound Tenses	
Singular	Plural	Singular	Plural

1   présent de l'indicatif

		8 passé composé	
garde	gardons	ai gardé	avons gardé
gardes	gardez	as gardé	avez gardé
garde	gardent	a gardé	ont gardé

2   imparfait de l'indicatif

		9 plus-que-parfait de l'indicatif	
gardais	gardions	avais gardé	avions gardé
gardais	gardiez	avais gardé	aviez gardé
gardait	gardaient	avait gardé	avaient gardé

3   passé simple

		10 passé antérieur	
gardai	gardâmes	eus gardé	eûmes gardé
gardas	gardâtes	eus gardé	eûtes gardé
garda	gardèrent	eut gardé	eurent gardé

4   futur

		11 futur antérieur	
garderai	garderons	aurai gardé	aurons gardé
garderas	garderez	auras gardé	aurez gardé
gardera	garderont	aura gardé	auront gardé

5   conditionnel

		12 conditionnel passé	
garderais	garderions	aurais gardé	aurions gardé
garderais	garderiez	aurais gardé	auriez gardé
garderait	garderaient	aurait gardé	auraient gardé

6   présent du subjonctif

		13 passé du subjonctif	
garde	gardions	aie gardé	ayons gardé
gardes	gardiez	aies gardé	ayez gardé
garde	gardent	ait gardé	aient gardé

7   imparfait du subjonctif

		14 plus-que-parfait du subjonctif	
gardasse	gardassions	eusse gardé	eussions gardé
gardasses	gardassiez	eusses gardé	eussiez gardé
gardât	gardassent	eût gardé	eussent gardé

Impératif
garde
gardons
gardez

Garder is an essential French verb because it is used in many everyday situations and idiomatic expressions.

Sentences using garder

Madame Dupont a mis son enfant chez une gardienne d'enfants parce qu'elle va travailler aujourd'hui. Mrs. Dupont left her child with a babysitter because she is going to work today.

Françoise a besoin d'acheter une nouvelle garde-robe. Françoise needs to buy a new wardrobe.

Garde-à-vous! Attention! (military)

Dieu m'en garde! God forbid!

Raoul garde tout son argent dans son matelas. Ralph keeps all his money in his mattress.

Je garde de très beaux souvenirs de cette ville. I have many beautiful memories of this city.

Words and expressions related to this verb

se garder de tomber **to take care not to fall**

un gardien, une gardienne **guardian**

un gardien de but, une gardienne de but **goalie**

une gardienne d'enfants **babysitter**

la garderie **day care**

une garde-robe **wardrobe (closet)**

un garde-fou **guardrail**

un garde-manger **pantry**

un garde-vue **eyeshade (visor)**

un chien de garde, une chienne de garde **guard dog**

à bien des égards **in many regards/respects**

sans égard pour **without regard for**

If you can conjugate **garder** you can also conjugate the following verbs (along with other regular **-er** verbs):

se garder **to protect oneself (Use** être **as auxiliary)**

regarder **to look at, to watch, to consider, to regard**

se regarder **to look at oneself, each other (Use** être **as auxiliary)**

sauvegarder **to protect, to save (computer)**

Regular **-er** verb   to spoil, to damage

The Seven Simple Tenses		The Seven Compound Tenses	
Singular	Plural	Singular	Plural
1 présent de l'indicatif		8 passé composé	
gâte	gâtons	ai gâté	avons gâté
gâtes	gâtez	as gâté	avez gâté
gâte	gâtent	a gâté	ont gâté
2 imparfait de l'indicatif		9 plus-que-parfait de l'indicatif	
gâtais	gâtions	avais gâté	avions gâté
gâtais	gâtiez	avais gâté	aviez gâté
gâtait	gâtaient	avait gâté	avaient gâté
3 passé simple		10 passé antérieur	
gâtai	gâtâmes	eus gâté	eûmes gâté
gâtas	gâtâtes	eus gâté	eûtes gâté
gâta	gâtèrent	eut gâté	eurent gâté
4 futur		11 futur antérieur	
gâterai	gâterons	aurai gâté	aurons gâté
gâteras	gâterez	auras gâté	aurez gâté
gâtera	gâteront	aura gâté	auront gâté
5 conditionnel		12 conditionnel passé	
gâterais	gâterions	aurais gâté	aurions gâté
gâterais	gâteriez	aurais gâté	auriez gâté
gâterait	gâteraient	aurait gâté	auraient gâté
6 présent du subjonctif		13 passé du subjonctif	
gâte	gâtions	aie gâté	ayons gâté
gâtes	gâtiez	aies gâté	ayez gâté
gâte	gâtent	ait gâté	aient gâté
7 imparfait du subjonctif		14 plus-que-parfait du subjonctif	
gâtasse	gâtassions	eusse gâté	eussions gâté
gâtasses	gâtassiez	eusses gâté	eussiez gâté
gâtât	gâtassent	eût gâté	eussent gâté

G

Impératif
gâte
gâtons
gâtez

Sentences using this verb and words related to it
Marcel est un enfant gâté. Je n'aime pas jouer avec lui. Il gâte tout. Il demande toujours des gâteries.

gâter un enfant   to spoil a child
se gâter   to pamper oneself
faire des dégâts   to cause damage

un enfant gâté   a spoiled child
une gâterie   a treat

Can't remember the French verb you need? Check the back pages of this book for the English-French verb index!

The subject pronouns are found on page 103.   **377**

to freeze

Regular **-er** verb endings; spelling change:
e changes to **è** before syllable with mute **e**

The Seven Simple Tenses		The Seven Compound Tenses	
Singular	Plural	Singular	Plural
1 présent de l'indicatif		8 passé composé	
gèle	gelons	ai gelé	avons gelé
gèles	gelez	as gelé	avez gelé
gèle	gèlent	a gelé	ont gelé
2 imparfait de l'indicatif		9 plus-que-parfait de l'indicatif	
gelais	gelions	avais gelé	avions gelé
gelais	geliez	avais gelé	aviez gelé
gelait	gelaient	avait gelé	avaient gelé
3 passé simple		10 passé antérieur	
gelai	gelâmes	eus gelé	eûmes gelé
gelas	gelâtes	eus gelé	eûtes gelé
gela	gelèrent	eut gelé	eurent gelé
4 futur		11 futur antérieur	
gèlerai	gèlerons	aurai gelé	aurons gelé
gèleras	gèlerez	auras gelé	aurez gelé
gèlera	gèleront	aura gelé	auront gelé
5 conditionnel		12 conditionnel passé	
gèlerais	gèlerions	aurais gelé	aurions gelé
gèlerais	gèleriez	aurais gelé	auriez gelé
gèlerait	gèleraient	aurait gelé	auraient gelé
6 présent du subjonctif		13 passé du subjonctif	
gèle	gelions	aie gelé	ayons gelé
gèles	geliez	aies gelé	ayez gelé
gèle	gèlent	ait gelé	aient gelé
7 imparfait du subjonctif		14 plus-que-parfait du subjonctif	
gelasse	gelassions	eusse gelé	eussions gelé
gelasses	gelassiez	eusses gelé	eussiez gelé
gelât	gelassent	eût gelé	eussent gelé

Impératif
gèle
gelons
gelez

Sentences using this verb and words related to it

Je ne veux pas sortir aujourd'hui parce qu'il gèle. Quand je me suis levé ce matin, j'ai regardé par la fenêtre et j'ai vu de la gelée partout.

Il gèle! It's freezing!	la congélation congelation, freezing, icing
Qu'il gèle! Let it freeze!	le point de congélation freezing point
le gel frost, freezing	à la gelée jellied
la gelée frost; jello; jelly	le congélateur freezer
congeler to congeal, to freeze	

Soak up some verbs used in weather expressions. There's a list in the Appendixes!

378

Regular **-er** verb

to bother, to hamper, to constrict, to embarrass,
to hinder, to impede, to inconvenience

The Seven Simple Tenses

The Seven Compound Tenses

Singular	Plural	Singular	Plural
1 présent de l'indicatif		8 passé composé	
gêne	gênons	ai gêné	avons gêné
gênes	gênez	as gêné	avez gêné
gêne	gênent	a gêné	ont gêné
2 imparfait de l'indicatif		9 plus-que-parfait de l'indicatif	
gênais	gênions	avais gêné	avions gêné
gênais	gêniez	avais gêné	aviez gêné
gênait	gênaient	avait gêné	avaient gêné
3 passé simple		10 passé antérieur	
gênai	gênâmes	eus gêné	eûmes gêné
gênas	gênâtes	eus gêné	eûtes gêné
gêna	gênèrent	eut gêné	eurent gêné
4 futur		11 futur antérieur	
gênerai	gênerons	aurai gêné	aurons gêné
gêneras	gênerez	auras gêné	aurez gêné
gênera	gêneront	aura gêné	auront gêné
5 conditionnel		12 conditionnel passé	
gênerais	gênerions	aurais gêné	aurions gêné
gênerais	gêneriez	aurais gêné	auriez gêné
gênerait	gêneraient	aurait gêné	auraient gêné
6 présent du subjonctif		13 passé du subjonctif	
gêne	gênions	aie gêné	ayons gêné
gênes	gêniez	aies gêné	ayez gêné
gêne	gênent	ait gêné	aient gêné
7 imparfait du subjonctif		14 plus-que-parfait du subjonctif	
gênasse	gênassions	eusse gêné	eussions gêné
gênasses	gênassiez	eusses gêné	eussiez gêné
gênât	gênassent	eût gêné	eussent gêné

Impératif
gêne
gênons
gênez

Words and expressions related to this verb
se gêner   to inconvenience oneself
Ne vous gênez pas!   Put yourself at ease!
   Don't trouble yourself!
gêné, gênée   bothered, uncomfortable
un gêneur, une gêneuse   nuisance (person)

C'est gênant!   It's bothersome!
Cela vous gêne?   Does that bother you?
la gêne   embarrassment, discomfort
sans gêne   inconsiderate

Don't forget to check the list of 2,600 additional verbs keyed to the 501 model verbs. It's in the Appendixes!

to taste, to have a snack, to enjoy

Regular **-er** verb

The Seven Simple Tenses		The Seven Compound Tenses	
Singular	Plural	Singular	Plural
1 présent de l'indicatif		8 passé composé	
goûte	goûtons	ai goûté	avons goûté
goûtes	goûtez	as goûté	avez goûté
goûte	goûtent	a goûté	ont goûté
2 imparfait de l'indicatif		9 plus-que-parfait de l'indicatif	
goûtais	goûtions	avais goûté	avions goûté
goûtais	goûtiez	avais goûté	aviez goûté
goûtait	goûtaient	avait goûté	avaient goûté
3 passé simple		10 passé antérieur	
goûtai	goûtâmes	eus goûté	eûmes goûté
goûtas	goûtâtes	eus goûté	eûtes goûté
goûta	goûtèrent	eut goûté	eurent goûté
4 futur		11 futur antérieur	
goûterai	goûterons	aurai goûté	aurons goûté
goûteras	goûterez	auras goûté	aurez goûté
goûtera	goûteront	aura goûté	auront goûté
5 conditionnel		12 conditionnel passé	
goûterais	goûterions	aurais goûté	aurions goûté
goûterais	goûteriez	aurais goûté	auriez goûté
goûterait	goûteraient	aurait goûté	auraient goûté
6 présent du subjonctif		13 passé du subjonctif	
goûte	goûtions	aie goûté	ayons goûté
goûtes	goûtiez	aies goûté	ayez goûté
goûte	goûtent	ait goûté	aient goûté
7 imparfait du subjonctif		14 plus-que-parfait du subjonctif	
goûtasse	goûtassions	eusse goûté	eussions goûté
goûtasses	goûtassiez	eusses goûté	eussiez goûté
goûtât	goûtassent	eût goûté	eussent goûté

Impératif
goûte
goûtons
goûtez

Common idiomatic expressions using this verb

Quand j'arrive chez moi de l'école l'après-midi, j'ai l'habitude de prendre le goûter à quatre heures.

le goûter   snack, bite to eat
goûter sur l'herbe   to have a picnic
à chacun son goût   To each his own
goûter à   to drink or eat only a small quantity
le goût   taste
de mauvais goût   in bad taste

avoir un goût de   to taste like
goûter de   to eat or drink something for the first time
dégoûter   to disgust
C'est dégoûtant!   It's disgusting!

380

Regular **-ir** verb   to grow (up, taller), to increase

The Seven Simple Tenses		The Seven Compound Tenses	
Singular	Plural	Singular	Plural
1 présent de l'indicatif		8 passé composé	
grandis	**grandissons**	**ai grandi**	**avons grandi**
grandis	**grandissez**	**as grandi**	**avez grandi**
grandit	**grandissent**	**a grandi**	**ont grandi**
2 imparfait de l'indicatif		9 plus-que-parfait de l'indicatif	
grandissais	**grandissions**	**avais grandi**	**avions grandi**
grandissais	**grandissiez**	**avais grandi**	**aviez grandi**
grandissait	**grandissaient**	**avait grandi**	**avaient grandi**
3 passé simple		10 passé antérieur	
grandis	**grandîmes**	**eus grandi**	**eûmes grandi**
grandis	**grandîtes**	**eus grandi**	**eûtes grandi**
grandit	**grandirent**	**eut grandi**	**eurent grandi**
4 futur		11 futur antérieur	
grandirai	**grandirons**	**aurai grandi**	**aurons grandi**
grandiras	**grandirez**	**auras grandi**	**aurez grandi**
grandira	**grandiront**	**aura grandi**	**auront grandi**
5 conditionnel		12 conditionnel passé	
grandirais	**grandirions**	**aurais grandi**	**aurions grandi**
grandirais	**grandiriez**	**aurais grandi**	**auriez grandi**
grandirait	**grandiraient**	**aurait grandi**	**auraient grandi**
6 présent du subjonctif		13 passé du subjonctif	
grandisse	**grandissions**	**aie grandi**	**ayons grandi**
grandisses	**grandissiez**	**aies grandi**	**ayez grandi**
grandisse	**grandissent**	**ait grandi**	**aient grandi**
7 imparfait du subjonctif		14 plus-que-parfait du subjonctif	
grandisse	**grandissions**	**eusse grandi**	**eussions grandi**
grandisses	**grandissiez**	**eusses grandi**	**eussiez grandi**
grandît	**grandissent**	**eût grandi**	**eussent grandi**

Impératif
grandis
grandissons
grandissez

Sentences using this verb and words related to it
Voyez-vous comme Joseph et Joséphine ont grandi? C'est incroyable! Quel âge ont-ils maintenant?

le grandissement   growth
grandiose   grandiose, grand
grand, grande   tall
la grandeur   size, greatness, grandeur
grandiosement   grandiosely

agrandir   to expand, to enlarge
un agrandissement   enlargement, extension, aggrandizement
un enfant grandi trop vite   a lanky child (grew tall too fast)

Can't find the verb you're looking for? Check the back pages of this book for a list of over 2,600 additional verbs!

The subject pronouns are found on page 103.   **381**

gratter (246)

Part. pr. **grattant**   Part. passé **gratté**

to grate, to scrape, to scratch

Regular **-er** verb

The Seven Simple Tenses		The Seven Compound Tenses	
Singular	Plural	Singular	Plural

1 présent de l'indicatif		8 passé composé	
gratte	grattons	ai gratté	avons gratté
grattes	grattez	as gratté	avez gratté
gratte	grattent	a gratté	ont gratté

2 imparfait de l'indicatif		9 plus-que-parfait de l'indicatif	
grattais	grattions	avais gratté	avions gratté
grattais	grattiez	avais gratté	aviez gratté
grattait	grattaient	avait gratté	avaient gratté

3 passé simple		10 passé antérieur	
grattai	grattâmes	eus gratté	eûmes gratté
grattas	grattâtes	eus gratté	eûtes gratté
gratta	grattèrent	eut gratté	eurent gratté

4 futur		11 futur antérieur	
gratterai	gratterons	aurai gratté	aurons gratté
gratteras	gratterez	auras gratté	aurez gratté
grattera	gratteront	aura gratté	auront gratté

5 conditionnel		12 conditionnel passé	
gratterais	gratterions	aurais gratté	aurions gratté
gratterais	gratteriez	aurais gratté	auriez gratté
gratterait	gratteraient	aurait gratté	auraient gratté

6 présent du subjonctif		13 passé du subjonctif	
gratte	grattions	aie gratté	ayons gratté
grattes	grattiez	aies gratté	ayez gratté
gratte	grattent	ait gratté	aient gratté

7 imparfait du subjonctif		14 plus-que-parfait du subjonctif	
grattasse	grattassions	eusse gratté	eussions gratté
grattasses	grattassiez	eusses gratté	eussiez gratté
grattât	grattassent	eût gratté	eussent gratté

Impératif
gratte
grattons
grattez

Words and expressions related to this verb

le grattement	scratching	**le grattage**	scratching, scraping
un gratte-ciel	skyscraper (**des gratte-ciel**)	**un grattoir**	scraper, grater
un gratte-dos	back scratcher (**des gratte-dos**)	**se gratter**	to scratch oneself

Grammar putting you in a tense mood? Review the definitions of basic grammatical terms with examples on pages 35–49.

Regular **-er** verb   to climb

The Seven Simple Tenses		The Seven Compound Tenses	
Singular	Plural	Singular	Plural
1 présent de l'indicatif		8 passé composé	
grimpe	**grimpons**	**ai grimpé**	**avons grimpé**
grimpes	**grimpez**	**as grimpé**	**avez grimpé**
grimpe	**grimpent**	**a grimpé**	**ont grimpé**
2 imparfait de l'indicatif		9 plus-que-parfait de l'indicatif	
grimpais	**grimpions**	**avais grimpé**	**avions grimpé**
grimpais	**grimpiez**	**avais grimpé**	**aviez grimpé**
grimpait	**grimpaient**	**avait grimpé**	**avaient grimpé**
3 passé simple		10 passé antérieur	
grimpai	**grimpâmes**	**eus grimpé**	**eûmes grimpé**
grimpas	**grimpâtes**	**eus grimpé**	**eûtes grimpé**
grimpa	**grimpèrent**	**eut grimpé**	**eurent grimpé**
4 futur		11 futur antérieur	
grimperai	**grimperons**	**aurai grimpé**	**aurons grimpé**
grimperas	**grimperez**	**auras grimpé**	**aurez grimpé**
grimpera	**grimperont**	**aura grimpé**	**auront grimpé**
5 conditionnel		12 conditionnel passé	
grimperais	**grimperions**	**aurais grimpé**	**aurions grimpé**
grimperais	**grimperiez**	**aurais grimpé**	**auriez grimpé**
grimperait	**grimperaient**	**aurait grimpé**	**auraient grimpé**
6 présent du subjonctif		13 passé du subjonctif	
grimpe	**grimpions**	**aie grimpé**	**ayons grimpé**
grimpes	**grimpiez**	**aies grimpé**	**ayez grimpé**
grimpe	**grimpent**	**ait grimpé**	**aient grimpé**
7 imparfait du subjonctif		14 plus-que-parfait du subjonctif	
grimpasse	**grimpassions**	**eusse grimpé**	**eussions grimpé**
grimpasses	**grimpassiez**	**eusses grimpé**	**eussiez grimpé**
grimpât	**grimpassent**	**eût grimpé**	**eussent grimpé**

G

Impératif
grimpe
grimpons
grimpez

Words and expressions related to this verb
grimper à l'échelle   to climb a ladder
une plante grimpante   climbing plant
une grimpée, une grimpette   steep climb

un grimpeur, une grimpeuse   climber
grimper aux arbres   to climb trees

Use the guide to French pronunciation. It's in the Appendixes.

The subject pronouns are found on page 103.   **383**

to chide, to reprimand, to scold

Regular **-er** verb

The Seven Simple Tenses | The Seven Compound Tenses

Singular	Plural	Singular	Plural
1 présent de l'indicatif		8 passé composé	
gronde	grondons	ai grondé	avons grondé
grondes	grondez	as grondé	avez grondé
gronde	grondent	a grondé	ont grondé
2 imparfait de l'indicatif		9 plus-que-parfait de l'indicatif	
grondais	grondions	avais grondé	avions grondé
grondais	grondiez	avais grondé	aviez grondé
grondait	grondaient	avait grondé	avaient grondé
3 passé simple		10 passé antérieur	
grondai	grondâmes	eus grondé	eûmes grondé
grondas	grondâtes	eus grondé	eûtes grondé
gronda	grondèrent	eut grondé	eurent grondé
4 futur		11 futur antérieur	
gronderai	gronderons	aurai grondé	aurons grondé
gronderas	gronderez	auras grondé	aurez grondé
grondera	gronderont	aura grondé	auront grondé
5 conditionnel		12 conditionnel passé	
gronderais	gronderions	aurais grondé	aurions grondé
gronderais	gronderiez	aurais grondé	auriez grondé
gronderait	gronderaient	aurait grondé	auraient grondé
6 présent du subjonctif		13 passé du subjonctif	
gronde	grondions	aie grondé	ayons grondé
grondes	grondiez	aies grondé	ayez grondé
gronde	grondent	ait grondé	aient grondé
7 imparfait du subjonctif		14 plus-que-parfait du subjonctif	
grondasse	grondassions	eusse grondé	eussions grondé
grondasses	grondassiez	eusses grondé	eussiez grondé
grondât	grondassent	eût grondé	eussent grondé

Impératif
gronde
grondons
grondez

Sentences using this verb and words related to it

—**Victor, pourquoi pleures-tu?**
—**La maîtresse de mathématiques m'a grondé.**
—**Pourquoi est-ce qu'elle t'a grondé? Qu'est-ce que tu as fait?**
—**Ce n'est pas parce que j'ai fait quelque chose. C'est parce que je n'ai rien fait. Je n'ai pas préparé la leçon.**
—**Alors, tu mérites une gronderie et une réprimande.**
—**C'est une grondeuse. Elle gronde à chaque instant. C'est une criarde.**

une grondeuse a scolder		**une gronderie** a scolding	
une criarde a nag, nagger		**à chaque instant** constantly	

Regular **-ir** verb   to cure, to heal, to remedy, to recover

The Seven Simple Tenses		The Seven Compound Tenses	
Singular	Plural	Singular	Plural
1 présent de l'indicatif		8 passé composé	
guéris	**guérissons**	**ai guéri**	**avons guéri**
guéris	**guérissez**	**as guéri**	**avez guéri**
guérit	**guérissent**	**a guéri**	**ont guéri**
2 imparfait de l'indicatif		9 plus-que-parfait de l'indicatif	
guérissais	**guérissions**	**avais guéri**	**avions guéri**
guérissais	**guérissiez**	**avais guéri**	**aviez guéri**
guérissait	**guérissaient**	**avait guéri**	**avaient guéri**
3 passé simple		10 passé antérieur	
guéris	**guérîmes**	**eus guéri**	**eûmes guéri**
guéris	**guérîtes**	**eus guéri**	**eûtes guéri**
guérit	**guérirent**	**eut guéri**	**eurent guéri**
4 futur		11 futur antérieur	
guérirai	**guérirons**	**aurai guéri**	**aurons guéri**
guériras	**guérirez**	**auras guéri**	**aurez guéri**
guérira	**guériront**	**aura guéri**	**auront guéri**
5 conditionnel		12 conditionnel passé	
guérirais	**guéririons**	**aurais guéri**	**aurions guéri**
guérirais	**guéririez**	**aurais guéri**	**auriez guéri**
guérirait	**guériraient**	**aurait guéri**	**auraient guéri**
6 présent du subjonctif		13 passé du subjonctif	
guérisse	**guérissions**	**aie guéri**	**ayons guéri**
guérisses	**guérissiez**	**aies guéri**	**ayez guéri**
guérisse	**guérissent**	**ait guéri**	**aient guéri**
7 imparfait du subjonctif		14 plus-que-parfait du subjonctif	
guérisse	**guérissions**	**eusse guéri**	**eussions guéri**
guérisses	**guérissiez**	**eusses guéri**	**eussiez guéri**
guérît	**guérissent**	**eût guéri**	**eussent guéri**

Impératif
guéris
guérissons
guérissez

Sentences using this verb and words related to it

Madame Gérard est tombée dans l'escalier la semaine dernière et elle a reçu une blessure au genou. Elle est allée chez le médecin et maintenant elle est guérie.

une guérison   healing, cure
guérisseur, guérisseuse   healer
guérissable   curable

guérir de   to recover from, to cure of
la guérison par la foi   faith healing

How are you doing? Find out with the verb drills and tests with answers explained on pages 50–101.

s'habiller (250)

to get dressed, to dress (oneself)

Part. pr. **s'habillant**   Part. passé **habillé(e)(s)**

Reflexieve regular **-er** verb

The Seven Simple Tenses		The Seven Compound Tenses	
Singular	Plural	Singular	Plural
1 présent de l'indicatif		**8 passé composé**	
m'habille	**nous habillons**	**me suis habillé(e)**	**nous sommes habillé(e)s**
t'habilles	**vous habillez**	**t'es habillé(e)**	**vous êtes habillé(e)(s)**
s'habille	**s'habillent**	**s'est habillé(e)**	**se sont habillé(e)s**
2 imparfait de l'indicatif		**9 plus-que-parfait de l'indicatif**	
m'habillais	**nous habillions**	**m'étais habillé(e)**	**nous étions habillé(e)s**
t'habillais	**vous habilliez**	**t'étais habillé(e)**	**vous étiez habillé(e)(s)**
s'habillait	**s'habillaient**	**s'était habillé(e)**	**s'étaient habillé(e)s**
3 passé simple		**10 passé antérieur**	
m'habillai	**nous habillâmes**	**me fus habillé(e)**	**nous fûmes habillé(e)s**
t'habillas	**vous habillâtes**	**te fus habillé(e)**	**vous fûtes habillé(e)(s)**
s'habilla	**s'habillèrent**	**se fut habillé(e)**	**se furent habillé(e)s**
4 futur		**11 futur antérieur**	
m'habillerai	**nous habillerons**	**me serai habillé(e)**	**nous serons habillé(e)s**
t'habilleras	**vous habillerez**	**te seras habillé(e)**	**vous serez habillé(e)(s)**
s'habillera	**s'habilleront**	**se sera habillé(e)**	**se seront habillé(e)s**
5 conditionnel		**12 conditionnel passé**	
m'habillerais	**nous habillerions**	**me serais habillé(e)**	**nous serions habillé(e)s**
t'habillerais	**vous habilleriez**	**te serais habillé(e)**	**vous seriez habillé(e)(s)**
s'habillerait	**s'habilleraient**	**se serait habillé(e)**	**se seraient habillé(e)s**
6 présent du subjonctif		**13 passé du subjonctif**	
m'habille	**nous habillions**	**me sois habillé(e)**	**nous soyons habillé(e)s**
t'habilles	**vous habilliez**	**te sois habillé(e)**	**vous soyez habillé(e)(s)**
s'habille	**s'habillent**	**se soit habillé(e)**	**se soient habillé(e)s**
7 imparfait du subjonctif		**14 plus-que-parfait du subjonctif**	
m'habillasse	**nous habillassions**	**me fusse habillé(e)**	**nous fussions habillé(e)s**
t'habillasses	**vous habillassiez**	**te fusses habillé(e)**	**vous fussiez habillé(e)(s)**
s'habillât	**s'habillassent**	**se fût habillé(e)**	**se fussent habillé(e)s**

Impératif
habille-toi; ne t'habille pas
habillons-nous; ne nous habillons pas
habillez-vous; ne vous habillez pas

Sentences using this verb and words related to it
un habit   costume, outfit
les habits   clothes
habiller qqn   to dress someone
habillement *m.*   garment, wearing apparel
L'habit ne fait pas le moine.   Clothes don't make the person (the monk).

déshabiller   to undress
se déshabiller   to undress oneself, to get undressed
habiller de   to clothe with
l'habit de gala   formal wear
l'habit militaire   military dress

See also **vêtir.**

Don't miss the definitions of basic grammatical terms with examples in English and French on pages 35–49.

Regular **-er** verb   to live (in), to dwell (in), to inhabit

The Seven Simple Tenses		The Seven Compound Tenses	
Singular	Plural	Singular	Plural
1 présent de l'indicatif		8 passé composé	
habite	**habitons**	**ai habité**	**avons habité**
habites	**habitez**	**as habité**	**avez habité**
habite	**habitent**	**a habité**	**ont habité**
2 imparfait de l'indicatif		9 plus-que-parfait de l'indicatif	
habitais	**habitions**	**avais habité**	**avions habité**
habitais	**habitiez**	**avais habité**	**aviez habité**
habitait	**habitaient**	**avait habité**	**avaient habité**
3 passé simple		10 passé antérieur	
habitai	**habitâmes**	**eus habité**	**eûmes habité**
habitas	**habitâtes**	**eus habité**	**eûtes habité**
habita	**habitèrent**	**eut habité**	**eurent habité**
4 futur		11 futur antérieur	
habiterai	**habiterons**	**aurai habité**	**aurons habité**
habiteras	**habiterez**	**auras habité**	**aurez habité**
habitera	**habiteront**	**aura habité**	**auront habité**
5 conditionnel		12 conditionnel passé	
habiterais	**habiterions**	**aurais habité**	**aurions habité**
habiterais	**habiteriez**	**aurais habité**	**auriez habité**
habiterait	**habiteraient**	**aurait habité**	**auraient habité**
6 présent du subjonctif		13 passé du subjonctif	
habite	**habitions**	**aie habité**	**ayons habité**
habites	**habitiez**	**aies habité**	**ayez habité**
habite	**habitent**	**ait habité**	**aient habité**
7 imparfait du subjonctif		14 plus-que-parfait du subjonctif	
habitasse	**habitassions**	**eusse habité**	**eussions habité**
habitasses	**habitassiez**	**eusses habité**	**eussiez habité**
habitât	**habitassent**	**eût habité**	**eussent habité**

Impératif
habite
habitons
habitez

Sentences using this verb and words related to it
    —Où habitez-vous?
    —J'habite 27 rue Duparc dans une petite maison blanche.
    —Avec qui habitez-vous?
    —J'habite avec mes parents, mes frères, mes soeurs, et mon chien.

une habitation   dwelling, residence, abode
un habitat   habitat
un habitant   inhabitant
H.L.M. (habitation à loyer modéré)   lodging at a moderate rental

l'amélioration de l'habitat   improvement of living conditions
habiter à la campagne   to live in the country
habiter la banlieue   to live in the suburbs

Be careful! **Habitable** means *habitable* or *inhabitable*. But **inhabitable** means *uninhabitable*.

The subject pronouns are found on page 103.   **387**

to hate

The Seven Simple Tenses		The Seven Compound Tenses	
Singular	Plural	Singular	Plural

1 présent de l'indicatif

hais	haïssons		
hais	haïssez		
hait	haïssent		

8 passé composé

ai haï	avons haï		
as haï	avez haï		
a haï	ont haï		

2 imparfait de l'indicatif

haïssais	haïssions
haïssais	haïssiez
haïssait	haïssaient

9 plus-que-parfait de l'indicatif

avais haï	avions haï
avais haï	aviez haï
avait haï	avaient haï

3 passé simple

haïs	haïmes
haïs	haïtes
haït	haïrent

10 passé antérieur

eus haï	eûmes haï
eus haï	eûtes haï
eut haï	eurent haï

4 futur

haïrai	haïrons
haïras	haïrez
haïra	haïront

11 futur antérieur

aurai haï	aurons haï
auras haï	aurez haï
aura haï	auront haï

5 conditionnel

haïrais	haïrions
haïrais	haïriez
haïrait	haïraient

12 conditionnel passé

aurais haï	aurions haï
aurais haï	auriez haï
aurait haï	auraient haï

6 présent du subjonctif

haïsse	haïssions
haïsses	haïssiez
haïsse	haïssent

13 passé du subjonctif

aie haï	ayons haï
aies haï	ayez haï
ait haï	aient haï

7 imparfait du subjonctif

haïsse	haïssions
haïsses	haïssiez
haït	haïssent

14 plus-que-parfait du subjonctif

eusse haï	eussions haï
eusses haï	eussiez haï
eût haï	eussent haï

Impératif
hais
haïssons
haïssez

Sentences using this verb and words related to it
Je hais le mensonge, je hais la médiocrité, et je hais la calomnie. Ces choses sont haïssables.
Je hais Marguerite et Jeanne; elles sont haineuses.

haïssable detestable, hateful	**haïr qqn comme la peste** to hate somebody
la haine hatred, hate	like poison
haineux, haineuse hateful, heinous	**des haines mesquines** petty hatreds

This verb begins with aspirate *h*; make no liaison and use *je* instead of *j'*.

The Seven Simple Tenses		The Seven Compound Tenses	
Singular	Plural	Singular	Plural
1 présent de l'indicatif		**8 passé composé**	
hésite	hésitons	ai hésité	avons hésité
hésites	hésitez	as hésité	avez hésité
hésite	hésitent	a hésité	ont hésité
2 imparfait de l'indicatif		**9 plus-que-parfait de l'indicatif**	
hésitais	hésitions	avais hésité	avions hésité
hésitais	hésitiez	avais hésité	aviez hésité
hésitait	hésitaient	avait hésité	avaient hésité
3 passé simple		**10 passé antérieur**	
hésitai	hésitâmes	eus hésité	eûmes hésité
hésitas	hésitâtes	eus hésité	eûtes hésité
hésita	hésitèrent	eut hésité	eurent hésité
4 futur		**11 futur antérieur**	
hésiterai	hésiterons	aurai hésité	aurons hésité
hésiteras	hésiterez	auras hésité	aurez hésité
hésitera	hésiteront	aura hésité	auront hésité
5 conditionnel		**12 conditionnel passé**	
hésiterais	hésiterions	aurais hésité	aurions hésité
hésiterais	hésiteriez	aurais hésité	auriez hésité
hésiterait	hésiteraient	aurait hésité	auraient hésité
6 présent du subjonctif		**13 passé du subjonctif**	
hésite	hésitions	aie hésité	ayons hésité
hésites	hésitiez	aies hésité	ayez hésité
hésite	hésitent	ait hésité	aient hésité
7 imparfait du subjonctif		**14 plus-que-parfait du subjonctif**	
hésitasse	hésitassions	eusse hésité	eussions hésité
hésitasses	hésitassiez	eusses hésité	eussiez hésité
hésitât	hésitassent	eût hésité	eussent hésité

Impératif
hésite
hésitons
hésitez

Words and expressions related to this verb
hésiter à faire qqch   to hesitate to do something
une hésitation   hesitation
hésitant, hésitante   undecided, hesitating
sans hésitation   unhesitatingly, without hesitation

Get acquainted with what preposition goes with what verb. See *Verbs with prepositions* in the Appendixes.

The subject pronouns are found on page 103.   **389**

to impose

Regular **-er** verb

The Seven Simple Tenses		The Seven Compound Tenses	
Singular	Plural	Singular	Plural
1 présent de l'indicatif		8 passé composé	
impose	imposons	ai imposé	avons imposé
imposes	imposez	as imposé	avez imposé
impose	imposent	a imposé	ont imposé
2 imparfait de l'indicatif		9 plus-que-parfait de l'indicatif	
imposais	imposions	avais imposé	avions imposé
imposais	imposiez	avais imposé	aviez imposé
imposait	imposaient	avait imposé	avaient imposé
3 passé simple		10 passé antérieur	
imposai	imposâmes	eus imposé	eûmes imposé
imposas	imposâtes	eus imposé	eûtes imposé
imposa	imposèrent	eut imposé	eurent imposé
4 futur		11 futur antérieur	
imposerai	imposerons	aurai imposé	aurons imposé
imposeras	imposerez	auras imposé	aurez imposé
imposera	imposeront	aura imposé	auront imposé
5 conditionnel		12 conditionnel passé	
imposerais	imposerions	aurais imposé	aurions imposé
imposerais	imposeriez	aurais imposé	auriez imposé
imposerait	imposeraient	aurait imposé	auraient imposé
6 présent du subjonctif		13 passé du subjonctif	
impose	imposions	aie imposé	ayons imposé
imposes	imposiez	aies imposé	ayez impoé
impose	imposent	ait imposé	aient imposé
7 imparfait du subjonctif		14 plus-que-parfait du subjonctif	
imposasse	imposassions	eusse imposé	eussions imposé
imposasses	imposassiez	eusses imposé	eussiez imposé
imposât	imposassent	eût imposé	eussent imposé

Impératif
impose
imposons
imposez

Words and expressions related to this verb

s'imposer   to assert oneself
s'imposer à   to intrude on
imposable   taxable
un impôt   tax; l'impôt sur le revenu
    income tax

une imposition   imposition
imposant, imposante   imposing, impressive
imposer le respect   to compel respect
imposer une règle   to lay down a rule

Can't remember the French verb you need? Check the back pages of this book for the English-French verb index!

The Seven Simple Tenses		The Seven Compound Tenses	
Singular	Plural	Singular	Plural
1 présent de l'indicatif		8 passé composé	
inclus	**incluons**	**ai inclus**	**avons inclus**
inclus	**incluez**	**as inclus**	**avez inclus**
inclut	**incluent**	**a inclus**	**ont inclus**
2 imparfait de l'indicatif		9 plus-que-parfait de l'indicatif	
incluais	**incluions**	**avais inclus**	**avions inclus**
incluais	**incluiez**	**avais inclus**	**aviez inclus**
incluait	**incluaient**	**avait inclus**	**avaient inclus**
3 passé simple		10 passé antérieur	
inclus	**inclûmes**	**eus inclus**	**eûmes inclus**
inclus	**inclûtes**	**eus inclus**	**eûtes inclus**
inclut	**inclurent**	**eut inclus**	**eurent inclus**
4 futur		11 futur antérieur	
inclurai	**inclurons**	**aurai inclus**	**aurons inclus**
incluras	**inclurez**	**auras inclus**	**aurez inclus**
inclura	**incluront**	**aura inclus**	**auront inclus**
5 conditionnel		12 conditionnel passé	
inclurais	**inclurions**	**aurais inclus**	**aurions inclus**
inclurais	**incluriez**	**aurais inclus**	**auriez inclus**
inclurait	**incluraient**	**aurait inclus**	**auraient inclus**
6 présent du subjonctif		13 passé du subjonctif	
inclue	**incluions**	**aie inclus**	**ayons inclus**
inclues	**incluiez**	**aies inclus**	**ayez inclus**
inclue	**incluent**	**ait inclus**	**aient inclus**
7 imparfait du subjonctif		14 plus-que-parfait du subjonctif	
inclusse	**inclussions**	**eusse inclus**	**eussions inclus**
inclusses	**inclussiez**	**eusses inclus**	**eussiez inclus**
inclût	**inclussent**	**eût inclus**	**eussent inclus**

Impératif
inclus
incluons
incluez

Words and expressions related to this verb

la lettre ci-incluse   the letter enclosed
  herewith
l'argent ci-inclus   the money enclosed
  herewith
une inclusion   inclusion
inclusif, inclusive   inclusive

See also **conclure.**

inclusivement   inclusively
service inclus   service included (no tip necessary)
exclure   to exclude
exclusivement   exclusively
exclusif, exclusive   exclusive
une exclusion   exclusion
exclu, exclue   excluded

Don't forget to study the section on defective and impersonal verbs. It's right after this main list.

The subject pronouns are found on page 103.
391

indiquer (256)   Part. pr. **indiquant**   Part. passé **indiqué**

to indicate, to point out, to show

Regular **-er** verb

The Seven Simple Tenses		The Seven Compound Tenses	
Singular	Plural	Singular	Plural
1 présent de l'indicatif		8 passé composé	
indique	**indiquons**	**ai indiqué**	**avons indiqué**
indiques	**indiquez**	**as indiqué**	**avez indiqué**
indique	**indiquent**	**a indiqué**	**ont indiqué**
2 imparfait de l'indicatif		9 plus-que-parfait de l'indicatif	
indiquais	**indiquions**	**avais indiqué**	**avions indiqué**
indiquais	**indiquiez**	**avais indiqué**	**aviez indiqué**
indiquait	**indiquaient**	**avait indiqué**	**avaient indiqué**
3 passé simple		10 passé antérieur	
indiquai	**indiquâmes**	**eus indiqué**	**eûmes indiqué**
indiquas	**indiquâtes**	**eus indiqué**	**eûtes indiqué**
indiqua	**indiquèrent**	**eut indiqué**	**eurent indiqué**
4 futur		11 futur antérieur	
indiquerai	**indiquerons**	**aurai indiqué**	**aurons indiqué**
indiqueras	**indiquerez**	**auras indiqué**	**aurez indiqué**
indiquera	**indiqueront**	**aura indiqué**	**auront indiqué**
5 conditionnel		12 conditionnel passé	
indiquerais	**indiquerions**	**aurais indiqué**	**aurions indiqué**
indiquerais	**indiqueriez**	**aurais indiqué**	**auriez indiqué**
indiquerait	**indiqueraient**	**aurait indiqué**	**auraient indiqué**
6 présent du subjonctif		13 passé du subjonctif	
indique	**indiquions**	**aie indiqué**	**ayons indiqué**
indiques	**indiquiez**	**aies indiqué**	**ayez indiqué**
indique	**indiquent**	**ait indiqué**	**aient indiqué**
7 imparfait du subjonctif		14 plus-que-parfait du subjonctif	
indiquasse	**indiquassions**	**eusse indiqué**	**eussions indiqué**
indiquasses	**indiquassiez**	**eusses indiqué**	**eussiez indiqué**
indiquât	**indiquassent**	**eût indiqué**	**eussent indiqué**

Impératif
indique
indiquons
indiquez

Words and expressions related to this verb
indiquer du doigt   to point out (with one's finger)
indiquer un bon médecin   to recommend a good doctor
une indication   indication
indicatif, indicative   indicative
un indice   index
indicateur, indicatrice   indicator
un indicateur de vitesse   speedometer

How are you doing? Find out with the verb drills and tests with answers explained on pages 50–101.

Reflexive regular **-er** verb

to find out, to inquire, to make
inquiries, to inform oneself

The Seven Simple Tenses		The Seven Compound Tenses	
Singular	Plural	Singular	Plural
1 présent de l'indicatif		8 passé composé	
m'informe	**nous informons**	**me suis informé(e)**	**nous sommes informé(e)s**
t'informes	**vous informez**	**t'es informé(e)**	**vous êtes informé(e)(s)**
s'informe	**s'informent**	**s'est informé(e)**	**se sont informé(e)s**
2 imparfait de l'indicatif		9 plus-que-parfait de l'indicatif	
m'informais	**nous informions**	**m'étais informé(e)**	**nous étions informé(e)s**
t'informais	**vous informiez**	**t'étais informé(e)**	**vous étiez informé(e)(s)**
s'informait	**s'informaient**	**s'était informé(e)**	**s'étaient informé(e)s**
3 passé simple		10 passé antérieur	
m'informai	**nous informâmes**	**me fus informé(e)**	**nous fûmes informé(e)s**
t'informas	**vous informâtes**	**te fus informé(e)**	**vous fûtes informé(e)(s)**
s'informa	**s'informèrent**	**se fut informé(e)**	**se furent informé(e)s**
4 futur		11 futur antérieur	
m'informerai	**nous informerons**	**me serai informé(e)**	**nous serons informé(e)s**
t'informeras	**vous informerez**	**te seras informé(e)**	**vous serez informé(e)(s)**
s'informera	**s'informeront**	**se sera informé(e)**	**se seront informé(e)s**
5 conditionnel		12 conditionnel passé	
m'informerais	**nous informerions**	**me serais informé(e)**	**nous serions informé(e)s**
t'informerais	**vous informeriez**	**te serais informé(e)**	**vous seriez informé(e)(s)**
s'informerait	**s'informeraient**	**se serait informé(e)**	**se seraient informé(e)s**
6 présent du subjonctif		13 passé du subjonctif	
m'informe	**nous informions**	**me sois informé(e)**	**nous soyons informé(e)s**
t'informes	**vous informiez**	**te sois informé(e)**	**vous soyez informé(e)(s)**
s'informe	**s'informent**	**se soit informé(e)**	**se soient informé(e)s**
7 imparfait du subjonctif		14 plus-que-parfait du subjonctif	
m'informasse	**nous informassions**	**me fusse informé(e)**	**nous fussions informé(e)s**
t'informasses	**vous informassiez**	**te fusses informé(e)**	**vous fussiez informé(e)(s)**
s'informât	**s'informassent**	**se fût informé(e)**	**se fussent informé(e)s**

Impératif
informe-toi; ne t'informe pas
informons-nous; ne nous informons pas
informez-vous; ne vous informez pas

Words and expressions related to this verb
informer to inform, to advise
Je vous informe que . . . I am informing you
    that . . .
les informations *f.* new items, news bulletins
informatif, informative informative
informationnel, informationnelle
    informational
l'informatique *f.* computer science
s'informer de to inquire about

prendre des informations sur qqn to make
    inquiries about someone
un informateur, une informatrice informer,
    informant
une information officielle official
    investigation
former to form
un informaticien, une informaticienne
    computer scientist

Don't forget to check the list of 2,600 additional verbs keyed to the 501 model verbs. It's in the
Appendixes!

The subject pronouns are found on page 103.
393

to worry, to be upset

Reflexive regular **-er** verb endings; spelling change:
é changes to **è** before syllable with mute **e**

The Seven Simple Tenses		The Seven Compound Tenses	
Singular	Plural	Singular	Plural

1 présent de l'indicatif

		8 passé composé	
m'inquiète	**nous inquiétons**	**me suis inquiété(e)**	**nous sommes inquiété(e)s**
t'inquiètes	**vous inquiétez**	**t'es inquiété(e)**	**vous êtes inquiété(e)(s)**
s'inquiète	**s'inquiètent**	**s'est inquiété(e)**	**se sont inquiété(e)s**

2 imparfait de l'indicatif

		9 plus-que-parfait de l'indicatif	
m'inquiétais	**nous inquiétions**	**m'étais inquiété(e)**	**nous étions inquiété(e)s**
t'inquiétais	**vous inquiétiez**	**t'étais inquiété(e)**	**vous étiez inquiété(e)(s)**
s'inquiétait	**s'inquiétaient**	**s'était inquiété(e)**	**s'étaient inquiété(e)s**

3 passé simple

		10 passé antérieur	
m'inquiétai	**nous inquiétâmes**	**me fus inquiété(e)**	**nous fûmes inquiété(e)s**
t'inquiétas	**vous inquiétâtes**	**te fus inquiété(e)**	**vous fûtes inquiété(e)(s)**
s'inquiéta	**s'inquiétèrent**	**se fut inquiété(e)**	**se furent inquiété(e)s**

4 futur

		11 futur antérieur	
m'inquiéterai	**nous inquiéterons**	**me serai inquiété(e)**	**nous serons inquiété(e)s**
t'inquiéteras	**vous inquiéterez**	**te seras inquiété(e)**	**vous serez inquiété(e)(s)**
s'inquiétera	**s'inquiéteront**	**se sera inquiété(e)**	**se seront inquiété(e)s**

5 conditionnel

		12 conditionnel passé	
m'inquiéterais	**nous inquiéterions**	**me serais inquiété(e)**	**nous serions inquiété(e)s**
t'inquiéterais	**vous inquiéteriez**	**te serais inquiété(e)**	**vous seriez inquiété(e)(s)**
s'inquiéterait	**s'inquiéteraient**	**se serait inquiété(e)**	**se seraient inquiété(e)s**

6 présent du subjonctif

		13 passé du subjonctif	
m'inquiète	**nous inquiétions**	**me sois inquiété(e)**	**nous soyons inquiété(e)s**
t'inquiètes	**vous inquiétiez**	**te sois inquiété(e)**	**vous soyez inquiété(e)(s)**
s'inquiète	**s'inquiètent**	**se soit inquiété(e)**	**se soient inquiété(e)s**

7 imparfait du subjonctif

		14 plus-que-parfait du subjonctif	
m'inquiétasse	**nous inquiétassions**	**me fusse inquiété(e)**	**nous fussions inquiété(e)s**
t'inquiétasses	**vous inquiétassiez**	**te fusses inquiété(e)**	**vous fussiez inquiété(e)(s)**
s'inquiétât	**s'inquiétassent**	**se fût inquiété(e)**	**se fussent inquiété(e)s**

Impératif
inquiète-toi; ne t'inquiète pas
inquiétons-nous; ne nous inquiétons pas
inquiétez-vous; ne vous inquiétez pas

Words related to this verb
s'inquiéter de   to worry about
inquiéter   to trouble, to worry
une inquiétude   restlessness, anxiety, uneasiness
inquiétant, inquiétante   disturbing, alarming
inquiet, inquiète   restless, alarmed, disturbed, worried

Grammar putting you in a tense mood? Review the definitions of basic grammatical terms with examples on pages 35–49.

Regular **-er** verb   to insist

The Seven Simple Tenses		The Seven Compound Tenses	
Singular	Plural	Singular	Plural
1 présent de l'indicatif		8 passé composé	
insiste	**insistons**	**ai insisté**	**avons insisté**
insistes	**insistez**	**as insisté**	**avez insisté**
insiste	**insistent**	**a insisté**	**ont insisté**
2 imparfait de l'indicatif		9 plus-que-parfait de l'indicatif	
insistais	**insistions**	**avais insisté**	**avions insisté**
insistais	**insistiez**	**avais insisté**	**aviez insisté**
insistait	**insistaient**	**avait insisté**	**avaient insisté**
3 passé simple		10 passé antérieur	
insistai	**insistâmes**	**eus insisté**	**eûmes insisté**
insistas	**insistâtes**	**eus insisté**	**eûtes insisté**
insista	**insistèrent**	**eut insisté**	**eurent insisté**
4 futur		11 futur antérieur	
insisterai	**insisterons**	**aurai insisté**	**aurons insisté**
insisteras	**insisterez**	**auras insisté**	**aurez insisté**
insistera	**insisteront**	**aura insisté**	**auront insisté**
5 conditionnel		12 conditionnel passé	
insisterais	**insisterions**	**aurais insisté**	**aurions insisté**
insisterais	**insisteriez**	**aurais insisté**	**auriez insisté**
insisterait	**insisteraient**	**aurait insisté**	**auraient insisté**
6 présent du subjonctif		13 passé du subjonctif	
insiste	**insistions**	**aie insisté**	**ayons insisté**
insistes	**insistiez**	**aies insisté**	**ayez insisté**
insiste	**insistent**	**ait insisté**	**aient insisté**
7 imparfait du subjonctif		14 plus-que-parfait du subjonctif	
insistasse	**insistassions**	**eusse insisté**	**eussions insisté**
insistasses	**insistassiez**	**eusses insisté**	**eussiez insisté**
insistât	**insistassent**	**eût insisté**	**eussent insisté**

Impératif
insiste
insistons
insistez

Sentences using this verb and words related to it
Madame Albertine, maîtresse de français, insiste beaucoup sur la discipline dans cette école.

insistant, insistante   insistent, persistent   **insister sur**   to insist on
l'insistance *f.*   insistence   **inutile d'insister**   useless to insist

It's important that you be familiar with the Subjunctive. See pages 26–31.

instruire (260)

to instruct

Part. pr. **instruisant**   Part. passé **instruit**

Irregular verb

The Seven Simple Tenses		The Seven Compound Tenses	
Singular	Plural	Singular	Plural
1 présent de l'indicatif		8 passé composé	
instruis	**instruisons**	**ai instruit**	**avons instruit**
instruis	**instruisez**	**as instruit**	**avez instruit**
instruit	**instruisent**	**a instruit**	**ont instruit**
2 imparfait de l'indicatif		9 plus-que-parfait de l'indicatif	
instruisais	**instruisions**	**avais instruit**	**avions instruit**
instruisais	**instruisiez**	**avais instruit**	**aviez instruit**
instruisait	**instruisaient**	**avait instruit**	**avaient instruit**
3 passé simple		10 passé antérieur	
instruisis	**instruisîmes**	**eus instruit**	**eûmes instruit**
instruisis	**instruisîtes**	**eus instruit**	**eûtes instruit**
instruisit	**instruisirent**	**eut instruit**	**eurent instruit**
4 futur		11 futur antérieur	
instruirai	**instruirons**	**aurai instruit**	**aurons instruit**
instruiras	**instruirez**	**auras instruit**	**aurez instruit**
instruira	**instruiront**	**aura instruit**	**auront instruit**
5 conditionnel		12 conditionnel passé	
instruirais	**instruirions**	**aurais instruit**	**aurions instruit**
instruirais	**instruiriez**	**aurais instruit**	**auriez instruit**
instruirait	**instruiraient**	**aurait instruit**	**auraient instruit**
6 présent du subjonctif		13 passé du subjonctif	
instruise	**instruisions**	**aie instruit**	**ayons instruit**
instruises	**instruisiez**	**aies instruit**	**ayez instruit**
instruise	**instruisent**	**ait instruit**	**aient instruit**
7 imparfait du subjonctif		14 plus-que-parfait du subjonctif	
instruisisse	**instruisissions**	**eusse instruit**	**eussions instruit**
instruisisses	**instruisissiez**	**eusses instruit**	**eussiez instruit**
instruisît	**instruisissent**	**eût instruit**	**eussent instruit**

Impératif
instruis
instruisons
instruisez

Words and expressions related to this verb

instruit, instruite   educated
instruction f.   instruction, teaching
sans instruction   uneducated
instructeur, instructrice   instructor
instructif, instructive   instructive

les instructions   instructions
s'instruire   to teach oneself, to educate oneself
l'instruction publique   public education
bien instruit (instruite), fort instruit
   (instruite)   well educated

Get acquainted with what preposition goes with what verb. See *Verbs with prepositions* in the Appendixes.

396

Irregular verb   to forbid, to prohibit

The Seven Simple Tenses		The Seven Compound Tenses	
Singular	Plural	Singular	Plural

1 présent de l'indicatif		8 passé composé	
interdis	interdisons	ai interdit	avons interdit
interdis	interdisez	as interdit	avez interdit
interdit	interdisent	a interdit	ont interdit

2 imparfait de l'indicatif		9 plus-que-parfait de l'indicatif	
interdisais	interdisions	avais interdit	avions interdit
interdisais	interdisiez	avais interdit	aviez interdit
interdisait	interdisaient	avait interdit	avaient interdit

3 passé simple		10 passé antérieur	
interdis	interdîmes	eus interdit	eûmes interdit
interdis	interdîtes	eus interdit	eûtes interdit
interdit	interdirent	eut interdit	eurent interdit

4 futur		11 futur antérieur	
interdirai	interdirons	aurai interdit	aurons interdit
interdiras	interdirez	auras interdit	aurez interdit
interdira	interdiront	aura interdit	auront interdit

5 conditionnel		12 conditionnel passé	
interdirais	interdirions	aurais interdit	aurions interdit
interdirais	interdiriez	aurais interdit	auriez interdit
interdirait	interdiraient	aurait interdit	auraient interdit

6 présent du subjonctif		13 passé du subjonctif	
interdise	interdisions	aie interdit	ayons interdit
interdises	interdisiez	aies interdit	ayez interdit
interdise	interdisent	ait interdit	aient interdit

7 imparfait du subjonctif		14 plus-que-parfait du subjonctif	
interdisse	interdissions	eusse interdit	eussions interdit
interdisses	interdissiez	eusses interdit	eussiez interdit
interdît	interdissent	eût interdit	eussent interdit

Impératif
interdis
interdisons
interdisez

Sentences using this verb and words and expressions related to it
Je vous interdis de m'interrompre constamment.   I forbid you to interrupt me constantly.
Il est interdit de marcher sur l'herbe.   Do not walk on the grass.

interdire qqch à qqn   to forbid someone something
l'interdit *m.*   interdict; *adj.* **les jeux interdits**   forbidden games
l'interdiction *f.*   interdiction, prohibition
interdire à qqn de faire qqch   to forbid someone from doing something
STATIONNEMENT INTERDIT   NO PARKING

See also **contredire, dire, maudire, médire,** and **prédire.**

The subject pronouns are found on page 103.   **397**

The Seven Simple Tenses | The Seven Compound Tenses

Singular	Plural	Singular	Plural
1 présent de l'indicatif		8 passé composé	
m'intéresse	nous intéressons	me suis intéressé(e)	nous sommes intéressé(e)s
t'intéresses	vous intéressez	t'es intéressé(e)	vous êtes intéressé(e)(s)
s'intéresse	s'intéressent	s'est intéressé(e)	se sont intéressé(e)s
2 imparfait de l'indicatif		9 plus-que-parfait de l'indicatif	
m'intéressais	nous intéressions	m'étais intéressé(e)	nous étions intéressé(e)s
t'intéressais	vous intéressiez	t'étais intéressé(e)	vous étiez intéressé(e)(s)
s'intéressait	s'intéressaient	s'était intéressé(e)	s'étaient intéressé(e)s
3 passé simple		10 passé antérieur	
m'intéressai	nous intéressâmes	me fus intéressé(e)	nous fûmes intéressé(e)s
t'intéressas	vous intéressâtes	te fus intéressé(e)	vous fûtes intéressé(e)(s)
s'intéressa	s'intéressèrent	se fut intéressé(e)	se furent intéressé(e)s
4 futur		11 futur antérieur	
m'intéresserai	nous intéresserons	me serai intéressé(e)	nous serons intéressé(e)s
t'intéresseras	vous intéresserez	te seras intéressé(e)	vous serez intéressé(e)(s)
s'intéressera	s'intéresseront	se sera intéressé(e)	se seront intéressé(e)s
5 conditionnel		12 conditionnel passé	
m'intéresserais	nous intéresserions	me serais intéressé(e)	nous serions intéressé(e)s
t'intéresserais	vous intéresseriez	te serais intéressé(e)	vous seriez intéressé(e)(s)
s'intéresserait	s'intéresseraient	se serait intéressé(e)	se seraient intéressé(e)s
6 présent du subjonctif		13 passé du subjonctif	
m'intéresse	nous intéressions	me sois intéressé(e)	nous soyons intéressé(e)s
t'intéresses	vous intéressiez	te sois intéressé(e)	vous soyez intéressé(e)(s)
s'intéresse	s'intéressent	se soit intéressé(e)	se soient intéressé(e)s
7 imparfait du subjonctif		14 plus-que-parfait du subjonctif	
m'intéressasse	nous intéressassions	me fusse intéressé(e)	nous fussions intéressé(e)s
t'intéressasses	vous intéressassiez	te fusses intéressé(e)	vous fussiez intéressé(e)(s)
s'intéressât	s'intéressassent	se fût intéressé(e)	se fussent intéressé(e)s

Impératif
intéresse-toi; ne t'intéresse pas
intéressons-nous; ne nous intéressons pas
intéressez-vous; ne vous intéressez pas

Words and expressions related to this verb
s'intéresser à qqch   to be interested in something, to concern oneself with
Je m'intéresse aux sports.   I am interested in sports.
s'intéresser à qqn   to be interested in someone
Janine s'intéresse à lui.   Janine is interested in him.
intéresser qqn à qqch   to interest someone in something
Je m'intéresse à tout.   I am interested in everything.
Cela ne m'intéresse pas du tout.   That does not interest me at all.
un intérêt   interest
intéressant, intéressante   interesting
Rien ne m'intéresse.   Nothing interests me.

Regular **-er** verb endings; spelling change: retain the
ge before **a** or **o** to keep the soft **g** sound of the verb

to interrogate,
to question

The Seven Simple Tenses		The Seven Compound Tenses	
Singular	Plural	Singular	Plural
1 présent de l'indicatif		8 passé composé	
interroge	interrogeons	ai interrogé	avons interrogé
interroges	interrogez	as interrogé	avez interrogé
interroge	interrogent	a interrogé	ont interrogé
2 imparfait de l'indicatif		9 plus-que-parfait de l'indicatif	
interrogeais	interrogions	avais interrogé	avions interrogé
interrogeais	interrogiez	avais interrogé	aviez interrogé
interrogeait	interrogeaient	avait interrogé	avaient interrogé
3 passé simple		10 passé antérieur	
interrogeai	interrogeâmes	eus interrogé	eûmes interrogé
interrogeas	interrogeâtes	eus interrogé	eûtes interrogé
interrogea	interrogèrent	eut interrogé	eurent interrogé
4 futur		11 futur antérieur	
interrogerai	interrogerons	aurai interrogé	aurons interrogé
interrogeras	interrogerez	auras interrogé	aurez interrogé
interrogera	interrogeront	aura interrogé	auront interrogé
5 conditionnel		12 conditionnel passé	
interrogerais	interrogerions	aurais interrogé	aurions interrogé
interrogerais	interrogeriez	aurais interrogé	auriez interrogé
interrogerait	interrogeraient	aurait interrogé	auraient interrogé
6 présent du subjonctif		13 passé du subjonctif	
interroge	interrogions	aie interrogé	ayons interrogé
interroges	interrogiez	aies interrogé	ayez interrogé
interroge	interrogent	ait interrogé	aient interrogé
7 imparfait du subjonctif		14 plus-que-parfait du subjonctif	
interrogeasse	interrogeassions	eusse interrogé	eussions interrogé
interrogeasses	interrogeassiez	eusses interrogé	eussiez interrogé
interrogeât	interrogeassent	eût interrogé	eussent interrogé

Impératif
interroge
interrogeons
interrogez

Words and expressions related to this verb
une interrogation   interrogation, questioning
un point d'interrogation   question mark
un interrogateur, une interrogatrice
   interrogator

interrogatif, interrogative   interrogative
interrogativement   interrogatively
un interrogatoire   interrogation
dérogatoire   derogatory

How are you doing? Find out with the verb drills and tests with answers explained on pages
50–101.

The subject pronouns are found on page 103.

to interrupt

Regular **-re** verb endings; spelling change:
3d person sing. of Tense No. 1 adds **t**

The Seven Simple Tenses		The Seven Compound Tenses	
Singular	Plural	Singular	Plural

1 présent de l'indicatif		8 passé composé	
interromps	interrompons	ai interrompu	avons interrompu
interromps	interrompez	as interrompu	avez interrompu
interrompt	interrompent	a interrompu	ont interrompu

2 imparfait de l'indicatif		9 plus-que-parfait de l'indicatif	
interrompais	interrompions	avais interrompu	avions interrompu
interrompais	interrompiez	avais interrompu	aviez interrompu
interrompait	interrompaient	avait interrompu	avaient interrompu

3 passé simple		10 passé antérieur	
interrompis	interrompîmes	eus interrompu	eûmes interrompu
interrompis	interrompîtes	eus interrompu	eûtes interrompu
interrompit	interrompirent	eut interrompu	eurent interrompu

4 futur		11 futur antérieur	
interromprai	interromprons	aurai interrompu	aurons interrompu
interrompras	interromprez	auras interrompu	aurez interrompu
interrompra	interrompront	aura interrompu	auront interrompu

5 conditionnel		12 conditionnel passé	
interromprais	interromprions	aurais interrompu	aurions interrompu
interromprais	interrompriez	aurais interrompu	auriez interrompu
interromprait	interrompraient	aurait interrompu	auraient interrompu

6 présent du subjonctif		13 passé du subjonctif	
interrompe	interrompions	aie interrompu	ayons interrompu
interrompes	interrompiez	aies interrompu	ayez interrompu
interrompe	interrompent	ait interrompu	aient interrompu

7 imparfait du subjonctif		14 plus-que-parfait du subjonctif	
interrompisse	interrompissions	eusse interrompu	eussions interrompu
interrompisses	interrompissiez	eusses interrompu	eussiez interrompu
interrompît	interrompissent	eût interrompu	eussent interrompu

Impératif
interromps
interrompons
interrompez

Sentences using this verb and words related to it

—Maurice, tu m'interromps à chaque instant. Cesse de m'interrompre, s'il te plaît! C'est une mauvaise habitude et je ne l'aime pas. Est-ce que tu l'aimes quand on t'interrompt continuellement?

une interruption   interruption
interrompu, interrompue   interrupted

See also **corrompre** and **rompre**.

un interrupteur, une interruptrice
  interrupter
un interrupteur   light switch

The Seven Simple Tenses		The Seven Compound Tenses	
Singular	Plural	Singular	Plural

1 présent de l'indicatif

		8 passé composé	
introduis	introduisons	ai introduit	avons introduit
introduis	introduisez	as introduit	avez introduit
introduit	introduisent	a introduit	ont introduit

2 imparfait de l'indicatif

		9 plus-que-parfait de l'indicatif	
introduisais	introduisions	avais introduit	avions introduit
introduisais	introduisiez	avais introduit	aviez introduit
introduisait	introduisaient	avait introduit	avaient introduit

3 passé simple

		10 passé antérieur	
introduisis	introduisîmes	eus introduit	eûmes introduit
introduisis	introduisîtes	eus introduit	eûtes introduit
introduisit	introduisirent	eut introduit	eurent introduit

4 futur

		11 futur antérieur	
introduirai	introduirons	aurai introduit	aurons introduit
introduiras	introduirez	auras introduit	aurez introduit
introduira	introduiront	aura introduit	auront introduit

5 conditionnel

		12 conditionnel passé	
introduirais	introduirions	aurais introduit	aurions introduit
introduirais	introduiriez	aurais introduit	auriez introduit
introduirait	introduiraient	aurait introduit	auraient introduit

6 présent du subjonctif

		13 passé du subjonctif	
introduise	introduisions	aie introduit	ayons introduit
introduises	introduisiez	aies introduit	ayez introduit
introduise	introduisent	ait introduit	aient introduit

7 imparfait du subjonctif

		14 plus-que-parfait du subjonctif	
introduisisse	introduisissions	eusse introduit	eussions introduit
introduisisses	introduisissiez	eusses introduit	eussiez introduit
introduisît	introduisissent	eût introduit	eussent introduit

Impératif
introduis
introduisons
introduisez

Words related to this verb
introducteur, introductrice introducer, initiator
introductif, introductive introductory
introduction *f.* introduction; **les paroles d'introduction** introductory words

See also **conduire, déduire, produire, réduire, reproduire, séduire,** and **traduire.**

Can't remember the French verb you need? Check the back pages of this book for the English-French verb index!

The Seven Simple Tenses		The Seven Compound Tenses	
Singular	Plural	Singular	Plural
1 présent de l'indicatif		8 passé composé	
invite	**invitons**	**ai invité**	**avons invité**
invites	**invitez**	**as invité**	**avez invité**
invite	**invitent**	**a invité**	**ont invité**
2 imparfait de l'indicatif		9 plus-que-parfait de l'indicatif	
invitais	**invitions**	**avais invité**	**avions invité**
invitais	**invitiez**	**avais invité**	**aviez invité**
invitait	**invitaient**	**avait invité**	**avaient invité**
3 passé simple		10 passé antérieur	
invitai	**invitâmes**	**eus invité**	**eûmes invité**
invitas	**invitâtes**	**eus invité**	**eûtes invité**
invita	**invitèrent**	**eut invité**	**eurent invité**
4 futur		11 futur antérieur	
inviterai	**inviterons**	**aurai invité**	**aurons invité**
inviteras	**inviterez**	**auras invité**	**aurez invité**
invitera	**inviteront**	**aura invité**	**auront invité**
5 conditionnel		12 conditionnel passé	
inviterais	**inviterions**	**aurais invité**	**aurions invité**
inviterais	**inviteriez**	**aurais invité**	**auriez invité**
inviterait	**inviteraient**	**aurait invité**	**auraient invité**
6 présent du subjonctif		13 passé du subjonctif	
invite	**invitions**	**aie invité**	**ayons invité**
invites	**invitiez**	**aies invité**	**ayez invité**
invite	**invitent**	**ait invité**	**aient invité**
7 imparfait du subjonctif		14 plus-que-parfait du subjonctif	
invitasse	**invitassions**	**eusse invité**	**eussions invité**
invitasses	**invitassiez**	**eusses invité**	**eussiez invité**
invitât	**invitassent**	**eût invité**	**eussent invité**

Impératif
invite
invitons
invitez

Sentences using this verb and words related to it

J'ai reçu une invitation à dîner chez les Martin. C'est pour samedi soir. J'ai accepté avec plaisir et maintenant je vais en ville acheter un cadeau pour eux.

l'invitation *f.*   invitation
les invités   the guests
sur l'invitation de   at the invitation of
sans invitation   without invitation, uninvited

inviter qqn à faire qqch   to invite someone to
  do something
Elle s'est invitée.   She invited herself.
C'est moi qui invite!   My treat!

Can't find the verb you're looking for? Check the back pages of this book for a list of over 2,600 additional verbs!

to throw, to cast

Regular **-er** verb endings; spelling change:
t becomes **tt** before syllable with mute **e**

The Seven Simple Tenses		The Seven Compound Tenses	
Singular	Plural	Singular	Plural
1 présent de l'indicatif		8 passé composé	
jette	jetons	ai jeté	avons jeté
jettes	jetez	as jeté	avez jeté
jette	jettent	a jeté	ont jeté
2 imparfait de l'indicatif		9 plus-que-parfait de l'indicatif	
jetais	jetions	avais jeté	avions jeté
jetais	jetiez	avais jeté	aviez jeté
jetait	jetaient	avait jeté	avaient jeté
3 passé simple		10 passé antérieur	
jetai	jetâmes	eus jeté	eûmes jeté
jetas	jetâtes	eus jeté	eûtes jeté
jeta	jetèrent	eut jeté	eurent jeté
4 futur		11 futur antérieur	
jetterai	jetterons	aurai jeté	aurons jeté
jetteras	jetterez	auras jeté	aurez jeté
jettera	jetteront	aura jeté	auront jeté
5 conditionnel		12 conditionnel passé	
jetterais	jetterions	aurais jeté	aurions jeté
jetterais	jetteriez	aurais jeté	auriez jeté
jetterait	jetteraient	aurait jeté	auraient jeté
6 présent du subjonctif		13 passé du subjonctif	
jette	jetions	aie jeté	ayons jeté
jettes	jetiez	aies jeté	ayez jeté
jette	jettent	ait jeté	aient jeté
7 imparfait du subjonctif		14 plus-que-parfait du subjonctif	
jetasse	jetassions	eusse jeté	eussions jeté
jetasses	jetassiez	eusses jeté	eussiez jeté
jetât	jetassent	eût jeté	eussent jeté

Impératif
jette
jetons
jetez

Common idiomatic expressions using this verb
jeter un cri   to utter a cry
jeter son argent par la fenêtre   to throw one's money out the window
se jeter sur (contre)   to throw oneself at (against)
un jeton de téléphone   telephone slug, token
une jetée   jetty
un jet d'eau   fountain
jeter un coup d'oeil à   to glance at; **se jeter au cou de qqn**   to throw oneself at somebody
rejeter   to reject, to throw back; **projeter**   to plan, to project
jetable   disposable
Ne jetez rien par la fenêtre.   Do not throw anything out the window.

Don't miss orthographically changing verbs on pages 32–34.

The subject pronouns are found on page 103.   **403**

to join, to contact

Irregular verb

The Seven Simple Tenses		The Seven Compound Tenses	
Singular	Plural	Singular	Plural
1 présent de l'indicatif		**8 passé composé**	
joins	joignons	ai joint	avons joint
joins	joignez	as joint	avez joint
joint	joignent	a joint	ont joint
2 imparfait de l'indicatif		**9 plus-que-parfait de l'indicatif**	
joignais	joignions	avais joint	avions joint
joignais	joigniez	avais joint	aviez joint
joignait	joignaient	avait joint	avaient joint
3 passé simple		**10 passé antérieur**	
joignis	joignîmes	eus joint	eûmes joint
joignis	joignîtes	eus joint	eûtes joint
joignit	joignirent	eut joint	eurent joint
4 futur		**11 futur antérieur**	
joindrai	joindrons	aurai joint	aurons joint
joindras	joindrez	auras joint	aurez joint
joindra	joindront	aura joint	auront joint
5 conditionnel		**12 conditionnel passé**	
joindrais	joindrions	aurais joint	aurions joint
joindrais	joindriez	aurais joint	auriez joint
joindrait	joindraient	aurait joint	auraient joint
6 présent du subjonctif		**13 passé du subjonctif**	
joigne	joignions	aie joint	ayons joint
joignes	joigniez	aies joint	ayez joint
joigne	joignent	ait joint	aient joint
7 imparfait du subjonctif		**14 plus-que-parfait du subjonctif**	
joignisse	joignissions	eusse joint	eussions joint
joignisses	joignissiez	eusses joint	eussiez joint
joignît	joignissent	eût joint	eussent joint

Impératif
joins
joignons
joignez

Common idiomatic expressions using this verb and words related to it

joindre les deux bouts to make ends meet
les jointures des doigts knuckles
joint, jointe joined
les talons joints heels together
ci-joint herewith, attached
joindre à to join to, to add to

rejoindre to rejoin, to join together
se rejoindre to meet, to come together again
se joindre à la discussion to join in the
    discussion
joindre par téléphone to reach by telephone

Use the guide to French pronunciation. It's in the Appendixes.

404

Regular **-er** verb   to play, to act (in a play), to gamble

The Seven Simple Tenses		The Seven Compound Tenses	
Singular	Plural	Singular	Plural

1   présent de l'indicatif

		8 passé composé	
joue	**jouons**	**ai joué**	**avons joué**
joues	**jouez**	**as joué**	**avez joué**
joue	**jouent**	**a joué**	**ont joué**

2   imparfait de l'indicatif

		9 plus-que-parfait de l'indicatif	
jouais	**jouions**	**avais joué**	**avions joué**
jouais	**jouiez**	**avais joué**	**aviez joué**
jouait	**jouaient**	**avait joué**	**avaient joué**

3   passé simple

		10 passé antérieur	
jouai	**jouâmes**	**eus joué**	**eûmes joué**
jouas	**jouâtes**	**eus joué**	**eûtes joué**
joua	**jouèrent**	**eut joué**	**eurent joué**

4   futur

		11 futur antérieur	
jouerai	**jouerons**	**aurai joué**	**aurons joué**
joueras	**jouerez**	**auras joué**	**aurez joué**
jouera	**joueront**	**aura joué**	**auront joué**

5   conditionnel

		12 conditionnel passé	
jouerais	**jouerions**	**aurais joué**	**aurions joué**
jouerais	**joueriez**	**aurais joué**	**auriez joué**
jouerait	**joueraient**	**aurait joué**	**auraient joué**

6   présent du subjonctif

		13 passé du subjonctif	
joue	**jouions**	**aie joué**	**ayons joué**
joues	**jouiez**	**aies joué**	**ayez joué**
joue	**jouent**	**ait joué**	**aient joué**

7   imparfait du subjonctif

		14 plus-que-parfait du subjonctif	
jouasse	**jouassions**	**eusse joué**	**eussions joué**
jouasses	**jouassiez**	**eusses joué**	**eussiez joué**
jouât	**jouassent**	**eût joué**	**eussent joué**

Impératif
joue
jouons
jouez

Jouer

Jouer is an essential French verb because it is very useful for a student, especially when talking about sports and music.

Sentences using jouer

Madeleine a joué un tour au voisin. Madeleine played a trick on the neighbor.

Cela va se jouer ce soir. That will be settled tonight.

Tu dois arrêter de fumer. Ta santé est en jeu! You must stop smoking. Your health is at stake!

Sports

Paul et ses frères jouent au foot tous les jours. Paul and his brothers play soccer every day.

Claire jouait au tennis quand elle est tombée. Claire was playing tennis when she fell down.

Fred et moi, nous jouons au squash demain soir. Tomorrow evening Fred and I will play squash.

James jouera dans le championnat du polo. James will play in the polo championship.

Music

Ma tante joue du piano. My aunt plays the piano.

Jean a joué de la flûte dans un concert à New York. John played the flute in a concert in New York.

Paul joue de la guitare après l'école. Paul plays guitar after school.

Words and expressions related to this verb

jouer un tour à qqn **to play a trick on someone**
un jouet **toy, plaything**
un joueur, une joueuse **player, gambler**
jouer sur les mots **to play with words**
un jeu de mots **word play, pun**
jouer un rôle **to play a part**
se jouer de **to make fun of, deride**
un joujou, des joujoux **toy, toys (child's language)**
jouer gros jeu **to play for high stakes**
un jeu **a game**
un jeu vidéo **video game**
en jeu **at stake**
enjoué, enjouée **playful**
un jeu de cartes **a deck of cards**
un jeu d'outils **a set of tools**
déjouer **to baffle, thwart**
rejouer **to replay, play again**

Sports and recreation
jouer au tennis **to play tennis**
jouer au squash **to play squash**
jouer au golf **to play golf**
jouer au foot **to play soccer**
jouer aux cartes **to play cards**

Music
jouer d'un instrument **to play an instrument**
jouer de la flûte **to play the flute**
jouer du piano **to play the piano**
jouer du violon **to play the violin**

The Seven Simple Tenses		The Seven Compound Tenses	
Singular	Plural	Singular	Plural

1 présent de l'indicatif

jouis	jouissons
jouis	jouissez
jouit	jouissent

8 passé composé

ai joui	avons joui
as joui	avez joui
a joui	ont joui

2 imparfait de l'indicatif

jouissais	jouissions
jouissais	jouissiez
jouissait	jouissaient

9 plus-que-parfait de l'indicatif

avais joui	avions joui
avais joui	aviez joui
avait joui	avaient joui

3 passé simple

jouis	jouîmes
jouis	jouîtes
jouit	jouirent

10 passé antérieur

eus joui	eûmes joui
eus joui	eûtes joui
eut joui	eurent joui

4 futur

jouirai	jouirons
jouiras	jouirez
jouira	jouiront

11 futur antérieur

aurai joui	aurons joui
auras joui	aurez joui
aura joui	auront joui

5 conditionnel

jouirais	jouirions
jouirais	jouiriez
jouirait	jouiraient

12 conditionnel passé

aurais joui	aurions joui
aurais joui	auriez joui
aurait joui	auraient joui

6 présent du subjonctif

jouisse	jouissions
jouisses	jouissiez
jouisse	jouissent

13 passé du subjonctif

aie joui	ayons joui
aies joui	ayez joui
ait joui	aient joui

7 imparfait du subjonctif

jouisse	jouissions
jouisses	jouissiez
jouît	jouissent

14 plus-que-parfait du subjonctif

eusse joui	eussions joui
eusses joui	eussiez joui
eût joui	eussent joui

Impératif
jouis
jouissons
jouissez

Words and expressions related to this verb
jouir de qqch   to enjoy something
la jouissance   delight, enjoyment
la joie   joy; **la joie de vivre**   joy of living;
   avec joie   gladly
la réjouissance   rejoicing
se réjouir de   to rejoice in, to be delighted at

réjouir   to cheer up, to gladden, to rejoice
réjouir la vue   to be pleasing to the eye
réjouir le coeur   to gladden the heart
réjouissant, réjouissante   entertaining,
   amusing

Don't forget to study the section on defective and impersonal verbs. It's right after this main list.

Part. pr. **jugeant**   Part. passé **jugé**

to judge, to deem

Regular **-er** verb endings; spelling change: retain the
ge before **a** or **o** to keep the soft **g** sound of the verb

The Seven Simple Tenses		The Seven Compound Tenses	
Singular	Plural	Singular	Plural
1 présent de l'indicatif		8 passé composé	
juge	jugeons	ai jugé	avons jugé
juges	jugez	as jugé	avez jugé
juge	jugent	a jugé	ont jugé
2 imparfait de l'indicatif		9 plus-que-parfait de l'indicatif	
jugeais	jugions	avais jugé	avions jugé
jugeais	jugiez	avais jugé	aviez jugé
jugeait	jugeaient	avait jugé	avaient jugé
3 passé simple		10 passé antérieur	
jugeai	jugeâmes	eus jugé	eûmes jugé
jugeas	jugeâtes	eus jugé	eûtes jugé
jugea	jugèrent	eut jugé	eurent jugé
4 futur		11 futur antérieur	
jugerai	jugerons	aurai jugé	aurons jugé
jugeras	jugerez	auras jugé	aurez jugé
jugera	jugeront	aura jugé	auront jugé
5 conditionnel		12 conditionnel passé	
jugerais	jugerions	aurais jugé	aurions jugé
jugerais	jugeriez	aurais jugé	auriez jugé
jugerait	jugeraient	aurait jugé	auraient jugé
6 présent du subjonctif		13 passé du subjonctif	
juge	jugions	aie jugé	ayons jugé
juges	jugiez	aies jugé	ayez jugé
juge	jugent	ait jugé	aient jugé
7 imparfait du subjonctif		14 plus-que-parfait du subjonctif	
jugeasse	jugeassions	eusse jugé	eussions jugé
jugeasses	jugeassiez	eusses jugé	eussiez jugé
jugeât	jugeassent	eût jugé	eussent jugé

Impératif
juge
jugeons
jugez

Words and expressions related to this verb
juger de   to judge (of); **Jugez de ma joie!**
   You can imagine my joy!
à en juger par . . .   judging by . . .
juger par . . .   to judge by . . .
mal juger qqn   to misjudge someone

juger bon de faire qqch   to think it wise to do
   something
un juge   judge, magistrate; **un juge de paix**
   justice of the peace
un jugement   judgment

Get acquainted with what preposition goes with what. See *Verbs with prepositions* in the Appendixes.

Regular **-er** verb

The Seven Simple Tenses		The Seven Compound Tenses	
Singular	Plural	Singular	Plural
1 présent de l'indicatif		8 passé composé	
jure	jurons	ai juré	avons juré
jures	jurez	as juré	avez juré
jure	jurent	a juré	ont juré
2 imparfait de l'indicatif		9 plus-que-parfait de l'indicatif	
jurais	jurions	avais juré	avions juré
jurais	juriez	avais juré	aviez juré
jurait	juraient	avait juré	avaient juré
3 passé simple		10 passé antérieur	
jurai	jurâmes	eus juré	eûmes juré
juras	jurâtes	eus juré	eûtes juré
jura	jurèrent	eut juré	eurent juré
4 futur		11 futur antérieur	
jurerai	jurerons	aurai juré	aurons juré
jureras	jurerez	auras juré	aurez juré
jurera	jureront	aura juré	auront juré
5 conditionnel		12 conditionnel passé	
jurerais	jurerions	aurais juré	aurions juré
jurerais	jureriez	aurais juré	auriez juré
jurerait	jureraient	aurait juré	auraient juré
6 présent du subjonctif		13 passé du subjonctif	
jure	jurions	aie juré	ayons juré
jures	juriez	aies juré	ayez juré
jure	jurent	ait juré	aient juré
7 imparfait du subjonctif		14 plus-que-parfait du subjonctif	
jurasse	jurassions	eusse juré	eussions juré
jurasses	jurassiez	eusses juré	eussiez juré
jurât	jurassent	eût juré	eussent juré

Impératif
jure
jurons
jurez

Words and expressions related to this verb
jurer sur la Bible to swear on the Bible
un juriste jurist
la jurisprudence jurisprudence
un jureur swearer
jurer contre to swear against
abjurer to abjure, renounce

un juron curse, oath
un jury jury
un jurisconsulte legal expert
Je vous le jure! I swear it!
dire des jurons to swear, to curse

It's important that you be familiar with the Subjunctive. See pages 26–31.

The subject pronouns are found on page 103.   **409**

to loosen, to unleash, to let go

Regular **-er** verb

The Seven Simple Tenses		The Seven Compound Tenses	
Singular	Plural	Singular	Plural
1 présent de l'indicatif		8 passé composé	
lâche	**lâchons**	**ai lâché**	**avons lâché**
lâches	**lâchez**	**as lâché**	**avez lâché**
lâche	**lâchent**	**a lâché**	**ont lâché**
2 imparfait de l'indicatif		9 plus-que-parfait de l'indicatif	
lâchais	**lâchions**	**avais lâché**	**avions lâché**
lâchais	**lâchiez**	**avais lâché**	**aviez lâché**
lâchait	**lâchaient**	**avait lâché**	**avaient lâché**
3 passé simple		10 passé antérieur	
lâchai	**lâchâmes**	**eus lâché**	**eûmes lâché**
lâchas	**lâchâtes**	**eus lâché**	**eûtes lâché**
lâcha	**lâchèrent**	**eut lâché**	**eurent lâché**
4 futur		11 futur antérieur	
lâcherai	**lâcherons**	**aurai lâché**	**aurons lâché**
lâcheras	**lâcherez**	**auras lâché**	**aurez lâché**
lâchera	**lâcheront**	**aura lâché**	**auront lâché**
5 conditionnel		12 conditionnel passé	
lâcherais	**lâcherions**	**aurais lâché**	**aurions lâché**
lâcherais	**lâcheriez**	**aurais lâché**	**auriez lâché**
lâcherait	**lâcheraient**	**aurait lâché**	**auraient lâché**
6 présent du subjonctif		13 passé du subjonctif	
lâche	**lâchions**	**aie lâché**	**ayons lâché**
lâches	**lâchiez**	**aies lâché**	**ayez lâché**
lâche	**lâchent**	**ait lâché**	**aient lâché**
7 imparfait du subjonctif		14 plus-que-parfait du subjonctif	
lâchasse	**lâchassions**	**eusse lâché**	**eussions lâché**
lâchasses	**lâchassiez**	**eusses lâché**	**eussiez lâché**
lâchât	**lâchassent**	**eût lâché**	**eussent lâché**

Impératif
lâche
lâchons
lâchez

Words and expressions related to this verb
lâcher prise   to let go
un lâcheur, une lâcheuse   quitter
lâche   cowardly; **lâchement**   in a cowardly way
la lâcheté   cowardice
un vêtement lâche   flowing, loose garment

un relâche   rest, relaxation, respite, temporary closing of a theater
relâcher   to abate, to loosen, to relax, to slacken
Lâchez-moi!   Let go of me!

Grammar putting you in a tense mood? Review the definitions of basic grammatical terms with examples on pages 35–49.

Regular **-er** verb   to let, to allow, to leave

The Seven Simple Tenses		The Seven Compound Tenses	
Singular	Plural	Singular	Plural
1 présent de l'indicatif		**8 passé composé**	
laisse	laissons	ai laissé	avons laissé
laisses	laissez	as laissé	avez laissé
laisse	laissent	a laissé	ont laissé
2 imparfait de l'indicatif		**9 plus-que-parfait de l'indicatif**	
laissais	laissions	avais laissé	avions laissé
laissais	laissiez	avais laissé	aviez laissé
laissait	laissaient	avait laissé	avaient laissé
3 passé simple		**10 passé antérieur**	
laissai	laissâmes	eus laissé	eûmes laissé
laissas	laissâtes	eus laissé	eûtes laissé
laissa	laissèrent	eut laissé	eurent laissé
4 futur		**11 futur antérieur**	
laisserai	laisserons	aurai laissé	aurons laissé
laisseras	laisserez	auras laissé	aurez laissé
laissera	laisseront	aura laissé	auront laissé
5 conditionnel		**12 conditionnel passé**	
laisserais	laisserions	aurais laissé	aurions laissé
laisserais	laisseriez	aurais laissé	auriez laissé
laisserait	laisseraient	aurait laissé	auraient laissé
6 présent du subjonctif		**13 passé du subjonctif**	
laisse	laissions	aie laissé	ayons laissé
laisses	laissiez	aies laissé	ayez laissé
laisse	laissent	ait laissé	aient laissé
7 imparfait du subjonctif		**14 plus-que-parfait du subjonctif**	
laissasse	laissassions	eusse laissé	eussions laissé
laissasses	laissassiez	eusses laissé	eussiez laissé
laissât	laissassent	eût laissé	eussent laissé

Impératif
laisse
laissons
laissez

Sentences using this verb and words related to it
J'ai laissé mes devoirs chez moi.   I left my homework at home.
Laissez-moi tranquille!   Leave me alone!
Laissez-moi passer, s'il vous plaît.   Please let me get by.

laissez-faire   do not interfere;   Laissez-moi faire.   Let me do as I please.
une laisse   a leash
laisser entrer   to let in, to allow to enter;   laisser tomber   to drop
laisser aller   to let go;   se laisser aller   to let oneself go
délaisser   to abandon, to forsake

The subject pronouns are found on page 103.   **411**

lancer (275)

to hurl, to launch, to throw

Part. Pr. **lançant**   Part. passé **lancé**

Regular **-er** verb endings; spelling change:
c changes to **ç** before **a** or **o** to keep **s** sound

The Seven Simple Tenses		The Seven Compound Tenses	
Singular	Plural	Singular	Plural
1 présent de l'indicatif		8 passé composé	
lance	lançons	ai lancé	avons lancé
lances	lancez	as lancé	avez lancé
lance	lancent	a lancé	ont lancé
2 imparfait de l'indicatif		9 plus-que-parfait de l'indicatif	
lançais	lancions	avais lancé	avions lancé
lançais	lanciez	avais lancé	aviez lancé
lançait	lançaient	avait lancé	avaient lancé
3 passé simple		10 passé antérieur	
lançai	lançâmes	eus lancé	eûmes lancé
lanças	lançâtes	eus lancé	eûtes lancé
lança	lancèrent	eut lancé	eurent lancé
4 futur		11 futur antérieur	
lancerai	lancerons	aurai lancé	aurons lancé
lanceras	lancerez	auras lancé	aurez lancé
lancera	lanceront	aura lancé	auront lancé
5 conditionnel		12 conditionnel passé	
lancerais	lancerions	aurais lancé	aurions lancé
lancerais	lanceriez	aurais lancé	auriez lancé
lancerait	lanceraient	aurait lancé	auraient lancé
6 présent du subjonctif		13 passé du subjonctif	
lance	lancions	aie lancé	ayons lancé
lances	lanciez	aies lancé	ayez lancé
lance	lancent	ait lancé	aient lancé
7 imparfait du subjonctif		14 plus-que-parfait du subjonctif	
lançasse	lançassions	eusse lancé	eussions lancé
lançasses	lançassiez	eusses lancé	eussiez lancé
lançât	lançassent	eût lancé	eussent lancé

Impératif
lance
lançons
lancez

Words and expressions related to this verb

se lancer contre   to throw oneself at, against
un départ lancé   a flying start (sports)
une lance   a spear
le lancement d'un disque, d'un livre, etc.
   ceremony to launch a new record, book, etc.

un lancement   hurling, casting
un lanceur   thrower, pitcher (sports)
lancer un cri   to cry out
une rampe de lancement   launching pad

Can't remember the French verb you need? Check the back pages of this book for the English-French verb index!

Regular **-er** verb   to wash

The Seven Simple Tenses		The Seven Compound Tenses	
Singular	Plural	Singular	Plural
1 présent de l'indicatif		**8 passé composé**	
lave	lavons	ai lavé	avons lavé
laves	lavez	as lavé	avez lavé
lave	lavent	a lavé	ont lavé
2 imparfait de l'indicatif		**9 plus-que-parfait de l'indicatif**	
lavais	lavions	avais lavé	avions lavé
lavais	laviez	avais lavé	aviez lavé
lavait	lavaient	avait lavé	avaient lavé
3 passé simple		**10 passé antérieur**	
lavai	lavâmes	eus lavé	eûmes lavé
lavas	lavâtes	eus lavé	eûtes lavé
lava	lavèrent	eut lavé	eurent lavé
4 futur		**11 futur antérieur**	
laverai	laverons	aurai lavé	aurons lavé
laveras	laverez	auras lavé	aurez lavé
lavera	laveront	aura lavé	auront lavé
5 conditionnel		**12 conditionnel passé**	
laverais	laverions	aurais lavé	aurions lavé
laverais	laveriez	aurais lavé	auriez lavé
laverait	laveraient	aurait lavé	auraient lavé
6 présent du subjonctif		**13 passé du subjonctif**	
lave	lavions	aie lavé	ayons lavé
laves	laviez	aies lavé	ayez lavé
lave	lavent	ait lavé	aient lavé
7 imparfait du subjonctif		**14 plus-que-parfait du subjonctif**	
lavasse	lavassions	eusse lavé	eussions lavé
lavasses	lavassiez	eusses lavé	eussiez lavé
lavât	lavassent	eût lavé	eussent lavé

Impératif
lave
lavons
lavez

AN ESSENTIAL
55 VERB

Laver and Se laver

Laver and **se laver** are essential verbs for you to learn because they can help you to understand the agreement of past participles.

Examples in the *présent*

Marie lave la voiture. (Marie is washing the car.) Note: **la voiture** is the direct object.

Marie se lave. (Marie is washing herself.) Note: **se** is the direct object pronoun.

Marie se lave les mains. (Marie is washing her hands.) Note: **les mains** is the direct object; **se** is an indirect object in this case.

Examples in the *passé composé*

Marie a lavé la voiture. (Marie washed the car.) Note: **la voiture** is the direct object.

Marie l'a lavée. (Marie washed it.) Note: **l'** stands for **la voiture**, so **lavée** agrees with the preceding direct object pronoun.

Marie s'est lavée. (Marie washed herself.) Note: **s'** is the direct object. What did Marie wash? She washed herself.

Marie s'est lavé les mains. (Marie washed her hands.) Note: **les mains** is the direct object; there is no feminine agreement on **lavé** because the direct object comes after; there is no preceding direct object pronoun. What did Marie wash? She washed her hands.

Sentences using se laver

—**Henriette, est-ce que tu t'es bien lavée?** Henrietta, did you wash yourself well?

—**Oui, maman, je me suis lavée! Je me suis bien lavé les mains!** Yes, Mother, I washed myself! I washed my hands well!

Lave-toi les mains, Marie. On va manger. Wash your hands, Marie. We're going to eat.

Words and expressions related to these verbs

un lavabo **washbasin, sink**

une douche **shower**

la salle de bains **bathroom**

se laver les mains de qqch **to wash one's hands of something**

lavable (en machine) **(machine) washable**

un lave-auto **car wash**

une laverie **laundry (room), launderette**

le lave-glace **windshield washer**

un lave-vaisselle **dishwasher**

une machine à laver, un lave-linge **washing machine**

laver en machine **to machine wash**

laver à la main **to hand wash**

un laveur, une laveuse **washer**

un raton laveur **raccoon**

se laver les dents (se brosser les dents) **to clean/brush one's teeth**

la lessive **laundry, laundry detergent**

le lavage **washing**

le lavement **enema**

la lavette **dish mop**

la lavure **dishwater**

For more information on **agreement of past participles**, read the entries in the section on definitions of basic grammatical terms with examples on pages 35–49.

Reflexive regular **-er** verb

The Seven Simple Tenses		The Seven Compound Tenses	
Singular	Plural	Singular	Plural
1 présent de l'indicatif		**8 passé composé**	
me lave	nous lavons	me suis lavé(e)	nous sommes lavé(e)s
te laves	vous lavez	t'es lavé(e)	vous êtes lavé(e)(s)
se lave	se lavent	s'est lavé(e)	se sont lavé(e)s
2 imparfait de l'indicatif		**9 plus-que-parfait de l'indicatif**	
me lavais	nous lavions	m'étais lavé(e)	nous étions lavé(e)s
te lavais	vous laviez	t'étais lavé(e)	vous étiez lavé(e)(s)
se lavait	se lavaient	s'était lavé(e)	s'étaient lavé(e)s
3 passé simple		**10 passé antérieur**	
me lavai	nous lavâmes	me fus lavé(e)	nous fûmes lavé(e)s
te lavas	vous lavâtes	te fus lavé(e)	vous fûtes lavé(e)(s)
se lava	se lavèrent	se fut lavé(e)	se furent lavé(e)s
4 futur		**11 futur antérieur**	
me laverai	nous laverons	me serai lavé(e)	nous serons lavé(e)s
te laveras	vous laverez	te seras lavé(e)	vous serez lavé(e)(s)
se lavera	se laveront	se sera lavé(e)	se seront lavé(e)s
5 conditionnel		**12 conditionnel passé**	
me laverais	nous laverions	me serais lavé(e)	nous serions lavé(e)s
te laverais	vous laveriez	te serais lavé(e)	vous seriez lavé(e)(s)
se laverait	se laveraient	se serait lavé(e)	se seraient lavé(e)s
6 présent du subjonctif		**13 passé du subjonctif**	
me lave	nous lavions	me sois lavé(e)	nous soyons lavé(e)s
te laves	vous laviez	te sois lavé(e)	vous soyez lavé(e)(s)
se lave	se lavent	se soit lavé(e)	se soient lavé(e)s
7 imparfait du subjonctif		**14 plus-que-parfait du subjonctif**	
me lavasse	nous lavassions	me fusse lavé(e)	nous fussions lavé(e)s
te lavasses	vous lavassiez	te fusses lavé(e)	vous fussiez lavé(e)(s)
se lavât	se lavassent	se fût lavé(e)	se fussent lavé(e)s

Impératif
lave-toi; ne te lave pas
lavons-nous; ne nous lavons pas
lavez-vous; ne vous lavez pas

to lift, to raise

Regular **-er** verb; spelling change: **e** changes to **è** before syllable with mute **e**

The Seven Simple Tenses		The Seven Compound Tenses	
Singular	Plural	Singular	Plural
1 présent de l'indicatif		**8 passé composé**	
lève	**levons**	**ai levé**	**avons levé**
lèves	**levez**	**as levé**	**avez levé**
lève	**lèvent**	**a levé**	**ont levé**
2 imparfait de l'indicatif		**9 plus-que-parfait de l'indicatif**	
levais	**levions**	**avais levé**	**avions levé**
levais	**leviez**	**avais levé**	**aviez levé**
levait	**levaient**	**avait levé**	**avaient levé**
3 passé simple		**10 passé antérieur**	
levai	**levâmes**	**eus levé**	**eûmes levé**
levas	**levâtes**	**eus levé**	**eûtes levé**
leva	**levèrent**	**eut levé**	**eurent levé**
4 futur		**11 futur antérieur**	
lèverai	**lèverons**	**aurai levé**	**aurons levé**
lèveras	**lèverez**	**auras levé**	**aurez levé**
lèvera	**lèveront**	**aura levé**	**auront levé**
5 conditionnel		**12 conditionnel passé**	
lèverais	**lèverions**	**aurais levé**	**aurions levé**
lèverais	**lèveriez**	**aurais levé**	**auriez levé**
lèverait	**lèveraient**	**aurait levé**	**auraient levé**
6 présent du subjonctif		**13 passé du subjonctif**	
lève	**levions**	**aie levé**	**ayons levé**
lèves	**leviez**	**aies levé**	**ayez levé**
lève	**lèvent**	**ait levé**	**aient levé**
7 imparfait du subjonctif		**14 plus-que-parfait du subjonctif**	
levasse	**levassions**	**eusse levé**	**eussions levé**
levasses	**levassiez**	**eusses levé**	**eussiez levé**
levât	**levassent**	**eût levé**	**eussent levé**

Impératif
lève
levons
levez

Words and expressions related to this verb

voter à main levée   to vote by a show of hands
le levage   raising, lifting
faire lever qqn   to get someone out of bed
le levant   the East
le levain   leaven
du pain sans levain   unleavened bread
le lever du soleil   sunrise

se relever   to get up on one's feet
lever la main   to raise one's hand
élever   to raise, to rear, to bring up
enlever   to remove
relever   to raise again, to pick up
La séance est levée.   The meeting is adjourned.
prélever   to take a sample, to withdraw

See also **élever, enlever,** and **se lever.**

Reflexive verb; regular **-er** verb endings; spelling change: to get up
e changes to **è** before syllable with mute **e**

The Seven Simple Tenses		The Seven Compound Tenses	
Singular	Plural	Singular	Plural
1 présent de l'indicatif		8 passé composé	
me lève	nous levons	me suis levé(e)	nous sommes levé(e)s
te lèves	vous levez	t'es levé(e)	vous êtes levé(e)(s)
se lève	se lèvent	s'est levé(e)	se sont levé(e)s
2 imparfait de l'indicatif		9 plus-que-parfait de l'indicatif	
me levais	nous levions	m'étais levé(e)	nous étions levé(e)s
te levais	vous leviez	t'étais levé(e)	vous étiez levé(e)(s)
se levait	se levaient	s'était levé(e)	s'étaient levé(e)s
3 passé simple		10 passé antérieur	
me levai	nous levâmes	me fus levé(e)	nous fûmes levé(e)s
te levas	vous levâtes	te fus levé(e)	vous fûtes levé(e)(s)
se leva	se levèrent	se fut levé(e)	se furent levé(e)s
4 futur		11 futur antérieur	
me lèverai	nous lèverons	me serai levé(e)	nous serons levé(e)s
te lèveras	vous lèverez	te seras levé(e)	vous serez levé(e)(s)
se lèvera	se lèveront	se sera levé(e)	se seront levé(e)s
5 conditionnel		12 conditionnel passé	
me lèverais	nous lèverions	me serais levé(e)	nous serions levé(e)s
te lèverais	vous lèveriez	te serais levé(e)	vous seriez levé(e)(s)
se lèverait	se lèveraient	se serait levé(e)	se seraient levé(e)s
6 présent du subjonctif		13 passé du subjonctif	
me lève	nous levions	me sois levé(e)	nous soyons levé(e)s
te lèves	vous leviez	te sois levé(e)	vous soyez levé(e)(s)
se lève	se lèvent	se soit levé(e)	se soient levé(e)s
7 imparfait du subjonctif		14 plus-que-parfait du subjonctif	
me levasse	nous levassions	me fusse levé(e)	nous fussions levé(e)s
te levasses	vous levassiez	te fusses levé(e)	vous fussiez levé(e)(s)
se levât	se levassent	se fût levé(e)	se fussent levé(e)s

Impératif
lève-toi; ne te lève pas
levons-nous; ne nous levons pas
levez-vous; ne vous levez pas

Se lever is a very useful reflexive verb with a tricky spelling change.

Sentences using se lever

Caroline s'est levée après le petit déjeuner.
  Caroline got up after breakfast.

Après s'être levée, elle a quitté la maison. After
  getting up, she left the house.

Lève-toi! Il est temps de partir! Get up! It's time
  to leave!

Le soleil se lève aussi. The sun also rises.

Mon camarade de chambre est un lève-tôt. Moi,
  je fais souvent la grasse matinée. Je suis un
  lève-tard. My roommate is an early riser. As
  for me, I often sleep in. I'm a late riser.

Il faut que tu te lèves de bonne heure demain.
  You must get up early tomorrow.

Words and expressions related to this verb

le lever du soleil **sunrise**

un lève-tôt, une lève-tôt **early riser**

un lève-tard, une lève-tard **late riser**

se lever de bonne heure **to get up early**

If you can conjugate se lever you can also conjugate the following verbs:

s'élever **to rise, go up**

enlever **to remove**

relever **to raise**

se relever **to rise again (use être as auxiliary)**

élever **to raise, bring up**

soulever **to lift up**

Review the entry **agreement of past participle of a reflexive verb with its reflexive pronoun** in the section on definitions of basic grammatical terms with examples on pages 35–49.

418

The Seven Simple Tenses		The Seven Compound Tenses	
Singular	Plural	Singular	Plural
1 présent de l'indicatif		8 passé composé	
lis	**lisons**	**ai lu**	**avons lu**
lis	**lisez**	**as lu**	**avez lu**
lit	**lisent**	**a lu**	**ont lu**
2 imparfait de l'indicatif		9 plus-que-parfait de l'indicatif	
lisais	**lisions**	**avais lu**	**avions lu**
lisais	**lisiez**	**avais lu**	**aviez lu**
lisait	**lisaient**	**avait lu**	**avaient lu**
3 passé simple		10 passé antérieur	
lus	**lûmes**	**eus lu**	**eûmes lu**
lus	**lûtes**	**eus lu**	**eûtes lu**
lut	**lurent**	**eut lu**	**eurent lu**
4 futur		11 futur antérieur	
lirai	**lirons**	**aurai lu**	**aurons lu**
liras	**lirez**	**auras lu**	**aurez lu**
lira	**liront**	**aura lu**	**auront lu**
5 conditionnel		12 conditionnel passé	
lirais	**lirions**	**aurais lu**	**aurions lu**
lirais	**liriez**	**aurais lu**	**auriez lu**
lirait	**liraient**	**aurait lu**	**auraient lu**
6 présent du subjonctif		13 passé du subjonctif	
lise	**lisions**	**aie lu**	**ayons lu**
lises	**lisiez**	**aies lu**	**ayez lu**
lise	**lisent**	**ait lu**	**aient lu**
7 imparfait du subjonctif		14 plus-que-parfait du subjonctif	
lusse	**lussions**	**eusse lu**	**eussions lu**
lusses	**lussiez**	**eusses lu**	**eussiez lu**
lût	**lussent**	**eût lu**	**eussent lu**

L

Impératif
lis
lisons
lisez

AN ESSENTIAL
55 VERB

Lire

Lire is used in many everyday situations and idiomatic expressions. It is a very useful verb for a beginning French student.

Sentences using lire

C'est un livre à lire. It's a book worth reading.

Frédéric, lis la prochaine phrase dans le livre. Lis-la à haute voix. Frederick, read the next sentence in the book. Read it aloud.

Guillaume, cette composition est complètement illisible. William, this essay is completely unreadable.

Lily lit un livre dans son lit. Lily is reading a book in her bed.

Anne lisait le journal quand Marie a frappé à la porte. Anne was reading the newspaper when Marie knocked on the door.

If you can conjugate lire you can also conjugate the following verbs:

élire **to elect**

réélire **to reelect**

relire **to reread**

Words and expressions related to this verb

lisible **legible, readable**

la lisibilité **legibility**

lisiblement **legibly**

illisible **illegible**

l'illisibilité *f.* **illegibility**

lecteur, lectrice **reader (a person who reads)**

un lecteur d'épreuves, une lectrice d'épreuves **proofreader**

la lecture **reading**

le livre **book**

livres pour la jeunesse **books for young readers**

Dans l'espoir de vous lire . . . **Hoping to receive a letter from you soon . . .**

lire à haute voix **to read aloud**

lire à voix basse **to read in a low voice**

lire tout bas **to read to oneself**

le lectorat **readership**

le lutrin **lectern**

Regular **-er** verb   to praise, to rent, to rent out

The Seven Simple Tenses		The Seven Compound Tenses	
Singular	Plural	Singular	Plural
1 présent de l'indicatif		8 passé composé	
loue	louons	ai loué	avons loué
loues	louez	as loué	avez loué
loue	louent	a loué	ont loué
2 imparfait de l'indicatif		9 plus-que-parfait de l'indicatif	
louais	louions	avais loué	avions loué
louais	louiez	avais loué	aviez loué
louait	louaient	avait loué	avaient loué
3 passé simple		10 passé antérieur	
louai	louâmes	eus loué	eûmes loué
louas	louâtes	eus loué	eûtes loué
loua	louèrent	eut loué	eurent loué
4 futur		11 futur antérieur	
louerai	louerons	aurai loué	aurons loué
loueras	louerez	auras loué	aurez loué
louera	loueront	aura loué	auront loué
5 conditionnel		12 conditionnel passé	
louerais	louerions	aurais loué	aurions loué
louerais	loueriez	aurais loué	auriez loué
louerait	loueraient	aurait loué	auraient loué
6 présent du subjonctif		13 passé du subjonctif	
loue	louions	aie loué	ayons loué
loues	louiez	aies loué	ayez loué
loue	louent	ait loué	aient loué
7 imparfait du subjonctif		14 plus-que-parfait du subjonctif	
louasse	louassions	eusse loué	eussions loué
louasses	louassiez	eusses loué	eussiez loué
louât	louassent	eût loué	eussent loué

Impératif
loue
louons
louez

Words and expressions related to this verb
une place louée   reserved seat
maison à louer   house for rent (to let)
se louer de   to congratulate oneself on
allouer   to allot, to allocate
Dieu soit loué!   God be praised!
la location   rental
le loyer   rent

un loueur, une loueuse   a person who rents
   something to someone
un loueur de voitures   car rental agent
le louage   renting, hiring out
la louange   praise
le/la locataire   renter

This verb has two very different meanings because it developed from two different Latin verbs:
locāre (to lend) and **laudāre** (to praise).

The subject pronouns are found on page 103.   **421**

to reduce (one's weight), to grow thin, to lose weight   Regular **-ir** verb

The Seven Simple Tenses		The Seven Compound Tenses	
Singular	Plural	Singular	Plural
1 présent de l'indicatif		8 passé composé	
maigris	maigrissons	ai maigri	avons maigri
maigris	maigrissez	as maigri	avez maigri
maigrit	maigrissent	a maigri	ont maigri
2 imparfait de l'indicatif		9 plus-que-parfait de l'indicatif	
maigrissais	maigrissions	avais maigri	avions maigri
maigrissais	maigrissiez	avais maigri	aviez maigri
maigrissait	maigrissaient	avait maigri	avaient maigri
3 passé simple		10 passé antérieur	
maigris	maigrîmes	eus maigri	eûmes maigri
maigris	maigrîtes	eus maigri	eûtes maigri
maigrit	maigrirent	eut maigri	eurent maigri
4 futur		11 futur antérieur	
maigrirai	maigrirons	aurai maigri	aurons maigri
maigriras	maigrirez	auras maigri	aurez maigri
maigrira	maigriront	aura maigri	auront maigri
5 conditionnel		12 conditionnel passé	
maigrirais	maigririons	aurais maigri	aurions maigri
maigrirais	maigririez	aurais maigri	auriez maigri
maigrirait	maigriraient	aurait maigri	auraient maigri
6 présent du subjonctif		13 passé du subjonctif	
maigrisse	maigrissions	aie maigri	ayons maigri
maigrisses	maigrissiez	aies maigri	ayez maigri
maigrisse	maigrissent	ait maigri	aient maigri
7 imparfait du subjonctif		14 plus-que-parfait du subjonctif	
maigrisse	maigrissions	eusse maigri	eussions maigri
maigrisses	maigrissiez	eusses maigri	eussiez maigri
maigrît	maigrissent	eût maigri	eussent maigri

Impératif
maigris
maigrissons
maigrissez

Words and expressions related to this verb
maigre thin
la maigreur thinness
maigrement meagerly
se faire maigrir to slim down one's weight
être au régime pour maigrir to be on a diet
  to lose weight

s'amaigrir to lose weight
maigre comme un clou as thin as a nail
faire maigre to abstain from meat
un gamin maigrelet a skinny kid
amaigri, amaigrie gaunt
amaigrissant reducing

to eat

Regular **-er** verb endings; spelling change: retain the
ge before **a** or **o** to keep the soft **g** sound of the verb

The Seven Simple Tenses		The Seven Compound Tenses	
Singular	Plural	Singular	Plural
1 présent de l'indicatif		8 passé composé	
mange	mangeons	ai mangé	avons mangé
manges	mangez	as mangé	avez mangé
mange	mangent	a mangé	ont mangé
2 imparfait de l'indicatif		9 plus-que-parfait de l'indicatif	
mangeais	mangions	avais mangé	avions mangé
mangeais	mangiez	avais mangé	aviez mangé
mangeait	mangeaient	avait mangé	avaient mangé
3 passé simple		10 passé antérieur	
mangeai	mangeâmes	eus mangé	eûmes mangé
mangeas	mangeâtes	eus mangé	eûtes mangé
mangea	mangèrent	eut mangé	eurent mangé
4 futur		11 futur antérieur	
mangerai	mangerons	aurai mangé	aurons mangé
mangeras	mangerez	auras mangé	aurez mangé
mangera	mangeront	aura mangé	auront mangé
5 conditionnel		12 conditionnel passé	
mangerais	mangerions	aurais mangé	aurions mangé
mangerais	mangeriez	aurais mangé	auriez mangé
mangerait	mangeraient	aurait mangé	auraient mangé
6 présent du subjonctif		13 passé du subjonctif	
mange	mangions	aie mangé	ayons mangé
manges	mangiez	aies mangé	ayez mangé
mange	mangent	ait mangé	aient mangé
7 imparfait du subjonctif		14 plus-que-parfait du subjonctif	
mangeasse	mangeassions	eusse mangé	eussions mangé
mangeasses	mangeassiez	eusses mangé	eussiez mangé
mangeât	mangeassent	eût mangé	eussent mangé

M

Impératif
mange
mangeons
mangez

AN ESSENTIAL
55 VERB

Manger is an essential verb for beginning French students because it has an important spelling change that also appears in several other verbs. You must keep the e after the g in order to retain the soft sound of g in the infinitive.

Sentences using manger

Y a-t-il de quoi manger? Is there something to eat?

Avez-vous quelque chose pour une démangeaison? Do you have something for an itch?

Dis-moi ce que tu manges, je te dirai ce que tu es. (Brillat-Savarin) Tell me what you eat, I'll tell you what you are.

Il faut manger pour vivre, et non pas vivre pour manger. (Molière) It is necessary to eat to live, and not to live to eat.

Proverbs

L'appétit vient en mangeant. **The more you have, the more you want. (Literally: Appetite comes while eating.)**

Les loups ne se mangent pas entre eux. **Wolves do not eat each other.**

Words and expressions related to this verb

la salle à manger **dining room**

une démangeaison **itch**

de quoi manger **something to eat**

le manger **food**

gros mangeur **big eater**

manger de l'argent **to spend money foolishly**

ne pas manger à sa faim **not to have much to eat**

manger à sa faim **to eat until filled**

manger comme quatre **to eat like a horse**

une mangeoire **manger**

mangeable **edible, eatable**

la mangeaille **disgusting food**

immangeable **inedible**

manger comme un oiseau **to eat like a bird**

If you can conjugate manger you can also conjugate the following verbs:

allonger **to lengthen**

démanger **to itch**

déménager **to move**

échanger **to exchange**

engranger **to gather, store**

mélanger **to mix**

The Seven Simple Tenses		The Seven Compound Tenses	
Singular	Plural	Singular	Plural
1 présent de l'indicatif		**8 passé composé**	
manque	manquons	ai manqué	avons manqué
manques	manquez	as manqué	avez manqué
manque	manquent	a manqué	ont manqué
2 imparfait de l'indicatif		**9 plus-que-parfait de l'indicatif**	
manquais	manquions	avais manqué	avions manqué
manquais	manquiez	avais manqué	aviez manqué
manquait	manquaient	avait manqué	avaient manqué
3 passé simple		**10 passé antérieur**	
manquai	manquâmes	eus manqué	eûmes manqué
manquas	manquâtes	eus manqué	eûtes manqué
manqua	manquèrent	eut manqué	eurent manqué
4 futur		**11 futur antérieur**	
manquerai	manquerons	aurai manqué	aurons manqué
manqueras	manquerez	auras manqué	aurez manqué
manquera	manqueront	aura manqué	auront manqué
5 conditionnel		**12 conditionnel passé**	
manquerais	manquerions	aurais manqué	aurions manqué
manquerais	manqueriez	aurais manqué	auriez manqué
manquerait	manqueraient	aurait manqué	auraient manqué
6 présent du subjonctif		**13 passé du subjonctif**	
manque	manquions	aie manqué	ayons manqué
manques	manquiez	aies manqué	ayez manqué
manque	manquent	ait manqué	aient manqué
7 imparfait du subjonctif		**14 plus-que-parfait du subjonctif**	
manquasse	manquassions	eusse manqué	eussions manqué
manquasses	manquassiez	eusses manqué	eussiez manqué
manquât	manquassent	eût manqué	eussent manqué

M

Impératif
manque
manquons
manquez

Common idiomatic expressions using this verb

manquer à   to lack;   Le courage lui manque   He lacks courage.

Elle me manque.   I miss her.

Est-ce que je te manque?   Do you miss me?

manquer de qqch   to be lacking something;   manquer de sucre   to be out of sugar

Ne manquez pas de venir.   Don't fail to come.

un mariage manqué   a broken engagement

un héros manqué   a would-be hero

Il me manque un euro   I am lacking (I need) one euro.

manquer de + inf.   to fail to, to almost do something

J'ai manqué de tomber.   I almost fell.

Paul a manqué de venir.   Paul failed to come.

manquer à sa parole   to go back on one's word

The subject pronouns are found on page 103.   **425**

to walk, to march, to run (machine), to function

Regular **-er** verb

The Seven Simple Tenses		The Seven Compound Tenses	
Singular	Plural	Singular	Plural
1 présent de l'indicatif		8 passé composé	
marche	**marchons**	**ai marché**	**avons marché**
marches	**marchez**	**as marché**	**avez marché**
marche	**marchent**	**a marché**	**ont marché**
2 imparfait de l'indicatif		9 plus-que-parfait de l'indicatif	
marchais	**marchions**	**avais marché**	**avions marché**
marchais	**marchiez**	**avais marché**	**aviez marché**
marchait	**marchaient**	**avait marché**	**avaient marché**
3 passé simple		10 passé antérieur	
marchai	**marchâmes**	**eus marché**	**eûmes marché**
marchas	**marchâtes**	**eus marché**	**eûtes marché**
marcha	**marchèrent**	**eut marché**	**eurent marché**
4 futur		11 futur antérieur	
marcherai	**marcherons**	**aurai marché**	**aurons marché**
marcheras	**marcherez**	**auras marché**	**aurez marché**
marchera	**marcheront**	**aura marché**	**auront marché**
5 conditionnel		12 conditionnel passé	
marcherais	**marcherions**	**aurais marché**	**aurions marché**
marcherais	**marcheriez**	**aurais marché**	**auriez marché**
marcherait	**marcheraient**	**aurait marché**	**auraient marché**
6 présent du subjonctif		13 passé du subjonctif	
marche	**marchions**	**aie marché**	**ayons marché**
marches	**marchiez**	**aies marché**	**ayez marché**
marche	**marchent**	**ait marché**	**aient marché**
7 imparfait du subjonctif		14 plus-que-parfait du subjonctif	
marchasse	**marchassions**	**eusse marché**	**eussions marché**
marchasses	**marchassiez**	**eusses marché**	**eussiez marché**
marchât	**marchassent**	**eût marché**	**eussent marché**

Impératif
marche
marchons
marchez

Words and expressions related to this verb
la marche march, walking
ralentir sa marche to slow down one's pace
le marché market
le marché aux fleurs flower market
le marché aux puces flea market
à bon marché cheap
faire marcher qqn to put someone on
une démarche gait, walk

faire une démarche to take a step
marcher bien to function (go, run, work) well
marcher sur les pas de qqn to follow in someone's footsteps
faire marcher qqch to make something go (run, function)
Ça ne marche plus. It's out of order.
la course et la marche running and walking

The Seven Simple Tenses		The Seven Compound Tenses	
Singular	Plural	Singular	Plural
1 présent de l'indicatif		**8 passé composé**	
maudis	maudissons	ai maudit	avons maudit
maudis	maudissez	as maudit	avez maudit
maudit	maudissent	a maudit	ont maudit
2 imparfait de l'indicatif		**9 plus-que-parfait de l'indicatif**	
maudissais	maudissions	avais maudit	avions maudit
maudissais	maudissiez	avais maudit	aviez maudit
maudissait	maudissaient	avait maudit	avaient maudit
3 passé simple		**10 passé antérieur**	
maudis	maudîmes	eus maudit	eûmes maudit
maudis	maudîtes	eus maudit	eûtes maudit
maudit	maudirent	eut maudit	eurent maudit
4 futur		**11 futur antérieur**	
maudirai	maudirons	aurai maudit	aurons maudit
maudiras	maudirez	auras maudit	aurez maudit
maudira	maudiront	aura maudit	auront maudit
5 conditionnel		**12 conditionnel passé**	
maudirais	maudirions	aurais maudit	aurions maudit
maudirais	maudiriez	aurais maudit	auriez maudit
maudirait	maudiraient	aurait maudit	auraient maudit
6 présent du subjonctif		**13 passé du subjonctif**	
maudisse	maudissions	aie maudit	ayons maudit
maudisses	maudissiez	aies maudit	ayez maudit
maudisse	maudissent	ait maudit	aient maudit
7 imparfait du subjonctif		**14 plus-que-parfait du subjonctif**	
maudisse	maudissions	eusse maudit	eussions maudit
maudisses	maudissiez	eusses maudit	eussiez maudit
maudît	maudissent	eût maudit	eussent maudit

M

Impératif
maudis
maudissons
maudissez

Words and expressions related to this verb
maudit, maudite   cursed
Quel maudit temps!   What rotten weather!
maudire un ennemi   to curse an enemy
les maudits   the damned

le Maudit   Demon
dire   to say, to tell; dire du mal de qqn   to
   say something evil about someone

Careful! Although **maudire** looks like it should be conjugated like **dire**, it is conjugated like a
regular **-ir** verb—and its past participle has a **t** added to it: **maudit**.

to misjudge, to misunderstand, not to know, not to recognize   Irregular verb

The Seven Simple Tenses		The Seven Compound Tenses	
Singular	Plural	Singular	Plural
1 présent de l'indicatif		8 passé composé	
méconnais	méconnaissons	ai méconnu	avons méconnu
méconnais	méconnaissez	as méconnu	avez méconnu
méconnaît	méconnaissent	a méconnu	ont méconnu
2 imparfait de l'indicatif		9 plus-que-parfait de l'indicatif	
méconnaissais	méconnaissions	avais méconnu	avions méconnu
méconnaissais	méconnaissiez	avais méconnu	aviez méconnu
méconnaissait	méconnaissaient	avait méconnu	avaient méconnu
3 passé simple		10 passé antérieur	
méconnus	méconnûmes	eus méconnu	eûmes méconnu
méconnus	méconnûtes	eus méconnu	eûtes méconnu
méconnut	méconnurent	eut méconnu	eurent méconnu
4 futur		11 futur antérieur	
méconnaîtrai	méconnaîtrons	aurai méconnu	aurons méconnu
méconnaîtras	méconnaîtrez	auras méconnu	aurez méconnu
méconnaîtra	méconnaîtront	aura méconnu	auront méconnu
5 conditionnel		12 conditionnel passé	
méconnaîtrais	méconnaîtrions	aurais méconnu	aurions méconnu
méconnaîtrais	méconnaîtriez	aurais méconnu	auriez méconnu
méconnaîtrait	méconnaîtraient	aurait méconnu	auraient méconnu
6 présent du subjonctif		13 passé du subjonctif	
méconnaisse	méconnaissions	aie méconnu	ayons méconnu
méconnaisses	méconnaissiez	aies méconnu	ayez méconnu
méconnaisse	méconnaissent	ait méconnu	aient méconnu
7 imparfait du subjonctif		14 plus-que-parfait du subjonctif	
méconnusse	méconnussions	eusse méconnu	eussions méconnu
méconnusses	méconnussiez	eusses méconnu	eussiez méconnu
méconnût	méconnussent	eût méconnu	eussent méconnu

Impératif
méconnais
méconnaissons
méconnaissez

Words related to this verb
méconnaissable unrecognizable
méconnu, méconnue misunderstood

la méconnaissance misappreciation
se méconnaître to underrate (underestimate) oneself

See also **connaître** and **reconnaître**.

Can't remember the French verb you need? Check the back pages of this book for the English-French verb index!

The Seven Simple Tenses		The Seven Compound Tenses	
Singular	Plural	Singular	Plural
1 présent de l'indicatif		8 passé composé	
médis	**médisons**	**ai médit**	**avons médit**
médis	**médisez**	**as médit**	**avez médit**
médit	**médisent**	**a médit**	**ont médit**
2 imparfait de l'indicatif		9 plus-que-parfait de l'indicatif	
médisais	**médisions**	**avais médit**	**avions médit**
médisais	**médisiez**	**avais médit**	**aviez médit**
médisait	**médisaient**	**avait médit**	**avaient médit**
3 passé simple		10 passé antérieur	
médis	**médîmes**	**eus médit**	**eûmes médit**
médis	**médîtes**	**eus médit**	**eûtes médit**
médit	**médirent**	**eut médit**	**eurent médit**
4 futur		11 futur antérieur	
médirai	**médirons**	**aurai médit**	**aurons médit**
médiras	**médirez**	**auras médit**	**aurez médit**
médira	**médiront**	**aura médit**	**auront médit**
5 conditionnel		12 conditionnel passé	
médirais	**médirions**	**aurais médit**	**aurions médit**
médirais	**médiriez**	**aurais médit**	**auriez médit**
médirait	**médiraient**	**aurait médit**	**auraient médit**
6 présent du subjonctif		13 passé du subjonctif	
médise	**médisions**	**aie médit**	**ayons médit**
médises	**médisiez**	**aies médit**	**ayez médit**
médise	**médisent**	**ait médit**	**aient médit**
7 imparfait du subjonctif		14 plus-que-parfait du subjonctif	
médisse	**médissions**	**eusse médit**	**eussions médit**
médisses	**médissiez**	**eusses médit**	**eussiez médit**
médît	**médissent**	**eût médit**	**eussent médit**

M

Impératif
médis
médisons
médisez

Words and expressions related to this verb
la médisance   slander
dire des médisances   to say scandalous things

un médisant, une médisante   slanderer
médire de   to speak ill of, to slander

See also **contredire, dire, interdire, maudire,** and **prédire.**

Careful! Although **médire** is conjugated like **dire**, the present tense **vous** form is **médisez** and the imperative for **vous** is: **médisez**.

The subject pronouns are found on page 103.
                                                                   429

to beware, to distrust, to mistrust

Reflexive regular **-er** verb

The Seven Simple Tenses		The Seven Compound Tenses	
Singular	Plural	Singular	Plural
1 présent de l'indicatif		8 passé composé	
me méfie	nous méfions	me suis méfié(e)	nous sommes méfié(e)s
te méfies	vous méfiez	t'es méfié(e)	vous êtes méfié(e)(s)
se méfie	se méfient	s'est méfié(e)	se sont méfié(e)s
2 imparfait de l'indicatif		9 plus-que-parfait de l'indicatif	
me méfiais	nous méfiions	m'étais méfié(e)	nous étions méfié(e)s
te méfiais	vous méfiiez	t'étais méfié(e)	vous étiez méfié(e)(s)
se méfiait	se méfiaient	s'était méfié(e)	s'étaient méfié(e)s
3 passé simple		10 passé antérieur	
me méfiai	nous méfiâmes	me fus méfié(e)	nous fûmes méfié(e)s
te méfias	vous méfiâtes	te fus méfié(e)	vous fûtes méfié(e)(s)
se méfia	se méfièrent	se fut méfié(e)	se furent méfié(e)s
4 futur		11 futur antérieur	
me méfierai	nous méfierons	me serai méfié(e)	nous serons méfié(e)s
te méfieras	vous méfierez	te seras méfié(e)	vous serez méfié(e)(s)
se méfiera	se méfieront	se sera méfié(e)	se seront méfié(e)s
5 conditionnel		12 conditionnel passé	
me méfierais	nous méfierions	me serais méfié(e)	nous serions méfié(e)s
te méfierais	vous méfieriez	te serais méfié(e)	vous seriez méfié(e)(s)
se méfierait	se méfieraient	se serait méfié(e)	se seraient méfié(e)s
6 présent du subjonctif		13 passé du subjonctif	
me méfie	nous méfiions	me sois méfié(e)	nous soyons méfié(e)s
te méfies	vous méfiiez	te sois méfié(e)	vous soyez méfié(e)(s)
se méfie	se méfient	se soit méfié(e)	se soient méfié(e)s
7 imparfait du subjonctif		14 plus-que-parfait du subjonctif	
me méfiasse	nous méfiassions	me fusse méfié(e)	nous fussions méfié(e)s
te méfiasses	vous méfiassiez	te fusses méfié(e)	vous fussiez méfié(e)(s)
se méfiât	se méfiassent	se fût méfié(e)	se fussent méfié(e)s

Impératif
méfie-toi; ne te méfie pas
méfions-nous; ne nous méfions pas
méfiez-vous; ne vous méfiez pas

Words and expressions related to this verb
se méfier de   to distrust, to mistrust
Méfiez-vous!   Watch out!
méfiant, méfiante   distrustful
la méfiance   distrust, mistrust
un méfait   misdeed, wrongdoing
Il faut vous méfier.   You must be careful.

être sans méfiance   to be completely trusting
Méfiez-vous de lui (d'elle).   Do not trust him (her).
avoir de la méfiance envers quelqu'un   to distrust someone

It's important that you be familiar with the Subjunctive. See pages 26–31.

Regular **-er** verb; spelling change: **e** changes
to **è** before syllable with mute **e**   to lead, to control

The Seven Simple Tenses		The Seven Compound Tenses	
Singular	Plural	Singular	Plural
1 présent de l'indicatif		**8 passé composé**	
mène	**menons**	**ai mené**	**avons mené**
mènes	**menez**	**as mené**	**avez mené**
mène	**mènent**	**a mené**	**ont mené**
2 imparfait de l'indicatif		**9 plus-que-parfait de l'indicatif**	
menais	**menions**	**avais mené**	**avions mené**
menais	**meniez**	**avais mené**	**aviez mené**
menait	**menaient**	**avait mené**	**avaient mené**
3 passé simple		**10 passé antérieur**	
menai	**menâmes**	**eus mené**	**eûmes mené**
menas	**menâtes**	**eus mené**	**eûtes mené**
mena	**menèrent**	**eut mené**	**eurent mené**
4 futur		**11 futur antérieur**	
mènerai	**mènerons**	**aurai mené**	**aurons mené**
mèneras	**mènerez**	**auras mené**	**aurez mené**
mènera	**mèneront**	**aura mené**	**auront mené**
5 conditionnel		**12 conditionnel passé**	
mènerais	**mènerions**	**aurais mené**	**aurions mené**
mènerais	**mèneriez**	**aurais mené**	**auriez mené**
mènerait	**mèneraient**	**aurait mené**	**auraient mené**
6 présent du subjonctif		**13 passé du subjonctif**	
mène	**menions**	**aie mené**	**ayons mené**
mènes	**meniez**	**aies mené**	**ayez mené**
mène	**mènent**	**ait mené**	**aient mené**
7 imparfait du subjonctif		**14 plus-que-parfait du subjonctif**	
menasse	**menassions**	**eusse mené**	**eussions mené**
menasses	**menassiez**	**eusses mené**	**eussiez mené**
menât	**menassent**	**eût mené**	**eussent mené**

M

Impératif
mène
menons
menez

Words and expressions related to this verb
un meneur, une meneuse   leader
Cela ne mène à rien.   That leads to nothing.
mener qqn par le bout du nez   to lead someone around by the nose
mener une vie vagabonde   to lead a vagabond life
mener tout le monde   to be bossy with everyone
mener la bande   to lead the group
Cela vous mènera loin.   That will take you a long way.
malmener   to bully

See also **amener**, **emmener**, and **promener**.

The subject pronouns are found on page 103.
                                          431

to lie, to tell a lie

The Seven Simple Tenses		The Seven Compound Tenses	
Singular	Plural	Singular	Plural

1   présent de l'indicatif

mens	mentons	**8 passé composé**	
mens	mentez	ai menti	avons menti
ment	mentent	as menti	avez menti
		a menti	ont menti

2   imparfait de l'indicatif

mentais	mentions	**9 plus-que-parfait de l'indicatif**	
mentais	mentiez	avais menti	avions menti
mentait	mentaient	avais menti	aviez menti
		avait menti	avaient menti

3   passé simple

mentis	mentîmes	**10 passé antérieur**	
mentis	mentîtes	eus menti	eûmes menti
mentit	mentirent	eus menti	eûtes menti
		eut menti	eurent menti

4   futur

mentirai	mentirons	**11 futur antérieur**	
mentiras	mentirez	aurai menti	aurons menti
mentira	mentiront	auras menti	aurez menti
		aura menti	auront menti

5   conditionnel

mentirais	mentirions	**12 conditionnel passé**	
mentirais	mentiriez	aurais menti	aurions menti
mentirait	mentiraient	aurais menti	auriez menti
		aurait menti	auraient menti

6   présent du subjonctif

mente	mentions	**13 passé du subjonctif**	
mentes	mentiez	aie menti	ayons menti
mente	mentent	aies menti	ayez menti
		ait menti	aient menti

7   imparfait du subjonctif

mentisse	mentissions	**14 plus-que-parfait du subjonctif**	
mentisses	mentissiez	eusse menti	eussions menti
mentît	mentissent	eusses menti	eussiez menti
		eût menti	eussent menti

Impératif
mens
mentons
mentez

Words and expressions related to this verb

un mensonge   a lie
dire des mensonges   to tell lies
un menteur, une menteuse   a liar
Elle vit dans le mensonge.   Her whole life is
a lie.

Ce sont des mensonges.   It's all a pack of lies.
Tu mens!   You're a liar!
sans mentir   quite honestly
démentir   to belie, to deny, to falsify, to refute
une menterie   fib

How are you doing? Find out with the verb drills and tests with answers explained on pages 50–101.

Reflexive irregular verb

to be mistaken, to mistake

The Seven Simple Tenses		The Seven Compound Tenses	
Singular	Plural	Singular	Plural
1 présent de l'indicatif		8 passé composé	
me méprends	**nous méprenons**	**me suis mépris(e)**	**nous sommes mépris(es)**
te méprends	**vous méprenez**	**t'es mépris(e)**	**vous êtes mépris(e)(es)**
se méprend	**se méprennent**	**s'est mépris(e)**	**se sont mépris(es)**
2 imparfait de l'indicatif		9 plus-que-parfait de l'indicatif	
me méprenais	**nous méprenions**	**m'étais mépris(e)**	**nous étions mépris(es)**
te méprenais	**vous mépreniez**	**t'étais mépris(e)**	**vous étiez mépris(e)(es)**
se méprenait	**se méprenaient**	**s'était mépris(e)**	**s'étaient mépris(es)**
3 passé simple		10 passé antérieur	
me mépris	**nous méprîmes**	**me fus mépris(e)**	**nous fûmes mépris(es)**
te mépris	**vous méprîtes**	**te fus mépris(e)**	**vous fûtes mépris(e)(es)**
se méprit	**se méprirent**	**se fut mépris(e)**	**se furent mépris(es)**
4 futur		11 futur antérieur	
me méprendrai	**nous méprendrons**	**me serai mépris(e)**	**nous serons mépris(es)**
te méprendras	**vous méprendrez**	**te seras mépris(e)**	**vous serez mépris(e)(es)**
se méprendra	**se méprendront**	**se sera mépris(e)**	**se seront mépris(es)**
5 conditionnel		12 conditionnel passé	
me méprendrais	**nous méprendrions**	**me serais mépris(e)**	**nous serions mépris(es)**
te méprendrais	**vous méprendriez**	**te serais mépris(e)**	**vous seriez mépris(e)(es)**
se méprendrait	**se méprendraient**	**se serait mépris(e)**	**se seraient mépris(es)**
6 présent du subjonctif		13 passé du subjonctif	
me méprenne	**nous méprenions**	**me sois mépris(e)**	**nous soyons mépris(es)**
te méprennes	**vous mépreniez**	**te sois mépris(e)**	**vous soyez mépris(e)(es)**
se méprenne	**se méprennent**	**se soit mépris(e)**	**se soient mépris(es)**
7 imparfait du subjonctif		14 plus-que-parfait du subjonctif	
me méprisse	**nous méprissions**	**me fusse mépris(e)**	**nous fussions mépris(es)**
te méprisses	**vous méprissiez**	**te fusses mépris(e)**	**vous fussiez mépris(e)(es)**
se méprît	**se méprissent**	**se fût mépris(e)**	**se fussent mépris(es)**

M

Impératif
méprends-toi; ne te méprends pas
méprenons-nous; ne nous méprenons pas
méprenez-vous; ne vous méprenez pas

Common idiomatic expressions using this verb
se méprendre sur qqn   to be mistaken about someone; to take someone for someone else

se méprendre au sujet de qqch   to be mistaken about something; to take something for something else

See also apprendre, comprendre, entreprendre, prendre, reprendre, and surprendre.

Can't remember the French verb you need? Check the back pages of this book for the English-French verb index!

The Seven Simple Tenses		The Seven Compound Tenses	
Singular	Plural	Singular	Plural
1 présent de l'indicatif		**8 passé composé**	
mérite	méritons	ai mérité	avons mérité
mérites	méritez	as mérité	avez mérité
mérite	méritent	a mérité	ont mérité
2 imparfait de l'indicatif		**9 plus-que-parfait de l'indicatif**	
méritais	méritions	avais mérité	avions mérité
méritais	méritiez	avais mérité	aviez mérité
méritait	méritaient	avait mérité	avaient mérité
3 passé simple		**10 passé antérieur**	
méritai	méritâmes	eus mérité	eûmes mérité
méritas	méritâtes	eus mérité	eûtes mérité
mérita	méritèrent	eut mérité	eurent mérité
4 futur		**11 futur antérieur**	
mériterai	mériterons	aurai mérité	aurons mérité
mériteras	mériterez	auras mérité	aurez mérité
méritera	mériteront	aura mérité	auront mérité
5 conditionnel		**12 conditionnel passé**	
mériterais	mériterions	aurais mérité	aurions mérité
mériterais	mériteriez	aurais mérité	auriez mérité
mériterait	mériteraient	aurait mérité	auraient mérité
6 présent du subjonctif		**13 passé du subjonctif**	
mérite	méritions	aie mérité	ayons mérité
mérites	méritiez	aies mérité	ayez mérité
mérite	méritent	ait mérité	aient mérité
7 imparfait du subjonctif		**14 plus-que-parfait du subjonctif**	
méritasse	méritassions	eusse mérité	eussions mérité
méritasses	méritassiez	eusses mérité	eussiez mérité
méritât	méritassent	eût mérité	eussent mérité

Impératif
mérite
méritons
méritez

Words and expressions related to this verb
un mérite   merit, worthiness
méritant, méritante   deserving (person)
une femme de mérite, un homme de mérite
  a woman, a man of merit

méritoire   meritorious, commendable,
  deserving (things, acts, deeds)
sans mérite   undeserving

Don't forget to study the section on defective and impersonal verbs. It's right after this main list.

Irregular verb   to put, to place, to put on (clothing)

The Seven Simple Tenses		The Seven Compound Tenses	
Singular	Plural	Singular	Plural
1 présent de l'indicatif		**8 passé composé**	
mets	mettons	ai mis	avons mis
mets	mettez	as mis	avez mis
met	mettent	a mis	ont mis
2 imparfait de l'indicatif		**9 plus-que-parfait de l'indicatif**	
mettais	mettions	avais mis	avions mis
mettais	mettiez	avais mis	aviez mis
mettait	mettaient	avait mis	avaient mis
3 passé simple		**10 passé antérieur**	
mis	mîmes	eus mis	eûmes mis
mis	mîtes	eus mis	eûtes mis
mit	mirent	eut mis	eurent mis
4 futur		**11 futur antérieur**	
mettrai	mettrons	aurai mis	aurons mis
mettras	mettrez	auras mis	aurez mis
mettra	mettront	aura mis	auront mis
5 conditionnel		**12 conditionnel passé**	
mettrais	mettrions	aurais mis	aurions mis
mettrais	mettriez	aurais mis	auriez mis
mettrait	mettraient	aurait mis	auraient mis
6 présent du subjonctif		**13 passé du subjonctif**	
mette	mettions	aie mis	ayons mis
mettes	mettiez	aies mis	ayez mis
mette	mettent	ait mis	aient mis
7 imparfait du subjonctif		**14 plus-que-parfait du subjonctif**	
misse	missions	eusse mis	eussions mis
misses	missiez	eusses mis	eussiez mis
mît	missent	eût mis	eussent mis

M

Impératif
mets
mettons
mettez

AN ESSENTIAL
55 VERB

Mettre and se mettre

Mettre and se mettre are a very useful pair of French verbs because there are many expressions related to them. Pay special attention to the differences between these two verbs.

Sentences using mettre

Mimi a mis ses souliers blancs. Mimi put on her white shoes.

Roger était si fâché contre Julie qu'il a mis sa lettre en morceaux. Roger was so angry at Julie that he tore her letter to pieces.

Mme Petrie n'était pas contente parce que Paul avait mis douze ans pour finir ses études. Mrs. Petrie was not pleased because Paul had taken twelve years to finish his studies.

Ne remets pas à demain ce que tu peux faire après-demain. (Alphonse Allais) Don't put off until tomorrow what you can do the day after tomorrow.

M. Dupont a mis la table et a annoncé: Venez, tout le monde; mettez-vous à table! Mr. Dupont set the table and announced: Come, everybody; sit down at the table!

Proverb

Il ne faut pas se mettre à l'eau de peur de la pluie. **One shouldn't jump in the water out of fear of the rain.**

Words and expressions related to these verbs

mettre la table **to set the table**

mettre le couvert **to set the table**

mettre de côté **to lay aside, to save**

mettre en cause **to question**

mettre qqn à la porte **to kick somebody out (the door)**

mettre au courant (de) **to inform (about)**

mettre au point **to make clear**

mettre en pièces **to tear to pieces, to break into pieces**

mettre en scène **to stage**

un metteur en scène **director of a film**

mettre la télé **to turn on the TV**

mettre la radio **to turn on the radio**

mettre à la poste **to mail, post**

mettre fin à qqch **to put an end to something**

se mettre à + inf. **to begin, to start + inf.**

se mettre à table **to go sit at the table**

se mettre en colère **to get angry**

se mettre en grande toilette **to dress for an occasion**

se mettre en smoking **to put on a dinner jacket**

Can't remember the French verb you need? Check the back pages of this book for the English-French verb index!

Reflexive irregular verb

to begin, to start, to place oneself

The Seven Simple Tenses		The Seven Compound Tenses	
Singular	Plural	Singular	Plural

1 présent de l'indicatif

me mets	nous mettons		
te mets	vous mettez		
se met	se mettent		

8 passé composé

me suis mis(e)	nous sommes mis(es)
t'es mis(e)	vous êtes mis(e)(es)
s'est mis(e)	se sont mis(es)

2 imparfait de l'indicatif

me mettais	nous mettions
te mettais	vous mettiez
se mettait	se mettaient

9 plus-que-parfait de l'indicatif

m'étais mis(e)	nous étions mis(es)
t'étais mis(e)	vous étiez mis(e)(es)
s'était mis(e)	s'étaient mis(es)

3 passé simple

me mis	nous mîmes
te mis	vous mîtes
se mit	se mirent

10 passé antérieur

me fus mis(e)	nous fûmes mis(es)
te fus mis(e)	vous fûtes mis(e)(es)
se fut mis(e)	se furent mis(es)

4 futur

me mettrai	nous mettrons
te mettras	vous mettrez
se mettra	se mettront

11 futur antérieur

me serai mis(e)	nous serons mis(es)
te seras mis(e)	vous serez mis(e)(es)
se sera mis(e)	se seront mis(es)

5 conditionnel

me mettrais	nous mettrions
te mettrais	vous mettriez
se mettrait	se mettraient

12 conditionnel passé

me serais mis(e)	nous serions mis(es)
te serais mis(e)	vous seriez mis(e)(es)
se serait mis(e)	se seraient mis(es)

6 présent du subjonctif

me mette	nous mettions
te mettes	vous mettiez
se mette	se mettent

13 passé du subjonctif

me sois mis(e)	nous soyons mis(es)
te sois mis(e)	vous soyez mis(e)(es)
se soit mis(e)	se soient mis(es)

7 imparfait du subjonctif

me misse	nous missions
te misses	vous missiez
se mît	se missent

14 plus-que-parfait du subjonctif

me fusse mis(e)	nous fussions mis(es)
te fusses mis(e)	vous fussiez mis(e)(es)
se fût mis(e)	se fussent mis(es)

Impératif
mets-toi; ne te mets pas
mettons-nous; ne nous mettons pas
mettez-vous; ne vous mettez pas

See also admettre, commetre, mettre, omettre, permettre, promettre, soumettre, and transmettre.

AN ESSENTIAL
55 VERB

to mirror

The Seven Simple Tenses		The Seven Compound Tenses	
Singular	Plural	Singular	Plural
1 présent de l'indicatif		**8 passé composé**	
mire	**mirons**	**ai miré**	**avons miré**
mires	**mirez**	**as miré**	**avez miré**
mire	**mirent**	**a miré**	**ont miré**
2 imparfait de l'indicatif		**9 plus-que-parfait de l'indicatif**	
mirais	**mirions**	**avais miré**	**avions miré**
mirais	**miriez**	**avais miré**	**aviez miré**
mirait	**miraient**	**avait miré**	**avaient miré**
3 passé simple		**10 passé antérieur**	
mirai	**mirâmes**	**eus miré**	**eûmes miré**
miras	**mirâtes**	**eus miré**	**eûtes miré**
mira	**mirèrent**	**eut miré**	**eurent miré**
4 futur		**11 futur antérieur**	
mirerai	**mirerons**	**aurai miré**	**aurons miré**
mireras	**mirerez**	**auras miré**	**aurez miré**
mirera	**mireront**	**aura miré**	**auront miré**
5 conditionnel		**12 conditionnel passé**	
mirerais	**mirerions**	**aurais miré**	**aurions miré**
mirerais	**mireriez**	**aurais miré**	**auriez miré**
mirerait	**mireraient**	**aurait miré**	**auraient miré**
6 présent du subjonctif		**13 passé du subjonctif**	
mire	**mirions**	**aie miré**	**ayons miré**
mires	**miriez**	**aies miré**	**ayez miré**
mire	**mirent**	**ait miré**	**aient miré**
7 imparfait du subjonctif		**14 plus-que-parfait du subjonctif**	
mirasse	**mirassions**	**eusse miré**	**eussions miré**
mirasses	**mirassiez**	**eusses miré**	**eussiez miré**
mirât	**mirassent**	**eût miré**	**eussent miré**

	Impératif
	mire
	mirons
	mirez

Words and expressions related to this verb

la mire aim, aiming; **point de mire** point aimed at; **prendre sa mire (viser)** to take aim

le mirage mirage; illusion
un miroir mirror

miroiter to gleam, glisten, sparkle
se mirer dans to look at oneself in (a mirror, a pool of water, a shiny surface)
admirer to admire

See also **admirer.**

Soak up some verbs used in weather expressions. There's a list in the Appendixes!

438

Regular **-er** verb endings; spelling change:
e changes to **è** before syllable with mute **e**

to model, to shape

The Seven Simple Tenses | The Seven Compound Tenses

Singular	Plural	Singular	Plural
1 présent de l'indicatif		**8 passé composé**	
modèle	modelons	ai modelé	avons modelé
modèles	modelez	as modelé	avez modelé
modèle	modèlent	a modelé	ont modelé
2 imparfait de l'indicatif		**9 plus-que-parfait de l'indicatif**	
modelais	modelions	avais modelé	avions modelé
modelais	modeliez	avais modelé	aviez modelé
modelait	modelaient	avait modelé	avaient modelé
3 passé simple		**10 passé antérieur**	
modelai	modelâmes	eus modelé	eûmes modelé
modelas	modelâtes	eus modelé	eûtes modelé
modela	modelèrent	eut modelé	eurent modelé
4 futur		**11 futur antérieur**	
modèlerai	modèlerons	aurai modelé	aurons modelé
modèleras	modèlerez	auras modelé	aurez modelé
modèlera	modèleront	aura modelé	auront modelé
5 conditionnel		**12 conditionnel passé**	
modèlerais	modèlerions	aurais modelé	aurions modelé
modèlerais	modèleriez	aurais modelé	auriez modelé
modèlerait	modèleraient	aurait modelé	auraient modelé
6 présent du subjonctif		**13 passé du subjonctif**	
modèle	modelions	aie modelé	ayons modelé
modèles	modeliez	aies modelé	ayez modelé
modèle	modèlent	ait modelé	aient modelé
7 imparfait du subjonctif		**14 plus-que-parfait du subjonctif**	
modelasse	modelassions	eusse modelé	eussions modelé
modelasses	modelassiez	eusses modelé	eussiez modelé
modelât	modelassent	eût modelé	eussent modelé

M

Impératif
modèle
modelons
modelez

Sentences using this verb

J'aime bien ta voiture, mais le nouveau modèle est plus économique.   I like your car, but the new model is more economical.

La ville de Washington est modelée sur la ville de Paris.   Washington, D.C., is modeled after the city of Paris.

Words and expressions related to this verb

le modelage   modeling
le modèle   model, example
un mannequin   fashion model
un modèle réduit   scale model
la pâte à modeler   modeling clay
se modeler sur   to model oneself on
un modéliste, une modéliste   model maker

Don't forget to study the section on defective and impersonal verbs. It's right after this main list.

The subject pronouns are found on page 103.

to go up, to ascend, to take up, to bring up, to mount

Regular **-er** verb

The Seven Simple Tenses		The Seven Compound Tenses	
Singular	Plural	Singular	Plural
1 présent de l'indicatif		**8 passé composé**	
monte	montons	suis monté(e)	sommes monté(e)s
montes	montez	es monté(e)	êtes monté(e)(s)
monte	montent	est monté(e)	sont monté(e)s
2 imparfait de l'indicatif		**9 plus-que-parfait de l'indicatif**	
montais	montions	étais monté(e)	étions monté(e)s
montais	montiez	étais monté(e)	étiez monté(e)(s)
montait	montaient	était monté(e)	étaient monté(e)s
3 passé simple		**10 passé antérieur**	
montai	montâmes	fus monté(e)	fûmes monté(e)s
montas	montâtes	fus monté(e)	fûtes monté(e)(s)
monta	montèrent	fut monté(e)	furent monté(e)s
4 futur		**11 futur antérieur**	
monterai	monterons	serai monté(e)	serons monté(e)s
monteras	monterez	seras monté(e)	serez monté(e)(s)
montera	monteront	sera monté(e)	seront monté(e)s
5 conditionnel		**12 conditionnel passé**	
monterais	monterions	serais monté(e)	serions monté(e)s
monterais	monteriez	serais monté(e)	seriez monté(e)(s)
monterait	monteraient	serait monté(e)	seraient monté(e)s
6 présent du subjonctif		**13 passé du subjonctif**	
monte	montions	sois monté(e)	soyons monté(e)s
montes	montiez	sois monté(e)	soyez monté(e)(s)
monte	montent	soit monté(e)	soient monté(e)s
7 imparfait du subjonctif		**14 plus-que-parfait du subjonctif**	
montasse	montassions	fusse monté(e)	fussions monté(e)s
montasses	montassiez	fusses monté(e)	fussiez monté(e)(s)
montât	montassent	fût monté(e)	fussent monté(e)s

Impératif
monte
montons
montez

AN ESSENTIAL 55 VERB

Monter

Monter is a very important verb for you to learn because it can take either avoir or être as auxiliary in the compound tenses (tenses 8–14).

This verb is conjugated with *avoir* when it has a direct object.

Examples: J'ai monté l'escalier. I went up the stairs.
　　　　　　J'ai monté les valises. I brought up the suitcases.

BUT: Elle est montée vite. She went up quickly.

Sentences using monter and related words

La température va remonter au cours de la semaine. The temperature will go back up during the week.

J'ai pris l'ascenseur pour monter. I took the elevator to go up.

Le prix de l'essence est monté en flèche pendant l'été. The price of gasoline shot up during the summer.

Les enfants ont monté une pièce de théâtre dans le garage. The children put on a play in the garage.

Words and expressions related to this verb

monter à bicyclette **to ride a bicycle**

monter dans un train **to get on a train**

monter une pièce de théâtre **to stage a play**

monter à cheval **to mount a horse**

monter à bord d'un navire **to get on board a ship**

monter les prix **to push prices up**

monter en flèche **to shoot up (like an arrow)**

M

If you can conjugate monter you can also conjugate the following verbs (as well as other regular -er verbs):

démonter **to dismantle**

remonter **to go back up**

surmonter **to overcome**

Can't find the verb you're looking for? Check the back pages of this book for a list of over 2,600 additional verbs!

The subject pronouns are found on page 103.

to show, to display, to exhibit, to point out

The Seven Simple Tenses		The Seven Compound Tenses	
Singular	Plural	Singular	Plural
1 présent de l'indicatif		8 passé composé	
montre	montrons	ai montré	avons montré
montres	montrez	as montré	avez montré
montre	montrent	a montré	ont montré
2 imparfait de l'indicatif		9 plus-que-parfait de l'indicatif	
montrais	montrions	avais montré	avions montré
montrais	montriez	avais montré	aviez montré
montrait	montraient	avait montré	avaient montré
3 passé simple		10 passé antérieur	
montrai	montrâmes	eus montré	eûmes montré
montras	montrâtes	eus montré	eûtes montré
montra	montrèrent	eut montré	eurent montré
4 futur		11 futur antérieur	
montrerai	montrerons	aurai montré	aurons montré
montreras	montrerez	auras montré	aurez montré
montrera	montreront	aura montré	auront montré
5 conditionnel		12 conditionnel passé	
montrerais	montrerions	aurais montré	aurions montré
montrerais	montreriez	aurais montré	auriez montré
montrerait	montreraient	aurait montré	auraient montré
6 présent du subjonctif		13 passé du subjonctif	
montre	montrions	aie montré	ayons montré
montres	montriez	aies montré	ayez montré
montre	montrent	ait montré	aient montré
7 imparfait du subjonctif		14 plus-que-parfait du subjonctif	
montrasse	montrassions	eusse montré	eussions montré
montrasses	montrassiez	eusses montré	eussiez montré
montrât	montrassent	eût montré	eussent montré

Impératif
montre
montrons
montrez

Words and expressions related to this verb
une montre   a watch, display
une montre-bracelet   wristwatch
faire montre de sa richesse   to display, to
show off one's wealth
Quelle heure est-il à votre montre?   What
time is it on your watch?

se faire montrer la porte   to be put out the
door, to be shown out the door
démontrer   to demonstrate
se démontrer   to be proved
se montrer   to show oneself, to appear
montrer du doigt   to point out, to show, to
indicate by pointing

Don't miss the definitions of basic grammatical terms on pages 35–49.

442

Reflexive regular **-er** verb

to make fun

The Seven Simple Tenses		The Seven Compound Tenses	
Singular	Plural	Singular	Plural
1 présent de l'indicatif		8 passé composé	
me moque	nous moquons	me suis moqué(e)	nous sommes moqué(e)s
te moques	vous moquez	t'es moqué(e)	vous êtes moqué(e)(s)
se moque	se moquent	s'est moqué(e)	se sont moqué(e)s
2 imparfait de l'indicatif		9 plus-que-parfait de l'indicatif	
me moquais	nous moquions	m'étais moqué(e)	nous étions moqué(e)s
te moquais	vous moquiez	t'étais moqué(e)	vous étiez moqué(e)(s)
se moquais	se moquaient	s'était moqué(e)	s'étaient moqué(e)s
3 passé simple		10 passé antérieur	
me moquai	nous moquâmes	me fus moqué(e)	nous fûmes moqué(e)s
te moquas	vous moquâtes	te fus moqué(e)	vous fûtes moqué(e)(s)
se moqua	se moquèrent	se fut moqué(e)	se furent moqué(e)s
4 futur		11 futur antérieur	
me moquerai	nous moquerons	me serai moqué(e)	nous serons moqué(e)s
te moqueras	vous moquerez	te seras moqué(e)	vous serez moqué(e)(s)
se moquera	se moqueront	se sera moqué(e)	se seront moqué(e)s
5 conditionnel		12 conditionnel passé	
me moquerais	nous moquerions	me serais moqué(e)	nous serions moqué(e)s
te moquerais	vous moqueriez	te serais moqué(e)	vous seriez moqué(e)(s)
se moquerait	se moqueraient	se serait moqué(e)	se seraient moqué(e)s
6 présent du subjonctif		13 passé du subjonctif	
me moque	nous moquions	me sois moqué(e)	nous soyons moqué(e)s
te moques	vous moquiez	te sois moqué(e)	vous soyez moqué(e)(s)
se moque	se moquent	se soit moqué(e)	se soient moqué(e)s
7 imparfait du subjonctif		14 plus-que-parfait du subjonctif	
me moquasse	nous moquassions	me fusse moqué(e)	nous fussions moqué(e)s
te moquasses	vous moquassiez	te fusses moqué(e)	vous fussiez moqué(e)(s)
se moquât	se moquassent	se fût moqué(e)	se fussent moqué(e)s

Impératif
moque-toi; ne te moque pas
moquons-nous; ne nous moquons pas
moquez-vous; ne vous moquez pas

Words and expressions related to this verb
se moquer de   to make fun of, to laugh at
Je m'en moque!   I don't give a hoot!
moquer   to mock
d'un ton moqueur   in a mocking way

une moquerie   mockery
un moqueur, une moqueuse   mocker
moqueusement   mockingly

Can't remember the French verb you need? Check the back pages of this book for the English-French verb index!

The subject pronouns are found on page 103.

mordre (301)
to bite

Regular **-re** verb

The Seven Simple Tenses		The Seven Compound Tenses	
Singular	Plural	Singular	Plural
1 présent de l'indicatif		8 passé composé	
mords	mordons	ai mordu	avons mordu
mords	mordez	as mordu	avez mordu
mord	mordent	a mordu	ont mordu
2 imparfait de l'indicatif		9 plus-que-parfait de l'indicatif	
mordais	mordions	avais mordu	avions mordu
mordais	mordiez	avais mordu	aviez mordu
mordait	mordaient	avait mordu	avaient mordu
3 passé simple		10 passé antérieur	
mordis	mordîmes	eus mordu	eûmes mordu
mordis	mordîtes	eus mordu	eûtes mordu
mordit	mordirent	eut mordu	eurent mordu
4 futur		11 futur antérieur	
mordrai	mordrons	aurai mordu	aurons mordu
mordras	mordrez	auras mordu	aurez mordu
mordra	mordront	aura mordu	auront mordu
5 conditionnel		12 conditionnel passé	
mordrais	mordrions	aurais mordu	aurions mordu
mordrais	mordriez	aurais mordu	auriez mordu
mordrait	mordraient	aurait mordu	auraient mordu
6 présent du subjonctif		13 passé du subjonctif	
morde	mordions	aie mordu	ayons mordu
mordes	mordiez	aies mordu	ayez mordu
morde	mordent	ait mordu	aient mordu
7 imparfait du subjonctif		14 plus-que-parfait du subjonctif	
mordisse	mordissions	eusse mordu	eussions mordu
mordisses	mordissiez	eusses mordu	eussiez mordu
mordît	mordissent	eût mordu	eussent mordu

Impératif
mords
mordons
mordez

Words and expressions related to this verb

Chien qui aboie ne mord pas.   A barking dog does not bite. (His bark is worse than his bite.)

Tous les chiens qui aboient ne mordent pas.   All dogs that bark do not bite.

mordre la poussière   to bite the dust
se mordre les lèvres   to bite one's lips
mordeur, mordeuse   biter (one who bites)
mordiller   to bite playfully, to nibble

mordant, mordante   biting, trenchant
une morsure   bite
mordre dans une pomme   to bite into an apple
un mordu de l'ordinateur   a computer fanatic, buff
C'est un mordu du jazz.   He's jazz crazy.

M

The Seven Simple Tenses		The Seven Compound Tenses	
Singular	Plural	Singular	Plural

1 présent de l'indicatif

mouds	moulons
mouds	moulez
moud	moulent

8 passé composé

ai moulu	avons moulu
as moulu	avez moulu
a moulu	ont moulu

2 imparfait de l'indicatif

moulais	moulions
moulais	mouliez
moulait	moulaient

9 plus-que-parfait de l'indicatif

avais moulu	avions moulu
avais moulu	aviez moulu
avait moulu	avaient moulu

3 passé simple

moulus	moulûmes
moulus	moulûtes
moulut	moulurent

10 passé antérieur

eus moulu	eûmes moulu
eus moulu	eûtes moulu
eut moulu	eurent moulu

4 futur

moudrai	moudrons
moudras	moudrez
moudra	moudront

11 futur antérieur

aurai moulu	aurons moulu
auras moulu	aurez moulu
aura moulu	auront moulu

5 conditionnel

moudrais	moudrions
moudrais	moudriez
moudrait	moudraient

12 conditionnel passé

aurais moulu	aurions moulu
aurais moulu	auriez moulu
aurait moulu	auraient moulu

6 présent du subjonctif

moule	moulions
moules	mouliez
moule	moulent

13 passé du subjonctif

aie moulu	ayons moulu
aies moulu	ayez moulu
ait moulu	aient moulu

7 imparfait du subjonctif

moulusse	moulussions
moulusses	moulussiez
moulût	moulussent

14 plus-que-parfait du subjonctif

eusse moulu	eussions moulu
eusses moulu	eussiez moulu
eût moulu	eussent moulu

Impératif
mouds
moulons
moulez

Words and expressions related to this verb
moudre du café   to grind coffee;
   moudre du poivre   to grind pepper
un moulin à café   coffee mill, coffee grinder
un petit moulin à légumes   vegetable blender

un moulin   mill; un moulin à eau   watermill;
   un moulin à vent   windmill; un moulin rouge   red mill
un moulin à paroles   person who talks constantly without ever stopping; excessively talkative; chatterbox

Don't forget to check the list of 2,600 additional verbs keyed to the 501 model verbs. It's in the Appendixes!

mourir (303)
to die

Part. pr. **mourant**   Part. passé **mort(e)(s)**

Irregular verb

The Seven Simple Tenses		The Seven Compound Tenses	
Singular	Plural	Singular	Plural
1 présent de l'indicatif		**8 passé composé**	
meurs	mourons	suis mort(e)	sommes mort(e)s
meurs	mourez	es mort(e)	êtes mort(e)(s)
meurt	meurent	est mort(e)	sont mort(e)s
2 imparfait de l'indicatif		**9 plus-que-parfait de l'indicatif**	
mourais	mourions	étais mort(e)	étions mort(e)s
mourais	mouriez	étais mort(e)	étiez mort(e)(s)
mourait	mouraient	était mort(e)	étaient mort(e)s
3 passé simple		**10 passé antérieur**	
mourus	mourûmes	fus mort(e)	fûmes mort(e)s
mourus	mourûtes	fus mort(e)	fûtes mort(e)(s)
mourut	moururent	fut mort(e)	furent mort(e)s
4 futur		**11 futur antérieur**	
mourrai	mourrons	serai mort(e)	serons mort(e)s
mourras	mourrez	seras mort(e)	serez mort(e)(s)
mourra	mourront	sera mort(e)	seront mort(e)s
5 conditionnel		**12 conditionnel passé**	
mourrais	mourrions	serais mort(e)	serions mort(e)s
mourrais	mourriez	serais mort(e)	seriez mort(e)(s)
mourrait	mourraient	serait mort(e)	seraient mort(e)s
6 présent du subjonctif		**13 passé du subjonctif**	
meure	mourions	sois mort(e)	soyons mort(e)s
meures	mouriez	sois mort(e)	soyez mort(e)(s)
meure	meurent	soit mort(e)	soient mort(e)s
7 imparfait du subjonctif		**14 plus-que-parfait du subjonctif**	
mourusse	mourussions	fusse mort(e)	fussions mort(e)s
mourusses	mourussiez	fusses mort(e)	fussiez mort(e)(s)
mourût	mourussent	fût mort(e)	fussent mort(e)s

Impératif
meurs
mourons
mourez

Words and expressions related to this verb
mourir de faim   to starve to death
la mort   death
Elle est mourante.   She is dying; **Elle se meurt.**   She is dying.
mourir d'ennui   to be bored to tears
mourir de chagrin   to die of a broken heart
mourir de soif   to die of thirst
mourir de rire   to die laughing
mourir d'envie de faire qqch   to be very eager to do something
C'est triste à mourir.   It's horribly sad.

Can't recognize an irregular verb form? Check out the index of common irregular French verb forms in the Appendixes.

Irregular verb   to move

The Seven Simple Tenses

Singular	Plural

1   présent de l'indicatif

meus	**mouvons**
meus	**mouvez**
meut	**meuvent**

2   imparfait de l'indicatif

mouvais	**mouvions**
mouvais	**mouviez**
mouvait	**mouvaient**

3   passé simple

mus	**mûmes**
mus	**mûtes**
mut	**murent**

4   futur

mouvrai	**mouvrons**
mouvras	**mouvrez**
mouvra	**mouvront**

5   conditionnel

mouvrais	**mouvrions**
mouvrais	**mouvriez**
mouvrait	**mouvraient**

6   présent du subjonctif

meuve	**mouvions**
meuves	**mouviez**
meuve	**meuvent**

7   imparfait du subjonctif

musse	**mussions**
musses	**mussiez**
mût	**mussent**

The Seven Compound Tenses

Singular	Plural

8   passé composé

ai mû	**avons mû**
as mû	**avez mû**
a mû	**ont mû**

9   plus-que-parfait de l'indicatif

avais mû	**avions mû**
avais mû	**aviez mû**
avait mû	**avaient mû**

10   passé antérieur

eus mû	**eûmes mû**
eus mû	**eûtes mû**
eut mû	**eurent mû**

11   futur antérieur

aurai mû	**aurons mû**
auras mû	**aurez mû**
aura mû	**auront mû**

12   conditionnel passé

aurais mû	**aurions mû**
aurais mû	**auriez mû**
aurait mû	**auraient mû**

13   passé du subjonctif

aie mû	**ayons mû**
aies mû	**ayez mû**
ait mû	**aient mû**

14   plus-que-parfait du subjonctif

eusse mû	**eussions mû**
eusses mû	**eussiez mû**
eût mû	**eussent mû**

Impératif

meus
mouvons
mouvez

Words and expressions related to this verb
émouvoir   to move, to affect (emotionally)
s'émouvoir   to be moved, to be touched, to be affected (emotionally)
faire mouvoir   to move, to set in motion
promouvoir   to promote

Do not confuse this verb with **déménager**, which means to move from one dwelling to another or from one city to another.

The subject pronouns are found on page 103.   **447**

to swim

Regular **-er** verb endings; spelling change: retain the **ge** before **a** or **o** to keep the soft **g** sound of the verb

The Seven Simple Tenses		The Seven Compound Tenses	
Singular	Plural	Singular	Plural

1 présent de l'indicatif		8 passé composé	
nage	nageons	ai nagé	avons nagé
nages	nagez	as nagé	avez nagé
nage	nagent	a nagé	ont nagé

2 imparfait de l'indicatif		9 plus-que-parfait de l'indicatif	
nageais	nagions	avais nagé	avions nagé
nageais	nagiez	avais nagé	aviez nagé
nageait	nageaient	avait nagé	avaient nagé

3 passé simple		10 passé antérieur	
nageai	nageâmes	eus nagé	eûmes nagé
nageas	nageâtes	eus nagé	eûtes nagé
nagea	nagèrent	eut nagé	eurent nagé

4 futur		11 futur antérieur	
nagerai	nagerons	aurai nagé	aurons nagé
nageras	nagerez	auras nagé	aurez nagé
nagera	nageront	aura nagé	auront nagé

5 conditionnel		12 conditionnel passé	
nagerais	nagerions	aurais nagé	aurions nagé
nagerais	nageriez	aurais nagé	auriez nagé
nagerait	nageraient	aurait nagé	auraient nagé

6 présent du subjonctif		13 passé du subjonctif	
nage	nagions	aie nagé	ayons nagé
nages	nagiez	aies nagé	ayez nagé
nage	nagent	ait nagé	aient nagé

7 imparfait du subjonctif		14 plus-que-parfait du subjonctif	
nageasse	nageassions	eusse nagé	eussions nagé
nageasses	nageassiez	eusses nagé	eussiez nagé
nageât	nageassent	eût nagé	eussent nagé

Impératif
nage
nageons
nagez

Words and expressions related to this verb

un nageur, une nageuse   swimmer
la piscine   swimming pool
savoir nager   to know how to swim
la natation   swimming
nager entre deux eaux   to sit on the fence
la nage   swimming; la nage libre   free style
   swimming
se sauver à la nage   to swim to safety

nager sous l'eau   to swim underwater
Il nage dans ses vêtements.   His clothes are
   too big on him.
un maillot de bain   swimsuit
nager comme un poisson   to swim like a fish
nager dans l'opulence   to be rolling in money
aller nager   to go swimming
faire de la natation   to swim

Don't miss orthographically changing verbs on pages 32–34.

448

Irregular verb

The Seven Simple Tenses		The Seven Compound Tenses	
Singular	Plural	Singular	Plural
1 présent de l'indicatif		8 passé composé	
nais	**naissons**	**suis né(e)**	**sommes né(e)s**
nais	**naissez**	**es né(e)**	**êtes né(e)(s)**
naît	**naissent**	**est né(e)**	**sont né(e)s**
2 imparfait de l'indicatif		9 plus-que-parfait de l'indicatif	
naissais	**naissions**	**étais né(e)**	**étions né(e)s**
naissais	**naissiez**	**étais né(e)**	**étiez né(e)(s)**
naissait	**naissaient**	**était né(e)**	**étaient né(e)s**
3 passé simple		10 passé antérieur	
naquis	**naquîmes**	**fus né(e)**	**fûmes né(e)s**
naquis	**naquîtes**	**fus né(e)**	**fûtes né(e)(s)**
naquit	**naquirent**	**fut né(e)**	**furent né(e)s**
4 futur		11 futur antérieur	
naîtrai	**naîtrons**	**serai né(e)**	**serons né(e)s**
naîtras	**naîtrez**	**seras né(e)**	**serez né(e)(s)**
naîtra	**naîtront**	**sera né(e)**	**seront né(e)s**
5 conditionnel		12 conditionnel passé	
naîtrais	**naîtrions**	**serais né(e)**	**serions né(e)s**
naîtrais	**naîtriez**	**serais né(e)**	**seriez né(e)(s)**
naîtrait	**naîtraient**	**serait né(e)**	**seraient né(e)s**
6 présent du subjonctif		13 passé du subjonctif	
naisse	**naissions**	**sois né(e)**	**soyons né(e)s**
naisses	**naissiez**	**sois né(e)**	**soyez né(e)(s)**
naisse	**naissent**	**soit né(e)**	**soient né(e)s**
7 imparfait du subjonctif		14 plus-que-parfait du subjonctif	
naquisse	**naquissions**	**fusse né(e)**	**fussions né(e)s**
naquisses	**naquissiez**	**fusses né(e)**	**fussiez né(e)(s)**
naquît	**naquissent**	**fût né(e)**	**fussent né(e)s**

N

Impératif
nais
naissons
naissez

Words and expressions related to this verb
la naissance   birth
un anniversaire de naissance   a birthday anniversary
donner naissance à   to give birth to; **la naissance du monde**   beginning of the world
Anne est Française de naissance.   Anne was born French.
renaître   to be born again
faire naître   to cause, to give rise to
Je ne suis pas né(e) d'hier!   I wasn't born yesterday!
la Nativité   Nativity

Don't forget to study the section on defective and impersonal verbs. It's right after this main list.

The subject pronouns are found on page 103.

Part. pr. **naviguant**   Part. passé **navigué**

to navigate, to sail; to browse, to surf (Internet)

Regular **-er** verb

The Seven Simple Tenses		The Seven Compound Tenses	
Singular	Plural	Singular	Plural
1 présent de l'indicatif		8 passé composé	
navigue	naviguons	ai navigué	avons navigué
navigues	naviguez	as navigué	avez navigué
navigue	naviguent	a navigué	ont navigué
2 imparfait de l'indicatif		9 plus-que-parfait de l'indicatif	
naviguais	naviguions	avais navigué	avions navigué
naviguais	naviguiez	avais navigué	aviez navigué
naviguait	naviguaient	avait navigué	avaient navigué
3 passé simple		10 passé antérieur	
naviguai	naviguâmes	eus navigué	eûmes navigué
naviguas	naviguâtes	eus navigué	eûtes navigué
navigua	naviguèrent	eut navigué	eurent navigué
4 futur		11 futur antérieur	
naviguerai	naviguerons	aurai navigué	aurons navigué
navigueras	naviguerez	auras navigué	aurez navigué
naviguera	navigueront	aura navigué	auront navigué
5 conditionnel		12 conditionnel passé	
naviguerais	naviguerions	aurais navigué	aurions navigué
naviguerais	navigueriez	aurais navigué	auriez navigué
naviguerait	navigueraient	aurait navigué	auraient navigué
6 présent du subjonctif		13 passé du subjonctif	
navigue	naviguions	aie navigué	ayons navigué
navigues	naviguiez	aies navigué	ayez navigué
navigue	naviguent	ait navigué	aient navigué
7 imparfait du subjonctif		14 plus-que-parfait du subjonctif	
naviguasse	naviguassions	eusse navigué	eussions navigué
naviguasses	naviguassiez	eusses navigué	eussiez navigué
naviguât	naviguassent	eût navigué	eussent navigué

Impératif
navigue
naviguons
naviguez

Sentences using this verb and words related to it
Je naviguais sur le Web quand mon ordinateur est tombé en panne. I was surfing the Web when my computer crashed.
Jacques Cartier est le navigateur qui a découvert le Saint-Laurent. Jacques Cartier is the navigator who discovered the Saint Lawrence River.

Words and expressions related to this verb
un navigateur, une navigatrice navigator, sailor
un navigateur Web Web browser
la navigation navigation, sailing
navigable *adj*. navigable
naviguer sur Internet, naviguer sur le Web to surf the Internet (You can also use **surfer**.)
un navire ship
naviguer à vue to fly visually (VFR)

Can't find the verb you're looking for? Check the back pages of this book for a list of over 2,600 additional verbs!

to clean

Regular **-er** verb endings; spelling change: **-oyer**
verbs must change **y** to **i** in front of a mute **e**

The Seven Simple Tenses		The Seven Compound Tenses	
Singular	Plural	Singular	Plural
1 présent de l'indicatif		8 passé composé	
nettoie	nettoyons	ai nettoyé	avons nettoyé
nettoies	nettoyez	as nettoyé	avez nettoyé
nettoie	nettoient	a nettoyé	ont nettoyé
2 imparfait de l'indicatif		9 plus-que-parfait de l'indicatif	
nettoyais	nettoyions	avais nettoyé	avions nettoyé
nettoyais	nettoyiez	avais nettoyé	aviez nettoyé
nettoyait	nettoyaient	avait nettoyé	avaient nettoyé
3 passé simple		10 passé antérieur	
nettoyai	nettoyâmes	eus nettoyé	eûmes nettoyé
nettoyas	nettoyâtes	eus nettoyé	eûtes nettoyé
nettoya	nettoyèrent	eut nettoyé	eurent nettoyé
4 futur		11 futur antérieur	
nettoierai	nettoierons	aurai nettoyé	aurons nettoyé
nettoieras	nettoierez	auras nettoyé	aurez nettoyé
nettoiera	nettoieront	aura nettoyé	auront nettoyé
5 conditionnel		12 conditionnel passé	
nettoierais	nettoierions	aurais nettoyé	aurions nettoyé
nettoierais	nettoieriez	aurais nettoyé	auriez nettoyé
nettoierait	nettoieraient	aurait nettoyé	auraient nettoyé
6 présent du subjonctif		13 passé du subjonctif	
nettoie	nettoyions	aie nettoyé	ayons nettoyé
nettoies	nettoyiez	aies nettoyé	ayez nettoyé
nettoie	nettoient	ait nettoyé	aient nettoyé
7 imparfait du subjonctif		14 plus-que-parfait du subjonctif	
nettoyasse	nettoyassions	eusse nettoyé	eussions nettoyé
nettoyasses	nettoyassiez	eusses nettoyé	eussiez nettoyé
nettoyât	nettoyassent	eût nettoyé	eussent nettoyé

Impératif
nettoie
nettoyons
nettoyez

Words and expressions related to this verb
le **nettoyage**   cleaning; le **nettoyage à sec**
   dry cleaning
nettoyer à sec   to dry clean
une **nettoyeuse**   cleaning machine
un **nettoyant**   cleanser

un **nettoyeur de fenêtres**   window cleaner
Elle refuse nettement.   She flatly refuses.
se faire nettoyer au jeu   to be cleaned out at
   gambling

The subject pronouns are found on page 103.

451

to deny

The Seven Simple Tenses		The Seven Compound Tenses	
Singular	Plural	Singular	Plural

1 présent de l'indicatif		8 passé composé	
nie	**nions**	**ai nié**	**avons nié**
nies	**niez**	**as nié**	**avez nié**
nie	**nient**	**a nié**	**ont nié**

2 imparfait de l'indicatif		9 plus-que-parfait de l'indicatif	
niais	**niions**	**avais nié**	**avions nié**
niais	**niiez**	**avais nié**	**aviez nié**
niait	**niaient**	**avait nié**	**avaient nié**

3 passé simple		10 passé antérieur	
niai	**niâmes**	**eus nié**	**eûmes nié**
nias	**niâtes**	**eus nié**	**eûtes nié**
nia	**nièrent**	**eut nié**	**eurent nié**

4 futur		11 futur antérieur	
nierai	**nierons**	**aurai nié**	**aurons nié**
nieras	**nierez**	**auras nié**	**aurez nié**
niera	**nieront**	**aura nié**	**auront nié**

5 conditionnel		12 conditionnel passé	
nierais	**nierions**	**aurais nié**	**aurions nié**
nierais	**nieriez**	**aurais nié**	**auriez nié**
nierait	**nieraient**	**aurait nié**	**auraient nié**

6 présent du subjonctif		13 passé du subjonctif	
nie	**niions**	**aie nié**	**ayons nié**
nies	**niiez**	**aies nié**	**ayez nié**
nie	**nient**	**ait nié**	**aient nié**

7 imparfait du subjonctif		14 plus-que-parfait du subjonctif	
niasse	**niassions**	**eusse nié**	**eussions nié**
niasses	**niassiez**	**eusses nié**	**eussiez nié**
niât	**niassent**	**eût nié**	**eussent nié**

Impératif
nie
nions
niez

Words and expressions related to this verb

nier un fait   to deny a fact
dénier qqch à qqn   to deny someone something, to refuse someone something
un déni   denial; **un déni de justice**   denial of justice
renier   to deny openly, to reject

renier un ami   to reject a friend
renier sa promesse   to go back on, to break one's promise
un renégat, une renégate   renegade
un reniement   denial
indéniable   undeniable

Get acquainted with what preposition goes with what verb. See *Verbs with prepositions* in the Appendixes.

The Seven Simple Tenses		The Seven Compound Tenses	
Singular	Plural	Singular	Plural
1 présent de l'indicatif		8 passé composé	
nomme	nommons	ai nommé	avons nommé
nommes	nommez	as nommé	avez nommé
nomme	nomment	a nommé	ont nommé
2 imparfait de l'indicatif		9 plus-que-parfait de l'indicatif	
nommais	nommions	avais nommé	avions nommé
nommais	nommiez	avais nommé	aviez nommé
nommait	nommaient	avait nommé	avaient nommé
3 passé simple		10 passé antérieur	
nommai	nommâmes	eus nommé	eûmes nommé
nommas	nommâtes	eus nommé	eûtes nommé
nomma	nommèrent	eut nommé	eurent nommé
4 futur		11 futur antérieur	
nommerai	nommerons	aurai nommé	aurons nommé
nommeras	nommerez	auras nommé	aurez nommé
nommera	nommeront	aura nommé	auront nommé
5 conditionnel		12 conditionnel passé	
nommerais	nommerions	aurais nommé	aurions nommé
nommerais	nommeriez	aurais nommé	auriez nommé
nommerait	nommeraient	aurait nommé	auraient nommé
6 présent du subjonctif		13 passé du subjonctif	
nomme	nommions	aie nommé	ayons nommé
nommes	nommiez	aies nommé	ayez nommé
nomme	nomment	ait nommé	aient nommé
7 imparfait du subjonctif		14 plus-que-parfait du subjonctif	
nommasse	nommassions	eusse nommé	eussions nommé
nommasses	nommassiez	eusses nommé	eussiez nommé
nommât	nommassent	eût nommé	eussent nommé

N

Impératif
nomme
nommons
nommez

Common idiomatic expressions using this verb and words related to it

nommément   namely, by name
un pronom   a pronoun
un pseudonyme   pseudonym
un nom de théâtre   stage name
le petit nom   a person's first name
appeler les choses par leur nom   to call a
  spade a spade
anonyme   anonymous

un nom de plume   pen name (a name used by
  an author other than the real name)
un nom de guerre   false (assumed) name
nominalement   nominally
au nom du Père, du Fils, et du Saint-Esprit
  in the name of the Father, the Son, and the
  Holy Spirit
le renom   renown

The subject pronouns are found on page 103.   **453**

to feed, to nourish

Regular **-ir** verb

The Seven Simple Tenses		The Seven Compound Tenses	
Singular	Plural	Singular	Plural
1 présent de l'indicatif		8 passé composé	
nourris	**nourrissons**	**ai nourri**	**avons nourri**
nourris	**nourrissez**	**as nourri**	**avez nourri**
nourrit	**nourrissent**	**a nourri**	**ont nourri**
2 imparfait de l'indicatif		9 plus-que-parfait de l'indicatif	
nourrissais	**nourrissions**	**avais nourri**	**avions nourri**
nourrissais	**nourrissiez**	**avais nourri**	**aviez nourri**
nourrissait	**nourrissaient**	**avait nourri**	**avaient nourri**
3 passé simple		10 passé antérieur	
nourris	**nourrîmes**	**eus nourri**	**eûmes nourri**
nourris	**nourrîtes**	**eus nourri**	**eûtes nourri**
nourrit	**nourrirent**	**eut nourri**	**eurent nourri**
4 futur		11 futur antérieur	
nourrirai	**nourrirons**	**aurai nourri**	**aurons nourri**
nourriras	**nourrirez**	**auras nourri**	**aurez nourri**
nourrira	**nourriront**	**aura nourri**	**auront nourri**
5 conditionnel		12 conditionnel passé	
nourrirais	**nourririons**	**aurais nourri**	**aurions nourri**
nourrirais	**nourririez**	**aurais nourri**	**auriez nourri**
nourrirait	**nourriraient**	**aurait nourri**	**auraient nourri**
6 présent du subjonctif		13 passé du subjonctif	
nourrisse	**nourrissions**	**aie nourri**	**ayons nourri**
nourrisses	**nourrissiez**	**aies nourri**	**ayez nourri**
nourrisse	**nourrissent**	**ait nourri**	**aient nourri**
7 imparfait du subjonctif		14 plus-que-parfait du subjonctif	
nourrisse	**nourrissions**	**eusse nourri**	**eussions nourri**
nourrisses	**nourrissiez**	**eusses nourri**	**eussiez nourri**
nourrît	**nourrissent**	**eût nourri**	**eussent nourri**

Impératif
nourris
nourrissons
nourrissez

Words and expressions related to this verb
la nourriture nourishment, food
une nourrice wet nurse
bien nourri well fed
mal nourri poorly fed
nourrissant, nourrissante nourishing

un nourrisson infant
nourricier, nourricière nutritious
une mère nourricière foster mother
un père nourricier foster father
se nourrir to feed oneself

Grammar putting you in a tense mood? Review the definitions of basic grammatical terms with examples on pages 35–49.

Reflexive regular **-er** verb endings; spelling change:
-oyer verbs must change **y** to **i** in front of a mute **e**

The Seven Simple Tenses		The Seven Compound Tenses	
Singular	Plural	Singular	Plural
1 présent de l'indicatif		8 passé composé	
me noie	nous noyons	me suis noyé(e)	nous sommes noyé(e)s
te noies	vous noyez	t'es noyé(e)	vous êtes noyé(e)(s)
se noie	se noient	s'est noyé(e)	se sont noyé(e)s
2 imparfait de l'indicatif		9 plus-que-parfait de l'indicatif	
me noyais	nous noyions	m'étais noyé(e)	nous étions noyé(e)s
te noyais	vous noyiez	t'étais noyé(e)	vous étiez noyé(e)(s)
se noyait	se noyaient	s'était noyé(e)	s'étaient noyé(e)s
3 passé simple		10 passé antérieur	
me noyai	nous noyâmes	me fus noyé(e)	nous fûmes noyé(e)s
te noyas	vous noyâtes	te fus noyé(e)	vous fûtes noyé(e)(s)
se noya	se noyèrent	se fut noyé(e)	se furent noyé(e)s
4 futur		11 futur antérieur	
me noierai	nous noierons	me serai noyé(e)	nous serons noyé(e)s
te noieras	vous noierez	te seras noyé(e)	vous serez noyé(e)(s)
se noiera	se noieront	se sera noyé(e)	se seront noyé(e)s
5 conditionnel		12 conditionnel passé	
me noierais	nous noierions	me serais noyé(e)	nous serions noyé(e)s
te noierais	vous noieriez	te serais noyé(e)	vous seriez noyé(e)(s)
se noierait	se noieraient	se serait noyé(e)	se seraient noyé(e)s
6 présent du subjonctif		13 passé du subjonctif	
me noie	nous noyions	me sois noyé(e)	nous soyons noyé(e)s
te noies	vous noyiez	te sois noyé(e)	vous soyez noyé(e)(s)
se noie	se noient	se soit noyé(e)	se soient noyé(e)s
7 imparfait du subjonctif		14 plus-que-parfait du subjonctif	
me noyasse	nous noyassions	me fusse noyé(e)	nous fussions noyé(e)s
te noyasses	vous noyassiez	te fusses noyé(e)	vous fussiez noyé(e)(s)
se noyât	se noyassent	se fût noyé(e)	se fussent noyé(e)s

Impératif
noie-toi; ne te noie pas
noyons-nous; ne nous noyons pas
noyez-vous; ne vous noyez pas

Words and expressions related to this verb
Suzanne se noyait quand le maître-nageur est arrivé lui sauver la vie.
   Suzanne was drowning when the lifeguard arrived to save her life.

une noyade   drowning
noyer   to drown (an animal or person), to water down (liquid)
se noyer dans   to get bogged down in
le noyé, la noyée   drowned person

Can't remember the French verb you need? Check the back pages of this book for the
English-French verb index!

N

to harm, to hinder

Irregular verb

The Seven Simple Tenses		The Seven Compound Tenses	
Singular	Plural	Singular	Plural
1 présent de l'indicatif		8 passé composé	
nuis	**nuisons**	**ai nui**	**avons nui**
nuis	**nuisez**	**as nui**	**avez nui**
nuit	**nuisent**	**a nui**	**ont nui**
2 imparfait de l'indicatif		9 plus-que-parfait de l'indicatif	
nuisais	**nuisions**	**avais nui**	**avions nui**
nuisais	**nuisiez**	**avais nui**	**aviez nui**
nuisait	**nuisaient**	**avait nui**	**avaient nui**
3 passé simple		10 passé antérieur	
nuisis	**nuisîmes**	**eus nui**	**eûmes nui**
nuisis	**nuisîtes**	**eus nui**	**eûtes nui**
nuisit	**nuisirent**	**eut nui**	**eurent nui**
4 futur		11 futur antérieur	
nuirai	**nuirons**	**aurai nui**	**aurons nui**
nuiras	**nuirez**	**auras nui**	**aurez nui**
nuira	**nuiront**	**aura nui**	**auront nui**
5 conditionnel		12 conditionnel passé	
nuirais	**nuirions**	**aurais nui**	**aurions nui**
nuirais	**nuiriez**	**aurais nui**	**auriez nui**
nuirait	**nuiraient**	**aurait nui**	**auraient nui**
6 présent du subjonctif		13 passé du subjonctif	
nuise	**nuisions**	**aie nui**	**ayons nui**
nuises	**nuisiez**	**aies nui**	**ayez nui**
nuise	**nuisent**	**ait nui**	**aient nui**
7 imparfait du subjonctif		14 plus-que-parfait du subjonctif	
nuisisse	**nuisissions**	**eusse nui**	**eussions nui**
nuisisses	**nuisissiez**	**eusses nui**	**eussiez nui**
nuisît	**nuisissent**	**eût nui**	**eussent nui**

Impératif
nuis
nuisons
nuisez

Words and expressions related to this verb
la **nuisance**   nuisance
les **nuisances sonores**   noise pollution
nuisible   harmful
nuire à   to do harm to, to be injurious to, to be harmful to

Cela peut nuire à la réputation de votre famille.   That may harm the reputation of your family.

How are you doing? Find out with the verb drills and tests with answers explained on pages 50–101.

Regular **-ir** verb   to obey

The Seven Simple Tenses		The Seven Compound Tenses	
Singular	Plural	Singular	Plural

1 présent de l'indicatif		8 passé composé	
obéis	obéissons	ai obéi	avons obéi
obéis	obéissez	as obéi	avez obéi
obéit	obéissent	a obéi	ont obéi

2 imparfait de l'indicatif		9 plus-que-parfait de l'indicatif	
obéissais	obéissions	avais obéi	avions obéi
obéissais	obéissiez	avais obéi	aviez obéi
obéissait	obéissaient	avait obéi	avaient obéi

3 passé simple		10 passé antérieur	
obéis	obéîmes	eus obéi	eûmes obéi
obéis	obéîtes	eus obéi	eûtes obéi
obéit	obéirent	eut obéi	eurent obéi

4 futur		11 futur antérieur	
obéirai	obéirons	aurai obéi	aurons obéi
obéiras	obéirez	auras obéi	aurez obéi
obéira	obéiront	aura obéi	auront obéi

5 conditionnel		12 conditionnel passé	
obéirais	obéirions	aurais obéi	aurions obéi
obéirais	obéiriez	aurais obéi	auriez obéi
obéirait	obéiraient	aurait obéi	auraient obéi

6 présent du subjonctif		13 passé du subjonctif	
obéisse	obéissions	aie obéi	ayons obéi
obéisses	obéissiez	aies obéi	ayez obéi
obéisse	obéissent	ait obéi	aient obéi

7 imparfait du subjonctif		14 plus-que-parfait du subjonctif	
obéisse	obéissions	eusse obéi	eussions obéi
obéisses	obéissiez	eusses obéi	eussiez obéi
obéît	obéissent	eût obéi	eussent obéi

Impératif
obéis
obéissons
obéissez

Words and expressions related to this verb
obéir à qqn   to obey someone
désobéir à qqn   to disobey someone
l'obéissance *f.*   obedience

obéissant, obéissante   obedient
désobéissant, désobéissante   disobedient
obéir à ses instincts   to obey one's instincts

Get acquainted with what preposition goes with what verb. See *Verbs with prepositions* in the Appendixes.

The subject pronouns are found on page 103.

to oblige

Regular -**er** verb endings; spelling change: retain the
ge before **a** or **o** to keep the soft **g** sound of the verb

The Seven Simple Tenses		The Seven Compound Tenses	
Singular	Plural	Singular	Plural
1 présent de l'indicatif		8 passé composé	
oblige	obligeons	ai obligé	avons obligé
obliges	obligez	as obligé	avez obligé
oblige	obligent	a obligé	ont obligé
2 imparfait de l'indicatif		9 plus-que-parfait de l'indicatif	
obligeais	obligions	avais obligé	avions obligé
obligeais	obligiez	avais obligé	aviez obligé
obligeait	obligeaient	avait obligé	avaient obligé
3 passé simple		10 passé antérieur	
obligeai	obligeâmes	eus obligé	eûmes obligé
obligeas	obligeâtes	eus obligé	eûtes obligé
obligea	obligèrent	eut obligé	eurent obligé
4 futur		11 futur antérieur	
obligerai	obligerons	aurai obligé	aurons obligé
obligeras	obligerez	auras obligé	aurez obligé
obligera	obligeront	aura obligé	auront obligé
5 conditionnel		12 conditionnel passé	
obligerais	obligerions	aurais obligé	aurions obligé
obligerais	obligeriez	aurais obligé	auriez obligé
obligerait	obligeraient	aurait obligé	auraient obligé
6 présent du subjonctif		13 passé du subjonctif	
oblige	obligions	aie obligé	ayons obligé
obliges	obligiez	aies obligé	ayez obligé
oblige	obligent	ait obligé	aient obligé
7 imparfait du subjonctif		14 plus-que-parfait du subjonctif	
obligeasse	obligeassions	eusse obligé	eussions obligé
obligeasses	obligeassiez	eusses obligé	eussiez obligé
obligeât	obligeassent	eût obligé	eussent obligé

Impératif
oblige
obligeons
obligez

Words and expressions related to this verb
obligatoire obligatory
l'obligation *f.* obligation
avoir beaucoup d'obligation à qqn to be
much obliged to someone
obligeant, obligeante obliging
se montrer obligeant envers qqn to show
kindness to someone

obligé, obligée obliged
Noblesse oblige. Nobility obliges. (*i.e.*, the
moral obligation of a highborn person is to
show honorable conduct)

If you want to see a sample English verb fully conjugated in all the tenses, check out pages 8
and 9.

Irregular verb

The Seven Simple Tenses		The Seven Compound Tenses	
Singular	Plural	Singular	Plural
1 présent de l'indicatif		**8 passé composé**	
obtiens	obtenons	ai obtenu	avons obtenu
obtiens	obtenez	as obtenu	avez obtenu
obtient	obtiennent	a obtenu	ont obtenu
2 imparfait de l'indicatif		**9 plus-que-parfait de l'indicatif**	
obtenais	obtenions	avais obtenu	avions obtenu
obtenais	obteniez	avais obtenu	aviez obtenu
obtenait	obtenaient	avait obtenu	avaient obtenu
3 passé simple		**10 passé antérieur**	
obtins	obtînmes	eus obtenu	eûmes obtenu
obtins	obtîntes	eus obtenu	eûtes obtenu
obtint	obtinrent	eut obtenu	eurent obtenu
4 futur		**11 futur antérieur**	
obtiendrai	obtiendrons	aurai obtenu	aurons obtenu
obtiendras	obtiendrez	auras obtenu	aurez obtenu
obtiendra	obtiendront	aura obtenu	auront obtenu
5 conditionnel		**12 conditionnel passé**	
obtiendrais	obtiendrions	aurais obtenu	aurions obtenu
obtiendrais	obtiendriez	aurais obtenu	auriez obtenu
obtiendrait	obtiendraient	aurait obtenu	auraient obtenu
6 présent du subjonctif		**13 passé du subjonctif**	
obtienne	obtenions	aie obtenu	ayons obtenu
obtiennes	obteniez	aies obtenu	ayez obtenu
obtienne	obtiennent	ait obtenu	aient obtenu
7 imparfait du subjonctif		**14 plus-que-parfait du subjonctif**	
obtinsse	obtinssions	eusse obtenu	eussions obtenu
obtinsses	obtinssiez	eusses obtenu	eussiez obtenu
obtînt	obtinssent	eût obtenu	eussent obtenu

O

Impératif
obtiens
obtenons
obtenez

Words and expressions related to this verb

l'obtention *f.*   obtainment

obtenir de qqn qqch de force   to get something out of someone by force

s'obtenir de   to be obtained from

See also **contenir, retenir,** and **tenir.**

It's important that you be familiar with the Subjunctive. See pages 26–31.

occuper (317)

to occupy

Part. pr. **occupant**   Part. passé **occupé**

Regular **-er** verb

The Seven Simple Tenses		The Seven Compound Tenses	
Singular	Plural	Singular	Plural

1 présent de l'indicatif

occupe	occupons		
occupes	occupez		
occupe	occupent		

8 passé composé

ai occupé		avons occupé	
as occupé		avez occupé	
a occupé		ont occupé	

2 imparfait de l'indicatif

occupais	occupions
occupais	occupiez
occupait	occupaient

9 plus-que-parfait de l'indicatif

avais occupé	avions occupé
avais occupé	aviez occupé
avait occupé	avaient occupé

3 passé simple

occupai	occupâmes
occupas	occupâtes
occupa	occupèrent

10 passé antérieur

eus occupé	eûmes occupé
eus occupé	eûtes occupé
eut occupé	eurent occupé

4 futur

occuperai	occuperons
occuperas	occuperez
occupera	occuperont

11 futur antérieur

aurai occupé	aurons occupé
auras occupé	aurez occupé
aura occupé	auront occupé

5 conditionnel

occuperais	occuperions
occuperais	occuperiez
occuperait	occuperaient

12 conditionnel passé

aurais occupé	aurions occupé
aurais occupé	auriez occupé
aurait occupé	auraient occupé

6 présent du subjonctif

occupe	occupions
occupes	occupiez
occupe	occupent

13 passé du subjonctif

aie occupé	ayons occupé
aies occupé	ayez occupé
ait occupé	aient occupé

7 imparfait du subjonctif

occupasse	occupassions
occupasses	occupassiez
occupât	occupassent

14 plus-que-parfait du subjonctif

eusse occupé	eussions occupé
eusses occupé	eussiez occupé
eût occupé	eussent occupé

Impératif
occupe
occupons
occupez

Words and expressions related to this verb
l'occupation *f.*   occupation
être occupé(e)   to be busy
occuper qqn   to keep someone busy
occuper trop de place   to take up too much room
occupant, occupante   occupying; **du travail occupant**   engrossing work
occuper l'attention de qqn   to hold someone's attention
préoccuper   to preoccupy; **une préoccupation**   preoccupation
La ligne est occupée.   The line is busy.

See also **s'occuper.**

Reflexive regular **-er** verb

to be busy, to keep oneself busy

The Seven Simple Tenses		The Seven Compound Tenses	
Singular	Plural	Singular	Plural
1 présent de l'indicatif		**8 passé composé**	
m'occupe	nous occupons	me suis occupé(e)	nous sommes occupé(e)s
t'occupes	vous occupez	t'es occupé(e)	vous êtes occupé(e)(s)
s'occupe	s'occupent	s'est occupé(e)	se sont occupé(e)s
2 imparfait de l'indicatif		**9 plus-que-parfait de l'indicatif**	
m'occupais	nous occupions	m'étais occupé(e)	nous étions occupé(e)s
t'occupais	vous occupiez	t'étais occupé(e)	vous étiez occupé(e)(s)
s'occupait	s'occupaient	s'était occupé(e)	s'étaient occupé(e)s
3 passé simple		**10 passé antérieur**	
m'occupai	nous occupâmes	me fus occupé(e)	nous fûmes occupé(e)s
t'occupas	vous occupâtes	te fus occupé(e)	vous fûtes occupé(e)(s)
s'occupa	s'occupèrent	se fut occupé(e)	se furent occupé(e)s
4 futur		**11 futur antérieur**	
m'occuperai	nous occuperons	me serai occupé(e)	nous serons occupé(e)s
t'occuperas	vous occuperez	te seras occupé(e)	vous serez occupé(e)(s)
s'occupera	s'occuperont	se sera occupé(e)	se seront occupé(e)s
5 conditionnel		**12 conditionnel passé**	
m'occuperais	nous occuperions	me serais occupé(e)	nous serions occupé(e)s
t'occuperais	vous occuperiez	te serais occupé(e)	vous seriez occupé(e)(s)
s'occuperait	s'occuperaient	se serait occupé(e)	se seraient occupé(e)s
6 présent du subjonctif		**13 passé du subjonctif**	
m'occupe	nous occupions	me sois occupé(e)	nous soyons occupé(e)s
t'occupes	vous occupiez	te sois occupé(e)	vous soyez occupé(e)(s)
s'occupe	s'occupent	se soit occupé(e)	se soient occupé(e)s
7 imparfait du subjonctif		**14 plus-que-parfait du subjonctif**	
m'occupasse	nous occupassions	me fusse occupé(e)	nous fussions occupé(e)s
t'occupasses	vous occupassiez	te fusses occupé(e)	vous fussiez occupé(e)(s)
s'occupât	s'occupassent	se fût occupé(e)	se fussent occupé(e)s

O

Impératif
occupe-toi; ne t'occupe pas
occupons-nous; ne nous occupons pas
occupez-vous; ne vous occupez pas

Words and expressions related to this verb
s'occuper de ses affaires to mind one's own business
Je m'occupe de mes affaires. I mind my own business.
s'occuper des enfants to look after children
s'occuper de to look after, to tend to
s'occuper à to be engaged in

Occupez-vous de vos affaires! Mind your own business!
Ne vous occupez pas de mes affaires! Don't mind my business!
Est-ce qu'on s'occupe de vous? Is someone helping you?

See also the verb **occuper.**

Don't forget to study the section on defective and impersonal verbs. It's right after this main list.

to offer

The Seven Simple Tenses		The Seven Compound Tenses	
Singular	Plural	Singular	Plural
1 présent de l'indicatif		**8 passé composé**	
offre	offrons	ai offert	avons offert
offres	offrez	as offert	avez offert
offre	offrent	a offert	ont offert
2 imparfait de l'indicatif		**9 plus-que-parfait de l'indicatif**	
offrais	offrions	avais offert	avions offert
offrais	offriez	avais offert	aviez offert
offrait	offraient	avait offert	avaient offert
3 passé simple		**10 passé antérieur**	
offris	offrîmes	eus offert	eûmes offert
offris	offrîtes	eus offert	eûtes offert
offrit	offrirent	eut offert	eurent offert
4 futur		**11 futur antérieur**	
offrirai	offrirons	aurai offert	aurons offert
offriras	offrirez	auras offert	aurez offert
offrira	offriront	aura offert	auront offert
5 conditionnel		**12 conditionnel passé**	
offrirais	offririons	aurais offert	aurions offert
offrirais	offririez	aurais offert	auriez offert
offrirait	offriraient	aurait offert	auraient offert
6 présent du subjonctif		**13 passé du subjonctif**	
offre	offrions	aie offert	ayons offert
offres	offriez	aies offert	ayez offert
offre	offrent	ait offert	aient offert
7 imparfait du subjonctif		**14 plus-que-parfait du subjonctif**	
offrisse	offrissions	eusse offert	eussions offert
offrisses	offrissiez	eusses offert	eussiez offert
offrît	offrissent	eût offert	eussent offert

Impératif
offre
offrons
offrez

Words and expressions related to this verb
offrir qqch à qqn   to offer (to present)
   something to someone
une offre   an offer, a proposal
une offrande   gift, offering

l'offre et la demande   supply and demand
une offre d'emploi   a job offer
les offres d'emploi   employment opportunities
C'est pour offrir?   Is it to give as a gift?

Get acquainted with what preposition goes with what verb. See *Verbs with prepositions* in the Appendixes.

462

The Seven Simple Tenses		The Seven Compound Tenses	
Singular	Plural	Singular	Plural

1   présent de l'indicatif

		8 passé composé	
omets	omettons	ai omis	avons omis
omets	omettez	as omis	avez omis
omet	omettent	a omis	ont omis

2   imparfait de l'indicatif

		9 plus-que-parfait de l'indicatif	
omettais	omettions	avais omis	avions omis
omettais	omettiez	avais omis	aviez omis
omettait	omettaient	avait omis	avaient omis

3   passé simple

		10 passé antérieur	
omis	omîmes	eus omis	eûmes omis
omis	omîtes	eus omis	eûtes omis
omit	omirent	eut omis	eurent omis

4   futur

		11 futur antérieur	
omettrai	omettrons	aurai omis	aurons omis
omettras	omettrez	auras omis	aurez omis
omettra	omettront	aura omis	auront omis

5   conditionnel

		12 conditionnel passé	
omettrais	omettrions	aurais omis	aurions omis
omettrais	omettriez	aurais omis	auriez omis
omettrait	omettraient	aurait omis	auraient omis

6   présent du subjonctif

		13 passé du subjonctif	
omette	omettions	aie omis	ayons omis
omettes	omettiez	aies omis	ayez omis
omette	omettent	ait omis	aient omis

7   imparfait du subjonctif

		14 plus-que-parfait du subjonctif	
omisse	omissions	eusse omis	eussions omis
omisses	omissiez	eusses omis	eussiez omis
omît	omissent	eût omis	eussent omis

Impératif
omets
omettons
omettez

Words and expressions related to this verb
omettre de faire qqch   to neglect to do something
une omission   an omission
omis, omise   omitted
commettre   to commit

See also **admettre, commettre, mettre, permettre, promettre, remettre, soumettre,** and **transmettre.**

Don't forget to check the list of 2,600 additional verbs keyed to the 501 model verbs. It's in the Appendixes!

The subject pronouns are found on page 103.   **463**

Regular **-er** verb

The Seven Simple Tenses		The Seven Compound Tenses	
Singular	Plural	Singular	Plural
1 présent de l'indicatif		**8 passé composé**	
ose	osons	ai osé	avons osé
oses	osez	as osé	avez osé
ose	osent	a osé	ont osé
2 imparfait de l'indicatif		**9 plus-que-parfait de l'indicatif**	
osais	osions	avais osé	avions osé
osais	osiez	avais osé	aviez osé
osait	osaient	avait osé	avaient osé
3 passé simple		**10 passé antérieur**	
osai	osâmes	eus osé	eûmes osé
osas	osâtes	eus osé	eûtes osé
osa	osèrent	eut osé	eurent osé
4 futur		**11 futur antérieur**	
oserai	oserons	aurai osé	aurons osé
oseras	oserez	auras osé	aurez osé
osera	oseront	aura osé	auront osé
5 conditionnel		**12 conditionnel passé**	
oserais	oserions	aurais osé	aurions osé
oserais	oseriez	aurais osé	auriez osé
oserait	oseraient	aurait osé	auraient osé
6 présent du subjonctif		**13 passé du subjonctif**	
ose	osions	aie osé	ayons osé
oses	osiez	aies osé	ayez osé
ose	osent	ait osé	aient osé
7 imparfait du subjonctif		**14 plus-que-parfait du subjonctif**	
osasse	osassions	eusse osé	eussions osé
osasses	osassiez	eusses osé	eussiez osé
osât	osassent	eût osé	eussent osé

	Impératif
	ose
	osons
	osez

Words and expressions related to this verb
Si j'ose dire . . .   If I may be so bold as to say . . .
Je n'ose le dire.   I dare not say so.
oser faire qqch   to dare to do something; to have the courage, audacity to do something
Je n'ose rien dire.   I don't dare say anything.
osé, osée   bold, daring

Can't remember the French verb you need? Check the back pages of this book for the
English-French verb index!

Regular **-er** verb

to forget

The Seven Simple Tenses		The Seven Compound Tenses	
Singular	Plural	Singular	Plural
1 présent de l'indicatif		8 passé composé	
oublie	**oublions**	**ai oublié**	**avons oublié**
oublies	**oubliez**	**as oublié**	**avez oublié**
oublie	**oublient**	**a oublié**	**ont oublié**
2 imparfait de l'indicatif		9 plus-que-parfait de l'indicatif	
oubliais	**oubliions**	**avais oublié**	**avions oublié**
oubliais	**oubliiez**	**avais oublié**	**aviez oublié**
oubliait	**oubliaient**	**avait oublié**	**avaient oublié**
3 passé simple		10 passé antérieur	
oubliai	**oubliâmes**	**eus oublié**	**eûmes oublié**
oublias	**oubliâtes**	**eus oublié**	**eûtes oublié**
oublia	**oublièrent**	**eut oublié**	**eurent oublié**
4 futur		11 futur antérieur	
oublierai	**oublierons**	**aurai oublié**	**aurons oublié**
oublieras	**oublierez**	**auras oublié**	**aurez oublié**
oubliera	**oublieront**	**aura oublié**	**auront oublié**
5 conditionnel		12 conditionnel passé	
oublierais	**oublierions**	**aurais oublié**	**aurions oublié**
oublierais	**oublieriez**	**aurais oublié**	**auriez oublié**
oublierait	**oublieraient**	**aurait oublié**	**auraient oublié**
6 présent du subjonctif		13 passé du subjonctif	
oublie	**oubliions**	**aie oublié**	**ayons oublié**
oublies	**oubliiez**	**aies oublié**	**ayez oublié**
oublie	**oublient**	**ait oublié**	**aient oublié**
7 imparfait du subjonctif		14 plus-que-parfait du subjonctif	
oubliasse	**oubliassions**	**eusse oublié**	**eussions oublié**
oubliasses	**oubliassiez**	**eusses oublié**	**eussiez oublié**
oubliât	**oubliassent**	**eût oublié**	**eussent oublié**

Impératif
oublie
oublions
oubliez

Words and expressions related to this verb
un oubli   oversight; oblivion
tomber dans l'oubli   to be forgotten (over
   time)
oubliable   forgettable
inoubliable   unforgettable
s'oublier   to forget oneself, to be unmindful of
   oneself

oublier de faire qqch   to forget to do
   something
oublieux, oublieuse   oblivious; **oublieux de**
   unmindful of; forgetful
Nous n'oublierons jamais.   We will never
   forget.

How are you doing? Find out with the verb drills and tests with answers explained on pages
50–101.

The subject pronouns are found on page 103.

465

to open

The Seven Simple Tenses		The Seven Compound Tenses	
Singular	Plural	Singular	Plural
1 présent de l'indicatif		**8 passé composé**	
ouvre	ouvrons	ai ouvert	avons ouvert
ouvres	ouvrez	as ouvert	avez ouvert
ouvre	ouvrent	a ouvert	ont ouvert
2 imparfait de l'indicatif		**9 plus-que-parfait de l'indicatif**	
ouvrais	ouvrions	avais ouvert	avions ouvert
ouvrais	ouvriez	avais ouvert	aviez ouvert
ouvrait	ouvraient	avait ouvert	avaient ouvert
3 passé simple		**10 passé antérieur**	
ouvris	ouvrîmes	eus ouvert	eûmes ouvert
ouvris	ouvrîtes	eus ouvert	eûtes ouvert
ouvrit	ouvrirent	eut ouvert	eurent ouvert
4 futur		**11 futur antérieur**	
ouvrirai	ouvrirons	aurai ouvert	aurons ouvert
ouvriras	ouvrirez	auras ouvert	aurez ouvert
ouvrira	ouvriront	aura ouvert	auront ouvert
5 conditionnel		**12 conditionnel passé**	
ouvrirais	ouvririons	aurais ouvert	aurions ouvert
ouvrirais	ouvririez	aurais ouvert	auriez ouvert
ouvrirait	ouvriraient	aurait ouvert	auraient ouvert
6 présent du subjonctif		**13 passé du subjonctif**	
ouvre	ouvrions	aie ouvert	ayons ouvert
ouvres	ouvriez	aies ouvert	ayez ouvert
ouvre	ouvrent	ait ouvert	aient ouvert
7 imparfait du subjonctif		**14 plus-que-parfait du subjonctif**	
ouvrisse	ouvrissions	eusse ouvert	eussions ouvert
ouvrisses	ouvrissiez	eusses ouvert	eussiez ouvert
ouvrît	ouvrissent	eût ouvert	eussent ouvert

Impératif
ouvre
ouvrons
ouvrez

Words and expressions related to this verb
ouvert, ouverte   open
l'ouverture *f.*   opening
ouvrir le gaz   to turn on the gas
ouvrir de force   to force open
un ouvre-boîte (des ouvre-boîtes)   can opener
entrouvert, entrouverte   ajar
un ouvre-bouteille (des ouvre-bouteilles)
  bottle opener

rouvrir   to reopen, to open again
entrouvrir   to open just a bit
s'ouvrir à   to confide in
les heures ouvrables   business hours
ouvrir une session   to log in, log on
  (computer)

Irregular verb

The Seven Simple Tenses		The Seven Compound Tenses	
Singular	Plural	Singular	Plural

1 présent de l'indicatif		8 passé composé	
parais	**paraissons**	**ai paru**	**avons paru**
parais	**paraissez**	**as paru**	**avez paru**
paraît	**paraissent**	**a paru**	**ont paru**

2 imparfait de l'indicatif		9 plus-que-parfait de l'indicatif	
paraissais	**paraissions**	**avais paru**	**avions paru**
paraissais	**paraissiez**	**avais paru**	**aviez paru**
paraissait	**paraissaient**	**avait paru**	**avaient paru**

3 passé simple		10 passé antérieur	
parus	**parûmes**	**eus paru**	**eûmes paru**
parus	**parûtes**	**eus paru**	**eûtes paru**
parut	**parurent**	**eut paru**	**eurent paru**

4 futur		11 futur antérieur	
paraîtrai	**paraîtrons**	**aurai paru**	**aurons paru**
paraîtras	**paraîtrez**	**auras paru**	**aurez paru**
paraîtra	**paraîtront**	**aura paru**	**auront paru**

5 conditionnel		12 conditionnel passé	
paraîtrais	**paraîtrions**	**aurais paru**	**aurions paru**
paraîtrais	**paraîtriez**	**aurais paru**	**auriez paru**
paraîtrait	**paraîtraient**	**aurait paru**	**auraient paru**

6 présent du subjonctif		13 passé du subjonctif	
paraisse	**paraissions**	**aie paru**	**ayons paru**
paraisses	**paraissiez**	**aies paru**	**ayez paru**
paraisse	**paraissent**	**ait paru**	**aient paru**

7 imparfait du subjonctif		14 plus-que-parfait du subjonctif	
parusse	**parussions**	**eusse paru**	**eussions paru**
parusses	**parussiez**	**eusses paru**	**eussiez paru**
parût	**parussent**	**eût paru**	**eussent paru**

Impératif
parais
paraissons
paraissez

P

Words and expressions related to this verb
l'apparition *f.*   apparition, appearance
Cela me paraît incroyable.   That seems unbelievable to me.
Le jour paraît.   Day is breaking.
apparaître   to appear, to come into view
disparaître   to disappear
réapparaître   to reappear
Ce livre vient de paraître.   This book has just been published.
la parution   (act of) publication

See also **apparaître, disparaître,** and **reparaître.**

Review the Subjunctive clearly and simply on pages 26–31.

The subject pronouns are found on page 103.   **467**

to pardon, to forgive

Regular **-er** verb

The Seven Simple Tenses		The Seven Compound Tenses	
Singular	Plural	Singular	Plural
1 présent de l'indicatif		**8 passé composé**	
pardonne	pardonnons	ai pardonné	avons pardonné
pardonnes	pardonnez	as pardonné	avez pardonné
pardonne	pardonnent	a pardonné	ont pardonné
2 imparfait de l'indicatif		**9 plus-que-parfait de l'indicatif**	
pardonnais	pardonnions	avais pardonné	avions pardonné
pardonnais	pardonniez	avais pardonné	aviez pardonné
pardonnait	pardonnaient	avait pardonné	avaient pardonné
3 passé simple		**10 passé antérieur**	
pardonnai	pardonnâmes	eus pardonné	eûmes pardonné
pardonnas	pardonnâtes	eus pardonné	eûtes pardonné
pardonna	pardonnèrent	eut pardonné	eurent pardonné
4 futur		**11 futur antérieur**	
pardonnerai	pardonnerons	aurai pardonné	aurons pardonné
pardonneras	pardonnerez	auras pardonné	aurez pardonné
pardonnera	pardonneront	aura pardonné	auront pardonné
5 conditionnel		**12 conditionnel passé**	
pardonnerais	pardonnerions	aurais pardonné	aurions pardonné
pardonnerais	pardonneriez	aurais pardonné	auriez pardonné
pardonnerait	pardonneraient	aurait pardonné	auraient pardonné
6 présent du subjonctif		**13 passé du subjonctif**	
pardonne	pardonnions	aie pardonné	ayons pardonné
pardonnes	pardonniez	aies pardonné	ayez pardonné
pardonne	pardonnent	ait pardonné	aient pardonné
7 imparfait du subjonctif		**14 plus-que-parfait du subjonctif**	
pardonnasse	pardonnassions	eusse pardonné	eussions pardonné
pardonnasses	pardonnassiez	eusses pardonné	eussiez pardonné
pardonnât	pardonnassent	eût pardonné	eussent pardonné

Impératif
pardonne
pardonnons
pardonnez

Sentences using this verb and words related to it

pardonner à qqn de qqch   to forgive
   someone for something
**J'ai pardonné à mon ami d'être arrivé en
   retard.**   I forgave my friend for having
   arrived late.
un pardon   forgiveness, pardon

un don   gift
pardonnable   forgivable, pardonable
Pardonnez-moi.   Pardon me.
Marie-Thérèse, ce que vous venez de faire est
   impardonnable.   Marie-Thérèse, what you
   just did is unforgivable.

See also **donner.**

Can't find the verb you're looking for? Check the back pages of this book for a list of over 2,600
additional verbs!

Regular **-er** verb

to talk, to speak

The Seven Simple Tenses		The Seven Compound Tenses	
Singular	Plural	Singular	Plural

1 présent de l'indicatif		8 passé composé	
parle	**parlons**	**ai parlé**	**avons parlé**
parles	**parlez**	**as parlé**	**avez parlé**
parle	**parlent**	**a parlé**	**ont parlé**

2 imparfait de l'indicatif		9 plus-que-parfait de l'indicatif	
parlais	**parlions**	**avais parlé**	**avions parlé**
parlais	**parliez**	**avais parlé**	**aviez parlé**
parlait	**parlaient**	**avait parlé**	**avaient parlé**

3 passé simple		10 passé antérieur	
parlai	**parlâmes**	**eus parlé**	**eûmes parlé**
parlas	**parlâtes**	**eus parlé**	**eûtes parlé**
parla	**parlèrent**	**eut parlé**	**eurent parlé**

4 futur		11 futur antérieur	
parlerai	**parlerons**	**aurai parlé**	**aurons parlé**
parleras	**parlerez**	**auras parlé**	**aurez parlé**
parlera	**parleront**	**aura parlé**	**auront parlé**

5 conditionnel		12 conditionnel passé	
parlerais	**parlerions**	**aurais parlé**	**aurions parlé**
parlerais	**parleriez**	**aurais parlé**	**auriez parlé**
parlerait	**parleraient**	**aurait parlé**	**auraient parlé**

6 présent du subjonctif		13 passé du subjonctif	
parle	**parlions**	**aie parlé**	**ayons parlé**
parles	**parliez**	**aies parlé**	**ayez parlé**
parle	**parlent**	**ait parlé**	**aient parlé**

7 imparfait du subjonctif		14 plus-que-parfait du subjonctif	
parlasse	**parlassions**	**eusse parlé**	**eussions parlé**
parlasses	**parlassiez**	**eusses parlé**	**eussiez parlé**
parlât	**parlassent**	**eût parlé**	**eussent parlé**

P

Impératif
parle
parlons
parlez

AN ESSENTIAL
55 VERB

The subject pronouns are found on page 103.   **469**

Parler

Parler is an essential verb because it is used in many everyday situations and idiomatic expressions. It is an essential verb for a beginning student.

Sentences using parler

Ce n'est qu'une façon de parler. It's just a way of speaking.

Avez-vous jamais entendu parler de cela? Have you ever heard of that?

Je ne peux pas vous entendre. Parlez plus fort, s'il vous plaît. I can't hear you. Please speak more loudly.

Écoutez, le professeur va nous adresser la parole. Listen, the professor is going to speak to us.

Ici on parle français. French is spoken here.

Grand parleur, petit faiseur. All talk no action.

Words and expressions related to this verb

parler à haute voix **to speak in a loud voice**

parler haut **to speak loudly**

parler bas **to speak softly**

la parole **spoken word**

parler à **to talk to**

parler de **to talk about (of)**

le don de la parole **the gift of gab**

les pourparlers **negotiations**

francophone **French-speaking**

anglophone **English-speaking**

hispanophone **Spanish-speaking**

parler affaires **to talk business, to talk shop**

sans parler de . . . **not to mention . . .**

parler pour qqn **to speak for someone**

parler contre qqn **to speak against someone**

un parloir **parlor (room where people talk)**

le franc-parler **outspokenness**

à proprement parler **strictly speaking**

adresser la parole à **to speak to, to direct one's words at**

entendre parler de **to hear about**

reparler **to speak again**

le parleur, la parleuse **talker**

Proverbs and expressions

Il est bon de parler et meilleur de se taire. **(La Fontaine) Speech is silver; silence is golden.**

Toute parole n'est pas bonne à dire. **Not everything is worth saying.**

J'en parlerai à mon cheval. **I don't care what you're talking about. (Literally: I'll talk to my horse about it.)**

Irregular verb

to leave, to depart

The Seven Simple Tenses		The Seven Compound Tenses	
Singular	Plural	Singular	Plural
1 présent de l'indicatif		**8 passé composé**	
pars	partons	suis parti(e)	sommes parti(e)s
pars	partez	es parti(e)	êtes parti(e)(s)
part	partent	est parti(e)	sont parti(e)s
2 imparfait de l'indicatif		**9 plus-que-parfait de l'indicatif**	
partais	partions	étais parti(e)	étions parti(e)s
partais	partiez	étais parti(e)	étiez parti(e)(s)
partait	partaient	était parti(e)	étaient parti(e)s
3 passé simple		**10 passé antérieur**	
partis	partîmes	fus parti(e)	fûmes parti(e)s
partis	partîtes	fus parti(e)	fûtes parti(e)(s)
partit	partirent	fut parti(e)	furent parti(e)s
4 futur		**11 futur antérieur**	
partirai	partirons	serai parti(e)	serons parti(e)s
partiras	partirez	seras parti(e)	serez parti(e)(s)
partira	partiront	sera parti(e)	seront parti(e)s
5 conditionnel		**12 conditionnel passé**	
partirais	partirions	serais parti(e)	serions parti(e)s
partirais	partiriez	serais parti(e)	seriez parti(e)(s)
partirait	partiraient	serait parti(e)	seraient parti(e)s
6 présent du subjonctif		**13 passé du subjonctif**	
parte	partions	sois parti(e)	soyons parti(e)s
partes	partiez	sois parti(e)	soyez parti(e)(s)
parte	partent	soit parti(e)	soient parti(e)s
7 imparfait du subjonctif		**14 plus-que-parfait du subjonctif**	
partisse	partissions	fusse parti(e)	fussions parti(e)s
partisses	partissiez	fusses parti(e)	fussiez parti(e)(s)
partît	partissent	fût parti(e)	fussent parti(e)s

Impératif
pars
partons
partez

AN ESSENTIAL
55 VERB

The subject pronouns are found on page 103.   **471**

AN ESSENTIAL 55 VERB

Partir

Partir is an important verb for a beginning student because there are many words and idiomatic expressions that are based on it.

Sentences using partir

À quelle heure part le train pour Paris? At what time does the train for Paris leave?

Le train en partance pour Paris est sur la voie deux. The train leaving for Paris is on track two.

Dépêche-toi, Nathalie, nous partons tout de suite. Hurry up, Nathalie, we're leaving right away.

À partir de cet instant, tu vas faire tes devoirs avant de regarder la télévision. From this moment on, you are going to do your homework before watching television.

Je voudrais savoir à quelle heure l'avion part pour Montréal. I would like to know at what time the plane leaves for Montreal.

Words and expressions related to this verb

en partance **due to depart**

à partir de **beginning with**

à partir de maintenant **from now on**

à partir d'aujourd'hui **from today on**

partir en voyage **to go on a trip**

partir en vacances **to leave for a vacation**

un département **department**

départir **to assign (regular -ir verb)**

se départir de **to depart from (Use** être **as auxiliary)**

repartir **to leave again, to set out again (Use** être **as auxiliary); to reply (Use** avoir **as auxiliary)**

Careful! répartir (to divide up, share) is a regular -ir verb.

un faux départ **false start**

Proverbs

Le chat parti, les souris dansent. **When the cat is away, the mice will play.**

Rien ne sert de courir; il faut partir à point. (La Fontaine, *le Lièvre et la Tortue*) **There's no point in running; you have to leave at the right moment.**

Regular **-er** verb   to pass, to spend (time)

The Seven Simple Tenses		The Seven Compound Tenses	
Singular	Plural	Singular	Plural
1 présent de l'indicatif		8 passé composé	
passe	**passons**	**ai passé**	**avons passé**
passes	**passez**	**as passé**	**avez passé**
passe	**passent**	**a passé**	**ont passé**
2 imparfait de l'indicatif		9 plus-que-parfait de l'indicatif	
passais	**passions**	**avais passé**	**avions passé**
passais	**passiez**	**avais passé**	**aviez passé**
passait	**passaient**	**avait passé**	**avaient passé**
3 passé simple		10 passé antérieur	
passai	**passâmes**	**eus passé**	**eûmes passé**
passas	**passâtes**	**eus passé**	**eûtes passé**
passa	**passèrent**	**eut passé**	**eurent passé**
4 futur		11 futur antérieur	
passerai	**passerons**	**aurai passé**	**aurons passé**
passeras	**passerez**	**auras passé**	**aurez passé**
passera	**passeront**	**aura passé**	**auront passé**
5 conditionnel		12 conditionnel passé	
passerais	**passerions**	**aurais passé**	**aurions passé**
passerais	**passeriez**	**aurais passé**	**auriez passé**
passerait	**passeraient**	**aurait passé**	**auraient passé**
6 présent du subjonctif		13 passé du subjonctif	
passe	**passions**	**aie passé**	**ayons passé**
passes	**passiez**	**aies passé**	**ayez passé**
passe	**passent**	**ait passé**	**aient passé**
7 imparfait du subjonctif		14 plus-que-parfait du subjonctif	
passasse	**passassions**	**eusse passé**	**eussions passé**
passasses	**passassiez**	**eusses passé**	**eussiez passé**
passât	**passassent**	**eût passé**	**eussent passé**

Impératif
passe
passons
passez

P

This verb is conjugated with **être** to indicate a state.
Example: **Ses soupçons sont passés en certitudes.**
This verb is conjugated with **être** when it means *to pass by, go by.*
Example: **Elle est passée chez moi.**   She came by my house.
BUT This verb is conjugated with **avoir** when it has a direct object.
Examples: **Elle m'a passé le sel.**   She passed me the salt.
Elle a passé un examen.   She took an exam.

Passez une bonne journée! Au revoir!   Have a nice day! Good bye!
repasser   to pass again; to iron
dépasser   to protrude, to exceed, to surpass, to pass (a vehicle)
passable   acceptable
passer un examen   to take an exam
passer chez qqn   to drop in on someone
passer un coup de fil à qqn   to give someone a ring (a telephone call)

See also **repasser** and **se passer**.   Review page 6.

The subject pronouns are found on page 103.

Part. pr. **patinant**   Part. passé **patiné**

to skate

Regular **-er** verb

The Seven Simple Tenses		The Seven Compound Tenses	
Singular	Plural	Singular	Plural
1 présent de l'indicatif		**8 passé composé**	
patine	patinons	ai patiné	avons patiné
patines	patinez	as patiné	avez patiné
patine	patinent	a patiné	ont patiné
2 imparfait de l'indicatif		**9 plus-que-parfait de l'indicatif**	
patinais	patinions	avais patiné	avions patiné
patinais	patiniez	avais patiné	aviez patiné
patinait	patinaient	avait patiné	avaient patiné
3 passé simple		**10 passé antérieur**	
patinai	patinâmes	eus patiné	eûmes patiné
patinas	patinâtes	eus patiné	eûtes patiné
patina	patinèrent	eut patiné	eurent patiné
4 futur		**11 futur antérieur**	
patinerai	patinerons	aurai patiné	aurons patiné
patineras	patinerez	auras patiné	aurez patiné
patinera	patineront	aura patiné	auront patiné
5 conditionnel		**12 conditionnel passé**	
patinerais	patinerions	aurais patiné	aurions patiné
patinerais	patineriez	aurais patiné	auriez patiné
patinerait	patineraient	aurait patiné	auraient patiné
6 présent du subjonctif		**13 passé du subjonctif**	
patine	patinions	aie patiné	ayons patiné
patines	patiniez	aies patiné	ayez patiné
patine	patinent	ait patiné	aient patiné
7 imparfait du subjonctif		**14 plus-que-parfait du subjonctif**	
patinasse	patinassions	eusse patiné	eussions patiné
patinasses	patinassiez	eusses patiné	eussiez patiné
patinât	patinassent	eût patiné	eussent patiné

Impératif
patine
patinons
patinez

Words and expressions related to this verb
patiner sur glace   to skate on ice
une patinette   scooter
un patineur, une patineuse   skater
le patinage   skating
le patinage artistique   figure skating
les patins à roues alignées   inline skates

une patinoire   skating rink
patiner sur roulettes, patiner à roulettes   to roller-skate
le patinage à roulettes   roller-skating
le patinage de vitesse   speed skating

Soak up some verbs used in weather expressions. There's a list in the Appendixes!

Regular **-er** verb endings; spelling change: **-ayer** verbs
may change **y** to **i** before a mute **e** or may keep **y**

The Seven Simple Tenses		The Seven Compound Tenses	
Singular	Plural	Singular	Plural

1 présent de l'indicatif		8 passé composé	
paye	payons	ai payé	avons payé
payes	payez	as payé	avez payé
paye	payent	a payé	ont payé

2 imparfait de l'indicatif		9 plus-que-parfait de l'indicatif	
payais	payions	avais payé	avions payé
payais	payiez	avais payé	aviez payé
payait	payaient	avait payé	avaient payé

3 passé simple		10 passé antérieur	
payai	payâmes	eus payé	eûmes payé
payas	payâtes	eus payé	eûtes payé
paya	payèrent	eut payé	eurent payé

4 futur		11 futur antérieur	
payerai	payerons	aurai payé	aurons payé
payeras	payerez	auras payé	aurez payé
payera	payeront	aura payé	auront payé

5 conditionnel		12 conditionnel passé	
payerais	payerions	aurais payé	aurions payé
payerais	payeriez	aurais payé	auriez payé
payerait	payeraient	aurait payé	auraient payé

6 présent du subjonctif		13 passé du subjonctif	
paye	payions	aie payé	ayons payé
payes	payiez	aies payé	ayez payé
paye	payent	ait payé	aient payé

7 imparfait du subjonctif		14 plus-que-parfait du subjonctif	
payasse	payassions	eusse payé	eussions payé
payasses	payassiez	eusses payé	eussiez payé
payât	payassent	eût payé	eussent payé

Impératif
paye
payons
payez

P

AN ESSENTIAL
55 VERB

Payer is an important verb for you to know because of its spelling change before a mute e. Payer is also useful for shopping when you travel!

Sentences using payer and related words

Payez à la caisse, s'il vous plaît. Please pay at the cashier.

Nous payons toutes nos factures à la fin du mois. We pay all our bills at the end of the month.

Roland paye par carte bancaire, mais Olivier paye comptant. Roland pays by credit card, but Olivier pays cash.

If you can conjugate payer you can also conjugate the following verbs:

débrayer **to disengage the clutch**

défrayer **to pay expenses**

repayer **to pay again**

sous-payer **to underpay**

surpayer **to overpay**

Words and expressions related to this verb

un paiement (or paiement) **payment**

avoir de quoi payer **to have the means to pay**

payable **payable**

se faire payer à dîner par qqn **to get your dinner paid for by someone**

payer cher **to pay a lot**

payer peu **to pay little**

payer comptant, payer en espèces **to pay in cash**

payer l'addition **to pay the check**

payer à la caisse **to pay at the counter (cashier's desk)**

Proverb

Les gens payent bien quand ils payent comptant. **People pay well when they pay cash.**

Can't find the verb you're looking for? Check the back pages of this book for a list of over 2,600 additional verbs!

Regular **-er** verb endings; spelling change:
é changes to **è** before syllable with mute **e**

to sin, to commit a sin

The Seven Simple Tenses

The Seven Compound Tenses

Singular	Plural	Singular	Plural
1 présent de l'indicatif		8 passé composé	
pèche	péchons	ai péché	avons péché
pèches	péchez	as péché	avez péché
pèche	pèchent	a péché	ont péché
2 imparfait de l'indicatif		9 plus-que-parfait de l'indicatif	
péchais	péchions	avais péché	avions péché
péchais	péchiez	avais péché	aviez péché
péchait	péchaient	avait péché	avaient péché
3 passé simple		10 passé antérieur	
péchai	péchâmes	eus péché	eûmes péché
péchas	péchâtes	eus péché	eûtes péché
pécha	péchèrent	eut péché	eurent péché
4 futur		11 futur antérieur	
pécherai	pécherons	aurai péché	aurons péché
pécheras	pécherez	auras péché	aurez péché
péchera	pécheront	aura péché	auront péché
5 conditionnel		12 conditionnel passé	
pécherais	pécherions	aurais péché	aurions péché
pécherais	pécheriez	aurais péché	auriez péché
pécherait	pécheraient	aurait péché	auraient péché
6 présent du subjonctif		13 passé du subjonctif	
pèche	péchions	aie péché	ayons péché
pèches	péchiez	aies péché	ayez péché
pèche	pèchent	ait péché	aient péché
7 imparfait du subjonctif		14 plus-que-parfait du subjonctif	
péchasse	péchassions	eusse péché	eussions péché
péchasses	péchassiez	eusses péché	eussiez péché
péchât	péchassent	eût péché	eussent péché

Impératif
pèche
péchons
péchez

Words and expressions related to this verb

le péché   sin
un pécheur, une pécheresse   sinner
à tout péché miséricorde   forgiveness for every sin

commettre, faire un péché   to commit sin
vivre dans le péché   to lead a sinful life
les sept péchés capitaux   the seven deadly sins

Do not confuse this verb with **pêcher,** *to fish.*

Don't forget to study the section on defective and impersonal verbs. It's right after this main list.

The subject pronouns are found on page 103.   **477**

Part. pr. **pêchant**   Part. passé **pêché**

Regular **-er** verb

The Seven Simple Tenses		The Seven Compound Tenses	
Singular	Plural	Singular	Plural
1 présent de l'indicatif		8 passé composé	
pêche	pêchons	ai pêché	avons pêché
pêches	pêchez	as pêché	avez pêché
pêche	pêchent	a pêché	ont pêché
2 imparfait de l'indicatif		9 plus-que-parfait de l'indicatif	
pêchais	pêchions	avais pêché	avions pêché
pêchais	pêchiez	avais pêché	aviez pêché
pêchait	pêchaient	avait pêché	avaient pêché
3 passé simple		10 passé antérieur	
pêchai	pêchâmes	eus pêché	eûmes pêché
pêchas	pêchâtes	eus pêché	eûtes pêché
pâcha	pêchèrent	eut pêché	eurent pêché
4 futur		11 futur antérieur	
pêcherai	pêcherons	aurai pêché	aurons pêché
pêcheras	pêcherez	auras pêché	aurez pêché
pêchera	pêcheront	aura pêché	auront pêché
5 conditionnel		12 conditionnel passé	
pêcherais	pêcherions	aurais pêché	aurions pêché
pêcherais	pêcheriez	aurais pêché	auriez pêché
pêcherait	pêcheraient	aurait pêché	auraient pêché
6 présent du subjonctif		13 passé du subjonctif	
pêche	pêchions	aie pêché	ayons pêché
pêches	pêchiez	aies pêché	ayez pêché
pêche	pêchent	ait pêché	aient pêché
7 imparfait du subjonctif		14 plus-que-parfait du subjonctif	
pêchasse	pêchassions	eusse pêché	eussions pêché
pêchasses	pêchassiez	eusses pêché	eussiez pêché
pêchât	pêchassent	eût pêché	eussent pêché

Impératif
pêche
pêchons
pêchez

Common idiomatic expressions using this verb

Samedi nous irons à la pêche. Je connais un lac à la campagne où il y a beaucoup de poissons.

aller à la pêche   to go fishing
un pêcheur   fisherman; **une pêcheuse**
  fisherwoman
un bateau pêcheur   fishing boat

le repêchage   recovery, (act of) fishing out
la pêche au filet   net fishing
un pêcheur de perles   pearl diver
repêcher   to fish out

Do not confuse this verb with **pécher,** *to sin.* And do not confuse **une pêche** (*peach*), which is a

Reflexive regular -er verb   to comb one's hair

The Seven Simple Tenses		The Seven Compound Tenses	
Singular	Plural	Singular	Plural

1 présent de l'indicatif

me peigne	nous peignons	
te peignes	vous peignez	
se peigne	se peignent	

8 passé composé

me suis peigné(e)	nous sommes peigné(e)s
t'es peigné(e)	vous êtes peigné(e)(s)
s'est peigné(e)	se sont peigné(e)s

2 imparfait de l'indicatif

me peignais	nous peignions
te peignais	vous peigniez
se peignait	se peignaient

9 plus-que-parfait de l'indicatif

m'étais peigné(e)	nous étions peigné(e)s
t'étais peigné(e)	vous étiez peigné(e)(s)
s'était peigné(e)	s'étaient peigné(e)s

3 passé simple

me peignai	nous peignâmes
te peignas	vous peignâtes
se peigna	se peignèrent

10 passé antérieur

me fus peigné(e)	nous fûmes peigné(e)s
te fus peigné(e)	vous fûtes peigné(e)(s)
se fut peigné(e)	se furent peigné(e)s

4 futur

me peignerai	nous peignerons
te peigneras	vous peignerez
se peignera	se peigneront

11 futur antérieur

me serai peigné(e)	nous serons peigné(e)s
te seras peigné(e)	vous serez peigné(e)(s)
se sera peigné(e)	se seront peigné(e)s

5 conditionnel

me peignerais	nous peignerions
te peignerais	vous peigneriez
se peignerait	se peigneraient

12 conditionnel passé

me serais peigné(e)	nous serions peigné(e)s
te serais peigné(e)	vous seriez peigné(e)(s)
se serait peigné(e)	se seraient peigné(e)s

6 présent du subjonctif

me peigne	nous peignions
te peignes	vous peigniez
se peigne	se peignent

13 passé du subjonctif

me sois peigné(e)	nous soyons peigné(e)s
te sois peigné(e)	vous soyez peigné(e)(s)
se soit peigné(e)	se soient peigné(e)s

7 imparfait du subjonctif

me peignasse	nous peignassions
te peignasses	vous peignassiez
se peignât	se peignassent

14 plus-que-parfait du subjonctif

me fusse peigné(e)	nous fussions peigné(e)s
te fusses peigné(e)	vous fussiez peigné(e)(s)
se fût peigné(e)	se fussent peigné(e)s

Impératif
peigne-toi; ne te peigne pas
peignons-nous; ne nous peignons pas
peignez-vous; ne vous peignez pas

Sentences using this verb and words related to it

Mon frère a peigné notre petit chien. Ma mère a lavé les cheveux de ma petite soeur et elle l'a peignée. Après cela, elle s'est lavé les cheveux et elle s'est peignée.

peigner qqn	to comb someone	mal peigné(e)(s)	untidy hair, dishevelled
un peigne	a comb	bien peigné(e)(s)	well combed
un peignoir	dressing gown	un peignoir de bain	bathrobe

Review the entry agreement of past participle of a reflexive verb with its reflexive pronoun in the section on definitions of basic grammatical terms with examples on pages 35–49.

to paint, to portray   Irregular verb

The Seven Simple Tenses		The Seven Compound Tenses	
Singular	Plural	Singular	Plural
1 présent de l'indicatif		8 passé composé	
peins	peignons	ai peint	avons peint
peins	peignez	as peint	avez peint
peint	peignent	a peint	ont peint
2 imparfait de l'indicatif		9 plus-que-parfait de l'indicatif	
peignais	peignions	avais peint	avions peint
peignais	peigniez	avais peint	aviez peint
peignait	peignaient	avait peint	avaient peint
3 passé simple		10 passé antérieur	
peignis	peignîmes	eus peint	eûmes peint
peignis	peignîtes	eus peint	eûtes peint
peignit	peignirent	eut peint	eurent peint
4 futur		11 futur antérieur	
peindrai	peindrons	aurai peint	aurons peint
peindras	peindrez	auras peint	aurez peint
peindra	peindront	aura peint	auront peint
5 conditionnel		12 conditionnel passé	
peindrais	peindrions	aurais peint	aurions peint
peindrais	peindriez	aurais peint	auriez peint
peindrait	peindraient	aurait peint	auraient peint
6 présent du subjonctif		13 passé du subjonctif	
peigne	peignions	aie peint	ayons peint
peignes	peigniez	aies peint	ayez peint
peigne	peignent	ait peint	aient peint
7 imparfait du subjonctif		14 plus-que-parfait du subjonctif	
peignisse	peignissions	eusse peint	eussions peint
peignisses	peignissiez	eusses peint	eussiez peint
peignît	peignissent	eût peint	eussent peint

Impératif
peins
peignons
peignez

Sentences using this verb and words related to it
—Qui a peint ce tableau? Mon fils. Il est artiste peintre.
—Est-ce que Renoir a jamais peint une reine noire?

une peinture   painting, picture
un tableau   painting, picture
une peinture à l'huile   oil painting
peintre en bâtiments   house painter
dépeindre   to depict, to describe
PEINTURE FRAÎCHE   WET PAINT

un peintre   painter
un artiste peintre   artist
une femme peintre   woman artist
une palette de peintre   artist's palette
se faire peindre   to have one's portrait painted

See also **dépeindre**.

480

Regular **-re** verb   to hang, to suspend

The Seven Simple Tenses		The Seven Compound Tenses	
Singular	Plural	Singular	Plural
1 présent de l'indicatif		8 passé composé	
pends	pendons	ai pendu	avons pendu
pends	pendez	as pendu	avez pendu
pend	pendent	a pendu	ont pendu
2 imparfait de l'indicatif		9 plus-que-parfait de l'indicatif	
pendais	pendions	avais pendu	avions pendu
pendais	pendiez	avais pendu	aviez pendu
pendait	pendaient	avait pendu	avaient pendu
3 passé simple		10 passé antérieur	
pendis	pendîmes	eus pendu	eûmes pendu
pendis	pendîtes	eus pendu	eûtes pendu
pendit	pendirent	eut pendu	eurent pendu
4 futur		11 futur antérieur	
pendrai	pendrons	aurai pendu	aurons pendu
pendras	pendrez	auras pendu	aurez pendu
pendra	pendront	aura pendu	auront pendu
5 conditionnel		12 conditionnel passé	
pendrais	pendrions	aurais pendu	aurions pendu
pendrais	pendriez	aurais pendu	auriez pendu
pendrait	pendraient	aurait pendu	auraient pendu
6 présent du subjonctif		13 passé du subjonctif	
pende	pendions	aie pendu	ayons pendu
pendes	pendiez	aies pendu	ayez pendu
pende	pendent	ait pendu	aient pendu
7 imparfait du subjonctif		14 plus-que-parfait du subjonctif	
pendisse	pendissions	eusse pendu	eussions pendu
pendisses	pendissiez	eusses pendu	eussiez pendu
pendît	pendissent	eût pendu	eussent pendu

Impératif
pends
pendons
pendez

P

Words and expressions related to this verb
pendre des rideaux   to hang curtains
pendre qqch   to hang something
pendre qqn   to hang someone
se pendre   to hang oneself
dépendre de   to depend on
pendant   during; pendant que   while
un pendant   pendant, main piece of a
   necklace, hanging ornament

suspendre un lustre   to hang a chandelier
   (ceiling lighting fixture)
pendu, pendue *adj.*   hung (thing); hanged
   (person)
un pendule   pendulum
une pendule   clock
un pendant d'oreille   pendant earring, drop
   earring

See also dépendre.

For an explanation of meanings and uses of French and English verb tenses and moods, see pages 10–21.

penser (336)
to think

Part. pr. **pensant**   Part. passé **pensé**

Regular **-er** verb

The Seven Simple Tenses

Singular	Plural
1 présent de l'indicatif	
pense	pensons
penses	pensez
pense	pensent
2 imparfait de l'indicatif	
pensais	pensions
pensais	pensiez
pensait	pensaient
3 passé simple	
pensai	pensâmes
pensas	pensâtes
pensa	pensèrent
4 futur	
penserai	penserons
penseras	penserez
pensera	penseront
5 conditionnel	
penserais	penserions
penserais	penseriez
penserait	penseraient
6 présent du subjonctif	
pense	pensions
penses	pensiez
pense	pensent
7 imparfait du subjonctif	
pensasse	pensassions
pensasses	pensassiez
pensât	pensassent

The Seven Compound Tenses

Singular	Plural
8 passé composé	
ai pensé	avons pensé
as pensé	avez pensé
a pensé	ont pensé
9 plus-que-parfait de l'indicatif	
avais pensé	avions pensé
avais pensé	aviez pensé
avait pensé	avaient pensé
10 passé antérieur	
eus pensé	eûmes pensé
eus pensé	eûtes pensé
eut pensé	eurent pensé
11 futur antérieur	
aurai pensé	aurons pensé
auras pensé	aurez pensé
aura pensé	auront pensé
12 conditionnel passé	
aurais pensé	aurions pensé
aurais pensé	auriez pensé
aurait pensé	auraient pensé
13 passé du subjonctif	
aie pensé	ayons pensé
aies pensé	ayez pensé
ait pensé	aient pensé
14 plus-que-parfait du subjonctif	
eusse pensé	eussions pensé
eusses pensé	eussiez pensé
eût pensé	eussent pensé

Impératif
pense
pensons
pensez

Common idiomatic expressions using this verb

—**Robert, tu as l'air pensif; à quoi penses-tu?**
—**Je pense à mon examen de français.**
—**Moi, je pense aux vacances de Noël.**
—**Que penses-tu de cette classe de français?**
—**Je trouve que cette classe est excellente.**
—**Penses-tu continuer à étudier le français l'année prochaine?**
—**Certainement.**

penser à   to think of, to think about; **penser de**   to think about (*i.e.*, to have an opinion about);
   un pense-bête   reminder (*e.g.*, string around one's finger); **repenser**   to rethink

Note: If you want to say that you're making up your mind (reflecting on something) use **réfléchir.**

The Seven Simple Tenses		The Seven Compound Tenses	
Singular	Plural	Singular	Plural
1 présent de l'indicatif		**8 passé composé**	
perds	perdons	ai perdu	avons perdu
perds	perdez	as perdu	avez perdu
perd	perdent	a perdu	ont perdu
2 imparfait de l'indicatif		**9 plus-que-parfait de l'indicatif**	
perdais	perdions	avais perdu	avions perdu
perdais	perdiez	avais perdu	aviez perdu
perdait	perdaient	avait perdu	avaient perdu
3 passé simple		**10 passé antérieur**	
perdis	perdîmes	eus perdu	eûmes perdu
perdis	perdîtes	eus perdu	eûtes perdu
perdit	perdirent	eut perdu	eurent perdu
4 futur		**11 futur antérieur**	
perdrai	perdrons	aurai perdu	aurons perdu
perdras	perdrez	auras perdu	aurez perdu
perdra	perdront	aura perdu	auront perdu
5 conditionnel		**12 conditionnel passé**	
perdrais	perdrions	aurais perdu	aurions perdu
perdrais	perdriez	aurais perdu	auriez perdu
perdrait	perdraient	aurait perdu	auraient perdu
6 présent du subjonctif		**13 passé du subjonctif**	
perde	perdions	aie perdu	ayons perdu
perdes	perdiez	aies perdu	ayez perdu
perde	perdent	ait perdu	aient perdu
7 imparfait du subjonctif		**14 plus-que-parfait du subjonctif**	
perdisse	perdissions	eusse perdu	eussions perdu
perdisses	perdissiez	eusses perdu	eussiez perdu
perdît	perdissent	eût perdu	eussent perdu

P

Impératif
perds
perdons
perdez

AN ESSENTIAL
55 VERB

Perdre is an important verb for a beginning French student because it is a regular -re verb and because it is used in numerous everyday situations and idiomatic expressions.

Sentences using perdre

Vous n'avez rien à perdre. You have nothing to lose.

Je me suis perdu(e). I'm lost.

À cause du verglas, le chauffeur a perdu la maîtrise de sa voiture. Because of the black ice, the driver lost control of his car.

Quand on n'a rien à perdre, on peut bien tout risquer. (Jean-Louis Laya) When one has nothing to lose, one can risk everything.

Words and expressions related to this verb

se perdre **to lose oneself, to lose one's way, to be ruined**

perdre son temps **to waste one's time**

perdre son chemin **to lose one's way**

perdre pied **to lose one's footing**

perdre les pédales **to lose one's head**

perdre le nord, perdre la boule **to go crazy**

perdre connaissance **to faint**

perdre l'esprit **to go out of one's mind**

une perte **loss**

perdre de vue **to lose sight of**

perdre la raison **to take leave of one's senses**

éperdu, éperdue **distraught, overcome**

éperdument **passionately**

reperdre **to lose again**

Can't remember the French verb you need? Check the back pages of this book for the English-French verb index!

Regular **-ir** verb

to perish, to die

The Seven Simple Tenses		The Seven Compound Tenses	
Singular	Plural	Singular	Plural

1 présent de l'indicatif		8 passé composé	
péris	**périssons**	**ai péri**	**avons péri**
péris	**périssez**	**as péri**	**avez péri**
périt	**périssent**	**a péri**	**ont péri**

2 imparfait de l'indicatif		9 plus-que-parfait de l'indicatif	
périssais	**périssions**	**avais péri**	**avions péri**
périssais	**périssiez**	**avais péri**	**aviez péri**
périssait	**périssaient**	**avait péri**	**avaient péri**

3 passé simple		10 passé antérieur	
péris	**pérîmes**	**eus péri**	**eûmes péri**
péris	**pérîtes**	**eus péri**	**eûtes péri**
périt	**périrent**	**eut péri**	**eurent péri**

4 futur		11 futur antérieur	
périrai	**périrons**	**aurai péri**	**aurons péri**
périras	**périrez**	**auras péri**	**aurez péri**
périra	**périront**	**aura péri**	**auront péri**

5 conditionnel		12 conditionnel passé	
périrais	**péririons**	**aurais péri**	**aurions péri**
périrais	**péririez**	**aurais péri**	**auriez péri**
périrait	**périraient**	**aurait péri**	**auraient péri**

6 présent du subjonctif		13 passé du subjonctif	
périsse	**périssions**	**aie péri**	**ayons péri**
périsses	**périssiez**	**aies péri**	**ayez péri**
périsse	**périssent**	**ait péri**	**aient péri**

7 imparfait du subjonctif		14 plus-que-parfait du subjonctif	
périsse	**périssions**	**eusse péri**	**eussions péri**
périsses	**périssiez**	**eusses péri**	**eussiez péri**
pérît	**périssent**	**eût péri**	**eussent péri**

Impératif
péris
périssons
périssez

Common idiomatic expressions using this verb
faire périr to kill
s'ennuyer à périr to be bored to death
périssable perishable
périr d'ennui to be bored to death

péri en mer lost at sea
périr de froid to freeze to death
les denrées périssables perishable foods
impérissable imperishable, eternal

Can't find the verb you're looking for? Check the back pages of this book for a list of over 2,600 additional verbs!

The subject pronouns are found on page 103.   **485**

to permit, to allow, to let

Irregular verb

The Seven Simple Tenses		The Seven Compound Tenses	
Singular	Plural	Singular	Plural
1 présent de l'indicatif		**8 passé composé**	
permets	permettons	ai permis	avons permis
permets	permettez	as permis	avez permis
permet	permettent	a permis	ont permis
2 imparfait de l'indicatif		**9 plus-que-parfait de l'indicatif**	
permettais	permettions	avais permis	avions permis
permettais	permettiez	avais permis	aviez permis
permettait	permettaient	avait permis	avaient permis
3 passé simple		**10 passé antérieur**	
permis	permîmes	eus permis	eûmes permis
permis	permîtes	eus permis	eûtes permis
permit	permirent	eut permis	eurent permis
4 futur		**11 futur antérieur**	
permettrai	permettrons	aurai permis	aurons permis
permettras	permettrez	auras permis	aurez permis
permettra	permettront	aura permis	auront permis
5 conditionnel		**12 conditionnel passé**	
permettrais	permettrions	aurais permis	aurions permis
permettrais	permettriez	aurais permis	auriez permis
permettrait	permettraient	aurait permis	auraient permis
6 présent du subjonctif		**13 passé du subjonctif**	
permette	permettions	aie permis	ayons permis
permettes	permettiez	aies permis	ayez permis
permette	permettent	ait permis	aient permis
7 imparfait du subjonctif		**14 plus-que-parfait du subjonctif**	
permisse	permissions	eusse permis	eussions permis
permisses	permissiez	eusses permis	eussiez permis
permît	permissent	eût permis	eussent permis

Impératif
permets
permettons
permettez

Common idiomatic expressions using this verb and words related to it

La maîtresse de français a permis à l'élève de quitter la salle de classe quelques minutes avant la fin de la leçon.

permettre à qqn de faire qqch   to permit (to allow) someone to do something
Vous permettez?   May I? Do you mind?
s'il est permis   if it is allowed, permitted
un permis   permit

un permis de conduire   driving license
la permission   permission
se permettre de faire qqch   to take the liberty to do something; to venture to do something
un permis de construction   building permit

See also **commettre, mettre, omettre, promettre, remettre, soumettre,** and **transmettre.**

Regular **-er** verb   to persuade, to convince, to induce

The Seven Simple Tenses		The Seven Compound Tenses	
Singular	Plural	Singular	Plural
1 présent de l'indicatif		8 passé composé	
persuade	**persuadons**	**ai persuadé**	**avons persuadé**
persuades	**persuadez**	**as persuadé**	**avez persuadé**
persuade	**persuadent**	**a persuadé**	**ont persuadé**
2 imparfait de l'indicatif		9 plus-que-parfait de l'indicatif	
persuadais	**persuadions**	**avais persuadé**	**avions persuadé**
persuadais	**persuadiez**	**avais persuadé**	**aviez persuadé**
persuadait	**persuadaient**	**avait persuadé**	**avaient persuadé**
3 passé simple		10 passé antérieur	
persuadai	**persuadâmes**	**eus persuadé**	**eûmes persuadé**
persuadas	**persuadâtes**	**eus persuadé**	**eûtes persuadé**
persuada	**persuadèrent**	**eut persuadé**	**eurent persuadé**
4 futur		11 futur antérieur	
persuaderai	**persuaderons**	**aurai persuadé**	**aurons persuadé**
persuaderas	**persuaderez**	**auras persuadé**	**aurez persuadé**
persuadera	**persuaderont**	**aura persuadé**	**auront persuadé**
5 conditionnel		12 conditionnel passé	
persuaderais	**persuaderions**	**aurais persuadé**	**aurions persuadé**
persuaderais	**persuaderiez**	**aurais persuadé**	**auriez persuadé**
persuaderait	**persuaderaient**	**aurait persuadé**	**auraient persuadé**
6 présent du subjonctif		13 passé du subjonctif	
persuade	**persuadions**	**aie persuadé**	**ayons persuadé**
persuades	**persuadiez**	**aies persuadé**	**ayez persuadé**
persuade	**persuadent**	**ait persuadé**	**aient persuadé**
7 imparfait du subjonctif		14 plus-que-parfait du subjonctif	
persuadasse	**persuadassions**	**eusse persuadé**	**eussions persuadé**
persuadasses	**persuadassiez**	**eusses persuadé**	**eussiez persuadé**
persuadât	**persuadassent**	**eût persuadé**	**eussent persuadé**

Impératif
persuade
persuadons
persuadez

P

Words and expressions related to this verb

persuader à qqn de faire qqch   to induce
  someone to do something
persuader qqn de qqch   to persuade someone
  of something

dissuader de   to dissuade from
la persuasion   persuasion
persuasif, persuasive   persuasive
persuasivement   persuasively

se persuader de qqch   to persuade (convince) oneself of something

Can't remember the French verb you need? Check the back pages of this book for the
English-French verb index!

The subject pronouns are found on page 103.
                                                                    487

Part. pr. **pesant**   Part. passé **pesé**

to weigh

Regular **-er** verb endings; spelling change:
e changes to **è** before syllable with mute **e**

The Seven Simple Tenses		The Seven Compound Tenses	
Singular	Plural	Singular	Plural
1 présent de l'indicatif		8 passé composé	
pèse	pesons	ai pesé	avons pesé
pèses	pesez	as pesé	avez pesé
pèse	pèsent	a pesé	ont pesé
2 imparfait de l'indicatif		9 plus-que-parfait de l'indicatif	
pesais	pesions	avais pesé	avions pesé
pesais	pesiez	avais pesé	aviez pesé
pesait	pesaient	avait pesé	avaient pesé
3 passé simple		10 passé antérieur	
pesai	pesâmes	eus pesé	eûmes pesé
pesas	pesâtes	eus pesé	eûtes pesé
pesa	pesèrent	eut pesé	eurent pesé
4 futur		11 futur antérieur	
pèserai	pèserons	aurai pesé	aurons pesé
pèseras	pèserez	auras pesé	aurez pesé
pèsera	pèseront	aura pesé	auront pesé
5 conditionnel		12 conditionnel passé	
pèserais	pèserions	aurais pesé	aurions pesé
pèserais	pèseriez	aurais pesé	auriez pesé
pèserait	pèseraient	aurait pesé	auraient pesé
6 présent du subjonctif		13 passé du subjonctif	
pèse	pesions	aie pesé	ayons pesé
pèses	pesiez	aies pesé	ayez pesé
pèse	pèsent	ait pesé	aient pesé
7 imparfait du subjonctif		14 plus-que-parfait du subjonctif	
pesasse	pesassions	eusse pesé	eussions pesé
pesasses	pesassiez	eusses pesé	eussiez pesé
pesât	pesassent	eût pesé	eussent pesé

Impératif
pèse
pesons
pesez

Words and expressions related to this verb

peser qqch   to weigh something; to ponder; to think out, to consider
peser sur   to weigh upon
se peser   to weigh oneself
pesamment   heavily
un pèse-lettre   weight scale for letters
   (des pèse-lettres)

le poids   weight (measured)
la pesanteur   weight, gravity
pesant, pesante   heavy, weighty
poids et mesures   weights and measures
perdre du poids   to lose weight
un pèse-personne   a bathroom scale

Grammar putting you in a tense mood? Review the definitions of basic grammatical terms on pages 35–49.

Regular **-er** verb endings; spelling change:
c changes to **ç** before **a** or **o** to keep **s** sound

to place, to put

The Seven Simple Tenses		The Seven Compound Tenses	
Singular	Plural	Singular	Plural
1 présent de l'indicatif		**8 passé composé**	
place	plaçons	ai placé	avons placé
places	placez	as placé	avez placé
place	placent	a placé	ont placé
2 imparfait de l'indicatif		**9 plus-que-parfait de l'indicatif**	
plaçais	placions	avais placé	avions placé
plaçais	placiez	avais placé	aviez placé
plaçait	plaçaient	avait placé	avaient placé
3 passé simple		**10 passé antérieur**	
plaçai	plaçâmes	eus placé	eûmes placé
plaças	plaçâtes	eus placé	eûtes placé
plaça	placèrent	eut placé	eurent placé
4 futur		**11 futur antérieur**	
placerai	placerons	aurai placé	aurons placé
placeras	placerez	auras placé	aurez placé
placera	placeront	aura placé	auront placé
5 conditionnel		**12 conditionnel passé**	
placerais	placerions	aurais placé	aurions placé
placerais	placeriez	aurais placé	auriez placé
placerait	placeraient	aurait placé	auraient placé
6 présent du subjonctif		**13 passé du subjonctif**	
place	placions	aie placé	ayons placé
places	placiez	aies placé	ayez placé
place	placent	ait placé	aient placé
7 imparfait du subjonctif		**14 plus-que-parfait du subjonctif**	
plaçasse	plaçassions	eusse placé	eussions placé
plaçasses	plaçassiez	eusses placé	eussiez placé
plaçât	plaçassent	eût placé	eussent placé

Impératif
place
plaçons
placez

P

Sentences using this verb and words related to it

Nous pouvons déjeuner maintenant. Ma place est ici près de la fenêtre, ta place est là-bas près de la porte. Marie, place-toi à côté de Pierre. Combien de places y a-t-il? Y a-t-il assez de places pour tout le monde?

une place   a seat, a place
chaque chose à sa place   everything in its place
un placement   placing
un bureau de placement   employment agency
se placer   to place oneself, to take a seat, to find employment
replacer   to replace, put back

See also **remplacer**.

The subject pronouns are found on page 103.

to pity

Irregular verb

The Seven Simple Tenses		The Seven Compound Tenses	
Singular	Plural	Singular	Plural
1 présent de l'indicatif		8 passé composé	
plains	plaignons	ai plaint	avons plaint
plains	plaignez	as plaint	avez plaint
plaint	plaignent	a plaint	ont plaint
2 imparfait de l'indicatif		9 plus-que-parfait de l'indicatif	
plaignais	plaignions	avais plaint	avions plaint
plaignais	plaigniez	avais plaint	aviez plaint
plaignait	plaignaient	avait plaint	avaient plaint
3 passé simple		10 passé antérieur	
plaignis	plaignîmes	eus plaint	eûmes plaint
plaignis	plaignîtes	eus plaint	eûtes plaint
plaignit	plaignirent	eut plaint	eurent plaint
4 futur		11 futur antérieur	
plaindrai	plaindrons	aurai plaint	aurons plaint
plaindras	plaindrez	auras plaint	aurez plaint
plaindra	plaindront	aura plaint	auront plaint
5 conditionnel		12 conditionnel passé	
plaindrais	plaindrions	aurais plaint	aurions plaint
plaindrais	plaindriez	aurais plaint	auriez plaint
plaindrait	plaindraient	aurait plaint	auraient plaint
6 présent du subjonctif		13 passé du subjonctif	
plaigne	plaignions	aie plaint	ayons plaint
plaignes	plaigniez	aies plaint	ayez plaint
plaigne	plaignent	ait plaint	aient plaint
7 imparfait du subjonctif		14 plus-que-parfait du subjonctif	
plaignisse	plaignissions	eusse plaint	eussions plaint
plaignisses	plaignissiez	eusses plaint	eussiez plaint
plaignît	plaignissent	eût plaint	eussent plaint

Impératif
plains
plaignons
plaignez

Sentences using this verb and words related to it
   Pauvre Madame Bayou! Elle a des ennuis et je la plains.

une plainte   groan, moan, protest, complaint
porter plainte contre   to bring charges against
déposer/faire une plainte   to file a complaint
plaintif, plaintive   plaintive
plaintivement   plaintively, mournfully

Je te plains.   I feel for you; I feel sorry for
   you; I pity you.
être à plaindre   to be pitied
Elle est à plaindre.   She is to be pitied.
For additional related words, see se plaindre.

Soak up some verbs used in weather expressions. There's a list in the Appendixes.

Reflexive irregular verb

to complain, to lament, to moan

The Seven Simple Tenses		The Seven Compound Tenses	
Singular	Plural	Singular	Plural
1 présent de l'indicatif		8 passé composé	
me plains	nous plaignons	me suis plaint(e)	nous sommes plaint(e)s
te plains	vous plaignez	t'es plaint(e)	vous êtes plaint(e)(s)
se plaint	se plaignent	s'est plaint(e)	se sont plaint(e)s
2 imparfait de l'indicatif		9 plus-que-parfait de l'indicatif	
me plaignais	nous plaignions	m'étais plaint(e)	nous étions plaint(e)s
te plaignais	vous plaigniez	t'étais plaint(e)	vous étiez plaint(e)(s)
se plaignait	se plaignaient	s'était plaint(e)	s'étaient plaint(e)s
3 passé simple		10 passé antérieur	
me plaignis	nous plaignîmes	me fus plaint(e)	nous fûmes plaint(e)s
te plaignis	vous plaignîtes	te fus plaint(e)	vous fûtes plaint(e)(s)
se plaignit	se plaignirent	se fut plaint(e)	se furent plaint(e)s
4 futur		11 futur antérieur	
me plaindrai	nous plaindrons	me serai plaint(e)	nous serons plaint(e)s
te plaindras	vous plaindrez	te seras plaint(e)	vous serez plaint(e)(s)
se plaindra	se plaindront	se sera plaint(e)	se seront plaint(e)s
5 conditionnel		12 conditionnel passé	
me plaindrais	nous plaindrions	me serais plaint(e)	nous serions plaint(e)s
te plaindrais	vous plaindriez	te serais plaint(e)	vous seriez plaint(e)(s)
se plaindrait	se plaindraient	se serait plaint(e)	se seraient plaint(e)s
6 présent du subjonctif		13 passé du subjonctif	
me plaigne	nous plaignions	me sois plaint(e)	nous soyons plaint(e)s
te plaignes	vous plaigniez	te sois plaint(e)	vous soyez plaint(e)(s)
se plaigne	se plaignent	se soit plaint(e)	se soient plaint(e)s
7 imparfait du subjonctif		14 plus-que-parfait du subjonctif	
me plaignisse	nous plaignissions	me fusse plaint(e)	nous fussions plaint(e)s
te plaignisses	vous plaignissiez	te fusses plaint(e)	vous fussiez plaint(e)(s)
se plaignît	se plaignissent	se fût plaint(e)	se fussent plaint(e)s

P

Impératif
plains-toi; ne te plains pas
plaignons-nous; ne nous plaignons pas
plaignez-vous; ne vous plaignez pas

Common idiomatic expressions using this verb

   Quelle jeune fille! Elle se plaint toujours de tout! Hier elle s'est plainte de son professeur de français, aujourd'hui elle se plaint de ses devoirs, et je suis certain que demain elle se plaindra du temps.

se plaindre du temps   to complain about the weather
se plaindre de qqn ou de qqch   to complain of, to find fault with, someone or something
avoir bonne raison de se plaindre   to have a good reason to complain

For other words related to this verb, see **plaindre**.

It's important that you be familiar with the Subjunctive. See pages 26–31.

Part. pr. **plaisant**   Part. passé **plu**

The Seven Simple Tenses		The Seven Compound Tenses	
Singular	Plural	Singular	Plural
1 présent de l'indicatif		8 passé composé	
plais	**plaisons**	**ai plu**	**avons plu**
plais	**plaisez**	**as plu**	**avez plu**
plaît	**plaisent**	**a plu**	**ont plu**
2 imparfait de l'indicatif		9 plus-que-parfait de l'indicatif	
plaisais	**plaisions**	**avais plu**	**avions plu**
plaisais	**plaisiez**	**avais plu**	**aviez plu**
plaisait	**plaisaient**	**avait plu**	**avaient plu**
3 passé simple		10 passé antérieur	
plus	**plûmes**	**eus plu**	**eûmes plu**
plus	**plûtes**	**eus plu**	**eûtes plu**
plut	**plurent**	**eut plu**	**eurent plu**
4 futur		11 futur antérieur	
plairai	**plairons**	**aurai plu**	**aurons plu**
plairas	**plairez**	**auras plu**	**aurez plu**
plaira	**plairont**	**aura plu**	**auront plu**
5 conditionnel		12 conditionnel passé	
plairais	**plairions**	**aurais plu**	**aurions plu**
plairais	**plairiez**	**aurais plu**	**auriez plu**
plairait	**plairaient**	**aurait plu**	**auraient plu**
6 présent du subjonctif		13 passé du subjonctif	
plaise	**plaisions**	**aie plu**	**ayons plu**
plaises	**plaisiez**	**aies plu**	**ayez plu**
plaise	**plaisent**	**ait plu**	**aient plu**
7 imparfait du subjonctif		14 plus-que-parfait du subjonctif	
plusse	**plussions**	**eusse plu**	**eussions plu**
plusses	**plussiez**	**eusses plu**	**eussiez plu**
plût	**plussent**	**eût plu**	**eussent plu**

Impératif
plais
plaisons
plaisez

Common idiomatic expressions using this verb

plaire à qqn   to please, to be pleasing to someone; **Son mariage a plu à sa famille.**   Her (his) marriage pleased her (his) family. **Est-ce que ce cadeau lui plaira?**   Will this present please her (him)? Will this gift be pleasing to her (to him)?

se plaire à   to take pleasure in; **Robert se plaît à ennuyer son petit frère.**   Robert takes pleasure in bothering his little brother.

le plaisir   delight, pleasure; **complaire à**   to please; **déplaire à**   to displease

s'il vous plaît; s'il te plaît   please (if it is pleasing to you); **avec plaisir**   with pleasure

Il a beaucoup plu hier et cela m'a beaucoup plu.   It rained a lot yesterday and that pleased me a great deal. (See **pleuvoir**)

See also **déplaire**.

Can't recognize an irregular verb form? Check out the index of common irregular French verb forms in the Appendixes.

Regular **-er** verb   to joke

The Seven Simple Tenses		The Seven Compound Tenses	
Singular	Plural	Singular	Plural

1   présent de l'indicatif

		8 passé composé	
plaisante	plaisantons	ai plaisanté	avons plaisanté
plaisantes	plaisantez	as plaisanté	avez plaisanté
plaisante	plaisantent	a plaisanté	ont plaisanté

2   imparfait de l'indicatif

		9 plus-que-parfait de l'indicatif	
plaisantais	plaisantions	avais plaisanté	avions plaisanté
plaisantais	plaisantiez	avais plaisanté	aviez plaisanté
plaisantait	plaisantaient	avait plaisanté	avaient plaisanté

3   passé simple

		10 passé antérieur	
plaisantai	plaisantâmes	eus plaisanté	eûmes plaisanté
plaisantas	plaisantâtes	eus plaisanté	eûtes plaisanté
plaisanta	plaisantèrent	eut plaisanté	eurent plaisanté

4   futur

		11 futur antérieur	
plaisanterai	plaisanterons	aurai plaisanté	aurons plaisanté
plaisanteras	plaisanterez	auras plaisanté	aurez plaisanté
plaisantera	plaisanteront	aura plaisanté	auront plaisanté

5   conditionnel

		12 conditionnel passé	
plaisanterais	plaisanterions	aurais plaisanté	aurions plaisanté
plaisanterais	plaisanteriez	aurais plaisanté	auriez plaisanté
plaisanterait	plaisanteraient	aurait plaisanté	auraient plaisanté

6   présent du subjonctif

		13 passé du subjonctif	
plaisante	plaisantions	aie plaisanté	ayons plaisanté
plaisantes	plaisantiez	aies plaisanté	ayez plaisanté
plaisante	plaisantent	ait plaisanté	aient plaisanté

7   imparfait du subjonctif

		14 plus-que-parfait du subjonctif	
plaisantasse	plaisantassions	eusse plaisanté	eussions plaisanté
plaisantasses	plaisantassiez	eusses plaisanté	eussiez plaisanté
plaisantât	plaisantassent	eût plaisanté	eussent plaisanté

Impératif
plaisante
plaisantons
plaisantez

P

Words and expressions related to this verb
pour plaisanter   for fun
une plaisanterie   joke, joking
dire des plaisanteries   to crack jokes
en plaisantant   in fun

dire une chose par plaisanterie   to say something in a joking way
prendre bien une plaisanterie   to know how to take a joke

Can't find the verb you're looking for? Check the back pages of this book for a list of over 2,600 additional verbs!

The subject pronouns are found on page 103.

pleurer (347)

Part. pr. pleurant   **Part. passé** pleuré

to cry, to weep, to mourn

Regular -**er** verb

The Seven Simple Tenses		The Seven Compound Tenses	
Singular	Plural	Singular	Plural

1 présent de l'indicatif

		8 passé composé	
pleure	pleurons	ai pleuré	avons pleuré
pleures	pleurez	as pleuré	avez pleuré
pleure	pleurent	a pleuré	ont pleuré

2 imparfait de l'indicatif

		9 plus-que-parfait de l'indicatif	
pleurais	pleurions	avais pleuré	avions pleuré
pleurais	pleuriez	avais pleuré	aviez pleuré
pleurait	pleuraient	avait pleuré	avaient pleuré

3 passé simple

		10 passé antérieur	
pleurai	pleurâmes	eus pleuré	eûmes pleuré
pleuras	pleurâtes	eus pleuré	eûtes pleuré
pleura	pleurèrent	eut pleuré	eurent pleuré

4 futur

		11 futur antérieur	
pleurerai	pleurerons	aurai pleuré	aurons pleuré
pleureras	pleurerez	auras pleuré	aurez pleuré
pleurera	pleureront	aura pleuré	auront pleuré

5 conditionnel

		12 conditionnel passé	
pleurerais	pleurerions	aurais pleuré	aurions pleuré
pleurerais	pleureriez	aurais pleuré	auriez pleuré
pleurerait	pleureraient	aurait pleuré	auraient pleuré

6 présent du subjonctif

		13 passé du subjonctif	
pleure	pleurions	aie pleuré	ayons pleuré
pleures	pleuriez	aies pleuré	ayez pleuré
pleure	pleurent	ait pleuré	aient pleuré

7 imparfait du subjonctif

		14 plus-que-parfait du subjonctif	
pleurasse	pleurassions	eusse pleuré	eussions pleuré
pleurasses	pleurassiez	eusses pleuré	eussiez pleuré
pleurât	pleurassent	eût pleuré	eussent pleuré

Impératif
pleure
pleurons
pleurez

Common idiomatic expressions using this verb and words related to it

pleurer toutes les larmes de son corps to cry one's eyes out
une larme a tear
un pleur a tear
pleurard, pleurarde whimpering person

une pièce pleurnicharde soap opera
larmoyant, larmoyante tearful, lachrymose
pleurnicher to snivel, to whine
un pleurnicheur, une pleurnicheuse crybaby

How are you doing? Find out with the verb drills and tests with answers explained on pages 50–101.

Regular **-er** verb   to fold, to bend

The Seven Simple Tenses | The Seven Compound Tenses

Singular	Plural	Singular	Plural

1   présent de l'indicatif

plie	plions		
plies	pliez		
plie	plient		

8   passé composé

ai plié	avons plié
as plié	avez plié
a plié	ont plié

2   imparfait de l'indicatif

pliais	pliions
pliais	pliiez
pliait	pliaient

9   plus-que-parfait de l'indicatif

avais plié	avions plié
avais plié	aviez plié
avait plié	avaient plié

3   passé simple

pliai	pliâmes
plias	pliâtes
plia	plièrent

10   passé antérieur

eus plié	eûmes plié
eus plié	eûtes plié
eut plié	eurent plié

4   futur

plierai	plierons
plieras	plierez
pliera	plieront

11   futur antérieur

aurai plié	aurons plié
auras plié	aurez plié
aura plié	auront plié

5   conditionnel

plierais	plierions
plierais	plieriez
plierait	plieraient

12   conditionnel passé

aurais plié	aurions plié
aurais plié	auriez plié
aurait plié	auraient plié

6   présent du subjonctif

plie	pliions
plies	pliiez
plie	plient

13   passé du subjonctif

aie plié	ayons plié
aies plié	ayez plié
ait plié	aient plié

7   imparfait du subjonctif

pliasse	pliassions
pliasses	pliassiez
pliât	pliassent

14   plus-que-parfait du subjonctif

eusse plié	eussions plié
eusses plié	eussiez plié
eût plié	eussent plié

Impératif
plie
plions
pliez

Sentences using this verb and words related to it

En pliant un morceau de papier ainsi, tu peux faire un petit avion en papier.   By folding a
   piece of paper in this way, you can make a little paper airplane.
Je plie et ne romps pas. (La Fontaine, le roseau dans "Le Chêne et le Roseau")   I bend and do
   not break. (La Fontaine, the reed in "The Oak and the Reed")

Words and expressions related to this verb

plier en deux to double over	**un dépliant** brochure
un pli fold, wrinkle, crease	**plier bagage** to pack up, to pack one's bags
sous pli séparé under separate cover	**un plié** plié (ballet)
se plier à to submit to	**replier** to fold up
plier devant qqn to submit to someone	**se replier** to fold back

porter (349)   Part. pr. **portant**   Part. passé **porté**

to wear, to carry

Regular -**er** verb

The Seven Simple Tenses		The Seven Compound Tenses	
Singular	Plural	Singular	Plural
1 présent de l'indicatif		8 passé composé	
porte	portons	ai porté	avons porté
portes	portez	as porté	avez porté
porte	portent	a porté	ont porté
2 imparfait de l'indicatif		9 plus-que-parfait de l'indicatif	
portais	portions	avais porté	avions porté
portais	portiez	avais porté	aviez porté
portait	portaient	avait porté	avaient porté
3 passé simple		10 passé antérieur	
portai	portâmes	eus porté	eûmes porté
portas	portâtes	eus porté	eûtes porté
porta	portèrent	eut porté	eurent porté
4 futur		11 futur antérieur	
porterai	porterons	aurai porté	aurons porté
porteras	porterez	auras porté	aurez porté
portera	porteront	aura porté	auront porté
5 conditionnel		12 conditionnel passé	
porterais	porterions	aurais porté	aurions porté
porterais	porteriez	aurais porté	auriez porté
porterait	porteraient	aurait porté	auraient porté
6 présent du subjonctif		13 passé du subjonctif	
porte	portions	aie porté	ayons porté
portes	portiez	aies porté	ayez porté
porte	portent	ait porté	aient porté
7 imparfait du subjonctif		14 plus-que-parfait du subjonctif	
portasse	portassions	eusse porté	eussions porté
portasses	portassiez	eusses porté	eussiez porté
portât	portassent	eût porté	eussent porté

Impératif
porte
portons
portez

Common idiomatic expressions using this verb and words related to it

porter la main sur qqn to raise one's hand
  against someone
porter son âge to look one's age
se porter to feel (health); **Comment vous
  portez-vous aujourd'hui?** How do you
  feel today?
apporter to bring; **rapporter** to bring back
exporter to export
importer to import; to matter, to be of
  importance

un porte-monnaie change purse
  (**des porte-monnaie**)
comporter to comprise
déporter to deport
se comporter to behave
emporter to carry away; *Autant en emporte
  le vent* (*Gone with the Wind*)
Elle porte de jolies robes. She wears pretty
  dresses.
un portable cell phone, laptop computer

See also **apporter** and **supporter.**

Regular **-er** verb   to lay, to place, to put, to set, to pose

The Seven Simple Tenses		The Seven Compound Tenses	
Singular	Plural	Singular	Plural
1 présent de l'indicatif		**8 passé composé**	
pose	posons	ai posé	avons posé
poses	posez	as posé	avez posé
pose	posent	a posé	ont posé
2 imparfait de l'indicatif		**9 plus-que-parfait de l'indicatif**	
posais	posions	avais posé	avions posé
posais	posiez	avais posé	aviez posé
posait	posaient	avait posé	avaient posé
3 passé simple		**10 passé antérieur**	
posai	posâmes	eus posé	eûmes posé
posas	posâtes	eus posé	eûtes posé
posa	posèrent	eut posé	eurent posé
4 futur		**11 futur antérieur**	
poserai	poserons	aurai posé	aurons posé
poseras	poserez	auras posé	aurez posé
posera	poseront	aura posé	auront posé
5 conditionnel		**12 conditionnel passé**	
poserais	poserions	aurais posé	aurions posé
poserais	poseriez	aurais posé	auriez posé
poserait	poseraient	aurait posé	auraient posé
6 présent du subjonctif		**13 passé du subjonctif**	
pose	posions	aie posé	ayons posé
poses	posiez	aies posé	ayez posé
pose	posent	ait posé	aient posé
7 imparfait du subjonctif		**14 plus-que-parfait du subjonctif**	
posasse	posassions	eusse posé	eussions posé
posasses	posassiez	eusses posé	eussiez posé
posât	posassent	eût posé	eussent posé

Impératif
pose
posons
posez

Words and expressions related to this verb
poser une question   to ask a question
poser pour son portrait   to sit for a portrait painting
faire poser qqn   to keep someone waiting
déposer   to deposit, to set (put) down
composer   to compose
supposer   to suppose
opposer   to oppose; s'opposer à   to be opposed to
reposer   to set down again; se reposer to rest
exposer   to exhibit, to expose

Can't find the verb you're looking for? Check the back pages of this book for a list of over 2,600 additional verbs!

The subject pronouns are found on page 103.   **497**

to possess, to own, to master

Regular **-er** verb endings; spelling change:
é changes to **è** before syllable with mute **e**

The Seven Simple Tenses		The Seven Compound Tenses	
Singular	Plural	Singular	Plural

1 présent de l'indicatif

| | | |
---|---|---|---
possède | **possédons** | **ai possédé** | **avons possédé**
possèdes | **possédez** | **as possédé** | **avez possédé**
possède | **possèdent** | **a possédé** | **ont possédé**

2 imparfait de l'indicatif

8 passé composé

9 plus-que-parfait de l'indicatif

| | | |
---|---|---|---
possédais | **possédions** | **avais possédé** | **avions possédé**
possédais | **possédiez** | **avais possédé** | **aviez possédé**
possédait | **possédaient** | **avait possédé** | **avaient possédé**

3 passé simple

10 passé antérieur

| | | |
---|---|---|---
possédai | **possédâmes** | **eus possédé** | **eûmes possédé**
possédas | **possédâtes** | **eus possédé** | **eûtes possédé**
posséda | **possédèrent** | **eut possédé** | **eurent possédé**

4 futur

11 futur antérieur

| | | |
---|---|---|---
posséderai | **posséderons** | **aurai possédé** | **aurons possédé**
posséderas | **posséderez** | **auras possédé** | **aurez possédé**
possédera | **posséderont** | **aura possédé** | **auront possédé**

5 conditionnel

12 conditionnel passé

| | | |
---|---|---|---
posséderais | **posséderions** | **aurais possédé** | **aurions possédé**
posséderais | **posséderiez** | **aurais possédé** | **auriez possédé**
posséderait | **posséderaient** | **aurait possédé** | **auraient possédé**

6 présent du subjonctif

13 passé du subjonctif

| | | |
---|---|---|---
possède | **possédions** | **aie possédé** | **ayons possédé**
possèdes | **possédiez** | **aies possédé** | **ayez possédé**
possède | **possèdent** | **ait possédé** | **aient possédé**

7 imparfait du subjonctif

14 plus-que-parfait du subjonctif

| | | |
---|---|---|---
possédasse | **possédassions** | **eusse possédé** | **eussions possédé**
possédasses | **possédassiez** | **eusses possédé** | **eussiez possédé**
possédât | **possédassent** | **eût possédé** | **eussent possédé**

Impératif
possède
possédons
possédez

Words and expressions related to this verb

se faire posséder   to be taken in
la possession   possession, ownership
possessif, possessive   possessive
se posséder   to have control of oneself

un possesseur   possessor, owner; Madame
   Goulu est possesseur d'un grand château.
déposséder de   to dispossess of (from)
une dépossession   dispossession

Don't forget to study the section on defective and impersonal verbs. It's right after this main list.

Irregular verb

to pursue, to prosecute

The Seven Simple Tenses		The Seven Compound Tenses	
Singular	Plural	Singular	Plural
1 présent de l'indicatif		8 passé composé	
poursuis	**poursuivons**	**ai poursuivi**	**avons poursuivi**
poursuis	**poursuivez**	**as poursuivi**	**avez poursuivi**
poursuit	**poursuivent**	**a poursuivi**	**ont poursuivi**
2 imparfait de l'indicatif		9 plus-que-parfait de l'indicatif	
poursuivais	**poursuivions**	**avais poursuivi**	**avions poursuivi**
poursuivais	**poursuiviez**	**avais poursuivi**	**aviez poursuivi**
poursuivait	**poursuivaient**	**avait poursuivi**	**avaient poursuivi**
3 passé simple		10 passé antérieur	
poursuivis	**poursuivîmes**	**eus poursuivi**	**eûmes poursuivi**
poursuivis	**poursuivîtes**	**eus poursuivi**	**eûtes poursuivi**
poursuivit	**poursuivirent**	**eut poursuivi**	**eurent poursuivi**
4 futur		11 futur antérieur	
poursuivrai	**poursuivrons**	**aurai poursuivi**	**aurons poursuivi**
poursuivras	**poursuivrez**	**auras poursuivi**	**aurez poursuivi**
poursuivra	**poursuivront**	**aura poursuivi**	**auront poursuivi**
5 conditionnel		12 conditionnel passé	
poursuivrais	**poursuivrions**	**aurais poursuivi**	**aurions poursuivi**
poursuivrais	**poursuivriez**	**aurais poursuivi**	**auriez poursuivi**
poursuivrait	**poursuivraient**	**aurait poursuivi**	**auraient poursuivi**
6 présent du subjonctif		13 passé du subjonctif	
poursuive	**poursuivions**	**aie poursuivi**	**ayons poursuivi**
poursuives	**poursuiviez**	**aies poursuivi**	**ayez poursuivi**
poursuive	**poursuivent**	**ait poursuivi**	**aient poursuivi**
7 imparfait du subjonctif		14 plus-que-parfait du subjonctif	
poursuivisse	**poursuivissions**	**eusse poursuivi**	**eussions poursuivi**
poursuivisses	**poursuivissiez**	**eusses poursuivi**	**eussiez poursuivi**
poursuivît	**poursuivissent**	**eût poursuivi**	**eussent poursuivi**

	Impératif
	poursuis
	poursuivons
	poursuivez

Words and expressions related to this verb

se **poursuivre**   to pursue each other

poursuivre qqn en justice   to sue someone, to prosecute

poursuivre ses études   to carry on one's studies

une **poursuite**   pursuit

à la **poursuite de**   in pursuit of

poursuivre son chemin   to continue on one's way

See also **suivre**.

Can't remember the French verb you need? Check the back pages of this book for the English-French verb index!

The subject pronouns are found on page 103.

to push, to grow

Regular **-er** verb

The Seven Simple Tenses		The Seven Compound Tenses	
Singular	Plural	Singular	Plural

1 présent de l'indicatif

pousse	poussons	ai poussé	avons poussé
pousses	poussez	as poussé	avez poussé
pousse	poussent	a poussé	ont poussé

8 passé composé (Singular/Plural headings above)

2 imparfait de l'indicatif

poussais	poussions	avais poussé	avions poussé
poussais	poussiez	avais poussé	aviez poussé
poussait	poussaient	avait poussé	avaient poussé

9 plus-que-parfait de l'indicatif

3 passé simple

poussai	poussâmes	eus poussé	eûmes poussé
poussas	poussâtes	eus poussé	eûtes poussé
poussa	poussèrent	eut poussé	eurent poussé

10 passé antérieur

4 futur

pousserai	pousserons	aurai poussé	aurons poussé
pousseras	pousserez	auras poussé	aurez poussé
poussera	pousseront	aura poussé	auront poussé

11 futur antérieur

5 conditionnel

pousserais	pousserions	aurais poussé	aurions poussé
pousserais	pousseriez	aurais poussé	auriez poussé
pousserait	pousseraient	aurait poussé	auraient poussé

12 conditionnel passé

6 présent du subjonctif

pousse	poussions	aie poussé	ayons poussé
pousses	poussiez	aies poussé	ayez poussé
pousse	poussent	ait poussé	aient poussé

13 passé du subjonctif

7 imparfait du subjonctif

poussasse	poussassions	eusse poussé	eussions poussé
poussasses	poussassiez	eusses poussé	eussiez poussé
poussât	poussassent	eût poussé	eussent poussé

14 plus-que-parfait du subjonctif

Impératif
pousse
poussons
poussez

Common idiomatic expressions using this verb

une poussée   a push, a thrust

pousser qqn à faire qqch   to egg someone on to do something

Robert pousse une barbe.   Robert is growing a beard.

pousser un cri   to utter a cry; pousser un soupir   to heave a sigh

repousser   to repulse, to drive back; to grow in again, to grow back in

se pousser   to push oneself; to push each other

un pousse-pousse   rickshaw

pousser qqn à bout   to corner someone

une poussette   a stroller

Don't forget to study the section on defective and impersonal verbs. It's right after this main list.

The Seven Simple Tenses		The Seven Compound Tenses	
Singular	Plural	Singular	Plural
1 présent de l'indicatif		8 passé composé	
peux *or* **puis**	**pouvons**	**ai pu**	**avons pu**
peux	**pouvez**	**as pu**	**avez pu**
peut	**peuvent**	**a pu**	**ont pu**
2 imparfait de l'indicatif		9 plus-que-parfait de l'indicatif	
pouvais	**pouvions**	**avais pu**	**avions pu**
pouvais	**pouviez**	**avais pu**	**aviez pu**
pouvait	**pouvaient**	**avait pu**	**avaient pu**
3 passé simple		10 passé antérieur	
pus	**pûmes**	**eus pu**	**eûmes pu**
pus	**pûtes**	**eus pu**	**eûtes pu**
put	**purent**	**eut pu**	**eurent pu**
4 futur		11 futur antérieur	
pourrai	**pourrons**	**aurai pu**	**aurons pu**
pourras	**pourrez**	**auras pu**	**aurez pu**
pourra	**pourront**	**aura pu**	**auront pu**
5 conditionnel		12 conditionnel passé	
pourrais	**pourrions**	**aurais pu**	**aurions pu**
pourrais	**pourriez**	**aurais pu**	**auriez pu**
pourrait	**pourraient**	**aurait pu**	**auraient pu**
6 présent du subjonctif		13 passé du subjonctif	
puisse	**puissions**	**aie pu**	**ayons pu**
puisses	**puissiez**	**aies pu**	**ayez pu**
puisse	**puissent**	**ait pu**	**aient pu**
7 imparfait du subjonctif		14 plus-que-parfait du subjonctif	
pusse	**pussions**	**eusse pu**	**eussions pu**
pusses	**pussiez**	**eusses pu**	**eussiez pu**
pût	**pussent**	**eût pu**	**eussent pu**

P

Impératif
[not in use]

AN ESSENTIAL
55 VERB

Pouvoir is a very important verb for a beginning French student because it is useful in many everyday situations and idiomatic expressions.

Sentences using pouvoir

Que me voulez-vous? What do you want from me?

Je n'y peux rien. I can't help it; I can't do anything about it.

Puis-je entrer?/Est-ce que je peux entrer? May I come in?

Cela se peut. That may be./That's possible.

Sauve qui peut! Run for your life!

Vouloir, c'est pouvoir. Where there's a will, there's a way.

Pouvez-vous me dire où se trouvent les toilettes? Can you tell me where the restrooms are located?

Je ne peux pas vous entendre. Parlez plus fort, s'il vous plaît. I cannot hear you. Please speak more loudly.

Où est-ce que je peux envoyer un courriel? Where can I send an e-mail?

Words and expressions related to this verb

le pouvoir **power**

la puissance **power**

si l'on peut dire **if one may say so**

se pouvoir **to be possible**

la course au pouvoir **the race for power**

le sauve-qui-peut **panic**

avoir du pouvoir sur soi-même **to have self-control**

n'y pouvoir rien **not to be able to do anything about it**

Do you need more drills? Have fun with the *501 French Verbs* CD-ROM!

Irregular verb

to predict, to foretell

The Seven Simple Tenses		The Seven Compound Tenses	
Singular	Plural	Singular	Plural
1 présent de l'indicatif		8 passé composé	
prédis	**prédisons**	**ai prédit**	**avons prédit**
prédis	**prédisez**	**as prédit**	**avez prédit**
prédit	**prédisent**	**a prédit**	**ont prédit**
2 imparfait de l'indicatif		9 plus-que-parfait de l'indicatif	
prédisais	**prédisions**	**avais prédit**	**avions prédit**
prédisais	**prédisiez**	**avais prédit**	**aviez prédit**
prédisait	**prédisaient**	**avait prédit**	**avaient prédit**
3 passé simple		10 passé antérieur	
prédis	**prédîmes**	**eus prédit**	**eûmes prédit**
prédis	**prédîtes**	**eus prédit**	**eûtes prédit**
prédit	**prédirent**	**eut prédit**	**eurent prédit**
4 futur		11 futur antérieur	
prédirai	**prédirons**	**aurai prédit**	**aurons prédit**
prédiras	**prédirez**	**auras prédit**	**aurez prédit**
prédira	**prédiront**	**aura prédit**	**auront prédit**
5 conditionnel		12 conditionnel passé	
prédirais	**prédirions**	**aurais prédit**	**aurions prédit**
prédirais	**prédiriez**	**aurais prédit**	**auriez prédit**
prédirait	**prédiraient**	**aurait prédit**	**auraient prédit**
6 présent du subjonctif		13 passé du subjonctif	
prédise	**prédisions**	**aie prédit**	**ayons prédit**
prédises	**prédisiez**	**aies prédit**	**ayez prédit**
prédise	**prédisent**	**ait prédit**	**aient prédit**
7 imparfait du subjonctif		14 plus-que-parfait du subjonctif	
prédisse	**prédissions**	**eusse prédit**	**eussions prédit**
prédisses	**prédissiez**	**eusses prédit**	**eussiez prédit**
prédît	**prédissent**	**eût prédit**	**eussent prédit**

Impératif
prédis
prédisons
prédisez

Words related to this verb
une prédiction   prediction
prédire l'avenir   to predict the future

See also **contredire, dire, interdire, maudire,** and **médire.**

Compare **(vous) prédisez** with **(vous) dites** of **dire** on page 290.

Can't find the verb you're looking for? Check the back pages of this book for a list of over 2,600 additional verbs!

préférer (356)
to prefer

Part. pr. préférant   Part. passé préféré

Regular **-er** verb endings; spelling change:
é changes to **è** before syllable with mute **e**

The Seven Simple Tenses		The Seven Compound Tenses	
Singular	Plural	Singular	Plural
1 présent de l'indicatif		**8 passé composé**	
préfère	préférons	ai préféré	avons préféré
préfères	préférez	as préféré	avez préféré
préfère	préfèrent	a préféré	ont préféré
2 imparfait de l'indicatif		**9 plus-que-parfait de l'indicatif**	
préférais	préférions	avais préféré	avions préféré
préférais	préfériez	avais préféré	aviez préféré
préférait	préféraient	avait préféré	avaient préféré
3 passé simple		**10 passé antérieur**	
préférai	préférâmes	eus préféré	eûmes préféré
préféras	préférâtes	eus préféré	eûtes préféré
préféra	préférèrent	eut préféré	eurent préféré
4 futur		**11 futur antérieur**	
préférerai	préférerons	aurai préféré	aurons préféré
préféreras	préférerez	auras préféré	aurez préféré
préférera	préféreront	aura préféré	auront préféré
5 conditionnel		**12 conditionnel passé**	
préférerais	préférerions	aurais préféré	aurions préféré
préférerais	préféreriez	aurais préféré	auriez préféré
préférerait	préféreraient	aurait préféré	auraient préféré
6 présent du subjonctif		**13 passé du subjonctif**	
préfère	préférions	aie préféré	ayons préféré
préfères	préfériez	aies préféré	ayez préféré
préfère	préfèrent	ait préféré	aient préféré
7 imparfait du subjonctif		**14 plus-que-parfait du subjonctif**	
préférasse	préférassions	eusse préféré	eussions préféré
préférasses	préférassiez	eusses préféré	eussiez préféré
préférât	préférassent	eût préféré	eussent préféré

Impératif
préfère
préférons
préférez

Sentences using this verb and words related to it

—Qu'est-ce que vous préférez faire ce soir?
—Je préfère aller voir un bon film. Et vous?
—Je préfère rester à la maison. Ne préféreriez-vous pas rester ici avec moi?
Mon père préfère monter l'escalier. Il n'aime pas les ascenseurs! My father prefers to walk up the stairs. He doesn't like elevators!

une préférence   a preference
préférentiel, préférentielle   preferential
préférable   preferable
préférablement   preferably
de préférence à   in preference to

Je n'ai pas de préférence.   I have no preference.
par ordre de préférence   in order of preference

Don't miss orthographically changing verbs on pages 32–34.

504

Irregular verb   to take

The Seven Simple Tenses		The Seven Compound Tenses	
Singular	Plural	Singular	Plural
1 présent de l'indicatif		**8 passé composé**	
prends	prenons	ai pris	avons pris
prends	prenez	as pris	avez pris
prend	prennent	a pris	ont pris
2 imparfait de l'indicatif		**9 plus-que-parfait de l'indicatif**	
prenais	prenions	avais pris	avions pris
prenais	preniez	avais pris	aviez pris
prenait	prenaient	avait pris	avaient pris
3 passé simple		**10 passé antérieur**	
pris	prîmes	eus pris	eûmes pris
pris	prîtes	eus pris	eûtes pris
prit	prirent	eut pris	eurent pris
4 futur		**11 futur antérieur**	
prendrai	prendrons	aurai pris	aurons pris
prendras	prendrez	auras pris	aurez pris
prendra	prendront	aura pris	auront pris
5 conditionnel		**12 conditionnel passé**	
prendrais	prendrions	aurais pris	aurions pris
prendrais	prendriez	aurais pris	auriez pris
prendrait	prendraient	aurait pris	auraient pris
6 présent du subjonctif		**13 passé du subjonctif**	
prenne	prenions	aie pris	ayons pris
prennes	preniez	aies pris	ayez pris
prenne	prennent	ait pris	aient pris
7 imparfait du subjonctif		**14 plus-que-parfait du subjonctif**	
prisse	prissions	eusse pris	eussions pris
prisses	prissiez	eusses pris	eussiez pris
prît	prissent	eût pris	eussent pris

P

Impératif
prends
prenons
prenez

AN ESSENTIAL
55 VERB

The subject pronouns are found on page 103.
                                                                                                505

Prendre

Prendre is a very useful French verb because, although it is irregular, many verbs are conjugated like it. It is used in numerous everyday situations and idiomatic expressions.

Sentences using prendre

Qu'est-ce qui vous prend? What's got into you?

J'ai pris assez de soleil. Je vais nager maintenant. I've had enough sun. I'm going to swim now.

Prenez garde de ne pas tomber. Take care not to fall.

Prenez garde de tomber. Avoid falling.

C'est à prendre ou à laisser. Take it or leave it.

Je ne sais comment m'y prendre. I don't know how to go about it.

—Qui a pris les fleurs qui étaient sur la table?
—C'est moi qui les ai prises.

—Who took the flowers that were on the table?
—I took them. (It is I who took them.)

Tel est pris qui croyait prendre. (La Fontaine, "Le Rat et l'Huître") He who believed he would take is taken. (That is, one can be hurt by one's own ignorance. La Fontaine, "The Rat and the Oyster")

Words and expressions related to this verb

à tout prendre **on the whole, all in all**

un preneur, une preneuse **taker, purchaser**

s'y prendre **to go about it, to handle it, to set about it**

prendre à témoin **to call to witness**

la prise **seize, capture;** La Prise de la Bastille **The Storming of the Bastille (July 14, 1789)**

prendre un bain **to take a bath**

prendre des photos **to take pictures**

prendre un bain de soleil **to sunbathe**

prendre garde de + inf. **to avoid + pres. part., to take care not + inf.**

prendre le parti de + inf. **to decide + inf.**

prendre un billet **to buy a ticket**

If you can conjugate **prendre** you can also conjugate the following verbs:

apprendre **to learn**

comprendre **to understand**

se déprendre de qqn/qqch **to give up someone/something (Use** être **as auxiliary)**

désapprendre **to unlearn, forget**

entreprendre **to undertake**

s'éprendre de qqn **to fall for someone (Use** être **as auxiliary)**

se méprendre **to be mistaken (Use** être **as auxiliary)**

réapprendre **to relearn, learn again**

Regular **-er** verb   to prepare

The Seven Simple Tenses		The Seven Compound Tenses	
Singular	Plural	Singular	Plural

1 présent de l'indicatif

		8 passé composé	
prépare	**préparons**	**ai préparé**	**avons préparé**
prépares	**préparez**	**as préparé**	**avez préparé**
prépare	**préparent**	**a préparé**	**ont préparé**

2 imparfait de l'indicatif

		9 plus-que-parfait de l'indicatif	
préparais	**préparions**	**avais préparé**	**avions préparé**
préparais	**prépariez**	**avais préparé**	**aviez préparé**
préparait	**préparaient**	**avait préparé**	**avaient préparé**

3 passé simple

		10 passé antérieur	
préparai	**préparâmes**	**eus préparé**	**eûmes préparé**
préparas	**préparâtes**	**eus préparé**	**eûtes préparé**
prépara	**préparèrent**	**eut préparé**	**eurent préparé**

4 futur

		11 futur antérieur	
préparerai	**préparerons**	**aurai préparé**	**aurons préparé**
prépareras	**préparerez**	**auras préparé**	**aurez préparé**
préparera	**prépareront**	**aura préparé**	**auront préparé**

5 conditionnel

		12 conditionnel passé	
préparerais	**préparerions**	**aurais préparé**	**aurions préparé**
préparerais	**prépareriez**	**aurais préparé**	**auriez préparé**
préparerait	**prépareraient**	**aurait préparé**	**auraient préparé**

6 présent du subjonctif

		13 passé du subjonctif	
prépare	**préparions**	**aie préparé**	**ayons préparé**
prépares	**prépariez**	**aies préparé**	**ayez préparé**
prépare	**préparent**	**ait préparé**	**aient préparé**

7 imparfait du subjonctif

		14 plus-que-parfait du subjonctif	
préparasse	**préparassions**	**eusse préparé**	**eussions préparé**
préparasses	**préparassiez**	**eusses préparé**	**eussiez préparé**
préparât	**préparassent**	**eût préparé**	**eussent préparé**

P

Impératif
prépare
préparons
préparez

Sentences using this verb and words related to it
    Si Albert avait préparé sa leçon, il aurait reçu une bonne note. Il prépare toujours ses leçons, mais, cette fois, il ne les a pas préparées.

la préparation preparation
les préparatifs *m.* preparations
préparatoire preparatory
se préparer to prepare oneself
préparer un examen to study for an exam

Get acquainted with what preposition goes with what verb. See *Verbs with prepositions* in the Appendixes.

The subject pronouns are found on page 103.
507

to present, to introduce

Regular **-er** verb

The Seven Simple Tenses		The Seven Compound Tenses	
Singular	Plural	Singular	Plural

1 présent de l'indicatif

présente	présentons		
présentes	présentez		
présente	présentent		

8 passé composé

ai présenté	avons présenté
as présenté	avez présenté
a présenté	ont présenté

2 imparfait de l'indicatif

présentais	présentions
présentais	présentiez
présentait	présentaient

9 plus-que-parfait de l'indicatif

avais présenté	avions présenté
avais présenté	aviez présenté
avait présenté	avaient présenté

3 passé simple

présentai	présentâmes
présentas	présentâtes
présenta	présentèrent

10 passé antérieur

eus présenté	eûmes présenté
eus présenté	eûtes présenté
eut présenté	eurent présenté

4 futur

présenterai	présenterons
présenteras	présenterez
présentera	présenteront

11 futur antérieur

aurai présenté	aurons présenté
auras présenté	aurez présenté
aura présenté	auront présenté

5 conditionnel

présenterais	présenterions
présenterais	présenteriez
présenterait	présenteraient

12 conditionnel passé

aurais présenté	aurions présenté
aurais présenté	auriez présenté
aurait présenté	auraient présenté

6 présent du subjonctif

présente	présentions
présentes	présentiez
présente	présentent

13 passé du subjonctif

aie présenté	ayons présenté
aies présenté	ayez présenté
ait présenté	aient présenté

7 imparfait du subjonctif

présentasse	présentassions
présentasses	présentassiez
présentât	présentassent

14 plus-que-parfait du subjonctif

eusse présenté	eussions présenté
eusses présenté	eussiez présenté
eût présenté	eussent présenté

Impératif
présente
présentons
présentez

Common idiomatic expressions using this verb
présenter qqn à qqn to introduce someone to someone
Je vous présente à mon professeur de français. May I introduce you to my French teacher?
un présentateur, une présentatrice newscaster, announcer
se présenter to introduce oneself
Permettez-moi de me présenter. Allow me to introduce myself.
présenter bien to make a good impression
présenter mal to make a bad impression
un présentoir display

Do you need more drills? Have fun with the *501 French Verbs* CD-ROM!

The Seven Simple Tenses		The Seven Compound Tenses	
Singular	Plural	Singular	Plural
1 présent de l'indicatif		**8 passé composé**	
presse	pressons	ai pressé	avons pressé
presses	pressez	as pressé	avez pressé
presse	pressent	a pressé	ont pressé
2 imparfait de l'indicatif		**9 plus-que-parfait de l'indicatif**	
pressais	pressions	avais pressé	avions pressé
pressais	pressiez	avais pressé	aviez pressé
pressait	pressaient	avait pressé	avaient pressé
3 passé simple		**10 passé antérieur**	
pressai	pressâmes	eus pressé	eûmes pressé
pressas	pressâtes	eus pressé	eûtes pressé
pressa	pressèrent	eut pressé	eurent pressé
4 futur		**11 futur antérieur**	
presserai	presserons	aurai pressé	aurons pressé
presseras	presserez	auras pressé	aurez pressé
pressera	presseront	aura pressé	auront pressé
5 conditionnel		**12 conditionnel passé**	
presserais	presserions	aurais pressé	aurions pressé
presserais	presseriez	aurais pressé	auriez pressé
presserait	presseraient	aurait pressé	auraient pressé
6 présent du subjonctif		**13 passé du subjonctif**	
presse	pressions	aie pressé	ayons pressé
presses	pressiez	aies pressé	ayez pressé
presse	pressent	ait pressé	aient pressé
7 imparfait du subjonctif		**14 plus-que-parfait du subjonctif**	
pressasse	pressassions	eusse pressé	eussions pressé
pressasses	pressassiez	eusses pressé	eussiez pressé
pressât	pressassent	eût pressé	eussent pressé

Impératif
presse
pressons
pressez

P

Words and expressions related to this verb

presser qqn to hurry someone
la pression pressure
un presse-bouton push button
  (**presse-bouton** *adj. pl.*)
un presse-papiers paperweight
  (**des presse-papiers**)
un pressoir press
un presseur, une presseuse press worker

presser qqn de se décider to urge someone to
  make a decision
être sous pression to be under pressure
un presse-citron lemon squeezer (**des
  presse-citrons**)
faire le coup du presse-citron à qqn to put
  the squeeze on someone
le pressing steam pressing (dry cleaner's)

Get acquainted with what preposition goes with what verb. See *Verbs with prepositions*
in the Appendixes.

The subject pronouns are found on page 103.
                                                                      509

to be in a hurry, to make haste, to rush, to crowd   Reflexive regular **-er** verb

The Seven Simple Tenses		The Seven Compound Tenses	
Singular	Plural	Singular	Plural
1 présent de l'indicatif		8 passé composé	
me presse	**nous pressons**	**me suis pressé(e)**	**nous sommes pressé(e)s**
te presses	**vous pressez**	**t'es pressé(e)**	**vous êtes pressé(e)(s)**
se presse	**se pressent**	**s'est pressé(e)**	**se sont pressé(e)s**
2 imparfait de l'indicatif		9 plus-que-parfait de l'indicatif	
me pressais	**nous pressions**	**m'étais pressé(e)**	**nous étions pressé(e)s**
te pressais	**vous pressiez**	**t'étais pressé(e)**	**vous étiez pressé(e)(s)**
se pressait	**se pressaient**	**s'était pressé(e)**	**s'étaient pressé(e)s**
3 passé simple		10 passé antérieur	
me pressai	**nous pressâmes**	**me fus pressé(e)**	**nous fûmes pressé(e)s**
te pressas	**vous pressâtes**	**te fus pressé(e)**	**vous fûtes pressé(e)(s)**
se pressa	**se pressèrent**	**se fut pressé(e)**	**se furent pressé(e)s**
4 futur		11 futur antérieur	
me presserai	**nous presserons**	**me serai pressé(e)**	**nous serons pressé(e)s**
te presseras	**vous presserez**	**te seras pressé(e)**	**vous serez pressé(e)(s)**
se pressera	**se presseront**	**se sera pressé(e)**	**se seront pressé(e)s**
5 conditionnel		12 conditionnel passé	
me presserais	**nous presserions**	**me serais pressé(e)**	**nous serions pressé(e)s**
te presserais	**vous presseriez**	**te serais pressé(e)**	**vous seriez pressé(e)(s)**
se presserait	**se presseraient**	**se serait pressé(e)**	**se seraient pressé(e)s**
6 présent du subjonctif		13 passé du subjonctif	
me presse	**nous pressions**	**me sois pressé(e)**	**nous soyons pressé(e)s**
te presses	**vous pressiez**	**te sois pressé(e)**	**vous soyez pressé(e)(s)**
se presse	**se pressent**	**se soit pressé(e)**	**se soient pressé(e)s**
7 imparfait du subjonctif		14 plus-que-parfait du subjonctif	
me pressasse	**nous pressassions**	**me fusse pressé(e)**	**nous fussions pressé(e)s**
te pressasses	**vous pressassiez**	**te fusses pressé(e)**	**vous fussiez pressé(e)(s)**
se pressât	**se pressassent**	**se fût pressé(e)**	**se fussent pressé(e)s**

Impératif
presse-toi; ne te presse pas
pressons-nous; ne nous pressons pas
pressez-vous; ne vous pressez pas

Words and expressions related to this verb

se presser contre qqn   to press oneself against someone

se presser de faire qqch   to hurry to do something

se presser en foule   to press against each other in a crowd

presser   to press, to squeeze

presser le pas   to walk more quickly

presser qqn   to urge someone, to hurry someone

une pression   pressure

faire pression sur qqn   to exert pressure on someone

Get acquainted with what preposition goes with what verb. See *Verbs with prepositions* in the Appendixes.

Regular **-re** verb   to pretend, to claim, to lay claim, to maintain

The Seven Simple Tenses		The Seven Compound Tenses	
Singular	Plural	Singular	Plural
1 présent de l'indicatif		8 passé composé	
prétends	**prétendons**	**ai prétendu**	**avons prétendu**
prétends	**prétendez**	**as prétendu**	**avez prétendu**
prétend	**prétendent**	**a prétendu**	**ont prétendu**
2 imparfait de l'indicatif		9 plus-que-parfait de l'indicatif	
prétendais	**prétendions**	**avais prétendu**	**avions prétendu**
prétendais	**prétendiez**	**avais prétendu**	**aviez prétendu**
prétendait	**prétendaient**	**avait prétendu**	**avaient prétendu**
3 passé simple		10 passé antérieur	
prétendis	**prétendîmes**	**eus prétendu**	**eûmes prétendu**
prétendis	**prétendîtes**	**eus prétendu**	**eûtes prétendu**
prétendit	**prétendirent**	**eut prétendu**	**eurent prétendu**
4 futur		11 futur antérieur	
prétendrai	**prétendrons**	**aurai prétendu**	**aurons prétendu**
prétendras	**prétendrez**	**auras prétendu**	**aurez prétendu**
prétendra	**prétendront**	**aura prétendu**	**auront prétendu**
5 conditionnel		12 conditionnel passé	
prétendrais	**prétendrions**	**aurais prétendu**	**aurions prétendu**
prétendrais	**prétendriez**	**aurais prétendu**	**auriez prétendu**
prétendrait	**prétendraient**	**aurait prétendu**	**auraient prétendu**
6 présent du subjonctif		13 passé du subjonctif	
prétende	**prétendions**	**aie prétendu**	**ayons prétendu**
prétendes	**prétendiez**	**aies prétendu**	**ayez prétendu**
prétende	**prétendent**	**ait prétendu**	**aient prétendu**
7 imparfait du subjonctif		14 plus-que-parfait du subjonctif	
prétendisse	**prétendissions**	**eusse prétendu**	**eussions prétendu**
prétendisses	**prétendissiez**	**eusses prétendu**	**eussiez prétendu**
prétendît	**prétendissent**	**eût prétendu**	**eussent prétendu**

P

Impératif
prétends
prétendons
prétendez

Words and expressions related to this verb
prétendre savoir qqch   to claim to know
    something
prétentieux, prétentieuse   pretentious
un prétendu spécialiste   self-styled specialist
prétendre à   to lay claim to

la prétention   pretention
sans prétentions   unpretentious,
    unpretentiously
prétentieusement   pretentiously

How are you doing? Find out with the verb drills and tests with answers explained on pages 50–101.

prêter (363)

to lend

Regular **-er** verb

The Seven Simple Tenses		The Seven Compound Tenses	
Singular	Plural	Singular	Plural
1 présent de l'indicatif		8 passé composé	
prête	prêtons	ai prêté	avons prêté
prêtes	prêtez	as prêté	avez prêté
prête	prêtent	a prêté	ont prêté
2 imparfait de l'indicatif		9 plus-que-parfait de l'indicatif	
prêtais	prêtions	avais prêté	avions prêté
prêtais	prêtiez	avais prêté	aviez prêté
prêtait	prêtaient	avait prêté	avaient prêté
3 passé simple		10 passé antérieur	
prêtai	prêtâmes	eus prêté	eûmes prêté
prêtas	prêtâtes	eus prêté	eûtes prêté
prêta	prêtèrent	eut prêté	eurent prêté
4 futur		11 futur antérieur	
prêterai	prêterons	aurai prêté	aurons prêté
prêteras	prêterez	auras prêté	aurez prêté
prêtera	prêteront	aura prêté	auront prêté
5 conditionnel		12 conditionnel passé	
prêterais	prêterions	aurais prêté	aurions prêté
prêterais	prêteriez	aurais prêté	auriez prêté
prêterait	prêteraient	aurait prêté	auraient prêté
6 présent du subjonctif		13 passé du subjonctif	
prête	prêtions	aie prêté	ayons prêté
prêtes	prêtiez	aies prêté	ayez prêté
prête	prêtent	ait prêté	aient prêté
7 imparfait du subjonctif		14 plus-que-parfait du subjonctif	
prêtasse	prêtassions	eusse prêté	eussions prêté
prêtasses	prêtassiez	eusses prêté	eussiez prêté
prêtât	prêtassent	eût prêté	eussent prêté

Impératif
prête
prêtons
prêtez

Common idiomatic expressions using this verb
prêter à intérêt to lend at interest
prêter attention à qqn ou à qqch to pay attention to someone or something
un prêteur sur gages pawnbroker
prêter la main à qqn to give a helping hand to someone

prêter secours à qqn to go to someone's rescue (help)
apprêter to prepare, to get (something) ready
s'apprêter to get oneself ready
prêter l'oreille to listen, to lend an ear

NOTE: Don't confuse **prêter** with **emprunter** (to borrow).

Irregular verb   to warn, to forestall, to ward off

The Seven Simple Tenses		The Seven Compound Tenses	
Singular	Plural	Singular	Plural

1   présent de l'indicatif
préviens	**prévenons**
préviens	**prévenez**
prévient	**préviennent**

8   passé composé
ai prévenu	**avons prévenu**
as prévenu	**avez prévenu**
a prévenu	**ont prévenu**

2   imparfait de l'indicatif
prévenais	**prévenions**
prévenais	**préveniez**
prévenait	**prévenaient**

9   plus-que-parfait de l'indicatif
avais prévenu	**avions prévenu**
avais prévenu	**aviez prévenu**
avait prévenu	**avaient prévenu**

3   passé simple
prévins	**prévînmes**
prévins	**prévîntes**
prévint	**prévinrent**

10   passé antérieur
eus prévenu	**eûmes prévenu**
eus prévenu	**eûtes prévenu**
eut prévenu	**eurent prévenu**

4   futur
préviendrai	**préviendrons**
préviendras	**préviendrez**
préviendra	**préviendront**

11   futur antérieur
aurai prévenu	**aurons prévenu**
auras prévenu	**aurez prévenu**
aura prévenu	**auront prévenu**

5   conditionnel
préviendrais	**préviendrions**
préviendrais	**préviendriez**
préviendrait	**préviendraient**

12   conditionnel passé
aurais prévenu	**aurions prévenu**
aurais prévenu	**auriez prévenu**
aurait prévenu	**auraient prévenu**

6   présent du subjonctif
prévienne	**prévenions**
préviennes	**préveniez**
prévienne	**préviennent**

13   passé du subjonctif
aie prévenu	**ayons prévenu**
aies prévenu	**ayez prévenu**
ait prévenu	**aient prévenu**

7   imparfait du subjonctif
prévinsse	**prévinssions**
prévinsses	**prévinssiez**
prévînt	**prévinssent**

14   plus-que-parfait du subjonctif
eusse prévenu	**eussions prévenu**
eusses prévenu	**eussiez prévenu**
eût prévenu	**eussent prévenu**

Impératif
préviens
prévenons
prévenez

Words and expressions related to this verb

Mieux vaut prévenir que guérir.   Prevention is better than cure.

la prévenance   considerateness, kindness

la prévention   prevention

prévenant, prévenante   considerate, kind, thoughtful

entourer qqn de prévenances   to shower someone with kindness, attention

See also **convenir, devenir, revenir, se souvenir,** and **venir.**

Can't find the verb you're looking for? Check the back pages of this book for a list of over 2,600 additional verbs!

to foresee

The Seven Simple Tenses | The Seven Compound Tenses

Singular	Plural	Singular	Plural
1 présent de l'indicatif		**8 passé composé**	
prévois	**prévoyons**	**ai prévu**	**avons prévu**
prévois	**prévoyez**	**as prévu**	**avez prévu**
prévoit	**prévoient**	**a prévu**	**ont prévu**
2 imparfait de l'indicatif		**9 plus-que-parfait de l'indicatif**	
prévoyais	**prévoyions**	**avais prévu**	**avions prévu**
prévoyais	**prévoyiez**	**avais prévu**	**aviez prévu**
prévoyait	**prévoyaient**	**avait prévu**	**avaient prévu**
3 passé simple		**10 passé antérieur**	
prévis	**prévîmes**	**eus prévu**	**eûmes prévu**
prévis	**prévîtes**	**eus prévu**	**eûtes prévu**
prévit	**prévirent**	**eut prévu**	**eurent prévu**
4 futur		**11 futur antérieur**	
prévoirai	**prévoirons**	**aurai prévu**	**aurons prévu**
prévoiras	**prévoirez**	**auras prévu**	**aurez prévu**
prévoira	**prévoiront**	**aura prévu**	**auront prévu**
5 conditionnel		**12 conditionnel passé**	
prévoirais	**prévoirions**	**aurais prévu**	**aurions prévu**
prévoirais	**prévoiriez**	**aurais prévu**	**auriez prévu**
prévoirait	**prévoiraient**	**aurait prévu**	**auraient prévu**
6 présent du subjonctif		**13 passé du subjonctif**	
prévoie	**prévoyions**	**aie prévu**	**ayons prévu**
prévoies	**prévoyiez**	**aies prévu**	**ayez prévu**
prévoie	**prévoient**	**ait prévu**	**aient prévu**
7 imparfait du subjonctif		**14 plus-que-parfait du subjonctif**	
prévisse	**prévissions**	**eusse prévu**	**eussions prévu**
prévisses	**prévissiez**	**eusses prévu**	**eussiez prévu**
prévît	**prévissent**	**eût prévu**	**eussent prévu**

Impératif
prévois
prévoyons
prévoyez

Words and expressions related to this verb
la prévision forecast
en prévision de in anticipation of
prévisible foreseeable; **visible** visible
la prévoyance foresight
une avant-première preview

prévoir le temps to forecast the weather
les prévisions météorologiques weather
  forecasts
voir to see
prévoyant, prévoyante provident

See also **voir**.

Soak up some verbs used in weather expressions. There's a list in the Appendixes!

Regular **-er** verb   to pray, to supplicate, to entreat, to beg, to request

The Seven Simple Tenses		The Seven Compound Tenses	
Singular	Plural	Singular	Plural
1 présent de l'indicatif		8 passé composé	
prie	**prions**	**ai prié**	**avons prié**
pries	**priez**	**as prié**	**avez prié**
prie	**prient**	**a prié**	**ont prié**
2 imparfait de l'indicatif		9 plus-que-parfait de l'indicatif	
priais	**priions**	**avais prié**	**avions prié**
priais	**priiez**	**avais prié**	**aviez prié**
priait	**priaient**	**avait prié**	**avaient prié**
3 passé simple		10 passé antérieur	
priai	**priâmes**	**eus prié**	**eûmes prié**
prias	**priâtes**	**eus prié**	**eûtes prié**
pria	**prièrent**	**eut prié**	**eurent prié**
4 futur		11 futur antérieur	
prierai	**prierons**	**aurai prié**	**aurons prié**
prieras	**prierez**	**auras prié**	**aurez prié**
priera	**prieront**	**aura prié**	**auront prié**
5 conditionnel		12 conditionnel passé	
prierais	**prierions**	**aurais prié**	**aurions prié**
prierais	**prieriez**	**aurais prié**	**auriez prié**
prierait	**prieraient**	**aurait prié**	**auraient prié**
6 présent du subjonctif		13 passé du subjonctif	
prie	**priions**	**aie prié**	**ayons prié**
pries	**priiez**	**aies prié**	**ayez prié**
prie	**prient**	**ait prié**	**aient prié**
7 imparfait du subjonctif		14 plus-que-parfait du subjonctif	
priasse	**priassions**	**eusse prié**	**eussions prié**
priasses	**priassiez**	**eusses prié**	**eussiez prié**
priât	**priassent**	**eût prié**	**eussent prié**

Impératif
prie
prions
priez

Words and expressions related to this verb
prier qqn de faire qqch to beg (entreat, request) someone to do something
Je vous en prie! You're welcome! I beg of you!
On vous prie de + inf. You are requested + inf.
prier qqn à faire qqch to invite someone to do something
une prière prayer; **Prière d'entrer sans frapper.** Please enter without knocking.

Prière de ne pas fumer. You are requested not to smoke.
Puis-je entrer? May I come in?—**Je vous en prie!** Please do! (I beg you to do so)
vouloir se faire prier to desire to be urged; **Madame Duchemin veut toujours se faire prier.** Mrs. Duchemin always wants to be urged.
sans se faire prier willingly

The subject pronouns are found on page 103.   **515**

to produce   Irregular verb

The Seven Simple Tenses		The Seven Compound Tenses	
Singular	Plural	Singular	Plural
1 présent de l'indicatif		8 passé composé	
produis	produisons	ai produit	avons produit
produis	produisez	as produit	avez produit
produit	produisent	a produit	ont produit
2 imparfait de l'indicatif		9 plus-que-parfait de l'indicatif	
produisais	produisions	avais produit	avions produit
produisais	produisiez	avais produit	aviez produit
produisait	produisaient	avait produit	avaient produit
3 passé simple		10 passé antérieur	
produisis	produisîmes	eus produit	eûmes produit
produisis	produisîtes	eus produit	eûtes produit
produisit	produisirent	eut produit	eurent produit
4 futur		11 futur antérieur	
produirai	produirons	aurai produit	aurons produit
produiras	produirez	auras produit	aurez produit
produira	produiront	aura produit	auront produit
5 conditionnel		12 conditionnel passé	
produirais	produirions	aurais produit	aurions produit
produirais	produiriez	aurais produit	auriez produit
produirait	produiraient	aurait produit	auraient produit
6 présent du subjonctif		13 passé du subjonctif	
produise	produisions	aie produit	ayons produit
produises	produisiez	aies produit	ayez produit
produise	produisent	ait produit	aient produit
7 imparfait du subjonctif		14 plus-que-parfait du subjonctif	
produisisse	produisissions	eusse produit	eussions produit
produisisses	produisissiez	eusses produit	eussiez produit
produisît	produisissent	eût produit	eussent produit

Impératif
produis
produisons
produisez

Words related to this verb
un produit product
la production production
productible producible
productif, productive productive
le produit national brut the gross national
  product

la productivité productivity
se produire to happen, to occur, to be brought
  about
les produits alimentaires food products
se produire en public to appear in public

See also **conduire, déduire, introduire, réduire, reproduire, séduire,** and **traduire.**

Get acquainted with what preposition goes with what verb. See *Verbs with prepositions* in the Appendixes.

Regular **-er** verb   to program, to plan

The Seven Simple Tenses		The Seven Compound Tenses	
Singular	Plural	Singular	Plural
1 présent de l'indicatif		**8 passé composé**	
programme	programmons	ai programmé	avons programmé
programmes	programmez	as programmé	avez programmé
programme	programment	a programmé	ont programmé
2 imparfait de l'indicatif		**9 plus-que-parfait de l'indicatif**	
programmais	programmions	avais programmé	avions programmé
programmais	programmiez	avais programmé	aviez programmé
programmait	programmaient	avait programmé	avaient programmé
3 passé simple		**10 passé antérieur**	
programmai	programmâmes	eus programmé	eûmes programmé
programmas	programmâtes	eus programmé	eûtes programmé
programma	programmèrent	eut programmé	eurent programmé
4 futur		**11 futur antérieur**	
programmerai	programmerons	aurai programmé	aurons programmé
programmeras	programmerez	auras programmé	aurez programmé
programmera	programmeront	aura programmé	auront programmé
5 conditionnel		**12 conditionnel passé**	
programmerais	programmerions	aurais programmé	aurions programmé
programmerais	programmeriez	aurais programmé	auriez programmé
programmerait	programmeraient	aurait programmé	auraient programmé
6 présent du subjonctif		**13 passé du subjonctif**	
programme	programmions	aie programmé	ayons programmé
programmes	programmiez	aies programmé	ayez programmé
programme	programment	ait programmé	aient programmé
7 imparfait du subjonctif		**14 plus-que-parfait du subjonctif**	
programmasse	programmassions	eusse programmé	eussions programmé
programmasses	programmassiez	eusses programmé	eussiez programmé
programmât	programmassent	eût programmé	eussent programmé

P

Impératif
programme
programmons
programmez

Sentences using this verb and words related to it

Marie est programmeuse. Elle a créé et programmé un site Web pour son entreprise.
  Marie is a programmer. She created and programmed a web site for her company.
Qu'est-ce que tu as au programme demain?   What's on your schedule for tomorrow?

Words and expressions related to this verb

un programmateur, une programmatrice
  programmer (radio and television)
un programmeur, une programmeuse
  programmer (computer)
un programme   program, schedule, curriculum
la programmation   programming

déprogrammer   to remove from a program,
  schedule
programmable *adj.*   programmable
programmé, programmée   computerized
une émission   radio, television broadcast
un logiciel   software

to take a walk

Regular **-er** verb endings; spelling change:
e changes to **è** before syllable with mute **e**

The Seven Simple Tenses		The Seven Compound Tenses	
Singular	Plural	Singular	Plural
1 présent de l'indicatif		8 passé composé	
me promène	nous promenons	me suis promené(e)	nous sommes promené(e)s
te promènes	vous promenez	t'es promené(e)	vous êtes promené(e)(s)
se promène	se promènent	s'est promené(e)	se sont promené(e)s
2 imparfait de l'indicatif		9 plus-que-parfait de l'indicatif	
me promenais	nous promenions	m'étais promené(e)	nous étions promené(e)s
te promenais	vous promeniez	t'étais promené(e)	vous étiez promené(e)(s)
se promenait	se promenaient	s'était promené(e)	s'étaient promené(e)s
3 passé simple		10 passé antérieur	
me promenai	nous promenâmes	me fus promené(e)	nous fûmes promené(e)s
te promenas	vous promenâtes	te fus promené(e)	vous fûtes promené(e)(s)
se promena	se promenèrent	se fut promené(e)	se furent promené(e)s
4 futur		11 futur antérieur	
me promènerai	nous promènerons	me serai promené(e)	nous serons promené(e)s
te promèneras	vous promènerez	te seras promené(e)	vous serez promené(e)(s)
se promènera	se promèneront	se sera promené(e)	se seront promené(e)s
5 conditionnel		12 conditionnel passé	
me promènerais	nous promènerions	me serais promené(e)	nous serions promené(e)s
te promènerais	vous promèneriez	te serais promené(e)	vous seriez promené(e)(s)
se promènerait	se promèneraient	se serait promené(e)	se seraient promené(e)s
6 présent du subjonctif		13 passé du subjonctif	
me promène	nous promenions	me sois promené(e)	nous soyons promené(e)s
te promènes	vous promeniez	te sois promené(e)	vous soyez promené(e)(s)
se promène	se promènent	se soit promené(e)	se soient promené(e)s
7 imparfait du subjonctif		14 plus-que-parfait du subjonctif	
me promenasse	nous promenassions	me fusse promené(e)	nous fussions promené(e)s
te promenasses	vous promenassiez	te fusses promené(e)	vous fussiez promené(e)(s)
se promenât	se promenassent	se fût promené(e)	se fussent promené(e)s

Impératif
promène-toi; ne te promène pas
promenons-nous; ne nous promenons pas
promenez-vous; ne vous promenez pas

Common idiomatic expressions using this verb

Je me promène tous les matins.   I take a walk every morning.

Cette promenade est merveilleuse.   This walk is marvelous.

Janine et Robert se sont promenés dans le parc.   Janine and Robert took a walk in the park.

faire une promenade   to take a walk

faire une promenade en voiture   to go for a drive

promener son chien   to take one's dog out for a walk

promener ses regards sur   to cast one's eyes on, to look over

un promenoir   indoor mall for walking, strolling

See also **amener, emmener,** and **mener.**

518

The Seven Simple Tenses		The Seven Compound Tenses	
Singular	Plural	Singular	Plural
1 présent de l'indicatif		8 passé composé	
promets	**promettons**	**ai promis**	**avons promis**
promets	**promettez**	**as promis**	**avez promis**
promet	**promettent**	**a promis**	**ont promis**
2 imparfait de l'indicatif		9 plus-que-parfait de l'indicatif	
promettais	**promettions**	**avais promis**	**avions promis**
promettais	**promettiez**	**avais promis**	**aviez promis**
promettait	**promettaient**	**avait promis**	**avaient promis**
3 passé simple		10 passé antérieur	
promis	**promîmes**	**eus promis**	**eûmes promis**
promis	**promîtes**	**eus promis**	**eûtes promis**
promit	**promirent**	**eut promis**	**eurent promis**
4 futur		11 futur antérieur	
promettrai	**promettrons**	**aurai promis**	**aurons promis**
promettras	**promettrez**	**auras promis**	**aurez promis**
promettra	**promettront**	**aura promis**	**auront promis**
5 conditionnel		12 conditionnel passé	
promettrais	**promettrions**	**aurais promis**	**aurions promis**
promettrais	**promettriez**	**aurais promis**	**auriez promis**
promettrait	**promettraient**	**aurait promis**	**auraient promis**
6 présent du subjonctif		13 passé du subjonctif	
promette	**promettions**	**aie promis**	**ayons promis**
promettes	**promettiez**	**aies promis**	**ayez promis**
promette	**promettent**	**ait promis**	**aient promis**
7 imparfait du subjonctif		14 plus-que-parfait du subjonctif	
promisse	**promissions**	**eusse promis**	**eussions promis**
promisses	**promissiez**	**eusses promis**	**eussiez promis**
promît	**promissent**	**eût promis**	**eussent promis**

Impératif
promets
promettons
promettez

Common idiomatic expressions using this verb
promettre de faire qqch   to promise to do something
une promesse   promise
tenir sa promesse   to keep one's promise
promettre à qqn de faire qqch   to promise someone to do something
Ça promet!   It looks promising!
se promettre   to promise oneself
compromettre   to compromise

See also **commettre, mettre, se mettre, omettre, permettre, remettre, soumettre,** and **transmettre.**

to pronounce, to declare

Regular **-er** verb endings; spelling change:
c changes to **ç** before **a** or **o** to keep **s** sound

The Seven Simple Tenses		The Seven Compound Tenses	
Singular	Plural	Singular	Plural
1 présent de l'indicatif		**8 passé composé**	
prononce	prononçons	ai prononcé	avons prononcé
prononces	prononcez	as prononcé	avez prononcé
prononce	prononcent	a prononcé	ont prononcé
2 imparfait de l'indicatif		**9 plus-que-parfait de l'indicatif**	
prononçais	prononcions	avais prononcé	avions prononcé
prononçais	prononciez	avais prononcé	aviez prononcé
prononçait	prononçaient	avait prononcé	avaient prononcé
3 passé simple		**10 passé antérieur**	
prononçai	prononçâmes	eus prononcé	eûmes prononcé
prononças	prononçâtes	eus prononcé	eûtes prononcé
prononça	prononcèrent	eut prononcé	eurent prononcé
4 futur		**11 futur antérieur**	
prononcerai	prononcerons	aurai prononcé	aurons prononcé
prononceras	prononcerez	auras prononcé	aurez prononcé
prononcera	prononceront	aura prononcé	auront prononcé
5 conditionnel		**12 conditionnel passé**	
prononcerais	prononcerions	aurais prononcé	aurions prononcé
prononcerais	prononceriez	aurais prononcé	auriez prononcé
prononcerait	prononceraient	aurait prononcé	auraient prononcé
6 présent du subjonctif		**13 passé du subjonctif**	
prononce	prononcions	aie prononcé	ayons prononcé
prononces	prononciez	aies prononcé	ayez prononcé
prononce	prononcent	ait prononcé	aient prononcé
7 imparfait du subjonctif		**14 plus-que-parfait du subjonctif**	
prononçasse	prononçassions	eusse prononcé	eussions prononcé
prononçasses	prononçassiez	eusses prononcé	eussiez prononcé
prononçât	prononçassent	eût prononcé	eussent prononcé

Impératif
prononce
prononçons
prononcez

Words and expressions related to this verb
prononcer un discours   to deliver a speech
la prononciation   pronunciation
prononçable   pronounceable
se prononcer pour   to decide in favor of
énoncer   to enunciate

annoncer   to announce
dénoncer   to denounce
se prononcer   to declare, to be pronounced
  (as a word)
se prononcer contre   to decide against

See also annoncer.

Don't miss orthographically changing verbs on pages 32–34.

Use the guide to French pronunciation. It's in the Appendixes!

520

Regular **-er** verb   to prove

The Seven Simple Tenses		The Seven Compound Tenses	
Singular	Plural	Singular	Plural
1 présent de l'indicatif		8 passé composé	
prouve	prouvons	ai prouvé	avons prouvé
prouves	prouvez	as prouvé	avez prouvé
prouve	prouvent	a prouvé	ont prouvé
2 imparfait de l'indicatif		9 plus-que-parfait de l'indicatif	
prouvais	prouvions	avais prouvé	avions prouvé
prouvais	prouviez	avais prouvé	aviez prouvé
prouvait	prouvaient	avait prouvé	avaient prouvé
3 passé simple		10 passé antérieur	
prouvai	prouvâmes	eus prouvé	eûmes prouvé
prouvas	prouvâtes	eus prouvé	eûtes prouvé
prouva	prouvèrent	eut prouvé	eurent prouvé
4 futur		11 futur antérieur	
prouverai	prouverons	aurai prouvé	aurons prouvé
prouveras	prouverez	auras prouvé	aurez prouvé
prouvera	prouveront	aura prouvé	auront prouvé
5 conditionnel		12 conditionnel passé	
prouverais	prouverions	aurais prouvé	aurions prouvé
prouverais	prouveriez	aurais prouvé	auriez prouvé
prouverait	prouveraient	aurait prouvé	auraient prouvé
6 présent du subjonctif		13 passé du subjonctif	
prouve	prouvions	aie prouvé	ayons prouvé
prouves	prouviez	aies prouvé	ayez prouvé
prouve	prouvent	ait prouvé	aient prouvé
7 imparfait du subjonctif		14 plus-que-parfait du subjonctif	
prouvasse	prouvassions	eusse prouvé	eussions prouvé
prouvasses	prouvassiez	eusses prouvé	eussiez prouvé
prouvât	prouvassent	eût prouvé	eussent prouvé

Impératif
prouve
prouvons
prouvez

P

Words and expressions related to this verb
une preuve   proof
comme preuve   by way of proof
prouvable   provable
une épreuve   test, proof
faire la preuve de qqch   to prove something
éprouver   to test, to try, to experience

éprouver de la sympathie pour   to feel
   sympathy for
mettre à l'épreuve   to put to the test
avoir la preuve de   to have proof of
désapprouver   to disapprove of

See also **approuver** and **éprouver**.

It's important that you be familiar with the Subjunctive. See pages 26–31.

to punish

The Seven Simple Tenses		The Seven Compound Tenses	
Singular	Plural	Singular	Plural
1 présent de l'indicatif		**8 passé composé**	
punis	punissons	ai puni	avons puni
punis	punissez	as puni	avez puni
punit	punissent	a puni	ont puni
2 imparfait de l'indicatif		**9 plus-que-parfait de l'indicatif**	
punissais	punissions	avais puni	avions puni
punissais	punissiez	avais puni	aviez puni
punissait	punissaient	avait puni	avaient puni
3 passé simple		**10 passé antérieur**	
punis	punîmes	eus puni	eûmes puni
punis	punîtes	eus puni	eûtes puni
punit	punirent	eut puni	eurent puni
4 futur		**11 futur antérieur**	
punirai	punirons	aurai puni	aurons puni
puniras	punirez	auras puni	aurez puni
punira	puniront	aura puni	auront puni
5 conditionnel		**12 conditionnel passé**	
punirais	punirions	aurais puni	aurions puni
punirais	puniriez	aurais puni	auriez puni
punirait	puniraient	aurait puni	auraient puni
6 présent du subjonctif		**13 passé du subjonctif**	
punisse	punissions	aie puni	ayons puni
punisses	punissiez	aies puni	ayez puni
punisse	punissent	ait puni	aient puni
7 imparfait du subjonctif		**14 plus-que-parfait du subjonctif**	
punisse	punissions	eusse puni	eussions puni
punisses	punissiez	eusses puni	eussiez puni
punît	punissent	eût puni	eussent puni

Impératif
punis
punissons
punissez

Words and expressions related to this verb
punisseur, punisseuse punisher
punissable punishable
la punition punishment
punitif, punitive punitive

échapper à la punition to escape punishment
la peine capitale capital punishment
en punition as a punishment

Grammar putting you in a tense mood? Review the definitions of basic grammatical terms with examples on pages 35–49.

Regular **-er** verb   to leave

The Seven Simple Tenses		The Seven Compound Tenses	
Singular	Plural	Singular	Plural
1 présent de l'indicatif		**8 passé composé**	
quitte	quittons	ai quitté	avons quitté
quittes	quittez	as quitté	avez quitté
quitte	quittent	a quitté	ont quitté
2 imparfait de l'indicatif		**9 plus-que-parfait de l'indicatif**	
quittais	quittions	avais quitté	avions quitté
quittais	quittiez	avais quitté	aviez quitté
quittait	quittaient	avait quitté	avaient quitté
3 passé simple		**10 passé antérieur**	
quittai	quittâmes	eus quitté	eûmes quitté
quittas	quittâtes	eus quitté	eûtes quitté
quitta	quittèrent	eut quitté	eurent quitté
4 futur		**11 futur antérieur**	
quitterai	quitterons	aurai quitté	aurons quitté
quitteras	quitterez	auras quitté	aurez quitté
quittera	quitteront	aura quitté	auront quitté
5 conditionnel		**12 conditionnel passé**	
quitterais	quitterions	aurais quitté	aurions quitté
quitterais	quitteriez	aurais quitté	auriez quitté
quitterait	quitteraient	aurait quitté	auraient quitté
6 présent du subjonctif		**13 passé du subjonctif**	
quitte	quittions	aie quitté	ayons quitté
quittes	quittiez	aies quitté	ayez quitté
quitte	quittent	ait quitté	aient quitté
7 imparfait du subjonctif		**14 plus-que-parfait du subjonctif**	
quittasse	quittassions	eusse quitté	eussions quitté
quittasses	quittassiez	eusses quitté	eussiez quitté
quittât	quittassent	eût quitté	eussent quitté

Impératif
quitte
quittons
quittez

Q

Words and expressions related to this verb
une quittance acquittance, discharge
quitter son chapeau to take off one's hat
se quitter to separate, to leave each other
Ne quittez pas, s'il vous plaît! Hold the line, please! (on the phone)
être quitte to be free of an obligation
quitte ou double double or nothing
Elle a quitté son mari. She left her husband.
Avant quelle heure dois-je quitter la chambre? Before what time must I leave the room?

acquitter to acquit
s'acquitter de to fulfill
un acquittement acquittal, payment
Je vous ai payé la dette; maintenant nous sommes quittes! I paid you the debt; now we're even!
Il a quitté sa femme. He left his wife.

The subject pronouns are found on page 103.   **523**

to relate, to tell about, to tell (a story)

The Seven Simple Tenses		The Seven Compound Tenses	
Singular	Plural	Singular	Plural
1 présent de l'indicatif		8 passé composé	
raconte	racontons	ai raconté	avons raconté
racontes	racontez	as raconté	avez raconté
raconte	racontent	a raconté	ont raconté
2 imparfait de l'indicatif		9 plus-que-parfait de l'indicatif	
racontais	racontions	avais raconté	avions raconté
racontais	racontiez	avais raconté	aviez raconté
racontait	racontaient	avait raconté	avaient raconté
3 passé simple		10 passé antérieur	
racontai	racontâmes	eus raconté	eûmes raconté
racontas	racontâtes	eus raconté	eûtes raconté
raconta	racontèrent	eut raconté	eurent raconté
4 futur		11 futur antérieur	
raconterai	raconterons	aurai raconté	aurons raconté
raconteras	raconterez	auras raconté	aurez raconté
racontera	raconteront	aura raconté	auront raconté
5 conditionnel		12 conditionnel passé	
raconterais	raconterions	aurais raconté	aurions raconté
raconterais	raconteriez	aurais raconté	auriez raconté
raconterait	raconteraient	aurait raconté	auraient raconté
6 présent du subjonctif		13 passé du subjonctif	
raconte	racontions	aie raconté	ayons raconté
racontes	racontiez	aies raconté	ayez raconté
raconte	racontent	ait raconté	aient raconté
7 imparfait du subjonctif		14 plus-que-parfait du subjonctif	
racontasse	racontassions	eusse raconté	eussions raconté
racontasses	racontassiez	eusses raconté	eussiez raconté
racontât	racontassent	eût raconté	eussent raconté

Impératif
raconte
racontons
racontez

Sentences using this verb and words related to it

Mon professeur de français aime nous raconter des anecdotes en français dans la classe de français. C'est un bon raconteur.

un raconteur, une raconteuse storyteller
Qu'est-ce que vous racontez? What are you talking about?

See also **conter**.

Can't find the verb you're looking for? Check the back pages of this book for a list of over 2,600 additional verbs!

Regular **-er** verb endings; spelling change: retain the **ge** before **a** or **o** to keep the soft **g** sound of the verb

to set (put) in order,
to tidy up

The Seven Simple Tenses		The Seven Compound Tenses	
Singular	Plural	Singular	Plural
1 présent de l'indicatif		8 passé composé	
range	rangeons	ai rangé	avons rangé
ranges	rangez	as rangé	avez rangé
range	rangent	a rangé	ont rangé
2 imparfait de l'indicatif		9 plus-que-parfait de l'indicatif	
rangeais	rangions	avais rangé	avions rangé
rangeais	rangiez	avais rangé	aviez rangé
rangeait	rangeaient	avait rangé	avaient rangé
3 passé simple		10 passé antérieur	
rangeai	rangeâmes	eus rangé	eûmes rangé
rangeas	rangeâtes	eus rangé	eûtes rangé
rangea	rangèrent	eut rangé	eurent rangé
4 futur		11 futur antérieur	
rangerai	rangerons	aurai rangé	aurons rangé
rangeras	rangerez	auras rangé	aurez rangé
rangera	rangeront	aura rangé	auront rangé
5 conditionnel		12 conditionnel passé	
rangerais	rangerions	aurais rangé	aurions rangé
rangerais	rangeriez	aurais rangé	auriez rangé
rangerait	rangeraient	aurait rangé	auraient rangé
6 présent du subjonctif		13 passé du subjonctif	
range	rangions	aie rangé	ayons rangé
ranges	rangiez	aies rangé	ayez rangé
range	rangent	ait rangé	aient rangé
7 imparfait du subjonctif		14 plus-que-parfait du subjonctif	
rangeasse	rangeassions	eusse rangé	eussions rangé
rangeasses	rangeassiez	eusses rangé	eussiez rangé
rangeât	rangeassent	eût rangé	eussent rangé

R

Impératif
range
rangeons
rangez

Words and expressions related to this verb
un rang   row; rank
sortir du rang   to rise from the ranks
une rangée d'arbres   a line of trees
déranger   to disturb
se déranger   to inconvenience oneself
de premier rang   first-rate

se mettre sur les rangs   to join the ranks
se ranger   to stand back (out of the way)
arranger   to arrange; **s'arranger avec**   to come to terms with, to come to an agreement with; to manage

The subject pronouns are found on page 103.

525

to call again, to call back,
to recall, to remind

Regular **-er** verb endings; spelling change:
l becomes **ll** before syllable with a mute **e**

The Seven Simple Tenses

The Seven Compound Tenses

Singular	Plural	Singular	Plural
1 présent de l'indicatif		8 passé composé	
rappelle	rappelons	ai rappelé	avons rappelé
rappelles	rappelez	as rappelé	avez rappelé
rappelle	rappellent	a rappelé	ont rappelé
2 imparfait de l'indicatif		9 plus-que-parfait de l'indicatif	
rappelais	rappelions	avais rappelé	avions rappelé
rappelais	rappeliez	avais rappelé	aviez rappelé
rappelait	rappelaient	avait rappelé	avaient rappelé
3 passé simple		10 passé antérieur	
rappelai	rappelâmes	eus rappelé	eûmes rappelé
rappelas	rappelâtes	eus rappelé	eûtes rappelé
rappela	rappelèrent	eut rappelé	eurent rappelé
4 futur		11 futur antérieur	
rappellerai	rappellerons	aurai rappelé	aurons rappelé
rappelleras	rappellerez	auras rappelé	aurez rappelé
rappellera	rappelleront	aura rappelé	auront rappelé
5 conditionnel		12 conditionnel passé	
rappellerais	rappellerions	aurais rappelé	aurions rappelé
rappellerais	rappelleriez	aurais rappelé	auriez rappelé
rappellerait	rappelleraient	aurait rappelé	auraient rappelé
6 présent du subjonctif		13 passé du subjonctif	
rappelle	rappelions	aie rappelé	ayons rappelé
rappelles	rappeliez	aies rappelé	ayez rappelé
rappelle	rappellent	ait rappelé	aient rappelé
7 imparfait du subjonctif		14 plus-que-parfait du subjonctif	
rappelasse	rappelassions	eusse rappelé	eussions rappelé
rappelasses	rappelassiez	eusses rappelé	eussiez rappelé
rappelât	rappelassent	eût rappelé	eussent rappelé

Impératif
rappelle
rappelons
rappelez

Sentences using this verb and words related to it
—Je ne peux pas vous parler maintenant. Rappelez-moi demain.
—D'accord. Je vous rappellerai demain.

un rappel   recall, call back, recalling
rappeler à la vie   to restore to life
Rappelez-moi votre nom.   Remind me of your name.
rappeler qqn à l'ordre   to call someone to order

See also appeler, s'appeler, and se rappeler.

Don't miss orthographically changing verbs on pages 32–34.

Regular **-er** verb endings; spelling change:
l becomes **ll** before syllable with a mute **e**

to remember, to recall,
to recollect

The Seven Simple Tenses		The Seven Compound Tenses	
Singular	Plural	Singular	Plural

1 présent de l'indicatif

me rappelle	nous rappelons	
te rappelles	vous rappelez	
se rappelle	se rappellent	

8 passé composé

me suis rappelé(e)	nous sommes rappelé(e)s
t'es rappelé(e)	vous êtes rappelé(e)(s)
s'est rappelé(e)	se sont rappelé(e)s

2 imparfait de l'indicatif

me rappelais	nous rappelions
te rappelais	vous rappeliez
se rappelait	se rappelaient

9 plus-que-parfait de l'indicatif

m'étais rappelé(e)	nous étions rappelé(e)s
t'étais rappelé(e)	vous étiez rappelé(e)(s)
s'était rappelé(e)	s'étaient rappelé(e)s

3 passé simple

me rappelai	nous rappelâmes
te rappelas	vous rappelâtes
se rappela	se rappelèrent

10 passé antérieur

me fus rappelé(e)	nous fûmes rappelé(e)s
te fus rappelé(e)	vous fûtes rappelé(e)(s)
se fut rappelé(e)	se furent rappelé(e)s

4 futur

me rappellerai	nous rappellerons
te rappelleras	vous rappellerez
se rappellera	se rappelleront

11 futur antérieur

me serai rappelé(e)	nous serons rappelé(e)s
te seras rappelé(e)	vous serez rappelé(e)(s)
se sera rappelé(e)	se seront rappelé(e)s

5 conditionnel

me rappellerais	nous rappellerions
te rappellerais	vous rappelleriez
se rappellerait	se rappelleraient

12 conditionnel passé

me serais rappelé(e)	nous serions rappelé(e)s
te serais rappelé(e)	vous seriez rappelé(e)(s)
se serait rappelé(e)	se seraient rappelé(e)s

6 présent du subjonctif

me rappelle	nous rappelions
te rappelles	vous rappeliez
se rappelle	se rappellent

13 passé du subjonctif

me sois rappelé(e)	nous soyons rappelé(e)s
te sois rappelé(e)	vous soyez rappelé(e)(s)
se soit rappelé(e)	se soient rappelé(e)s

7 imparfait du subjonctif

me rappelasse	nous rappelassions
te rappelasses	vous rappelassiez
se rappelât	se rappelassent

14 plus-que-parfait du subjonctif

me fusse rappelé(e)	nous fussions rappelé(e)
te fusses rappelé(e)	vous fussiez rappelé(e)(s)
se fût rappelé(e)	se fussent rappelé(e)s

R

Impératif
rappelle-toi; ne te rappelle pas
rappelons-nous; ne nous rappelons pas
rappelez-vous; ne vous rappelez pas

Sentences using this verb and words related to it
   Je me rappelle bien le premier jour où j'ai vu la belle Hélène. C'était un jour inoubliable.

See also **appeler, s'appeler,** and **rappeler.**

How are you doing? Find out with the verb drills and tests with answers explained on pages
50–101.

The subject pronouns are found on page 103.   **527**

to receive, to get

Irregular verb with spelling change: **c** changes
to **ç** before **a** or **u** to keep **s** sound

The Seven Simple Tenses		The Seven Compound Tenses	
Singular	Plural	Singular	Plural

1　présent de l'indicatif

reçois	recevons
reçois	recevez
reçoit	reçoivent

8　passé composé

ai reçu	avons reçu
as reçu	avez reçu
a reçu	ont reçu

2　imparfait de l'indicatif

recevais	recevions
recevais	receviez
recevait	recevaient

9　plus-que-parfait de l'indicatif

avais reçu	avions reçu
avais reçu	aviez reçu
avait reçu	avaient reçu

3　passé simple

reçus	reçûmes
reçus	reçûtes
reçut	reçurent

10　passé antérieur

eus reçu	eûmes reçu
eus reçu	eûtes reçu
eut reçu	eurent reçu

4　futur

recevrai	recevrons
recevras	recevrez
recevra	recevront

11　futur antérieur

aurai reçu	aurons reçu
auras reçu	aurez reçu
aura reçu	auront reçu

5　conditionnel

recevrais	recevrions
recevrais	recevriez
recevrait	recevraient

12　conditionnel passé

aurais reçu	aurions reçu
aurais reçu	auriez reçu
aurait reçu	auraient reçu

6　présent du subjonctif

reçoive	recevions
reçoives	receviez
reçoive	reçoivent

13　passé du subjonctif

aie reçu	ayons reçu
aies reçu	ayez reçu
ait reçu	aient reçu

7　imparfait du subjonctif

reçusse	reçussions
reçusses	reçussiez
reçût	reçussent

14　plus-que-parfait du subjonctif

eusse reçu	eussions reçu
eusses reçu	eussiez reçu
eût reçu	eussent reçu

Impératif
reçois
recevons
recevez

Words and expressions related to this verb

réceptif, réceptive receptive
une réception reception, welcome
un, une réceptionniste receptionist
un reçu a receipt
au reçu de on receipt of

recevable receivable
un receveur, une receveuse receiver
être reçu à un examen to pass an exam
Est-ce que tu as reçu mon courriel? Did you
　receive my e-mail?

Proverb:
Il y a plus de bonheur à donner qu'à recevoir. It is better to give than to receive.

Don't miss the definitions of basic grammatical terms on pages 35–49.

Irregular verb

to recognize, to acknowledge

The Seven Simple Tenses	The Seven Compound Tenses

Singular	Plural	Singular	Plural
1 présent de l'indicatif		**8 passé composé**	
reconnais	reconnaissons	ai reconnu	avons reconnu
reconnais	reconnaissez	as reconnu	avez reconnu
reconnaît	reconnaissent	a reconnu	ont reconnu
2 imparfait de l'indicatif		**9 plus-que-parfait de l'indicatif**	
reconnaissais	reconnaissions	avais reconnu	avions reconnu
reconnaissais	reconnaissiez	avais reconnu	aviez reconnu
reconnaissait	reconnaissaient	avait reconnu	avaient reconnu
3 passé simple		**10 passé antérieur**	
reconnus	reconnûmes	eus reconnu	eûmes reconnu
reconnus	reconnûtes	eus reconnu	eûtes reconnu
reconnut	reconnurent	eut reconnu	eurent reconnu
4 futur		**11 futur antérieur**	
reconnaîtrai	reconnaîtrons	aurai reconnu	aurons reconnu
reconnaîtras	reconnaîtrez	auras reconnu	aurez reconnu
reconnaîtra	reconnaîtront	aura reconnu	auront reconnu
5 conditionnel		**12 conditionnel passé**	
reconnaîtrais	reconnaîtrions	aurais reconnu	aurions reconnu
reconnaîtrais	reconnaîtriez	aurais reconnu	auriez reconnu
reconnaîtrait	reconnaîtraient	aurait reconnu	auraient reconnu
6 présent du subjonctif		**13 passé du subjonctif**	
reconnaisse	reconnaissions	aie reconnu	ayons reconnu
reconnaisses	reconnaissiez	aies reconnu	ayez reconnu
reconnaisse	reconnaissent	ait reconnu	aient reconnu
7 imparfait du subjonctif		**14 plus-que-parfait du subjonctif**	
reconnusse	reconnussions	eusse reconnu	eussions reconnu
reconnusses	reconnussiez	eusses reconnu	eussiez reconnu
reconnût	reconnussent	eût reconnu	eussent reconnu

R

Impératif
reconnais
reconnaissons
reconnaissez

Words and expressions related to this verb

la reconnaissance   gratitude, gratefulness, recognition

être reconnaissant à qqn de   to be grateful (thankful, obliged) to someone for

See also **connaître** and **méconnaître**.

la reconnaissance vocale   speech/voice recognition (computer)

se reconnaître   to recognize oneself, to recognize each other

reconnaissable   recognizable

Don't forget to study the section on defective and impersonal verbs. It's right after this main list.

to collect, to gather, to harvest

Irregular verb

The Seven Simple Tenses		The Seven Compound Tenses	
Singular	Plural	Singular	Plural
1 présent de l'indicatif		8 passé composé	
recueille	recueillons	ai recueilli	avons recueilli
recueilles	recueillez	as recueilli	avez recueilli
recueille	recueillent	a recueilli	ont recueilli
2 imparfait de l'indicatif		9 plus-que-parfait de l'indicatif	
recueillais	recueillions	avais recueilli	avions recueilli
recueillais	recueilliez	avais recueilli	aviez recueilli
recueillait	recueillaient	avait recueilli	avaient recueilli
3 passé simple		10 passé antérieur	
recueillis	recueillîmes	eus recueilli	eûmes recueilli
recueillis	recueillîtes	eus recueilli	eûtes recueilli
recueillit	recueillirent	eut recueilli	eurent recueilli
4 futur		11 futur antérieur	
recueillerai	recueillerons	aurai recueilli	aurons recueilli
recueilleras	recueillerez	auras recueilli	aurez recueilli
recueillera	recueilleront	aura recueilli	auront recueilli
5 conditionnel		12 conditionnel passé	
recueillerais	recueillerions	aurais recueilli	aurions recueilli
recueillerais	recueilleriez	aurais recueilli	auriez recueilli
recueillerait	recueilleraient	aurait recueilli	auraient recueilli
6 présent du subjonctif		13 passé du subjonctif	
recueille	recueillions	aie recueilli	ayons recueilli
recueilles	recueilliez	aies recueilli	ayez recueilli
recueille	recueillent	ait recueilli	aient recueilli
7 imparfait du subjonctif		14 plus-que-parfait du subjonctif	
recueillisse	recueillissions	eusse recueilli	eussions recueilli
recueillisses	recueillissiez	eusses recueilli	eussiez recueilli
recueillît	recueillissent	eût recueilli	eussent recueilli

Impératif
recueille
recueillons
recueillez

Words and expressions related to this verb

recueillir le fruit de son travail   to reap the fruit of one's labor

un recueil   collection; **un recueil de contes** collection of stories

le recueillement   meditation, contemplation

See also **accueillir** and **cueillir**.

se recueillir   to meditate, to collect one's thoughts

Avez-vous jamais lu le poème *Recueillement* de Charles Baudelaire?   Have you ever read the poem *Recueillement* by Charles Baudelaire?

Irregular verb

to reduce, to decrease, to diminish

The Seven Simple Tenses		The Seven Compound Tenses	
Singular	Plural	Singular	Plural
1 présent de l'indicatif		8 passé composé	
réduis	**réduisons**	**ai réduit**	**avons réduit**
réduis	**réduisez**	**as réduit**	**avez réduit**
réduit	**réduisent**	**a réduit**	**ont réduit**
2 imparfait de l'indicatif		9 plus-que-parfait de l'indicatif	
réduisais	**réduisions**	**avais réduit**	**avions réduit**
réduisais	**réduisiez**	**avais réduit**	**aviez réduit**
réduisait	**réduisaient**	**avait réduit**	**avaient réduit**
3 passé simple		10 passé antérieur	
réduisis	**réduisîmes**	**eus réduit**	**eûmes réduit**
réduisis	**réduisîtes**	**eus réduit**	**eûtes réduit**
réduisit	**réduisirent**	**eut réduit**	**eurent réduit**
4 futur		11 futur antérieur	
réduirai	**réduirons**	**aurai réduit**	**aurons réduit**
réduiras	**réduirez**	**auras réduit**	**aurez réduit**
réduira	**réduiront**	**aura réduit**	**auront réduit**
5 conditionnel		12 conditionnel passé	
réduirais	**réduirions**	**aurais réduit**	**aurions réduit**
réduirais	**réduiriez**	**aurais réduit**	**auriez réduit**
réduirait	**réduiraient**	**aurait réduit**	**auraient réduit**
6 présent du subjonctif		13 passé du subjonctif	
réduise	**réduisions**	**aie réduit**	**ayons réduit**
réduises	**réduisiez**	**aies réduit**	**ayez réduit**
réduise	**réduisent**	**ait réduit**	**aient réduit**
7 imparfait du subjonctif		14 plus-que-parfait du subjonctif	
réduisisse	**réduisissions**	**eusse réduit**	**eussions réduit**
réduisisses	**réduisissiez**	**eusses réduit**	**eussiez réduit**
réduisît	**réduisissent**	**eût réduit**	**eussent réduit**

Impératif
réduis
réduisons
réduisez

R

Words and expressions related to this verb
une réduction   reduction, decrease
réductible   reducible
une tête réduite   shrunken head

la réductibilité   reductibility
se réduire à   to be reduced to
à prix réduit   at a reduced price

See also **conduire, déduire, introduire, produire, reproduire, séduire,** and **traduire.**

Consult the back pages for over 2,600 verbs conjugated like model verbs among the 501 in this book.

How are you doing? Find out with the verb drills and tests with answers explained on pages 50–101.

The subject pronouns are found on page 103.

réfléchir (383)

Part. pr. **réfléchissant**   Part. passé **réfléchi**

to think, to meditate, to reflect, to ponder

Regular **-ir** verb

The Seven Simple Tenses

The Seven Compound Tenses

Singular	Plural	Singular	Plural
1 présent de l'indicatif		**8 passé composé**	
réfléchis	réfléchissons	ai réfléchi	avons réfléchi
réfléchis	réfléchissez	as réfléchi	avez réfléchi
réfléchit	réfléchissent	a réfléchi	ont réfléchi
2 imparfait de l'indicatif		**9 plus-que-parfait de l'indicatif**	
réfléchissais	réfléchissions	avais réfléchi	avions réfléchi
réfléchissais	réfléchissiez	avais réfléchi	aviez réfléchi
réfléchissait	réfléchissaient	avait réfléchi	avaient réfléchi
3 passé simple		**10 passé antérieur**	
réfléchis	réfléchîmes	eus réfléchi	eûmes réfléchi
réfléchis	réfléchîtes	eus réfléchi	eûtes réfléchi
réfléchit	réfléchirent	eut réfléchi	eurent réfléchi
4 futur		**11 futur antérieur**	
réfléchirai	réfléchirons	aurai réfléchi	aurons réfléchi
réfléchiras	réfléchirez	auras réfléchi	aurez réfléchi
réfléchira	réfléchiront	aura réfléchi	auront réfléchi
5 conditionnel		**12 conditionnel passé**	
réfléchirais	réfléchirions	aurais réfléchi	aurions réfléchi
réfléchirais	réfléchiriez	aurais réfléchi	auriez réfléchi
réfléchirait	réfléchiraient	aurait réfléchi	auraient réfléchi
6 présent du subjonctif		**13 passé du subjonctif**	
réfléchisse	réfléchissions	aie réfléchi	ayons réfléchi
réfléchisses	réfléchissiez	aies réfléchi	ayez réfléchi
réfléchisse	réfléchissent	ait réfléchi	aient réfléchi
7 imparfait du subjonctif		**14 plus-que-parfait du subjonctif**	
réfléchisse	réfléchissions	eusse réfléchi	eussions réfléchi
réfléchisses	réfléchissiez	eusses réfléchi	eussiez réfléchi
réfléchît	réfléchissent	eût réfléchi	eussent réfléchi

Impératif
réfléchis
réfléchissons
réfléchissez

Sentences using this verb and expressions related to it
Mathide: **Yvette, vas-tu au bal samedi soir?**
Yvette: **Je ne sais pas si j'y vais. Je demande à réfléchir.**
Mathilde: **Bon, alors, réfléchis avant de me donner ta réponse.**

réfléchir à qqch   to think over (ponder) something
Il faut que j'y réfléchisse.   I must think it over.
réfléchir avant de parler   to think before speaking
La mer réfléchit le ciel.   The sea reflects the sky.
un reflet   reflection
tout bien réfléchi   after careful thought

Review the Subjunctive clearly and simply on pages 26–31.

532

The Seven Simple Tenses		The Seven Compound Tenses	
Singular	Plural	Singular	Plural
1 présent de l'indicatif		8 passé composé	
refuse	refusons	ai refusé	avons refusé
refuses	refusez	as refusé	avez refusé
refuse	refusent	a refusé	ont refusé
2 imparfait de l'indicatif		9 plus-que-parfait de l'indicatif	
refusais	refusions	avais refusé	avions refusé
refusais	refusiez	avais refusé	aviez refusé
refusait	refusaient	avait refusé	avaient refusé
3 passé simple		10 passé antérieur	
refusai	refusâmes	eus refusé	eûmes refusé
refusas	refusâtes	eus refusé	eûtes refusé
refusa	refusèrent	eut refusé	eurent refusé
4 futur		11 futur antérieur	
refuserai	refuserons	aurai refusé	aurons refusé
refuseras	refuserez	auras refusé	aurez refusé
refusera	refuseront	aura refusé	auront refusé
5 conditionnel		12 conditionnel passé	
refuserais	refuserions	aurais refusé	aurions refusé
refuserais	refuseriez	aurais refusé	auriez refusé
refuserait	refuseraient	aurait refusé	auraient refusé
6 présent du subjonctif		13 passé du subjonctif	
refuse	refusions	aie refusé	ayons refusé
refuses	refusiez	aies refusé	ayez refusé
refuse	refusent	ait refusé	aient refusé
7 imparfait du subjonctif		14 plus-que-parfait du subjonctif	
refusasse	refusassions	eusse refusé	eussions refusé
refusasses	refusassiez	eusses refusé	eussiez refusé
refusât	refusassent	eût refusé	eussent refusé

Impératif
refuse
refusons
refusez

R

Sentences using this verb and words related to it
   **Je refuse absolument de vous écouter. Sortez, s'il vous plaît! Si vous refusez, vous le
regretterez.**

refuser de faire qqch   to refuse to do
   something
se refuser qqch   to deny oneself something
refusable   refusable
un refus   refusal

refuser l'entrée à qqn   to turn someone away
refuser la vie routinière   to refuse a routine
   life
Elle a été refusée.   She was refused.

Use the guide to French pronunciation. It's in the Appendixes.

to look (at), to watch

The Seven Simple Tenses | The Seven Compound Tenses

Singular	Plural	Singular	Plural
1 présent de l'indicatif		8 passé composé	
regarde	regardons	ai regardé	avons regardé
regardes	regardez	as regardé	avez regardé
regarde	regardent	a regardé	ont regardé
2 imparfait de l'indicatif		9 plus-que-parfait de l'indicatif	
regardais	regardions	avais regardé	avions regardé
regardais	regardiez	avais regardé	aviez regardé
regardait	regardaient	avait regardé	avaient regardé
3 passé simple		10 passé antérieur	
regardai	regardâmes	eus regardé	eûmes regardé
regardas	regardâtes	eus regardé	eûtes regardé
regarda	regardèrent	eut regardé	eurent regardé
4 futur		11 futur antérieur	
regarderai	regarderons	aurai regardé	aurons regardé
regarderas	regarderez	auras regardé	aurez regardé
regardera	regarderont	aura regardé	auront regardé
5 conditionnel		12 conditionnel passé	
regarderais	regarderions	aurais regardé	aurions regardé
regarderais	regarderiez	aurais regardé	auriez regardé
regarderait	regarderaient	aurait regardé	auraient regardé
6 présent du subjonctif		13 passé du subjonctif	
regarde	regardions	aie regardé	ayons regardé
regardes	regardiez	aies regardé	ayez regardé
regarde	regardent	ait regardé	aient regardé
7 imparfait du subjonctif		14 plus-que-parfait du subjonctif	
regardasse	regardassions	eusse regardé	eussions regardé
regardasses	regardassiez	eusses regardé	eussiez regardé
regardât	regardassent	eût regardé	eussent regardé

Impératif
regarde
regardons
regardez

Sentences using this verb and words related to it
—Qu'est-ce que tu regardes, Bernard?
—Je regarde le ciel. Il est beau et clair.
—Pourquoi ne me regardes-tu pas?
Cela ne vous regarde pas.   That's none of your business.

regarder qqch   to look at (to watch) something;   **regarder la télé**   to watch TV
un regard   glance, look;   **au regard de**   compared to, with regard to

See *Verbs with prepositions* in the Appendixes.

Regular **-er** verb

to regret, to miss

The Seven Simple Tenses

The Seven Compound Tenses

Singular	Plural	Singular	Plural
1 présent de l'indicatif		8 passé composé	
regrette	**regrettons**	**ai regretté**	**avons regretté**
regrettes	**regrettez**	**as regretté**	**avez regretté**
regrette	**regrettent**	**a regretté**	**ont regretté**
2 imparfait de l'indicatif		9 plus-que-parfait de l'indicatif	
regrettais	**regrettions**	**avais regretté**	**avions regretté**
regrettais	**regrettiez**	**avais regretté**	**aviez regretté**
regrettait	**regrettaient**	**avait regretté**	**avaient regretté**
3 passé simple		10 passé antérieur	
regrettai	**regrettâmes**	**eus regretté**	**eûmes regretté**
regrettas	**regrettâtes**	**eus regretté**	**eûtes regretté**
regretta	**regrettèrent**	**eut regretté**	**eurent regretté**
4 futur		11 futur antérieur	
regretterai	**regretterons**	**aurai regretté**	**aurons regretté**
regretteras	**regretterez**	**auras regretté**	**aurez regretté**
regrettera	**regretteront**	**aura regretté**	**auront regretté**
5 conditionnel		12 conditionnel passé	
regretterais	**regretterions**	**aurais regretté**	**aurions regretté**
regretterais	**regretteriez**	**aurais regretté**	**auriez regretté**
regretterait	**regretteraient**	**aurait regretté**	**auraient regretté**
6 présent du subjonctif		13 passé du subjonctif	
regrette	**regrettions**	**aie regretté**	**ayons regretté**
regrettes	**regrettiez**	**aies regretté**	**ayez regretté**
regrette	**regrettent**	**ait regretté**	**aient regretté**
7 imparfait du subjonctif		14 plus-que-parfait du subjonctif	
regrettasse	**regrettassions**	**eusse regretté**	**eussions regretté**
regrettasses	**regrettassiez**	**eusses regretté**	**eussiez regretté**
regrettât	**regrettassent**	**eût regretté**	**eussent regretté**

R

Impératif
regrette
regrettons
regrettez

Common idiomatic expressions using this verb and words related to it
regretter d'avoir fait qqch   to regret (to be sorry for) having done something
regrettable   regrettable; **Il est regrettable que + subjunctive**   It is regrettable (It is a pity)
    that . . .
Je ne regrette rien.   I regret nothing.
Je le regrette.   I'm sorry. (I regret it.)
un regret   regret; **avoir regret de qqch**   to regret something, to feel sorry about something

It's important that you be familiar with the Subjunctive. See pages 26–31.

to read again, to reread

The Seven Simple Tenses		The Seven Compound Tenses	
Singular	Plural	Singular	Plural
1 présent de l'indicatif		8 passé composé	
relis	**relisons**	**ai relu**	**avons relu**
relis	**relisez**	**as relu**	**avez relu**
relit	**relisent**	**a relu**	**ont relu**
2 imparfait de l'indicatif		9 plus-que-parfait de l'indicatif	
relisais	**relisions**	**avais relu**	**avions relu**
relisais	**relisiez**	**avais relu**	**aviez relu**
relisait	**relisaient**	**avait relu**	**avaient relu**
3 passé simple		10 passé antérieur	
relus	**relûmes**	**eus relu**	**eûmes relu**
relus	**relûtes**	**eus relu**	**eûtes relu**
relut	**relurent**	**eut relu**	**eurent relu**
4 futur		11 futur antérieur	
relirai	**relirons**	**aurai relu**	**aurons relu**
reliras	**relirez**	**auras relu**	**aurez relu**
relira	**reliront**	**aura relu**	**auront relu**
5 conditionnel		12 conditionnel passé	
relirais	**relirions**	**aurais relu**	**aurions relu**
relirais	**reliriez**	**aurais relu**	**auriez relu**
relirait	**reliraient**	**aurait relu**	**auraient relu**
6 présent du subjonctif		13 passé du subjonctif	
relise	**relisions**	**aie relu**	**ayons relu**
relises	**relisiez**	**aies relu**	**ayez relu**
relise	**relisent**	**ait relu**	**aient relu**
7 imparfait du subjonctif		14 plus-que-parfait du subjonctif	
relusse	**relussions**	**eusse relu**	**eussions relu**
relusses	**relussiez**	**eusses relu**	**eussiez relu**
relût	**relussent**	**eût relu**	**eussent relu**

Impératif
relis
relisons
relisez

Words and expressions related to this verb
lire   to read
la lecture   reading; reading selection
la relecture   rereading

For other words related to this verb see lire.

relire une composition en vue de la corriger
to reread a composition for the purpose of
correcting it

Grammar putting you in a tense mood? Review the definitions of basic grammatical terms with examples on pages 35–49.

Regular **-er** verb   to remark, to notice, to observe, to distinguish

The Seven Simple Tenses		The Seven Compound Tenses	
Singular	Plural	Singular	Plural

1   présent de l'indicatif

remarque	remarquons
remarques	remarquez
remarque	remarquent

8   passé composé

ai remarqué	avons remarqué
as remarqué	avez remarqué
a remarqué	ont remarqué

2   imparfait de l'indicatif

remarquais	remarquions
remarquais	remarquiez
remarquait	remarquaient

9   plus-que-parfait de l'indicatif

avais remarqué	avions remarqué
avais remarqué	aviez remarqué
avait remarqué	avaient remarqué

3   passé simple

remarquai	remarquâmes
remarquas	remarquâtes
remarqua	remarquèrent

10   passé antérieur

eus remarqué	eûmes remarqué
eus remarqué	eûtes remarqué
eut remarqué	eurent remarqué

4   futur

remarquerai	remarquerons
remarqueras	remarquerez
remarquera	remarqueront

11   futur antérieur

aurai remarqué	aurons remarqué
auras remarqué	aurez remarqué
aura remarqué	auront remarqué

5   conditionnel

remarquerais	remarquerions
remarquerais	remarqueriez
remarquerait	remarqueraient

12   conditionnel passé

aurais remarqué	aurions remarqué
aurais remarqué	auriez remarqué
aurait remarqué	auraient remarqué

6   présent du subjonctif

remarque	remarquions
remarques	remarquiez
remarque	remarquent

13   passé du subjonctif

aie remarqué	ayons remarqué
aies remarqué	ayez remarqué
ait remarqué	aient remarqué

7   imparfait du subjonctif

remarquasse	remarquassions
remarquasses	remarquassiez
remarquât	remarquassent

14   plus-que-parfait du subjonctif

eusse remarqué	eussions remarqué
eusses remarqué	eussiez remarqué
eût remarqué	eussent remarqué

R

Impératif
remarque
remarquons
remarquez

Words and expressions related to this verb
une remarque   remark, observation, comment
marquer   to mark
faire remarquer qqch à qqn   to bring
   something to someone's attention, to point
   out something to someone

se faire remarquer   to make oneself noticed,
   draw attention
remarquable   remarkable

Can't find the verb you're looking for? Check the back pages of this book for a list of over 2,600
additional verbs!

The subject pronouns are found on page 103.   **537**

The Seven Simple Tenses		The Seven Compound Tenses	
Singular	Plural	Singular	Plural
1 présent de l'indicatif		**8 passé composé**	
remercie	remercions	ai remercié	avons remercié
remercies	remerciez	as remercié	avez remercié
remercie	remercient	a remercié	ont remercié
2 imparfait de l'indicatif		**9 plus-que-parfait de l'indicatif**	
remerciais	remerciions	avais remercié	avions remercié
remerciais	remerciiez	avais remercié	aviez remercié
remerciait	remerciaient	avait remercié	avaient remercié
3 passé simple		**10 passé antérieur**	
remerciai	remerciâmes	eus remercié	eûmes remercié
remercias	remerciâtes	eus remercié	eûtes remercié
remercia	remercièrent	eut remercié	eurent remercié
4 futur		**11 futur antérieur**	
remercierai	remercierons	aurai remercié	aurons remercié
remercieras	remercierez	auras remercié	aurez remercié
remerciera	remercieront	aura remercié	auront remercié
5 conditionnel		**12 conditionnel passé**	
remercierais	remercierions	aurais remercié	aurions remercié
remercierais	remercieriez	aurais remercié	auriez remercié
remercierait	remercieraient	aurait remercié	auraient remercié
6 présent du subjonctif		**13 passé du subjonctif**	
remercie	remerciions	aie remercié	ayons remercié
remercies	remerciiez	aies remercié	ayez remercié
remercie	remercient	ait remercié	aient remercié
7 imparfait du subjonctif		**14 plus-que-parfait du subjonctif**	
remerciasse	remerciassions	eusse remercié	eussions remercié
remerciasses	remerciassiez	eusses remercié	eussiez remercié
remerciât	remerciassent	eût remercié	eussent remercié

Impératif
remercie
remercions
remerciez

Common idiomatic expressions using this verb and words related to it

remercier qqn de qqch to thank someone for something; **Je vous remercie de votre aimable invitation.** I thank you for your kind invitation.

un remerciement acknowledgment, thanks

Merci! Thank you!
Merci bien! Thank you very much!
sans merci without mercy, mercilessly
être à la merci de to be at the mercy of;
la merci mercy, good will

Can't remember the French verb you need? Check the back pages of this book for the English-French verb index!

Irregular verb

to put (on) again, to replace, to put back,
to give back, to postpone

The Seven Simple Tenses | The Seven Compound Tenses

Singular	Plural	Singular	Plural
1 présent de l'indicatif		8 passé composé	
remets	**remettons**	**ai remis**	**avons remis**
remets	**remettez**	**as remis**	**avez remis**
remet	**remettent**	**a remis**	**ont remis**
2 imparfait de l'indicatif		9 plus-que-parfait de l'indicatif	
remettais	**remettions**	**avais remis**	**avions remis**
remettais	**remettiez**	**avais remis**	**aviez remis**
remettait	**remettaient**	**avait remis**	**avaient remis**
3 passé simple		10 passé antérieur	
remis	**remîmes**	**eus remis**	**eûmes remis**
remis	**remîtes**	**eus remis**	**eûtes remis**
remit	**remirent**	**eut remis**	**eurent remis**
4 futur		11 futur antérieur	
remettrai	**remettrons**	**aurai remis**	**aurons remis**
remettras	**remettrez**	**auras remis**	**aurez remis**
remettra	**remettront**	**aura remis**	**auront remis**
5 conditionnel		12 conditionnel passé	
remettrais	**remettrions**	**aurais remis**	**aurions remis**
remettrais	**remettriez**	**aurais remis**	**auriez remis**
remettrait	**remettraient**	**aurait remis**	**auraient remis**
6 présent du subjonctif		13 passé du subjonctif	
remette	**remettions**	**aie remis**	**ayons remis**
remettes	**remettiez**	**aies remis**	**ayez remis**
remette	**remettent**	**ait remis**	**aient remis**
7 imparfait du subjonctif		14 plus-que-parfait du subjonctif	
remisse	**remissions**	**eusse remis**	**eussions remis**
remisses	**remissiez**	**eusses remis**	**eussiez remis**
remît	**remissent**	**eût remis**	**eussent remis**

R

Impératif
remets
remettons
remettez

Sentences using this verb and words and expressions related to it
—Où avez-vous remis les fleurs que je vous ai données?
—Je les ai remises là-bas. Ne les voyez-vous pas?

se remettre de   to recover from
se remettre à faire qqch   to start to do
   something again
s'en remettre à   to depend on, to rely on

Remettez-vous!   Pull yourself together!
une remise   remittance, postponement,
   discount

See also **commettre, mettre, se mettre, omettre, permettre, promettre, soumettre,** and
transmettre.

The subject pronouns are found on page 103.   **539**

remplacer (391)

to replace

Part. pr. remplaçant   **Part. passé remplacé**

The Seven Simple Tenses		The Seven Compound Tenses	
Singular	Plural	Singular	Plural
1 présent de l'indicatif		**8 passé composé**	
remplace	remplaçons	ai remplacé	avons remplacé
remplaces	remplacez	as remplacé	avez remplacé
remplace	remplacent	a remplacé	ont remplacé
2 imparfait de l'indicatif		**9 plus-que-parfait de l'indicatif**	
remplaçais	remplacions	avais remplacé	avions remplacé
remplaçais	remplaciez	avais remplacé	aviez remplacé
remplaçait	remplaçaient	avait remplacé	avaient remplacé
3 passé simple		**10 passé antérieur**	
remplaçai	remplaçâmes	eus remplacé	eûmes remplacé
remplaças	remplaçâtes	eus remplacé	eûtes remplacé
remplaça	remplacèrent	eut remplacé	eurent remplacé
4 futur		**11 futur antérieur**	
remplacerai	remplacerons	aurai remplacé	aurons remplacé
remplaceras	remplacerez	auras remplacé	aurez remplacé
remplacera	remplaceront	aura remplacé	auront remplacé
5 conditionnel		**12 conditionnel passé**	
remplacerais	remplacerions	aurais remplacé	aurions remplacé
remplacerais	remplaceriez	aurais remplacé	auriez remplacé
remplacerait	remplaceraient	aurait remplacé	auraient remplacé
6 présent du subjonctif		**13 passé du subjonctif**	
remplace	remplacions	aie remplacé	ayons remplacé
remplaces	remplaciez	aies remplacé	ayez remplacé
remplace	remplacent	ait remplacé	aient remplacé
7 imparfait du subjonctif		**14 plus-que-parfait du subjonctif**	
remplaçasse	remplaçassions	eusse remplacé	eussions remplacé
remplaçasses	remplaçassiez	eusses remplacé	eussiez remplacé
remplaçât	remplaçassent	eût remplacé	eussent remplacé

Impératif
remplace
remplaçons
remplacez

Words and expressions related to this verb

remplacer par   to replace with
un remplacement   replacement (thing)
un remplaçant, une remplaçante
  replacement (person), substitute

remplaçable   replaceable; irremplaçable
  irreplaceable
en remplacement de   in place of

See also placer.

Use the guide to French pronunciation. It's in the Appendixes!

540

Regular **-ir** verb   to fill, to fulfill, to fill in, to fill out

The Seven Simple Tenses		The Seven Compound Tenses	
Singular	Plural	Singular	Plural
1 présent de l'indicatif		8 passé composé	
remplis	remplissons	ai rempli	avons rempli
remplis	remplissez	as rempli	avez rempli
remplit	remplissent	a rempli	ont rempli
2 imparfait de l'indicatif		9 plus-que-parfait de l'indicatif	
remplissais	remplissions	avais rempli	avions rempli
remplissais	remplissiez	avais rempli	aviez rempli
remplissait	remplissaient	avait rempli	avaient rempli
3 passé simple		10 passé antérieur	
remplis	remplîmes	eus rempli	eûmes rempli
remplis	remplîtes	eus rempli	eûtes rempli
remplit	remplirent	eut rempli	eurent rempli
4 futur		11 futur antérieur	
remplirai	remplirons	aurai rempli	aurons rempli
rempliras	remplirez	auras rempli	aurez rempli
remplira	rempliront	aura rempli	auront rempli
5 conditionnel		12 conditionnel passé	
remplirais	remplirions	aurais rempli	aurions rempli
remplirais	rempliriez	aurais rempli	auriez rempli
remplirait	rempliraient	aurait rempli	auraient rempli
6 présent du subjonctif		13 passé du subjonctif	
remplisse	remplissions	aie rempli	ayons rempli
remplisses	remplissiez	aies rempli	ayez rempli
remplisse	remplissent	ait rempli	aient rempli
7 imparfait du subjonctif		14 plus-que-parfait du subjonctif	
remplisse	remplissions	eusse rempli	eussions rempli
remplisses	remplissiez	eusses rempli	eussiez rempli
remplît	remplissent	eût rempli	eussent rempli

R

Impératif
remplis
remplissons
remplissez

Words and expressions related to this verb

remplir de   to fill with
remplir qqch de qqch   to fill something with
  something
se remplir   to fill up
un remplissage   filling up
emplir   to fill

remplir des conditions   to fulfill
  requirements, conditions
remplir une tâche   to carry out (perform) a
  task
remplir quelqu'un d'admiration   to fill
  someone with admiration

Grammar putting you in a tense mood? Review the definitions of basic grammatical terms with examples on pages 35–49.

to meet, to encounter   Regular **-er** verb

The Seven Simple Tenses		The Seven Compound Tenses	
Singular	Plural	Singular	Plural
1 présent de l'indicatif		8 passé composé	
rencontre	rencontrons	ai rencontré	avons rencontré
rencontres	rencontrez	as rencontré	avez rencontré
rencontre	rencontrent	a rencontré	ont rencontré
2 imparfait de l'indicatif		9 plus-que-parfait de l'indicatif	
rencontrais	rencontrions	avais rencontré	avions rencontré
rencontrais	rencontriez	avais rencontré	aviez rencontré
rencontrait	rencontraient	avait rencontré	avaient rencontré
3 passé simple		10 passé antérieur	
rencontrai	rencontrâmes	eus rencontré	eûmes rencontré
rencontras	rencontrâtes	eus rencontré	eûtes rencontré
rencontra	rencontrèrent	eut rencontré	eurent rencontré
4 futur		11 futur antérieur	
rencontrerai	rencontrerons	aurai rencontré	aurons rencontré
rencontreras	rencontrerez	auras rencontré	aurez rencontré
rencontrera	rencontreront	aura rencontré	auront rencontré
5 conditionnel		12 conditionnel passé	
rencontrerais	rencontrerions	aurais rencontré	aurions rencontré
rencontrerais	rencontreriez	aurais rencontré	auriez rencontré
rencontrerait	rencontreraient	aurait rencontré	auraient rencontré
6 présent du subjonctif		13 passé du subjonctif	
rencontre	rencontrions	aie rencontré	ayons rencontré
rencontres	rencontriez	aies rencontré	ayez rencontré
rencontre	rencontrent	ait rencontré	aient rencontré
7 imparfait du subjonctif		14 plus-que-parfait du subjonctif	
rencontrasse	rencontrassions	eusse rencontré	eussions rencontré
rencontrasses	rencontrassiez	eusses rencontré	eussiez rencontré
rencontrât	rencontrassent	eût rencontré	eussent rencontré

Impératif
rencontre
rencontrons
rencontrez

Words and expressions related to this verb

se rencontrer   to meet each other
une rencontre   encounter, meeting
aller à la rencontre de qqn   to go to meet someone
rencontrer par hasard   to meet someone by chance (bump into)

une rencontre au sommet   summit meeting
faire une rencontre inattendue   to have an unexpected encounter
de mauvaises rencontres   the wrong sort of people

Do you need more drills? Have fun with the *501 French Verbs* CD-ROM!

Regular **-re** verb   to give back, to return (something), to render; to vomit

The Seven Simple Tenses		The Seven Compound Tenses	
Singular	Plural	Singular	Plural
1 présent de l'indicatif		8 passé composé	
rends	**rendons**	**ai rendu**	**avons rendu**
rends	**rendez**	**as rendu**	**avez rendu**
rend	**rendent**	**a rendu**	**ont rendu**
2 imparfait de l'indicatif		9 plus-que-parfait de l'indicatif	
rendais	**rendions**	**avais rendu**	**avions rendu**
rendais	**rendiez**	**avais rendu**	**aviez rendu**
rendait	**rendaient**	**avait rendu**	**avaient rendu**
3 passé simple		10 passé antérieur	
rendis	**rendîmes**	**eus rendu**	**eûmes rendu**
rendis	**rendîtes**	**eus rendu**	**eûtes rendu**
rendit	**rendirent**	**eut rendu**	**eurent rendu**
4 futur		11 futur antérieur	
rendrai	**rendrons**	**aurai rendu**	**aurons rendu**
rendras	**rendrez**	**auras rendu**	**aurez rendu**
rendra	**rendront**	**aura rendu**	**auront rendu**
5 conditionnel		12 conditionnel passé	
rendrais	**rendrions**	**aurais rendu**	**aurions rendu**
rendrais	**rendriez**	**aurais rendu**	**auriez rendu**
rendrait	**rendraient**	**aurait rendu**	**auraient rendu**
6 présent du subjonctif		13 passé du subjonctif	
rende	**rendions**	**aie rendu**	**ayons rendu**
rendes	**rendiez**	**aies rendu**	**ayez rendu**
rende	**rendent**	**ait rendu**	**aient rendu**
7 imparfait du subjonctif		14 plus-que-parfait du subjonctif	
rendisse	**rendissions**	**eusse rendu**	**eussions rendu**
rendisses	**rendissiez**	**eusses rendu**	**eussiez rendu**
rendît	**rendissent**	**eût rendu**	**eussent rendu**

R

Impératif
rends
rendons
rendez

AN ESSENTIAL
55 VERB

Rendre

Rendre is a very useful verb for beginning students because it is used in numerous everyday situations and idiomatic expressions. It is a regular -re verb.

Sentences using rendre

J'ai rendu le livre à la bibliothèque. I returned the book to the library.

Elle a rendu tout ce qu'elle a mangé. She vomited everything she ate.

Prière de rendre la clé de la chambre avant de partir. Please return the room key before leaving. (When going out for the day or checking out of a hotel.)

Tous les citoyens se sont rendus aux urnes afin d'élire un nouveau président. All the citizens voted in order to elect a new president.

Rendez à César ce qui est à César, et à Dieu ce qui est à Dieu. (Luc 20, 25) Render unto Caesar that which is Caesar's, and unto God that which is God's. (Luke 20, 25)

Pendant les vacances nous rendrons visite à notre grand-père. During vacation we will pay a visit to our grandfather.

Words and expressions related to this verb

un rendez-vous **appointment, date**

fixer un rendez-vous **to make an appointment, a date**

un compte rendu **report, account**

se rendre à **to go to, to surrender to**

rendre un service à qqn **to do someone a favor**

rendre service à qqn **to be of service to someone**

rendre qqn + adj. **to make someone + adj.**

rendre grâce à qqn **to give thanks to someone**

rendre compte de qqch **to give an account of something**

se rendre compte de **to realize**

rendre justice **to uphold justice**

rendre qqch **to return something**

se rendre aux urnes **to vote**

rendre hommage à qqn/qqch **to pay someone/something homage**

rendre visite à **to pay a visit to**

Can't remember the French verb you need? Check the back pages of this book for the English-French verb index!

Regular **-er** verb

The Seven Simple Tenses		The Seven Compound Tenses	
Singular	Plural	Singular	Plural
1 présent de l'indicatif		8 passé composé	
rentre	rentrons	suis rentré(e)	sommes rentré(e)s
rentres	rentrez	es rentré(e)	êtes rentré(e)(s)
rentre	rentrent	est rentré(e)	sont rentré(e)s
2 imparfait de l'indicatif		9 plus-que-parfait de l'indicatif	
rentrais	rentrions	étais rentré(e)	étions rentré(e)s
rentrais	rentriez	étais rentré(e)	étiez rentré(e)(s)
rentrait	rentraient	était rentré(e)	étaient rentré(e)s
3 passé simple		10 passé antérieur	
rentrai	rentrâmes	fus rentré(e)	fûmes rentré(e)s
rentras	rentrâtes	fus rentré(e)	fûtes rentré(e)(s)
rentra	rentrèrent	fut rentré(e)	furent rentré(e)s
4 futur		11 futur antérieur	
rentrerai	rentrerons	serai rentré(e)	serons rentré(e)s
rentreras	rentrerez	seras rentré(e)	serez rentré(e)(s)
rentrera	rentreront	sera rentré(e)	seront rentré(e)s
5 conditionnel		12 conditionnel passé	
rentrerais	rentrerions	serais rentré(e)	serions rentré(e)s
rentrerais	rentreriez	serais rentré(e)	seriez rentré(e)(s)
rentrerait	rentreraient	serait rentré(e)	seraient rentré(e)s
6 présent du subjonctif		13 passé du subjonctif	
rentre	rentrions	sois rentré(e)	soyons rentré(e)s
rentres	rentriez	sois rentré(e)	soyez rentré(e)(s)
rentre	rentrent	soit rentré(e)	soient rentré(e)s
7 imparfait du subjonctif		14 plus-que-parfait du subjonctif	
rentrasse	rentrassions	fusse rentré(e)	fussions rentré(e)s
rentrasses	rentrassiez	fusses rentré(e)	fussiez rentré(e)(s)
rentrât	rentrassent	fût rentré(e)	fussent rentré(e)s

R

Impératif
rentre
rentrons
rentrez

AN ESSENTIAL
55 VERB

Rentrer

Rentrer is an important verb because it is used in many everyday situations and because it is a non-reflexive verb that takes être as an auxiliary (see page 6).

This verb is conjugated with avoir when it has a direct object.

Example: Elle a rentré le chat dans la maison. She brought (took) the cat into the house.
BUT: Elle est rentrée tôt. She returned home early.

Sentences using rentrer

—À quelle heure es-tu rentré à la maison, Alexandre?
—Je suis rentré à dix heures du soir, maman.

—What time did you get home, Alexander?
—I got home at ten in the evening, Mom.

Aide-moi, s'il te plaît, je ne parviens pas à faire rentrer ce téléviseur dans le coffre de ma voiture. Please help me, I cannot manage to make this television set fit in the trunk of my car.

J'ai hâte de voir tous mes amis à la rentrée des classes. I can't wait to see all my friends when we go back to school.

Words and expressions related to this verb

rentrer chez soi **to go back home**

rentrer les enfants **to take the children home**

rentrer ses larmes **to hold back one's tears**

la rentrée **return, homecoming**

la rentrée des classes, la rentrée scolaire **back to school**

rentrer ses griffes **to calm down (Literally, to pull in one's claws)**

rentrer dans **to crash into**

Can't find the verb you're looking for? Check the back pages of this book for a list of over 2,600 additional verbs!

Regular **-re** verb   to spread, to scatter, to spill

The Seven Simple Tenses		The Seven Compound Tenses	
Singular	Plural	Singular	Plural
1 présent de l'indicatif		8 passé composé	
répands	**répandons**	**ai répandu**	**avons répandu**
répands	**répandez**	**as répandu**	**avez répandu**
répand	**répandent**	**a répandu**	**ont répandu**
2 imparfait de l'indicatif		9 plus-que-parfait de l'indicatif	
répandais	**répandions**	**avais répandu**	**avions répandu**
répandais	**répandiez**	**avais répandu**	**aviez répandu**
répandait	**répandaient**	**avait répandu**	**avaient répandu**
3 passé simple		10 passé antérieur	
répandis	**répandîmes**	**eus répandu**	**eûmes répandu**
répandis	**répandîtes**	**eus répandu**	**eûtes répandu**
répandit	**répandirent**	**eut répandu**	**eurent répandu**
4 futur		11 futur antérieur	
répandrai	**répandrons**	**aurai répandu**	**aurons répandu**
répandras	**répandrez**	**auras répandu**	**aurez répandu**
répandra	**répandront**	**aura répandu**	**auront répandu**
5 conditionnel		12 conditionnel passé	
répandrais	**répandrions**	**aurais répandu**	**aurions répandu**
répandrais	**répandriez**	**aurais répandu**	**auriez répandu**
répandrait	**répandraient**	**aurait répandu**	**auraient répandu**
6 présent du subjonctif		13 passé du subjonctif	
répande	**répandions**	**aie répandu**	**ayons répandu**
répandes	**répandiez**	**aies répandu**	**ayez répandu**
répande	**répandent**	**ait répandu**	**aient répandu**
7 imparfait du subjonctif		14 plus-que-parfait du subjonctif	
répandisse	**répandissions**	**eusse répandu**	**eussions répandu**
répandisses	**répandissiez**	**eusses répandu**	**eussiez répandu**
répandît	**répandissent**	**eût répandu**	**eussent répandu**

Impératif
répands
répandons
répandez

Words and expressions related to this verb
répandre l'effroi   to spread fear
une personne répandue   widely known
   person
une opinion répandue   widely accepted
   opinion

répandre du sang   to shed blood
répandre une nouvelle   to spread news
se répandre en injures   to pour out insults
répandre la joie   to spread joy

Don't forget to study the section on defective and impersonal verbs. It's right after this main list.

to reappear, to appear again

Irregular verb

The Seven Simple Tenses		The Seven Compound Tenses	
Singular	Plural	Singular	Plural
1 présent de l'indicatif		**8 passé composé**	
reparais	reparaissons	ai reparu	avons reparu
reparais	reparaissez	as reparu	avez reparu
reparaît	reparaissent	a reparu	ont reparu
2 imparfait de l'indicatif		**9 plus-que-parfait de l'indicatif**	
reparaissais	reparaissions	avais reparu	avions reparu
reparaissais	reparaissiez	avais reparu	aviez reparu
reparaissait	reparaissaient	avait reparu	avaient reparu
3 passé simple		**10 passé antérieur**	
reparus	reparûmes	eus reparu	eûmes reparu
reparus	reparûtes	eus reparu	eûtes reparu
reparut	reparurent	eut reparu	eurent reparu
4 futur		**11 futur antérieur**	
reparaîtrai	reparaîtrons	aurai reparu	aurons reparu
reparaîtras	reparaîtrez	auras reparu	aurez reparu
reparaîtra	reparaîtront	aura reparu	auront reparu
5 conditionnel		**12 conditionnel passé**	
reparaîtrais	reparaîtrions	aurais reparu	aurions reparu
reparaîtrais	reparaîtriez	aurais reparu	auriez reparu
reparaîtrait	reparaîtraient	aurait reparu	auraient reparu
6 présent du subjonctif		**13 passé du subjonctif**	
reparaisse	reparaissions	aie reparu	ayons reparu
reparaisses	reparaissiez	aies reparu	ayez reparu
reparaisse	reparaissent	ait reparu	aient reparu
7 imparfait du subjonctif		**14 plus-que-parfait du subjonctif**	
reparusse	reparussions	eusse reparu	eussions reparu
reparusses	reparussiez	eusses reparu	eussiez reparu
reparût	reparussent	eût reparu	eussent reparu

Impératif
reparais
reparaissons
reparaissez

Words related to this verb
paraître   to appear, to seem
réapparaître   to appear again, to reappear
la réapparition   reappearance

disparaître   to disappear
apparaître   to appear, to come into view

See also apparaître, disparaître, and paraître.

Do you need more drills? Have fun with the *501 French Verbs* CD-ROM!

Regular **-er** verb   to repair

The Seven Simple Tenses		The Seven Compound Tenses	
Singular	Plural	Singular	Plural
1 présent de l'indicatif		8 passé composé	
répare	**réparons**	**ai réparé**	**avons réparé**
répares	**réparez**	**as réparé**	**avez réparé**
répare	**réparent**	**a réparé**	**ont réparé**
2 imparfait de l'indicatif		9 plus-que-parfait de l'indicatif	
réparais	**réparions**	**avais réparé**	**avions réparé**
réparais	**répariez**	**avais réparé**	**aviez réparé**
réparait	**réparaient**	**avait réparé**	**avaient réparé**
3 passé simple		10 passé antérieur	
réparai	**réparâmes**	**eus réparé**	**eûmes réparé**
réparas	**réparâtes**	**eus réparé**	**eûtes réparé**
répara	**réparèrent**	**eut réparé**	**eurent réparé**
4 futur		11 futur antérieur	
réparerai	**réparerons**	**aurai réparé**	**aurons réparé**
répareras	**réparerez**	**auras réparé**	**aurez réparé**
réparera	**répareront**	**aura réparé**	**auront réparé**
5 conditionnel		12 conditionnel passé	
réparerais	**réparerions**	**aurais réparé**	**aurions réparé**
réparerais	**répareriez**	**aurais réparé**	**auriez réparé**
réparerait	**répareraient**	**aurait réparé**	**auraient réparé**
6 présent du subjonctif		13 passé du subjonctif	
répare	**réparions**	**aie réparé**	**ayons réparé**
répares	**répariez**	**aies réparé**	**ayez réparé**
répare	**réparent**	**ait réparé**	**aient réparé**
7 imparfait du subjonctif		14 plus-que-parfait du subjonctif	
réparasse	**réparassions**	**eusse réparé**	**eussions réparé**
réparasses	**réparassiez**	**eusses réparé**	**eussiez réparé**
réparât	**réparassent**	**eût réparé**	**eussent réparé**

R

Impératif
répare
réparons
réparez

Words and expressions related to this verb

faire réparer ses chaussures   to have one's shoes repaired
un réparateur, une réparatrice   repairer
réparable   reparable
irréparable   irreparable

réparer une maison   to restore a house
la réparation   repair, repairing; **en réparation** in repair, under repair
réparer une offense   to correct an offense
irréparablement   irreparably

How are you doing? Find out with the verb drills and tests with answers explained on pages 50–101.

The subject pronouns are found on page 103.   **549**

to iron, to pass again, to pass by again   Regular **-er** verb

The Seven Simple Tenses		The Seven Compound Tenses	
Singular	Plural	Singular	Plural
1 présent de l'indicatif		8 passé composé	
repasse	repassons	ai repassé	avons repassé
repasses	repassez	as repassé	avez repassé
repasse	repassent	a repassé	ont repassé
2 imparfait de l'indicatif		9 plus-que-parfait de l'indicatif	
repassais	repassions	avais repassé	avions repassé
repassais	repassiez	avais repassé	aviez repassé
repassait	repassaient	avait repassé	avaient repassé
3 passé simple		10 passé antérieur	
repassai	repassâmes	eus repassé	eûmes repassé
repassas	repassâtes	eus repassé	eûtes repassé
repassa	repassèrent	eut repassé	eurent repassé
4 futur		11 futur antérieur	
repasserai	repasserons	aurai repassé	aurons repassé
repasseras	repasserez	auras repassé	aurez repassé
repassera	repasseront	aura repassé	auront repassé
5 conditionnel		12 conditionnel passé	
repasserais	repasserions	aurais repassé	aurions repassé
repasserais	repasseriez	aurais repassé	auriez repassé
repasserait	repasseraient	aurait repassé	auraient repassé
6 présent du subjonctif		13 passé du subjonctif	
repasse	repassions	aie repassé	ayons repassé
repasses	repassiez	aies repassé	ayez repassé
repasse	repassent	ait repassé	aient repassé
7 imparfait du subjonctif		14 plus-que-parfait du subjonctif	
repassasse	repassassions	eusse repassé	eussions repassé
repassasses	repassassiez	eusses repassé	eussiez repassé
repassât	repassassent	eût repassé	eussent repassé

Impératif
repasse
repassons
repassez

Common idiomatic expressions using this verb and words related to it

une planche à repasser ironing board
un fer à repasser flat iron (for ironing clothes)
passer un examen to take (sit for) an exam
repasser un examen to take an exam over again

repasser un couteau, des ciseaux to sharpen a knife, scissors
repasser une leçon to review a lesson
repasser une chemise to iron a shirt
repasser un autre jour to stop in again another day
du linge à repasser laundry to iron

See also **passer**.

Can't remember the French verb you need? Check the back pages of this book for the English-French verb index!

Regular **-er** verb with spelling change: **é** changes   to repeat, to rehearse
to **è** before syllable with mute **e**

The Seven Simple Tenses		The Seven Compound Tenses	
Singular	Plural	Singular	Plural
1 présent de l'indicatif		**8 passé composé**	
répète	**répétons**	**ai répété**	**avons répété**
répètes	**répétez**	**as répété**	**avez répété**
répète	**répètent**	**a répété**	**ont répété**
2 imparfait de l'indicatif		**9 plus-que-parfait de l'indicatif**	
répétais	**répétions**	**avais répété**	**avions répété**
répétais	**répétiez**	**avais répété**	**aviez répété**
répétait	**répétaient**	**avait répété**	**avaient répété**
3 passé simple		**10 passé antérieur**	
répétai	**répétâmes**	**eus répété**	**eûmes répété**
répétas	**répétâtes**	**eus répété**	**eûtes répété**
répéta	**répétèrent**	**eut répété**	**eurent répété**
4 futur		**11 futur antérieur**	
répéterai	**répéterons**	**aurai répété**	**aurons répété**
répéteras	**répéterez**	**auras répété**	**aurez répété**
répétera	**répéteront**	**aura répété**	**auront répété**
5 conditionnel		**12 conditionnel passé**	
répéterais	**répéterions**	**aurais répété**	**aurions répété**
répéterais	**répéteriez**	**aurais répété**	**auriez répété**
répéterait	**répéteraient**	**aurait répété**	**auraient répété**
6 présent du subjonctif		**13 passé du subjonctif**	
répète	**répétions**	**aie répété**	**ayons répété**
répètes	**répétiez**	**aies répété**	**ayez répété**
répète	**répètent**	**ait répété**	**aient répété**
7 imparfait du subjonctif		**14 plus-que-parfait du subjonctif**	
répétasse	**répétassions**	**eusse répété**	**eussions répété**
répétasses	**répétassiez**	**eusses répété**	**eussiez répété**
répétât	**répétassent**	**eût répété**	**eussent répété**

R

Impératif
répète
répétons
répétez

Words and expressions related to this verb

répéter une pièce de théâtre   to rehearse a play

une répétition   repetition

La pièce est en répétition.   The play is in rehearsal.

se répéter   to repeat oneself; to recur

Soak up some verbs used in weather expressions. There's a list in the Appendixes!

to respond, to reply, to answer

Regular **-re** verb

The Seven Simple Tenses		The Seven Compound Tenses	
Singular	Plural	Singular	Plural
1 présent de l'indicatif		8 passé composé	
réponds	répondons	ai répondu	avons répondu
réponds	répondez	as répondu	avez répondu
répond	répondent	a répondu	ont répondu
2 imparfait de l'indicatif		9 plus-que-parfait de l'indicatif	
répondais	répondions	avais répondu	avions répondu
répondais	répondiez	avais répondu	aviez répondu
répondait	répondaient	avait répondu	avaient répondu
3 passé simple		10 passé antérieur	
répondis	répondîmes	eus répondu	eûmes répondu
répondis	répondîtes	eus répondu	eûtes répondu
répondit	répondirent	eut répondu	eurent répondu
4 futur		11 futur antérieur	
répondrai	répondrons	aurai répondu	aurons répondu
répondras	répondrez	auras répondu	aurez répondu
répondra	répondront	aura répondu	auront répondu
5 conditionnel		12 conditionnel passé	
répondrais	répondrions	aurais répondu	aurions répondu
répondrais	répondriez	aurais répondu	auriez répondu
répondrait	répondraient	aurait répondu	auraient répondu
6 présent du subjonctif		13 passé du subjonctif	
réponde	répondions	aie répondu	ayons répondu
répondes	répondiez	aies répondu	ayez répondu
réponde	répondent	ait répondu	aient répondu
7 imparfait du subjonctif		14 plus-que-parfait du subjonctif	
répondisse	répondissions	eusse répondu	eussions répondu
répondisses	répondissiez	eusses répondu	eussiez répondu
répondît	répondissent	eût répondu	eussent répondu

Impératif
réponds
répondons
répondez

Words and expressions related to this verb

répondre à qqn   to answer someone; to reply to someone

répondre de qqn   to be responsible for, to vouch for someone

répondre de qqch   to vouch for something, to guarantee something

une **réponse**   answer, reply; **en réponse à votre lettre . . .**   in reply to your letter . . .

pour répondre à la question de . . .   in answer to the question of . . .

un **répondeur téléphonique**   telephone answering machine

Elle m'a répondu en claquant la porte.   She answered me by slamming the door.

un **coupon-réponse**   reply coupon

Get acquainted with what preposition goes with what verb. See *Verbs with prepositions* in the Appendixes.

The Seven Simple Tenses		The Seven Compound Tenses	
Singular	Plural	Singular	Plural
1 présent de l'indicatif		8 passé composé	
me repose	**nous reposons**	**me suis reposé(e)**	**nous sommes reposé(e)s**
te reposes	**vous reposez**	**t'es reposé(e)**	**vous êtes reposé(e)(s)**
se repose	**se reposent**	**s'est reposé(e)**	**se sont reposé(e)s**
2 imparfait de l'indicatif		9 plus-que-parfait de l'indicatif	
me reposais	**nous reposions**	**m'étais reposé(e)**	**nous étions reposé(e)s**
te reposais	**vous reposiez**	**t'étais reposé(e)**	**vous étiez reposé(e)(s)**
se reposait	**se reposaient**	**s'était reposé(e)**	**s'étaient reposé(e)s**
3 passé simple		10 passé antérieur	
me reposai	**nous reposâmes**	**me fus reposé(e)**	**nous fûmes reposé(e)s**
te reposas	**vous reposâtes**	**te fus reposé(e)**	**vous fûtes reposé(e)(s)**
se reposa	**se reposèrent**	**se fut reposé(e)**	**se furent reposé(e)s**
4 futur		11 futur antérieur	
me reposerai	**nous reposerons**	**me serai reposé(e)**	**nous serons reposé(e)s**
te reposeras	**vous reposerez**	**te seras reposé(e)**	**vous serez reposé(e)(s)**
se reposera	**se reposeront**	**se sera reposé(e)**	**se seront reposé(e)s**
5 conditionnel		12 conditionnel passé	
me reposerais	**nous reposerions**	**me serais reposé(e)**	**nous serions reposé(e)s**
te reposerais	**vous reposeriez**	**te serais reposé(e)**	**vous seriez reposé(e)(s)**
se reposerait	**se reposeraient**	**se serait reposé(e)**	**se seraient reposé(e)s**
6 présent du subjonctif		13 passé du subjonctif	
me repose	**nous reposions**	**me sois reposé(e)**	**nous soyons reposé(e)s**
te reposes	**vous reposiez**	**te sois reposé(e)**	**vous soyez reposé(e)(s)**
se repose	**se reposent**	**se soit reposé(e)**	**se soient reposé(e)s**
7 imparfait du subjonctif		14 plus-que-parfait du subjonctif	
me reposasse	**nous reposassions**	**me fusse reposé(e)**	**nous fussions reposé(e)s**
te reposasses	**vous reposassiez**	**te fusses reposé(e)**	**vous fussiez reposé(e)(s)**
se reposât	**se reposassent**	**se fût reposé(e)**	**se fussent reposé(e)s**

R

Impératif
repose-toi; ne te repose pas
reposons-nous; ne nous reposons pas
reposez-vous; ne vous reposez pas

Words and expressions related to this verb
reposer   to put down again; **reposer la tête**
  sur   to rest one's head on; **reposer sur**
  to be based on
le repos   rest, repose; **Au repos!**   At ease!
se reposer sur qqn, qqch   to put one's trust in
  someone, something

un repose-pied   footrest; **un repose-bras**
  armrest
Je suis fatigué; je vais me reposer.   I'm tired;
  I'm going to rest.

Do you need more drills? Have fun with the *501 French Verbs* CD-ROM!

The subject pronouns are found on page 103.   **553**

to take again, to take back, to recover, to resume   Irregular verb

The Seven Simple Tenses		The Seven Compound Tenses	
Singular	Plural	Singular	Plural
1 présent de l'indicatif		8 passé composé	
reprends	reprenons	ai repris	avons repris
reprends	reprenez	as repris	avez repris
reprend	reprennent	a repris	ont repris
2 imparfait de l'indicatif		9 plus-que-parfait de l'indicatif	
reprenais	reprenions	avais repris	avions repris
reprenais	repreniez	avais repris	aviez repris
reprenait	reprenaient	avait repris	avaient repris
3 passé simple		10 passé antérieur	
repris	reprîmes	eus repris	eûmes repris
repris	reprîtes	eus repris	eûtes repris
reprit	reprirent	eut repris	eurent repris
4 futur		11 futur antérieur	
reprendrai	reprendrons	aurai repris	aurons repris
reprendras	reprendrez	auras repris	aurez repris
reprendra	reprendront	aura repris	auront repris
5 conditionnel		12 conditionnel passé	
reprendrais	reprendrions	aurais repris	aurions repris
reprendrais	reprendriez	aurais repris	auriez repris
reprendrait	reprendraient	aurait repris	auraient repris
6 présent du subjonctif		13 passé du subjonctif	
reprenne	reprenions	aie repris	ayons repris
reprennes	repreniez	aies repris	ayez repris
reprenne	reprennent	ait repris	aient repris
7 imparfait du subjonctif		14 plus-que-parfait du subjonctif	
reprisse	reprissions	eusse repris	eussions repris
reprisses	reprissiez	eusses repris	eussiez repris
reprît	reprissent	eût repris	eussent repris

Impératif
reprends
reprenons
reprenez

Words and expressions related to this verb
reprendre froid to catch cold again
reprendre ses esprits to recover one's senses
reprendre le dessus to regain the upper hand
reprendre ses forces to recover one's strength
se reprendre to take hold of oneself, to recover oneself

une reprise resumption, renewal, repetition (*music*)
à maintes reprises over and over again
reprendre la parole to go on speaking, to resume speaking

See also **apprendre, comprendre, entreprendre, se méprendre, prendre,** and **surprendre.**

Don't forget to study the section on defective and impersonal verbs. It's right after this main list.

Regular **-er** verb

to reprimand, to rebuke

The Seven Simple Tenses		The Seven Compound Tenses	
Singular	Plural	Singular	Plural
1 présent de l'indicatif		8 passé composé	
réprimande	réprimandons	ai réprimandé	avons réprimandé
réprimandes	réprimandez	as réprimandé	avez réprimandé
réprimande	réprimandent	a réprimandé	ont réprimandé
2 imparfait de l'indicatif		9 plus-que-parfait de l'indicatif	
réprimandais	réprimandions	avais réprimandé	avions réprimandé
réprimandais	réprimandiez	avais réprimandé	aviez réprimandé
réprimandait	réprimandaient	avait réprimandé	avaient réprimandé
3 passé simple		10 passé antérieur	
réprimandai	réprimandâmes	eus réprimandé	eûmes réprimandé
réprimandas	réprimandâtes	eus réprimandé	eûtes réprimandé
réprimanda	réprimandèrent	eut réprimandé	eurent réprimandé
4 futur		11 futur antérieur	
réprimanderai	réprimanderons	aurai réprimandé	aurons réprimandé
réprimanderas	réprimanderez	auras réprimandé	aurez réprimandé
réprimandera	réprimanderont	aura réprimandé	auront réprimandé
5 conditionnel		12 conditionnel passé	
réprimanderais	réprimanderions	aurais réprimandé	aurions réprimandé
réprimanderais	réprimanderiez	aurais réprimandé	auriez réprimandé
réprimanderait	réprimanderaient	aurait réprimandé	auraient réprimandé
6 présent du subjonctif		13 passé du subjonctif	
réprimande	réprimandions	aie réprimandé	ayons réprimandé
réprimandes	réprimandiez	aies réprimandé	ayez réprimandé
réprimande	réprimandent	ait réprimandé	aient réprimandé
7 imparfait du subjonctif		14 plus-que-parfait du subjonctif	
réprimandasse	réprimandassions	eusse réprimandé	eussions réprimandé
réprimandasses	réprimandassiez	eusses réprimandé	eussiez réprimandé
réprimandât	réprimandassent	eût réprimandé	eussent réprimandé

Impératif
réprimande
réprimandons
réprimandez

Words and expressions related to this verb
une **réprimande**   reprimand, rebuke
faire des **réprimandes**   to make rebukes

réprimandable   blameworthy
prononcer une réprimande   to issue a reprimand

If you want to see a sample English verb fully conjugated in all the tenses, check out pages 8 and 9.

The subject pronouns are found on page 103.

to reproduce

Irregular verb

The Seven Simple Tenses		The Seven Compound Tenses	
Singular	Plural	Singular	Plural

1 présent de l'indicatif

reproduis	reproduisons		
reproduis	reproduisez		
reproduit	reproduisent		

8 passé composé

ai reproduit	avons reproduit
as reproduit	avez reproduit
a reproduit	ont reproduit

2 imparfait de l'indicatif

reproduisais	reproduisions
reproduisais	reproduisiez
reproduisait	reproduisaient

9 plus-que-parfait de l'indicatif

avais reproduit	avions reproduit
avais reproduit	aviez reproduit
avait reproduit	avaient reproduit

3 passé simple

reproduisis	reproduisîmes
reproduisis	reproduisîtes
reproduisit	reproduisirent

10 passé antérieur

eus reproduit	eûmes reproduit
eus reproduit	eûtes reproduit
eut reproduit	eurent reproduit

4 futur

reproduirai	reproduirons
reproduiras	reproduirez
reproduira	reproduiront

11 futur antérieur

aurai reproduit	aurons reproduit
auras reproduit	aurez reproduit
aura reproduit	auront reproduit

5 conditionnel

reproduirais	reproduirions
reproduirais	reproduiriez
reproduirait	reproduiraient

12 conditionnel passé

aurais reproduit	aurions reproduit
aurais reproduit	auriez reproduit
aurait reproduit	auraient reproduit

6 présent du subjonctif

reproduise	reproduisions
reproduises	reproduisiez
reproduise	reproduisent

13 passé du subjonctif

aie reproduit	ayons reproduit
aies reproduit	ayez reproduit
ait reproduit	aient reproduit

7 imparfait du subjonctif

reproduisisse	reproduisissions
reproduisisses	reproduisissiez
reproduisît	reproduisissent

14 plus-que-parfait du subjonctif

eusse reproduit	eussions reproduit
eusses reproduit	eussiez reproduit
eût reproduit	eussent reproduit

Impératif
reproduis
reproduisons
reproduisez

Words and expressions related to this verb

se reproduire   to reproduce itself, to multiply,
   to recur, to happen again
une reproduction   reproduction; les droits de
   reproduction   copyright

reproductif, reproductive   reproductive
reproductible   reproductible
le clonage   cloning
cloner   to clone

See also conduire, déduire, introduire, produire, réduire, séduire, and traduire.

Grammar putting you in a tense mood? Review the definitions of basic grammatical terms with examples on pages 35–49.

Irregular verb

The Seven Simple Tenses		The Seven Compound Tenses	
Singular	Plural	Singular	Plural

1 présent de l'indicatif

résous	résolvons		
résous	résolvez		
résout	résolvent		

8 passé composé

ai résolu	avons résolu
as résolu	avez résolu
a résolu	ont résolu

2 imparfait de l'indicatif

résolvais	résolvions
résolvais	résolviez
résolvait	résolvaient

9 plus-que-parfait de l'indicatif

avais résolu	avions résolu
avais résolu	aviez résolu
avait résolu	avaient résolu

3 passé simple

résolus	résolûmes
résolus	résolûtes
résolut	résolurent

10 passé antérieur

eus résolu	eûmes résolu
eus résolu	eûtes résolu
eut résolu	eurent résolu

4 futur

résoudrai	résoudrons
résoudras	résoudrez
résoudra	résoudront

11 futur antérieur

aurai résolu	aurons résolu
auras résolu	aurez résolu
aura résolu	auront résolu

5 conditionnel

résoudrais	résoudrions
résoudrais	résoudriez
résoudrait	résoudraient

12 conditionnel passé

aurais résolu	aurions résolu
aurais résolu	auriez résolu
aurait résolu	auraient résolu

6 présent du subjonctif

résolve	résolvions
résolves	résolviez
résolve	résolvent

13 passé du subjonctif

aie résolu	ayons résolu
aies résolu	ayez résolu
ait résolu	aient résolu

7 imparfait du subjonctif

résolusse	résolussions
résolusses	résolussiez
résolût	résolussent

14 plus-que-parfait du subjonctif

eusse résolu	eussions résolu
eusses résolu	eussiez résolu
eût résolu	eussent résolu

Impératif
résous
résolvons
résolvez

Words and expressions related to this verb
se résoudre à to make up one's mind to
résoudre qqn à faire qqch to induce someone to do something
résoudre un problème mathématique to solve a math problem
une résolution resolution

See also **absoudre**.

être résolu(e) à faire qqch to be resolved to doing something
Le feu a résous le bois en cendres. The fire has changed the wood into ashes. (The past part. **résous** is used for things that have undergone a physical change.)

Soak up some verbs used in weather expressions. There's a list in the Appendixes!

The subject pronouns are found on page 103.   **557**

to resemble, to be like, to look like   Regular **-er** verb

The Seven Simple Tenses		The Seven Compound Tenses	
Singular	Plural	Singular	Plural

1   présent de l'indicatif

ressemble	ressemblons	ai ressemblé	avons ressemblé
ressembles	ressemblez	as ressemblé	avez ressemblé
ressemble	ressemblent	a ressemblé	ont ressemblé

8   passé composé (in right column header)

2   imparfait de l'indicatif   **9   plus-que-parfait de l'indicatif**

ressemblais	ressemblions	avais ressemblé	avions ressemblé
ressemblais	ressembliez	avais ressemblé	aviez ressemblé
ressemblait	ressemblaient	avait ressemblé	avaient ressemblé

3   passé simple   **10   passé antérieur**

ressemblai	ressemblâmes	eus ressemblé	eûmes ressemblé
ressemblas	ressemblâtes	eus ressemblé	eûtes ressemblé
ressembla	ressemblèrent	eut ressemblé	eurent ressemblé

4   futur   **11   futur antérieur**

ressemblerai	ressemblerons	aurai ressemblé	aurons ressemblé
ressembleras	ressemblerez	auras ressemblé	aurez ressemblé
ressemblera	ressembleront	aura ressemblé	auront ressemblé

5   conditionnel   **12   conditionnel passé**

ressemblerais	ressemblerions	aurais ressemblé	aurions ressemblé
ressemblerais	ressembleriez	aurais ressemblé	auriez ressemblé
ressemblerait	ressembleraient	aurait ressemblé	auraient ressemblé

6   présent du subjonctif   **13   passé du subjonctif**

ressemble	ressemblions	aie ressemblé	ayons ressemblé
ressembles	ressembliez	aies ressemblé	ayez ressemblé
ressemble	ressemblent	ait ressemblé	aient ressemblé

7   imparfait du subjonctif   **14   plus-que-parfait du subjonctif**

ressemblasse	ressemblassions	eusse ressemblé	eussions ressemblé
ressemblasses	ressemblassiez	eusses ressemblé	eussiez ressemblé
ressemblât	ressemblassent	eût ressemblé	eussent ressemblé

Impératif
ressemble
ressemblons
ressemblez

Words and expressions related to this verb
ressembler à qqn   to resemble someone
Paulette ressemble beaucoup à sa mère.
    Paulette looks very much like her mother.
se ressembler   to resemble each other, to look
    alike
Qui se ressemble s'assemble.   Birds of a
    feather flock together.

sembler   to seem, to appear
une ressemblance   resemblance
Cela ne te ressemble pas!   That's not like
    you!
Ils se ressemblent comme deux gouttes d'eau.
    They are as alike as two peas in a pod (like
    two drops of water).

Regular **-er** verb   to remain, to stay; to be left (over)

The Seven Simple Tenses | The Seven Compound Tenses

Singular	Plural	Singular	Plural
1 présent de l'indicatif		**8 passé composé**	
reste	restons	suis resté(e)	sommes resté(e)s
restes	restez	es resté(e)	êtes resté(e)(s)
reste	restent	est resté(e)	sont resté(e)s
2 imparfait de l'indicatif		**9 plus-que-parfait de l'indicatif**	
restais	restions	étais resté(e)	étions resté(e)s
restais	restiez	étais resté(e)	étiez resté(e)(s)
restait	restaient	était resté(e)	étaient resté(e)s
3 passé simple		**10 passé antérieur**	
restai	restâmes	fus resté(e)	fûmes resté(e)s
restas	restâtes	fus resté(e)	fûtes resté(e)(s)
resta	restèrent	fut resté(e)	furent resté(e)s
4 futur		**11 futur antérieur**	
resterai	resterons	serai resté(e)	serons resté(e)s
resteras	resterez	seras resté(e)	serez resté(e)(s)
restera	resteront	sera resté(e)	seront resté(e)s
5 conditionnel		**12 conditionnel passé**	
resterais	resterions	serais resté(e)	serions resté(e)s
resterais	resteriez	serais resté(e)	seriez resté(e)(s)
resterait	resteraient	serait resté(e)	seraient resté(e)s
6 présent du subjonctif		**13 passé du subjonctif**	
reste	restions	sois resté(e)	soyons resté(e)s
restes	restiez	sois resté(e)	soyez resté(e)(s)
reste	restent	soit resté(e)	soient resté(e)s
7 imparfait du subjonctif		**14 plus-que-parfait du subjonctif**	
restasse	restassions	fusse resté(e)	fussions resté(e)s
restasses	restassiez	fusses resté(e)	fussiez resté(e)(s)
restât	restassent	fût resté(e)	fussent resté(e)s

Impératif
reste
restons
restez

Sentences using this verb and words related to it

Combien d'argent vous reste-t-il?   How much money do you have left (over)?
   Il me reste deux cents euros.   I have two hundred euros left.
Restez là; je reviens tout de suite.   Stay there; I'll be right back.

Simone est restée au lit toute la journée.   Simone stayed in bed all day.
les restes   leftovers; **le reste du temps** the rest of the time
le restant   remainder
rester au lit   to stay in bed

Can't find the verb you're looking for? Check the back pages of this book for a list of over 2,600 additional verbs!

to retain, to keep, to detain, to hold back

Irregular verb

The Seven Simple Tenses		The Seven Compound Tenses	
Singular	Plural	Singular	Plural
1 présent de l'indicatif		8 passé composé	
retiens	retenons	ai retenu	avons retenu
retiens	retenez	as retenu	avez retenu
retient	retiennent	a retenu	ont retenu
2 imparfait de l'indicatif		9 plus-que-parfait de l'indicatif	
retenais	retenions	avais retenu	avions retenu
retenais	reteniez	avais retenu	aviez retenu
retenait	retenaient	avait retenu	avaient retenu
3 passé simple		10 passé antérieur	
retins	retînmes	eus retenu	eûmes retenu
retins	retîntes	eus retenu	eûtes retenu
retint	retinrent	eut retenu	eurent retenu
4 futur		11 futur antérieur	
retiendrai	retiendrons	aurai retenu	aurons retenu
retiendras	retiendrez	auras retenu	aurez retenu
retiendra	retiendront	aura retenu	auront retenu
5 conditionnel		12 conditionnel passé	
retiendrais	retiendrions	aurais retenu	aurions retenu
retiendrais	retiendriez	aurais retenu	auriez retenu
retiendrait	retiendraient	aurait retenu	auraient retenu
6 présent du subjonctif		13 passé du subjonctif	
retienne	retenions	aie retenu	ayons retenu
retiennes	reteniez	aies retenu	ayez retenu
retienne	retiennent	ait retenu	aient retenu
7 imparfait du subjonctif		14 plus-que-parfait du subjonctif	
retinsse	retinssions	eusse retenu	eussions retenu
retinsses	retinssiez	eusses retenu	eussiez retenu
retînt	retinssent	eût retenu	eussent retenu

Impératif
retiens
retenons
retenez

Words and expressions related to this verb

retenir au lit   to confine to bed
retenir qqn   to detain someone
se retenir   to restrain oneself
retenir une chambre   to reserve a room

retenir une place   to reserve a place, a seat
une rétention   retention
une retenue   deduction, detention (in school)

See also contenir, obtenir, and tenir.

Do you need more drills? Have fun with the *501 French Verbs* CD-ROM!

The Seven Simple Tenses		The Seven Compound Tenses	
Singular	Plural	Singular	Plural

1 présent de l'indicatif		8 passé composé	
retire	retirons	ai retiré	avons retiré
retires	retirez	as retiré	avez retiré
retire	retirent	a retiré	ont retiré

2 imparfait de l'indicatif		9 plus-que-parfait de l'indicatif	
retirais	retirions	avais retiré	avions retiré
retirais	retiriez	avais retiré	aviez retiré
retirait	retiraient	avait retiré	avaient retiré

3 passé simple		10 passé antérieur	
retirai	retirâmes	eus retiré	eûmes retiré
retiras	retirâtes	eus retiré	eûtes retiré
retira	retirèrent	eut retiré	eurent retiré

4 futur		11 futur antérieur	
retirerai	retirerons	aurai retiré	aurons retiré
retireras	retirerez	auras retiré	aurez retiré
retirera	retireront	aura retiré	auront retiré

5 conditionnel		12 conditionnel passé	
retirerais	retirerions	aurais retiré	aurions retiré
retirerais	retireriez	aurais retiré	auriez retiré
retirerait	retireraient	aurait retiré	auraient retiré

6 présent du subjonctif		13 passé du subjonctif	
retire	retirions	aie retiré	ayons retiré
retires	retiriez	aies retiré	ayez retiré
retire	retirent	ait retiré	aient retiré

7 imparfait du subjonctif		14 plus-que-parfait du subjonctif	
retirasse	retirassions	eusse retiré	eussions retiré
retirasses	retirassiez	eusses retiré	eussiez retiré
retirât	retirassent	eût retiré	eussent retiré

	Impératif	
	retire	
	retirons	
	retirez	

R

Words and expressions related to this verb

retirer qqch à qqn   to take something back from someone

retirer qqn de   to take someone out of, to withdraw someone from

retirer une promesse   to take back a promise

retirer ses chaussures   to take off one's shoes

retirer qqch de   to take something out of

retirer ses paroles   to withdraw, to take back one's words

la carte de retrait   debit card

See also **attirer, se retirer,** and **tirer.**

How are you doing? Find out with the verb drills and tests with answers explained on pages 50–101.

to retire, to withdraw

The Seven Simple Tenses		The Seven Compound Tenses	
Singular	Plural	Singular	Plural
1 présent de l'indicatif		**8 passé composé**	
me retire	**nous retirons**	**me suis retiré(e)**	**nous sommes retiré(e)s**
te retires	**vous retirez**	**t'es retiré(e)**	**vous êtes retiré(e)(s)**
se retire	**se retirent**	**s'est retiré(e)**	**se sont retiré(e)s**
2 imparfait de l'indicatif		**9 plus-que-parfait de l'indicatif**	
me retirais	**nous retirions**	**m'étais retiré(e)**	**nous étions retiré(e)s**
te retirais	**vous retiriez**	**t'étais retiré(e)**	**vous étiez retiré(e)(s)**
se retirait	**se retiraient**	**s'était retiré(e)**	**s'étaient retiré(e)s**
3 passé simple		**10 passé antérieur**	
me retirai	**nous retirâmes**	**me fus retiré(e)**	**nous fûmes retiré(e)s**
te retiras	**vous retirâtes**	**te fus retiré(e)**	**vous fûtes retiré(e)(s)**
se retira	**se retirèrent**	**se fut retiré(e)**	**se furent retiré(e)s**
4 futur		**11 futur antérieur**	
me retirerai	**nous retirerons**	**me serai retiré(e)**	**nous serons retiré(e)s**
te retireras	**vous retirerez**	**te seras retiré(e)**	**vous serez retiré(e)(s)**
se retirera	**se retireront**	**se sera retiré(e)**	**se seront retiré(e)s**
5 conditionnel		**12 conditionnel passé**	
me retirerais	**nous retirerions**	**me serais retiré(e)**	**nous serions retiré(e)s**
te retirerais	**vous retireriez**	**te serais retiré(e)**	**vous seriez retiré(e)(s)**
se retirerait	**se retireraient**	**se serait retiré(e)**	**se seraient retiré(e)s**
6 présent du subjonctif		**13 passé du subjonctif**	
me retire	**nous retirions**	**me sois retiré(e)**	**nous soyons retiré(e)s**
te retires	**vous retiriez**	**te sois retiré(e)**	**vous soyez retiré(e)(s)**
se retire	**se retirent**	**se soit retiré(e)**	**se soient retiré(e)s**
7 imparfait du subjonctif		**14 plus-que-parfait du subjonctif**	
me retirasse	**nous retirassions**	**me fusse retiré(e)**	**nous fussions retiré(e)s**
te retirasses	**vous retirassiez**	**te fusses retiré(e)**	**vous fussiez retiré(e)(s)**
se retirât	**se retirassent**	**se fût retiré(e)**	**se fussent retiré(e)s**

Impératif
retire-toi; ne te retire pas
retirons-nous; ne nous retirons pas
retirez-vous; ne vous retirez pas

Words and expressions related to this verb
se retirer des affaires to retire from business
retraité, retraitée retired, pensioned off
un officier en retraite retired officer
une retraite retreat, retirement; **vivre à la retraite** to live in retirement

un retrait withdrawal; **en retrait** set back; out of line; **un mur en retrait** recess of a wall

See also **attirer, retirer,** and **tirer.**

It's important that you be familiar with the Subjunctive. See pages 26–31.

Regular **-er** verb   to return, to go back, to turn again

The Seven Simple Tenses		The Seven Compound Tenses	
Singular	Plural	Singular	Plural
1 présent de l'indicatif		8 passé composé	
retourne	**retournons**	**suis retourné(e)**	**sommes retourné(e)s**
retournes	**retournez**	**es retourné(e)**	**êtes retourné(e)(s)**
retourne	**retournent**	**est retourné(e)**	**sont retourné(e)s**
2 imparfait de l'indicatif		9 plus-que-parfait de l'indicatif	
retournais	**retournions**	**étais retourné(e)**	**étions retourné(e)s**
retournais	**retourniez**	**étais retourné(e)**	**étiez retourné(e)(s)**
retournait	**retournaient**	**était retourné(e)**	**étaient retourné(e)s**
3 passé simple		10 passé antérieur	
retournai	**retournâmes**	**fus retourné(e)**	**fûmes retourné(e)s**
retournas	**retournâtes**	**fus retourné(e)**	**fûtes retourné(e)(s)**
retourna	**retournèrent**	**fut retourné(e)**	**furent retourné(e)s**
4 futur		11 futur antérieur	
retournerai	**retournerons**	**serai retourné(e)**	**serons retourné(e)s**
retourneras	**retournerez**	**seras retourné(e)**	**serez retourné(e)(s)**
retournera	**retourneront**	**sera retourné(e)**	**seront retourné(e)s**
5 conditionnel		12 conditionnel passé	
retournerais	**retournerions**	**serais retourné(e)**	**serions retourné(e)s**
retournerais	**retourneriez**	**serais retourné(e)**	**seriez retourné(e)(s)**
retournerait	**retourneraient**	**serait retourné(e)**	**seraient retourné(e)s**
6 présent du subjonctif		13 passé du subjonctif	
retourne	**retournions**	**sois retourné(e)**	**soyons retourné(e)s**
retournes	**retourniez**	**sois retourné(e)**	**soyez retourné(e)(s)**
retourne	**retournent**	**soit retourné(e)**	**soient retourné(e)s**
7 imparfait du subjonctif		14 plus-que-parfait du subjonctif	
retournasse	**retournassions**	**fusse retourné(e)**	**fussions retourné(e)s**
retournasses	**retournassiez**	**fusses retourné(e)**	**fussiez retourné(e)(s)**
retournât	**retournassent**	**fût retourné(e)**	**fussent retourné(e)s**

Impératif
retourne
retournons
retournez

R

Words and expressions related to this verb

retourner une chaussette   to turn a sock inside out
retourner un matelas   to turn over a mattress
retourner qqn   to change someone's mind
se retourner   to turn around; **se retourner sur le dos**   to turn over on one's back

un retour   return; **un billet de retour**   return ticket
un billet d'aller et retour   a round trip ticket
être de retour   to be back; **Madame Dupin sera de retour demain.**   Mrs. Dupin will be back tomorrow.

See also **détourner** and **tourner**.

Can't remember the French verb you need? Check the back pages of this book for the English-French verb index.

to succeed, to result

Regular **-ir** verb

The Seven Simple Tenses		The Seven Compound Tenses	
Singular	Plural	Singular	Plural
1 présent de l'indicatif		8 passé composé	
réussis	**réussissons**	**ai réussi**	**avons réussi**
réussis	**réussissez**	**as réussi**	**avez réussi**
réussit	**réussissent**	**a réussi**	**ont réussi**
2 imparfait de l'indicatif		9 plus-que-parfait de l'indicatif	
réussissais	**réussissions**	**avais réussi**	**avions réussi**
réussissais	**réussissiez**	**avais réussi**	**aviez réussi**
réussissait	**réussissaient**	**avait réussi**	**avaient réussi**
3 passé simple		10 passé antérieur	
réussis	**réussîmes**	**eus réussi**	**eûmes réussi**
réussis	**réussîtes**	**eus réussi**	**eûtes réussi**
réussit	**réussirent**	**eut réussi**	**eurent réussi**
4 futur		11 futur antérieur	
réussirai	**réussirons**	**aurai réussi**	**aurons réussi**
réussiras	**réussirez**	**auras réussi**	**aurez réussi**
réussira	**réussiront**	**aura réussi**	**auront réussi**
5 conditionnel		12 conditionnel passé	
réussirais	**réussirions**	**aurais réussi**	**aurions réussi**
réussirais	**réussiriez**	**aurais réussi**	**auriez réussi**
réussirait	**réussiraient**	**aurait réussi**	**auraient réussi**
6 présent du subjonctif		13 passé du subjonctif	
réussisse	**réussissions**	**aie réussi**	**ayons réussi**
réussisses	**réussissiez**	**aies réussi**	**ayez réussi**
réussisse	**réussissent**	**ait réussi**	**aient réussi**
7 imparfait du subjonctif		14 plus-que-parfait du subjonctif	
réussisse	**réussissions**	**eusse réussi**	**eussions réussi**
réussisses	**réussissiez**	**eusses réussi**	**eussiez réussi**
réussît	**réussissent**	**eût réussi**	**eussent réussi**

Impératif
réussis
réussissons
réussissez

Words and expressions related to this verb
réussir à qqch   to succeed in something
réussir à un examen   to pass an exam
une réussite   success; une réussite sociale
   social success
réussir   to result; Le projet a mal réussi.
   The plan turned out badly; Le projet a bien
   réussi.   The plan turned out well.

une soirée réussie   a successful evening
réussir dans la vie   to succeed in life
Les fritures ne me réussissent pas.   Fried
   food doesn't agree with me.

Get acquainted with what preposition goes with what verb. See *Verbs with prepositions* in the Appendixes.

Reflexive regular **-er** verb

The Seven Simple Tenses		The Seven Compound Tenses

Singular	Plural	Singular	Plural
1 présent de l'indicatif		**8 passé composé**	
me réveille	nous réveillons	me suis réveillé(e)	nous sommes réveillé(e)s
te réveilles	vous réveillez	t'es réveillé(e)	vous êtes réveillé(e)(s)
se réveille	se réveillent	s'est réveillé(e)	se sont réveillé(e)s
2 imparfait de l'indicatif		**9 plus-que-parfait de l'indicatif**	
me réveillais	nous réveillions	m'étais réveillé(e)	nous étions réveillé(e)s
te réveillais	vous réveilliez	t'étais réveillé(e)	vous étiez réveillé(e)(s)
se réveillait	se réveillaient	s'était réveillé(e)	s'étaient réveillé(e)s
3 passé simple		**10 passé antérieur**	
me réveillai	nous réveillâmes	me fus réveillé(e)	nous fûmes réveillé(e)s
te réveillas	vous réveillâtes	te fus réveillé(e)	vous fûtes réveillé(e)(s)
se réveilla	se réveillèrent	se fut réveillé(e)	se furent réveillé(e)s
4 futur		**11 futur antérieur**	
me réveillerai	nous réveillerons	me serai réveillé(e)	nous serons réveillé(e)s
te réveilleras	vous réveillerez	te seras réveillé(e)	vous serez réveillé(e)(s)
se réveillera	se réveilleront	se sera réveillé(e)	se seront réveillé(e)s
5 conditionnel		**12 conditionnel passé**	
me réveillerais	nous réveillerions	me serais réveillé(e)	nous serions réveillé(e)s
te réveillerais	vous réveilleriez	te serais réveillé(e)	vous seriez réveillé(e)(s)
se réveillerait	se réveilleraient	se serait réveillé(e)	se seraient réveillé(e)s
6 présent du subjonctif		**13 passé du subjonctif**	
me réveille	nous réveillions	me sois réveillé(e)	nous soyons réveillé(e)s
te réveilles	vous réveilliez	te sois réveillé(e)	vous soyez réveillé(e)(s)
se réveille	se réveillent	se soit réveillé(e)	se soient réveillé(e)s
7 imparfait du subjonctif		**14 plus-que-parfait du subjonctif**	
me réveillasse	nous réveillassions	me fusse réveillé(e)	nous fussions réveillé(e)s
te réveillasses	vous réveillassiez	te fusses réveillé(e)	vous fussiez réveillé(e)(s)
se réveillât	se réveillassent	se fût réveillé(e)	se fussent réveillé(e)s

Impératif
réveille-toi; ne te réveille pas
réveillons-nous; ne nous réveillons pas
réveillez-vous; ne vous réveillez pas

R

Words and expressions related to this verb
le réveillon   Christmas or New Year's Eve
  party
faire réveillon   to see the New Year in, to see
  Christmas in on Christmas Eve
un réveille-matin   alarm clock
éveiller (réveiller) qqn   to wake up, awaken
  someone; **éveiller**   implies to awaken or
  wake up gently; **réveiller**   suggests with
  some effort

veiller   to stay awake; **veiller à**   to look after
veiller sur   to watch over; **surveiller**   to keep
  an eye on
la veille de Noël   Christmas Eve
La tempête a réveillé le chien.   The storm
  woke up the dog.
Marie s'est réveillée à six heures.   Mary
  woke up at six o'clock.

The subject pronouns are found on page 103.

to come back

The Seven Simple Tenses		The Seven Compound Tenses	
Singular	Plural	Singular	Plural
1 présent de l'indicatif		8 passé composé	
reviens	revenons	suis revenu(e)	sommes revenu(e)s
reviens	revenez	es revenu(e)	êtes revenu(e)(s)
revient	reviennent	est revenu(e)	sont revenu(e)s
2 imparfait de l'indicatif		9 plus-que-parfait de l'indicatif	
revenais	revenions	étais revenu(e)	étions revenu(e)s
revenais	reveniez	étais revenu(e)	étiez revenu(e)(s)
revenait	revenaient	était revenu(e)	étaient revenu(e)s
3 passé simple		10 passé antérieur	
revins	revînmes	fus revenu(e)	fûmes revenu(e)s
revins	revîntes	fus revenu(e)	fûtes revenu(e)(s)
revint	revinrent	fut revenu(e)	furent revenu(e)s
4 futur		11 futur antérieur	
reviendrai	reviendrons	serai revenu(e)	serons revenu(e)s
reviendras	reviendrez	seras revenu(e)	serez revenu(e)(s)
reviendra	reviendront	sera revenu(e)	seront revenu(e)s
5 conditionnel		12 conditionnel passé	
reviendrais	reviendrions	serais revenu(e)	serions revenu(e)s
reviendrais	reviendriez	serais revenu(e)	seriez revenu(e)(s)
reviendrait	reviendraient	serait revenu(e)	seraient revenu(e)s
6 présent du subjonctif		13 passé du subjonctif	
revienne	revenions	sois revenu(e)	soyons revenu(e)s
reviennes	reveniez	sois revenu(e)	soyez revenu(e)(s)
revienne	reviennent	soit revenu(e)	soient revenu(e)s
7 imparfait du subjonctif		14 plus-que-parfait du subjonctif	
revinsse	revinssions	fusse revenu(e)	fussions revenu(e)s
revinsses	revinssiez	fusses revenu(e)	fussiez revenu(e)(s)
revînt	revinssent	fût revenu(e)	fussent revenu(e)s

Impératif
reviens
revenons
revenez

Words and expressions related to this verb

le revenu   revenue, income
à revenu fixe   fixed interest
revenir d'une erreur   to realize one's mistake
revenir au même   to amount to the same thing
revenir sur ses pas   to retrace one's steps
revenir sur le sujet   to get back to the subject
revenir sur sa parole   to go back on one's word

Tout revient à ceci . . .   It all boils down to this . . .

Il/Elle s'appelle "reviens."   Make sure you return it (*m.* or *f.* object that is being lent to someone). (Literally: Its name is "come back.")

See also **convenir, devenir, prévenir, se souvenir,** and **venir.**

Regular **-er** verb   to dream

The Seven Simple Tenses		The Seven Compound Tenses	
Singular	Plural	Singular	Plural
1 présent de l'indicatif		8 passé composé	
rêve	**rêvons**	**ai rêvé**	**avons rêvé**
rêves	**rêvez**	**as rêvé**	**avez rêvé**
rêve	**rêvent**	**a rêvé**	**ont rêvé**
2 imparfait de l'indicatif		9 plus-que-parfait de l'indicatif	
rêvais	**rêvions**	**avais rêvé**	**avions rêvé**
rêvais	**rêviez**	**avais rêvé**	**aviez rêvé**
rêvait	**rêvaient**	**avait rêvé**	**avaient rêvé**
3 passé simple		10 passé antérieur	
rêvai	**rêvâmes**	**eus rêvé**	**eûmes rêvé**
rêvas	**rêvâtes**	**eus rêvé**	**eûtes rêvé**
rêva	**rêvèrent**	**eut rêvé**	**eurent rêvé**
4 futur		11 futur antérieur	
rêverai	**rêverons**	**aurai rêvé**	**aurons rêvé**
rêveras	**rêverez**	**auras rêvé**	**aurez rêvé**
rêvera	**rêveront**	**aura rêvé**	**auront rêvé**
5 conditionnel		12 conditionnel passé	
rêverais	**rêverions**	**aurais rêvé**	**aurions rêvé**
rêverais	**rêveriez**	**aurais rêvé**	**auriez rêvé**
rêverait	**rêveraient**	**aurait rêvé**	**auraient rêvé**
6 présent du subjonctif		13 passé du subjonctif	
rêve	**rêvions**	**aie rêvé**	**ayons rêvé**
rêves	**rêviez**	**aies rêvé**	**ayez rêvé**
rêve	**rêvent**	**ait rêvé**	**aient rêvé**
7 imparfait du subjonctif		14 plus-que-parfait du subjonctif	
rêvasse	**rêvassions**	**eusse rêvé**	**eussions rêvé**
rêvasses	**rêvassiez**	**eusses rêvé**	**eussiez rêvé**
rêvât	**rêvassent**	**eût rêvé**	**eussent rêvé**

R

Impératif
rêve
rêvons
rêvez

Common idiomatic expressions using this verb and words related to it

rêver de   to dream of, to dream about, to yearn for

J'ai rêvé de toi toute la nuit.   I dreamt of you all night long.

rêver tout éveillé(e)   to daydream

rêver à   to imagine, to think vaguely about something, to daydream

Janine, tu ne fais pas attention! A quoi rêves-tu?   Janine, you are not paying attention! What are you dreaming about?

un rêveur, une rêveuse   dreamer

une rêverie   reverie, meditation

un rêve   dream

Use the guide to French pronunciation. It's in the Appendixes.

The subject pronouns are found on page 103.
567

to see again, to see once more

Irregular verb

The Seven Simple Tenses		The Seven Compound Tenses	
Singular	Plural	Singular	Plural
1 présent de l'indicatif		8 passé composé	
revois	**revoyons**	**ai revu**	**avons revu**
revois	**revoyez**	**as revu**	**avez revu**
revoit	**revoient**	**a revu**	**ont revu**
2 imparfait de l'indicatif		9 plus-que-parfait de l'indicatif	
revoyais	**revoyions**	**avais revu**	**avions revu**
revoyais	**revoyiez**	**avais revu**	**aviez revu**
revoyait	**revoyaient**	**avait revu**	**avaient revu**
3 passé simple		10 passé antérieur	
revis	**revîmes**	**eus revu**	**eûmes revu**
revis	**revîtes**	**eus revu**	**eûtes revu**
revit	**revirent**	**eut revu**	**eurent revu**
4 futur		11 futur antérieur	
reverrai	**reverrons**	**aurai revu**	**aurons revu**
reverras	**reverrez**	**auras revu**	**aurez revu**
reverra	**reverront**	**aura revu**	**auront revu**
5 conditionnel		12 conditionnel passé	
reverrais	**reverrions**	**aurais revu**	**aurions revu**
reverrais	**reverriez**	**aurais revu**	**auriez revu**
reverrait	**reverraient**	**aurait revu**	**auraient revu**
6 présent du subjonctif		13 passé du subjonctif	
revoie	**revoyions**	**aie revu**	**ayons revu**
revoies	**revoyiez**	**aies revu**	**ayez revu**
revoie	**revoient**	**ait revu**	**aient revu**
7 imparfait du subjonctif		14 plus-que-parfait du subjonctif	
revisse	**revissions**	**eusse revu**	**eussions revu**
revisses	**revissiez**	**eusses revu**	**eussiez revu**
revît	**revissent**	**eût revu**	**eussent revu**

Impératif
revois
revoyons
revoyez

Words and expressions related to this verb
au revoir good-bye, see you again, until we meet again
se revoir to see each other again
une revue review, magazine

un, une revuiste a writer of reviews
une révision revision; à revoir to be revised
passer en revue to review, look through

See also prévoir and voir.

Irregular verb   to laugh

The Seven Simple Tenses		The Seven Compound Tenses	
Singular	Plural	Singular	Plural
1 présent de l'indicatif		8 passé composé	
ris	rions	ai ri	avons ri
ris	riez	as ri	avez ri
rit	rient	a ri	ont ri
2 imparfait de l'indicatif		9 plus-que-parfait de l'indicatif	
riais	riions	avais ri	avions ri
riais	riiez	avais ri	aviez ri
riait	riaient	avait ri	avaient ri
3 passé simple		10 passé antérieur	
ris	rîmes	eus ri	eûmes ri
ris	rîtes	eus ri	eûtes ri
rit	rirent	eut ri	eurent ri
4 futur		11 futur antérieur	
rirai	rirons	aurai ri	aurons ri
riras	rirez	auras ri	aurez ri
rira	riront	aura ri	auront ri
5 conditionnel		12 conditionnel passé	
rirais	ririons	aurais ri	aurions ri
rirais	ririez	aurais ri	auriez ri
rirait	riraient	aurait ri	auraient ri
6 présent du subjonctif		13 passé du subjonctif	
rie	riions	aie ri	ayons ri
ries	riiez	aies ri	ayez ri
rie	rient	ait ri	aient ri
7 imparfait du subjonctif		14 plus-que-parfait du subjonctif	
risse	rissions	eusse ri	eussions ri
risses	rissiez	eusses ri	eussiez ri
rît	rissent	eût ri	eussent ri

Impératif
ris
rions
riez

Words and expressions related to this verb

éclater de rire   to burst out laughing; **rire de**
  to laugh at
dire qqch pour rire   to say something just for
  a laugh
rire au nez de qqn   to laugh in someone's face
rire de bon coeur   to laugh heartily
le rire   laughter; **un sourire**   smile; **risible**
  laughable

See also **sourire**.

le fou rire   fit of laughter, giggles
rire aux éclats   to roar with laughter
le rire franc   a hearty laugh, an open laugh
se rire de   to make fun of
la risette   a little smile (as a child's smile)
Rira bien qui rira le dernier.   Whoever
  laughs last laughs best.

Grammar putting you in a tense mood? Review the definitions of basic grammatical terms with
examples on pages 35–49.

The subject pronouns are found on page 103.   **569**

rompre (419)

to break, to burst,
to shatter, to break off

Regular **-re** verb endings; spelling change:
3rd person sing. of Tense No. 1 adds **t**

The Seven Simple Tenses		The Seven Compound Tenses	
Singular	Plural	Singular	Plural
1 présent de l'indicatif		**8 passé composé**	
romps	rompons	ai rompu	avons rompu
romps	rompez	as rompu	avez rompu
rompt	rompent	a rompu	ont rompu
2 imparfait de l'indicatif		**9 plus-que-parfait de l'indicatif**	
rompais	rompions	avais rompu	avions rompu
rompais	rompiez	avais rompu	aviez rompu
rompait	rompaient	avait rompu	avaient rompu
3 passé simple		**10 passé antérieur**	
rompis	rompîmes	eus rompu	eûmes rompu
rompis	rompîtes	eus rompu	eûtes rompu
rompit	rompirent	eut rompu	eurent rompu
4 futur		**11 futur antérieur**	
romprai	romprons	aurai rompu	aurons rompu
rompras	romprez	auras rompu	aurez rompu
rompra	rompront	aura rompu	auront rompu
5 conditionnel		**12 conditionnel passé**	
romprais	romprions	aurais rompu	aurions rompu
romprais	rompriez	aurais rompu	auriez rompu
romprait	rompraient	aurait rompu	auraient rompu
6 présent du subjonctif		**13 passé du subjonctif**	
rompe	rompions	aie rompu	ayons rompu
rompes	rompiez	aies rompu	ayez rompu
rompe	rompent	ait rompu	aient rompu
7 imparfait du subjonctif		**14 plus-que-parfait du subjonctif**	
rompisse	rompissions	eusse rompu	eussions rompu
rompisses	rompissiez	eusses rompu	eussiez rompu
rompît	rompissent	eût rompu	eussent rompu

Impératif
romps
rompons
rompez

Common idiomatic expressions using this verb and words related to it

rompu de fatigue   worn out
rompu aux affaires   experienced in
   business
se rompre à   to get used to
se rompre la tête   to rack one's brains
une rupture de contrat   breach of contract

corrompre   to corrupt
interrompre   to interrupt
une rupture   rupture, bursting
un rupteur   circuit breaker
rompre avec qqn   to have a falling out with
   someone

See also **corrompre** and **interrompre**.

How are you doing? Find out with the verb drills and tests with answers explained on pages 50–101.

Regular **-ir** verb   to blush, to redden

The Seven Simple Tenses		The Seven Compound Tenses	
Singular	Plural	Singular	Plural
1 présent de l'indicatif		**8 passé composé**	
rougis	rougissons	ai rougi	avons rougi
rougis	rougissez	as rougi	avez rougi
rougit	rougissent	a rougi	ont rougi
2 imparfait de l'indicatif		**9 plus-que-parfait de l'indicatif**	
rougissais	rougissions	avais rougi	avions rougi
rougissais	rougissiez	avais rougi	aviez rougi
rougissait	rougissaient	avait rougi	avaient rougi
3 passé simple		**10 passé antérieur**	
rougis	rougîmes	eus rougi	eûmes rougi
rougis	rougîtes	eus rougi	eûtes rougi
rougit	rougirent	eut rougi	eurent rougi
4 futur		**11 futur antérieur**	
rougirai	rougirons	aurai rougi	aurons rougi
rougiras	rougirez	auras rougi	aurez rougi
rougira	rougiront	aura rougi	auront rougi
5 conditionnel		**12 conditionnel passé**	
rougirais	rougirions	aurais rougi	aurions rougi
rougirais	rougiriez	aurais rougi	auriez rougi
rougirait	rougiraient	aurait rougi	auraient rougi
6 présent du subjonctif		**13 passé du subjonctif**	
rougisse	rougissions	aie rougi	ayons rougi
rougisses	rougissiez	aies rougi	ayez rougi
rougisse	rougissent	ait rougi	aient rougi
7 imparfait du subjonctif		**14 plus-que-parfait du subjonctif**	
rougisse	rougissions	eusse rougi	eussions rougi
rougisses	rougissiez	eusses rougi	eussiez rougi
rougît	rougissent	eût rougi	eussent rougi

Impératif
rougis
rougissons
rougissez

R

Words and expressions related to this verb
faire rougir qqn   to make someone blush
le rouge   red; **rougeâtre**   reddish
un rouge-gorge   robin redbreast;
  (des rouges-gorges)
rougir de qqn   to feel shame for someone
la rougeole   measles

rougeaud, rougeaude   ruddy complexion
le rouge à lèvres   lipstick; **le rouge à joues**
  rouge (for cheeks)
voir rouge   to see red
une jeune mariée rougissante   a blushing
  bride

Can't find the verb you're looking for? Check the back pages of this book for a list of over 2,600 additional verbs!

The subject pronouns are found on page 103.

rouler (421)

Part. pr. **roulant**   Part. passé **roulé**

to roll, to roll along, to drive (a car), to ride along

Regular **-er** verb

The Seven Simple Tenses		The Seven Compound Tenses	
Singular	Plural	Singular	Plural
1 présent de l'indicatif		**8 passé composé**	
roule	roulons	ai roulé	avons roulé
roules	roulez	as roulé	avez roulé
roule	roulent	a roulé	ont roulé
2 imparfait de l'indicatif		**9 plus-que-parfait de l'indicatif**	
roulais	roulions	avais roulé	avions roulé
roulais	rouliez	avais roulé	aviez roulé
roulait	roulaient	avait roulé	avaient roulé
3 passé simple		**10 passé antérieur**	
roulai	roulâmes	eus roulé	eûmes roulé
roulas	roulâtes	eus roulé	eûtes roulé
roula	roulèrent	eut roulé	eurent roulé
4 futur		**11 futur antérieur**	
roulerai	roulerons	aurai roulé	aurons roulé
rouleras	roulerez	auras roulé	aurez roulé
roulera	rouleront	aura roulé	auront roulé
5 conditionnel		**12 conditionnel passé**	
roulerais	roulerions	aurais roulé	aurions roulé
roulerais	rouleriez	aurais roulé	auriez roulé
roulerait	rouleraient	aurait roulé	auraient roulé
6 présent du subjonctif		**13 passé du subjonctif**	
roule	roulions	aie roulé	ayons roulé
roules	rouliez	aies roulé	ayez roulé
roule	roulent	ait roulé	aient roulé
7 imparfait du subjonctif		**14 plus-que-parfait du subjonctif**	
roulasse	roulassions	eusse roulé	eussions roulé
roulasses	roulassiez	eusses roulé	eussiez roulé
roulât	roulassent	eût roulé	eussent roulé

Impératif
roule
roulons
roulez

Words and expressions related to this verb

rouler les *r*   to roll one's r's
rouler sur l'or   to be rolling in dough (money)
se rouler   to roll over
dérouler   to unroll
un rouleau   roll; **un rouleau de papier peint**
  roll of wallpaper

un rouleau de pièces de monnaie   a roll of
  coins
un rouleau de pellicule   roll of film
un rouleau à pâtisserie   rolling pin
se dérouler   to take place, to develop, to
  unfold

Review the Subjunctive clearly and simply on pages 26–31.

Regular **-ir** verb   to seize, to grasp, to comprehend

The Seven Simple Tenses		The Seven Compound Tenses	
Singular	Plural	Singular	Plural
1 présent de l'indicatif		8 passé composé	
saisis	saisissons	ai saisi	avons saisi
saisis	saisissez	as saisi	avez saisi
saisit	saisissent	a saisi	ont saisi
2 imparfait de l'indicatif		9 plus-que-parfait de l'indicatif	
saisissais	saisissions	avais saisi	avions saisi
saisissais	saisissiez	avais saisi	aviez saisi
saisissait	saisissaient	avait saisi	avaient saisi
3 passé simple		10 passé antérieur	
saisis	saisîmes	eus saisi	eûmes saisi
saisis	saisîtes	eus saisi	eûtes saisi
saisit	saisirent	eut saisi	eurent saisi
4 futur		11 futur antérieur	
saisirai	saisirons	aurai saisi	aurons saisi
saisiras	saisirez	auras saisi	aurez saisi
saisira	saisiront	aura saisi	auront saisi
5 conditionnel		12 conditionnel passé	
saisirais	saisirions	aurais saisi	aurions saisi
saisirais	saisiriez	aurais saisi	auriez saisi
saisirait	saisiraient	aurait saisi	auraient saisi
6 présent du subjonctif		13 passé du subjonctif	
saisisse	saisissions	aie saisi	ayons saisi
saisisses	saisissiez	aies saisi	ayez saisi
saisisse	saisissent	ait saisi	aient saisi
7 imparfait du subjonctif		14 plus-que-parfait du subjonctif	
saisisse	saisissions	eusse saisi	eussions saisi
saisisses	saisissiez	eusses saisi	eussiez saisi
saisît	saisissent	eût saisi	eussent saisi

S

Impératif
saisis
saisissons
saisissez

Words and expressions related to this verb
un saisissement   shock
saisissable   seizable
saisissant, saisissante   thrilling, piercing
une saisie   seizure
saisir des données   to input data (comp.)
la saisie de données   data input (comp.)

saisir l'occasion   to seize the opportunity
saisi de joie   overcome with joy
saisir la signification de qqch   to grasp the
   meaning of something
insaisissable   elusive
se saisir de   to take possession of

Seize the opportunity! Read pages 26–31 and grasp the basics of the Subjunctive.

The subject pronouns are found on page 103.   **573**

to soil, to dirty

The Seven Simple Tenses		The Seven Compound Tenses	
Singular	Plural	Singular	Plural
1 présent de l'indicatif		8 passé composé	
salis	salissons	ai sali	avons sali
salis	salissez	as sali	avez sali
salit	salissent	a sali	ont sali
2 imparfait de l'indicatif		9 plus-que-parfait de l'indicatif	
salissais	salissions	avais sali	avions sali
salissais	salissiez	avais sali	aviez sali
salissait	salissaient	avait sali	avaient sali
3 passé simple		10 passé antérieur	
salis	salîmes	eus sali	eûmes sali
salis	salîtes	eus sali	eûtes sali
salit	salirent	eut sali	eurent sali
4 futur		11 futur antérieur	
salirai	salirons	aurai sali	aurons sali
saliras	salirez	auras sali	aurez sali
salira	saliront	aura sali	auront sali
5 conditionnel		12 conditionnel passé	
salirais	salirions	aurais sali	aurions sali
salirais	saliriez	aurais sali	auriez sali
salirait	saliraient	aurait sali	auraient sali
6 présent du subjonctif		13 passé du subjonctif	
salisse	salissions	aie sali	ayons sali
salisses	salissiez	aies sali	ayez sali
salisse	salissent	ait sali	aient sali
7 imparfait du subjonctif		14 plus-que-parfait du subjonctif	
salisse	salissions	eusse sali	eussions sali
salisses	salissiez	eusses sali	eussiez sali
salît	salissent	eût sali	eussent sali

Impératif
salis
salissons
salissez

Words and expressions related to this verb
sale   dirty, soiled
salement   disgustingly
la saleté   filth
dire des saletés   to use filthy language
se salir   to get dirty

une réputation salie   a tarnished reputation
les mains sales   soiled hands
Avez-vous jamais lu ou vu la pièce de théâtre
   Les Mains sales **de Jean-Paul Sartre?**

How are you doing? Find out with the verb drills and tests with answers explained on pages
50–101.

Irregular verb   to satisfy

The Seven Simple Tenses		The Seven Compound Tenses	
Singular	Plural	Singular	Plural
1 présent de l'indicatif		8 passé composé	
satisfais	**satisfaisons**	**ai satisfait**	**avons satisfait**
satisfais	**satisfaites**	**as satisfait**	**avez satisfait**
satisfait	**satisfont**	**a satisfait**	**ont satisfait**
2 imparfait de l'indicatif		9 plus-que-parfait de l'indicatif	
satisfaisais	**satisfaisions**	**avais satisfait**	**avions satisfait**
satisfaisais	**satisfaisiez**	**avais satisfait**	**aviez satisfait**
satisfaisait	**satisfaisaient**	**avait satisfait**	**avaient satisfait**
3 passé simple		10 passé antérieur	
satisfis	**satisfîmes**	**eus satisfait**	**eûmes satisfait**
satisfis	**satisfîtes**	**eus satisfait**	**eûtes satisfait**
satisfit	**satisfirent**	**eut satisfait**	**eurent satisfait**
4 futur		11 futur antérieur	
satisferai	**satisferons**	**aurai satisfait**	**aurons satisfait**
satisferas	**satisferez**	**auras satisfait**	**aurez satisfait**
satisfera	**satisferont**	**aura satisfait**	**auront satisfait**
5 conditionnel		12 conditionnel passé	
satisferais	**satisferions**	**aurais satisfait**	**aurions satisfait**
satisferais	**satisferiez**	**aurais satisfait**	**auriez satisfait**
satisferait	**satisferaient**	**aurait satisfait**	**auraient satisfait**
6 présent du subjonctif		13 passé du subjonctif	
satisfasse	**satisfassions**	**aie satisfait**	**ayons satisfait**
satisfasses	**satisfassiez**	**aies satisfait**	**ayez satisfait**
satisfasse	**satisfassent**	**ait satisfait**	**aient satisfait**
7 imparfait du subjonctif		14 plus-que-parfait du subjonctif	
satisfisse	**satisfissions**	**eusse satisfait**	**eussions satisfait**
satisfisses	**satisfissiez**	**eusses satisfait**	**eussiez satisfait**
satisfît	**satisfissent**	**eût satisfait**	**eussent satisfait**

Impératif
satisfais
satisfaisons
satisfaites

Words and expressions related to this verb
satisfaire sa faim   to satisfy one's hunger;
   satisfaire sa soif   to satisfy one's thirst
satisfaisant, satisfaisante   satisfying
la satisfaction   satisfaction

demander satisfaction à   to demand
   satisfaction from
être satisfait (satisfaite) de   to be satisfied
   with

See also **défaire** and **faire.**

Do you need more drills? Have fun with the *501 French Verbs* CD-ROM!

Part. pr. **sautant**   Part. passé **sauté**

to jump, to leap

Regular **-er** verb

The Seven Simple Tenses		The Seven Compound Tenses	
Singular	Plural	Singular	Plural
1 présent de l'indicatif		8 passé composé	
saute	**sautons**	**ai sauté**	**avons sauté**
sautes	**sautez**	**as sauté**	**avez sauté**
saute	**sautent**	**a sauté**	**ont sauté**
2 imparfait de l'indicatif		9 plus-que-parfait de l'indicatif	
sautais	**sautions**	**avais sauté**	**avions sauté**
sautais	**sautiez**	**avais sauté**	**aviez sauté**
sautait	**sautaient**	**avait sauté**	**avaient sauté**
3 passé simple		10 passé antérieur	
sautai	**sautâmes**	**eus sauté**	**eûmes sauté**
sautas	**sautâtes**	**eus sauté**	**eûtes sauté**
sauta	**sautèrent**	**eut sauté**	**eurent sauté**
4 futur		11 futur antérieur	
sauterai	**sauterons**	**aurai sauté**	**aurons sauté**
sauteras	**sauterez**	**auras sauté**	**aurez sauté**
sautera	**sauteront**	**aura sauté**	**auront sauté**
5 conditionnel		12 conditionnel passé	
sauterais	**sauterions**	**aurais sauté**	**aurions sauté**
sauterais	**sauteriez**	**aurais sauté**	**auriez sauté**
sauterait	**sauteraient**	**aurait sauté**	**auraient sauté**
6 présent du subjonctif		13 passé du subjonctif	
saute	**sautions**	**aie sauté**	**ayons sauté**
sautes	**sautiez**	**aies sauté**	**ayez sauté**
saute	**sautent**	**ait sauté**	**aient sauté**
7 imparfait du subjonctif		14 plus-que-parfait du subjonctif	
sautasse	**sautassions**	**eusse sauté**	**eussions sauté**
sautasses	**sautassiez**	**eusses sauté**	**eussiez sauté**
sautât	**sautassent**	**eût sauté**	**eussent sauté**

Impératif
saute
sautons
sautez

Words and expressions related to this verb
un saut   leap, jump
une sauterelle   grasshopper
sautiller   to skip, to hop
sauter à la corde   to jump (skip) rope
sauter au bas du lit   to jump out of bed

faire sauter une crêpe   to toss a pancake
sauter aux yeux   to be evident, self-evident
Cela saute aux yeux.   That's obvious.
sursauter   to jump, start

Don't forget to study the section on defective and impersonal verbs. It's right after this main list.

Regular **-er** verb

to rescue, to save

The Seven Simple Tenses		The Seven Compound Tenses	
Singular	Plural	Singular	Plural
1 présent de l'indicatif		**8 passé composé**	
sauve	**sauvons**	**ai sauvé**	**avons sauvé**
sauves	**sauvez**	**as sauvé**	**avez sauvé**
sauve	**sauvent**	**a sauvé**	**ont sauvé**
2 imparfait de l'indicatif		**9 plus-que-parfait de l'indicatif**	
sauvais	**sauvions**	**avais sauvé**	**avions sauvé**
sauvais	**sauviez**	**avais sauvé**	**aviez sauvé**
sauvait	**sauvaient**	**avait sauvé**	**avaient sauvé**
3 passé simple		**10 passé antérieur**	
sauvai	**sauvâmes**	**eus sauvé**	**eûmes sauvé**
sauvas	**sauvâtes**	**eus sauvé**	**eûtes sauvé**
sauva	**sauvèrent**	**eut sauvé**	**eurent sauvé**
4 futur		**11 futur antérieur**	
sauverai	**sauverons**	**aurai sauvé**	**aurons sauvé**
sauveras	**sauverez**	**auras sauvé**	**aurez sauvé**
sauvera	**sauveront**	**aura sauvé**	**auront sauvé**
5 conditionnel		**12 conditionnel passé**	
sauverais	**sauverions**	**aurais sauvé**	**aurions sauvé**
sauverais	**sauveriez**	**aurais sauvé**	**auriez sauvé**
sauverait	**sauveraient**	**aurait sauvé**	**auraient sauvé**
6 présent du subjonctif		**13 passé du subjonctif**	
sauve	**sauvions**	**aie sauvé**	**ayons sauvé**
sauves	**sauviez**	**aies sauvé**	**ayez sauvé**
sauve	**sauvent**	**ait sauvé**	**aient sauvé**
7 imparfait du subjonctif		**14 plus-que-parfait du subjonctif**	
sauvasse	**sauvassions**	**eusse sauvé**	**eussions sauvé**
sauvasses	**sauvassiez**	**eusses sauvé**	**eussiez sauvé**
sauvât	**sauvassent**	**eût sauvé**	**eussent sauvé**

Impératif
sauve
sauvons
sauvez

Words and expressions related to this verb
sauvegarder   to safeguard
le sauvetage   life-saving, rescue
Sauve qui peut!   Run for your life!
le sauve-qui-peut   panic
sauver les apparences   to preserve
  appearances

se sauver   to run away, to escape, to rush off
sauver la vie à qqn   to save someone's life
une échelle de sauvetage   fire escape
un gilet de sauvetage   a life jacket

See also **se sauver.**

Grammar putting you in a tense mood? Review the definitions of basic grammatical terms with examples on pages 35–49.

The subject pronouns are found on page 103.

to run away, to rush off, to escape   Reflexive regular **-er** verb

The Seven Simple Tenses		The Seven Compound Tenses	
Singular	Plural	Singular	Plural
1 présent de l'indicatif		8 passé composé	
me sauve	nous sauvons	me suis sauvé(e)	nous sommes sauvé(e)s
te sauves	vous sauvez	t'es sauvé(e)	vous êtes sauvé(e)(s)
se sauve	se sauvent	s'est sauvé(e)	se sont sauvé(e)s
2 imparfait de l'indicatif		9 plus-que-parfait de l'indicatif	
me sauvais	nous sauvions	m'étais sauvé(e)	nous étions sauvé(e)s
te sauvais	vous sauviez	t'étais sauvé(e)	vous étiez sauvé(e)(s)
se sauvait	se sauvaient	s'était sauvé(e)	s'étaient sauvé(e)s
3 passé simple		10 passé antérieur	
me sauvai	nous sauvâmes	me fus sauvé(e)	nous fûmes sauvé(e)s
te sauvas	vous sauvâtes	te fus sauvé(e)	vous fûtes sauvé(e)(s)
se sauva	se sauvèrent	se fut sauvé(e)	se furent sauvé(e)s
4 futur		11 futur antérieur	
me sauverai	nous sauverons	me serai sauvé(e)	nous serons sauvé(e)s
te sauveras	vous sauverez	te seras sauvé(e)	vous serez sauvé(e)(s)
se sauvera	se sauveront	se sera sauvé(e)	se seront sauvé(e)s
5 conditionnel		12 conditionnel passé	
me sauverais	nous sauverions	me serais sauvé(e)	nous serions sauvé(e)s
te sauverais	vous sauveriez	te serais sauvé(e)	vous seriez sauvé(e)(s)
se sauverait	se sauveraient	se serait sauvé(e)	se seraient sauvé(e)s
6 présent du subjonctif		13 passé du subjonctif	
me sauve	nous sauvions	me sois sauvé(e)	nous soyons sauvé(e)s
te sauves	vous sauviez	te sois sauvé(e)	vous soyez sauvé(e)(s)
se sauve	se sauvent	se soit sauvé(e)	se soient sauvé(e)s
7 imparfait du subjonctif		14 plus-que-parfait du subjonctif	
me sauvasse	nous sauvassions	me fusse sauvé(e)	nous fussions sauvé(e)s
te sauvasses	vous sauvassiez	te fusses sauvé(e)	vous fussiez sauvé(e)(s)
se sauvât	se sauvassent	se fût sauvé(e)	se fussent sauvé(e)s

Impératif
sauve-toi; ne te sauve pas
sauvons-nous; ne nous sauvons pas
sauvez-vous; ne vous sauvez pas

Words and expressions related to this verb
se sauver de prison to get out of prison
sauvegarder to safeguard
le sauvetage life-saving, rescue
Sauve qui peut! Run for your life!
Je me sauve! I'm out of here!

sauver to rescue, to save
sauver la vie à qqn to save someone's life
vendre à la sauvette to peddle in the streets
une vente à la sauvette street peddling

See also **sauver.**

Get acquainted with what preposition goes with what verb. See *Verbs with prepositions* in the Appendixes.

Part. pr. **sachant**   Part. passé **su**

Irregular verb

The Seven Simple Tenses		The Seven Compou...
Singular	Plural	Singular
1 présent de l'indicatif		**8 passé compos...**
sais	savons	ai su
sais	savez	as su
sait	savent	a su
2 imparfait de l'indicatif		**9 plus-que-parfa...**
savais	savions	avais su	avions su
savais	saviez	avais su	aviez su
savait	savaient	avait su	avaient su
3 passé simple		**10 passé antérieur**
sus	sûmes	eus su	eûmes su
sus	sûtes	eus su	eûtes su
sut	surent	eut su	eurent su
4 futur		**11 futur antérieur**
saurai	saurons	aurai su	aurons su
sauras	saurez	auras su	aurez su
saura	sauront	aura su	auront su
5 conditionnel		**12 conditionnel passé**
saurais	saurions	aurais su	aurions su
saurais	sauriez	aurais su	auriez su
saurait	sauraient	aurait su	auraient su
6 présent du subjonctif		**13 passé du subjonctif**
sache	sachions	aie su	ayons su
saches	sachiez	aies su	ayez su
sache	sachent	ait su	aient su
7 imparfait du subjonctif		**14 plus-que-parfait du subjonctif**
susse	sussions	eusse su	eussions su
susses	sussiez	eusses su	eussiez su
sût	sussent	eût su	eussent su

Impératif
sache
sachons
sachez

voir is an important verb to know, especially if you are a beginning student. It is used in many idiomatic expressions and everyday situations.

Sentences using savoir

Savez-vous jouer du piano? Do you know how to play the piano?

C'est à savoir. That remains to be seen.

Pas que je sache. Not to my knowledge.

Je voudrais savoir à quelle heure l'avion va partir pour Toronto. I would like to know at what time the plane is going to leave for Toronto.

—Sais-tu que nous déménageons en Europe?
—Oui, je l'ai su hier.

—Do you know that we're moving to Europe?
—Yes, I found out yesterday.

Généralement, les gens qui savent peu parlent beaucoup, et les gens qui savent beaucoup parlent peu. (Rousseau) In general, people who know little talk a lot, and people who know a lot talk little.

Words and expressions related to this verb

le savoir knowledge

le savoir-faire know-how, tact, ability

savoir faire qqch to know how to do something

avoir le savoir-vivre to be well-mannered, well-bred

faire savoir to inform

sans le savoir without knowing it

savoir bon gré à qqn to be thankful, grateful to someone

Proverb

Savoir, c'est pouvoir. Knowledge is power.

Tongue Twister

Le chasseur, sachant chasser sans son chien, chassera. The hunter, knowing how to hunt without his dog, will hunt.

Careful! If you're talking about knowing a person, use connaître:

Je le connais. I know him.

Can't remember the French verb you need? Check the back pages of this book for the English-French verb index!

to dry

Regular **-er** verb endings; spelling change:
é changes to **è** before syllable with mute **e**

The Seven Simple Tenses		The Seven Compound Tenses	
Singular	Plural	Singular	Plural
1 présent de l'indicatif		**8 passé composé**	
sèche	séchons	ai séché	avons séché
sèches	séchez	as séché	avez séché
sèche	sèchent	a séché	ont séché
2 imparfait de l'indicatif		**9 plus-que-parfait de l'indicatif**	
séchais	séchions	avais séché	avions séché
séchais	séchiez	avais séché	aviez séché
séchait	séchaient	avait séché	avaient séché
3 passé simple		**10 passé antérieur**	
séchai	séchâmes	eus séché	eûmes séché
séchas	séchâtes	eus séché	eûtes séché
sécha	séchèrent	eut séché	eurent séché
4 futur		**11 futur antérieur**	
sécherai	sécherons	aurai séché	aurons séché
sécheras	sécherez	auras séché	aurez séché
séchera	sécheront	aura séché	auront séché
5 conditionnel		**12 conditionnel passé**	
sécherais	sécherions	aurais séché	aurions séché
sécherais	sécheriez	aurais séché	auriez séché
sécherait	sécheraient	aurait séché	auraient séché
6 présent du subjonctif		**13 passé du subjonctif**	
sèche	séchions	aie séché	ayons séché
sèches	séchiez	aies séché	ayez séché
sèche	sèchent	ait séché	aient séché
7 imparfait du subjonctif		**14 plus-que-parfait du subjonctif**	
séchasse	séchassions	eusse séché	eussions séché
séchasses	séchassiez	eusses séché	eussiez séché
séchât	séchassent	eût séché	eussent séché

Impératif
sèche
séchons
séchez

S

Sentences using this verb and words related to it

Les fermiers ont perdu la moitié de leur récolte à cause de la sécheresse. The farmers lost half of their harvest because of the drought.

Sèche tes pleurs, sèche tes pleurs, je t'en prie sèche tes pleurs. Dry your tears, dry your tears, please (I beg of you) dry your tears. ("Sèche tes pleurs," song by Daniel Bélanger)

Words and expressions related to this verb

sec, sèche   dry
sèchement   dryly, tersely
sécher un cours   to skip a class
la sécheresse   dryness, drought
mettre à sec   to drain, dry up

le séchage   drying
un sèche-cheveux, un séchoir à cheveux
  hair dryer
une sécheuse   clothes dryer

The subject pronouns are found on page 103.

to shake, to shake down (off)

Regular **-er** verb

The Seven Simple Tenses		The Seven Compound Tenses	
Singular	Plural	Singular	Plural
1 présent de l'indicatif		**8 passé composé**	
secoue	secouons	ai secoué	avons secoué
secoues	secouez	as secoué	avez secoué
secoue	secouent	a secoué	ont secoué
2 imparfait de l'indicatif		**9 plus-que-parfait de l'indicatif**	
secouais	secouions	avais secoué	avions secoué
secouais	secouiez	avais secoué	aviez secoué
secouait	secouaient	avait secoué	avaient secoué
3 passé simple		**10 passé antérieur**	
secouai	secouâmes	eus secoué	eûmes secoué
secouas	secouâtes	eus secoué	eûtes secoué
secoua	secouèrent	eut secoué	eurent secoué
4 futur		**11 futur antérieur**	
secouerai	secouerons	aurai secoué	aurons secoué
secoueras	secouerez	auras secoué	aurez secoué
secouera	secoueront	aura secoué	auront secoué
5 conditionnel		**12 conditionnel passé**	
secouerais	secouerions	aurais secoué	aurions secoué
secouerais	secoueriez	aurais secoué	auriez secoué
secouerait	secoueraient	aurait secoué	auraient secoué
6 présent du subjonctif		**13 passé du subjonctif**	
secoue	secouions	aie secoué	ayons secoué
secoues	secouiez	aies secoué	ayez secoué
secoue	secouent	ait secoué	aient secoué
7 imparfait du subjonctif		**14 plus-que-parfait du subjonctif**	
secouasse	secouassions	eusse secoué	eussions secoué
secouasses	secouassiez	eusses secoué	eussiez secoué
secouât	secouassent	eût secoué	eussent secoué

Impératif
secoue
secouons
secouez

Words and expressions related to this verb
secouer la tête   to shake one's head   **secouer la poussière**   to shake off the dust
le secouement   shaking   **une secousse**   jolt; **sans secousse**   smoothly

Do you need more drills? Have fun with the *501 French Verbs* CD-ROM!

Irregular verb   to help, to relieve, to succor

The Seven Simple Tenses		The Seven Compound Tenses	
Singular	Plural	Singular	Plural
1 présent de l'indicatif		**8 passé composé**	
secours	secourons	ai secouru	avons secouru
secours	secourez	as secouru	avez secouru
secourt	secourent	a secouru	ont secouru
2 imparfait de l'indicatif		**9 plus-que-parfait de l'indicatif**	
secourais	secourions	avais secouru	avions secouru
secourais	secouriez	avais secouru	aviez secouru
secourait	secouraient	avait secouru	avaient secouru
3 passé simple		**10 passé antérieur**	
secourus	secourûmes	eus secouru	eûmes secouru
secourus	secourûtes	eus secouru	eûtes secouru
secourut	secoururent	eut secouru	eurent secouru
4 futur		**11 futur antérieur**	
secourrai	secourrons	aurai secouru	aurons secouru
secourras	secourrez	auras secouru	aurez secouru
secourra	secourront	aura secouru	auront secouru
5 conditionnel		**12 conditionnel passé**	
secourrais	secourrions	aurais secouru	aurions secouru
secourrais	secourriez	aurais secouru	auriez secouru
secourrait	secourraient	aurait secouru	auraient secouru
6 présent du subjonctif		**13 passé du subjonctif**	
secoure	secourions	aie secouru	ayons secouru
secoures	secouriez	aies secouru	ayez secouru
secoure	secourent	ait secouru	aient secouru
7 imparfait du subjonctif		**14 plus-que-parfait du subjonctif**	
secourusse	secourussions	eusse secouru	eussions secouru
secourusses	secourussiez	eusses secouru	eussiez secouru
secourût	secourussent	eût secouru	eussent secouru

S

Impératif
secours
secourons
secourez

Common idiomatic expressions using this verb and words related to it

le secours help, assistance
Au secours! Help!
crier au secours to shout for help
une roue de secours spare wheel
une sortie de secours emergency exit
secourir qqn contre un ennemi to help
someone from an enemy

aller au secours de qqn to go to someone's aid
prêter secours à qqn to go to someone's rescue, assistance
une équipe de secours rescue squad
courir to run

Don't forget to study the section on defective and impersonal verbs. It's right after this main list.

to seduce   Irregular verb

The Seven Simple Tenses		The Seven Compound Tenses	
Singular	Plural	Singular	Plural
1 présent de l'indicatif		8 passé composé	
séduis	**séduisons**	**ai séduit**	**avons séduit**
séduis	**séduisez**	**as séduit**	**avez séduit**
séduit	**séduisent**	**a séduit**	**ont séduit**
2 imparfait de l'indicatif		9 plus-que-parfait de l'indicatif	
séduisais	**séduisions**	**avais séduit**	**avions séduit**
séduisais	**séduisiez**	**avais séduit**	**aviez séduit**
séduisait	**séduisaient**	**avait séduit**	**avaient séduit**
3 passé simple		10 passé antérieur	
séduisis	**séduisîmes**	**eus séduit**	**eûmes séduit**
séduisis	**séduisîtes**	**eus séduit**	**eûtes séduit**
séduisit	**séduisirent**	**eut séduit**	**eurent séduit**
4 futur		11 futur antérieur	
séduirai	**séduirons**	**aurai séduit**	**aurons séduit**
séduiras	**séduirez**	**auras séduit**	**aurez séduit**
séduira	**séduiront**	**aura séduit**	**auront séduit**
5 conditionnel		12 conditionnel passé	
séduirais	**séduirions**	**aurais séduit**	**aurions séduit**
séduirais	**séduiriez**	**aurais séduit**	**auriez séduit**
séduirait	**séduiraient**	**aurait séduit**	**auraient séduit**
6 présent du subjonctif		13 passé du subjonctif	
séduise	**séduisions**	**aie séduit**	**ayons séduit**
séduises	**séduisiez**	**aies séduit**	**ayez séduit**
séduise	**séduisent**	**ait séduit**	**aient séduit**
7 imparfait du subjonctif		14 plus-que-parfait du subjonctif	
séduisisse	**séduisissions**	**eusse séduit**	**eussions séduit**
séduisisses	**séduisissiez**	**eusses séduit**	**eussiez séduit**
séduisît	**séduisissent**	**eût séduit**	**eussent séduit**

Impératif
séduis
séduisons
séduisez

Words related to this verb
séduisant, séduisante   fascinating, seductive, attractive
un séducteur, une séductrice   tempter (temptress), seducer (seductress)
une séduction   seduction, enticement

See also **conduire, déduire, introduire, produire, réduire, reproduire,** and **traduire.**

Soak up some verbs used in weather expressions. There's a list in the Appendixes!

Regular **-er** verb

to sojourn, to live somewhere temporarily

The Seven Simple Tenses		The Seven Compound Tenses	
Singular	Plural	Singular	Plural
1 présent de l'indicatif		**8 passé composé**	
séjourne	séjournons	ai séjourné	avons séjourné
séjournes	séjournez	as séjourné	avez séjourné
séjourne	séjournent	a séjourné	ont séjourné
2 imparfait de l'indicatif		**9 plus-que-parfait de l'indicatif**	
séjournais	séjournions	avais séjourné	avions séjourné
séjournais	séjourniez	avais séjourné	aviez séjourné
séjournait	séjournaient	avait séjourné	avaient séjourné
3 passé simple		**10 passé antérieur**	
séjournai	séjournâmes	eus séjourné	eûmes séjourné
séjournas	séjournâtes	eus séjourné	eûtes séjourné
séjourna	séjournèrent	eut séjourné	eurent séjourné
4 futur		**11 futur antérieur**	
séjournerai	séjournerons	aurai séjourné	aurons séjourné
séjourneras	séjournerez	auras séjourné	aurez séjourné
séjournera	séjourneront	aura séjourné	auront séjourné
5 conditionnel		**12 conditionnel passé**	
séjournerais	séjournerions	aurais séjourné	aurions séjourné
séjournerais	séjourneriez	aurais séjourné	auriez séjourné
séjournerait	séjourneraient	aurait séjourné	auraient séjourné
6 présent du subjonctif		**13 passé du subjonctif**	
séjourne	séjournions	aie séjourné	ayons séjourné
séjournes	séjourniez	aies séjourné	ayez séjourné
séjourne	séjournent	ait séjourné	aient séjourné
7 imparfait du subjonctif		**14 plus-que-parfait du subjonctif**	
séjournasse	séjournassions	eusse séjourné	eussions séjourné
séjournasses	séjournassiez	eusses séjourné	eussiez séjourné
séjournât	séjournassent	eût séjourné	eussent séjourné

Impératif
séjourne
séjournons
séjournez

S

Words and expressions related to this verb

séjourner à un hôtel to stay (stop) at a hotel
un séjour sojourn, stay
faire un séjour à la campagne to stay in the country
séjourner chez des amis to stay with friends
le jour day

une salle de séjour living room
un bref séjour a brief stay
Mon séjour dans votre hôtel a été très agréable. My stay in your hotel has been very pleasuant.

Can't find the verb you're looking for? Check the back pages of this book for a list of over 2,600 additional verbs!

The subject pronouns are found on page 103.   **585**

to feel, to smell, to perceive

Irregular verb

The Seven Simple Tenses		The Seven Compound Tenses	
Singular	Plural	Singular	Plural
1 présent de l'indicatif		8 passé composé	
sens	sentons	ai senti	avons senti
sens	sentez	as senti	avez senti
sent	sentent	a senti	ont senti
2 imparfait de l'indicatif		9 plus-que-parfait de l'indicatif	
sentais	sentions	avais senti	avions senti
sentais	sentiez	avais senti	aviez senti
sentait	sentaient	avait senti	avaient senti
3 passé simple		10 passé antérieur	
sentis	sentîmes	eus senti	eûmes senti
sentis	sentîtes	eus senti	eûtes senti
sentit	sentirent	eut senti	eurent senti
4 futur		11 futur antérieur	
sentirai	sentirons	aurai senti	aurons senti
sentiras	sentirez	auras senti	aurez senti
sentira	sentiront	aura senti	auront senti
5 conditionnel		12 conditionnel passé	
sentirais	sentirions	aurais senti	aurions senti
sentirais	sentiriez	aurais senti	auriez senti
sentirait	sentiraient	aurait senti	auraient senti
6 présent du subjonctif		13 passé du subjonctif	
sente	sentions	aie senti	ayons senti
sentes	sentiez	aies senti	ayez senti
sente	sentent	ait senti	aient senti
7 imparfait du subjonctif		14 plus-que-parfait du subjonctif	
sentisse	sentissions	eusse senti	eussions senti
sentisses	sentissiez	eusses senti	eussiez senti
sentît	sentissent	eût senti	eussent senti

Impératif
sens
sentons
sentez

Sentir

Sentir is a very improtant verb for a beginning student because, although it is irregular, several useful verbs are conjugated like it. There are also many idiomatic expressions related to sentir.

Sentences using sentir

Qu'est-ce que tu fais pour le dîner? Ça sent bon!
What are you making for dinner? That smells good!

Je me sens mal. I feel ill.

Je ne me sens pas bien. I don't feel well.

Ouvre la fenêtre, Claire. Ça sent le renfermé ici!
Open the window, Claire. It smells stuffy here!

If you can conjugate sentir you can also conjugate the following verbs:

consentir **to allow;** consentir à **to agree to**

pressentir **to sense**

Words and expressions related to this verb

un sentiment **feeling, sense, impression**

un sentiment d'appartenance **feeling of membership, belonging**

sentimental, sentimentale **sentimental**

la sentimentalité **sentimentality**

le sentimentalisme **sentimentalism**

sentir le chagrin **to feel sorrow**

se sentir + adj. **to feel + adj.**

ressentir **to feel**

le ressentiment **resentment**

sentir bon **to smell good**

sentir mauvais **to smell bad**

faire sentir qqch à qqn **to make someone feel something**

se faire sentir **to make itself felt**

ne se sentir pas bien **not to feel well**

S

Don't forget to study the section on defective and impersonal verbs. It's right after this main list.

The subject pronouns are found on page 103.

to separate

The Seven Simple Tenses		The Seven Compound Tenses	
Singular	Plural	Singular	Plural
1 présent de l'indicatif		8 passé composé	
sépare	**séparons**	**ai séparé**	**avons séparé**
sépares	**séparez**	**as séparé**	**avez séparé**
sépare	**séparent**	**a séparé**	**ont séparé**
2 imparfait de l'indicatif		9 plus-que-parfait de l'indicatif	
séparais	**séparions**	**avais séparé**	**avions séparé**
séparais	**sépariez**	**avais séparé**	**aviez séparé**
séparait	**séparaient**	**avait séparé**	**avaient séparé**
3 passé simple		10 passé antérieur	
séparai	**séparâmes**	**eus séparé**	**eûmes séparé**
séparas	**séparâtes**	**eus séparé**	**eûtes séparé**
sépara	**séparèrent**	**eut séparé**	**eurent séparé**
4 futur		11 futur antérieur	
séparerai	**séparerons**	**aurai séparé**	**aurons séparé**
sépareras	**séparerez**	**auras séparé**	**aurez séparé**
séparera	**sépareront**	**aura séparé**	**auront séparé**
5 conditionnel		12 conditionnel passé	
séparerais	**séparerions**	**aurais séparé**	**aurions séparé**
séparerais	**sépareriez**	**aurais séparé**	**auriez séparé**
séparerait	**sépareraient**	**aurait séparé**	**auraient séparé**
6 présent du subjonctif		13 passé du subjonctif	
sépare	**séparions**	**aie séparé**	**ayons séparé**
sépares	**sépariez**	**aies séparé**	**ayez séparé**
sépare	**séparent**	**ait séparé**	**aient séparé**
7 imparfait du subjonctif		14 plus-que-parfait du subjonctif	
séparasse	**séparassions**	**eusse séparé**	**eussions séparé**
séparasses	**séparassiez**	**eusses séparé**	**eussiez séparé**
séparât	**séparassent**	**eût séparé**	**eussent séparé**

Impératif
sépare
séparons
séparez

Words and expressions related to this verb
séparer de   to sever from, to separate from
Les Pyrénées séparent la France et l'Espagne.   France is separated from Spain by the Pyrenees.

se séparer de   to be separated from, to separate oneself from
Madame Dubois se sépare de son mari.   Mrs. Dubois is separating from her husband.
une séparation   separation, parting

Get acquainted with what preposition goes with what verb. See *Verbs with prepositions* in the Appendixes.

Regular **-er** verb   to grasp, to press, to squeeze, to shake (hands)

The Seven Simple Tenses		The Seven Compound Tenses	
Singular	Plural	Singular	Plural
1 présent de l'indicatif		8 passé composé	
serre	serrons	ai serré	avons serré
serres	serrez	as serré	avez serré
serre	serrent	a serré	ont serré
2 imparfait de l'indicatif		9 plus-que-parfait de l'indicatif	
serrais	serrions	avais serré	avions serré
serrais	serriez	avais serré	aviez serré
serrait	serraient	avait serré	avaient serré
3 passé simple		10 passé antérieur	
serrai	serrâmes	eus serré	eûmes serré
serras	serrâtes	eus serré	eûtes serré
serra	serrèrent	eut serré	eurent serré
4 futur		11 futur antérieur	
serrerai	serrerons	aurai serré	aurons serré
serreras	serrerez	auras serré	aurez serré
serrera	serreront	aura serré	auront serré
5 conditionnel		12 conditionnel passé	
serrerais	serrerions	aurais serré	aurions serré
serrerais	serreriez	aurais serré	auriez serré
serrerait	serreraient	aurait serré	auraient serré
6 présent du subjonctif		13 passé du subjonctif	
serre	serrions	aie serré	ayons serré
serres	serriez	aies serré	ayez serré
serre	serrent	ait serré	aient serré
7 imparfait du subjonctif		14 plus-que-parfait du subjonctif	
serrasse	serrassions	eusse serré	eussions serré
serrasses	serrassiez	eusses serré	eussiez serré
serrât	serrassent	eût serré	eussent serré

Impératif
serre
serrons
serrez

Words and expressions related to this verb
serrer la main à qqn   to shake hands with
  someone
serrer un noeud   to tighten a knot
un serre-livres   book end (**des serre-livres**)
serrer les rangs   to close up ranks
serrer le coeur   to wring one's heart

serrés comme des harengs   packed like
  sardines
une serrure   lock; **le trou de la serrure**
  keyhole
Serrez à droite./Serrez à gauche.   Keep
  (Squeeze) right/left.

Grammar putting you in a tense mood? Review the definitions of basic grammatical terms with
examples on pages 35–49.

to serve, to be useful

The Seven Simple Tenses		The Seven Compound Tenses	
Singular	Plural	Singular	Plural
1 présent de l'indicatif		8 passé composé	
sers	servons	ai servi	avons servi
sers	servez	as servi	avez servi
sert	servent	a servi	ont servi
2 imparfait de l'indicatif		9 plus-que-parfait de l'indicatif	
servais	servions	avais servi	avions servi
servais	serviez	avais servi	aviez servi
servait	servaient	avait servi	avaient servi
3 passé simple		10 passé antérieur	
servis	servîmes	eus servi	eûmes servi
servis	servîtes	eus servi	eûtes servi
servit	servirent	eut servi	eurent servi
4 futur		11 futur antérieur	
servirai	servirons	aurai servi	aurons servi
serviras	servirez	auras servi	aurez servi
servira	serviront	aura servi	auront servi
5 conditionnel		12 conditionnel passé	
servirais	servirions	aurais servi	aurions servi
servirais	serviriez	aurais servi	auriez servi
servirait	serviraient	aurait servi	auraient servi
6 présent du subjonctif		13 passé du subjonctif	
serve	servions	aie servi	ayons servi
serves	serviez	aies servi	ayez servi
serve	servent	ait servi	aient servi
7 imparfait du subjonctif		14 plus-que-parfait du subjonctif	
servisse	servissions	eusse servi	eussions servi
servisses	servissiez	eusses servi	eussiez servi
servît	servissent	eût servi	eussent servi

Impératif
sers
servons
servez

Words and expressions related to this verb

le serveur   waiter
la serveuse   waitress
le service   service
une serviette   napkin
un serviteur   servant
la servitude   servitude
desservir   to clear off the table
un serveur   server (computer)

se servir   to serve oneself, to help oneself
se servir de qqch   to use something, to avail oneself of something, to make use of something
servir à qqch   to be of some use
servir à rien   to be of no use; Cela ne sert à rien.   That serves no purpose.

See also se servir.

590

Refelxive irregular verb

to serve oneself, to help oneself
(to food and drink)

The Seven Simple Tenses		The Seven Compound Tenses	
Singular	Plural	Singular	Plural
1 présent de l'indicatif		8 passé composé	
me sers	nous servons	me suis servi(e)	nous sommes servi(e)s
te sers	vous servez	t'es servi(e)	vous êtes servi(e)(s)
se sert	se servent	s'est servi(e)	se sont servi(e)s
2 imparfait de l'indicatif		9 plus-que-parfait de l'indicatif	
me servais	nous servions	m'étais servi(e)	nous étions servi(e)s
te servais	vous serviez	t'étais servi(e)	vous étiez servi(e)(s)
se servait	se servaient	s'était servi(e)	s'étaient servi(e)s
3 passé simple		10 passé antérieur	
me servis	nous servîmes	me fus servi(e)	nous fûmes servi(e)s
te servis	vous servîtes	te fus servi(e)	vous fûtes servi(e)(s)
se servit	se servirent	se fut servi(e)	se furent servi(e)s
4 futur		11 futur antérieur	
me servirai	nous servirons	me serai servi(e)	nous serons servi(e)s
te serviras	vous servirez	te seras servi(e)	vous serez servi(e)(s)
se servira	se serviront	se sera servi(e)	se seront servi(e)s
5 conditionnel		12 conditionnel passé	
me servirais	nous servirions	me serais servi(e)	nous serions servi(e)s
te servirais	vous serviriez	te serais servi(e)	vous seriez servi(e)(s)
se servirait	se serviraient	se serait servi(e)	se seraient servi(e)s
6 présent du subjonctif		13 passé du subjonctif	
me serve	nous servions	me sois servi(e)	nous soyons servi(e)s
te serves	vous serviez	te sois servi(e)	vous soyez servi(e)(s)
se serve	se servent	se soit servi(e)	se soient servi(e)s
7 imparfait du subjonctif		14 plus-que-parfait du subjonctif	
me servisse	nous servissions	me fusse servi(e)	nous fussions servi(e)s
te servisses	vous servissiez	te fusses servi(e)	vous fussiez servi(e)(s)
se servît	se servissent	se fût servi(e)	se fussent servi(e)s

Impératif
sers-toi; ne te sers pas
servons-nous; ne nous servons pas
servez-vous; ne vous servez pas

S

Words and expressions related to this verb

un serviteur servant
la servitude servitude
le serveur waiter
la serveuse waitress
le service service
une serviette napkin

See also **servir.**

se servir de qqch   to use something, to make use of something
Servez-vous, je vous en prie!   Help yourself, please!
Est-ce qu'on se sert seul dans ce restaurant?—Oui, c'est un restaurant self-service.

Can't find the verb you're looking for? Check the back pages of this book for a list of over 2,600 additional verbs!

Part. pr. **sifflant**   Part. passé **sifflé**

to whistle, to hiss, to boo

Regular **-er** verb

The Seven Simple Tenses		The Seven Compound Tenses	
Singular	Plural	Singular	Plural
1 présent de l'indicatif		8 passé composé	
siffle	**sifflons**	**ai sifflé**	**avons sifflé**
siffles	**sifflez**	**as sifflé**	**avez sifflé**
siffle	**sifflent**	**a sifflé**	**ont sifflé**
2 imparfait de l'indicatif		9 plus-que-parfait de l'indicatif	
sifflais	**sifflions**	**avais sifflé**	**avions sifflé**
sifflais	**siffliez**	**avais sifflé**	**aviez sifflé**
sifflait	**sifflaient**	**avait sifflé**	**avaient sifflé**
3 passé simple		10 passé antérieur	
sifflai	**sifflâmes**	**eus sifflé**	**eûmes sifflé**
sifflas	**sifflâtes**	**eus sifflé**	**eûtes sifflé**
siffla	**sifflèrent**	**eut sifflé**	**eurent sifflé**
4 futur		11 futur antérieur	
sifflerai	**sifflerons**	**aurai sifflé**	**aurons sifflé**
siffleras	**sifflerez**	**auras sifflé**	**aurez sifflé**
sifflera	**siffleront**	**aura sifflé**	**auront sifflé**
5 conditionnel		12 conditionnel passé	
sifflerais	**sifflerions**	**aurais sifflé**	**aurions sifflé**
sifflerais	**siffleriez**	**aurais sifflé**	**auriez sifflé**
sifflerait	**siffleraient**	**aurait sifflé**	**auraient sifflé**
6 présent du subjonctif		13 passé du subjonctif	
siffle	**sifflions**	**aie sifflé**	**ayons sifflé**
siffles	**siffliez**	**aies sifflé**	**ayez sifflé**
siffle	**sifflent**	**ait sifflé**	**aient sifflé**
7 imparfait du subjonctif		14 plus-que-parfait du subjonctif	
sifflasse	**sifflassions**	**eusse sifflé**	**eussions sifflé**
sifflasses	**sifflassiez**	**eusses sifflé**	**eussiez sifflé**
sifflât	**sifflassent**	**eût sifflé**	**eussent sifflé**

Impératif
siffle
sifflons
sifflez

Words and expressions related to this verb
un sifflet   whistle
un sifflet d'alarme   alarm whistle
un siffleur, une siffleuse   whistler, booer, hisser

le sifflet d'un agent de police   policeman's whistle
le sifflement   whistling, hissing

Do you need more drills? Have fun with the *501 French Verbs* CD-ROM!

The Seven Simple Tenses		The Seven Compound Tenses	
Singular	Plural	Singular	Plural
1 présent de l'indicatif		**8 passé composé**	
signale	signalons	ai signalé	avons signalé
signales	signalez	as signalé	avez signalé
signale	signalent	a signalé	ont signalé
2 imparfait de l'indicatif		**9 plus-que-parfait de l'indicatif**	
signalais	signalions	avais signalé	avions signalé
signalais	signaliez	avais signalé	aviez signalé
signalait	signalaient	avait signalé	avaient signalé
3 passé simple		**10 passé antérieur**	
signalai	signalâmes	eus signalé	eûmes signalé
signalas	signalâtes	eus signalé	eûtes signalé
signala	signalèrent	eut signalé	eurent signalé
4 futur		**11 futur antérieur**	
signalerai	signalerons	aurai signalé	aurons signalé
signaleras	signalerez	auras signalé	aurez signalé
signalera	signaleront	aura signalé	auront signalé
5 conditionnel		**12 conditionnel passé**	
signalerais	signalerions	aurais signalé	aurions signalé
signaierais	signaleriez	aurais signalé	auriez signalé
signalerait	signaleraient	aurait signalé	auraient signalé
6 présent du subjonctif		**13 passé du subjonctif**	
signale	signalions	aie signalé	ayons signalé
signales	signaliez	aies signalé	ayez signalé
signale	signalent	ait signalé	aient signalé
7 imparfait du subjonctif		**14 plus-que-parfait du subjonctif**	
signalasse	signalassions	eusse signalé	eussions signalé
signalasses	signalassiez	eusses signalé	eussiez signalé
signalât	signalassent	eût signalé	eussent signalé

Impératif
signale
signalons
signalez

S

Words and expressions related to this verb
se signaler to distinguish oneself
un signal signal
le signal d'alarme alarm signal
les signaux de route road signs
signaliser to mark with signs

le signal de détresse distress signal
tirer le signal d'alarme to pull the alarm
les moyens de signalisation means of signaling

Don't forget to study the section on defective and impersonal verbs. It's right after this main list.

to sign

Regular **-er** verb

The Seven Simple Tenses		The Seven Compound Tenses	
Singular	Plural	Singular	Plural
1 présent de l'indicatif		**8 passé composé**	
signe	signons	ai signé	avons signé
signes	signez	as signé	avez signé
signe	signent	a signé	ont signé
2 imparfait de l'indicatif		**9 plus-que-parfait de l'indicatif**	
signais	signions	avais signé	avions signé
signais	signiez	avais signé	aviez signé
signait	signaient	avait signé	avaient signé
3 passé simple		**10 passé antérieur**	
signai	signâmes	eus signé	eûmes signé
signas	signâtes	eus signé	eûtes signé
signa	signèrent	eut signé	eurent signé
4 futur		**11 futur antérieur**	
signerai	signerons	aurai signé	aurons signé
signeras	signerez	auras signé	aurez signé
signera	signeront	aura signé	auront signé
5 conditionnel		**12 conditionnel passé**	
signerais	signerions	aurais signé	aurions signé
signerais	signeriez	aurais signé	auriez signé
signerait	signeraient	aurait signé	auraient signé
6 présent du subjonctif		**13 passé du subjonctif**	
signe	signions	aie signé	ayons signé
signes	signiez	aies signé	ayez signé
signe	signent	ait signé	aient signé
7 imparfait du subjonctif		**14 plus-que-parfait du subjonctif**	
signasse	signassions	eusse signé	eussions signé
signasses	signassiez	eusses signé	eussiez signé
signât	signassent	eût signé	eussent signé

Impératif
signe
signons
signez

Words and expressions related to this verb

se signer to cross oneself (to make the sign of the Cross)
un signe gesture, sign; **un signe de tête** nod
faire le signe de la Croix to make the sign of the Cross
la signature signature, signing
assigner to assign

consigner to deposit (money); to consign (merchandise)
la consignation consignment, deposit
le, la consignataire consignee
le, la signataire signer
les signes de vie signs of life
Veuillez signer le document ici. Please sign the document here.

If you don't know the French verb for an English verb you have in mind, try the index in the Appendixes.

Regular **-er** verb endings; spelling change: retain the
ge before **a** or **o** to keep the soft **g** sound of the verb

The Seven Simple Tenses		The Seven Compound Tenses	
Singular	Plural	Singular	Plural
1 présent de l'indicatif		**8 passé composé**	
songe	songeons	ai songé	avons songé
songes	songez	as songé	avez songé
songe	songent	a songé	ont songé
2 imparfait de l'indicatif		**9 plus-que-parfait de l'indicatif**	
songeais	songions	avais songé	avions songé
songeais	songiez	avais songé	aviez songé
songeait	songeaient	avait songé	avaient songé
3 passé simple		**10 passé antérieur**	
songeai	songeâmes	eus songé	eûmes songé
songeas	songeâtes	eus songé	eûtes songé
songea	songèrent	eut songé	eurent songé
4 futur		**11 futur antérieur**	
songerai	songerons	aurai songe	aurons songé
songeras	songerez	auras songé	aurez songé
songera	songeront	aura songé	auront songé
5 conditionnel		**12 conditionnel passé**	
songerais	songerions	aurais songé	aurions songé
songerais	songeriez	aurais songé	auriez songé
songerait	songeraient	aurait songé	auraient songé
6 présent du subjonctif		**13 passé du subjonctif**	
songe	songions	aie songé	ayons songé
songes	songiez	aies songé	ayez songé
songe	songent	ait songé	aient songé
7 imparfait du subjonctif		**14 plus-que-parfait du subjonctif**	
songeasse	songeassions	eusse songé	eussions songé
songeasses	songeassiez	eusses songé	eussiez songé
songeât	songeassent	eût songé	eussent songé

Impératif
songe
songeons
songez

Words and expressions related to this verb
un songe   dream
un songeur, une songeuse   dreamer
songer à l'avenir   to think of the future
faire un songe   to have a dream

songer à   to think of something, to give thought to something
Songez-y bien!   Think it over carefully!
songer à faire qqch   to contemplate doing something

Get acquainted with what preposition goes with what. See *Verbs with prepositions* in the Appendixes.

to ring

The Seven Simple Tenses		The Seven Compound Tenses	
Singular	Plural	Singular	Plural
1 présent de l'indicatif		8 passé composé	
sonne	**sonnons**	**ai sonné**	**avons sonné**
sonnes	**sonnez**	**as sonné**	**avez sonné**
sonne	**sonnent**	**a sonné**	**ont sonné**
2 imparfait de l'indicatif		9 plus-que-parfait de l'indicatif	
sonnais	**sonnions**	**avais sonné**	**avions sonné**
sonnais	**sonniez**	**avais sonné**	**aviez sonné**
sonnait	**sonnaient**	**avait sonné**	**avaient sonné**
3 passé simple		10 passé antérieur	
sonnai	**sonnâmes**	**eus sonné**	**eûmes sonné**
sonnas	**sonnâtes**	**eus sonné**	**eûtes sonné**
sonna	**sonnèrent**	**eut sonné**	**eurent sonné**
4 futur		11 futur antérieur	
sonnerai	**sonnerons**	**aurai sonné**	**aurons sonné**
sonneras	**sonnerez**	**auras sonné**	**aurez sonné**
sonnera	**sonneront**	**aura sonné**	**auront sonné**
5 conditionnel		12 conditionnel passé	
sonnerais	**sonnerions**	**aurais sonné**	**aurions sonné**
sonnerais	**sonneriez**	**aurais sonné**	**auriez sonné**
sonnerait	**sonneraient**	**aurait sonné**	**auraient sonné**
6 présent du subjonctif		13 passé du subjonctif	
sonne	**sonnions**	**aie sonné**	**ayons sonné**
sonnes	**sonniez**	**aies sonné**	**ayez sonné**
sonne	**sonnent**	**ait sonné**	**aient sonné**
7 imparfait du subjonctif		14 plus-que-parfait du subjonctif	
sonnasse	**sonnassions**	**eusse sonné**	**eussions sonné**
sonnasses	**sonnassiez**	**eusses sonné**	**eussiez sonné**
sonnât	**sonnassent**	**eût sonné**	**eussent sonné**

Impératif
sonne
sonnons
sonnez

Words and expressions related to this verb

une **sonnerie**   ringing, chiming
une **sonnette**   house bell, doorbell
une **sonnette électrique**   electric bell
le **son**   sound, ringing
une **sonnette de nuit**   night bell
sonner creux   to sound hollow

une **sonnette d'alarme**   alarm bell
faire sonner un mot   to emphasize a word
une **clochette**   hand bell
la **sonnerie du téléphone**   the ringing of the
    telephone

Use the guide to French pronunciation. It's in the Appendixes.

Irregular verb

The Seven Simple Tenses		The Seven Compound Tenses	
Singular	Plural	Singular	Plural

1 présent de l'indicatif		8 passé composé	
sors	**sortons**	**suis sorti(e)**	**sommes sorti(e)s**
sors	**sortez**	**es sorti(e)**	**êtes sorti(e)(s)**
sort	**sortent**	**est sorti(e)**	**sont sorti(e)s**

2 imparfait de l'indicatif		9 plus-que-parfait de l'indicatif	
sortais	**sortions**	**étais sorti(e)**	**étions sorti(e)s**
sortais	**sortiez**	**étais sorti(e)**	**étiez sorti(e)(s)**
sortait	**sortaient**	**était sorti(e)**	**étaient sorti(e)s**

3 passé simple		10 passé antérieur	
sortis	**sortîmes**	**fus sorti(e)**	**fûmes sorti(e)s**
sortis	**sortîtes**	**fus sorti(e)**	**fûtes sorti(e)(s)**
sortit	**sortirent**	**fut sorti(e)**	**furent sorti(e)s**

4 futur		11 futur antérieur	
sortirai	**sortirons**	**serai sorti(e)**	**serons sorti(e)s**
sortiras	**sortirez**	**seras sorti(e)**	**serez sorti(e)(s)**
sortira	**sortiront**	**sera sorti(e)**	**seront sorti(e)s**

5 conditionnel		12 conditionnel passé	
sortirais	**sortirions**	**serais sorti(e)**	**serions sorti(e)s**
sortirais	**sortiriez**	**serais sorti(e)**	**seriez sorti(e)(s)**
sortirait	**sortiraient**	**serait sorti(e)**	**seraient sorti(e)s**

6 présent du subjonctif		13 passé du subjonctif	
sorte	**sortions**	**sois sorti(e)**	**soyons sorti(e)s**
sortes	**sortiez**	**sois sorti(e)**	**soyez sorti(e)(s)**
sorte	**sortent**	**soit sorti(e)**	**soient sorti(e)s**

7 imparfait du subjonctif		14 plus-que-parfait du subjonctif	
sortisse	**sortissions**	**fusse sorti(e)**	**fussions sorti(e)s**
sortisses	**sortissiez**	**fusses sorti(e)**	**fussiez sorti(e)(s)**
sortît	**sortissent**	**fût sorti(e)**	**fussent sorti(e)s**

Impératif
sors
sortons
sortez

AN ESSENTIAL
55 VERB

Sortir

Sortir is useful in many everyday situations and idiomatic expressions. Although sortir is an irregular verb, many verbs are conjugated like it.

This verb is conjugated with avoir when it has a direct object. Review page 6.

Example: Elle a sorti son mouchoir. She took out her handkerchief.
BUT: Elle est sortie hier soir. She went out last night.

Sentences using sortir

Le cambrioleur est entré par la fenêtre, mais il est sorti par la porte. The burglar came in through the window, but he left through the door.

René et Nathalie sortent ensemble depuis longtemps. René and Nathalie have been going out for a long time.

Le magicien a sorti un lapin de son chapeau haut-de-forme. The magician took a rabbit out of his top hat.

Words and expressions related to this verb

une sortie **exit**

une sortie de secours **emergency exit**

sortir du lit **to get out of bed**

se sortir d'une situation **to get oneself out of a situation**

sortir d'une bonne famille **to come from a good family**

If you can conjugate sortir you can also conjugate the following verbs:

Careful! Assortir (to match) looks like it should be conjugated like sortir, but it is a regular -ir verb.

démentir **to contradict**

partir **to leave**

ressortir **to go out again (Note:** Ressortir à **means "to pertain to." In this usage** ressortir **is conjugated like a regular -ir verb.)**

Proverb

La faim fait sortir le loup du bois. **Hunger makes the wolf leave the woods.**

Can't remember the French verb you need? Check the back pages of this book for the English-French verb index!

Regular **-er** verb   to blow, to pant, to prompt (an actor/actress with a cue)

The Seven Simple Tenses		The Seven Compound Tenses	
Singular	Plural	Singular	Plural
1 présent de l'indicatif		8 passé composé	
souffle	**soufflons**	**ai soufflé**	**avons soufflé**
souffles	**soufflez**	**as soufflé**	**avez soufflé**
souffle	**soufflent**	**a soufflé**	**ont soufflé**
2 imparfait de l'indicatif		9 plus-que-parfait de l'indicatif	
soufflais	**soufflions**	**avais soufflé**	**avions soufflé**
soufflais	**souffliez**	**avais soufflé**	**aviez soufflé**
soufflait	**soufflaient**	**avait soufflé**	**avaient soufflé**
3 passé simple		10 passé antérieur	
soufflai	**soufflâmes**	**eus soufflé**	**eûmes soufflé**
soufflas	**soufflâtes**	**eus soufflé**	**eûtes soufflé**
souffla	**soufflèrent**	**eut soufflé**	**eurent soufflé**
4 futur		11 futur antérieur	
soufflerai	**soufflerons**	**aurai soufflé**	**aurons soufflé**
souffleras	**soufflerez**	**auras soufflé**	**aurez soufflé**
soufflera	**souffleront**	**aura soufflé**	**auront soufflé**
5 conditionnel		12 conditionnel passé	
soufflerais	**soufflerions**	**aurais soufflé**	**aurions soufflé**
soufflerais	**souffleriez**	**aurais soufflé**	**auriez soufflé**
soufflerait	**souffleraient**	**aurait soufflé**	**auraient soufflé**
6 présent du subjonctif		13 passé du subjonctif	
souffle	**soufflions**	**aie soufflé**	**ayons soufflé**
souffles	**souffliez**	**aies soufflé**	**ayez soufflé**
souffle	**soufflent**	**ait soufflé**	**aient soufflé**
7 imparfait du subjonctif		14 plus-que-parfait du subjonctif	
soufflasse	**soufflassions**	**eusse soufflé**	**eussions soufflé**
soufflasses	**soufflassiez**	**eusses soufflé**	**eussiez soufflé**
soufflât	**soufflassent**	**eût soufflé**	**eussent soufflé**

Impératif
souffle
soufflons
soufflez

S

Words and expressions related to this verb
le souffle   breath, breathing
à bout de souffle   out of breath
retenir son souffle   to hold one's breath
couper le souffle à qqn   to take someone's
   breath away

un soufflé au fromage   cheese soufflé
souffler le verre   to blow glass
le souffle cardiaque   heart murmur
une souffleuse   snowblower

Do you need more drills? Have fun with the *501 French Verbs* CD-ROM!

to suffer, to endure

Irregular verb

The Seven Simple Tenses		The Seven Compound Tenses	
Singular	Plural	Singular	Plural
1 présent de l'indicatif		8 passé composé	
souffre	souffrons	ai souffert	avons souffert
souffres	souffrez	as souffert	avez souffert
souffre	souffrent	a souffert	ont souffert
2 imparfait de l'indicatif		9 plus-que-parfait de l'indicatif	
souffrais	souffrions	avais souffert	avions souffert
souffrais	souffriez	avais souffert	aviez souffert
souffrait	souffraient	avait souffert	avaient souffert
3 passé simple		10 passé antérieur	
souffris	souffrîmes	eus souffert	eûmes souffert
souffris	souffrîtes	eus souffert	eûtes souffert
souffrit	souffrirent	eut souffert	eurent souffert
4 futur		11 futur antérieur	
souffrirai	souffrirons	aurai souffert	aurons souffert
souffriras	souffrirez	auras souffert	aurez souffert
souffrira	souffriront	aura souffert	auront souffert
5 conditionnel		12 conditionnel passé	
souffrirais	souffririons	aurais souffert	aurions souffert
souffrirais	souffririez	aurais souffert	auriez souffert
souffrirait	souffriraient	aurait souffert	auraient souffert
6 présent du subjonctif		13 passé du subjonctif	
souffre	souffrions	aie souffert	ayons souffert
souffres	souffriez	aies souffert	ayez souffert
souffre	souffrent	ait souffert	aient souffert
7 imparfait du subjonctif		14 plus-que-parfait du subjonctif	
souffrisse	souffrissions	eusse souffert	eussions souffert
souffrisses	souffrissiez	eusses souffert	eussiez souffert
souffrît	souffrissent	eût souffert	eussent souffert

Impératif
souffre
souffrons
souffrez

Words and expressions related to this verb
la souffrance   suffering
souffrant, souffrante   ailing, sick
souffreteux, souffreteuse   sickly, feeble

souffrir le froid   to withstand the cold
Cela me fait souffrir.   That hurts me.

Regular **-er** verb   to wish

The Seven Simple Tenses		The Seven Compound Tenses	
Singular	Plural	Singular	Plural
1 présent de l'indicatif		8 passé composé	
souhaite	souhaitons	ai souhaité	avons souhaité
souhaites	souhaitez	as souhaité	avez souhaité
souhaite	souhaitent	a souhaité	ont souhaité
2 imparfait de l'indicatif		9 plus-que-parfait de l'indicatif	
souhaitais	souhaitions	avais souhaité	avions souhaité
souhaitais	souhaitiez	avais souhaité	aviez souhaité
souhaitait	souhaitaient	avait souhaité	avaient souhaité
3 passé simple		10 passé antérieur	
souhaitai	souhaitâmes	eus souhaité	eûmes souhaité
souhaitas	souhaitâtes	eus souhaité	eûtes souhaité
souhaita	souhaitèrent	eut souhaité	eurent souhaité
4 futur		11 futur antérieur	
souhaiterai	souhaiterons	aurai souhaité	aurons souhaité
souhaiteras	souhaiterez	auras souhaité	aurez souhaité
souhaitera	souhaiteront	aura souhaité	auront souhaité
5 conditionnel		12 conditionnel passé	
souhaiterais	souhaiterions	aurais souhaité	aurions souhaité
souhaiterais	souhaiteriez	aurais souhaité	auriez souhaité
souhaiterait	souhaiteraient	aurait souhaité	auraient souhaité
6 présent du subjonctif		13 passé du subjonctif	
souhaite	souhaitions	aie souhaité	ayons souhaité
souhaites	souhaitiez	aies souhaité	ayez souhaité
souhaite	souhaitent	ait souhaité	aient souhaité
7 imparfait du subjonctif		14 plus-que-parfait du subjonctif	
souhaitasse	souhaitassions	eusse souhaité	eussions souhaité
souhaitasses	souhaitassiez	eusses souhaité	eussiez souhaité
souhaitât	souhaitassent	eût souhaité	eussent souhaité

S

Impératif
souhaite
souhaitons
souhaitez

Words and expressions related to this verb
un souhait a wish
à souhait to one's liking
souhaits de bonne année New Year's
  greetings
souhaiter bon voyage à qqn to wish someone
  a good trip

souhaiter la bienvenue à qqn to welcome
  someone
souhaiter le bonjour à qqn to greet someone
souhaitable desirable

Don't miss the definitions of basic grammatical terms with examples in English and French on
pages 35–49.

The subject pronouns are found on page 103.
                                                601

to dirty, to muddy, to soil

Regular **-er** verb

The Seven Simple Tenses		The Seven Compound Tenses	
Singular	Plural	Singular	Plural
1 présent de l'indicatif		8 passé composé	
souille	souillons	ai souillé	avons souillé
souilles	souillez	as souillé	avez souillé
souille	souillent	a souillé	ont souillé
2 imparfait de l'indicatif		9 plus-que-parfait de l'indicatif	
souillais	souillions	avais souillé	avions souillé
souillais	souilliez	avais souillé	aviez souillé
souillait	souillaient	avait souillé	avaient souillé
3 passé simple		10 passé antérieur	
souillai	souillâmes	eus souillé	eûmes souillé
souillas	souillâtes	eus souillé	eûtes souillé
souilla	souillèrent	eut souillé	eurent souillé
4 futur		11 futur antérieur	
souillerai	souillerons	aurai souillé	aurons souillé
souilleras	souillerez	auras souillé	aurez souillé
souillera	souilleront	aura souillé	auront souillé
5 conditionnel		12 conditionnel passé	
souillerais	souillerions	aurais souillé	aurions souillé
souillerais	souilleriez	aurais souillé	auriez souillé
souillerait	souilleraient	aurait souillé	auraient souillé
6 présent du subjonctif		13 passé du subjonctif	
souille	souillions	aie souillé	ayons souillé
souilles	souilliez	aies souillé	ayez souillé
souille	souillent	ait souillé	aient souillé
7 imparfait du subjonctif		14 plus-que-parfait du subjonctif	
souillasse	souillassions	eusse souillé	eussions souillé
souillasses	souillassiez	eusses souillé	eussiez souillé
souillât	souillassent	eût souillé	eussent souillé

Impératif
souille
souillons
souillez

Sentences using this verb and words related to it

Monsieur Beauregard dîne seul dans un restaurant. Le garçon lui apporte du poisson et après quelques minutes il demande au monsieur.

—Eh bien, monsieur. Comment trouvez-vous le poisson? Il est bon, n'est-ce pas?
—Non, je le trouve dégoûtant. Ce poisson salé est souillé. Emportez-le!

dégoûtant, dégoûtante   disgusting
salé, salée   salty
Comment trouvez-vous le poisson?   How do
  you like the fish?

souillé, souillée   dirty, soiled
Emportez-le!   Take it away!
un, une souillon   filthy slob
une souillure   spot, stain

Irregular verb   to submit

The Seven Simple Tenses

The Seven Compound Tenses

Singular	Plural	Singular	Plural

1   présent de l'indicatif

		8 passé composé	
soumets	**soumettons**	**ai soumis**	**avons soumis**
soumets	**soumettez**	**as soumis**	**avez soumis**
soumet	**soumettent**	**a soumis**	**ont soumis**

2   imparfait de l'indicatif

		9 plus-que-parfait de l'indicatif	
soumettais	**soumettions**	**avais soumis**	**avions soumis**
soumettais	**soumettiez**	**avais soumis**	**aviez soumis**
soumettait	**soumettaient**	**avait soumis**	**avaient soumis**

3   passé simple

		10 passé antérieur	
soumis	**soumîmes**	**eus soumis**	**eûmes soumis**
soumis	**soumîtes**	**eus soumis**	**eûtes soumis**
soumit	**soumirent**	**eut soumis**	**eurent soumis**

4   futur

		11 futur antérieur	
soumettrai	**soumettrons**	**aurai soumis**	**aurons soumis**
soumettras	**soumettrez**	**auras soumis**	**aurez soumis**
soumettra	**soumettront**	**aura soumis**	**auront soumis**

5   conditionnel

		12 conditionnel passé	
soumettrais	**soumettrions**	**aurais soumis**	**aurions soumis**
soumettrais	**soumettriez**	**aurais soumis**	**auriez soumis**
soumettrait	**soumettraient**	**aurait soumis**	**auraient soumis**

6   présent du subjonctif

		13 passé du subjonctif	
soumette	**soumettions**	**aie soumis**	**ayons soumis**
soumettes	**soumettiez**	**aies soumis**	**ayez soumis**
soumette	**soumettent**	**ait soumis**	**aient soumis**

7   imparfait du subjonctif

		14 plus-que-parfait du subjonctif	
soumisse	**soumissions**	**eusse soumis**	**eussions soumis**
soumisses	**soumissiez**	**eusses soumis**	**eussiez soumis**
soumît	**soumissent**	**eût soumis**	**eussent soumis**

Impératif
soumets
soumettons
soumettez

S

Words and expressions related to this verb
se **soumettre à**   to give in to, to comply with
se **soumettre à une décision**   to comply with a decision
la soumission   submission

See also **commettre, mettre, se mettre, permettre, promettre, remettre,** and **transmettre.**

It's important that you be familiar with the Subjunctive. See pages 26–31.

The subject pronouns are found on page 103.   **603**

The Seven Simple Tenses		The Seven Compound Tenses	
Singular	Plural	Singular	Plural
1 présent de l'indicatif		**8 passé composé**	
souris	sourions	ai souri	avons souri
souris	souriez	as souri	avez souri
sourit	sourient	a souri	ont souri
2 imparfait de l'indicatif		**9 plus-que-parfait de l'indicatif**	
souriais	souriions	avais souri	avions souri
souriais	souriiez	avais souri	aviez souri
souriait	souriaient	avait souri	avaient souri
3 passé simple		**10 passé antérieur**	
souris	sourîmes	eus souri	eûmes souri
souris	sourîtes	eus souri	eûtes souri
sourit	sourirent	eut souri	eurent souri
4 futur		**11 futur antérieur**	
sourirai	sourirons	aurai souri	aurons souri
souriras	sourirez	auras souri	aurez souri
sourira	souriront	aura souri	auront souri
5 conditionnel		**12 conditionnel passé**	
sourirais	souririons	aurais souri	aurions souri
sourirais	souririez	aurais souri	auriez souri
sourirait	souriraient	aurait souri	auraient souri
6 présent du subjonctif		**13 passé du subjonctif**	
sourie	souriions	aie souri	ayons souri
souries	souriiez	aies souri	ayez souri
sourie	sourient	ait souri	aient souri
7 imparfait du subjonctif		**14 plus-que-parfait du subjonctif**	
sourisse	sourissions	eusse souri	eussions souri
sourisses	sourissiez	eusses souri	eussiez souri
sourît	sourissent	eût souri	eussent souri

Impératif
souris
sourions
souriez

Words and expressions related to this verb
un sourire a smile
Gardez le sourire! Keep smiling!
un large sourire a broad smile
le rire laughter
sourire à to favor, to be favorable to, to smile on; **Claudine est heureuse; la vie lui sourit.**

faire un sourire à qqn to give someone a smile
Souris à la vie, et la vie te sourira. Smile at life and life will smile at you.

See also **rire.**

Don't forget to study the section on defective and impersonal verbs. It's right after this main list.

The Seven Simple Tenses | The Seven Compound Tenses

Singular	Plural	Singular	Plural

1 présent de l'indicatif

me souviens	nous souvenons
te souviens	vous souvenez
se souvient	se souviennent

8 passé composé

me suis souvenu(e)	nous sommes souvenu(e)s
t'es souvenu(e)	vous êtes souvenu(e)(s)
s'est souvenu(e)	se sont souvenu(e)s

2 imparfait de l'indicatif

me souvenais	nous souvenions
te souvenais	vous souveniez
se souvenait	se souvenaient

9 plus-que-parfait de l'indicatif

m'étais souvenu(e)	nous étions souvenu(e)s
t'étais souvenu(e)	vous étiez souvenu(e)(s)
s'était souvenu(e)	s'étaient souvenu(e)s

3 passé simple

me souvins	nous souvînmes
te souvins	vous souvîntes
se souvint	se souvinrent

10 passé antérieur

me fus souvenu(e)	nous fûmes souvenu(e)s
te fus souvenu(e)	vous fûtes souvenu(e)(s)
se fut souvenu(e)	se furent souvenu(e)s

4 futur

me souviendrai	nous souviendrons
te souviendras	vous souviendrez
se souviendra	se souviendront

11 futur antérieur

me serai souvenu(e)	nous serons souvenu(e)s
te seras souvenu(e)	vous serez souvenu(e)(s)
se sera souvenu(e)	se seront souvenu(e)s

5 conditionnel

me souviendrais	nous souviendrions
te souviendrais	vous souviendriez
se souviendrait	se souviendraient

12 conditionnel passé

me serais souvenu(e)	nous serions souvenu(e)s
te serais souvenu(e)	vous seriez souvenu(e)(s)
se serait souvenu(e)	se seraient souvenu(e)s

6 présent du subjonctif

me souvienne	nous souvenions
te souviennes	vous souveniez
se souvienne	se souviennent

13 passé du subjonctif

me sois souvenu(e)	nous soyons souvenu(e)s
te sois souvenu(e)	vous soyez souvenu(e)(s)
se soit souvenu(e)	se soient souvenu(e)s

7 imparfait du subjonctif

me souvinsse	nous souvinssions
te souvinsses	vous souvinssiez
se souvînt	se souvinssent

14 plus-que-parfait du subjonctif

me fusse souvenu(e)	nous fussions souvenu(e)s
te fusses souvenu(e)	vous fussiez souvenu(e)(s)
se fût souvenu(e)	se fussent souvenu(e)s

S

Impératif
souviens-toi; ne te souviens pas
souvenons-nous; ne nous souvenons pas
souvenez-vous; ne vous souvenez pas

Words and expressions related to this verb
un souvenir souvenir, remembrance
Je m'en souviendrai! I'll remember that! I won't forget that!
se souvenir de qqn ou de qqch to remember someone or something
conserver le souvenir de qqch to retain the memory of something

raconter des souvenirs d'enfance to recount memories of one's childhood
les souvenirs memoirs
en souvenir de in remembrance of
Je me souviens. I remember. (Motto of the Province of Québec)

See also **convenir, devenir, prévenir, revenir,** and **venir.**

The subject pronouns are found on page 103.   **605**

to suck

Regular **-er** verb endings; spelling change:
c changes to **ç** before **a** or **o** to keep **s** sound

The Seven Simple Tenses		The Seven Compound Tenses	
Singular	Plural	Singular	Plural
1 présent de l'indicatif		8 passé composé	
suce	**suçons**	**ai sucé**	**avons sucé**
suces	**sucez**	**as sucé**	**avez sucé**
suce	**sucent**	**a sucé**	**ont sucé**
2 imparfait de l'indicatif		9 plus-que-parfait de l'indicatif	
suçais	**sucions**	**avais sucé**	**avions sucé**
suçais	**suciez**	**avais sucé**	**aviez sucé**
suçait	**suçaient**	**avait sucé**	**avaient sucé**
3 passé simple		10 passé antérieur	
suçai	**suçâmes**	**eus sucé**	**eûmes sucé**
suças	**suçâtes**	**eus sucé**	**eûtes sucé**
suça	**sucèrent**	**eut sucé**	**eurent sucé**
4 futur		11 futur antérieur	
sucerai	**sucerons**	**aurai sucé**	**aurons sucé**
suceras	**sucerez**	**auras sucé**	**aurez sucé**
sucera	**suceront**	**aura sucé**	**auront sucé**
5 conditionnel		12 conditionnel passé	
sucerais	**sucerions**	**aurais sucé**	**aurions sucé**
sucerais	**suceriez**	**aurais sucé**	**auriez sucé**
sucerait	**suceraient**	**aurait sucé**	**auraient sucé**
6 présent du subjonctif		13 passé du subjonctif	
suce	**sucions**	**aie sucé**	**ayons sucé**
suces	**suciez**	**aies sucé**	**ayez sucé**
suce	**sucent**	**ait sucé**	**aient sucé**
7 imparfait du subjonctif		14 plus-que-parfait du subjonctif	
suçasse	**suçassions**	**eusse sucé**	**eussions sucé**
suçasses	**suçassiez**	**eusses sucé**	**eussiez sucé**
suçât	**suçassent**	**eût sucé**	**eussent sucé**

Impératif
suce
suçons
sucez

Words and expressions related to this verb
une sucette lollipop; **une sucette de bébé** teething ring
sucer le jus d'une orange to suck the juice of an orange
un suceur, une suceuse sucker; **suceur de sang** bloodsucker

suçoter to suck away on a candy; **toujours à sucer des bonbons** always sucking candies
un suçon hickey

Don't miss the definitions of basic grammatical terms with examples in English and French on pages 35–49.

The Seven Simple Tenses | The Seven Compound Tenses

Singular	Plural	Singular	Plural
1 présent de l'indicatif		**8 passé composé**	
suis	suivons	ai suivi	avons suivi
suis	suivez	as suivi	avez suivi
suit	suivent	a suivi	ont suivi
2 imparfait de l'indicatif		**9 plus-que-parfait de l'indicatif**	
suivais	suivions	avais suivi	avions suivi
suivais	suiviez	avais suivi	aviez suivi
suivait	suivaient	avait suivi	avaient suivi
3 passé simple		**10 passe antérieur**	
suivis	suivîmes	eus suivi	eûmes suivi
suivis	suivîtes	eus suivi	eûtes suivi
suivit	suivirent	eut suivi	eurent suivi
4 futur		**11 futur antérieur**	
suivrai	suivrons	aurai suivi	aurons suivi
suivras	suivrez	auras suivi	aurez suivi
suivra	suivront	aura suivi	auront suivi
5 conditionnel		**12 conditionnel passé**	
suivrais	suivrions	aurais suivi	aurions suivi
suivrais	suivriez	aurais suivi	auriez suivi
suivrait	suivraient	aurait suivi	auraient suivi
6 présent du subjonctif		**13 passé du subjonctif**	
suive	suivions	aie suivi	ayons suivi
suives	suiviez	aies suivi	ayez suivi
suive	suivent	ait suivi	aient suivi
7 imparfait du subjonctif		**14 plus-que-parfait du subjonctif**	
suivisse	suivissions	eusse suivi	eussions suivi
suivisses	suivissiez	eusses suivi	eussiez suivi
suivît	suivissent	eût suivi	eussent suivi

Impératif
suis
suivons
suivez

Words and expressions related to this verb
suivant   according to
suivant que ...   according as ...
la suite   continuation
à la suite de   coming after
de suite   in succession, right away
à suivre   to be continued
Je vais suivre un cours de français cet été.
   I'm going to take a course in French this summer.

Pourquoi me suivez-vous?   Why are you following me?
le jour suivant   on the following day
les questions suivantes   the following questions
tout de suite   immediately
suivre un cours   to take a course
suivre un régime   to be on a diet

See also **poursuivre**.

to beg, to beseech, to implore, to supplicate

Regular **-er** verb

The Seven Simple Tenses		The Seven Compound Tenses	
Singular	Plural	Singular	Plural
1 présent de l'indicatif		8 passé composé	
supplie	**supplions**	**ai supplié**	**avons supplié**
supplies	**suppliez**	**as supplié**	**avez supplié**
supplie	**supplient**	**a supplié**	**ont supplié**
2 imparfait de l'indicatif		9 plus-que-parfait de l'indicatif	
suppliais	**suppliions**	**avais supplié**	**avions supplié**
suppliais	**suppliiez**	**avais supplié**	**aviez supplié**
suppliait	**suppliaient**	**avait supplié**	**avaient supplié**
3 passé simple		10 passé antérieur	
suppliai	**suppliâmes**	**eus supplié**	**eûmes supplié**
supplias	**suppliâtes**	**eus supplié**	**eûtes supplié**
supplia	**supplièrent**	**eut supplié**	**eurent supplié**
4 futur		11 futur antérieur	
supplierai	**supplierons**	**aurai supplié**	**aurons supplié**
supplieras	**supplierez**	**auras supplié**	**aurez supplié**
suppliera	**supplieront**	**aura supplié**	**auront supplié**
5 conditionnel		12 conditionnel passé	
supplierais	**supplierions**	**aurais supplié**	**aurions supplié**
supplierais	**supplieriez**	**aurais supplié**	**auriez supplié**
supplierait	**supplieraient**	**aurait supplié**	**auraient supplié**
6 présent du subjonctif		13 passé du subjonctif	
supplie	**suppliions**	**aie supplié**	**ayons supplié**
supplies	**suppliiez**	**aies supplié**	**ayez supplié**
supplie	**supplient**	**ait supplié**	**aient supplié**
7 imparfait du subjonctif		14 plus-que-parfait du subjonctif	
suppliasse	**suppliassions**	**eusse supplié**	**eussions supplié**
suppliasses	**suppliassiez**	**eusses supplié**	**eussiez supplié**
suppliât	**suppliassent**	**eût supplié**	**eussent supplié**

Impératif
supplie
supplions
suppliez

Words and expressions related to this verb
une supplique request, petition
suppliant, suppliante imploring, supplicating
supplicier to torture
un supplice torture

une supplication supplication, plea
supplier qqn à genoux to beg someone on hands and knees

Try the verb drills and verb tests with answers explained on pages 50–101.

Regular **-er** verb   to hold up, to prop up, to support, to endure, to tolerate

The Seven Simple Tenses		The Seven Compound Tenses	
Singular	Plural	Singular	Plural
1 présent de l'indicatif		8 passé composé	
supporte	supportons	ai supporté	avons supporté
supportes	supportez	as supporté	avez supporté
supporte	supportent	a supporté	ont supporté
2 imparfait de l'indicatif		9 plus-que-parfait de l'indicatif	
supportais	supportions	avais supporté	avions supporté
supportais	supportiez	avais supporté	aviez supporté
supportait	supportaient	avait supporté	avaient supporté
3 passé simple		10 passé antérieur	
supportai	supportâmes	eus supporté	eûmes supporté
supportas	supportâtes	eus supporté	eûtes supporté
supporta	supportèrent	eut supporté	eurent supporté
4 futur		11 futur antérieur	
supporterai	supporterons	aurai supporté	aurons supporté
supporteras	supporterez	auras supporté	aurez supporté
supportera	supporteront	aura supporté	auront supporté
5 conditionnel		12 conditionnel passé	
supporterais	supporterions	aurais supporté	aurions supporté
supporterais	supporteriez	aurais supporté	auriez supporté
supporterait	supporteraient	aurait supporté	auraient supporté
6 présent du subjonctif		13 passé du subjonctif	
supporte	supportions	aie supporté	ayons supporté
supportes	supportiez	aies supporté	ayez supporté
supporte	supportent	ait supporté	aient supporté
7 imparfait du subjonctif		14 plus-que-parfait du subjonctif	
supportasse	supportassions	eusse supporté	eussions supporté
supportasses	supportassiez	eusses supporté	eussiez supporté
supportât	supportassent	eût supporté	eussent supporté

Impératif
supporte
supportons
supportez

Words and expressions related to this verb
supportable   endurable, bearable, supportable
porter   to carry
insupportable   unbearable, insufferable

un support   support, prop
un support-chaussette   elastic band support
(for socks) (**des supports-chaussettes**)

See also **apporter** and **porter**.

Grammar putting you in a tense mood? Review the definitions of basic grammatical terms with examples on pages 35–49.

to surprise   Irregular verb

The Seven Simple Tenses		The Seven Compound Tenses	
Singular	Plural	Singular	Plural
1 présent de l'indicatif		8 passé composé	
surprends	**surprenons**	**ai surpris**	**avons surpris**
surprends	**surprenez**	**as surpris**	**avez surpris**
surprend	**surprennent**	**a surpris**	**ont surpris**
2 imparfait de l'indicatif		9 plus-que-parfait de l'indicatif	
surprenais	**surprenions**	**avais surpris**	**avions surpris**
surprenais	**surpreniez**	**avais surpris**	**aviez surpris**
surprenait	**surprenaient**	**avait surpris**	**avaient surpris**
3 passé simple		10 passé antérieur	
surpris	**surprîmes**	**eus surpris**	**eûmes surpris**
surpris	**surprîtes**	**eus surpris**	**eûtes surpris**
surprit	**surprirent**	**eut surpris**	**eurent surpris**
4 futur		11 futur antérieur	
surprendrai	**surprendrons**	**aurai surpris**	**aurons surpris**
surprendras	**surprendrez**	**auras surpris**	**aurez surpris**
surprendra	**surprendront**	**aura surpris**	**auront surpris**
5 conditionnel		12 conditionnel passé	
surprendrais	**surprendrions**	**aurais surpris**	**aurions aurpris**
surprendrais	**surprendriez**	**aurais surpris**	**auriez surpris**
surprendrait	**surprendraient**	**aurait surpris**	**auraient surpris**
6 présent du subjonctif		13 passé du subjonctif	
surprenne	**surprenions**	**aie surpris**	**ayons surpris**
surprennes	**surpreniez**	**aies surpirs**	**ayez surpris**
surprenne	**surprennent**	**ait surpris**	**aient surpris**
7 imparfait du subjonctif		14 plus-que-parfait du subjonctif	
surprisse	**surprissions**	**eusse surpris**	**eussions surpris**
surprisses	**surprissiez**	**eusses surpris**	**eussiez surpris**
surprît	**surprissent**	**eût surpris**	**eussent surpris**

Impératif
surprends
surprenons
surprenez

Words and expressions related to this verb

surprendre qqn chez soi   to surprise someone
   at home
une surprise   surprise
surprenant, surprenante   surprising
une boîte à surprise   jack-in-the-box
surpris par qqn   surprised by someone

surpris par qqch   surprised by something
par surprise   by surprise
à ma grande surprise   to my great surprise
une surprise partie (une surprise-party)
   surprise party; **des surprises-parties**

See also **apprendre, comprendre, entreprendre, se méprendre, prendre,** and **reprendre.**

The Seven Simple Tenses		The Seven Compound Tenses	
Singular	Plural	Singular	Plural
1 présent de l'indicatif		8 passé composé	
survis	**survivons**	**ai survécu**	**avons survécu**
survis	**survivez**	**as survécu**	**avez survécu**
survit	**survivent**	**a survécu**	**ont survécu**
2 imparfait de l'indicatif		9 plus-que-parfait de l'indicatif	
survivais	**survivions**	**avais survécu**	**avions survécu**
survivais	**surviviez**	**avais survécu**	**aviez survécu**
survivait	**survivaient**	**avait survécu**	**avaient survécu**
3 passé simple		10 passé antérieur	
survécus	**survécûmes**	**eus survécu**	**eûmes survécu**
survécus	**survécûtes**	**eus survécu**	**eûtes survécu**
survécut	**survécurent**	**eut survécu**	**eurent survécu**
4 futur		11 futur antérieur	
survivrai	**survivrons**	**aurai survécu**	**aurons survécu**
survivras	**survivrez**	**auras survécu**	**aurez survécu**
survivra	**survivront**	**aura survécu**	**auront survécu**
5 conditionnel		12 conditionnel passé	
survivrais	**survivrions**	**aurais survécu**	**aurions survécu**
survivrais	**survivriez**	**aurais survécu**	**auriez survécu**
survivrait	**survivraient**	**aurait survécu**	**auraient survécu**
6 présent du subjonctif		13 passé du subjonctif	
survive	**survivions**	**aie survécu**	**ayons survécu**
survives	**surviviez**	**aies survécu**	**ayez survécu**
survive	**survivent**	**ait survécu**	**aient survécu**
7 imparfait du subjonctif		14 plus-que-parfait du subjonctif	
survécusse	**survécussions**	**eusse survécu**	**eussions survécu**
survécusses	**survécussiez**	**eusses survécu**	**eussiez survécu**
survécût	**survécussent**	**eût survécu**	**eussent survécu**

	Impératif
	survis
	survivons
	survivez

Words and expressions related to this verb
survivre à qqn   to survive someone
survivant, survivante   surviving; survivor
la survivance   survival
se survivre   to live on

survivre à l'humiliation   to survive
humiliation
la survie   survival

See also **vivre.**

For an explanation of meanings and uses of French and English verb tenses and moods, see pages
10–21.

to fly over

The Seven Simple Tenses		The Seven Compound Tenses	
Singular	Plural	Singular	Plural
1 présent de l'indicatif		**8 passé composé**	
survole	survolons	ai survolé	avons survolé
survoles	survolez	as survolé	avez survolé
survole	survolent	a survolé	ont survolé
2 imparfait de l'indicatif		**9 plus-que-parfait de l'indicatif**	
survolais	survolions	avais survolé	avions survolé
survolais	survoliez	avais survolé	aviez survolé
survolait	survolaient	avait survolé	avaient survolé
3 passé simple		**10 passé antérieur**	
survolai	survolâmes	eus survolé	eûmes survolé
survolas	survolâtes	eus survolé	eûtes survolé
survola	survolèrent	eut survolé	eurent survolé
4 futur		**11 futur antérieur**	
survolerai	survolerons	aurai survolé	aurons survolé
survoleras	survolerez	auras survolé	aurez survolé
survolera	survoleront	aura survolé	auront survolé
5 conditionnel		**12 conditionnel passé**	
survolerais	survolerions	aurais survolé	aurions survolé
survolerais	survoleriez	aurais survolé	auriez survolé
survolerait	survoleraient	aurait survolé	auraient survolé
6 présent du subjonctif		**13 passé du subjonctif**	
survole	survolions	aie survolé	ayons survolé
survoles	survoliez	aies survolé	ayez survolé
survole	survolent	ait survolé	aient survolé
7 imparfait du subjonctif		**14 plus-que-parfait du subjonctif**	
survolasse	survolassions	eusse survolé	eussions survolé
survolasses	survolassiez	eusses survolé	eussiez survolé
survolât	survolassent	eût survolé	eussent survolé

Impératif
survole
survolons
survolez

Words and expressions related to this verb
le survol   flying over
voler   to fly, to steal
le vol   flight, theft
faire un survol à basse altitude   to make a low flight

See also **voler.**

If you want to see a sample English verb fully conjugated in all the tenses, check out pages 8 and 9.

Reflexive irregular verb   to be silent, to be quiet, not to speak

The Seven Simple Tenses		The Seven Compound Tenses	
Singular	Plural	Singular	Plural
1 présent de l'indicatif		**8 passé composé**	
me tais	**nous taisons**	**me suis tu(e)**	**nous sommes tu(e)s**
te tais	**vous taisez**	**t'es tu(e)**	**vous êtes tu(e)(s)**
se tait	**se taisent**	**s'est tu(e)**	**se sont tu(e)s**
2 imparfait de l'indicatif		**9 plus-que-parfait de l'indicatif**	
me taisais	**nous taisions**	**m'étais tu(e)**	**nous étions tu(e)s**
te taisais	**vous taisiez**	**t'étais tu(e)**	**vous étiez tu(e)(s)**
se taisait	**se taisaient**	**s'était tu(e)**	**s'étaient tu(e)s**
3 passé simple		**10 passé antérieur**	
me tus	**nous tûmes**	**me fus tu(e)**	**nous fûmes tu(e)s**
te tus	**vous tûtes**	**te fus tu(e)**	**vous fûtes tu(e)(s)**
se tut	**se turent**	**se fut tu(e)**	**se furent tu(e)s**
4 futur		**11 futur antérieur**	
me tairai	**nous tairons**	**me serai tu(e)**	**nous serons tu(e)s**
te tairas	**vous tairez**	**te seras tu(e)**	**vous serez tu(e)(s)**
se taira	**se tairont**	**se sera tu(e)**	**se seront tu(e)s**
5 conditionnel		**12 conditionnel passé**	
me tairais	**nous tairions**	**me serais tu(e)**	**nous serions tu(e)s**
te tairais	**vous tairiez**	**te serais tu(e)**	**vous seriez tu(e)(s)**
se tairait	**se tairaient**	**se serait tu(e)**	**se seraient tu(e)s**
6 présent du subjonctif		**13 passé du subjonctif**	
me taise	**nous taisions**	**me sois tu(e)**	**nous soyons tu(e)s**
te taises	**vous taisiez**	**te sois tu(e)**	**vous soyez tu(e)(s)**
se taise	**se taisent**	**se soit tu(e)**	**se soient tu(e)s**
7 imparfait du subjonctif		**14 plus-que-parfait du subjonctif**	
me tusse	**nous tussions**	**me fusse tu(e)**	**nous fussions tu(e)s**
te tusses	**vous tussiez**	**te fusses tu(e)**	**vous fussiez tu(e)(s)**
se tût	**se tussent**	**se fût tu(e)**	**se fussent tu(e)s**

Impératif
tais-toi; ne te tais pas
taisons-nous; ne nous taisons pas
taisez-vous; ne vous taisez pas

Sentences using this verb
—**Marie, veux-tu te taire! Tu es trop bavarde. Et toi, Hélène, tais-toi aussi.**
   Les deux élèves ne se taisent pas. La maîtresse de chimie continue:
   —**Taisez-vous, je vous dis, toutes les deux; autrement, vous resterez dans cette salle après**
la classe.
   Les deux jeunes filles se sont tues.
Il est bon de parler et meilleur de se taire.   Speech is silver, silence is golden.

See also **bavarder** and **cesser.**

For an explanation of meanings and uses of French and English verb tenses and moods, see pages 10–21.

to dye   Irregular verb

The Seven Simple Tenses		The Seven Compound Tenses	
Singular	Plural	Singular	Plural
1 présent de l'indicatif		8 passé composé	
teins	**teignons**	**ai teint**	**avons teint**
teins	**teignez**	**as teint**	**avez teint**
teint	**teignent**	**a teint**	**ont teint**
2 imparfait de l'indicatif		9 plus-que-parfait de l'indicatif	
teignais	**teignions**	**avais teint**	**avions teint**
teignais	**teigniez**	**avais teint**	**aviez teint**
teignait	**teignaient**	**avait teint**	**avaient teint**
3 passé simple		10 passé antérieur	
teignis	**teignîmes**	**eus teint**	**eûmes teint**
teignis	**teignîtes**	**eus teint**	**eûtes teint**
teignit	**teignirent**	**eut teint**	**eurent teint**
4 futur		11 futur antérieur	
teindrai	**teindrons**	**aurai teint**	**aurons teint**
teindras	**teindrez**	**auras teint**	**aurez teint**
teindra	**teindront**	**aura teint**	**auront teint**
5 conditionnel		12 conditionnel passé	
teindrais	**teindrions**	**aurais teint**	**aurions teint**
teindrais	**teindriez**	**aurais teint**	**auriez teint**
teindrait	**teindraient**	**aurait teint**	**auraient teint**
6 présent du subjonctif		13 passé du subjonctif	
teigne	**teignions**	**aie teint**	**ayons teint**
teignes	**teigniez**	**aies teint**	**ayez teint**
teigne	**teignent**	**ait teint**	**aient teint**
7 imparfait du subjonctif		14 plus-que-parfait du subjonctif	
teignisse	**teignissions**	**eusse teint**	**eussions teint**
teignisses	**teignissiez**	**eusses teint**	**eussiez teint**
teignît	**teignissent**	**eût teint**	**eussent teint**

Impératif
teins
teignons
teignez

Words and expressions related to this verb
déteindre   to fade, to lose color, to remove the color
faire teindre qqch   to have something dyed
la teinture   dyeing
un teinturier, une teinturière   dyer
des cheveux teints   dyed hair

teindre en noir   to dye black
le teint   color, dye; complexion
teinter   to tint
la teinturerie   cleaning and dyeing
des lunettes à verres teintés   tinted eyeglasses
se teindre les cheveux   to dye one's hair

Use the guide to French pronunciation. It's in the Appendixes.

Regular **-er** verb

to telephone

The Seven Simple Tenses		The Seven Compound Tenses	
Singular	Plural	Singular	Plural
1 présent de l'indicatif		8 passé composé	
téléphone	**téléphonons**	**ai téléphoné**	**avons téléphoné**
téléphones	**téléphonez**	**as téléphoné**	**avez téléphoné**
téléphone	**téléphonent**	**a téléphoné**	**ont téléphoné**
2 imparfait de l'indicatif		9 plus-que-parfait de l'indicatif	
téléphonais	**téléphonions**	**avais téléphoné**	**avions téléphoné**
téléphonais	**téléphoniez**	**avais téléphoné**	**aviez téléphoné**
téléphonait	**téléphonaient**	**avait téléphoné**	**avaient téléphoné**
3 passé simple		10 passé antérieur	
téléphonai	**téléphonâmes**	**eus téléphoné**	**eûmes téléphoné**
téléphonas	**téléphonâtes**	**eus téléphoné**	**eûtes téléphoné**
téléphona	**téléphonèrent**	**eut téléphoné**	**eurent téléphoné**
4 futur		11 futur antérieur	
téléphonerai	**téléphonerons**	**aurai téléphoné**	**aurons téléphoné**
téléphoneras	**téléphonerez**	**auras téléphoné**	**aurez téléphoné**
téléphonera	**téléphoneront**	**aura téléphoné**	**auront téléphoné**
5 conditionnel		12 conditionnel passé	
téléphonerais	**téléphonerions**	**aurais téléphoné**	**aurions téléphoné**
téléphonerais	**téléphoneriez**	**aurais téléphoné**	**auriez téléphoné**
téléphonerait	**téléphoneraient**	**aurait téléphoné**	**auraient téléphoné**
6 présent du subjonctif		13 passé du subjonctif	
téléphone	**téléphonions**	**aie téléphoné**	**ayons téléphoné**
téléphones	**téléphoniez**	**aies téléphoné**	**ayez téléphoné**
téléphone	**téléphonent**	**ait téléphoné**	**aient téléphoné**
7 imparfait du subjonctif		14 plus-que-parfait du subjonctif	
téléphonasse	**téléphonassions**	**eusse téléphoné**	**eussions téléphoné**
téléphonasses	**téléphonassiez**	**eusses téléphoné**	**eussiez téléphoné**
téléphonât	**téléphonassent**	**eût téléphoné**	**eussent téléphoné**

Impératif
téléphone
téléphonons
téléphonez

T

Words and expressions related to this verb

le **téléphone**   telephone
téléphonique   telephonic
téléphoniquement   telephonically (by telephone)
un, une **téléphoniste**   telephone operator
téléphoner à qqn   to telephone someone

Marie? Je lui ai téléphoné hier   Mary? I telephoned her yesterday.
le **téléphone rouge**   hot line
un **téléphone cellulaire, un téléphone portable** cell phone
faire un appel téléphonique   to make a telephone call

Check out the principal parts of some important French verbs on page 7.

tendre (462)   Part. pr. **tendant**   Part. passé **tendu**

to strain, to stretch, to tighten, to tend

Regular **-re** verb

The Seven Simple Tenses		The Seven Compound Tenses	
Singular	Plural	Singular	Plural
1 présent de l'indicatif		8 passé composé	
tends	tendons	ai tendu	avons tendu
tends	tendez	as tendu	avez tendu
tend	tendent	a tendu	ont tendu
2 imparfait de l'indicatif		9 plus-que-parfait de l'indicatif	
tendais	tendions	avais tendu	avions tendu
tendais	tendiez	avais tendu	aviez tendu
tendait	tendaient	avait tendu	avaient tendu
3 passé simple		10 passé antérieur	
tendis	tendîmes	eus tendu	eûmes tendu
tendis	tendîtes	eus tendu	eûtes tendu
tendit	tendirent	eut tendu	eurent tendu
4 futur		11 futur antérieur	
tendrai	tendrons	aurai tendu	aurons tendu
tendras	tendrez	auras tendu	aurez tendu
tendra	tendront	aura tendu	auront tendu
5 conditionnel		12 conditionnel passé	
tendrais	tendrions	aurais tendu	aurions tendu
tendrais	tendriez	aurais tendu	auriez tendu
tendrait	tendraient	aurait tendu	auraient tendu
6 présent du subjonctif		13 passé du subjonctif	
tende	tendions	aie tendu	ayons tendu
tendes	tendiez	aies tendu	ayez tendu
tende	tendent	ait tendu	aient tendu
7 imparfait du subjonctif		14 plus-que-parfait du subjonctif	
tendisse	tendissions	eusse tendu	eussions tendu
tendisses	tendissiez	eusses tendu	eussiez tendu
tendît	tendissent	eût tendu	eussent tendu

Impératif
tends
tendons
tendez

Words and expressions related to this verb

tendre la main à qqn   to hold out one's hand
  to someone
attendre   to wait (for)
détendre   to slacken
se détendre   to bend, to relax
étendre   to extend, to spread
une détente   relaxing, slackening, release of
  tension

s'attendre à   to expect
entendre   to hear, to understand
s'entendre avec qqn   to get along with
  someone, to understand each other, to agree
s'étendre   to stretch out, to lie down
tendre l'autre joue   to turn the other cheek
tendre l'oreille   to prick up one's ears
tendre un piège   to set a trap

See the summary of sequence of tenses with *si* (if) clauses on page 26.

616

Irregular verb   to hold, to grasp

The Seven Simple Tenses		The Seven Compound Tenses	
Singular	Plural	Singular	Plural
1 présent de l'indicatif		8 passé composé	
tiens	tenons	ai tenu	avons tenu
tiens	tenez	as tenu	avez tenu
tient	tiennent	a tenu	ont tenu
2 imparfait de l'indicatif		9 plus-que-parfait de l'indicatif	
tenais	tenions	avais tenu	avions tenu
tenais	teniez	avais tenu	aviez tenu
tenait	tenaient	avait tenu	avaient tenu
3 passé simple		10 passé antérieur	
tins	tînmes	eus tenu	eûmes tenu
tins	tîntes	eus tenu	eûtes tenu
tint	tinrent	eut tenu	eurent tenu
4 futur		11 futur antérieur	
tiendrai	tiendrons	aurai tenu	aurons tenu
tiendras	tiendrez	auras tenu	aurez tenu
tiendra	tiendront	aura tenu	auront tenu
5 conditionnel		12 conditionnel passé	
tiendrais	tiendrions	aurais tenu	aurions tenu
tiendrais	tiendriez	aurais tenu	auriez tenu
tiendrait	tiendraient	aurait tenu	auraient tenu
6 présent du subjonctif		13 passé du subjonctif	
tienne	tenions	aie tenu	ayons tenu
tiennes	teniez	aies tenu	ayez tenu
tienne	tiennent	ait tenu	aient tenu
7 imparfait du subjonctif		14 plus-que-parfait du subjonctif	
tinsse	tinssions	eusse tenu	eussions tenu
tinsses	tinssiez	eusses tenu	eussiez tenu
tînt	tinssent	eût tenu	eussent tenu

Impératif
tiens
tenons
tenez

T

Tenir is an essential verb for beginning students because it is used in many idiomatic expressions and because there are several useful verbs that are conjugated like it.

Sentences using tenir

Robert tient de son père. Robert takes after his father.

Cette maîtresse tient bien sa classe. This teacher controls her class well.

Tiens! Voilà Bob! Look! There's Bob!

Ma nouvelle voiture a une excellente tenue de route. My new car holds the road very well.

Tenez votre droite. Keep to your right.

Proverb

Il vaut mieux "je tiens" que "je tiendrai."
It's better to say "I hold" than "I will hold." (Similar to: A bird in the hand is worth two in the bush.)

If you can conjugate **tenir** you can also conjugate these verbs:

entretenir **to maintain**

s'entretenir avec **to talk with (Use être as auxiliary)**

maintenir **to keep, to maintain**

soutenir **to support**

Words and expressions related to this verb

tenir de qqn **to take after (to favor) someone**

tenir de bonne source **to have on good authority**

tenir à qqch **to cherish something**

tenir qqn au courant **to keep someone informed**

tenir sa promsesse **to keep one's promise**

tenir le pari **to take on the bet**

tenir les bras levés **to keep one's arms up**

tenir les yeux fermés **to keep one's eyes closed**

tenir un chien en laisse **to keep a dog on a leash**

la tenue **behavior, attitude, uniform**

bien tenu, bien tenue **well-kept**

Tiens, tiens! **Well, well! Fancy that!**

Regular **-er** verb   to tempt, to attempt, to try

The Seven Simple Tenses		The Seven Compound Tenses	
Singular	Plural	Singular	Plural
1 présent de l'indicatif		8 passé composé	
tente	**tentons**	**ai tenté**	**avons tenté**
tentes	**tentez**	**as tenté**	**avez tenté**
tente	**tentent**	**a tenté**	**ont tenté**
2 imparfait de l'indicatif		9 plus-que-parfait de l'indicatif	
tentais	**tentions**	**avais tenté**	**avions tenté**
tentais	**tentiez**	**avais tenté**	**aviez tenté**
tentait	**tentaient**	**avait tenté**	**avaient tenté**
3 passé simple		10 passé antérieur	
tentai	**tentâmes**	**eus tenté**	**eûmes tenté**
tentas	**tentâtes**	**eus tenté**	**eûtes tenté**
tenta	**tentèrent**	**eut tenté**	**eurent tenté**
4 futur		11 futur antérieur	
tenterai	**tenterons**	**aurai tenté**	**aurons tenté**
tenteras	**tenterez**	**auras tenté**	**aurez tenté**
tentera	**tenteront**	**aura tenté**	**auront tenté**
5 conditionnel		12 conditionnel passé	
tenterais	**tenterions**	**aurais tenté**	**aurions tenté**
tenterais	**tenteriez**	**aurais tenté**	**auriez tenté**
tenterait	**tenteraient**	**aurait tenté**	**auraient tenté**
6 présent du subjonctif		13 passé du subjonctif	
tente	**tentions**	**aie tenté**	**ayons tenté**
tentes	**tentiez**	**aies tenté**	**ayez tenté**
tente	**tentent**	**ait tenté**	**aient tenté**
7 imparfait du subjonctif		14 plus-que-parfait du subjonctif	
tentasse	**tentassions**	**eusse tenté**	**eussions tenté**
tentasses	**tentassiez**	**eusses tenté**	**eussiez tenté**
tentât	**tentassent**	**eût tenté**	**eussent tenté**

Impératif
tente
tentons
tentez

Words and expressions related to this verb

se laisser tenter   to allow oneself to be tempted

une tentative   attempt

tenter sa chance   to try one's luck

un tentateur, une tentatrice   tempter, temptress

tenter de faire qqch   to try, to attempt to do something

tentant, tentante   tempting, inviting

Tongue twister:

Tas de riz, tas de rats. Tas de riz tentant, tas de rats tentés.   Pile of rice, pile of rats. Tempting pile of rice, pile of tempted rats.

Use the guide to French pronunciation. It's in the Appendixes.

The subject pronouns are found on page 103.   **619**

to terminate, to finish, to end

Regular **-er** verb

The Seven Simple Tenses		The Seven Compound Tenses	
Singular	Plural	Singular	Plural
1 présent de l'indicatif		8 passé composé	
termine	**terminons**	**ai terminé**	**avons terminé**
termines	**terminez**	**as terminé**	**avez terminé**
termine	**terminent**	**a terminé**	**ont terminé**
2 imparfait de l'indicatif		9 plus-que-parfait de l'indicatif	
terminais	**terminions**	**avais terminé**	**avions terminé**
terminais	**terminiez**	**avais terminé**	**aviez terminé**
terminait	**terminaient**	**avait terminé**	**avaient terminé**
3 passé simple		10 passé antérieur	
terminai	**terminâmes**	**eus terminé**	**eûmes terminé**
terminas	**terminâtes**	**eus terminé**	**eûtes terminé**
termina	**terminèrent**	**eut terminé**	**eurent terminé**
4 futur		11 futur antérieur	
terminerai	**terminerons**	**aurai terminé**	**aurons terminé**
termineras	**terminerez**	**auras terminé**	**aurez terminé**
terminera	**termineront**	**aura terminé**	**auront terminé**
5 conditionnel		12 conditionnel passé	
terminerais	**terminerions**	**aurais terminé**	**aurions terminé**
terminerais	**termineriez**	**aurais terminé**	**auriez terminé**
terminerait	**termineraient**	**aurait terminé**	**auraient terminé**
6 présent du subjonctif		13 passé du subjonctif	
termine	**terminions**	**aie terminé**	**ayons terminé**
termines	**terminiez**	**aies terminé**	**ayez terminé**
termine	**terminent**	**ait terminé**	**aient terminé**
7 imparfait du subjonctif		14 plus-que-parfait du subjonctif	
terminasse	**terminassions**	**eusse terminé**	**eussions terminé**
terminasses	**terminassiez**	**eusses terminé**	**eussiez terminé**
terminât	**terminassent**	**eût terminé**	**eussent terminé**

Impératif
termine
terminons
terminez

Words and expressions related to this verb
terminal, terminale terminal
la terminaison ending, termination
terminable terminable
interminable interminable, endless
exterminer to exterminate
terminer la journée chez un ami to end the
  day at a friend's house
terminer une session to log off (computer)

J'attends qu'elle termine le travail. I'm
  waiting for her to finish the work.
Les vacances de Noël se terminent demain.
  Christmas vacation ends tomorrow.
se terminer to end (itself)
se terminer en to end in; **un verbe qui se**
  termine en *er . . .* a verb that ends in *er . . .*
terminer un repas to finish a meal

Check out the principal parts of some important French verbs on page 7.

Regular **-er** verb   to draw out, to shoot, to pull

The Seven Simple Tenses		The Seven Compound Tenses	
Singular	Plural	Singular	Plural
1 présent de l'indicatif		8 passé composé	
tire	**tirons**	**ai tiré**	**avons tiré**
tires	**tirez**	**as tiré**	**avez tiré**
tire	**tirent**	**a tiré**	**ont tiré**
2 imparfait de l'indicatif		9 plus-que-parfait de l'indicatif	
tirais	**tirions**	**avais tiré**	**avions tiré**
tirais	**tiriez**	**avais tiré**	**aviez tiré**
tirait	**tiraient**	**avait tiré**	**avaient tiré**
3 passé simple		10 passé antérieur	
tirai	**tirâmes**	**eus tiré**	**eûmes tiré**
tiras	**tirâtes**	**eus tiré**	**eûtes tiré**
tira	**tirèrent**	**eut tiré**	**eurent tiré**
4 futur		11 futur antérieur	
tirerai	**tirerons**	**aurai tiré**	**aurons tiré**
tireras	**tirerez**	**auras tiré**	**aurez tiré**
tirera	**tireront**	**aura tiré**	**auront tiré**
5 conditionnel		12 conditionnel passé	
tirerais	**tirerions**	**aurais tiré**	**aurions tiré**
tirerais	**tireriez**	**aurais tiré**	**auriez tiré**
tirerait	**tireraient**	**aurait tiré**	**auraient tiré**
6 présent du subjonctif		13 passé du subjonctif	
tire	**tirions**	**aie tiré**	**ayons tiré**
tires	**tiriez**	**aies tiré**	**ayez tiré**
tire	**tirent**	**ait tiré**	**aient tiré**
7 imparfait du subjonctif		14 plus-que-parfait du subjonctif	
tirasse	**tirassions**	**eusse tiré**	**eussions tiré**
tirasses	**tirassiez**	**eusses tiré**	**eussiez tiré**
tirât	**tirassent**	**eût tiré**	**eussent tiré**

Impératif
tire
tirons
tirez

Words and expressions related to this verb
tirer une affaire au clair   to clear up a matter
tirer parti de   to take advantage of, to make
  the best of
un tireur, une tireuse   marksman,
  markswoman
un tire-bouchon   corkscrew (**des
  tire-bouchons**)
Tirez la langue.   Stick out your tongue.

s'en tirer   to pull through
s'en tirer bien   to get off well, to come
  through well
tirer sur   to fire (shoot) at
un tiroir   drawer (of a desk, etc.)
se tirer d'affaire   to get out of a jam
un tire-clou   nail puller (**des tire-clous**)

See also **attirer, retirer,** and **se retirer.**

The subject pronouns are found on page 103.   **621**

tomber (467)   Part. pr. **tombant**   Part. passé **tombé(e)(s)**

to fall

The Seven Simple Tenses		The Seven Compound Tenses	
Singular	Plural	Singular	Plural
1 présent de l'indicatif		8 passé composé	
tombe	**tombons**	**suis tombé(e)**	**sommes tombé(e)s**
tombes	**tombez**	**es tombé(e)**	**êtes tombé(e)(s)**
tombe	**tombent**	**est tombé(e)**	**sont tombé(e)s**
2 imparfait de l'indicatif		9 plus-que-parfait de l'indicatif	
tombais	**tombions**	**étais tombé(e)**	**étions tombé(e)s**
tombais	**tombiez**	**étais tombé(e)**	**étiez tombé(e)(s)**
tombait	**tombaient**	**était tombé(e)**	**étaient tombé(e)s**
3 passé simple		10 passé antérieur	
tombai	**tombâmes**	**fus tombé(e)**	**fûmes tombé(e)s**
tombas	**tombâtes**	**fus tombé(e)**	**fûtes tombé(e)(s)**
tomba	**tombèrent**	**fut tombé(e)**	**furent tombé(e)s**
4 futur		11 futur antérieur	
tomberai	**tomberons**	**serai tombé(e)**	**serons tombé(e)s**
tomberas	**tomberez**	**seras tombé(e)**	**serez tombé(e)(s)**
tombera	**tomberont**	**sera tombé(e)**	**seront tombé(e)s**
5 conditionnel		12 conditionnel passé	
tomberais	**tomberions**	**serais tombé(e)**	**serions tombé(e)s**
tomberais	**tomberiez**	**serais tombé(e)**	**seriez tombé(e)(s)**
tomberait	**tomberaient**	**serait tombé(e)**	**seraient tombé(e)s**
6 présent du subjonctif		13 passé du subjonctif	
tombe	**tombions**	**sois tombé(e)**	**soyons tombé(e)s**
tombes	**tombiez**	**sois tombé(e)**	**soyez tombé(e)(s)**
tombe	**tombent**	**soit tombé(e)**	**soient tombé(e)s**
7 imparfait du subjonctif		14 plus-que-parfait du subjonctif	
tombasse	**tombassions**	**fusse tombé(e)**	**fussions tombé(e)s**
tombasses	**tombassiez**	**fusses tombé(e)**	**fussiez tombé(e)(s)**
tombât	**tombassent**	**fût tombé(e)**	**fussent tombé(e)s**

Impératif
tombe
tombons
tombez

Tomber

Tomber is a very useful verb for a beginning French student. Note that it is one of the nonreflexive verbs that take être as an auxiliary in the compound tenses (see page 6).

Sentences using tomber

Oups! J'ai laissé tomber mes clés. Oops! I dropped my keys.

David est tombé de l'échelle et il s'est cassé le bras. David fell from the ladder and broke his arm.

Cela tombe bien. That's fortunate.

Nous nous sommes pressés pour arriver avant la tombée du jour. We hurried to arrive before nightfall.

Il tombe des clous. It's raining cats and dogs. (Literally: Nails are falling.)

Words and expressions related to this verb

tomber amoureux (amoureuse) de qqn **to fall in love with someone**

tomber sur **to run into, to come across**

laisser tomber **to drop**

tomber malade **to fall sick**

faire tomber **to knock down**

tomber en panne **to break down, to crash (computer)**

tomber dans les pommes **to pass out, to faint**

tomber à la renverse **to fall backward**

tomber à pic **to fall/come at the right time**

retomber **to fall again**

la tombée du jour **nightfall**

T

Can't find the verb you're looking for? Check the back pages of this book for a list of over 2,600 additional verbs!

The subject pronouns are found on page 103.

to twist

The Seven Simple Tenses		The Seven Compound Tenses	
Singular	Plural	Singular	Plural
1 présent de l'indicatif		8 passé composé	
tords	tordons	ai tordu	avons tordu
tords	tordez	as tordu	avez tordu
tord	tordent	a tordu	ont tordu
2 imparfait de l'indicatif		9 plus-que-parfait de l'indicatif	
tordais	tordions	avais tordu	avions tordu
tordais	tordiez	avais tordu	aviez tordu
tordait	tordaient	avait tordu	avaient tordu
3 passé simple		10 passé antérieur	
tordis	tordîmes	eus tordu	eûmes tordu
tordis	tordîtes	eus tordu	eûtes tordu
tordit	tordirent	eut tordu	eurent tordu
4 futur		11 futur antérieur	
tordrai	tordrons	aurai tordu	aurons tordu
tordras	tordrez	auras tordu	aurez tordu
tordra	tordront	aura tordu	auront tordu
5 conditionnel		12 conditionnel passé	
tordrais	tordrions	aurais tordu	aurions tordu
tordrais	tordriez	aurais tordu	auriez tordu
tordrait	tordraient	aurait tordu	auraient tordu
6 présent du subjonctif		13 passé du subjonctif	
torde	tordions	aie tordu	ayons tordu
tordes	tordiez	aies tordu	ayez tordu
torde	tordent	ait tordu	aient tordu
7 imparfait du subjonctif		14 plus-que-parfait du subjonctif	
tordisse	tordissions	eusse tordu	eussions tordu
tordisses	tordissiez	eusses tordu	eussiez tordu
tordît	tordissent	eût tordu	eussent tordu

Impératif
tords
tordons
tordez

Words and expressions related to this verb

tordre le cou à qqn   to twist someone's neck
tordu, tordue   twisted
tortueux   twisting
être tordu (tordue)   to be crazy
une rue tortueuse   winding street

se tordre les mains   to wring one's hands
se tordre de rire   to split one's sides laughing
avoir la gueule tordue   to have an ugly puss
(face)
avoir l'esprit tordu   to have a twisted mind

How are you doing? Find out with the verb drills and tests with answers explained on pages 50–101.

Regular **-er** verb

to touch, to affect

The Seven Simple Tenses		The Seven Compound Tenses	
Singular	Plural	Singular	Plural
1 présent de l'indicatif		8 passé composé	
touche	touchons	ai touché	avons touché
touches	touchez	as touché	avez touché
touche	touchent	a touché	ont touché
2 imparfait de l'indicatif		9 plus-que-parfait de l'indicatif	
touchais	touchions	avais touché	avions touché
touchais	touchiez	avais touché	aviez touché
touchait	touchaient	avait touché	avaient touché
3 passé simple		10 passé antérieur	
touchai	touchâmes	eus touché	eûmes touché
touchas	touchâtes	eus touché	eûtes touché
toucha	touchèrent	eut touché	eurent touché
4 futur		11 futur antérieur	
toucherai	toucherons	aurai touché	aurons touché
toucheras	toucherez	auras touché	aurez touché
touchera	toucheront	aura touché	auront touché
5 conditionnel		12 conditionnel passé	
toucherais	toucherions	aurais touché	aurions touché
toucherais	toucheriez	aurais touché	auriez touché
toucherait	toucheraient	aurait touché	auraient touché
6 présent du subjonctif		13 passé du subjonctif	
touche	touchions	aie touché	ayons touché
touches	touchiez	aies touché	ayez touché
touche	touchent	ait touché	aient touché
7 imparfait du subjonctif		14 plus-que-parfait du subjonctif	
touchasse	touchassions	eusse touché	eussions touché
touchasses	touchassiez	eusses touché	eussiez touché
touchât	touchassent	eût touché	eussent touché

Impératif
touche
touchons
touchez

T

Words and expressions related to this verb

une personne qui touche à tout
   a meddlesome person
Touchez là!   Put it there! Shake!
toucher à qqch   to touch something
N'y touchez pas!   Don't touch!
retoucher   to touch up

le toucher   touch, feeling, sense of touch
toucher de l'argent   to get some money
toucher un chèque   to cash a check
Cela me touche profondément.   That touches
   me deeply.
un, une touche-à-tout   meddler

to turn

Regular **-er** verb

The Seven Simple Tenses		The Seven Compound Tenses	
Singular	Plural	Singular	Plural
1 présent de l'indicatif		8 passé composé	
tourne	tournons	ai tourné	avons tourné
tournes	tournez	as tourné	avez tourné
tourne	tournent	a tourné	ont tourné
2 imparfait de l'indicatif		9 plus-que-parfait de l'indicatif	
tournais	tournions	avais tourné	avions tourné
tournais	tourniez	avais tourné	aviez tourné
tournait	tournaient	avait tourné	avaient tourné
3 passé simple		10 passé antérieur	
tournai	tournâmes	eus tourné	eûmes tourné
tournas	tournâtes	eus tourné	eûtes tourné
tourna	tournèrent	eut tourné	eurent tourné
4 futur		11 futur antérieur	
tournerai	tournerons	aurai tourné	aurons tourné
tourneras	tournerez	auras tourné	aurez tourné
tournera	tourneront	aura tourné	auront tourné
5 conditionnel		12 conditionnel passé	
tournerais	tournerions	aurais tourné	aurions tourné
tournerais	tourneriez	aurais tourné	auriez tourné
tournerait	tourneraient	aurait tourné	auraient tourné
6 présent du subjonctif		13 passé du subjonctif	
tourne	tournions	aie tourné	ayons tourné
tournes	tourniez	aies tourné	ayez tourné
tourne	tournent	ait tourné	aient tourné
7 imparfait du subjonctif		14 plus-que-parfait du subjonctif	
tournasse	tournassions	eusse tourné	eussions tourné
tournasses	tournassiez	eusses tourné	eussiez tourné
tournât	tournassent	eût tourné	eussent tourné

Impératif
tourne
tournons
tournez

Words and expressions related to this verb
se **tourner** to turn around
tourner qqn en ridicule to ridicule someone
un tourne-disque record player
  (des **tourne-disques**)
un tournevis screwdriver
retourner to return

tourner l'estomac à qqn to turn someone's stomach
faire une tournée to go on a tour
tourner autour du pot to beat around the bush

See also **détourner** and **retourner**.

If you don't know the French verb for an English verb you have in mind, try the index in the Appendixes.

Regular **-er** verb   to cough

The Seven Simple Tenses		The Seven Compound Tenses	
Singular	Plural	Singular	Plural
1 présent de l'indicatif		8 passé composé	
tousse	toussons	ai toussé	avons toussé
tousses	toussez	as toussé	avez toussé
tousse	toussent	a toussé	ont toussé
2 imparfait de l'indicatif		9 plus-que-parfait de l'indicatif	
toussais	toussions	avais toussé	avions toussé
toussais	toussiez	avais toussé	aviez toussé
toussait	toussaient	avait toussé	avaient toussé
3 passé simple		10 passé antérieur	
toussai	toussâmes	eus toussé	eûmes toussé
toussas	toussâtes	eus toussé	eûtes toussé
toussa	toussèrent	eut toussé	eurent toussé
4 futur		11 futur antérieur	
tousserai	tousserons	aurai toussé	aurons toussé
tousseras	tousserez	auras toussé	aurez toussé
toussera	tousseront	aura toussé	auront toussé
5 conditionnel		12 conditionnel passé	
tousserais	tousserions	aurais toussé	aurions toussé
tousserais	tousseriez	aurais toussé	auriez toussé
tousserait	tousseraient	aurait toussé	auraient toussé
6 présent du subjonctif		13 passé du subjonctif	
tousse	toussions	aie toussé	ayons toussé
tousses	toussiez	aies toussé	ayez toussé
tousse	toussent	ait toussé	aient toussé
7 imparfait du subjonctif		14 plus-que-parfait du subjonctif	
toussasse	toussassions	eusse toussé	eussions toussé
toussasses	toussassiez	eusses toussé	eussiez toussé
toussât	toussassent	eût toussé	eussent toussé

Impératif
tousse
toussons
toussez

Words and expressions related to this verb

une toux   cough; **une toux grasse**   crackling
   cough, heavy cough; **une toux sèche**   dry
   cough
une toux nerveuse   nervous cough
toussoter   to have a minor, slight cough

un tousseur, une tousseuse   cougher
un toussotement   slight cough
**Je voudrais acheter des pastilles contre
   la toux.**   I would also like to buy some
   cough drops.

How are you doing? Find out with the verb drills and tests with answers explained on pages
50–101.

traduire (472)
to translate

Part. pr. **traduisant**   Part. passé **traduit**

Irregular verb

The Seven Simple Tenses		The Seven Compound Tenses	
Singular	Plural	Singular	Plural
1 présent de l'indicatif		**8 passé composé**	
traduis	traduisons	ai traduit	avons traduit
traduis	traduisez	as traduit	avez traduit
traduit	traduisent	a traduit	ont traduit
2 imparfait de l'indicatif		**9 plus-que-parfait de l'indicatif**	
traduisais	traduisions	avais traduit	avions traduit
traduisais	traduisiez	avais traduit	aviez traduit
traduisait	traduisaient	avait traduit	avaient traduit
3 passé simple		**10 passé antérieur**	
traduisis	traduisîmes	eus traduit	eûmes traduit
traduisis	traduisîtes	eus traduit	eûtes traduit
traduisit	traduisirent	eut traduit	eurent traduit
4 futur		**11 futur antérieur**	
traduirai	traduirons	aurai traduit	aurons traduit
traduiras	traduirez	auras traduit	aurez traduit
traduira	traduiront	aura traduit	auront traduit
5 conditionnel		**12 conditionnel passé**	
traduirais	traduirions	aurais traduit	aurions traduit
traduirais	traduiriez	aurais traduit	auriez traduit
traduirait	traduiraient	aurait traduit	auraient traduit
6 présent du subjonctif		**13 passé du subjonctif**	
traduise	traduisions	aie traduit	ayons traduit
traduises	tradusiez	aies traduit	ayez traduit
traduise	traduisent	ait traduit	aient traduit
7 imparfait du subjonctif		**14 plus-que-parfait du subjonctif**	
traduisisse	traduisissions	eusse traduit	eussions traduit
traduisisses	traduisissiez	eusses traduit	eussiez traduit
traduisît	traduisissent	eût traduit	eussent traduit

Impératif
traduis
traduisons
traduisez

Words and expressions related to this verb
un traducteur, une traductrice translator
une traduction a translation
traduisible translatable
une traduction littérale a literal translation
une traduction libre a free translation
traduire du français en anglais to translate from French to English

se traduire to be translated; **Cette phrase se traduit facilement.** This sentence is easily translated.
une traduction fidèle a faithful translation
traduire de l'anglais en français to translate from English to French

See also **conduire, déduire, introduire, produire, réduire, reproduire,** and **séduire.**

628

Regular **-ir** verb

The Seven Simple Tenses		The Seven Compound Tenses	
Singular	Plural	Singular	Plural
1 présent de l'indicatif		**8 passé composé**	
trahis	trahissons	ai trahi	avons trahi
trahis	trahissez	as trahi	avez trahi
trahit	trahissent	a trahi	ont trahi
2 imparfait de l'indicatif		**9 plus-que-parfait de l'indicatif**	
trahissais	trahissions	avais trahi	avions trahi
trahissais	trahissiez	avais trahi	aviez trahi
trahissait	trahissaient	avait trahi	avaient trahi
3 passé simple		**10 passé antérieur**	
trahis	trahîmes	eus trahi	eûmes trahi
trahis	trahîtes	eus trahi	eûtes trahi
trahit	trahirent	eut trahi	eurent trahi
4 futur		**11 futur antérieur**	
trahirai	trahirons	aurai trahi	aurons trahi
trahiras	trahirez	auras trahi	aurez trahi
trahira	trahiront	aura trahi	auront trahi
5 conditionnel		**12 conditionnel passé**	
trahirais	trahirions	aurais trahi	aurions trahi
trahirais	trahiriez	aurais trahi	auriez trahi
trahirait	trahiraient	aurait trahi	auraient trahi
6 présent du subjonctif		**13 passé du subjonctif**	
trahisse	trahissions	aie trahi	ayons trahi
trahisses	trahissiez	aies trahi	ayez trahi
trahisse	trahissent	ait trahi	aient trahi
7 imparfait du subjonctif		**14 plus-que-parfait du subjonctif**	
trahisse	trahissions	eusse trahi	eussions trahi
trahisses	trahissiez	eusses trahi	eussiez trahi
trahît	trahissent	eût trahi	eussent trahi

Impératif
trahis
trahissons
trahissez

T

Words and expressions related to this verb

se **trahir**   to give oneself away, to betray each
    other, to deceive each other
traîtreusement   treacherously
la **trahison**   betrayal, treason

la haute **trahison**   high treason
un **traître**   traitor, betrayer
une **traîtresse**   traitress, betrayer

Don't miss the definitions of basic grammatical terms with examples in English and French on pages 35–49.

to milk, to draw (milk)

The Seven Simple Tenses		The Seven Compound Tenses	
Singular	Plural	Singular	Plural
1 présent de l'indicatif		8 passé composé	
trais	**trayons**	**ai trait**	**avons trait**
trais	**trayez**	**as trait**	**avez trait**
trait	**traient**	**a trait**	**ont trait**
2 imparfait de l'indicatif		9 plus-que-parfait de l'indicatif	
trayais	**trayions**	**avais trait**	**avions trait**
trayais	**trayiez**	**avais trait**	**aviez trait**
trayait	**trayaient**	**avait trait**	**avaient trait**
3 passé simple		10 passé antérieur	
—		**eus trait**	**eûmes trait**
—		**eus trait**	**eûtes trait**
		eut trait	**eurent trait**
4 futur		11 futur antérieur	
trairai	**trairons**	**aurai trait**	**aurons trait**
trairas	**trairez**	**auras trait**	**aurez trait**
traira	**trairont**	**aura trait**	**auront trait**
5 conditionnel		12 conditionnel passé	
trairais	**trairions**	**aurais trait**	**aurions trait**
trairais	**trairiez**	**aurais trait**	**auriez trait**
trairait	**trairaient**	**aurait trait**	**auraient trait**
6 présent du subjonctif		13 passé du subjonctif	
traie	**trayions**	**aie trait**	**ayons trait**
traies	**trayiez**	**aies trait**	**ayez trait**
traie	**traient**	**ait trait**	**aient trait**
7 imparfait du subjonctif		14 plus-que-parfait du subjonctif	
—		**eusse trait**	**eussions trait**
—		**eusses trait**	**eussiez trait**
		eût trait	**eussent trait**

Impératif
trais
trayons
trayez

Sentences using this verb and words related to it
M. Verjean se lève tôt pour traire les vaches.   Mr. Verjean gets up early to milk the cows.
Le trayeur trait les vaches deux fois par jour.   The milker milks the cows twice a day.

Words and expressions related to this verb

traire les vaches, traire les chèvres   to milk
  the cows, milk the goats
une trayeuse, une machine à traire   milking
  machine
un trayeur   milker, milkman
une trayeuse   milker, milkwoman

le laitier   milkman (delivery)
la laitière   milkwoman (delivery)
la traite   milking
la laiterie   dairy
un tabouret à traire   milking stool

Part. pr. **traitant**   Part. passé **traité**   **traiter (475)**

Regular -er verb   to treat, to negotiate

The Seven Simple Tenses		The Seven Compound Tenses	
Singular	Plural	Singular	Plural

1 présent de l'indicatif

traite	traitons		
traites	traitez		
traite	traitent		

8 passé composé

ai traité	avons traité		
as traité	avez traité		
a traité	ont traité		

2 imparfait de l'indicatif

traitais	traitions
traitais	traitiez
traitait	traitaient

9 plus-que-parfait de l'indicatif

avais traité	avions traité
avais traité	aviez traité
avait traité	avaient traité

3 passé simple

traitai	traitâmes
traitas	traitâtes
traita	traitèrent

10 passé antérieur

eus traité	eûmes traité
eus traité	eûtes traité
eut traité	eurent traité

4 futur

traiterai	traiterons
traiteras	traiterez
traitera	traiteront

11 futur antérieur

aurai traité	aurons traité
auras traité	aurez traité
aura traité	auront traité

5 conditionnel

traiterais	traiterions
traiterais	traiteriez
traiterait	traiteraient

12 conditionnel passé

aurais traité	aurions traité
aurais traité	auriez traité
aurait traité	auraient traité

6 présent du subjonctif

traite	traitions
traites	traitiez
traite	traitent

13 passé du subjonctif

aie traité	ayons traité
aies traité	ayez traité
ait traité	aient traité

7 imparfait du subjonctif

traitasse	traitassions
traitasses	traitassiez
traitât	traitassent

14 plus-que-parfait du subjonctif

eusse traité	eussions traité
eusses traité	eussiez traité
eût traité	eussent traité

Impératif
traite
traitons
traitez

Words and expressions related to this verb
traiter qqn mal   to treat someone badly;
  traiter qqn bien   to treat someone well
maltraiter   to maltreat, to mistreat; **traiter de**
  to deal with
traiter qqn de qqch   to call someone
  something; **traiter qqn de menteur**   to call
  someone a liar

un traitement   treatment; salary
un traité   treatise; treaty
boire d'une seule traite   to drink in one
  gulp
le traitement de texte   word processing

Do you need more drills? Have fun with the *501 French Verbs* CD-ROM!

The subject pronouns are found on page 103.   **631**

to transmit, to transfer

Irregular verb

The Seven Simple Tenses		The Seven Compound Tenses	
Singular	Plural	Singular	Plural

1 présent de l'indicatif

transmets	transmettons
transmets	transmettez
transmet	transmettent

8 passé composé

ai transmis	avons transmis
as transmis	avez transmis
a transmis	ont transmis

2 imparfait de l'indicatif

transmettais	transmettions
transmettais	transmettiez
transmettait	transmettaient

9 plus-que-parfait de l'indicatif

avais transmis	avions transmis
avais transmis	aviez transmis
avait transmis	avaient transmis

3 passé simple

transmis	transmîmes
transmis	transmîtes
transmit	transmirent

10 passé antérieur

eus transmis	eûmes transmis
eus transmis	eûtes transmis
eut transmis	eurent transmis

4 futur

transmettrai	transmettrons
transmettras	transmettrez
transmettra	transmettront

11 futur antérieur

aurai transmis	aurons transmis
auras transmis	aurez transmis
aura transmis	auront transmis

5 conditionnel

transmettrais	transmettrions
transmettrais	transmettriez
transmettrait	transmettraient

12 conditionnel passé

aurais transmis	aurions transmis
aurais transmis	auriez transmis
aurait transmis	auraient transmis

6 présent du subjonctif

transmette	transmettions
transmettes	transmettiez
transmette	transmettent

13 passé du subjonctif

aie transmis	ayons transmis
aies transmis	ayez transmis
ait transmis	aient transmis

7 imparfait du subjonctif

transmisse	transmissions
transmisses	transmissiez
transmît	transmissent

14 plus-que-parfait du subjonctif

eusse transmis	eussions transmis
eusses transmis	eussiez transmis
eût transmis	eussent transmis

Impératif
transmets
transmettons
transmettez

Words and expressions related to this verb

transmettre une maladie to transmit an illness

transmettre un message to relay, to transmit a message

transmettre son autorité to transfer one's authority

transmettre une lettre to forward a letter

une transmission transmission

transmissible transmissible, transferable

une maladie transmissible contagious disease

Le SIDA est une maladie transmissible. AIDS is a transmittable disease.

See also commettre, mettre, se mettre, omettre, permettre, promettre, remettre, and soumettre.

Regular **-er** verb   to work

The Seven Simple Tenses		The Seven Compound Tenses	
Singular	Plural	Singular	Plural
1 présent de l'indicatif		8 passé composé	
travaille	travaillons	ai travaillé	avons travaillé
travailles	travaillez	as travaillé	avez travaillé
travaille	travaillent	a travaillé	ont travaillé
2 imparfait de l'indicatif		9 plus-que-parfait de l'indicatif	
travaillais	travaillions	avais travaillé	avions travaillé
travaillais	travailliez	avais travaillé	aviez travaillé
travaillait	travaillaient	avait travaillé	avaient travaillé
3 passé simple		10 passé antérieur	
travaillai	travaillâmes	eus travaillé	eûmes travaillé
travaillas	travaillâtes	eus travaillé	eûtes travaillé
travailla	travaillèrent	eut travaillé	eurent travaillé
4 futur		11 futur antérieur	
travaillerai	travaillerons	aurai travaillé	aurons travaillé
travailleras	travaillerez	auras travaillé	aurez travaillé
travaillera	travailleront	aura travaillé	auront travaillé
5 conditionnel		12 conditionnel passé	
travaillerais	travaillerions	aurais travaillé	aurions travaillé
travaillerais	travailleriez	aurais travaillé	auriez travaillé
travaillerait	travailleraient	aurait travaillé	auraient travaillé
6 présent du subjonctif		13 passé du subjonctif	
travaille	travaillions	aie travaillé	ayons travaillé
travailles	travailliez	aies travaillé	ayez travaillé
travaille	travaillent	ait travaillé	aient travaillé
7 imparfait du subjonctif		14 plus-que-parfait du subjonctif	
travaillasse	travaillassions	eusse travaillé	eussions travaillé
travaillasses	travaillassiez	eusses travaillé	eussiez travaillé
travaillât	travaillassent	eût travaillé	eussent travaillé

Impératif
travaille
travaillons
travaillez

Words and expressions related to this verb

travailleur, travailleuse   industrious, worker
être sans travail   to be out of work
faire travailler son argent   to put one's money to work (to earn interest)

Madame Reed fait travailler ses élèves dans la classe de français.   Mrs. Reed makes her students work in French class.
le travail   work, labor, travail (les travaux)
les travaux publics   public works
les vêtements de travail   work clothes

Proverb:

Choisissez un travail que vous aimez et vous n'aurez pas à travailler un seul jour de votre vie.   Choose a job you love and you will never have to work a day in your life. (Confucius)

Consult the entry *causative* **faire** (page 37) in the section on definitions of basic grammatical terms.

The subject pronouns are found on page 103.

to traverse, to cross

The Seven Simple Tenses		The Seven Compound Tenses	
Singular	Plural	Singular	Plural
1　présent de l'indicatif		8　passé composé	
traverse	traversons	ai traversé	avons traversé
traverses	traversez	as traversé	avez traversé
traverse	traversent	a traversé	ont traversé
2　imparfait de l'indicatif		9　plus-que-parfait de l'indicatif	
traversais	traversions	avais traversé	avions traversé
traversais	traversiez	avais traversé	aviez traversé
traversait	traversaient	avait traversé	avaient traversé
3　passé simple		10　passé antérieur	
traversai	traversâmes	eus traversé	eûmes traversé
traversas	traversâtes	eus traversé	eûtes traversé
traversa	traversèrent	eut traversé	eurent traversé
4　futur		11　futur antérieur	
traverserai	traverserons	aurai traversé	aurons traversé
traverseras	traverserez	auras traversé	aurez traversé
traversera	traverseront	aura traversé	auront traversé
5　conditionnel		12　conditionnel passé	
traverserais	traverserions	aurais traversé	aurions traversé
traverserais	traverseriez	aurais traversé	auriez traversé
traverserait	traverseraient	aurait traversé	auraient traversé
6　présent du subjonctif		13　passé du subjonctif	
traverse	traversions	aie traversé	ayons traversé
traverses	traversiez	aies traversé	ayez traversé
traverse	traversent	ait traversé	aient traversé
7　imparfait du subjonctif		14　plus-que-parfait du subjonctif	
traversasse	traversassions	eusse traversé	eussions traversé
traversasses	traversassiez	eusses traversé	eussiez traversé
traversât	traversassent	eût traversé	eussent traversé

Impératif
traverse
traversons
traversez

Words and expressions related to this verb
la traversée　the crossing
à travers　through
de travers　askew, awry, crooked

une traversée de voie　railroad crossing
marcher de travers　to stagger

Check out the principal parts of some important French verbs on page 7.

634

Regular **-er** verb   to cheat, to trick

The Seven Simple Tenses   The Seven Compound Tenses

Singular	Plural	Singular	Plural
1 présent de l'indicatif		8 passé composé	
triche	**trichons**	**ai triché**	**avons triché**
triches	**trichez**	**as triché**	**avez triché**
triche	**trichent**	**a triché**	**ont triché**
2 imparfait de l'indicatif		9 plus-que-parfait de l'indicatif	
trichais	**trichions**	**avais triché**	**avions triché**
trichais	**trichiez**	**avais triché**	**aviez triché**
trichait	**trichaient**	**avait triché**	**avaient triché**
3 passé simple		10 passé antérieur	
trichai	**trichâmes**	**eus triché**	**eûmes triché**
trichas	**trichâtes**	**eus triché**	**eûtes triché**
tricha	**trichèrent**	**eut triché**	**eurent triché**
4 futur		11 futur antérieur	
tricherai	**tricherons**	**aurai triché**	**aurons triché**
tricheras	**tricherez**	**auras triché**	**aurez triché**
trichera	**tricheront**	**aura triché**	**auront triché**
5 conditionnel		12 conditionnel passé	
tricherais	**tricherions**	**aurais triché**	**aurions triché**
tricherais	**tricheriez**	**aurais triché**	**auriez triché**
tricherait	**tricheraient**	**aurait triché**	**auraient triché**
6 présent du subjonctif		13 passé du subjonctif	
triche	**trichions**	**aie triché**	**ayons triché**
triches	**trichiez**	**aies triché**	**ayez triché**
triche	**trichent**	**ait triché**	**aient triché**
7 imparfait du subjonctif		14 plus-que-parfait du subjonctif	
trichasse	**trichassions**	**eusse triché**	**eussions triché**
trichasses	**trichassiez**	**eusses triché**	**eussiez triché**
trichât	**trichassent**	**eût triché**	**eussent triché**

Impératif
triche
trichons
trichez

Words and expressions related to this verb
une tricherie cheating
gagner par tricherie to win by cheating
une triche cheating

un tricheur, une tricheuse cheater
tricher aux cartes to cheat at cards

If you want to see a sample English verb fully conjugated in all the tenses, check out pages 8 and 9.

to be mistaken, to be wrong (about something)   Reflexive regular **-er** verb

The Seven Simple Tenses		The Seven Compound Tenses	
Singular	Plural	Singular	Plural
1 présent de l'indicatif		8 passé composé	
me trompe	nous trompons	me suis trompé(e)	nous sommes trompé(e)s
te trompes	vous trompez	t'es trompé(e)	vous êtes trompé(e)(s)
se trompe	se trompent	s'est trompé(e)	se sont trompé(e)s
2 imparfait de l'indicatif		9 plus-que-parfait de l'indicatif	
me trompais	nous trompions	m'étais trompé(e)	nous étions trompé(e)s
te trompais	vous trompiez	t'étais trompé(e)	vous étiez trompé(e)(s)
se trompait	se trompaient	s'était trompé(e)	s'étaient trompé(e)s
3 passé simple		10 passé antérieur	
me trompai	nous trompâmes	me fus trompé(e)	nous fûmes trompé(e)s
te trompas	vous trompâtes	te fus trompé(e)	vous fûtes trompé(e)(s)
se trompa	se trompèrent	se fut trompé(e)	se furent trompé(e)s
4 futur		11 futur antérieur	
me tromperai	nous tromperons	me serai trompé(e)	nous serons trompé(e)s
te tromperas	vous tromperez	te seras trompé(e)	vous serez trompé(e)(s)
se trompera	se tromperont	se sera trompé(e)	se seront trompé(e)s
5 conditionnel		12 conditionnel passé	
me tromperais	nous tromperions	me serais trompé(e)	nous serions trompé(e)s
te tromperais	vous tromperiez	te serais trompé(e)	vous seriez trompé(e)(s)
se tromperait	se tromperaient	se serait trompé(e)	se seraient trompé(e)s
6 présent du subjonctif		13 passé du subjonctif	
me trompe	nous trompions	me sois trompé(e)	nous soyons trompé(e)s
te trompes	vous trompiez	te sois trompé(e)	vous soyez trompé(e)(s)
se trompe	se trompent	se soit trompé(e)	se soient trompé(e)s
7 imparfait du subjonctif		14 plus-que-parfait du subjonctif	
me trompasse	nous trompassions	me fusse trompé(e)	nous fussions trompé(e)s
te trompasses	vous trompassiez	te fusses trompé(e)	vous fussiez trompé(e)(s)
se trompât	se trompassent	se fût trompé(e)	se fussent trompé(e)s

Impératif
trompe-toi; ne te trompe pas
trompons-nous; ne nous trompons pas
trompez-vous; ne vous trompez pas

Words and expressions related to this verb
tromper to cheat, to deceive
détromper to free from deception, to set a matter straight
se laisser tromper to be taken in (fooled, deceived)

un trompeur, une trompeuse deceiver
se détromper to see the truth about a matter
se tromper de chemin to take the wrong route
une tromperie deceit, deception

For an explanation of meanings and uses of French and English verb tenses and moods, see pages 10–21.

Regular **-er** verb   to find

The Seven Simple Tenses		The Seven Compound Tenses	
Singular	Plural	Singular	Plural
1 présent de l'indicatif		8 passé composé	
trouve	**trouvons**	**ai trouvé**	**avons trouvé**
trouves	**trouvez**	**as trouvé**	**avez trouvé**
trouve	**trouvent**	**a trouvé**	**ont trouvé**
2 imparfait de l'indicatif		9 plus-que-parfait de l'indicatif	
trouvais	**trouvions**	**avais trouvé**	**avions trouvé**
trouvais	**trouviez**	**avais trouvé**	**aviez trouvé**
trouvait	**trouvaient**	**avait trouvé**	**avaient trouvé**
3 passé simple		10 passé antérieur	
trouvai	**trouvâmes**	**eus trouvé**	**eûmes trouvé**
trouvas	**trouvâtes**	**eus trouvé**	**eûtes trouvé**
trouva	**trouvèrent**	**eut trouvé**	**eurent trouvé**
4 futur		11 futur antérieur	
trouverai	**trouverons**	**aurai trouvé**	**aurons trouvé**
trouveras	**trouverez**	**auras trouvé**	**aurez trouvé**
trouvera	**trouveront**	**aura trouvé**	**auront trouvé**
5 conditionnel		12 conditionnel passé	
trouverais	**trouverions**	**aurais trouvé**	**aurions trouvé**
trouverais	**trouveriez**	**aurais trouvé**	**auriez trouvé**
trouverait	**trouveraient**	**aurait trouvé**	**auraient trouvé**
6 présent du subjonctif		13 passé du subjonctif	
trouve	**trouvions**	**aie trouvé**	**ayons trouvé**
trouves	**trouviez**	**aies trouvé**	**ayez trouvé**
trouve	**trouvent**	**ait trouvé**	**aient trouvé**
7 imparfait du subjonctif		14 plus-que-parfait du subjonctif	
trouvasse	**trouvassions**	**eusse trouvé**	**eussions trouvé**
trouvasses	**trouvassiez**	**eusses trouvé**	**eussiez trouvé**
trouvât	**trouvassent**	**eût trouvé**	**eussent trouvé**

Impératif
trouve
trouvons
trouvez

Words and expressions related to this verb

**J'ai une nouvelle voiture; comment la
   trouvez-vous?**   I have a new car; how do
   you like it?

trouver un emploi   to find a job
trouver bon de faire qqch   to think fit to do
   something
retrouver   to find again, to recover, to retrieve

trouver porte close, trouver visage de bois
   not to find anyone answering the door after
   knocking
une trouvaille   a discovery, a find
les retrouvailles *f.*   reunion, rediscovery
le bueau d'objets trouvés   lost and found

See also **se trouver.**

Review the Subjunctive clearly and simply on pages 26–31.

The subject pronouns are found on page 103.   **637**

to be located, to be situated

The Seven Simple Tenses		The Seven Compound Tenses	
Singular	Plural	Singular	Plural
1 présent de l'indicatif		**8 passé composé**	
me trouve	nous trouvons	me suis trouvé(e)	nous sommes trouvé(e)s
te trouves	vous trouvez	t'es trouvé(e)	vous êtes trouvé(e)(s)
se trouve	se trouvent	s'est trouvé(e)	se sont trouvé(e)s
2 imparfait de l'indicatif		**9 plus-que-parfait de l'indicatif**	
me trouvais	nous trouvions	m'étais trouvé(e)	nous étions trouvé(e)s
te trouvais	vous trouviez	t'étais trouvé(e)	vous étiez trouvé(e)(s)
se trouvait	se trouvaient	s'était trouvé(e)	s'étaient trouvé(e)s
3 passé simple		**10 passé antérieur**	
me trouvai	nous trouvâmes	me fus trouvé(e)	nous fûmes trouvé(e)s
te trouvas	vous trouvâtes	te fus trouvé(e)	vous fûtes trouvé(e)(s)
se trouva	se trouvèrent	se fut trouvé(e)	se furent trouvé(e)s
4 futur		**11 futur antérieur**	
me trouverai	nous trouverons	me serai trouvé(e)	nous serons trouvé(e)s
te trouveras	vous trouverez	te seras trouvé(e)	vous serez trouvé(e)(s)
se trouvera	se trouveront	se sera trouvé(e)	se seront trouvé(e)s
5 conditionnel		**12 conditionnel passé**	
me trouverais	nous trouverions	me serais trouvé(e)	nous serions trouvé(e)s
te trouverais	vous trouveriez	te serais trouvé(e)	vous seriez trouvé(e)(s)
se trouverait	se trouveraient	se serait trouvé(e)	se seraient trouvé(e)s
6 présent du subjonctif		**13 passé du subjonctif**	
me trouve	nous trouvions	me sois trouvé(e)	nous soyons trouvé(e)s
te trouves	vous trouviez	te sois trouvé(e)	vous soyez trouvé(e)(s)
se trouve	se trouvent	se soit trouvé(e)	se soient trouvé(e)s
7 imparfait du subjonctif		**14 plus-que-parfait du subjonctif**	
me trouvasse	nous trouvassions	me fusse trouvé(e)	nous fussions trouvé(e)s
te trouvasses	vous trouvassiez	te fusses trouvé(e)	vous fussiez trouvé(e)(s)
se trouvât	se trouvassent	se fût trouvé(e)	se fussent trouvé(e)s

Impératif
trouve-toi; ne te trouve pas
trouvons-nous; ne nous trouvons pas
trouvez-vous; ne vous trouvez pas

Words and expressions related to this verb
Où se trouve le bureau de poste? Where is the post office located?
Pouvez-vous me dire où se trouvent les toilettes? Can you tell me where the rest rooms are located?
Trouve-toi dans ce café à huit heures ce soir. Be in this café at 8 o'clock tonight.

Vous avez été malade; allez-vous mieux maintenant?—Oui, je me trouve mieux, merci! You have been sick; are you feeling better now?—Yes, I'm feeling better, thank you!

See also **trouver.**

The Seven Simple Tenses		The Seven Compound Tenses	
Singular	Plural	Singular	Plural
1 présent de l'indicatif		8 passé composé	
tue	**tuons**	**ai tué**	**avons tué**
tues	**tuez**	**as tué**	**avez tué**
tue	**tuent**	**a tué**	**ont tué**
2 imparfait de l'indicatif		9 plus-que-parfait de l'indicatif	
tuais	**tuions**	**avais tué**	**avions tué**
tuais	**tuiez**	**avais tué**	**aviez tué**
tuait	**tuaient**	**avait tué**	**avaient tué**
3 passé simple		10 passé antérieur	
tuai	**tuâmes**	**eus tué**	**eûmes tué**
tuas	**tuâtes**	**eus tué**	**eûtes tué**
tua	**tuèrent**	**eut tué**	**eurent tué**
4 futur		11 futur antérieur	
tuerai	**tuerons**	**aurai tué**	**aurons tué**
tueras	**tuerez**	**auras tué**	**aurez tué**
tuera	**tueront**	**aura tué**	**auront tué**
5 conditionnel		12 conditionnel passé	
tuerais	**tuerions**	**aurais tué**	**aurions tué**
tuerais	**tueriez**	**aurais tué**	**auriez tué**
tuerait	**tueraient**	**aurait tué**	**auraient tué**
6 présent du subjonctif		13 passé du subjonctif	
tue	**tuions**	**aie tué**	**ayons tué**
tues	**tuiez**	**aies tué**	**ayez tué**
tue	**tuent**	**ait tué**	**aient tué**
7 imparfait du subjonctif		14 plus-que-parfait du subjonctif	
tuasse	**tuassions**	**eusse tué**	**eussions tué**
tuasses	**tuassiez**	**eusses tué**	**eussiez tué**
tuât	**tuassent**	**eût tué**	**eussent tué**

Impératif
tue
tuons
tuez

Words and expressions related to this verb
tuer le temps   to kill time
Ce travail me tue!   This work is killing me!
se tuer   to kill oneself; to get killed
un tueur, une tueuse   killer
une tuerie   slaughter
La drogue tue.   Drugs kill.

un tue-mouche   fly swatter (**des tue-mouches**)
crier à tue-tête   to shout at the top of one's voice.
chanter à tue-tête   to sing at the top of one's voice

French Proverb:
Il ne faut pas vendre la peau de l'ours avant de l'avoir tué.   Don't count your chickens before they're hatched. (Lit.: Don't sell the bear's pelt before you've killed it.)

The subject pronouns are found on page 103.   **639**

to use **tu** when speaking, to be on familiar terms with someone

Regular **-er** verb endings; spelling change: **-oyer** verbs must change **y** to **i** in front of a mute **e**

The Seven Simple Tenses		The Seven Compound Tenses	
Singular	Plural	Singular	Plural
1 présent de l'indicatif		**8 passé composé**	
tutoie	tutoyons	ai tutoyé	avons tutoyé
tutoies	tutoyez	as tutoyé	avez tutoyé
tutoie	tutoient	a tutoyé	ont tutoyé
2 imparfait de l'indicatif		**9 plus-que-parfait de l'indicatif**	
tutoyais	tutoyions	avais tutoyé	avions tutoyé
tutoyais	tutoyiez	avais tutoyé	aviez tutoyé
tutoyait	tutoyaient	avait tutoyé	avaient tutoyé
3 passé simple		**10 passé antérieur**	
tutoyai	tutoyâmes	eus tutoyé	eûmes tutoyé
tutoyas	tutoyâtes	eus tutoyé	eûtes tutoyé
tutoya	tutoyèrent	eut tutoyé	eurent tutoyé
4 futur		**11 futur antérieur**	
tutoierai	tutoierons	aurai tutoyé	aurons tutoyé
tutoieras	tutoierez	auras tutoyé	aurez tutoyé
tutoiera	tutoieront	aura tutoyé	auront tutoyé
5 conditionnel		**12 conditionnel passé**	
tutoierais	tutoierions	aurais tutoyé	aurions tutoyé
tutoierais	tutoieriez	aurais tutoyé	auriez tutoyé
tutoierait	tutoieraient	aurait tutoyé	auraient tutoyé
6 présent du subjonctif		**13 passé du subjonctif**	
tutoie	tutoyions	aie tutoyé	ayons tutoyé
tutoies	tutoyiez	aies tutoyé	ayez tutoyé
tutoie	tutoient	ait tutoyé	aient tutoyé
7 imparfait du subjonctif		**14 plus-que-parfait du subjonctif**	
tutoyasse	tutoyassions	eusse tutoyé	eussions tutoyé
tutoyasses	tutoyassiez	eusses tutoyé	eussiez tutoyé
tutoyât	tutoyassent	eût tutoyé	eussent tutoyé

Impératif
tutoie
tutoyons
tutoyez

Sentences using this verb and words related to it

Est-ce que cela vous dérangerait si on se tutoyait? (Cela vous dérange si on se tutoie?)
    Would it bother you if we used **tu** with each other?

Words and expressions related to this verb

le tutoiement   use of **tu** when speaking with   **se tutoyer**   to use **tu** with each other
  someone   See **vouvoyer**.

In French, **tu** is used when you are speaking to a member of your family, a close friend, a classmate, or someone younger than you. **Tu** is also used when speaking to an animal. **Vous** is the polite form of *you* and is used at all other times. **Vous** is also the plural of **tu**; when you are speaking to two or more strangers, two or more members of your family at the same time, or two or more close friends at the same time, use **vous**. If you're not sure, use **vous** until someone tells you otherwise!

Regular **-ir** verb   to unite, to join

The Seven Simple Tenses		The Seven Compound Tenses	
Singular	Plural	Singular	Plural

1 présent de l'indicatif		8 passé composé	
unis	unissons	ai uni	avons uni
unis	unissez	as uni	avez uni
unit	unissent	a uni	ont uni

2 imparfait de l'indicatif		9 plus-que-parfait de l'indicatif	
unissais	unissions	avais uni	avions uni
unissais	unissiez	avais uni	aviez uni
unissait	unissaient	avait uni	avaient uni

3 passé simple		10 passé antérieur	
unis	unîmes	eus uni	eûmes uni
unis	unîtes	eus uni	eûtes uni
unit	unirent	eut uni	eurent uni

4 futur		11 futur antérieur	
unirai	unirons	aurai uni	aurons uni
uniras	unirez	auras uni	aurez uni
unira	uniront	aura uni	auront uni

5 conditionnel		12 conditionnel passé	
unirais	unirions	aurais uni	aurions uni
unirais	uniriez	aurais uni	auriez uni
unirait	uniraient	aurait uni	auraient uni

6 présent du subjonctif		13 passé du subjonctif	
unisse	unissions	aie uni	ayons uni
unisses	unissiez	aies uni	ayez uni
unisse	unissent	ait uni	aient uni

7 imparfait du subjonctif		14 plus-que-parfait du subjonctif	
unisse	unissions	eusse uni	eussions uni
unisses	unissiez	eusses uni	eussiez uni
unît	unissent	eût uni	eussent uni

Impératif
unis
unissons
unissez

U

Words and expressions related to this verb
s'unir to join together, to marry
réunir to reunite; **se réunir** to meet together
les Etats-Unis the United States
les Nations-Unies (l'ONU) the United
  Nations

une union union, alliance
un trait d'union hyphen
unisexe unisex
unir ses forces to combine one's forces
chanter à l'unisson to sing in unison

Don't forget to study the section on defective and impersonal verbs. It's right after this main list.

The subject pronouns are found on page 103.   **641**

to utilize, to use, to make use of, to put to use

Regular **-er** verb

The Seven Simple Tenses		The Seven Compound Tenses	
Singular	Plural	Singular	Plural
1 présent de l'indicatif		8 passé composé	
utilise	**utilisons**	**ai utilisé**	**avons utilisé**
utilises	**utilisez**	**as utilisé**	**avez utilisé**
utilise	**utilisent**	**a utilisé**	**ont utilisé**
2 imparfait de l'indicatif		9 plus-que-parfait de l'indicatif	
utilisais	**utilisions**	**avais utilisé**	**avions utilisé**
utilisais	**utilisiez**	**avais utilisé**	**aviez utilisé**
utilisait	**utilisaient**	**avait utilisé**	**avaient utilisé**
3 passé simple		10 passé antérieur	
utilisai	**utilisâmes**	**eus utilisé**	**eûmes utilisé**
utilisas	**utilisâtes**	**eus utilisé**	**eûtes utilisé**
utilisa	**utilisèrent**	**eut utilisé**	**eurent utilisé**
4 futur		11 futur antérieur	
utiliserai	**utiliserons**	**aurai utilisé**	**aurons utilisé**
utiliseras	**utiliserez**	**auras utilisé**	**aurez utilisé**
utilisera	**utiliseront**	**aura utilisé**	**auront utilisé**
5 conditionnel		12 conditionnel passé	
utiliserais	**utiliserions**	**aurais utilisé**	**aurions utilisé**
utiliserais	**utiliseriez**	**aurais utilisé**	**auriez utilisé**
utiliserait	**utiliseraient**	**aurait utilisé**	**auraient utilisé**
6 présent du subjonctif		13 passé du subjonctif	
utilise	**utilisions**	**aie utilisé**	**ayons utilisé**
utilises	**utilisiez**	**aies utilisé**	**ayez utilisé**
utilise	**utilisent**	**ait utilisé**	**aient utilisé**
7 imparfait du subjonctif		14 plus-que-parfait du subjonctif	
utilisasse	**utilisassions**	**eusse utilisé**	**eussions utilisé**
utilisasses	**utilisassiez**	**eusses utilisé**	**eussiez utilisé**
utilisât	**utilisassent**	**eût utilisé**	**eussent utilisé**

Impératif
utilise
utilisons
utilisez

Words and expressions related to this verb
utile useful
inutile useless
une utilité utility, usefulness
un utilisateur, une utilisatrice user

utilitaire utilitarian
une utilisation utilization
Il est utile de + inf. It is useful + inf.
utilement usefully

Get acquainted with what preposition (if any) goes with what verb. See *Verbs with prepositions* in the Appendixes.

The Seven Simple Tenses		The Seven Compound Tenses	
Singular	Plural	Singular	Plural
1 présent de l'indicatif		8 passé composé	
vaincs	**vainquons**	**ai vaincu**	**avons vaincu**
vaincs	**vainquez**	**as vaincu**	**avez vaincu**
vainc	**vainquent**	**a vaincu**	**ont vaincu**
2 imparfait de l'indicatif		9 plus-que-parfait de l'indicatif	
vainquais	**vainquions**	**avais vaincu**	**avions vaincu**
vainquais	**vainquiez**	**avais vaincu**	**aviez vaincu**
vainquait	**vainquaient**	**avait vaincu**	**avaient vaincu**
3 passé simple		10 passé antérieur	
vainquis	**vainquîmes**	**eus vaincu**	**eûmes vaincu**
vainquis	**vainquîtes**	**eus vaincu**	**eûtes vaincu**
vainquit	**vainquirent**	**eut vaincu**	**eurent vaincu**
4 futur		11 futur antérieur	
vaincrai	**vaincrons**	**aurai vaincu**	**aurons vaincu**
vaincras	**vaincrez**	**auras vaincu**	**aurez vaincu**
vaincra	**vaincront**	**aura vaincu**	**auront vaincu**
5 conditionnel		12 conditionnel passé	
vaincrais	**vaincrions**	**aurais vaincu**	**aurions vaincu**
vaincrais	**vaincriez**	**aurais vaincu**	**auriez vaincu**
vaincrait	**vaincraient**	**aurait vaincu**	**auraient vaincu**
6 présent du subjonctif		13 passé du subjonctif	
vainque	**vainquions**	**aie vaincu**	**ayons vaincu**
vainques	**vainquiez**	**aies vaincu**	**ayez vaincu**
vainque	**vainquent**	**ait vaincu**	**aient vaincu**
7 imparfait du subjonctif		14 plus-que-parfait du subjonctif	
vainquisse	**vainquissions**	**eusse vaincu**	**eussions vaincu**
vainquisses	**vainquissiez**	**eusses vaincu**	**eussiez vaincu**
vainquît	**vainquissent**	**eût vaincu**	**eussent vaincu**

Impératif
vaincs
vainquons
vainquez

V

Words and expressions related to this verb
convaincre qqn de qqch   to convince, to
    persuade someone of something
vainqueur   victor, victorious; conqueror,
    conquering

convaincant, convaincante   convincing
vaincu   defeated

See also **convaincre.**

How are you doing? Find out with the verb drills and tests with answers explained on pages
50–101.

to be worth, to be as good as, to deserve,   Irregular verb
to merit, to be equal to

The Seven Simple Tenses		The Seven Compound Tenses	
Singular	Plural	Singular	Plural
1 présent de l'indicatif		8 passé composé	
vaux	**valons**	**ai valu**	**avons valu**
vaux	**valez**	**as valu**	**avez valu**
vaut	**valent**	**a valu**	**ont valu**
2 imparfait de l'indicatif		9 plus-que-parfait de l'indicatif	
valais	**valions**	**avais valu**	**avions valu**
valais	**valiez**	**avais valu**	**aviez valu**
valait	**valaient**	**avait valu**	**avaient valu**
3 passé simple		10 passé antérieur	
valus	**valûmes**	**eus valu**	**eûmes valu**
valus	**valûtes**	**eus valu**	**eûtes valu**
valut	**valurent**	**eut valu**	**eurent valu**
4 futur		11 futur antérieur	
vaudrai	**vaudrons**	**aurai valu**	**aurons valu**
vaudras	**vaudrez**	**auras valu**	**aurez valu**
vaudra	**vaudront**	**aura valu**	**auront valu**
5 conditionnel		12 conditionnel passé	
vaudrais	**vaudrions**	**aurais valu**	**aurions valu**
vaudrais	**vaudriez**	**aurais valu**	**auriez valu**
vaudrait	**vaudraient**	**aurait valu**	**auraient valu**
6 présent du subjonctif		13 passé du subjonctif	
vaille	**valions**	**aie valu**	**ayons valu**
vailles	**valiez**	**aies valu**	**ayez valu**
vaille	**vaillent**	**ait valu**	**aient valu**
7 imparfait du subjonctif		14 plus-que-parfait du subjonctif	
valusse	**valussions**	**eusse valu**	**eussions valu**
valusses	**valussiez**	**eusses valu**	**eussiez valu**
valût	**valussent**	**eût valu**	**eussent valu**

Impératif
vaux
valons
valez

Words and expressions related to this verb
la valeur value, worth
valeureusement valorously
valeureux, valeureuse valorous
la validation validation
valide valid
Mieux vaut tard que jamais. Better late than never.

Cela vaut la peine. It's worth the trouble.
faire valoir to make the most of, to invest one's money
valoir cher to be worth a lot
valoir de l'argent to be worth money

Can't recognize an irregular verb form? Check out the index of common irregular French verb forms in the Appendixes.

Regular **-re** verb   to sell

The Seven Simple Tenses		The Seven Compound Tenses	
Singular	Plural	Singular	Plural
1 présent de l'indicatif		**8 passé composé**	
vends	vendons	ai vendu	avons vendu
vends	vendez	as vendu	avez vendu
vend	vendent	a vendu	ont vendu
2 imparfait de l'indicatif		**9 plus-que-parfait de l'indicatif**	
vendais	vendions	avais vendu	avions vendu
vendais	vendiez	avais vendu	aviez vendu
vendait	vendaient	avait vendu	avaient vendu
3 passé simple		**10 passé antérieur**	
vendis	vendîmes	eus vendu	eûmes vendu
vendis	vendîtes	eus vendu	eûtes vendu
vendit	vendirent	eut vendu	eurent vendu
4 futur		**11 futur antérieur**	
vendrai	vendrons	aurai vendu	aurons vendu
vendras	vendrez	auras vendu	aurez vendu
vendra	vendront	aura vendu	auront vendu
5 conditionnel		**12 conditionnel passé**	
vendrais	vendrions	aurais vendu	aurions vendu
vendrais	vendriez	aurais vendu	auriez vendu
vendrait	vendraient	aurait vendu	auraient vendu
6 présent du subjonctif		**13 passé du subjonctif**	
vende	vendions	aie vendu	ayons vendu
vendes	vendiez	aies vendu	ayez vendu
vende	vendent	ait vendu	aient vendu
7 imparfait du subjonctif		**14 plus-que-parfait du subjonctif**	
vendisse	vendissions	eusse vendu	eussions vendu
vendisses	vendissiez	eusses vendu	eussiez vendu
vendît	vendissent	eût vendu	eussent vendu

|
|---|
| Impératif |
| **vends** |
| **vendons** |
| **vendez** |

V

AN ESSENTIAL 55 VERB

Vendre

Vendre is an important verb because of its usefulness in many idiomatic expressions and everyday situations. **Vendre** is a regular **-re** verb, so many verbs are conjugated like it.

Sentences using vendre

Ce comédien a commencé sa carrière comme vendeur de chaussures. This actor began his career as a shoe salesman.

On vend des livres ici. Books are sold here.

Proverb

Il ne faut pas vendre la peau de l'ours avant de l'avoir tué. **Don't count your chickens before they're hatched. (Literally: Don't sell the bear's pelt before you've killed it.)**

Words and expressions related to this verb

un vendeur, une vendeuse **salesperson**

une vente **sale**

en vente **on sale**

maison à vendre **house for sale**

une salle de ventes **salesroom**

vendre à bon marché **to sell at a reasonably low price (a good buy)**

une vente aux enchères **auction**

vendre au rabais **to sell at a discount**

vendre à la sauvette **to peddle on the streets**

une vente à la sauvette **street peddling**

la mévente **a drop in sales, a sale at a loss**

À Vendre
Ordinateur portable, 512 Mo, 80 Gig, graveur CD, 700€.

For Sale
Laptop computer, 512 Meg, 80 Gig, CD burner, 700€.

If you can conjugate **vendre** you can also conjugate the following verbs (as well as other regular **-re** verbs):

fendre **to split**

revendre **to resell**

suspendre **to hang**

to avenge

Regular **-er** verb endings; spelling change: retain the
ge before **a** or **o** to keep the soft **g** sound of the verb

The Seven Simple Tenses		The Seven Compound Tenses	
Singular	Plural	Singular	Plural
1 présent de l'indicatif		8 passé composé	
venge	**vengeons**	**ai vengé**	**avons vengé**
venges	**vengez**	**as vengé**	**avez vengé**
venge	**vengent**	**a vengé**	**ont vengé**
2 imparfait de l'indicatif		9 plus-que-parfait de l'indicatif	
vengeais	**vengions**	**avais vengé**	**avions vengé**
vengeais	**vengiez**	**avais vengé**	**aviez vengé**
vengeait	**vengeaient**	**avait vengé**	**avaient vengé**
3 passé simple		10 passé antérieur	
vengeai	**vengeâmes**	**eus vengé**	**eûmes vengé**
vengeas	**vengeâtes**	**eus vengé**	**eûtes vengé**
vengea	**vengèrent**	**eut vengé**	**eurent vengé**
4 futur		11 futur antérieur	
vengerai	**vengerons**	**aurai vengé**	**aurons vengé**
vengeras	**vengerez**	**auras vengé**	**aurez vengé**
vengera	**vengeront**	**aura vengé**	**auront vengé**
5 conditionnel		12 conditionnel passé	
vengerais	**vengerions**	**aurais vengé**	**aurions vengé**
vengerais	**vengeriez**	**aurais vengé**	**auriez vengé**
vengerait	**vengeraient**	**aurait vengé**	**auraient vengé**
6 présent du subjonctif		13 passé du subjonctif	
venge	**vengions**	**aie vengé**	**ayons vengé**
venges	**vengiez**	**aies vengé**	**ayez vengé**
venge	**vengent**	**ait vengé**	**aient vengé**
7 imparfait du subjonctif		14 plus-que-parfait du subjonctif	
vengeasse	**vengeassions**	**eusse vengé**	**eussions vengé**
vengeasses	**vengeassiez**	**eusses vengé**	**eussiez vengé**
vengeât	**vengeassent**	**eût vengé**	**eussent vengé**

V

Impératif
venge
vengeons
vengez

Words and expressions related to this verb
se venger   to avenge oneself
venger son honneur   to avenge one's honor
par vengeance   out of revenge
un vengeur, une vengeresse   avenger

se venger de   to avenge oneself for
la vengeance   vengeance, revenge
la vengeance divine   divine vengeance

Don't miss orthographically changing verbs on pages 32–34.

The subject pronouns are found on page 103.   **647**

to come

Irregular verb

The Seven Simple Tenses		The Seven Compound Tenses	
Singular	Plural	Singular	Plural
1 présent de l'indicatif		8 passé composé	
viens	**venons**	**suis venu(e)**	**sommes venu(e)s**
viens	**venez**	**es venu(e)**	**êtes venu(e)(s)**
vient	**viennent**	**est venu(e)**	**sont venu(e)s**
2 imparfait de l'indicatif		9 plus-que-parfait de l'indicatif	
venais	**venions**	**étais venu(e)**	**étions venu(e)s**
venais	**veniez**	**étais venu(e)**	**étiez venu(e)(s)**
venait	**venaient**	**était venu(e)**	**étaient venu(e)s**
3 passé simple		10 passé antérieur	
vins	**vînmes**	**fus venu(e)**	**fûmes venu(e)s**
vins	**vîntes**	**fus venu(e)**	**fûtes venu(e)(s)**
vint	**vinrent**	**fut venu(e)**	**furent venu(e)s**
4 futur		11 futur antérieur	
viendrai	**viendrons**	**serai venu(e)**	**serons venu(e)s**
viendras	**viendrez**	**seras venu(e)**	**serez venu(e)(s)**
viendra	**viendront**	**sera venu(e)**	**seront venu(e)s**
5 conditionnel		12 conditionnel passé	
viendrais	**viendrions**	**serais venu(e)**	**serions venu(e)s**
viendrais	**viendriez**	**serais venu(e)**	**seriez venu(e)(s)**
viendrait	**viendraient**	**serait venu(e)**	**seraient venu(e)s**
6 présent du subjonctif		13 passé du subjonctif	
vienne	**venions**	**sois venu(e)**	**soyons venu(e)s**
viennes	**veniez**	**sois venu(e)**	**soyez venu(e)(s)**
vienne	**viennent**	**soit venu(e)**	**soient venu(e)s**
7 imparfait du subjonctif		14 plus-que-parfait du subjonctif	
vinsse	**vinssions**	**fusse venu(e)**	**fussions venu(e)s**
vinsses	**vinssiez**	**fusses venu(e)**	**fussiez venu(e)(s)**
vînt	**vinssent**	**fût venu(e)**	**fussent venu(e)s**

Impératif
viens
venons
venez

AN ESSENTIAL
55 VERB

AN ESSENTIAL 55 VERB

Venir

Venir is an important verb for a beginning student because it is used in numerous situations and idiomatic expressions. There are also many useful verbs that are conjugated like venir. Note that the auxiliary of venir is être (see page 6).

Sentences using venir

Je viens de manger. I have just eaten.

D'où vient cela? Where does that come from?

Venons-en au fait. Let's get to the point.

Si nous venons à nous voir en ville, nous pouvons prendre un café ensemble. If we happen to see each other downtown, we can have coffee together.

Tina venait de sortir avec Alexandre quand le téléphone a sonné. Tina had just gone out with Alexander when the telephone rang.

Tu viens avec moi? Are you coming with me?

Words and expressions related to this verb

venir de faire qqch **to have just done something**

venir à + inf. **to happen to;** Si je viens à devenir riche . . . **If I happen to become rich . . .**

venir à bout de + inf. **to manage, to succeed + inf.**

s'en venir **to come**

faire venir **to send for**

venir chercher **to call for, to come to get**

le va et vient **coming and going (of people, cars, etc.)**

Proverbs

Tout vient à temps (à point) à qui sait attendre. **Everything comes to him who waits.**

L'appétit vient en mangeant. **The more you have, the more you want. (Literally: Appetite comes while eating.)**

Note: If you want to tell someone that you're on the way, say "J'arrive!" (I'm on the way! I'm coming!)

V

If you can conjugate venir you can also conjugate the following verbs:

intervenir **to intervene**

parvenir à **to reach, succeed**

survenir **to occur, arise**

The subject pronouns are found on page 103.

to pour

Regular **-er** verb

The Seven Simple Tenses		The Seven Compound Tenses	
Singular	Plural	Singular	Plural
1 présent de l'indicatif		8 passé composé	
verse	versons	ai versé	avons versé
verses	versez	as versé	avez versé
verse	versent	a versé	ont versé
2 imparfait de l'indicatif		9 plus-que-parfait de l'indicatif	
versais	versions	avais versé	avions versé
versais	versiez	avais versé	aviez versé
versait	versaient	avait versé	avaient versé
3 passé simple		10 passé antérieur	
versai	versâmes	eus versé	eûmes versé
versas	versâtes	eus versé	eûtes versé
versa	versèrent	eut versé	eurent versé
4 futur		11 futur antérieur	
verserai	verserons	aurai versé	aurons versé
verseras	verserez	auras versé	aurez versé
versera	verseront	aura versé	auront versé
5 conditionnel		12 conditionnel passé	
verserais	verserions	aurais versé	aurions versé
verserais	verseriez	aurais versé	auriez versé
verserait	verseraient	aurait versé	auraient versé
6 présent du subjonctif		13 passé du subjonctif	
verse	versions	aie versé	ayons versé
verses	versiez	aies versé	ayez versé
verse	versent	ait versé	aient versé
7 imparfait du subjonctif		14 plus-que-parfait du subjonctif	
versasse	versassions	eusse versé	eussions versé
versasses	versassiez	eusses versé	eussiez versé
versât	versassent	eût versé	eussent versé

Impératif
verse
versons
versez

Common idiomatic expressions using this verb and words related to it

verser des larmes   to shed tears
verser de l'argent   to deposit money
verser des fonds   to invest capital
un versement   deposit, payment

verser du sang   to shed blood
verser à boire à qqn   to pour someone a drink
pleuvoir à verse   to rain hard

Soak up some verbs used in weather expressions. There's a list in the Appendixes!

Irregular verb   to clothe, to dress

The Seven Simple Tenses		The Seven Compound Tenses	
Singular	Plural	Singular	Plural

1 présent de l'indicatif

		8 passé composé	
vêts	vêtons	ai vêtu	avons vêtu
vêts	vêtez	as vêtu	avez vêtu
vêt	vêtent	a vêtu	ont vêtu

2 imparfait de l'indicatif

		9 plus-que-parfait de l'indicatif	
vêtais	vêtions	avais vêtu	avions vêtu
vêtais	vêtiez	avais vêtu	aviez vêtu
vêtait	vêtaient	avait vêtu	avaient vêtu

3 passé simple

		10 passé antérieur	
vêtis	vêtîmes	eus vêtu	eûmes vêtu
vêtis	vêtîtes	eus vêtu	eûtes vêtu
vêtit	vêtirent	eut vêtu	eurent vêtu

4 futur

		11 futur antérieur	
vêtirai	vêtirons	aurai vêtu	aurons vêtu
vêtiras	vêtirez	auras vêtu	aurez vêtu
vêtira	vêtiront	aura vêtu	auront vêtu

5 conditionnel

		12 conditionnel passé	
vêtirais	vêtirions	aurais vêtu	aurions vêtu
vêtirais	vêtiriez	aurais vêtu	auriez vêtu
vêtirait	vêtiraient	aurait vêtu	auraient vêtu

6 présent du subjonctif

		13 passé du subjonctif	
vête	vêtions	aie vêtu	ayons vêtu
vêtes	vêtiez	aies vêtu	ayez vêtu
vête	vêtent	ait vêtu	aient vêtu

7 imparfait du subjonctif

		14 plus-que-parfait du subjonctif	
vêtisse	vêtissions	eusse vêtu	eussions vêtu
vêtisses	vêtissiez	eusses vêtu	eussiez vêtu
vêtît	vêtissent	eût vêtu	eussent vêtu

V

Impératif
vêts
vêtons
vêtez

Words and expressions related to this verb
un vêtement garment, wearing apparel;
   des vêtements clothes
les vêtements de dessus outerwear
les sous-vêtements underwear
vêtir un enfant to dress a child
dévêtir to undress
mettre sur soi un vêtement to put on clothing
les vêtements de deuil mourning clothes

le vestiaire coatroom
les vêtements de travail work clothes
se vêtir to dress oneself
se dévêtir to undress oneself
être bien vêtu (vêtue) to be well dressed;
   mal vêtu badly dressed;
   à demi-vêtu half dressed

See also **s'habiller**.

The subject pronouns are found on page 103.

to grow old, to become old, to age

The Seven Simple Tenses		The Seven Compound Tenses	
Singular	Plural	Singular	Plural

1 présent de l'indicatif

		8 passé composé	
vieillis	**vieillissons**	**ai vieilli**	**avons vieilli**
vieillis	**vieillissez**	**as vieilli**	**avez vieilli**
vieillit	**vieillissent**	**a vieilli**	**ont vieilli**

2 imparfait de l'indicatif

		9 plus-que-parfait de l'indicatif	
vieillissais	**vieillissions**	**avais vieilli**	**avions vieilli**
vieillissais	**vieillissiez**	**avais vieilli**	**aviez vieilli**
vieillissait	**vieillissaient**	**avait vieilli**	**avaient vieilli**

3 passé simple

		10 passé antérieur	
vieillis	**vieillîmes**	**eus vieilli**	**eûmes vieilli**
vieillis	**vieillîtes**	**eus vieilli**	**eûtes vieilli**
vieillit	**vieillirent**	**eut vieilli**	**eurent vieilli**

4 futur

		11 futur antérieur	
vieillirai	**vieillirons**	**aurai vieilli**	**aurons vieilli**
vieilliras	**vieillirez**	**auras vieilli**	**aurez vieilli**
vieillira	**vieilliront**	**aura vieilli**	**auront vieilli**

5 conditionnel

		12 conditionnel passé	
vieillirais	**vieillirions**	**aurais vieilli**	**aurions vieilli**
vieillirais	**vieilliriez**	**aurais vieilli**	**auriez vieilli**
vieillirait	**vieilliraient**	**aurait vieilli**	**auraient vieilli**

6 présent du subjonctif

		13 passé du subjonctif	
vieillisse	**vieillissions**	**aie vieilli**	**ayons vieilli**
vieillisses	**vieillissiez**	**aies vieilli**	**ayez vieilli**
vieillisse	**vieillissent**	**ait vieilli**	**aient vieilli**

7 imparfait du subjonctif

		14 plus-que-parfait du subjonctif	
vieillisse	**vieillissions**	**eusse vieilli**	**eussions vieilli**
vieillisses	**vieillissiez**	**eusses vieilli**	**eussiez vieilli**
vieillît	**vieillissent**	**eût vieilli**	**eussent vieilli**

Impératif
vieillis
vieillissons
vieillissez

Words related to this verb

vieux, vieil, vieille   old
  un vieux chapeau   an old hat
  un vieil arbre   an old tree
  un vieil homme   an old man
  deux vieux hommes   two old men
  une vieille dame   an old lady

la vieillesse   old age
un vieillard   old man
une vieille   old woman
vieillissant, vieillissante *adj.*   aging
le vieillissement   aging, growing old

Can't find the verb you're looking for? Check the back pages of this book for a list of over 2,600 additional verbs!

The Seven Simple Tenses		The Seven Compound Tenses	
Singular	Plural	Singular	Plural
1 présent de l'indicatif		**8 passé composé**	
visite	visitons	ai visité	avons visité
visites	visitez	as visité	avez visité
visite	visitent	a visité	ont visité
2 imparfait de l'indicatif		**9 plus-que-parfait de l'indicatif**	
visitais	visitions	avais visité	avions visité
visitais	visitiez	avais visité	aviez visité
visitait	visitaient	avait visité	avaient visité
3 passé simple		**10 passé antérieur**	
visitai	visitâmes	eus visité	eûmes visité
visitas	visitâtes	eus visité	eûtes visité
visita	visitèrent	eut visité	eurent visité
4 futur		**11 futur antérieur**	
visiterai	visiterons	aurai visité	aurons visité
visiteras	visiterez	auras visité	aurez visité
visitera	visiteront	aura visité	auront visité
5 conditionnel		**12 conditionnel passé**	
visiterais	visiterions	aurais visité	aurions visité
visiterais	visiteriez	aurais visité	auriez visité
visiterait	visiteraient	aurait visité	auraient visité
6 présent du subjonctif		**13 passé du subjonctif**	
visite	visitions	aie visité	ayons visité
visites	visitiez	aies visité	ayez visité
visite	visitent	ait visité	aient visité
7 imparfait du subjonctif		**14 plus-que-parfait du subjonctif**	
visitasse	visitassions	eusse visité	eussions visité
visitasses	visitassiez	eusses visité	eussiez visité
visitât	visitassent	eût visité	eussent visité

Impératif
visite
visitons
visitez

Words and expressions related to this verb

rendre visite à qqn   to visit someone, to pay a call

un visiteur, une visiteuse   visitor, caller

une visite guidée   a guided tour

rendre une visite à qqn   to return a visit

les heures de visite   visiting hours

une visitation   visitation

Can't remember the French verb you need? Check the back pages of this book for the English-French verb index!

to live

The Seven Simple Tenses		The Seven Compound Tenses	
Singular	Plural	Singular	Plural
1 présent de l'indicatif		8 passé composé	
vis	vivons	ai vécu	avons vécu
vis	vivez	as vécu	avez vécu
vit	vivent	a vécu	ont vécu
2 imparfait de l'indicatif		9 plus-que-parfait de l'indicatif	
vivais	vivions	avais vécu	avions vécu
vivais	viviez	avais vécu	aviez vécu
vivait	vivaient	avait vécu	avaient vécu
3 passé simple		10 passé antérieur	
vécus	vécûmes	eus vécu	eûmes vécu
vécus	vécûtes	eus vécu	eûtes vécu
vécut	vécurent	eut vécu	eurent vécu
4 futur		11 futur antérieur	
vivrai	vivrons	aurai vécu	aurons vécu
vivras	vivrez	auras vécu	aurez vécu
vivra	vivront	aura vécu	auront vécu
5 conditionnel		12 conditionnel passé	
vivrais	vivrions	aurais vécu	aurions vécu
vivrais	vivriez	aurais vécu	auriez vécu
vivrait	vivraient	aurait vécu	auraient vécu
6 présent du subjonctif		13 passé du subjonctif	
vive	vivions	aie vécu	ayons vécu
vives	viviez	aies vécu	ayez vécu
vive	vivent	ait vécu	aient vécu
7 imparfait du subjonctif		14 plus-que-parfait du subjonctif	
vécusse	vécussions	eusse vécu	eussions vécu
vécusses	vécussiez	eusses vécu	eussiez vécu
vécût	vécussent	eût vécu	eussent vécu

Impératif
vis
vivons
vivez

Words and expressions related to this verb
revivre   to relive, to revive
survivre à   to survive
Vive la France!   Long live France!
avoir de quoi vivre   to have enough to live on
vivre de   to subsist on
savoir-vivre   to be well-mannered
Qui vivra verra.   Time will tell.

Vivent les Etats-Unis!   Long live the United States!
le vivre et le couvert   room and board
vivre largement   to live well
Nous vivons des temps troublés.   We are living in troubled times.

See also survivre.

Can't recognize an irregular verb form? Check out the index of common irregular French verb forms in the Appendixes.

Irregular verb   to see

The Seven Simple Tenses		The Seven Compound Tenses	
Singular	Plural	Singular	Plural
1 présent de l'indicatif		8 passé composé	
vois	voyons	ai vu	avons vu
vois	voyez	as vu	avez vu
voit	voient	a vu	ont uv
2 imparfait de l'indicatif		9 plus-que-parfait de l'indicatif	
voyais	voyions	avais vu	avions vu
voyais	voyiez	avais vu	aviez vu
voyait	voyaient	avait vu	avaient vu
3 passé simple		10 passé antérieur	
vis	vîmes	eus vu	eûmes vu
vis	vîtes	eus vu	eûtes vu
vit	virent	eut vu	eurent vu
4 futur		11 futur antérieur	
verrai	verrons	aurai vu	aurons vu
verras	verrez	auras vu	aurez vu
verra	verront	aura vu	auront vu
5 conditionnel		12 conditionnel passé	
verrais	verrions	aurais vu	aurions vu
verrais	verriez	aurais vu	auriez vu
verrait	verraient	aurait vu	auraient vu
6 présent du subjonctif		13 passé du subjonctif	
voie	voyions	aie vu	ayons vu
voies	voyiez	aies vu	ayez vu
voie	voient	ait vu	aient vu
7 imparfait du subjonctif		14 plus-que-parfait du subjonctif	
visse	vissions	eusse vu	eussions vu
visses	vissiez	eusses vu	eussiez vu
vît	vissent	eût vu	eussent vu

Impératif
vois
voyons
voyez

V

AN ESSENTIAL
55 VERB

Voir is an important verb for a beginning French student to learn because it is used in many everyday situations and idiomatic expressions.

Sentences using voir

Cela se voit. That's obvious.

Voyez vous-même! See for yourself!

C'est à voir. It remains to be seen.

Voir c'est croire. Seeing is believing

Il m'a frappé si fort que j'ai vu trente-six chandelles. He hit me so hard I saw stars.

Édith a tendance à voir la vie en rose. Edith tends to see life through rose-colored glasses.

Voyons! See here now!

Qu'est-ce que tu caches dans ton sac-à-dos? Fais voir. What are you hiding in your backpack? Show me.

Words and expressions related to this verb

à vue d'oeil **visibly**

voir de loin **to be farsighted**

faire voir **to show**

voir la vie en rose **to see the bright side of life, to see life through rose-colored glasses**

voir tout en rose **to see the bright side of things, to be optimistic**

If you can conjugate voir you can also conjugate the following verbs:

entrevoir **to glimpse, to catch a glimpse**

prévoir **to foresee (Note: The future and conditional stem is** prévoir-**)**

revoir **to see again**

Can't find the verb you're looking for? Check the back pages of this book for a list of over 2,600 additional verbs!

Regular **-er** verb

to fly, to steal

The Seven Simple Tenses		The Seven Compound Tenses	
Singular	Plural	Singular	Plural
1 présent de l'indicatif		8 passé composé	
vole	volons	ai volé	avons volé
voles	volez	as volé	avez volé
vole	volent	a volé	ont volé
2 imparfait de l'indicatif		9 plus-que-parfait de l'indicatif	
volais	volions	avais volé	avions volé
volais	voliez	avais volé	aviez volé
volait	volaient	avait volé	avaient volé
3 passé simple		10 passé antérieur	
volai	volâmes	eus volé	eûmes volé
volas	volâtes	eus volé	eûtes volé
vola	volèrent	eut volé	eurent volé
4 futur		11 futur antérieur	
volerai	volerons	aurai volé	aurons volé
voleras	volerez	auras volé	aurez volé
volera	voleront	aura volé	auront volé
5 conditionnel		12 conditionnel passé	
volerais	volerions	aurais volé	aurions volé
volerais	voleriez	aurais volé	auriez volé
volerait	voleraient	aurait volé	auraient volé
6 présent du subjonctif		13 passé du subjonctif	
vole	volions	aie volé	ayons volé
voles	voliez	aies volé	ayez volé
vole	volent	ait volé	aient volé
7 imparfait du subjonctif		14 plus-que-parfait du subjonctif	
volasse	volassions	eusse volé	eussions volé
volasses	volassiez	eusses volé	eussiez volé
volât	volassent	eût volé	eussent volé

Impératif
vole
volons
volez

Words and expressions related to this verb
un vol   flight, theft
le voleur   thief
Au voleur!   Stop thief!
à vol d'oiseau   as the crow flies
vol de nuit   night flying (airplane), night flight
New York à vol d'oiseau   bird's eye view of
  New York
survoler   to fly over

See also s'envoler and survoler.

le volant   steering wheel
se mettre au volant   to take the (steering)
  wheel
voler un baiser à qqn   to steal a kiss from
  someone
voler dans les bras de qqn   to fly into
  someone's arms

The subject pronouns are found on page 103.

to want

Irregular verb

The Seven Simple Tenses		The Seven Compound Tenses	
Singular	Plural	Singular	Plural
1 présent de l'indicatif		**8 passé composé**	
veux	**voulons**	**ai voulu**	**avons voulu**
veux	**voulez**	**as voulu**	**avez voulu**
veut	**veulent**	**a voulu**	**ont voulu**
2 imparfait de l'indicatif		**9 plus-que-parfait de l'indicatif**	
voulais	**voulions**	**avais voulu**	**avions voulu**
voulais	**vouliez**	**avais voulu**	**aviez voulu**
voulait	**voulaient**	**avait voulu**	**avaient voulu**
3 passé simple		**10 passé antérieur**	
voulus	**voulûmes**	**eus voulu**	**eûmes voulu**
voulus	**voulûtes**	**eus voulu**	**eûtes voulu**
voulut	**voulurent**	**eut voulu**	**eurent voulu**
4 futur		**11 futur antérieur**	
voudrai	**voudrons**	**aurai voulu**	**aurons voulu**
voudras	**voudrez**	**auras voulu**	**aurez voulu**
voudra	**voudront**	**aura voulu**	**auront voulu**
5 conditionnel		**12 conditionnel passé**	
voudrais	**voudrions**	**aurais voulu**	**aurions voulu**
voudrais	**voudriez**	**aurais voulu**	**auriez voulu**
voudrait	**voudraient**	**aurait voulu**	**auraient voulu**
6 présent du subjonctif		**13 passé du subjonctif**	
veuille	**voulions**	**aie voulu**	**ayons voulu**
veuilles	**vouliez**	**aies voulu**	**ayez voulu**
veuille	**veuillent**	**ait voulu**	**aient voulu**
7 imparfait du subjonctif		**14 plus-que-parfait du subjonctif**	
voulusse	**voulussions**	**eusse voulu**	**eussions voulu**
voulusses	**voulussiez**	**eusses voulu**	**eussiez voulu**
voulût	**voulussent**	**eût voulu**	**eussent voulu**

Impératif
veuille
veuillons
veuillez

AN ESSENTIAL
55 VERB

Vouloir

Vouloir is an important verb for beginning students because it is used in many everyday situations and idiomatic expressions.

Sentences using vouloir

Que voulez-vous dire par là? What do you mean by that remark?

Vouloir c'est pouvoir. Where there's a will there's a way.

Pourriez-vous m'aider? Je voudrais installer ce logiciel. Could you please help me? I would like to install this software.

—Est-ce que tu veux m'accompagner?
—Oui, je veux bien!

—Do you want to accompany me?
—Yes, I'd really like to!

Que voulez-vous? What do you expect?

Qu'est-ce que cela veut dire? What does that mean?

Veuillez éteindre vos téléphones cellulaires. Please turn off your cell phones.

Veuillez agréer, Monsieur (Madame), mes sincères salutations. Please be good enough, Sir (Madam) to accept my sincere greetings. (This is one of many possible closing statements in correspondence. Of course, in English we simply say: Sincerely.)

Words and expressions related to this verb

vouloir dire **to mean**

Que veut dire . . .? **What does . . . mean?**

un voeu **wish**

meilleurs voeux **best wishes**

vouloir bien faire qqch **to be willing to do something**

sans le vouloir **without meaning to, unintentionally**

en temps voulu **in due time**

en vouloir à qqn **to bear a grudge against someone**

vouloir du bien à qqn **to wish someone well**

V

Can't remember the French verb you need? Check the back pages of this book for the English-French verb index!

The subject pronouns are found on page 103.

vouvoyer (500)

Part. pr. vouvoyant   **Part. passé vouvoyé**

to use **vous** when speaking, to be on formal or polite terms with someone

Regular **-er** verb endings; spelling change: **-oyer** verbs must change **y** to **i** before a mute **e**

The Seven Simple Tenses		The Seven Compound Tenses	
Singular	Plural	Singular	Plural
1 présent de l'indicatif		**8 passé composé**	
vouvoie	vouvoyons	ai vouvoyé	avons vouvoyé
vouvoies	vouvoyez	as vouvoyé	avez vouvoyé
vouvoie	vouvoient	a vouvoyé	ont vouvoyé
2 imparfait de l'indicatif		**9 plus-que-parfait de l'indicatif**	
vouvoyais	vouvoyions	avais vouvoyé	avions vouvoyé
vouvoyais	vouvoyiez	avais vouvoyé	aviez vouvoyé
vouvoyait	vouvoyaient	avait vouvoyé	avaient vouvoyé
3 passé simple		**10 passé antérieur**	
vouvoyai	vouvoyâmes	eus vouvoyé	eûmes vouvoyé
vouvoyas	vouvoyâtes	eus vouvoyé	eûtes vouvoyé
vouvoya	vouvoyèrent	eut vouvoyé	eurent vouvoyé
4 futur		**11 futur antérieur**	
vouvoierai	vouvoierons	aurai vouvoyé	aurons vouvoyé
vouvoieras	vouvoierez	auras vouvoyé	aurez vouvoyé
vouvoiera	vouvoieront	aura vouvoyé	auront vouvoyé
5 conditionnel		**12 conditionnel passé**	
vouvoierais	vouvoierions	aurais vouvoyé	aurions vouvoyé
vouvoierais	vouvoieriez	aurais vouvoyé	auriez vouvoyé
vouvoierait	vouvoieraient	aurait vouvoyé	auraient vouvoyé
6 présent du subjonctif		**13 passé du subjonctif**	
vouvoie	vouvoyions	aie vouvoyé	ayons vouvoyé
vouvoies	vouvoyiez	aies vouvoyé	ayez vouvoyé
vouvoie	vouvoient	ait vouvoyé	aient vouvoyé
7 imparfait du subjonctif		**14 plus-que-parfait du subjonctif**	
vouvoyasse	vouvoyassions	eusse vouvoyé	eussions vouvoyé
vouvoyasses	vouvoyassiez	eusses vouvoyé	eussiez vouvoyé
vouvoyât	vouvoyassent	eût vouvoyé	eussent vouvoyé

Impératif
vouvoie
vouvoyons
vouvoyez

Sentences using this verb and words related to it

Quand je l'ai connu on se vouvoyait, mais maintenant je le tutoie.   When I met him we used **vous**, but now I use **tu** with him.

Words and expressions related to this verb
le vouvoiement   use of **vous** when speaking with someone

se vouvoyer   to use **vous** with each other

See **tutoyer.**

In French, **tu** is used when you are speaking to a member of your family, a close friend, a classmate, or someone younger than you. **Tu** is also used when speaking to an animal. **Vous** is the polite form of *you* and is used at all other times. **Vous** is also the plural of **tu**; when you are speaking to two or more strangers, two or more members of your family at the same time, or two or more close friends at the same time, use **vous**. If you're not sure, use **vous** until someone tells you otherwise!

to travel

Regular **-er** verb endings; spelling change: retain the **ge** before **a** or **o** to keep the soft **g** sound of the verb

The Seven Simple Tenses		The Seven Compound Tenses	
Singular	Plural	Singular	Plural
1 présent de l'indicatif		**8 passé composé**	
voyage	voyageons	ai voyagé	avons voyagé
voyages	voyagez	as voyagé	avez voyagé
voyage	voyagent	a voyagé	ont voyagé
2 imparfait de l'indicatif		**9 plus-que-parfait de l'indicatif**	
voyageais	voyagions	avais voyagé	avions voyagé
voyageais	voyagiez	avais voyagé	aviez voyagé
voyageait	voyageaient	avait voyagé	avaient voyagé
3 passé simple		**10 passé antérieur**	
voyageai	voyageâmes	eus voyagé	eûmes voyagé
voyageas	voyageâtes	eus voyagé	eûtes voyagé
voyagea	voyagèrent	eut voyagé	eurent voyagé
4 futur		**11 futur antérieur**	
voyagerai	voyagerons	aurai voyagé	aurons voyagé
voyageras	voyagerez	auras voyagé	aurez voyagé
voyagera	voyageront	aura voyagé	auront voyagé
5 conditionnel		**12 conditionnel passé**	
voyagerais	voyagerions	aurais voyagé	aurions voyagé
voyagerais	voyageriez	aurais voyagé	auriez voyagé
voyagerait	voyageraient	aurait voyagé	auraient voyagé
6 présent du subjonctif		**13 passé du subjonctif**	
voyage	voyagions	aie voyagé	ayons voyagé
voyages	voyagiez	aies voyagé	ayez voyagé
voyage	voyagent	ait voyagé	aient voyagé
7 imparfait du subjonctif		**14 plus-que-parfait du subjonctif**	
voyageasse	voyageassions	eusse voyagé	eussions voyagé
voyageasses	voyageassiez	eusses voyagé	eussiez voyagé
voyageât	voyageassent	eût voyagé	eussent voyagé

Impératif
voyage
voyageons
voyagez

V

Words and expressions related to this verb
un voyage   a trip
faire un voyage   to take a trip
un voyageur, une voyageuse   traveler
une agence de voyages   tourist agency
Bon voyage!   Have a good trip!
Bon voyage et bon retour!   Have a good trip and a safe return!

Les Voyages de Gulliver   *Gulliver's Travels*
les frais de voyage   travel expenses
un voyage d'affaires   business trip
un voyage d'agrément   pleasure trip
Quand je fais un voyage, j'envoie des cartes postales à mes amis.   When I take a trip, I send postcards to my friends.

Don't miss orthographically changing verbs on pages 32–34.

The subject pronouns are found on page 103.

Appendixes

Defective and impersonal verbs

Part. pr. *advenant* Part. passé *advenu* **advenir**

Irregular verb to happen, to occur, to come to pass

The Seven Simple Tenses		The Seven Compound Tenses	
Singular	Plural	Singular	Plural
1 présent de l'indicatif		8 passé composé	
il advient		**il est advenu**	
2 imparfait de l'indicatif		9 plus-que-parfait de l'indicatif	
il advenait		**il était advenu**	
3 passé simple		10 passé antérieur	
il advint		**il fut advenu**	
4 futur		11 futur antérieur	
il adviendra		**il sera advenu**	
5 conditionnel		12 conditionnel passé	
il adviendrait		**il serait advenu**	
6 présent du subjonctif		13 passé du subjonctif	
qu'il advienne		**qu'il soit advenu**	
7 imparfait du subjonctif		14 plus-que-parfait du subjonctif	
qu'il advînt		**qu'il fût advenu**	

Impératif
Qu'il advienne!
Let it come to pass!

Words and expressions related to this verb
Il advint que . . . It came to pass that . . .
Advienne que pourra . . . Come what may . . .
Voilà ce qu'il advint. That's what happened.
quoiqu'il advienne whatever may happen

This is an impersonal verb used in the third person singular only.

to be the matter, to be a question of

Reflexive regular **-ir** verb

The Seven Simple Tenses	The Seven Compound Tenses
Singular Plural	Singular Plural
1 présent de l'indicatif **il s'agit**	8 passé composé **il s'est agi**
2 imparfait de l'indicatif **il s'agissait**	9 plus-que-parfait de l'indicatif **il s'était agi**
3 passé simple **il s'agit**	10 passé antérieur **il se fut agi**
4 futur **il s'agira**	11 futur antérieur **il se sera agi**
5 conditionnel **il s'agirait**	12 conditionnel passé **il se serait agi**
6 présent du subjonctif **qu'il s'agisse**	13 passé du subjonctif **qu'il se soit agi**
7 imparfait du subjonctif **qu'il s'agît**	14 plus-que-parfait du subjonctif **qu'il se fût agi**

Impératif
[not in use]

Common idiomatic expressions using this verb
s'agir de   to have to do with, to be a matter of
De quoi s'agit-il?   What's the matter? What's up?
Voici ce dont il s'agit.   This is what it's about.
Il s'agit de mon vélo.   It's about my bike.

Note that this verb is impersonal and is used primarily in the tenses given above.

The Seven Simple Tenses		The Seven Compound Tenses	
Singular	Plural	Singular	Plural
1 présent de l'indicatif		8 passé composé	
il choit	**ils choient**	**ai chu**	**avons chu**
		as chu	**avez chu**
		a chu	**ont chu**
		9 plus-que-parfait de l'indicatif	
		avais chu	**avions chu**
		avais chu	**aviez chu**
		avait chu	**avaient chu**
3 passé simple		10 passé antérieur	
il chut	**ils churent**	**eus chu**	**eûmes chu**
		eus chu	**eûtes chu**
		eut chu	**eurent chu**
		11 futur antérieur	
		aurai chu	**aurons chu**
		auras chu	**aurez chu**
		aura chu	**auront chu**
		12 conditionnel passé	
		aurais chu	**aurions chu**
		aurais chu	**auriez chu**
		aurait chu	**auraient chu**

This is a defective verb. It is generally used in the above tenses.

Defective and impersonal verbs   **667**

clore
to close

The Seven Simple Tenses		The Seven Compound Tenses	
Singular	Plural	Singular	Plural
1 présent de l'indicatif		8 passé composé	
clos	—	**ai clos**	**avons clos**
clos	—	**as clos**	**avez clos**
clôt	**closent**	**a clos**	**ont clos**
		9 plus-que-parfait de l'indicatif	
		avais clos	**avions clos**
		avais clos	**aviez clos**
		avait clos	**avaient clos**
		10 passé antérieur	
		eus clos	**eûmes clos**
		eus clos	**eûtes clos**
		eut clos	**eurent clos**
4 futur		11 futur antérieur	
clorai	**clorons**	**aurai clos**	**aurons clos**
cloras	**clorez**	**auras clos**	**aurez clos**
clora	**cloront**	**aura clos**	**auront clos**
5 conditionnel		12 conditionnel passé	
clorais	**clorions**	**aurais clos**	**aurions clos**
clorais	**cloriez**	**aurais clos**	**auriez clos**
clorait	**cloraient**	**aurait clos**	**auraient clos**
6 présent du subjonctif		13 passé du subjonctif	
close	**closions**	**aie clos**	**ayons clos**
closes	**closiez**	**aies clos**	**ayez clos**
close	**closent**	**ait clos**	**aient clos**
		14 plus-que-parfait du subjonctif	
		eusse clos	**eussions clos**
		eusses clos	**eussiez clos**
		eût clos	**eussent clos**

Impératif
clos

This is a defective verb. It is generally used in the above tenses.

The Seven Simple Tenses		The Seven Compound Tenses	
Singular	Plural	Singular	Plural
1 présent de l'indicatif		8 passé composé	
il coûte	**ils coûtent**	**il a coûté**	**ils ont coûté**
2 imparfait de l'indicatif		9 plus-que-parfait de l'indicatif	
il coûtait	**ils coûtaient**	**il avait coûté**	**ils avaient coûté**
3 passé simple		10 passé antérieur	
il coûta	**ils coûtèrent**	**il eut coûté**	**ils eurent coûté**
4 futur		11 futur antérieur	
il coûtera	**ils coûteront**	**il aura coûté**	**ils auront coûté**
5 conditionnel		12 conditionnel passé	
il coûterait	**ils coûteraient**	**il aurait coûté**	**ils auraient coûté**
6 présent du subjonctif		13 passé du subjonctif	
qu'il coûte	**qu'ils coûtent**	**qu'il ait coûté**	**qu'ils aient coûté**
7 imparfait du subjonctif		14 plus-que-parfait du subjonctif	
qu'il coûtât	**qu'ils coûtassent**	**qu'il eût coûté**	**qu'ils eussent coûté**

Impératif
[not in use]

Sentences using this verb and words related to it
—Combien coûte cette table?
—Elle coûte dix mille euros.
—Et combien coûte ce lit?
—Il coûte dix mille euros aussi.
—Ils coûtent joliment cher!

coûteusement expensively, dearly
coûte que coûte at any cost
coûteux, coûteuse costly, expensive
Cela coûte joliment cher. That costs a pretty penny.
coûter cher, coûter peu to be expensive, inexpensive

coûter à qqn to cost someone;
Cela lui en a coûté la vie. That cost him his life.
coûter les yeux de la tête to be very expensive
le coût de la vie the cost of living

This verb is generally regarded as impersonal and is used primarily in the third person singular and plural.

Defective and impersonal verbs   669

échoir   Part. pr. **échéant**   Part. passé **échu**

to fall due

The Seven Simple Tenses		The Seven Compound Tenses	
Singular	Plural	Singular	Plural
1 présent de l'indicatif		8 passé composé	
échoit	**échoient**	**est échu**	**sont échus**
2 imparfait de l'indicatif		9 plus-que-parfait de l'indicatif	
échoyait	**échoyaient**	**était échu**	**étaient échus**
3 passé simple		10 passé antérieur	
échut	**échurent**	**fut échu**	**furent échus**
4 futur		11 futur antérieur	
échoira	**échoiront**	**sera échu**	**seront échus**
5 conditionnel		12 conditionnel passé	
échoirait	**échoiraient**	**serait échu**	**seraient échus**
6 présent du subjonctif		13 passé du subjonctif	
échoie	**échoient**	**soit échu**	**soient échus**
7 imparfait du subjonctif		14 plus-que-parfait du subjonctif	
échût	**échussent**	**fût échu**	**fussent échus**

Expression related to this verb
échoir à   to fall to

This verb is used only in the third person singular and plural.

to be necessary, must, to be lacking to (à), to need

The Seven Simple Tenses		The Seven Compound Tenses	
Singular	Plural	Singular	Plural
1 présent de l'indicatif **il faut**		8 passé composé **il a fallu**	
2 imparfait de l'indicatif **il fallait**		9 plus-que-parfait de l'indicatif **il avait fallu**	
3 passé simple **il fallut**		10 passé antérieur **il eut fallu**	
4 futur **il faudra**		11 futur antérieur **il aura fallu**	
5 conditionnel **il faudrait**		12 conditionnel passé **il aurait fallu**	
6 présent du subjonctif **qu'il faille**		13 passé du subjonctif **qu'il ait fallu**	
7 imparfait du subjonctif **qu'il fallût**		14 plus-que-parfait du subjonctif **qu'il eût fallu**	

Impératif
[not in use]

Common idiomatic expressions using this verb

comme il faut   as is proper
agir comme il faut   to behave properly
Il me faut de l'argent.   I need some money.
Il faut manger pour vivre.   It is necessary to eat in order to live.

Il ne faut pas parler sans politesse.   One must not talk impolitely.
Il faut . . .   It is necessary; one must
Il ne faut pas . . .   One must not . . .
Peu s'en faut . . .   It takes only a little . . .
s'en falloir   to be lacking
Il s'en faut de beaucoup . . .   It takes a lot . . .

This is an impersonal verb and it is used in the tenses given above with the subject *il*.

to fry

The Seven Simple Tenses		The Seven Compound Tenses	
Singular	Plural	Singular	Plural
1 présent de l'indicatif		8 passé composé	
fris		**ai frit**	**avons frit**
fris		**as frit**	**avez frit**
frit		**a frit**	**ont frit**
		9 plus-que-parfait de l'indicatif	
		avais frit	**avions frit**
		avais frit	**aviez frit**
		avait frit	**avaient frit**
		10 passé antérieur	
		eus frit	**eûmes frit**
		eus frit	**eûtes frit**
		eut frit	**eurent frit**
4 futur		11 futur antérieur	
frirai	**frirons**	**aurai frit**	**aurons frit**
friras	**frirez**	**auras frit**	**aurez frit**
frira	**friront**	**aura frit**	**auront frit**
5 conditionnel		12 conditionnel passé	
frirais	**fririons**	**aurais frit**	**aurions frit**
frirais	**fririez**	**aurais frit**	**auriez frit**
frirait	**friraient**	**aurait frit**	**auraient frit**
		13 passé du subjonctif	
		aie frit	**ayons frit**
		aies frit	**ayez frit**
		ait frit	**aient frit**
		14 plus-que-parfait du subjonctif	
		eusse frit	**eussions frit**
		eusses frit	**eussiez frit**
		eût frit	**eussent frit**

Impératif
fris
faisons frire
faites frire

Words and expressions related to this verb
faire frire   to fry (see note below)
pommes frites   French fries
une friteuse   frying basket
la friture   frying

des pommes de terre frites   fried potatoes
   (French style)
un bifteck-frites, un steak-frites   steak with
   French fries

This verb is generally used only in the persons and tenses given above. To supply the forms that are lacking, use the appropriate form of **faire** plus the infinitive **frire**, *e.g.*, the plural of the present indicative is: **nous faisons frire, vous faites frire, ils font frire**.

to lie down, to be lying down

The Seven Simple Tenses		The Seven Compound Tenses	
Singular	Plural	Singular	Plural

1 présent de l'indicatif

gis	gisons
gis	gisez
gît	gisent

2 imparfait de l'indicatif

gisais	gisions
gisais	gisiez
gisait	gisaient

Words and expressions related to this verb
un gisement   layer, deposit
un gisement de charbon   coal field
Ci-gît . . .   Here lies . . .
Ci-gisent . . .   Here lie . . .

gisant, gisante   lying, fallen, felled
un gîte   lodging, refuge, shelter
gîter   to lodge

This is a defective verb. It is generally used only in the above tenses. **Gésir** is used primarily in reference to the dead, to sick persons lying down, and to inanimate objects that have been felled.

grêler

Part. pr. grêlant   **Part. passé grêlé**

to hail (weather)

The Seven Simple Tenses	The Seven Compound Tenses
Singular Plural	Singular Plural
1 présent de l'indicatif **il grêle**	8 passé composé **il a grêlé**
2 imparfait de l'indicatif **il grêlait**	9 plus-que-parfait de l'indicatif **il avait grêlé**
3 passé simple **il grêla**	10 passé antérieur **il eut grêlé**
4 futur **il grêlera**	11 futur antérieur **il aura grêlé**
5 conditionnel **il grêlerait**	12 conditionnel passé **il aurait grêlé**
6 présent du subjonctif **qu'il grêle**	13 passé du subjonctif **qu'il ait grêlé**
7 imparfait du subjonctif **qu'il grêlât**	14 plus-que-parfait du subjonctif **qu'il eût grêlé**

Impératif
Qu'il grêle!   Let it hail!

Words and expressions related to this verb
la grêle   hail (weather)
une averse de grêle   hail storm
un grêlon   hailstone

grêle *adj.*   thin, slender, slim; **un bras grêle**
thin arm; **une voix grêle**   shrill voice

to shine, to gleam, to glisten

The Seven Simple Tenses		The Seven Compound Tenses	
Singular	Plural	Singular	Plural
1 présent de l'indicatif **il luit**		8 passé composé **il a lui**	
2 imparfait de l'indicatif **il luisait**		9 plus-que-parfait de l'indicatif **il avait lui**	
3 passé simple **il luisit**		10 passé antérieur **il eut lui**	
4 futur **il luira**		11 futur antérieur **il aura lui**	
5 conditionnel **il luirait**		12 conditionnel passé **il aurait lui**	
6 présent du subjonctif **qu'il luise**		13 passé du subjonctif **qu'il ait lui**	
7 imparfait du subjonctif **qu'il luisît**		14 plus-que-parfait du subjonctif **qu'il eût lui**	

Impératif
Qu'il luise!   Let it shine!

Words and expressions related to this verb
la lueur   glimmer, gleam, glow
luisant, luisante   shining
à la lueur d'une bougie   by candlelight
l'espoir luit encore   there is still a glimmer of
   hope

le lac luisait au soleil du matin   the lake
   glistened in the morning sunlight
Le soleil luit.   The sun is shining.
J'ai le nez qui luit.   My nose is shiny.
une lueur d'espoir   a glimmer of hope

messeoir (à)   Part. pr. **messéant**   Part. passé [not in use]

to be unbecoming to

The Seven Simple Tenses		The Seven Compound Tenses	
Singular	Plural	Singular	Plural
1 présent de l'indicatif			
messied	**messiéent**		
2 imparfait de l'indicatif			
messeyait	**messeyaient**		
4 futur			
messiéra	**messiéront**		
5 conditionnel			
messiérait	**messiéraient**		
6 présent du subjonctif			
messiée	**messiéent**		

This verb is defective and it is only used in the third person singular and plural.

The Seven Simple Tenses		The Seven Compound Tenses	
Singular	Plural	Singular	Plural
1 présent de l'indicatif **il neige**		8 passé composé **il a neigé**	
2 imparfait de l'indicatif **il neigeait**		9 plus-que-parfait de l'indicatif **il avait neigé**	
3 passé simple **il neigea**		10 passé antérieur **il eut neigé**	
4 futur **il neigera**		11 futur antérieur **il aura neigé**	
5 conditionnel **il neigerait**		12 conditionnel passé **il aurait neigé**	
6 présent du subjonctif **qu'il neige**		13 passé du subjonctif **qu'il ait neigé**	
7 imparfait du subjonctif **qu'il neigeât**		14 plus-que-parfait du subjonctif **qu'il eût neigé**	

Impératif
Qu'il neige!   Let it snow!

Words and expressions related to this verb
la neige   snow
un bonhomme de neige   a snowman
neige fondue   slush
neigeux, neigeuse   snowy
Blanche-Neige   Snow White
une boule de neige   snowball
lancer des boules de neige   to throw
    snowballs
une chute de neige   snowfall
déneiger   to clear the snow

la neige artificielle   artificial snow
la neige poudreuse   dusting of snow
la bataille de boules de neige   snowball fight
être submergé de travail   to be snowed under
    with work
les conditions d'enneigement   snow
    conditions
le bulletin d'enneigement   snow report
un chasse-neige   snowplow

Defective and impersonal verbs   **677**

paître

Part. pr. **paissant**   Part. passé [not in use]

to graze, to feed

The Seven Simple Tenses		The Seven Compound Tenses	
Singular	Plural	Singular	Plural

1   présent de l'indicatif

pais   **paissons**
pais   **paissez**
paît   **paissent**

2   imparfait de l'indicatif

paissais   **paissions**
paissais   **paissiez**
paissait   **paissaient**

4   futur

paîtrai   **paîtrons**
paîtras   **paîtrez**
paîtra   **paîtront**

5   conditionnel

paîtrais   **paîtrions**
paîtrais   **paîtriez**
paîtrait   **paîtraient**

6   présent du subjonctif

paisse   **paissions**
paisses   **paissiez**
paisse   **paissent**

Impératif
pais
paissons
paissez

This verb is used only in the above tenses.

to happen, to take place

The Seven Simple Tenses	The Seven Compound Tenses
Singular Plural	Singular Plural
1 présent de l'indicatif **il se passe**	8 passé composé **il s'est passé**
2 imparfait de l'indicatif **il se passait**	9 plus-que-parfait de l'indicatif **il s'était passé**
3 passé simple **il se passa**	10 passé antérieur **il se fut passé**
4 futur **il se passera**	11 futur antérieur **il se sera passé**
5 conditionnel **il se passerait**	12 conditionnel passé **il se serait passé**
6 présent du subjonctif **qu'il se passe**	13 passé du subjonctif **qu'il se soit passé**
7 imparfait du subjonctif **qu'il se passât**	14 plus-que-parfait du subjonctif **qu'il se fût passé**

Impératif
Qu'il se passe!   Let it happen!

Words and expressions related to this verb
Que se passe-t-il?   What's going on? What's happening?
Qu'est-ce qui se passe?   What's going on? What's happening?
Qu'est-ce qui s'est passé?   What happened?
se passer de qqch   to do without something
Je peux me passer de fumer.   I can do without smoking.

See also **passer** and **repasser.**

This verb is impersonal and is generally used in the third person singular only.

Defective and impersonal verbs   **679**

to rain

The Seven Simple Tenses	The Seven Compound Tenses
Singular Plural	Singular Plural
1 présent de l'indicatif **il pleut**	8 passé composé **il a plu**
2 imparfait de l'indicatif **il pleuvait**	9 plus-que-parfait de l'indicatif **il avait plu**
3 passé simple **il plut**	10 passé antérieur **il eut plu**
4 futur **il pleuvra**	11 futur antérieur **il aura plu**
5 conditionnel **il pleuvrait**	12 conditionnel passé **il aurait plu**
6 présent du subjonctif **qu'il pleuve**	13 passé du subjonctif **qu'il ait plu**
7 imparfait du subjonctif **qu'il plût**	14 plus-que-parfait du subjonctif **qu'il eût plu**

Impératif
Qu'il pleuve! Let it rain!

Sentences using this verb and words related to it
  Hier il a plu, il pleut maintenant, et je suis certain qu'il pleuvra demain.

la pluie   the rain
pluvieux, pluvieuse   rainy
pleuvoter   to drizzle
bruiner   to drizzle; un parapluie   umbrella
Il pleut à seaux.   It's raining buckets.

Il pleut à verse.   It's raining hard.
Il a beaucoup plu hier et cela m'a beaucoup plu.   It rained a lot yesterday and that pleased me a great deal. (See plaire)

Do not confuse the past part. of this verb with the past part. of **plaire**, which is identical.

The Seven Simple Tenses

Singular	Plural

1 présent de l'indicatif

pue	puons
pues	puez
pue	puent

2 imparfait de l'indicatif

puais	puions
puais	puiez
puait	puaient

4 futur

puerai	puerons
pueras	puerez
puera	pueront

5 conditionnel

puerais	puerions
puerais	pueriez
puerait	pueraient

Words and expressions related to this verb

puant, puante stinking; conceited

la puanteur stink, foul smell

Robert est un type puant. Robert is a stinker.

Cet ivrogne pue l'alcool; je me bouche le nez. This drunkard stinks of alcohol; I'm plugging my nose.

Joseph, ta chambre pue la porcherie. Joseph, your room smells like a pigsty.

This verb is used mainly in the above tenses.

If you have the need to use this verb in all the 14 tenses and the imperative, the forms are the same as for the verb **tuer** among the 501 verbs. Just replace the letter **t** with the letter **p**.

to seem

The Seven Simple Tenses	The Seven Compound Tenses
Singular Plural	Singular Plural
1 présent de l'indicatif **il semble**	8 passé composé **il a semblé**
2 imparfait de l'indicatif **il semblait**	9 plus-que-parfait de l'indicatif **il avait semblé**
3 passé simple **il sembla**	10 passé antérieur **il eut semblé**
4 futur **il semblera**	11 futur antérieur **il aura semblé**
5 conditionnel **il semblerait**	12 conditionnel passé **il aurait semblé**
6 présent du subjonctif **qu'il semble**	13 passé du subjonctif **qu'il ait semblé**
7 imparfait du subjonctif **qu'il semblât**	14 plus-que-parfait du subjonctif **qu'il eût semblé**

Impératif
[not in use]

Words and expressions related to this verb

Il me semble difficile.   It seems difficult to me.

Il me semble que . . .   It seems to me that . . .

Il semble bon   It seems good.

Il semble inutile.   It seems useless.

à ce qu'il me semble . . .   to my mind . . .

C'est ce qui me semble.   That's what it looks like to me.

This verb has regular forms in all the tenses (like **ressembler** among the 501 verbs in this book) but much of the time it is used impersonally in the forms given above with **il** (*it*) as the subject.

to be becoming, to suit

The Seven Simple Tenses

Singular	Plural

1   présent de l'indicatif
il sied   **ils siéent**

2   imparfait de l'indicatif
il seyait   **ils seyaient**

4   futur
il siéra   **ils siéront**

5   conditionnel
il siérait   **ils siéraient**

6   présent du subjonctif
qu'il siée   **qu'ils siéent**

This verb is defective and it is generally used only in the above persons and tenses.
Cela vous sied.   That suits you well.
Ce chapeau te sied si bien!   That hat looks so good on you!
Connaissez-vous la pièce *Le Deuil sied à Electre* **d'Eugene O'Neill?**   Do you know the play
   Mourning Becomes Electra by Eugene O'Neill?
seoir à   to be becoming to

See also **s'asseoir.**

The form **séant** is used as an adj.: **Il n'est pas séant de faire cela.**   It's unbecoming to do that.

Defective and impersonal verbs   683

to suffice, to be sufficient, to be enough

The Seven Simple Tenses		The Seven Compound Tenses	
Singular	Plural	Singular	Plural
1 présent de l'indicatif **il suffit**		8 passé composé **il a suffi**	
2 imparfait de l'indicatif **il suffisait**		9 plus-que-parfait de l'indicatif **il avait suffi**	
3 passé simple **il suffit**		10 passé antérieur **il eut suffi**	
4 futur **il suffira**		11 futur antérieur **il aura suffi**	
5 conditionnel **il suffirait**		12 conditionnel passé **il aurait suffi**	
6 présent du subjonctif **qu'il suffise**		13 passé du subjonctif **qu'il ait suffi**	
7 imparfait du subjonctif **qu'il suffît**		14 plus-que-parfait du subjonctif **qu'il eût suffi**	

Impératif
Qu'il suffise!

Words and expressions related to this verb
la **suffisance**   sufficiency
suffisamment   sufficiently
Cela suffit!   That's quite enough!
Suffit!   Enough! Stop it!
Ma famille suffit à mon bonheur.   My family
   is enough for my happiness.

Ça ne te suffit pas?   That's not enough for
   you?
Y a-t-il suffisamment à manger?   Is there
   enough to eat?

This verb is generally impersonal and is used in the third person singular as given in the above tenses.

The Seven Simple Tenses	The Seven Compound Tenses
Singular Plural	Singular Plural
1 présent de l'indicatif **il tonne**	8 passé composé **il a tonné**
2 imparfait de l'indicatif **il tonnait**	9 plus-que-parfait de l'indicatif **il avait tonné**
3 passé simple **il tonna**	10 passé antérieur **il eut tonné**
4 futur **il tonnera**	11 futur antérieur **il aura tonné**
5 conditionnel **il tonnerait**	12 conditionnel passé **il aurait tonné**
6 présent du subjonctif **qu'il tonne**	13 passé du subjonctif **qu'il ait tonné**
7 imparfait du subjonctif **qu'il tonnât**	14 plus-que-parfait du subjonctif **qu'il eût tonné**

Impératif
Qu'il tonne!   Let it thunder!

Common idiomatic expressions using this verb and words related to it

le tonnerre   thunder
Tonnerre!   By thunder!
C'est du tonnerre!   That's terrific!

un coup de tonnerre   a clap of thunder
un tonnerre d'acclamations   thundering
   applause

This verb is impersonal and is used in the third person singular.

Guide to French pronunciation

The purpose of the guide on the next page is to help you pronounce French words as correctly as possible. However, the best way to improve your pronunciation is to imitate spoken French that you hear from speakers who pronounce French accurately. To accomplish this, you may want to consult the Barron's book *Pronounce It Perfectly in French*, which comes with three CDs that give you practice, during pauses, in imitating French spoken by French speakers.

In French there are several spellings for the same sound; for example, the following spellings are all pronounced ay, as in the English word *say*.

et   (j')ai   (parl)é   (av)ez   (all)er   (l)es

Consonant sounds are approximately the same in French and English. When speaking French, you must raise your voice slightly on the last sound when there is more than one in a group; for example, in pronouncing s'il vous plaît (please), raise your voice slightly on *plaît*.

There are only four nasal vowel sounds in French. They are expressed in the following catchy phrase, which means "a good white wine."

un   bon   vin   blanc

How do you nasalize a vowel in French? Instead of letting breath (air) out your mouth, you must push it up your nose so that it does not come out your mouth.

Now, become familiar with the guide to French pronunciation. Practice pronouncing each sound first and then try it out by reading aloud some of the words and expressions on the pages that follow.

Approximate pronunciation

IPA Phonetic Symbol	English Word	French Word
[a]	something like the vowel sound in T**o**m	l**a**
[ɑ]	**ah**!	p**a**s
[e]	s**ay**	**ai**
[ə]	**the**	l**e**
[i]	s**ee**	**i**c**i**
[ɛ]	**e**gg	m**è**re
[y]	(not an English sound, but close to the sound of f**ew** without pronouncing the y sound that comes before the **u** sound or the **w** that comes after it)	l**u**
[ɥ]	(not an English sound, but close to "**you + ee**" without the y sound)	h**ui**t
[ɲ]	can**y**on	monta**gne**
[o]	als**o**	h**ô**tel
[ɔ]	d**o**ne	d**o**nne
[u]	t**oo**	**ou**
[ʃ]	**sh**ip	**ch**ose
[s]	ki**ss**	**c**e**ss**e
[ø]	(not an English sound, but close to p**u**dding)	p**eu**x
[œ]	(not an English sound, but close to p**ur**r)	h**eu**re
[j]	**y**es	jo**y**eux
[z]	**z**ero	**z**éro
[ʒ]	mea**s**ure	**j**e

Nasal Vowels

[œ̃]	(not an English sound, but close to s**ung**)	**un**
[ɔ̃]	(not an English sound, but close to s**ong**)	b**on**
[ɛ̃]	(not an English sound, but close to s**ang**)	v**in**
[ɑ̃]	(not an English sound, but close to thr**ong**)	bl**anc**

Verbs used in weather expressions

Quel temps fait-il? / What's the weather like?

(a) With **Il fait** . . .

Il fait beau / The weather is fine; The weather is beautiful.
Il fait beau temps / The weather is beautiful.
Il fait bon / It's nice; It's good.
Il fait brumeux / It's misty.
Il fait chaud / It's warm.
Il fait clair / It is clear.
Il fait de l'orage / It's storming; there is a thunderstorm.
Il fait des éclairs / There's lightning.
Il fait doux / It's mild.
Il fait du soleil / It's sunny.
Il fait du tonnerre / It's thundering. (You can also say: **Il tonne.**)
Il fait du vent / It's windy.
Il fait frais / It is cool.
Il fait froid / It's cold.
Il fait glissant / It is slippery.
Il fait humide / It's humid.
Il fait jour / It is daylight.
Il fait lourd / The weather is sultry.
Il fait mauvais / The weather is bad.
Il fait nuit / It is dark.
Il fait sec / It's dry.
Il fait une chaleur épouvantable / It's awfully (frightfully) hot.

(b) With **Il fait un temps** . . .

Il fait un temps affreux / The weather is frightful.
Il fait un temps calme / The weather is calm.
Il fait un temps couvert / The weather is cloudy.
Il fait un temps de saison / The weather is seasonal.
Il fait un temps épouvantable / The weather is frightful.
Il fait un temps lourd / It's muggy.
Il fait un temps magnifique / The weather is magnificent.
Il fait un temps pourri / The weather is rotten.
Il fait un temps serein / The weather is serene.
Il fait un temps superbe / The weather is superb.

(c) With **Le temps + verb** . . .

Le temps menace / The weather is threatening.
Le temps s'éclaircit / The weather is clearing up.
Le temps se couvre / The sky is overcast.
Le temps se gâte / The weather is getting bad.
Le temps se met au beau / The weather is getting beautiful.
Le temps se met au froid / It's getting cold.
Le temps se radoucit / The weather is getting nice again.

Le temps se rafraîchit / The weather is getting cold.
Le temps se remet / The weather is clearing up.

(d) With Le ciel est . . .

Le ciel est bleu / The sky is blue.
Le ciel est calme / The sky is calm.
Le ciel est couvert / The sky is cloudy.
Le ciel est gris / The sky is gray.
Le ciel est serein / The sky is serene.

(e) With other verbs

Il gèle / It's freezing.
Il grêle / It's hailing.
Il neige / It's snowing.
Il pleut / It's raining.
Il pleut à verse / It's raining hard.
Il tombe de la grêle / It's hailing.
Il va grêler / It's going to hail.
Il tonne / It's thundering.
Je sors par tous les temps / I go out in all kinds of weather.
Quelle est la prévision scientifique du temps? Quelle est la météo? / What is the
weather forecast?

Verbs with prepositions

French verbs are used with certain prepositions or no preposition at all. At times, the preposition used with a particular verb changes the meaning entirely, *e.g.*, **se passer** means *to happen* and **se passer de** means *to do without*.

When you look up a verb among the 501 to find its verb forms (or in the section of over 2,600 verbs), also consult the following categories so that you will learn what preposition that verb requires, if any.

Consult all the categories that are given below; *e.g.*, verbs that take à + noun, verbs that take à + inf., verbs that take **de** + noun, verbs that take **de** + inf., verbs that take à + noun + **de** + inf., verbs that take prepositions other than à or **de**, verbs that require no preposition, and verbs that do not require any preposition in French whereas in English a preposition is used.

The following are used frequently in French readings and in conversation.

A. *The following verbs take* à + *noun*

assister à qqch (à une assemblée, à une réunion, à un spectacle, *etc.***)** to attend a gathering, a meeting, a theatrical presentation, *etc.*, or to be present at: **Allez-vous assister à la conférence du professeur Godard?** Are you going to attend (to be present at) Prof. Godard's lecture? **Oui, je vais y assister.** Yes, I am going to attend it.

convenir à qqn ou à qqch to please (to be pleasing to), to suit (to be suitable to): **Cette robe ne convient pas à la circonstance.** This dress does not suit the occasion. **Cela ne convient pas à mon père.** That is not suitable to my father.

demander à qqn to ask someone: **Demandez à la dame où s'arrête l'autobus.** Ask the lady where the bus stops.

déplaire à qqn to displease someone, to be displeasing to someone: **Cet homme-là déplaît à ma soeur.** That man is displeasing to my sister. **Cet homme-là lui déplaît.** That man is displeasing to her.

désobéir à qqn to disobey someone: **Ce chien ne désobéit jamais à son maître.** This dog never disobeys his master. **Il ne lui désobéit jamais.** He never disobeys him.

être à qqn to belong to someone: **Ce livre est à Victor.** This book belongs to Victor. [Note this special possessive meaning when you use être + à.]

faire attention à qqn ou à qqch to pay attention to someone or to something: **Faites attention au professeur.** Pay attention to the professor. **Faites attention aux marches.** Pay attention to the steps.

se fier à qqn to trust someone: **Je me fie à mes parents.** I trust my parents. **Je me fie à eux.** I trust them.

goûter à qqch to taste a little, to sample a little something: **Goûtez à ce gâteau; il est délicieux et vous m'en direz des nouvelles.** Taste a little of this cake; it is delicious and you will rave about it. **Goûtez-y!** Taste it!

s'habituer à qqn ou à qqch to get used to someone or something: **Je m'habitue à mon nouveau professeur.** I am getting used to my new teacher. **Je m'habitue à lui.** I am getting used to him. **Je m'habitue à ce travail.** I am getting used to this work. **Je m'y habitue.** I am getting used to it.

s'intéresser à qqn ou à qqch to be interested in someone or something: **Je m'intéresse aux sports.** I am interested in sports.

jouer à to play (a game or sport): **Il aime bien jouer à la balle.** He likes to play ball. **Elle aime bien jouer au tennis.** She likes to play tennis.

manquer à qqn to miss someone (because of an absence): **Vous me manquez.** I miss you. **Ses enfants lui manquent.** He (or She) misses his (or her) children.

se mêler à qqch to mingle with, to mix with, to join in: **Il se mêle à tous les groupes à l'école.** He mixes with all the groups at school.

nuire à qqn ou à qqch to harm someone or something: **Ce que vous faites peut nuire à la réputation de votre famille.** What you are doing may harm the reputation of your family.

obéir à qqn to obey someone: **Une personne honorable obéit à ses parents.** An honorable person obeys his (her) parents.

s'opposer à qqn ou à qqch to oppose someone or something: **Je m'oppose aux idées du président.** I am opposed to the president's ideas.

penser à qqn ou à qqch to think of (about) someone or something: **Je pense à mes amis.** I am thinking of my friends. **Je pense à eux.** I am thinking of them. **Je pense à mon travail.** I am thinking about my work. **J'y pense.** I am thinking about it. BUT: **Que pensez-vous de cela?** What do you think of that?

plaire à qqn to please, to be pleasing to someone: **Mon mariage plaît à ma famille.** My marriage pleases my family. **Mon mariage leur plaît.** My marriage pleases them (is pleasing to them).

réfléchir à qqch to think over something: **Il faut que j'y réfléchisse.** I must think it over.

répondre à qqn ou à qqch to answer someone or something: **J'ai répondu au professeur.** I answered the teacher. **Je lui ai répondu.** I answered him. **J'ai répondu à la lettre.** I answered the letter. **J'y ai répondu.** I answered it.

résister à qqn ou à qqch to resist someone or something: **Le criminel a résisté à l'agent de police.** The criminal resisted the police officer.

ressembler à qqn to resemble someone: **Il ressemble beaucoup à sa mère.** He resembles his mother a lot.

réussir à qqch   to succeed in something.   réussir à un examen   to pass an examination: Il a réussi à l'examen.   He passed the exam.

serrer la main à qqn   to shake hands with someone: Bobby, va serrer la main à la
dame.   Bobby, go shake hands with the lady.

songer à qqn ou à qqch   to dream (to think) of someone or something: Je songe aux
grandes vacances.   I'm dreaming of the summer vacation.

survivre à qqn ou à qqch   to survive someone or something: Il a survécu à
l'ouragan.   He survived the hurricane.

téléphoner à qqn   to telephone someone: Marie a téléphoné à Paul.   Marie telephoned Paul.   Elle lui a téléphoné.   She telephoned him.

B. *The following verbs take* à + *inf.*

aider à   to help: Roger aide son petit frère à faire sa leçon de mathématiques.
Roger is helping his little brother do the math lesson.

aimer à   to like: J'aime à lire.   I like to read. [Note that aimer à + inf. is used primarily in literary style; ordinarily, use aimer + inf.]

s'amuser à   to amuse oneself, to enjoy, to have fun: Il y a des élèves qui s'amusent
à mettre le professeur en colère.   There are pupils who have fun making the
teacher angry.

apprendre à   to learn: J'apprends à lire.   I am learning to read.

s'apprêter à   to get ready: Je m'apprête à aller au bal.   I am getting ready to go to
the dance.

arriver à   to succeed in: Jacques arrive à comprendre le subjonctif.   Jack is
succeeding in learning the subjunctive.

s'attendre à   to expect: Je m'attendais à trouver une salle de classe vide.   I was
expecting to find an empty classroom.

autoriser à   to authorize, to allow: Je vous autorise à quitter cette salle de classe
tout de suite.   I authorize you to leave this classroom immediately.

avoir à   to have, to be obliged (to do something):   J'ai à faire mes devoirs ce soir.
I have to do my homework tonight.

commencer à   to begin: Il commence à pleuvoir.   It is beginning to rain. [Note that
commencer de + inf. is also correct.]

consentir à   to consent: Je consens à venir chez vous après le dîner.   I consent
(agree) to come to your house after dinner.

continuer à   to continue: Je continue à étudier le français.   I am continuing to
study French. [Note that continuer de + inf. is also correct.]

décider qqn à to persuade someone: **J'ai décidé mon père à me prêter quelques euros.** I persuaded my father to lend me a few euros.

se décider à to make up one's mind: **Il s'est décidé à l'épouser.** He made up his mind to marry her.

demander à to ask, to request: **Elle demande à parler.** She asks to speak. [Note that here the subjects are the same—she is the one who is asking to speak. If the subjects are different, use **demander de**: **Je vous demande de parler.** I am asking you to talk.]

encourager à to encourage: **Je l'ai encouragé à suivre un cours de français.** I encouraged him to take a course in French.

s'engager à to get oneself around (to doing something): **Je ne peux pas m'engager à accepter ses idées frivoles.** I can't get myself around to accepting his (her) frivolous ideas.

enseigner à to teach: **Je vous enseigne à lire en français.** I am teaching you to read in French.

s'habituer à to get used (to): **Je m'habitue à parler français couramment.** I am getting used to speaking French fluently.

hésiter à to hesitate: **J'hésite à répondre à sa lettre.** I hesitate to reply to her (his) letter.

inviter à to invite: **Monsieur et Madame Boivin ont invité les Béry à dîner chez eux.** Mr. and Mrs. Boivin invited the Bérys to have dinner at their house.

se mettre à to begin: **L'enfant se met à rire.** The child is beginning to laugh.

parvenir à to succeed: **Elle est parvenue à devenir docteur.** She succeeded in becoming a doctor.

persister à to persist: **Je persiste à croire que cet homme est innocent.** I persist in believing that this man is innocent.

se plaire à to take pleasure in: **Il se plaît à taquiner ses amis.** He takes pleasure in teasing his friends.

recommencer à to begin again: **Il recommence à pleuvoir.** It is beginning to rain again.

résister à to resist: **Je résiste à croire qu'il est malhonnête.** I resist believing that he is dishonest.

réussir à to succeed in: **Henri a réussi à me convaincre.** Henry succeeded in convincing me.

songer à to dream, to think: **Elle songe à trouver un millionnaire.** She is dreaming of finding a millionaire.

tarder à to delay: **Mes amis tardent à venir.** My friends are late in coming.

tenir à to insist, to be anxious: *Je tiens absolument à voir mon enfant cet instant.* I am very anxious to see my child this instant.

venir à to happen (to): *Si je viens à voir mes amis en ville, je vous le dirai.* If I happen to see my friends downtown, I will tell you (so).

C. *The following verbs take* de + *noun*

s'agir de to be a question of, to be a matter of: *Il s'agit de l'amour.* It is a matter of love.

s'approcher de to approach: *La dame s'approche de la porte et elle l'ouvre.* The lady approaches the door and opens it.

changer de to change: *Je dois changer de train à Paris.* I have to change trains in Paris.

dépendre de to depend on: *Je veux sortir avec toi mais cela dépend des circonstances.* I want to go out with you but that depends on the circumstances.

douter de to doubt: *Je doute de la véracité de ce que vous dites.* I doubt the veracity of what you are saying.

se douter de to suspect: *Je me doute de ses actions.* I suspect his (her) actions.

féliciter de to congratulate on: *Je vous félicite de vos progrès.* I congratulate you on your progress.

jouer de to play (a musical instrument): *Je sais jouer du piano.* I know how to play the piano.

jouir de to enjoy: *Mon père jouit d'une bonne santé.* My father enjoys good health.

manquer de to lack: *Cette personne manque de politesse.* This person lacks courtesy. *Mon frère manque de bon sens.* My brother lacks common sense.

se méfier de to distrust, to mistrust, to beware of: *Je me méfie des personnes que je ne connais pas.* I distrust persons whom I do not know.

se moquer de to make fun of: *Les enfants aiment se moquer d'un singe.* Children like to make fun of a monkey.

s'occuper de to be busy with: *Madame Boulanger s'occupe de son mari infirme.* Mrs. Boulanger is busy with her disabled husband. *Je m'occupe de mes affaires.* I mind my own business. *Occupez-vous de vos affaires!* Mind your own business!

partir de to leave: *Il est parti de la maison à 8 h.* He left the house at 8 o'clock.

se passer de to do without: *Je me passe de sel.* I do without salt.

se plaindre de to complain about: *Il se plaint toujours de son travail.* He always complains about his work.

remercier de   to thank: **Je vous remercie de votre bonté.**   I thank you for your kindness. [Use **remercier de** + an abstract noun or + inf.;   Use **remercier pour** + a concrete object; *e.g.*,   **Je vous remercie pour le cadeau.**   I thank you for the present.]

se rendre compte de   to realize: **Je me rends compte de la condition de cette personne.**   I realize the condition of this person.

rire de   to laugh at;   **Tout le monde rit de cette personne.**   Everybody laughs at this person.

se servir de   to employ, to use, to make use of: **Je me sers d'un stylo quand j'écris une lettre.**   I use a pen when I write a letter.

se soucier de   to care about, to be concerned about: **Marc se soucie de ses amis.**   Marc cares about his friends.

se souvenir de   to remember: **Oui, je me souviens de Gervaise.**   Yes, I remember Gervaise.   **Je me souviens de lui.**   I remember him.   **Je me souviens d'elle.**   I remember her.   **Je me souviens de l'été passé.**   I remember last summer.   **Je m'en souviens.**   I remember it.

tenir de   to take after (to resemble):   **Julie tient de sa mère.**   Julie takes after her mother.

D. *The following verbs take* **de** + *inf.*

s'agir de   to be a question of, to be a matter of: **Il s'agit de faire les devoirs tous les jours.**   It is a matter of doing the homework every day.

avoir peur de   to be afraid of: **Le petit garçon a peur de traverser la rue seul.**   The little boy is afraid of crossing the street alone.

cesser de   to stop, to cease: **Il a cessé de pleuvoir.**   It has stopped raining.

commencer de   to begin: **Il a commencé de pleuvoir.**   It has started to rain. [Note that **commencer à** + inf. is also correct.]

continuer de   to continue: **Il continue de pleuvoir.**   It's still raining OR It's continuing to rain. [Note that **continuer à** + inf. is also correct.]

convenir de faire qqch   to agree to do something: **Nous avons convenu de venir chez vous.**   We agreed to coming to your place.

craindre de   to be afraid of, to fear: **La petite fille craint de traverser la rue seule.**   The little girl is afraid of crossing the street alone.

décider de   to decide: **J'ai décidé de partir tout de suite.**   I decided to leave immediately.   **Il a décidé d'acheter la maison.**   He decided to buy the house.

demander de   to ask, to request: **Je vous demande de parler.**   I am asking you to speak. [Note that here the subjects are different: I am asking you to speak; whereas, when the subjects are the same, use damander à: Elle demande à parler. She is asking to speak. Je demande à parler. I am asking to speak.]

se dépêcher de to hurry: Je me suis dépêché de venir chez vous pour vous dire quelque chose. I hurried to come to your place in order to tell you something.

empêcher de to keep from, to prevent: Je vous empêche de sortir. I prevent you from going out.

s'empresser de to hurry: Je m'empresse de venir chez toi. I am hurrying to come to your place.

essayer de to try: J'essaye d'ouvrir la porte mais je ne peux pas. I'm trying to open the door but I can't.

féliciter de to congratulate: On m'a félicité d'avoir gagné le prix. I was congratulated on having won the prize.

finir de to finish: J'ai fini de travailler sur cette composition. I have finished working on this composition.

gronder de to scold: La maîtresse a grondé l'élève d'avoir fait beaucoup de fautes dans le devoir. The teacher scolded the pupil for having made many errors in the homework.

se hâter de to hurry: Je me hâte de venir chez toi. I am hurrying to come to your house.

manquer de to neglect to, to fail to, to forget to: Guy a manqué de compléter sa leçon de français. Guy neglected to complete his French lesson.

offrir de to offer: J'ai offert d'écrire une lettre pour elle. I offered to write a letter for her.

oublier de to forget: J'ai oublié de vous donner la monnaie. I forgot to give you the change.

persuader de to persuade: J'ai persuadé mon père de me prêter quelques euros. I persuaded my father to lend me a few euros.

prendre garde de to take care not to: Prenez garde de tomber. Be careful not to fall.

prendre le parti de faire qqch to decide to do something: Théodore n'a pas hésité à prendre le parti de voter pour elle. Theodore did not hesitate to decide to vote for her.

prier de to beg: Je vous prie d'arrêter. I beg you to stop.

promettre de to promise: J'ai promis de venir chez toi à 8 h. I promised to come to your place at 8 o'clock.

refuser de to refuse: Je refuse de le croire. I refuse to believe it.

regretter de to regret, to be sorry: Je regrette d'être obligé de vous dire cela. I am sorry to be obliged to tell you that.

remercier de to thank: *Je vous remercie d'être venu si vite.* I thank you for coming (having come) so quickly. [Use remercier de + inf. or + abstract noun. Use remercier pour + concrete object.]

se souvenir de to remember: *Tu vois? Je me suis souvenu de venir chez toi.* You see? I remembered to come to your house.

tâcher de to try: *Tâche de finir tes devoirs avant de sortir.* Try to finish your homework before going out.

venir de to have just (done something): *Je viens de manger.* I have just eaten *or* I just ate.

E. *The following verbs commonly take* à + *noun* + de + *inf.*

The model to follow is: *J'ai conseillé à Robert de suivre un cours de français.* I advised Robert to take a course in French.

conseiller à to advise: *J'ai conseillé à Jeanne de se marier.* I advised Joan to get married.

défendre à to forbid: *Mon père défend à mon frère de fumer.* My father forbids my brother to smoke.

demander à to ask, to request: *J'ai demandé à Marie de venir.* I asked Mary to come.

dire à to say, to tell: *J'ai dit à Charles de venir.* I told Charles to come.

interdire à to forbid: *Mon père interdit à mon frère de fumer.* My father forbids my brother to smoke.

ordonner à to order: *J'ai ordonné au chauffeur de ralentir.* I ordered the driver to slow down.

permettre à to permit: *J'ai permis à l'étudiant de partir quelques minutes avant la fin de la classe.* I permitted the student to leave a few minutes before the end of class.

promettre à to promise: *J'ai promis à mon ami d'arriver à l'heure.* I promised my friend to arrive on time.

téléphoner à to telephone: *J'ai téléphoné à Marcel de venir me voir.* I phoned Marcel to come to see me.

F. *The following verbs take prepositions other than* à *or* de

commencer par + inf. to begin by + present participle: *La présidente a commencé par discuter les problèmes de la société.* The president began by discussing the problems in society.

continuer par + inf. to continue by + pres. part.: *La maîtresse a continué la conférence par lire un poème.* The teacher continued the lecture by reading a poem.

entrer dans + noun   to enter, to go in: **Elle est entrée dans le restaurant.**   She went in the restaurant.

être en colère contre qqn   to be angry with someone: **Monsieur Laroche est toujours en colère contre ses voisins.**   Mr. Laroche is always angry with his neighbors.

finir par + inf.   to end up by + pres. part.:   **Clément a fini par épouser une femme plus âgée que lui.**   Clement ended up marrying a woman older than he.

s'incliner devant qqn   to bow to someone: **La princesse s'incline devant la reine.**   The princess is bowing to the queen.

insister pour + inf.   to insist on, upon: **J'insiste pour obtenir tous mes droits.**   I insist on obtaining all my rights.

se marier avec qqn   to marry someone: **Elle va se marier avec lui.**   She is going to marry him.

se mettre en colère   to become angry, upset: **Monsieur Leduc se met en colère facilement.**   Mr. Leduc gets angry easily.

se mettre en route   to start out, to set out: **Ils se sont mis en route dès l'aube.**   They started out at dawn.

remercier pour + a concrete noun   to thank for: **Je vous remercie pour le joli cadeau.**   I thank you for the pretty present. [Remember to use **remercier pour + a concrete object**; use **remercier de + an abstract noun** or **+ inf.**   **Je vous remercie de votre bonté.**   I thank you for your kindness.   **Je vous remercie d'être venue si vite.**   I thank you for coming so quickly.]

G. *The following verbs require no preposition before the infinitive*

adorer + inf.   to adore, to love: **Madame Morin adore mettre tous ses bijoux avant de sortir.**   Mrs. Morin loves to put on all her jewelry before going out.

aimer + inf.   to like: **J'aime lire.**   I like to read. [You may also say: **J'aime à lire**, but **aimer + à + inf.** is used primarily in literary style.]

aimer mieux + inf.   to prefer: **J'aime mieux rester ici.**   I prefer to stay here.

aller + inf.   to go: **Je vais faire mes devoirs maintenant.**   I am going to do my homework now.

apercevoir + inf.   to perceive: **J'aperçois avancer l'ouragan.**   I notice the hurricane advancing. [This is a verb of perception. You may also say: **J'aperçois l'ouragan qui s'avance.**]

compter + inf.   to intend: **Je compte aller en France l'été prochain.**   I intend to go to France next summer.

croire + inf.   to believe: **Il croit être innocent.**   He believes he is innocent.

désirer + inf.   to desire, to wish: **Je désire prendre une tasse de café.**   I desire to have a cup of coffee.

devoir + inf.   to have to, ought to: **Je dois faire mes devoirs avant de sortir.**   I have to do my homework before going out.

écouter + inf.   to listen to: **J'écoute chanter les enfants.**   I am listening to the children singing. [This is a verb of perception. You may also say: **J'écoute les enfants qui chantent.**]

entendre + inf.   to hear: **J'entends chanter les enfants.**   I hear the children singing. [This is a verb of perception. You may also say: **J'entends les enfants qui chantent.**]

espérer + inf.   to hope: **J'espère aller en France.**   I hope to go to France.

faire + inf.   to cause, to make, to have something done by someone: **Le professeur fait travailler les élèves dans la salle de classe.**   The teacher has the pupils work in the classroom. (See **causative faire**, page 676.)

falloir + inf.   to be necessary: **Il faut être honnête.**   One must be honest.

laisser + inf.   to let, to allow: **Je vous laisse partir.**   I am letting you go.

oser + inf.   to dare: **Ce garçon ose dire n'importe quoi.**   This boy dares to say anything.

paraître + inf.   to appear, to seem: **Elle paraît être capable.**   She appears to be capable.

penser + inf.   to think, to plan, to intend: **Je pense aller à Paris.**   I intend to go to Paris.

pouvoir + inf.   to be able, can: **Je peux marcher mieux maintenant après l'accident.**   I can walk better now after the accident.

préférer + inf.   to prefer: **Je préfère manger maintenant.**   I prefer to eat now.

regarder + inf.   to look at: **Je regarde voler les oiseaux.**   I am looking at the birds flying. [This is a verb of perception. You may also say: **Je regarde les oiseaux qui volent.**]

savoir + inf.   to know, to know how: **Je sais nager.**   I know how to swim.

sentir + inf.   to feel: **Je sens s'approcher l'ouragan.**   I feel the hurricane approaching. [This is a verb of perception. You can also say: **Je sens l'ouragan qui s'approche.**]

sentir + inf.   to smell: **Je sens venir une odeur agréable du jardin.**   I smell a pleasant fragrance coming from the garden. [This is another verb of perception. You may also say: **Je sens une odeur agréable qui vient du jardin.**]

valoir mieux + inf.   to be better: **Il vaut mieux être honnête.**   It is better to be honest.

venir + inf.   to come: Gérard vient voir ma nouvelle voiture.   Gerard is coming to see my new car.

voir + inf.   to see: Je vois courir les enfants.   I see the children running. [This is another verb of perception. You may also say: Je vois les enfants qui courent.]

vouloir + inf.   to want: Je veux venir chez vous.   I want to come to your house.

H. *The following verbs do not require a preposition, whereas in English a preposition is used*

---

approuver   to approve of: J'approuve votre décision.   I approve of your decision.

attendre   to wait for: J'attends l'autobus depuis vingt minutes.   I have been waiting for the bus for twenty minutes.

chercher   to look for: Je cherche mon livre.   I'm looking for my book.

demander   to ask for: Je demande une réponse.   I am asking for a reply

écouter   to listen to: J'écoute la musique.   I am listening to the music.   J'écoute le professeur.   I am listening to the teacher.

envoyer chercher   to send for: J'ai envoyé chercher le docteur.   I sent for the doctor.

essayer   to try on: Elle a essayé une jolie robe.   She tried on a pretty dress.

habiter   to live in: J'habite cette maison.   I live in this house.

ignorer   to be unaware of: J'ignore ce fait.   I am unaware of this fact.

mettre   to put on: Elle a mis la robe rouge.   She put on the red dress.

payer   to pay for: J'ai payé le dîner.   I paid for the dinner.

pleurer   to cry about, to cry over: Elle pleure la perte de son petit chien.   She is crying over the loss of her little dog.

prier   to pray to: Elle prie le ciel.   She is praying to the heavens.   Elle prie la Vierge.   She is praying to the Holy Mother.

puer   to stink of: Cet ivrogne pue l'alcool.   This drunkard stinks of alcohol.

regarder   to look at: Je regarde le ciel.   I am looking at the sky.

sentir   to smell of: Robert, ta chambre sent la porcherie.   Robert, your room smells like a pigsty (pigpen).

soigner   to take care of: Cette personne soigne les pauvres.   This person takes care of (cares for) poor people.

Index of common irregular French verb forms identified by infinitive

The purpose of this index is to help you identify those verb forms that cannot be readily identified because they are irregular in some way. For example, if you come across the verb form *fut* (which is very common) in your French readings, this index will tell you that *fut* is a form of être. Then you look up être in this book and you will find that verb form on the page where all the forms of être are given.

Verb forms whose first few letters are the same as the infinitive have not been included because they can easily be identified by referring to the alphabetical listing of the 501 verbs in this book.

After you find the verb of an irregular verb form, if it is not among the 501 verbs, consult the list of over 2,600 French verbs conjugated like model verbs.

A

a   avoir
ai   avoir
aie   avoir
aient   avoir
aies   avoir
aille   aller
ait   avoir
as   avoir
asseyais, *etc.*   asseoir
assieds   asseoir
assiérai, *etc.*   asseoir
assis   asseoir
assoie   asseoir
assoirai, *etc.*   asseoir
assoyais, *etc.*   asseoir
aurai, *etc.*   avoir
avaient   avoir
avais   avoir
avait   avoir
avez   avoir
aviez   avoir
avions   avoir
avons   avoir
ayant   avoir
ayons, *etc.*   avoir

B

bats   battre
bois   boire

boivent   boire
bu   boire
bûmes   boire
burent   boire
bus, bût   boire
busse, *etc.*   boire
but   boire
bûtes   boire
buvant   boire
buvez   boire
buvons   boire

C

connu   connaître
craignis, *etc.*   craindre
crois   croire
croîs   croître
croissais, *etc.*   croître
croit   croire
croît   croître
croyais, *etc.*   croire
cru   croire
crû, crue   croître
crûmes   croire, croître
crurent   croire
crûrent   croître
crus   croire
crûs   croître
crûsse, *etc.*   croître
crût   croire, croître

D

devais, *etc.* devoir
dîmes dire
dis, disais, *etc.* dire
disse, *etc.* dire
dit, dît dire
dois, *etc.* devoir
doive, *etc.* devoir
dors, *etc.* dormir
dû, due devoir
dûmes devoir
dus, dussent devoir
dut, dût, dûtes devoir

E

es être
est être
étais, *etc.* être
été être
êtes être
étiez être
eu avoir
eûmes avoir
eurent avoir
eus avoir
eusse, *etc.* avoir
eut, eût avoir
eûtes avoir

F

faille faillir, falloir (Def. and Imp.)
fais, *etc.* faire
fallut, *etc.* falloir (Def. and Imp.)
fasse, *etc.* faire
faudra faillir, falloir (Def. and Imp.)
faudrait faillir, falloir (Def. and Imp.)
faut faillir, falloir (Def. and Imp.)
faux faillir
ferai, *etc.* faire
fîmes faire
firent faire
fis, *etc.* faire
font faire
fûmes être

furent être
fus, *etc.* être
fut, fût être
fuyais, *etc.* fuir

G

gis, gisons, *etc.* gésir (Def. and Imp.)
gît gésir (Def. and Imp.)

I

ira, irai, iras, *etc.* aller

L

lis, *etc.* lire
lu lire
lus, *etc.* lire

M

mens mentir
mets mettre
meure, *etc.* mourir
meus, *etc.* mouvoir
mîmes mettre
mirent mettre, mirer
mis mettre
misses, *etc.* mettre
mit mettre
mort mourir
moulons, *etc.* moudre
moulu moudre
mû, mue mouvoir
mussent mouvoir
mut mouvoir

N

nais, *etc.* naître
naquîmes, *etc.* naître
né naître
nuis, nuit, *etc.* nuire

O

offert   offrir
omis   omettre
ont   avoir

P

paie (paye)   payer
pars   partir
paru, *etc.*   paraître
peignis, *etc.*   peindre
peins, *etc.*   peindre
pendant   pendre
peut, *etc.*   pouvoir
peuvent   pouvoir
plaigne, *etc.*   plaindre
plu   plaire, pleuvoir (Def. and Imp.)
plurent   plaire
plut, plût, *etc.*   plaire, pleuvoir
    (Def. and Imp.)
plûtes   plaire
pourrai, *etc.*   pouvoir
prenne, *etc.*   prendre
prîmes   prendre
prirent   prendre
pris   prendre
prisse, *etc.*   prendre
pu   pouvoir
puis   pouvoir
puisse, *etc.*   pouvoir
pûmes, *etc.*   pouvoir
purent   pouvoir
pus   pouvoir
pusse   pouvoir
put, pût   pouvoir

R

reçois, *etc.*   recevoir
reçûmes, *etc.*   recevoir
relu   relire
résolu, *etc.*   résoudre
reviens, *etc.*   revenir
revins, *etc.*   revenir
ri, rie, riant, *etc.*   rire
riiez   rire
ris, *etc.*   rire

S

sache, *etc.*   savoir
sais, *etc.*   savoir
saurai, *etc.*   savoir
séant   seoir (Def. and Imp.)
sens, *etc.*   sentir
serai, *etc.*   être
sers, *etc.*   servir
seyant   seoir (Def. and Imp.)
sied   seoir (Def. and Imp.)
siéent   seoir (Def. and Imp.)
siéra, *etc.*   seoir (Def. and Imp.)
sois, *etc.*   être
sommes   être
sont   être
sors, *etc.*   sortir
soyez   être
soyons   être
su   savoir
suis   être, suivre
suit   suivre
sûmes   savoir
surent   savoir
survécu   survivre
sus, susse, *etc.*   savoir
sut, sût   savoir

T

tais, *etc.*   se taire
teigne, *etc.*   teindre
tiendrai, *etc.*   tenir
tienne, *etc.*   tenir
tînmes   tenir
tins, *etc.*   tenir
trayant   traire
tu   se taire
tûmes   se taire
turent   se taire
tus   se taire
tusse, *etc.*   se taire
tut, tût   se taire

V

va aller
vaille valoir
vainque, *etc.* vaincre
vais aller
vas aller
vaudrai, *etc.* valoir
vaux, *etc.* valoir
vécu, *etc.* vivre
vécûmes, *etc.* vivre
verrai, *etc.* voir
veuille, *etc.* vouloir
veulent vouloir
veut, *etc.* vouloir
viendrai, *etc.* venir
vienne, *etc.* venir

viens, *etc.* venir
vîmes voir
vînmes venir
vinrent venir
vins, *etc.* venir
virent voir
vis vivre, voir
visse, *etc.* voir
vit vivre, voir
vît voir
vîtes voir
voie, *etc.* voir
vont aller
voudrai, *etc.* vouloir
voulu, *etc.* vouloir
voyais, *etc.* voir
vu voir

English-French verb index

The purpose of this index is to give you instantly the French verb for the English verb you have in mind to use. We have listed the most common definition to save you time if you do not have at your fingertips a standard English-French dictionary.

If the French verb you want is reflexive (*e.g.*, s'appeler or se lever), you will find it listed alphabetically under the first letter of the verb and not under the reflexive pronoun *s'* or *se*.

When you find the French verb you need, look up the form of the model verb that has a similar conjugation (*e.g.*, bark is aboyer, which is conjugated like verb 187, which is envoyer). If there is no verb number listed (*e.g.*, amuser) that means that the French verb is one of the 501 model verbs.

Note: The mark * in front of the letter *h* in a French verb denotes that it is aspirate; make no liaison and use *je* instead of *j'*; *me* instead of *m'*.

A

abandon   abandonner (171)
abandon, quit   délaisser (274)
abdicate   abdiquer (219)
abhor   exécrer (203)
abhor   abhorrer (27)
abjure   abjurer (148)
able, to be   pouvoir
abolish   abolir
abominate   abominer (465)
abort   avorter (27)
abound   affluer (114)
abound   foisonner (171)
abound   surabonder (27)
abound in   abonder en (26)
abound in   regorger de (283)
abrade   abraser (27)
abridge   abréger (52)
absent oneself from   s'absenter de (26)
absolve   absoudre
absorb   absorber (385)
absorb   résorber (240)
abstain   s'abstenir
abstract   abstraire (474) (no passé simple or imp. subj.)
abuse   injurier (389)
abuse   abuser de qqch (32)
abuse   maltraiter (475)

accelerate   accélérer (356)
accentuate, stress   accentuer (483)
accept   agréer (128)
accept   accepter
accessorize   accessoiriser (486)
acclaim   acclamer
acclimate   acclimater (27)
accommodate   accommoder (147)
accompany   accompagner
accomplish   accomplir (392)
accord   accorder
accost   accoster (160)
accost   aborder (26)
accredit   accréditer (251)
acculturate   acculturer (27)
accumulate   accumuler (81)
accuse   accuser
accuse oneself   s'accuser (16, 33)
accustom   habituer (483)
accustom oneself   s'habituer (33, 483)
achieve   achever
acquire   aquérir
acquit   acquitter (de) (374)
act   agir
activate   actionner (171)

activist/militant, to be an   militer (251)
adapt to   adapter à (8)
add   ajouter
add a sound track   sonoriser (486)
add more   rajouter (28)
add up   additionner (171)
address   adresser
address someone   s'adresser à qqn (33, 79)
adhere to   adhérer à (87)
adjust   ajuster (28)
administer   administrer (26)
admire   admirer
admit   avouer (269)
admit   admettre
admonish   admonester (27)
adopt   adopter (8)
adore   adorer
adorn   parer (435)
adulate   aduler (81)
advance   avancer
advance (oneself)   s'avancer (33, 61)
advise   conseiller
advise against   déconseiller (109)
advocate   préconiser (486)

advocate prôner (27)
aerate aérer (87)
affiliate to s'affilier à (33, 41)
affirm affirmer (227)
afflict with affliger de (119)
age vieillir
agglutinate agglutiner (329)
aggravate exacerber (27)
aggravate aggraver (276)
agree consentir
agree acquiescer (342)
agree with concorder avec (11)
aid aider
aim at viser à (486)
aim, point braquer (284)
air aérer (87)
air condition climatiser (486)
alarm alarmer (310)
alarm effarer (22)
alienate aliéner (87)
align aligner (26)
allocate allouer (281)
allow laisser
allow permettre
ally allier (41)
almost (do something) faillir
alter altérer (87)
alternate alterner (27)
amass amasser (92)
amass amonceler (38)
amaze épater (241)
ambush s'embusquer (33, 284)
amend amender (27)
Americanize américaniser (32)
amplify with/by amplifier de (322)
amputate amputer (251)
amuse amuser
amuse divertir (210)
amuse récréer (128)
amuse oneself s'amuser
analyze analyser (32)
anchor ancrer (27)
anger courroucer (342)
anger someone fâcher qqn (82) (See 216; aux. avoir)

anglicize angliciser (23)
angry, to become se fâcher
anguish, to cause angoisser (27)
animate animer (27)
annex annexer (27)
annihilate anéantir (229)
annihilate annihiler (27)
announce annoncer
annoy agacer
annoy enquiquiner (329)
annoy contrarier (41)
annoy embêter (47)
annoy vexer (27)
annoyed, to become s'énerver (33, 276)
annul annuler (81)
anoint oindre (268)
answer répondre
antedate antidater (28)
anticipate anticiper (329)
ape singer (283)
apologize s'excuser
appall consterner (27)
appear apparaître
appear paraître
appear before court comparaître (324)
applaud for applaudir de (229)
apply appliquer (219)
apply for (a position) postuler (81)
apply makeup to one's own face se farder (83, 240)
apply makeup to someone's face farder (240)
appoint mandater (241)
appoint to préposer à (350)
appreciate apprécier
apprehend (legal term) appréhender (27)
approach approcher
approach s'approcher (33, 43)
appropriate s'approprier (83, 212)
approve homologuer (307)
approve (of) approuver
arabize arabiser (486)
arbitrate arbitrer (27)
arch cambrer (27)

arch arquer (284)
arch cintrer (27)
archive archiver (27)
argue bagarrer (435)
arise survenir (491)
arise procéder de (87)
arm armer (238)
arrange disposer (350)
arrange arranger
arrange agencer (342)
arrange ordonner (171)
arrest arrêter
arrive arriver
arrive ahead of devancer (61)
articulate articuler (81)
ascend monter
ask (for) demander
ask again redemander (147)
ask for réclamer (71)
asphyxiate asphyxier (41)
aspire to ambitionner de (171)
assail assaillir
assassinate assassiner (159)
assemble assembler (407)
assemble rassembler (407)
assign assigner (441)
assimilate assimiler (27)
assist seconder (240)
associate (something with) associer (qqch à) (41)
associate (with) adjoindre à (268)
assume assumer (27)
assure assurer
astonish étonner
astound ahurir (229)
atomize atomiser (486)
atone se racheter (17, 122)
attach again rattacher (82)
attack agresser (23)
attack attaquer (219)
attack assaillir
attain atteindre
attain accéder à (87)
attend assister (à)
attract attirer
attribute to attribuer à (114)
authorize autoriser (16)

authorize **habiliter** (251)

automate **automatiser** (486)

avenge **venger**

avoid **esquiver** (276)

avoid **éviter**

awaken **éveiller** (109)

award **adjuger** (283)

award **décerner** (470)

B

back, to give **rendre**

backdate **antidater** (28)

badger, pester someone **tanner qqn** (171)

balance **équilibrer** (158)

balance **pondérer** (203)

balance **balancer**

ban **proscrire** (177)

bandage **panser** (134)

bandage **bander** (27)

bang **claquer** (284)

banish from **bannir de** (229)

banter **marivauder** (27)

banter, to exchange **badiner** (167)

baptize **baptiser** (32)

bar **barrer** (21)

bark **aboyer** (187)

base upon **baser sur** (32)

bathe **baigner** (10)

battle **batailler** (477)

bawl, cry **brailler** (477)

be **être**

be green **verdoyer** (187)

bead **perler** (326)

beat **battre**

beat up **rouer (de coups)** (269)

beat with a stick **bâtonner** (171)

beautify **embellir** (229)

become **devenir**

become again **redevenir** (164)

becoming, to be **seoir** (Def. and Imp.)

bed, to go back to **se recoucher** (122)

bed, to go to **se coucher**

bed, to put to **coucher**

beg **mendier** (212)

beg **prier**

beg **supplier**

begin **débuter** (173)

begin **commencer**

begin **se mettre**

begin **entamer** (71)

begin again **recommencer** (99)

behave **se comporter** (80, 349)

belch **éructer** (28)

believe **croire**

belong **appartenir**

bend **courber** (481)

bend **recourber** (240)

bend **plier**

bend **fléchir** (383)

bend **ployer** (187)

bequeath **léguer** (87, 307)

beseech **conjurer** (54)

besiege **assiéger**

bet **miser** (486)

bet **gager** (305)

bet on **parier sur** (129)

betray **trahir**

beware **se méfier**

bewitch **ensorceler** (38)

bid, to increase **renchérir** (94)

bifurcate **bifurquer** (284)

bill **facturer** (54)

billet **cantonner** (171)

bite **mordre**

bivouac **bivouaquer** (219)

black, to stain **mâchurer** (54)

blacken **noircir** (229)

blame **blâmer**

blame **reprocher qqch à qqn** (43)

blaspheme **blasphémer** (356)

blaze **flamboyer** (187)

bleach **javelliser** (486)

bleach hair **blondir** (210)

bleed **saigner** (441)

blend **malaxer** (27)

bless **bénir**

blind **aveugler** (27)

blindfold **bander** (27)

blink **cligner** (10)

blink **clignoter** (27)

bloat **boursoufler** (445)

block **enrayer** (330)

block up **bloquer** (219)

block up **boucher** (469)

blog **bloguer** (307)

blond, to become **blondir** (210)

bloody **ensanglanter** (90)

bloom **s'épanouir** (214)

blow **souffler**

blow away (slang) **flinguer** (307)

blow one's nose **se moucher** (122)

blow up **péter** (87)

bluff **bluffer** (26)

blur **estomper** (247)

blur **brouiller** (233)

blush **rougir**

boast **se targuer de** (122, 307)

boil **bouillir**

bold, to make **enhardir** (210)

bombard **bombarder** (385)

bone (remove bones) **désosser** (79)

boo ***huer** (483)

boot (computer) **démarrer** (27)

boot (computer) **amorcer** (342)

border **border** (248)

bore **barber** (27)

bore **ennuyer**

bored, to be **s'ennuyer** (55, 192)

bored, to be **s'ennuyer**

born, to be **naître**

borrow **emprunter**

borrow again **remprunter** (188)

botch **torchonner** (171)

botch up **bâcler** (445)

bother **contrarier** (41)

bother **embêter** (47)

bother **gêner**

bother   emmerder   (240)
bother   incommoder   (96)
bother   tracasser   (84)
bow down before   s'incliner
    devant   (33, 329)
box   boxer   (26)
boycott   boycotter   (373)
brag   se vanter   (90, 122)
braid   tresser   (73)
braid   natter   (246)
brake   freiner   (329)
brandish   brandir   (210)
bread   paner   (27)
break   casser
break   rompre
break   briser   (32)
break (body part)   se casser
break (wave)   déferler
    (326)
break in (mechanical)   roder
    (96)
break one's pledge   se
    parjurer   (122, 272)
break through   poindre
    (268)
breakfast, to have   déjeuner
breast-feed   allaiter   (27)
breathe   respirer   (466)
brew   brasser   (79)
bridle   brider   (329)
brighten with sunlight
    ensoleiller   (109)
bring   amener
bring   apporter
bring back   ramener   (31)
bring back   rapporter   (40)
bring back   remmener
    (290)
bring closer to   rapprocher
    de   (43)
bring up to date   actualiser
    (16)
bristle   se *hérisser   (122,
    486)
broadcast   retransmettre
    (294)
broadcast   diffuser   (32)
broadcast   radiodiffuser
    (32)
bronze   bronzer   (134)
brown   brunir   (229)
brown   rissoler   (498)

browse books   bouquiner
    (329)
bruise   contusionner   (171)
bruise   meurtrir   (249)
brush   brosser
brush   effleurer   (466)
brush against   frôler   (498)
brush oneself   se brosser
brutalize, bully   brutaliser
    (486)
bubble   bouillonner   (171)
bubble   pétiller   (477)
buckle   boucler   (469)
bud   bourgeonner   (171)
build   bâtir
build   construire
build   édifier   (41)
build (with masonry)
    maçonner   (171)
bully   brimer   (27)
bump into someone   croiser
    (86)
bump off   zigouiller   (233)
burglarize   cambrioler   (26)
burn   flamber   (240)
burn   brûler
burn up   consumer   (32)
burn up   carboniser   (486)
burp   éructer   (28)
burp   roter   (96)
burst forth   fuser   (32)
burst into   éclater en   (176)
burst with   crever de   (278)
bury   enfouir   (270)
bury   ensevelir   (229)
bury   inhumer   (238)
bury   enterrer
busy, to be   s'occuper
butter   beurrer   (26)
button   boutonner   (171)
buy   acheter
buy back   racheter   (17)
buzz   bourdonner   (171)
by, to get   se débrouiller
bypass   contourner   (470)

C

cackle   caqueter   (267)
cajole   enjôler   (498)
cajole   cajoler   (27)
calcify   calcifier   (41)
calculate   calculer   (81)
calibrate   calibrer   (27)

call   appeler
call again   rappeler
call onself   s'appeler
calm   calmer   (27)
calm down   se calmer   (27)
calm down, pacify   apaiser
    (27)
camouflage   camoufler
    (445)
camp   camper   (235)
can   pouvoir
cancel   annuler   (81)
cancel an order
    décommander   (98)
canonize   canoniser   (486)
capitalize   capitaliser   (486)
capitulate   capituler   (81)
capsize   chavirer   (27)
captivate   captiver   (167)
capture   capturer   (27)
capture   accaparer   (27)
carbonate   gazéifier   (212)
care about   se soucier de
    (41 (aux. être))
caress   caresser   (353)
caricature   caricaturer   (21)
carry   porter
carry away   emporter   (349)
carry away   entraîner   (27)
carry forward   reporter
    (349)
carry out   réaliser   (486)
cart (something) around
    trimbaler   (326)
cash   encaisser   (274)
castrate   castrer   (27)
catalog   cataloguer   (307)
catch (a ball)   réceptionner
    (443)
catch a cold   s'enrhumer
    (33, 238)
catch a glimpse   entrevoir
    (497)
catch on   piger   (218)
catch up   rattraper   (59)
catechize   catéchiser   (486)
cause   occasionner   (171)
cause   causer
cease   cesser
celebrate   célébrer   (356)
celebrate   fêter   (363)
celebrate at a carnival (Qué.)
    carnavaler   (27)

compensate compenser (336)

compensate dédommager (305)

compete concurrencer (342)

compete with concourir avec (125)

compile compiler (251)

complain rouspéter (87)

complain se plaindre

complete compléter (87)

complicate compliquer (219)

complicate embrouiller (233)

compliment complimenter (60)

comply with obtempérer à (203)

compose composer (350)

comprise comporter (349)

compromise compromettre (294)

compromise transiger (218)

computerize informatiser (486)

conceal celer (297)

conceal dissimuler (81)

concede concéder (87)

conceive concevoir

concentrate (oneself) on se concentrer sur (80, 299)

concentrate on concentrer sur (299)

conclude conclure

concoct concocter (349)

condemn condamner (98)

condescend to condescendre à (394)

condition conditionner (171)

conduct conduire

confer conférer (356)

confess confesser (73)

configure configurer (27)

confine confiner (329)

confirm confirmer (227)

confiscate confisquer (219)

conform to se conformer à (122, 227)

confound confondre (231)

confront affronter (113)

confront confronter (113)

confuse tournebouler (421)

confuse troubler (407)

congratulate féliciter (251)

conjecture conjecturer (54)

conjugate conjuguer (307)

connect connecter (349)

connect brancher

connect (Internet) se connecter à (122, 349)

connect to raccorder à (11)

conquer conquérir

conquer vaincre

consecrate consacrer (54)

consecrate sacrer (22)

consent consentir

consider considérer (87)

consist of consister en (215)

console consoler (27)

consolidate consolider (329)

conspire conspirer (21)

constitute constituer (483)

constrain contraindre

construct bâtir

construct construire

consult compulser (32)

consult consulter (375)

consume consommer (310)

contact contacter (28)

contain contenir

contaminate contaminer (329)

contemplate contempler (407)

content contenter (464)

continue continuer

contradict contredire

contrast with contraster avec (160)

contribute contribuer (114)

contribute cotiser (32)

control contrôler (498)

control by radio téléguider (27)

convene convoquer (219)

converge converger (283)

converge confluer (114)

converse converser (492)

converse dialoguer (307)

convert convertir (229)

convince convaincre

convulse convulser (336)

coo roucouler (421)

cook cuisiner (159)

cook cuire

cool refroidir (229)

cooler, to get fraîchir (383)

cooperate coopérer (356)

coordinate coordonner (171)

cope se débrouiller (122, 233)

copy copier (212)

corner somebody acculer (81)

correct amender (27)

correct corriger

correspond correspondre (401)

correspond (with) cadrer (27)

corroborate corroborer (27)

corrupt corrompre

corset corseter (297)

cost coûter (Def. and Imp.)

cough tousser

cough, to have a slight toussoter (96)

cough, to have a slight toussailler (477)

counsel conseiller

count dénombrer (407)

count nombrer (22)

count compter

count again recompter (103)

count on tabler sur (407)

counterfeit contrefaire (223)

couple accoupler (27)

couple coupler (421)

couple jumeler (38)

cover couvrir

cover again recouvrir (126)

cover in sand ensabler (407)

covet convoiter (447)

crack craquer (219)

crack fendiller (477)

crack crevasser (84)

crackle pétiller (477)

crackle (object) craqueler (38)

crackle (sound) crépiter (215)

cram (for a test) potasser (84)

cram for an exam bachoter (96)

cram, shove in fourrer (22)

crawl ramper (247)

crazy about, to be raffoler de (498)

creak, grind grincer (99)

crease froisser (353)

crease plisser (73)

create créer

create an uproar chahuter (8)

credit with créditer de (251)

crisscross quadriller (477)

criticize critiquer (219)

crochet crocheter (17)

cross traverser

cross croiser (86)

cross off (a list) radier (212)

cross out raturer (54)

cross out rayer (330)

crossbreed métisser (274)

crouch se tapir (66) (aux. être)

crown couronner (171)

crucify crucifier (212)

crumple chiffonner (171)

crumple froisser (353)

crunch croquer (219)

crush concasser (84)

crush écrabouiller (233)

crush écraser (183)

crush broyer (187)

cry chialer (421)

cry pleurer

cry out s'écrier (33, 41)

cry out s'exclamer (9)

cry out crier

crystallize cristalliser (486)

cuddle se blottir (214, 229)

cuddle câliner (329)

culminate culminer (329)

cultivate cultiver (329)

curl friser (486)

curl up se recroqueviller (414)

curse pester (27)

curse maudire

curve arquer (284)

curve cintrer (27)

cushion amortir (229)

cut couper

cut tailler (477)

cut again recouper (124)

cut down trees (Qué.) bûcher (285)

cut into sections tronçonner (483)

cut the head off of something étêter (47)

cut the throat of égorger (283)

cut up découper (124)

D

damage endommager (305)

damage accidenter (27)

damage abîmer (27)

damn damner (239)

dance dancer

dare oser

darken assombrir (229)

darken obscurcir (229)

darken foncer (371)

date from dater de (241)

daub (with) barbouiller (de) (233)

dawdle lambiner (329)

dawdle s'attarder (33)

daydream rêvasser (84)

dazzle éblouir (229)

deafen assourdir (229)

debit débiter (251)

debug (computer) déboguer (307)

decalcify décalcifier (41)

decamp décamper (27)

decant soutirer (466)

decapitate décapiter (251)

deceive leurrer (22)

deceive tromper (247) (See 480)

deceive décevoir

decide décider

decimate décimer (27)

decipher déchiffrer (27)

declaim déclamer (71)

declare déclarer (69)

decline décliner (465)

decolorize décolorer (22)

decompose décomposer (350)

decongest décongestionner (171)

deconstruct déconstruire (133)

decorate with décorer de (22)

decorate with orner de (470)

decrease décroître

decrease diminuer

decree décréter (87)

decry décrier (129)

dedicate (a book) dédicacer à (342)

dedicate to dédier à (212)

deduce déduire

deduct déduire

deepen approfondir (229)

defame diffamer (71)

defend défendre

defer to déférer à (356)

define définir (229)

deflate dégonfler (498)

deforest déboiser (486)

deform déformer (227)

defraud frauder (27)

defrost dégivrer (27)

defuse désamorcer (342)

defy braver (276)

degrade dégrader (27)

degrade avilir (423)

dehydrate déshydrater (241)

deign daigner (10)

delay attarder (240)

delay retarder (240)

delay tarder (240)

delay temporiser (486)

delegate déléguer (87, 307)

deliberate délibérer (356)

delight ravir (422)

delight réjouir (270)

delist (Internet) délister (160)

deliver to livrer à (27)

demand revendiquer (256)

demand ransom rançonner (443)

demobilize démobiliser (486)

democratize démocratiser (486)

demolish démolir

demonstrate démontrer (299)

demote destituer (483)

denationalize dénationaliser (486)

denigrate dénigrer (21)

denote dénoter (498)

denounce dénoncer (371)

dent cabosser (79)

deny nier

deny démentir (291)

depart partir

depart from se départir de (434)

depend (on) dépendre

depend on se fier

depict dépeindre

depilate épiler (329)

deplore déplorer (22)

deploy déployer (187)

depoliticize dépolitiser (486)

depopulate dépeupler (326)

deport déporter (349)

deposit consigner (441)

deposit déposer (350)

deprave dépraver (276)

depreciate déprécier (41)

depress déprimer (220)

deprive priver (276)

derive from dériver de (329)

desalinate dessaler (326)

descend descendre

describe décrire

desert déserter (40)

deserve mériter

designate désigner (441)

desire désirer

despair désespérer (203)

despise mépriser (486)

destabilize déstabiliser (486)

destine/intend for destiner à (329)

destroy détruire

detail détailler (477)

detain détenir (463)

detect détecter (160)

deteriorate détériorer (27)

determine déterminer (329)

detest détester

detonate détoner (461)

detoxify désintoxiquer (219)

devalue dévaluer (114)

devastate dévaster (259)

devastate saccager (305)

develop évoluer (213)

develop développer

deviate dévier (41)

devote dévouer (269)

devote oneself to se consacrer à (54, 122)

devour dévorer (27)

diagnose diagnostiquer (219)

dial (a number) composer (350)

dictate dicter (253)

die mourir

die périr

differ différer (203)

dig creuser (32)

dig again recreuser (32)

dig out/up bêcher (285)

dig up déterrer (196)

dig, study hard piocher (82)

digest digérer (203)

digitize numériser (486)

dine dîner

direct diriger (119)

direct towards acheminer (465)

dirty encrasser (84)

dirty souiller

disabuse of détromper de (317) (See 480)

disadvantage défavoriser (486)

disadvantage désavantager (305)

disappear disparaître

disappoint décevoir

disapprove of désapprouver (44)

disarm désarmer (238)

discern discerner (27)

disconcert déconcerter (160)

disconnect déconnecter (27)

disconnect débrancher (285)

discontinue discontinuer (114)

discount (financial) escompter (103)

discourage from décourager de (305)

discover découvrir

discover, reveal déceler (297)

discredit déconsidérer (356)

discredit discréditer (215)

discriminate discriminer (465)

discuss débattre (67)

discuss discuter

disdain dédaigner (10)

disembark from débarquer de (219)

disentangle débrouiller (233)

disfigure déparer (27)

disguise oneself se déguiser (122, 486)

disgust dégoûter (244)

disgust écoeurer

dishevel écheveler (38)

dishonor déshonorer (22)

disillusioned, to become déchanter (90)

disinfect désinfecter (160)

disintegrate désintégrer (356)

disjoint désarticuler (81)

dislocate démettre (294)

dislodge déloger (305)

dismantle something démonter qqch (298) (aux. avoir)

dismay consterner (27)

dismiss congédier (212)

disobey désobéir à (314)

disorient déboussoler (498)

disorient dépayser (486)

dispatch dépêcher (27)

disperse disperser (478)

displace déplacer (342)

display afficher (94)

displease déplaire

dispossess déposséder (87)

dispute contester (160)

dispute something disputer de qqch (425)

disqualify disqualifier (212)

dissect disséquer (87, 284)

disseminate disséminer (465)

dissipate dissiper (251)

dissociate dissocier (41)

dissolve dissoudre (6)

dissuade from dissuader de (340)

distinguish discriminer (465)

distinguish distinguer (307)

distort fausser (353)

distract distraire (474)

distress navrer (27)

distress chagriner (329)

distribute distribuer (114)

disturb déranger

disturb dérégler (87)

diverge diverger (283)

diversify diversifier (41)

divert dériver (329)

divert détourner (470)

divide into diviser en (32)

divide up lotir (66)

divide up répartir (229)

divide up into pieces morceler (38)

divulge divulguer (307)

divulge a secret ébruiter (215)

do faire

do one's own hair se coiffer (122)

do someone's hair coiffer qqn (443)

do without something se priver de qqch (276)

document documenter (60)

dog someone s'acharner contre qqn (27, 33)

domesticate domestiquer (219)

dominant over, to be primer sur (220)

dominate dominer (329)

don (clothing) affubler (407)

doodle, scribble crayonner (171)

dose, to measure doser (321)

double doubler (481)

doubt douter

down, to go descendre

down, to go back redescendre (157)

down, to take descendre

download télécharger (91)

doze sommeiller (109)

doze somnoler (498)

drag traîner (167)

drain drainer (27)

drain égoutter (374)

drain, dry assécher (429)

draw dessiner

draw again retirer

draw from puiser (486)

draw up, erect dresser (23)

draw/incite a crowd ameuter (374)

dread, fear redouter de (173)

dream rêver

dream songer

dredge draguer (307)

dress (someone) vêtir

dress again rhabiller (477)

dress someone, something habiller qqn, qqch (477) (See 250; aux. avoir)

dressed again, to get se rhabiller (250)

dressed, to get s'habiller

dribble (sports) dribbler (326)

drink boire

drip dégoutter (244)

drive away bouter (28)

drivel radoter (96)

drizzle bruiner (27)

drone ânonner (171)

drool baver (276)

drown se noyer

drug droguer (307)

drum tambouriner (329)

drunk, to get se soûler (122, 421)

dry sécher

dry out dessécher (87)

dry out essorer (22)

dry up tarir (249)

dub (audio) doubler (481)

dull, to make affadir (229)

dupe duper (317)

duplicate dupliquer (219)

dust épousseter (267)

dye teindre

dynamite dynamiter (251)

E

earn gagner

ease alléger (52)

eat manger

economize économiser (486)

edit éditer (251)

educate éduquer (219)

effect effectuer (483)

egosurf egosurfer (27)

elect élire

electrify électriser (486)

elide élider (251)

eliminate éliminer (465)

elucidate élucider (26)
elude éluder (32)
emanate from émaner de (27)
emasculate émasculer (81)
embalm embaumer (27)
embark embarquer (219)
embarrass embarrasser (84)
embellish with agrémenter de (60)
embroider broder (96)
emigrate émigrer (21)
emit émettre (294)
emit dégager
empty vidanger (283)
empty vider (251)
empty out dévaliser (486)
enchant enchanter (90)
encircle encercler (27)
encircle with ceindre de (334)
encircle with cercler de (27)
enclose enclaver (276)
enclose renfermer (227)
encompass englober (27)
encourage encourager
encrust encroûter (244)
end terminer
end up in aboutir à/dans (229)
endorse endosser (79)
endow douer (269)
endure endurer (54)
engage engager (305)
engaged, to get se fiancer (122, 342)
engrave buriner (465)
engrave graver (276)
engulf engloutir (66)
enjoy jouir
enjoy oneself s'amuser
enlarge agrandir (245)
enlarge élargir (229)
enliven aviver (486)
ennoble anoblir (423)
enough, to be suffire
enraged, to be enrager (305)
enrich enrichir (229)
entangle s'empêtrer (33, 299)

enter entrer
entertain divertir (210)
entertain récréer (128)
entertain égayer
enthuse enthousiasmer (27)
entice aguicher (285)
entrust confier (212)
entwine enlacer (342)
enumerate énumérer (356)
envelope envelopper (235)
envisage envisager (305)
envy envier (212)
equal égaler (326)
equalize égaliser (486)
equip with équiper de (215)
equip with tools outiller (477)
equivalent, to be équivaloir (488)
eradicate éradiquer (219)
erase effacer (342)
erase gommer (310)
erect ériger (119)
erode s'effriter (33, 215)
erode éroder (96)
escape s'échapper (27, 33)
escape échapper
escape s'enfuir
escape se sauver
escape from s'évader de (26, 33)
establish établir
establish fonder
esteem estimer (27)
estimate estimer (27)
evacuate évacuer (114)
evade escamoter (96)
evaluate évaluer
evaporate s'évaporer (22, 33)
evoke évoquer (219)
exaggerate exagérer (356)
exalt exalter (28)
examine examiner (465)
exasperate exaspérer (203)
exceed excéder (87)
exceed dépasser
excel exceller (326)
except excepter (8)
exchange échanger (89)
excite exciter (251)

exclude exclure (105)
excommunicate excommunier (309)
excuse excuser
excuse oneself s'excuser
execute exécuter (169)
exempt dispenser (336)
exercise exercer (342)
exert exercer (342)
exhale expirer (466)
exhaust abrutir (229)
exhaust épuiser (486)
exhaust éreinter (90)
exhaust *harasser (183)
exhibit exhiber (251)
exhume exhumer (238)
exist exister (349)
exonerate disculper (27)
exonerate exonérer (203)
expect s'attendre à (208)
expect to compter
expel expulser (336)
experience éprouver
expire expirer (466)
expire se périmer (122, 220)
explain expliquer
explode exploser (321)
exploit exploiter (251)
explore explorer (22)
export exporter (349)
expose exposer (350)
express exprimer
expropriate exproprier (41)
exterminate exterminer (465)
extinguish éteindre
extract extraire (474)
extricate dépêtrer (349)
eye lorgner (441)
eye (someone) zieuter (27)

F

fabricate fabuler (81)
facilitate faciliter (225)
fact, to make a statement of constater (241)
fade se faner (122)
fade flétrir (383)
fail recaler (326)
fail échouer
fail faillir

English-French verb index

715

fun time, to have a se marrer (122)

fun, to have se divertir (210, 214)

fun, to make se moquer

function fonctionner (171)

furnish fournir

furnish with meubler de (27)

furrow sillonner (171)

G

gab papoter (96)

gag bâillonner (171)

gallicize franciser (486)

gallop galoper (163)

garden jardiner (167)

gargle se gargariser (85, 486)

garnish garnir de (229)

gather cueillir

gather recueillir

gauge jauger (76)

generate engendrer (299)

gesticulate gesticuler (32)

get along (with) s'entendre (avec) (195) (aux. être)

get bigger grossir (282)

get by se débrouiller (122, 233)

get on well with sympathiser avec (486)

get something for someone procurer qqch à qqn (54)

giggle ricaner (27)

gild dorer (22)

give donner

give a first name prénommer (310)

give a nickname surnommer (310)

give again redonner (171)

give back redonner (171)

give back rendre

give birth to accoucher de (121)

give someone responsibility responsabiliser (486)

gleam rutiler (27)

glean glaner (27)

glisten reluire (See luire) (Def. and Imp.)

glisten luire (Def. and Imp.)

glisten chatoyer (187)

glorify glorifier (212)

glorify magnifier (212)

gnaw ronger (442)

go aller

go along longer (283)

go away s'en aller

go boating canoter (26)

go out sortir

go out again ressortir (444)

go past, beyond dépasser (328)

go up again remonter (298)

goad aiguillonner (171)

gobble up bouffer (235)

gossip potiner (329)

gossip about babiller sur (27)

govern gouverner (167)

grab by the collar colleter (267)

grant octroyer (187)

grant accorder

grasp serrer

grasp tenir

grate râper (59)

graze brouter (28)

graze pâturer (54)

greet saluer (114)

grill (meat, fish), toast (bread) griller (477)

grimace (one's face) grimacer (342)

grind piler (27)

grind moudre

grip agripper (163)

groan gémir (229)

groan geindre (334)

groom toiletter (246)

grope tâtonner (171)

group grouper (124)

group together regrouper (59)

grow croître

grow grandir

grumble grogner (10)

grumble bougonner (171)

grumble rechigner (441)

guarantee cautionner (171)

guarantee garantir (229)

guard against prémunir contre (229)

guess deviner (329)

guide guider (26)

guillotine guillotiner (329)

gush forth jaillir (423)

gut étriper (215)

guzzle bâfrer (82)

H

habitual offender, to be an récidiver (276)

hack (computer) pirater (241)

haggle marchander (147)

haggle, quibble chicaner (147)

hail grêler (Def. and Imp.)

hail, call to *héler (87)

hallucinate halluciner (329)

hammer marteler (297)

handicap *handicaper (59)

handle manier (212)

handle roughly maltraiter (475)

handle roughly malmener (290)

hang pendre

hang (up) accrocher

hang around poireauter (27)

hang on se cramponner (122, 171)

hang on s'accrocher (13)

hang up raccrocher (469)

happen advenir (Def. and Imp.)

happen se passer (Def. and Imp.)

harass *harceler (297)

harden durcir (95)

harden, toughen endurcir (95)

harm nuire

harm léser (87)

harness (horses) atteler (38)

harp on, repeat over and over
  rabâcher (82)
harvest (grapes) vendanger
  (283)
harvest, gather récolter
  (27)
hassle someone emmerder
  (240)
hasten s'empresser de
  (361)
hatch éclore (See clore)
  (Def. and Imp.)
hatch (with hatch marks)
  *hachurer (54)
hate détester
hate haïr
haunt *hanter (90)
have avoir
have a slimming effect
  amincir (229)
have to devoir
hazard *hasarder (240)
heal guérir
healthier, to make assainir
  (229)
hear entendre
heat échauffer (171)
heat up chauffer (235)
hebraize hébraïser (486)
help aider
help secourir
help oneself se servir
help out dépanner (171)
hem ourler (326)
hesitate hésiter
hesitate tergiverser (492)
hide cacher
hide (something) planquer
  (284)
hide oneself se cacher
hierarchize *hiérarchiser
  (486)
hinder entraver (276)
hinder empêcher
hire engager (305)
hire embaucher (285)
hit cogner (10)
hit frapper
hit *heurter (246)
hoist *hisser (84)
hold tenir
hold receler (297)

hold back endiguer (307)
hold up supporter
hole, to make a trouer
  (269)
honor honorer (22)
hoot *hululer, ululer (81)
hoot, toot, sound a horn
  klaxonner (171)
hope espérer
horn, to remove a décorner
  (470)
horn, to sound a corner
  (349)
horrify horrifier (212)
hospitalize hospitaliser
  (486)
host (Internet) héberger
  (283)
hover over planer sur (71)
howl *hurler (326)
hug étreindre (334)
hum fredonner (171)
hum, buzz vrombir (229)
humble oneself s'abaisser
hunt chasser
hurry se dépêcher
hurry oneself se *hâter
  (74, 241)
hurry, to be in a se presser
hurt onself se blesser
hyperlink (Internet)
  hyperlier (454)
hypertrophy
  s'hypertrophier (212)
  (aux. être)
hypnotize hypnotiser
  (486)

I

idealize idéaliser (486)
identify identifier (212)
idolize idolâtrer (299)
illuminate illuminer
  (465)
illustrate illustrer (299)
imagine imaginer (329)
imitate imiter (251)
immerse immerger (91)
immigrate immigrer (93)
immobilize immobiliser
  (486)
immolate immoler (498)

immortalize immortaliser
  (486)
immunize immuniser
  (486)
impatient, to get
  s'impatienter (33, 464)
implicate impliquer (219)
implore implorer (22)
implore supplier
implore adjurer (272)
imply impliquer (219)
import importer (349)
importune importuner
  (32)
impose imposer (350)
impoverish appauvrir
  (229)
impress impressionner
  (171)
imprison incarcérer (203)
improve bonifier (41)
improve améliorer (22)
improvise improviser
  (486)
improvise se débrouiller
inaugurate inaugurer
  (54)
incinerate incinérer (356)
incite inciter (251)
incline incliner (329)
include inclure
incorporate in incorporer à
  (22)
increase redoubler (407)
increase acroître
increase augmenter
increase croître
increase the value
  valoriser (486)
incur encourir (125)
indicate indiquer
indifferent to, to become
  se blaser de (33,
  122)
indignant, to become
  s'indigner (33, 441)
indoctrinate
  endoctriner (329)
induce (to) induire (à)
  (106)
industrialize
  industrialiser (486)

infect with **infecter de** (113)

infer from **inférer de** (356)

infest with **infester de** (259)

infiltrate **s'infiltrer dans** (299, 262)

inflate **gonfler** (445)

inflict on **infliger à** (218)

influence **influencer** (99)

inform **informer** (227)

inform **renseigner** (194)

inform oneself **s'informer**

infringe **enfreindre** (334)

infuse **infuser** (32)

ingest **ingérer** (203)

inhale **aspirer** (21)

inhale **inspirer** (466)

inherit **hériter** (293)

inhibit **inhiber** (215)

initiate into **initier à** (389)

inject **injecter** (8)

injure **blesser**

injure oneself **se blesser**

inoculate **inoculer** (81)

inquire about **s'enquérir de** (19) (aux. être)

inscribe **inscrire** (177)

insert **insérer** (203)

insert **intercaler** (326)

insinuate **insinuer** (114)

insist **insister**

inspect **inspecter** (113)

inspire **inspirer** (466)

install **installer** (27)

install glass **vitrer** (22)

install signals **signaliser** (486)

institute **instituer** (483)

instruct **instruire**

insulate **isoler** (498)

insult **insulter** (176)

integrate **intégrer** (203)

intensify **s'intensifier** (212) (aux. être)

intercede **intercéder** (87)

intercept **intercepter** (8)

interest someone in something **intéresser qqn à qqch** (88)

interested, to be **s'intéresser**

interfere **interférer** (356)

interfere in **s'ingérer dans** (33, 203)

intermingle **entremêler** (82)

interpolate **interpoler** (498)

interpose between **interposer entre** (350)

interpret **interpréter** (87)

interrogate **interroger**

interrupt **interrompre**

intersperse with **entrecouper de** (124)

intertwine **entrelacer** (342)

intervene **intervenir** (491)

intervene **s'entremettre** (295)

interview **interviewer** (27)

intimidate by **intimider par** (266)

intoxicate **griser** (486)

intoxicated, to become **s'enivrer** (33)

introduce **introduire**

invade **envahir** (229)

invalidate **invalider** (266)

invent **inventer** (90)

inventory **recenser** (27)

invert **invertir** (66)

invest **investir** (66)

investigate **enquêter (sur)** (47)

invite **convier** (41)

invite **inviter**

invoke, call upon **invoquer** (219)

iron **repasser**

irradiate, radiate **irradier** (389)

irritate **irriter** (266)

irritate, tingle **picoter** (96)

isolate **isoler** (498)

isolate (from) **isoler (de)** (498)

italianize **italianiser** (486)

J

jabber **jacter** (8)

jabber **jargonner** (171)

jabber **baragouiner** (329)

jam **coincer** (342)

join **joindre**

join **unir**

join (member) **adhérer** (87)

join in marriage **conjoindre** (268)

join tip to tip, end to end **abouter** (173)

joke **blaguer** (307)

joke **plaisanter**

joke **rigoler** (498)

jolt **cahoter** (28)

jolt, bounce around **ballotter** (171)

judge **juger**

juggle **jongler** (326)

jump **sauter**

jump **tressaillir** (50)

jump **sursauter** (425)

justify **justifier** (389)

jut out **saillir** (50) (3^{d} pers.); (229) (if **saillir** means "mate," 3^{d} pers.)

K

keep **garder**

keep away from **éloigner de** (194)

kidnap **kidnapper** (235)

kill **tuer**

kill each other **s'entretuer** (33, 483)

kiss **embrasser**

knead **pétrir** (249)

kneel **s'agenouiller** (233)

knit **tricoter** (96)

knit (brow) **froncer** (34)

knock **toquer** (219)

knock down **abattre**

knock down **défoncer** (371)

knock out **assommer** (310)

know **connaître**

know (how) **savoir**

L

label **étiqueter** (267)

lace **lacer** (342)

lacerate **lacérer** (356)

laicize **laïciser** (486)

lament **se lamenter sur qqch** (60)

land **atterrir** (229)

land on the moon **alunir** (229)

languish **languir** (229)

lapidate **lapider** (251)

English-French verb index

719

maximize
  maximaliser/maximiser
  (486)
mean   signifier   (212)
measure   mesurer   (54)
measure time   minuter   (32)
mechanize   mécaniser
  (486)
meddle in   se mêler de   (83)
meddle with   se mêler à
  (83)
meditate   méditer   (251)
meet   rencontrer
meet with   se retrouver
  (122, 481)
melt   fondre
membership, to renew one's
  se réabonner   (122, 171)
memorize   mémoriser
  (486)
mend   raccommoder   (147)
mention   mentionner   (171)
merit   mériter
migrate   migrer   (22)
milder, to get   radoucir
  (95)
milk   traire
mime   mimer   (220)
mine   miner   (465)
minimize
  minimaliser/minimiser
  (486)
mint   monnayer   (330)
mirror   mirer
misjudge   méconnaître
mislead   fourvoyer   (187)
misrepresent   travestir   (66)
miss   manquer
miss   louper   (124)
miss   rater   (241)
mist up   embuer   (114)
mistaken, to be   se
  méprendre
mistaken, to be   se tromper
mistreat   maltraiter   (475)
misuse   abuser de qqch
  (32)
misuse   maltraiter   (475)
mix   mélanger   (283)
mix up   brouiller   (233)
mix with   mêler à/avec
  (82)

mixed up, to get   cafouiller
  (233)
moan   râler   (498)
mobilize   mobiliser   (486)
mock   se gausser   (122,
  353)
mock   railler   (477)
mock   persifler   (439)
model   modeler
moderate   modérer   (203)
modernize   moderniser
  (486)
modify   modifier   (389)
modulate   moduler   (81)
moisten   humecter   (60)
moisturize   hydrater   (241)
mold   mouler   (421)
moldy, to make/go   moisir
  (95)
molest   molester   (160)
molt   muer   (483)
monopolize   monopoliser
  (486)
monopolize (manipulate the
  market)   truster   (27)
moo   meugler   (326)
moor   amarrer   (27)
moralize   moraliser   (486)
mortgage   hypothéquer
  (87, 219)
mortify   mortifier   (389)
motivate   motiver   (26)
mount   enfourcher   (285)
move   bouger
move   mouvoir
move (emotionally)
  émouvoir
move away   s'éloigner
move back   reculer   (81)
move belongings from one
  residence to another
  déménager   (305)
move in   emménager   (305)
move out of line   décaler
  (326)
move over (Qué.)   se tasser
  (84, 122)
multiply   multiplier   (454)
mumble   bredouiller   (233)
mumble   marmonner   (171)
mummify   momifier   (212)
murmur   murmurer   (54)
must   devoir

mutilate   mutiler   (27)
mutiny   se mutiner   (329)
muzzle   museler   (38)
mystify   mystifier   (129)

N

nail   clouer   (269)
name   dénommer   (310)
name   nommer
named, to be   s'appeler
nap, to take a   roupiller
  (477)
narrate   narrer   (22)
narrate   conter
navigate   naviguer
necessary, to be   falloir
  (Def. and Imp.)
neglect   négliger   (119)
negotiate   négocier   (389)
neutralize   neutraliser
  (486)
next to, to be   côtoyer
  (187)
nibble at; snack   grignoter
  (96)
nod (one's head)   *hocher
  (82)
nod off   s'assoupir   (229)
normalize   normaliser
  (486)
note   noter   (176)
notice   remarquer
notice   s'aviser   (32, 33)
notify   aviser   (32)
notify   notifier   (322)
nuance   nuancer
numb   engourdir   (210)
number   chiffrer   (27)
number   numéroter   (96)
nurse (baby)   téter   (87)
nurse (infant)   allaiter   (27)

O

obey   obéir
objectify   objectiver   (276)
objection, to make an
  objecter   (160)
oblige   obliger
obliterate   oblitérer   (356)
observe   observer   (481)
obsess   obséder   (87)
obstruct   obstruer   (114)
obtain   obtenir

phrase (in music) **phraser** (32)

pick **cueillir**

pick someone up (fig.) **draguer** (307)

pick up **ramasser** (92)

pierce **percer** (275)

pierce **transpercer** (342)

pile up **amasser** (92)

pile up **amonceler** (38)

pile up **empiler** (329)

pilfer **chaparder** (27)

pillage **piller** (477)

pilot **piloter** (96)

pin **épingler** (326)

pinch **pincer** (99)

pirate **pirater** (241)

pity **plaindre**

pity, to inspire **apitoyer** (187)

pity, to inspire **attendrir** (229)

pivot **pivoter** (96)

place **mettre**

place **placer**

place **poser**

plagiarize **plagier** (389)

plan **planifier** (212)

plan **programmer**

plane **raboter** (96)

plant **planter** (90)

plaster **plâtrer** (22)

plaster, to remove **déplâtrer** (349)

play **jouer**

play the piano **pianoter** (96)

plead **plaider** (26)

please **plaire**

pleat **plisser** (73)

plot **comploter** (349)

plot **manigancer** (342)

plot **tramer** (71)

plow **labourer** (481)

plug **tamponner** (171)

plug in **brancher**

plug up **colmater** (28)

plumb **plomber** (240)

plunge **plonger** (442)

plunge in, smash down **enfoncer** (371)

poach (cooking) **pocher** (82)

pocket **empocher** (285)

pocket again **rempocher** (82)

point **pointer** (464)

poison **empoisonner** (171)

poison **intoxiquer** (219)

poison **envenimer** (27)

polish **dégrossir** (282)

polish **polir** (423)

polish **fignoler** (498)

polish **peaufiner** (329)

politicize **politiser** (486)

poll **sonder** (27)

pollute with **polluer de** (114)

pomade, to put on **pommader** (240)

pontificate **pontifier** (212)

populate **peupler** (326)

position **positionner** (171)

possess **posséder**

postpone **reporter** (349)

postpone **ajourner** (433)

pour **verser**

pour again **reverser** (492)

pour out **épancher** (78)

pour out **déverser** (492)

powder **poudrer** (299)

practice **pratiquer** (219)

praise **louanger** (283)

praise **louer**

pray **prier**

preach **prêcher** (332)

precede **précéder** (87)

predestine **prédestiner** (329)

predict **présager** (305)

predict **prédire**

predispose **prédisposer** (350)

preexist **préexister à** (27)

preface **préfacer** (342)

prefer **préférer**

prejudge **préjuger** (271)

premeditate **préméditer** (251)

preoccupy **préoccuper** (317)

prepare **apprêter** (363)

prepare **préparer**

prescribe **prescrire** (177)

prescribe (medical) **ordonner** (171)

present **présenter**

preserve **conserver** (27)

preserve from **préserver de** (426)

preside (over) **présider** (251)

press **appuyer** (192)

press **presser**

presume **présumer** (238)

presuppose **présupposer** (350)

pretend **prétendre**

pretend to **affecter de** (8)

prevail over **prédominer sur** (465)

prevail over **prévaloir sur** (488)

prick **piquer** (219)

print **imprimer** (220)

privatize **privatiser** (486)

proceed from **procéder** (87)

proclaim **proclamer** (71)

proclaim **clamer** (9)

produce **produire**

profane **profaner** (27)

profess **professer** (73)

profile **profiler** (27)

profit from **profiter de** (251)

profit from/by **bénéficier de** (389)

profitable, to make **rentabiliser** (486)

program **programmer**

progress **progresser** (73)

prohibit **prohiber** (251)

prohibit **défendre**

project **projeter** (267)

prolong by **prolonger de** (442)

promise **promettre**

promote **promouvoir** (304) (*part. passé* promu, promue)

promulgate **promulguer** (307)

pronounce **prononcer**

prop up **étayer** (330)

propagate **propager** (305)

proportionate, to make **proportionner** (171)

propose **proposer** (350)

proscribe **proscrire** (177)

prosper prospérer (203)

prostitute oneself se prostituer (122, 483)

protect protéger (52)

protest protester (160)

proud of (something), to be enorgueillir de (229)

prove prouver

prove/turn out be s'avérer (33, 87)

provide pourvoir (497) (except Tenses 4 & 5, stem: pourvoir-; Tense 3 pourvus, pourvus, pourvut...; Tense 7 pourvusse, pourvusses, pourvût...)

provide nantir (66)

provide for subvenir à (491)

provoke provoquer (219)

prowl rôder (96)

prune émonder (240)

psychoanalyze psychanalyser (32)

publish publier (212)

publish éditer (251)

pull tirer

pull again retirer

pull down rabattre (67)

pull off leaves effeuiller (477)

pull on tirailler (477)

pulverize pulvériser (486)

pump pomper (59)

punch (a ticket) composter (349)

punch (ticket) poinçonner (171)

punctuate ponctuer (483)

puncture ponctionner (171)

puncture (tire) crever (278)

punish châtier (212)

punish punir

purge purger (283)

purify purifier (212)

purple, to become se violacer (342)

pursue pourchasser (92)

pursue chasser

pursue poursuivre

push pousser

push away repousser (353)

push back refouler (421)

push further in renfoncer (342)

put mettre

put poser

put a slipcover on *housser (353)

put again remettre

put back reposer (350)

put makeup on one's face se maquiller (122)

put out of order détraquer (219)

put topspin on a ball lifter (27)

put up posters placarder (240)

Q

quadruple quadrupler (326)

qualify qualifier (212)

quantify quantifier (212)

quarrel with each other se quereller (122, 477)

quebecize, make Québécois québéciser (486)

question questionner (171)

question interroger

question (police) interpeller (27)

quibble ergoter (96)

quibble ratiociner (329)

quiet, to be se taire

quintuple quintupler (326)

quote citer (251)

R

radicalize radicaliser (486)

rage rager (305)

rain pleuvoir (Def. and Imp.)

raise exhausser (353)

raise *hausser (92)

raise soulever (278)

raise surélever (278)

raise élever

raise rehausser (353)

raise a bid surenchérir (94)

raise again relever (278)

rake ratisser (486)

rally rallier (212)

ramify se ramifier (212) (aux. être)

rancid, to get rancir (95)

rant and rave déblatérer (356)

rarefy raréfier (212)

ratify homologuer (307)

ratify entériner (329)

ratify ratifier (212)

ration rationner (171)

ravage ravager (305)

reaccustom réaccoutumer (238)

reach parvenir à (491)

react réagir (25)

read lire

read again relire

readjust réadapter (8)

readmit réadmettre (294)

ready, to get oneself s'apprêter à qqch (48, 363)

reappear réapparaître (324)

reappear reparaître

reappear ressurgir/resurgir (229)

reappoint renommer (310)

rear up cabrer (27)

rear up regimber (240)

rearm réarmer (227)

reason raisonner (443)

reassure rassurer (54)

reassure sécuriser (486)

reassure tranquilliser (486)

rebel se rebeller (122)

reborn, to be renaître (306)

rebroadcast rediffuser (32)

rebuild reconstituer (483)

recall rappeler

receive recevoir

recite réciter (251)

reclassify reclasser (84)

recognize reconnaître

recommend recommander (98)

reconcile concilier (212)

reconcile réconcilier (212)

reconcile (with) rabibocher (285)

reconquer reconquérir (19)

reconsider reconsidérer (203)

reconstruct reconstruire (111)

reconstruct recomposer (350)

reconvert reconvertir (229)

recorrect recorriger (218)

recount retracer (342)

recover recouvrer (466)

recreate recréer (128)

recross retraverser (492)

recruit recruter (32)

rectify rectifier (389)

recycle recycler (326)

redden rougeoyer (187)

redefine redéfinir (229)

rediscover redécouvrir (139)

redo refaire (223)

reduce réduire

reduce rabaisser (63)

redye reteindre (334)

reeducate rééduquer (219)

reelect réélire (280)

reembark rembarquer (284)

reemerge ressurgir/resurgir (229)

reestablish rétablir (206)

reexamine réexaminer (465)

refer to se référer à (122, 356)

referee arbitrer (27)

refine raffiner (329)

reflect refléter (87)

reflect (thought) réfléchir

refract réfracter (27)

refresh rafraîchir (383)

refresh désaltérer (356)

refrigerate réfrigérer (203)

refund ristourner (27)

refuse refuser

refute démentir (291)

refute réfuter (425)

regain regagner (239)

regenerate régénérer (356)

register s'inscrire (177) (aux. être)

register enregistrer (393)

register immatriculer (81)

regret regretter

regulate régulariser (486)

regulate régler (87)

rehabilitate réhabiliter (251)

rehearse répéter

reheat réchauffer (84)

reign régner (87)

reimburse rembourser (27)

reimprison réincarcérer (356)

reincarnated, to be se réincarner (122)

reinforce renforcer (342)

reinstall réinstaller (326)

reinstate réintégrer (356)

reinvent réinventer (464)

reiterate réitérer (356)

reject rejeter (267)

rejoin rejoindre (268)

rejuvenate rajeunir (229)

relapse rechuter (32)

relate relater (241)

relativize relativiser (486)

relaunch relancer (342)

relax délasser (79)

relax se détendre (394)

relax relaxer (27)

relay relayer (330)

relearn rapprendre, réapprendre (42)

release lâcher (82)

relet relouer (269)

relieve atténuer (114)

relieve of soulager de (305)

reload recharger (91)

remain rester

remark remarquer

remedy remédier à (212)

remelt, recast refondre (394)

remember se remémorer (22, 122)

remember se rappeler

remember se souvenir

remodel refaçonner (443)

remove enlever

remove retrancher (78)

remove bandages débander (27)

remove one's makeup se démaquiller (477)

remunerate rémunérer (203)

renew renouveler (38)

renounce renier (309)

renounce, give up renoncer (371)

renovate rénover (276)

rent louer

reopen rouvrir (323)

repaint repeindre (334)

repair réparer

repatriate rapatrier (212)

repave repaver (276)

repeat répéter

repel rebuter (32)

repent se repentir

replace suppléer (128)

replace remettre

replace replacer (342)

replay rejouer (269)

reply répliquer (219)

repolish repolir (229)

repopulate repeupler (326)

represent figurer (54)

represent représenter (60)

repress réprimer (220)

reprimand *houspiller (477)

reprimand réprimander

reprint réimprimer (220)

reproach someone for something reprocher qqch à qqn (43)

reproduce reproduire

reprogram reprogrammer (368)

reprove réprouver (481)

republish rééditer (215)

repudiate répudier (212)

request demander

require nécessiter (251)

require exiger

require, demand requérir (19)

requisition réquisitionner (171)

reread relire

reroute dérouter (28)

resell revendre (489)

resemble ressembler

reserve réserver (276)

resheath rengainer (329)

reside résider (251)

reside demeurer

resign from démissionner de (171)

resign oneself to se résigner à (122, 441)

resist résister (259)

resoak retremper (247)

resolder ressouder (27)

resolve résoudre

resonate résonner (443)

resort to something recourir à qqch (125)

respect respecter (8)

respond répondre

respond riposter (27)

rest se reposer

restick recoller (326)

restock regarnir (229)

restore restaurer (347)

restrict restreindre (334)

restring recorder (27)

result from provenir de (491)

result from résulter de (27)

retain retenir

retie renouer (269)

retighten resserrer (22)

retighten retendre (394)

retire se retirer

retort rétorquer (284)

retouch retoucher (469)

retract rétracter (60)

retranscribe retranscrire (177)

retread (tire) rechaper (59)

return rentrer

return retourner

return, restore restituer (483)

retype retaper (59)

reunify réunifier (212)

reunite with réunir à (485)

reuse réemployer/remployer (187)

reuse réutiliser (486)

revalue revaloriser (486)

reveal révéler (356)

reverberate réverbérer (203)

revere révérer (203)

reverse inverser (492)

revise remanier (309)

revise réviser (486)

revitalize revitaliser (486)

revive ranimer (220)

revive raviver (276)

revoke révoquer (219)

revolt révolter (27)

revolutionize révolutionner (171)

reward récompenser (336)

rewind rembobiner (329)

rewrap remballer (326)

rewrite récrire (177)

rewrite réécrire (177)

rhyme rimer (220)

ricochet ricocher (82)

rid of, to get se débarrasser de (79, 122)

ridicule ridiculiser (486)

rifle through trifouiller dans (233)

ring carillonner (171)

ring tinter (464)

ring sonner

rinse rincer (99)

ripen mûrir (249)

rise up against s'insurger contre (33, 283)

risk risquer (219)

rival rivaliser (486)

rivet river (276)

roam around vadrouiller (233)

roam, wander vaguer (307)

roar mugir (229)

roar rugir (229)

roar with laughter se bidonner (122, 171)

roast rôtir (229)

rock bercer (99)

rock climb varapper (235)

roll bouler (421)

roll rouler

roll up enrouler (421)

romanize romaniser (486)

round (off) arrondir (229)

row ramer (27)

rub frotter (79)

rub elbows with coudoyer (187)

rubberize caoutchouter (28)

ruin bousiller (477)

ruin délabrer (407)

ruin ruiner (329)

ruin, smash up esquinter (90)

rule over régenter (464)

run courir

run away déguerpir (95)

run away fuguer (307)

run away se sauver

run off filer (27)

run out of breath s'essouffler (122, 445)

run to accourir

rush se précipiter (122, 251)

rush brusquer (219)

rush forward s'élancer (33, 342)

rush toward se ruer sur/vers (114, 122)

rust rouiller (233)

S

sabotage saboter (96)

sacrifice sacrifier (212)

sadden attrister (28)

sadden désoler (421)

saddle seller (326)

safeguard sauvegarder (240)

sail naviguer

sail, drift voguer (307)

sale, to put on solder (27)

salivate saliver (426)

salt saler (326)

salvage récupérer (203)

sample   échantillonner
(171)
sanctify   sanctifier   (212)
sanction (law)   sanctionner
(443)
sand   poncer   (342)
sand, to get buried in
s'ensabler   (33, 407)
satisfy   satisfaire
saturate   saturer   (54)
save   sauver
save   épargner   (10)
save (computer)
sauvegarder   (240)
saw   scier   (41)
say   dire
scaffolding, to put up
échafauder   (447)
scan (image)   scanner
(171)
scan (verse)   scander   (240)
scandalize   scandaliser
(486)
scare away   effaroucher
(285)
scatter   éparpiller   (477)
scatter   parsemer   (341)
schematize   schématiser
(486)
school   scolariser   (486)
scoff at   narguer   (307)
scold   quereller   (477)
scold   gronder
scold   engueuler   (421)
scorn   bafouer qqn   (269)
scrape   racler   (326)
scratch   égratigner   (441)
scratch   érafler   (439)
scratch   griffer   (439)
scratch   gratter
screen (medical)   dépister
(215)
screw on   visser   (486)
scribble   griffonner   (171)
scrub   briquer   (219)
scrub   récurer   (54)
scrutinize   scruter   (32)
sculpt   sculpter   (8)
scuttle   saborder   (27)
seal   cacheter   (267)
search   fureter   (17)
search   perquisitionner
(171)

search   fouiller
search   rechercher   (93)
season   assaisonner   (171)
season (soldiers)   aguerrir
(229)
secrete   sécréter   (87)
seduce   séduire
see   voir
see again   revoir
see someone home
reconduire   (106)
see someone off, home
raccompagner   (441)
seek   chercher
seek after   quêter   (47)
seem   sembler   (Def. and
Imp.)
seem   paraître
seem   sembler   (Def. and
Imp.)
segment   segmenter   (60)
seize   s'emparer de   (33,
101)
seize   saisir
seize   pogner   (441)
select   sélectionner   (171)
sell   vendre
sell out of   écouler   (421)
send   expédier   (212)
send   envoyer
send back   renvoyer   (200)
sensitize   sensibiliser   (486)
separate   disjoindre   (268)
separate   séparer
separate in two   dédoubler
(407)
sermonize   sermonner
(171)
serve   servir
serve again   resservir   (437)
serve oneself   se servir
session, to be in   siéger
(52)
set   fixer   (27)
set free   délivrer   (21)
set free   affranchir   (72)
set on fire   incendier   (212)
set up   aménager   (305)
settle (debt)   s'acquitter de
(33, 374)
settle down, subside;   se
tasser   (84, 122)

settle in   s'implanter   (33,
90)
sew   coudre
sew up again   recoudre
(123)
sextuple   sextupler   (326)
shade   ombrager   (189)
shade   ombrer   (22)
shake   ébranler   (326)
shake   secouer
shake   branler   (498)
shake   agiter   (251)
share   partager   (501)
sharpen   affûter   (173)
sharpen   aiguiser   (486)
shave   raser   (86)
shave oneself   se raser   (86,
122)
shear   tondre   (394)
sheath   gainer   (329)
shell (military)   canonner
(171)
shell (remove a shell)
décortiquer   (219)
shelter from   abriter
de/contre   (251)
shield   blinder   (27)
shift ahead/back (hour)
décaler   (326)
shine   briller   (477)
shine   resplendir   (229)
shine   rayonner   (171)
shine   luire   (Def. and Imp.)
shiny, to make   lustrer
(299)
shiver   frissonner   (171)
shiver   grelotter   (79)
shock   choquer   (284)
shock   estomaquer   (219)
shoes, to put back on   se
rechausser   (85)
shoes, to put on   chausser
(79)
shoot   fusiller   (477)
shop   magasiner   (159)
shopping (online), to go
magasiner en ligne
short-circuit   court-circuiter
(215)
shorten   écourter   (160)
shorten   raccourcir   (95)
shoulder   épauler   (421)
shout   crier

shove, bump **bousculer** (81)

shovel **pelleter** (267)

show **montrer**

show **manifester** (299)

show again **remontrer** (299)

shrink **rétrécir** (95)

shrink **se ratatiner** (122, 329)

shrivel up **se rabougrir** (214, 249)

shudder **frémir**

sift **cribler** (326)

sift **tamiser** (486)

sigh **soupirer** (21)

sign **signer**

signal **signaler**

signify **signifier** (212)

silent, to be **se taire**

silhouette **silhouetter** (386)

simmer **mijoter** (96)

simplify **simplifier** (212)

simulate **simuler** (81)

sin **pécher**

sing **chanter**

sing oneself **chantonner** (171)

sink **s'affaisser** (33, 274)

sink **sombrer** (22)

sip **siroter** (96)

sit down **s'asseoir**

sit down again **se rasseoir** (51) (aux. être; *part. passé* rassis, rassise)

sit down at a table (for a meal) **s'attabler** (33)

sit on (eggs) **couver** (28)

situate **situer** (483)

skate **patiner**

sketch **ébaucher** (469)

sketch **esquisser** (183)

ski **skier** (129)

skim (reading) **parcourir** (125)

skim off **écrémer** (87)

skimp **mégoter** (96)

skimp on **lésiner sur** (159)

skip **sautiller** (477)

slalom **slalomer** (71)

slander **diffamer** (71)

slander **médire**

slander **calomnier** (212)

slap **gifler** (439)

slash **balafrer** (27)

slash **sabrer** (22)

slash **taillader** (27)

slaughter **abattre**

sled **luger** (271)

sleep **dormir**

slice **trancher** (78)

slide **glisser** (73)

slow down **ralentir** (95)

smaller, to make/get **rapetisser** (486)

smash in (car, train) **télescoper** (163)

smash into **percuter** (169)

smash, shatter **fracasser** (84)

smear **enduire** (133)

smell **flairer** (22)

smell **sentir**

smell up **empuantir** (210)

smile **sourire**

smoke **fumer**

smooth **lisser** (73)

snake, meander **serpenter** (60)

sneak in without paying **resquiller** (477)

sneak through **se faufiler** (27, 122)

sneeze **éternuer** (114)

sniffle **renifler** (439)

snore **ronfler** (445)

snow **neiger** (Def. and Imp.)

snub **snober** (27)

soak **détremper** (464)

soak **imbiber** (215)

soak **tremper** (247)

sob **sangloter** (96)

sober up **dégriser** (486)

socialize **socialiser** (486)

soften **amollir** (229)

soften **assouplir** (423)

soften **mollir** (229)

soften **se velouter** (28, 122)

soften **adoucir** (229)

soften **ramollir** (229)

soil **entacher** (82)

soil **salir**

soil **souiller**

sojourn **séjourner**

solder **souder** (27)

solicit **solliciter** (251)

solidify **solidifier** (212)

solubilize **solubiliser** (486)

solve **résoudre**

somersault **culbuter** (28)

sort **trier** (129)

soundproof **insonoriser** (486)

sour **aigrir** (229)

sow **semer** (341)

space **échelonner** (171)

sparing in the use of, to be **ménager** (305)

sparkle **scintiller** (477)

spatialize **spatialiser** (486)

speak **parler**

speak patois **patoiser** (486)

speak with a nasal twang **nasiller** (477)

specialize **se spécialiser** (486)

specify **préciser** (486)

specify **spécifier** (212)

speculate **spéculer** (81)

spell **épeler** (38)

spell **orthographier** (212)

spend (money) **dépenser**

spend (time) **passer**

spend the night away from one's house **découcher** (121)

spice up **épicer** (342)

spin **vriller** (477)

spin around **virevolter** (27)

spiritualize **spiritualiser** (486)

spit **cracher** (82)

splash **éclabousser** (79)

split **scinder** (240)

split **fendre**

split up **désunir** (229)

split up **sectionner** (171)

spoil **gâcher** (82)

spoil **gâter**

spoil **pourrir** (249)

sponge **éponger** (283)

spool   embobiner   (329)
spool   bobiner   (329)
spray   vaporiser   (486)
spread   répandre
spread (butter, pâté)   tartiner
   (329)
spread apart   écarter   (69)
spread out   étendre   (462)
spread out, display   étaler
   (326)
sprinkle   asperger   (283)
sprinkle   saupoudrer   (299)
sprint   sprinter   (464)
spurt   gicler   (326)
spurt up   rejaillir   (423)
spy on   épier   (212)
spy on   espionner   (171)
squat   s'accroupir   (214)
squeeze   serrer
squint   loucher   (469)
stab   zigouiller   (233)
stab   poignarder   (240)
stabilize   stabiliser   (486)
stack   superposer   (350)
stagger   chanceler   (38)
stagger   tituber   (32)
stagnate   croupir   (229)
stagnate   stagner   (441)
stagnate   vivoter   (96)
stain   maculer   (81)
stain with   tacher de   (82)
stall   caler   (27)
stammer   bafouiller   (233)
stammer   balbutier   (212)
stammer   bégayer   (179)
stamp   estamper   (247)
stamp   timbrer   (466)
stand someone up   plaquer
   (219)
stand up   se dresser   (23,
   122)
staple   agrafer   (27)
staple (Qué.)   brocher
   (285)
starch   amidonner   (171)
stare at someone   dévisager
   (305)
start   commencer
start   amorcer   (342)
start again   redémarrer
   (22)
start again   repartir   (327)
   (aux. être)

start out   démarrer   (27)
starve   affamer   (71)
state   énoncer   (371)
stay   demeurer
stay   rester
stay up   veiller   (109)
steal   choper   (163)
steal   faucher   (82)
steal   chiper   (251)
steal   dérober   (498)
steal   subtiliser   (486)
steal   voler
steep   macérer   (203)
step over   enjamber   (240)
sterilize   stériliser   (486)
stick to   coller à   (445)
stick together   agglutiner
   (329)
stiffen   raidir   (229)
stigmatize   stigmatiser
   (486)
stimulate   stimuler   (81)
stimulate someone's appetite
   allécher   (87)
stink   puer   (Def. and Imp.)
stipulate   stipuler   (81)
stir   remuer   (483)
stitch   brocher   (285)
stock   stocker   (27)
stockpile   emmagasiner
   (159)
stone   lapider   (251)
stop   stopper   (163)
stop   arrêter
stop (oneself)   s'arrêter
store in a warehouse
   entreposer   (350)
storm   tempêter   (47)
straddle, ride   chevaucher
   (285)
straighten up   redresser
   (353)
strain   peiner   (329)
strangle   étrangler   (326)
stratify   stratifier   (212)
stream   ruisseler   (38)
strengthen   affermir   (229)
strengthen   raffermir   (229)
stress   stresser   (353)
stretch   (étirer)   (466)
stretch   tendre
stretch one's legs   se
   dégourdir   (210, 214)

stretch oneself   s'étirer
   (182, 466)
stretch oneself   s'étendre
stretch out   allonger   (442)
strew something with
   joncher qqch de   (93)
striate   strier   (129)
strike (lightning)   foudroyer
   (187)
strike down   terrasser   (84)
strip   dépouiller   (233)
strip (paint, wood)   décaper
   (235)
stripe with   zébrer de   (356)
stroll   se balader   (26, 122)
stroll   flâner   (443)
structure   structurer   (54)
struggle   se démener   (122,
   290)
struggle   lutter   (425)
struggle   vasouiller   (233)
strut around   se pavaner
   (122)
stubborn, to be   s'opiniâtrer
   (33)
stuck, to get   s'enliser   (33,
   486)
study   étudier
study hard   bûcher   (285)
stuff   bourrer   (22)
stuff oneself   s'empiffrer
   (33, 466)
stuff with (cooking), cram with
   farcir de   (229)
stumble, trip   trébucher
   (82)
stun   ébahir   (95)
stun   sidérer   (203)
stun   abasoudir
stun   étourdir
stupefy   abasourdir
stupefy   stupéfier   (212)
style, to go out of   se
   démoder   (27)
stylize   styliser   (486)
subjugate   asservir   (229)
sublimate   sublimer   (220)
submerge   submerger
   (283)
submit   soumettre
subordinate   subordonner
   (171)

tan (leather) tanner (171)
tangle enchevêtrer (299)
tangle up embrouiller
  (233)
tap tapoter (96)
tap taper (235)
target cibler (27)
tarnish galvauder (26)
tarnish ternir (229)
taste goûter
taste, sample food déguster
  (53)
tattoo tatouer (175)
tax taxer (27)
teach enseigner
teach someone to read and
  write alphabétiser (486)
tear déchirer
tear pieces écharper (59)
tease taquiner (329)
telegraph télégraphier
  (212)
telephone téléphoner
televise télédiffuser (32)
televise téléviser (486)
tell (a story) raconter
temper tempérer (203)
temper, to be in a bad
  décolérer (356)
tempt tenter
tense crisper (27)
tenure, to give titulariser
  (486)
terminate terminer
terrify épouvanter (90)
terrify terrifier (212)
terrorize terroriser (486)
test expérimenter (464)
test éprouver
test tester (160)
testify attester (160)
testify témoigner (10)
thank remercier
thaw dégeler (242)
theorize théoriser (486)
thicken épaissir (95)
thin, to make amaigrir
  (282)
think penser
think réfléchir
thinner, to get mincir (95)
thread enfiler (329)

threaten with menacer de
  (342)
throw jeter
throw lancer
thunder fulminer (465)
thunder tonner (Def. and
  Imp.)
tickle chatouiller (233)
tidy up ranger
tie lier (129)
tie nouer (269)
tie down arrimer (27)
tie up attacher (82)
tie up ligoter (96)
tile carreler (38)
tilt pencher (93)
time chronométrer (87)
tinker bricoler (32)
tint teinter (464)
tintinnabulate tintinnabuler
  (81)
tip off tuyauter (27)
tip off rancarder (27)
tire fatiguer (307)
tired, to get se lasser (84,
  122)
title titrer (466)
toast (drink) trinquer
  (284)
tolerate tolérer (356)
tolerate supporter
tone up tonifier (212)
tonsure tonsurer (54)
topple over basculer (81)
torment tenailler (477)
torment tourmenter (60)
torpedo torpiller (477)
torture supplicier (41)
torture torturer (54)
toss around tanguer (307)
total totaliser (486)
touch toucher
tousle someone's hair
  ébouriffer (215)
tousle someone's hair
  décoiffer qqn (443)
tow remorquer (284)
tow tracter
trace tracer (342)
track traquer (219)
track pister (27)
trade with commercer avec
  (99)

traffic trafiquer (219)
trample piétiner (329)
trample on fouler (421)
transcribe transcrire (177)
transfer transborder
transfer transférer (356)
transfer (funds) virer (21)
transform into transformer
  en (227)
transfuse transfuser (32)
transgress transgresser
  (353)
translate traduire
transmit transmettre
transmute transmuer
  (483)
transplant transhumer
  (238)
transplant transplanter
  (90)
transport transporter
  (349)
transport véhiculer (81)
transpose transposer (350)
trap piéger (52)
traumatize traumatiser
  (486)
travel voyager
travel through parcourir
  (125)
traverse traverser
treat traiter
tremble trembloter (96)
tremble with trembler de
  (407)
trick tricher
trickle down dégouliner
  (329)
trigger déclencher (285)
trim tailler (477)
trim rogner (441)
trip buter (173)
triple tripler (326)
triumph triompher (27)
trivialize banaliser (486)
trot trotter (246)
trot along trottiner (329)
trumpet trompeter (267)
truncate tronquer (284)
truth about a matter, to see the
  se détromper (480)
try tâcher (82)
try essayer

try   tenter
try again   réessayer   (204)
try one's best   s'ingénier à
(309) (aux. être)
try to please   complaire à
(345)
tu, to use   tutoyer
tumble   dégringoler   (498)
tumble down   dévaler   (27)
turn   tourner
turn aside   détourner
turn back   rebrousser   (353)
turn blue   bleuir   (229)
turn brown   roussir   (95)
turn green again   reverdir
turn oneself away from   se
détourner   (122, 161)
turn over, collapse   capoter
turn pale   pâlir   (423)
turn pink   rosir   (95)
turn up   retrousser   (353)
twist   entortiller   (477)
twist   tordre
type   taper   (235)
type   dactylographier
(366)
tyrannize   tyranniser   (486)

U

ugly, to make   enlaidir
(210)
ulcerate   ulcérer   (203)
unaware of, to be   ignorer
(22)
unblock   dégorger   (283)
unblock   débloquer   (219)
unbolt   déboulonner   (171)
unbridle   débrider   (251)
unbuckle   déboucler   (326)
unbutton   déboutonner
(171)
unchain   déchaîner   (329)
unclench   décontracter
(160)
unclog   déboucher   (285)
uncross (arms, legs)
décroiser   (486)
undergo   subir   (95)
underline   souligner   (10)
undermine   saper   (59)
understand   comprendre
undertake   entreprendre
undo   défaire

undress   dévêtir   (493)
undress oneself   se
déshabiller   (250)
undress oneself   se dévêtir
(250, 493)
undulate   ondoyer   (187)
undulate   onduler   (81)
unearth   déterrer   (196)
unearth   dénicher   (285)
unemployed, to be   chômer
(27)
unfasten   dégrafer   (27)
unfold   déplier   (389)
unhook   décrocher   (82)
uniform, to make
uniformiser   (486)
unify   unifier   (212)
unionize   syndicaliser
(486)
unionize   syndiquer   (219)
unite   unir
unlace   délacer   (342)
unlearn   désapprendre   (42)
unload   décharger   (91)
unlock   déverrouiller   (233)
unpack   déballer   (498)
unplug   débrancher   (285)
unroll   dérouler   (421)
unscrew   dévisser   (486)
unseal   décacheter   (267)
unstick   décoller   (385)
unstitch   découdre   (123)
untangle   démêler   (82)
untie   délier   (389)
untie   dénouer   (269)
untie   détacher   (285)
unveil   dévoiler   (498)
unwind   se défouler   (122,
421)
unwind   dévider   (251)
unworthy of, to show oneself
démériter de   (293)
up, to get   se lever
up, to go   monter
up, to take   monter
upload   télécharger vers le
serveur   (91)
uproot   déraciner   (159)
uproot   arracher
upset   vexer   (27)
upset, to be   s'inquiéter
urbanize   urbaniser   (486)
urinate   uriner   (465)

use   employer
use   utiliser
use trickery   ruser   (32)
use up   user   (32)
used again, to become   se
réhabituer   (33, 483)
used to, to get   s'habituer
(33, 483)
used to, to get   accoutumer
(238)
usurp   usurper   (59)
utilize   utiliser

V

vaccinate against   vacciner
contre   (329)
vacillate   vaciller   (477)
validate   valider   (251)
value   priser   (486)
vanquish   vaincre
vaporize   vaporiser   (486)
varnish   vernir   (229)
vary   varier   (129)
vaunt, praise   vanter   (90)
vegetate   végéter   (356)
veil   voiler   (27)
venerate   vénérer   (356)
ventilate   ventiler   (266)
venture   aventurer   (148)
verbalize   verbaliser   (486)
verify   vérifier   (212)
versify   versifier   (41)
vibrate   vibrer   (22)
view, look at   visionner
(171)
violate, rape   violer
(498)
visit   visiter
visualize   visualiser
(486)
vituperate   vitupérer
(203)
vocalize   vocaliser
(486)
vomit   vomir   (229)
vote again   revoter
(96)
vote for/against   voter
pour/contre   (96)
vous, to use   vouvoyer
vow   vouer à   (269)
vulgarize, popularize
vulgariser   (486)

W

waddle like a duck se dandiner (122, 329)
wade patauger (305)
wait attendre
wake up se réveiller
wake up (someone who's asleep) réveiller (109) (See 414)
walk marcher
walk along cheminer (465)
walk, to take a se promener
wall in emmurer (32)
wall in/up murer (54)
wallow se vautrer (122)
waltz valser (492)
wander errer (27)
wander vagabonder (248)
want vouloir
warm oneself up se chauffer (122, 235)
warm up se réchauffer (85)
warn prévenir
warn about alerter de (173)
warn about avertir de (229)
wash laver
wash one's face (w/washcloth) se débarbouiller (33, 233)
wash oneself se laver
waste dilapider (215)
waste gaspiller (477)
watch guetter (386)
watch surveiller (109)
watch regarder
water arroser (79)
water (animals) abreuver (26)
water (eye) larmoyer (187)
water down délayer (330)
waterproof, to make étancher (78)
wax cirer (466)
weaken affaiblir (229)

weaken faiblir (392)
weaken défaillir (222)
wear porter
wear down vanner (171)
wear thin élimer (27)
weave tisser (73)
weed désherber (27)
weigh peser
weigh down alourdir de (229)
weigh down appesantir (229)
weigh down oppresser (360)
weight, to lose maigrir
weight, to put back on regrossir (282)
weight, to put on grossir (282)
welcome accueillir
westernize occidentaliser (486)
wet mouiller (233)
wet, to get oneself se mouiller (83, 233)
whimper pleurnicher (285)
whinny, bray *hennir (229)
whip flageller (326)
whip fouetter (447)
whirl tournoyer (308)
whisper susurrer (22)
whisper chuchoter
whistle siffloter (96)
whistle siffler
whiten blanchir
wiggle tortiller (477)
wiggle frétiller (477)
will, to make out a (legal term) tester (160)
win remporter (349)
win gagner
wipe torcher (285)
wipe essuyer
wish souhaiter
withdraw se retirer

withdraw (in someone's favor) se désister de (en faveur de qqn) (53)
wobble flageoler (498)
wonder se demander (122, 147)
word libeller (27)
work travailler
work hard besogner (441)
work hard bosser (79)
worry s'inquiéter
worry someone inquiéter qqn (87) (See 258)
worsen empirer (466)
worth, to be valoir
wrap emballer (421)
wriggle gigoter (96)
wrinkle rider (27)
write écrire
write rédiger (218)
write about disserter sur (160)
write badly écrivasser (84)
wrong, to be clocher (285)
wrong, to be se tromper

X

x-ray radiographier (212)

Y

yap, yelp japper (235)
yawn bâiller (477)
yell gueuler (421)
yell vociférer (356)
yell at the top of one's lungs s'époumoner (461)
yellow, turn yellow jaunir (229)
yield céder
yodel yodler (326)

Z

zigzag zigzaguer (307)
zip up zipper (235)
zone zoner (461)
zoom in, zoom out zoomer (71)

Index of 2,600 additional verbs keyed to listing of 501 French verbs

The number after each verb is the number of the fully conjugated model verb in the main section. If the French verb you want is reflexive (for example, s'appeler or se lever), you will find it listed alphabetically under the first letter of the verb. The reflexive pronoun s' or se is given in parentheses after the verb: appeler (s'), lever (se). Sometimes two verb numbers are listed for a reflexive verb. For example, s'abonner is keyed to verb 171 (donner) and to verb 83 (se cacher) because it is a reflexive regular -er verb. If a verb is in the Defective and Impersonal verb section it will be marked Def. and Imp. Several verbs in this list are keyed to two verbs because you need to make two spelling changes.

Note: The English definitions are a guide to the most common meanings. In some cases we have also included a preposition when it is likely that you will use it along with the verb. There are obviously many more definitions for the verbs in this list. Think of the definitions as a way to make sure you're looking up the right word!

A

abandonner   to abandon (171)

abdiquer   to abdicate (219)

abhorrer   to abhor, loathe (27)

abîmer   to damage, spoil (27)

abjurer   to abjure, renounce (148)

abominer   to abominate, loathe (465)

abonder en   to abound in, be plentiful (26)

abonner (s') à   to subscribe to (83, 171)

abonner à   to subscribe for someone to (171)

aborder   to accost, approach (26)

abouter   to join tip to tip, end to end (173)

aboutir à/dans   to succeed, end up in (229)

aboyer   to bark (187)

abraser   to abrade (27)

abréger   to shorten, abridge (52)

abreuver   to water (animals) (26)

abriter de/contre   to shelter from (251)

abriter (s') de   to take shelter (from) (122, 251)

abrutir   to exhaust (229)

absenter (s') de   to absent oneself from (26)

absorber   to absorb (385)

abstraire   to abstract, isolate (474) (no *passé simple* or imp. subj.)

abuser de qqch   to abuse, misuse (32)

accabler   to overwhelm (407)

accaparer   to capture, monopolize (27)

accéder à   to get to, attain (87)

accélérer   to accelerate (356)

accentuer   to accentuate, stress (483)

accessoiriser   to accessorize (486)

accidenter   to damage, injure (27)

acclimater   to acclimate (27)

accommoder   to accommodate (147)

accomplir   to accomplish (392)

accoster   to accost (160)

accoucher de   to give birth to (121)

accouder (s') sur   to lean one's elbow on (33, 421)

accoupler   to couple (27)

accoutumer   to get used to (238)

accréditer   to accredit (251)

accrocher (s')   to hang on, collide (13)

accroupir (s')   to squat, crouch (214)

acculer   to corner somebody (81)

acculturer   to acculturate (27)

accumuler   to accumulate (81)

accuser (s')   to accuse oneself (16, 33)

acharner (s') contre qqn   to dog someone (27, 33)

acheminer   to direct towards (465)

acquiescer   to agree, approve (342)

acquitter (de)   to acquit, release (from)   (374)

acquitter (s') de   to pay off (duty), settle (debt)   (33, 374)

actionner   to activate   (171)

activer   to speed up, pep up   (26)

actualiser   to bring up to date   (16)

adapter à   to fit, adapt to   (8)

additionner   to add up   (171)

adhérer   to join, be a member   (87)

adhérer à   to adhere to   (87)

adjoindre à   to associate (with)   (268)

adjuger   to award   (283)

adjurer   to implore, beg   (272)

administrer   to administer   (26)

admonester   to admonish   (27)

adopter   to adopt   (8)

adosser   to lean against   (79)

adoucir   to soften, sweeten   (229)

adresser (s') à qqn   to speak to someone, address someone   (33, 79)

aduler   to adulate, flatter   (81)

advenir   to happen, occur, come to pass   (Def. and Imp.)

aérer   to air, aerate   (87)

affadir   to make (something) dull   (229)

affaiblir   to weaken   (229)

affaisser (s')   to collapse, sink   (33, 274)

affamer   to starve   (71)

affecter de   to pretend to   (8)

affectionner   to have a liking for   (171)

affermer   to lease, rent   (227)

affermir   to strengthen   (229)

afficher   to display   (94)

affilier (s') à   to affiliate to   (33, 41)

affirmer   to affirm   (227)

affliger de   to afflict with   (119)

affluer   to abound   (114)

affoler (s')   to panic   (33, 421)

affranchir   to set free; to stamp (frank)   (72)

affréter   to charter (boat, plane)   (87)

affronter   to confront   (113)

affubler   to don (clothing)   (407)

affûter   to hone, sharpen   (173)

agencer   to arrange, combine   (342)

agenouiller (s')   to kneel   (233)

agglutiner   to agglutinate, stick together   (329)

aggraver   to aggravate, make worse   (276)

agiter   to wag, wave, shake   (251)

agrafer   to staple, fasten   (27)

agrandir   to enlarge   (245)

agréer   to accept   (128)

agrémenter de   to embellish with   (60)

agresser   to attack   (23)

agripper   to grab, grip   (163)

aguerrir   to harden, season (soldiers)   (229)

aguicher   to entice, seduce   (285)

aiguiser   to sharpen   (486)

ahurir   to astound, stun   (229)

aigrir   to sour   (229)

aiguiller   to orient, steer   (477)

aiguillonner   to goad   (171)

aimanter   to magnetize   (90)

ajourner   to postpone   (433)

ajuster   to adjust   (28)

alarmer   to alarm   (310)

alerter de   to warn about   (173)

aliéner   to alienate   (87)

aligner   to align   (26)

alimenter de   to feed with   (60)

allaiter   to breast-feed, nurse (infant), suckle (animal)   (27)

allécher   to stimulate someone's appetite   (87)

alléger   to ease, lighten   (52)

allier   to ally, tie together   (41)

allonger   to stretch out   (442)

allouer   to allocate, grant   (281)

allumer   to light, turn on   (238)

alourdir de   to weigh down   (229)

alphabétiser   to teach someone to read and write   (486)

altérer   to alter, spoil   (87)

alterner   to alternate   (27)

alunir   to land on the moon   (229)

amadouer   to coax   (269)

amaigrir   to make thin   (282)

amarrer   to moor, tie down   (27)

amasser   to amass, pile up   (92)

ambitionner de   to aspire to   (171)

améliorer   to improve, ameliorate   (22)

aménager   to set up, install   (305)

amender   to amend, correct   (27)

américaniser   to Americanize   (32)

ameuter   to draw/incite a crowd   (374)

amidonner   to starch   (171)

amincir   to have a slimming effect   (229)

amoindrir   to lessen   (229)

amollir   to soften   (229)

amonceler   to amass, pile up (38)

amorcer   to start, boot (computer) (342)

amortir   to cushion, soften (229)

amplifier de   to amplify with/by (322)

amputer   to amputate (251)

analyser   to analyze (32)

ancrer   to anchor (27)

anéantir   to annihilate (229)

angliciser   to anglicize (23)

angoisser   to cause anguish, distress (27)

animer   to animate (27)

annexer   to annex (27)

annihiler   to annihilate (27)

annuler   to annul, cancel (81)

anoblir   to ennoble (423)

ânonner   to drone, stumble through a public reading (171)

anticiper   to anticipate (329)

antidater   to antedate, backdate (28)

apaiser   to calm down, pacify (27)

apitoyer   to inspire pity (187)

aplanir   to make level, smooth (229)

aplatir   to flatten (229)

appauvrir   to impoverish (229)

applaudir de   to applaud for (229)

appliquer   to apply (219)

appesantir   to weigh down (229)

appréhender   to fear, grasp, apprehend (legal term) (27)

apprêter (s') à qqch   to get oneself ready for (48, 363)

apprêter   to get ready, prepare (363)

apprivoiser   to tame (486)

approcher (s')   to approach, come near (33, 43)

approfondir   to deepen (229)

approprier (s')   to appropriate (83, 212)

approvisionner   to supply (171)

appuyer   to lean, press (192)

arabiser   to arabize (486)

arbitrer   to arbitrate, referee (27)

arc-bouter (s') à   to lean against (33)

archiver   to archive (27)

armer   to arm (238)

arnaquer   to cheat, swindle (284)

arpenter   to pace, survey (land) (28)

arquer   to arch, curve (284)

arranger (s')   to come to an agreement (33, 46)

arrimer   to secure, tie down (27)

arroger (s')   to claim falsely (33, 305)

arrondir   to round (off) (229)

arroser   to water (79)

articuler   to articulate (81)

asperger   to spray, sprinkle (283)

asphyxier   to asphyxiate, suffocate (41)

aspirer   to inhale (21)

assainir   to clean, make healthier (229)

assaisonner   to season (171)

assassiner   to murder, assassinate (159)

assécher   to drain, dry (429)

assembler   to assemble (407)

assermenter   to swear in (374)

asservir   to subjugate (229)

assigner   to assign (441)

assimiler   to assimilate, take in (27)

assimiler qqn/qqch à   to compare someone/something to (27)

associer (qqch à)   to link (something with), associate (41)

assombrir   to darken (229)

assommer   to knock out, stun (310)

assortir   to match (229)

assoupir (s')   to nod off (229)

assouplir   to soften (423)

assourdir   to deafen (229)

assumer   to assume, accept (27)

atomiser   to atomize (486)

attabler (s')   to sit down at a table (for a meal) (33)

attacher   to tie up (82)

attaquer   to attack (219)

attarder   to delay (240)

attarder (s')   to dawdle, fall behind schedule (33)

atteler   to harness (horses) (38)

attendre (s') à   to expect (208)

attendrir   to inspire pity, tenderize (meat) (229)

atténuer   to relieve, lighten, ease (114)

atterrir   to land (229)

attester   to testify (160)

attiédir   to make lukewarm (229)

attribuer à   to attribute to (114)

attrister   to sadden (28)

ausculter   to auscultate, listen to someone's chest (28)

automatiser   to automate (486)

autoriser   to authorize (16)

avaler   to swallow (27)

avancer (s')   to advance (oneself) (33, 61)

avantager   to favor (305)

aventurer   to venture (148)

avérer (s') to prove/turn out to be (33, 87)

avertir de to warn about (229)

aveugler to blind (27)

avilir to degrade, depreciate (423)

aviser to notify (32)

aviser (s') to notice, become aware (32, 33)

aviver to enliven, excite (486)

avoisiner to be close to, border (159)

avorter to abort (27)

avouer to admit (269)

B

babiller sur to gossip about (27)

bachoter to cram for an exam (96)

bâcler to botch up (445)

badiner to exchange banter, jest (167)

bafouer qqn to flout, scorn (269)

bafouiller to stammer (233)

bâfrer to guzzle, eat like a pig (82)

bagarrer to argue, wrangle (435)

baigner to bathe (10)

bâiller to yawn (477)

bâillonner to gag, muzzle (171)

baiser to kiss, have intercourse (Watch out! Unless you're kissing someone's cheek or hand, avoid *baiser*!) (27)

balader to take for a walk (26)

balader (se) to stroll (26, 122)

balafrer to slash (27)

balbutier to stammer (212)

baliser to mark a path, mark off (486)

ballotter to jolt, bounce around (171)

banaliser to make commonplace, trivialize (486)

bander to bandage, blindfold (27)

bannir de to banish from (229)

baptiser to baptize (32)

baragouiner to jabber, speak badly (329)

baratiner to sweet-talk (329)

barber to bore (27)

barbouiller (de) to daub (with) (233)

barrer to bar (21)

basculer to topple over (81)

baser sur to base upon (32)

batailler to battle (477)

bâtonner to beat with a stick (171)

baver to drool, dribble (276)

bêcher to dig out/up (285)

becqueter to peck (267)

bégayer to stammer (179)

bénéficier de to profit from/by (389)

bercer to rock (99)

besogner to drudge, work hard (441)

beugler to low, bellow (27)

beurrer to butter (26)

bidonner (se) to roar with laughter (122, 171)

bifurquer to bifurcate, fork (284)

bivouaquer to bivouac (219)

blaguer to joke (307)

blaser (se) de to become indifferent to (33, 122)

blasphémer to blaspheme (356)

blêmir to become pale (229)

bleuir to turn blue (229)

blinder to shield, armor (27)

bloguer to blog (307)

blondir to become blond, bleach hair (210)

bloquer to block up (219)

blottir (se) to cuddle (214, 229)

bluffer to bluff (26)

bobiner to wind, spool (329)

boiter to limp (26)

bombarder to bombard (385)

bondir to leap (229)

bonifier to improve (41)

border to border (248)

borner to limit (27)

bosser to work hard (79)

boucher to block up (469)

boucler to buckle (469)

bouder to sulk (240)

bouffer to gobble up (235)

bougonner to grumble (171)

bouillonner to bubble (171)

bouler to roll (421)

bouleverser to overwhelm (492)

bouquiner to read (329)

bourdonner to buzz (171)

bourgeonner to bud (171)

bourrer to stuff (22)

boursoufler to bloat, puff up (445)

bousculer to shove, bump (81)

bousiller to ruin (477)

bouter to drive away (28)

boutonner to button (171)

boxer to box (26)

boycotter to boycott (373)

brailler to bawl, cry (477)

brandir to brandish (210)

branler to shake (Watch out! Avoid using this verb pronominally!) (498)

braquer to aim, point (284)

brasser to brew, stir (79)

braver to defy (276)

bredouiller to mumble (233)

bricoler to tinker, fix (32)

brider to bridle, restrain (329)

briller to shine (477)

brimer to bully (27)

briquer to scrub (219)

briser   to break, smash   (32)

brocher   to stitch, staple (Qué.)   (285)

broder   to embroider   (96)

bronzer   to bronze, tan   (134)

brouiller   to blur, mix up   (233)

brouter   to graze   (28)

broyer   to crush, grind   (187)

bruiner   to drizzle   (27)

brunir   to brown   (229)

brusquer   to rush, hasten   (219)

brutaliser   to brutalize, bully   (486)

bûcher   to study hard, cut down trees (Qué.)   (285)

buriner   to engrave   (465)

buter   to trip   (173)

C

cabosser   to dent   (79)

cabrer   to rear up   (27)

cacheter   to seal   (267)

cadrer   to correspond (with)   (27)

cafouiller   to get mixed up   (233)

cahoter   to jolt   (28)

cajoler   to cajole, coax   (27)

calcifier   to calcify   (41)

calciner   to char   (329)

calculer   to calculate   (81)

caler   to stall, wedge   (27)

calibrer   to calibrate   (27)

câliner   to cuddle   (329)

calmer   to calm   (27)

calmer (se)   to calm down   (27)

calomnier   to slander, libel (in writing)   (212)

cambrer   to arch   (27)

cambrioler   to break into, burglarize   (26)

camoufler   to camouflage   (445)

camper   to camp   (235)

canaliser   to channel, funnel   (26)

canoniser   to canonize   (486)

canonner   to shell (military)   (171)

canoter   to go boating, rowing   (26)

cantonner   to station, billet   (171)

caoutchouter   to rubberize   (28)

capitaliser   to capitalize   (486)

capoter   to turn over, collapse, go crazy (Qué.)

capituler   to capitulate, surrender   (81)

captiver   to captivate   (167)

capturer   to capture   (27)

caqueter   to cackle, gossip   (267)

caractériser   to characterize   (486)

carboniser   to carbonize, burn up   (486)

caresser   to caress   (353)

caricaturer   to caricature   (21)

carillonner   to ring   (171)

carnavaler   to celebrate at a carnival (Qué.)   (27)

carreler   to tile   (38)

caser   to fit (something) in   (32)

castrer   to castrate   (27)

cataloguer   to catalog   (307)

catéchiser   to catechize   (486)

cautionner   to guarantee   (171)

caviarder   to censor   (27)

ceindre de   to encircle with   (334)

célébrer   to celebrate   (356)

celer   to conceal   (297)

censurer   to censure   (54)

centraliser   to centralize   (486)

cercler de   to encircle with   (27)

cerner   to surround, define   (27)

certifier   to certify   (212)

chagriner   to grieve, distress   (329)

chahuter   to create an uproar   (8)

chaîner   to chain   (167)

chanceler   to stagger   (38)

chantonner   to sing to oneself   (171)

chaparder   to pilfer, swipe   (27)

chaperonner   to chaperon   (171)

charmer   to charm   (238)

châtier   to punish   (212)

chatouiller   to tickle   (233)

chatoyer   to glisten, glimmer   (187)

chauffer   to warm up, heat up   (235)

chauffer (se)   to warm oneself up   (122, 235)

chausser   to put on shoes   (79)

chavirer   to capsize   (27)

cheminer   to walk along   (465)

chevaucher   to straddle, ride   (285)

chialer   to bawl   (421)

chicaner   to haggle, quibble   (147)

chiffonner   to crumple   (171)

chiffrer   to number   (27)

chiper   to steal   (251)

choir   to fall   (Def. and Imp.)

choper   to catch, snatch, steal   (163)

chloroformer   to chloroform   (227)

chômer   to be unemployed   (27)

choquer   to shock   (284)

choyer   to pamper   (187)

chronométrer   to time   (87)

chuter   to fall, flop   (28)

cibler   to target   (27)

cimenter   to cement   (464)

cintrer   to arch, curve   (27)

circonscrire   to circumscribe, delimit, set limits   (177)

circonvenir   to circumvent   (491)

circuler   to circulate   (81)

cirer   to wax   (466)

ciseler   to chisel, engrave   (297)

citer   to quote   (251)

civiliser   to civilize   (486)

clamer   to proclaim, clamor   (9)

clapper (de la langue)   to click (one's tongue)   (235)

claquer   to bang, click (one's tongue)   (284)

clarifier   to clarify   (212)

classer   to classify   (84)

classifier   to classify   (212)

clavarder   to chat (Internet)   (69)

cligner   to blink   (10)

clignoter   to blink, flash, twinkle   (27)

climatiser   to air condition   (486)

cliquer   to click   (219)

clocher   to be wrong   (285)

cloisonner   to partition   (171)

cloner   to clone   (461)

clouer   to nail, tack down   (269)

cocher   to check off   (121)

coder   to code   (26)

codifier   to codify   (41)

coexister   to coexist   (259)

cogiter   to cogitate, ponder   (215)

cogner   to hit   (10)

coiffer qqn   to do someone's hair   (443)

coiffer (se)   to do one's own hair   (122)

coincer   to jam, corner   (342)

collaborer   to collaborate   (22)

collationner   to collate   (171)

collectionner   to collect   (171)

coller à   to stick to   (445)

colleter   to grab by the collar   (267)

colmater   to plug up   (28)

coloniser   to colonize, settle   (486)

colorer   to color   (22)

colorier   to color (in)   (212)

colporter   to peddle   (349)

combiner   to combine   (329)

combler de   to fill up with   (407)

commanditer   to finance   (215)

commémorer   to commemorate   (22)

commercer avec   to trade with   (99)

commercialiser   to commercialize   (486)

commuer   to commute (legal term)   (114)

communier   to receive communion   (389)

communiquer   to communicate   (219)

commuter   to commute (mathematics)   (173)

comparaître   to appear before court   (324)

compatir   to sympathize   (95)

compenser   to compensate, make up for   (336)

compiler   to compile   (251)

complaire à   to try to please   (345)

compléter   to complete   (87)

complimenter   to compliment   (60)

compliquer   to complicate   (219)

comploter   to plot   (349)

comporter (se)   to behave   (80, 349)

comporter   to comprise   (349)

composer   to compose, dial (a number)   (350)

composter   to punch (a ticket)   (349)

compromettre   to compromise   (294)

compulser   to consult   (32)

concasser   to crush   (84)

concéder   to concede   (87)

concentrer (se) sur   to concentrate (oneself) on   (80, 299)

concentrer sur   to concentrate on   (299)

concilier   to reconcile   (212)

concocter   to concoct   (349)

concorder avec   to agree with   (11)

concourir avec   to compete with   (125)

concurrencer   to compete   (342)

condamner   to condemn   (98)

condescendre à   to condescend to   (394)

conditionner   to condition   (171)

confectionner   to make   (171)

conférer   to confer, bestow on   (356)

confesser   to confess   (73)

confier   to entrust   (212)

configurer   to configure   (27)

confiner   to confine   (329)

confirmer   to confirm   (227)

confisquer   to confiscate   (219)

confluer   to converge, flow together   (114)

confondre   to confound   (231)

conformer (se) à   to conform to   (122, 227)

confronter   to confront   (113)

congédier   to dismiss   (212)

congeler   to freeze   (242)

conjecturer   to conjecture, speculate   (54)

conjoindre   to join in marriage   (268)

conjuguer   to conjugate   (307)

conjurer   to beseech   (54)

connecter   to connect   (349)

Index of 2,600 additional verbs

déblatérer   to rant and rave (356)

déblayer   to clear off (snow, dirt) (330)

débloquer   to unblock (219)

déboguer   to debug (computer) (307)

déboiser   to deforest (486)

déborder   to overflow (26)

déboucher   to uncork, unclog (285)

déboucler   to unbuckle (326)

déboulonner   to unbolt (171)

déboussoler   to disorient (498)

déboutonner   to unbutton (171)

débrancher   to disconnect, unplug (285)

débrayer   to disengage the clutch, declutch (330)

débrider   to unbridle (251)

débrouiller   to disentangle (233)

débrouiller (se)   to cope, get by, manage (122, 233)

débuter   to begin (173)

décacheter   to unseal (267)

décalcifier   to decalcify, delime (41)

décaler   to move out of line, to shift ahead/back (hour) (326)

décamper   to decamp, run away (27)

décaper   to strip (paint, wood) (235)

décapiter   to decapitate (251)

décéder   to pass away (87)

déceler   to discover, reveal (297)

décerner   to award (470)

déchaîner   to unchain (329)

déchanter   to become disillusioned (90)

décharger   to unload (91)

déchausser (se)   to take off one's shoes (80, 122)

déchiffrer   to decipher (27)

décimer   to decimate (27)

déclamer   to declaim (71)

déclarer   to declare (69)

déclencher   to trigger, set off (285)

décliner   to decline (465)

décoiffer qqn   to tousle, mess up someone's hair (443)

décoincer   to free up, loosen (342)

décolérer   to be in a (bad) temper (356)

décoller   to unstick, take off (airplane) (385)

décolorer   to decolorize, to bleach (22)

décommander   to cancel an order (98)

décomposer   to decompose (350)

déconcerter   to disconcert (160)

décongestionner   to decongest, relieve congestion (traffic) (171)

déconnecter   to disconnect (27)

déconseiller   to advise against (109)

déconsidérer   to discredit (356)

déconstruire   to deconstruct (133)

décontracter   to unclench, relax (160)

décorer de   to decorate with (22)

décorner   to remove a horn, smooth out (paper) (470)

décortiquer   to shell (remove a shell), analyze (219)

découcher   to spend the night away from one's house (121)

découdre   to unstitch (123)

découler de   to follow from (usually impers.) (421)

découper   to cut up (124)

décourager de   to discourage from (305)

décrasser   to clean, scrub (79)

décréter   to decree (87)

décrier   to decry (129)

décroiser   to uncross (arms, legs) (486)

décrocher   to unhook; to get; to drop out of school (82)

décrotter   to clean mud off (163)

dédaigner   to disdain (10)

dédicacer à   to dedicate to (a book) (342)

dédier à   to dedicate to (212)

dédommager   to compensate, make up for (305)

dédoubler   to separate in two (407)

défaillir   to weaken, faint (222)

défavoriser   to disadvantage (486)

déférer à   to defer to (356)

déferler   to break (wave), unfurl (326)

défier   to challenge (212)

définir   to define (229)

défoncer   to push the bottom out, knock down (371)

déformer   to deform (227)

défouler (se)   to unwind (122, 421)

défricher   to clear (land) (285)

dégarnir   to empty, take away objects/decorations (229)

dégeler   to thaw (242)

dégivrer   to defrost, deice (27)

dégonfler   to deflate, reduce swelling (498)

dégorger   to disgorge, unblock (283)

dégouliner   to drip, trickle down (329)

dégourdir (se)   to stretch one's legs, relieve stiffness (210, 214)

dégoûter   to disgust (244)

dégoutter   to drip (244)

dégrader   to damage, degrade (27)

dégrafer   to unfasten, unstaple (27)

dégraisser to remove/trim fat (274)

dégringoler to tumble (498)

dégriser to sober up (486)

dégrossir to polish (282)

déguerpir to run away (95)

déguiser (se) to disguise oneself (122, 486)

déguster to taste, sample food (53)

déjouer to foil, thwart (269)

délabrer to ruin (407)

délacer to unlace (342)

délaisser to abandon, quit (274)

délasser to relax (79)

délayer to mix, water down (330)

déléguer to delegate (87, 307)

délibérer to deliberate (356)

délier to untie (389)

délister to delist (Internet) (160)

délivrer to set free (21)

déloger to dislodge, move out (305)

demander (se) to wonder (122, 147)

démanger to feel an itch (283)

démaquiller (se) to remove one's makeup (477)

démarrer to start out, to boot (computer) (27)

démêler to untangle (82)

déménager to move belongings from one residence to another (305)

démener (se) to struggle (122, 290)

démentir to deny, refute (291)

démériter de to show oneself unworthy of (293)

démettre to dislocate (294)

démissionner de to resign from (171)

démobiliser to demobilize, demotivate (486)

démocratiser to democratize (486)

démoder (se) to go out of style (27)

démonter qqch to dismantle something (298) (aux. avoir)

démontrer to demonstrate (299)

dénationaliser to denationalize (486)

dénicher to unearth, spot (285)

dénigrer to denigrate (21)

dénombrer to count (407)

dénommer to name (310)

dénoncer to denounce (371)

dénoter to denote (498)

dénouer to untie (269)

dépanner to fix, help out (171)

déparer to spoil, disfigure (27)

départir de (se) to depart from, stray from (434)

dépasser to go past, beyond (328)

dépayser to make a change of scenery, to disorient (486)

dépêcher to dispatch (27)

dépêtrer to extricate, free someone (349)

dépeupler to depopulate (326)

dépister to track down, screen (medical) (215)

déplacer to move, shift, displace (342)

déplâtrer to remove plaster, remove a cast (medical) (349)

déplier to unfold (389)

déplorer to deplore (22)

déployer to deploy, spread out, exhibit (187)

dépolitiser to depoliticize (486)

déporter to deport (349)

déposer to put down, set down, deposit (350)

déposséder to dispossess, deprive (87)

dépouiller to strip, skim, despoil (233)

dépraver to corrupt, deprave (276)

déprécier to depreciate (41)

déprimer to depress (220)

déraciner to uproot (159)

dérégler to disturb, throw out of whack (87)

dériver to divert (329)

dériver de to derive from (329)

dérober to steal (498)

dérouler to unwind, roll out, unroll (421)

dérouler (se) to unwind, take place (421)

dérouter to reroute, disconcert (28)

désaltérer to refresh, slake/quench thirst (356)

désamorcer to defuse (342)

désapprendre to unlearn, forget (42)

désapprouver to disapprove of (44)

désarmer to disarm (238)

désarticuler to disjoint (81)

désavantager to disadvantage (305)

déserter to desert, abandon (40)

désespérer to despair (203)

déshabiller (se) to undress oneself (250)

désherber to weed (27)

déshonorer to dishonor (22)

déshydrater to dehydrate (241)

désigner to designate, point out (441)

désinfecter to disinfect (160)

désintégrer to disintegrate (356)

désintoxiquer to detoxify (219)

désister (se) de (en faveur de qqn) to withdraw (in someone's favor) (53)

désobéir à to disobey (314)

désoler to sadden (421)

désosser to bone (remove bones) (79)

dessaler to desalinate (326)

dessécher to dry out (87)

desservir to clear away (la table/the table); to provide a service (437)

déstabiliser to destabilize (486)

destiner à to destine/intend for (329)

destituer to dismiss, demote (483)

désunir to split up (229)

détacher to untie (285)

détailler to detail, sell retail (477)

détecter to detect (160)

déteindre to take out the color (207)

détendre to loosen, slacken (462)

détendre (se) to relax (394)

détenir to detain (463)

détériorer to deteriorate (27)

déterminer to determine (329)

déterrer to dig up, unearth (196)

détoner to detonate (461)

détourner to divert (470)

détourner (se) to turn oneself away from (122, 161)

détraquer to put out of order (219)

détremper to soak (464)

détromper (se) to see the truth about a matter (480)

détromper de to disabuse of, free someone from a misconception (317) (See 480)

dévaler to tumble down (27)

dévaliser to rob, empty out (486)

dévaluer to devalue (114)

devancer to arrive ahead of, precede, anticipate (61)

dévaster to devastate (259)

déverrouiller to unlock, unbolt (233)

déverser to pour, pour out (492)

dévêtir to undress (493)

dévêtir (se) to undress oneself (250, 493)

dévider to unwind, reel off (251)

dévier to deviate (41)

deviner to guess (329)

dévisager to stare at someone (305)

dévisser to unscrew (486)

dévoiler to unveil (498)

dévorer to devour (27)

dévouer to devote (269)

diagnostiquer to diagnose (219)

dialoguer (avec un ordinateur) to converse; to interact with a computer (307)

dicter to dictate (253)

diffamer to defame, slander (71)

différer to differ, defer (203)

diffuser to broadcast, diffuse (32)

digérer to digest (203)

dilapider to waste (215)

diriger to direct (119)

discerner to discern, distinguish (27)

discontinuer to discontinue (114)

discourir sur to expatiate on, talk at length (125)

discréditer to discredit (215)

discriminer to discriminate, distinguish (465)

disculper to exonerate (27)

disjoindre to separate (268)

dispenser to exempt, excuse (336)

disperser to disperse (478)

disposer to arrange (350)

disputer de qqch to dispute something (425)

disqualifier to disqualify (212)

disséminer to disseminate, scatter (465)

disséquer to dissect, analyze (87, 284)

disserter sur to write about (160)

dissimuler to conceal, hide (81)

dissiper to dissipate, disperse (251)

dissocier to separate, dissociate (41)

dissoudre to dissolve (6)

dissuader de to dissuade from (340)

distancer to outdistance (342)

distraire to distract, entertain (474)

distinguer to distinguish (307)

distribuer to distribute (114)

diverger to diverge (283)

diversifier to diversify (41)

divertir to amuse, entertain (210)

divertir (se) to have fun (210, 214)

diviser en to divide into (32)

divulguer to divulge (307)

documenter to document (60)

domestiquer to domesticate (219)

dominer to control, dominate (329)

dompter to tame (107)

dorer to gild (22)

dorloter to pamper (96)

doser to measure/determine a dose (321)

doubler to double, to pass (auto), to dub (audio) (481)

douer to endow (269)

douter (se) to suspect (122, 173)

draguer to dredge (literal), to try to pick someone up (figurative) (307)

drainer to drain (27)

dresser to draw up, erect (23)

dresser (se) to stand up (23, 122)

dribbler to dribble (sports) (326)

droguer to drug (307)

duper to dupe, trick (317)

dupliquer to duplicate (219)

durcir to harden (95)

durer to last (272)

dynamiter dynamite (251)

E

ébahir to stun (95)

ébaucher to sketch (469)

éblouir to dazzle (229)

ébouriffer to tousle someone's hair, stun (215)

ébranler to shake (326)

ébruiter to divulge a secret (215)

écarter to separate, spread apart (69)

échafauder to build up, put up scaffolding (447)

échanger to exchange (89)

échantillonner to sample (171)

échapper (s') to escape (27, 33)

écharper to tear to pieces (59)

échauffer to heat, overheat (171)

échelonner to space, spread out at even intervals (171)

écheveler to dishevel (38)

éclabousser to splash (79)

éclaircir to clear up (229)

éclairer to light (21)

éclater en to burst into (176)

éclore to hatch (See clore) (Def. and Imp.)

écoeurer to disgust, make someone sick (466)

économiser to save, economize (486)

écouler to sell out of (421)

écourter to shorten (160)

écrabouiller to crush (233)

écraser to crush (183)

écrémer to skim off (87)

écrier (s') to cry out (33, 41)

écrivasser to write badly (84)

écrouler (s') to collapse (33, 421)

écumer to foam, lather, skim off (27)

édifier to build, edify (41)

éditer to publish, edit (251)

édulcorer to sweeten (22)

éduquer to educate (219)

effacer to efface, erase (342)

effarer to alarm (22)

effaroucher to scare away (285)

effectuer to effect, bring about (483)

effeuiller to pull off leaves, petals (477)

effleurer to brush, touch lightly (466)

efforcer (s') to force oneself, try (33, 342)

effriter (s') to erode (33, 215)

égaler to equal (326)

égaliser to equalize (486)

égarer (s') to get lost, wander (33, 101)

égorger to cut the throat of (283)

egosurfer to egosurf (27)

égoutter to drain (374)

égratigner to scratch (441)

élancer (s') to rush forward (33, 342)

élargir to enlarge, widen (229)

électriser to electrify (486)

élider to elide (251)

élimer to wear out, wear thin (27)

éliminer to eliminate (465)

éloigner de to move, keep away from (194)

élucider to elucidate (26)

éluder to elude (32)

émaner de to emanate from (27)

émasculer to emasculate (81)

emballer to pack, wrap (421)

embarquer to embark (219)

embarrasser to embarrass, clutter, hinder (84)

embaucher to hire (285)

embaumer to embalm, make fragrant (27)

embellir to beautify, embellish (229)

embêter to annoy, bother, worry (47)

embobiner to spool, wind, wrap someone around one's finger (329)

emboîter to fit together (251)

embrayer to engage the clutch (330)

embrouiller to complicate, tangle up (233)

embuer to mist up (114)

embusquer (s') to ambush (33, 284)

émettre to emit (294)

émigrer to emigrate (21)

emmagasiner to store, stockpile (159)

emménager to move in (305)

emmerder to bother, hassle someone (240)

emmurer to wall in (32)

émonder to prune (240)

empaqueter to wrap up, package (267)

emparer (s') de to seize (33, 101)

empêtrer (s') to trap, entangle (33, 299)

empiffrer (s') to stuff oneself, make a pig of oneself (33, 466) empiler to pile up (329)

empirer to worsen (466)

emplir to fill (95)

empocher to pocket (285)

empoisonner to poison (171)

emporter to carry away (349)

empresser (s') de to make haste, hasten (361)

empuantir to smell/stink up (210)

encadrer to frame (299)

encaisser to cash (274)

encercler to encircle (27)

enchaîner to put in chains, to link/string together (167)

enchanter to enchant (90)

enchevêtrer to tangle, confuse (299)

enclaver to enclose (276)

encourir to incur (125)

encrasser to dirty (84)

encroûter to encrust (244)

endiguer to hold back (307)

endoctriner to indoctrinate (329)

endommager to damage (305)

endormir (s') to fall asleep (172, 257)

endosser to put on, endorse (79)

enduire to smear (133)

endurcir to harden, toughen (95)

endurer to endure (54)

énerver (s') to become annoyed (33, 276)

enfermer to shut away, lock up (227)

enfiler to thread, put on (329)

enfler (s') to swell (361, 445)

enfoncer to plunge in, smash down (371)

enfouir to bury (270)

enfourcher to mount, straddle (285)

enfreindre to infringe (334)

enfumer to fill (a place) with smoke (238)

engager (s') to commit oneself to do (305, 318)

engager to engage, start up, to hire (305)

engendrer to generate, beget (299)

englober to encompass, include (27)

engloutir to engulf, swallow up (66)

engouffrer to swallow up (445)

engourdir to numb (210)

engraisser to fatten (274)

engueuler to scold, chew someone out (421)

enhardir to make bold (210)

enivrer (s') to become intoxicated (33)

enjamber to stride, step over (240)

enjoindre à qqn de faire to charge someone to do (268)

enjôler to cajole (498)

enlacer to entwine, embrace (342)

enlaidir to make ugly (210)

enliser (s') to get stuck, bogged down (33, 486)

ennuyer (s') to be bored (55, 192)

énoncer to state, express (371)

enorgueillir de to be proud of (something) (229)

enquérir (s') de to inquire about (19) (aux. être)

enquêter (sur) to investigate (47)

enquiquiner to annoy, bore (329)

enraciner (s') to take root (33, 329)

enrager to be enraged, furious (305)

enrayer to block, curb (330)

enregistrer to record, register (393)

enrhumer (s') to catch a cold (33, 238)

enrichir to enrich (229)

enrouler to wind, roll up (421)

ensabler to cover in sand (407)

ensabler (s') to get stuck, buried in sand (33, 407)

ensanglanter to bloody (90)

ensevelir to bury (229)

ensoleiller to brighten with sunlight (109)

ensorceler to bewitch (38)

ensuivre (s') to follow (453) (3ᵈ pers. sing. and pl.)

entacher to soil (82)

entamer to begin, start (71)

entendre (s') (avec) to get along (with) (195) (aux. être)

entériner to ratify (329)

entêter (s') to persist in, be stubborn (33, 47)

enthousiasmer to enthuse (27)

entôler to fleece (498)

entortiller to twist (477)

entourer de to surround with (21)

entraîner to carry away (27)

entraver to hinder (276)

entrebâiller to open halfway (477)

entrecouper de to intersperse, interrupt with (124)

entrelacer to intertwine, interlace (342)

entremêler to intermingle (82)

entremettre (s') to intervene, meddle (295)

entreposer to store in a warehouse (350)

entretenir to maintain, support (463)

entretuer (s') to kill each other (33, 483)

entrevoir to catch a glimpse (497)

entrouvrir to half open, open halfway (323)

énumérer to enumerate (356)

envahir to invade (229)

envelopper to envelope, wrap up (235)

envenimer to poison, inflame (27)

envier to envy (212)

environner to surround (171)

envisager to envisage, contemplate (305)

épaissir to thicken (95)

épancher to pour out, vent (78)

épanouir (s') to bloom, blossom (214)

épargner to save, economize (10)

éparpiller to scatter (477)

épater to amaze, shock (241)

épauler to shoulder, support (421)

épeler to spell (38)

épicer to spice up (342)

épier to spy on (212)

épiler to depilate, remove unwanted hair (329)

épingler to pin (326)

éplucher to peel (82)

éponger to sponge (283)

époumoner (s') to yell at the top of one's lungs (461)

épousseter to dust (267)

époustoufler to flabbergast, stun (445)

épouvanter to terrify (90)

éprendre de (s') to fall for someone (357)

épuiser to exhaust (486)

épurer to filter, refine (54)

équilibrer to balance (158)

équiper de to equip with (215)

équivaloir to be equivalent (488)

éradiquer to eradicate (219)

érafler to scratch (439)

éreinter to exhaust (90)

ergoter to quibble (96)

ériger to erect (119)

éroder to erode (96)

errer to wander (27)

éructer to belch, burp (28)

escamoter to evade, dodge (96)

escompter to discount (financial), to count on (103)

escroquer to cheat (219)

espionner to spy on (171)

esquinter to ruin, smash up (90)

esquisser to sketch (183)

esquiver to avoid (276)

essorer dry out (22)

essouffler (s') to run out of breath (122, 445)

estamper to stamp (247)

estimer to esteem, estimate (27)

estomaquer to shock (219)

estomper to blur (247)

étaler to spread out, display (326)

étancher to make something waterproof, watertight (78)

étayer to prop up (330)

étendre to roll out, spread out (462)

éternuer to sneeze (114)

étêter to cut the head off of something (47)

étiqueter to label (267)

étirer to stretch 466)

étirer (s') to stretch oneself (182, 466)

étouffer to suffocate (353)

étrangler to strangle (326)

étreindre to embrace, hug (334)

étriper to gut (215)

évacuer to evacuate (114)

évader (s') de to escape from (26, 33)

évaporer (s') to evaporate (22, 33)

éveiller to awaken (109)

éventer to fan (90)

évoluer to develop (213)

évoquer to evoke (219)

exacerber to aggravate, exacerbate (27)

exagérer to exaggerate (356)

exalter to exalt, excite (28)

examiner to examine (465)

exaspérer to exasperate (203)

excéder to exceed (87)

exceller to excel (326)

excepter to except (8)

exciter to excite (251)

exclamer (s') to cry out (9)

exclure to exclude (105)

excommunier to excommunicate (309)

exécrer to abhor, detest (203)

exécuter to execute, carry out (169)

exercer to exercise, exert (342)

exhausser to raise (353)

exhiber to exhibit (251)

exhumer to exhume (238)

exister to exist (349)

exonérer to exonerate, exempt (203)

expédier to send (212)

expérimenter test (464)

expirer to exhale; to expire, die (466)

exploiter to exploit (251)

explorer to explore (22)

exploser to explode (321)

exporter to export (349)

exposer to expose (350)

exproprier to expropriate (41)

expulser to expel (336)

exterminer to exterminate (465)

extraire to extract (474)

F

fabriquer to manufacture (219)

fabuler to fabricate, make up stories (81)

fâcher qqn to annoy, offend, anger someone (82) (See 216; aux. avoir)

faciliter to facilitate (225)

façonner to shape, fashion (171)
facturer to bill (54)
faiblir to weaken (392)
falloir to be necessary, must, to be lacking (à), to need (Def. and Imp.)
falsifier to falsify (212)
familiariser to familiarize (486)
faner (se) to fade, wither (122)
farcir de to stuff with (cooking), cram with (229)
farder to apply makeup to someone's face (240)
farder (se) to apply makeup to one's own face (83, 240)
fasciner to fascinate (329)
fatiguer to tire, get weary (307)
faucher to reap, mow; to steal (82)
faufiler (se) to sneak through, slip through (27, 122)
fausser to distort, twist (353)
favoriser to favor (486)
fédérer to federate (203)
féliciter to congratulate (251)
fendiller to crack (477)
fertiliser to fertilize (486)
fêter to celebrate (363)
feuilleter to leaf through (267)
fiancer (se) to get engaged (122, 342)
figer (se) to coagulate, freeze up (119)
fignoler to polish, perfect (498)
figurer to represent (54)
filer to spin, dash off, run off (27)
filmer to film (227)
filtrer to filter (299)
fixer to fix, set, arrange (27)
flageller whip (326)
flageoler to wobble (498)
flairer to smell (22)
flamber to burn (240)

flamboyer to blaze (187)
flâner to stroll (443)
flanquer to fling (284)
flatter to flatter, to stroke/pet (an animal) (27)
fléchir to bend, flex (383)
flétrir to fade, wither (383)
fleurir to flourish (249)
flinguer to blow away (slang), to flame (Internet) (307)
flirter to flirt (425)
flotter to float (79)
foisonner to abound (171)
foncer to dash along, run along, to darken (371)
fonctionner to function, work (171)
forger to forge (283)
formaliser to formalize (486)
formater to format (computer) (176)
former to form (227)
formuler to formulate (32)
fortifier to fortify (212)
foudroyer to strike (lightning), strike down (187)
fouetter to whip (447)
fouler to press, trample on (421)
fourmiller to swarm, tingle (477)
fourrager to forage, rummage (305)
fourrer to cram, shove in (22)
fourvoyer to mislead (187)
fracasser to smash, shatter (84)
fragmenter to fragment, split (464)
fraîchir to get cooler (383)
franchir to clear, cross (383)
franciser to gallicize (486)
fraterniser to fraternize (486)
frauder to defraud, cheat (27)
frayer to clear (330)
fredonner to hum (171)

freiner to brake, slow down (329)
fréquenter to frequent (60)
frétiller to wiggle (477)
friser to curl (486)
frissonner to shiver (171)
froisser to crumple, crease (353)
frôler to brush against, come close to (498)
froncer to knit (brow), wrinkle (nose) (34)
frotter to rub (79)
frustrer to frustrate (22)
fuguer to run away (307)
fulminer to fulminate, thunder (465)
fureter to ferret out, pry into, snoop, search (17)
fuser to burst forth, melt (32)
fusiller to shoot (477)

G

gâcher to spoil (82)
gager to bet, wager (305)
gainer to sheath (329)
galoper to gallop (163)
galvauder to tarnish (26)
gambader to leap about, gambol (26)
garantir to guarantee (229)
garer to park (435)
gargariser (se) to gargle (85, 486)
garnir de to garnish, provide with (229)
gaspiller to waste (477)
gausser (se) to mock (122, 353)
gazéifier to carbonate, aerate (212)
gazouiller to chirp, warble (233)
geindre to groan, moan (334)
gémir to groan (229)
gercer to chap (342)
gérer to manage (203)
gesticuler to gesticulate, make gestures while talking (32)

gicler   to spurt   (326)
gifler   to slap   (439)
gigoter   to wriggle   (96)
givrer   to frost   (466)
glacer   to freeze   (342)
glaner   to glean   (27)
glisser   to glide, slide   (73)
glorifier   to glorify   (212)
glousser   to cluck   (353)
gober   to swallow   (27)
gommer   to erase; to gum   (310)
gonfler   to inflate   (445)
gouverner   to govern   (167)
graver   to engrave   (276)
gravir   to climb   (95)
grelotter   to shiver   (79)
griffer   to scratch   (439)
griffonner   to scribble   (171)
grignoter   to nibble at; to snack   (96)
griller   to grill (meat, fish), toast (bread)   (477)
grimacer   to grimace (one's face)   (342)
grincer   to creak, grind   (99)
griser   to intoxicate, make tipsy   (486)
grogner   to growl, grumble   (10)
grossir   to get bigger, put on weight   (282)
grouiller   to swarm   (233)
grouper   to group   (124)
guetter   to watch   (386)
gueuler   to yell   (421)
guider   to guide   (26)
guillotiner   to guillotine   (329)

H

NOTE: The mark * in front of the letter *h* denotes that it is aspirate; make no liaison and use *je* instead of *j'*; *me* instead of *m'*.

habiliter   to authorize   (251)
habiller qqn, qqch   to dress someone, something   (477) (See 250; aux. **avoir**)

habituer (s')   to accustom oneself, get used to   (33, 483)
habituer   to accustom   (483)
*hacher   to chop up   (285)
*hachurer   to hatch (with hatch marks)   (54)
*haleter   to pant, gasp   (17)
halluciner   to hallucinate   (329)
hameçonner   to phish   (171)
*handicaper   to handicap   (59)
*hanter   to haunt   (90)
*harasser   to exhaust   (183)
*harceler   to harass   (297)
*hasarder   to hazard, risk   (240)
*hâter (se)   to hurry oneself   (74, 241)
*hausser   to raise   (92)
héberger   to lodge; to host (Internet)   (283)
hébraïser   to hebraize   (486)
*héler   to hail, call to   (87)
*hennir   to whinny, to bray   (229)
*hérisser (se)   to bristle, become annoyed   (122, 486)
hériter   to inherit   (293)
*heurter   to hit, bump   (246)
*hiérarchiser   to hierarchize, classify in a hierarchy   (486)
*hisser   to hoist   (84)
*hocher   to nod (one's head)   (82)
homologuer   to approve, ratify   (307)
honorer   to honor   (22)
horrifier   to horrify   (212)
hospitaliser   to hospitalize   (486)
*houspiller   to reprimand   (477)
*housser   to put a slipcover on   (353)
*huer   to boo   (483)
huiler   to oil   (27)

*hululer, ululer   to hoot, screech   (81)
humecter   to moisten, dampen   (60)
*hurler   to howl, yell   (326)
hydrater   to moisturize, hydrate   (241)
hyperlier   to hyperlink (Internet)   (454)
hypertrophier (s')   to hypertrophy, develop excessively   (212) (aux. être)
hypnotiser   to hypnotize   (486)
hypothéquer   to mortgage   (87, 219)

I

idéaliser   to idealize   (486)
identifier   to identify   (212)
idolâtrer   to idolize   (299)
ignorer   to be unaware of, not to know   (22)
illuminer   to illuminate   (465)
illustrer   to illustrate   (299)
imaginer   to imagine   (329)
imbiber   to soak   (215)
imbriquer (s')   to overlap, imbricate   (33, 219)
imiter   to imitate   (251)
immatriculer   to register   (81)
immerger   to immerse   (91)
immigrer   to immigrate   (93)
immobiliser   to immobilize   (486)
immoler   to immolate   (498)
immortaliser   to immortalize   (486)
immuniser   to immunize   (486)
impatienter (s')   to get impatient   (33, 464)
implanter (s')   to settle in, be located   (33, 90)
impliquer   to imply, implicate   (219)

implorer to implore (22)

importer to import, to matter (349)

importuner to importune, bother (32)

imposer to impose (350)

imprégner to permeate (87, 441)

impressionner to impress (171)

imprimer to print (220)

improviser to improvise (486)

inaugurer to inaugurate, initiate (54)

incarcérer to imprison (203)

incarner to personify, embody (27)

incendier to set on fire (212)

incinérer to incinerate (356)

inciter to incite (251)

incliner (s') devant to bow down before (33, 329)

incliner to incline (329)

incommoder to bother, inconvenience (96)

incorporer à to incorporate in (22)

indigner (s') to become indignant (33, 441)

induire (à) to induce (to) (106)

industrialiser to industrialize (486)

infecter de to infect with (113)

inférer de to infer from (356)

infester de to infest with (259)

infiltrer (s') dans to infiltrate, filter into (299, 262)

infliger à to inflict on (218)

influencer to influence (99)

informatiser to computerize (486)

informer to inform (227)

infuser to infuse (32)

ingénier (s') à to try one's best, use one's ingenuity (309) (aux. être)

ingérer to ingest (203)

ingérer (s') dans to interfere in (33, 203)

inhiber to inhibit (215)

inhumer to bury (238)

initier à to initiate into (389)

injecter to inject (8)

injurier to abuse (389)

inoculer to inoculate (81)

inonder to flood (336)

inquiéter qqn to worry, disturb someone (87) (See 258)

inscrire to inscribe, write down (177)

inscrire (s') to join, register (177) (aux. être)

insérer to insert (203)

insinuer to insinuate (114)

insonoriser to soundproof (486)

inspecter to inspect (113)

inspirer to inspire, to inhale (466)

installer to install (27)

instaurer to found (54)

instituer to institute (483)

insulter to insult (176)

insurger (s') contre to rise up against (33, 283)

intégrer to integrate, assimilate (203)

intensifier (s') to intensify (212) (aux. être)

intercaler to insert, intercalate (326)

intercéder to intercede (87)

intercepter to intercept (8)

intéresser qqn à qqch to interest someone in something (88)

interférer to interfere (356)

interpeller to hail, to question (police) (27)

interpoler to interpolate (498)

interposer entre to interpose between (350)

interpréter to interpret (87)

intervenir to intervene (491)

interviewer to interview (27)

intimider par to intimidate by (266)

intoxiquer to poison (219)

invalider to invalidate (266)

inventer to invent (90)

inverser to reverse (492)

invertir to invert (66)

investir to invest (66)

invoquer to invoke, call upon (219)

irradier to irradiate, radiate (389)

irriter to irritate (266)

isoler to isolate, insulate (498)

isoler (de) to isolate (from) (498)

italianiser to italianize (486)

J

jacasser to chatter, jabber (84)

jacter to jabber (8)

jaillir to gush forth, spurt out (423)

jalonner to mark off (171)

japper to yap, yelp (235)

jardiner to garden (167)

jargonner to jabber (171)

jaser to chatter, prattle (84)

jauger to gauge, size up (76)

jaunir to yellow, turn yellow (229)

javelliser to bleach, chlorinate (486)

jeûner to fast, go without food (146)

joncher qqch de to strew something with (93)

jongler to juggle (326)

jucher sur to perch on (469)

jumeler to twin, couple (38)

justifier to justify (389)

K

kidnapper to kidnap (235)
klaxonner to hoot, toot, sound a horn (171)

L

labourer to plow (481)
lacer to lace (342)
lacérer to lacerate (356)
lâcher to loosen, let go, release (82)
laïciser to laicize, secularize (486)
lambiner to dawdle, dillydally (329)
lamenter (se) sur qqch to lament, moan over something (60)
langer to swaddle (283)
languir to languish (229)
lapider to lapidate, stone (251)
larmoyer to water (eye), to whimper (187)
lasser (se) to get tired (84, 122)
latiniser to latinize (486)
lécher to lick (87)
légiférer to legislate (356)
léguer to bequeath (87, 307)
léser to harm, injure (87)
lésiner sur to skimp on (159)
leurrer to deceive (22)
libeller to word, draw up, make out a check (27)
libérer to liberate, to move out (203)
libérer de to free from (203)
licencier to fire (41)
lier to tie (129)
lifter to put topspin on a ball (27)
ligoter to tie up (96)
limer to file (220)
limiter to limit (251)
liquider to liquidate (251)
lisser to smooth (73)
lister to list (27)
livrer à to deliver to (27)
localiser to locate (486)
loger chez to live with (263)

loger dans to live in (263)
longer to go/run along, border (283)
lorgner to eye (441)
lotir to divide up (66)
louanger to praise (283)
loucher to squint (469)
louper to miss, fail (124)
luger to sled, toboggan (271)
luire to shine, gleam, glisten (Def. and Imp.)
lustrer to shine, make shiny (299)
lutter to struggle (425)
lyncher to lynch (78)

M

macérer to steep (203)
mâcher to chew (82)
machiner to machinate, plot (329)
mâchonner to chew (171)
mâchurer to stain black, blacken, blur (54)
maçonner to build (with masonry) (171)
maculer to stain, spatter (81)
magasiner (en ligne) to shop, go shopping (online) (159)
magnétiser to magnetize, hypnotize (486)
magnifier to glorify, magnify (exalt) (212)
maintenir to maintain (463)
maîtriser to control, master (486)
malaxer to blend, knead (27)
malmener to handle roughly (290)
maltraiter to abuse, misuse, handle roughly, mistreat (475)
mandater to appoint; to pay by money order (241)
mander to command, summon (147)
manier to handle (212)
manifester to show, demonstrate (299)

manigancer to plot (342)
manipuler to manipulate (81)
manoeuvrer to maneuver, operate a machine, manipulate a person (26)
manufacturer to manufacture (54)
maquiller (se) to put makeup on one's face (122)
marauder to maraud, prowl, cruise (27)
marchander to haggle, bargain over (147)
marginaliser to marginalize (486)
marier to marry (someone to someone) (389)
marier (se) à/avec qqn to get married to someone (122)
marivauder to banter (27)
marmonner to mumble (171)
marquer de to mark with (219)
marrer (se) to have a fun time, good time (122)
marteler to hammer (297)
martyriser to martyr, mistreat (486)
masquer à to mask, conceal from (219)
massacrer to massacre (299)
masser to massage, gather together (84)
mastiquer to chew (219)
matelasser to pad (274)
mater to checkmate, curb (241)
matraquer to club (219)
maximaliser/maximiser to maximize (486)
mécaniser to mechanize (486)
méditer to meditate (251)
mégoter to skimp (96)
mélanger to mix (283)

mêler à/avec   to mix with (82)

mêler (se) à   to join in, meddle with, get mixed up in (83)

mêler (se) de   to meddle in (83)

mémoriser   to memorize (486)

menacer de   to threaten with (342)

ménager   to be sparing in the use of (305)

mendier   to beg (212)

mentionner   to mention (171)

mépriser   to despise, scorn (486)

mesurer   to measure (54)

métisser   to crossbreed (274)

meubler de   to furnish with (27)

meugler   to moo (326)

meurtrir   to bruise (249)

migrer   to migrate (22)

mijoter   to simmer (96)

militer   to be an activist/militant (251)

mimer   to mime (220)

mincir   to get thinner (95)

miner   to mine, undermine, erode (465)

minimaliser/minimiser   to minimize (486)

minuter   to measure time (32)

miser   to bet (486)

mitrailler   to machine-gun (477)

mobiliser   to mobilize (486)

modérer   to moderate, reduce (203)

moderniser   to modernize (486)

modifier   to modify (389)

moduler   to modulate (81)

moisir   to make moldy; to go moldy (95)

molester   to molest (160)

mollir   to soften (229)

momifier   to mummify (212)

monnayer   to mint, sell (330)

monopoliser   to monopolize (486)

moraliser   to moralize (486)

morceler   to divide up into pieces (38)

mortifier   to mortify (389)

motiver   to motivate (26)

moucher (se)   to blow one's nose (122)

mouiller (se)   to get oneself wet (83, 233)

mouiller   to wet (233)

mouler   to mold, make a cast (421)

mousser   to bubble, lather, froth (353)

muer   to molt; to have a change of voice (483)

mugir   to moo, roar (229)

multiplier   to multiply (454)

munir de   to supply with (229)

murer   to wall in/up (54)

mûrir   to ripen (249)

murmurer   to murmur (54)

museler   to muzzle (38)

mutiler   to mutilate (27)

mutiner (se)   to mutiny (329)

mystifier   to deceive, mystify (129)

N

nantir   to provide, supply (66)

napper de   to coat, top with (59)

narguer   to scoff at (307)

narrer   to narrate (22)

nasiller   to speak with a nasal twang; to quack (477)

natter   to braid, interweave (246)

navrer   to distress (27)

nécessiter   to require (251)

négliger   to neglect (119)

négocier   to negotiate (389)

neiger   to snow   (Def. and Imp.)

neutraliser   to neutralize (486)

niveler   to level (38)

noircir   to blacken (229)

noliser   to charter (boat, plane) (486)

nombrer   to count (22)

normaliser   to normalize, standardize (486)

noter   to note (176)

notifier   to notify (322)

nouer   to tie (269)

nuancer   to nuance (342)

numériser   to digitize (486)

numéroter   to number, paginate (96)

O

objecter   to make an objection (160)

objectiver   to objectify (276)

oblitérer   to obliterate (356)

obscurcir   to darken, make obscure (229)

obséder   to obsess (87)

observer   to observe (481)

obstiner (s') à   to persist in (318, 329)

obstruer   to obstruct (114)

obtempérer à   to comply with (203)

occasionner   to cause (171)

occidentaliser   to westernize (486)

octroyer   to grant (187)

offenser   to offend (336)

offusquer   to offend (219)

oindre   to anoint, rub with oil (268)

ombrager   to shade (189)

ombrer   to shade (22)

ondoyer   to undulate (187)

onduler   to undulate (81)

opérer   to operate (356)

opiniâtrer (s')   to be stubborn, persist in (33)

opposer   to oppose (350)

oppresser   to weigh down, suffocate (360)

opprimer   to oppress (220)

opter pour   to opt for (113)

orchestrer   to orchestrate (22)

ordonner to arrange, organize, order, to prescribe (medical) (171)

organiser to organize (486)

orienter (s') vers to orient, direct towards (113)

orner de to decorate with (470)

orthographier to spell (212)

osciller to oscillate (477)

ôter to take off, remove (498)

ourler to hem (326)

outiller to equip with tools (477)

outrager to outrage (305)

outrer to exaggerate, outrage (22)

P

pacifier to pacify (389)

pactiser to make a pact (486)

palataliser to palatalize (486)

pâlir to turn pale (423)

palpiter to palpitate (251)

pâmer (se) to swoon (71, 122)

paner to bread, coat with bread crumbs (27)

paniquer to panic (219)

panser to bandage (134)

papillonner to flutter around (171)

papoter to gab, chatter (96)

parachuter to parachute (425)

parcourir to travel through; to skim (reading) (125)

parer to adorn (435)

parfaire to perfect (223)

parfumer to perfume (238)

parier sur to bet on (129)

parjurer (se) to break one's pledge (122, 272)

parodier to parody (212)

parquer to park; to confine (284)

parsemer to scatter (341)

partager to share (501)

participer à to participate in (251)

parvenir à to get to, reach (491)

passer (se) to happen, take place (Def. and Imp.)

passionner to fascinate (171)

patauger to splash, wade (305)

patienter to be patient, wait (26)

patoiser to speak patois (486)

patronner to sponsor, patronize (171)

patrouiller to patrol (233)

pâturer to graze (54)

paumer to lose (27)

paupériser to pauperize, impoverish (486)

pavaner (se) to strut around (122)

paver to pave (276)

peaufiner to polish, put on the finishing touches (329)

pédaler to pedal (326)

peiner to upset; to strain (329)

peler to peel (297)

pelleter to shovel (267)

pencher (se) to lean over (122)

pencher to tilt, tip up (93)

pénétrer to penetrate (356)

percer to pierce (275)

percevoir to notice, perceive (379)

percher to perch (93)

percuter to strike, smash into (169)

perdre (se) to get lost, lose one's way (122, 337)

perfectionner to perfect (171)

perforer to perforate (22)

périmer (se) to expire, lapse (legal term) (122, 220)

perler to bead (326)

permuter to permutate, swap (32)

perpétrer to perpetrate (356)

perquisitionner to search (171)

persécuter to persecute (32)

persévérer to persevere (356)

persifler to mock, scoff (439)

persister to persist (259)

personnaliser to personalize (486)

personnifier to personify (389)

pervertir to pervert (66)

pester to complain, curse (27)

péter to break, blow up, break wind (87)

pétiller to bubble, crackle (477)

pétrifier to petrify (212)

pétrir to knead (249)

peupler to populate (326)

philosopher to philosophize (27)

photocopier to photocopy (212)

photographier to photograph (212)

phraser to phrase (in music) (32)

pianoter to play the piano, tickle the ivory (96)

picoter to irritate, tingle (96)

piéger to trap (52)

piétiner to trample (329)

piger to catch on, understand, freelance (218)

piler to grind (27)

piller to pillage (477)

piloter to pilot (96)

pincer to pinch (99)

piocher to dig, study hard (82)

piquer to prick, sting, to steal (219)

pirater to pirate, hack (computer) (241)

pister to track, follow (27)

pivoter   to pivot, revolve (96)

placarder   to put up posters, cover up (240)

plafonner   to peak (171)

plagier   to plagiarize (389)

plaider   to plead (26)

planer sur   to hover over (71)

planifier   to plan (212)

planquer   to hide (something) (284)

planter   to plant (90)

plaquer   to jilt, stand up (219)

plâtrer   to plaster, put in a cast (medical) (22)

pleurnicher   to whimper, whine (285)

pleuvoir   to rain (Def. and Imp.)

plisser   to pleat, crease (73)

plomber   to plumb, put in a filling (dentist) (240)

plonger   to plunge, dive (442)

ployer   to bend, flex (187)

pocher   to poach (cooking) (82)

pogner   to take, seize, understand (Qué.) (441)

poignarder   to stab (240)

poinçonner   to punch (ticket) (171)

poindre   to dawn, break through (268)

pointer   to point (464)

poireauter   to hang around (27)

poivrer   to pepper (466)

polir   to polish (423)

politiser   to politicize (486)

polluer de   to pollute with (114)

pommader   to put on pomade, ointment (240)

pomper   to pump (59)

poncer   to sand (342)

ponctionner   to puncture (171)

ponctuer   to punctuate (483)

pondérer   to balance (203)

pondre   to lay (eggs), produce (394)

pontifier   to pontificate (212)

porter (se)   to feel well/unwell (122, 349)

positionner   to position (171)

poster   to mail (27)

postuler   to apply for (a position), postulate (81)

potasser   to cram (for a test) (84)

potiner   to gossip (329)

poudrer   to powder (299)

pourchasser   to pursue (92)

pourrir   to spoil, rot (249)

pourvoir   to provide (497) (except Tenses 4 & 5, stem: pourvoir-; Tense 3 pourvus, pourvus, pourvut...; Tense 7 pourvusse, pourvusses, pourvût...)

pratiquer   to practice, drill (a hole) (219)

précéder   to precede (87)

prêcher   to preach (332)

précipiter (se)   to rush (122, 251)

préciser   to specify (486)

préconiser   to advocate (486)

prédestiner   to predestine (329)

prédisposer   to predispose (350)

prédominer sur   to prevail over (465)

préexister à   to preexist, come before (27)

préfacer   to preface (342)

préjuger   to prejudge (271)

prélever   to take a sample (278)

préméditer   to premeditate (251)

prémunir contre   to guard against (229)

prénommer   to give a first name (310)

préoccuper   to preoccupy, worry (317)

préposer à   to appoint to (350)

présager   to predict (305)

prescrire   to prescribe (177)

préserver de   to preserve from (426)

présider   to preside (over) (251)

présumer   to presume (238)

présupposer   to presuppose (350)

prévaloir sur   to prevail over (488)

primer sur   to be dominant over (220)

priser   to value (486)

privatiser   to privatize (486)

priver   to deprive (276)

priver de (se) qqch   to do without something (276)

privilégier   to favor, give an advantage to (41)

procéder de   to arise, proceed from (87)

proclamer   to proclaim (71)

procurer qqch à qqn   to get something for someone (54)

profaner   to profane (27)

professer   to profess (73)

profiler   to profile, outline (27)

profiter de   to profit from, enjoy (251)

progresser   to progress (73)

prohiber   to prohibit (251)

projeter   to project (267)

prolonger de   to prolong by (442)

promener   to take for a walk (290)

promouvoir   to promote (304) (part. passé promu, promue)

promulguer   to promulgate (307)

prôner   to advocate (27)

propager   to propagate, spread (305)

proportionner   to make something match/be proportionate (171) proposer   to propose   (350)

proscrire   to proscribe, ban, outlaw   (177)

prospérer   to prosper   (203)

prostituer (se)   to prostitute oneself   (122, 483)

protéger   to protect   (52)

protester   to protest   (160)

provenir de   to result from   (491)

provoquer   to provoke   (219)

psalmodier   to chant   (212)

psychanalyser   to psychoanalyze   (32)

publier   to publish   (212)

puer   to stink   (Def. and Imp.)

puiser   to draw from   (486)

pulvériser   to pulverize   (486)

purger   to purge   (283)

purifier   to purify   (212)

Q

quadriller   to crisscross   (477)

quadrupler   to quadruple   (326)

qualifier   to qualify, consider, describe as   (212)

quantifier   to quantify   (212)

québéciser   to quebecize, make Québécois   (486)

quereller (se)   to quarrel with each other   (122, 477)

quereller   to scold   (477)

questionner   to question   (171)

quêter   to collect (money); to seek after   (47)

quintupler   to quintuple   (326)

R

rabâcher   to harp on, repeat over and over   (82)

rabaisser   to reduce, decrease, devalue   (63)

rabattre   to pull down   (67)

rabibocher   to reconcile (with)   (285)

raboter   to plane   (96)

rabougrir (se)   to shrivel up   (214, 249)

raccommoder   to mend   (147)

raccompagner   to see someone off, home   (441)

raccorder à   to connect to, link up   (11)

raccourcir   to shorten   (95)

raccrocher   to hang up   (469)

racheter   to buy back   (17)

racheter (se)   to redeem oneself   (17, 122)

racler   to scrape   (326)

radicaliser   to radicalize   (486)

radier   to cross off (a list)   (212)

radiodiffuser   to broadcast, radiocast   (32)

radiographier   to x-ray   (212)

radoter   to drivel   (96)

radoucir   to soften, get milder   (95)

raffermir   to strengthen, tone up   (229)

raffiner   to refine   (329)

raffoler de   to be crazy about   (498)

rafistoler   to patch up   (498)

rafler   to swipe   (439)

rafraîchir   to cool, refresh   (383)

ragaillardir   to perk up   (210)

rager   to rage, be infuriated   (305)

raidir   to stiffen   (229)

railler   to mock, jeer at   (477)

raisonner   to reason   (443)

rajeunir   to rejuvenate   (229)

rajouter   to add more   (28)

ralentir   to slow down   (95)

râler   to moan   (498)

rallier   to rally   (212)

rallonger   to lengthen   (442)

rallumer   to light again   (238)

ramasser   to pick up   (92)

ramener   to bring back   (31)

ramer   to row   (27)

ramifier (se)   to ramify, split   (212) (aux. être)

ramollir   to soften, weaken   (229)

ramoner   to sweep a chimney   (461)

ramper   to crawl   (247)

rancarder   to tip off, arrange a meeting with   (27)

rancir   to get stale/rancid   (95)

rançonner   to demand ransom   (443)

ranimer   to revive   (220)

rapatrier   to repatriate   (212)

râper   to grate   (59)

rapetisser   to make/get smaller   (486)

rappliquer   to come back   (219)

rapporter   to bring back   (40)

rapprendre, réapprendre   to learn again, relearn   (42)

rapprocher de   to bring closer to   (43)

raréfier   to rarefy   (212)

raser (se)   to shave oneself   (86, 122)

raser   to shave   (86)

rassembler   to assemble   (407)

rasseoir (se)   to take one's seat again, sit down again   (51) (aux. être; *part. passé* rassis, rassise)

rassurer   to reassure   (54)

ratatiner (se)   to shrink, shrivel   (122, 329)

rater   to miss, fail   (241)

ratifier   to ratify   (212)

ratiociner   to quibble   (329)

rationner   to ration   (171)

ratisser   to rake   (486)

rattacher   to attach again, link together   (82)

rattraper   to catch up   (59)

raturer   to cross out   (54)

ravager   to ravage   (305)

ravaler   to clean; to swallow   (326)

ravir   to delight   (422)

raviser (se)   to change one's mind   (122, 486)

ravitailler   to supply   (477)

raviver   to revive   (276)

rayer   to cross out   (330)

rayonner   to shine, be radiant   (171)

réabonner (se)   to renew one's membership/ subscription   (122, 171)

réaccoutumer   to reaccustom   (238)

réadapter   to readjust   (8)

réadmettre   to readmit   (294)

réagir   to react   (25)

réaliser   to carry out, realize   (486)

réapparaître   to reappear   (324)

réapprendre, rapprendre   to learn again, relearn   (42)

réarmer   to rearm   (227)

rebaisser   to lower   (63)

rebeller (se)   to rebel   (122)

rebrousser   to turn back; to brush the wrong way   (353)

rebuter   to repel, put off   (32)

recaler   to fail   (326)

receler   to hold, receive, harbor (someone)   (297)

recenser   to inventory, take a census   (27)

réceptionner   to catch, trap (a ball)   (443)

rechaper   to retread (tire)   (59)

recharger   to reload, refill   (91)

réchauffer   to reheat   (84)

réchauffer (se)   to warm up   (85)

rechausser (se)   to put one's shoes back on   (85)

rechercher   to search, hunt for   (93)

réciter   to recite   (251)

rechigner   to grumble, frown   (441)

rechuter   to relapse   (32)

récidiver   to be an habitual offender/recidivist   (276)

réclamer   to ask for, reclaim   (71)

reclasser   to reclassify   (84)

recoller   to restick   (326)

récolter   to harvest, gather   (27)

recommander   to recommend; to register (a letter)   (98)

recommencer   to begin again   (99)

récompenser   to reward   (336)

recomposer   to reconstruct, to redial a number   (350)

recompter   to recount, count again   (103)

réconcilier   to reconcile   (212)

reconduire   to see someone home, escort   (106)

réconforter   to comfort   (349)

reconquérir   to reconquer   (19)

reconsidérer   to reconsider   (203)

reconstituer   to rebuild, reconstruct   (483)

reconstruire   to reconstruct   (111)

reconvertir   to reconvert   (229)

recorder   to restring   (27)

recorriger   to recorrect   (218)

recoucher (se)   to go back to bed   (122)

recoudre   to sew up again   (123)

recouper   to cut again   (124)

recourber   to bend   (240)

recourir à qqn/qqch   to turn to someone, resort to something   (125)

recouvrer   to recover   (466)

recouvrir   to cover, cover again   (126)

recréer   to recreate   (128)

récréer   to amuse, entertain   (128)

recreuser   to dig again   (32)

récrire   to rewrite   (177)

recroqueviller (se)   to curl up   (414)

recruter   to recruit   (32)

rectifier   to rectify, correct   (389)

reculer   to step back, move back   (81)

récupérer   to salvage, recover   (203)

récurer   to scrub   (54)

recycler   to recycle   (326)

redécouvrir   to rediscover   (139)

redéfinir   to redefine   (229)

redemander   to ask again   (147)

redémarrer   to start again   (22)

redescendre   to go back down   (157)

redevenir   to become again   (164)

rediffuser   to rebroadcast   (32)

rédiger   to write, compose   (218)

redonner   to give again, give back   (171)

redoubler   to increase   (407)

redouter de   to dread, fear   (173)

redresser   to straighten up   (353)

réécrire   to rewrite   (177)

rééditer   to republish   (215)

rééduquer   to reeducate   (219)

réélire   to reelect   (280)

réemployer/remployer   to reuse   (187)

réessayer   to try again   (204)

réexaminer   to reexamine   (465)

réexpédier   to return/forward mail   (212)

refaçonner   to remodel (443)

refaire   to redo   (223)

référer (se) à   to refer to, consult   (122, 356)

refléter   to reflect   (87)

refleurir   to flower again (249)

refondre   to remelt, recast (394)

refouler   to push back, force back   (421)

réfracter   to refract   (27)

réfrigérer   to refrigerate (203)

refroidir   to cool   (229)

réfuter   to refute   (425)

regagner   to regain, win back, get back   (239)

regarnir   to restock   (229)

regeler   to freeze again, refreeze   (242)

régénérer   to regenerate (356)

régenter   to rule over   (464)

regimber   to rear up, rebel (240)

régler   to regulate, settle (87)

régner   to reign, rule   (87)

regorger de   to abound in, overflow with   (283)

regrossir   to put weight back on   (282)

regrouper   to group together (59)

régulariser   to regulate (486)

réhabiliter   to rehabilitate (251)

réhabituer (se)   to become used to again   (33, 483)

rehausser   to raise, increase (353)

réimprimer   to reprint (220)

réincarcérer   to reimprison (356)

réincarner (se)   to be reincarnated   (122)

réinstaller   to reinstall (326)

réintégrer   to reinstate (356)

réinventer   to reinvent (464)

réitérer   to reiterate   (356)

rejaillir   to splash up, spurt up   (423)

rejeter   to reject, throw up, spew   (267)

rejoindre   to rejoin, meet up with   (268)

rejouer   to replay   (269)

réjouir   to delight, gladden (270)

relancer   to throw again, relaunch   (342)

relater   to relate   (241)

relativiser   to relativize (486)

relaxer   to relax, release (27)

relayer   to relieve, relay (330)

relever   to raise again   (278)

relouer   to relet   (269)

reluire   to glisten   (See luire) (Def. and Imp.)

remanier   to revise   (309)

remballer   to repack, rewrap (326)

rembarquer   to reembark (284)

rembobiner   to rewind (329)

rembourser   to reimburse (27)

remédier à   to remedy (212)

remémorer (se)   to remember   (22, 122)

remmener   to take/bring back   (290)

remonter   to go up again; à date back to   (298)

remontrer   to show again (299)

remorquer   to tow   (284)

remployer/réemployer   to reuse   (187)

rempocher   to pocket again (82)

remporter   to take back, win (349)

remprunter   to borrow again (188)

remuer   to move, stir   (483)

rémunérer   to remunerate (203)

renaître   to be reborn, recover   (306)

renchérir   to go further, increase a bid   (94)

rendormir (se)   to fall asleep again   (172) (aux. être)

renfermer   to enclose, shut again, contain   (227)

renfoncer   to plunge/push further in   (342)

renforcer   to reinforce (342)

renfrogner (se)   to frown (122, 441)

rengainer   to resheath (329)

renier   to renounce   (309)

renifler   to sniff, sniffle (439)

renommer   to reappoint (310)

renoncer   to renounce, give up   (371)

renouer   to retie   (269)

renouveler   to renew   (38)

rénover   to renovate   (276)

renseigner   to inform   (194)

rentabiliser   to make something profitable   (486)

renverser   to knock over, turn upside down, overturn (492)

renvoyer   to send back (200)

repartir   to start again (aux. être); to reply (aux. avoir)   (327)

répartir   to divide up, share   (229)

repaver   to repave (276)

repêcher   to fish out, recover   (332)

repeindre   to repaint (334)

repentir (se)   to repent ()

répercuter sur   to pass on to   (169)

repérer   to locate, discover   (203)

repeupler   to repopulate (326)

replacer   to replace, put back (342)

replier   to fold again   (129)

répliquer   to retort, reply (219)

repolir   to repolish   (229)

reporter   to carry forward, postpone, take back   (349)

reposer   to put back, rest on, ask a question again   (350)

repousser   to push away (353)

reprendre   to take back, resume   (357)

représenter   to represent (60)

réprimer   to repress   (220)

reprocher qqch à qqn   to blame, reproach someone for something   (43)

reprogrammer   to reprogram (368)

réprouver   to reprove, condemn   (481)

répudier   to repudiate (212)

requérir   to require, demand (19)

réquisitionner   to requisition (171)

réserver   to reserve   (276)

résider   to reside   (251)

résigner (se) à   to resign oneself to   (122, 441)

résister   to resist   (259)

résonner   to resonate, resound   (443)

résorber   to reduce, absorb (240)

respecter   to respect   (8)

respirer   to breathe   (466)

resplendir   to shine   (229)

responsabiliser   to give someone responsibility (486)

resquiller   to sneak in without paying   (477)

ressentir   to feel, experience (434)

resserrer   to retighten   (22)

resservir   to serve again (437)

ressortir   to go out again, take out again   (444)

ressouder   to resolder   (27)

ressurgir/resurgir   to reemerge, reappear   (229)

restaurer   to restore   (347)

restituer   to return, restore (483)

restreindre   to restrict (334)

résulter de   to result from (27)

résumer   to summarize (238)

resurgir/ressurgir   to reemerge, reappear   (229)

rétablir   to reestablish (206)

retaper   to retype, fix up (59)

retarder   to delay   (240)

reteindre   to redye   (334)

retendre   to retighten   (394)

retomber   to fall again (467)

rétorquer   to retort   (284)

retoucher   to retouch   (469)

retracer   to recount   (342)

rétracter   to retract   (60)

retrancher   to remove, deduct   (78)

retranscrire   to retranscribe (177)

retransmettre   to broadcast (294)

retraverser   to recross (492)

rétrécir   to shrink   (95)

retremper   to resoak   (247)

rétribuer   to pay   (114)

retrousser   to roll up, turn up (353)

retrouver   to find (again) (481)

retrouver (se)   to meet with, get together   (122, 481)

réunifier   to reunify   (212)

réunir à   to reunite with (485)

réutiliser   to reuse   (486)

revaloriser   to revalue (486)

rêvasser   to daydream   (84)

réveiller   to wake up (someone who's asleep) (109) (See 414)

réveillonner   to celebrate on Christmas Eve or New Year's Eve   (171)

révéler   to reveal   (356)

revendiquer   to claim, demand   (256)

revendre   to resell   (489)

réverbérer   to reverberate, reflect   (203)

reverdir   to turn green again (229)

révérer   to revere   (203)

reverser   to pour again, pour back   (492)

revêtir   to pave, take on a certain appearance   (493)

réviser   to revise   (486)

revitaliser   to revitalize (486)

revivre   to live again, come alive again   (496)

révolter   to revolt   (27)

révolutionner   to revolutionize   (171)

révoquer   to revoke   (219)

revoter   to vote again   (96)

rhabiller   to dress again (477)

rhabiller (se)   to get dressed again   (250)

ricaner   to giggle   (27)

ricocher   to ricochet   (82)

rider   to wrinkle   (27)

ridiculiser   to ridicule (486)

rigoler   to laugh, joke   (498)

rimer   to rhyme, create poetry   (220)

rincer   to rinse   (99)

riposter   to respond, answer (27)

risquer   to risk   (219)

rissoler   to brown   (498)

ristourner   to refund   (27)

rivaliser   to rival   (486)

river   to rivet   (276)

roder   to break in (mechanical)   (96)

rôder   to prowl   (96)

rogner   to trim   (441)

romaniser to romanize (486)

ronfler to snore (445)

ronger to gnaw (442)

rosir to turn pink (95)

roter to burp (96)

rôtir to roast (229)

roucouler to coo (421)

rouer (de coups) to beat up (269)

rougeoyer to redden (187)

rouiller to rust (233)

roupiller to take a nap, sleep (477)

rouspéter to complain (87)

roussir to turn brown (95)

rouvrir to reopen (323)

ruer (se) sur/vers to rush toward (114, 122)

rugir to roar (229)

ruiner to ruin (329)

ruisseler to stream (38)

ruser to use trickery (32)

rutiler to gleam (27)

S

saborder to scuttle (27)

saboter to sabotage (96)

sabrer to slash (22)

saccager to devastate (305)

sacquer to fire, flunk (284)

sacrer to consecrate, swear (22)

sacrifier to sacrifice (212)

saigner to bleed (441)

saillir to jut out (50) (3ᵈ pers.); (229) (if saillir, means "to mate," 3ᵈ pers.)

saler to salt (326)

saliver to salivate (426)

saluer to greet, salute (114)

sanctifier to sanctify (212)

sanctionner to punish, to sanction (law) (443)

sangloter to sob (96)

saper to undermine (59)

saturer to saturate (54)

saupoudrer to sprinkle (299)

sautiller to skip (477)

sauvegarder to safeguard, to safe (computer) (240)

scandaliser to scandalize (486)

scander to scan (verse) (240)

scanner to scan (image) (171)

schématiser to schematize (486)

scier to saw (41)

scinder to split (240)

scintiller to sparkle (477)

scolariser to school, educate (486)

scruter to scrutinize (32)

sculpter to sculpt (8)

seconder to assist (240)

sécréter to secrete (87)

sectionner to split up (171)

sécuriser to reassure (486)

segmenter to segment (60)

sélectionner to select (171)

seller to saddle (326)

sembler to seem (Def. and Imp.)

semer to sow (341)

sensibiliser to sensitize, make aware (486)

seoir to be becoming, suit (Def. and Imp.)

sermonner to sermonize (171)

serpenter to snake, meander (60)

sextupler to sextuple (326)

sidérer to stun (203)

siéger to be in session (52)

siffloter to whistle (96)

signaliser to install signals/markings (486)

signifier to mean, signify (212)

silhouetter to silhouette (386)

sillonner to furrow, crisscross (171)

simplifier to simplify (212)

simuler to simulate (81)

singer to ape (283)

siroter to sip (96)

situer to situate, locate (483)

situer (se) to be located (122, 483)

skier to ski (129)

slalomer to slalom (71)

snober to snub (27)

socialiser to socialize, collectivize (486)

soigner qqn to take care of, look after someone (10)

solder to settle a debt, put on sale (27)

solidifier to solidify (212)

solliciter to solicit (251)

solubiliser to solubilize (486)

sombrer to sink (22)

sommeiller to doze (109)

sommer to summon (310)

somnoler to doze (498)

sonder to poll (27)

sonoriser to add a sound track (486)

soucier (se) de to care about (41) (aux. être)

souder to solder (27)

soulager de to relieve of (305)

soûler (se) to get drunk (122, 421)

soulever to raise (278)

souligner to underline (10)

soupçonner de to suspect of (443)

souper to have supper (124)

soupirer to sigh (21)

souscrire à to subscribe to (177)

soustraire to subtract (474) (no *passé simple* or imp. subj.)

soutenir to support (463)

soutirer to decant (466)

spatialiser to spatialize (486)

spécialiser (se) to specialize (486)

spécifier to specify (212)

spéculer to speculate (81)

spiritualiser to spiritualize (486)

sprinter to sprint (464)

stabiliser to stabilize (486)

stagner to stagnate (441)

stationner to park (171)

sténographier to take shorthand (212)

stériliser to sterilize (486)

stigmatiser to stigmatize (486)

stimuler to stimulate (81)

stipuler to stipulate (81)

stocker to stock (27)

stopper to stop (163)

stratifier to stratify (212)

stresser to stress (353)

strier to striate (129)

structurer to structure (54)

stupéfier to stupefy, stun (212)

styliser to stylize (486)

subir to undergo (95)

sublimer to sublimate (220)

submerger to submerge (283)

subordonner to subordinate (171)

subsister de to live on (53)

subtiliser to steal (486)

substituer à to substitute for (483)

subvenir à to provide for (491)

subventionner to subsidize (171)

subvertir to subvert, overthrow (229)

succéder à to succeed (87)

succomber to succumb (240)

suçoter to suck (96)

sucrer to sweeten (21)

suer to sweat (483)

suffire to suffice, be sufficient, be enough (Def. and Imp.)

suffoquer (de) to suffocate, choke (with) (219)

suggérer to suggest (356)

suinter to ooze (464)

superposer to stack, superimpose (350)

superviser to supervise (486)

suppléer to replace (128)

supplicier to torture (41)

supposer to suppose (350)

supprimer to suppress (220)

surabonder to abound (27)

surbaisser to lower (63)

surcharger to overload (283)

surélever to raise (278)

surenchérir to raise a bid (94)

suréquiper to overquip (215)

surestimer to overestimate (220)

surévaluer to overvalue (213)

surexposer to overexpose (350)

surfer to surf, netsurf (Internet) (27)

surgeler to freeze (242)

surgir to loom up, spring up (229)

surimposer to overtax (350)

surmener to overwork (290)

surmonter to overcome, surmount (298) (aux. avoir)

surnommer to give a nickname (310)

surpasser to surpass (84)

surpayer to overpay (17)

surplomber to overhang (240)

sursauter to jump, give a start (425)

surtaxer to surcharge (27)

surveiller to watch (109)

survenir to arise, occur (491)

suspecter de to suspect of (113)

suspendre to suspend (335)

susurrer to whisper (22)

suturer to suture (54)

symboliser to symbolize (486)

sympathiser avec to get on well with (486)

synchroniser to synchronize (486)

syndicaliser to unionize (486)

syndiquer to unionize (219)

synthétiser to synthesize (486)

systématiser to systematize (486)

T

tabler sur to count on (407)

tacher de to stain with (82)

tâcher to try (82)

tacheter to fleck (267)

taillader to slash (27)

tailler to cut, sharpen, trim (477)

talonner to tail, follow on someone's heels (171)

tambouriner to drum (329)

tamiser to sift (486)

tamponner to dab, mop up, plug (171)

tanguer to toss around, rock (the boat) (307)

tanner to tan (leather) (171)

tanner qqn to badger, pester someone (171)

taper to tap, type, strike, slap (235)

tapir (se) to crouch, hunker down (66) (aux. être)

tapoter to tap, pat (96)

taquiner to tease (329)

tarder to delay (240)

targuer (se) de to boast (122, 307)

tarir to dry up (249)

tartiner to spread (butter, pâté) (329)

tasser to tamp down, pack down (84)

tasser (se) to settle down, subside; to move over, step aside (Qué.) (84, 122) tâter   to feel by touching (241)

tâtonner   to grope (171)

tatouer   to tattoo (175)

taxer   to tax (27)

teinter   to tint (464)

télécharger   to download (91)

télécharger vers le serveur   to upload (91)

télécommander   to operate by remote control (98)

télécopier   to fax (212)

télédiffuser   to televise (32)

télégraphier   to telegraph (212)

téléguider   to control by radio (27)

téléscoper   to smash into (car, train) (163)

téléviser   to televise (486)

témoigner   to testify, show (10)

tempérer   to temper (203)

tempêter   to rant, storm (47)

temporiser   to delay (486)

tenailler   to torment (477)

tergiverser   to procrastinate, hesitate (492)

ternir   to tarnish (229)

terrasser   to strike down (84)

terrer (se)   to lie low, hide (122, 196)

terrifier   to terrify (212)

terroriser   to terrorize (486)

tester   to test, make out a will (legal term) (160)

téter   to nurse (baby) (87)

théoriser   to theorize (486)

tiédir   to become lukewarm (hotter or colder) (210)

timbrer   to stamp (466)

tinter   to ring (464)

tintinnabuler   to tintinnabulate, jingle (81)

tirailler   to pull on (477)

tisser   to weave (73)

titrer   to title, entitle, titrate (466)

tituber   to stagger (32)

titulariser   to give tenure, a contract (486)

toiletter   to groom (246)

tolérer   to tolerate (356)

tondre   to mow, shear (394)

tonifier   to tone up (212)

tonsurer   to tonsure (54)

toquer   to knock, rap, tap (219)

torcher   to wipe (Watch out! se torcher = to wipe one's bottom) (285)

torchonner   to botch (171)

torpiller   to torpedo (477)

tortiller   to twiddle, wiggle (477)

torturer   to torture (54)

totaliser   to total (486)

tourbillonner   to swirl, whirl (171)

tourmenter   to torment (60)

tournebouler   to confuse (421)

tournoyer   to whirl (308)

toussailler   to have a slight persistent cough (477)

toussoter   to have a slight cough (96)

tracasser   to bother, worry (84)

tracer   to trace (342)

tracter   to tow ()

trafiquer   to traffic, tamper with something (219)

traîner   to drag (167)

tramer   to plot (71)

trancher   to slice (78)

tranquilliser   to reassure (486)

transborder   to transfer (27)

transcrire   to transcribe (177)

transférer   to transfer (356)

transformer en   to transform into (227)

transfuser   to transfuse (32)

transgresser   to transgress (353)

transhumer   to move, transplant (238)

transiger   to compromise (218)

transiter   to pass through (251)

transmuer   to transmute (483)

transpercer   to pierce (342)

transpirer   to sweat, perspire (466)

transplanter   to transplant (90)

transporter   to transport (349)

transposer   to transpose (350)

traquer   to track (219)

traumatiser   to traumatize (486)

travestir   to dress up, misrepresent (66)

trébucher   to stumble, trip (82)

trembler de   to tremble with (407)

trembloter   to tremble (96)

tremper   to soak (247)

trépasser   to pass away (84) (aux. être or avoir)

tressaillir   to jump, flinch (50)

tresser   to braid (73)

tricoter   to knit (96)

trier   to select, sort (129)

trifouiller dans   to rifle through (233)

trimbaler   to cart (something) around (326)

trinquer   to toast (drink) (284)

triompher   to triumph (27)

tripatouiller   to tamper with (233)

tripler   to triple (326)

tripoter   to fiddle with (96)

tromper   to deceive (247) (See 480)

trompeter   to trumpet (267)

tronçonner   to cut into sections (483)

trôner   to take the place of honor   (27)

tronquer   to truncate   (284)

troquer   to swap, trade   (219)

trotter   to trot   (246)

trottiner   to trot along   (329)

troubler   to confuse   (407)

trouer   to make a hole in   (269)

truquer   to fake, rig   (219)

truster   to monopolize (manipulate the market)   (27)

tuméfier (se)   to swell up   (212) (aux. être)

tuyauter   to tip off   (27)

tyranniser   to tyrannize   (486)

U

ulcérer   to ulcerate   (203)

ululer, hululer   to hoot, screech   (81)

unifier   to unify   (212)

uniformiser   to make uniform, standardize   (486)

urbaniser   to urbanize   (486)

uriner   to urinate   (465)

user   to wear out, use up   (32)

usurper   to usurp   (59)

V

vacciner contre   to vaccinate against   (329)

vaciller   to sway, stagger, vacillate   (477)

vadrouiller   to roam around, wander   (233)

vagabonder   to wander   (248)

vaguer   to roam, wander   (307)

valider   to validate   (251)

valoriser   to increase the value, standing of someone/thing   (486)

valser   to waltz   (492)

vanner   to winnow, wear down   (171)

vanter   to vaunt, praise   (90)

vanter (se)   to brag   (90, 122)

vaporiser   to spray, vaporize   (486)

varapper   to rock climb   (235)

varier   to vary   (129)

vasouiller   to struggle   (233)

vautrer (se)   to wallow   (122)

végéter   to vegetate   (356)

véhiculer   to transport   (81)

veiller   to stay up, keep watch   (109)

velouter (se)   to soften   (28, 122)

vendanger   to harvest (grapes)   (283)

vénérer   to venerate   (356)

ventiler   to ventilate   (266)

verbaliser   to verbalize   (486)

verdoyer   to be green   (187)

vérifier   to verify   (212)

vernir   to varnish   (229)

verrouiller   to lock   (233)

versifier   to versify   (41)

vexer   to annoy, offend, upset   (27)

vibrer   to vibrate   (22)

vidanger   to empty   (283)

vider   to empty   (251)

violacer (se)   to become purple   (342)

violer   to violate, rape   (498)

virer   to turn, transfer (funds)   (21)

virevolter   to spin around   (27)

viser à   to aim at   (486)

visionner   to view, look at   (171)

visser   to screw on   (486)

visualiser   to visualize   (486)

vitrer   to install glass   (22)

vitupérer   to vituperate   (203)

vivifier   to give/bring life to   (212)

vivoter   to stagnate, barely get by   (96)

vocaliser   to vocalize   (486)

vociférer   to yell   (356)

voguer   to sail, drift   (307)

voiler   to veil   (27)

voisiner   to be close to   (159)

voleter   to flutter   (267)

voltiger   to flutter   (218)

vomir   to vomit   (229)

voter pour/contre   to vote for/against   (96)

vouer à   to dedicate to, to vow   (269)

vriller   to spin, whirl   (477)

vrombir   to hum, buzz   (229)

vulgariser   to vulgarize, popularize   (486)

Y

yodler   to yodel   (326)

Z

zapper   to zap, change channels   (235)

zébrer de   to streak, stripe with   (356)

zézayer   to lisp   (330)

zieuter   to eye (someone)   (27)

zigouiller   to bump off, stab   (233)

zigzaguer   to zigzag   (307)

zipper   to zip up   (235)

zoner   to zone   (461)

zoomer   to zoom in, zoom out   (71)

3 Foreign Language Series From Barron's!

The VERB SERIES offers more than 300 of the most frequently used verbs.
The GRAMMAR SERIES provides complete coverage of the elements of grammar.
The VOCABULARY SERIES offers more than 3500 words and phrases with their foreign language translations. Each book: paperback.

FRENCH
GRAMMAR
ISBN: 0-7641-1351-8
$6.99, Can. $9.99

GERMAN
GRAMMAR
ISBN: 0-8120-4296-4
$7.99, Can. $11.50

ITALIAN
GRAMMAR
ISBN: 0-7641-2060-3
$6.99, Can. $9.99

JAPANESE
GRAMMAR
ISBN: 0-7641-2061-1
$6.95, Can. $9.95

RUSSIAN
GRAMMAR
ISBN: 0-8120-4902-0
$6.95, Can. $8.95

SPANISH
GRAMMAR
ISBN: 0-7641-1615-0
$6.99, Can. $9.99

FRENCH
VERBS
ISBN: 0-7641-1356-9
$6.99, Can. $9.99

GERMAN
VERBS
ISBN: 0-8120-4310-3
$8.99, Can. $12.99

ITALIAN
VERBS
ISBN: 0-7641-2063-8
$6.99, Can. $8.75

SPANISH
VERBS
ISBN: 0-7641-1357-7
$5.95, Can. $8.50

FRENCH
VOCABULARY
ISBN: 0-7641-1999-0
$6.99, Can. $9.99

GERMAN
VOCABULARY
ISBN: 0-8120-4497-5
$7.95, Can. $11.50

ITALIAN
VOCABULARY
ISBN: 0-7641-2190-1
$6.95, Can. $9.95

JAPANESE
VOCABULARY
ISBN: 0-8120-4743-5
$8.99, Can. $11.99

RUSSIAN
VOCABULARY
ISBN: 0-8120-1554-1
$6.95, Can. $8.95

SPANISH
VOCABULARY
ISBN: 0-7641-1985-3
$6.95, Can. $9.95

BARRON'S

Barron's Educational Series, Inc.
250 Wireless Blvd., Hauppauge, NY 11788 •
Call toll-free: 1-800-645-3476
In Canada: Georgetown Book Warehouse
34 Armstrong Ave., Georgetown, Ontario L7G 4R9 •
Call toll-free: 1-800-247-7160
www.barronseduc.com
Can. $ = Canadian dollars

Books may be purchased at your bookstore or by mail from Barron's. Enclose check or money order for total amount plus sales tax where applicable and 18% for postage and handling (minimum charge $5.95 U.S. and Canada). Prices subject to change without notice. New York, New Jersey, Michigan, Tennessee, and California residents, please add sales tax to total after postage and handling.

Minimum Systems Requirement for the Flash Standalone Executable

Windows:
- Pentium II or higher recommended
- Windows 98, ME, NT4, 2000, XP
- 64 MB of installed RAM, 128 MB recommended
- 1024 × 768 color display

Apple:
- Power Macintosh Power PC processor (G3 or higher recommended)
- Mac OS® X 10.2–10.4 64 MB of installed RAM
- 128 MB recommended
- CD-ROM drive
- 1024 × 768 color display

Launching Instructions for the PC

Windows Users:
Insert the CD-ROM into your CD-ROM drive. The application should start in a few moments. If it doesn't, follow the steps below.

1. Click on the Start button on the Desktop and select Run.
2. Type "D:/501Verbs" (where D is the letter of your CD-ROM drive).
3. Click OK.

Launching Instructions for the Mac

Macintosh Users:
The CD will open to the desktop automatically when inserted into the CD drive. Double click the 501 Verbs Flash icon to launch the program.